2003 | WORLD DEVELOPMENT INDICATORS

The World Bank

2003 | WORLD DEVELOPMENT INDICATORS

This volume is a product of the staff of the Development Data Group of the World Bank's Development Economics Vice Presidency, and the judgments herein do not necessarily reflect the views of the World Bank's Board of Executive Directors or the countries they represent.

The World Bank does not guarantee the accuracy of the data included in this publication and accepts no responsibility whatsoever for any consequence of their use. The boundaries, colors, denominations, and other information shown on any map in this volume do not imply on the part of the World Bank any judgment on the legal status of any territory or the endorsement or acceptance of such boundaries. This publication uses the Robinson projection for maps, which represents both area and shape reasonably well for most of the earth's surface. Nevertheless, some distortions of area, shape, distance, and direction remain.

Photo credits: Front cover, from top to bottom and left to right, PhotoDisc, Alex Baluyut/World Bank, PhotoDisc, Demi/UNEP/Still Pictures, PhotoDisc, PhotoDisc; Back cover, Curt Carnemark/World Bank, PhotoDisc; Page 178, Curt Carnemark/World Bank.

If you have questions or comments about this product, please contact:

Development Data Group

The World Bank

1818 H Street NW, Room MC2-812, Washington, DC 20433, USA

Hotline: 800 590 1906 or 202 473 7824; fax 202 522 1498

Email: data@worldbank.org

Web site: www.worldbank.org or www.worldbank.org/data

ISBN 0-8213-5422-1

FOREWORD

When the world's nations adopted the Millennium Declaration in September 2000, they made a commitment to quicken the pace of development and ensure that its benefits reach all people. We at the World Bank share that commitment. The challenge now is to scale up our efforts to meet the goals that we have set for ourselves.

The Millennium Development Goals set specific targets for achieving development progress. We know what this effort will require. First, good development outcomes require good policies and institutions that are country owned and driven. Second, the global economic environment, including trade and financial systems, must be open, fair, and supportive. Third, when these conditions are met, development assistance can be highly effective. But the poorest countries will need substantial increases in assistance if they are to reach the Millennium Development Goals.

In the past three years our partners—developing countries, high-income countries, and international agencies—have shaped an unprecedented consensus on how to achieve progress. In Doha, Qatar, in November 2001 the members of the World Trade Organization declared that the next round of trade negotiations would place the interests of the developing countries at the top of the agenda. In Monterrey, Mexico, in March 2002 developing countries committed to improving their governance, institutions, and policies, and rich countries committed to increasing aid, opening trade, and supporting capacity building. And in Johannesburg, South Africa, in August 2002 the international community addressed the challenges of achieving sustainable development and protecting the environment. Together, these agreements provide the foundations for a global partnership for development.

Over the past 40 years the developing world has seen tangible but uneven growth and poverty reduction. The *World Development Indicators* documents much of that story. In 1962 the list of the 20 poorest countries in the world included the Republic of Korea, Botswana, China, and India. Today Korea has joined the ranks of the high-income economies. Botswana's average real income has doubled almost four times, placing it among upper-middle-income countries. China, where poverty is falling rapidly, is now the sixth largest economy in the world. And India, after opening its economy and accelerating growth, has moved well above the 20 poorest.

Still, the *World Development Indicators* reminds us that growth alone will not be enough to achieve the Millennium Development Goals. Hundreds of millions of people suffer illnesses and early deaths that could be prevented if basic health services were widely available. Each year more than 10 million children die before their fifth birthday. More than 100 million children do not attend primary school. And more than a billion people lack access to a safe source of water. These figures pose enormous challenges. Speaking plainly, many of the poorest countries will not reach the Millennium Development Goals unless all development partners take decisive action without further delay.

One more thing we need to do: continue to measure our efforts using the best statistics available and to use that information wisely to set policies, guide programs, and monitor outcomes. The *World Development Indicators* is the result of a worldwide effort shared by many people and agencies. It is another example of development partnership, something very important to us. Our focus is on scaling up support for capacity building in statistics and working with our partners to improve the internationally comparable data set that is needed to monitor development policies, actions, and outcomes. Statistics are not the most glamorous work. But without them we would not know how far we have come—or how far we have to go.

James D. Wolfensohn
President
The World Bank Group

ACKNOWLEDGMENTS

This book and its companion volumes, *The World Bank Atlas* and *The Little Data Book*, were prepared by a team coordinated by David Cieslikowski. The team consisted of Mehdi Akhlaghi, Mona Fetouh, Richard Fix, Amy Heyman, Masako Hiraga, M. H. Saeed Ordoubadi, Sulekha Patel, Eric Swanson, K. M. Vijayalakshmi, Vivienne Wang, and Estela Zamora, working closely with other teams in the Development Economics Vice Presidency's Development Data Group. The CD-ROM development team included Azita Amjadi, Elizabeth Crayford, Ramgopal Erobelly, Reza Farivari, and William Prince. The work was carried out under the management of Shaida Badiee.

The choice of indicators and textual content was shaped through close consultation with and substantial contributions from staff in the World Bank's four thematic networks—Environmentally and Socially Sustainable Development, Human Development, Poverty Reduction and Economic Management, and Private Sector Development and Infrastructure—and staff of the International Finance Corporation and the Multilateral Investment Guarantee Agency. Most important, the team received substantial help, guidance, and data from external partners. For individual acknowledgments of contributions to the book's content, please see the *Credits* section. For a listing of our key partners, see the *Partners* section.

Communications Development Incorporated provided overall design direction, editing, and layout, led by Meta de Coquereaumont and Bruce Ross-Larson. The editing and production team consisted of Joseph Costello, Wendy Guyette, Paul Holtz, Elizabeth McCrocklin, Alison Strong, and Elaine Wilson. Communications Development's London partner, Grundy & Northedge, provided art direction and design. Staff from External Affairs oversaw publication and dissemination of the book.

PREFACE

When launched more than a quarter century ago, the *World Development Indicators* presented a statistical snapshot of the world as seen by development economists. As our understanding of the development process has grown, so has the *World Development Indicators*. It now encompasses more than 500 indicators covering 152 countries, selected from a database spanning 40 years with more than 800 indicators for 208 countries. It provides a larger picture of poverty trends and social welfare, the use of environmental resources, the performance of the public sector, and the integration of the global economy.

The availability of internationally comparable statistics has encouraged a new focus on measuring development outcomes. The Millennium Development Goals, adopted by all members of the United Nations, set specific, quantified targets for reducing poverty and achieving progress in health, education, and the use of environmental resources. (The *World view* section reports on these goals and on the commitments by richer countries to help poorer countries achieve them.) These goals and the growing emphasis on results-focused development strategies have in turn increased the demand for timely, reliable, and relevant data.

But many countries still lack the capacity to produce and use reliable statistical information. A shortage of skills, resources, and technology has often led to incomplete or erroneous data. And the unreliability of data has meant less demand from potential users and fewer resources for statistical agencies. The result: a long history of underinvestment in the most public of all goods—information.

In the past several years the World Bank has expanded its efforts to help developing countries break out of this vicious cycle. Working in partnership with national agencies and international donors, we are helping to build the capacity of statistical systems to collect, compile, and disseminate reliable statistics. We also support training programs to increase the use of statistics to inform public choices. And by participating in the international statistical system, we help to provide frameworks and standards to guide practitioners.

Improving statistics requires real resources. The World Bank's Trust Fund for Statistical Capacity Building, supported by contributions from bilateral aid agencies, provides grants to support planning of statistical systems. For larger, long-term projects a new lending facility will provide funding for reforming and expanding statistical services.

But making long-term improvements in statistics requires more than money. We work closely with the International Monetary Fund on the implementation of the General Data Dissemination System and Data Quality Assessment Framework, both of which encourage countries to improve the quality of official statistics. The World Bank is an active member of the Partnership in Statistics for the 21st Century—the PARIS21 consortium—which helps to build awareness of statistics and provides a forum where statisticians, policymakers, and other users of data can interact and articulate needs. And we are leading the work of the International Comparison Programme in non-OECD countries to produce a new set of international price data.

The *World Development Indicators* reflects the efforts of many people and organizations. We have tried to acknowledge our debts in the *Partners* section and the *About the data* pages that accompany each table. Our purpose is to serve you, the user of statistics, whether a policymaker, researcher, commentator, or interested citizen. We hope that the *World Development Indicators* goes some way toward meeting your needs. You can find out more about our products at http://www.worldbank.org/data. And you can send queries and comments to data@worldbank.org.

Shaida Badiee
Director
Development Data Group

TABLE OF CONTENTS

FRONT

1. WORLD VIEW

2. PEOPLE

3. ENVIRONMENT

TABLE OF CONTENTS

4. ECONOMY

5. STATES AND MARKETS

6. GLOBAL LINKS

BACK

PARTNERS

Defining, gathering, and disseminating international statistics is a collective effort of many people and organizations. The indicators presented in the *World Development Indicators* are the fruit of decades of work at many levels, from the field workers who administer censuses and household surveys to the committees and working parties of the national and international statistical agencies that develop the nomenclature, classifications, and standards fundamental to an international statistical system. Nongovernmental organizations and the private sector have also made important contributions, both in gathering primary data and in organizing and publishing their results. And academic researchers have played a crucial role in developing statistical methods and carrying on a continuing dialogue about the quality and interpretation of statistical indicators. All these contributors have a strong belief that available, accurate data will improve the quality of public and private decisionmaking.

The organizations listed here have made the *World Development Indicators* possible by sharing their data and their expertise with us. More important, their collaboration contributes to the World Bank's efforts, and to those of many others, to improve the quality of life of the world's people. We acknowledge our debt and gratitude to all who have helped to build a base of comprehensive, quantitative information about the world and its people.

For your easy reference we have included URLs (Web addresses) for organizations that maintain Web sites. The addresses shown were active on 1 March 2003. Information about the World Bank is also provided.

International and government agencies

Bureau of Verification and Compliance, U.S. Department of State

The Bureau of Verification and Compliance, U.S. Department of State, is responsible for international agreements on conventional, chemical, and biological weapons and on strategic forces; treaty verification and compliance; and support to ongoing negotiations, policymaking, and interagency implementation efforts.

For information, contact the Public Affairs Officer, Bureau of Verification and Compliance, U.S. Department of State, 2201 C Street NW, Washington, DC 20520, USA; telephone: 202 647 6946; Web site: www.state.gov/t/vc.

Carbon Dioxide Information Analysis Center

The Carbon Dioxide Information Analysis Center (CDIAC) is the primary global change data and information analysis center of the U.S. Department of Energy. The CDIAC's scope includes potentially anything that would be of value to those concerned with the greenhouse effect and global climate change, including concentrations of carbon dioxide and other radiatively active gases in the atmosphere; the role of the terrestrial biosphere and the oceans in the biogeochemical cycles of greenhouse gases; emissions of carbon dioxide to the atmosphere; long-term climate trends; the effects of elevated carbon dioxide on vegetation; and the vulnerability of coastal areas to rising sea levels.

For information, contact the CDIAC, Oak Ridge National Laboratory, PO Box 2008, Oak Ridge, TN 37831-6335, USA; telephone: 865 574 0390; fax: 865 574 2232; email: cdiac@ornl.gov; Web site: cdiac.esd.ornl.gov.

Deutsche Gesellschaft für Technische Zusammenarbeit

The Deutsche Gesellschaft für Technische Zusammenarbeit (GTZ) GmbH is a German government-owned corporation for international cooperation with worldwide operations. GTZ's aim is to positively shape the political, economic, ecological and social development in partner countries, thereby improving people's living conditions and prospects.

The organization has more than 10,000 employees in some 130 countries of Africa, Asia, Latin America, and Eastern Europe.

For publications, contact Deutsche Gesellschaft für Technische Zusammenarbeit (GTZ) GmbH Corporate Communications, Dag-Hammarskjöld-Weg 1-5, 65760 Eschborn. Germany; telephone: + 49 (0) 6196 79 1174, fax: + 49 (0) 6196 79 6196, email: presse@gtz.de, Web site: www.gtz.de

Food and Agriculture Organization

The Food and Agriculture Organization (FAO), a specialized agency of the United Nations, was founded in October 1945 with a mandate to raise nutrition levels and living standards, to increase agricultural productivity, and to better the condition of rural populations. The organization provides direct development assistance; collects, analyzes, and disseminates information; offers policy and planning advice to governments; and serves as an international forum for debate on food and agricultural issues.

Statistical publications of the FAO include the *Production Yearbook*, *Trade Yearbook*, and *Fertilizer Yearbook*. The FAO makes much of its data available online through its FAOSTAT and AQUASTAT systems.

FAO publications can be ordered from national sales agents or directly from the FAO Sales and Marketing Group, Viale delle Terme di Caracalla, 00100 Rome, Italy; telephone: 39 06 5705 5727; fax: 39 06 5705 3360; email: Publications-sales@fao.org; Web site: www.fao.org.

International Civil Aviation Organization

The International Civil Aviation Organization (ICAO), a specialized agency of the United Nations, was founded on December 7, 1944. It is responsible for establishing international standards and recommended practices and procedures for the technical, economic, and legal aspects of international civil aviation operations. The ICAO works to achieve the highest practicable degree of uniformity worldwide in civil aviation issues whenever this will facilitate and improve air safety, efficiency, and regularity.

To obtain ICAO publications, contact the ICAO, Document Sales Unit, 999 University Street, Montreal, Quebec H3C 5H7, Canada; telephone: 514 954 8022; fax: 514 954 6769; email: sales_unit@icao.int; Web site: www.icao.int.

International Labour Organization

The International Labour Organization (ILO), a specialized agency of the United Nations, seeks the promotion of social justice and internationally recognized human and labor rights. Founded in 1919, it is the only surviving major creation of the Treaty of Versailles, which brought the League of Nations into being. It became the first specialized agency of the United Nations in 1946. Unique within the United Nations system, the ILO's tripartite structure has workers and employers participating as equal partners with governments in the work of its governing organs.

As part of its mandate, the ILO maintains an extensive statistical publication program. The *Yearbook of Labour Statistics* is its most comprehensive collection of labor force data.

Publications can be ordered from the International Labour Organization Publications, 4 route des

Morillons, CH-1211 Geneva 22, Switzerland, or from sales agents and major booksellers throughout the world and ILO offices in many countries. telephone: 41 22 799 6111; fax: 41 22 798 8685; email: publns@ilo.org; Web site: www.ilo.org.

International Monetary Fund

The International Monetary Fund (IMF) was established at a conference in Bretton Woods, New Hampshire, United States, on July 1–22, 1944. (The conference also established the World Bank.) The IMF came into official existence on December 27, 1945, and commenced financial operations on March 1, 1947. It currently has 184 member countries.

The statutory purposes of the IMF are to promote international monetary cooperation, facilitate the expansion and balanced growth of international trade, promote exchange rate stability, help to establish a multilateral payments system, make the general resources of the IMF temporarily available to its members under adequate safeguards, and shorten the duration and lessen the degree of disequilibrium in the international balances of payments of members.

The IMF maintains an extensive program for the development and compilation of international statistics and is responsible for collecting and reporting statistics on international financial transactions and the balance of payments. In April 1996 it undertook an important initiative to improve the quality of international statistics, establishing the Special Data Dissemination Standard (SDDS) to guide members that have, or seek, access to international capital markets in providing economic and financial data to the public. In 1997 the IMF established the General Data Dissemination System (GDDS) to guide countries in providing the public with comprehensive, timely, accessible, and reliable economic, financial, and sociodemographic data. Building on this work, the IMF established the Data Quality Assessment Framework (DQAF) to assess data quality in subject areas such as debt and poverty. The DQAF comprises dimensions of data quality such as methodological soundness, accuracy, serviceability, and accessibility. In 1999 work began on Reports on the Observance of Standards and Codes (ROSC), which summarize the extent to which countries observe certain internationally recognized standards and codes in areas including data, monetary and financial policy transparency, fiscal transparency, banking supervision, securities, insurance, payments systems, corporate governance, accounting, auditing, and insolvency and creditor rights.

The IMF's major statistical publications include *International Financial Statistics*, *Balance of Payments Statistics Yearbook*, *Government Finance Statistics Yearbook*, and *Direction of Trade Statistics Yearbook*.

For more information on IMF statistical publications, contact the International Monetary Fund, Publications Services, Catalog Orders, 700 19th Street NW, Washington, DC 20431, USA; telephone: 202 623 7430; fax: 202 623 7201; telex: RCA 248331 IMF UR; email: pub-web@imf.org; Web site: www.imf.org; SDDS and GDDS bulletin board: dsbb.imf.org.

International Telecommunication Union

Founded in Paris in 1865 as the International Telegraph Union, the International Telecommunication Union (ITU) took its current name in 1934 and became a specialized agency of the United Nations in 1947. The ITU is an intergovernmental organization in which the public and private sectors cooperate for the development of telecommunications. The ITU adopts international regulations and treaties governing all terrestrial and space uses of the frequency spectrum and the use of the geostationary satellite orbit. It also develops standards for the interconnection of telecommunications systems worldwide.

The ITU fosters the development of telecommunications in developing countries by establishing medium-term development policies and strategies in consultation with other partners in the sector and providing specialized technical assistance in management, telecommunications policy, human resource management, research and development, technology choice and transfer, network installation and maintenance, and investment financing and resource mobilization. The ITU's main statistical publication is the *ITU Yearbook of Statistics*.

Publications can be ordered from ITU Sales and Marketing Service, Web site: www.itu.int/ITU-D/ict/publications/index.htm; telephone: 41 22 730 6141 (English), 41 22 730 6142 (French), and 41 22 730 6143 (Spanish); fax: 41 22 730 5194; email: sales@itu.int; telex: 421 000 uit ch; telegram: ITU GENEVE; Web site: www.itu.int.

National Science Foundation

The National Science Foundation (NSF) is an independent U.S. government agency whose mission is to promote the progress of science; to advance the national health, prosperity, and welfare; and to secure the national defense. It is responsible for promoting science and engineering through almost 20,000 research and education projects. In addition, the NSF fosters the exchange of scientific information among scientists and engineers in the United States and other countries, supports programs to strengthen scientific and engineering research potential, and evaluates the impact of research on industrial development and general welfare.

As part of its mandate, the NSF biennially publishes *Science and Engineering Indicators*, which tracks national and international trends in science and engineering research and education.

Electronic copies of NSF documents can be obtained from the NSF's online document system (www.nsf.gov/pubsys/ods/index.html) or requested by email from its automated mailserver (getpub@nsf.gov). Documents can also be requested from the NSF Publications Clearinghouse by mail, at PO Box 218, Jessup, MD 20794-0218, USA, or by telephone, at 301 947 2722.

For more information, contact the National Science Foundation, 4201 Wilson Boulevard, Arlington, VA 22230, USA; telephone: 703 292 5111; Web site: www.nsf.gov.

Organisation for Economic Co-operation and Development

The Organisation for Economic Co-operation and Development (OECD) was set up in 1948 as the Organisation for European Economic Co-operation (OEEC) to administer Marshall Plan funding in Europe. In 1960, when the Marshall Plan had completed its task, the OEEC's member countries agreed to bring in Canada and the United States to form an organization to coordinate policy among industrial countries. The OECD is the international organization of the industrialized, market economy countries.

Representatives of member countries meet at the OECD to exchange information and harmonize policy with a view to maximizing economic growth in member countries and helping nonmember countries develop more rapidly. The OECD has set up a number of specialized committees to further its aims. One of these is the Development Assistance Committee (DAC), whose members have agreed to coordinate their policies on assistance to developing and transition economies.

Also associated with the OECD are several agencies or bodies that have their own governing statutes, including the International Energy Agency and the Centre for Co-operation with Economies in Transition.

The OECD's main statistical publications include *Geographical Distribution of Financial Flows to Aid Recipients*, *National Accounts of OECD Countries*, *Labour Force Statistics*, *Revenue Statistics of OECD Member Countries*, *International Direct Investment Statistics Yearbook*, *Basic Science and Technology*

Statistics, *Industrial Structure Statistics*, and *Services: Statistics on International Transactions*.

For information on OECD publications, contact the OECD, 2, rue André Pascal, F-75775 Paris Cedex 16, France; telephone: 33 1 45 24 81 67; fax: 33 1 45 24 19 50; email: sales@oecd.org; Web sites: www.oecd.org and www.oecd.org/bookshop.

United Nations

The United Nations and its specialized agencies maintain a number of programs for the collection of international statistics, some of which are described elsewhere in this book. At United Nations headquarters the Statistics Division provides a wide range of statistical outputs and services for producers and users of statistics worldwide.

The Statistics Division publishes statistics on international trade, national accounts, demography and population, gender, industry, energy, environment, human settlements, and disability.

Its major statistical publications include the *International Trade Statistics Yearbook*, *Yearbook of National Accounts*, and *Monthly Bulletin of Statistics*, along with general statistics compendiums such as the *Statistical Yearbook* and *World Statistics Pocketbook*.

For publications, contact United Nations Publications, Room DC2-853, Department I004, 2 UN Plaza, New York, NY 10017, USA; telephone: 212 963 8302 or 800 253 9646 (toll free); fax: 212 963 3489; email: publications@un.org; Web site: www.un.org.

United Nations Centre for Human Settlements (Habitat), Global Urban Observatory

The Urban Indicators Programme of the United Nations Centre for Human Settlements (Habitat) was established to address the urgent global need to improve the urban knowledge base by helping countries and cities design, collect, and apply policy-oriented indicators related to urban development at the city level. In 1997 the Urban Indicators Programme was integrated into the Global Urban Observatory, the principal United Nations program for monitoring urban conditions and trends and for tracking progress in implementing the goals of the Habitat Agenda. With the Urban Indicators and Best Practices programs, the Global Urban Observatory is establishing a worldwide information, assessment, and capacity building network to help governments, local authorities, the private sector, and nongovernmental and other civil society organizations.

Contact the Co-ordinator, Global Urban Observatory and Statistics, Urban Secretariat, UN-HABITAT, PO Box 30030, Nairobi, Kenya; telephone: 254 2 623119; fax: 254 2 623080; email: habitat.publications@unhabitat.org or guo@unhabitat.org; Web site: www.unhabitat.org.

United Nations Children's Fund

The United Nations Children's Fund (UNICEF), the only organization of the United Nations dedicated exclusively to children, works with other United Nations bodies and with governments and non-governmental organizations to improve children's lives in more than 140 developing countries through community-based services in primary health care, basic education, and safe water and sanitation.

UNICEF's major publications include *The State of the World's Children* and *The Progress of Nations*.

For information on UNICEF publications, contact the Chief, EPS, Division of Communication, UNICEF, 3 United Nations Plaza, New York, NY 10017, USA; telephone: 212 326 7000; fax: 212 303 7985; email: pubdoc@unicef.org; Web site: www.unicef.org and www.un.org/Publications.

United Nations Conference on Trade and Development

The United Nations Conference on Trade and Development (UNCTAD) is the principal organ of the United Nations General Assembly in the field of trade and development. It was established as a permanent intergovernmental body in 1964 in Geneva with a view to accelerating economic growth and development, particularly in developing countries. UNCTAD discharges its mandate through policy analysis; intergovernmental deliberations, consensus building, and negotiation; monitoring, implementation, and follow-up; and technical cooperation.

UNCTAD produces a number of publications containing trade and economic statistics, including the *Handbook of International Trade and Development Statistics*.

For information, contact UNCTAD, Palais des Nations, 8-14, Avenue de la Paix, 1211 Geneva 10, Switzerland; telephone: 41 22 907 1234; fax: 41 22 907 0043; email: info@unctad.org; Web site: www.unctad.org.

United Nations Educational, Scientific, and Cultural Organization, Institute for Statistics (UIS)

The United Nations Educational, Scientific, and Cultural Organization (UNESCO) is a specialized agency of the United Nations established in 1945 to promote "collaboration among nations through education, science, and culture in order to further universal respect for justice, for the rule of law, and for the human rights and fundamental freedoms . . . for the peoples of the world, without distinction of race, sex, language, or religion."

UNESCO's principal statistical publications are the *World Education Report* (biennial) and *Basic Education and Literacy: World Statistical Indicators*. They are produced by the UNESCO Institute for Statistics.

For publications, contact the UNESCO Institute for Statistics, C.P. 6128, Succursale Centre-ville, Montreal, Quebec, H3C 3J7, Canada; telephone: 1 514 343 6880; fax: 1 514 343 6882; email: uis@unesco.org; Web site: www.unesco.org; and for the Institute for Statistics: www.uis.unesco.org/.

United Nations Environment Programme

The mandate of the United Nations Environment Programme (UNEP) is to provide leadership and encourage partnership in caring for the environment by inspiring, informing, and enabling nations and people to improve their quality of life without compromising that of future generations.

UNEP publications include *Global Environment Outlook* and *Our Planet* (a bimonthly magazine).

For information, contact the UNEP, PO Box 30552, Nairobi, Kenya; telephone: 254 2 621234; fax: 254 2 624489/90; email: eisinfo@unep.org; Web site: www.unep.org.

United Nations Industrial Development Organization

The United Nations Industrial Development Organization (UNIDO) was established in 1966 to act as the central coordinating body for industrial activities and to promote industrial development and cooperation at the global, regional, national, and sectoral levels. In 1985 UNIDO became the 16th specialized agency of the United Nations, with a mandate to help develop scientific and technological plans and programs for industrialization in the public, cooperative, and private sectors.

UNIDO's databases and information services include the Industrial Statistics Database (INDSTAT), Commodity Balance Statistics Database (COMBAL), Industrial Development Abstracts (IDA), and the International Referral System on Sources of Information. Among its publications is the *International Yearbook of Industrial Statistics*.

For information, contact UNIDO Public Information Section, Vienna International Centre, PO Box 300, A-1400 Vienna, Austria; telephone: 43 1 26026 5031; fax: 43 1 21346 5031 or 26026 6843; email: publications@unido.org; Web site: www.unido.org.

World Bank Group

The World Bank Group is made up of five organizations: the International Bank for Reconstruction and Development (IBRD), the International Development Association (IDA), the International Finance Corporation (IFC), the Multilateral Investment Guarantee Agency (MIGA), and the International Centre for Settlement of Investment Disputes (ICSID).

Established in 1944 at a conference of world leaders in Bretton Woods, New Hampshire, United States, the World Bank is the world's largest source of development assistance, providing $19.5 billion in loans to its client countries. It uses its financial resources, trained staff, and extensive knowledge base to help each developing country onto a path of stable, sustainable, and equitable growth in the fight against poverty. The World Bank Group has 184 member countries.

For information about the World Bank, visit its Web site at www.worldbank.org. For more information about development data, contact the Development Data Group, World Bank, 1818 H Street NW, Washington, DC 20433, USA; telephone: 800 590 1906 or 202 473 7824; fax: 202 522 1498; email: data@worldbank.org; Web site: www.worldbank.org/data.

World Health Organization

The constitution of the World Health Organization (WHO) was adopted on July 22, 1946, by the International Health Conference, convened in New York by the Economic and Social Council of the United Nations. The objective of the WHO, a specialized agency of the United Nations, is the attainment by all people of the highest possible level of health.

The WHO carries out a wide range of functions, including coordinating international health work; helping governments strengthen health services; providing technical assistance and emergency aid; working for the prevention and control of disease; promoting improved nutrition, housing, sanitation, recreation, and economic and working conditions; promoting and coordinating biomedical and health services research; promoting improved standards of teaching and training in health and medical professions; establishing international standards for biological, pharmaceutical, and similar products; and standardizing diagnostic procedures.

The WHO publishes the *World Health Statistics Annual* and many other technical and statistical publications.

For publications, contact the World Health Organization, Marketing and Dissemination, CH-1211 Geneva 27, Switzerland; telephone: 41 22 791 2476; fax: 41 22 791 4857; email: publications@who.int; Web site: www.who.int.

World Intellectual Property Organization

The World Intellectual Property Organization (WIPO) is a specialized agency of the United Nations based in Geneva, Switzerland. The objectives of WIPO are to promote the protection of intellectual property throughout the world through cooperation among states and, where appropriate, in collaboration with other international organizations and to ensure administrative cooperation among the intellectual property unions—that is, the "unions" created by the Paris and Berne Conventions and several subtreaties concluded by members of the Paris Union. WIPO is responsible for administering various multilateral treaties dealing with the legal and administrative aspects of intellectual property. A substantial part of its activities and resources is devoted to development cooperation with developing countries.

For information, contact the World Intellectual Property Organization, 34, chemin des Colombettes, CH-1211 Geneva 20, Switzerland; telephone: 41 22 338 9734; fax: 41 22 740 1812; email: ebookshop@wipo.int; Web site: www.wipo.int.

World Tourism Organization

The World Tourism Organization is an intergovernmental body entrusted by the United Nations with promoting and developing tourism. It serves as a global forum for tourism policy issues and a source of tourism know-how. The organization began as the International Union of Official Tourist Publicity Organizations, set up in 1925 in The Hague. Renamed the World Tourism Organization, it held its first general assembly in Madrid in May 1975. Its membership includes 139 countries and territories and more than 350 affiliate members representing local governments, tourism associations, and private companies, including airlines, hotel groups, and tour operators.

The World Tourism Organization publishes the *Yearbook of Tourism Statistics*, *Compendium of Tourism Statistics*, and *Travel and Tourism Barometer* (triannual).

For information, contact the World Tourism Organization, Calle Capitán Haya, 42, 28020 Madrid, Spain; telephone: 34 91 567 8100; fax: 34 91 571 3733; email: infoshop@world-tourism.org; Web site: www.world-tourism.org.

World Trade Organization

The World Trade Organization (WTO), established on January 1, 1995, is the successor to the General Agreement on Tariffs and Trade (GATT). The WTO has 144 member countries, and is the only international organization dealing with the global rules of trade between nations. Its main function is to ensure that trade flows as smoothly, predictably and freely as possible. It does this by administering trade agreements, acting as a forum for trade negotiations, settling trade disputes, reviewing national trade policies, assisting developing countries in trade policy issues—through technical assistance and training programs—and cooperating with other international organizations. At the heart of the system—known as the multilateral trading system—are WTO's agreements, negotiated and signed by a large majority of the world's trading nations and ratified by their parliaments.

The WTO's *International Trade Statistics* is its main statistical publication, providing comprehensive, comparable, and up-to-date statistics on trade.

For publications, contact the World Trade Organization, Publications Services, Centre William Rappard, rue de Lausanne 154, CH-1211, Geneva 21, Switzerland; telephone: 41 22 739 5208 or 5308; fax: 41 22 739 5792; email: publications@wto.org; Web site: www.wto.org.

Private and nongovernmental organizations

Containerisation International

Containerisation International Yearbook is the most concise, yet comprehensive, single reference source on the container transport industry. Now in its 34th year, the *Yearbook* is known worldwide as "the bible of the industry." It has more than 850 pages of data, including detailed information on more than 560 container ports in more than 150 countries and a review section that features two-year rankings for 350 ports. The information can be accessed on the Web at www.ci-online.co.uk, which also provides a comprehensive online daily business news and information service for the container industry.

For more information, contact Informa UK at 69-77 Paul Street, London, EC2A 4LQ, UK; telephone: 44 1206 772061; fax: 44 1206 772563; email: webtechhelp@informa.com.

Euromoney Publications PLC

Euromoney Publications PLC provides a wide range of financial, legal, and general business information. The monthly magazine *Euromoney* carries a semiannual rating of country creditworthiness.

For information, contact Euromoney Publications PLC, Nestor House, Playhouse Yard, London EC4V 5EX, UK; telephone: 44 870 90 62 600; email: customerservice@euromoney.com; Web site: www.euromoney.com.

Institutional Investor, Inc.

Institutional Investor, Inc., develops country credit ratings every six months based on information provided by leading international banks. It publishes the magazine *Institutional Investor* monthly.

For information, contact Institutional Investor, Inc., 225 Park Avenue South, New York, NY 10003, USA; telephone: 212 224 3800; email: info@iiplatinum.com; Web site: www.institutionalinvestor.com.

International Road Federation

The International Road Federation (IRF) is a not-for-profit, nonpolitical service organization. Its purpose is to encourage better road and transport systems worldwide and to help apply technology and management practices that will maximize economic and social returns from national road investments.

The IRF has led global road infrastructure developments and is the international point of affiliation for about 600 member companies, associations, and governments.

The IRF's mission is to promote road development as a key factor in social and economic growth, to provide governments and financial institutions with professional ideas and expertise, to facilitate business exchange among members, to establish links between members and external institutions and agencies, to support national road federations, and to give information to professional groups.

The IRF publishes *World Road Statistics*.

Contact the Geneva office at chemin de Blandonnet 2, CH-1214 Vernier, Geneva, Switzerland; telephone: 41 22 306 0260; fax: 41 22 306 0270; or the Washington, DC, office at 1010 Massachusetts Avenue NW, Suite 410, Washington, DC 20001, USA; telephone: 202 371 5544; fax: 202 371 5565; email: info@irfnet.com; Web site: www.irfnet.org.

Moody's Investors Service

Moody's Investors Service is a global credit analysis and financial opinion firm. It provides the international investment community with globally consistent credit ratings on debt and other securities issued by North American state and regional government entities, by corporations worldwide, and by some sovereign issuers. It also publishes extensive financial data in both print and electronic form. Its clients include investment banks, brokerage firms, insurance companies, public utilities, research libraries, manufacturers, and government agencies and departments.

Moody's Investors Service

Moody's publishes *Sovereign, Subnational and Sovereign-Guaranteed Issuers*. For information, contact Moody's Investors Service, 99 Church Street, New York, NY 10007, USA; telephone: 212 553 0377; fax: 212 553 0882; Web site: www.moodys.com.

Netcraft

Netcraft is an Internet consultancy based in Bath, England. Most of its work relates to the development of Internet services for its clients or for itself acting as principal.

For information, visit its Web site: www.netcraft.com.

PricewaterhouseCoopers

Drawing on the talents of 125,000 people in more than 142 countries, PricewaterhouseCoopers provides a full range of business advisory services to leading global, national, and local companies and public institutions. Its service offerings have been organized into four lines of service, each staffed with highly qualified, experienced professionals and leaders. These services include audit, assurance, and business advisory services; business process outsourcing; corporate finance and recovery services; and global tax services.

PricewaterhouseCoopers publishes *Corporate Taxes: Worldwide Summaries* and *Individual Taxes: Worldwide Summaries*.

For information, contact PricewaterhouseCoopers, 1177 Avenue of the Americas, New York, NY 10036, USA; telephone: 646 471 4000; fax: 646 471 3188; Web site: www.pwcglobal.com.

The PRS Group, Inc.

The PRS Group, Inc., is a global leader in political and economic risk forecasting and market analysis and has served international companies large and small for over 20 years. The data it contributed to this year's *World Development Indicators* come from the *International Country Risk Guide* monthly publication that monitors and rates political, financial, and economic risk in 140 countries.

The guide's data series and commitment to independent and unbiased analysis make it the standard for any organization practicing effective risk management.

For information, contact The PRS Group, Inc., 6320 Fly Road, Suite 102, PO Box 248, East Syracuse, NY 13057-0248, USA; telephone: 315 431 0511; fax: 315 431 0200; email: custserv@PRSgroup.com; Web site: www.prsgroup.com or www.ICRGOnline.com.

Standard & Poor's Equity Indexes and Rating Services

Standard & Poor's, a division of the McGraw-Hill Companies, has provided independent and objective financial information, analysis, and research for more than 140 years. The S&P 500 index, one of its most popular products, is calculated and maintained by Standard & Poor's Index Services, a leading provider of equity indexes. Standard & Poor's indexes are used by investors around the world for measuring investment performance and as the basis for a wide range of financial instruments.

Standard & Poor's *Sovereign Ratings* provides issuer and local and foreign currency debt ratings for sovereign governments and for sovereign-supported and supranational issuers worldwide. Standard & Poor's Rating Services monitors the credit quality of $1.5 trillion worth of bonds and other financial instruments and offers investors global coverage of debt issuers. Standard & Poor's also has ratings on commercial paper, mutual funds, and the financial condition of insurance companies worldwide.

For information on equity indexes, contact Standard & Poor's Index Services, 22 Water Street, New York, NY 10041, USA; telephone: 212 438 7280; fax: 212 438 3523; email: index_services@sandp.com; Web site: www.spglobal.com.

For information on ratings contact the McGraw-Hill Companies, Inc., Executive Offices, 1221 Avenue of the Americas, New York, NY 10020, USA; telephone: 212 512 4105 or 800 352 3566 (toll free); fax: 212 512 4105; email: ratingsdirect@standardandpoors.com; Web site: http://www.ratingsdirect.com.

World Conservation Monitoring Centre

The World Conservation Monitoring Centre (WCMC) provides information on the conservation and sustainable use of the world's living resources and helps others to develop information systems of their own. It works in close collaboration with a wide range of people and organizations to increase access to the information needed for wise management of the world's living resources. Committed to the principle of data exchange with other centers and noncommercial users, the WCMC, whenever possible, places the data it manages in the public domain.

For information, contact the World Conservation Monitoring Centre, 219 Huntington Road, Cambridge CB3 0DL, UK; telephone: 44 12 2327 7314; fax: 44 12 2327 7136; email: info@unep-wcmc.org; Web site: www.unep-wcmc.org.

WORLD CONSERVATION
MONITORING CENTRE

World Information Technology and Services Alliance

The World Information Technology and Services Alliance (WITSA) is a consortium of 41 information technology industry associations from around the world. WITSA members represent more than 97 percent of the world information technology market. As the global voice of the information technology industry, WITSA is dedicated to advocating policies that advance the industry's growth and development; facilitating international trade and investment in information technology products and services; strengthening WITSA's national industry associations by sharing knowledge, experience, and information; providing members with a network of contacts in nearly every region; and hosting the World Congress on Information Technology.

WITSA's publication, *Digital Planet 2002: The Global Information Economy*, uses data provided by the International Data Corporation.

For information, contact WITSA, 1401 Wilson Boulevard, Suite 1100, Arlington, VA 22209, USA; telephone: 703 284 5333; fax: 617 687 6590; email: ahalvorsen@itaa.org; Web site: www.witsa.org.

World Resources Institute

The World Resources Institute is an independent center for policy research and technical assistance on global environmental and development issues. The institute provides—and helps other institutions provide—objective information and practical proposals for policy and institutional change that will foster environmentally sound, socially equitable development. The institute's current areas of work include trade, forests, energy, economics, technology, biodiversity, human health, climate change, sustainable agriculture, resource and environmental information, and national strategies for environmental and resource management.

For information, contact the World Resources Institute, Suite 800, 10 G Street NE, Washington, DC 20002, USA; telephone: 202 729 7600; fax: 202 729 7610; email: front@wri.org; Web site: www.wri.org.

USERS GUIDE

Tables

The tables are numbered by section and display the identifying icon of the section. Countries and economies are listed alphabetically (except for Hong Kong, China, which appears after China). Data are shown for 152 economies with populations of more than 1 million, as well as for Taiwan, China, in selected tables. Selected indicators for 56 other economies—small economies with populations between 30,000 and 1 million and smaller economies if they are members of the International Bank for Reconstruction and Development (IBRD) or, as it is commonly known, the World Bank—are shown in table 1.6. The term *country*, used interchangeably with *economy*, does not imply political independence, but refers to any territory for which authorities report separate social or economic statistics. When available, aggregate measures for income and regional groups appear at the end of each table.

Indicators are shown for the most recent year or period for which data are available and, in most tables, for an earlier year or period (usually 1990 in this edition). Time-series data are available on the *World Development Indicators* CD-ROM.

Known deviations from standard definitions or breaks in comparability over time or across countries are either footnoted in the tables or noted in *About the data*. When available data are deemed to be too weak to provide reliable measures of levels and trends or do not adequately adhere to international standards, the data are not shown.

Aggregate measures for income groups

The aggregate measures for income groups include 208 economies (the economies listed in the main tables plus those in table 1.6) wherever data are available. To maintain consistency in the aggregate measures over time and between tables, missing data are imputed where possible. The aggregates are totals (designated by a *t* if the aggregates include gap-filled estimates for missing data and by an *s*, for simple totals, where they do not), median values (*m*), or weighted averages (*w*). Gap filling of amounts not allocated to countries may result in discrepancies between subgroup aggregates and overall totals. For further discussion of aggregation methods, see *Statistical methods*.

Aggregate measures for regions

The aggregate measures for regions include only low- and middle-income economies (note that these measures include developing economies with populations of less than 1 million, including those listed in table 1.6).

The country composition of regions is based on the World Bank's analytical regions and may differ from common geographic usage. For regional classifications, see the map on the inside back cover and the list on the back cover flap. For further discussion of aggregation methods, see *Statistical methods*.

Statistics

Data are shown for economies as they were constituted in 2001, and historical data are revised to reflect current political arrangements. Exceptions are noted throughout the tables.

Additional information about the data is provided in *Primary data documentation*. That section summarizes national and international efforts to improve basic data collection and gives information on primary sources, census years, fiscal years, and other background. *Statistical methods* provides technical information on some of the general calculations and formulas used throughout the book.

Data consistency and reliability

Considerable effort has been made to standardize the data, but full comparability cannot be assured, and care must be taken in interpreting the indicators. Many factors affect data availability, comparability, and reliability: statistical systems in many developing economies are still weak; statistical methods, coverage, practices, and definitions differ widely; and cross-country and inter-temporal comparisons involve complex technical and conceptual problems that cannot be unequivocally resolved. Data coverage may not be complete for economies experiencing problems (such as those stemming from internal or external conflicts) affecting the collection and reporting of data. For these reasons, although data are drawn from the sources thought to be most authoritative, they should

be construed only as indicating trends and characterizing major differences among economies rather than offering precise quantitative measures of those differences. Discrepancies in data presented in different editions of the *World Development Indicators* reflect updates by countries as well as revisions to historical series and changes in methodology. Thus readers are advised not to compare data series between editions of the *World Development Indicators* or between different World Bank publications. Consistent time-series data for 1960–2001 are available on the *World Development Indicators* CD-ROM.

Except where otherwise noted, growth rates are in real terms. (See *Statistical methods* for information on the methods used to calculate growth rates.) Data for some economic indicators for some economies are presented in fiscal years rather than calendar years; see *Primary data documentation*. All dollar figures are current U.S. dollars unless otherwise stated. The methods used for converting national currencies are described in *Statistical methods*.

China

On July 1, 1997, China resumed its exercise of sovereignty over Hong Kong, and on December 20, 1999, it resumed its exercise of sovereignty over Macao. Unless otherwise noted, data for China do not include data for Hong Kong, China; Taiwan, China; or Macao, China.

Democratic Republic of Congo

Data for the Democratic Republic of Congo (Congo, Dem. Rep., in the table listings) refer to the former Zaire. The Republic of Congo is referred to as Congo, Rep., in the table listings.

Czech Republic and Slovak Republic

Data are shown whenever possible for the individual countries formed from the former Czechoslovakia—the Czech Republic and the Slovak Republic.

Eritrea

Data are shown for Eritrea whenever possible, but in most cases before 1992 Eritrea is included in the data for Ethiopia.

Germany

Data for Germany refer to the unified Germany unless otherwise noted.

Jordan

Data for Jordan refer to the East Bank only unless otherwise noted.

Timor-Leste

On May 20, 2002, Timor-Leste became an independent country. Data for Indonesia include Timor-Leste through 1999 unless otherwise noted.

Union of Soviet Socialist Republics

In 1991 the Union of Soviet Socialist Republics came to an end. Available data are shown for the individual countries now existing on its former territory (Armenia, Azerbaijan, Belarus, Estonia, Georgia, Kazakhstan, the Kyrgyz Republic, Latvia, Lithuania, Moldova, the Russian Federation, Tajikistan, Turkmenistan, Ukraine, and Uzbekistan). External debt data presented for the Russian Federation prior to 1992 are for the former Soviet Union. The debt of the former Soviet Union is included in the Russian Federation data after 1992 on the assumption that 100 percent of all outstanding external debt as of December 1991 has become a liability of the Russian Federation. Beginning in 1993, the data for the Russian Federation have been revised to include obligations to members of the former Council for Mutual Economic Assistance and other countries in the form of trade-related credits amounting to $15.4 billion as of the end of 1996.

República Bolivariana de Venezuela

In December 1999 the official name of Venezuela was changed to República Bolivariana de Venezuela (Venezuela, RB, in the table listings).

Republic of Yemen

Data for the Republic of Yemen refer to that country from 1990 onward; data for previous years refer to aggregated data for the former People's Democratic Republic of Yemen and the former Yemen Arab Republic unless otherwise noted.

Former Socialist Federal Republic of Yugoslavia

Available data are shown for the individual countries formed from the former Socialist Federal Republic of Yugoslavia—Bosnia and Herzegovina, Croatia, the former Yugoslav Republic of Macedonia, Slovenia, and the Federal Republic of Yugoslavia. Note that on February 4, 2003, the Federal Republic of Yugoslavia changed its name to Serbia and Montenegro.

Changes in the System of National Accounts

The *World Development Indicators* uses terminology in line with the 1993 System of National Accounts (SNA). For example, in the 1993 SNA *gross national income* replaces *gross national product*. See *About the data* for tables 1.1 and 4.9.

Most countries continue to compile their national accounts according to the 1968 SNA, but more and more are adopting the 1993 SNA. Countries that use the 1993 SNA are identified in *Primary data documentation*. A few low-income countries still use concepts from older SNA guidelines, including valuations such as factor cost, in describing major economic aggregates.

Classification of economies

For operational and analytical purposes the World Bank's main criterion for classifying economies is gross national income (GNI) per capita. Every economy is classified as low income, middle income (subdivided into lower middle and upper middle), or high income. For income classifications, see the map on the inside front cover and the list on the front cover flap. Low- and middle-income economies are sometimes referred to as developing economies. The use of the term is convenient; it is not intended to imply that all economies in the group are experiencing similar development or that other economies have reached a preferred or final stage of development. Note that classification by income does not necessarily reflect development status. Because GNI per capita changes over time, the country composition of income groups may change from one edition of the *World Development*

Indicators to the next. Once the classification is fixed for an edition, based on GNI per capita in the most recent year for which data are available (2001 in this edition), all historical data presented are based on the same country grouping.

Low-income economies are those with a GNI per capita of $745 or less in 2001. Middle-income economies are those with a GNI per capita of more than $745 but less than $9,206. Lower-middle-income and upper-middle-income economies are separated at a GNI per capita of $2,975. High-income economies are those with a GNI per capita of $9,206 or more. The 12 participating member countries of the European Monetary Union (EMU) are presented as a subgroup under high-income economies.

Symbols

..

means that data are not available or that aggregates cannot be calculated because of missing data in the years shown.

0 or 0.0

means zero or less than half the unit shown.

/

in dates, as in 1990/91, means that the period of time, usually 12 months, straddles two calendar years and refers to a crop year, a survey year, or a fiscal year.

$

means current U.S. dollars unless otherwise noted.

>

means more than.

<

means less than.

Data presentation conventions

- A blank means not applicable or, for an aggregate, not analytically meaningful.
- A billion is 1,000 million.
- A trillion is 1,000 billion.
- Figures in italics refer to years or periods other than those specified.
- Data for years that are more than three years from the range shown are footnoted.

The cutoff date for data is February 1, 2003.

1 WORLD VIEW

The Millennium Development Goals summarize and give substance to the commitments embodied in the Millennium Declaration, adopted unanimously by the members of the United Nations in September 2000. They reinforce the paramount task of development as improving the welfare of all people on earth—to help them realize their human potential, to reduce insecurity and increase opportunity, and to ensure that the benefits secured in the current generation are sustained and augmented in the next.

The Millennium Development Goals set specific targets for improving income poverty, education, the status of women, health, the environment, and global development cooperation. Now widely accepted as a framework for measuring development progress, the goals focus the efforts of the world community on achieving significant, measurable improvements in people's lives. They establish yardsticks for measuring results—not just for developing countries but for rich countries that help to fund development programs and for the multilateral institutions that help countries implement these programs.

Each of the goals is important by itself, but they should be viewed together because they are mutually reinforcing. Better health care increases school enrollment and reduces poverty. Better education leads to better health. And increasing income gives people more resources to pursue better education and health care and a cleaner environment.

① Eradicate extreme poverty . . .

The first Millennium Development Goal calls for cutting in half the proportion of people living in extreme poverty—and those suffering from hunger—between 1990 and 2015. In 1990, 30 percent of the people in low- and middle-income countries lived on less than $1 a day. By 1999 the share had fallen to 23 percent, representing 1,170 million people living in extreme poverty. During the same period the population of low- and middle-income countries grew by 15 percent to 5 billion, and their gross domestic product (GDP) grew by 31 percent.

Progress was far from uniform. The fastest economic growth and the greatest poverty reduction were in East Asia and Pacific, where GDP per capita rose by 75 percent while the share of people in extreme poverty fell from 31 percent to 16 percent. But in Sub-Saharan Africa, where GDP per capita fell by 5 percent, the poverty rate rose from 47 percent in 1990 to 49 percent in 1999, and the number of people living in extreme poverty increased by 74 million. The transition economies of Europe and Central Asia experienced an even sharper drop in income, and their poverty rate more than doubled.

Despite these setbacks, there were at least 123 million fewer people living in extreme poverty at the decade's end than at its beginning. And if projected growth remains on track, global poverty rates will fall to 13 percent—less than half the 1990 level—and 360 million more people will avert extreme poverty. But rapid progress in Asia and a return to pretransition poverty levels in Europe and Central Asia will do nothing to alleviate the crushing burden of poverty in Sub-Saharan Africa, where more than 400 million people will continue to live on less than $1 a day.

A poverty line set at $1 a day ($1.08 in 1993 purchasing power parity terms), has been accepted as the working definition of extreme poverty in low-income countries. Although many people in low-income countries live on less than $1 a day, in middle-income countries a poverty line of $2 a day ($2.15 in 1993 purchasing power parity terms) is closer to a practical minimum, and national poverty lines may be set even higher. In 1999 an estimated 2.8 billion people were living on less than $2 a day—more than half the population of the developing world. The numbers living on less than $2 a day will continue to rise in South Asia and Sub-Saharan Africa. Improvements will be greatest in East Asia and Pacific. But by 2015, if present trends continue, the poverty rate measured at this higher line will have fallen by no more than 40 percent from its 1990 level.

1a

Asia has reduced poverty the most over the past decade

Share of people living on less than $1 (or $2) a day (%)

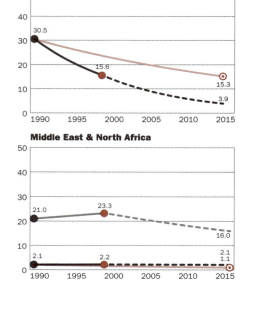

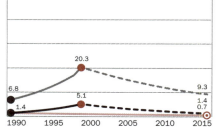

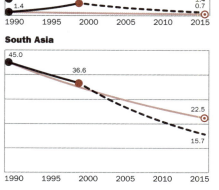

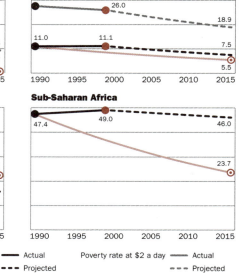

Source: World Bank staff estimates.

1b

Measuring poverty

There is almost never just one way to measure an economic indicator and poverty is no exception. Judgments are required about the design and conduct of the household survey, the processing of the data, and the subsequent data analysis that results in estimates of the level and distribution of income or consumption. Comparisons over time or between countries or even between regions in the same country require additional judgments and data.

The World Bank's poverty measure, based on a "dollar a day" poverty line began with the 1990 World Development Report (World Bank 1990). That report provided estimates for developing countries taken as a whole and by region centered on 1985. Those estimates were based on 22 household surveys, one for each of 22 countries, and model-based extrapolations for other countries. (Ravallion, Datt, and van de Walle 1991). Since then the data set has expanded to include more than 300 representative household surveys from more than 90 countries. The surveys all have national coverage. Most measure consumption, including consumption from own-production—a key feature in many developing countries. Consumption is preferred to income for measuring poverty, but income is used when consumption is not available.

Most countries set their own poverty lines. But to measure poverty between countries, an international poverty line is needed. The dollar-a-day poverty line was originally chosen as representative of typical poverty lines prevailing in a sample of low-income countries. It has since been updated to $1.08 a day in 1993 prices. Poverty measured at this level is sometimes called "extreme poverty." To estimate poverty in a country, the dollar-day-line is converted to local currency units using the purchasing power parity (PPP) exchange rates. The PPP rates, based on the relative prices of consumption goods in each country, are more representative of the actual purchasing power of a dollar than market exchange rates, especially in very poor countries. However, PPP rates are themselves a product of a complex and error-prone data collection process. Furthermore, different methods of deriving PPP rates can change the relative value of expenditures between countries.

The international poverty line is applied to distributions of consumption per person (or income per person if consumption is not available) constructed from the household survey data. Adjustments to the data are often required. For example, population weights are needed to obtain an estimate of the distribution of individual consumption per person from household consumption data. Because surveys are not conducted at the same time or at regular intervals in all countries, it is necessary to adjust consumption estimates to a common, reference year when calculating regional and global aggregates.

Aggregate poverty measures based on international poverty lines should not be confused with estimates based national poverty lines. Most of the poverty analysis work done at the World Bank is based on national poverty lines. The PPP-based international poverty line is required only to form aggregate poverty estimates across countries, for which the judgment is made than people with the same command over the purchase of goods and services should be treated the same no matter where they live. National poverty lines are set in a variety of ways: some are calculated from minimum consumption levels and some are based on relative consumption levels. As a general rule, national poverty lines tend to increase in purchasing power with the average level of income of a country. So the dollar-a-day line, while representative of poverty lines in very poor countries, underestimates the national poverty lines of richer countries, which may be set at the equivalent of two or three dollars-a-day or higher.

Source: Adapted from Ravallion (2002).

1c

Despite progress, millions remain in extreme poverty

	People living on less than $1 a day (millions)			Share of people living on less than $1 a day (%)		
	1990	**1999**	**2015**	**1990**	**1999**	**2015**
East Asia & Pacific	486	279	80	30.5	15.6	3.9
Excluding China	110	57	7	24.2	10.6	1.1
Europe & Central Asia	6	24	7	1.4	5.1	1.4
Latin America & Caribbean	48	57	47	11.0	11.1	7.5
Middle East & North Africa	5	6	8	2.1	2.2	2.1
South Asia	506	488	264	45.0	36.6	15.7
Sub-Saharan Africa	241	315	404	47.4	49.0	46.0
Total	**1,292**	**1,169**	**809**	**29.6**	**23.2**	**13.3**
Excluding China	917	945	735	28.5	25.0	15.7

Source: World Bank 2002d.

1d

And millions more live on less than $2 a day

	People living on less than $2 a day (millions)			Share of people living on less than $2 a day (%)		
	1990	**1999**	**2015**	**1990**	**1999**	**2015**
East Asia & Pacific	1,114	897	339	69.7	50.1	16.6
Excluding China	295	269	120	64.9	50.2	18.4
Europe & Central Asia	31	97	45	6.8	20.3	9.3
Latin America & Caribbean	121	132	117	27.6	26.0	18.9
Middle East & North Africa	50	68	62	21.0	23.3	16.0
South Asia	1,010	1,128	1,139	89.8	84.8	68.0
Sub-Saharan Africa	386	480	618	76.0	74.7	70.4
Total	**2,712**	**2,802**	**2,320**	**62.1**	**55.6**	**38.1**
Excluding China	1,892	2,173	2,101	58.7	57.5	44.7

Source: World Bank 2002d.

① ... and reduce hunger and malnutrition

The Millennium Development Goals also call for halving the proportion of people who suffer from hunger. Of the many ways to measure hunger, the goals refer to two: the prevalence of undernourishment in the general population and the prevalence of underweight children under five.

Undernourishment means consuming too little food to maintain normal levels of activity. The Food and Agriculture Organization (FAO) sets the average requirement at 1,900 calories a day. Among the less severely affected, the average daily shortfall is less than 200 calories a person. In the FAO's estimation, extreme hunger occurs with a shortfall of more than 300 calories, but the needs of individuals vary with age, sex, and height. Adding to the problems of undernourishment are diets that lack essential nutrients and illnesses that deplete those nutrients.

For 1998–2000 the FAO estimates that 799 million people, or 17 percent of the population in developing countries, were undernourished. This does not include the 30 million undernourished people in the transition economies of Eastern Europe and the former Soviet Union and the 11 million more in high-income countries. Since 1990–92 the number of undernourished people in developing countries has fallen by 20 million, and the prevalence of undernourishment by 3 percentage points. Regional trends show the greatest progress in East Asia and Pacific, but the rates of malnutrition remain high in South Asia, and they are rising in Sub-Saharan Africa.

Malnutrition among children is measured by comparing their weight and height with those of a well-nourished reference population. Such data must be obtained from surveys, which are costly and infrequently carried out. So it is difficult to assess progress toward the malnutrition target. A comparison of median malnutrition rates in 1990–95 and 1996–2001 shows small signs of progress in all regions except South Asia. But some large countries, such as Brazil, India, Pakistan, and the Russian Federation, are not included in the analysis. Coverage of countries in Africa, where donors have taken a greater interest in measuring child malnutrition, tends to be better than in other regions.

1e

Undernourishment is rising in Sub-Saharan Africa

Prevalence of undernourishment (% of population)

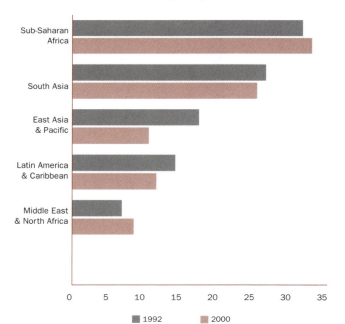

Source: FAO 2001, *The State of Food Insecurity in the World*. Rome.

1f

Child malnutrition remains highest in South Asia

Median child malnutrition rate (% of children under five)

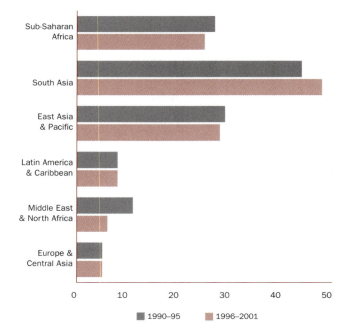

Source: World Health Organization and World Bank staff estimates.

② Achieve universal primary education

In 1990 the United Nations Conference on Education for All called for universal primary education. The original target date of 2000 has come and gone—and an estimated 115 million children remain out of school. In 2000 the Millennium Declaration resolved to ensure, by 2015, that all children would be able to complete a course of primary education. This target can be achieved—and it must be, if all developing countries are to compete in the global economy.

Progress toward the primary education target is commonly measured by the net enrollment ratio—the ratio of enrolled children of official school age to the number of children of the same age in the population. Net enrollment ratios at or near 100 percent imply that all children will receive a full primary education, though repetition may delay completion of their schooling. But lower ratios are ambiguous. They may show that schools fail to enroll all students in the first grade or that many students drop out in later grades. For example, Bangladesh has increased its enrollment ratio to 96 percent, but only 45 percent complete the final year of primary education.

The charts here show the primary school completion rate, the number of students successfully completing the last year of (or graduating from) primary school divided by the number of children of official graduation age in the population. This indicator directly measures progress toward the primary education target.

Three regions—East Asia and the Pacific, Europe and Central Asia, and Latin America and the Caribbean—are on track to achieving the goal. But three more, with 150 million primary-school-age children, are in danger of falling short. Sub-Saharan Africa lags farthest behind, with little progress since 1990. South Asia is the other region with chronically low enrollment and completion rates. Some countries have made large gains. Azerbaijan, Guinea, Haiti, and Malawi doubled their completion rates in the 1990s. Removing impediments and reducing costs can help boost enrollments. Malawi and Uganda lowered school fees but lost part of their gains when they could not provide spaces for all the new students. Many countries face the challenge of improving school quality while attracting and keeping more children in school.

1g

Education for all can be achieved, but sustained effort is required

Primary completion rate (% of relevant age group)

East Asia & Pacific; Europe & Central Asia; Latin America & the Caribbean; Middle East & North Africa; South Asia; Sub-Saharan Africa — primary completion rate charts

Goal: 1990, 2000, 2015. Primary completion rate: Actual, Path to goal

Source: World Bank staff estimates.

③ Promote gender equality and empower women

Gender disparities exist everywhere in the world. Women are underrepresented in local and national decisionmaking bodies. They earn less than men and are less likely to participate in wage employment. And in many low-income countries girls are less likely to attend school.

The Millennium Development Goals call for eliminating gender disparities in primary and secondary education by 2005 and at all levels of education by 2015. But all regions except Latin America are still short of the first target. The differences between boys' and girls' schooling are greatest in regions with the lowest primary school completion rates and lowest average incomes. In Sub-Saharan Africa the ratio of girls' to boys' enrollments in primary and secondary school has barely changed since 1990, and in 1998 it stood at 80 percent. In South Asia progress has been greater, but girls' enrollments reached only 78 percent of boys' in 1998.

The failure to enroll girls and keep them in school has long-term effects. In South Asia, where only 61 percent of girls complete primary school, the average woman has 3.4 years of schooling, almost 2.5 years less than a man. Even so, there has been remarkable progress in many countries over the past decade. Gender differences at the primary level have been eliminated or greatly reduced in Algeria, Angola, Bangladesh, China, the Arab Republic of Egypt, The Gambia, and India. In some countries girls' secondary school enrollments now exceed those of boys.

What does improving girls' enrollments require? Mainly overcoming the social and economic obstacles that stop parents from sending their daughters to school. Concerns about girls' safety and lack of suitable toilet facilities inhibit attendance. And for many poor families the economic value of girls' work at home exceeds the perceived returns to schooling. Improving the quality of schools is a first step. Overcoming women's disadvantages in the labor force and increasing their representation in public life will also help encourage girls to attend and stay in school.

Increasing opportunities for women will also contribute toward other goals for reducing poverty, educating children, improving health, and managing environmental resources. For example, there is strong evidence that the children of mothers with less education are more likely to be malnourished and have higher mortality rates—and that educated women make better decisions in seeking health care for themselves and their families.

1h

Recent estimates show more girls in school

Girls' enrollments in primary and secondary education as % of boys'

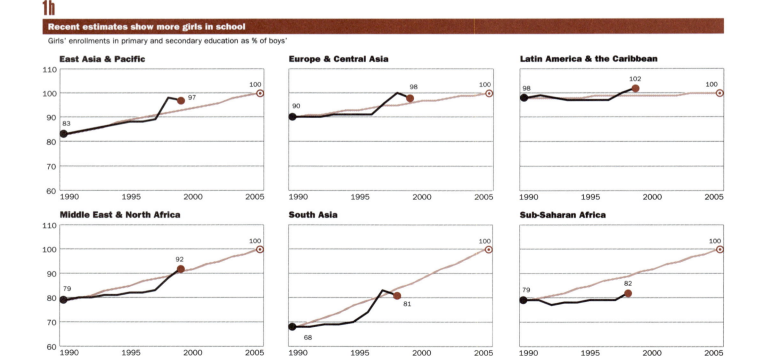

Note: A break in the series between 1997 and 1998, due to the change from the International Standard Classification of Education, 1976 (ISCED76), to ISCED97, may affect comparability over time.
Source: United Nations and UNESCO data.

④ Reduce child mortality

Rapid improvements before 1990 gave hope that mortality rates for infants and children under five could be cut by two-thirds in the following 25 years. But progress slowed almost everywhere in the 1990s. And no region, except possibly Latin America and the Caribbean, is on track to achieve that target. Progress has been particularly slow in Sub-Saharan Africa, where civil disturbances and the HIV/AIDS epidemic have driven up rates of infant and child mortality in several countries.

Child mortality is closely linked to poverty. In 2001 the average under-five mortality rate was 121 deaths per 1,000 live births in low-income countries, 41 in lower-middle-income countries, and 27 in upper-middle-income countries. In high-income countries the rate was less than 7. For 70 percent of the deaths before age five, the cause is a disease or a combination of diseases and malnutrition that would be preventable in a high-income country: acute respiratory infections, diarrhea, measles, and malaria.

Improvements in infant and child mortality have come slowly in low-income countries, where mortality rates have fallen by only 12 percent since 1990. Upper-middle-income countries have made the greatest improvement, reducing average mortality rates by 36 percent. But even this falls short of the rate needed to reach the target. Within countries there is evidence that improvements in child mortality have been greatest among the better off. In Bolivia, which is nearly on track to achieve the target, under-five mortality rates fell by 34 percent in the wealthiest quintile but by only 8 percent in the poorest. In Vietnam mortality rates also fell among the better off but scarcely changed for the poor. Trends such as these raise the possibility that without greater effort to ensure that health care and other public services reach the poor, success in reaching the Millennium Development Goals will make little difference for many of the poor.

Just as child deaths are the result of many causes, reducing child mortality will require multiple, complementary interventions. Raising incomes will help. So will increasing public spending on health services. But more is needed. Access to safe water, better sanitation facilities, and improvements in education, especially for girls and mothers, are closely linked to reduced mortality. Also needed are roads to improve access to health facilities and modern forms of energy to reduce dependence on traditional fuels, which cause damaging indoor air pollution.

1i

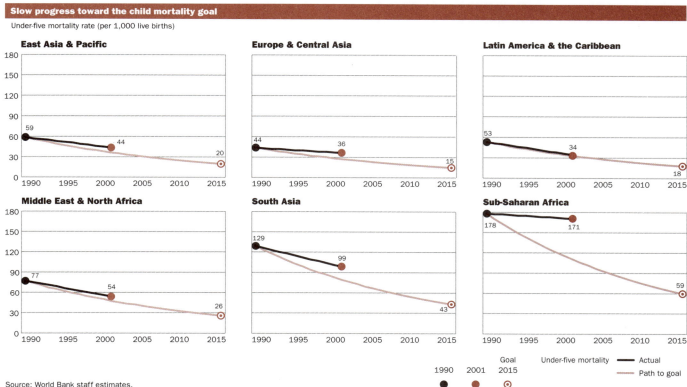

Slow progress toward the child mortality goal

Under-five mortality rate (per 1,000 live births)

Source: World Bank staff estimates.

⑤ Improve the health of mothers

The most recent global estimates of maternal mortality suggest that about 500,000 women died during pregnancy and childbirth in 2000, most of them in developing countries. What makes maternal mortality such a compelling problem is that it strikes young women undergoing what should be a normal process. The difference in outcomes is enormous between those who live in rich countries, where the average maternal mortality ratio is around 21 deaths per 100,000 live births—and those who live in poor countries, where the ratio may be as high as 1,000 deaths per 100,000 live births.

The Millennium Development Goals call for reducing the maternal mortality ratio by three-quarters between 1990 and 2015. For this to be possible, women need access to modern health services. The share of births attended by skilled health staff provides a good index of where the need is greatest. Only 58 percent of women in developing countries give birth with the assistance of a trained midwife or doctor. In Latin America, where the share of births attended by skilled health personnel is high, maternal mortality is relatively low. But in Africa, where skilled attendants and health facilities are not readily available, it is very high.

Maternal mortality is difficult to measure accurately. Deaths resulting from pregnancy or childbirth are relatively rare and may not be captured in general-purpose surveys or those with small sample sizes. Moreover, maternal deaths may be underreported in countries that lack good administrative statistics or where many births take place outside the formal health system.

Significant progress in reducing maternal mortality will require a comprehensive approach to health care: deaths in childbirth often involve complications, such as hemorrhaging, that require fully equipped medical facilities. Causes of complications during pregnancy and childbirth include inadequate nutrition, unsafe sex, and poor health care. Gender inequality in controlling household resources and making decisions also contributes to poor maternal health. Early childbearing and closely spaced pregnancies increase the risks for mothers and children. Access to family planning services helps women plan whether and when to have children.

1j

Skilled attendants reduce maternal deaths

Births attended by skilled health personnel (% of total)

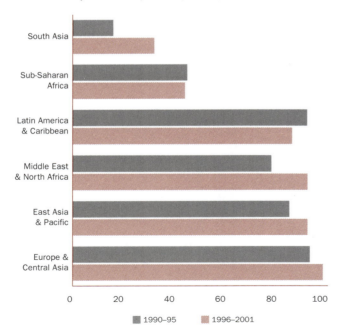

Source: World Health Organization and World Bank staff estimates.

1k

Young mothers at risk

Adolescent fertility rate (births per 1,000 women ages 15–19), 2000

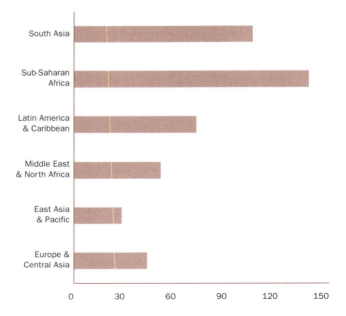

Source: World Bank staff estimates.

⑥ **Combat HIV/AIDS, malaria, and other diseases**

Epidemic diseases exact a huge toll in human suffering and lost opportunities for development. Poverty, civil disturbances, and natural disasters all contribute to, and are made worse by, the spread of diseases. In Africa the spread of HIV/AIDS has reversed decades of improvements in life expectancy and left millions of children orphaned. It is draining the supply of teachers and eroding the quality of education.

In 2002, 42 million adults and 5 million children were living with HIV/AIDS—more than 95 percent of them in developing countries and 70 percent in Sub-Saharan Africa. There were almost a million new cases in South and East Asia, where more than 7 million people are now living with HIV/AIDS. Current projections suggest that by 2010, 45 million more people in low- and middle-income countries will become infected unless the world mounts an effective campaign to halt the disease's spread.

Malaria is endemic in large parts of the developing world, particularly in tropical and subtropical regions. Because many cases of malaria are not clinically diagnosed or reported to official agencies, it is hard to gauge the full extent of the epidemic. The World Health Organization estimates that 300–500 million cases occur each year, leading to 1.1 million deaths (WHO 2002). Almost 90 percent of all cases occur in Sub-Saharan Africa, where children are the most affected and malaria may account for as much as 25 percent of child mortality. The emergence of drug-resistant strains of malaria has

increased the urgency of finding new and effective means of treatment and prevention.

Because children bear the greatest burden of the disease, the Millennium Development Goals call for a monitoring effort focusing on children under five. An effective means of preventing new infections is the use of insecticide-treated bed nets. Vietnam, where more than 25 percent of children sleep under treated bed nets, has made significant strides in controlling malaria. But in Africa, only 3 of 24 countries with survey data reported rates of bed net use greater than 5 percent.

Tuberculosis kills around 2 million people a year. The emergence of drug-resistant strains of tuberculosis, the spread of HIV/AIDS, which reduces resistance to tuberculosis, and the growing number of refugees and displaced persons have allowed the disease to spread. Each year there are about 8 million new cases—2 million in Sub-Saharan Africa, 3 million in Southeast Asia, and more than a quarter million in Eastern Europe and the former Soviet Union.

Poorly managed tuberculosis programs allow drug-resistant strains to spread. The World Health Organization has developed a treatment strategy—directly observed treatment, short course (DOTS)—that emphasizes positive diagnosis followed by an effective course of treatment and follow-up care. DOTS produces cure rates of up to 95 percent, even in poor countries. That is why the Millennium Development Goals include an indicator of the proportion of tuberculosis cases detected and cured under DOTS.

1l

No end in sight for the HIV/AIDS epidemic

Adults and children newly infected with HIV (millions), 2002

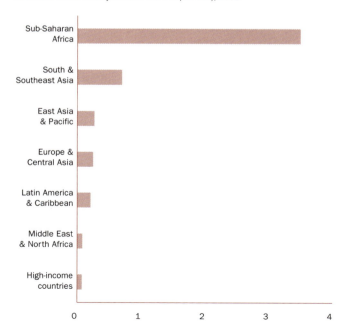

Note: UNAIDS regions differ from World Bank definitions.

Source: UNAIDS 2002.

1m

More global cooperation needed against tuberculosis

Incidence of tuberculosis (per 100,000 people), 2000

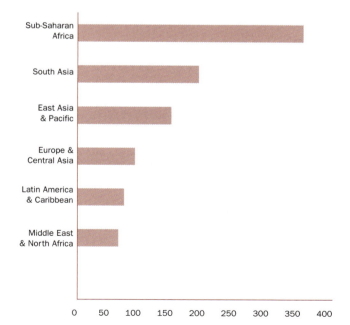

Source: WHO 2002, *World Health Report 2002*. Geneva.

⑦ Ensure environmental sustainability

Sustainable development can be ensured only by protecting the environment and using its resources wisely. The Millennium Development Goals draw attention to some of the environmental conditions that need to be closely monitored—changes in forest coverage and biological diversity, energy use and the emission of greenhouse gases, the plight of slum dwellers in rapidly growing cities, and the availability of adequate water and sanitation services. But the Millennium Development Goals cannot cover all aspects of the environment. Nor can they capture all the ways environmental factors interact with the other development goals.

Lack of clean water and basic sanitation is the main reason diseases transmitted by feces are so common in developing countries. In 1990 diarrhea led to 3 million deaths, 85 percent of them among children. Between 1990 and 2000 about 900 million people obtained access to improved water sources, gains just sufficient to keep pace with population growth.

An improved water source is any form of water collection or piping used to make water regularly available. It is not the same as "safe water," but there is no practical measure of whether water supplies are safe. Connecting all households to a reliable source of water that is reasonably protected from contamination would be an important step toward improving health and reducing the time spent collecting water.

Along with safe water sources, improved sanitation services and good hygiene practices are needed to reduce the risk of disease. A basic sanitation system provides disposal facilities that can effectively prevent human, animal, and insect contact with excreta. Such systems do not, however, ensure that effluents are treated to remove harmful substances before they are released into the environment.

In 2000, 1.2 billion people still lacked access to an improved water source, 40 percent of them in East Asia and Pacific and 25 percent in Sub-Saharan Africa. Meeting the Millennium Development Goals will require providing about 1.5 billion people with access to safe water and 2 billion with access to basic sanitation facilities between 2000 and 2015.

Rapid urbanization is exposing more people in developing countries to polluted air. Poor people, who live in crowded neighborhoods close to traffic corridors and industrial plants, are likely to suffer the most. Every year an estimated 0.5–1.0 million people die prematurely from respiratory and other illnesses associated with urban air pollution (World Bank 2002i). But not all sources of air pollution are outside the home. The use of traditional fuels for cooking and heating—wood, dung, charcoal, crop residues—is associated with blindness, chronic lung disease, complications during pregnancy, and acute respiratory infections in children.

Because poor people are often those most dependent on environmental resources for their livelihood, they are most affected by environmental degradation and by natural disasters, such as fires, storms, and earthquakes, whose effects are worsened by environmental mismanagement.

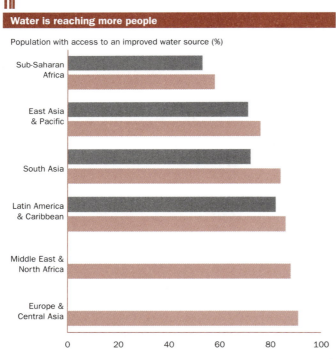

1n

Water is reaching more people

Population with access to an improved water source (%)

- Sub-Saharan Africa
- East Asia & Pacific
- South Asia
- Latin America & Caribbean
- Middle East & North Africa
- Europe & Central Asia

0 20 40 60 80 100

■ 1990 ■ 2000

Source: World Health Organization, UNICEF, and World Bank staff estimates.

1o

Many still lack access to sanitation

% of population with access to improved sanitation facilities

- Sub-Saharan Africa
- East Asia & Pacific
- South Asia
- Latin America & Caribbean
- Middle East & North Africa

0 20 40 60 80 100

■ 1990 ■ 2000

Source: World Health Organization.

⑧ Develop a global partnership for development

To achieve the Millennium Development Goals, economies need to grow to provide more jobs and more income for poor people. And growth requires investment in plants and equipment, in energy and transport systems, in human skills and knowledge. Growth is fastest in a good investment climate where good economic policies and good governance assure investors and workers of the rewards for their efforts.

But growth alone will not be enough to achieve the Millennium Development Goals. Also needed are health and education systems that deliver services to everyone, men and women, rich and poor. Infrastructure that works and is accessible to all. And policies that empower people to participate in the development process. While success depends on the actions of developing countries, which must direct their own development, there is also much that rich countries must do to help.

Goal 8 complements the first seven. It commits wealthy countries to work with developing countries to create an environment in which rapid, sustainable development is possible. It calls for an open, rule-based trading and financial system, more generous aid to countries committed to poverty reduction, and relief for the debt problems of developing countries. It draws attention to the problems of the least developed countries and of landlocked countries and small island developing states, which have greater difficulty competing in the global economy. And it calls for cooperation with the private sector to address youth unemployment, ensure access to affordable, essential drugs, and make available the benefits of new technologies.

- *Providing effective development assistance.* Aid is most effective in reducing poverty when it goes to poor countries with good economic policies and sound governance and advances country-owned poverty reduction programs. Aid levels have been falling, both in comparison with the size of donor country economies and in nominal terms. In 2001 only 56 percent of all aid went to low-income economies with per capita income of $745 or less. To help the poorest countries reach the Millennium Development Goals, official development assistance will need to double from its current level of $52 billion a year and developing counties will have to supply several times more than that.
- *Easing the burden of debt.* The Debt Initiative for Heavily Indebted Poor Countries (HIPCs) provides debt relief to the world's poorest and most heavily indebted countries. By November 2002, 26 countries had qualified for debt relief amounting to about $40 billion. The savings in debt service have allowed average annual social spending in these countries to rise from 6 percent of GDP to 8 percent.
- *Increasing market access.* Tariffs and quotas on textile exports to high-income countries cost developing countries 27 million jobs. And rich countries' agricultural subsidies, more than $300 billion a year in 2001, hurt growth in the agricultural sector, where many of the poorest people work. The World Bank estimates that full liberalization of trade could increase growth enough to lift 300 million more people out of poverty by 2015.

1p
Aid to the poorest countries has increased

Aid to low- and middle-income economies (2000 $ billions)

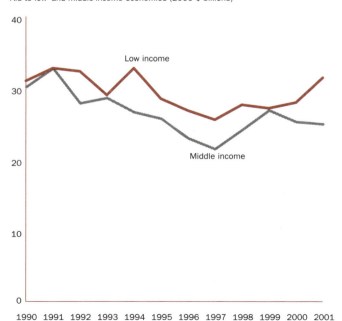

Source: OECD, Development Assistance Committee data.

1q
HIPCs have improved debt service ratios

Ratio of debt service to exports for heavily indebted poor countries (%)

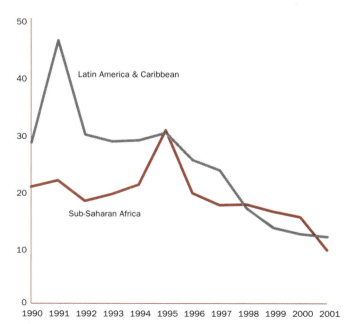

Source: World Bank staff estimates.

Size of the economy

	Population	Surface area	Population density	Gross national income		Gross national income per capita		PPP gross national income [a]			Gross domestic product	
									Per capita			Per capita
	millions	thousand sq. km	people per sq. km	$ billions	Rank	$	Rank	$ billions	$	Rank	% growth	% growth
	2001	2001	2001	2001 [b]	2001	2001 [b]	2001	2001	2001	2001	2000–01	2000–01
Afghanistan	27 [c]	652	42	..	..	.. [d]	..	..	..	..	..	..
Albania	3	29	115	4.2	119	1,340	123	12	3,810	130	6.5	5.5
Algeria	31	2,382	13	51.0	48	1,650	114	182 [e]	5,910 [e]	99	2.1	0.6
Angola	14	1,247	11	6.7	102	500	158	23 [e]	1,690 [e]	171	3.2	0.3
Argentina	37	2,780	14	260.3	17	6,940	60	412	10,980	63	–4.5	–5.6
Armenia	4	30	135	2.2	143	570	154	10	2,730	145	9.6	9.4
Australia	19	7,741	3	385.9	15	19,900	29	478	24,630	24	3.9	2.8
Austria	8	84	98	194.7	21	23,940	17	215	26,380	17	1.0	0.8
Azerbaijan	8	87	94	5.3	111	650	146	23	2,890	141	9.9	9.0
Bangladesh	133	144	1,024	48.6	51	360	172	213	1,600	173	5.3	3.5
Belarus	10	208	48	12.9	81	1,290	126	76	7,630	83	4.1	4.5
Belgium	10	31	313	245.3	19	23,850	18	269	26,150	18	1.0	0.7
Benin	6	113	58	2.4	142	380	169	6	970	190	5.0	2.3
Bolivia	9	1,099	8	8.1	96	950	134	19	2,240	155	1.2	–1.0
Bosnia and Herzegovina	4	51	80	5.0	114	1,240	127	25	6,250	92	6.0	3.8
Botswana	2	582	3	5.3	112	3,100	89	13	7,410	84	6.3	5.1
Brazil	172	8,547	20	528.9	11	3,070	90	1,219	7,070	86	1.5	0.2
Bulgaria	8	111	73	13.2	79	1,650	114	54	6,740	89	4.0	5.9
Burkina Faso	12	274	42	2.5	141	220	192	13 [e]	1,120 [e]	185	5.6	3.1
Burundi	7	28	270	0.7	178	100	206	5 [e]	680 [e]	203	3.2	1.3
Cambodia	12	181	69	3.3	131	270	184	22	1,790	168	6.3	4.2
Cameroon	15	475	33	8.7	91	580	152	24	1,580	174	5.3	3.1
Canada	31	9,971	3	681.6	8	21,930	25	825 [e]	26,530 [e]	15	1.5	0.4
Central African Republic	4	623	6	1.0	170	260	187	5 [e]	1,300 [e]	181	1.5	0.1
Chad	8	1,284	6	1.6	154	200	195	8	1,060	187	8.5	5.5
Chile	15	757	21	70.6	43	4,590	73	136	8,840	76	2.8	1.5
China	1,272	9,598 [f]	136	1,131.2	6	890	138	5,027	3,950	127	7.3	6.5
Hong Kong, China	7	..	..	170.3	23	25,330	13	172	25,560	19	0.1	–0.7
Colombia	43	1,139	41	81.6	40	1,890	106	292	6,790	88	1.4	–0.3
Congo, Dem. Rep.	52	2,345	23	4.2	122	80	208	33	630	205	–4.5	–7.1
Congo, Rep.	3	342	9	2.0	146	640	147	2	680	203	2.9	0.1
Costa Rica	4	51	76	15.7	74	4,060	76	36	9,260	74	0.9	–0.7
Côte d'Ivoire	16	322	52	10.3	85	630	149	23	1,400	179	–0.9	–3.3
Croatia	4	57	78	19.9	64	4,550	74	39	8,930	75	4.1	4.1
Cuba	11	111	102	..	..	.. [g]	..	..	..	..	..	..
Czech Republic	10	79	132	54.3	45	5,310	70	146	14,320	55	3.3	3.8
Denmark	5	43	126	164.0	25	30,600	8	153	28,490	9	1.0	0.6
Dominican Republic	9	49	176	19.0	68	2,230	96	57	6,650	90	2.7	1.1
Ecuador	13	284	47	14.0	77	1,080	129	38	2,960	140	5.6	3.7
Egypt, Arab Rep.	65	1,001	65	99.6	37	1,530	116	232	3,560	131	2.9	1.0
El Salvador	6	21	309	13.0	80	2,040	101	33	5,160	107	1.8	–0.1
Eritrea	4	118	42	0.7	179	160	199	4	1,030	189	9.7	6.9
Estonia	1	45	32	5.3	110	3,870	79	13	9,650	71	5.0	5.5
Ethiopia	66	1,104	66	6.7	103	100	206	53	800	198	7.7	5.2
Finland	5	338	17	123.4	29	23,780	19	125	24,030	28	0.7	0.4
France	59	552	108	1,380.7 [h]	5	22,730 [h]	23	1,425	24,080	27	1.8	1.3
Gabon	1	268	5	4.0	125	3,160	88	7	5,190	105	2.5	0.0
Gambia, The	1	11	134	0.4	191	320	176	3 [e]	2,010 [e]	160	6.0	3.0
Georgia	5	70	76	3.1	136	590	150	14	2,580	148	4.5	6.2
Germany	82	357	231	1,939.6	3	23,560	20	2,078	25,240	21	0.6	0.4
Ghana	20	239	87	5.7	109	290	179	43 [e]	2,170 [e]	157	4.0	1.9
Greece	11	132	82	121.0	31	11,430	47	186	17,520	47	4.1	3.8
Guatemala	12	109	108	19.6	65	1,680	112	51	4,380	120	2.1	–0.5
Guinea	8	246	31	3.1	135	410	165	14	1,900	164	3.6	1.3
Guinea-Bissau	1	36	44	0.2	203	160	199	1	890	193	0.2	–2.0
Haiti	8	28	295	3.9	126	480	160	15 [e]	1,870 [e]	166	–1.7	–3.8

	Population	Surface area	Population density	Gross national income		Gross national income per capita		PPP gross national income [a]			Gross domestic product	
									Per capita			Per capita
	millions	thousand sq. km	people per sq. km	$ billions	Rank	$	Rank	$ billions	$	Rank	% growth	% growth
	2001	2001	2001	2001 [b]	2001	2001 [b]	2001	2001	2001	2001	2000–01	2000–01
Honduras	7	112	59	5.9	106	900	137	18	2,760	144	2.6	0.0
Hungary	10	93	110	49.2	50	4,830	71	122	11,990	59	3.8	3.1
India	1,032	3,287	347	477.4	12	460	162	2,913	2,820	143	5.4	3.7
Indonesia	209	1,905	115	144.7	28	690	145	591	2,830	142	3.3	2.0
Iran, Islamic Rep.	65	1,648	39	108.7	35	1,680	112	383	5,940	98	4.8	3.4
Iraq	24	438	54	..		.. [g]	..	..	..	..	..	..
Ireland	4	70	56	87.7	39	22,850	22	104	27,170	14	5.8	4.6
Israel	6	21	309	106.6	36	16,750	35	125	19,630	40	–0.9	–2.9
Italy	58	301	197	1,123.8	7	19,390	30	1,422	24,530	25	1.8	1.3
Jamaica	3	11	239	7.3	100	2,800	93	9	3,490	133	1.7	1.1
Japan	127	378	349	4,523.3	2	35,610	5	3,246	25,550	20	–0.6	–0.7
Jordan	5	89	57	8.8	90	1,750	108	20	3,880	128	4.2	1.2
Kazakhstan	15	2,725	6	20.1	62	1,350	120	92	6,150	94	13.2	14.4
Kenya	31	580	54	10.7	84	350	174	30	970	190	1.1	–1.0
Korea, Dem. Rep.	22	121	186	..		.. [d]	..	..	..	..	..	..
Korea, Rep.	47	99	480	447.6	13	9,460	54	713	15,060	54	3.0	2.3
Kuwait	2	18	115	37.4	54	18,270	31	44	21,530	35	–1.0	–3.9
Kyrgyz Republic	5	200	26	1.4	158	280	182	13	2,630	147	5.3	4.5
Lao PDR	5	237	23	1.6	153	300	178	8 [e]	1,540 [e]	175	5.7	3.3
Latvia	2	65	38	7.6	98	3,230	86	18	7,760	82	7.6	8.2
Lebanon	4	10	429	17.6	69	4,010	77	19	4,400	119	1.3	0.0
Lesotho	2	30	68	1.1	166	530	156	6 [e]	2,980 [e]	139	4.0	2.6
Liberia	3	111	33	0.5	190	140	203	..	..	196	5.3	2.6
Libya	5	1,760	3	..	..	.. [i]	..	..	..	..	..	..
Lithuania	3	65	54	11.7	82	3,350	83	29	8,350	78	5.9	6.6
Macedonia, FYR	2	26	80	3.5	130	1,690	111	12	6,040	97	–4.1	–4.7
Madagascar	16	587	27	4.2	120	260	187	13	820	197	6.0	3.0
Malawi	11	118	112	1.7	151	160	199	6	560	206	–1.5	–3.5
Malaysia	24	330	72	79.3	42	3,330	84	188	7,910	81	0.4	–1.9
Mali	11	1,240	9	2.5	139	230	191	9	770	200	1.4	–0.9
Mauritania	3	1,026	3	1.0	169	360	172	5	1,940	162	4.6	1.4
Mauritius	1	2	591	4.6	117	3,830	80	12	9,860	70	7.2	6.0
Mexico	99	1,958	52	550.2	10	5,530	69	820	8,240	80	–0.3	–1.8
Moldova	4	34	130	1.5	156	400	167	10	2,300	154	6.1	6.3
Mongolia	2	1,567	2	1.0	172	400	167	4	1,710	170	1.4	0.4
Morocco	29	447	65	34.7	57	1,190	128	102	3,500	132	6.5	4.8
Mozambique	18	802	23	3.8	127	210	194	19 [e]	1,050 [e]	188	13.9	11.5
Myanmar	48	677	73	..		.. [d]	..	..	..	..	..	..
Namibia	2	824	2	3.5	129	1,960	104	13 [e]	7,410 [e]	85	2.7	0.7
Nepal	24	147	165	5.8	108	250	190	32	1,360	180	4.8	2.4
Netherlands	16	42	473	390.3	14	24,330	16	439	27,390	13	1.1	0.4
New Zealand	4	271	14	51.0	49	13,250	44	70	18,250	43	3.2	2.7
Nicaragua	5	130	43	..	148	..	171	..	..	158	..	..
Niger	11	1,267	9	2.0	147	180	197	10 [e]	880 [e]	194	7.6	4.2
Nigeria	130	924	143	37.1	55	290	179	102	790	199	3.9	1.5
Norway	5	324	15	160.8	27	35,630	4	132	29,340	7	1.4	0.9
Oman	2	310	8	..	..	.. [i]	..	..	..	..	..	..
Pakistan	141	796	183	60.0	44	420	164	263	1,860	167	2.7	0.3
Panama	3	76	39	9.5	87	3,260	85	16 [e]	5,440 [e]	104	0.3	–1.2
Papua New Guinea	5	463	12	3.0	137	580	152	13 [e]	2,450 [e]	149	–3.5	–5.8
Paraguay	6	407	14	7.6	99	1,350	120	29 [e]	5,180 [e]	106	2.7	0.2
Peru	26	1,285	21	52.2	47	1,980	103	118	4,470	117	0.2	–1.3
Philippines	78	300	263	80.8	41	1,030	132	319	4,070	125	3.4	1.2
Poland	39	323	127	163.6	26	4,230	75	362	9,370	73	1.0	1.0
Portugal	10	92	110	109.3	34	10,900	51	178	17,710	46	1.7	1.5
Puerto Rico	4	9	433	42.1	52	10,950 [j]	50	69	18,090	44	5.6	4.9

1.1 Size of the economy

	Population	Surface area	Population density	Gross national income		Gross national income per capita		PPP gross national income[a]			Gross domestic product	
									Per capita			Per capita
	millions	thousand sq. km	people per sq. km	$ billions	Rank	$	Rank	$ billions	$	Rank	% growth	% growth
	2001	2001	2001	2001[b]	2001	2001[b]	2001	2001	2001	2001	2000–01	2000–01
Romania	22	238	97	38.6	53	1,720	110	130	5,780	101	5.3	5.4
Russian Federation	145	17,075	9	253.4	18	1,750	108	995	6,880	87	5.0	5.6
Rwanda	9	26	352	1.9	149	220	192	11	1,240	183	6.7	4.5
Saudi Arabia	21	2,150	10	181.1	22	8,460	57	284	13,290	56	1.2	–2.0
Senegal	10	197	51	4.7	115	490	159	14	1,480	176	5.7	3.2
Sierra Leone	5	72	72	0.7	177	140	203	2	460	208	5.4	3.3
Singapore	4	1	6,772	88.8	38	21,500	26	94	22,850	32	–2.0	–4.7
Slovak Republic	5	49	112	20.3	61	3,760	81	64	11,780	60	3.3	3.2
Slovenia	2	20	99	19.4	66	9,760	52	34	17,060	49	3.0	2.8
Somalia	9	638	14	..	..	..[d]	..	..	..	..	..	..
South Africa	43	1,221	35	121.9	30	2,820	92	472[e]	10,910[e]	64	2.2	1.2
Spain	41	506	82	588.0	9	14,300	41	816	19,860	39	2.8	1.2
Sri Lanka	19	66	290	16.4	73	880	140	61	3,260	134	–1.4	–2.8
Sudan	32	2,506	13	10.7	83	340	175	56	1,750	169	6.9	4.9
Swaziland	1	17	62	1.4	157	1,300	125	5	4,430	118	1.6	–0.6
Sweden	9	450	22	225.9	20	25,400	12	212	23,800	29	1.2	0.9
Switzerland	7	41	183	277.2	16	38,330	3	224	30,970	5	1.3	0.6
Syrian Arab Republic	17	185	90	17.3	71	1,040	131	52	3,160	136	2.8	0.3
Tajikistan	6	143	44	1.1	165	180	197	7	1,140	184	10.2	9.3
Tanzania	34	945	39	9.4[k]	88	270[k]	184	18	520	207	5.7	3.4
Thailand	61	513	120	118.5	32	1,940	105	381	6,230	93	1.8	1.0
Togo	5	57	86	1.3	159	270	184	8	1,620	172	2.7	–0.1
Trinidad and Tobago	1	5	255	7.8	97	5,960	66	11	8,620	77	5.0	4.3
Tunisia	10	164	62	20.0	63	2,070	100	59	6,090	96	4.9	3.7
Turkey	66	775	86	167.3	24	2,530	95	386	5,830	100	–7.4	–8.7
Turkmenistan	5	488	12	5.1	113	950	134	23	4,240	124	20.5	17.2
Uganda	23	241	116	5.9	107	260	187	33[e]	1,460[e]	177	4.6	2.0
Ukraine	49	604	85	35.2	56	720	143	210	4,270	123	9.1	10.0
United Arab Emirates	3	84	36	..	..	..[l]	..	..	..	..	..	..
United Kingdom	59	243	244	1,476.8	4	25,120	14	1,431	24,340	26	2.2	2.1
United States	285	9,629	31	9,780.8	1	34,280	7	9,781	34,280	3	0.3	–0.8
Uruguay	3	176	19	19.2	67	5,710	68	28	8,250	79	–3.1	–3.8
Uzbekistan	25	447	61	13.8	78	550	155	60	2,410	152	4.5	3.2
Venezuela, RB	25	912	28	117.2	33	4,760	72	138	5,590	102	2.7	0.7
Vietnam	80	332	244	32.8	58	410	165	164	2,070	159	6.8	5.5
West Bank and Gaza	3	..	..	4.2	121	1,350	120	..	..	129	–11.9	–15.4
Yemen, Rep.	18	528	34	8.2	93	450	163	13	730	202	3.1	0.0
Yugoslavia, Fed. Rep.	11	102	108	9.9	86	930	136	..	..	..	..	..
Zambia	10	753	14	3.3	132	320	176	8	750	201	4.9	2.9
Zimbabwe	13	391	33	6.2	105	480	160	28	2,220	156	–8.4	–9.8
World	6,130 s	133,883 s	47 w	31,400 t		5,120 w		45,183 t	7,370 w		1.1 w	–0.2 w
Low income	2,506	34,246	76	1,069		430		5,494	2,190		4.7	2.8
Middle income	2,667	67,224	40	4,957		1,860		14,373	5,390		2.5	1.6
Lower middle income	2,164	45,811	48	2,672		1,230		10,178	4,700		4.1	3.2
Upper middle income	504	21,413	24	2,291		4,550		4,282	8,500		0.7	–0.6
Low & middle income	5,172	101,470	52	6,025		1,160		19,823	3,830		2.9	1.5
East Asia & Pacific	1,823	16,301	115	1,640		900		6,899	3,790		5.5	4.5
Europe & Central Asia	475	24,168	20	935		1,970		2,998	6,320		2.3	2.3
Latin America & Carib.	524	20,460	26	1,876		3,580		3,613	6,900		0.4	–1.1
Middle East & N. Africa	301	11,135	27	669		2,220		1,631	5,430		3.0	1.0
South Asia	1,378	5,140	288	618		450		3,535	2,570		4.9	3.1
Sub-Saharan Africa	674	24,267	29	311		460		1,178	1,750		2.9	0.7
High income	957	32,414	31	25,372		26,510		25,506	26,650		0.7	0.0
Europe EMU	307	2,569	121	6,339		20,670		7,298	23,800		1.4	0.9

a. PPP is purchasing power parity; see *Definitions*. b. Calculated using the World Bank Atlas method. c. Estimate does not account for recent refugee flows. d. Estimated to be low income ($745 or less). e. The estimate is based on regression; others are extrapolated from the latest International Comparison Programme benchmark estimates. f. Includes Taiwan, China; Macao, China; and Hong Kong, China. g. Estimated to be lower middle income ($746–$2,975). h. GNI and GNI per capita estimates include the French overseas departments of French Guiana, Guadeloupe, Martinique, and Réunion. i. Estimated to be upper middle income ($2,976–$9,205). j. Included in the aggregates for upper-middle-income economies on the basis of earlier data. k. Data refer to mainland Tanzania only. l. Estimated to be high income ($9,206 or more).

About the data

Population, land area, income, and output are basic measures of the size of an economy. They also provide a broad indication of actual and potential resources. Population, land area, income—as measured by gross national income (GNI)—and output—as measured by gross domestic product (GDP)—are therefore used throughout the *World Development Indicators* to normalize other indicators.

Population estimates are generally based on extrapolations from the most recent national census. For further discussion of the measurement of population and population growth, see *About the data* for table 2.1 and *Statistical methods*.

The surface area of a country or economy includes inland bodies of water and some coastal waterways. Surface area thus differs from land area, which excludes bodies of water, and from gross area, which may include offshore territorial waters. Land area is particularly important for understanding the agricultural capacity of an economy and the effects of human activity on the environment. (For measures of land area and data on rural population density, land use, and agricultural productivity, see tables 3.1–3.3.) Recent innovations in satellite mapping techniques and computer databases have resulted in more precise measurements of land and water areas.

GNI (gross national product, or GNP, in the terminology of the 1968 United Nations System of National Accounts) measures the total domestic and foreign value added claimed by residents. GNI comprises GDP plus net receipts of primary income (compensation of employees and property income) from nonresident sources.

The World Bank uses GNI per capita in U.S. dollars to classify countries for analytical purposes and to determine borrowing eligibility. See the *Users guide* for definitions of the income groups used in the *World Development Indicators*. For further discussion of the usefulness of national income as a measure of productivity or welfare, see *About the data* for tables 4.1 and 4.2.

When calculating GNI in U.S. dollars from GNI reported in national currencies, the World Bank follows its Atlas conversion method. This involves using a three-year average of exchange rates to smooth the effects of transitory exchange rate fluctuations. (For further discussion of the Atlas method, see *Statistical methods*.) Note that growth rates are calculated from data in constant prices and national currency units, not from the Atlas estimates.

Because exchange rates do not always reflect international differences in relative prices, this table also shows GNI and GNI per capita estimates converted into international dollars using purchasing power parity (PPP) rates. PPP rates provide a standard measure allowing comparison of real price levels between countries, just as conventional price indexes allow comparison of real values over time. The PPP conversion factors used here are derived from price surveys covering 118 countries conducted by the International Comparison Programme. For Organisation for Economic Co-operation and Development countries data come from the most recent round of surveys, completed in 1999; the rest are either from the 1996 survey, or data from the 1993 or earlier round, which have been extrapolated to the 1996 benchmark. Estimates for countries not included in the surveys are derived from statistical models using available data.

All economies shown in the *World Development Indicators* are ranked by size, including those that appear in table 1.6. Ranks are shown only in table 1.1. (The *World Bank Atlas* includes a table comparing the GNI per capita rankings based on the Atlas method with those based on the PPP method for all economies with available data.) No rank is shown for economies for which numerical estimates of GNI per capita are not published. Economies with missing data are included in the ranking process at their approximate level, so that the relative order of other economies remains consistent. Where available, rankings for small economies are shown in the *World Bank Atlas*.

Growth in GDP and growth in GDP per capita are based on GDP measured in constant prices. Growth in GDP is considered a broad measure of the growth of an economy, as GDP in constant prices can be estimated by measuring the total quantity of goods and services produced in a period, valuing them at an agreed set of base year prices, and subtracting the cost of intermediate inputs, also in constant prices. For further discussion of the measurement of economic growth, see *About the data* for table 4.1.

Definitions

• **Population** is based on the de facto definition of population, which counts all residents regardless of legal status or citizenship—except for refugees not permanently settled in the country of asylum, who are generally considered part of the population of their country of origin. The values shown are midyear estimates for 2001. See also table 2.1. • **Surface area** is a country's total area, including areas under inland bodies of water and some coastal waterways. • **Population density** is midyear population divided by land area in square kilometers. • **Gross national income** (GNI) is the sum of value added by all resident producers plus any product taxes (less subsidies) not included in the valuation of output plus net receipts of primary income (compensation of employees and property income) from abroad. Data are in current U.S. dollars converted using the World Bank Atlas method (see *Statistical methods*). • **GNI per capita** is gross national income divided by midyear population. GNI per capita in U.S. dollars is converted using the World Bank Atlas method. • **PPP GNI** is gross national income converted to international dollars using purchasing power parity rates. An international dollar has the same purchasing power over GNI as a U.S. dollar has in the United States. • **Gross domestic product** (GDP) is the sum of value added by all resident producers plus any product taxes (less subsidies) not included in the valuation of output. Growth is calculated from constant price GDP data in local currency. • **GDP per capita** is gross domestic product divided by midyear population.

Data sources

Population estimates are prepared by World Bank staff from a variety of sources (see *Data sources* for table 2.1). The data on surface and land area are from the Food and Agriculture Organization (see *Data sources* for table 3.1). GNI, GNI per capita, GDP growth, and GDP per capita growth are estimated by World Bank staff based on national accounts data collected by Bank staff during economic missions or reported by national statistical offices to other international organizations such as the Organisation for Economic Co-operation and Development. Purchasing power parity conversion factors are estimates by World Bank staff based on data collected by the International Comparison Program.

	Eradicate extreme poverty and hunger		Achieve universal primary education		Promote gender equality		Reduce child mortality		Improve maternal health		
	Share of poorest quintile in national income or consumption [a] %	Prevalence of child malnutrition % of children under 5	Primary completion rate %		Ratio of female to male enrollments in primary and secondary school [c, d] %		Under-five mortality rate per 1,000		Maternal mortality ratio per 100,000 live births Modeled estimates	Births attended by skilled health staff % of total	
	1987–2001 [b]	1990	2001	1990	2001	1990	2000	1990	2001	1995	1990	2000
Afghanistan	..	..	..	22	8	50	..	260	257	..	9	..
Albania	..	..	14	101	..	90	102	42	25	31	..	99
Algeria	7.0	9	6	82	..	80	98	69	49	150	77	92
Angola	..	20	..	..	28	..	84	260	260	1,300	17	..
Argentina	..	..	..	..	96	..	103	28	19	85	..	98
Armenia	6.7	..	3	..	..	..	106	58	35	29	..	97
Australia	5.9	..	..	..	..	96	100	10	6	6	100	100
Austria	7.0	..	..	..	..	90	97	9	5	11	..	..
Azerbaijan	7.4	..	17	47	100	94	101	106	96	37	..	88
Bangladesh	9.0	66	48	50	70	72	103	144	77	600	7	12
Belarus	8.4	..	..	97	..	..	101	21	20	33	..	..
Belgium	8.3	..	..	..	..	97	106	9	6	8	..	..
Benin	..	..	23	23	39	..	62	185	158	880	38	..
Bolivia	4.0	11	8	55	72	89	97	122	77	550	43	59
Bosnia and Herzegovina	..	..	4	..	88	..	..	22	18	15	..	100
Botswana	2.2	..	13	114	..	107	102	58	110	480	79	99
Brazil	2.0	7	..	48	71	..	103	60	36	260	..	..
Bulgaria	6.7	..	..	90	..	94	97	19	16	23	..	99
Burkina Faso	4.5	..	34	19	25	61	70	210	197	1,400	30	27
Burundi	5.1	..	45	46	43	82	79	190	190	1,900	20	25
Cambodia	6.9	..	45	71	70	..	83	115	138	590	47	34
Cameroon	4.6	15	22	57	43	82	81	139	155	720	58	56
Canada	7.3	..	..	..	..	94	101	8	7	6	..	..
Central African Republic	2.0	..	..	28	19	61	..	180	180	1,200	66	44
Chad	..	..	28	19	19	..	56	203	200	1,500	15	16
Chile	3.2	..	1	94	99	98	88	19	12	33	..	..
China	5.9	17	10	99	..	81	98	49	39	60	..	..
Hong Kong, China	5.3	..	..	..	..	..	..	..	..	..	100	100
Colombia	1.4	10	7	72	85	104	104	36	23	120	94	86
Congo, Dem. Rep.	..	..	..	48	40	69	80	205	205	940	..	70
Congo, Rep.	..	..	..	61	44	88	89	110	108	1,100	..	..
Costa Rica	2.6	3	..	73	89	96	101	17	11	35	97	98
Côte d'Ivoire	7.1	..	21	44	40	..	71	155	175	1,200	50	47
Croatia	8.3	..	..	86	..	97	..	13	8	18	..	..
Cuba	..	..	..	..	..	101	100	13	9	24	..	100
Czech Republic	10.3	1	..	89	..	94	101	12	5	14	..	..
Denmark	8.3	..	..	..	..	96	103	9	4	15	..	..
Dominican Republic	5.1	10	5	..	82	..	106	65	47	110	92	..
Ecuador	3.3	..	14	99	96	97	100	57	30	210	56	69
Egypt, Arab Rep.	8.6	10	4	77	..	78	94	104	41	170	37	61
El Salvador	3.3	15	12	61	80	100	98	60	39	180	90	90
Eritrea	..	..	..	22	35	82	77	155	111	1,100	..	..
Estonia	7.0	..	..	93	..	99	99	17	12	80	..	..
Ethiopia	2.4	48	47	22	24	68	68	193	172	1,800	8	10
Finland	10.1	..	..	..	..	105	106	7	5	6	..	..
France	7.2	..	..	..	..	98	100	10	6	20	..	..
Gabon	..	..	12	71	..	..	98	90	90	620	79	86
Gambia, The	4.0	..	17	40	70	64	85	154	126	1,100	44	51
Georgia	6.0	..	3	..	90	94	102	29	29	22	..	96
Germany	5.7	..	..	..	..	94	99	9	5	12	..	..
Ghana	5.6	30	25	63	64	..	88	126	100	590	55	44
Greece	7.1	..	..	..	..	93	101	11	5	2	..	..
Guatemala	2.6	..	24	43	52	..	92	82	58	270	30	41
Guinea	6.4	..	33	16	34	43	57	240	169	1,200	31	35
Guinea-Bissau	5.2	..	25	16	31	..	65	253	211	910	..	35
Haiti	..	27	17	28	70	..	..	150	123	1,100	78	24

Millennium Development Goals: eradicating poverty and improving lives

	Eradicate extreme poverty and hunger			Achieve universal primary education		Promote gender equality		Reduce child mortality		Improve maternal health		
	Share of poorest quintile in national income or consumption [a] %	Prevalence of child malnutrition % of children under 5		Primary completion rate %		Ratio of female to male enrollments in primary and secondary school [c, d] %		Under-five mortality rate per 1,000		Maternal mortality ratio per 100,000 live births Modeled estimates	Births attended by skilled health staff % of total	
	1987–2001 [b]	1990	2001	1990	2001	1990	2000	1990	2001	1995	1990	2000
Honduras	2.0	18	17	66	67	103	..	61	38	220	47	..
Hungary	10.0	2	..	93	..	96	100	17	9	23	..	..
India	8.1	64	..	70	76	68	78	123	93	440	44	42
Indonesia	8.4	..	25	92	91	91	98	91	45	470	47	56
Iran, Islamic Rep.	5.1	..	11	94	..	80	95	72	42	130	78	..
Iraq	..	12	..	63	..	75	77	50	133	370	50	..
Ireland	6.7	..	..	..	..	99	..	9	6	9	..	..
Israel	6.9	..	..	..	..	99	100	12	6	8	..	..
Italy	6.0	..	..	..	..	95	98	10	6	11	..	..
Jamaica	6.7	5	4	90	94	97	101	20	20	120	92	95
Japan	10.6	..	..	..	..	96	101	6	5	12	100	..
Jordan	7.6	6	..	102	104	93	101	43	33	41	87	..
Kazakhstan	8.2	..	4	..	..	..	98	52	99	80	..	98
Kenya	5.6	..	22	87	63	..	97	97	122	1,300	50	44
Korea, Dem. Rep.	..	..	28	..	..	..	..	55	55	35	..	..
Korea, Rep.	7.9	..	..	96	96	93	100	9	5	20	95	..
Kuwait	..	..	..	56	..	97	101	16	10	25	..	..
Kyrgyz Republic	9.1	..	..	..	100	100	99	81	61	80	..	98
Lao PDR	7.6	..	40	44	69	75	82	163	100	650	..	21
Latvia	7.6	..	..	76	..	96	101	18	21	70	..	..
Lebanon	..	..	..	..	..	..	102	37	32	130	95	95
Lesotho	1.4	16	18	75	68	124	107	148	132	530	40	60
Liberia	..	..	..	..	..	..	70	235	235	..	..	..
Libya	..	..	..	..	..	..	103	42	19	120	76	..
Lithuania	7.9	..	..	88	..	93	99	14	9	27	..	..
Macedonia, FYR	8.4	..	6	89	..	94	98	33	26	17	88	..
Madagascar	6.4	41	..	34	26	..	97	168	136	580	57	47
Malawi	4.9	28	25	33	64	79	94	241	183	580	50	56
Malaysia	4.4	25	..	91	..	98	105	21	8	39	..	96
Mali	4.6	..	..	11	23	57	66	254	231	630	..	..
Mauritania	6.4	48	32	34	46	67	93	183	183	870	40	57
Mauritius	..	..	..	136	..	98	97	25	19	45	92	..
Mexico	3.4	17	8	89	100	96	101	46	29	65	..	..
Moldova	7.1	..	..	67	79	103	102	37	32	65	..	..
Mongolia	5.6	12	13	..	82	107	112	107	76	65	100	97
Morocco	6.5	10	..	47	..	67	83	85	44	390	31	..
Mozambique	6.5	..	..	30	36	73	75	235	197	980	..	..
Myanmar	..	32	..	..	..	95	98	130	109	170	94	..
Namibia	1.4	26	..	70	..	111	104	84	67	370	68	76
Nepal	7.6	..	48	51	65	53	82	145	91	830	..	12
Netherlands	7.3	..	..	..	..	93	97	8	6	10	100	..
New Zealand	6.4	..	..	..	..	96	103	11	6	15	..	..
Nicaragua	2.3	..	12	45	65	..	105	66	43	250	..	61
Niger	2.6	43	40	18	20	54	67	320	265	920	15	16
Nigeria	4.4	35	31	72	67	76	..	190	183	1,100	31	42
Norway	9.7	..	..	..	..	97	101	9	4	9	..	..
Oman	..	24	..	67	..	86	97	30	13	120	87	..
Pakistan	8.8	40	..	44	59	47	61	128	109	200	40	20
Panama	3.6	6	..	87	94	96	100	34	25	100	..	90
Papua New Guinea	4.5	..	..	53	..	77	90	101	94	390	40	..
Paraguay	1.9	4	..	65	78	95	99	37	30	170	71	71
Peru	4.4	11	7	85	98	93	97	75	39	240	78	..
Philippines	5.4	34	32	89	..	..	103	66	38	240	..	56
Poland	7.8	..	..	100	..	96	98	22	9	12	..	..
Portugal	5.8	..	..	99	..	99	102	15	6	12	98	100
Puerto Rico	..	..	..	..	..	..	..	..	..	30	..	..

	Eradicate extreme poverty and hunger		Achieve universal primary education		Promote gender equality		Reduce child mortality		Improve maternal health		
	Share of poorest quintile in national income or consumption [a] %	Prevalence of child malnutrition % of children under 5	Primary completion rate %		Ratio of female to male enrollments in primary and secondary school [c, d] %		Under-five mortality rate per 1,000		Maternal mortality ratio per 100,000 live births Modeled estimates	Births attended by skilled health staff % of total	
	1987–2001 [b]	1990	2001	1990	2001	1990	2000	1990	2001	1995	1990	2000
Romania	8.2	6	..	96	..	95	100	36	21	60	..	98
Russian Federation	4.9	..	..	..	96	..	..	21	21	75	..	99
Rwanda	..	29	24	34	28	98	97	178	183	2,300	22	31
Saudi Arabia	..	..	..	60	..	82	94	44	28	23	88	91
Senegal	6.4	22	18	45	41	69	84	148	138	1,200	42	51
Sierra Leone	1.1	29	27	..	32	67	77	323	316	2,100	..	42
Singapore	5.0	..	..	..	..	89	..	8	4	9	..	100
Slovak Republic	8.8	..	..	96	..	98	101	14	9	14	..	..
Slovenia	9.1	..	..	99	..	97	..	10	5	17	..	..
Somalia	..	..	26	..	..	..	..	225	225	..	..	34
South Africa	2.0	..	..	76	..	103	100	60	71	340	..	84
Spain	7.5	..	..	..	..	99	103	9	6	8	..	..
Sri Lanka	8.0	..	33	100	111	99	102	23	19	60	85	..
Sudan	..	..	11	59	46	75	102	123	107	1,500	69	..
Swaziland	2.7	..	10	71	..	..	96	110	149	..	55	..
Sweden	9.1	..	..	..	..	97	115	7	3	8	..	..
Switzerland	6.9	..	..	..	..	92	96	8	6	8	..	..
Syrian Arab Republic	..	..	..	98	..	82	92	44	28	200	64	..
Tajikistan	8.0	..	..	..	95	..	87	127	116	120	..	77
Tanzania	6.8	29	29	65	60	97	99	163	165	1,100	44	35
Thailand	6.1	..	..	93	90	94	95	40	28	44	71	..
Togo	..	25	25	41	63	59	70	152	141	980	32	51
Trinidad and Tobago	5.5	..	..	100	81	98	102	24	20	65	..	..
Tunisia	5.7	10	4	75	..	82	100	52	27	70	80	90
Turkey	6.1	..	8	90	..	77	84	74	43	55	77	81
Turkmenistan	6.1	..	12	..	..	..	..	98	87	65	..	97
Uganda	7.1	23	23	49	65	..	89	165	124	1,100	38	..
Ukraine	8.8	..	3	58	..	..	92	22	20	45	..	99
United Arab Emirates	..	..	..	94	..	96	105	14	9	30	96	..
United Kingdom	6.1	..	..	..	..	97	111	9	7	10	100	99
United States	5.2	..	..	..	..	95	100	11	8	12	..	99
Uruguay	4.5	6	..	95	98	..	105	24	16	50	..	..
Uzbekistan	9.2	..	..	..	100	..	..	65	68	60	..	96
Venezuela, RB	3.0	8	4	91	78	101	105	27	22	43	97	..
Vietnam	8.0	45	34	..	101	..	..	50	38	95	95	70
West Bank and Gaza	..	..	..	..	..	..	..	53	25	..	..	..
Yemen, Rep.	7.4	30	..	..	58	..	50	142	107	850	16	22
Yugoslavia, Fed. Rep.	..	..	2	72	96	96	..	26	19	15	..	93
Zambia	3.3	25	..	91	73	..	92	192	202	870	41	..
Zimbabwe	4.6	12	13	97	..	96	94	80	123	610	62	84
World	.. w	.. w	.. w	.. w	.. w	84 w	93 w	93 w	81 w	.. w	.. w	.. w
Low income	..	..	..	68	..	74	84	139	121	43	..	..
Middle income	..	..	..	94	..	84	98	52	38	..	..	..
Lower middle income	..	18	10	95	..	82	97	54	41	..	..	..
Upper middle income	..	..	..	..	..	..	101	43	27	..	..	..
Low & middle income	..	..	..	83	..	80	92	101	88	..	..	..
East Asia & Pacific	..	19	15	98	..	83	97	59	44	..	..	..
Europe & Central Asia	..	..	..	..	..	..	98	44	38	..	..	..
Latin America & Carib.	..	..	..	..	..	..	102	53	34	..	..	..
Middle East & N. Africa	..	..	..	81	..	79	95	77	54	..	..	..
South Asia	..	64	..	70	74	68	81	129	99	..	39	42
Sub-Saharan Africa	..	..	..	57	..	79	82	178	171	..	..	..
High income	..	..	..	..	..	96	101	10	7	..	..	..
Europe EMU	..	..	..	..	..	97	100	10	6	..	..	..

a. See table 2.8 for survey year and whether share is based on income or consumption expenditure. b. Data are for the most recent year available. c. Break in series between 1997 and 1998 due to change from International Standard Classification of Education 1976 (ISCED76) to ISCED97. d. Data are provisional for Organisation for Economic Co-operation and Development and World Education Indicators (WEI) countries. For a list of WEI countries, see *About the data* for table 2.10.

About the data

This table and the following two present indicators for 17 of the 18 targets specified by the Millennium Development Goals. Each of the eight goals comprises one or more targets, and each target has associated with it several indicators by which progress toward the target can be monitored. Most of the targets are set as a value of a specific indicator to be attained by a certain date. In some cases the target value is set relative to a level in 1990. In others it is set at an absolute level. Some of the targets for goals 7 and 8 have not yet been quantified.

The indicators in this table relate to goals 1–5. Goal 1 has two targets between 1990 and 2015: to reduce by half the proportion of people whose income is less than $1 a day and to reduce by half the proportion of people who suffer from hunger. Estimates of poverty rates can be found in table 2.6. The indicator shown here, the share of the poorest quintile in national consumption, is a distributional measure. Countries with less equal distributions of consumption (or income) will have a higher rate of poverty for a given average income. No single indicator captures the concept of suffering from hunger. Child malnutrition is a symptom of inadequate food supply, lack of essential nutrients, illnesses that deplete these nutrients, and undernourished mothers who give birth to underweight children.

In previous editions of the *World Development Indicators* progress toward achieving universal primary education was measured by net enrollment ratios. But official enrollments sometimes differ significantly from actual attendance, and even school systems with high average enrollment ratios may have poor completion rates. New estimates of primary school completion rates have been calculated by World Bank staff using data provided by the United Nations Educational, Scientific, and Cultural Organization (UNESCO) and national sources.

Eliminating gender disparities in education would help to increase the status and capabilities of women. The ratio of girls' to boys' enrollments in primary and secondary school provides an imperfect measure of the relative accessibility of schooling for girls. With a target date of 2005, this is the first of the targets to fall due.

The targets for reducing under-five and maternal mortality are among the most challenging. Although estimates of under-five mortality rates are available at regular intervals for most countries, maternal mortality is difficult to measure, in part because it is relatively rare.

Most of the 48 indicators relating to the Millennium Development Goals can be found in the *World Development Indicators*. Table 1.2a shows where to find the indicators for the first five goals. For more information about data collection methods and limitations, see *About the data* for the tables listed there. For information about the indicators for goals 6, 7, and 8, see *About the data* for tables 1.3 and 1.4.

Definitions

- **Share of poorest quintile in national consumption** is the share of consumption (or, in some cases, income) that accrues to the poorest 20 percent of the population.
- **Prevalence of child malnutrition** is the percentage of children under five whose weight for age is more than two standard deviations below the median for the international reference population ages 0–59 months. The reference population, adopted by the World Health Organization in 1983, is based on children from the United States, who are assumed to be well nourished.
- **Primary completion rate** is the number of students successfully completing (or graduating from) the last year of primary school in a given year, divided by the number of children of official graduation age in the population.
- **Ratio of female to male enrollments in primary and secondary school** is the ratio of female students enrolled in primary and secondary school to male students. • **Under-five mortality rate** is the probability that a newborn baby will die before reaching age five, if subject to current age-specific mortality rates. The probability is expressed as a rate per 1,000. • **Maternal mortality ratio** is the number of women who die from pregnancy-related causes during pregnancy and childbirth, per 100,000 live births. The data shown here have been collected in various years and adjusted to a common 1995 base year. The values are modeled estimates (see *About the data* for table 2.17). • **Births attended by skilled health staff** are the percentage of deliveries attended by personnel trained to give the necessary supervision, care, and advice to women during pregnancy, labor, and the postpartum period, to conduct deliveries on their own, and to care for newborns.

1.2a

Location of indicators for Millennium Development Goals 1–5

Goal 1. Eradicate extreme poverty and hunger

1. Proportion of population below $1 a day (table 2.6)
2. Poverty gap ratio (table 2.6)
3. Share of poorest quintile in national consumption (tables 1.2 and 2.8)
4. Prevalence of underweight in children under five (tables 1.2 and 2.18)
5. Proportion of population below minimum level of dietary energy consumption (table 2.18)

Goal 2. Achieve universal primary education

6. Net enrollment ratio (table 2.12)
7. Proportion of pupils starting grade 1 who reach grade 5 (table 2.13)
8. Literacy rate of 15- to 24-year-olds (table 2.14)

Goal 3. Promote gender equality and empower women

9. Ratio of girls to boys in primary, secondary, and tertiary education (see ratio of girls to boys in primary and secondary education in table 1.2)
10. Ratio of literate females to males among 15- to 24-year-olds (tables 1.5 and 2.14)
11. Share of women in wage employment in the nonagricultural sector (table 2.3)
12. Proportion of seats held by women in national parliament (see women in decisionmaking positions in table 1.5)

Goal 4. Reduce child mortality

13. Under-five mortality rate (tables 1.2 and 2.20)
14. Infant mortality rate (table 2.20)
15. Proportion of one-year-old children immunized against measles (table 2.16)

Goal 5. Improve maternal health

16. Maternal mortality ratio (tables 1.2 and 2.17)
17. Proportion of births attended by skilled health personnel (tables 1.2 and 2.17)

Data sources

The indicators here and throughout the rest of the book have been compiled by World Bank staff from primary and secondary sources. Efforts have been made to harmonize these data series with those published by the United Nations Millennium Development Goals Web site (www.un.org/millenniumgoals), but some differences in timing, sources, and definitions remain.

	Combat HIV/AIDS and other diseases			Ensure environmental sustainability						Develop a global partnership for development	
	Prevalence of HIV		Incidence of tuberculosis per 100,000 people	Carbon dioxide emissions per capita metric tons		Access to an improved water source % of population		Access to improved sanitation facilities % of population		Unemployment % ages 15–24	Fixed line and mobile phone subscribers per 1,000 people [b]
	Males % ages 15–24 [a]	Females % ages 15–24 [a]									
	2001	2001	2000	1990	1999	1990	2000	1990	2000	2000	2001
Afghanistan	..	..	321	0.1	0.0	..	13	..	12	..	..
Albania	..	..	29	2.2	0.5	..	97	..	91	..	138
Algeria	..	..	46	3.2	3.0	..	89	..	92	..	64
Angola	2.2	5.7	275	0.5	0.8	..	38	..	44	..	12
Argentina	0.9	0.3	48	3.4	3.8	94	..	82	..	..	416
Armenia	0.2	0.1	69	1.0	0.8	..	..	..	..	..	147
Australia	0.1	0.0 [c]	8	15.6	18.2	100	100	100	100	12	1,095
Austria	0.2	0.1	15	7.4	7.6	100	100	100	100	6	1,275
Azerbaijan	0.1	0.0 [c]	74	6.4	4.2	..	78	..	81	..	191
Bangladesh	0.0 [c]	0.0 [c]	242	0.1	0.2	94	97	41	48	..	8
Belarus	0.6	0.2	88	9.3	5.7	..	100	..	..	..	292
Belgium	0.1	0.1	14	10.1	10.2	..	..	..	..	23	..
Benin	1.2	3.7	259	0.1	0.2	..	63	20	23	..	29
Bolivia	0.1	0.1	230	0.8	1.4	71	83	52	70	..	152
Bosnia and Herzegovina	..	..	91	1.1	1.2	..	..	..	..	..	168
Botswana	16.1	37.5	757	1.7	2.4	93	95	60	66	..	..
Brazil	0.6	0.5	68	1.4	1.8	83	87	71	76	18	385
Bulgaria	..	..	41 [d]	8.6	5.1	..	100	..	100	34	551
Burkina Faso	4.0	9.7	324	0.1	0.1	..	42	..	29	..	11
Burundi	5.0	11.0	406	0.0	0.0	69	78	87	88	..	6
Cambodia	1.0	2.5	572	0.0	0.1	..	30	..	17	..	19
Cameroon	5.4	12.7	341	0.1	0.3	51	58	77	79	..	27
Canada	0.3	0.2	7	15.4	14.4	100	100	100	100	14	1,038
Central African Republic	5.8	13.5	445	0.1	0.1	48	70	24	25	..	5
Chad	2.4	4.3	274	0.0	0.0	..	27	18	29	..	4
Chile	0.4	0.1	25	2.7	4.2	90	93	97	96	21	575
China	0.2	0.1	107	2.1	2.3	71	75	29	38	3	248
Hong Kong, China	0.0	0.0	91	4.6	6.2	..	..	..	..	10	1,439
Colombia	0.9	0.2	50	1.6	1.5	94	91	83	86	36	247
Congo, Dem. Rep.	2.9	5.9	320	0.1	0.0	..	45	..	21	..	3
Congo, Rep.	3.3	7.8	338	0.9	0.8	..	51	..	..	..	55
Costa Rica	0.6	0.3	16	1.0	1.6	..	95	..	93	12	305
Côte d'Ivoire	2.9	8.3	389	1.0	0.8	80	81	46	52	..	63
Croatia	0.0	0.0	59	3.5	4.8	..	..	..	..	30	742
Cuba	0.1	0.0 [c]	14	3.0	2.3	..	91	..	98	..	52
Czech Republic	0.0	0.0	19	13.1	10.6	..	..	..	..	17	1,050
Denmark	0.1	0.1	13	9.9	9.3	..	100	..	..	10	1,457
Dominican Republic	2.1	2.8	147	1.3	2.8	83	86	66	67	..	257
Ecuador	0.3	0.2	176	1.6	1.9	71	85	70	86	24	170
Egypt, Arab Rep.	..	..	39	1.4	2.0	94	97	87	98	..	147
El Salvador	0.8	0.4	64	0.5	0.9	66	77	73	82	..	218
Eritrea	2.8	4.3	289	..	0.1	..	46	..	13	..	..
Estonia	2.5	0.6	67	16.1	11.7	..	..	..	..	16	808
Ethiopia	4.4	7.8	397	0.1	0.1	25	24	8	12	..	5
Finland	0.0 [c]	0.0 [c]	11	10.6	11.3	100	100	100	100	22	1,326
France	0.3	0.2	15	6.3	6.1	..	..	..	..	27	1,179
Gabon	2.3	4.7	293	7.1	3.0	..	86	..	53	..	234
Gambia, The	0.5	1.4	264	0.2	0.2	..	62	..	37	..	67
Georgia	0.1	0.0 [c]	75	2.8	1.0	..	79	..	100	..	213
Germany	0.1	0.0 [c]	12	11.1	9.7	..	..	..	..	8	1,317
Ghana	1.4	3.0	286	0.2	0.3	53	73	61	72	..	21
Greece	0.1	0.1	22	7.1	8.2	..	..	..	..	30	1,281
Guatemala	0.9	0.8	85	0.6	0.9	76	92	70	81	..	162
Guinea	0.6	1.4	270	0.2	0.2	45	48	55	58	..	10
Guinea-Bissau	1.1	3.0	271	0.8	0.2	..	56	44	56	..	..
Haiti	4.1	5.0	350	0.2	0.2	53	46	23	28	..	21

	Combat HIV/AIDS and other diseases			Ensure environmental sustainability						Develop a global partnership for development	
	Prevalence of HIV		Incidence of tuberculosis per 100,000 people	Carbon dioxide emissions per capita metric tons		Access to an improved water source % of population		Access to improved sanitation facilities % of population		Unemployment % ages 15–24	Fixed line and mobile phone subscribers per 1,000 people [b]
	Males % ages 15–24 [a]	Females % ages 15–24 [a]									
	2001	**2001**	**2000**	**1990**	**1999**	**1990**	**2000**	**1990**	**2000**	**2000**	**2001**
Honduras	1.2	1.5	91	0.5	0.8	83	88	61	75	*6*	83
Hungary	0.1	0.0 [c]	41	5.6	5.6	99	99	99	99	*12*	872
India	0.3	0.7	184	0.8	1.1	68	84	16	28	..	44
Indonesia	0.1	0.1	280	0.9	1.2	71	78	47	55	..	66
Iran, Islamic Rep.	0.0 [c]	0.0 [c]	53	3.9	4.8	..	92	..	83	..	201
Iraq	..	..	132	2.7	3.3	..	85	..	79	..	..
Ireland	0.1	0.1	14	8.5	10.8	..	..	..	..	*9*	1,214
Israel	*0.1*	*0.1*	11	7.4	10.0	..	..	..	..	*17*	1,285
Italy	0.3	0.3	9	7.0	7.3	..	..	..	..	*33*	1,311
Jamaica	0.8	0.9	8	3.3	4.0	93	92	99	99	*34*	467
Japan	0.0 [c]	0.0 [c]	36	8.7	9.1	..	..	..	..	*9*	1,185
Jordan	..	..	10	3.2	3.1	97	96	98	99	..	294
Kazakhstan	0.1	0.0 [c]	152	*15.3*	7.4	..	91	..	99	..	..
Kenya	6.0	15.6	484	0.2	0.3	45	57	80	87	..	30
Korea, Dem. Rep.	..	..	175	12.3	9.4	..	100	..	99	..	..
Korea, Rep.	0.0 [c]	0.0 [c]	62	5.6	8.4	..	92	..	63	*14*	1,106
Kuwait	..	..	31	19.9	24.9	..	..	..	..	..	685
Kyrgyz Republic	0.0	0.0	153	*2.4*	1.0	..	77	..	100	..	83
Lao PDR	0.0 [c]	0.0 [c]	160	0.1	0.1	..	37	..	30	..	15
Latvia	0.9	0.2	118	*4.8*	2.8	..	..	..	..	*23*	588
Lebanon	..	..	22	2.5	4.0	..	100	..	99	..	..
Lesotho	17.4	38.1	578	..	..	..	78	..	49	..	..
Liberia	..	..	275	0.2	0.1	..	..	..	..	..	3
Libya	..	..	24	8.8	8.3	71	72	97	97	..	118
Lithuania	0.2	0.0 [c]	111	*5.8*	3.8	..	*67*	..	*67*	*25*	566
Macedonia, FYR	0.0	0.0	52	*5.5*	5.6	..	..	..	..	..	373
Madagascar	0.1	0.2	254	0.1	0.1	44	47	36	42	..	13
Malawi	6.3	14.9	447	0.1	0.1	49	57	73	76	..	11
Malaysia	0.7	0.1	111	3.0	5.4	..	..	..	..	..	510
Mali	1.4	2.1	267	0.0	0.0	55	65	70	69	..	8
Mauritania	*0.4*	*0.6*	226	1.3	1.2	37	37	30	33	..	..
Mauritius	*0.0* [c]	*0.0* [c]	69	1.1	2.1	100	100	100	99	..	509
Mexico	0.4	0.1	38	3.7	3.9	80	88	70	74	*3*	354
Moldova	0.5	0.1	135	*4.8*	1.5	..	92	..	99	..	202
Mongolia	..	..	216	4.7	3.2	..	60	..	30	..	133
Morocco	..	..	118	1.0	1.3	75	80	58	68	*35*	204
Mozambique	6.1	14.7	433	0.1	0.1	..	57	..	43	..	13
Myanmar	*1.0*	*1.7*	168	0.1	0.2	..	72	..	64	..	6
Namibia	11.1	24.3	521	..	0.1	72	77	33	41	..	122
Nepal	0.3	0.3	208	0.0	0.1	67	88	20	28	..	14
Netherlands	0.2	0.1	9	10.0	8.5	100	100	100	100	*7*	1,388
New Zealand	0.1	0.0 [c]	11	6.9	8.1	..	..	..	..	*13*	1,076
Nicaragua	0.2	0.1	85	0.7	0.8	70	77	76	85	..	..
Niger	*0.9*	*1.5*	256	0.1	0.1	53	59	15	20	..	2
Nigeria	3.0	5.8	305	0.9	0.3	53	62	53	54	..	9
Norway	0.1	0.0 [c]	6	7.5	8.7	100	100	..	..	*10*	1,546
Oman	..	..	9	7.1	8.5	37	39	84	92	..	213
Pakistan	0.1	0.1	175	0.6	0.7	83	90	36	62	..	29
Panama	1.9	1.3	52	1.3	2.9	..	90	..	92	*29*	355
Papua New Guinea	0.3	0.4	262	0.6	0.5	40	42	82	82	..	14
Paraguay	*0.1*	*0.0* [c]	66	0.5	0.8	63	78	93	94	..	255
Peru	0.4	0.2	212	1.0	1.2	74	80	60	71	*21*	192
Philippines	0.0 [c]	0.0 [c]	330	0.7	1.0	87	86	74	83	*30*	555
Poland	0.1	0.0 [c]	36	9.1	8.1	..	..	..	..	*9*	1,201
Portugal	0.4	0.2	52	4.3	6.0	..	..	..	..	*9*	1,201
Puerto Rico	..	..	9	3.3	2.7	..	..	..	..	*20*	643

	Combat HIV/AIDS and other diseases			Ensure environmental sustainability						Develop a global partnership for development	
	Prevalence of HIV		Incidence of tuberculosis	Carbon dioxide emissions		Access to an improved water source		Access to improved sanitation facilities		Unemployment	Fixed line and mobile phone subscribers
	Males % ages 15–24[a]	Females % ages 15–24[a]	per 100,000 people	per capita metric tons		% of population		% of population		% ages 15–24	per 1,000 people[b]
	2001	2001	2000	1990	1999	1990	2000	1990	2000	2000	2001
Romania	0.0[c]	0.0[c]	135	6.7	3.6	..	58	..	53	20	356
Russian Federation	1.9	0.7	132	13.3	9.8	..	99	..	..	27	281
Rwanda	4.9	11.2	405	0.1	0.1	..	41	..	8	..	11
Saudi Arabia	..	..	45	11.3	11.7	..	95	..	100	..	258
Senegal	0.2	0.5	261	0.4	0.4	72	78	57	70	..	56
Sierra Leone	2.5	7.5	278	0.1	0.1	..	57	..	66	..	10
Singapore	0.1	0.2	48	13.8	13.7	100	100	100	100	7	1,196
Slovak Republic	0.0	0.0	25	8.1	7.2	..	100	..	100	32	685
Slovenia	0.0	0.0	26	6.1	7.3	100	100	..	..	18	1,161
Somalia	..	..	360	0.0	0.0	..	..	..	..	..	..
South Africa	10.7	25.6	526	8.3	7.9	86	86	86	87	56	364
Spain	0.5	0.2	34	5.5	6.8	..	..	..	..	29	1,086
Sri Lanka	0.0[c]	0.0[c]	58	0.2	0.5	68	77	85	94	28	80
Sudan	1.1	3.1	193	0.1	0.1	67	75	58	62	..	18
Swaziland	15.2	39.5	600	0.6	0.4	..	..	..	..	..	96
Sweden	0.1	0.0[c]	5	5.7	5.3	100	100	100[b]	100	14	1,529
Switzerland	0.5	0.4	11	6.4	5.7	100	100	100	100	6	1,476
Syrian Arab Republic	..	..	85	3.0	3.4	..	80	..	90	..	115
Tajikistan	0.0	0.0	160	3.7	0.8	..	60	..	90	..	36
Tanzania	3.5	8.1	359	0.1	0.1	38	68	84	90	..	16
Thailand	1.1	1.7	140	1.7	3.3	80	84	79	96	7	222
Togo	2.0	5.9	317	0.2	0.3	51	54	37	34	..	31
Trinidad and Tobago	2.4	3.2	13	13.9	19.4	91	90	99	99	25	437
Tunisia	..	..	37	1.6	1.8	75	80	76	84	..	149
Turkey	..	..	36	2.6	3.1	79	82	87	90	15	587
Turkmenistan	0.0	0.0	84	6.9	6.4	..	..	..	..	..	..
Uganda	2.0	4.6	351	0.0	0.1	45	52	..	79	..	17
Ukraine	2.0	0.9	79	11.5	7.5	..	98	..	99	23	256
United Arab Emirates	..	..	21	33.0	31.3	..	..	..	..	..	956
United Kingdom	0.1	0.1	12	9.9	9.2	100	100	100	100	12	1,358
United States	0.5	0.2	5	19.3	19.7	100	100	100	100	10	1,118
Uruguay	0.5	0.2	28	1.3	2.0	..	98	..	94	24	438
Uzbekistan	0.0[c]	0.0	104	5.3	4.8	..	85	..	89	..	68
Venezuela, RB	0.7	0.1	42	5.8	5.3	..	83	..	68	26	373
Vietnam	0.3	0.2	189	0.3	0.6	55	77	29	47	..	53
West Bank and Gaza	..	..	28	..	..	..	..	..	..	..	168
Yemen, Rep.	..	..	107	0.7	1.1	..	69	32	38	..	30
Yugoslavia, Fed. Rep.	..	..	45	12.4	3.7	..	98	..	100	..	416
Zambia	8.1	21.0	529	0.3	0.2	52	64	63	78	..	19
Zimbabwe	12.4	33.0	584	1.6	1.4	78	83	56	62	..	43
World	**0.77 w**	**1.34 w**	**145 w**	**3.4 w**	**3.8 w**	**74 w**	**81 w**	**45 w**	**55 w**		**330 w**
Low income	1.13	2.37	233	0.7	1.0	66	76	30	44		40
Middle income	0.61	0.77	107	2.6	3.2	76	82	47	59		281
Lower middle income	0.62	0.85	119	2.3	3.0	74	80	42	55		246
Upper middle income	0.57	0.43	55	3.7	4.3	84	88	75	79		432
Low & middle income	0.87	1.58	168	1.7	2.2	71	79	39	51		166
East Asia & Pacific	0.19	0.16	147	1.9	2.1	71	76	35	46		207
Europe & Central Asia	1.08	0.41	91	9.1	6.6	..	91	..	..		375
Latin America & Carib.	0.68	0.46	73	2.2	2.5	82	86	72	77		326
Middle East & N. Africa	..	..	64	3.3	3.7	..	88	..	85		153
South Asia	0.27	0.55	190	0.7	0.9	72	84	22	34		38
Sub-Saharan Africa	4.12	9.34	354	0.9	0.8	53	58	54	53		41
High income	0.26	0.14	18	11.8	12.3	..	..	..	..		1,202
Europe EMU	0.24	0.15	17	6.9	7.9	..	..	..	..		1,251

a. Data are an average of high and low estimates. b. Data are from the International Telecommunications Union's (ITU) *World Telecommunication Development Report 2002*. Please cite the ITU for third-party use of these data. c. Less than 0.05. d. Data are for 2001.

About the data

The Millennium Development Goals address issues of common concern to people of all nations. Diseases and environmental degradation do not respect national boundaries. Epidemic diseases, wherever they persist, pose a threat to people everywhere. And damage done to the environment in one location may affect the well-being of plants, animals, and human beings in distant locations.

The indicators in the table relate to goals 6 and 7 and the targets of goal 8 that address youth employment and access to new technologies. For the other targets of goal 8, see table 1.4.

Measuring the prevalence or incidence of a disease can be difficult. Much of the developing world lacks reporting systems needed for monitoring the course of a disease. Estimates are often derived from surveys and reports from sentinel sites that must be extrapolated to the general population. Tracking diseases such as HIV/AIDS, which has a long latency between contraction of the virus and the appearance of outward symptoms, or malaria, which has periods of dormancy, can be particularly difficult. For some of the most serious illnesses international organizations have formed coalitions such as the Joint United Nations Programme on HIV/AIDS (UNAIDS) and the Roll Back Malaria campaign to gather information and coordinate global efforts to treat victims and prevent the spread of disease.

Antenatal care clinics are a key site for monitoring sexually transmitted diseases such as HIV and syphilis. The prevalence of HIV in young people provides an indicator of the spread of the epidemic. Prevalence rates in the older population can be affected by life-prolonging treatment. The table shows the estimated prevalence among men and women ages 15–24.

The incidence of tuberculosis is based on data on case notifications and estimates of the proportion of cases detected in the population.

Carbon dioxide emissions are the primary source of greenhouse gases, which are believed to contribute to global warming.

Access to reliable supplies of safe drinking water and sanitary disposal of excrement are two of the most important means of improving human health and protecting the environment. There is no widespread program for testing the quality of water. The indicator shown here measures the proportion of households with access to an improved source, such as piped water or protected wells. Improved sanitation facilities prevent human, animal, and insect contact with excreta but do not include treatment to render sewage outflows innocuous.

The eighth goal—to develop a global partnership for development—takes note of the need for decent and productive work for youth. Labor market information, such as unemployment rates, is still generally unavailable for most low- and middle-income economies. Fixed telephone lines and mobile phones are among the telecommunications technologies that are changing the way the global economy works. For more information on goal 8, see table 1.4.

Definitions

- **Prevalence of HIV** is the percentage of people ages 15–24 who are infected with HIV. • **Incidence of tuberculosis** is the estimated number of new tuberculosis cases (pulmonary, smear positive, extrapulmonary). • **Carbon dioxide emissions** are those stemming from the burning of fossil fuels and the manufacture of cement. They include carbon dioxide produced during consumption of solid, liquid, and gas fuels and gas flaring. • **Access to an improved water source** refers to the percentage of the population with reasonable access to an adequate amount of water from an improved source, such as a household connection, public standpipe, borehole, protected well or spring, or rainwater collection. Unimproved sources include vendors, tanker trucks, and unprotected wells and springs. Reasonable access is defined as the availability of at least 20 liters a person a day from a source within one kilometer of the dwelling. • **Access to improved sanitation facilities** refers to the percentage of the population with access to at least adequate excreta disposal facilities (private or shared but not public) that can effectively prevent human, animal, and insect contact with excreta. Improved facilities range from simple but protected pit latrines to flush toilets with a sewerage connection. To be effective, facilities must be correctly constructed and properly maintained. • **Unemployment** refers to the share of the labor force without work but available for and seeking employment. Definitions of labor force and unemployment differ by country. • **Fixed line and mobile phone subscribers** are telephone mainlines connecting a customer's equipment to the public switched telephone network, and users of portable telephones subscribing to an automatic public mobile telephone service using cellular technology that provides access to the public switched telephone network.

1.3a

Location of indicators for Millennium Development Goals 6–7

Goal 6. Combat HIV/AIDS, malaria, and other diseases

18. HIV prevalence among 15- to 24-year-old pregnant women (tables 1.3 and 2.19)

19. Condom use rate of the contraceptive prevalence rate (see contraceptive prevalence rate in table 2.17)

20. Number of children orphaned by HIV/AIDS*

21. Prevalence and death rates associated with malaria*

22. Proportion of population in malaria-risk areas using effective malaria prevention and treatment measures*

23. Tuberculosis prevalence and death rates (see incidence of tuberculosis in tables 1.2 and 2.19)

24. Proportion of tuberculosis cases detected and cured under directly observed treatment, short course (table 2.16)

Goal 7. Ensure environmental sustainability

25. Proportion of land area covered by forest (table 3.4)

26. Ratio of area protected to maintain biological diversity to surface area (table 3.4)

27. Energy use (kilograms of oil equivalent) per $1 of GDP (PPP) (see GDP per unit of energy use in table 3.8)

28. Carbon dioxide emissions per capita (table 3.8) and consumption of ozone-depleting chlorofluorocarbons*

29. Proportion of population using solid fuels (see traditional fuel use in table 3.8)

30. Proportion of population with sustainable access to an improved water source (tables 2.16 and 3.5)

31. Proportion of urban population with access to improved sanitation (table 2.16)

32. Proportion of population with access to secure tenure (table 3.11)

* No data available in the World Development Indicators database.

Data sources

The indicators here, and where they appear throughout the rest of the book, have been compiled by World Bank staff from primary and secondary sources. Efforts have been made to harmonize these data series with those published on the United Nations Millennium Development Goals Web site (http://www.un.org/ millenniumgoals), but some differences in timing, sources, and definitions remain.

Development Assistance Committee members

	Official development assistance (ODA) by donor		Market access to high-income countries						Support to agriculture
	Net ODA	ODA for basic social services[a]	Goods (excluding arms) admitted free of tariffs		Average tariff on exports of low- and middle-income economies				
					Agricultural products		Textiles and clothing		
	% of donor GNI	% of total ODA commitments	%		%		%		% of GDP
	2001	**2000–01**	**1990**	**2000**	**1990**	**2000**	**1990**	**2000**	**2001**
Australia	0.25	19.0	*38.8*	42.7	*1.9*	1.6	*29.3*	14.6	0.3
Canada	0.22	19.4	*27.8*	65.2	*3.6*	2.7	*20.0*	11.5	0.7
European Union			48.2	72.9	11.1	4.9	6.3	4.3	1.4
Austria	0.29	20.5	..	..	..	..	..	..	..
Belgium	0.37	14.6	..	..	..	..	..	..	..
Denmark	1.03	8.7	..	..	..	..	..	..	..
Finland	0.32	11.6	..	..	..	..	..	..	..
France	0.32	..	..	..	..	..	..	..	..
Germany	0.27	9.7	..	..	..	..	..	..	..
Greece	0.17	4.6	..	..	..	..	..	..	..
Ireland	0.33	20.5	..	..	..	..	..	..	..
Italy	0.15	6.1	..	..	..	..	..	..	..
Luxembourg	0.82	21.2	..	..	..	..	..	..	..
Netherlands	0.82	22.5	..	..	..	..	..	..	..
Portugal	0.25	2.8	..	..	..	..	..	..	..
Spain	0.30	11.7	..	..	..	..	..	..	..
Sweden	0.81	13.6	..	..	..	..	..	..	..
United Kingdom	0.32	27.0	..	..	..	..	..	..	..
Japan	0.23	6.8	42.2	57.2	9.4	9.1	5.0	4.1	1.4
New Zealand	0.25	8.4	*54.4*	52.4	*5.7*	1.7	*18.4*	8.2	0.3
Norway	0.83	9.1	*87.1*	71.7	*0.5*	15.2	*14.0*	11.6	1.4
Switzerland	0.34	10.9	*2.6*	61.8	..	..	..	..	1.9
United States	0.11	21.5	20.3	56.2	3.7	4.4	11.8	10.2	0.9

Heavily indebted poor countries (HIPCs)

	HIPC decision point[b]	HIPC completion point[c]	Estimated total nominal debt service relief		HIPC decision point[b]	HIPC completion point[c]	Estimated total nominal debt service relief
			$ millions				$ millions
Benin	Jul. 2000	Floating	460	Malawi	Dec. 2000	Floating	1,000
Bolivia	Feb. 2000	Jun. 2001	2,060	Mali	Sep. 2000	Floating	870
Burkina Faso	Jul. 2000	Apr. 2002	930	Mauritania	Feb. 2000	Jun. 2002	1,100
Cameroon	Oct. 2000	Floating	2,000	Mozambique	Apr. 2000	Sep. 2001	4,300
Chad	May 2001	Floating	260	Nicaragua	Dec. 2000	Floating	4,500
Côte d'Ivoire	Mar. 1998	..	800	Niger	Dec. 2000	Floating	900
Ethiopia	Nov. 2001	Floating	1,930	Rwanda	Dec. 2000	Floating	810
Gambia, The	Dec. 2000	Floating	90	São Tomé and Principe	Dec. 2000	Floating	200
Ghana	Feb. 2002	Floating	3,700	Senegal	Jun. 2000	Floating	850
Guinea	Dec. 2000	Floating	800	Sierra Leone	Mar. 2002	Floating	950
Guinea-Bissau	Dec. 2000	Floating	790	Tanzania	Apr. 2000	Nov. 2001	3,000
Guyana	Nov. 2000	Floating	1,030	Uganda	Feb. 2000	May 2000	1,950
Honduras	Jul. 2000	Floating	900	Zambia	Dec. 2000	Floating	3,820
Madagascar	Dec. 2000	Floating	1,500				

a. Includes basic health, education, nutrition, and water and sanitation services. b. Except for Côte d'Ivoire, Ghana, and Sierra Leone, the date refers to the enhanced framework. The following countries also reached decision points under the original framework: Bolivia in September 1997, Burkina Faso in September 1997, Guyana in December 1997, Mali in September 1998, Mozambique in April 1998, and Uganda in April 1997. c. Except for Côte d'Ivoire, Ghana, and Sierra Leone, the date refers to the enhanced framework. The following countries also reached completion points under the original framework: Bolivia in September 1998, Burkina Faso in July 2000, Guyana in May 1999, Mali in September 2000, Mozambique in July 1999, and Uganda in April 1998.

About the data

Achieving the Millennium Development Goals will require an open, rule-based global economy in which all countries, rich and poor, participate. Many poor countries, lacking the resources to finance their development, burdened by unsustainable levels of debt, and unable to compete in the global marketplace, need assistance from rich countries. For goal 8—develop a global partnership for development—many of the indicators therefore monitor the actions of members of the Development Assistance Committee (DAC) of the Organisation for Economic Co-operation and Development (OECD).

Official development assistance (ODA) has declined in recent years as a share of donor countries' gross national income (GNI). The poorest countries will need additional assistance to achieve the Millennium Development Goals. Recent estimates suggest that $40–60 billion more a year, a doubling of current aid levels, would allow most of them to achieve the goals, if the aid goes to countries with good policies. At the United Nations International Conference on Financing for Development in 2002 many donor countries made new commitments that, if fulfilled, would add $15 billion to ODA.

One of the most important things that high-income economies can do to help is to reduce barriers to the exports of low- and middle-income economies. The European Union has announced a program to eliminate tariffs on developing country exports of "everything but arms." The data in the table reflect the tariff schedules applied by high-income OECD members to exports of low- and middle-income economies. Agricultural commodities and textiles and clothing are two of the most important categories of goods exported by developing economies. Although average tariffs have been falling, averages may disguise high tariffs targeted at specific goods (see table 6.6 for estimates of the share of lines with "international peaks" in each country's tariff schedule). The averages in the table include only ad valorem duties. No data are shown for Switzerland, which applies specific duties almost exclusively. The World Trade Organization is preparing new estimates of trade flows and average tariffs; the data shown here are from last year's edition of the *World Development Indicators*.

Subsidies to agricultural producers and exporters in OECD countries are another form of barrier to developing economies' exports. The table shows the value of total support to agriculture as a share of the economy's gross domestic product (GDP). In 2001 agricultural subsidies in OECD economies totaled $311 billion.

The Debt Initiative for Heavily Indebted Poor Countries (HIPCs) is the first comprehensive approach to reducing the external debt of the world's poorest, most heavily indebted countries. It represents an important step forward in placing debt relief within an overall framework of poverty reduction. While the initiative yielded significant early progress, multilateral organizations, bilateral creditors, HIPC governments, and civil society have engaged in an intensive dialogue about its strengths and weaknesses. A major review in 1999 led to an enhancement of the original framework.

Definitions

• **Net official development assistance** (ODA) comprises grants and loans (net of repayments of principal) that meet the DAC definition of ODA and are made to countries and territories in part I of the DAC list of recipient countries. • **ODA for basic social services** is aid reported by DAC donors for basic health, education, nutrition, and water and sanitation services. • **Goods admitted free of tariffs** are the value of exports of goods (excluding arms) from developing countries admitted without tariff, as a share of total exports from developing countries. • **Average tariff** is the simple mean tariff, the unweighted average of the effectively applied rates for all products subject to tariffs. • **Agricultural products** comprise plant and animal products, including tree crops but excluding timber and fish products. • **Textiles and clothing** include natural and man-made fibers and fabrics and articles of clothing made from them. • **Support to agriculture** is the value of subsidies to the agricultural sector. • **HIPC decision point** is the date at which a heavily indebted poor country with an established track record of good performance under adjustment programs supported by the International Monetary Fund and the World Bank commits to undertake additional reforms and to develop and implement a poverty reduction strategy. • **HIPC completion point** is the date at which the country successfully completes the key structural reforms agreed on at the decision point, including developing and implementing its poverty reduction strategy. The country then receives the bulk of debt relief under the HIPC Debt Initiative without further policy conditions. • **Estimated total nominal debt service relief** is the amount of debt service relief, calculated at the decision point, that will allow the country to achieve debt sustainability at the completion point.

1.4a

Location of indicators for Millennium Development Goal 8

Goal 8. Develop a global partnership for development

33. Net ODA as a percentage of DAC donors' gross national income (table 6.9)
34. Proportion of ODA for basic social services (table 1.4)
35. Proportion of ODA that is untied (table 6.9)
36. Proportion of ODA received in landlocked countries as a percentage of GNI*
37. Proportion of ODA received in small island developing states as a percentage of GNI*
38. Proportion of developing country exports (by value, excluding arms) admitted free of duties and quotas (table 1.4)
39. Average tariffs and quotas on agricultural products and textiles and clothing (see related indicators in table 6.6)
40. Agricultural support estimate for OECD countries as a percentage of GDP (table 1.4)
41. Proportion of ODA provided to help build trade capacity*
42. Number of countries reaching HIPC decision and completion points (table 1.4)
43. Debt relief committed under new HIPC initiative (table 1.4)
44. Debt service as a percentage of exports of goods and services (table 4.17)
45. Unemployment rate of 15- to 24-year-olds (see table 2.4 for related indicators)
46. Proportion of population with access to affordable, essential drugs on a sustainable basis*
47. Telephone lines and mobile subscribers per 1,000 people (tables 1.3 and 5.10)
48. Personal computers and Internet users per 1,000 people (table 5.11)

* No data available in the World Development Indicators database.

Data sources

The indicators here, and where they appear throughout the rest of the book, have been compiled by World Bank staff from primary and secondary sources. Efforts have been made to harmonize these data series with those published on the United Nations Millennium Development Goals Web site (http://www.un.org/millenniumgoals), but some differences in timing, sources, and definitions remain.

	Female population	Life expectancy at birth		Pregnant women receiving prenatal care	Literacy gender parity index	Labor force gender parity index		Maternity leave benefits	Women in decision-making positions	
								% of wages paid in covered period	% of total at ministerial level	
	% of total 2001	Male years 2001	Female years 2001	% 1996	ages 15–24 2001	1990	2001	1998	1994	1998
Afghanistan	49.0	43	43	..	..	0.5	0.6	..	..	..
Albania	48.9	72	76	..	1.0	0.7	0.7	..	0	11
Algeria	49.4	69	72	58	0.9	0.3	0.4	100	4	0
Angola	50.5	45	48	25	..	0.9	0.9	100	7	14
Argentina	50.9	71	78	..	1.0	0.4	0.5	100	0	8
Armenia	51.4	71	78	95	1.0	0.9	0.9	..	3	0
Australia	50.1	76	82	..	..	0.7	0.8	0	13	14
Austria	51.4	76	81	..	..	0.7	0.7	100	16	20
Azerbaijan	50.9	62	69	95	..	0.8	0.8	..	5	10
Bangladesh	49.6	61	62	23	0.7	0.7	0.7	100	8	5
Belarus	53.1	62	74	..	1.0	1.0	1.0	100	3	3
Belgium	50.9	75	82	..	..	0.7	0.7	82[a]	11	3
Benin	50.7	51	55	60	0.5	0.9	0.9	100	10	13
Bolivia	50.2	61	65	52	1.0	0.6	0.6	70[b]	0	6
Bosnia and Herzegovina	50.5	71	76	..	..	0.6	0.6	..	0	6
Botswana	50.2	39	38	92	1.1	0.9	0.8	25	6	14
Brazil	50.6	64	72	74	1.0	0.5	0.6	100	5	4
Bulgaria	51.3	68	75	..	1.0	0.9	0.9	100	0	..
Burkina Faso	50.5	43	44	59	0.5	0.9	0.9	100	7	10
Burundi	51.0	41	42	88	1.0	1.0	0.9	50	7	8
Cambodia	51.3	52	55	52	0.9	1.2	1.1	50	0	..
Cameroon	50.0	48	50	73	1.0	0.6	0.6	100	3	6
Canada	50.5	76	82	..	..	0.8	0.8	55[c]	14	..
Central African Republic	51.2	42	43	67	0.8	..	..	50	5	4
Chad	50.5	47	50	30	0.8	0.8	0.8	50	5	0
Chile	50.5	73	79	91	1.0	0.4	0.5	100	13	13
China	49.0	69	72	79	1.0	0.8	0.8	100	6	..
Hong Kong, China	50.8	77	83	100	1.0	0.6	0.6	..	..	..
Colombia	50.5	69	75	83	1.0	0.6	0.6	100	11	18
Congo, Dem. Rep.	50.5	45	46	66	0.9	0.8	0.8	67	6	..
Congo, Rep.	51.0	49	54	55	1.0	0.8	0.8	100	6	6
Costa Rica	50.1	75	80	95	1.0	0.4	0.5	100	10	15
Côte d'Ivoire	49.2	45	46	83	0.8	0.5	0.5	100	8	3
Croatia	51.7	69	78	..	1.0	0.7	0.8	..	4	12
Cuba	50.0	75	79	100	1.0	0.6	0.7	100	0	5
Czech Republic	51.2	72	78	..	..	0.9	0.9	..	0	17
Denmark	50.5	74	79	..	..	0.9	0.9	100[d]	29	41
Dominican Republic	49.2	65	70	97	1.0	0.4	0.5	100	4	10
Ecuador	49.8	69	72	75	1.0	0.3	0.4	100	6	20
Egypt, Arab Rep.	49.1	67	70	53	0.8	0.4	0.4	100	4	6
El Salvador	50.9	67	73	69	1.0	0.5	0.6	75	10	6
Eritrea	50.4	50	52	19	0.8	0.9	0.9	..	7	5
Estonia	53.5	65	76	..	1.0	1.0	1.0	..	15	12
Ethiopia	49.8	41	43	20	0.8	0.7	0.7	100	10	5
Finland	51.2	75	82	..	..	0.9	0.9	80	39	29
France	51.4	76	83	..	..	0.8	0.8	100	7	12
Gabon	50.5	52	54	86	..	0.8	0.8	100	7	3
Gambia, The	50.5	52	55	91	0.8	0.8	0.8	100	0	29
Georgia	52.5	69	77	95	..	0.9	0.9	..	0	4
Germany	50.9	75	81	..	..	0.7	0.7	100	16	8
Ghana	50.2	55	57	86	1.0	1.0	1.0	50	11	9
Greece	50.8	75	81	..	1.0	0.5	0.6	75	4	5
Guatemala	49.6	62	68	53	0.9	0.3	0.4	100	19	0
Guinea	49.7	46	47	59	..	0.9	0.9	100	9	8
Guinea-Bissau	50.7	44	47	50	0.6	0.7	0.7	100	4	18
Haiti	50.9	50	55	68	1.0	0.8	0.8	100[d]	13	0

	Female population	Life expectancy at birth		Pregnant women receiving prenatal care	Literacy gender parity index	Labor force gender parity index		Maternity leave benefits	Women in decision-making positions	
	% of total	Male years	Female years	%	ages 15–24			% of wages paid in covered period	% of total at ministerial level	
	2001	**2001**	**2001**	**1996**	**2001**	**1990**	**2001**	**1998**	**1994**	**1998**
Honduras	49.7	63	69	73	1.0	0.4	0.5	100 e	11	11
Hungary	52.3	67	76	..	1.0	0.8	0.8	100	0	5
India	48.4	62	64	62	0.8	0.5	0.5	100	3	..
Indonesia	50.1	65	68	82	1.0	0.6	0.7	100	6	3
Iran, Islamic Rep.	49.8	68	70	62	1.0	0.3	0.4	67	0	0
Iraq	49.2	61	63	59	0.5	0.2	0.3	100	0	0
Ireland	50.5	74	79	..	..	0.5	0.5	70 f	16	21
Israel	50.3	77	81	90	1.0	0.6	0.7	75	4	0
Italy	51.5	75	82	..	1.0	0.6	0.6	80	12	13
Jamaica	50.8	74	78	98	1.1	0.9	0.9	100 g	5	12
Japan	51.1	78	85	..	..	0.7	0.7	60	6	0
Jordan	48.3	70	73	80	1.0	0.2	0.3	100	3	2
Kazakhstan	51.6	58	68	92	1.0	0.9	0.9	..	6	5
Kenya	49.9	46	47	95	1.0	0.8	0.9	100	0	0
Korea, Dem. Rep.	49.8	60	63	100	..	0.8	0.8	..	0	..
Korea, Rep.	49.7	70	77	96	1.0	0.6	0.7	100	4	..
Kuwait	46.8	75	79	99	1.0	0.3	0.5	100	0	0
Kyrgyz Republic	51.1	62	70	90	..	0.9	0.9	..	0	4
Lao PDR	50.0	53	55	25	0.8	..	..	100	0	0
Latvia	54.1	65	76	..	1.0	1.0	1.0	..	0	7
Lebanon	50.8	69	72	85	1.0	0.4	0.4	100	0	0
Lesotho	50.4	43	44	91	1.2	0.6	0.6	0	6	6
Liberia	49.7	46	48	0	0.6	0.6	0.7	0	0	0
Libya	48.2	70	74	100	0.9	0.2	0.3	50	0	7
Lithuania	52.8	68	78	..	1.0	0.9	0.9	..	0	6
Macedonia, FYR	50.0	71	75	..	..	0.7	0.7	..	8	9
Madagascar	50.1	54	57	78	0.9	0.8	0.8	100 f	0	19
Malawi	50.8	38	39	90	0.8	1.0	0.9	..	9	4
Malaysia	49.4	70	75	90	1.0	0.6	0.6	100	7	16
Mali	51.0	40	43	25	0.5	0.9	0.9	100	10	21
Mauritania	50.4	49	53	49	0.7	0.8	0.8	100	0	4
Mauritius	50.5	69	76	99	1.0	0.4	0.5	100	3	..
Mexico	51.4	70	76	71	1.0	0.4	0.5	100	5	5
Moldova	52.4	64	71	..	1.0	0.9	0.9	..	0	0
Mongolia	50.4	64	67	90	1.0	0.9	0.9	..	0	0
Morocco	50.0	66	70	45	0.8	0.5	0.5	100	0	0
Mozambique	51.4	41	43	54	0.6	0.9	0.9	100	4	0
Myanmar	50.3	54	60	80	1.0	0.8	0.7	67	0	0
Namibia	50.5	44	44	88	1.0	0.7	0.7	..	10	8
Nepal	48.7	60	59	15	0.6	0.7	0.7	100	0	3
Netherlands	50.5	75	81	..	..	0.6	0.7	100	31	28
New Zealand	51.1	76	81	..	..	0.8	0.8	0	8	8
Nicaragua	50.2	66	71	71	1.0	0.5	0.6	60	10	5
Niger	50.6	44	48	30	0.4	0.8	0.8	50	5	10
Nigeria	50.6	45	47	60	0.9	0.5	0.6	50	3	6
Norway	50.5	76	81	..	..	0.8	0.9	100	35	20
Oman	47.4	72	75	98	1.0	0.1	0.2	..	0	0
Pakistan	48.2	62	65	27	0.6	0.3	0.4	100	4	7
Panama	49.6	72	77	72	1.0	0.5	0.6	100	13	6
Papua New Guinea	48.5	56	58	70	0.9	0.7	0.7	0	0	0
Paraguay	49.6	68	73	83	1.0	0.4	0.4	50 h	0	7
Peru	49.7	67	72	64	1.0	0.4	0.5	100	6	10
Philippines	49.6	68	72	83	1.0	0.6	0.6	100	8	10
Poland	51.4	69	78	..	1.0	0.8	0.9	100	17	12
Portugal	52.0	73	79	..	1.0	0.7	0.8	100	10	10
Puerto Rico	51.9	72	81	99	1.0	0.5	0.6	..	..	..

	Female population	Life expectancy at birth		Pregnant women receiving prenatal care	Literacy gender parity index	Labor force gender parity index		Maternity leave benefits	Women in decision-making positions	
	% of total	Male years	Female years	%	ages 15–24			% of wages paid in covered period	% of total at ministerial level	
	2001	2001	2001	1996	2001	1990	2001	1998	1994	1998
Romania	51.1	66	74	..	1.0	0.8	0.8	50–94	0	8
Russian Federation	53.3	59	72	..	1.0	0.9	1.0	100	0	8
Rwanda	50.5	39	40	94	1.0	1.0	1.0	67	9	5
Saudi Arabia	45.8	71	75	87	1.0	0.1	0.2	50–100	0	0
Senegal	50.2	51	54	74	0.7	0.7	0.7	100	7	7
Sierra Leone	50.9	36	39	30	..	0.6	0.6	..	0	10
Singapore	48.7	76	80	100	1.0	0.6	0.6	100	0	0
Slovak Republic	51.3	69	77	..	..	0.9	0.9	..	5	19
Slovenia	51.3	72	79	..	1.0	0.9	0.9	..	5	0
Somalia	50.4	46	49	0	..	0.8	0.8	0	0	0
South Africa	51.7	46	48	89	1.0	0.6	0.6	45	6	..
Spain	51.1	75	82	..	1.0	0.5	0.6	100	14	18
Sri Lanka	50.6	71	76	100	1.0	0.5	0.6	100	3	13
Sudan	49.7	57	59	54	0.9	0.4	0.4	100	0	0
Swaziland	51.8	44	45	0	1.0	0.6	0.6	0	0	0
Sweden	50.4	78	82	..	..	0.9	0.9	75	30	43
Switzerland	50.4	77	83	..	..	0.6	0.7	100	17	17
Syrian Arab Republic	49.5	68	72	33	0.8	0.3	0.4	100	7	8
Tajikistan	50.2	64	70	90	1.0	0.7	0.8	..	3	6
Tanzania	50.4	43	44	92	0.9	1.0	1.0	100	13	13
Thailand	50.8	67	71	77	1.0	0.9	0.9	100 [i]	0	4
Togo	50.3	48	51	43	0.7	0.7	0.7	100	5	9
Trinidad and Tobago	50.1	70	75	98	1.0	0.5	0.5	60–100	19	14
Tunisia	49.5	70	74	71	0.9	0.4	0.5	67	4	3
Turkey	49.5	67	72	62	1.0	0.5	0.6	67	5	5
Turkmenistan	50.5	61	69	90	..	0.8	0.8	..	3	4
Uganda	50.0	43	43	87	0.9	0.9	0.9	100 [j]	10	13
Ukraine	53.5	63	74	..	1.0	1.0	1.0	100	0	5
United Arab Emirates	34.2	74	77	95	1.1	0.1	0.2	100	0	0
United Kingdom	50.9	75	80	..	..	0.7	0.8	90 [k]	9	24
United States	51.1	75	81	..	..	0.8	0.9	0	14	26
Uruguay	51.5	71	79	80	1.0	0.6	0.7	100	0	7
Uzbekistan	50.3	64	71	90	1.0	0.8	0.9	..	3	3
Venezuela, RB	49.7	71	77	74	1.0	0.5	0.5	100	11	3
Vietnam	50.6	67	72	78	1.0	1.0	1.0	100	5	0
West Bank and Gaza	49.3	70	75	..	..	..	..	..	..	..
Yemen, Rep.	49.0	56	58	26	0.6	0.4	0.4	100	0	0
Yugoslavia, Fed. Rep.	50.2	70	75	..	..	0.7	0.8	..	..	5
Zambia	50.3	37	38	92	0.9	0.8	0.8	100	5	3
Zimbabwe	49.9	40	39	93	1.0	0.8	0.8	60–75	3	12
World	**49.6 w**	**65 w**	**69 w**	**70 w**	**.. w**	**0.7 w**	**0.7 w**		**6 w**	**.. w**
Low income	49.3	58	60	62	0.9	0.6	0.6		4	6
Middle income	49.5	67	72	77	1.0	0.7	0.7		5	..
Lower middle income	49.3	67	71	76	1.0	0.8	0.8		4	..
Upper middle income	50.5	68	75	80	1.0	0.5	0.6		6	8
Low & middle income	49.4	63	66	70	0.9	0.7	0.7		5	..
East Asia & Pacific	48.9	67	71	80	1.0	0.8	0.8		3	..
Europe & Central Asia	51.8	64	73	..	1.0	0.8	0.9		3	7
Latin America & Carib.	50.6	67	74	75	1.0	0.5	0.5		8	8
Middle East & N. Africa	49.2	67	70	58	0.9	0.3	0.4		2	2
South Asia	48.5	62	63	55	0.8	0.5	0.5		4	..
Sub-Saharan Africa	50.3	45	47	65	0.9	0.7	0.7		5	8
High income	50.7	75	81	..	..	0.7	0.8		13	13
Europe EMU	51.0	75	82	..	..	0.7	0.7		16	15

a. For 30 days; 75 percent thereafter. b. Benefit is 70 percent of wages above the minimum wage and 100 percent of the national minimum wage. c. For 15 weeks. d. For 6 weeks. e. For 84 days. f. Up to a ceiling. g. For 8 weeks. h. For 9 weeks. i. Benefit is 100 percent for the first 45 days, then 50 percent for 15 days. j. For 1 month. k. For 6 weeks; flat rate thereafter.

About the data

Despite much progress in recent decades, gender inequalities remain pervasive in many dimensions of life—worldwide. But while disparities exist throughout the world, they are most prevalent in poor developing countries. The differences in outcomes between men and women—and between boys and girls—are a consequence of differences in the opportunities and resources available to them. Inequalities in the allocation of such resources as education, health care, and nutrition matter because of the strong association of these resources with well-being, productivity, and economic growth. This pattern of inequality begins at an early age, with boys routinely receiving a larger share of education and health spending than girls do, for example.

Life expectancy has increased for both men and women in all regions, but female morbidity and mortality rates sometimes exceed male rates, particularly during early childhood and the reproductive years. In high-income countries women tend to outlive men by four to eight years on average, while in low-income countries the difference is narrower—about two to three years. The female disadvantage is best reflected in differences in child mortality rates (see table 2.20). Child mortality captures the effect of preferences for boys because adequate nutrition and medical interventions are particularly important for the age group 1–5. Because of the natural female biological advantage, when female child mortality is as high as or higher than male child mortality, there is good reason to believe that girls are discriminated against.

Female disadvantage in mortality is carried into adolescence and the reproductive years. Serious health risks for adolescents arise when they become sexually active. And while in high-income countries women have universal access to health care during pregnancy, in developing countries it is estimated that 35 percent of pregnant women—some 45 million each year—receive no care at all (United Nations 2000b). Prenatal care is essential for recognizing, diagnosing, and promptly treating complications that arise during pregnancy.

Girls in many developing countries are allowed less education by their families than boys are—a disparity reflected in lower female primary enrollment (see table 1.2) and higher female illiteracy. As a result, women have fewer employment opportunities, especially in the formal sector. A labor force gender parity index of less than 1.0 shows that women's labor force participation in the formal sector is lower than men's. (A ratio of 1.0 indicates gender equality.)

Women who work outside the home continue to bear a disproportionate share of the responsibility for housework and child rearing. They also face discriminatory practices in the workplace, especially relating to equal pay and benefits. The maternity benefits data in the table relate only to legislated benefits and do not include contractual benefits negotiated through labor union contracts. The benefits generally apply only in the formal sector, leaving out the vast majority of working women in developing countries. As a result, while the situation in the United States is much better than the data indicate, the situation in Thailand is likely to be much worse.

Women are vastly underrepresented in decision-making positions in government, although there is some evidence of recent improvement. While 6 percent of the world's cabinet ministers were women in 1994, 8 percent were in 1998. Without representation at this level, it is difficult for women to influence policy.

For information on other aspects of gender, see tables 1.2 (Millennium Development Goals: eradicating poverty and improving lives), 2.3 (employment by economic activity), 2.4 (unemployment), 2.13 (education efficiency), 2.14 (education outcomes), 2.17 (reproductive health), 2.19 (health: risk factors and future challenges), and 2.20 (mortality).

Definitions

• **Female population** is the percentage of the population that is female. • **Life expectancy at birth** is the number of years a newborn infant would live if prevailing patterns of mortality at the time of its birth were to stay the same throughout its life. • **Pregnant women receiving prenatal care** are the percentage of women attended at least once during pregnancy by skilled health personnel for reasons related to pregnancy. • **Literacy gender parity index** is the ratio of the female literacy rate to the male rate, for the age group 15–24. • **Labor force gender parity index** is the ratio of the percentage of women who are economically active to the percentage of men who are. According to the International Labour Organization's (ILO) definition, the economically active population is all those who supply labor for the production of goods and services during a specified period. It includes both the employed and the unemployed. While national practices vary in the treatment of such groups as the armed forces and seasonal or part-time workers, in general the labor force includes the armed forces, the unemployed, and first-time job seekers, but excludes homemakers and other unpaid caregivers and workers in the informal sector. • **Maternity leave benefits** refer to the compensation provided to women during maternity leave, as a share of their full wages. • **Women in decisionmaking positions** are those in ministerial or equivalent positions in the government.

Data sources

The data are from the World Bank's population database; electronic databases of the United Nations Educational, Scientific, and Cultural Organization (UNESCO); the ILO database Estimates and Projections of the Economically Active Population, 1950–2010; and the United Nations' *World's Women: Trends and Statistics 2000*.

	Population	Surface area	Population density	Gross national income				Gross domestic product		Life expectancy at birth	Adult illiteracy rate	Carbon dioxide emissions
						PPP [a]						
					Per capita		Per capita		Per capita		% ages 15 and above	
	thousands	thousand sq. km	people per sq. km	$ millions	$	$ millions	$	% growth	% growth	years		thousand metric tons
	2001	2001	2001	2001 [b]	2001 [b]	2001	2001	2000–01	2000–01	2001	2001	1999
American Samoa	70	0.2	350	..	.. [c]	..	..	..	..	..	..	286
Andorra	70	0.5	140	..	.. [d]	..	..	..	..	..	..	..
Antigua and Barbuda	68	0.4	156	627	9,150	654	9,550	0.2	–0.5	..	..	348
Aruba	90	0.2	474	..	.. [d]	..	..	..	..	..	..	1,905
Bahamas, The	310	13.9	31	..	.. [d]	..	..	..	..	70	5	1,795
Bahrain	651	0.7	917	7,246	11,130	10,020	15,390	0.0	–0.4	73	12	19,012
Barbados	268	0.4	624	2,614	9,750 [e]	4,052	15,110	1.5	1.0	75	0	2,034
Belize	247	23.0	11	727	2,940	1,273	5,150	5.1	2.1	74	7	619
Bermuda	60	0.1	1,200	..	.. [d]	..	..	..	..	..	..	462
Bhutan	828	47.0	18	529	640			7.0	4.0	63	..	385
Brunei	344	5.8	65	..	.. [d]	..	..	..	..	76	8	4,668
Cape Verde	446	4.0	111	596	1,340	2,471 [f]	5,540 [f]	3.3	0.6	69	25	139
Cayman Islands	35	0.3	135	..	.. [d]	..	..	..	..	..	..	282
Channel Islands	149	0.2	768	..	..	..	..	..	..	79	..	..
Comoros	572	2.2	256	219	380	1,080	1,890	1.9	–0.5	61	44	81
Cyprus	761	9.3	82	9,372	12,320	16,060 [f]	21,110 [f]	4.0	3.5	78	3	6,020
Djibouti	644	23.2	28	572	890	1,562	2,420	1.6	–0.4	45	35	385
Dominica	72	0.8	96	230	3,200	354	4,920	–4.3	–4.1	76	..	81
Equatorial Guinea	469	28.1	17	327	700	..	..	1.3	–1.3	51	16	649
Faeroe Islands	50	1.4	36	..	.. [d]	..	..	..	..	..	..	649
Fiji	817	18.3	45	1,755	2,150	4,017	4,920	2.6	2.0	69	7	725
French Polynesia	237	4.0	65	..	.. [d]	..	..	..	..	73	..	542
Greenland	60	341.7	0	..	.. [d]	..	..	..	..	..	..	539
Grenada	100	0.3	295	363	3,610	632	6,290	–4.7	–6.0	73	..	213
Guam	157	0.6	285	..	.. [d]	..	..	..	..	78	..	4,071
Guyana	766	215.0	4	641	840	3,280	4,280	1.5	0.8	63	1	1,685
Iceland	282	103.0	3	8,152	28,910	8,135	28,850	3.0	2.3	80	..	2,066
Isle of Man	80	0.6	133	..	.. [c]	..	..	..	..	..	..	..

About the data

This table shows data for 56 economies—small economies with populations between 30,000 and 1 million and smaller economies if they are members of the World Bank. Where data on gross national income (GNI) per capita are not available, the estimated range is given. For more information on the calculation of GNI (gross national product, or GNP, in the 1968 United Nations System of National Accounts) and purchasing power parity (PPP) conversion factors, see *About the data* for table 1.1. Since 2000 this table has excluded France's overseas departments—French Guiana, Guadeloupe, Martinique, and Réunion—for which GNI and other economic measures are now included in the French national accounts.

Definitions

• **Population** is based on the de facto definition of population, which counts all residents regardless of legal status or citizenship—except for refugees not permanently settled in the country of asylum, who are generally considered part of the population of their country of origin. The values shown are midyear estimates for 2001. See also table 2.1. • **Surface area** is a country's total area, including areas under inland bodies of water and some coastal waterways. • **Population density** is midyear population divided by land area in square kilometers. • **Gross national income** (GNI) is the sum of value added by all resident producers plus any product taxes (less subsidies) not included in the valuation of output plus net receipts of primary income (compensation of employees and property income) from abroad. Data are in current

U.S. dollars converted using the World Bank Atlas method (see *Statistical methods*). • **GNI per capita** is gross national income divided by midyear population. GNI per capita in U.S. dollars is converted using the World Bank Atlas method. • **PPP GNI** is gross national income converted to international dollars using purchasing power parity rates. An international dollar has the same purchasing power over GNI as a U.S. dollar has in the United States. • **Gross domestic product** (GDP) is the sum of value added by all resident producers plus any product taxes (less subsidies) not included in the valuation of output. Growth is calculated from constant price GDP data in local currency. • **GDP per capita** is gross domestic product divided by midyear population. • **Life expectancy at birth** is the number of years a newborn infant would live if prevail-

Key indicators for other economies | 1.6

	Population	Surface area	Population density	Gross national income				Gross domestic product		Life expectancy at birth	Adult illiteracy rate	Carbon dioxide emissions
						PPP [a]						
					Per capita		Per capita		Per capita		% ages 15	
	thousands	thousand sq. km	people per sq. km	$ millions	$	$ millions	$	% growth	% growth	years	and above	thousand metric tons
	2001	2001	2001	2001 [b]	2001 [b]	2001	2001	2000–01	2000–01	2001	2001	1999
Kiribati	93	0.7	127	77	830	..	..	1.6	–0.7	62	..	26
Liechtenstein	30	0.2	188	..	.. [d]	..	..	..	..	..	..	..
Luxembourg	441	2.6	170	17,571	39,840	21,416	48,560	1.0	0.3	77	..	8,024
Macao, China	440	..	..	6,329 [g]	14,380 [g]	9,518	21,630	2.1	1.7	79	6	1,517
Maldives	280	0.3	934	562	2,000	..	..	2.1	–0.2	69	3	465
Malta	395	0.3	1,234	3,637	9,210 [e]	5,192	13,140	–0.7	–2.0	78	8	3,422
Marshall Islands	53	0.2	263	115	2,190	..	..	0.6	–0.7	..	..	..
Mayotte	145	0.4	388	..	.. [c]	..	..	..	..	..	..	..
Micronesia, Fed. Sts.	120	0.7	172	258	2,150	..	..	0.9	–0.9	68	..	..
Monaco	30	0.0	15,789	..	.. [d]	..	..	..	..	..	..	..
Netherlands Antilles	220	0.8	275	..	.. [d]	..	..	..	..	..	3	5,606
New Caledonia	216	18.6	12	..	.. [d]	..	..	..	..	73	..	1,667
Northern Mariana Islands	80	0.5	160	..	.. [d]	..	..	..	..	..	..	..
Palau	20	0.5	42	132	6,780	..	..	1.0	–1.1	..	..	242
Qatar	598	11.0	54	..	.. [d]	..	..	..	..	75	18	51,699
Samoa	174	2.8	61	260	1,490	1,067	6,130	10.0	8.7	69	1	139
São Tomé and Principe	151	1.0	157	43	280	..	..	3.0	0.9	65	..	88
Seychelles	82	0.5	183	538	6,530	..	..	–8.1	–9.4	73	..	216
Solomon Islands	431	28.9	15	253	590	825 [f]	1,910 [f]	–9.0	–11.5	69	..	165
San Marino	30	0.1	300	..	.. [d]	..	..	..	..	..	..	..
St. Kitts and Nevis	45	0.4	125	299	6,630	459	10,190	1.7	–0.7	71	..	103
St. Lucia	157	0.6	257	619	3,950	778	4,960	–3.7	–4.6	72	..	322
St. Vincent and the Grenadines	116	0.4	297	317	2,740	577	4,980	–0.6	–1.3	73	..	161
Suriname	420	163.3	3	761	1,810	..	..	5.9	5.2	70	..	2,151
Timor-Leste	753	14.9	51	391	520	..	..	..	..	..	..	..
Tonga	101	0.8	140	154	1,530	..	..	3.1	2.6	71	..	121
Vanuatu	201	12.2	17	212	1,050	626	3,110	–4.0	–6.0	68	..	81
Virgin Islands (U.S.)	109	0.3	322	..	.. [d]	..	..	..	..	78	..	13,106

a. PPP is purchasing power parity; see *Definitions*. b. Calculated using the World Bank Atlas method. c. Estimated to be upper middle income ($2,976–9,205). d. Estimated to be high income ($9,206 or more). e. Included in the aggregates for upper-middle-income economies on the basis of earlier data. f. The estimate is based on regression; others are extrapolated from the latest International Comparison Programme benchmark estimates. g. Refers to GDP or GDP per capita.

ing patterns of mortality at the time of its birth were to stay the same throughout its life. • **Adult illiteracy rate** is the percentage of people ages 15 and above who cannot, with understanding, read and write a short, simple statement about their everyday life. • **Carbon dioxide emissions** are those stemming from the burning of fossil fuels and the manufacture of cement. They include carbon dioxide produced during consumption of solid, liquid, and gas fuels and gas flaring.

Data sources

The indicators here and throughout the rest of the book have been compiled by World Bank staff from primary and secondary sources. More information about the indicators and their sources can be found in *About the data*, *Definitions*, and *Data sources* for tables in subsequent sections.

2 | PEOPLE

Development has often bypassed the poorest people—and sometimes increased their disadvantage. Attacking poverty directly has therefore become an urgent global priority.

Poverty is commonly measured by income, but it has many other dimensions. Poor people not only lack money, but they also lack resources, opportunities, and access to services such as health and education. So to help people move out of poverty, countries need to take action in three areas: They need to stimulate growth and make markets work for the poor. They need to invest in health, nutrition, and education—increasing human capital. And they need to provide effective mechanisms for reducing vulnerability to economic shocks, natural disasters, ill health, and disability.

This section measures income poverty and tracks the progress countries have made in developing their human capital and in reducing the vulnerability of their people.

Boosting growth to lift people out of poverty

A paradox of the second half of the 20th century is that the world population underwent unprecedented growth—from 2.5 billion in 1950 to more than 6 billion in 2001—even as the population growth rate was declining (figure 2a). The decline was triggered largely by a drop in fertility rates. Between 1952 and 2001 fertility rates fell from 5.1 to 2.7 births per woman. Thus while the population grew by 1.5 percent a year in 1980–2001, the growth rate is expected to drop to 1 percent in 2001–15 (table 2.1).

During the transition from high fertility and rapid population growth to lower fertility and slower growth, the working-age population expands relative to the dependent (younger and older) population, opening a demographic window of opportunity for economic growth. Countries can take advantage of this one-time opportunity if they invest appropriately in their human and physical capital and create employment opportunities for youth and for those who have not been working for wages. Several countries in East Asia, such as the Republic of Korea and Thailand, and a few in Latin America, such as Brazil and Mexico, have done so (figure 2b). But South Asian countries that are now moving into the later stage of their transition to low fertility may not benefit from the demographic transition if they do not encourage growth, investment, and human capital development. The demographic window for these countries will close within a generation.

In many developing countries agriculture is still the main economic activity (table 2.3). As economies grow, more people work for wages. In most countries wages are rising steadily, increasing prosperity and raising standards of living (table 2.5).

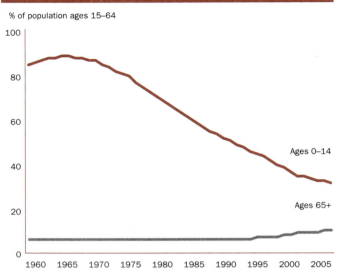

2b

Thailand's child dependency ratio fell quickly in the 1970s and 1980s, before the old-age dependency rose

% of population ages 15–64

Ages 0–14

Ages 65+

Source: World Bank data.

In developing countries gross domestic product (GDP) grew by 3.3 percent a year in the 1990s, and the share of people living on less than $1 a day fell from 29 percent to 23 percent. By 1999, 125 million fewer people were living in extreme poverty. But the poorest are often excluded from all but the lowest level of economic activity.

Progress in reducing poverty has been uneven. Within countries, the large gaps in social indicators between rich and poor confirm the persistence of deprivation (table 2.7). Globally, much of the decline in income poverty took place in East Asia, where sustained growth in China has lifted nearly 150 million people out of poverty since 1990. And faster growth in India has led to a modest decline in the number of poor people in South Asia. But in other regions the number of poor people has increased even as their share in the population has declined—and in Europe and Central Asia both the number and the share of poor people have risen. Unemployment is high in many of the formerly centrally planned economies, with long-term unemployment hovering around 50 percent of total unemployment in the Czech Republic, Estonia, and Latvia in 1998–2001 (table 2.4).

Enhancing security for poor people

Poor people face many risks. They face labor market risks, often having to take precarious jobs in the informal sector and put their children to work to increase household income. In Sub-Saharan Africa one in three children ages 10–14 was in the labor force in 2001 (table 2.9). Poor people also face health risks, with illness and injury having both direct and opportunity costs. In South Asia nearly 80 percent of all spending on health comes from private sources, much of it out of pocket, exposing

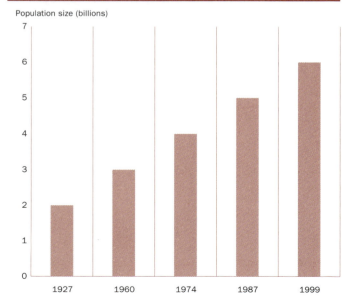

2a

The world population boomed in the second half of the 20th century

Population size (billions)

Source: World Bank staff estimates.

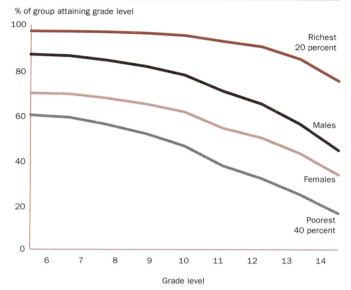

In India educational attainment is sharply lower for the poor—and for girls

% of group attaining grade level

Richest 20 percent

Males

Females

Poorest 40 percent

Grade level

Source: Demographic and Health Survey.

many poor households to the impoverishing effects of needed health care (table 2.9).

Enhancing security for poor people means reducing their vulnerability to ill health and economic shocks. Market-based insurance and pension schemes can reduce risk significantly, but they play only a minor role in many developing countries. In 16 developing countries public spending on pensions amounted to less than 0.5 percent of GDP in the 1990s (table 2.10). To increase the security of poor people, national poverty reduction strategies must support their immediate consumption needs and protect their assets by ensuring access to basic services. Literacy training and health and nutrition services are often the most needed and most valued by poor people. Yet government spending in these areas remains low in many countries. In 2000 low-income countries' public spending on health averaged 1 percent of GDP, compared with 6 percent for high-income countries (table 2.10).

Building human capital through education and health services

Poor people lack the means to escape poverty. Increasing the productivity of their labor through investments in education and health is often the most effective way to improve their welfare.

Investments in education widen horizons, making it easier for people to take advantage of new opportunities and helping them to participate in social and economic life. But despite increased spending on education, particularly primary education (table 2.11), enrollment rates remain low in many countries. In Sub-Saharan Africa primary enrollment rates declined between 1980 and 2000 (table 2.12). Low primary enrollment typically reflects

low participation by poor people. But in many poor countries it also has a gender dimension, reflecting traditional biases against girls' education and reliance on girls' contributions to the household (figure 2c; table 2.13). One consequence of this imbalance: higher rates of illiteracy among women (table 2.14).

The public sector is the main provider of health care in developing countries—training medical personnel, investing in hospitals, and directly providing medical care (table 2.15). To reduce inequities, many countries have emphasized primary health care, including immunization, provision of sanitation, access to safe drinking water, and safe motherhood initiatives (tables 2.16 and 2.17). Even so, much remains to be done. Child malnutrition remains a burden, with 22 countries having rates of more than 30 percent in the 1990s (table 2.18). An estimated 40 million people are living with HIV/AIDS, an unprecedented public health challenge (table 2.19). And the reemergence of old diseases such as tuberculosis in Europe and Central Asia and parts of South and East Asia has put severe strains on health budgets. A high prevalence of disease in a country goes hand-in-hand with poor economic performance (figure 2d).

* * *

There are many ways to measure poverty and its effects on people's lives. The indicators reported here suffer from many shortcomings, noted in *About the data* for each table. But taken together, the indicators provide a broad picture of how well different economies are doing in reducing poverty, enhancing human security, and building human capital—and how large a task still faces many developing countries.

2d

Where per capita income is low, so is life expectancy

GNI per capita ($ thousands), 2001

Life expectancy (years), 2001

Source: World Bank data.

2.1 Population dynamics

	Total population (millions)			Average annual population growth rate (%)		Population age composition			Dependency ratio (dependents as proportion of working–age population)		Crude death rate (per 1,000 people)	Crude birth rate (per 1,000 people)
						Ages 0–14 %	Ages 15–64 %	Ages 65+ %	Young	Old		
	1980	2001	2015	1980–2001	2001–15	2001	2001	2001	2001	2001	2001	2001
Afghanistan	16.0	27.2 [a]	38.8	2.6	2.5	43.7	53.5	2.8	0.8	0.1	21	48
Albania	2.7	3.2	3.6	0.8	1.0	28.6	64.5	6.9	0.5	0.1	6	17
Algeria	18.7	30.8	38.3	2.4	1.5	35.4	60.7	3.9	0.6	0.1	5	23
Angola	7.1	13.5	19.6	3.1	2.6	47.4	49.7	2.9	1.0	0.1	19	47
Argentina	28.1	37.5	42.8	1.4	1.1	27.5	62.8	9.7	0.4	0.2	8	19
Armenia	3.1	3.8	4.0	1.0	0.3	23.0	67.7	9.3	0.4	0.1	7	11
Australia	14.7	19.4	21.5	1.3	0.7	20.5	67.5	12.0	0.3	0.2	7	13
Austria	7.6	8.1	8.0	0.4	–0.1	16.5	67.8	15.7	0.2	0.2	9	9
Azerbaijan	6.2	8.1	8.9	1.3	0.7	28.4	64.4	7.2	0.5	0.1	6	16
Bangladesh	85.4	133.3	166.0	2.1	1.6	37.0	59.7	3.3	0.6	0.1	9	28
Belarus	9.6	10.0	9.3	0.2	–0.5	18.0	68.3	13.6	0.3	0.2	14	9
Belgium	9.8	10.3	10.4	0.2	0.0	17.2	66.1	16.6	0.3	0.3	10	11
Benin	3.5	6.4	9.0	3.0	2.4	45.9	51.4	2.7	0.9	0.1	13	39
Bolivia	5.4	8.5	10.9	2.2	1.8	39.1	56.5	4.4	0.7	0.1	8	30
Bosnia and Herzegovina	4.1	4.1	4.4	0.0	0.5	18.6	71.3	10.2	0.3	0.1	8	12
Botswana	0.9	1.7	1.8	3.0	0.5	42.0	55.7	2.2	0.8	0.0	21	31
Brazil	121.6	172.4	201.0	1.7	1.1	28.4	66.4	5.2	0.4	0.1	7	19
Bulgaria	8.9	8.0	7.3	–0.5	–0.7	15.2	68.6	16.2	0.2	0.2	14	9
Burkina Faso	7.0	11.6	15.6	2.4	2.1	47.1	50.2	2.7	0.9	0.1	19	44
Burundi	4.1	6.9	8.8	2.5	1.7	46.0	51.4	2.6	0.9	0.1	20	39
Cambodia	6.8	12.3	15.1	2.8	1.5	43.0	54.2	2.8	0.8	0.1	12	29
Cameroon	8.7	15.2	19.4	2.6	1.7	41.6	54.8	3.7	0.8	0.1	15	36
Canada	24.6	31.1	33.7	1.1	0.6	18.8	68.6	12.6	0.3	0.2	7	11
Central African Republic	2.3	3.8	4.6	2.3	1.5	42.3	54.2	3.5	0.8	0.1	20	36
Chad	4.5	7.9	11.8	2.7	2.9	49.6	47.4	3.0	1.1	0.1	16	45
Chile	11.1	15.4	17.7	1.5	1.0	27.8	65.0	7.2	0.4	0.1	6	17
China	981.2	1,271.8	1,392.6	1.2	0.6	24.8	68.1	7.1	0.4	0.1	7	15
Hong Kong, China	5.0	6.7	7.0	1.4	0.3	16.7	72.0	11.2	0.2	0.2	5	7
Colombia	28.4	43.0	51.5	2.0	1.3	32.4	62.9	4.7	0.5	0.1	6	22
Congo, Dem. Rep.	26.9	52.4	75.7	3.2	2.6	47.6	49.8	2.6	1.0	0.1	17	45
Congo, Rep.	1.7	3.1	4.6	3.0	2.7	46.3	50.5	3.2	0.9	0.1	14	42
Costa Rica	2.3	3.9	4.7	2.5	1.4	31.2	63.1	5.7	0.5	0.1	4	20
Côte d'Ivoire	8.2	16.4	20.5	3.3	1.6	42.1	55.3	2.6	0.8	0.0	17	37
Croatia	4.6	4.4	4.2	–0.2	–0.3	16.7	68.1	15.2	0.2	0.2	11	9
Cuba	9.7	11.2	11.7	0.7	0.3	21.1	68.8	10.1	0.3	0.1	7	12
Czech Republic	10.2	10.2	9.9	0.0	–0.2	16.1	70.1	13.8	0.2	0.2	11	9
Denmark	5.1	5.4	5.4	0.2	0.1	18.4	66.7	14.9	0.3	0.2	11	12
Dominican Republic	5.7	8.5	10.1	1.9	1.3	33.0	62.7	4.4	0.5	0.1	7	23
Ecuador	8.0	12.9	15.8	2.3	1.5	33.4	61.9	4.7	0.6	0.1	6	24
Egypt, Arab Rep.	40.9	65.2	80.9	2.2	1.5	34.7	61.1	4.2	0.6	0.1	6	25
El Salvador	4.6	6.4	8.0	1.6	1.6	35.3	59.7	5.0	0.6	0.1	6	26
Eritrea	2.4	4.2	5.8	2.7	2.3	45.2	52.2	2.6	0.9	0.1	13	38
Estonia	1.5	1.4	1.3	–0.4	–0.5	17.1	68.0	14.9	0.3	0.2	14	9
Ethiopia	37.7	65.8	88.2	2.7	2.1	46.0	51.2	2.8	0.9	0.1	20	43
Finland	4.8	5.2	5.3	0.4	0.1	17.9	67.0	15.0	0.3	0.2	9	11
France	53.9	59.2	61.8	0.4	0.3	18.7	65.1	16.1	0.3	0.2	9	13
Gabon	0.7	1.3	1.7	2.9	2.2	40.3	54.1	5.7	0.7	0.1	15	35
Gambia, The	0.6	1.3	1.8	3.5	2.0	40.3	56.5	3.2	0.7	0.1	14	38
Georgia	5.1	5.3	4.8	0.2	–0.7	20.1	66.8	13.1	0.3	0.2	10	8
Germany	78.3	82.3	80.1	0.2	–0.2	15.3	68.3	16.4	0.2	0.2	10	9
Ghana	10.7	19.7	24.7	2.9	1.6	43.3	52.2	4.6	0.9	0.1	12	29
Greece	9.6	10.6	10.7	0.4	0.1	14.9	67.0	18.1	0.2	0.3	11	11
Guatemala	6.8	11.7	16.3	2.6	2.4	43.2	53.3	3.5	0.8	0.1	7	33
Guinea	4.5	7.6	9.8	2.5	1.9	44.3	53.1	2.6	0.8	0.1	17	38
Guinea-Bissau	0.8	1.2	1.7	2.3	2.2	43.6	52.9	3.6	0.8	0.1	20	40
Haiti	5.4	8.1	10.3	2.0	1.7	40.2	56.3	3.5	0.7	0.1	13	32

	Total population (millions)			Average annual population growth rate (%)		Population age composition			Dependency ratio (dependents as proportion of working-age population)		Crude death rate (per 1,000 people)	Crude birth rate (per 1,000 people)
						Ages 0–14 %	Ages 15–64 %	Ages 65+ %	Young	Old		
	1980	2001	2015	1980–2001	2001–15	2001	2001	2001	2001	2001	2001	2001
Honduras	3.6	6.6	8.9	2.9	2.1	41.4	55.2	3.4	0.8	0.1	6	30
Hungary	10.7	10.2	9.4	–0.2	–0.6	16.8	68.7	14.5	0.2	0.2	13	10
India	687.3	1,032.4	1,227.9	1.9	1.2	33.1	61.9	5.0	0.5	0.1	9	25
Indonesia	148.3	209.0	245.5	1.6	1.1	30.2	65.1	4.7	0.5	0.1	7	21
Iran, Islamic Rep.	39.1	64.5	80.4	2.4	1.6	32.6	62.7	4.7	0.6	0.1	6	22
Iraq	13.0	23.8	31.2	2.9	1.9	40.9	56.2	2.9	0.8	0.1	8	30
Ireland	3.4	3.8	4.3	0.6	0.8	21.5	67.2	11.2	0.3	0.2	8	15
Israel	3.9	6.4	7.9	2.4	1.5	27.6	62.6	9.7	0.4	0.2	6	21
Italy	56.4	57.9	55.0	0.1	–0.4	14.2	67.4	18.4	0.2	0.3	10	9
Jamaica	2.1	2.6	3.0	0.9	1.1	30.6	62.4	7.0	0.5	0.1	7	21
Japan	116.8	127.0	124.1	0.4	–0.2	14.5	67.9	17.6	0.2	0.3	9	9
Jordan	2.2	5.0	6.8	4.0	2.2	38.2	58.7	3.1	0.7	0.1	4	29
Kazakhstan	14.9	14.9	15.1	0.0	0.1	26.1	66.4	7.5	0.4	0.1	10	15
Kenya	16.6	30.7	37.5	2.9	1.4	43.0	54.3	2.7	0.8	0.1	15	35
Korea, Dem. Rep.	17.2	22.4	24.2	1.3	0.6	27.1	67.1	5.8	0.4	0.1	11	18
Korea, Rep.	38.1	47.3	50.3	1.0	0.4	21.3	71.8	7.0	0.3	0.1	6	13
Kuwait	1.4	2.0	2.7	1.9	2.1	32.2	65.5	2.3	0.5	0.0	2	20
Kyrgyz Republic	3.6	5.0	5.8	1.5	1.1	33.4	60.6	6.0	0.6	0.1	7	20
Lao PDR	3.2	5.4	7.3	2.5	2.2	42.4	54.1	3.5	0.8	0.1	13	36
Latvia	2.5	2.4	2.1	–0.4	–0.7	16.5	68.6	14.9	0.3	0.2	14	8
Lebanon	3.0	4.4	5.2	1.8	1.2	31.5	62.6	5.9	0.5	0.1	6	20
Lesotho	1.4	2.1	2.3	2.0	0.8	39.7	56.1	4.3	0.7	0.1	18	32
Liberia	1.9	3.2	4.4	2.6	2.3	44.5	52.8	2.8	0.8	0.1	19	44
Libya	3.0	5.4	7.0	2.7	1.9	33.6	62.9	3.5	0.5	0.1	4	27
Lithuania	3.4	3.5	3.4	0.1	–0.2	18.9	67.4	13.7	0.3	0.2	12	9
Macedonia, FYR	1.9	2.0	2.2	0.4	0.4	22.2	67.5	10.2	0.3	0.1	8	13
Madagascar	8.9	16.0	22.5	2.8	2.5	44.8	52.2	3.0	0.9	0.1	12	39
Malawi	6.2	10.5	13.6	2.5	1.8	44.4	52.0	3.6	0.8	0.1	24	45
Malaysia	13.8	23.8	29.6	2.6	1.5	33.7	62.1	4.2	0.5	0.1	4	22
Mali	6.6	11.1	14.9	2.5	2.1	47.1	49.9	3.0	0.9	0.1	21	46
Mauritania	1.6	2.7	3.8	2.7	2.3	43.9	52.9	3.2	0.8	0.1	15	41
Mauritius	1.0	1.2	1.4	1.0	0.9	25.5	68.3	6.2	0.4	0.1	7	16
Mexico	67.6	99.4	121.1	1.8	1.4	33.6	61.4	5.0	0.6	0.1	5	24
Moldova	4.0	4.3	4.1	0.3	–0.2	21.8	67.1	11.0	0.3	0.2	9	9
Mongolia	1.7	2.4	2.9	1.8	1.3	33.2	62.7	4.0	0.5	0.1	6	22
Morocco	19.4	29.2	35.4	1.9	1.4	34.1	61.7	4.2	0.6	0.1	6	22
Mozambique	12.1	18.1	22.7	1.9	1.6	42.8	53.5	3.7	0.8	0.1	21	40
Myanmar	33.7	48.3	55.9	1.7	1.0	32.7	62.7	4.6	0.5	0.1	12	24
Namibia	1.0	1.8	2.1	2.8	1.2	41.7	54.6	3.8	0.8	0.1	19	35
Nepal	14.6	23.6	31.1	2.3	2.0	40.7	55.5	3.8	0.7	0.1	10	32
Netherlands	14.2	16.0	16.9	0.6	0.4	18.5	67.9	13.7	0.3	0.2	9	13
New Zealand	3.1	3.8	4.1	1.0	0.5	22.3	65.9	11.8	0.3	0.2	7	15
Nicaragua	2.9	5.2	7.0	2.8	2.1	42.1	54.9	3.1	0.8	0.1	5	30
Niger	5.6	11.2	16.6	3.3	2.8	49.0	48.7	2.4	1.0	0.0	20	50
Nigeria	71.1	129.9	169.4	2.9	1.9	43.9	53.5	2.6	0.8	0.0	17	39
Norway	4.1	4.5	4.8	0.5	0.4	20.0	65.0	15.1	0.3	0.2	10	13
Oman	1.1	2.5	3.4	3.9	2.2	43.2	54.2	2.5	0.8	0.0	3	27
Pakistan	82.7	141.5	192.8	2.6	2.2	41.2	55.5	3.3	0.8	0.1	8	33
Panama	2.0	2.9	3.5	1.9	1.3	30.9	63.5	5.6	0.5	0.1	5	21
Papua New Guinea	3.1	5.3	6.8	2.5	1.9	39.9	57.6	2.5	0.7	0.0	10	32
Paraguay	3.1	5.6	7.5	2.8	2.1	39.1	57.3	3.5	0.7	0.1	5	30
Peru	17.3	26.3	31.6	2.0	1.3	32.9	62.2	4.9	0.5	0.1	6	24
Philippines	48.0	78.3	98.2	2.3	1.6	36.9	59.2	3.9	0.6	0.1	6	26
Poland	35.6	38.6	38.4	0.4	0.0	18.8	69.0	12.2	0.3	0.2	9	10
Portugal	9.8	10.0	9.9	0.1	–0.1	17.1	67.6	15.2	0.3	0.2	10	11
Puerto Rico	3.2	3.8	4.2	0.9	0.7	23.8	66.1	10.1	0.4	0.2	8	15

	Total population (millions)			Average annual population growth rate (%)		Population age composition			Dependency ratio (dependents as proportion of working–age population)		Crude death rate (per 1,000 people)	Crude birth rate (per 1,000 people)
						Ages 0–14 %	Ages 15–64 %	Ages 65+ %	Young	Old		
	1980	2001	2015	1980–2001	2001–15	2001	2001	2001	2001	2001	2001	2001
Romania	22.2	22.4	21.4	0.0	−0.3	17.7	68.8	13.5	0.3	0.2	12	10
Russian Federation	139.0	144.8	134.5	0.2	−0.5	17.5	69.9	12.5	0.3	0.2	16	9
Rwanda	5.2	8.7	10.9	2.5	1.6	47.6	49.3	3.1	1.0	0.1	22	44
Saudi Arabia	9.4	21.4	32.1	3.9	2.9	40.9	56.2	2.9	0.7	0.1	4	33
Senegal	5.5	9.8	13.0	2.7	2.0	44.4	52.9	2.7	0.9	0.1	13	36
Sierra Leone	3.2	5.1	6.7	2.2	1.9	44.6	52.9	2.6	0.9	0.0	25	44
Singapore	2.4	4.1	4.8	2.6	1.1	21.5	71.2	7.3	0.3	0.1	4	12
Slovak Republic	5.0	5.4	5.4	0.4	0.0	19.3	69.3	11.3	0.3	0.2	10	10
Slovenia	1.9	2.0	1.9	0.2	−0.2	15.7	70.2	14.2	0.2	0.2	9	9
Somalia	6.5	9.1	14.0	1.6	3.1	47.9	49.7	2.4	1.0	0.0	17	50
South Africa	27.6	43.2	45.8	2.1	0.4	32.3	63.1	4.6	0.5	0.1	18	25
Spain	37.4	41.1	41.4	0.5	0.0	15.0	68.1	16.9	0.2	0.2	9	10
Sri Lanka	14.6	18.7	21.9	1.2	1.1	26.0	67.6	6.4	0.4	0.1	6	18
Sudan	19.3	31.7	42.1	2.4	2.0	39.9	56.6	3.5	0.7	0.1	11	34
Swaziland	0.6	1.1	1.3	3.0	1.2	42.2	55.0	2.8	0.8	0.1	17	35
Sweden	8.3	8.9	8.9	0.3	0.0	17.9	64.6	17.5	0.3	0.3	10	10
Switzerland	6.3	7.2	7.2	0.6	−0.1	16.8	67.8	15.4	0.3	0.2	8	10
Syrian Arab Republic	8.7	16.6	22.1	3.1	2.1	40.0	56.9	3.1	0.7	0.1	4	29
Tajikistan	4.0	6.2	7.7	2.2	1.5	38.6	57.0	4.4	0.7	0.1	6	21
Tanzania	18.6	34.4	43.9	2.9	1.7	45.2	52.4	2.4	0.9	0.0	18	39
Thailand	46.7	61.2	66.3	1.3	0.6	23.6	70.1	6.3	0.3	0.1	8	15
Togo	2.5	4.7	6.0	2.9	1.9	43.9	53.0	3.2	0.8	0.1	15	35
Trinidad and Tobago	1.1	1.3	1.5	0.9	0.8	24.9	68.8	6.3	0.4	0.1	7	15
Tunisia	6.4	9.7	11.6	2.0	1.3	28.9	65.1	5.9	0.5	0.1	6	17
Turkey	44.5	66.2	77.7	1.9	1.1	28.3	65.9	5.8	0.4	0.1	7	20
Turkmenistan	2.9	5.4	6.4	3.1	1.1	36.6	59.1	4.3	0.6	0.1	7	20
Uganda	12.8	22.8	32.0	2.7	2.4	49.0	49.1	1.9	1.0	0.0	18	45
Ukraine	50.0	49.1	44.7	−0.1	−0.7	17.1	68.6	14.3	0.3	0.2	15	8
United Arab Emirates	1.0	3.0	3.8	5.0	1.8	26.1	71.2	2.7	0.4	0.0	4	17
United Kingdom	56.3	58.8	58.9	0.2	0.0	18.6	65.4	16.1	0.3	0.2	11	11
United States	227.2	285.3	319.9	1.1	0.8	21.2	66.2	12.6	0.3	0.2	9	15
Uruguay	2.9	3.4	3.7	0.7	0.6	24.7	62.7	12.6	0.4	0.2	10	16
Uzbekistan	16.0	25.1	30.0	2.2	1.3	36.5	59.0	4.5	0.6	0.1	6	21
Venezuela, RB	15.1	24.6	30.3	2.3	1.5	33.5	62.1	4.4	0.6	0.1	5	23
Vietnam	53.7	79.5	94.4	1.9	1.2	32.4	62.3	5.3	0.5	0.1	6	19
West Bank and Gaza	..	3.1	4.8	..	3.2	46.6	50.1	3.3	1.0	0.1	4	37
Yemen, Rep.	8.5	18.0	27.3	3.6	3.0	46.2	51.0	2.8	0.9	0.1	11	41
Yugoslavia, Fed. Rep.	9.8	10.7	10.7	0.4	0.1	20.1	66.2	13.7	0.3	0.2	11	12
Zambia	5.7	10.3	12.2	2.8	1.2	45.1	52.7	2.2	0.9	0.0	22	39
Zimbabwe	7.1	12.8	14.0	2.8	0.6	44.6	52.2	3.2	0.9	0.1	20	29
World	**4,429.6 s**	**6,130.1 s**	**7,093.9 s**	**1.5 w**	**1.0 w**	**29.6 w**	**63.4 w**	**7.0 w**	**0.5 w**	**0.1 w**	**9 w**	**21 w**
Low income	1,613.4	2,505.9	3,090.9	2.1	1.5	36.4	59.2	4.4	0.6	0.1	11	29
Middle income	1,988.8	2,667.2	3,001.1	1.4	0.8	27.1	66.0	6.9	0.4	0.1	8	17
Lower middle income	1,626.4	2,163.5	2,413.0	1.4	0.8	26.7	66.4	6.9	0.4	0.1	8	17
Upper middle income	362.4	503.6	588.1	1.6	1.1	29.0	64.4	6.6	0.4	0.1	7	20
Low & middle income	3,601.6	5,172.3	6,091.9	1.7	1.2	31.6	62.7	5.7	0.5	0.1	9	23
East Asia & Pacific	1,359.4	1,822.5	2,041.3	1.4	0.8	26.8	66.8	6.4	0.4	0.1	7	17
Europe & Central Asia	425.8	474.6	476.6	0.5	0.0	21.4	67.6	11.0	0.3	0.2	12	12
Latin America & Carib.	359.9	523.6	625.7	1.8	1.3	31.3	63.2	5.5	0.5	0.1	6	22
Middle East & N. Africa	174.0	300.6	387.7	2.6	1.8	36.2	59.8	4.0	0.6	0.1	6	26
South Asia	901.3	1,377.8	1,680.0	2.0	1.4	34.6	60.8	4.6	0.6	0.1	9	26
Sub-Saharan Africa	381.7	673.9	880.6	2.7	1.9	44.0	53.0	3.0	0.8	0.1	17	39
High income	827.4	957.0	1,001.9	0.7	0.3	18.4	67.3	14.3	0.3	0.2	9	12
Europe EMU	286.7	306.7	306.0	0.3	0.0	16.2	67.3	16.5	0.2	0.2	10	10

a. Estimate does not account for recent refugee flows.

Population dynamics | **2.1**

Population estimates are usually based on national population censuses, but the frequency and quality of these vary by country. Most countries conduct a complete enumeration no more than once a decade. Pre- and postcensus estimates are interpolations or extrapolations based on demographic models. Errors and undercounting occur even in high-income countries; in developing countries such errors may be substantial because of limits in the transport, communications, and other resources required to conduct a full census. The quality and reliability of official demographic data are also affected by the public trust in the government, the government's commitment to full and accurate enumeration, the confidentiality and protection against misuse accorded to census data, and the independence of census agencies from undue political influence. Moreover, the international comparability of population indicators is limited by differences in the concepts, definitions, data collection procedures, and estimation methods used by national statistical agencies and other organizations that collect population data.

Of the 152 economies listed in the table, 123 (about 81 percent) conducted a census between 1995 and 2002. The currentness of a census, along with the availability of complementary data from surveys or registration systems, is one of many objective ways to judge the quality of demographic data. In some European countries registration systems offer complete information on population in the absence of a census. See *Primary data documentation* for the most recent census or survey year and for the completeness of registration.

Current population estimates for developing countries that lack recent census-based data, and pre- and postcensus estimates for countries with census data, are provided by national statistical offices, the United Nations Population Division, and other agencies. The standard estimation method requires fertility, mortality, and net migration data, which are often collected from sample surveys, some of which may be small or limited in coverage. The population estimates are the product of demographic modeling and so are susceptible to biases and errors because of shortcomings in the model as well as in the data. Population projections are made using the cohort component method.

The growth rate of the total population conceals the fact that different age groups may grow at very different rates. In many developing countries the population under 15 was earlier growing rapidly but is now starting to shrink. Previously high fertility rates and declining mortality rates are now reflected in the larger share of the working-age population.

Dependency ratios take into account the variations in the proportions of children, elderly people, and working-age people in the population. Separate calculations of young-age and old-age dependency suggest the burden of dependency that the working-age population must bear in relation to children and the elderly. But dependency ratios show the age composition of a population, not economic dependency. Some children and elderly people are part of the labor force, and many working-age people are not.

The vital rates shown in the table are based on data derived from birth and death registration systems, censuses, and sample surveys conducted by national statistical offices, United Nations agencies, and other organizations. The estimates for 2001 for many countries are based on extrapolations of levels and trends measured in earlier years.

Vital registers are the preferred source of these data, but in many developing countries systems for registering births and deaths do not exist or are incomplete because of deficiencies in the coverage of events or of geographic areas. Many developing countries carry out special household surveys that estimate vital rates by asking respondents about births and deaths in the recent past. Estimates derived in this way are subject to sampling errors as well as errors due to inaccurate recall by the respondents.

The United Nations Statistics Division monitors the completeness of vital registration systems. The share of countries with at least 90 percent complete vital registration increased from 45 percent in 1988 to 55 percent in 2001. Still, some of the most populous developing countries—China, India, Indonesia, Brazil, Pakistan, Bangladesh, Nigeria—do not have complete vital registration systems. Fewer than 30 percent of births and 40 percent of deaths worldwide are thought to be registered and reported.

International migration is the only other factor besides birth and death rates that directly determines a country's population growth. In the high-income countries about 40 percent of annual population growth in 1990–95 was due to migration, while in the developing countries migration reduced population growth by about 3 percent. Estimating international migration is difficult. At any time many people are located outside their home country as tourists, workers, or refugees or for other reasons. Standards relating to the duration and purpose of international moves that qualify as migration vary, and accurate estimates require information on flows into and out of countries that is difficult to collect.

• **Total population** of an economy includes all residents regardless of legal status or citizenship—except for refugees not permanently settled in the country of asylum, who are generally considered part of the population of their country of origin. The values shown are midyear estimates for 1980 and 2001 and projections for 2015. • **Average annual population growth rate** is the exponential change for the period indicated. See *Statistical methods* for more information. • **Population age composition** refers to the percentage of the total population that is in specific age groups. • **Dependency ratio** is the ratio of dependents—people younger than 15 or older than 64—to the working-age population—those ages 15–64. • **Crude death rate** and **crude birth rate** are the number of deaths and the number of live births occurring during the year, per 1,000 population estimated at midyear. Subtracting the crude death rate from the crude birth rate provides the rate of natural increase, which is equal to the population growth rate in the absence of migration.

The World Bank's population estimates are produced by its Human Development Network and Development Data Group in consultation with its operational staff and country offices. Important inputs to the World Bank's demographic work come from the following sources: census reports and other statistical publications from national statistical offices; Demographic and Health Surveys conducted by national agencies, Macro International, and the U.S. Centers for Disease Control and Prevention; United Nations Statistics Division, *Population and Vital Statistics Report* (quarterly); United Nations Population Division, *World Population Prospects: The 2000 Revision*; Eurostat, *Demographic Statistics* (various years); Centro Latinoamericano de Demografía, *Boletín Demográfico* (various years); and U.S. Bureau of the Census, International Database.

	Population ages 15–64		Labor force						
	millions		Total millions			Average annual growth rate %		Female % of labor force	
	1980	2001	1980	2001	2010	1980–2001	2001–10	1980	2001
Afghanistan	8.5	14.6 ᵃ	6.8	11.4 ᵃ	14.1	2.5	2.3	34.8	35.7
Albania	1.6	2.0	1.2	1.6	1.8	1.3	1.5	38.8	41.4
Algeria	9.3	18.7	4.8	10.6	14.3	3.7	3.4	21.4	28.3
Angola	3.7	6.7	3.5	6.2	8.1	2.7	3.0	47.0	46.3
Argentina	17.2	23.5	10.7	15.4	18.5	1.7	2.1	27.6	33.8
Armenia	2.0	2.6	1.4	1.9	2.2	1.4	1.2	47.9	48.6
Australia	9.6	13.1	6.7	9.9	10.6	1.8	0.7	36.8	43.9
Austria	4.8	5.5	3.4	3.8	3.8	0.5	0.0	40.5	40.4
Azerbaijan	3.7	5.2	2.7	3.7	4.3	1.4	1.7	47.5	44.6
Bangladesh	44.8	79.6	40.3	70.8	86.0	2.7	2.2	42.3	42.4
Belarus	6.4	6.8	5.1	5.3	5.3	0.2	0.0	49.9	49.0
Belgium	6.5	6.8	3.9	4.3	4.2	0.4	–0.1	33.9	41.0
Benin	1.8	3.3	1.7	2.9	3.7	2.7	2.8	47.0	48.3
Bolivia	2.9	4.8	2.0	3.5	4.3	2.6	2.4	33.3	37.9
Bosnia and Herzegovina	2.7	2.9	1.6	1.9	2.0	0.8	0.7	32.8	38.1
Botswana	0.4	0.9	0.4	0.8	0.8	3.1	0.8	50.1	45.2
Brazil	70.3	114.3	47.7	80.7	89.9	2.5	1.2	28.4	35.5
Bulgaria	5.8	5.6	4.6	4.1	3.8	–0.6	–0.7	45.3	48.1
Burkina Faso	3.4	5.8	3.8	5.7	6.7	1.9	1.9	47.6	46.5
Burundi	2.1	3.6	2.3	3.8	4.6	2.5	2.2	50.2	48.6
Cambodia	3.9	6.6	3.7	6.5	7.9	2.7	2.2	55.4	51.6
Cameroon	4.5	8.4	3.6	6.2	7.5	2.5	2.1	36.8	38.1
Canada	16.7	21.3	12.2	16.7	17.5	1.5	0.6	39.5	45.9
Central African Republic	1.3	2.0	1.2	1.8	2.1	1.9	1.5	..	..
Chad	2.3	3.7	2.2	3.8	5.0	2.6	3.0	43.4	44.8
Chile	6.8	10.0	3.8	6.3	7.5	2.4	1.9	26.3	34.1
China	586.3	865.4	538.7	763.2	818.3	1.7	0.8	43.2	45.2
Hong Kong, China	3.4	4.8	2.5	3.6	3.7	1.7	0.5	34.3	37.2
Colombia	15.8	27.0	9.4	18.9	23.0	3.3	2.1	26.2	38.9
Congo, Dem. Rep.	13.8	26.1	12.0	21.6	28.2	2.8	2.9	44.5	43.4
Congo, Rep.	0.9	1.6	0.7	1.3	1.7	2.9	3.0	42.4	43.5
Costa Rica	1.3	2.4	0.8	1.6	1.9	3.2	2.0	20.8	31.4
Côte d'Ivoire	4.2	9.0	3.3	6.6	8.0	3.3	2.2	32.2	33.5
Croatia	3.1	3.0	2.2	2.1	2.0	–0.2	–0.3	40.2	44.3
Cuba	5.9	7.7	3.7	5.6	5.9	1.9	0.7	31.4	39.7
Czech Republic	6.5	7.2	5.3	5.7	5.5	0.4	–0.4	47.1	47.3
Denmark	3.3	3.6	2.7	2.9	2.8	0.4	–0.5	44.0	46.4
Dominican Republic	3.1	5.3	2.1	3.8	4.6	2.8	2.2	24.7	31.1
Ecuador	4.2	8.0	2.5	5.1	6.5	3.3	2.6	20.1	28.4
Egypt, Arab Rep.	23.1	39.8	14.3	25.2	32.2	2.7	2.7	26.5	30.7
El Salvador	2.4	3.8	1.6	2.8	3.6	2.8	2.8	26.5	36.9
Eritrea	1.3	2.2	1.2	2.1	2.7	2.6	2.6	47.4	47.4
Estonia	1.0	0.9	0.8	0.8	0.8	–0.3	–0.2	50.6	49.0
Ethiopia	19.9	33.6	16.9	28.3	34.6	2.4	2.2	42.3	40.9
Finland	3.2	3.5	2.4	2.6	2.5	0.3	–0.6	46.5	48.1
France	34.4	38.5	23.8	26.8	27.6	0.6	0.3	40.1	45.2
Gabon	0.4	0.7	0.4	0.6	0.7	2.2	1.9	45.0	44.7
Gambia, The	0.3	0.8	0.3	0.7	0.8	3.4	2.2	44.8	45.1
Georgia	3.3	3.3	2.6	..	2.5	..	..	49.3	46.8
Germany	51.6	56.1	37.5	41.0	40.9	0.4	0.0	40.1	42.4
Ghana	5.5	10.2	5.1	9.4	11.2	2.9	2.0	51.0	50.4
Greece	6.2	7.1	3.8	4.6	4.7	0.9	0.4	27.9	38.0
Guatemala	3.5	6.2	2.3	4.4	6.0	3.0	3.5	22.4	29.5
Guinea	2.3	4.0	2.3	3.6	4.3	2.1	2.0	47.1	47.2
Guinea-Bissau	0.4	0.6	0.4	0.6	0.7	1.9	2.3	39.9	40.5
Haiti	2.9	4.6	2.5	3.6	4.2	1.6	1.7	44.6	42.9

Labor force structure

	Population ages 15–64		Labor force						
	millions		Total millions			Average annual growth rate %		Female % of labor force	
	1980	2001	1980	2001	2010	1980–2001	2001–10	1980	2001
Honduras	1.8	3.6	1.2	2.5	3.5	3.5	3.6	25.2	32.2
Hungary	6.9	6.9	5.1	4.9	4.6	−0.2	−0.8	43.3	44.7
India	394.5	637.9	299.5	460.5	543.6	2.0	1.8	33.7	32.4
Indonesia	83.2	136.1	58.6	102.0	122.0	2.6	2.0	35.2	41.0
Iran, Islamic Rep.	20.5	40.5	11.7	20.4	27.7	2.6	3.4	20.4	27.8
Iraq	6.7	13.3	3.5	6.6	8.6	3.0	2.8	17.3	20.0
Ireland	2.0	2.6	1.3	1.6	1.9	1.3	1.4	28.1	34.8
Israel	2.3	4.0	1.5	2.8	3.5	3.1	2.5	33.7	41.5
Italy	36.4	38.8	22.6	25.8	24.8	0.6	−0.4	32.9	38.6
Jamaica	1.1	1.6	1.0	1.4	1.6	1.7	1.5	46.3	46.2
Japan	78.7	86.2	57.2	68.2	66.0	0.8	−0.4	37.9	41.6
Jordan	1.0	2.9	0.5	1.5	2.0	5.1	3.4	14.7	25.1
Kazakhstan	9.1	10.0	7.0	7.3	7.7	0.2	0.5	47.6	47.1
Kenya	7.8	16.6	7.8	15.9	19.0	3.4	2.0	46.0	46.1
Korea, Dem. Rep.	10.5	15.0	7.5	11.7	12.3	2.1	0.6	44.8	43.3
Korea, Rep.	23.7	34.1	15.5	24.3	26.6	2.1	1.0	38.7	41.6
Kuwait	0.8	1.3	0.5	0.8	1.2	2.5	3.9	13.1	31.7
Kyrgyz Republic	2.1	3.0	1.5	2.2	2.6	1.6	2.0	47.5	47.3
Lao PDR	1.8	2.9	1.7	2.6	3.3	2.1	2.6	..	..
Latvia	1.7	1.6	1.4	1.3	1.3	−0.5	−0.4	50.8	50.5
Lebanon	1.6	2.7	0.8	1.6	2.0	2.9	2.6	22.6	29.9
Lesotho	0.7	1.2	0.6	0.9	0.9	1.9	1.2	37.9	37.0
Liberia	1.0	1.7	0.8	1.3	1.5	2.3	1.9	38.4	39.6
Libya	1.6	3.4	0.9	1.6	1.9	2.4	2.4	18.6	23.6
Lithuania	2.2	2.4	1.8	1.8	1.8	0.0	0.1	49.7	48.0
Macedonia, FYR	1.2	1.4	0.8	1.0	1.0	0.8	0.6	36.1	41.8
Madagascar	4.6	8.3	4.3	7.6	9.7	2.7	2.8	45.2	44.7
Malawi	3.1	5.5	3.1	5.1	6.0	2.3	1.9	50.6	48.5
Malaysia	7.8	14.7	5.3	10.0	12.8	3.0	2.8	33.7	38.1
Mali	3.3	5.5	3.4	5.4	6.6	2.2	2.2	46.7	46.2
Mauritania	0.8	1.4	0.7	1.3	1.6	2.5	2.5	45.0	43.5
Mauritius	0.6	0.8	0.3	0.5	0.6	2.0	1.1	25.7	32.8
Mexico	34.5	61.0	22.0	41.3	50.9	3.0	2.3	26.9	33.5
Moldova	2.6	2.9	2.1	2.2	2.2	0.1	0.1	50.3	48.5
Mongolia	0.9	1.5	0.8	1.2	1.5	2.2	2.1	45.7	47.1
Morocco	10.2	18.0	7.0	11.8	14.7	2.5	2.5	33.5	34.8
Mozambique	6.4	9.6	6.7	9.4	11.1	1.6	1.9	49.0	48.4
Myanmar	18.6	30.3	17.1	25.8	29.4	2.0	1.5	43.7	43.4
Namibia	0.5	1.0	0.4	0.7	0.8	2.6	1.3	40.1	40.9
Nepal	8.1	13.1	7.1	11.0	13.6	2.1	2.4	38.8	40.5
Netherlands	9.4	10.9	5.6	7.4	7.6	1.3	0.2	31.5	40.8
New Zealand	2.0	2.5	1.3	1.9	2.0	1.8	0.6	34.3	45.1
Nicaragua	1.5	2.8	1.0	2.1	2.9	3.6	3.4	27.6	36.3
Niger	2.7	5.4	2.8	5.3	6.9	3.0	3.0	44.6	44.3
Nigeria	37.0	69.4	29.5	51.6	63.1	2.7	2.2	36.2	36.6
Norway	2.6	2.9	1.9	2.3	2.4	0.9	0.3	40.5	46.5
Oman	0.6	1.3	0.3	0.7	0.8	3.3	2.6	6.2	18.0
Pakistan	45.4	78.5	29.3	53.5	71.4	2.9	3.2	22.7	29.0
Panama	1.1	1.8	0.7	1.2	1.5	2.8	2.0	29.9	35.5
Papua New Guinea	1.7	3.0	1.5	2.6	3.1	2.5	2.2	41.7	42.3
Paraguay	1.7	3.2	1.1	2.1	2.8	3.0	2.9	26.7	30.2
Peru	9.4	16.4	5.4	10.1	12.7	3.0	2.5	23.9	31.6
Philippines	25.8	46.2	18.7	33.3	41.5	2.7	2.4	35.0	37.9
Poland	23.3	26.7	18.5	19.9	20.1	0.3	0.1	45.3	46.4
Portugal	6.2	6.8	4.6	5.1	5.0	0.5	−0.1	38.7	44.1
Puerto Rico	1.9	2.5	1.0	1.5	1.6	1.7	1.2	31.8	37.5

	Population ages 15–64		Labor force							
	millions		Total millions			Average annual growth rate %		Female % of labor force	
	1980	**2001**	**1980**	**2001**	**2010**	**1980–2001**	**2001–10**	**1980**	**2001**
Romania	14.0	15.4	10.9	10.8	10.6	–0.1	–0.1	45.8	44.5
Russian Federation	94.7	101.3	76.0	77.6	77.0	0.1	–0.1	49.4	49.2
Rwanda	2.5	4.3	2.6	4.7	5.6	2.8	1.9	49.1	48.8
Saudi Arabia	5.0	12.0	2.8	7.1	9.6	4.5	3.4	7.6	16.9
Senegal	2.9	5.2	2.5	4.4	5.3	2.6	2.2	42.2	42.6
Sierra Leone	1.7	2.7	1.2	1.9	2.3	2.0	2.2	35.5	37.0
Singapore	1.6	2.9	1.1	2.0	2.2	2.9	0.9	34.6	39.2
Slovak Republic	3.2	3.7	2.5	3.0	3.0	0.9	0.2	45.3	47.7
Slovenia	1.2	1.4	1.0	1.0	1.0	0.3	–0.3	45.8	46.5
Somalia	3.3	4.5	3.0	3.9	5.2	1.3	3.2	43.4	43.4
South Africa	15.2	27.2	10.3	17.2	18.4	2.4	0.7	35.1	37.9
Spain	23.5	27.7	14.0	18.2	18.6	1.3	0.3	28.3	37.3
Sri Lanka	8.9	12.6	5.4	8.3	9.6	2.0	1.7	26.9	36.8
Sudan	10.2	18.0	7.1	12.7	16.2	2.8	2.7	26.9	29.8
Swaziland	0.3	0.6	0.2	0.4	0.5	3.2	1.9	33.5	37.8
Sweden	5.3	5.7	4.2	4.8	4.7	0.6	–0.2	43.8	48.0
Switzerland	4.2	4.9	3.1	3.9	3.9	1.2	0.0	36.7	40.6
Syrian Arab Republic	4.2	9.4	2.5	5.4	7.5	3.7	3.8	23.5	27.3
Tajikistan	2.1	3.6	1.5	2.5	3.3	2.3	3.0	46.9	45.0
Tanzania	9.3	18.0	9.5	17.7	21.1	3.0	2.0	49.8	49.0
Thailand	26.9	42.8	24.4	37.2	39.7	2.0	0.7	47.4	46.3
Togo	1.3	2.4	1.1	1.9	2.3	2.7	2.2	39.3	40.0
Trinidad and Tobago	0.7	0.9	0.4	0.6	0.7	1.6	1.6	31.4	34.6
Tunisia	3.5	6.3	2.2	3.9	4.8	2.7	2.4	28.9	31.9
Turkey	24.9	43.6	18.7	31.9	37.1	2.5	1.7	35.5	37.8
Turkmenistan	1.6	3.2	1.2	2.4	2.9	3.3	2.0	47.0	45.9
Uganda	6.4	11.2	6.6	11.2	14.1	2.5	2.6	47.9	47.6
Ukraine	33.4	33.7	26.4	25.0	24.3	–0.3	–0.3	50.2	48.8
United Arab Emirates	0.7	2.1	0.6	1.5	1.7	4.6	1.8	5.1	15.3
United Kingdom	36.1	38.4	26.9	29.4	29.3	0.4	–0.1	38.9	44.2
United States	150.6	188.6	110.1	146.7	159.0	1.4	0.9	41.0	46.1
Uruguay	1.8	2.1	1.2	1.5	1.7	1.4	0.9	30.8	42.0
Uzbekistan	8.6	14.8	6.5	10.7	13.2	2.4	2.3	48.0	46.9
Venezuela, RB	8.5	15.3	5.2	10.2	12.8	3.2	2.5	26.7	35.1
Vietnam	28.6	49.5	25.6	41.1	48.0	2.3	1.7	48.1	48.8
West Bank and Gaza	..	1.5	..	..	..	..	..	..	..
Yemen, Rep.	4.0	9.2	2.5	5.7	7.8	4.0	3.4	32.5	28.2
Yugoslavia, Fed. Rep.	6.5	7.0	4.5	5.1	5.2	0.6	0.3	38.7	43.0
Zambia	2.9	5.4	2.4	4.4	5.1	2.9	1.8	45.4	44.7
Zimbabwe	3.5	6.6	3.2	5.9	6.6	2.9	1.1	44.4	44.5
World	**2,600.4 s**	**3,882.1 s**	**2,036.0 s**	**2,983.4 s**	**3,376.7 s**	**1.8 w**	**1.4 w**	**39.1 w**	**40.7 w**
Low income	896.5	1,480.4	710.3	1,138.4	1,367.5	2.2	2.0	37.8	37.9
Middle income	1,174.6	1,759.5	952.2	1,378.4	1,526.5	1.8	1.1	40.2	42.1
Lower middle income	964.2	1,435.8	809.6	1,155.8	1,271.1	1.7	1.1	41.6	43.2
Upper middle income	210.4	323.7	142.6	222.6	255.4	2.1	1.5	32.3	36.3
Low & middle income	2,071.2	3,239.9	1,662.5	2,516.8	2,894.0	2.0	1.6	39.2	40.2
East Asia & Pacific	796.7	1,215.4	703.8	1,037.6	1,140.5	1.8	1.1	42.6	44.5
Europe & Central Asia	274.2	320.4	214.1	236.5	248.1	0.5	0.5	46.7	46.3
Latin America & Carib.	201.1	330.6	129.9	226.8	269.2	2.7	1.9	27.8	35.0
Middle East & N. Africa	91.6	179.9	54.1	102.0	134.1	3.0	3.0	23.8	28.1
South Asia	510.6	836.9	388.7	616.0	738.9	2.2	2.0	33.8	33.5
Sub-Saharan Africa	197.0	356.8	172.0	297.9	363.2	2.6	2.2	42.0	42.0
High income	529.3	642.2	373.4	466.6	482.7	1.1	0.4	38.4	43.3
Europe EMU	184.8	205.6	123.4	142.2	142.6	0.7	0.0	36.4	41.3

a. Estimate does not account for recent refugee flows.

Labor force structure | 2.2

About the data

The labor force is the supply of labor available for the production of goods and services in an economy. It includes people who are currently employed and people who are unemployed but seeking work as well as first-time job-seekers. Not everyone who works is included, however. Unpaid workers, family workers, and students are among those usually omitted, and in some countries members of the military are not counted. The size of the labor force tends to vary during the year as seasonal workers enter and leave it.

Data on the labor force are compiled by the International Labour Organization (ILO) from censuses or labor force surveys. For some countries a combination of sources is used, including establishment surveys and data on job-seekers. While the resulting statistics may provide rough estimates of the labor force, they are not comparable across countries because of the noncomparability of the original data.

For international comparisons the most comprehensive source is labor force surveys. Despite the ILO's efforts to encourage the use of international standards, labor force data are not fully comparable, however, because of differences among countries, and sometimes within countries, in their scope and coverage. In some countries data on the labor force refer to people above a specific age, while in others there is no specific age provision. The reference period of the census or survey is another important source of differences: in some countries data refer to people's status on the day of the census or survey or during a specific period before the inquiry date, while in others the data are recorded without reference to any period. In developing countries,

where the household is often the basic unit of production and all members contribute to output, but some at low intensity or irregular intervals, the estimated labor force may be significantly smaller than the numbers actually working (ILO, *Yearbook of Labour Statistics 1997*).

The labor force estimates in the table were calculated by World Bank staff by applying economic activity rates from the ILO database to World Bank population estimates to create a series consistent with these population estimates. This procedure sometimes results in estimates of labor force size that differ slightly from those in the ILO's *Yearbook of Labour Statistics*. The population ages 15–64 is often used to provide a rough estimate of the potential labor force. But in many developing countries children under 15 work full or part time. And in some high-income countries many workers postpone retirement past age 65. As a result, labor force participation rates calculated in this way may systematically over- or underestimate actual rates.

In general, estimates of women in the labor force are lower than those of men and are not comparable internationally, reflecting the fact that for women, demographic, social, legal, and cultural trends and norms determine whether their activities are regarded as economic. In many countries large numbers of women work on farms or in other family enterprises without pay, while others work in or near their homes, mixing work and family activities during the day. Countries differ in the criteria used to determine the extent to which such workers are to be counted as part of the labor force. In most economies the gap between male and female labor force participation rates has been narrowing since 1980.

Definitions

• **Population ages 15–64** is the number of people who could potentially be economically active. • **Total labor force** comprises people who meet the ILO definition of the economically active population: all people who supply labor for the production of goods and services during a specified period. It includes both the employed and the unemployed. While national practices vary in the treatment of such groups as the armed forces and seasonal or part-time workers, the labor force generally includes the armed forces, the unemployed, and first-time job-seekers, but excludes homemakers and other unpaid caregivers and workers in the informal sector. • **Average annual growth rate of the labor force** is calculated using the exponential endpoint method (see *Statistical methods* for more information). • **Females as a percentage of the labor force** show the extent to which women are active in the labor force.

2.2a

Women are clustered in unpaid family work

Contributing family workers as % of employment, 1996–2000

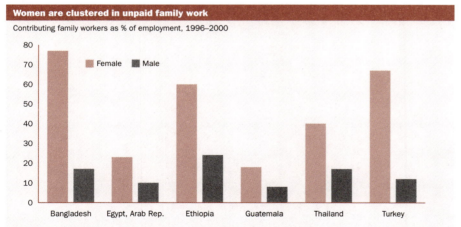

Women's participation in the labor force has increased in almost all regions. But more women than men continue to be employed in unpaid family work, with the largest shares being in Africa and Asia.

Note: Data are for most recent year available between 1996 and 2000.
Source: International Labour Organization, Key Indicators of the Labour Market (2001–02 issue).

Data sources

The population estimates are from the World Bank's population database. The economic activity rates are from the ILO database Estimates and Projections of the Economically Active Population, 1950–2010. The ILO publishes estimates of the economically active population in its *Yearbook of Labour Statistics*.

Employment by economic activity

	Agriculture [a]				Industry [a]				Services [a]			
	Male % of male employment		Female % of female employment		Male % of male employment		Female % of female employment		Male % of male employment		Female % of female employment	
	1980–82 [b]	1998–2001 [b]	1980–82 [b]	1998–2001 [b]	1980–82 [b]	1998–2001 [b]	1980–82 [b]	1998–2001 [b]	1980–82 [b]	1998–2001 [b]	1980–82 [b]	1998–2001 [b]
Afghanistan	66	..	86	..	9	..	12	..	26	..	2	..
Albania	..	..	..	..	..	..	..	..	..	..	..	..
Algeria	27	..	69	..	33	..	6	..	40	..	25	..
Angola	67	..	87	..	13	..	1	..	20	..	11	..
Argentina	..	1	..	0 [c]	..	34	..	10	..	65	..	89
Armenia	..	..	..	..	..	..	..	..	..	..	..	..
Australia	8	6	4	3	38	31	16	10	54	63	80	86
Austria	..	6	..	7	..	43	..	14	..	52	..	79
Azerbaijan	..	..	..	..	..	..	..	..	..	..	..	..
Bangladesh	..	52	..	48	..	11	..	20	..	37	..	32
Belarus	..	..	..	..	..	..	..	..	..	..	..	..
Belgium	..	3	..	2	..	37	..	13	..	60	..	86
Benin	66	..	69	..	10	..	4	..	24	..	27	..
Bolivia	52	..	28	..	21	..	19	..	27	..	53	..
Bosnia and Herzegovina	26	..	38	..	45	..	24	..	30	..	39	..
Botswana	6	..	3	..	41	..	8	..	53	..	89	..
Brazil	34	26	19	19	28	27	13	10	37	47	68	71
Bulgaria	..	..	..	..	..	..	..	..	..	..	..	..
Burkina Faso	92	..	93	..	3	..	2	..	5	..	5	..
Burundi	..	..	..	..	..	..	..	..	..	..	..	..
Cambodia	..	..	..	..	..	..	..	..	..	..	..	..
Cameroon	65	..	87	..	11	..	2	..	24	..	11	..
Canada	7	5	3	2	35	32	14	11	58	63	83	87
Central African Republic	79	..	90	..	5	..	1	..	15	..	9	..
Chad	82	..	95	..	6	..	0 [c]	..	12	..	4	..
Chile	22	19	3	5	21	31	12	14	57	49	86	82
China	..	..	..	..	..	..	..	..	..	..	..	..
Hong Kong, China	1	0 [c]	1	0 [c]	44	28	52	12	55	71	47	88
Colombia	2	2	1	1	39	30	26	20	59	68	74	80
Congo, Dem. Rep.	62	..	84	..	18	..	4	..	20	..	12	..
Congo, Rep.	42	..	81	..	20	..	2	..	38	..	17	..
Costa Rica	38	22	6	4	21	27	20	17	40	51	73	79
Côte d'Ivoire	60	..	75	..	10	..	5	..	30	..	20	..
Croatia	..	16	..	17	..	38	..	22	..	46	..	61
Cuba	30	..	10	..	32	..	22	..	39	..	68	..
Czech Republic	13	6	11	4	57	49	39	28	30	48	50	69
Denmark	11	5	4	2	41	37	16	15	48	58	80	83
Dominican Republic	..	24	..	3	..	27	..	20	..	49	..	77
Ecuador	..	11	..	2	..	26	..	14	..	63	..	84
Egypt, Arab Rep.	42	29	9	35	23	25	13	9	35	46	72	56
El Salvador	51	37	10	6	21	24	21	25	28	38	69	69
Eritrea	79	..	88	..	7	..	2	..	14	..	11	..
Estonia	..	11	..	7	..	40	..	23	..	49	..	70
Ethiopia	..	..	..	..	..	..	..	..	..	..	..	..
Finland	15	8	11	4	44	40	22	14	41	52	68	82
France	2	2	1	1	49	35	23	13	49	63	76	86
Gabon	59	..	74	..	18	..	6	..	24	..	21	..
Gambia, The	78	..	93	..	10	..	3	..	13	..	5	..
Georgia	..	..	..	..	..	..	..	..	..	..	..	..
Germany	..	3	..	2	..	46	..	19	..	50	..	79
Ghana	..	..	..	..	..	..	..	..	..	..	..	..
Greece	25	16	38	20	34	29	18	12	41	54	43	67
Guatemala	..	37	..	14	..	26	..	19	..	38	..	68
Guinea	86	..	97	..	2	..	1	..	12	..	3	..
Guinea-Bissau	81	..	98	..	3	..	0	..	17	..	3	..
Haiti	81	..	53	..	8	..	8	..	11	..	39	..

Employment by economic activity

	Agriculture [a]				Industry [a]				Services [a]			
	Male		Female		Male		Female		Male		Female	
	% of male employment		% of female employment		% of male employment		% of female employment		% of male employment		% of female employment	
	1980–82 [b]	1998–2001 [b]	1980–82 [b]	1998–2001 [b]	1980–82 [b]	1998–2001 [b]	1980–82 [b]	1998–2001 [b]	1980–82 [b]	1998–2001 [b]	1980–82 [b]	1998–2001 [b]
Honduras	..	50	..	9	..	21	..	25	..	30	..	67
Hungary	26	9	18	4	44	42	32	25	31	48	41	71
India	..	..	..	..	..	..	..	..	..	..	..	..
Indonesia	55	..	54	..	15	..	14	..	30	..	32	..
Iran, Islamic Rep.	..	..	..	..	..	..	..	..	..	..	..	..
Iraq	21	..	62	..	24	..	11	..	55	..	28	..
Ireland	..	12	..	2	..	38	..	15	..	50	..	83
Israel	7	3	3	1	39	35	15	13	54	61	81	86
Italy	12	6	13	5	42	39	27	21	46	55	60	74
Jamaica	47	30	23	10	20	26	8	9	33	45	69	81
Japan	8	5	12	6	39	38	28	22	52	57	60	73
Jordan	..	..	..	..	..	..	..	..	..	..	..	..
Kazakhstan	..	..	..	..	..	..	..	..	..	..	..	..
Kenya	23	20	25	16	24	23	9	10	53	57	65	75
Korea, Dem. Rep.	39	..	52	..	37	..	20	..	24	..	28	..
Korea, Rep.	30	10	36	13	32	34	22	19	39	56	42	68
Kuwait	2	..	0	..	36	..	3	..	62	..	97	..
Kyrgyz Republic	..	52	..	53	..	14	..	8	..	34	..	38
Lao PDR	77	..	82	..	7	..	4	..	16	..	13	..
Latvia	..	17	..	14	..	35	..	18	..	49	..	69
Lebanon	13	..	20	..	29	..	21	..	58	..	59	..
Lesotho	26	..	64	..	52	..	5	..	22	..	31	..
Liberia	69	..	89	..	9	..	1	..	22	..	10	..
Libya	16	..	63	..	29	..	3	..	55	..	34	..
Lithuania	..	24	..	16	..	33	..	40	..	43	..	63
Macedonia, FYR	..	..	..	..	..	..	..	..	..	..	..	..
Madagascar	73	..	93	..	9	..	2	..	19	..	5	..
Malawi	..	..	..	..	..	..	..	..	..	..	..	..
Malaysia	28	21	37	13	26	33	21	29	46	46	42	58
Mali	86	..	92	..	2	..	1	..	12	..	7	..
Mauritania	65	..	79	..	11	..	2	..	25	..	19	..
Mauritius	29	..	30	..	19	..	40	..	47	..	31	..
Mexico	..	23	..	7	..	29	..	22	..	47	..	71
Moldova	..	..	..	..	..	..	..	..	..	..	..	..
Mongolia	..	..	..	..	..	..	..	..	..	..	..	..
Morocco	..	6	..	6	..	32	..	40	..	63	..	54
Mozambique	72	..	97	..	14	..	1	..	14	..	2	..
Myanmar	..	..	..	..	..	..	..	..	..	..	..	..
Namibia	52	..	42	..	22	..	10	..	27	..	47	..
Nepal	..	..	..	..	..	..	..	..	..	..	..	..
Netherlands	7	4	3	2	39	31	13	9	54	63	84	84
New Zealand	..	11	..	6	..	32	..	12	..	56	..	81
Nicaragua	..	..	..	..	..	..	..	..	..	..	..	..
Niger	7	..	6	..	69	..	29	..	25	..	66	..
Nigeria	..	..	..	..	..	..	..	..	..	..	..	..
Norway	10	6	6	2	40	33	13	9	50	61	82	88
Oman	52	..	24	..	21	..	33	..	27	..	43	..
Pakistan	..	..	..	..	..	..	..	..	..	..	..	..
Panama	37	25	6	2	21	22	12	10	39	52	81	88
Papua New Guinea	76	..	92	..	8	..	2	..	16	..	6	..
Paraguay	2	..	0 [c]	..	35	..	13	..	63	..	86	..
Peru	..	8	..	3	..	25	..	11	..	67	..	86
Philippines	60	47	39	27	15	18	13	13	25	36	48	61
Poland	..	19	..	19	..	41	..	21	..	39	..	60
Portugal	21	11	32	14	45	44	26	24	35	45	42	62
Puerto Rico	8	3	0 [c]	0 [c]	25	28	25	14	67	69	75	85

| | Agriculture [a] | | | | Industry [a] | | | | Services [a] | | | |
| | Male % of male employment | | Female % of female employment | | Male % of male employment | | Female % of female employment | | Male % of male employment | | Female % of female employment | |
	1980–82 [b]	1998–2001 [b]	1980–82 [b]	1998–2001 [b]	1980–82 [b]	1998–2001 [b]	1980–82 [b]	1998–2001 [b]	1980–82 [b]	1998–2001 [b]	1980–82 [b]	1998–2001 [b]
Romania	22	39	38	45	52	33	35	22	27	29	27	33
Russian Federation	19	15	13	8	50	36	37	23	31	49	50	69
Rwanda	88	..	98	..	5	..	1	..	7	..	1	..
Saudi Arabia	45	..	25	..	17	..	5	..	39	..	70	..
Senegal	74	..	90	..	9	..	2	..	17	..	8	..
Sierra Leone	63	..	82	..	20	..	4	..	17	..	14	..
Singapore	1	0 [c]	1	0 [c]	36	33	38	23	63	67	61	77
Slovak Republic	..	10	..	5	..	49	..	26	..	42	..	69
Slovenia	..	11	..	11	..	46	..	28	..	42	..	61
Somalia	69	..	90	..	12	..	2	..	19	..	8	..
South Africa	..	..	..	..	..	..	..	..	..	..	..	..
Spain	19	8	17	5	40	41	19	14	41	51	64	81
Sri Lanka	44	38	51	49	19	23	18	22	30	37	28	27
Sudan	66	..	88	..	9	..	4	..	24	..	8	..
Swaziland	40	..	38	..	29	..	14	..	30	..	48	..
Sweden	8	4	3	1	44	38	15	12	49	59	82	87
Switzerland	8	5	5	4	47	36	23	13	46	59	72	83
Syrian Arab Republic	..	..	..	..	..	..	..	..	..	..	..	..
Tajikistan	..	..	..	..	..	..	..	..	..	..	..	..
Tanzania	..	..	..	..	..	..	..	..	..	..	..	..
Thailand	60	50	64	47	16	20	11	17	24	31	25	36
Togo	70	..	67	..	12	..	7	..	19	..	26	..
Trinidad and Tobago	11	11	9	3	44	37	21	13	45	52	70	83
Tunisia	33	..	53	..	30	..	32	..	37	..	16	..
Turkey	4	34	9	72	36	25	31	10	60	41	60	18
Turkmenistan	..	..	..	..	..	..	..	..	..	..	..	..
Uganda	..	..	..	..	..	..	..	..	..	..	..	..
Ukraine	..	..	..	..	..	..	..	..	..	..	..	..
United Arab Emirates	5	..	0	..	40	..	7	..	55	..	93	..
United Kingdom	4	2	1	1	45	36	20	12	52	61	79	87
United States	5	4	2	1	37	32	17	12	58	64	81	86
Uruguay	..	6	..	1	..	34	..	14	..	61	..	85
Uzbekistan	..	..	..	..	..	..	..	..	..	..	..	..
Venezuela, RB	19	..	2	..	32	..	17	..	49	..	80	..
Vietnam	..	..	..	..	..	..	..	..	..	..	..	..
West Bank and Gaza	22	..	25	..	43	..	25	..	36	..	50	..
Yemen, Rep.	60	..	98	..	19	..	1	..	21	..	1	..
Yugoslavia, Fed. Rep.	..	..	..	..	..	..	..	..	..	..	..	..
Zambia	69	..	85	..	13	..	3	..	19	..	13	..
Zimbabwe	29	..	50	..	31	..	8	..	40	..	42	..
World	.. w	.. w	.. w	.. w	.. w	.. w	.. w	.. w	.. w	.. w	.. w	.. w
Low income	..	..	..	..	..	..	..	..	..	..	..	..
Middle income	..	..	..	..	..	..	..	..	..	..	..	..
Lower middle income	..	..	..	..	..	..	..	..	..	..	..	..
Upper middle income	..	21	..	13	..	31	..	16	..	48	..	70
Low & middle income	..	..	..	..	..	..	..	..	..	..	..	..
East Asia & Pacific	..	..	..	..	..	..	..	..	..	..	..	..
Europe & Central Asia	..	21	..	21	..	35	..	21	..	44	..	58
Latin America & Carib.	..	21	..	11	..	28	..	14	..	51	..	75
Middle East & N. Africa	..	..	..	..	..	..	..	..	..	..	..	..
South Asia	..	..	..	..	..	..	..	..	..	..	..	..
Sub-Saharan Africa	..	..	..	..	..	..	..	..	..	..	..	..
High income	9	4	7	3	39	36	21	15	52	59	71	81
Europe EMU	..	5	..	3	..	41	..	17	..	54	..	80

a. Data may not sum to 100 because of workers not classified by sectors. b. Data are for the most recent year available. c. Less than 0.5.

About the data

The International Labour Organization (ILO) classifies economic activity on the basis of the International Standard Industrial Classification (ISIC) of All Economic Activities. Because this classification is based on where work is performed (industry) rather than on what type of work is performed (occupation), all of an enterprise's employees are classified under the same industry, regardless of their trade or occupation. The categories should add up to 100 percent. Where they do not, the differences arise because of workers who cannot be classified by economic activity.

Data on employment are drawn from labor force surveys, establishment censuses and surveys, administrative records of social insurance schemes, and official national estimates. The concept of employment generally refers to people above a certain age who worked, or who held a job, during a reference period. Employment data include both full-time and part-time workers. There are, however, many differences in how countries define and measure employment status, particularly for students, part-time workers, members of the armed forces, and household or contributing family workers. Where the armed forces are included, they are allocated to the service sector, causing that sector to be somewhat overstated relative to the service sector in economies where they are excluded. Where data are obtained from establishment surveys, they cover only employees; thus self-employed and contributing family workers are excluded. In such cases the employment share of the agricultural sector is severely underreported.

Countries also take very different approaches to the treatment of unemployed people. In most countries unemployed people with previous job experience are classified according to their last job. But in some countries the unemployed and people seeking their first job are not classifiable by economic activity. Because of these differences, the size and distribution of employment by economic activity may not be fully comparable across countries (ILO, *Yearbook of Labour Statistics* 1996, p. 64).

The ILO's *Yearbook of Labour Statistics* and its database Key Indicators of the Labour Market report data by major divisions of the ISIC revision 2 or ISIC revision 3. In this table the reported divisions or categories are aggregated into three broad groups: agriculture, industry, and services. An increasing number of countries report economic activity according to the ISIC. Where data are supplied according to national classifications, however, industry definitions and descriptions may differ. In addition, classification into broad groups may obscure fundamental differences in countries' industrial patterns.

The distribution of economic activity by gender reveals some interesting patterns. Agriculture accounts for the largest share of female employment in much of Africa and Asia. Services account for much of the increase in women's labor force participation in North Africa, Latin America and the Caribbean, and high-income economies. Worldwide, women are underrepresented in industry.

Segregating one sex in a narrow range of occupations significantly reduces economic efficiency by reducing labor market flexibility and thus the economy's ability to adapt to change. This segregation is particularly harmful for women, who have a much narrower range of labor market choices and lower levels of pay than men. But it is also detrimental to men when job losses are concentrated in industries dominated by men and job growth is centered in service occupations, where women often dominate, as has been the recent experience in many countries.

There are several explanations for the rising importance of service jobs for women. Many service jobs—such as nursing and social and clerical work—are considered "feminine" because of a perceived similarity to women's traditional roles. Women often do not receive the training needed to take advantage of changing employment opportunities. And the greater availability of part-time work in service industries may lure more women, although it is not clear whether this is a cause or an effect.

Definitions

- **Agriculture** corresponds to division 1 (ISIC revision 2) or tabulation categories A and B (ISIC revision 3) and includes hunting, forestry, and fishing.
- **Industry** corresponds to divisions 2–5 (ISIC revision 2) or tabulation categories C–F (ISIC revision 3) and includes mining and quarrying (including oil production), manufacturing, construction, electricity, gas, and water. • **Services** correspond to divisions 6–9 (ISIC revision 2) or tabulation categories G–P (ISIC revision 3) and include wholesale and retail trade and restaurants and hotels; transport, storage, and communications; financing, insurance, real estate, and business services; and community, social, and personal services.

Data sources

The employment data are from the ILO database Key Indicators of the Labour Market (2001–02 issue).

	Unemployment						Long-term unemployment			Unemployment by level of educational attainment		
	Male % of male labor force		Female % of female labor force		Total % of total labor force		% of total unemployment			% of total unemployment		
							Male	Female	Total	Primary	Secondary	Tertiary
	1980–82[a]	1998–2001[a]	1980–82[a]	1998–2001[a]	1980–82[a]	1998–2001[a]	1998–2001[a]	1998–2001[a]	1998–2001[a]	1997–99[a]	1997–99[a]	1997–99[a]
Afghanistan	..	..	..	..	..	..	..	..	..	..	..	..
Albania	..	15.8	..	20.9	3.6	18.0	..	..	..	..	..	..
Algeria	..	..	..	..	..	..	..	..	..	..	..	..
Angola	..	..	..	..	..	..	..	..	..	..	..	..
Argentina	..	11.9	..	14.3	4.8	12.8	..	..	..	..	..	..
Armenia	..	4.9	..	15.0	..	9.3	..	..	..	..	..	..
Australia	6.3	7.2	7.5	6.7	6.7	6.4	30.6	24.0	27.9	53.3	32.1	11.8
Austria	3.8	4.7	3.5	4.8	3.7	4.7	28.1	36.1	31.7	35.2	60.3	4.6
Azerbaijan	..	1.0	..	1.4	..	1.2	..	..	..	6.7	30.8	62.5
Bangladesh	..	..	..	..	..	..	..	..	..	..	..	..
Belarus	..	..	..	..	..	2.0	..	..	..	7.8	15.5	76.7
Belgium	9.5	5.8	18.6	8.7	13.0	7.0	60.1	60.9	60.5	53.1	33.4	13.6
Benin	..	..	..	..	..	..	..	..	..	..	..	..
Bolivia	..	..	..	..	..	..	..	..	..	..	..	..
Bosnia and Herzegovina	..	..	..	..	..	..	..	..	..	..	..	..
Botswana	..	..	..	..	..	..	..	..	..	..	..	..
Brazil	3.9	7.2	4.0	11.6	3.9	9.6	..	..	..	..	..	..
Bulgaria	..	14.0	..	14.1	..	14.1	55.1	55.5	55.3	7.4	85.3	7.3
Burkina Faso	..	..	..	..	..	..	..	..	..	..	..	..
Burundi	..	..	..	..	..	..	..	..	..	..	..	..
Cambodia	..	..	..	..	..	..	..	..	..	..	..	..
Cameroon	..	..	..	..	..	..	..	..	..	..	..	..
Canada	11.2	6.9	10.6	6.7	11.0	6.8	11.7	9.5	10.7	25.9	31.2	35.6
Central African Republic	..	..	..	..	..	..	..	..	..	..	..	..
Chad	..	..	..	..	..	..	..	..	..	..	..	..
Chile	20.2	9.4	18.3	10.2	19.6	9.7	..	..	..	28.5	56.2	14.6
China	..	..	..	..	3.2	3.1	..	..	..	..	..	..
Hong Kong, China	4.0	5.1	3.1	4.0	3.6	5.0	..	..	..	..	..	..
Colombia	7.5	16.9	11.5	24.5	9.1	20.5	..	..	..	21.3	57.8	19.1
Congo, Dem. Rep.	..	..	..	..	..	..	..	..	..	..	..	..
Congo, Rep.	..	..	..	..	..	..	..	..	..	..	..	..
Costa Rica	8.6	5.2	11.4	7.6	9.4	6.1	..	..	..	75.1	12.7	8.1
Côte d'Ivoire	..	..	..	..	..	..	..	..	..	..	..	..
Croatia	3.9	12.8	9.1	14.5	6.0	20.6	..	..	..	19.5	69.1	11.4
Cuba	..	..	..	..	..	..	..	..	..	..	..	..
Czech Republic	..	7.3	..	10.6	..	8.8	47.5	49.8	48.8	24.2	72.1	3.7
Denmark	9.7	4.5	10.0	5.9	10.0	5.4	20.9	20.1	20.5	34.6	47.7	16.7
Dominican Republic	..	7.8	..	24.9	..	13.8	..	..	..	50.4	31.1	9.6
Ecuador	..	8.4	..	16.0	..	11.5	..	..	..	..	..	..
Egypt, Arab Rep.	4.1	5.1	20.5	19.9	5.7	8.2	..	..	..	..	..	..
El Salvador	..	8.2	..	6.0	12.9	7.3	..	..	..	57.1	23.4	7.5
Eritrea	..	..	..	..	..	..	..	..	..	..	..	..
Estonia	..	13.0	..	10.2	..	14.8	45.4	49.1	47.0	22.5	54.4	23.1
Ethiopia	3.6	..	9.5	..	5.2	..	..	..	..	26.9	61.3	8.1
Finland	5.5	9.7	5.2	10.7	5.4	9.8	30.1	25.2	27.6	41.1	49.8	9.1
France	5.8	8.5	10.5	11.9	7.8	10.0	41.1	43.6	42.5	..	..	..
Gabon	..	..	..	..	..	..	..	..	..	..	..	..
Gambia, The	..	15.3	..	12.2	..	13.8	..	..	..	3.9	32.4	60.8
Georgia	..	..	..	..	..	..	..	..	..	..	..	..
Germany	..	7.6	..	8.6	..	8.1	49.9	54.0	51.7	28.9	57.5	13.6
Ghana	..	..	..	..	..	..	..	..	..	..	..	..
Greece	4.8	7.0	8.1	16.5	5.8	10.8	44.7	61.5	54.9	36.9	40.5	21.9
Guatemala	..	..	..	..	..	..	..	..	..	..	..	..
Guinea	..	..	..	..	..	..	..	..	..	..	..	..
Guinea-Bissau	..	..	..	..	..	..	..	..	..	..	..	..
Haiti	..	..	..	..	..	..	..	..	..	..	..	..

	Unemployment						Long-term unemployment			Unemployment by level of educational attainment		
	Male % of male labor force		Female % of female labor force		Total % of total labor force		% of total unemployment			% of total unemployment		
							Male	Female	Total	Primary	Secondary	Tertiary
	1980–82[a]	1998–2001[a]	1980–82[a]	1998–2001[a]	1980–82[a]	1998–2001[a]	1998–2001[a]	1998–2001[a]	1998–2001[a]	1997–99[a]	1997–99[a]	1997–99[a]
Honduras	8.6	3.7	6.0	3.8	7.3	3.7	..	..	..	63.2	22.4	5.8
Hungary	..	7.5	..	6.3	..	6.5	45.0	43.2	44.3	35.2	61.6	3.2
India	..	..	..	..	..	..	..	..	..	..	..	..
Indonesia	..	..	..	..	..	6.1	..	..	..	38.3	47.9	9.2
Iran, Islamic Rep.	..	..	..	..	..	..	..	..	..	..	..	..
Iraq	..	..	..	..	..	..	..	..	..	..	..	..
Ireland	11.4	4.8	8.2	4.6	12.1	4.7	44.9	23.4	36.5	60.7	20.8	16.1
Israel	4.4	8.5	6.0	8.1	5.0	8.3	..	..	..	23.9	42.2	33.1
Italy	5.7	8.7	14.0	15.7	8.5	10.8	62.1	60.7	61.4	52.3	39.0	6.9
Jamaica	16.1	10.0	40.6	22.5	27.6	15.7	19.4	30.5	26.6	..	..	..
Japan	2.4	5.0	2.2	4.5	2.3	4.8	30.7	17.1	25.5	23.3	51.2	25.6
Jordan	..	11.8	..	20.7	..	13.2	..	..	..	..	..	..
Kazakhstan	..	..	..	..	..	13.7	..	..	..	7.2	52.5	40.3
Kenya	..	..	..	..	..	..	..	..	..	..	..	..
Korea, Dem. Rep.	..	..	..	..	..	..	..	..	..	..	..	..
Korea, Rep.	5.5	7.1	2.5	5.1	4.4	4.1	3.1	0.7	2.3	16.4	52.7	20.0
Kuwait	..	..	..	..	..	..	..	..	..	..	..	..
Kyrgyz Republic	..	..	..	..	..	..	..	..	..	33.4	55.7	10.9
Lao PDR	..	..	..	..	..	..	..	..	..	..	..	..
Latvia	..	15.5	..	13.3	..	8.4	50.5	52.8	51.5	20.8	68.1	8.5
Lebanon	..	..	..	..	..	..	..	..	..	..	..	..
Lesotho	..	..	..	..	..	..	..	..	..	..	..	..
Liberia	..	..	..	..	..	..	..	..	..	..	..	..
Libya	..	..	..	..	..	..	..	..	..	..	..	..
Lithuania	..	19.3	..	13.9	..	16.6	60.9	56.2	59.0	15.4	56.2	28.5
Macedonia, FYR	15.6	32.5	32.8	37.5	22.0	34.5	..	..	..	..	..	..
Madagascar	..	..	..	..	..	..	..	..	..	..	..	..
Malawi	..	..	..	..	..	..	..	..	..	..	..	..
Malaysia	..	..	..	..	..	3.0	..	..	..	..	..	..
Mali	..	..	..	..	..	..	..	..	..	..	..	..
Mauritania	..	..	..	..	..	..	..	..	..	..	..	..
Mauritius	..	..	..	..	..	..	..	..	..	33.2	66.1	..
Mexico	..	1.8	..	2.6	..	2.0	0.4	1.5	0.8	15.5	36.0	37.7
Moldova	..	..	..	..	..	11.1	..	..	..	..	..	..
Mongolia	..	5.2	..	6.3	..	5.7	..	..	..	47.9	24.1	17.3
Morocco	..	20.3	..	27.6	..	22.0	..	..	..	..	..	..
Mozambique	..	..	..	..	..	..	..	..	..	..	..	..
Myanmar	..	..	..	..	..	..	..	..	..	..	..	..
Namibia	..	..	..	..	..	..	..	..	..	38.4	50.1	0.5
Nepal	..	1.5	..	0.7	..	1.1	..	..	..	..	..	..
Netherlands	10.0	2.7	8.9	4.9	9.6	3.6	47.7	40.4	43.5	30.4	33.0	14.3
New Zealand	..	6.1	..	5.8	..	6.0	20.7	12.6	17.1	0.5	38.5	22.6
Nicaragua	..	8.8	..	14.5	..	13.3	..	..	..	54.9	24.7	14.9
Niger	..	..	..	..	..	..	..	..	..	..	..	..
Nigeria	..	..	..	..	..	..	..	..	..	..	..	..
Norway	2.5	3.7	3.0	3.2	2.7	3.4	6.7	2.9	5.0	25.3	54.7	17.3
Oman	..	..	..	..	..	..	..	..	..	..	..	..
Pakistan	3.0	4.2	7.5	14.9	3.6	5.9	..	..	..	..	..	..
Panama	6.3	10.8	13.3	17.9	8.4	13.3	..	..	..	..	..	..
Papua New Guinea	..	..	..	..	..	..	..	..	..	..	..	..
Paraguay	5.4	..	5.9	..	5.6	..	..	..	..	..	..	..
Peru	..	7.5	..	8.6	..	8.0	..	..	..	13.1	52.6	33.3
Philippines	3.6	9.8	8.6	10.5	5.5	10.1	..	..	..	..	..	..
Poland	..	15.2	..	18.5	..	16.7	34.2	41.4	37.9	33.1	64.8	2.0
Portugal	2.7	2.9	11.9	4.8	6.3	3.8	39.5	42.9	41.2	73.9	14.9	5.8
Puerto Rico	26.3	11.9	15.5	7.8	22.9	10.1	..	..	..	..	..	..

2.4 | Unemployment

	Unemployment						Long-term unemployment			Unemployment by level of educational attainment		
	Male % of male labor force		Female % of female labor force		Total % of total labor force		% of total unemployment			% of total unemployment		
							Male	Female	Total	Primary	Secondary	Tertiary
	1980–82[a]	1998–2001[a]	1980–82[a]	1998–2001[a]	1980–82[a]	1998–2001[a]	1998–2001[a]	1998–2001[a]	1998–2001[a]	1997–99[a]	1997–99[a]	1997–99[a]
Romania	..	7.4	..	6.2	..	10.8	41.0	48.4	44.0	21.7	70.6	6.4
Russian Federation	..	13.6	..	13.1	..	11.4	..	..	11.9	16.8	41.6	41.6
Rwanda	..	..	..	..	..	..	..	..	..	..	..	..
Saudi Arabia	..	..	..	..	..	..	..	..	..	..	..	..
Senegal	..	..	..	..	..	..	..	..	..	..	..	..
Sierra Leone	..	..	..	..	..	..	..	..	..	..	..	..
Singapore	2.4	4.5	2.9	4.6	2.6	4.4	..	..	..	26.8	27.4	28.6
Slovak Republic	..	15.9	..	16.4	..	18.9	43.2	49.7	46.1	..	75.6	3.0
Slovenia	..	7.5	..	7.4	..	7.5	44.3	36.8	40.7	28.2	64.8	7.0
Somalia	..	..	..	..	..	..	..	..	..	..	..	..
South Africa	..	19.8	..	27.8	..	23.3	..	..	..	..	..	..
Spain	14.4	9.7	18.7	20.5	15.6	14.1	39.5	52.4	46.8	52.3	19.1	21.5
Sri Lanka	..	7.1	..	16.2	..	10.6	..	..	..	49.8	..	50.2
Sudan	..	..	..	..	..	..	..	..	..	..	..	..
Swaziland	..	..	..	..	..	..	..	..	..	..	..	..
Sweden	3.3	7.4	3.8	6.7	3.5	5.1	33.3	26.1	30.1	32.0	50.6	15.8
Switzerland	0.4	2.3	0.6	3.1	0.4	2.7	27.5	29.1	28.3	..	..	..
Syrian Arab Republic	3.8	..	3.8	..	3.9	..	..	..	..	..	..	..
Tajikistan	..	..	..	..	..	..	..	..	..	10.6	83.2	6.3
Tanzania	..	..	..	..	..	..	..	..	..	..	..	..
Thailand	2.4	3.0	3.1	3.0	2.8	2.4	..	..	..	71.7	12.3	12.9
Togo	..	..	..	..	..	..	..	..	..	..	..	..
Trinidad and Tobago	8.3	10.9	13.8	16.8	10.0	13.1	19.0	33.8	26.2	38.2	60.7	0.8
Tunisia	..	..	..	..	..	..	..	..	..	..	33.7	4.1
Turkey	9.0	7.6	23.0	6.6	10.9	8.3	29.8	44.1	33.7	..	..	..
Turkmenistan	..	..	..	..	..	..	..	..	..	..	..	..
Uganda	..	..	..	..	..	..	..	..	..	..	..	..
Ukraine	..	12.2	..	11.5	..	11.9	..	..	..	9.4	27.2	63.4
United Arab Emirates	..	..	..	..	..	..	..	..	..	..	..	..
United Kingdom	13.1	6.7	7.5	5.1	10.9	5.3	34.8	21.6	29.8	9.3	43.4	12.1
United States	9.9	3.7	9.4	4.6	9.7	4.1	6.7	5.3	6.0	22.2	35.6	42.1
Uruguay	..	8.7	..	14.6	..	11.3	..	..	..	..	..	..
Uzbekistan	..	..	..	..	..	..	..	..	..	..	..	..
Venezuela, RB	..	..	..	..	7.1	14.9	..	..	..	..	..	..
Vietnam	..	..	..	..	..	..	..	..	..	..	..	..
West Bank and Gaza	..	..	..	..	..	14.1	..	..	..	..	..	..
Yemen, Rep.	..	..	..	..	..	..	..	..	..	..	..	..
Yugoslavia, Fed. Rep.	..	..	..	..	..	..	..	..	..	..	..	..
Zambia	32.7	..	59.0	..	42.2	..	..	..	..	..	..	..
Zimbabwe	..	7.3	..	4.6	..	6.0	..	..	..	..	..	..
World	.. w	.. w	.. w	.. w	.. w	.. w	.. w	.. w	.. w	.. w	.. w	.. w
Low income	..	..	..	..	..	..	..	..	..	..	..	..
Middle income	..	..	..	..	4.1	4.9	..	..	..	..	..	..
Lower middle income	..	..	..	..	3.6	4.3	..	..	..	..	..	..
Upper middle income	..	7.0	..	8.9	..	9.0	..	..	..	..	..	..
Low & middle income	..	..	..	..	..	..	..	..	..	..	..	..
East Asia & Pacific	..	..	..	..	3.3	3.7	..	..	..	..	..	..
Europe & Central Asia	..	11.3	..	11.1	..	11.1	..	..	27.1	17.6	47.3	34.8
Latin America & Carib.	..	7.2	..	10.5	..	9.2	..	..	..	..	..	..
Middle East & N. Africa	..	..	..	..	..	..	..	..	..	..	..	..
South Asia	..	..	..	..	..	..	..	..	..	..	..	..
Sub-Saharan Africa	..	..	..	..	..	..	..	..	..	..	..	..
High income	7.8	5.4	8.7	6.7	8.1	6.2	28.4	25.6	27.3	27.3	41.2	27.4
Europe EMU	7.5	7.9	12.8	11.6	9.5	9.8	48.5	50.9	49.8	42.3	42.9	12.9

a. Data are for the most recent year available.

Unemployment | **2.4**

Unemployment and total employment in an economy are the broadest indicators of economic activity as reflected by the labor market. The International Labour Organization (ILO) defines the unemployed as members of the economically active population who are without work but available for and seeking work, including people who have lost their jobs and those who have voluntarily left work. Some unemployment is unavoidable in all economies. At any time some workers are temporarily unemployed—between jobs as employers look for the right workers and workers search for better jobs. Such unemployment, often called frictional unemployment, results from the normal operation of labor markets.

Changes in unemployment over time may reflect changes in the demand for and supply of labor, but they may also reflect changes in reporting practices. Ironically, low unemployment rates can often disguise substantial poverty in a country, while high unemployment rates can occur in countries with a high level of economic development and low incidence of poverty. In countries without unemployment or welfare benefits, people eke out a living in the informal sector. In countries with well-developed safety nets, workers can afford to wait for suitable or desirable jobs. But high and sustained unemployment indicates serious inefficiencies in the allocation of resources.

The ILO definition of unemployment notwithstanding, reference periods, the criteria for those considered to be seeking work, and the treatment of people temporarily laid off and those seeking work for the first time vary across countries. In many developing countries it is especially difficult to measure employment and unemployment in agriculture. The timing of a survey, for example, can maximize the effects of seasonal unemployment in agriculture. And informal sector employment is difficult to quantify where informal activities are not registered and tracked.

Data on unemployment are drawn from labor force sample surveys and general household sample surveys, social insurance statistics, employment office statistics, and official estimates, which are usually based on information drawn from one or more of the above sources. Labor force surveys generally yield the most comprehensive data because they include groups not covered in other unemployment statistics, particularly people seeking work for the first time. These surveys generally use a definition of unemployment that follows the international recommendations more closely than that used by other sources and therefore generate statistics that are more comparable internationally.

In contrast, the quality and completeness of data from employment offices and social insurance programs vary widely. Where employment offices work closely with social insurance schemes and registration with such offices is a prerequisite for receipt of unemployment benefits, the two sets of unemployment estimates tend to be comparable. Where registration is voluntary and where employment offices function only in more populous areas, employment office statistics do not give a reliable indication of unemployment. Most commonly excluded from both these sources are discouraged workers who have given up their job search because they believe that no employment opportunities exist or do not register as unemployed after their benefits have been exhausted. Thus measured unemployment may be higher in countries that offer more or longer unemployment benefits.

Long-term unemployment is measured in terms of duration, that is, the length of time that an unemployed person has been without work and looking for a job. The underlying assumption is that shorter periods of joblessness are of less concern, especially when the unemployed are covered by unemployment benefits or similar forms of welfare support. The length of time a person has been unemployed is difficult to measure, because the ability to recall the length of that time diminishes as the period of joblessness extends. Women's long-term unemployment is likely to be lower in countries where women constitute a large share of the unpaid family workforce. Women in such countries have more access than men to nonmarket work and are more likely to drop out of the labor force and not be counted as unemployed.

No data are given in the table for economies for which unemployment data are not consistently available or are deemed unreliable.

• **Unemployment** refers to the share of the labor force without work but available for and seeking employment. Definitions of labor force and unemployment differ by country (see *About the data*). • **Long-term unemployment** refers to the number of people with continuous periods of unemployment extending for a year or longer, expressed as a percentage of the total unemployed. • **Unemployment by level of educational attainment** shows the unemployed by level of educational attainment, as a percentage of the total unemployed. The levels of educational attainment accord with the International Standard Classification of Education 1997, of the United Nations Educational, Cultural, and Scientific Organization (UNESCO).

2.4a

Youth unemployment does not always exceed adult unemployment

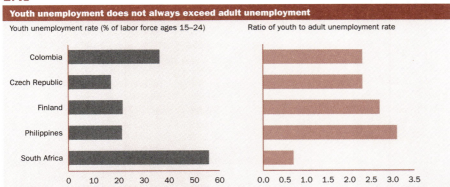

Youth unemployment rate (% of labor force ages 15–24)

Ratio of youth to adult unemployment rate

Unemployment among youth (ages 15–24) is an important policy issue for many economies, at all stages of development. Youth unemployment tends to exceed adult unemployment. But where the ratio of the youth unemployment rate to the adult rate is one or less, the problem of finding work is not limited to the young.

Source: ILO database Key Indicators of the Labour Market (2001–02 issue).

Data sources

The unemployment data are from the ILO database Key Indicators of the Labour Market (2001–02 issue).

	Average hours worked per week		Minimum wage		Agricultural wage		Labor cost per worker in manufacturing		Value added per worker in manufacturing	
			$ per year		$ per year		$ per year		$ per year	
	1980–84	1995–99[a]	1980–84	1995–99[a]	1980–84	1995–99[a]	1980–84	1995–99[a]	1980–84	1995–99[a]
Afghanistan	..	..	..	..	..	..	..	..	..	..
Albania	..	..	..	..	..	..	..	..	..	..
Algeria	..	..	..	1,340	..	..	6,242	2,638	11,306	..
Angola	..	..	..	..	..	..	..	..	..	..
Argentina	41	40	..	2,400	..	..	6,768	7,338	33,694	37,480
Armenia	..	..	..	..	..	..	..	..	..	..
Australia	37	39	..	12,712	11,212	15,124	14,749	26,087	27,801	57,857
Austria	33	32	..	b	..	..	11,949	28,342	20,956	53,061
Azerbaijan	..	..	..	..	..	..	..	..	..	..
Bangladesh	..	52	..	492	192	360	556	671	1,820	1,711
Belarus	..	..	..	..	1,641	410	2,233	754	..	..
Belgium	..	38	7,661	15,882	6,399	..	12,805	24,132	25,579	58,678
Benin	..	..	..	..	..	..	..	..	..	..
Bolivia	..	46	..	529	..	..	4,432	2,343	21,519	26,282
Bosnia and Herzegovina	..	..	..	..	..	..	..	..	..	..
Botswana	45	..	894	961	650	1,223	3,250	2,884	7,791	..
Brazil	..	..	1,690	1,308	..	..	10,080	14,134	43,232	61,595
Bulgaria	..	..	..	573	..	1,372	2,485	1,179	..	..
Burkina Faso	..	..	695	585	..	..	3,282	..	15,886	..
Burundi	..	..	..	..	..	..	..	..	..	..
Cambodia	..	..	..	..	..	..	..	..	..	..
Cameroon	..	..	..	..	..	..	..	..	..	..
Canada	38	38	4,974	7,897	20,429	30,625	17,710	28,424	36,903	60,712
Central African Republic	..	..	..	..	..	..	..	..	..	..
Chad	..	..	..	..	..	..	..	..	..	..
Chile	43	45	663	1,781	..	..	6,234	5,822	32,805	32,977
China	..	..	..	..	349	325	472	729	3,061	2,885
Hong Kong, China	48	46	..	..	..	..	4,127	10,353	7,886	32,611
Colombia	..	..	..	1,128	..	..	2,988	2,507	15,096	17,061
Congo, Dem. Rep.	..	..	..	..	..	..	..	..	..	..
Congo, Rep.	..	..	..	..	..	..	..	..	..	..
Costa Rica	..	47	1,042	1,638	982	1,697	2,433	2,829	7,185	7,184
Côte d'Ivoire	..	..	1,246	871	..	..	5,132	9,995	16,158	..
Croatia	..	..	..	..	..	..	..	..	..	..
Cuba	..	..	..	..	..	..	..	..	..	..
Czech Republic	43	43	..	942	2,277	3,090	2,306	3,815	5,782	5,094
Denmark	..	37	9,170	19,933	..	..	16,169	29,235	27,919	49,273
Dominican Republic	44	44	..	1,439	..	..	2,191	1,806	8,603	..
Ecuador	..	..	1,637	492	..	..	5,065	3,738	12,197	9,747
Egypt, Arab Rep.	58	..	343	415	..	..	2,210	1,863	3,691	5,976
El Salvador	..	..	..	790	..	..	3,654	..	14,423	..
Eritrea	..	..	..	..	..	..	..	..	..	..
Estonia	..	..	..	..	..	..	..	..	..	..
Ethiopia	..	..	..	..	..	..	..	1,596	..	7,094
Finland	..	38	..	b	..	..	11,522	26,615	25,945	55,037
France	40	39	6,053	12,072	..	..	18,488	..	26,751	61,019
Gabon	..	..	..	..	..	..	..	..	..	..
Gambia, The	..	..	..	..	..	..	..	..	..	..
Georgia	..	..	..	..	..	..	..	..	..	..
Germany	41	40	..	b	..	..	15,708	33,226	34,945	79,616
Ghana	..	..	..	..	1,470	..	2,306	..	12,130	..
Greece	39	41	..	6,057	..	..	6,461	12,296	14,561	30,429
Guatemala	..	..	..	459	..	..	2,605	1,802	11,144	9,235
Guinea	40		..	..	..	..	..	..	..	..
Guinea-Bissau	48		..	..	..	..	..	..	..	..
Haiti	..	..	..	..	..	..	..	..	..	..

	Average hours worked per week		Minimum wage		Agricultural wage		Labor cost per worker in manufacturing		Value added per worker in manufacturing	
			$ per year		$ per year		$ per year		$ per year	
	1980–84	1995–99[a]	1980–84	1995–99[a]	1980–84	1995–99[a]	1980–84	1995–99[a]	1980–84	1995–99[a]
Honduras	..	44	..	..	1,623	..	2,949	2,658	7,458	7,427
Hungary	35	33	1,186	1,132	1,186	2,676	1,410	3,755	4,307	10,918
India	46	..	..	408	205	245	1,035	1,192	2,108	3,118
Indonesia	40	43	..	241	..	639	898	3,054	3,807	5,139
Iran, Islamic Rep.	..	..	..	..	..	..	9,737	30,562	17,679	89,787
Iraq	..	..	..	..	..	..	4,624	13,288	13,599	34,316
Ireland	41	41	5,556	12,087	..	..	10,190	22,681	26,510	86,036
Israel	36	36	..	5,861	4,582	7,906	13,541	21,150	23,459	35,526
Italy	..	32	..	b	..	..	9,955	34,859	24,580	50,760
Jamaica	..	39	782	692	..	..	5,218	3,655	12,056	11,091
Japan	47	47	3,920	12,265	..	..	12,306	31,687	34,456	92,582
Jordan	..	50	b	b	..	..	4,643	2,082	16,337	11,906
Kazakhstan	..	..	..	..	..	..	..	..	..	..
Kenya	41	39	..	551	508	568	1,043	810	2,345	1,489
Korea, Dem. Rep.	..	..	..	..	..	..	..	..	..	..
Korea, Rep.	52	48	..	3,903	..	..	3,153	10,743	11,617	40,916
Kuwait	..	..	..	8,244	..	..	10,281	..	30,341	..
Kyrgyz Republic	..	..	..	65	1,695	168	2,287	687	..	..
Lao PDR	..	..	..	..	..	..	..	..	..	..
Latvia	..	..	..	..	..	..	..	366	..	..
Lebanon	..	..	..	..	..	..	..	..	..	..
Lesotho	..	45	..	..	..	..	1,442	..	6,047	..
Liberia	..	..	..	..	..	..	..	..	..	..
Libya	..	..	..	..	..	..	8,648	..	21,119	..
Lithuania	..	..	..	..	..	..	..	..	..	..
Macedonia, FYR	..	..	..	..	..	..	..	..	..	..
Madagascar	..	40	..	..	..	..	1,575	..	3,542	..
Malawi	..	..	..	..	..	..	..	..	..	..
Malaysia	..	..	..	b	1,435	..	2,519	3,429	8,454	12,661
Mali	..	..	321	459	..	..	2,983	..	10,477	..
Mauritania	..	..	..	..	..	..	..	..	..	..
Mauritius	..	..	..	..	..	..	1,465	1,973	2,969	4,217
Mexico	43	45	1,343	768	1,031	908	3,772	7,607	17,448	25,931
Moldova	..	..	..	..	..	..	..	..	..	..
Mongolia	..	..	..	..	..	..	..	..	..	..
Morocco	..	..	..	1,672	..	..	2,583	3,391	6,328	9,089
Mozambique	..	..	..	..	..	..	..	..	..	..
Myanmar	..	..	..	..	..	..	..	..	..	..
Namibia	..	..	..	..	..	..	..	..	..	..
Nepal	..	..	..	..	..	..	371	..	1,523	..
Netherlands	40	40	9,074	15,170	..	..	18,891	34,326	27,491	56,801
New Zealand	39	39	3,309	9,091	..	..	10,605	18,419	16,835	32,723
Nicaragua	..	44	..	..	..	..	..	..	..	..
Niger	40	..	..	..	..	..	4,074	..	22,477	..
Nigeria	..	..	..	300	..	..	4,812	..	20,000	..
Norway	33	35	9,074	b	..	..	14,935	38,415	24,905	51,510
Oman	..	..	..	..	..	..	..	3,099	..	61,422
Pakistan	48	..	..	600	427	416	1,264	..	6,214	..
Panama	..	..	..	..	..	..	4,768	6,351	15,327	17,320
Papua New Guinea	44	..	..	..	..	..	4,825	..	13,563	..
Paraguay	36	39	..	..	1,606	1,210	2,509	3,241	..	14,873
Peru	48	..	..	..	..	944	2,988	..	15,962	..
Philippines	47	43	915	1,472	382	..	1,240	2,450	5,266	10,781
Poland	36	33	320	1,584	1,726	1,301	1,682	1,714	6,242	7,637
Portugal	39	40	1,606	4,086	..	..	3,115	6,237	7,161	17,273
Puerto Rico	..	..	..	..	..	..	..	..	..	..

2.5 Wages and productivity

	Average hours worked per week		Minimum wage		Agricultural wage		Labor cost per worker in manufacturing		Value added per worker in manufacturing	
			$ per year		$ per year		$ per year		$ per year	
	1980–84	1995–99[a]	1980–84	1995–99[a]	1980–84	1995–99[a]	1980–84	1995–99[a]	1980–84	1995–99[a]
Romania	34	34	..	531	1,669	1,864	1,757	1,190	..	3,482
Russian Federation	..	..	863	297	2,417	659	2,524	1,528	..	..
Rwanda	..	..	..	..	..	..	1,871	..	9,835	..
Saudi Arabia	..	..	..	..	..	..	9,814	..	..	..
Senegal	..	..	993	848	..	..	2,828	7,754	6,415	..
Sierra Leone	44	..	..	..	..	..	1,624	..	7,807	..
Singapore	46	47	..	..	..	4,856	5,576	21,317	16,442	40,674
Slovak Republic	43	40	..	..	2,277	1,885	2,306	1,876	5,782	5,094
Slovenia	..	..	..	..	..	..	..	9,632	..	12,536
Somalia	..	..	..	..	..	..	..	..	..	..
South Africa	42	41	..	b	888	..	6,261	8,475	12,705	16,612
Spain	38	37	3,058	5,778	..	..	8,276	19,329	18,936	47,016
Sri Lanka	50	53	..	..	198	264	447	604	2,057	3,405
Sudan	..	..	..	..	..	..	..	..	..	..
Swaziland	..	..	..	..	..	..	..	..	..	..
Sweden	36	37	..	..	9,576	27,098	13,038	26,601	32,308	56,675
Switzerland	44	42	..	b	..	..	..	..	..	61,848
Syrian Arab Republic	..	..	..	..	..	..	2,844	4,338	9,607	9,918
Tajikistan	..	..	..	..	..	..	..	..	..	..
Tanzania	..	..	..	..	..	..	1,123	..	3,339	..
Thailand	50	47	749	1,159	..	..	2,305	3,868	11,072	19,946
Togo	..	..	..	..	..	..	..	..	..	..
Trinidad and Tobago	..	40	..	2,974	..	..	..	..	14,008	..
Tunisia	..	..	1,381	1,525	668	968	3,344	3,599	7,111	..
Turkey	..	48	594	1,254	1,015	2,896	3,582	7,958	13,994	32,961
Turkmenistan	..	..	..	..	..	..	..	..	..	..
Uganda	43	..	..	..	..	..	253	..	..	..
Ukraine	..	..	..	..	..	..	..	..	..	..
United Arab Emirates	..	..	..	..	..	..	6,968	..	20,344	..
United Kingdom	42	40	..	b	..	..	11,406	23,843	24,716	55,060
United States	40	41	6,006	8,056	..	..	19,103	28,907	47,276	81,353
Uruguay	48	42	1,262	1,027	1,289	..	4,128	3,738	13,722	16,028
Uzbekistan	..	..	..	..	..	..	..	..	..	..
Venezuela	41	..	1,869	1,463	..	..	11,188	4,667	37,063	24,867
Vietnam	..	47	..	134	..	442	..	711	..	..
West Bank and Gaza	..	..	..	..	..	..	..	..	..	..
Yemen, Rep.	..	..	..	..	..	..	4,492	1,291	17,935	5,782
Yugoslavia, Fed. Rep.	..	..	..	..	..	..	..	..	..	..
Zambia	..	45	..	..	..	..	3,183	4,292	11,753	16,615
Zimbabwe	..	..	..	..	1,065	..	4,097	3,422	9,625	11,944

a. Figures in italics refer to 1990–94. b. Country has sectoral minimum wage but no minimum wage policy.

Much of the available data on labor markets is collected through national reporting systems that depend on plant-level surveys. Even when these data are compiled and reported by international agencies such as the International Labour Organization or the United Nations Industrial Development Organization, differences in definitions, coverage, and units of account limit their comparability across countries. The data in this table are the result of a research project at the World Bank that has compiled results from more than 300 national and international sources in an effort to provide a set of uniform and representative labor market indicators. Nevertheless, many differences in reporting practices persist, some of which are described below.

Analyses of labor force participation, employment, and underemployment often rely on the number of hours of work per week. The indicator reported in the table is the time spent at the workplace working, preparing for work, or waiting for work to be supplied or for a machine to be fixed. It also includes the time spent at the workplace when no work is being performed but for which payment is made under a guaranteed work contract, or time spent in short periods of rest. Hours paid for but not spent at the place of work—such as paid annual and sick leave, paid holidays, paid meal breaks, and time spent in commuting between home and workplace—are not included. When this information is not available, the table reports the number of hours paid for, comprising the hours actually worked plus the hours paid for but not spent in the workplace. Data on hours worked are influenced by differences in methods of compilation and coverage as well as by national practices relating to the number of days worked and overtime, making comparisons across countries difficult.

Wages refer to remuneration in cash and in kind paid to employees at regular intervals. They exclude employers' contributions to social security and pension schemes as well as other benefits received by employees under these schemes. In some countries the national minimum wage represents a "floor," with higher minimum wages for particular skills and occupations set through collective bargaining. In those countries the agreements reached by trade unions and employers associations are extended by the government to all firms in the sector, or at least to large firms. Changes in the national minimum wage are generally associated with parallel changes in the minimum wages set through collective bargaining.

International comparisons of agricultural wages are subject to greater reservations than those of wages in other activities. The nature of the work carried out by different categories of agricultural workers and the length of the workday and workweek vary considerably from one country to another. Seasonal fluctuations in agricultural wages are more important in some countries than in others. And the methods followed in different countries for estimating the monetary value of payments in kind are not uniform. In many developing countries agricultural workers are hired on a casual or daily basis and lack any social security benefits.

Labor cost per worker in manufacturing is sometimes used as a measure of international competitiveness. The indicator reported in the table is the ratio of total compensation to the number of workers in the manufacturing sector. Compensation includes direct wages, salaries, and other remuneration paid directly by employers plus all contributions by employers to social security programs on behalf of their employees. But there are unavoidable differences in concepts, reference periods, and reporting practices. Remuneration for time not worked, bonuses and gratuities, and housing and family allowances should be considered part of the compensation costs, along with severance and termination pay. These indirect labor costs can vary substantially from country to country, depending on the labor laws and collective bargaining agreements in force.

International competitiveness also depends on productivity, which is often measured by value added per worker in manufacturing. The indicator reported in the table is the ratio of total value added in manufacturing to the number of employees engaged in that sector. Total value added is estimated as the difference between the value of industrial output and the value of materials and supplies for production (including fuel and purchased electricity) and cost of industrial services received.

Observations on labor costs and value added per worker are from plant-level surveys covering relatively large establishments, usually employing 10 or more workers and mostly in the formal sector. In high-income countries the coverage of these surveys tends to be quite good. In developing countries there is often a substantial bias toward very large establishments in the formal sector. As a result, the data may not be strictly comparable across countries. The data are converted into U.S. dollars using the average exchange rate for each year.

The data in the table are period averages and refer to workers of both sexes.

- **Average hours worked per week** refer to all workers (male and female) in nonagricultural activities or, if unavailable, in manufacturing. The data correspond to hours actually worked, to hours paid for, or to statutory hours of work in a normal workweek.
- **Minimum wage** corresponds to the most general regime for nonagricultural activities. When rates vary across sectors, only that for manufacturing (or commerce, if the manufacturing wage is unavailable) is reported. • **Agricultural wage** is based on daily wages in agriculture. To ensure comparability with the other wage series, full employment over the year is assumed, although many wage earners in agriculture are employed seasonally. • **Labor cost per worker in manufacturing** is obtained by dividing the total payroll by the number of employees, or the number of people engaged, in manufacturing establishments. • **Value added per worker in manufacturing** is obtained by dividing the value added of manufacturing establishments by the number of employees, or the number of people engaged, in those establishments.

Data sources

The data are drawn from Martin Rama and Raquel Artecona's "Database of Labor Market Indicators across Countries" (2002).

	National poverty line								International poverty line			
		Population below the poverty line				Population below the poverty line				Population below $1 a day	Poverty gap at $1 a day	Population below $2 a day	Poverty gap at $2 a day
	Survey year	Rural %	Urban %	National %	Survey year	Rural %	Urban %	National %	Survey year	%	%	%	%
Afghanistan		..	..	..		..	..	..		..	..	..	..
Albania		..	..	..		..	..	..		..	..	..	..
Algeria	1988	16.6	7.3	12.2	1995	30.3	14.7	22.6	1995	<2	<0.5	15.1	3.6
Angola		..	..	..		..	..	..		..	..	..	..
Argentina	1995	..	28.4	..	1998	..	29.9			..	..	..	..
Armenia	1998	..	..	55.0		..	..	..	1998	12.8	3.3	49.0	17.3
Australia		..	..	..		..	..	..		..	..	..	..
Austria		..	..	..		..	..	..		..	..	..	..
Azerbaijan	1995	..	..	68.1		..	..	..	2001	3.7	<1	9.1	3.5
Bangladesh	1995–96	38.5	13.7	34.4	2000	37.4	19.1	33.7	2000	36.0	8.1	82.8	36.3
Belarus	1998	..	..	33.0	2000	..	..	41.9	2000	<2	<0.5	<2	0.1
Belgium		..	..	..		..	..	..		..	..	..	..
Benin	1995	..	..	33.0		..	..	..		..	..	..	..
Bolivia	1997	77.3	..	63.2	1999	81.7	..	62.7	1999	14.4	5.4	34.3	14.9
Bosnia and Herzegovina	2001–02	19.9	13.8	19.5		..	..	..		..	..	..	..
Botswana		..	..	..		..	..	..	1993	23.5	7.7	50.1	22.8
Brazil	1990	32.6	13.1	17.4		..	..	..	1998	9.9	3.2	23.7	10.1
Bulgaria		..	..	..		..	..	..	2001	4.7	1.4	23.7	10.1
Burkina Faso	1994	51.0	10.4	44.5	1998	51.0	16.5	45.3	1994	61.2	25.5	85.8	50.9
Burundi	1990	..	..	36.2		..	..	..	1998	58.4	24.9	89.2	51.3
Cambodia	1993–94	43.1	24.8	39.0	1997	40.1	21.1	36.1		..	..	..	..
Cameroon	1984	32.4	44.4	40.0		..	..	..	1996	33.4	11.8	64.4	31.2
Canada		..	..	..		..	..	..		..	..	..	..
Central African Republic		..	..	..		..	..	..	1993	66.6	38.1	84.0	58.4
Chad	1995–96	67.0	63.0	64.0		..	..	..		..	..	..	..
Chile	1996	..	..	19.9	1998	..	..	17.0	1998	<2	<0.5	8.7	2.3
China	1996	7.9	<2	6.0	1998	4.6	<2	4.6	2000	16.1	3.7	47.3	18.3
Hong Kong, China		..	..	..		..	..	..		..	..	..	..
Colombia	1991	29.0	7.8	16.9	1992	31.2	8.0	17.7	1998	14.4	8.1	26.5	14.3
Congo, Dem. Rep.		..	..	..		..	..	..		..	..	..	..
Congo, Rep.		..	..	..		..	..	..		..	..	..	..
Costa Rica	1992	25.5	19.2	22.0		..	..	..	1998	6.9	3.4	14.3	7.0
Côte d'Ivoire	1995	..	..	36.8		..	..	..	1995	12.3	2.4	49.4	16.8
Croatia		..	..	..		..	..	..	2000	<2	<0.5	<2	<0.5
Cuba		..	..	..		..	..	..		..	..	..	..
Czech Republic		..	..	..		..	..	..	1996	<2	<0.5	<2	<0.5
Denmark		..	..	..		..	..	..		..	..	..	..
Djibouti	1996	86.5	..	45.1		..	..	..		..	..	..	..
Dominican Republic	1989	27.4	23.3	24.5	1992	29.8	10.9	20.6	1998	<2	<0.5	<2	<0.5
Ecuador	1994	47.0	25.0	35.0		..	..	..	1995	20.2	5.8	52.3	21.2
Egypt, Arab Rep.	1995–96	23.3	22.5	22.9	1999–2000	..	..	16.7	2000	3.1	<0.5	43.9	11.3
El Salvador	1992	55.7	43.1	48.3		..	..	..	1997	21.4	7.9	45.0	20.9
Eritrea	1993–94	..	..	53.0		..	..	..		..	..	..	..
Estonia	1995	14.7	6.8	8.9		..	..	..	1998	<2	<0.5	5.2	0.8
Ethiopia	1995–96	47.0	33.3	45.5	1999–2000	45.0	37.0	44.2	1999–2000	81.9	39.9	98.4	66.5
Finland		..	..	..		..	..	..		..	..	..	..
France		..	..	..		..	..	..		..	..	..	..
Gabon		..	..	..		..	..	..		..	..	..	..
Gambia, The	1992	..	..	64.0	1998	61.0	48.0	..	1998	59.3	28.8	82.9	51.1
Georgia	1997	9.9	12.1	11.1		..	..	..	1998	<2	<0.5	12.4	3.4
Germany		..	..	..		..	..	..		..	..	..	..
Ghana	1992	34.3	26.7	31.4		..	..	..	1999	44.8	17.3	78.5	40.8
Greece		..	..	..		..	..	..		..	..	..	..
Guatemala	1989	71.9	33.7	57.9		..	..	..	2000	16.0	4.6	37.4	16.0
Guinea	1994	..	..	40.0		..	..	..		..	..	..	..
Guinea-Bissau	1991	..	..	48.7		..	..	..		..	..	..	..

	National poverty line								International poverty line				
		Population below the poverty line				Population below the poverty line				Population below $1 a day	Poverty gap at $1 a day	Population below $2 a day	Poverty gap at $2 a day
	Survey year	Rural %	Urban %	National %	Survey year	Rural %	Urban %	National %	Survey year	%	%	%	%
Guyana	1993	..	..	43.2		..	..	..	1998	<2	<0.5	6.1	1.7
Haiti	1987	..	..	65.0	1995	66.0	..	..		..	..	..	..
Honduras	1992	46.0	56.0	50.0	1993	51.0	57.0	53.0	1998	23.8	11.6	44.4	23.1
Hungary	1993	..	..	14.5	1997	..	..	17.3	1998	<2	<0.5	7.3	1.7
India	1993–94	37.3	32.4	36.0	1999–2000	30.2	24.7	28.6	1999–2000	34.7	8.2	79.9	35.3
Indonesia	1996	..	..	15.7	1999	..	..	27.1	2000	7.2	1.0	55.4	16.4
Iran, Islamic Rep.		..	..	..		..	..	..	1998	<2	<0.5	7.3	1.5
Iraq		..	..	..		..	..	..		..	..	..	..
Ireland		..	..	..		..	..	..		..	..	..	..
Israel		..	..	..		..	..	..		..	..	..	..
Italy		..	..	..		..	..	..		..	..	..	..
Jamaica	1995	37.0	..	27.5	2000	25.1	..	18.7	2000	<2	<0.5	13.3	2.7
Japan		..	..	..		..	..	..		..	..	..	..
Jordan	1991	..	..	15.0	1997	..	..	11.7	1997	<2	<0.5	7.4	1.4
Kazakhstan	1996	39.0	30.0	34.6		..	..	..	1996	1.5	0.3	15.3	3.9
Kenya	1992	46.4	29.3	42.0		..	..	..	1997	23.0	6.0	58.6	24.1
Korea, Dem. Rep.		..	..	..		..	..	..		..	..	..	..
Korea, Rep.		..	..	..		..	..	..	1998	<2	<0.5	<2	<0.5
Kuwait		..	..	..		..	..	..		..	..	..	..
Kyrgyz Republic	1997	64.5	28.5	51.0	1999	69.7	49.0	64.1	2000	2.0	0.2	34.1	8.3
Lao PDR	1993	48.7	33.1	45.0	1997–98	41.0	26.9	38.6	1997–98	26.3	6.3	73.2	29.6
Latvia		..	..	..		..	..	..	1998	<2	<0.5	8.3	2.0
Lebanon		..	..	..		..	..	..		..	..	..	..
Lesotho	1993	53.9	27.8	49.2		..	..	..	1993	43.1	20.3	65.7	38.1
Liberia		..	..	..		..	..	..		..	..	..	..
Libya		..	..	..		..	..	..		..	..	..	..
Lithuania		..	..	..		..	..	..	2000	<2	<0.5	13.7	4.2
Macedonia, FYR		..	..	..		..	..	..	1998	<2	<0.5	4.0	0.6
Madagascar	1997	76.0	63.2	73.3	1999	76.7	52.1	71.3	1999	49.1	18.3	83.3	44.0
Malawi	1990–91	..	..	54.0	1997–98	66.5	54.9	65.3	1997–98	41.7	14.8	76.1	38.3
Malaysia	1989	..	..	15.5		..	..	..	1997	<2	<0.5	9.3	2.0
Mali		..	..	..		..	..	..	1994	72.8	37.4	90.6	60.5
Mauritania	1996	65.5	30.1	50.0	2000	61.2	25.4	46.3	1995	28.6	9.1	68.7	29.6
Mauritius	1992	..	..	10.6		..	..	..		..	..	..	..
Mexico	1988	..	..	10.1		..	..	..	1998	8.0	2.1	24.3	9.2
Moldova	1997	26.7	..	23.3		..	..	..	2001	22.0	5.8	63.7	25.1
Mongolia	1995	33.1	38.5	36.3		..	..	..	1995	13.9	3.1	50.0	17.5
Morocco	1990–91	18.0	7.6	13.1	1998–99	27.2	12.0	19.0	1999	<2	<0.5	14.3	3.1
Mozambique	1996–97	71.3	62.0	69.4		..	..	..	1996	37.9	12.0	78.4	36.8
Myanmar		..	..	..		..	..	..		..	..	..	..
Namibia		..	..	..		..	..	..	1993	34.9	14.0	55.8	30.4
Nepal	1995–96	44.0	23.0	42.0		..	..	..	1995	37.7	9.7	82.5	37.5
Netherlands		..	..	..		..	..	..		..	..	..	..
New Zealand		..	..	..		..	..	..		..	..	..	..
Nicaragua	1993	76.1	31.9	50.3	1998	68.5	30.5	47.9	1998	82.3	52.2	94.5	71.1
Niger	1989–93	66.0	52.0	63.0		..	..	..	1995	61.4	33.9	85.3	54.8
Nigeria	1985	49.5	31.7	43.0	1992–93	36.4	30.4	34.1	1997	70.2	34.9	90.8	59.0
Norway		..	..	..		..	..	..		..	..	..	..
Oman		..	..	..		..	..	..		..	..	..	..
Pakistan	1993	33.4	17.2	28.6	1998–99	35.9	24.2	32.6	1998	13.4	2.4	65.6	22.0
Panama	1997	64.9	15.3	37.3		..	..	..	1998	7.6	2.9	17.9	7.9
Papua New Guinea	1996	41.3	16.1	37.5		..	..	..	1998	19.5	9.8	49.3	26.3
Paraguay	1991	28.5	19.7	21.8		..	..	..	1996	15.5	5.4	41.4	17.1
Peru	1994	67.0	46.1	53.5	1997	64.7	40.4	49.0	2000	14.6	2.7	46.4	17.2
Philippines	1994	53.1	28.0	40.6	1997	50.7	21.5	36.8	1998	<2	<0.5	<2	<0.5
Poland	1993	..	..	23.8		..	..	..		..	..	..	..

	National poverty line								International poverty line			
		Population below the poverty line				Population below the poverty line				Population below $1 a day	Poverty gap at $1 a day	Population below $2 a day	Poverty gap at $2 a day
	Survey year	Rural %	Urban %	National %	Survey year	Rural %	Urban %	National %	Survey year	%	%	%	%
Portugal		..	..	..					1994	<2	<0.5	<0.5	<0.5
Puerto Rico		..	..	..		..	..	..		..	..	..	..
Romania	1994	27.9	20.4	21.5		..	..	..	2000	2.1	0.6	20.5	5.2
Russian Federation	1994	..	..	30.9		..	..	..	2000	6.1	1.2	23.8	8.0
Rwanda	1993	..	..	51.2		..	..	..	1983–85	35.7	7.7	84.6	36.7
Saudi Arabia		..	..	..		..	..	..		..	..	..	..
Senegal	1992	40.4	..	33.4		..	..	..	1995	26.3	7.0	67.8	28.2
Sierra Leone	1989	76.0	53.0	68.0		..	..	..	1989	57.0	39.5	74.5	51.8
Singapore		..	..	..		..	..	..		..	..	..	..
Slovak Republic		..	..	..		..	..	..	1996	<2	<0.5	2.4	0.7
Slovenia		..	..	..		..	..	..	1998	<2	<0.5	<2	<0.5
Somalia		..	..	..		..	..	..		..	..	..	..
South Africa		..	..	..		..	..	..	1995	<2	<0.5	14.5	2.8
Spain		..	..	..		..	..	..		..	..	..	..
Sri Lanka	1990–91	22.0	15.0	20.0	1995–96	27.0	15.0	25.0	1995–96	6.6	1.0	45.4	13.5
Sudan		..	..	..		..	..	..		..	..	..	..
Swaziland	1995	..	..	40.0		..	..	..		..	..	..	..
Sweden		..	..	..		..	..	..		..	..	..	..
Switzerland		..	..	..		..	..	..		..	..	..	..
Syrian Arab Republic		..	..	..		..	..	..		..	..	..	..
Tajikistan		..	..	..		..	..	..	1998	10.3	2.6	50.8	16.3
Tanzania	1991	..	..	51.1	1993	49.7	24.4	41.6	1993	19.9	4.8	59.7	23.0
Thailand	1990	..	..	18.0	1992	15.5	10.2	13.1	2000	<2	<0.5	32.5	9.0
Togo	1987–89	..	..	32.3		..	..	..		..	..	..	..
Trinidad and Tobago	1992	20.0	24.0	21.0		..	..	..	1992	12.4	3.5	39.0	14.6
Tunisia	1990	13.1	3.5	7.4	1995	13.9	3.6	7.6	1995	<2	<0.5	10.0	2.3
Turkey		..	..	..		..	..	..	2000	<2	<0.5	10.3	2.5
Turkmenistan		..	..	..		..	..	..	1998	12.1	2.6	44.0	15.4
Uganda	1993	..	..	55.0		..	..	..	1996	82.2	40.1	96.4	65.9
Ukraine	1995	..	..	31.7		..	..	..	1999	2.9	0.6	45.7	16.3
United Arab Emirates		..	..	..		..	..	..		..	..	..	..
United Kingdom		..	..	..		..	..	..		..	..	..	..
United States		..	..	..		..	..	..		..	..	..	..
Uruguay		..	..	..		..	..	..	1998	<2	<0.5	<2	<0.5
Uzbekistan		..	..	..		..	..	..	1998	19.1	8.1	44.2	19.9
Venezuela, RB	1989	..	..	31.3		..	..	..	1998	15.0	6.9	32.0	15.2
Vietnam	1993	57.2	25.9	50.9		..	..	..	1998	17.7	3.3	63.7	22.9
West Bank and Gaza		..	..	..		..	..	..		..	..	..	..
Yemen, Rep.	1998	45.0	30.8	41.8		..	..	..	1998	15.7	4.5	45.2	15.0
Yugoslavia, Fed. Rep.		..	..	..		..	..	..		..	..	..	..
Zambia	1996	82.8	46.0	69.2	1998	83.1	56.0	72.9	1998	63.7	32.7	87.4	55.4
Zimbabwe	1990–91	35.8	3.4	25.8	1995–96	48.0	7.9	34.9	1990–91	36.0	9.6	64.2	29.4

About the data

International comparisons of poverty data entail both conceptual and practical problems. Different countries have different definitions of poverty, and consistent comparisons between countries can be difficult. Local poverty lines tend to have higher purchasing power in rich countries, where more generous standards are used than in poor countries. Is it reasonable to treat two people with the same standard of living—in terms of their command over commodities—differently because one happens to live in a better-off country? Can we hold the real value of the poverty line constant across countries, just as we do when making comparisons over time?

Poverty measures based on an international poverty line attempt to do this. The commonly used $1 a day standard, measured in 1985 international prices and adjusted to local currency using purchasing power parities (PPPs), was chosen for the World Bank's *World Development Report 1990: Poverty* because it is typical of the poverty lines in low-income countries. PPP exchange rates, such as those from the Penn World Tables or the World Bank, are used because they take into account the local prices of goods and services not traded internationally. But PPP rates were designed not for making international poverty comparisons but for comparing aggregates from national accounts. Thus there is no certainty that an international poverty line measures the same degree of need or deprivation across countries.

This year's edition of the *World Development Indicators* (like those of the past three years) uses 1993 consumption PPP estimates produced by the World Bank. The international poverty line, set at $1 a day in 1985 PPP terms, has been recalculated in 1993 PPP terms at about $1.08 a day. Any revisions in the PPP of a country to incorporate better price indexes can produce dramatically different poverty lines in local currency.

Problems also exist in comparing poverty measures within countries. For example, the cost of living is typically higher in urban than in rural areas. So the urban monetary poverty line should be higher than the rural poverty line. But it is not always clear that the difference between urban and rural poverty lines found in practice properly reflects the difference in the cost of living. In some countries the urban poverty line in common use has a higher real value than does the rural poverty line. Sometimes the difference has been so large as to imply that the incidence of poverty is greater in urban than in rural areas, even though the reverse is found when adjustments are made only for differences in the cost of living. As with international comparisons, when the real value of the poverty line varies, it is not clear how meaningful such urban-rural comparisons are.

The problems of making poverty comparisons do not end there. More issues arise in measuring household living standards. The choice between income and consumption as a welfare indicator is one issue. Income is generally more difficult to measure accurately, and consumption accords better with the idea of the standard of living than does income, which can vary over time even if the standard of living does not. But consumption data are not always available, and when they are not there is little choice but to use income. There are still other problems. Household survey questionnaires can differ widely, for example, in the number of distinct categories of consumer goods they identify. Survey quality varies, and even similar surveys may not be strictly comparable.

Comparisons across countries at different levels of development also pose a potential problem, because of differences in the relative importance of consumption of nonmarket goods. The local market value of all consumption in kind (including consumption from own production, particularly important in underdeveloped rural economies) should be included in the measure of total consumption expenditure. Similarly, the imputed profit from production of nonmarket goods should be included in income. This is not always done, though such omissions were a far bigger problem in surveys before the 1980s. Most survey data now include valuations for consumption or income from own production. Nonetheless, valuation methods vary. For example, some surveys use the price in the nearest market, while others use the average farm gate selling price.

Wherever possible, consumption has been used as the welfare indicator for deciding who is poor. Where consumption data are unavailable, income data are used, though there is a change in this year's edition in how income surveys are used. In the past, average income was adjusted to accord with consumption and income data from national accounts. This approach was tested using data for more than 20 countries for which the surveys provided both income and consumption expenditure data. Income gave a higher mean than consumption but also greater income inequality. These two effects roughly canceled each other out when poverty measures based on consumption were compared with those based on income from the same survey; statistically, there was no significant difference. So this year's edition uses income data to estimate poverty directly and no longer adjusts the income mean.

In all cases the measures of poverty have been calculated from primary data sources (tabulations or household data) rather than existing estimates. Estimation from tabulations requires an interpolation method; the method chosen was Lorenz curves with flexible functional forms, which have proved reliable in past work. Empirical Lorenz curves were weighted by household size, so they are based on percentiles of population, not households.

Definitions

- **Survey year** is the year in which the underlying data were collected. • **Rural poverty rate** is the percentage of the rural population living below the national rural poverty line. • **Urban poverty rate** is the percentage of the urban population living below the national urban poverty line. • **National poverty rate** is the percentage of the population living below the national poverty line. National estimates are based on population-weighted subgroup estimates from household surveys. • **Population below $1 a day** and **population below $2 a day** are the percentages of the population living on less than $1.08 a day and $2.15 a day at 1993 international prices (equivalent to $1 and $2 in 1985 prices, adjusted for purchasing power parity). Poverty rates are comparable across countries, but as a result of revisions in PPP exchange rates, they cannot be compared with poverty rates reported in previous editions for individual countries. • **Poverty gap** is the mean shortfall from the poverty line (counting the nonpoor as having zero shortfall), expressed as a percentage of the poverty line. This measure reflects the depth of poverty as well as its incidence.

Data sources

The poverty measures are prepared by the World Bank's Development Research Group. The national poverty lines are based on the World Bank's country poverty assessments. The international poverty lines are based on nationally representative primary household surveys conducted by national statistical offices or by private agencies under the supervision of government or international agencies and obtained from government statistical offices and World Bank country departments. The World Bank has prepared an annual review of its poverty work since 1993. *Poverty Reduction and the World Bank: Progress in 2001/02* is forthcoming.

2.7 Social indicators of poverty

	Survey year	Infant mortality rate		Births attended by skilled health staff		Prevalence of child malnutrition		Women with low body mass index		Total fertility rate	
		per 1,000 live births		% of births in the five years prior to survey		% of children under five		%		births per woman	
		Poorest quintile	Richest quintile	Poorest quintile	Richest quintile	Poorest quintile	Richest quintile	Poorest quintile	Richest quintile	Poorest quintile	Richest quintile
Bangladesh	1996–97	96	57	2	30	60	28	64.4	32.6	3.8	2.2
Benin	1996	119	63	34	98	37	19	21.0	7.0	7.3	3.8
Bolivia	1998	107	26	20	98	17	3	0.5	2.2	7.4	2.1
Brazil	1996	83	29	72	99	12	3	8.8	5.4	4.8	1.7
Burkina Faso	1992–93	114	80	26	86	36	22	15.7	10.2	7.5	4.6
Cameroon	1991	104	51	32	95	25	6	..	..	6.2	4.8
Central African Republic	1994–95	132	54	14	82	37	20	16.3	11.2	5.1	4.9
Chad	1996–97	80	89	3	47	50	29	27.5	21.0	7.1	6.2
Colombia	1995	41	16	61	98	15	3	5.9	1.2	5.2	1.7
Comoros	1996	87	65	26	85	36	18	7.4	8.6	6.4	3.0
Côte d'Ivoire	1994	117	63	17	84	31	13	11.0	5.7	6.4	3.7
Dominican Republic	1996	67	23	89	98	13	1	8.9	3.0	5.1	2.1
Egypt, Arab Rep.	1995–96	110	32	21	86	17	8	2.9	0.4	4.4	2.7
Ghana	1993	78	46	25	85	33	13	11.3	7.2	6.7	3.4
Guatemala	1995	57	35	9	92	35	7	4.2	2.0	8.0	2.4
Haiti	1994–95	94	74	24	78	39	10	24.9	9.3	7.0	2.3
India	1992–93	109	44	12	79	60	34	..	..	4.1	2.1
Indonesia	1997	78	23	21	89	..	..	..	..	3.3	2.0
Kazakhstan	1995	35	29	99	100	11	3	7.9	3.8	3.2	1.3
Kenya	1998	103	50	23	80	32	10	17.6	6.0	6.6	3.0
Kyrgyz Republic	1997	83	46	96	100	13	8	5.6	3.7	4.6	2.0
Madagascar	1997	119	58	30	89	45	32	24.3	15.1	8.1	3.4
Malawi	1992	141	106	45	78	34	17	14.1	6.0	7.2	6.1
Mali	1995–96	151	93	11	81	47	28	15.9	12.2	6.9	5.1
Morocco	1993	80	35	5	78	17	2	6.2	1.8	6.7	2.3
Mozambique	1997	188	95	18	82	37	14	17.2	4.2	5.2	4.4
Namibia	1992	64	57	51	91	36	13	19.3	5.3	6.9	3.6
Nepal	1996	96	64	3	34	53	28	25.7	21.4	6.2	2.9
Nicaragua	1997–98	51	26	33	92	18	4	4.0	4.1	6.6	1.9
Niger	1998	131	86	4	63	52	37	26.7	12.8	8.4	5.7
Nigeria	1990	102	69	12	70	40	22	..	..	6.6	4.7
Pakistan	1990–91	89	63	5	55	54	26	..	..	5.1	4.0
Paraguay	1990	43	16	41	98	6	1	..	..	7.9	2.7
Peru	1996	78	20	14	97	17	1	1.3	1.1	6.6	1.7
Philippines	1998	49	21	21	92	..	..	..	..	6.5	2.1
Senegal	1997	85	45	20	86	..	..	..	..	7.4	3.6
Tanzania	1996	87	65	27	81	40	18	12.2	7.1	7.8	3.9
Togo	1998	84	66	25	91	32	12	13.3	7.9	7.3	2.9
Turkey	1993	100	25	43	99	22	3	2.7	3.2	3.7	1.5
Uganda	1995	109	63	23	70	31	16	12.7	5.8	7.5	5.4
Uzbekistan	1996	50	47	92	100	25	12	11.4	5.7	4.4	2.1
Vietnam	1997	43	17	49	99	..	..	..	..	3.1	1.6
Yemen, Rep.	1997	109	60	7	50	20	6	39.0	13.1	7.3	4.7
Zambia	1996	124	70	19	91	32	13	10.2	7.9	7.4	4.4
Zimbabwe	1994	52	42	55	93	19	9	5.7	1.2	6.2	2.8

Social indicators of poverty | **2.7**

The data in the table describe the health status of, and use of health services by, individuals in different socioeconomic groups within countries. The data are from Demographic and Health Surveys conducted by Macro International with the support of the U.S. Agency for International Development. These large-scale household sample surveys, conducted periodically in about 50 developing countries, collect information on a large number of health, nutrition, and population measures as well as on respondents' social, demographic, and economic characteristics using a standard set of questionnaires. The data presented here draw on responses to individual and household questionnaires.

In the table socioeconomic status is defined in terms of a household's assets, including ownership of consumer items, characteristics of the household's dwelling, and other characteristics related to wealth. Each household asset for which information was collected was assigned a weight generated through principal component analysis. The resulting scores were standardized in relation to a standard normal distribution with a mean of zero and a standard deviation of one. The standardized scores were then used to create break points defining wealth quintiles, expressed as quintiles of individuals in the population rather than quintiles of individuals at risk with respect to any one health indicator.

The choice of the asset index for defining socioeconomic status was based on pragmatic rather than conceptual considerations: Demographic and Health Surveys do not provide income or consumption data but do have detailed information on households' ownership of consumer goods and their access to a variety of goods and services. Like income or consumption, the asset index defines disparities in primarily economic terms. It therefore excludes other possibilities of disparities among groups, such as those based on gender, education, ethnic background, or other facets of social exclusion. To that extent the index provides only a partial view of the multidimensional concepts of poverty, inequality, and inequity.

Creating one index that includes all asset indicators limits the types of analysis that can be performed. In particular, the use of a unified index does not permit a disaggregated analysis to examine which asset indicators have a more or less important association with health status or use of health services. In addition, some asset indicators may reflect household wealth better in some countries than in others—or reflect different degrees of wealth in different countries. Taking such information into account and creating country-specific asset indexes with country-specific choices of asset indicators might produce a more effective and accurate index for each country. The asset index used in the table does not have this flexibility.

The analysis has been carried out for 45 countries, with the results issued in country reports. The table shows the estimates for the poorest and richest quintiles only; the full set of estimates for more than 20 indicators is available in the country reports (see *Data sources*).

• **Survey year** is the year in which the underlying data were collected. • **Infant mortality rate** is the number of infants dying before reaching one year of age, per 1,000 live births. The estimates are based on births in the 10 years preceding the survey and may therefore differ from the estimates in table 2.20. • **Births attended by skilled health staff** are the percentage of deliveries attended by personnel trained to give the necessary supervision, care, and advice to women during pregnancy, labor, and the postpartum period, to conduct deliveries on their own, and to care for newborns. • **Prevalence of child malnutrition** is the percentage of children whose weight is more than two standard deviations below the median reference standard for their age as established by the U.S. National Center for Health Statistics, the U.S. Centers for Disease Control and Prevention, and the World Health Organization. The data are based on a sample of children who survived to age three, four, or five years, depending on the country. • **Women with low body mass index** are the percentage of women whose body mass index (BMI) is less than 18.5, a cutoff point indicating acute malnutrition. The BMI is the weight in kilograms divided by the square of the height in meters. • **Total fertility rate** is the number of children that would be born to a woman if she were to live to the end of her childbearing years and bear children in accordance with current age-specific fertility rates. The estimates are based on births during the three years preceding the survey and may therefore differ from those in table 2.17.

2.7a

Poor women lack adequate access to reproductive health care in urban as well as rural areas

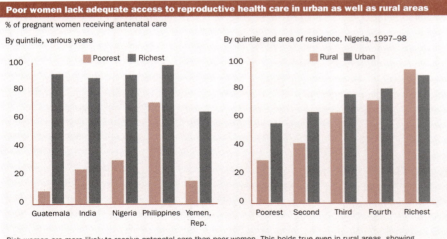

% of pregnant women receiving antenatal care

By quintile, various years — Poorest / Richest

By quintile and area of residence, Nigeria, 1997–98 — Rural / Urban

Rich women are more likely to receive antenatal care than poor women. This holds true even in rural areas, showing that poverty, not area of residence, has a greater effect on access to health care.

Source: Demographic and Health Survey data.

The data are from an analysis of Demographic and Health Surveys by the World Bank and Macro International. Country reports are available at http://www.worldbank.org/poverty/health/data/index.htm.

Distribution of income or consumption

	Survey year	Gini Index	Percentage share of income or consumption						
			Lowest 10%	Lowest 20%	Second 20%	Third 20%	Fourth 20%	Highest 20%	Highest 10%
Afghanistan		..	..	..	..	..	..	..	..
Albania		..	..	..	..	..	..	..	..
Algeria	1995 [a, b]	35.3	2.8	7.0	11.6	16.1	22.7	42.6	26.8
Angola		..	..	..	..	..	..	..	..
Argentina		..	..	..	..	..	..	..	..
Armenia	1998 [a, b]	37.9	2.6	6.7	11.3	15.4	21.6	45.1	29.7
Australia	1994 [c, d]	35.2	2.0	5.9	12.0	17.2	23.6	41.3	25.4
Austria	1995 [c, d]	30.5	2.3	7.0	13.2	17.9	24.0	37.9	22.4
Azerbaijan	2001 [a, b]	36.5	3.1	7.4	11.5	15.3	21.2	44.5	29.5
Bangladesh	2000 [a, b]	31.8	3.9	9.0	12.5	15.9	21.2	41.3	26.7
Belarus	2000 [a, b]	30.4	3.5	8.4	13.0	17.0	22.5	39.1	24.1
Belgium	1996 [c, d]	25.0	2.9	8.3	14.1	17.7	22.7	37.3	22.6
Benin		..	..	..	..	..	..	..	..
Bolivia	1999 [a, b]	44.7	1.3	4.0	9.2	14.8	22.9	49.1	32.0
Bosnia and Herzegovina		..	..	..	..	..	..	..	..
Botswana	1993 [a, b]	63.0	0.7	2.2	4.9	8.2	14.4	70.3	56.6
Brazil	1998 [c, d]	59.1	0.5	2.0	5.7	10.0	18.0	64.4	46.7
Bulgaria	2001 [c, d]	31.9	2.4	6.7	13.1	17.9	23.4	38.9	23.7
Burkina Faso	1998 [a, b]	48.2	1.8	4.5	7.4	10.6	16.7	60.7	46.3
Burundi	1998 [a, b]	33.3	1.7	5.1	10.3	15.1	21.5	48.0	32.8
Cambodia	1997 [a, b]	40.4	2.9	6.9	10.7	14.7	20.1	47.6	33.8
Cameroon	1996 [a, b]	47.7	1.8	4.6	8.3	13.0	21.0	53.0	36.5
Canada	1997 [c, d]	31.5	2.7	7.3	12.9	17.4	23.1	39.3	23.9
Central African Republic	1993 [a, b]	61.3	0.7	2.0	4.9	9.6	18.5	65.0	47.7
Chad		..	..	..	..	..	..	..	..
Chile	1998 [c, d]	57.5	1.1	3.2	6.7	10.7	18.1	61.3	45.4
China	1998 [c, d]	40.3	2.4	5.9	10.2	15.1	22.2	46.6	30.4
Hong Kong, China	1996 [c, d]	43.4	2.0	5.3	9.4	13.9	20.7	50.7	34.9
Colombia	1998 [c, d]	57.1	0.1	1.4	6.1	10.6	18.2	63.8	47.7
Congo, Dem. Rep.		..	..	..	..	..	..	..	..
Congo, Rep.		..	..	..	..	..	..	..	..
Costa Rica	1998 [c, d]	45.9	0.4	2.6	8.0	13.2	21.4	54.8	37.7
Côte d'Ivoire	1995 [a, b]	36.7	3.1	7.1	11.2	15.6	21.9	44.3	28.8
Croatia	2001 [a, b]	29.0	3.4	8.3	12.8	16.8	22.6	39.6	24.5
Cuba		..	..	..	..	..	..	..	..
Czech Republic	1996 [c, d]	25.4	4.3	10.3	14.5	17.7	21.7	35.9	22.4
Denmark	1997 [c, d]	24.7	2.6	8.3	14.7	18.2	22.9	35.8	21.3
Dominican Republic	1998 [c, d]	47.4	2.1	5.1	8.6	13.0	20.0	53.3	37.9
Ecuador	1998 [a, b]	43.7	0.9	3.3	7.5	11.7	19.4	58.0	41.6
Egypt, Arab Rep.	1999 [a, b]	34.4	3.7	8.6	12.1	15.4	20.4	43.6	29.5
El Salvador	1998 [c, d]	50.8	1.2	3.3	7.3	12.4	20.7	56.4	39.4
Eritrea		..	..	..	..	..	..	..	..
Estonia	1998 [c, d]	37.6	3.0	7.0	11.0	15.3	21.6	45.1	29.8
Ethiopia	2000 [a, b]	48.6	0.7	2.4	6.1	11.1	19.6	60.8	43.8
Finland	1995 [c, d]	25.6	4.1	10.1	14.7	17.9	22.3	35.0	20.9
France	1995 [c, d]	32.7	2.8	7.2	12.6	17.2	22.8	40.2	25.1
Gabon		..	..	..	..	..	..	..	..
Gambia, The	1998 [a, b]	47.8	1.5	4.0	7.6	12.3	20.8	55.2	38.0
Georgia	2000 [a, b]	38.9	2.2	6.0	10.8	15.6	22.4	45.2	29.3
Germany	1998 [c, d]	38.2	2.0	5.7	10.5	15.7	23.4	44.7	28.0
Ghana	1999 [a, b]	39.6	2.1	5.6	10.1	14.9	22.8	46.6	30.0
Greece	1998 [c, d]	35.4	2.9	7.1	11.4	15.8	22.0	43.6	28.5
Guatemala	2000 [c, d]	59.9	0.9	2.6	5.9	9.8	17.6	64.1	48.3
Guinea	1994 [a, b]	40.3	2.6	6.4	10.4	14.8	21.2	47.2	32.0
Guinea-Bissau	1993 [a, b]	47.0	2.1	5.2	8.8	13.1	19.4	53.4	39.3
Guyana	1999 [a, b]	44.6	1.3	4.5	9.9	14.5	21.4	49.7	33.8
Haiti		..	..	..	..	..	..	..	..

Distribution of income or consumption 2.8

	Survey year	Gini Index	Percentage share of income or consumption						
			Lowest 10%	Lowest 20%	Second 20%	Third 20%	Fourth 20%	Highest 20%	Highest 10%
Honduras	1998 [c, d]	59.0	0.5	2.0	6.2	11.3	19.5	61.0	44.4
Hungary	1998 [a, b]	24.4	4.1	10.0	14.7	18.3	22.7	34.4	20.5
India	1997 [a, b]	37.8	3.5	8.1	11.6	15.0	19.3	46.1	33.5
Indonesia	2000 [a, b]	30.3	3.6	8.4	11.9	15.4	21.0	43.3	28.5
Iran, Islamic Rep.	1998 [a, b]	43.0	2.0	5.1	9.4	14.1	21.5	49.9	33.7
Iraq		..	..	..	..	..	..	..	..
Ireland	1987 [c, d]	35.9	2.5	6.7	11.6	16.4	22.4	42.9	27.4
Israel	1997 [c, d]	35.5	2.4	6.9	11.4	16.3	22.9	44.3	28.2
Italy	1998 [c, d]	36.0	1.9	6.0	12.0	16.8	22.6	42.6	27.4
Jamaica	2000 [a, b]	37.9	2.7	6.7	10.7	15.0	21.7	46.0	30.3
Japan	1993 [c, d]	24.9	4.8	10.6	14.2	17.6	22.0	35.7	21.7
Jordan	1997 [a, b]	36.4	3.3	7.6	11.4	15.5	21.1	44.4	29.8
Kazakhstan	2001 [a, b]	31.2	3.4	8.2	12.5	16.8	22.9	39.6	24.2
Kenya	1997 [a, b]	44.5	2.3	5.6	9.3	13.6	20.2	51.2	36.1
Korea, Dem. Rep.		..	..	..	..	..	..	..	..
Korea, Rep.	1998 [c, d]	31.6	2.9	7.9	13.6	18.0	23.1	37.5	22.5
Kuwait		..	..	..	..	..	..	..	..
Kyrgyz Republic	2001 [a, b]	29.0	3.9	9.1	13.2	16.9	22.5	38.3	23.3
Lao PDR	1997 [a, b]	37.0	3.2	7.6	11.4	15.3	20.8	45.0	30.6
Latvia	1998 [c, d]	32.4	2.9	7.6	12.9	17.1	22.1	40.3	25.9
Lebanon		..	..	..	..	..	..	..	..
Lesotho	1995 [a, b]	56.0	0.5	1.4	3.7	7.7	16.5	70.7	53.6
Liberia		..	..	..	..	..	..	..	..
Libya		..	..	..	..	..	..	..	..
Lithuania	2000 [a, b]	36.3	3.2	7.9	12.7	16.9	22.6	40.0	24.9
Luxembourg	1998 [c, d]	30.8	3.2	8.0	12.8	16.9	22.5	39.7	24.7
Macedonia, FYR	1998 [a, b]	28.2	3.3	8.4	14.0	17.7	23.1	36.7	22.1
Madagascar	1999 [a, b]	46.0	2.5	6.4	10.7	15.5	22.7	44.8	28.6
Malawi	1997 [a, b]	50.3	1.9	4.9	8.5	12.3	18.3	56.1	42.2
Malaysia	1997 [c, d]	49.2	1.7	4.4	8.1	12.9	20.3	54.3	38.4
Mali	1994 [a, b]	50.5	1.8	4.6	8.0	11.9	19.3	56.2	40.4
Mauritania	1995 [a, b]	37.3	2.5	6.4	11.2	16.0	22.4	44.1	28.4
Mauritius		..	..	..	..	..	..	..	..
Mexico	1998 [c, d]	51.9	1.2	3.4	7.4	12.1	19.5	57.6	41.6
Moldova	2001 [a, b]	36.2	2.8	7.1	11.5	15.8	22.0	43.7	28.4
Mongolia	1998 [a, b]	44.0	2.1	5.6	10.0	13.8	19.4	51.2	37.0
Morocco	1998–99 [a, b]	39.5	2.6	6.5	10.6	14.8	21.3	46.6	30.9
Mozambique	1996–97 [a, b]	39.6	2.5	6.5	10.8	15.1	21.1	46.5	31.7
Myanmar		..	..	..	..	..	..	..	..
Namibia	1993 [c, d]	70.7	0.5	1.4	3.0	5.4	11.5	78.7	64.5
Nepal	1995–96 [a, b]	36.7	3.2	7.6	11.5	15.1	21.0	44.8	29.8
Netherlands	1994 [c, d]	32.6	2.8	7.3	12.7	17.2	22.8	40.1	25.1
New Zealand	1997 [c, d]	36.2	2.2	6.4	11.4	15.8	22.6	43.8	27.8
Nicaragua	1998 [a, b]	60.3	0.7	2.3	5.9	10.4	17.9	63.6	48.8
Niger	1995 [a, b]	50.5	0.8	2.6	7.1	13.9	23.1	53.3	35.4
Nigeria	1996–97 [a, b]	50.6	1.6	4.4	8.2	12.5	19.3	55.7	40.8
Norway	1995 [c, d]	25.8	4.1	9.7	14.3	17.9	22.2	35.8	21.8
Oman		..	..	..	..	..	..	..	..
Pakistan	1998–99 [a, b]	33.0	3.7	8.8	12.5	15.9	20.6	42.3	28.3
Panama	1997 [a, b]	48.5	1.2	3.6	8.1	13.6	21.9	52.8	35.7
Papua New Guinea	1996 [a, b]	50.9	1.7	4.5	7.9	11.9	19.2	56.5	40.5
Paraguay	1998 [c, d]	57.7	0.5	1.9	6.0	11.4	20.1	60.7	43.8
Peru	1996 [c, d]	46.2	1.6	4.4	9.1	14.1	21.3	51.2	35.4
Philippines	2000 [a, b]	46.1	2.2	5.4	8.8	13.1	20.5	52.3	36.3
Poland	1998 [a, b]	31.6	3.2	7.8	12.8	17.1	22.6	39.7	24.7
Portugal	1997 [c, d]	38.5	2.0	5.8	11.0	15.5	21.9	45.9	29.8
Puerto Rico		..	..	..	..	..	..	..	..

	Survey year	Gini Index	Percentage share of income or consumption						
			Lowest 10%	Lowest 20%	Second 20%	Third 20%	Fourth 20%	Highest 20%	Highest 10%
Romania	2000 [a, b]	30.3	3.3	8.2	13.1	17.4	22.9	38.4	23.6
Russian Federation	2000 [a, b]	45.6	1.8	4.9	9.5	14.1	20.3	51.3	36.0
Rwanda	1983–85 [a, b]	28.9	4.2	9.7	13.2	16.5	21.6	39.1	24.2
Saudi Arabia	..	..	..	..	..	..	..	..	..
Senegal	1995 [a, b]	41.3	2.6	6.4	10.3	14.5	20.6	48.2	33.5
Sierra Leone	1989 [a, b]	62.9	0.5	1.1	2.0	9.8	23.7	63.4	43.6
Singapore	1998 [c, d]	42.5	1.9	5.0	9.4	14.6	22.0	49.0	32.8
Slovak Republic	1996 [c, d]	25.8	3.1	8.8	14.9	18.7	22.8	34.8	20.9
Slovenia	1998 [c, d]	28.4	3.9	9.1	13.4	17.3	22.5	37.7	23.0
Somalia	..	..	..	..	..	..	..	..	..
South Africa	1995 [a, b]	59.3	0.7	2.0	4.3	8.3	18.9	66.5	46.9
Spain	1990 [c, d]	32.5	2.8	7.5	12.6	17.0	22.6	40.3	25.2
Sri Lanka	1995 [a, b]	34.4	3.5	8.0	11.8	15.8	21.5	42.8	28.0
St. Lucia	1995 [c, d]	42.6	2.0	5.2	9.9	14.8	21.8	48.3	32.5
Sudan	..	..	..	..	..	..	..	..	..
Swaziland	1994 [c, d]	60.9	1.0	2.7	5.8	10.0	17.1	64.4	50.2
Sweden	1995 [c, d]	25.0	3.4	9.1	14.5	18.4	23.4	34.5	20.1
Switzerland	1992 [c, d]	33.1	2.6	6.9	12.7	17.3	22.9	40.3	25.2
Syrian Arab Republic	..	..	..	..	..	..	..	..	..
Tajikistan	1998 [a, b]	34.7	3.2	8.0	12.9	17.0	22.1	40.0	25.2
Tanzania	1993 [a, b]	38.2	2.8	6.8	11.0	15.1	21.6	45.5	30.1
Thailand	2000 [a, b]	43.2	2.5	6.1	9.5	13.5	20.9	50.0	33.8
Togo	..	..	..	..	..	..	..	..	..
Trinidad and Tobago	1992 [c, d]	40.3	2.1	5.5	10.3	15.5	22.7	45.9	29.9
Tunisia	1995 [a, b]	41.7	2.3	5.7	9.9	14.7	21.8	47.9	31.8
Turkey	2000 [a, b]	40.0	2.3	6.1	10.6	14.9	21.8	46.7	30.7
Turkmenistan	1998 [a, b]	40.8	2.6	6.1	10.2	14.7	21.5	47.5	31.7
Uganda	1996 [a, b]	37.4	3.0	7.1	11.1	15.4	21.5	44.9	29.8
Ukraine	1999 [a, b]	29.0	3.7	8.8	13.3	17.4	22.7	37.8	23.2
United Arab Emirates	..	..	..	..	..	..	..	..	..
United Kingdom	1995 [c, d]	36.0	2.1	6.1	11.7	16.3	22.7	43.2	27.5
United States	1997 [c, d]	40.8	1.8	5.2	10.5	15.6	22.4	46.4	30.5
Uruguay [e]	1998 [c, d]	44.8	1.6	4.5	9.2	14.2	21.7	50.4	33.8
Uzbekistan	2000 [a, b]	26.8	3.6	9.2	14.1	17.9	22.6	36.3	22.0
Venezuela, RB	1998 [c, d]	49.1	0.6	3.0	8.4	13.7	21.6	53.4	36.3
Vietnam	1998 [a, b]	36.1	3.6	8.0	11.4	15.2	20.9	44.5	29.9
West Bank and Gaza	..	..	..	..	..	..	..	..	..
Yemen, Rep.	1998 [a, b]	33.4	3.0	7.4	12.2	16.7	22.5	41.2	25.9
Yugoslavia, Fed. Rep.	..	..	..	..	..	..	..	..	..
Zambia	1998 [a, b]	52.6	1.1	3.3	7.6	12.5	20.0	56.6	41.0
Zimbabwe	1995 [a, b]	56.8	1.8	4.6	8.1	12.2	19.3	55.7	40.3

a. Refers to expenditure shares by percentiles of population. b. Ranked by per capita expenditure. c. Refers to income shares by percentiles of population. d. Ranked by per capita income.
e. Urban data.

Inequality in the distribution of income is reflected in the percentage shares of income or consumption accruing to segments of the population ranked by income or consumption levels. The segments ranked lowest by personal income receive the smallest shares of total income. The Gini index provides a convenient summary measure of the degree of inequality.

Data on personal or household income or consumption come from nationally representative household surveys. The data in the table refer to different years between 1987 and 2001. Footnotes to the survey year indicate whether the rankings are based on per capita income or consumption. Each distribution is based on percentiles of population— rather than of households—with households ranked by income or expenditure per person.

Where the original data from the household survey were available, they have been used to directly calculate the income (or consumption) shares by quintile. Otherwise shares have been estimated from the best available grouped data.

The distribution data have been adjusted for household size, providing a more consistent measure of per capita income or consumption. No adjustment has been made for spatial differences in cost of living within countries, because the data needed for such calculations are generally unavailable. For further details on the estimation method for low- and middle-income economies, see Ravallion and Chen (1996).

Because the underlying household surveys differ in method and in the type of data collected, the distribution data are not strictly comparable across countries. These problems are diminishing as survey methods improve and become more standardized, but achieving strict comparability is still impossible (see *About the data* for table 2.6).

Two sources of noncomparability should be noted. First, the surveys can differ in many respects, including whether they use income or consumption expenditure as the living standard indicator. The distribution of income is typically more unequal than the distribution of consumption. In addition, the definitions of income used usually differ among surveys. Consumption is usually a much better welfare indicator, particularly in developing countries. Second, households differ in size (number of members) and in the extent of income sharing among members. And individuals differ in age and consumption needs. Differences among countries in these respects may bias comparisons of distribution.

World Bank staff have made an effort to ensure that the data are as comparable as possible. Wherever possible, consumption has been used rather than income. Income distribution and Gini indexes for high-income countries are calculated directly from the Luxembourg Income Study database, using an estimation method consistent with that applied for developing countries.

• **Survey year** is the year in which the underlying data were collected. • **Gini index** measures the extent to which the distribution of income (or, in some cases, consumption expenditure) among individuals or households within an economy deviates from a perfectly equal distribution. A Lorenz curve plots the cumulative percentages of total income received against the cumulative number of recipients, starting with the poorest individual or household. The Gini index measures the area between the Lorenz curve and a hypothetical line of absolute equality, expressed as a percentage of the maximum area under the line. Thus a Gini index of 0 represents perfect equality, while an index of 100 implies perfect inequality. • **Percentage share of income or consumption** is the share that accrues to subgroups of population indicated by deciles or quintiles. Percentage shares by quintile may not sum to 100 because of rounding.

The data on distribution are compiled by the World Bank's Development Research Group using primary household survey data obtained from government statistical agencies and World Bank country departments. The data for high-income economies are from the Luxembourg Income Study database.

	Urban informal sector employment			Children 10–14 in the labor force		Pension contributors			Private health expenditure
	% of urban employment							% of	% of
	Male	Female	Total	% of age group			% of	working-age	total
	1995–99[a]	1995–99[a]	1995–99[a]	1980	2001	Year	labor force	population	2000
Afghanistan	..	..	..	28	24		..	..	36.5
Albania	..	..	..	4	0	1995	32.0	31.0	37.9
Algeria	..	..	..	7	0	1997	31.0	23.0	17.8
Angola	..	..	..	30	26		..	..	44.1
Argentina	48	36	43	8	2	1995	53.0	39.0	45.0
Armenia	..	..	..	0	0	1995	66.6	49.4	57.7
Australia	..	..	..	0	0		..	..	27.6
Austria	..	..	..	0	0	1993	95.8	76.6	30.3
Azerbaijan	..	..	..	0	0	1996	52.0	46.0	24.9
Bangladesh	..	..	..	35	27	1993	3.5	2.6	63.6
Belarus	..	..	..	0	0	1992	97.0	94.0	17.2
Belgium	..	..	..	0	0	1995	86.2	65.9	28.8
Benin	..	..	..	30	26	1996	4.8	..	50.0
Bolivia	..	..	53	19	11	1999	14.8	13.3	27.6
Bosnia and Herzegovina	..	..	..	1	0		..	..	31.0
Botswana	12	28	19	26	14		..	..	36.9
Brazil	43	31	38	19	14	1996	36.0	31.0	59.2
Bulgaria	..	..	..	0	0	1994	64.0	63.0	22.4
Burkina Faso	..	..	..	71	42	1993	3.1	3.0	29.3
Burundi	..	..	..	50	48	1993	3.3	3.0	46.9
Cambodia	..	..	..	27	24		..	..	75.5
Cameroon	..	..	..	34	23	1993	13.7	11.5	75.3
Canada	..	..	..	0	0	1992	91.9	80.2	28.0
Central African Republic	..	..	..	..	..		..	..	51.6
Chad	..	..	..	42	36	1990	1.1	1.0	20.2
Chile	33	32	32	0	0	2001	54.8	34.9	57.4
China	..	..	..	30	7	1994	17.6	17.4	63.4
Hong Kong, China	..	..	..	6	0		..	..	..
Colombia	49	44	47	12	6	1999	35.0	29.3	44.2
Congo, Dem. Rep.	..	..	..	33	28		..	..	26.3
Congo, Rep.	..	..	..	27	25	1992	5.8	5.6	29.8
Costa Rica	43	36	40	10	4	1998	50.6	38.5	31.6
Côte d'Ivoire	37	73	53	28	18	1997	9.3	9.1	63.1
Croatia	6	7	6	0	0	1997	66.0	57.0	20.0
Cuba	..	..	..	0	0		..	..	10.8
Czech Republic	..	..	..	0	0	1995	85.0	67.2	8.6
Denmark	..	..	..	0	0	1993	89.6	88.0	17.9
Dominican Republic	..	..	..	25	13	2001	30.9	18.0	72.0
Ecuador	54	55	53	9	4	1999	43.1	33.8	49.6
Egypt, Arab Rep.	..	..	..	18	9	1994	50.0	34.2	53.9
El Salvador	..	..	..	17	13	1996	26.2	25.0	57.0
Eritrea	..	..	..	44	38		..	..	34.4
Estonia	..	..	..	0	0	1995	76.0	67.0	23.3
Ethiopia	19	53	33	46	41		..	..	60.6
Finland	..	..	..	0	0	1993	90.3	83.6	24.9
France	..	..	..	0	0	1993	88.4	74.6	24.0
Gabon	..	..	..	29	13	1995	15.0	14.0	31.4
Gambia, The	..	..	..	44	33		..	..	17.6
Georgia	..	..	..	0	0	2000	41.7	40.2	89.5
Germany	..	..	..	0	0	1995	94.2	82.3	24.9
Ghana	..	..	79	16	12	1993	7.2	9.0	46.5
Greece	..	..	..	5	0	1996	88.0	73.0	44.5
Guatemala	..	..	..	19	14	1999	22.8	19.3	52.1
Guinea	..	..	..	41	31	1993	1.5	1.8	42.9
Guinea-Bissau	..	..	..	43	36		..	..	34.6
Haiti	..	..	..	33	22		..	..	50.7

	Urban informal sector employment			Children 10–14 in the labor force		Pension contributors			Private health expenditure
	% of urban employment			% of age group				% of	% of
	Male	Female	Total				% of	working-age	total
	1995–99 [a]	**1995–99** [a]	**1995–99** [a]	**1980**	**2001**	Year	labor force	population	**2000**
Honduras	53	58	55	14	7	1999	20.6	17.7	36.9
Hungary	..	..	..	0	0	1996	77.0	65.0	24.3
India	..	..	..	21	12	1992	10.6	7.9	82.2
Indonesia	19	23	21	13	7	1995	8.0	7.0	76.3
Iran, Islamic Rep.	3	90	18	14	2	2000	48.2	25.2	53.7
Iraq	..	..	..	11	2		..	..	40.1
Ireland	..	..	..	1	0	1992	79.3	64.7	24.2
Israel	..	..	..	0	0	1992	82.0	63.0	24.1
Italy	..	..	..	2	0	1997	87.0	68.0	26.3
Jamaica	26	21	24	0	0	1999	44.4	45.8	53.0
Japan	..	..	..	0	0	1994	97.5	92.3	23.3
Jordan	..	..	..	4	0	1995	40.0	25.0	48.2
Kazakhstan	..	..	12	0	0	2001	38.3	28.3	26.8
Kenya	..	..	58	45	39	1995	18.0	24.0	77.8
Korea, Dem. Rep.	..	..	..	3	0		..	..	22.7
Korea, Rep.	..	..	..	0	0	1996	58.0	43.0	55.9
Kuwait	..	..	..	0	0		..	..	12.8
Kyrgyz Republic	..	..	12	0	0	1997	44.0	42.0	50.2
Lao PDR	..	..	..	31	25		..	..	62.0
Latvia	..	..	17	0	0	1995	60.5	52.3	40.0
Lebanon	..	..	..	5	0		..	..	*80.0*
Lesotho	..	..	..	28	20		..	..	17.7
Liberia	..	..	..	26	15		..	..	23.8
Libya	..	..	..	9	0		..	..	51.4
Lithuania	12	5	9	0	0		..	..	27.6
Macedonia, FYR	..	..	..	1	0	1995	49.0	47.0	15.5
Madagascar	..	..	58	40	34	1993	5.4	4.8	28.2
Malawi	..	..	..	45	31		..	..	52.2
Malaysia	..	..	..	8	2	1993	48.7	37.8	41.2
Mali	..	..	71	61	50	1990	2.5	2.0	54.5
Mauritania	..	..	..	30	22	1995	5.0	4.0	20.7
Mauritius	..	..	..	5	2	1995	60.0	57.0	43.7
Mexico	38	30	35	9	5	1997	30.0	31.0	53.6
Moldova	..	..	..	3	0		..	..	17.6
Mongolia	..	..	..	4	1		..	..	29.7
Morocco	..	..	..	21	1	2000	17.3	11.3	70.4
Mozambique	..	..	..	39	32	1995	2.0	2.1	36.6
Myanmar	53	57	54	28	23		..	..	82.9
Namibia	..	..	..	34	17		..	..	40.7
Nepal	..	..	..	56	41		..	..	..
Netherlands	..	..	..	0	0	1993	91.7	75.4	32.5
New Zealand	..	..	..	0	0		..	..	22.0
Nicaragua	..	..	..	19	12	1999	14.3	13.3	48.3
Niger	..	..	..	48	43	1992	1.3	1.5	55.1
Nigeria	..	..	..	29	24	1993	1.3	1.3	79.2
Norway	..	..	..	0	0	1993	94.0	85.8	14.8
Oman	..	..	..	6	0		..	..	17.1
Pakistan	..	..	..	23	15	1993	3.5	2.1	77.1
Panama	36	28	32	6	2	1998	51.6	40.7	30.8
Papua New Guinea	..	..	..	28	17		..	..	11.4
Paraguay	..	..	58	15	5	2001	14.2	9.2	61.7
Peru	45	53	48	4	2	2001	41.0	25.0	40.8
Philippines	16	19	17	14	5	1996	28.3	13.6	54.3
Poland	14	11	13	0	0	1996	68.0	64.0	30.3
Portugal	..	..	..	8	1	1996	84.3	80.0	28.8
Puerto Rico	..	..	..	0	0		..	..	..

	Urban informal sector employment			Children 10–14 in the labor force		Pension contributors			Private health expenditure
	% of urban employment			**% of age group**				**% of working-age population**	**% of total**
	Male 1995–99[a]	Female 1995–99[a]	Total 1995–99[a]	1980	2001	Year	% of labor force		2000
Romania	..	..	..	0	0	1994	55.0	48.0	36.2
Russian Federation	..	..	..	0	0				27.5
Rwanda	..	..	..	43	41	1993	9.3	13.3	48.7
Saudi Arabia	..	..	..	5	0		..	..	20.9
Senegal	..	..	..	43	26	1998	4.3	4.7	43.4
Sierra Leone	..	..	..	19	14		..	..	40.0
Singapore	..	..	..	2	0	1995	73.0	56.0	64.3
Slovak Republic	25	11	19	0	0	1996	73.0	72.0	10.4
Slovenia	..	..	..	0	0	1995	86.0	68.7	21.1
Somalia	..	..	..	38	31		..	..	28.6
South Africa	11	26	17	1	0		..	..	57.8
Spain	..	..	..	0	0	1994	85.3	61.4	30.1
Sri Lanka	..	..	..	4	2	1992	28.8	20.8	51.0
Sudan	..	..	..	33	27	1995	12.1	12.0	78.8
Swaziland	..	..	..	17	12		..	..	27.9
Sweden	..	..	..	0	0	1994	91.1	88.9	22.7
Switzerland	..	..	..	0	0	1994	98.1	96.8	44.4
Syrian Arab Republic	..	..	..	14	2		..	..	36.6
Tajikistan	..	..	..	0	0		..	..	*70.0*
Tanzania	60	85	67	43	36	1996	2.0	2.0	53.0
Thailand	75	79	77	25	11	1999	18.0	17.0	42.6
Togo	..	..	..	36	27	1997	15.9	15.0	45.7
Trinidad and Tobago	..	..	..	1	0		..	..	49.3
Tunisia	..	..	..	6	0	2000	40.0	23.0	*48.0*
Turkey	..	..	..	21	7	1997	37.1	27.4	28.9
Turkmenistan	..	..	..	0	0		..	..	15.1
Uganda	..	..	..	49	43	1994	8.2	..	62.0
Ukraine	5	5	5	0	0	1995	69.8	66.1	29.9
United Arab Emirates	..	..	..	0	0		..	..	22.3
United Kingdom	..	..	..	0	0	1994	89.7	84.5	19.0
United States	..	..	..	0	0	1993	94.0	91.9	55.7
Uruguay	39	41	36	4	1	1995	82.0	78.0	53.5
Uzbekistan	..	..	..	0	0		..	..	50.0
Venezuela, RB	47	46	47	4	0	1999	23.6	18.2	42.6
Vietnam	..	..	..	22	5	1998	8.4	10.0	74.2
West Bank and Gaza	..	..	..	..	..		..	..	..
Yemen, Rep.	..	..	..	26	18		..	..	*57.0*
Yugoslavia, Fed. Rep.	..	..	..	0	0		..	..	49.0
Zambia	..	..	..	19	15	1994	10.2	7.9	37.9
Zimbabwe	..	..	..	37	27	1995	12.0	10.0	57.4
World				**20 w**	**11 w**				**40.6 w**
Low income				25	18				72.9
Middle income				21	6				48.3
Lower middle income				24	6				50.6
Upper middle income				11	6				45.8
Low & middle income				23	12				52.4
East Asia & Pacific				27	8				61.4
Europe & Central Asia				3	1				27.6
Latin America & Carib.				13	8				52.4
Middle East & N. Africa				14	4				38.1
South Asia				23	15				79.2
Sub-Saharan Africa				35	29				57.6
High income				0	0				37.8
Europe EMU				1	0				26.6

a. Data are for the most recent year available.

About the data

As traditionally defined and measured, poverty is a static concept, and vulnerability a dynamic one. Vulnerability reflects a household's resilience in the face of shocks and the likelihood that a shock will lead to a decline in well-being. Thus it depends primarily on the household's asset endowment and insurance mechanisms. Because poor people have fewer assets and less diversified sources of income than the better-off, fluctuations in income affect them more.

Poor households face many risks, and vulnerability is thus multidimensional. The indicators in the table focus on individual risks—informal sector employment, child labor, income insecurity in old age—and the extent to which publicly provided services may be capable of mitigating some of these risks. Poor people face labor market risks, often having to take up precarious, low-quality jobs in the informal sector and to increase their household's labor market participation through their children. Income security is a prime concern for the elderly. And affordable access to health care is a primary concern for all poor people, for whom illness and injury have both direct and opportunity costs.

For informal sector employment the most common sources of data are labor force and special informal sector surveys, based on a mixed household and enterprise survey approach or an economic or establishment census approach. Other sources include multipurpose household surveys, household income and expenditure surveys, surveys of household industries or economic activities, surveys of small and micro enterprises, and official estimates. The international comparability of the data is affected by differences among countries in definitions and coverage and in the treatment of domestic workers and those who have a secondary job in the informal sector. The data in the table are based on national definitions of urban areas established by countries. For details on these definitions, see the notes in the data source.

Reliable estimates of child labor are difficult to obtain. In many countries child labor is officially presumed not to exist and so is not included in surveys or in official data. Underreporting also occurs because data exclude children engaged in agricultural or household activities with their families. Most child workers are in Asia. But the share of children working is highest in Africa, where, on average, one in three children ages 10–14 is engaged in some form of economic activity, mostly in agriculture (Fallon and Tzannatos 1998). Available statistics

suggest that more boys than girls work. But the number of girls working is often underestimated because surveys exclude those working as unregistered domestic help or doing full-time household work to enable their parents to work outside the home.

The data on pension contributors come from national sources, the International Labour Organization, and International Monetary Fund country reports. Coverage by pension schemes may be broad or even universal where eligibility is determined by citizenship, residency, or income status. In contribution-related schemes, however, eligibility is usually restricted to individuals who have made contributions for a minimum number of years. Definitional issues—relating to the labor force, for example—may arise in comparing coverage by contribution-related schemes over time and across countries (for country-specific information, see Palacios and Pallares-Miralles 2000). Coverage may be overstated in countries that do not attempt to count informal sector workers as part of the labor force.

The expenditure on health in a country can be divided into two main categories by source of funding: public and private. Public health expenditure consists of spending by central and local governments, including social health insurance funds. Private health expenditure includes private insurance, direct out-of-pocket payments by households, spending by nonprofit institutions serving households, and direct payments by private corporations. In countries where the share of out-of-pocket spending is large, poor households may be particularly vulnerable to the impoverishing effects of health care needs.

Definitions

• **Urban informal sector employment** is broadly characterized as employment in urban areas in units that produce goods or services on a small scale with the primary objective of generating employment and income for those concerned. These units typically operate at a low level of organization, with little or no division between labor and capital as factors of production. Labor relations are based on casual employment, kinship, or social relationships rather than contractual arrangements. • **Children 10–14 in the labor force** refer to the share of that age group active in the labor force. • **Pension contributors** are the share of the labor force or working-age population (here defined as ages 20–59) covered by a pension scheme. • **Private health expenditure** includes direct (out-of-pocket) spending by households, private insurance, spending by nonprofit institutions serving households (other than social insurance), and direct service payments by private corporations.

Data sources

The data on urban informal sector employment are from the International Labour Organization (ILO) database Key Indicators of the Labour Market (2001–02 issue). The child labor force participation rates are from the ILO database Estimates and Projections of the Economically Active Population, 1950–2010. The data on pension contributors are drawn from Robert Palacios and Montserrat Pallares-Miralles's "International Patterns of Pension Provision" (2000). For updates and further notes and sources, go to *Knowledge and Information* on the World Bank's Web site on pensions (http://www.worldbank.org/pensions). The data on private health expenditure for developing countries are largely from the World Health Organization's *World Health Report 2002*, from household surveys, and from World Bank poverty assessments and sector studies. The data on private health expenditure for member countries of the Organisation for Economic Co-operation and Development (OECD) are from the OECD.

		Public expenditure on pensions			Public expenditure on health	Public expenditure on education	
	Year	% of GDP	Year	Average pension % of per capita income	% of GDP 2000	% of GDP 2000 [a]	Per student % of GDP per capita 2000 [a]
Afghanistan		..		..	0.6	..	..
Albania	1995	5.1	1995	36.4	2.1	..	..
Algeria	1997	2.1	1991	75.0	3.0	..	..
Angola		..		..	2.0	2.7	..
Argentina	1994	6.2		..	4.7	4.0	14.7
Armenia	1996	3.1	1996	18.7	3.2	2.9	17.1
Australia	1997	5.9	1989	37.3	6.0	4.7	16.3
Austria	1995	14.9	1993	69.3	5.6	5.8	32.8
Azerbaijan	1996	2.5	1996	51.4	0.6	4.2	11.2
Bangladesh	1992	0.0		..	1.4	2.5	10.7
Belarus	1997	7.7	1995	31.2	4.7	6.0	..
Belgium	1997	12.9			6.2	5.9	..
Benin	1993	0.4	1993	189.7	1.6	3.2	11.4
Bolivia	1995	2.5		..	4.9	5.5	15.9
Bosnia and Herzegovina		..		..	3.1	..	..
Botswana		..		..	3.8	8.6	..
Brazil	1997	9.8		..	3.4	4.7	15.5
Bulgaria	1996	7.3	1995	39.3	3.0	3.4	16.1
Burkina Faso	1992	0.3	1992	207.3	3.0	..	..
Burundi	1991	0.2	1991	57.4	1.6	3.4	24.7
Cambodia		..		..	2.0	1.9	8.0
Cameroon	1993	0.4		..	1.1	3.2	12.7
Canada	1997	5.4	1994	54.3	6.6	5.5	..
Central African Republic	1990	0.3		..	1.4	1.9	..
Chad	1997	0.1		..	2.5	2.0	14.3
Chile	2001	2.9	1993	56.1	3.1	4.2	15.4
China	1996	2.7		..	1.9	2.9	10.8
Hong Kong, China		..		..	..	..	..
Colombia	1994	1.1	1989	72.2	5.4	..	..
Congo, Dem. Rep.		..		..	1.1	..	..
Congo, Rep.	1992	0.9		..	1.5	4.2	..
Costa Rica	1997	4.2	1993	76.1	4.4	4.4	19.1
CÙte d'Ivoire	1997	0.3		..	1.0	4.6	22.1
Croatia	1997	11.6			8.0	4.2	..
Cuba	1992	12.6			6.1	8.5	43.5
Czech Republic	1999	9.8	1996	37.0	6.6	4.4	20.9
Denmark	1997	8.8	1994	46.7	6.8	8.2	37.2
Dominican Republic	2000	0.8	2000	42.0	1.8	2.5	..
Ecuador	1997	1.0		..	1.2	1.6	..
Egypt, Arab Rep.	1994	2.5	1994	45.0	1.8	..	..
El Salvador	1997	1.3		..	3.8	2.3	9.4
Eritrea	2001	0.3		..	2.8	4.8	..
Estonia	1995	7.0	1995	56.7	4.7	7.5	28.5
Ethiopia	1993	0.9		..	1.8	4.8	..
Finland	1997	12.1	1994	57.4	5.0	6.1	26.1
France	1997	13.4		..	7.2	5.8	25.8
Gabon		..		..	2.1	3.9	8.4
Gambia, The		..		..	3.4	2.7	..
Georgia	2000	2.7	1996	12.6	0.7	..	..
Germany	1997	12.1	1995	62.8	8.0	4.6	23.1
Ghana	1996	1.1		..	2.2	4.1	..
Greece	1993	11.9	1990	85.6	4.6	3.8	19.3
Guatemala	1995	0.7	1995	27.6	2.3	1.7	..
Guinea		..		..	1.9	1.9	..
Guinea-Bissau		..		..	2.6	2.1	..
Haiti		..		..	2.4	1.1	..

	Public expenditure on pensions				Public expenditure on health	Public expenditure on education	
	Year	% of GDP	Year	Average pension % of per capita income	% of GDP **2000**	% of GDP **2000 [a]**	Per student % of GDP per capita **2000 [a]**
Honduras	1994	0.6		..	4.3	4.0	..
Hungary	1996	9.7	1996	33.6	5.1	5.0	20.4
India		..		..	0.9	4.1	..
Indonesia		..		..	0.6	..	..
Iran, Islamic Rep.	1994	1.5		..	2.5	4.4	14.0
Iraq		..		..	2.2	..	..
Ireland	1997	4.6	1993	77.9	5.1	4.4	16.5
Israel	1996	5.9	1992	48.1	8.3	7.3	23.4
Italy	1997	17.6		..	6.0	4.5	25.0
Jamaica	1996	..	1989	25.9	2.6	6.3	24.2
Japan	1997	6.9	1989	33.9	6.0	3.5	..
Jordan	1995	4.2	1995	144.0	4.2	5.0	16.3
Kazakhstan	2001	3.8	2001	23.0	2.7	..	..
Kenya	1993	0.5		..	1.8	6.4	3.8
Korea, Dem. Rep.		..		..	1.6	..	..
Korea, Rep.	1997	1.3		..	2.6	3.8	15.0
Kuwait	1990	3.5		..	2.6	..	..
Kyrgyz Republic	1997	6.4	2001	45.0	2.2	5.4	12.8
Lao PDR		..		..	1.3	2.3	9.1
Latvia	1995	10.2	1994	47.6	3.5	5.9	24.3
Lebanon		..		..	2.5	3.0	..
Lesotho		..		..	5.2	10.1	42.7
Liberia		..		..	3.0	..	..
Libya		..		..	1.6	..	..
Lithuania	1998	7.3	1995	21.3	4.3	6.4	..
Macedonia, FYR	1998	8.7	1996	91.6	5.1	4.1	..
Madagascar	1990	0.2		..	2.5	3.2	..
Malawi		..		..	3.6	4.1	..
Malaysia	1999	6.5		..	1.5	6.2	20.8
Mali	1991	0.4		..	2.2	2.8	..
Mauritania	1992	0.2		..	3.4	3.0	..
Mauritius	1999	4.4		..	1.9	3.5	..
Mexico	2000	0.3 [b]		..	2.5	4.4	15.0
Moldova	1996	7.5		..	2.9	4.0	18.8
Mongolia		..		..	4.6	2.3	..
Morocco	1994	1.8	1994	118.0	1.3	5.5	33.0
Mozambique	1996	0.0		..	2.7	2.4	..
Myanmar		..		..	0.4	0.5	2.6
Namibia		..		..	4.2	8.1	26.4
Nepal		..		..	0.9	3.7	16.3
Netherlands	1997	11.1	1989	48.5	5.5	4.8	22.5
New Zealand	1997	6.5		..	6.2	6.1	22.0
Nicaragua	1996	2.5		..	2.3	5.0	..
Niger	1992	0.1		..	1.8	2.7	37.5
Nigeria	1991	0.1	1991	40.5	0.5	..	..
Norway	1997	8.2	1994	49.9	6.6	6.8	..
Oman		..		..	2.3	3.9	..
Pakistan	1993	0.9		..	0.9	1.8	..
Panama	1996	4.3		..	5.3	5.9	22.2
Papua New Guinea		..		..	3.6	2.3	12.0
Paraguay		..		..	3.0	5.0	..
Peru	1996	1.2		..	2.8	3.3	9.9
Philippines	1993	1.0		..	1.6	4.2	14.8
Poland	1997	15.5	1995	61.2	4.2	5.0	19.0
Portugal	1997	10.0	1989	44.6	5.8	5.8	25.6
Puerto Rico		..		..	..	..	..

		Public expenditure on pensions			Public expenditure on health	Public expenditure on education	
	Year	% of GDP	Year	Average pension % of per capita income	% of GDP 2000	% of GDP 2000 [a]	Per student % of GDP per capita 2000 [a]
Romania	1996	5.1	1994	34.1	1.9	3.5	..
Russian Federation	1996	5.7	1995	18.3	3.8	4.4	..
Rwanda		..		..	2.7	2.8	..
Saudi Arabia		..		..	4.2	9.5	..
Senegal	1998	1.5	1997	85.0 [c]	2.6	3.2	21.1
Sierra Leone		..		..	2.6	1.0	..
Singapore	1996	1.4		..	1.2	3.7	..
Slovak Republic	1994	9.1	1994	44.5	5.3	4.2	18.3
Slovenia	1996	13.6	1996	49.3	6.8	..	..
Somalia		..		..	0.9	..	..
South Africa		..		..	3.7	5.5	18.6
Spain	1997	10.9	1995	54.1	5.4	4.5	21.9
Sri Lanka	1996	2.4		..	1.8	3.1	..
Sudan		..		..	1.0	..	..
Swaziland		..		..	3.0	1.5	18.1
Sweden	1997	11.1	1994	78.0	6.5	7.8	30.7
Switzerland	1997	13.4	1993	44.4	5.9	5.5	29.5
Syrian Arab Republic	1991	0.5		..	1.6	4.1	..
Tajikistan	1996	3.0		..	0.9	2.1	..
Tanzania		..		..	2.8	2.1	..
Thailand		..		..	2.1	5.4	15.9
Togo	1997	0.6	1993	178.8	1.5	4.8	15.9
Trinidad and Tobago	1996	0.6		..	2.6	4.0	16.2
Tunisia	2000	4.2	1991	89.5	2.9	6.8	26.1
Turkey	1997	4.5	1993	56.0	3.6	3.5	19.8
Turkmenistan	1996	2.3		..	4.6	..	..
Uganda	1997	0.8		..	1.5	2.3	..
Ukraine	1996	8.6	1995	30.9	2.9	4.4	..
United Arab Emirates		..		..	2.5	1.9	..
United Kingdom	1997	10.3		..	5.9	4.5	16.2
United States	1997	7.5	1989	33.0	5.8	4.8	..
Uruguay	1996	15.0	1996	64.1	5.1	2.8	11.3
Uzbekistan	1995	5.3	1995	45.8	2.6	..	..
Venezuela, RB	2001	2.7		..	2.7	..	..
Vietnam	1998	1.6		..	1.3	..	..
West Bank and Gaza		..		..	..	..	..
Yemen, Rep.	1994	0.1		..	2.1	10.0	..
Yugoslavia, Fed. Rep.		..		..	2.9	5.1	..
Zambia	1993	0.1		..	3.5	2.3	..
Zimbabwe		..		..	3.1	10.4	17.7
World					**5.4 w**	**4.4 m**	**17.1 m**
Low income					1.1	2.8	17.1
Middle income					3.0	4.5	19.1
Lower middle income					2.6	4.6	15.0
Upper middle income					3.5	4.4	24.3
Low & middle income					2.7	4.1	17.4
East Asia & Pacific					1.8	2.3	9.1
Europe & Central Asia					4.0	4.4	18.8
Latin America & Carib.					3.3	4.4	25.8
Middle East & N. Africa					2.9	5.3	14.0
South Asia					1.0	2.5	13.5
Sub-Saharan Africa					2.5	3.4	24.7
High income					6.0	5.3	16.3
Europe EMU					6.7	4.8	..

a. Data are provisional for Organisation for Economic Co-operation and Development and World Education Indicators (WEI) countries. For a list of WEI countries, see *About the Data*.
b. Refers only to the scheme for civil servants. c. Refers to system covering private sector workers.

Enhancing security for poor people means reducing their vulnerability to such risks as ill health, providing them the means to manage risk themselves, and strengthening market or public institutions for managing risk. The tools include microfinance programs, old age assistance and pensions, and public provision of basic health care and education.

Public interventions and institutions can provide services directly to poor people, although whether these work well for the poor is debated. State action is often ineffective, in part because governments can influence only a few of the many sources of well-being and in part because of difficulties in delivering goods and services. The effectiveness of public provision is further constrained by the fiscal resources at governments' disposal and the fact that state institutions may not be responsive to the needs of poor people.

The data on public pension spending are from national sources and cover all government expenditures, including the administrative costs of pension programs. They cover noncontributory pensions or social assistance targeted to the elderly and disabled and spending by social insurance schemes for which contributions had previously been made. The pattern of spending in a country is correlated with its demographic structure—spending increases as the population ages.

The lack of consistent national health accounting systems in most developing countries makes cross-country comparisons of health spending difficult. Compiling estimates of public health expenditures is complicated in countries where state or provincial and local governments are involved in financing and delivering health care because the data on public spending often are not aggregated. The data in the table are the product of an effort to collect all available information on health expenditures from national and local government budgets, national accounts, household surveys, insurance publications, international donors, and existing tabulations.

The data on education spending in the table refer solely to public spending—government spending on public education plus subsidies for private education. The data generally exclude foreign aid for education. They may also exclude spending by religious schools, which play a significant role in many developing countries. Data for some countries and for some years refer to spending by the ministry of education only (excluding education expenditures by other ministries and departments and local authorities). The share of gross domestic product (GDP) devoted to education can be interpreted as reflecting a country's effort in education. It often bears a weak relationship to the output of the education system as reflected in educational attainment. The pattern in this relationship suggests wide variations across countries in the efficiency with which the government's resources are translated into education outcomes.

For Organisation for Economic Co-operation and Development (OECD) and World Education Indicators (WEI) countries, education data for 1998–2000 are provisional. WEI is a joint UNESCO Institute for Statistics–OECD program that develops policy-relevant education indicators with national coordinators from 19 countries: Argentina, Brazil, Chile, China, Egypt, India, Indonesia, Jamaica, Jordan, Malaysia, Paraguay, Peru, the Philippines, the Russian Federation, Sri Lanka, Thailand, Tunisia, Uruguay, and Zimbabwe.

• **Public expenditure on pensions** includes all government expenditures on cash transfers to the elderly, the disabled, and survivors and the administrative costs of these programs. • **Average pension** is estimated by dividing total pension expenditure by the number of pensioners. • **Public expenditure on health** consists of recurrent and capital spending from government (central and local) budgets, external borrowings and grants (including donations from international agencies and nongovernmental organizations), and social (or compulsory) health insurance funds. • **Public expenditure on education** consists of public spending on public education plus subsidies to private education at the primary, secondary, and tertiary levels.

2.10a

% of total health expenditure, 2000

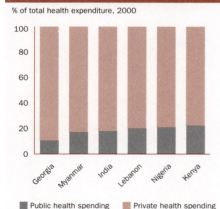

■ Public health spending   ■ Private health spending

In some developing countries private health spending accounts for more than 80 percent of the total. Out-of-pocket payments not only can impoverish people but also can deter the poor from obtaining care. To reduce the risks associated with out-of-pocket payments, some countries have exempted the poor from user fees at public facilities or used a sliding scale based on patients' socioeconomic characteristics. But such schemes can lead to high administrative costs and may end up having little effect on private health spending.

Source: WHO, *World Health Report 2002.*

The data on pension spending are drawn from Robert Palacios and Montserrat Pallares-Miralles's "International Patterns of Pension Provision" (2000). For updates and further notes and sources, go to *Knowledge and Information* on the World Bank's Web site on pensions (http://www.worldbank.org/pensions). The estimates of health expenditure come from the World Health Organization's *World Health Report 2002*, from the Organisation for Economic Co-operation and Development for its member countries, and from countries' national health accounts, supplemented by World Bank country and sector studies, including the Human Development Network's Sector Strategy, "Health, Nutrition, and Population" (World Bank 1997a). The data on education expenditure are from the UNESCO Institute for Statistics.

| | Public expenditure per student [a] | | | | | | Public expenditure on education | Trained teachers in primary education | Primary pupil-teacher ratio |
| | Primary % of GDP per capita | | Secondary % of GDP per capita | | Tertiary % of GDP per capita | | % of total government expenditure | % of total | pupils per teacher |
	1980	2000 [b]	1980	2000 [b]	1980	2000 [b]	2000 [b]	2000 [b]	2000 [b]
Afghanistan	10.8	..	46.7	..	..	..	..	..	43
Albania	..	..	..	..	..	..	..	..	22
Algeria	8.7	..	23.2	..	..	..	..	93.7	28
Angola	..	..	..	..	..	..	..	..	35
Argentina	..	12.5	11.0	16.4	29.8	17.7	11.8	..	22
Armenia	..	4.0	..	22.2	..	17.9	..	..	..
Australia	..	15.9	42.5	13.9	48.8	24.9	..	..	..
Austria	15.4	25.1	19.6	30.5	36.7	51.0	12.4	..	13
Azerbaijan	..	24.8	..	0.9	..	13.1	24.4	99.9	19
Bangladesh	..	7.3	9.3	14.1	33.9	38.9	15.7	65.0	57
Belarus	..	..	..	..	..	..	..	100.0	17
Belgium	..	17.0	32.4	..	50.3	..	11.6	..	12
Benin	..	10.3	..	12.1	..	108.2	..	65.0	54
Bolivia	..	13.3	..	11.0	..	45.2	23.1	74.2	24
Bosnia and Herzegovina	..	..	..	..	..	..	..	..	..
Botswana	..	..	..	..	..	..	..	89.2	27
Brazil	..	12.5	..	12.6	..	72.8	12.9	..	26
Bulgaria	17.2	15.2	..	17.1	50.5	14.5	..	..	18
Burkina Faso	..	..	102.9	..	2,938.5	..	..	80.4	47
Burundi	..	10.9	..	66.6	..	923.6	..	..	50
Cambodia	..	3.2	..	15.0	..	48.6	10.1	95.9	53
Cameroon	..	8.3	..	24.6	..	69.6	12.5	..	63
Canada	..	..	..	..	37.7	46.1	..	..	15
Central African Republic	..	..	23.9	..	938.8	..	..	..	74
Chad	..	9.5	..	28.5	..	423.7	..	37.2	71
Chile	9.2	13.9	15.7	15.2	107.8	21.9	17.5	..	25
China	3.8	6.1	12.4	12.1	246.2	85.8	..	..	22 [c]
Hong Kong, China	..	..	8.2	..	..	..	..	..	..
Colombia	5.2	..	7.7	..	43.6	..	..	..	26
Congo, Dem. Rep.	..	..	..	..	..	..	..	..	26
Congo, Rep.	..	9.9	15.4	..	334.4	..	12.6	64.6	51
Costa Rica	..	14.9	24.5	19.4	72.4	55.7	..	..	25
Côte d'Ivoire	..	14.7	..	35.7	357.4	139.6	21.5	99.1	48
Croatia	..	..	..	..	..	..	10.4	..	18
Cuba	..	34.7	..	41.9	..	101.7	15.1	100.0	11
Czech Republic	..	12.5	..	23.2	..	33.9	9.7	..	18
Denmark	..	23.4	11.0	37.2	48.7	65.1	15.3	..	10
Dominican Republic	..	..	5.8	..	..	..	15.7	..	40
Ecuador	..	4.3	12.5	8.9	23.0	..	8.0	..	23
Egypt, Arab Rep.	..	..	..	..	54.1	39.4	..	..	22
El Salvador	..	2.0	13.9	26.4	138.4	10.4	13.4	..	26
Eritrea	..	..	..	..	..	..	..	70.5	45
Estonia	..	24.5	..	30.8	..	33.0	..	..	14
Ethiopia	..	..	..	..	..	..	13.8	70.4	55
Finland	..	17.3	21.2	25.5	35.9	39.7	12.5	..	16
France	11.7	18.0	19.7	29.3	28.6	30.3	11.5	..	19
Gabon	..	4.6	..	18.5	..	50.9	..	95.3	49
Gambia, The	18.4	..	43.2	..	..	..	14.2	73.1	37
Georgia	..	..	..	..	..	..	..	..	16
Germany	..	17.8	..	20.5	..	42.5	9.7	..	15
Ghana	..	..	10.3	..	..	..	..	68.6	33
Greece	..	16.0	..	17.9	..	26.7	7.0	..	13
Guatemala	..	4.9	..	12.1	..	..	11.4	..	33
Guinea	..	9.5	..	..	..	..	25.6	..	44
Guinea-Bissau	19.0	..	63.5	..	..	..	4.8	35.1	44
Haiti	..	..	12.8	..	128.6	..	10.9	..	..

	Public expenditure per student [a]						Public expenditure on education	Trained teachers in primary education	Primary pupil-teacher ratio
	Primary % of GDP per capita		Secondary % of GDP per capita		Tertiary % of GDP per capita		% of total government expenditure	% of total	pupils per teacher
	1980	2000 [b]	1980	2000 [b]	1980	2000 [b]	2000 [b]	2000 [b]	2000 [b]
Honduras	..	..	13.8	..	73.2	..	..	..	34
Hungary	13.7	17.7	25.5	18.7	83.8	30.5	14.1	..	11
India	..	7.2	15.1	23.1	83.3	..	12.7	..	40
Indonesia	..	3.2	..	8.7	..	..	..	..	22
Iran, Islamic Rep.	22.6	10.3	36.4	11.8	..	81.6	20.4	96.5	25
Iraq	..	..	6.5	..	87.5	..	..	..	21
Ireland	10.7	13.3	22.5	15.2	55.6	27.8	13.2	..	20
Israel	15.6	21.2	41.7	22.5	71.6	31.6	..	..	12
Italy	..	21.2	..	27.1	..	26.0	9.5	..	11
Jamaica	12.7	16.2	..	26.8	185.5	80.0	11.1	..	36
Japan	14.6	21.3	16.4	..	20.7	..	9.3	..	20
Jordan	..	13.7	..	16.1	61.7	31.1	5.0	..	..
Kazakhstan	..	..	..	..	..	..	..	..	19
Kenya	..	0.4	35.2	1.2	899.2	496.9	22.5	96.6	30
Korea, Dem. Rep.	..	..	..	..	..	..	..	..	..
Korea, Rep.	..	18.3	9.1	16.8	15.7	8.0	17.4	..	32
Kuwait	..	..	..	..	43.8	..	..	100.0	14
Kyrgyz Republic	..	..	..	18.3	..	32.2	..	48.4	24
Lao PDR	..	6.5	..	8.7	..	145.3	8.8	76.2	30
Latvia	..	23.6	16.1	25.2	13.6	22.5	..	..	15
Lebanon	..	10.5	..	..	..	9.3	11.1	..	17
Lesotho	12.7	27.0	107.3	76.3	1,500.8	962.7	18.5	74.2	48
Liberia	..	..	..	..	..	..	..	..	36
Libya	..	..	..	..	..	..	..	..	8
Lithuania	..	61.4	..	..	..	40.4	..	..	16
Macedonia, FYR	..	..	..	30.6	..	44.8	..	..	22
Madagascar	..	3.9	..	..	397.9	76.2	10.2	..	50
Malawi	7.0	..	89.2	..	1,685.7	..	24.6	51.2	56
Malaysia	..	11.2	20.5	19.9	140.9	86.1	26.7	..	18
Mali	29.6	13.7	87.3	..	..	241.4	..	..	63
Mauritania	28.8	11.7	167.6	36.4	..	..	18.9	..	42
Mauritius	..	..	21.3	..	355.7	..	12.1	100.0	26
Mexico	4.2	11.7	10.0	13.8	25.5	45.2	22.6	..	27
Moldova	..	1.3	..	28.7	..	19.3	15.0	..	20
Mongolia	..	..	..	40.6	95.5	26.8	2.2	92.9	32
Morocco	..	20.5	53.6	49.9	150.3	102.7	26.1	..	28
Mozambique	..	..	..	..	..	..	12.3	61.8	64
Myanmar	..	1.6	..	1.9	..	19.4	9.0	85.4	32
Namibia	..	20.7	..	34.0	..	147.1	..	36.0	32
Nepal	..	14.2	..	15.6	274.9	98.7	14.1	44.5	37
Netherlands	13.2	15.4	22.3	21.8	70.1	43.0	10.7	..	10
New Zealand	14.7	19.9	13.4	22.3	58.5	25.5	..	..	16
Nicaragua	..	20.5	..	..	..	..	13.8	..	36
Niger	..	22.3	..	81.0	..	441.0	..	84.1	42
Nigeria	..	..	..	..	..	..	..	..	..
Norway	..	29.2	14.5	..	37.1	46.5	16.2	..	..
Oman	..	11.4	..	20.4	..	..	..	99.6	24
Pakistan	..	..	17.1	..	..	..	7.8	..	44
Panama	..	15.8	10.2	24.4	26.5	47.7	..	79.0	25
Papua New Guinea	..	11.1	..	18.0	..	40.4	17.5	..	36
Paraguay	..	..	..	18.1	..	..	11.2	..	20
Peru	6.9	8.0	8.0	10.6	4.7	22.0	21.1	..	25
Philippines	..	14.3	4.2	12.5	13.7	23.2	20.6	..	35
Poland	..	26.5	..	12.0	..	20.2	11.4	..	11
Portugal	..	20.5	19.2	29.4	34.4	28.2	13.1	..	13
Puerto Rico	..	..	..	..	..	..	..	..	..

	Public expenditure per student [a]						Public expenditure on education	Trained teachers in primary education	Primary pupil-teacher ratio
	Primary % of GDP per capita		Secondary % of GDP per capita		Tertiary % of GDP per capita		% of total government expenditure	% of total	pupils per teacher
	1980	2000 [b]	1980	2000 [b]	1980	2000 [b]	2000 [b]	2000 [b]	2000 [b]
Romania	..	..	..	..	..	..	..	..	20
Russian Federation	..	..	..	20.5	..	15.8	..	..	17
Rwanda	11.1	6.9	112.4	..	902.7	571.6	..	..	51
Saudi Arabia	..	..	..	..	109.5	86.9	..	..	12
Senegal	..	13.6	68.5	33.1	432.5	244.6	..	100.0	51
Sierra Leone	..	..	..	..	..	..	..	78.9	44
Singapore	..	..	12.4	..	41.5	..	23.6	..	..
Slovak Republic	..	10.8	..	19.2	..	30.8	13.8	..	19
Slovenia	..	..	..	..	..	..	..	..	14
Somalia	..	..	..	..	..	..	..	..	..
South Africa	..	14.0	..	17.9	..	61.3	25.8	67.9	33
Spain	..	18.8	..	25.5	..	19.8	11.3	..	14
Sri Lanka	..	..	..	..	..	..	..	..	..
Sudan	..	..	601.0	..	..	..	..	62.4	27
Swaziland	..	8.5	35.3	24.0	139.5	358.8	..	91.1	33
Sweden	41.7	23.5	14.0	28.3	33.9	53.5	13.4	..	11
Switzerland	..	23.2	31.0	28.2	60.8	55.8	15.2	..	14
Syrian Arab Republic	..	12.9	15.1	23.3	74.7	..	11.1	92.2	24
Tajikistan	..	..	..	..	..	9.9	11.8	..	22
Tanzania	..	..	..	..	..	..	..	44.1	40
Thailand	8.8	12.5	9.8	12.8	59.7	38.2	31.0	..	21
Togo	7.7	11.6	..	23.1	828.7	295.3	23.2	80.0	34
Trinidad and Tobago	..	16.2	12.4	14.8	56.4	147.9	16.7	78.1	20
Tunisia	..	16.2	36.4	28.4	188.1	89.8	17.4	..	23
Turkey	..	17.6	8.7	11.8	96.3	72.1	..	..	..
Turkmenistan	..	..	..	..	..	..	..	..	..
Uganda	..	..	..	..	..	..	..	45.0	59
Ukraine	2.1	..	1.2	21.2	2.0	28.2	15.7	..	20
United Arab Emirates	..	8.5	..	11.2	..	..	..	71.0	16
United Kingdom	..	14.0	22.2	14.9	80.1	26.3	11.4	..	18
United States	..	17.9	17.3	22.4	47.8	..	..	..	15
Uruguay	8.9	8.2	13.6	12.0	27.0	21.3	..	..	21
Uzbekistan	..	..	..	..	..	..	..	..	..
Venezuela, RB	5.8	..	..	..	71.4	..	..	..	..
Vietnam	..	..	..	..	..	..	..	84.9	28
West Bank and Gaza	..	..	..	..	..	..	..	..	..
Yemen, Rep.	..	..	..	..	..	..	32.8	..	30
Yugoslavia, Fed. Rep.	..	..	..	..	..	..	..	100.0	20
Zambia	9.8	..	56.4	..	..	..	17.6	100.0	45
Zimbabwe	19.5	13.2	103.8	20.1	326.8	200.9	..	..	37
World	..m	..m	..m	..m	..m	..m	..m	**94.3 m**	**27 m**
Low income	..	..	..	..	..	..	..	90.4	39
Middle income	..	..	..	..	72.4	..	..	95.5	22
Lower middle income	..	..	..	..	..	..	..	93.8	21
Upper middle income	..	11.7	..	..	63.9	..	..	98.2	23
Low & middle income	..	..	..	..	..	..	..	93.6	29
East Asia & Pacific	..	7.6	..	..	..	40.1	13.8	94.6	21
Europe & Central Asia	..	..	..	..	..	..	..	94.4	..
Latin America & Carib.	..	..	12.6	..	71.4	..	12.4	86.1	26
Middle East & N. Africa	..	..	..	..	87.5	..	..	83.7	24
South Asia	..	7.3	16.1	..	83.7	..	14.1	92.1	42
Sub-Saharan Africa	..	..	..	..	..	..	..	90.4	47
High income	..	..	19.7	..	48.7	..	12.0	..	17
Europe EMU	..	..	..	..	..	..	11.5	..	14

a. Break in series between 1997 and 1998 due to change from International Standard Classification of Education 1976 (ISCED76) to ISCED97. b. Data are provisional for Organisation for Economic Co-operation and Development and World Education Indicators (WEI) countries. For a list of WEI countries, see *About the Data* for table 2.10. c. Data are for 2001.

Data on education are compiled by the UNESCO Institute for Statistics from official responses to surveys and from reports provided by education authorities in each country. Such data are used for monitoring, policymaking, and resource allocation. For a variety of reasons, however, education statistics generally fail to provide a complete and accurate picture of a country's education system. Statistics often lag by two to three years, though an effort is being made to shorten the delay. Moreover, coverage and data collection methods vary across countries and over time within countries, so the results of comparisons should be interpreted with caution. (For further discussion of the reliability of education data, see Behrman and Rosenzweig 1994.)

The data on education spending in the table refer solely to public spending—government spending on public education plus subsidies for private education. The data generally exclude foreign aid for education. They may also exclude spending by religious schools, which play a significant role in many developing countries. Data for some countries and for some years refer to spending by the ministry of education only (excluding education expenditures by other ministries and departments and local authorities).

Many developing countries have sought to supplement public funds for education. Some countries have adopted tuition fees to recover part of the cost of providing education services or to encourage development of private schools. Charging fees raises difficult questions relating to equity, efficiency, access, and taxation, however, and some governments have used scholarships, vouchers, and other methods of public finance to counter criticism. Data for a few countries include private spending, although national practices vary with respect to whether parents or schools pay for books, uniforms, and other supplies. For greater detail, see the country- and indicator-specific notes in the source.

The share of public expenditure devoted to education allows an assessment of the priority a government assigns to education relative to other public investments. It also reflects a government's commitment to investing in human capital development.

The share of trained teachers in primary schools measures the quality of the teaching staff. It does not take account of competencies acquired by teachers through their professional experience or self-instruction, or of such factors as work experience, teaching methods and materials, or classroom conditions, all of which may affect the quality of teaching. Since the training teachers receive varies greatly, care should be taken in comparing across countries.

The comparability of pupil-teacher ratios across countries is affected by the definition of teachers and by differences in class size by grade and in the number of hours taught. Moreover, the underlying enrollment levels are subject to a variety of reporting errors (for further discussion of enrollment data, see *About the data* for table 2.12). While the pupil-teacher ratio is often used to compare the quality of schooling across countries, it is often weakly related to the value added of schooling systems (Behrman and Rosenzweig 1994).

For two decades the International Standard Classification of Education, 1976 (ISCED76), was used to assemble, compile, and present education statistics. In 1998 the United Nations Educational, Scientific, and Cultural Organization (UNESCO) introduced ISCED97 and adjusted its data collection program and country reporting of education statistics to this new classification. The adjustments were made to ease the international compilation and comparison of education statistics and to take into account new types of learning opportunities and activities for both children and adults. Thus the time-series data for the years through 1997 are not consistent with those for 1998 and later. Any time-series analysis should therefore be undertaken with extreme caution.

ISCED97 introduced a new level of education—level 4, or postsecondary nontertiary education. The students in this category are not counted as either secondary or tertiary.

• **Public expenditure per student** is public current spending on education divided by the number of students by level, as a percentage of gross domestic product (GDP) per capita. • **Public expenditure on education** is current and capital public expenditure on education. • **Trained teachers in primary education** are the percentage of primary school teachers who have received the minimum organized teacher training (preservice or in service) required for teaching. • **Primary pupil-teacher ratio** is the number of pupils enrolled in primary school divided by the number of primary school teachers (regardless of their teaching assignment).

2.11a

Even the poorest households in Indonesia contribute a significant share of education spending

Source of expenditure on primary education by quintile (%), 1999

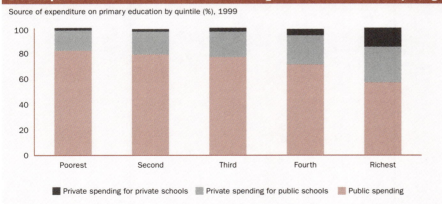

■ Private spending for private schools   ▓ Private spending for public schools   ▒ Public spending

Household surveys offer a valuable perspective on the private flows of education spending. According to the National Social and Economic Survey (SUSENAS) in Indonesia, poorer households benefit more than richer ones from public spending on primary schooling. But even the poorest households provide a significant share (16 percent) of the total expenditure on public primary education. Spending on private schools occurs in all income quintiles, possibly linked to enrollment in religious schools. But those in the richest quintile spend the most on private primary schools.

Source: UNESCO Institute for Statistics and OECD 2002.

The data are from the UNESCO Institute for Statistics, which compiles international data on education in cooperation with national commissions and national statistical services.

Participation in education

	Gross enrollment ratio [a]							Net enrollment ratio [b]			
	Preprimary % of relevant age group	Primary % of relevant age group		Secondary % of relevant age group		Tertiary % of relevant age group		Primary % of relevant age group		Secondary % of relevant age group	
	2000 [c]	1980	2000 [c]	1980	2000 [c]	1980	2000 [c]	1980	2000 [c]	1980	2000 [c]
Afghanistan	..	34	15	10	..	..	..	29	..	..	..
Albania	43	113	107	67	78	5	15	..	98	..	74
Algeria	3	94	112	33	71	6	15	81	98	31	62
Angola	..	175	74	21	15	0 [d]	1	..	37	..	..
Argentina	60	106	120	56	97	22	48	..	107	..	79
Armenia	21	..	78	..	73	..	20	..	69	..	64
Australia	98	112	102	71	161	25	63	100	96	70	90
Austria	81	99	104	93	99	22	58	87	91	..	89
Azerbaijan	23	115	98	95	80	24	22	..	91	..	78
Bangladesh	25	61	100	18	46	3	7	..	89	..	43
Belarus	86	104	109	98	84	39	56	..	108	..	76
Belgium	111	104	105	91	..	26	57	97	101	..	..
Benin	6	67	95	16	22	1	4	..	70	..	17
Bolivia	46	87	116	37	80	15	36	79	97	16	68
Bosnia and Herzegovina	..	..	..	..	..	..	..	..	..	..	..
Botswana	..	91	108	19	93	1	5	76	84	14	70
Brazil	63	98	162	33	108	11	17	80	97	14	71
Bulgaria	68	98	103	84	94	16	41	96	94	73	88
Burkina Faso	1	17	44	3	10	0 [d]	..	15	36	..	8
Burundi	1	26	65	3	10	0 [d]	1	20	54	..	..
Cambodia	7	139	110	..	19	0 [d]	3	..	95	..	17
Cameroon	14	98	108	18	20	2	5	..	..	15	..
Canada	64	99	99	88	103	57	60	..	99	..	98
Central African Republic	..	71	75	14	..	1	2	56	55	..	..
Chad	..	..	73	..	11	..	1	..	58	..	8
Chile	77	109	103	53	75	12	38	..	89	..	75
China	40	113	106	46	63	2	7	..	93	..	..
Hong Kong, China	..	107	..	64	..	10	..	95	..	61	..
Colombia	37	112	112	39	70	9	23	..	89	..	57
Congo, Dem. Rep.	1	92	47	24	18	1	1	..	33	..	12
Congo, Rep.	3	141	97	74	42	5	5	96	..	..	..
Costa Rica	87	105	107	47	60	21	16	89	91	39	49
Côte d'Ivoire	3	75	81	19	23	3	7	..	64	..	..
Croatia	..	..	..	77	..	19	..	..	..	..	..
Cuba	109	106	102	81	85	17	24	95	97	..	82
Czech Republic	92	95	104	99	95	17	30	..	90	..	..
Denmark	92	95	102	105	128	28	59	95	99	88	89
Dominican Republic	38	118	124	42	59	..	..	..	93	..	40
Ecuador	69	117	115	53	57	35	..	..	99	..	48
Egypt, Arab Rep.	12	73	100	50	86	16	39	..	93	..	79
El Salvador	44	75	109	24	54	9	18	..	81	..	39
Eritrea	6	..	59	..	28	..	2	..	41	..	22
Estonia	102	103	103	127	92	25	58	..	98	..	83
Ethiopia	2	37	64	9	18	0 [d]	2	..	47	..	13
Finland	49	96	102	100	126	32	..	..	100	..	95
France	114	111	105	85	108	25	54	100	100	79	92
Gabon	14	..	144	..	60	..	8	..	88	..	..
Gambia, The	20	53	82	11	36	..	..	50	69	..	35
Georgia	39	93	95	109	73	30	35	..	95	..	73
Germany	96	..	104	..	99	..	46	..	87	..	88
Ghana	59	79	80	41	36	2	3	..	58	..	31
Greece	72	103	99	81	98	17	..	96	97	..	87
Guatemala	51	71	102	19	37	8	..	59	84	13	26
Guinea	..	36	67	17	14	5	..	..	47	..	12
Guinea-Bissau	4	68	83	6	20	..	0 [d]	47	54	3	..
Haiti	..	77	..	14	..	1	..	38	..	..	..

Participation in education

	Gross enrollment ratio [a]							Net enrollment ratio [b]			
	Preprimary % of relevant age group	Primary % of relevant age group		Secondary % of relevant age group		Tertiary % of relevant age group		Primary % of relevant age group		Secondary % of relevant age group	
	2000 [c]	1980	2000 [c]	1980	2000 [c]	1980	2000 [c]	1980	2000 [c]	1980	2000 [c]
Honduras	21	98	106	30	..	7	15	78	88	..	..
Hungary	79	96	102	70	99	14	40	95	90	..	87
India	20	83	102	30	49	5	10	..	..	..	..
Indonesia	19	107	110	29	57	4	15	88	92	..	48
Iran, Islamic Rep.	17	87	86	42	78	..	10	..	74	..	..
Iraq	6	113	102	57	38	9	14	99	93	47	33
Ireland	..	100	119	90	..	18	48	90	90	78	..
Israel	113	95	114	73	93	29	53	..	101	..	88
Italy	95	100	101	72	96	27	50	..	100	..	91
Jamaica	88	103	100	67	83	7	16	96	95	64	74
Japan	84	101	101	93	102	31	48	100	101	93	101
Jordan	31	82	101	59	88	13	29	73	94	53	76
Kazakhstan	13	84	99	93	88	34	31	..	89	..	83
Kenya	42	115	94	20	31	1	3	91	69	..	23
Korea, Dem. Rep.	..	..	..	..	..	..	..	..	..	..	..
Korea, Rep.	80	110	101	78	94	15	78	100	99	70	91
Kuwait	98	102	85	80	56	11	21	85	66	..	50
Kyrgyz Republic	14	116	101	110	86	16	41	..	82	..	..
Lao PDR	8	113	113	21	38	0 [d]	3	..	81	..	30
Latvia	59	102	100	99	91	24	63	..	92	..	74
Lebanon	71	111	99	59	76	30	42	..	74	..	70
Lesotho	18	103	115	18	33	1	3	67	78	13	21
Liberia	70	48	118	22	38	..	..	..	83	..	25
Libya	8	125	116	76	90	8	49	..	..	62	..
Lithuania	52	79	101	114	95	35	52	..	95	..	89
Macedonia, FYR	29	100	99	61	84	28	24	..	92	..	81
Madagascar	3	130	103	..	14	3	2	..	68	..	11
Malawi	..	60	137	5	36	0 [d]	0 [d]	43	101	..	25
Malaysia	..	93	99	48	70	4	28	..	98	..	70
Mali	1	26	61	8	15	1	2	20	43	..	..
Mauritania	..	37	83	11	21	..	4	..	64	..	14
Mauritius	90	93	109	50	77	1	11	79	95	..	64
Mexico	76	120	113	49	75	14	21	..	103	..	60
Moldova	35	83	84	78	71	30	28	..	78	..	68
Mongolia	29	107	99	92	61	22	33	..	89	..	58
Morocco	53	83	94	26	39	6	10	62	78	20	30
Mozambique	..	99	92	5	12	0 [d]	1	36	54	..	9
Myanmar	2	91	89	22	39	5	12	..	83	..	37
Namibia	21	..	112	..	62	..	6	..	82	..	38
Nepal	13	86	118	22	51	3	5	..	72	..	..
Netherlands	98	100	108	93	124 [e]	29	55	93	100	81	90
New Zealand	..	111	100	83	112	27	69	..	99	81	92
Nicaragua	27	94	104	41	54	12	..	70	81	22	36
Niger	1	25	35	5	6	0 [d]	1	21	30	4	5
Nigeria	..	109	..	18	..	3	..	..	..	..	..
Norway	77	99	101	94	115	25	70	98	101	84	95
Oman	5	51	72	12	68	0 [d]	8	43	65	10	59
Pakistan	..	40	75	14	..	..	..	..	66	..	..
Panama	47	106	112	61	69	21	35	89	100	46	62
Papua New Guinea	18	59	84	12	21	2	2	..	84	..	21
Paraguay	83	106	111	27	60	9	..	89	92	..	47
Peru	59	114	128	59	81	17	29	86	104	..	61
Philippines	..	112	113	64	77	24	31	94	93	45	53
Poland	49	100	100	77	101	18	56	98	98	70	91
Portugal	68	123	121	37	114 [e]	11	50	98	..	..	85
Puerto Rico	..	..	..	..	..	42	..	..	..	..	..

	Gross enrollment ratio [a]								Net enrollment ratio [b]			
	Preprimary % of relevant age group	Primary % of relevant age group		Secondary % of relevant age group		Tertiary % of relevant age group			Primary % of relevant age group		Secondary % of relevant age group	
	2000 [c]	1980	2000 [c]	1980	2000 [c]	1980	2000 [c]		1980	2000 [c]	1980	2000 [c]
Romania	73	104	99	94	82	12	27		..	93	..	80
Russian Federation	..	102	..	96	83	46	64		..	..	..	..
Rwanda	3	63	119	3	12	0 [d]	2		59	97	..	..
Saudi Arabia	5	61	68	29	68	7	22		49	58	21	51
Senegal	4	46	75	11	18	3	4		37	63	..	..
Sierra Leone	4	52	93	14	26	1	2		..	..	..	26
Singapore	..	108	..	60	..	8	..		99	..	..	..
Slovak Republic	82	..	103	..	87	..	30		..	89	..	75
Slovenia	75	98	100	..	..	20	61		..	93	..	..
Somalia	..	21	..	9	..	..	..		16	..	5	..
South Africa	34	90	111	..	87	..	15		..	89	..	57
Spain	102	109	105	87	116	23	59		100	102	74	94
Sri Lanka	..	103	106	55	72	3	..		..	97	..	..
Sudan	22	50	55	16	29	2	7		..	46	..	..
Swaziland	..	103	125	38	60	4	5		80	93	..	44
Sweden	74	97	110	88	149 [e]	31	70		..	102	..	96
Switzerland	95	84	107	94	100	18	42		79	99	78	88
Syrian Arab Republic	10	100	109	46	43	17	6		89	96	39	39
Tajikistan	9	..	104	..	79	24	14		..	103	..	76
Tanzania	..	93	63	3	6	0 [d]	1		68	47	..	5
Thailand	83	99	95	29	82	15	35		..	85	..	..
Togo	2	118	124	33	39	2	4		..	92	..	23
Trinidad and Tobago	63	99	100	69	81	4	6		90	92	..	71
Tunisia	16	102	117	27	78	5	22		82	99	23	70
Turkey	..	96	101	35	58	5	15		..	..	..	..
Turkmenistan	..	..	..	..	..	22	..		..	..	..	..
Uganda	4	50	136	5	19	1	3		..	109	..	12
Ukraine	48	102	78	94	105	42	43		..	72	..	..
United Arab Emirates	84	89	99	52	75	3	12		74	87	..	67
United Kingdom	79	103	99	83	156 [e]	19	60		97	99	79	94
United States	57	99	101	91	95	56	73		..	95	..	88
Uruguay	63	107	109	62	98	17	36		..	90	..	70
Uzbekistan	..	81	..	105	..	28	..		..	..	..	..
Venezuela, RB	48	93	102	21	59	21	28		82	88	14	50
Vietnam	43	109	106	42	67	2	10		95	95	..	62
West Bank and Gaza	..	..	..	..	..	..	..		..	..	..	..
Yemen, Rep.	0 [d]	..	79	..	48	..	11		..	67	..	37
Yugoslavia, Fed. Rep.	..	..	..	..	..	..	..		..	..	..	..
Zambia	2	90	78	16	24	1	2		77	66	..	19
Zimbabwe	36	85	95	8	44	1	4		..	80	..	40
World	48 w	97 w	102 w	49 w	67 w	13 w	22 w		.. w	.. w	.. w	.. w
Low income	20	83	95	29	44	6	8		..	..	..	..
Middle income	47	106	109	51	70	10	17		..	93	..	..
Lower middle income	44	107	104	51	65	9	15		..	92	..	..
Upper middle income	61	102	125	49	91	15	26		..	96	..	69
Low & middle income	33	96	102	41	58	8	14		..	..	..	..
East Asia & Pacific	37	111	106	43	61	3	9		..	93	..	..
Europe & Central Asia	..	99	94	86	88	31	44		..	..	..	..
Latin America & Carib.	58	105	130	42	86	14	21		..	97	..	64
Middle East & N. Africa	16	87	95	42	76	11	22		..	82	..	..
South Asia	20	77	98	27	48	5	10		..	..	..	..
Sub-Saharan Africa	..	80	86	15	27	1	4		..	..	..	..
High income	79	102	102	86	106	35	62		..	98	..	92
Europe EMU	97	106	104	81	107	24	52		..	100	..	91

a. Break in series between 1997 and 1998 due to change from International Standard Classification of Education 1976 (ISCED76) to ISCED97. b. Net enrollment ratios exceeding 100 percent indicate discrepancies between estimates of the school-age population and reported enrollment data. c. Data are provisional for Organisation for Economic Co-operation and Development and World Education Indicators (WEI) countries. For a list of WEI countries, see *About the Data* for table 2.10. d. Less than 0.5. e. Includes training for the unemployed.

About the data

School enrollment data are reported to the UNESCO Institute for Statistics by national education authorities. Enrollment ratios help to monitor two important issues for universal primary education: a Millennium Development Goal that implies achieving a net primary enrollment ratio of 100 percent, and gross enrollment ratios help to assess whether an education system has sufficient capacity to meet the needs of universal primary education. Net enrollment ratios show the share of children of primary school age who are enrolled in school and thus also the share who are not.

Enrollment ratios, while a useful measure of participation in education, also have significant limitations. They are based on data collected during annual school surveys, which are typically conducted at the beginning of the school year. They do not reflect actual rates of attendance or dropouts during the school year. And school administrators may report exaggerated enrollments, especially if there is a financial incentive to do so. Often the number of teachers paid by the government is related to the number of pupils enrolled. Behrman and Rosenzweig (1994), comparing official school enrollment data for Malaysia in 1988 with gross school attendance rates from a household survey, found that the official statistics systematically overstated enrollment.

Overage or underage enrollments frequently occur, particularly when parents prefer, for cultural or economic reasons, to have children start school at other than the official age. Children's age at enrollment may be inaccurately estimated or misstated, especially in communities where registration of births is not strictly enforced. Parents who want to enroll their underage children in primary school may do so by overstating the age of the children. And in some education systems ages for children repeating a grade may be deliberately or inadvertently underreported.

As an international indicator, the gross primary enrollment ratio has been used to indicate broad levels of participation as well as school capacity. It has an inherent weakness: the length of primary education differs significantly across countries. A short duration tends to increase the ratio, and a long duration to decrease it (in part because there are more dropouts among older children).

Other problems affecting cross-country comparisons of enrollment data stem from errors in estimates of school-age populations. Age-gender structures from censuses or vital registration systems, the primary sources of data on school-age populations, are commonly subject to underenumeration (especially of young children) aimed at circumventing laws or regulations; errors are also introduced when parents round up children's ages. While census data are often adjusted for age bias, adjustments are rarely made for inadequate vital registration systems.

Compounding these problems, pre- and postcensus estimates of school-age children are interpolations or projections based on models that may miss important demographic events (see the discussion of demographic data in *About the data* for table 2.1).

In using enrollment data, it is also important to consider repetition rates. These rates are quite high in some developing countries, leading to a substantial number of overage children enrolled in each grade and raising the gross enrollment ratio. A common error that may also distort enrollment ratios is the lack of distinction between new entrants and repeaters, which, other things equal, leads to underreporting of repeaters and overestimation of dropouts.

Thus gross enrollment ratios indicate the capacity of each level of the education system, but a high ratio does not necessarily mean a successful education system. The net enrollment ratio excludes overage students in an attempt to capture more accurately the system's coverage and internal efficiency. It does not solve the problem completely, however, because some children fall outside the official school age because of late or early entry rather than because of grade repetition. The difference between gross and net enrollment ratios shows the incidence of overage and underage enrollments.

In 1998 the United Nations Educational, Scientific, and Cultural Organization (UNESCO) introduced the International Standard Classification of Education, 1997 (ISCED97), and adjusted its data collection program and

2.12a

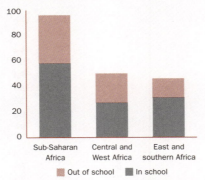

Nearly 40 million African children were out of school in 1998

Children of primary school age (millions)

In Sub-Saharan Africa an estimated 38 million children of primary school age (about 40 percent) were out of school in 1998. A large share (about 60 percent) of these children were in Central and West Africa. Unless countries in this region devise strategies to improve access to schools and create incentives to attend, they are unlikely to achieve the Millennium Development Goal of providing universal primary education by 2015.

Source: UNESCO Institute for Statistics 2001.

country reporting of education statistics to this new classification. The adjustments were made to ease the international compilation and comparison of education statistics and to take into account new types of learning opportunities and activities for both children and adults. Thus the time-series data for the years through 1997 are not consistent with those for 1998 and later. Any time-series analysis should therefore be undertaken with extreme caution.

ISCED97 introduced a new level of education—level 4, or postsecondary nontertiary education. The students in this category are not counted as either secondary or tertiary.

The years shown in the table usually refer to the beginning of the school year. In most countries the school year ends in the following year.

Definitions

- **Gross enrollment ratio** is the ratio of total enrollment, regardless of age, to the population of the age group that officially corresponds to the level of education shown.
- **Net enrollment ratio** is the ratio of children of official school age (as defined by the national education system) who are enrolled in school to the population of the corresponding official school age. Based on the International Standard Classification of Education, 1997 (ISCED97), • **Preprimary education** refers to the initial stage of organized instruction, designed primarily to introduce very young children to a school-type environment. • **Primary education** provides children with basic reading, writing, and mathematics skills along with an elementary understanding of such subjects as history, geography, natural science, social science, art, and music. • **Secondary education** completes the provision of basic education that began at the primary level, and aims at laying the foundations for lifelong learning and human development, by offering more subject- or skill-oriented instruction using more specialized teachers. • **Tertiary education**, whether or not leading to an advanced research qualification, normally requires, as a minimum condition of admission, the successful completion of education at the secondary level.

Data sources

The data are from the UNESCO Institute for Statistics.

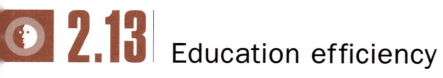
	Net intake rate in grade 1		Share of cohort reaching grade 5				Primary completion rate			Average years of schooling		
	% of school-age population		% of grade 1 students				% of relevant age group					
	Male	Female	Male		Female		Total	Male	Female	Total	Male	Female
	2000 [a]	2000 [a]	1980	1999 [a]	1980	1999 [a]	1995–2001 [b]	1995–2001 [b]	1995–2001 [b]	2000	2000	2000
Afghanistan	..	..	62	..	61	..	8	15	0 [c]	1.7	2.6	0.8
Albania	79	79	..	..	..	..	91	89	93	..	..	..
Algeria	82	80	90	97	85	98	91	93	88	5.4	6.2	4.5
Angola	18	17	..	..	..	..	28	..	..	..	..	..
Argentina	92	92	..	90	..	90	96	..	..	8.8	8.8	8.9
Armenia	57	58	..	..	..	..	82	70	95	..	..	..
Australia	..	..	..	..	..	..	..	..	..	10.9	11.2	10.7
Austria	..	..	..	..	..	..	..	..	..	8.4	9.2	7.6
Azerbaijan	84	86	..	..	..	..	100	99	101	..	..	..
Bangladesh	86	85	18	..	26	..	70	68	72	2.6	3.3	1.8
Belarus	87	85	..	..	..	..	93	95	92	..	..	..
Belgium	..	..	75	..	77	..	..	..	..	9.3	9.6	9.1
Benin	..	..	59	89	62	78	39	47	30	2.3	3.3	1.4
Bolivia	66	68	..	84	..	81	72	..	..	5.6	6.1	5.1
Bosnia and Herzegovina	..	..	..	..	..	..	88	..	..	..	..	..
Botswana	22	25	80	84	84	89	102	96	107	6.3	6.2	6.3
Brazil	..	..	..	..	..	..	71	..	..	4.9	5.4	4.4
Bulgaria	..	..	..	..	..	..	92	92	92	..	..	..
Burkina Faso	25	17	76	68	74	71	25	30	20	..	..	..
Burundi	32	28	100	59	96	58	43	31	28	..	..	..
Cambodia	70	67	..	63	..	63	70	68	51	..	..	..
Cameroon	..	..	70	72	69	93	43	46	39	3.5	4.2	2.9
Canada	..	..	..	..	..	..	..	..	..	11.6	11.7	11.6
Central African Republic	..	..	63	..	50	..	19	..	..	2.5	3.4	1.7
Chad	32	24	..	58	..	48	19	29	9	..	..	..
Chile	37	37	..	101	..	101	99	..	..	7.5	7.6	7.5
China	..	..	..	..	..	..	108	111	106	6.4	7.6	5.1
Hong Kong, China	..	..	98	..	99	..	..	..	..	9.4	9.9	8.9
Colombia	60	57	..	..	..	..	85	84	88	5.3	4.9	5.7
Congo, Dem. Rep.	21	23	56	..	59	..	40	45	34	3.0	4.1	2.0
Congo, Rep.	11	10	81	..	83	..	44	28	60	5.1	5.8	4.6
Costa Rica	61	61	77	77	82	84	89	91	88	6.0	6.1	6.0
CÙte d'Ivoire	30	24	..	91	..	90	40	48	33	..	..	..
Croatia	..	..	..	..	..	..	79	80	79	..	..	..
Cuba	94	93	..	95	..	96	..	..	..	..	..	..
Czech Republic	47	53	..	..	..	..	109	110	107	..	..	..
Denmark	86	88	99	..	99	..	..	..	..	9.7	9.8	9.5
Dominican Republic	63	63	..	71	..	79	82	78	86	4.9	4.9	5.0
Ecuador	80	83	..	76	..	79	96	96	96	6.4	6.4	6.4
Egypt, Arab Rep.	88	85	92	..	88	..	99	104	92	5.5	6.5	4.5
El Salvador	..	..	17	69	16	72	80	..	..	5.2	5.2	5.1
Eritrea	28	24	..	..	..	..	35	40	31	..	..	..
Estonia	..	..	..	100	..	99	88	89	86	..	..	..
Ethiopia	27	24	50	64	51	64	24	36	12	..	..	..
Finland	93	94	..	99	..	101	..	..	..	10.0	10.2	9.8
France	..	..	..	..	..	..	..	..	..	7.9	8.1	7.6
Gabon	..	..	57	..	56	..	80	79	80	..	..	..
Gambia, The	46	44	74	75	71	63	70	..	..	2.3	3.0	1.6
Georgia	73	72	..	..	..	..	90	..	..	..	..	..
Germany	..	..	..	..	..	..	..	..	..	10.2	10.5	9.9
Ghana	29	29	..	67	..	65	64	..	..	3.9	5.7	2.2
Greece	..	..	99	..	98	..	..	..	..	8.7	9.8	7.6
Guatemala	62	59	..	..	..	..	52	..	..	3.5	3.8	3.1
Guinea	22	19	..	90	..	77	34	44	24	..	..	..
Guinea-Bissau	38	29	25	41	17	34	31	40	24	0.8	0.9	0.7
Haiti			20	..	21	..	70	69	70	2.8	3.5	2.1

	Net intake rate in grade 1		Share of cohort reaching grade 5				Primary completion rate			Average years of schooling		
	% of school-age population		% of grade 1 students					% of relevant age group				
	Male	Female	Male		Female		Total	Male	Female	Total	Male	Female
	2000 [a]	2000 [a]	1980	1999 [a]	1980	1999 [a]	1995–2001 [b]	1995–2001 [b]	1995–2001 [b]	2000	2000	2000
Honduras	49	49	..	..	..	..	67	66	74	4.8	5.6	4.0
Hungary	..	..	96	..	97	..	102	102	102	9.1	9.6	8.7
India	..	..	..	70	..	65	76	88	63	5.1	6.3	3.7
Indonesia	45	44	..	92	..	102	91	90	92	5.0	5.5	4.5
Iran, Islamic Rep.	38	38	..	..	..	..	92	95	89	5.3	6.1	4.5
Iraq	76	71	..	..	..	..	55	59	51	4.0	4.6	3.3
Ireland	..	..	..	98	..	99	..	..	..	9.4	9.3	9.4
Israel	..	..	..	..	..	..	..	..	..	9.6	9.8	9.4
Italy	..	..	99	..	99	..	..	..	..	7.2	7.6	6.8
Jamaica	80	85	..	87	..	91	94	91	98	5.3	4.9	5.6
Japan	..	..	100	..	100	..	..	..	..	9.5	9.9	9.1
Jordan	70	71	100	98	98	97	104	102	106	6.9	7.7	6.0
Kazakhstan	69	67	..	..	..	..	100	99	101	..	..	..
Kenya	30	31	60	70	62	73	63	..	..	4.2	4.7	3.7
Korea, Dem. Rep.	..	..	..	..	..	..	..	..	..	..	..	..
Korea, Rep.	..	..	94	..	94	..	96	95	98	10.8	11.7	10.0
Kuwait	68	66	..	..	..	..	70	69	71	7.1	7.2	6.9
Kyrgyz Republic	..	..	..	..	..	..	100	..	..	..	..	..
Lao PDR	60	58	..	..	..	..	69	73	64	..	..	..
Latvia	..	..	..	..	..	..	86	87	84	..	..	..
Lebanon	5	7	..	95	..	99	70	..	..	..	..	..
Lesotho	53	56	50	68	68	80	68	65	92	4.2	3.6	4.8
Liberia	65	51	..	49	..	17	..	..	..	2.5	3.3	1.5
Libya	..	..	..	..	..	..	..	..	..	..	..	..
Lithuania	..	..	..	..	..	..	95	97	94	..	..	..
Macedonia, FYR	..	..	..	..	..	..	91	94	87	..	..	..
Madagascar	59	49	..	..	..	..	26	26	26	..	..	..
Malawi	..	..	48	55	40	43	64	72	58	3.2	3.6	2.8
Malaysia	..	..	97	..	97	..	90	89	90	6.8	7.4	6.2
Mali	..	..	..	100	..	86	23	29	18	0.9	1.2	0.6
Mauritania	28	27	..	68	..	55	46	48	43	..	..	..
Mauritius	24	25	..	..	..	..	111	115	108	6.0	6.5	5.6
Mexico	83	86	..	88	..	89	100	..	..	7.2	7.6	6.9
Moldova	..	..	..	..	..	..	79	..	..	..	..	..
Mongolia	71	71	..	..	..	..	82	..	..	..	..	..
Morocco	68	65	79	79	78	81	55	63	47	..	..	..
Mozambique	22	21	..	..	..	..	36	50	22	1.1	1.4	0.8
Myanmar	90	90	..	..	..	..	..	..	..	2.8	3.0	2.5
Namibia	57	60	..	92	..	93	90	86	94	..	..	..
Nepal	..	..	..	..	..	..	65	70	58	2.4	3.4	1.5
Netherlands	99	98	94	..	98	..	..	..	..	9.4	9.6	9.1
New Zealand	..	..	93	..	94	..	..	..	..	11.7	12.0	11.5
Nicaragua	41	39	..	45	..	53	65	61	70	4.6	4.5	4.6
Niger	36	25	74	76	72	71	20	24	16	1.0	1.4	0.7
Nigeria	..	..	..	..	..	..	67	73	61	..	..	..
Norway	..	..	100	..	100	..	..	..	..	11.8	12.2	11.6
Oman	54	54	..	95	..	97	76	76	76	..	..	..
Pakistan	..	..	..	..	..	..	59	..	..	3.9	5.1	2.5
Panama	86	87	74	92	79	92	94	..	..	8.6	8.6	8.5
Papua New Guinea	102	93	..	..	..	..	59	64	53	2.9	3.3	2.4
Paraguay	69	71	58	74	58	79	78	..	..	6.2	6.3	6.1
Peru	85	85	78	88	74	88	98	..	..	7.6	8.0	7.1
Philippines	46	49	..	..	..	..	92	..	..	8.2	8.2	8.2
Poland	..	..	..	99	..	99	96	96	97	9.8	10.0	9.7
Portugal	..	..	..	..	..	..	..	..	..	5.9	6.1	5.7
Puerto Rico	..	..	..	..	..	..	..	..	..	..	..	..

2.13 Education efficiency

	Net intake rate in grade 1		Share of cohort reaching grade 5				Primary completion rate			Average years of schooling		
	% of school-age population		% of grade 1 students				% of relevant age group					
	Male	Female	Male		Female		Total	Male	Female	Total	Male	Female
	2000 [a]	2000 [a]	1980	1999 [a]	1980	1999 [a]	1995–2001 [b]	1995–2001 [b]	1995–2001 [b]	2000	2000	2000
Romania	..	..	..	..	..	..	98	99	98	..	..	..
Russian Federation	..	..	..	..	..	..	96			..	..	..
Rwanda	63	67	69	38	74	40	28	..	..	2.6	3.0	2.2
Saudi Arabia	53	35	82	94	86	94	69	68	69	..	..	..
Senegal	..	..	89	75	82	69	41	49	34	2.6	3.1	2.0
Sierra Leone	82	79	..	..	..	..	32	36	30	2.4	3.1	1.7
Singapore	..	..	..	..	..	..	..	..	..	8.6 [d]	9.3 [d]	8.1 [d]
Slovak Republic	49	56	..	..	..	..	97	96	97	9.3	..	..
Slovenia	..	..	..	..	..	..	92	90	94	7.1	..	..
Somalia	..	..	..	..	..	..	..	..	..	..	..	..
South Africa	39	36	..	66	..	63	98	95	100	6.1	5.7	6.6
Spain	..	..	95	..	94	..	..	..	..	7.3	7.4	7.1
Sri Lanka	..	..	..	..	..	..	111	108	114	6.9	7.2	6.6
Sudan	30	26	68	86	71	88	46	..	..	2.1	2.7	1.6
Swaziland	49	51	77	83	81	85	81	78	85	6.0	5.8	6.2
Sweden	..	..	98	..	98	..	..	..	..	11.4	11.4	11.4
Switzerland	59	59	75	101	74	101	..	..	..	10.5	11.1	9.9
Syrian Arab Republic	63	61	93	..	88	..	90	95	86	5.8	6.8	4.8
Tajikistan	98	92	..	..	..	..	95	..	..	..	..	..
Tanzania	12	14	89	80	90	83	60	..	..	2.7	3.1	2.3
Thailand	56	52	..	96	..	99	90	..	..	6.5	7.0	6.0
Togo	50	44	59	78	44	69	63	73	52	3.3	4.6	2.1
Trinidad and Tobago	66	67	85	98	87	101	81	79	84	7.8	7.5	8.0
Tunisia	81	82	89	92	84	94	91	93	90	5.0	5.8	4.2
Turkey	..	..	..	..	..	..	92	95	89	5.3	6.2	4.3
Turkmenistan	..	..	..	..	..	..	..	..	..	..	..	..
Uganda	..	..	..	..	..	..	65	..	..	3.5	4.3	2.7
Ukraine	67	66	..	..	..	..	55	55	55	..	..	..
United Arab Emirates	59	62	100	98	100	98	80	76	86	..	..	..
United Kingdom	..	..	..	..	..	..	..	..	..	9.4	9.5	9.4
United States	..	..	..	..	..	..	..	..	..	12.0	12.1	12.0
Uruguay	35	38	..	93	..	88	98	95	101	7.6	7.2	7.9
Uzbekistan	..	..	..	..	..	..	100	..	..	..	..	..
Venezuela, RB	63	64	..	88	..	94	78	77	79	6.6	6.5	6.8
Vietnam	..	..	..	..	..	..	101	104	98	..	..	..
West Bank and Gaza	..	..	..	..	..	..	..	..	..	..	..	..
Yemen, Rep.	33	24	..	..	..	..	58	77	38	..	..	..
Yugoslavia, Fed. Rep.	..	..	..	..	..	..	96			..	..	..
Zambia	37	40	88	83	82	78	73	..	..	5.5	6.0	5.0
Zimbabwe	39	40	..	..	..	..	113	116	111	5.4	6.0	4.7
World	.. w	.. w	.. w	.. w	.. w	.. w	.. w	.. w	.. w	**6.5 w**	**7.2 w**	**5.7 w**
Low income	..	..	..	..	..	..	..	..	..	4.4	5.4	3.3
Middle income	..	..	..	..	..	..	102	105	100	6.3	7.3	5.5
Lower middle income	..	..	..	..	..	..	103	106	101	6.2	7.3	5.2
Upper middle income	..	..	..	..	..	..	..	..	..	6.7	7.3	6.5
Low & middle income	..	..	..	..	..	..	..	..	..	5.5	6.5	4.6
East Asia & Pacific	..	..	..	..	..	..	105	108	103	6.2	7.3	5.2
Europe & Central Asia	..	..	..	..	..	..	..	..	..	..	..	..
Latin America & Carib.	..	..	..	..	..	..	..	..	..	6.0	6.3	5.8
Middle East & N. Africa	62	58	..	..	..	..	86	90	83	5.3	6.1	4.4
South Asia	..	..	..	70	..	65	74	86	61	4.7	5.8	3.4
Sub-Saharan Africa	..	..	..	..	..	..	..	..	..	..	..	..
High income	..	..	..	..	..	..	..	..	..	10.0	10.2	9.8
Europe EMU	..	..	..	..	..	..	..	..	..	8.4	8.8	8.1

a. Data are provisional for Organisation for Economic Co-operation and Development and World Education Indicators (WEI) countries. For a list of WEI countries, see *About the Data* for table 2.10. b. Data are for the most recent year available. c. Less than 0.5. d. Data are for 2001.

About the data

Indicators of students' progress through school are estimated by the UNESCO Institute for Statistics and the World Bank. These indicators measure an education system's success in extending coverage to all students, maintaining the flow of students from one grade to the next, and, ultimately, imparting a particular level of education.

Low net intake rates in grade 1 reflect the fact that many children do not enter primary school at the official age, even though school attendance, at least through the primary level, is mandatory in all countries. Once enrolled, students drop out for a variety of reasons, including low quality of schooling, discouragement over poor performance, and the direct and indirect costs of schooling. Students' progress to higher grades may also be limited by the availability of teachers, classrooms, and educational materials.

The cohort survival rate is estimated as the proportion of an entering cohort of grade 1 students that eventually reaches grade 5. It measures the holding power and internal efficiency of an education system. Cohort survival rates approaching 100 percent indicate a high level of retention and a low level of dropout.

Cohort survival rates are typically estimated from data on enrollment and repetition by grade for two consecutive years, in a procedure called the reconstructed cohort method. This method makes three simplifying assumptions: dropouts never return to school; promotion, repetition, and dropout rates remain constant over the entire period in which the cohort is enrolled in school; and the same rates apply to all pupils enrolled in a given grade, regardless of whether they previously repeated a grade (Fredricksen 1993). Given these assumptions, cross-country comparisons should be made with caution, because other flows—caused by new entrants, reentrants, grade skipping, migration, or school transfers during the school year—are not considered.

The UNESCO Institute for Statistics measures cohort survival to grade 5 because research suggests that five to six years of schooling is a critical threshold for the achievement of sustainable basic literacy and numeracy skills. But the cohort survival rate only indirectly reflects the quality of schooling, and a high rate does not guarantee these learning outcomes. Measuring actual learning outcomes requires setting curriculum standards and measuring students' learning progress against those standards through standardized assessments or tests.

The primary completion rate is increasingly used as a core indicator of an education system's performance. Because it measures both the coverage of the education system and the educational attainment of students, the primary completion rate is a more accurate indicator of human capital formation and the quality and efficiency of the school system than are gross and net enrollment ratios. It is also the most direct measure of national progress toward the Millennium Development Goal of universal primary education.

The primary completion rate reflects the primary cycle as nationally defined, ranging from three or four years of primary education (in a very small number of countries) to five or six years (in most countries) and seven or eight years (in a relatively small number of countries). For any country it is therefore consistent with the gross and net enrollment ratios. The numerator may include overage children who have repeated one or more grades of primary school but are now graduating successfully as well as children who entered school early. The demoninator is the number of children of official graduation age, which could cause the primary completion rate to exceed 100 percent. There are other data limitations that contribute to completion rates exceeding 100 percent, such as the use of estimates for the population, different times of the year that the school and population surveys are conducted, and other discrepancies in the numbers used in the calculation.

For countries where the number of primary graduates is not reported, a proxy primary completion rate is calculated by subtracting the number of students who repeat the final grade in a typical year from the total number of students in that grade and dividing the result by the number of children of official graduation age in the population. Data limitations preclude adjusting this number for students who drop out during the final year of primary school. Thus proxy rates should be taken as an upper-bound estimate of the actual primary completion rate.

Average years of schooling measure the educational attainment of the population ages 15 and above, providing another indication of a country's human capital stock. But the data do not directly measure the human skills obtained in schools and do not take account of differences in the quality of schooling across countries. Average years of schooling are computed using a perpetual inventory method (for further details on this method, see Barro and Lee 2000).

Definitions

• **Net intake rate in grade 1** is the number of new entrants in the first grade of primary education who are of official primary school entrance age, expressed as a percentage of the population of the corresponding age. • **Share of cohort reaching grade 5** is the percentage of children enrolled in the first grade of primary school who eventually reach grade 5. The estimate is based on the reconstructed cohort method (see *About the data*). • **Primary completion rate** is the number of students successfully completing the last year of (or graduating from) primary school in a given year, divided by the number of children of official graduation age in the population. • **Average years of schooling** are the years of formal schooling received, on average, by adults ages 15 and above.

Data sources

The data on the net intake rate and the cohort reaching grade 5 are from the UNESCO Institute for Statistics. The data on the primary completion rate are compiled by staff in the education group of the World Bank's Human Development Network. The data on average years of schooling are from Robert Barro and Jong-Wha Lee's *International Data on Educational Attainment: Updates and Implications* (2000).

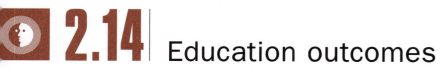

	Adult illiteracy rate				Youth illiteracy rate				Expected years of schooling			
	Male % ages 15 and above		Female % ages 15 and above		Male % ages 15–24		Female % ages 15–24		Males		Females	
	1990	2001	1990	2001	1990	2001	1990	2001	1990	2000 [a]	1990	2000 [a]
Afghanistan	..	..	..	..	..	..	..	..	..	..	..	..
Albania	13	8	33	22	3	1	8	3	..	11	..	11
Algeria	36	23	59	42	14	6	32	15	11	..	9	..
Angola	..	..	..	..	..	..	..	..	..	..	..	..
Argentina	4	3	4	3	2	2	2	1	..	14	..	15
Armenia	1	1	4	2	0 [b]	0 [b]	1	0 [b]	..	8	..	9
Australia	..	..	..	..	..	..	..	..	13	17	13	17
Austria	..	..	..	..	..	..	..	..	15	15	14	15
Azerbaijan	..	..	..	..	..	..	..	..	..	11	..	10
Bangladesh	56	50	76	69	49	43	67	60	6	8	4	8
Belarus	0 [b]	0 [b]	1	0 [b]	0 [b]	0 [b]	0 [b]	0 [b]	..	12	..	13
Belgium	..	..	..	..	..	..	..	..	14	16	14	16
Benin	62	47	85	75	43	28	75	63	..	9	..	5
Bolivia	13	8	30	20	4	2	11	6	..	..	..	..
Bosnia and Herzegovina	..	..	..	..	..	..	..	..	..	..	..	..
Botswana	34	25	30	19	21	15	13	8	10	12	11	12
Brazil	17	13	19	13	9	6	7	3	..	13	..	14
Bulgaria	2	1	4	2	0 [b]	0 [b]	1	0 [b]	12	13	12	13
Burkina Faso	75	65	92	85	64	53	86	75	3	..	2	..
Burundi	52	43	73	58	42	33	55	36	6	..	4	..
Cambodia	22	20	51	42	19	16	34	25	..	8	..	7
Cameroon	31	20	52	35	14	8	24	11	..	..	..	..
Canada	..	..	..	..	..	..	..	..	17	14	17	15
Central African Republic	53	39	79	63	34	23	61	39	..	..	..	..
Chad	63	47	81	64	42	25	62	38	..	7	..	4
Chile	6	4	6	4	2	1	2	1	..	14	..	13
China	13	7	31	21	3	1	7	3	..	..	..	..
Hong Kong, China	4	3	17	10	2	1	2	0 [b]	..	..	..	..
Colombia	11	8	12	8	6	4	4	2	..	11	..	11
Congo, Dem. Rep.	39	26	66	48	20	11	42	24	..	..	..	..
Congo, Rep.	23	12	42	24	5	2	10	3	..	..	..	..
Costa Rica	6	4	6	4	3	2	2	1	..	10	..	10
Côte d'Ivoire	49	40	74	62	35	29	60	46	..	..	..	..
Croatia	1	1	5	3	0 [b]	0 [b]	0 [b]	0 [b]	..	12	..	12
Cuba	5	3	5	3	1	0 [b]	1	0 [b]	12	12	13	12
Czech Republic	..	..	..	..	..	..	..	..	..	14	..	14
Denmark	..	..	..	..	..	..	..	..	14	15	14	16
Dominican Republic	20	16	21	16	13	9	12	8	..	..	..	..
Ecuador	10	7	15	10	4	2	5	3	..	..	..	..
Egypt, Arab Rep.	40	33	66	55	29	23	49	36	..	10	..	10
El Salvador	24	18	31	23	15	11	17	12	..	11	..	11
Eritrea	42	32	65	54	27	19	51	39	..	6	..	4
Estonia	0 [b]	0 [b]	0 [b]	0 [b]	0 [b]	0 [b]	0 [b]	0 [b]	12	14	12	15
Ethiopia	63	52	80	68	48	38	66	50	..	6	..	4
Finland	..	..	..	..	..	..	..	..	15	16	16	17
France	..	..	..	..	..	..	..	..	14	15	15	16
Gabon	..	..	..	..	..	..	..	..	..	..	..	..
Gambia, The	68	55	80	69	50	33	66	49	..	..	..	..
Georgia	..	..	..	..	..	..	..	..	..	6	..	6
Germany	..	..	..	..	..	..	..	..	15	15	14	15
Ghana	30	19	53	35	12	6	25	11	..	8	..	7
Greece	2	1	8	4	1	0 [b]	0 [b]	0 [b]	13	15	13	15
Guatemala	31	23	47	38	20	14	34	27	..	..	..	..
Guinea	..	..	..	..	..	..	..	..	..	..	..	..
Guinea-Bissau	58	45	87	75	38	26	74	54	..	..	..	..
Haiti	57	47	63	51	44	35	46	34	..	..	..	..

Education outcomes 2.14

	Adult illiteracy rate				Youth illiteracy rate				Expected years of schooling			
	Male		Female		Male		Female		Males		Females	
	% ages 15 and above		% ages 15 and above		% ages 15–24		% ages 15–24					
	1990	2001	1990	2001	1990	2001	1990	2001	1990	2000[a]	1990	2000[a]
Honduras	31	25	33	24	22	16	19	13	..	..	..	..
Hungary	1	1	1	1	0[b]	0[b]	0[b]	0[b]	11	13	11	14
India	38	31	64	54	27	20	46	34	..	..	..	..
Indonesia	13	8	27	17	3	2	7	3	10	..	9	..
Iran, Islamic Rep.	28	16	46	30	8	4	19	8	..	..	..	..
Iraq	49	45	80	76	44	40	75	70	..	10	..	8
Ireland	..	..	..	..	..	..	..	..	12	14	13	15
Israel	5	3	12	7	1	0[b]	2	1	..	14	..	15
Italy	2	1	3	2	0[b]	0[b]	0[b]	0[b]	..	15	..	15
Jamaica	22	17	14	9	13	9	5	2	11	11	11	11
Japan	..	..	..	..	..	..	..	..	..	14	..	14
Jordan	10	5	28	15	2	1	5	1	9	12	9	13
Kazakhstan	1	0[b]	2	1	0[b]	0[b]	0[b]	0[b]	..	12	..	12
Kenya	19	11	39	23	7	4	13	5	..	8	..	8
Korea, Dem. Rep.	..	..	..	..	..	..	..	..	..	..	..	..
Korea, Rep.	2	1	7	3	0[b]	0[b]	0[b]	0[b]	14	16	13	14
Kuwait	21	16	27	20	12	8	13	6	7	8	7	9
Kyrgyz Republic	..	..	..	..	..	..	..	..	..	..	..	..
Lao PDR	30	23	57	46	21	15	39	28	9	9	6	7
Latvia	0[b]	0[b]	0[b]	0[b]	0[b]	0[b]	0[b]	0[b]	..	12	..	14
Lebanon	12	8	27	19	5	3	11	7	..	13	..	13
Lesotho	35	27	11	6	23	17	3	1	9	10	11	10
Liberia	45	29	77	62	25	14	61	46	..	11	..	8
Libya	17	9	49	31	1	0[b]	17	6	..	..	..	..
Lithuania	0[b]	0[b]	1	0[b]	0[b]	0[b]	0[b]	0[b]	..	14	..	15
Macedonia, FYR	..	..	..	..	..	..	..	..	..	12	..	12
Madagascar	34	26	50	39	22	16	33	23	..	6	..	6
Malawi	31	25	64	52	24	19	49	38	..	..	..	..
Malaysia	13	8	26	16	5	2	6	2	..	12	..	12
Mali	72	63	90	83	62	52	83	74	3	..	1	..
Mauritania	54	49	76	69	44	43	64	59	..	7	..	6
Mauritius	15	12	25	18	9	6	9	5	..	12	..	12
Mexico	9	7	16	11	4	2	6	3	..	12	..	11
Moldova	1	0[b]	4	2	0[b]	0[b]	0[b]	0[b]	..	9	..	10
Mongolia	2	1	3	2	1	1	1	1	..	9	..	11
Morocco	47	37	75	63	32	23	58	40	..	9	..	7
Mozambique	51	39	82	70	34	24	68	52	4	7	3	5
Myanmar	13	11	26	19	10	9	14	9	..	7	..	7
Namibia	23	17	28	18	14	10	11	6	..	12	..	12
Nepal	53	39	86	75	33	23	73	56	..	..	..	..
Netherlands	..	..	..	..	..	..	..	..	15	16	15	16
New Zealand	..	..	..	..	..	..	..	..	14	16	15	17
Nicaragua	37	33	37	33	32	29	31	27	..	..	..	..
Niger	82	76	95	91	75	67	91	86	..	3	..	2
Nigeria	41	27	62	42	19	10	34	15	..	..	..	..
Norway	..	..	..	..	..	..	..	..	14	16	14	18
Oman	33	19	62	36	5	0[b]	25	3	10	9	9	9
Pakistan	51	42	80	71	37	28	69	57	..	..	..	..
Panama	10	7	12	9	4	3	5	4	..	12	..	13
Papua New Guinea	36	29	52	42	26	20	38	28	..	6	..	6
Paraguay	8	5	12	8	4	3	5	3	9	10	8	10
Peru	8	5	21	14	3	2	8	5	..	13	..	11
Philippines	8	5	9	5	3	1	3	1	..	11	..	12
Poland	0[b]	0[b]	0[b]	0[b]	0[b]	0[b]	0[b]	0[b]	12	14	12	15
Portugal	9	5	16	10	1	0[b]	0[b]	0[b]	13	15	14	16
Puerto Rico	8	6	9	6	5	3	3	2	..	..	..	..

2.14 Education outcomes

	Adult illiteracy rate				Youth illiteracy rate				Expected years of schooling			
	Male % ages 15 and above		Female % ages 15 and above		Male % ages 15–24		Female % ages 15–24		Males		Females	
	1990	2001	1990	2001	1990	2001	1990	2001	1990	2000 a	1990	2000 a
Romania	1	1	4	3	1	0 b	1	0 b	11	12	11	12
Russian Federation	0 b	0 b	1	1	0 b	0 b	0 b	0 b	..	..	..	..
Rwanda	37	26	56	38	22	14	33	17	..	..	..	..
Saudi Arabia	24	16	50	32	9	5	21	9	9	..	7	9
Senegal	62	52	81	71	50	40	70	57	..	..	..	..
Sierra Leone	..	..	..	..	..	..	..	..	..	7	..	5
Singapore	6	4	17	11	1	0 b	1	0 b	..	..	..	..
Slovak Republic	..	..	..	..	..	..	..	..	..	13	..	13
Slovenia	0 b	0 b	0 b	0 b	0 b	0 b	0 b	0 b	..	14	..	15
Somalia	..	..	..	..	..	..	..	..	..	..	..	..
South Africa	18	14	20	15	11	8	12	9	13	13	13	13
Spain	2	1	5	3	0 b	0 b	0 b	0 b	..	15	..	16
Sri Lanka	7	5	15	11	4	3	6	3	..	..	..	..
Sudan	40	30	68	52	24	17	46	27	..	..	..	..
Swaziland	26	19	30	21	15	10	15	8	11	13	10	12
Sweden	..	..	..	..	..	..	..	..	13	15	13	17
Switzerland	..	..	..	..	..	..	..	..	14	16	13	15
Syrian Arab Republic	18	11	52	38	8	4	33	20	11	..	9	..
Tajikistan	1	0 b	3	1	0 b	0 b	0 b	0 b	..	11	..	9
Tanzania	24	15	49	32	11	6	23	11	..	5	..	5
Thailand	5	3	11	6	1	1	2	2	..	11	..	11
Togo	40	27	71	56	21	12	52	35	11	12	6	8
Trinidad and Tobago	2	1	4	2	0 b	0 b	0 b	0 b	11	11	11	12
Tunisia	28	18	53	38	7	2	25	10	11	14	10	14
Turkey	11	6	34	23	3	1	12	6	..	..	..	..
Turkmenistan	..	..	..	..	..	..	..	..	..	..	..	..
Uganda	31	22	57	42	20	14	40	27	..	..	..	..
Ukraine	0 b	0 b	1	0 b	0 b	0 b	0 b	0 b	..	11	..	12
United Arab Emirates	29	25	29	20	18	12	11	5	10	..	11	..
United Kingdom	..	..	..	..	..	..	..	..	14	16	14	17
United States	..	..	..	..	..	..	..	..	15	16	16	16
Uruguay	4	3	3	2	2	1	1	1	..	13	..	14
Uzbekistan	1	0 b	2	1	0 b	0 b	0 b	0 b	..	..	..	..
Venezuela, RB	10	7	12	8	5	3	3	1	..	10	..	11
Vietnam	6	5	13	9	6	5	6	4	..	..	..	..
West Bank and Gaza	..	..	..	..	..	..	..	..	..	..	..	..
Yemen, Rep.	45	32	87	73	26	16	75	51	..	11	..	5
Yugoslavia, Fed. Rep.	..	..	..	..	..	..	..	..	..	10	..	11
Zambia	21	14	41	27	14	9	24	14	..	7	..	7
Zimbabwe	13	7	25	15	3	1	9	4	..	10	..	9
World	.. w	.. w	.. w	.. w	.. w	.. w	.. w	.. w	.. w	.. w	.. w	.. w
Low income	35	28	56	46	24	19	40	31	..	..	..	..
Middle income	13	9	25	18	5	4	9	6	..	..	..	..
Lower middle income	13	9	28	20	5	4	10	7	..	..	..	..
Upper middle income	11	8	14	10	6	4	6	3	..	..	..	..
Low & middle income	22	17	38	30	14	11	23	19	..	..	..	..
East Asia & Pacific	12	7	29	19	3	2	7	4	..	..	..	..
Europe & Central Asia	2	1	5	4	1	0 b	2	1	..	..	..	..
Latin America & Carib.	13	10	17	12	7	5	7	5	..	..	..	..
Middle East & N. Africa	34	25	60	46	19	14	39	26	..	..	..	..
South Asia	41	34	66	56	30	24	50	41	..	..	..	..
Sub-Saharan Africa	40	30	60	46	25	18	40	27	..	..	..	..
High income	..	..	..	..	..	..	..	..	15		15	
Europe EMU	..	..	..	..	..	..	..	..	15		15	

a. Data are provisional for Organisation for Economic Co-operation and Development and World Education Indicator (WEI) countries. For a list of WEI countries, see *About the data* for table 2.10. b. Less than 0.5.

About the data

Many governments collect and publish statistics that indicate how their education systems are working and developing—statistics on enrollment and on such efficiency indicators as repetition rates, pupil-teacher ratios, and cohort progression through school. But until recently, despite an obvious interest in what education achieves, few systems in high-income or developing countries had systematically collected information on outcomes of education.

Basic student outcomes include achievements in reading and mathematics judged against established standards. In many countries national learning assessments are enabling ministries of education to monitor progress in these outcomes. Internationally, the UNESCO Institute for Statistics has established literacy as an outcome indicator based on an internationally agreed definition. The rate of illiteracy is defined as the percentage of people who cannot, with understanding, read and write a short, simple statement about their everyday life. In practice, illiteracy is difficult to measure. To estimate illiteracy using such a definition requires census or survey measurements under controlled conditions. Many countries estimate the number of illiterate people from self-reported data or by taking people with no schooling as illiterate.

Literacy statistics for most countries cover the population ages 15 and above, by five-year age groups, but some include younger ages or are confined to age ranges that tend to inflate literacy rates. As an alternative, the UNESCO Institute for Statistics has proposed the narrower age range of 15–24, which better captures the ability of participants in the formal education system. The youth illiteracy rate reported in the table measures the accumulated outcomes of primary education over the previous 10 years or so by indicating the proportion of people who have passed through the primary education system without acquiring basic literacy and numeracy skills (or never entered the system). Reasons for this may include difficulties in attending school or dropping out before reaching grade 5 (see *About the data* for table 2.13) and thereby failing to achieve basic learning competencies.

The indicator expected years of schooling is an estimate of the total years of schooling that a typical child at the age of school entry will receive, including years spent on repetition, given the current patterns of enrollment across cycles of education. It may also be interpreted as an indicator of the total education resources, measured in school years, that a child will acquire over his or her "lifetime" in school—or as an indicator of an education system's overall level of development.

Because the calculation of this indicator assumes that the probability of a child's being enrolled in school at any future age is equal to the current enrollment ratio for that age, it does not account for changes and trends in future enrollment ratios. The expected number of years and the expected number of grades completed are not necessarily consistent, because the first includes years spent in repetition. Comparability across countries and over time may be affected by differences in the length of the school year or changes in policies on automatic promotions and grade repetition.

Definitions

• **Adult illiteracy rate** is the percentage of people ages 15 and above who cannot, with understanding, read and write a short, simple statement about their everyday life. • **Youth illiteracy rate** is the illiteracy rate among people ages 15–24. • **Expected years of schooling** are the average number of years of formal schooling that children are expected to receive, including university education and years spent in repetition. They reflect the underlying age-specific enrollment ratios for primary, secondary, and tertiary education.

Data sources

The data on illiteracy are based on estimates and projections by the UNESCO Institute for Statistics, assessed in 2002. The data on expected years of schooling are from the UNESCO Institute for Statistics.

Health expenditure, services, and use

	Health expenditure			Health expenditure per capita	Physicians		Hospital beds		Inpatient admission rate	Average length of stay	Outpatient visits per capita
	Total	% of total			per 1,000 people		per 1,000 people		% of population	days	
	% of GDP	Public	Private	$							
	1997–2000[a]	1997–2000[a]	1997–2000[a]	1997–2000[a]	1980	1995–2000[a]	1980	1995–2000[a]	1995–2000[a]	1995–2000[a]	1995–2000[a]
Afghanistan	1.0	63.5	36.5	8	..	0.1	..	..	..	..	..
Albania	3.4	62.1	37.9	41	..	1.3	..	3.2	..	..	..
Algeria	3.6	82.2	17.8	64	..	1.0	..	2.1	..	..	..
Angola	3.6	55.9	44.1	24	..	0.1	..	..	..	..	..
Argentina	8.6	55.0	45.0	658	..	2.7	..	3.3	..	..	..
Armenia	7.5	42.3	57.7	38	3.5	3.2	8.4	0.7	8	15	2
Australia	8.3	72.4	27.6	1,698	..	2.5	12.3	7.9	16	16	6
Austria	8.0	69.7	30.3	1,872	1.6	3.1	11.2	8.6	30	9	7
Azerbaijan	0.9	75.1	24.9	8	3.4	3.6	9.7	9.7	6	..	1
Bangladesh	3.8	36.4	63.6	14	0.1	0.2	0.2	..	..	..	..
Belarus	5.7	82.8	17.2	57	3.4	4.4	12.5	12.2	26	18	11
Belgium	8.7	71.2	28.8	1,936	2.3	3.9	9.4	7.3	20	11	8
Benin	3.2	50.0	50.0	11	0.1	0.1	1.5	..	..	..	..
Bolivia	6.7	72.4	27.6	67	..	1.3	..	1.7	..	..	..
Bosnia and Herzegovina	4.5	69.0	31.0	50	..	1.4	..	1.8	..	15	..
Botswana	6.0	63.1	36.9	191	0.1	..	2.4	..	..	..	..
Brazil	8.3	40.8	59.2	267	..	1.3	..	3.1	0[b]	..	2
Bulgaria	3.9	77.6	22.4	59	2.5	3.4	11.1	7.4	..	12	..
Burkina Faso	4.2	70.7	29.3	8	0.0[c]	0.0[c]	..	1.4	2	3	0[b]
Burundi	3.1	53.1	46.9	3	..	..	..	..	..	..	..
Cambodia	8.1	24.5	75.5	19	..	0.3	..	..	..	..	..
Cameroon	4.3	24.7	75.3	24	..	0.1	..	..	..	..	..
Canada	9.1	72.0	28.0	2,058	1.8	2.1	6.8	3.9	10	9	7
Central African Republic	2.9	48.4	51.6	8	0.0[c]	0.0[c]	1.6	..	..	..	..
Chad	3.1	79.8	20.2	6	..	..	..	..	..	..	..
Chile	7.2	42.6	57.4	336	..	1.1	3.4	2.7	..	..	..
China	5.3	36.6	63.4	45	0.9	1.7	2.0	2.4	4	12	..
Hong Kong, China	..	..	..	..	0.8	1.3	4.0	..	..	..	..
Colombia	9.6	55.8	44.2	186	..	1.2	1.6	1.5	..	..	..
Congo, Dem. Rep.	1.5	73.7	26.3	9	..	0.1	..	..	..	..	..
Congo, Rep.	2.2	70.2	29.8	22	..	0.3	..	..	..	..	..
Costa Rica	6.4	68.4	31.6	273	..	0.9	3.3	1.7	9	6	1
Côte d'Ivoire	2.7	36.9	63.1	16	..	0.1	..	..	..	..	..
Croatia	10.0	80.0	20.0	434	..	2.3	..	..	..	..	..
Cuba	6.8	89.2	10.8	169	..	5.3	..	5.1	..	..	..
Czech Republic	7.2	91.4	8.6	358	2.3	3.1	11.3	8.8	21	11	12
Denmark	8.3	82.1	17.9	2,512	2.2	3.4	8.1	4.5	20	7	6
Dominican Republic	6.3	28.0	72.0	151	..	2.2	..	1.5	..	..	..
Ecuador	2.4	50.4	49.6	26	..	1.7	1.9	1.6	..	..	..
Egypt, Arab Rep.	3.8	46.1	53.9	51	1.1	1.6	2.0	2.1	3	6	4
El Salvador	8.8	43.0	57.0	184	0.3	1.1	..	1.6	..	..	..
Eritrea	4.3	65.6	34.4	9	..	0.0[c]	..	..	..	..	..
Estonia	6.1	76.7	23.3	218	4.2	3.0	12.4	7.4	18	9	5
Ethiopia	4.6	39.4	60.6	5	0.0[c]	..	0.3	..	..	..	..
Finland	6.6	75.1	24.9	1,559	1.7	3.1	15.6	7.5	27	10	4
France	9.5	76.0	24.0	2,057	2.0	3.0	11.1	8.2	23	11	7
Gabon	3.0	68.6	31.4	120	..	..	..	..	..	..	..
Gambia, The	4.1	82.4	17.6	10	..	0.0[c]	..	..	..	..	..
Georgia	7.1	10.5	89.5	41	4.8	4.4	10.7	4.8	5	11	1
Germany	10.6	75.1	24.9	2,422	2.3	3.6	11.5	9.1	24	12	7
Ghana	4.2	53.5	46.5	11	..	0.1	..	..	..	..	..
Greece	8.3	55.5	44.5	884	2.4	4.4	6.2	4.9	15	8	..
Guatemala	4.7	47.9	52.1	79	..	0.9	..	1.0	..	..	..
Guinea	3.4	57.1	42.9	13	..	0.1	..	..	..	..	..
Guinea-Bissau	3.9	65.4	34.6	9	0.1	0.2	1.9	..	..	..	..
Haiti	4.9	49.3	50.7	21	..	0.2	0.7	0.7	..	..	..

Health expenditure, services, and use

	Health expenditure			Health expenditure per capita	Physicians		Hospital beds		Inpatient admission rate	Average length of stay	Outpatient visits per capita
	Total % of GDP	% of total Public	Private	$	per 1,000 people		per 1,000 people		% of population	days	
	1997–2000 a	1997–2000 a	1997–2000 a	1997–2000 a	1980	1995–2000 a	1980	1995–2000 a	1995–2000 a	1995–2000 a	1995–2000 a
Honduras	6.8	63.1	36.9	62	..	0.8	1.3	1.1	..	..	..
Hungary	6.8	75.7	24.3	315	2.3	3.2	9.1	8.2	24	10	15
India	4.9	17.8	82.2	23	0.4	..	0.8	..	..	..	..
Indonesia	2.7	23.7	76.3	19	..	..	..	..	..	..	..
Iran, Islamic Rep.	5.5	46.3	53.7	258	..	0.9	1.5	1.6	..	..	..
Iraq	3.7	59.9	40.1	375	0.6	0.6	1.9	1.5	..	..	..
Ireland	6.7	75.8	24.2	1,692	..	2.3	13.0	9.7	15	8	..
Israel	10.9	75.9	24.1	2,021	..	3.8	5.1	6.0	..	..	..
Italy	8.1	73.7	26.3	1,498	2.6	6.0	9.6	4.9	18	8	..
Jamaica	5.5	47.0	53.0	165	..	1.4	..	2.1	..	..	..
Japan	7.8	76.7	23.3	2,908	1.3	1.9	13.7	16.5	10	40	16
Jordan	8.1	51.8	48.2	137	0.8	1.7	1.3	1.8	11	4	..
Kazakhstan	3.7	73.2	26.8	44	3.2	3.5	13.2	8.5	15	16	0 b
Kenya	8.3	22.2	77.8	28	..	0.1	..	..	..	..	..
Korea, Dem. Rep.	2.1	77.3	22.7	18	..	3.0	..	..	..	..	..
Korea, Rep.	6.0	44.1	55.9	584	..	1.3	1.7	6.1	6	14	10
Kuwait	3.0	87.2	12.8	586	1.7	1.9	4.1	2.8	..	..	..
Kyrgyz Republic	4.3	49.8	50.2	12	2.9	3.0	12.0	9.5	21	15	1
Lao PDR	3.4	38.0	62.0	11	..	0.2	..	..	..	..	..
Latvia	5.9	60.0	40.0	174	4.1	2.8	13.7	10.3	21	14	4
Lebanon	12.4	20.0	80.0	499	..	2.1	..	2.7	17	4	..
Lesotho	6.3	82.3	17.7	28	..	0.1	..	..	..	..	..
Liberia	4.0	76.2	23.8	2	..	0.0 c	..	..	..	..	..
Libya	3.3	48.6	51.4	246	1.3	1.3	..	4.3	..	..	..
Lithuania	6.0	72.4	27.6	185	3.9	4.0	12.1	9.2	24	11	7
Macedonia, FYR	6.0	84.5	15.5	106	..	2.2	..	4.9 d	9	13	3
Madagascar	3.5	71.8	28.2	9	..	0.1	..	..	..	..	..
Malawi	7.6	47.8	52.2	11	..	..	..	1.3	..	..	2
Malaysia	2.5	58.8	41.2	101	0.3	0.7	..	2.0	..	..	..
Mali	4.9	45.5	54.5	10	0.0 c	0.1	..	0.2	1	7	0 b
Mauritania	4.3	79.3	20.7	14	..	0.1	..	..	..	..	..
Mauritius	3.4	56.3	43.7	134	0.5	0.9	3.1	..	..	..	..
Mexico	5.4	46.4	53.6	311	..	1.8	0.7	1.1	6	4	2
Moldova	3.5	82.4	17.6	11	3.1	3.5	12.0	12.1	19	18	8
Mongolia	6.6	70.3	29.7	23	..	2.4	11.2	..	..	..	..
Morocco	4.5	29.6	70.4	50	..	0.5	..	1.0	3	7	..
Mozambique	4.3	63.4	36.6	9	0.0 c	..	1.1	..	..	..	..
Myanmar	2.2	17.1	82.9	153	..	0.3	0.9	..	..	..	..
Namibia	7.1	59.3	40.7	136	..	0.3	..	..	..	..	..
Nepal	..	..	..	..	0.0 c	0.0 c	0.2	0.2	..	..	..
Netherlands	8.1	67.5	32.5	1,900	1.9	3.2	12.3	10.8	10	33	6
New Zealand	8.0	78.0	22.0	1,062	1.6	2.2	10.2	6.2	13	8	..
Nicaragua	4.4	51.7	48.3	43	0.4	0.9	..	1.5	..	..	..
Niger	3.9	44.9	55.1	5	..	0.0 c	..	0.1	28	5	0 b
Nigeria	2.2	20.8	79.2	8	0.1	..	0.9	..	..	..	..
Norway	7.8	85.2	14.8	2,832	2.0	2.9	16.5	14.6	17	9	..
Oman	2.8	82.9	17.1	295	0.5	1.3	1.6	2.2	9	4	4
Pakistan	4.1	22.9	77.1	18	0.3	0.6	0.6	..	..	..	..
Panama	7.6	69.2	30.8	268	..	1.7	..	2.2	..	..	..
Papua New Guinea	4.1	88.6	11.4	31	0.1	0.1	5.5	..	..	..	..
Paraguay	7.9	38.3	61.7	112	..	1.1	..	1.3	..	..	..
Peru	4.8	59.2	40.8	100	0.7	0.9	..	1.5	1	6	..
Philippines	3.4	45.7	54.3	33	0.1	1.2	1.7	..	..	..	..
Poland	6.0	69.7	30.3	246	1.8	2.2	5.6	4.9	16	9	5
Portugal	8.2	71.2	28.8	862	2.0	3.2	5.2	4.0	12	9	3
Puerto Rico	..	..	..	..	..	1.8	..	3.3	..	..	..

2.15 Health expenditure, services, and use

	Health expenditure Total % of GDP 1997–2000[a]	Health expenditure % of total Public 1997–2000[a]	Health expenditure % of total Private 1997–2000[a]	Health expenditure per capita $ 1997–2000[a]	Physicians per 1,000 people 1980	Physicians per 1,000 people 1995–2000[a]	Hospital beds per 1,000 people 1980	Hospital beds per 1,000 people 1995–2000[a]	Inpatient admission rate % of population 1995–2000[a]	Average length of stay days 1995–2000[a]	Outpatient visits per capita 1995–2000[a]
Romania	2.9	63.8	36.2	48	1.5	1.8	8.8	7.6	18	10	4
Russian Federation	5.3	72.5	27.5	92	4.0	4.2	13.0	12.1	22	17	8
Rwanda	5.2	51.3	48.7	12	0.0[c]	..	1.5	..	..	..	..
Saudi Arabia	5.3	79.1	20.9	448	..	1.7	..	2.3	11	4	1
Senegal	4.6	56.6	43.4	22	..	0.1	..	0.4	..	10	1
Sierra Leone	4.3	60.0	40.0	6	0.1	0.1	1.2	..	..	..	..
Singapore	3.5	35.7	64.3	814	0.9	1.6	4.0	..	..	..	..
Slovak Republic	5.9	89.6	10.4	210	..	3.5	..	7.1	20	10	4
Slovenia	8.6	78.9	21.1	788	..	2.3	7.0	5.7	..	..	..
Somalia	1.3	71.4	28.6	19	0.0[c]	0.0[c]	..	..	..	..	..
South Africa	8.8	42.2	57.8	255	..	0.6	..	..	..	..	..
Spain	7.7	69.9	30.1	1,073	..	3.3	5.4	4.1	12	10	..
Sri Lanka	3.6	49.0	51.0	31	0.1	0.4	2.9	..	..	..	..
Sudan	4.7	21.2	78.8	13	0.1	0.1	0.9	..	..	..	..
Swaziland	4.2	72.1	27.9	56	..	0.2	..	..	..	..	..
Sweden	8.4	77.3	22.7	2,179	2.2	2.9	15.1	3.6	18	6	3
Switzerland	10.7	55.6	44.4	3,573	2.4	3.5	..	17.9	15	13	..
Syrian Arab Republic	2.5	63.4	36.6	30	0.4	1.3	1.1	1.4	..	..	..
Tajikistan	3.3	30.0	70.0	6	2.4	2.0	10.0	..	..	..	..
Tanzania	5.9	47.0	53.0	12	..	0.0[c]	1.4	..	..	..	..
Thailand	3.7	57.4	42.6	71	0.1	0.4	1.5	2.0	..	..	1
Togo	2.8	54.3	45.7	8	0.1	0.1	..	..	..	..	..
Trinidad and Tobago	5.2	50.7	49.3	268	0.7	0.8	..	5.1	..	..	..
Tunisia	5.5	52.0	48.0	110	0.3	0.7	2.1	1.7	..	..	..
Turkey	5.0	71.1	28.9	150	0.6	1.3	2.2	2.6	8	6	2
Turkmenistan	5.4	84.9	15.1	52	2.9	3.0	10.6	..	..	..	..
Uganda	3.9	38.0	62.0	10	..	..	..	..	..	..	..
Ukraine	4.1	70.1	29.9	26	3.7	3.0	12.5	11.8	20	..	10
United Arab Emirates	3.2	77.7	22.3	767	1.1	1.8	2.8	2.6	..	..	..
United Kingdom	7.3	81.0	19.0	1,747	1.3	1.8	8.1	4.1	15	10	6
United States	13.0	44.3	55.7	4,499	2.0	2.8	6.0	3.6	12	7	6
Uruguay	10.9	46.5	53.5	653	..	3.7	..	4.4	..	..	..
Uzbekistan	5.3	50.0	50.0	29	2.9	3.1	11.5	8.3	..	..	..
Venezuela, RB	4.7	57.4	42.6	233	0.8	2.4	0.3	1.5	..	..	..
Vietnam	5.2	25.8	74.2	21	0.2	0.5	3.5	1.7	8	7	..
West Bank and Gaza	..	..	..	..	..	0.5	..	1.2	9	3	4
Yemen, Rep.	4.9	43.0	57.0	20	..	0.2	..	0.6	..	..	..
Yugoslavia, Fed. Rep.	5.6	51.0	49.0	50	..	2.0	..	5.3	..	12	2
Zambia	5.6	62.1	37.9	18	0.1	0.1	..	..	..	..	..
Zimbabwe	7.3	42.6	57.4	43	0.2	0.1	3.0	..	..	..	..
World	**9.3 w**	**59.4 w**	**40.6 w**	**482 w**	**1.1 w**	**.. w**	**4.0 w**	**.. w**	**9 w**	**.. w**	**.. w**
Low income	4.3	27.1	72.9	21	0.5	..	1.7	..	..	..	..
Middle income	5.9	51.8	48.2	116	1.2	1.9	3.4	3.3	6	11	..
Lower middle income	5.3	49.4	50.6	72	1.2	1.8	3.3	3.3	6	12	3
Upper middle income	6.6	54.2	45.8	309	..	1.6	..	3.2	6	..	..
Low & middle income	5.6	47.6	52.4	71	0.9	..	2.7	..	..	..	..
East Asia & Pacific	4.7	38.6	61.4	44	0.8	1.7	2.0	2.4	4	12	..
Europe & Central Asia	5.5	72.4	27.6	108	3.0	3.1	10.4	9.0	18	13	6
Latin America & Carib.	7.0	47.6	52.4	262	..	1.5	..	2.3	2	..	2
Middle East & N. Africa	4.6	61.9	38.1	171	..	..	..	..	..	..	..
South Asia	4.7	20.8	79.2	21	0.3	..	0.7	..	..	..	..
Sub-Saharan Africa	6.0	42.4	57.6	29	..	..	..	..	..	..	..
High income	10.2	62.2	37.8	2,736	1.9	3.0	8.6	7.4	15	14	8
Europe EMU	9.1	73.4	26.6	1,808	2.2	4.1	9.9	8.0	19	11	6

a. Data are for the most recent year available. b. Less than 0.5. c. Less than 0.05. d. Data are for 2001.

About the data

National health accounts track financial flows in the health sector, including public and private expenditures by source of funding. In contrast with high-income countries, few developing countries have health accounts that are methodologically consistent with national accounting approaches. The difficulties in creating national health accounts go beyond data collection. To establish a national health accounting system, a country needs to define the boundaries of the health care system and a taxonomy of health care delivery institutions. The accounting system should be comprehensive and standardized, providing not only accurate measures of financial flows but also information on the equity and efficiency of health financing to inform health policy.

The absence of consistent national health accounting systems in most developing countries makes cross-country comparisons of health spending difficult. Records of private out-of-pocket spending are often lacking. And compiling estimates of public health expenditures is complicated in countries where state or provincial and local governments are involved in financing and delivering health care because the data on public spending often are not aggregated. The data in the table are the product of an effort by the World Health Organization (WHO), the Organisation for Economic Co-operation and Development (OECD), and the World Bank to collect all available information on health expenditures from national and local government budgets, national accounts, household surveys, insurance publications, international donors, and existing tabulations.

Indicators on health services (physicians and hospital beds per 1,000 people) and health care utilization (inpatient admission rates, average length of stay, and outpatient visits) come from a variety of sources (see *Data sources*). Data are lacking for many countries, and for others comparability is limited by differences in definitions. In estimates of health personnel, for example, some countries incorrectly include retired physicians (because deletions are made only periodically) or those working outside the health sector. There is no universally accepted definition of hospital beds. Moreover, figures on physicians and hospital beds are indicators of availability, not of quality or use. They do not show how well trained the physicians are or how well equipped the hospitals or medical centers are. And physicians and hospital beds tend to be concentrated in urban areas, so these indicators give only a partial view of health services available to the entire population.

The average length of stay in hospitals is an indicator of the efficiency of resource use. Longer stays may reflect a waste of resources if patients are kept in hospitals beyond the time medically required, inflating demand for hospital beds and increasing hospital costs. Aside from differences in cases and financing methods, cross-country variations in average length of stay may result from differences in the role of hospitals. Many developing countries do not have separate extended care facilities, so hospitals become the source of both long-term and acute care. Other factors may also explain the variations. Data for some countries may not include all public and private hospitals. Admission rates may be overstated in some countries if outpatient surgeries are counted as hospital admissions. And in many countries outpatient visits, especially emergency visits, may result in double counting if a patient receives treatment in more than one department.

- **Total health expenditure** is the sum of public and private health expenditure. It covers the provision of health services (preventive and curative), family planning activities, nutrition activities, and emergency aid designated for health but does not include provision of water and sanitation. • **Public health expenditure** consists of recurrent and capital spending from government (central and local) budgets, external borrowings and grants (including donations from international agencies and nongovernmental organizations), and social (or compulsory) health insurance funds. • **Private health expenditure** includes direct (out-of-pocket) spending by households, private insurance, spending by nonprofit institutions serving households (other than social insurance), and direct service payments by private corporations. • **Physicians** are graduates of any faculty or school of medicine who are working in the country in any medical field (practice, teaching, research). • **Hospital beds** include inpatient beds available in public, private, general, and specialized hospitals and rehabilitation centers. In most cases beds for both acute and chronic care are included. • **Inpatient admission rate** is the percentage of the population admitted to hospitals during a year. • **Average length of stay** is the average duration of inpatient hospital admissions. • **Outpatient visits per capita** are the number of visits to health care facilities per capita, including repeat visits.

Data sources

The estimates of health expenditure come mostly from the WHO's *World Health Report 2002* and from the OECD for its member countries, supplemented by World Bank poverty assessments and country and sector studies, including the Human Development Network's *Sector Strategy: Health, Nutrition, and Population* (World Bank 1997a). Data are also drawn from World Bank public expenditure reviews, the International Monetary Fund's Government Finance Statistics database, and other studies. The data on private expenditure in developing countries are drawn largely from household surveys conducted by governments or by statistical or international organizations. The data on physicians, hospital beds, and utilization of health services are from the WHO and OECD, supplemented by country data.

	Access to an improved water source		Access to improved sanitation facilities		Tetanus vaccinations	Child immunization rate		Tuberculosis treatment success rate	DOTS detection rate
	% of population		% of population		% of pregnant women	% of children under age one		% of registered cases	% of estimated cases
						Measles	DPT		
	1990	2000	1990	2000	1996–2000[a]	2001	2001	1999	1998–2000[a]
Afghanistan	..	13	..	12	..	46	44	87	9
Albania	..	97	..	91	65	95	97	..	..
Algeria	..	89	..	92	52	83	89	87	129
Angola	..	38	..	44	24	72	41	..	..
Argentina	94	..	82	..	..	94	82	59	31
Armenia	..	..	..	..	..	93	94	88	39
Australia	100	100	100	100	..	93	92	84	18
Austria	100	100	100	100	..	79	84	77	58
Azerbaijan	..	78	..	81	..	99	98	88	6
Bangladesh	94	97	41	48	64	76	83	81	24
Belarus	..	100	..	..	..	99	99	..	..
Belgium	..	..	..	..	..	83	96	..	..
Benin	..	63	20	23	50	65	76	77	32
Bolivia	71	83	52	70	27	79	81	74	75
Bosnia and Herzegovina	..	..	..	..	..	92	91	90	47
Botswana	93	95	60	66	54	83	87	71	67
Brazil	83	87	71	76	45	99	97	11	1
Bulgaria	..	100	..	100	..	96	96	..	22
Burkina Faso	..	42	..	29	33	46	41	61	10
Burundi	69	78	87	88	9	75	74	..	30
Cambodia	..	30	..	17	31	59	60	93	44
Cameroon	51	58	77	79	49	62	43	75	16
Canada	100	100	100	100	..	96	97	..	..
Central African Republic	48	70	24	25	6	29	23	..	..
Chad	..	27	18	29	24	36	27	..	33
Chile	90	93	97	96	..	97	97	83	76
China	71	75	29	38	13	79	79	96	33
Hong Kong, China	..	..	..	..	..	..	..	78	33
Colombia	94	91	83	86	..	75	74	82	34
Congo, Dem. Rep.	..	45	..	21	10	46	40	69	51
Congo, Rep.	..	51	..	..	30	35	31	61	97
Costa Rica	..	95	..	93	..	82	88	81	147
Côte d'Ivoire	80	81	46	52	49	61	57	63	32
Croatia	..	..	..	..	..	94	94	..	..
Cuba	..	91	..	98	..	99	99	91	96
Czech Republic	..	..	..	..	..	97	98	78	49
Denmark	..	100	..	..	..	94	97	..	..
Dominican Republic	83	86	66	67	86	98	62	81	4
Ecuador	71	85	70	86	..	99	90	75	23
Egypt, Arab Rep.	94	97	87	98	36	97	99	87	36
El Salvador	66	77	73	82	..	99	99	78	56
Eritrea	..	46	..	13	34	88	93	44	13
Estonia	..	..	..	..	..	95	94	63	61
Ethiopia	25	24	8	12	17	52	56	76	29
Finland	100	100	100	100	..	96	99	..	..
France	..	..	..	..	..	84	98	..	..
Gabon	..	86	..	53	54	55	38	..	..
Gambia, The	..	62	..	37	96	90	96	..	67
Georgia	..	79	..	100	..	73	86	61	34
Germany	..	..	..	..	..	89	97	..	..
Ghana	53	73	61	72	51	81	80	55	29
Greece	..	..	..	..	..	88	88	..	..
Guatemala	76	92	70	81	39	90	82	81	47
Guinea	45	48	55	58	61	52	43	..	40
Guinea-Bissau	..	56	44	56	46	48	47	35	37
Haiti	53	46	23	28	52	53	43	70	22

	Access to an improved water source		Access to improved sanitation facilities		Tetanus vaccinations	Child immunization rate		Tuberculosis treatment success rate	DOTS detection rate
	% of population		% of population		% of pregnant women	% of children under age one		% of registered cases	% of estimated cases
						Measles	DPT		
	1990	2000	1990	2000	1996–2000 [a]	2001	2001	1999	1998–2000 [a]
Honduras	83	88	61	75	..	95	95	88	61
Hungary	99	99	99	99	..	99	99	..	22
India	68	84	16	28	67	56	64	82	11
Indonesia	71	78	47	55	54	59	60	50	19
Iran, Islamic Rep.	..	92	..	83	75	96	95	82	32
Iraq	..	85	..	79	56	90	81	85	23
Ireland	..	..	..	..	..	73	84	..	..
Israel	..	..	..	..	..	94	95	..	..
Italy	..	..	..	..	..	70	95	71	30
Jamaica	93	92	99	99	..	85	90	74	102
Japan	..	..	..	..	..	96	85	76	21
Jordan	97	96	98	99	15	99	99	88	40
Kazakhstan	..	91	..	99	..	96	96	79	80
Kenya	45	57	80	87	51	76	76	78	43
Korea, Dem. Rep.	..	100	..	99	5	34	37	94	26
Korea, Rep.	..	92	..	63	..	97	99	..	65
Kuwait	..	..	..	..	8	99	98	..	..
Kyrgyz Republic	..	77	..	100	..	99	99	83	37
Lao PDR	..	37	..	30	32	50	40	84	40
Latvia	..	..	..	..	..	98	97	74	50
Lebanon	..	100	..	99	..	94	93	96	57
Lesotho	..	78	..	49	17	77	85	69	64
Liberia	..	..	..	..	..	78	62	..	42
Libya	71	72	97	97	..	93	94	67	106
Lithuania	..	..	..	..	..	97	95	84	1
Macedonia, FYR	..	..	..	..	..	92	90	..	..
Madagascar	44	47	36	42	35	55	55	..	67
Malawi	49	57	73	76	81	82	90	71	40
Malaysia	..	..	..	..	71	92	97	90	74
Mali	55	65	70	69	32	37	51	68	17
Mauritania	37	37	30	33	63	58	61	..	..
Mauritius	100	100	100	99	78	90	92	87	32
Mexico	80	88	70	74	..	97	97	80	66
Moldova	..	92	..	99	..	81	90	..	..
Mongolia	..	60	..	30	..	95	95	86	57
Morocco	75	80	58	68	33	96	96	88	81
Mozambique	..	57	..	43	29	92	80	71	40
Myanmar	..	72	..	64	78	73	72	81	48
Namibia	72	77	33	41	70	58	63	50	105
Nepal	67	88	20	28	33	71	72	87	58
Netherlands	100	100	100	100	..	96	97	79	40
New Zealand	..	..	..	..	..	85	90	..	41
Nicaragua	70	77	76	85	42	99	92	81	76
Niger	53	59	15	20	41	51	31	60	22
Nigeria	53	62	53	54	44	40	26	75	12
Norway	100	100	..	..	..	93	95	77	31
Oman	37	39	84	92	96	100	99	67	159
Pakistan	83	90	36	62	58	54	56	70	3
Panama	..	90	..	92	..	97	98	80	45
Papua New Guinea	40	42	82	82	11	58	56	66	7
Paraguay	63	78	93	94	..	77	66	..	4
Peru	74	80	60	71	59	97	85	93	93
Philippines	87	86	74	83	35	75	70	87	45
Poland	..	..	..	..	..	97	98	69	3
Portugal	..	..	..	..	..	87	96	85	80
Puerto Rico	..	..	..	..	..	..	..	77	58

Disease prevention: coverage and quality

	Access to an improved water source		Access to improved sanitation facilities		Tetanus vaccinations	Child immunization rate		Tuberculosis treatment success rate	DOTS detection rate
	% of population		% of population		% of pregnant women	% of children under age one		% of registered cases	% of estimated cases
						Measles	DPT		
	1990	2000	1990	2000	1996–2000[a]	2001	2001	1999	1998–2000[a]
Romania	..	58	..	53	..	98	99	78	9
Russian Federation	..	99	..	..	..	98	96	65	3
Rwanda	..	41	..	8	43	78	86	67	29
Saudi Arabia	..	95	..	100	66	94	97	66	39
Senegal	72	78	57	70	64	48	52	..	49
Sierra Leone	..	57	..	66	42	37	44	75	46
Singapore	100	100	100	100	..	89	92	95	12
Slovak Republic	..	100	..	100	..	99	99	79	39
Slovenia	100	100	..	..	..	98	92	88	63
Somalia	..	..	..	..	..	38	33	88	27
South Africa	86	86	86	87	26	72	81	60	67
Spain	..	..	..	..	..	94	95	..	..
Sri Lanka	68	77	85	94	78	99	99	84	35
Sudan	67	75	58	62	55	67	46	81	37
Swaziland	..	..	..	..	..	72	77	..	..
Sweden	100	100	100	100	..	94	99	..	..
Switzerland	100	100	100	100	79	81	95	..	..
Syrian Arab Republic	..	80	..	90	53	93	92	84	24
Tajikistan	..	60	..	90	..	86	83	..	..
Tanzania	38	68	84	90	61	83	85	78	45
Thailand	80	84	79	96	81	94	96	77	46
Togo	51	54	37	34	41	58	64	76	16
Trinidad and Tobago	91	90	99	99	..	91	91	..	..
Tunisia	75	80	76	84	50	92	96	91	68
Turkey	79	82	87	90	30	90	88	..	..
Turkmenistan	..	..	..	..	..	98	95	..	18
Uganda	45	52	..	79	38	61	60	61	50
Ukraine	..	98	..	99	87	99	99	..	..
United Arab Emirates	..	..	..	..	..	94	94	..	29
United Kingdom	100	100	100	100	..	85	94	..	..
United States	100	100	100	100	..	91	94	76	89
Uruguay	..	98	..	94	..	94	94	83	83
Uzbekistan	..	85	..	89	..	99	97	79	4
Venezuela, RB	..	83	..	68	..	49	70	82	78
Vietnam	55	77	29	47	55	97	98	92	80
West Bank and Gaza	..	..	..	..	31	..	..	..	..
Yemen, Rep.	..	69	32	38	9	79	76	83	50
Yugoslavia, Fed. Rep.	..	98	..	100	..	90	93	..	..
Zambia	52	64	63	78	35	85	78	..	..
Zimbabwe	78	83	56	62	58	68	75	73	52
World	**74 w**	**81 w**	**45 w**	**55 w**		**72 w**	**73 w**		
Low income	66	76	30	44		60	61		
Middle income	76	82	47	59		86	85		
Lower middle income	74	80	42	55		84	83		
Upper middle income	84	88	75	79		94	94		
Low & middle income	71	79	39	51		71	71		
East Asia & Pacific	71	76	35	46		76	77		
Europe & Central Asia	..	91	..	..		95	94		
Latin America & Carib.	82	86	72	77		91	89		
Middle East & N. Africa	..	88	..	85		92	92		
South Asia	72	84	22	34		58	65		
Sub-Saharan Africa	53	58	54	53		58	53		
High income	..	..	..	..		90	94		
Europe EMU	..	..	..	..		85	96		

a. Data are for the most recent year available.

About the data

The indicators in the table are based on data provided to the World Health Organization (WHO) by member states as part of their efforts to monitor and evaluate progress in implementing national health strategies. Because reliable, observation-based statistical data for these indicators do not exist in some developing countries, the data are at times estimated.

People's health is influenced by the environment in which they live. Lack of clean water and basic sanitation is the main reason diseases transmitted by feces are so common in developing countries. Drinking water contaminated by feces deposited near homes and an inadequate water supply cause diseases accounting for 10 percent of the disease burden in developing countries (World Bank 1993c). The data on access to an improved water source measure the share of the population with ready access to water for domestic purposes. The data are based on surveys and estimates provided by governments to the Joint Monitoring Programme of the WHO and United Nations Children's Fund (UNICEF). The coverage rates for water and sanitation are based on information from service users on the facilities their households actually use rather than on information from service providers, who may include nonfunctioning systems. Access to drinking water from an improved source does not ensure that the water is safe or adequate, as these characteristics are not tested at the time of the surveys.

Neonatal tetanus is an important cause of infant mortality in some developing countries. It can be prevented through immunization of the mother during pregnancy. Recommended doses for full protection are generally two tetanus shots during the first pregnancy and one booster shot during each subsequent pregnancy, with five doses considered adequate for lifetime protection. Information on tetanus shots during pregnancy is collected through surveys in which pregnant respondents are asked to show antenatal cards on which tetanus shots have been recorded. Because not all women have antenatal cards, respondents are also asked about their receipt of these injections. Poor recall may result in a downward bias in estimates of the share of births protected. But in settings where receiving injections is common, respondents may erroneously report having received tetanus shots.

Governments in developing countries usually finance immunization against measles and diphtheria, pertussis (whooping cough), and tetanus (DPT) as part of the basic public health package. According to the World Bank's *World Development Report 1993: Investing in Health*, these diseases accounted for about 10 percent of the disease burden among children under five in 1990, compared with an expected 23 percent at 1970 levels of vaccination. In many developing countries, however, lack of precise information on the size of the cohort of children under one year of age makes immunization coverage difficult to estimate. The data shown here are based on an assessment of national immunization coverage rates carried out in 2002 by the WHO and UNICEF. The assessment considered both administrative data from service providers and household survey data on children's immunization histories. Based on the data available, consideration of potential biases, and contributions of local experts, the most likely true level of immunization coverage was determined for each year.

Data on the success rate of tuberculosis treatment are provided for countries that have implemented the recommended control strategy: directly observed treatment, short course (DOTS). Countries that have not adopted DOTS or have only recently done so are omitted because of lack of data or poor comparability or reliability of reported results. The treatment success rate for tuberculosis provides a useful indicator of the quality of health services. A low rate or no success suggests that infectious patients may not be receiving adequate treatment. An essential complement to the tuberculosis treatment success rate is the DOTS detection rate, which indicates whether there is adequate coverage by the recommended case detection and treatment strategy. A country with a high treatment success rate may still face big challenges if its DOTS detection rate remains low.

Definitions

• **Access to an improved water source** refers to the percentage of the population with reasonable access to an adequate amount of water from an improved source, such as a household connection, public standpipe, borehole, protected well or spring, or rainwater collection. Unimproved sources include vendors, tanker trucks, and unprotected wells and springs. Reasonable access is defined as the availability of at least 20 liters a person a day from a source within one kilometer of the dwelling. • **Access to improved sanitation facilities** refers to the percentage of the population with at least adequate access to excreta disposal facilities (private or shared but not public) that can effectively prevent human, animal, and insect contact with excreta. Improved facilities range from simple but protected pit latrines to flush toilets with a sewerage connection. To be effective, facilities must be correctly constructed and properly maintained. • **Tetanus vaccinations** refer to the percentage of pregnant women who receive two tetanus toxoid injections during their first pregnancy and one booster shot during each subsequent pregnancy. • **Child immunization rate** is the percentage of children under one year of age receiving vaccination coverage for four diseases—measles and diphtheria, pertussis (whooping cough), and tetanus (DPT). A child is considered adequately immunized against measles after receiving one dose of vaccine, and against DPT after receiving three doses. • **Tuberculosis treatment success rate** is the percentage of new, registered smear-positive (infectious) cases that were cured or in which a full course of treatment was completed. • **DOTS detection rate** is the percentage of estimated new infectious tuberculosis cases detected under the directly observed treatment, short-course (DOTS) case detection and treatment strategy.

Data sources

The table was produced using information provided to the WHO by countries, the WHO's EPI (Expanded Programme on Immunization) Information System, and its *Global Tuberculosis Control Report 2002*; UNICEF's *State of the World's Children 2003*; and the WHO and UNICEF's *Global Water Supply and Sanitation Assessment 2000 Report*.

	Total fertility rate		Adolescent fertility rate	Women at risk of unintended pregnancy	Contraceptive prevalence rate	Births attended by skilled health staff		Maternal mortality ratio	
	births per woman		births per 1,000 women ages 15–19	% of married women ages 15–49	% of women ages 15–49	% of total		per 100,000 live births National estimates	Modeled estimates
	1980	2001	2002	1990–2001[a]	1990–2001[a]	1982	1996–2000[a]	1990–98[a]	1995
Afghanistan	7.0	6.8	151	..	..	..	..	..	820
Albania	3.6	2.2	11	..	..	..	99	..	31
Algeria	6.7	2.9	17	..	51	..	92	220	150
Angola	6.9	6.6	209	..	..	34	23	..	1,300
Argentina	3.3	2.5	60	..	..	..	98	38	85
Armenia	2.3	1.4	44	12	..	..	97	35	29
Australia	1.9	1.8	18	..	..	99	100	..	6
Austria	1.6	1.3	20	..	..	..	..	..	11
Azerbaijan	3.2	2.1	44	..	55	..	88	43	37
Bangladesh	6.1	3.0	129	15	54	2	12	440	600
Belarus	2.0	1.3	21	..	..	..	100	28	33
Belgium	1.7	1.6	11	..	..	..	..	..	8
Benin	7.0	5.4	103	27	16	..	60	500	880
Bolivia	5.5	3.8	75	26	49	..	59	390	550
Bosnia and Herzegovina	2.1	1.6	29	..	..	..	100	10	15
Botswana	6.2	3.9	68	..	..	..	99	330	480
Brazil	3.9	2.2	68	7	77	98	88	160	260
Bulgaria	2.0	1.3	49	..	..	..	99	15	23
Burkina Faso	7.5	6.4	133	26	12	12	27	..	1,400
Burundi	6.8	5.9	50	..	..	..	25	..	1,900
Cambodia	5.7	3.9	57	33	24	..	34	470	590
Cameroon	6.4	4.7	127	20	19	..	56	430	720
Canada	1.7	1.5	20	..	..	..	..	..	6
Central African Republic	5.8	4.7	124	16	15	..	44	1,100	1,200
Chad	6.9	6.3	182	10	4	24	16	830	1,500
Chile	2.8	2.1	42	..	..	92	100	20	33
China	2.5	1.9	15	..	83	..	70	55	60
Hong Kong, China	2.0	0.9	6	..	..	89	100	..	..
Colombia	3.9	2.5	75	6	77	..	86	80	120
Congo, Dem. Rep.	6.6	6.1	210	..	..	..	70	..	940
Congo, Rep.	6.3	5.9	134	..	..	..	..	..	1,100
Costa Rica	3.6	2.4	69	..	..	..	98	29	35
Côte d'Ivoire	7.4	4.7	118	28	15	..	47	600	1,200
Croatia	1.9	1.4	18	..	..	..	100	6	18
Cuba	2.0	1.6	67	..	..	..	100	27	24
Czech Republic	2.1	1.2	23	..	69	..	..	9	14
Denmark	1.5	1.8	8	..	..	..	..	10	15
Dominican Republic	4.2	2.7	89	12	64	..	96	230	110
Ecuador	5.0	2.9	65	..	66	62	69	160	210
Egypt, Arab Rep.	5.1	3.2	46	11	56	..	61	170	170
El Salvador	4.9	3.0	87	..	60	..	90	120	180
Eritrea	7.5	5.4	110	28	8	..	..	1,000	1,100
Estonia	2.0	1.2	26	..	..	..	..	50	80
Ethiopia	6.6	5.6	143	36	8	10	10	870	1,800
Finland	1.6	1.7	10	..	..	..	..	6	6
France	2.0	1.9	10	..	71	..	..	10	20
Gabon	4.5	4.1	156	28	33	..	86	520	620
Gambia, The	6.5	4.9	139	..	..	41	51	..	1,100
Georgia	2.3	1.1	27	..	41	..	96	70	22
Germany	1.4	1.4	14	..	..	..	..	8	12
Ghana	6.5	4.1	79	23	22	..	44	210	590
Greece	2.2	1.3	17	..	..	..	..	1	2
Guatemala	6.3	4.4	100	23	38	..	41	190	270
Guinea	6.1	5.1	153	24	6	..	35	670	1,200
Guinea-Bissau	6.0	5.7	182	..	..	..	35	910	910
Haiti	5.9	4.3	72	40	28	34	24	525	1,100

	Total fertility rate		Adolescent fertility rate	Women at risk of unintended pregnancy	Contraceptive prevalence rate	Births attended by skilled health staff		Maternal mortality ratio	
	births per woman		births per 1,000 women ages 15–19	% of married women ages 15–49	% of women ages 15–49	% of total		per 100,000 live births National estimates	Modeled estimates
	1980	2001	2002	1990–2001[a]	1990–2001[a]	1982	1996–2000[a]	1990–98[a]	1995
Honduras	6.5	4.1	110	..	62	..	55	110	220
Hungary	1.9	1.3	27	..	73	99	..	15	23
India	4.9	3.0	104	16	52	23	42	410	440
Indonesia	4.3	2.4	52	9	57	27	56	450	470
Iran, Islamic Rep.	6.7	2.6	45	..	73	..	86	37	130
Iraq	6.4	4.2	35	..	..	..	..	..	370
Ireland	3.2	1.9	14	..	60	..	..	6	9
Israel	3.2	2.8	19	..	..	..	..	5	8
Italy	1.6	1.2	8	..	..	..	..	7	11
Jamaica	3.7	2.4	84	..	65	86	95	120	120
Japan	1.8	1.4	3	..	..	..	100	8	12
Jordan	6.8	3.6	30	14	50	..	97	41	41
Kazakhstan	2.9	1.8	35	9	66	..	98	70	80
Kenya	7.8	4.3	100	24	39	..	44	590	1,300
Korea, Dem. Rep.	2.8	2.1	2	..	..	..	99	110	35
Korea, Rep.	2.6	1.4	4	..	..	70	100	20	20
Kuwait	5.3	2.6	30	..	..	..	98	5	25
Kyrgyz Republic	4.1	2.5	29	12	60	..	95	65	80
Lao PDR	6.7	4.9	91	..	25	..	21	650	650
Latvia	1.9	1.2	32	..	..	..	..	45	70
Lebanon	4.0	2.3	23	..	61	..	95	100	130
Lesotho	5.5	4.3	75	..	23	..	60	..	530
Liberia	6.8	5.9	196	..	..	..	..	..	..
Libya	7.3	3.4	35	..	45	..	94	75	120
Lithuania	2.0	1.3	33	..	..	..	..	18	27
Macedonia, FYR	2.5	1.8	31	..	..	..	97	3	17
Madagascar	6.6	5.3	157	26	19	..	46	490	580
Malawi	7.6	6.2	137	30	31	..	56	1,120	580
Malaysia	4.2	2.9	23	..	..	88	96	39	39
Mali	7.1	6.2	167	26	7	14	24	580	630
Mauritania	6.4	4.5	135	32	8	..	57	550	870
Mauritius	2.7	2.0	39	..	75	..	99	50	45
Mexico	4.7	2.5	64	..	65	..	86	55	65
Moldova	2.4	1.4	44	..	74	..	99	42	65
Mongolia	5.3	2.5	45	..	60	..	97	150	65
Morocco	5.4	2.8	44	20	59	29	..	230	390
Mozambique	6.5	5.1	153	23	6	..	44	1,100	980
Myanmar	4.9	2.9	29	..	..	97	57	230	170
Namibia	5.9	4.9	103	22	29	..	76	230	370
Nepal	6.1	4.2	112	28	29	..	12	..	830
Netherlands	1.6	1.7	5	..	75	100	100	7	10
New Zealand	2.0	2.0	31	..	..	..	..	15	15
Nicaragua	6.3	3.5	124	15	60	..	61	150	250
Niger	8.0	7.2	205	17	8	26	16	590	920
Nigeria	6.9	5.2	111	17	15	..	42	700	1,100
Norway	1.7	1.8	12	..	..	..	..	6	9
Oman	9.9	4.1	54	..	24	..	91	19	120
Pakistan	7.0	4.6	62	32	28	..	20	..	200
Panama	3.7	2.5	75	..	..	80	90	70	100
Papua New Guinea	5.8	4.4	68	..	26	..	53	370	390
Paraguay	5.2	3.9	75	15	57	..	71	190	170
Peru	4.5	2.7	61	10	69	30	56	265	240
Philippines	4.8	3.3	33	19	47	..	56	170	240
Poland	2.3	1.3	17	..	..	..	..	8	12
Portugal	2.2	1.5	22	..	..	..	100	8	12
Puerto Rico	2.5	1.9	64	..	78	..	..	..	30

	Total fertility rate		Adolescent fertility rate	Women at risk of unintended pregnancy	Contraceptive prevalence rate	Births attended by skilled health staff		Maternal mortality ratio	
	births per woman		births per 1,000 women ages 15–19	% of married women ages 15–49	% of women ages 15–49	% of total		per 100,000 live births National estimates	Modeled estimates
	1980	2001	2002	1990–2001[a]	1990–2001[a]	1982	1996–2000[a]	1990–98[a]	1995
Romania	2.4	1.3	41	..	48	..	98	41	60
Russian Federation	1.9	1.2	46	..	34	..	99	50	75
Rwanda	8.3	5.8	52	39	13	20	31	..	2,300
Saudi Arabia	7.3	5.4	103	..	21	..	91	..	23
Senegal	6.8	5.0	89	35	11	..	51	560	1,200
Sierra Leone	6.5	5.7	182	..	..	..	42	..	2,100
Singapore	1.7	1.4	9	..	..	100	100	6	9
Slovak Republic	2.3	1.3	25	..	..	..	..	9	14
Slovenia	2.1	1.2	9	..	..	..	..	11	17
Somalia	7.3	7.0	204	..	..	2	34	..	..
South Africa	4.6	2.8	43	..	62	..	84	..	340
Spain	2.2	1.2	9	..	..	..	..	6	8
Sri Lanka	3.5	2.1	20	..	..	85	95	60	60
Sudan	6.1	4.5	56	..	10	23	..	500	1,500
Swaziland	6.2	4.3	103	..	..	..	..	..	..
Sweden	1.7	1.6	9	..	..	..	..	5	8
Switzerland	1.5	1.4	4	..	..	..	..	5	8
Syrian Arab Republic	7.4	3.6	39	..	45	43	..	110	200
Tajikistan	5.6	3.0	24	..	..	..	77	65	120
Tanzania	6.7	5.2	115	22	25	..	35	530	1,100
Thailand	3.5	1.8	72	..	72	40	95	44	44
Togo	6.8	5.0	81	32	24	..	51	480	980
Trinidad and Tobago	3.3	1.8	42	..	..	..	99	..	65
Tunisia	5.2	2.1	10	..	60	40	90	70	70
Turkey	4.3	2.3	51	10	64	70	81	130	55
Turkmenistan	4.9	2.3	14	10	..	..	97	65	65
Uganda	7.2	6.1	179	35	15	..	38	510	1,100
Ukraine	2.0	1.2	31	..	72	..	99	27	45
United Arab Emirates	5.4	3.1	64	..	..	..	99	3	30
United Kingdom	1.9	1.7	27	..	..	..	99	7	10
United States	1.8	2.1	48	..	64	..	99	8	12
Uruguay	2.7	2.2	64	..	..	..	..	26	50
Uzbekistan	4.8	2.5	37	14	56	..	96	21	60
Venezuela, RB	4.2	2.8	90	..	..	82	95	60	43
Vietnam	5.0	2.2	31	7	75	100	70	160	95
West Bank and Gaza	..	5.0	81	..	42	..	..	..	..
Yemen, Rep.	7.9	6.1	97	39	21	..	22	350	850
Yugoslavia, Fed. Rep.	2.3	1.7	32	..	..	..	93	10	15
Zambia	7.0	5.2	129	27	26	..	47	650	870
Zimbabwe	6.3	3.7	86	13	54	37	84	695	610
World	**3.7 w**	**2.6 w**	**69 w**		**44 w**				
Low income	5.3	3.6	104		44				
Middle income	3.2	2.2	40		61				
Lower middle income	3.1	2.1	34		61				
Upper middle income	3.7	2.4	62		..				
Low & middle income	4.1	2.8	74		44				
East Asia & Pacific	3.1	2.1	28		59				
Europe & Central Asia	2.5	1.6	43		64				
Latin America & Carib.	4.1	2.6	72		40				
Middle East & N. Africa	6.2	3.4	51		54				
South Asia	5.3	3.3	105		49				
Sub-Saharan Africa	6.6	5.2	138		21				
High income	1.9	1.7	24		..				
Europe EMU	1.8	1.5	11		..				

a. Data are for most recent year available.

About the data

Reproductive health is a state of physical and mental well-being in relation to the reproductive system and its functions and processes. Means of achieving reproductive health include education and services during pregnancy and childbirth, provision of safe and effective contraception, and prevention and treatment of sexually transmitted diseases. Health conditions related to sex and reproduction have been estimated to account for 25 percent of the global disease burden in women (Murray and Lopez 1998). Reproductive health services will need to expand rapidly over the next two decades, when the number of women and men of reproductive age is projected to increase by more than 300 million.

Total and adolescent fertility rates are based on data on registered live births from vital registration systems or, in the absence of such systems, from censuses or sample surveys. As long as the surveys are fairly recent, the estimated rates are generally considered reliable measures of fertility in the recent past. Where no empirical information on age-specific fertility rates is available, a model is used to estimate the share of births to adolescents. For countries without vital registration systems, fertility rates are generally based on extrapolations from trends observed in censuses or surveys from earlier years.

An increasing number of couples in the developing world want to limit or postpone childbearing but are not using effective contraceptive methods. These couples face the risk of unintended pregnancy, shown in the table as the percentage of married women of reproductive age who do not want to become pregnant but are not using contraception (Bulatao 1998). Information on this indicator is collected through surveys and excludes women not exposed to the risk of unintended pregnancy because of menopause, infertility, or postpartum anovulation. Common reasons for not using contraception are lack of knowledge about contraceptive methods and concerns about their possible health side-effects.

Contraceptive prevalence reflects all methods—ineffective traditional methods as well as highly effective modern methods. Contraceptive prevalence rates are obtained mainly from Demographic and Health Surveys and contraceptive prevalence surveys (see *Primary data documentation* for the most recent survey year). Unmarried women are often excluded from such surveys, which may bias the estimates.

The share of births attended by skilled health staff is an indicator of a health system's ability to provide adequate care for pregnant women. Good antenatal and postnatal care improves maternal health and

reduces maternal and infant mortality. But data may not reflect such improvements because health information systems are often weak, maternal deaths are underreported, and rates of maternal mortality are difficult to measure.

Maternal mortality ratios are generally of unknown reliability, as are many other cause-specific mortality indicators. Household surveys such as the Demographic and Health Surveys attempt to measure maternal mortality by asking respondents about survivorship of sisters. The main disadvantage of this method is that the estimates of maternal mortality that it produces pertain to 12 years or so before the survey, making them unsuitable for monitoring recent changes or observing the impact of interventions. In addition, measurement of maternal mortality is subject to many types of errors. Even in high-income countries with vital registration systems, misclassification of maternal deaths has been found to lead to serious underestimation.

The maternal mortality ratios shown in the table as national estimates are based on national surveys, vital registration, or surveillance or are derived from community and hospital records. Those shown as modeled estimates are based on an exercise carried out by the World Health Organization (WHO) and United Nations Children's Fund (UNICEF). In this exercise maternal mortality was estimated with a regression model using information on fertility, birth attendants, and HIV prevalence. Neither set of ratios can be assumed to provide an accurate estimate of maternal mortality in any of the countries in the table.

Definitions

• **Total fertility rate** is the number of children that would be born to a woman if she were to live to the end of her childbearing years and bear children in accordance with current age-specific fertility rates. • **Adolescent fertility rate** is the number of births per 1,000 women ages 15–19. • **Women at risk of unintended pregnancy** are fertile, married women of reproductive age who do not want to become pregnant and are not using contraception. • **Contraceptive prevalence rate** is the percentage of women who are practicing, or whose sexual partners are practicing, any form of contraception. It is usually measured for married women ages 15–49 only. • **Births attended by skilled health staff** are the percentage of deliveries attended by personnel trained to give the necessary supervision, care, and advice to women during pregnancy, labor, and the postpartum period, to conduct deliveries on their own, and to care for newborns. • **Maternal mortality ratio** is the number of women who die from pregnancy-related causes during pregnancy and childbirth, per 100,000 live births.

Data sources

The data on reproductive health come from Demographic and Health Surveys, the WHO's *Coverage of Maternity Care* (1997) and other WHO sources, UNICEF, and national statistical offices. Modeled estimates for maternal mortality ratios are from Kenneth Hill, Carla AbouZahr, and Tessa Wardlaw's "Estimates of Maternal Mortality for 1995" (2001).

	Prevalence of undernourishment		Prevalence of child malnutrition % of children under 5		Prevalence of overweight		Prevalence of anemia	Low-birthweight babies	Exclusive breastfeeding	Consumption of iodized salt	Vitamin A supplementation
	% of population		Weight for age 1993–2001[a]	Height for age 1993–2001[a]	Year	% of children under 5	% of pregnant women 1985–2000[a]	% of births 1992–2000[a]	% of children under 6 months 1995–2001[a]	% of households 1997–2002[a]	% of children 6–59 months 2000
	1990–92	1998–2000									
Afghanistan	63	70	49	48	1997	4	..	20	..	..	70
Albania	..	..	14	15	1996–98	6	..	8	6	56	..
Algeria	5	6	6	18	2000	10	42	..	13	69	..
Angola	61	50	41	53	1996	1	29	..	11	10	100
Argentina	..	..	5	12	1995–96	9	26	7	..	90	..
Armenia	..	..	3	13	1998	6	..	..	30	84	..
Australia	..	..	0	0	1995–96	5	..	7	..	..	..
Austria	..	..	..	..			..	6	..	..	..
Azerbaijan	..	..	17	20	1997	4	..	6	7	41	..
Bangladesh	35	35	48	45	1996–97	1	53	50	46	70	85
Belarus	..	..	..	..			..	6	..	37	..
Belgium	..	..	..	..			..	..	..	..	..
Benin	19	13	23	31	1996	1	41	9	38	72	96
Bolivia	26	23	8	27	1998	7	54	9	29	63	73
Bosnia and Herzegovina	..	..	4				..	..	..	..	..
Botswana	17	25	13	29			..	..	34	66	..
Brazil	13	10	6	11	1996	5	33	8	..	95	11
Bulgaria	..	..	..	..			..	..	9[b]	..	..	..
Burkina Faso	23	23	34	37	1998–99	1	24	..	6	23	93
Burundi	49	69	45	..	1987	1	68	16	62	68	96
Cambodia	43	36	45	45	1996	3	..	18	12	14	63
Cameroon	32	25	22	29	1998	5	44	..	12	84	100
Canada	..	..	..	..			..	6	..	..	..
Central African Republic	49	44	23	28	1995	1	67	..	17	87	100
Chad	58	32	28	29	1996–97	1	37	..	10	58	99
Chile	8	4	1	2	1999	8	13	5	73	100	..
China	16	9	10	14	2000	3	52	6	67	91	..
Hong Kong, China	..	..	..	..			..	5	..	..	..
Colombia	17	13	7	14	1995	3	24	17	32	92	..
Congo, Dem. Rep.	32	73	34	45			..	20	24	72	93
Congo, Rep.	37	32	..	..	1987	1	..	..	4	..	100
Costa Rica	6	5	5	6	1996	6	27	6	35	97	..
Côte d'Ivoire	18	15	21	25	1994	2	34	..	10	31	16
Croatia	..	..	1	1	1995–96	6	..	8	23	90	..
Cuba	5	13	..	..			..	47	8	41	0	..
Czech Republic	..	..	..	..	1991	4	23	6	..	..	..
Denmark	..	..	..	..			..	5	..	..	..
Dominican Republic	27	26	5	11	1996	5	..	14	11	18	9
Ecuador	8	5	14	26			..	17	17	29	99	25
Egypt, Arab Rep.	5	4	4	19	2000	9	24	9	57	28	..
El Salvador	12	14	12	23	1998	3	14	11	16	91	..
Eritrea	..	58	44	38	1995–96	1	..	..	59	97	74
Estonia	..	..	..	..			..	4	..	..	..
Ethiopia	..	44	47	52			..	42	9	55	28	65
Finland	..	..	..	..			..	4	..	..	..
France	..	..	..	..			..	6	..	..	..
Gabon	11	8	12	21			..	..	..	6	15	100
Gambia, The	21	21	17	30			..	80	..	26	8	87
Georgia	..	..	3	12	1999	13	..	5	18	8	..
Germany	..	..	..	..			..	..	..	..	..
Ghana	35	12	25	26	1998–99	2	64	8	31	28	89
Greece	..	..	..	..			..	..	..	..	..
Guatemala	14	25	24	46	1998–99	4	45	8	39	49	..
Guinea	40	32	33	41			..	..	13	11	12	99
Guinea-Bissau	..	..	25	..			..	74	..	37	2	91
Haiti	64	50	17	23	2000	3	64	15	24	11	32

	Prevalence of undernourishment		Prevalence of child malnutrition % of children under 5		Prevalence of overweight		Prevalence of anemia	Low-birthweight babies	Exclusive breastfeeding	Consumption of iodized salt	Vitamin A supplementation
	% of population		Weight for age	Height for age		% of children	% of pregnant women	% of births	% of children under 6 months	% of households	% of children 6–59 months
	1990–92	1998–2000	1993–2001[a]	1993–2001[a]	Year	under 5	1985–2000[a]	1992–2000[a]	1995–2001[a]	1997–2002[a]	2000
Honduras	23	21	17	39	1996	1	14	9	42	80	60
Hungary	..	..	..	..	1980–88	2	..	8	..	..	..
India	25	24	53	52	1998–99	2	88	34	37	49	22
Indonesia	..	6	25	42	1995	4	64	15	42	64	71
Iran, Islamic Rep.	4	5	11	15	1998	4	17	10	66	94	..
Iraq	7	27	..	..		..	18	24	..	40	..
Ireland	..	..	..	..		..	..	..	..	..	..
Israel	..	..	..	..		..	..	8	..	..	..
Italy	..	..	..	..		..	..	..	..	..	..
Jamaica	14	9	4	4	1997	4	40	11	..	100	..
Japan	..	..	..	..	1978–81	2	..	8	..	..	..
Jordan	4	6	5	8	1997	6	50	2	11	88	..
Kazakhstan	..	..	4	10	1999	3	27	9	36	20	..
Kenya	47	44	22	33	1998	4	35	..	5	91	90
Korea, Dem. Rep.	18	34	28	..		..	71	..	97	..	96
Korea, Rep.	..	..	..	..		..	..	..	..	..	..
Kuwait	22	4	2	3	1996–97	6	40	7	12	..	..
Kyrgyz Republic	..	..	11	25	1997	6	..	6	24	27	..
Lao PDR	29	24	40	41		..	62	60	23	76	58
Latvia	..	..	..	..		..	..	4	..	..	..
Lebanon	..	3	3	12		..	49	19	27	87	..
Lesotho	27	26	18	44		..	7	..	16	69	17
Liberia	33	39	..	..		..	78	..	73	..	83
Libya	..	..	5	15		..	..	4	..	90	..
Lithuania	..	..	..	..		..	..	4	..	..	..
Macedonia, FYR	..	..	6	7	1999	5	..	8	37	100	..
Madagascar	35	40	40	48	1997	2	..	15	41	76	58
Malawi	49	33	25	49	2000	7	55	..	44	49	54
Malaysia	3		20			..	56	8	..	..	..
Mali	25	20	27	49	1995–96	1	58	..	8	9	70
Mauritania	14	12	32	35		..	24	9	28	2	81
Mauritius	6	5	15	10	1995	4	29	..	16	0	..
Mexico	5	5	8	18	1998–99	5	41	9	38	90	..
Moldova	..	..	..	..		..	20	5	..	33	..
Mongolia	34	42	13	25	1999	5	45	11	51	68	87
Morocco	6	7	..	..	1992	7	45	4	31	..	..
Mozambique	69	55	26	36	1997	3	58	..	30	62	92
Myanmar	10	6	43	45	1997	8	58	24	11	46	67
Namibia	15	9	..	..	1992	3	16	12	14	63	81
Nepal	19	19	48	51	1997–98	1	65	23	69	63	82
Netherlands	..	..	..	..	1980	2	..	6	..	..	..
New Zealand	..	..	..	..		..	..	6	..	83	..
Nicaragua	30	29	12	25	1997–98	4	36	8	22	86	..
Niger	42	36	40	40	2000	1	41	..	1	44	92
Nigeria	13	7	31	34	1993	3	55	..	17	98	79
Norway	..	..	..	..		..	..	5	..	..	..
Oman	..	..	23	23	1994–95	1	54	8	31	61	..
Pakistan	25	19	38	36	1995	1	37	25	16	19	95
Panama	19	18	8	18	1997	4	..	8	25	95	..
Papua New Guinea	25	27	..	..	1982–83	2	16	16	59	..	..
Paraguay	18	14	..	..	1990	4	44	9	7	83	..
Peru	40	11	7	25	1996	6	53	6	71	93	..
Philippines	26	23	32	32	1998	1	48	11	37	22	90
Poland	..	..	..	..		..	..	8	..	..	..
Portugal	..	..	..	..		..	..	7	..	..	..
Puerto Rico	..	..	..	..		..	..	14	..	..	..

	Prevalence of undernourishment % of population		Prevalence of child malnutrition % of children under 5		Prevalence of overweight		Prevalence of anemia % of pregnant women	Low-birthweight babies % of births	Exclusive breastfeeding % of children under 6 months	Consumption of iodized salt % of households	Vitamin A supplementation % of children 6–59 months
	1990–92	1998–2000	Weight for age 1993–2001[a]	Height for age 1993–2001[a]	Year	% of children under 5	1985–2000[a]	1992–2000[a]	1995–2001[a]	1997–2002[a]	2000
Romania	..	..	..	..	1991	2	31	10	..	..	..
Russian Federation	..	..	3	13		..	30	5		30	..
Rwanda	34	40	24	43	1996	2	..	..	84	82	59
Saudi Arabia	4	3	..	..		..	..	5	31	..	..
Senegal	23	25	18	23	1996	3	26	..	24	31	93
Sierra Leone	46	47	27	..		..	31	..	4	23	77
Singapore	..	..	..	..		..	..	7	..	..	..
Slovak Republic	..	..	..	..		..	..	6	..	..	..
Slovenia	..	..	..	..		..	..	5	..	..	..
Somalia	67	71	26	23		..	78	..	9	..	100
South Africa	..	..	9	23	1994–95	7	37	..	6	62	..
Spain	..	..	..	..		..	..	..	..	..	..
Sri Lanka	29	23	33	20	1995	0	39	18	54	88	..
Sudan	31	21	11	34		..	36	15	13	1	99
Swaziland	10	12	10	..		..	..	..	24	54	..
Sweden	..	..	..	..		..	..	4	..	..	..
Switzerland	..	..	..	..		..	..	5	..	..	..
Syrian Arab Republic	5	3	13	21		..	..	7	..	40	7
Tajikistan	..	..	..	31		..	50	8	14	20	..
Tanzania	36	47	29	44	1999	3	59	17	32	67	45
Thailand	28	18	18	13	1995	3	57	7	4	74	..
Togo	28	23	25	22	1998	2	48	..	18	67	100
Trinidad and Tobago	13	12	..	..	1987	3	53	14	2	1	..
Tunisia	..	..	4	8	1998	5	38	16	12	97	..
Turkey	..	..	8	16	1998	2	74	..	7	64	..
Turkmenistan	..	..	12	22		..	..	5	13	75	..
Uganda	23	21	23	39	1995	3	30	..	65	95	42
Ukraine	..	..	3	16		..	..	8	..	5	..
United Arab Emirates	3	..	7	..		..	..	6	34	..	..
United Kingdom	..	..	..	..		..	..	6	..	..	..
United States	..	..	1	2	1988–94	5	..	7	..	..	..
Uruguay	6	3	4	10	1992–93	6	20	8	..	..	..
Uzbekistan	..	..	19	31	1996	14	..	6	16	19	..
Venezuela, RB	11	21	4	13	2000	3	29	12	7	90	..
Vietnam	27	18	34	37	2000	3	..	11	31	40	61
West Bank and Gaza	..	..	15	..		..	..	6	..	..	..
Yemen, Rep.	36	33	46	52	1997	6	..	26	18	39	95
Yugoslavia, Fed. Rep.	..	..	2	5	1996	13	..	..	11	73	..
Zambia	45	50	24	42	1996–97	3	34	10	11	54	86
Zimbabwe	43	38	13	27	1999	7	..	11	33	93	..
World	**21 w**	**18 w**	**.. w**	**.. w**			**57 w**	**18 w**		**67 w**	**.. w**
Low income	28	25	..	..			65	27		61	53
Middle income	15	10	13	25			44	8		69	..
Lower middle income	16	10	10	17			46	8		87	..
Upper middle income	9	9	9	..			36	8		67	..
Low & middle income	21	18	..	..			57	19		74	51
East Asia & Pacific	17	11	15	14			54	9		25	..
Europe & Central Asia	..	..	..	..			..	7		89	..
Latin America & Carib.	14	12	9	19			35	10		53	..
Middle East & N. Africa	7	8	15	..			28	11		66	..
South Asia	27	25	53	47			77	34		60	38
Sub-Saharan Africa	32	33	..	..			46	..		..	78
High income	..	..	..	..			..	7		..	..
Europe EMU	..	..	..	..			..	..		..	..

a. Data are for the most recent year available. b. Data are for 2001.

Data on undernourishment are produced by the Food and Agriculture Organization (FAO) based on the calories available from local food production, trade, and stocks; the number of calories needed by different age and gender groups; the proportion of the population represented by each age group; and a coefficient of distribution to take account of inequality in access to food (FAO 2000). From a policy and program standpoint, however, this measure has its limits. First, food insecurity exists even where food availability is not a problem because of inadequate access of poor households to food. Second, food insecurity is an individual or household phenomenon, and the average food available to each person, even corrected for possible effects of low income, is not a good predictor of food insecurity among the population. And third, nutrition security is determined not only by food security but also by the quality of care of mothers and children and the quality of the household's health environment (Smith and Haddad 2000).

Estimates of child malnutrition, based on weight for age (underweight) and height for age (stunting), are from national survey data. The proportion of children who are underweight is the most common indicator of malnutrition. Being underweight, even mildly, increases the risk of death and inhibits cognitive development in children. Moreover, it perpetuates the problem from one generation to the next, as malnourished women are more likely to have low-birthweight babies. Height for age reflects linear growth achieved pre- and postnatally, and a deficit indicates long-term, cumulative effects of inadequacies of health, diet, or care. It is often argued that stunting is a proxy for multifaceted deprivation.

Estimates of children who are overweight are also from national survey data. Overweight in children has become a growing concern in developing countries. Researchers show an association between obesity in childhood and a high prevalence of diabetes, respiratory disease, high blood pressure, and psychosocial and orthopedic disorders (de Onis and Blossner 2000). The survey data were analyzed in a standardized way by the World Health Organization (WHO) to allow comparisons across countries.

Adequate quantities of micronutrients (vitamins and minerals) are essential for healthy growth and development. Studies indicate that more people are deficient in iron (anemic) than any other micronutrient, and most are women of reproductive age. Anemia during pregnancy can harm both the mother and the fetus, causing loss of the baby, premature birth, or low birthweight. Estimates of the prevalence of anemia among pregnant women are generally drawn from clinical data, which suffer from two weaknesses: the sample is based on those who seek care and is therefore not random, and private clinics or hospitals may not be part of the reporting network.

Low birthweight, which is associated with maternal malnutrition, raises the risk of infant mortality and stunts growth in infancy and childhood. Estimates of low-birthweight infants are drawn mostly from hospital records. But many births in developing countries take place at home, and these births are seldom recorded. A hospital birth may indicate higher income and therefore better nutrition, or it could indicate a higher-risk birth, possibly skewing the data on birthweights downward. The data should therefore be treated with caution.

It is estimated that breastfeeding can save some 1.5 million children a year. Breast milk alone contains all the nutrients, antibodies, hormones, and antioxidants an infant needs to thrive. It protects babies from diarrhea and acute respiratory infections, stimulates their immune systems and response to vaccination, and, according to some studies, confers cognitive benefits as well. The data on breastfeeding are derived from national surveys.

Iodine deficiency is the single most important cause of preventable mental retardation, and it contributes significantly to the risk of stillbirth and miscarriage. Iodized salt is the best source of iodine, and a global campaign to iodize edible salt is significantly reducing the risks (UNICEF, *The State of the World's Children 1999*).

Vitamin A is essential for the functioning of the immune system. A child deficient in vitamin A faces a 25 percent greater risk of dying from a range of childhood ailments such as measles, malaria, or diarrhea. Improving the vitamin A status of pregnant women helps reduce anemia, improves their resistance to infection, and may reduce their risk of dying during pregnancy and childbirth. Giving vitamin A to new mothers who are breastfeeding helps to protect their children during the first months of life. Food fortification with vitamin A is being introduced in many developing countries.

• **Prevalence of undernourishment** is the percentage of the population that is undernourished. • **Prevalence of child malnutrition** is the percentage of children under five whose weight for age and height for age are more than two standard deviations below the median for the international reference population ages 0–59 months. For children up to two years of age, height is measured by recumbent length. For older children, height is measured by stature while standing. The reference population, adopted by the WHO in 1983, is based on children from the United States, who are assumed to be well nourished. • **Prevalence of overweight** is the percentage of children under five whose weight for height is more than two standard deviations above the median for the international reference population of the corresponding age, established by the U.S. National Center for Health Statistics and the WHO. • **Prevalence of anemia,** or iron deficiency, is the percentage of pregnant women with hemoglobin levels less than 11 grams per deciliter of blood. • **Low-birthweight babies** are newborns weighing less than 2,500 grams, with the measurement taken within the first hours of life, before significant postnatal weight loss has occurred. • **Exclusive breastfeeding** refers to the percentage of children less than 6 months old who are fed breast milk alone (no other liquids). • **Consumption of iodized salt** refers to the percentage of households that use edible salt fortified with iodine. • **Vitamin A supplementation** refers to the percentage of children ages 6–59 months who received at least one high-dose vitamin A capsule in the previous six months.

Data sources

Data are drawn from a variety of sources, including the FAO's *State of Food Insecurity in the World 2002*; the United Nations Administrative Committee on Coordination, Subcommittee on Nutrition's *Update on the Nutrition Situation*; the WHO's *World Health Report 2002*; and the United Nations Children's Fund's (UNICEF) *State of the World's Children 2003*.

Health: risk factors and future challenges

	Prevalence of smoking		Incidence of tuberculosis	Prevalence of HIV		
	% of adults		per 100,000	% of	% of ages 15–24 [a]	
	Males	Females	people	adults	Male	Female
	2000	**2000**	**2000**	**2001**	**2001**	**2001**
Afghanistan	..	..	321	*<0.01*	..	..
Albania	60	18	29	*<0.01*	..	..
Algeria	44	7	46	0.10	..	..
Angola	..	..	275	5.50	2.23	5.74
Argentina	47	34	48	0.70	0.86	0.34
Armenia	64	1	69	0.20	0.22	0.06
Australia	21	18	8	0.10	0.12	0.01
Austria	30	19	15	0.20	0.22	0.12
Azerbaijan	30	1	74	<0.10	0.06	0.01
Bangladesh	54	24	242	<0.10	0.01	0.01
Belarus	55	5	88	0.30	0.58	0.19
Belgium	30	26	14	0.20	0.12	0.12
Benin	..	..	259	3.60	1.17	3.71
Bolivia	43	18	230	<0.10	0.11	0.05
Bosnia and Herzegovina			91	0.10	..	..
Botswana	..	..	757	38.80	16.08	37.49
Brazil	38	29	68	0.70	0.64	0.48
Bulgaria	49	24	41 [b]	<0.10	..	..
Burkina Faso	..	..	324	6.50	3.97	9.73
Burundi	..	..	406	8.30	4.95	11.05
Cambodia	66	8	572	2.70	0.96	2.48
Cameroon	..	..	341	11.80	5.44	12.67
Canada	27	23	7	0.30	0.28	0.17
Central African Republic	..	..	445	12.90	5.82	13.54
Chad	24	..	274	3.60	2.38	4.28
Chile	26	18	25	0.30	0.35	0.13
China	67	4	107	0.10	0.16	0.09
Hong Kong, China	..	..	91	0.10	0.00	0.00
Colombia	24	21	50	0.40	0.85	0.19
Congo, Dem. Rep.	..	6	320	4.90	2.92	5.91
Congo, Rep.	..	..	338	7.20	3.28	7.80
Costa Rica	29	7	16	0.60	0.58	0.27
Côte d'Ivoire	42	2	389	9.70	2.91	8.31
Croatia	34	32	59	<0.10	0.00	0.00
Cuba	48	26	14	<0.10	0.09	0.05
Czech Republic	36	22	19	<0.10	0.00	0.00
Denmark	32	29	13	0.20	0.14	0.06
Dominican Republic	24	17	147	2.50	2.10	2.76
Ecuador	46	17	176	0.30	0.31	0.15
Egypt, Arab Rep.	35	2	39	<0.10	..	..
El Salvador	38	12	64	0.60	0.77	0.35
Eritrea	..	..	289	2.80	2.78	4.30
Estonia	44	20	67	1.00	2.48	0.62
Ethiopia	..	..	397	6.40	4.39	7.82
Finland	27	20	11	<0.10	0.04	0.03
France	39	30	15	0.30	0.26	0.17
Gabon	..	..	293	*4.16*	*2.32*	*4.72*
Gambia, The	34	2	264	1.60	0.52	1.35
Georgia	61	15	75	<0.10	0.08	0.02
Germany	39	31	12	0.10	0.10	0.05
Ghana	28	4	286	3.00	1.36	2.97
Greece	47	29	22	0.20	0.14	0.06
Guatemala	38	18	85	1.00	0.90	0.85
Guinea	60	44	270	*1.54*	*0.57*	*1.43*
Guinea-Bissau	..	..	271	2.80	1.06	2.98
Haiti	11	9	350	6.10	4.06	4.95

Health: risk factors and future challenges

	Prevalence of smoking		Incidence of tuberculosis	Prevalence of HIV		
	% of adults		per 100,000 people	% of adults	% of ages 15–24 [a]	
	Males	Females			Male	Female
	2000	**2000**	**2000**	**2001**	**2001**	**2001**
Honduras	36	11	91	1.60	1.20	1.50
Hungary	44	27	41	0.10	0.09	0.02
India	29	3	184	0.80	0.34	0.71
Indonesia	59	4	280	0.10	0.06	0.06
Iran, Islamic Rep.	27	3	53	<0.10	0.05	0.01
Iraq	40	5	132	<0.10	..	..
Ireland	32	31	14	0.10	0.06	0.05
Israel	33	24	11	0.10	*0.06*	*0.06*
Italy	32	17	9	0.40	0.28	0.26
Jamaica	..	..	8	1.20	0.82	0.86
Japan	53	13	36	<0.10	0.01	0.04
Jordan	48	10	10	<0.10	..	..
Kazakhstan	60	7	152	0.10	0.13	0.03
Kenya	67	32	484	15.00	6.01	15.56
Korea, Dem. Rep.	..	..	175	*<0.01*	..	..
Korea, Rep.	65	5	62	<0.10	0.03	0.01
Kuwait	30	2	31	*0.12*	..	..
Kyrgyz Republic	60	16	153	<0.10	0.00	0.00
Lao PDR	41	15	160	<0.10	0.05	0.03
Latvia	49	13	118	0.40	0.94	0.24
Lebanon	46	35	22	*0.09*	..	..
Lesotho	39	1	578	31.00	17.40	38.08
Liberia	..	..	275	*2.80*	..	..
Libya	..	..	24	0.20	..	..
Lithuania	51	16	111	0.10	0.16	0.05
Macedonia, FYR	40	33	52	<0.10	0.00	0.00
Madagascar	..	..	254	0.30	0.06	0.23
Malawi	20	9	447	15.00	6.35	14.89
Malaysia	49	4	111	0.40	0.70	0.12
Mali	..	..	267	1.70	1.37	2.08
Mauritania	..	..	226	*0.52*	*0.38*	*0.59*
Mauritius	45	3	69	0.10	*0.04*	*0.04*
Mexico	51	18	38	0.30	0.37	0.09
Moldova	46	18	135	0.20	0.46	0.14
Mongolia	68	26	216	<0.10	..	..
Morocco	35	2	118	0.10	..	..
Mozambique	..	..	433	13.00	6.13	14.67
Myanmar	44	22	168	*1.99*	*1.04*	*1.72*
Namibia	65	35	521	22.50	11.10	24.29
Nepal	48	29	208	0.50	0.26	0.28
Netherlands	37	29	9	0.20	0.20	0.09
New Zealand	25	25	11	0.10	0.05	0.01
Nicaragua	..	..	85	0.20	0.23	0.08
Niger	..	..	256	*1.35*	*0.95*	*1.50*
Nigeria	15	2	305	5.80	2.99	5.82
Norway	31	32	6	0.10	0.08	0.04
Oman	16	2	9	0.10	..	..
Pakistan	36	9	175	0.10	0.06	0.05
Panama	56	20	52	1.50	1.88	1.25
Papua New Guinea	46	28	262	0.70	0.33	0.39
Paraguay	24	6	66	*0.11*	*0.13*	*0.04*
Peru	42	16	212	0.40	0.41	0.18
Philippines	54	11	330	<0.10	0.01	0.01
Poland	44	25	36	0.10	0.09	0.05
Portugal	30	7	52	0.50	0.41	0.19
Puerto Rico	..	..	9	..	..	..

	Prevalence of smoking		Incidence of tuberculosis	Prevalence of HIV		
	% of adults		per 100,000	% of	% of ages 15–24 [a]	
	Males	Females	people	adults	Male	Female
	2000	2000	2000	2001	2001	2001
Romania	62	25	135	<0.10	*0.02*	*0.02*
Russian Federation	63	10	132	0.90	1.87	0.67
Rwanda	7	4	405	8.90	4.91	11.20
Saudi Arabia	22	1	45	*0.01*	..	..
Senegal	..	..	261	0.50	0.19	0.54
Sierra Leone	..	..	278	7.00	2.48	7.53
Singapore	27	3	48	0.20	0.14	0.16
Slovak Republic	55	30	25	<0.10	0.00	0.00
Slovenia	30	20	26	<0.10	0.00	0.00
Somalia	..	..	360	1.00	..	..
South Africa	42	11	526	20.10	10.66	25.64
Spain	42	25	34	0.50	0.51	0.24
Sri Lanka	26	2	58	<0.10	0.03	0.04
Sudan	24	1	193	2.60	1.08	3.13
Swaziland	25	2	600	33.40	15.23	39.49
Sweden	19	19	5	0.10	0.06	0.05
Switzerland	39	28	11	0.50	0.46	0.40
Syrian Arab Republic	51	10	85	*0.01*	..	..
Tajikistan	..	..	160	<0.10	0.00	0.00
Tanzania	50	12	359	7.80	3.55	8.06
Thailand	44	3	140	1.80	1.11	1.66
Togo	..	..	317	6.00	2.05	5.93
Trinidad and Tobago	42	8	13	2.50	2.41	3.23
Tunisia	62	8	37	*0.04*	..	..
Turkey	65	24	36	<0.10	..	..
Turkmenistan	27	1	84	<0.10	0.00	0.00
Uganda	52	17	351	5.00	1.99	4.63
Ukraine	51	19	79	1.00	1.96	0.88
United Arab Emirates	18	1	21	*0.18*	..	..
United Kingdom	27	26	12	0.10	0.10	0.05
United States	26	22	5	0.60	0.47	0.22
Uruguay	32	14	28	0.30	0.52	0.20
Uzbekistan	49	9	104	<0.10	0.01	0.00
Venezuela, RB	42	39	42	0.50	*0.65*	*0.15*
Vietnam	51	4	189	0.30	0.31	0.17
West Bank and Gaza	..	..	28	..	..	..
Yemen, Rep.	60	29	107	0.10	..	..
Yugoslavia, Fed. Rep.	52	42	45	0.20	..	..
Zambia	35	10	529	21.50	8.06	20.98
Zimbabwe	34	1	584	33.70	12.38	33.01
World	**46 w**	**11 w**	**145 w**	**1.27 w**	**0.77 w**	**1.34 w**
Low income	37	7	233	2.29	1.13	2.37
Middle income	56	10	107	0.67	0.61	0.77
Lower middle income	59	7	119	0.68	0.62	0.85
Upper middle income	42	24	55	0.62	0.57	0.43
Low & middle income	48	9	168	1.44	0.87	1.58
East Asia & Pacific	63	5	147	0.19	0.19	0.16
Europe & Central Asia	56	17	91	0.45	1.08	0.41
Latin America & Carib.	40	24	73	0.67	0.68	0.46
Middle East & N. Africa	37	6	64	0.10	..	..
South Asia	33	6	190	0.64	0.27	0.55
Sub-Saharan Africa	..	..	354	8.36	4.12	9.34
High income	36	21	18	0.33	0.26	0.14
Europe EMU	37	26	17	0.28	0.24	0.15

a. Data are an average of high and low estimates. b. Data are for 2001.

The limited availability of data on health status is a major constraint in assessing the health situation in developing countries. Surveillance data are lacking for many major public health concerns. Estimates of prevalence and incidence are available for some diseases but are often unreliable and incomplete. National health authorities differ widely in their capacity and willingness to collect or report information. To compensate for the paucity of data and ensure reasonable reliability and international comparability, the World Health Organization (WHO) prepares estimates in accordance with epidemiological models and statistical standards.

Smoking is the most common form of tobacco use in many countries, and the prevalence of smoking is therefore a good measure of the extent of the tobacco epidemic (Corrao and others 2000). While the prevalence of smoking has been declining in some high-income countries, it has been increasing in many developing countries. Tobacco use causes heart and other vascular diseases and cancers of the lung and other organs. Given the long delay between starting to smoke and the onset of disease, the health impact of smoking in developing countries will increase rapidly in the next few decades. Because the data present a one-time esti-

mate, with no information on the intensity or duration of smoking, they should be interpreted with caution.

Tuberculosis is the main cause of death from a single infectious agent among adults in developing countries. In high-income countries tuberculosis has reemerged largely as a result of cases among immigrants. The estimates of tuberculosis incidence in the table are based on a new approach in which reported cases are adjusted using the ratio of case notifications to the estimated share of cases detected by panels of 80 epidemiologists convened by the WHO.

Adult HIV prevalence rates reflect the rate of HIV infection in each country's population. Low national prevalence rates can be very misleading, however. They often disguise serious epidemics that are initially concentrated in certain localities or among specific population groups and threaten to spill over into the wider population. In many parts of the developing world most new infections occur in young adults, with young women especially vulnerable. About a third of those living with HIV/AIDS are in the age group 15–24. The estimates of HIV prevalence are based on extrapolations from data collected through surveys and surveillance of small, nonrepresentative groups.

Definitions

• **Prevalence of smoking** is the percentage of men and women who smoke cigarettes. The age range varies among countries but in most is 18 and above or 15 and above. • **Incidence of tuberculosis** is the estimated number of new tuberculosis cases (pulmonary, smear positive, extrapulmonary). • **Prevalence of HIV** is the percentage of people who are infected with HIV.

2.19a

In some regions more young women than men are living with HIV/AIDS

15- to 24-year-olds living with HIV/AIDS (millions), 2001

In regions where HIV/AIDS is spread mainly through heterosexual activity, young women are infected in far greater numbers than young men. For both biological and social reasons, young women are especially vulnerable to HIV infection. Adolescent girls have an immature reproductive tract that makes them susceptible to infection. Girls and young women often have older partners who have already been exposed to HIV, and they may lack the knowledge or self-confidence to resist sexual advances or persuade older men to use a condom. Poverty is also a factor, as girls and women may exchange sex for money or gifts.

Source: Population Reference Bureau 2002.

Data sources

The data are drawn from a variety of sources, including the WHO's *World Health Report 2002*, *Tobacco Atlas 2002*, and *Global Tuberculosis Control Report 2002*; the NATIONS (National Tobacco Information Online System) database (http://apps.nccd.cdc.gov/nations/); and the Joint United Nations Programme on HIV/AIDS (UNAIDS) and WHO's *AIDS Epidemic Update* (2002).

	Life expectancy at birth		Infant mortality rate		Under-five mortality rate		Child mortality rate		Adult mortality rate		Survival to age 65	
	years		per 1,000 live births		per 1,000		Male per 1,000	Female per 1,000	Male per 1,000	Female per 1,000	% of cohort	
							1997–2001[a]	1997–2001[a]	2000–2001[a]	2000–2001[a]	Male	Female
	1980	2001	1980	2001	1980	2001					2002	2002
Afghanistan	40	43	183	165	280	257	..	..	437	376	32	33
Albania	69	74	47	23	57	25	..	..	209	95	77	85
Algeria	59	71	94	39	134	49	..	..	155	119	73	79
Angola	41	47	158	154	265	260	..	..	492	386	34	39
Argentina	70	74	33	16	38	19	..	..	184	92	75	87
Armenia	73	74	48	31	..	35	5	3	223	106	70	83
Australia	74	79	11	6	13	6	..	..	100	53	84	92
Austria	73	78	14	5	17	5	..	..	124	59	83	91
Azerbaijan	68	65	76	77	107	96	..	..	261	150	58	72
Bangladesh	49	62	129	51	205	77	28	38	262	252	59	61
Belarus	71	68	21	17	26	20	..	..	381	133	54	81
Belgium	73	78	12	5	15	6	..	..	127	66	82	91
Benin	48	53	127	94	214	158	72	79	384	328	43	50
Bolivia	52	63	112	60	170	77	26	29	264	219	59	67
Bosnia and Herzegovina	70	74	31	15	..	18	..	..	200	93	75	86
Botswana	58	39	62	80	84	110	..	..	703	669	13	18
Brazil	63	68	70	31	92	36	..	..	259	136	62	79
Bulgaria	71	72	20	14	25	16	..	..	239	103	69	83
Burkina Faso	44	44	140	104	247	197	131	128	559	507	28	32
Burundi	47	42	116	114	195	190	..	..	648	603	26	29
Cambodia	39	54	110	97	190	138	34	30	373	264	42	48
Cameroon	50	49	105	96	173	155	69	75	488	440	35	41
Canada	75	79	10	5	13	7	..	..	101	57	83	92
Central African Republic	46	43	121	115	189	180	..	..	620	573	24	29
Chad	42	48	124	117	225	200	106	99	449	361	38	43
Chile	69	76	32	10	39	12	..	..	151	67	78	88
China	67	70	42	31	64	39	..	..	161	110	72	79
Hong Kong, China	74	80	11	3	..	..	..	..	99	51	85	92
Colombia	66	72	40	19	56	23	4	3	238	115	71	83
Congo, Dem. Rep.	49	45	130	129	210	205	..	..	571	493	31	35
Congo, Rep.	50	51	88	81	125	108	..	..	475	406	35	44
Costa Rica	73	78	19	9	26	11	..	..	131	78	82	90
Côte d'Ivoire	49	46	114	102	172	175	83	58	553	494	31	34
Croatia	70	74	21	7	23	8	..	..	152	114	71	87
Cuba	74	77	20	7	22	9	..	..	143	94	81	88
Czech Republic	70	75	16	4	19	5	..	..	167	75	75	88
Denmark	74	77	8	4	10	4	..	..	129	81	80	88
Dominican Republic	63	67	71	41	92	47	13	8	234	146	63	75
Ecuador	63	70	64	24	98	30	..	..	199	120	72	77
Egypt, Arab Rep.	56	68	119	35	175	41	15	16	210	147	69	75
El Salvador	57	70	84	33	120	39	..	..	250	148	68	81
Eritrea	44	51	112	72	200	111	..	..	493	441	37	42
Estonia	69	71	17	11	25	12	..	..	316	114	60	85
Ethiopia	42	42	143	116	213	172	83	86	594	535	26	30
Finland	73	78	8	4	9	5	..	..	144	61	80	91
France	74	79	10	4	14	6	..	..	137	59	82	92
Gabon	48	53	68	60	105	90	32	33	380	330	45	51
Gambia, The	40	53	144	91	231	126	..	..	373	320	40	47
Georgia	71	73	35	24	43	29	..	..	250	133	71	87
Germany	73	78	12	4	16	5	..	..	126	60	81	90
Ghana	53	56	92	57	157	100	53	51	379	326	47	51
Greece	74	78	18	5	23	5	..	..	114	47	82	90
Guatemala	57	65	97	43	139	58	15	18	286	182	58	72
Guinea	40	46	175	109	300	169	101	98	432	366	32	33
Guinea-Bissau	39	45	173	130	290	211	..	..	495	427	34	39
Haiti	51	52	132	79	195	123	52	54	524	373	38	47

	Life expectancy at birth		Infant mortality rate		Under-five mortality rate		Child mortality rate		Adult mortality rate		Survival to age 65	
							Male per 1,000	Female per 1,000	Male per 1,000	Female per 1,000	% of cohort	
	years		per 1,000 live births		per 1,000		1997–	1997–	2000–	2000–	Male	Female
	1980	2001	1980	2001	1980	2001	2001[a]	2001[a]	2001[a]	2001[a]	2002	2002
Honduras	60	66	75	31	103	38	..	..	221	157	59	72
Hungary	70	72	23	8	26	9	..	..	295	123	66	85
India	54	63	113	67	173	93	25	37	250	191	61	65
Indonesia	55	66	79	33	125	45	19	20	230	178	64	72
Iran, Islamic Rep.	58	69	92	35	130	42	..	..	170	139	71	75
Iraq	62	62	63	107	83	133	..	..	258	208	63	67
Ireland	73	77	11	6	14	6	..	..	108	62	80	89
Israel	73	79	16	6	19	6	..	..	99	56	84	90
Italy	74	79	15	4	17	6	..	..	110	53	81	91
Jamaica	71	76	28	17	34	20	..	..	169	127	80	87
Japan	76	81	8	3	10	5	..	..	98	44	86	94
Jordan	64	72	52	27	67	33	4	7	199	144	74	81
Kazakhstan	67	63	50	81	60	99	11	6	366	201	47	71
Kenya	55	46	73	78	115	122	36	38	578	529	28	33
Korea, Dem. Rep.	67	61	32	42	43	55	..	..	238	192	54	62
Korea, Rep.	67	74	16	5	18	5	..	..	186	71	72	86
Kuwait	71	77	27	9	35	10	..	..	100	68	82	88
Kyrgyz Republic	65	66	90	52	115	61	10	11	335	299	56	75
Lao PDR	45	54	135	87	200	100	..	..	355	299	45	50
Latvia	69	70	20	17	26	21	..	..	328	122	60	84
Lebanon	65	71	38	28	44	32	..	..	192	136	71	79
Lesotho	53	43	115	91	168	132	..	..	667	630	26	29
Liberia	51	47	157	157	235	235	..	..	448	385	33	37
Libya	60	72	55	16	70	19	..	..	210	157	73	83
Lithuania	71	73	20	8	24	9	..	..	286	106	66	87
Macedonia, FYR	..	73	54	22	69	26	..	..	160	89	75	84
Madagascar	51	55	106	84	175	136	75	68	385	322	49	55
Malawi	44	38	157	114	265	183	101	102	701	653	20	23
Malaysia	67	73	31	8	42	8	..	..	202	113	72	83
Mali	42	41	171	141	295	231	..	..	518	446	25	29
Mauritania	47	51	118	120	175	183	38	38	357	302	43	49
Mauritius	66	72	33	17	40	19	..	..	228	109	70	85
Mexico	67	73	56	24	74	29	..	..	180	101	75	85
Moldova	66	67	41	27	53	32	..	..	325	165	58	75
Mongolia	58	65	97	61	140	76	..	..	280	199	65	71
Morocco	58	68	99	39	144	44	..	..	174	113	68	76
Mozambique	44	42	140	125	230	197	85	82	674	612	25	30
Myanmar	51	57	94	77	134	109	..	..	343	245	46	58
Namibia	53	44	84	55	114	67	..	..	695	661	22	25
Nepal	48	59	133	66	195	91	28	40	314	314	58	56
Netherlands	76	78	9	5	11	6	..	..	95	64	82	90
New Zealand	73	78	13	6	16	6	..	..	108	69	83	90
Nicaragua	59	69	85	36	120	43	12	11	225	161	67	77
Niger	42	46	191	156	320	265	184	202	473	308	30	37
Nigeria	46	46	117	110	196	183	66	69	443	393	33	36
Norway	76	79	8	4	11	4	..	..	106	60	83	91
Oman	60	74	41	12	95	13	..	..	187	135	78	84
Pakistan	55	63	105	84	157	109	..	..	221	198	64	70
Panama	70	75	34	19	46	25	..	..	145	93	78	86
Papua New Guinea	51	57	79	70	108	94	..	..	359	329	49	53
Paraguay	67	71	46	26	61	30	..	..	173	129	70	80
Peru	60	70	81	30	126	39	19	17	190	139	69	78
Philippines	61	70	65	29	81	38	21	19	249	142	71	77
Poland	70	74	26	8	29	9	..	..	226	88	71	87
Portugal	71	76	24	5	31	6	..	..	164	66	77	89
Puerto Rico	74	76	19	10	..	..	..	..	149	56	76	91

	Life expectancy at birth (years)		Infant mortality rate (per 1,000 live births)		Under-five mortality rate (per 1,000)		Child mortality rate		Adult mortality rate		Survival to age 65 (% of cohort)	
							Male per 1,000 1997–2001[a]	Female per 1,000 1997–2001[a]	Male per 1,000 2000–2001[a]	Female per 1,000 2000–2001[a]	Male	Female
	1980	2001	1980	2001	1980	2001					2002	2002
Romania	69	70	29	19	36	21	..	..	260	117	64	81
Russian Federation	67	66	22	18	..	21	..	..	424	153	48	77
Rwanda	46	40	130	96	219	183	..	..	667	599	23	25
Saudi Arabia	61	73	65	23	85	28	..	..	181	116	76	83
Senegal	45	52	128	79	218	138	76	74	355	303	38	47
Sierra Leone	35	37	192	182	336	316	..	..	587	531	24	29
Singapore	71	78	12	3	13	4	..	..	114	61	83	89
Slovak Republic	70	73	21	8	23	9	..	..	210	83	70	86
Slovenia	70	76	15	4	18	5	..	..	170	76	76	89
Somalia	43	47	133	133	225	225	..	..	516	452	38	44
South Africa	57	47	65	56	90	71	..	..	594	543	27	33
Spain	76	78	12	4	16	6	..	..	122	49	82	92
Sri Lanka	68	73	35	17	48	19	..	..	244	124	76	84
Sudan	48	58	86	65	142	107	..	..	341	291	53	58
Swaziland	52	45	99	106	143	149	..	..	635	595	26	30
Sweden	76	80	7	3	8	3	..	..	89	56	86	92
Switzerland	76	80	9	5	11	6	..	..	99	58	85	92
Syrian Arab Republic	62	70	54	23	73	28	..	..	170	132	69	79
Tajikistan	66	67	..	91	..	116	..	..	293	204	62	75
Tanzania	50	44	106	104	175	165	61	58	569	520	27	31
Thailand	64	69	45	24	58	28	..	..	245	150	67	77
Togo	49	49	106	79	175	141	73	65	460	406	37	42
Trinidad and Tobago	68	72	35	17	40	20	..	..	209	133	74	82
Tunisia	62	72	72	21	100	27	..	..	169	99	75	83
Turkey	61	70	103	36	133	43	10	13	218	120	69	79
Turkmenistan	64	65	67	69	133	87	19	17	280	157	57	72
Uganda	48	43	108	79	180	124	78	70	617	567	25	28
Ukraine	69	68	22	17	27	20	..	..	365	135	56	80
United Arab Emirates	68	75	23	8	27	9	..	..	143	93	80	85
United Kingdom	74	77	12	6	14	7	..	..	109	66	81	89
United States	74	78	13	7	15	8	..	..	141	82	81	91
Uruguay	70	74	37	14	42	16	..	..	185	89	74	88
Uzbekistan	67	67	47	52	62	68	..	..	282	176	63	77
Venezuela, RB	68	74	34	19	42	22	..	..	178	99	75	85
Vietnam	60	69	50	30	70	38	10	13	203	139	68	78
West Bank and Gaza	..	72	..	21	..	25	..	..	157	100	74	83
Yemen, Rep.	49	57	135	79	205	107	33	36	278	226	50	53
Yugoslavia, Fed. Rep.	70	73	33	17	..	19	..	..	180	100	73	83
Zambia	50	37	92	112	149	202	..	..	725	687	16	21
Zimbabwe	55	39	69	76	108	123	35	31	650	612	18	20
World	**63 w**	**67 w**	**78 w**	**56 w**	**121 w**	**81 w**	**.. w**	**.. w**	**234 w**	**165 w**	**65 w**	**72 w**
Low income	53	59	109	80	171	121	..	..	312	256	55	60
Middle income	66	70	55	31	80	38	..	..	207	127	68	78
Lower middle income	65	69	55	33	83	41	..	..	205	130	68	77
Upper middle income	66	72	52	23	68	27	..	..	218	114	67	81
Low & middle income	60	64	86	61	132	88	..	..	255	186	62	69
East Asia & Pacific	64	69	53	34	79	44	..	..	184	129	69	75
Europe & Central Asia	68	69	43	30	..	36	..	..	317	137	60	80
Latin America & Carib.	65	71	61	28	84	34	..	..	221	124	66	80
Middle East & N. Africa	58	68	94	44	134	54	..	..	193	143	67	73
South Asia	54	63	115	71	176	99	25	37	252	202	61	64
Sub-Saharan Africa	48	46	118	105	192	171	..	..	520	461	39	44
High income	74	78	12	5	15	7	..	..	128	66	80	90
Europe EMU	74	78	13	4	16	6	..	..	125	58	80	90

a. Data are for the most recent year available.

Mortality rates for different age groups—infants, children, or adults—and overall indicators of mortality—life expectancy at birth or survival to a given age—are important indicators of health status in a country. Because data on the incidence and prevalence of diseases (morbidity data) are frequently unavailable, mortality rates are often used to identify vulnerable populations. And they are among the indicators most frequently used to compare levels of socioeconomic development across countries.

The main sources of mortality data are vital registration systems and direct or indirect estimates based on sample surveys or censuses. A "complete" vital registration system—one covering at least 90 percent of vital events in the population—is the best source of age-specific mortality data. But such systems are fairly uncommon in developing countries. Thus estimates must be obtained from sample surveys or derived by applying indirect estimation techniques to registration, census, or survey data. Survey data are subject to recall error, and surveys estimating infant deaths require large samples because households in which a birth or an infant death has occurred during a given year cannot ordinarily be preselected for sampling. Indirect estimates rely on estimated actuarial ("life") tables that may be inappropriate for the population concerned. Because life expectancy at birth is constructed using infant mortality data and model life tables, similar reliability issues arise for this indicator.

Life expectancy at birth and age-specific mortality rates for 2001 (or for the most recent year available) are generally estimates based on vital registration or the most recent census or survey available (see *Primary data documentation*). Extrapolations based on outdated surveys may not be reliable for monitoring changes in health status or for comparative analytical work.

To produce harmonized estimates of infant and under-five mortality rates that make use of all available information in a transparent way, a methodology that fits a regression line to the relationship between mortality rates and their reference dates using weighted least squares was developed and adopted by both UNICEF and the World Bank. (For further discussion of methodology for childhood mortality estimates, see Hill and others 1999.)

Infant and child mortality rates are higher for boys than for girls in countries in which parental gender preferences are insignificant. Child mortality captures the effect of gender discrimination better than does infant mortality, as malnutrition and medical interventions are more important in this age group. Where female child mortality is higher, as in some countries in South Asia, girls probably have unequal access to resources.

Adult mortality rates have increased in many countries in Sub-Saharan Africa and Europe and Central Asia. In Sub-Saharan Africa the increase stems from AIDS-related mortality and affects both men and women. In Europe and Central Asia the causes are more diverse and affect men more. They include a high prevalence of smoking, a high-fat diet, excessive alcohol use, and stressful conditions related to the economic transition.

The percentage of a cohort surviving to age 65 reflects both child and adult mortality rates. Like life expectancy, it is a synthetic measure based on current age-specific mortality rates and used in the construction of life tables. It shows that even in countries where mortality is high, a certain share of the current birth cohort will live well beyond the life expectancy at birth, while in low-mortality countries close to 90 percent will reach at least age 65.

• **Life expectancy at birth** is the number of years a newborn infant would live if prevailing patterns of mortality at the time of its birth were to stay the same throughout its life. • **Infant mortality rate** is the number of infants dying before reaching one year of age, per 1,000 live births in a given year. • **Under-five mortality rate** is the probability that a newborn baby will die before reaching age five, if subject to current age-specific mortality rates. The probability is expressed as a rate per 1,000. • **Child mortality rate** is the probability of dying between the ages of one and five, if subject to current age-specific mortality rates. The probability is expressed as a rate per 1,000. • **Adult mortality rate** is the probability of dying between the ages of 15 and 60—that is, the probability of a 15-year-old dying before reaching age 60, if subject to current age-specific mortality rates between ages 15 and 60. • **Survival to age 65** refers to the percentage of a cohort of newborn infants that would survive to age 65, if subject to current age-specific mortality rates.

2.20a

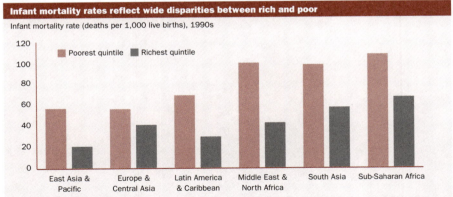

Infant mortality rates reflect wide disparities between rich and poor

Infant mortality rate (deaths per 1,000 live births), 1990s

Wide disparities between the rich and poor in many countries indicate the persistence of deprivation among poor people. They have less access to basic health services, safe drinking water, adequate nutrition, and safe motherhood and child initiatives. All this is reflected in higher infant mortality among the poor.

Note: The figure covers the 45 developing countries for which survey data for various years between 1990 and 1998 have been converted into quintiles.
Source: Demographic and Health surveys; World Bank data files.

Data sources

The data are from the United Nations Statistics Division's *Population and Vital Statistics Report*, publications and other releases from national statistical offices, Demographic and Health Surveys from national sources and Macro International, and the United Nations Children's Fund's (UNICEF) *State of the World's Children 2003*.

3|ENVIRONMENT

If the vision of a world without poverty is to be realized, sustainable development is the key. And whether the world continues to sustain itself depends in large part on proper management of its natural resources. The Millennium Development Goals call for integrating principles of environmental sustainability into country policies and programs and reversing environmental losses. This requires measuring and monitoring the state of the environment and its changes as well as the links between the economy and the environment.

Given the close links between economic activity and environmental change, there is a strong argument for developing indicators that integrate the economy and the environment more closely. One approach that appears to hold much promise is environmental accounting. Aimed at deriving "greener" measures of national income, savings, and wealth, environmental accounting adds natural resources and pollutants to the assets and liabilities measured in the standard national accounts. This approach forms the basis of the United Nations System of Environmental and Economic Accounts (United Nations 1993, 1999; Commission of the European Communities and others 2002). But preparing full-fledged environmental and economic accounts is costly, and not all countries are doing so. In the absence of such integrated accounts, physical indicators and descriptive statistics can provide useful information for monitoring the state of the environment.

Many such indicators are presented here, but despite greater awareness of the importance of environmental issues and efforts to improve environmental data, information on many aspects of the environment remains sparse. The data available are often of uneven quality, relate to different periods, and are sometimes out of date. The lack of adequate data hampers efforts to measure the state of the environment and design sound policies.

Another problem is that many environmental indicators are not meaningful at the national level. Climate change and air and water pollution have impacts that go beyond national boundaries. Other environmental issues are local. So global, regional, or city indicators are often more meaningful than national aggregates (tables 3.11 and 3.13).

Finite land resources

Three of every five people in developing countries—some 3 billion—live in rural areas (table 3.1). In many of these countries agriculture is still the main source of employment. Every $1 earned by a farmer increases incomes in other sectors by as much as $2.60. So the starting point for sustainable development for many developing countries is rural development and growth in sustainable farm and nonfarm activities.

But land resources are finite, fragile, and nonrenewable, so countries must meet their increased need for food and other agricultural products mainly by raising and sustaining crop and livestock yields and by using land more intensively. Low-income and lower-middle-income countries are increasing the land under cereal production, but their use of agricultural machinery lags far behind that in other countries (table 3.2). Low-income countries, where current cereal yields are a third those in high-income countries, will have to expand their arable land—not a strategy that can be sustained for long (table 3.3).

Shrinking forests and threatened biodiversity

Of the world's 1.2 billion extremely poor people—those living on less than $1 a day—90 percent depend on forests and their products for their livelihood. But the forests are shrinking, as is the diversity of the plants and animals they support. With growth and development, forests are being converted to agricultural land and urban areas. At the beginning of the 20th century the earth had about 5 billion hectares of forested area. Now it has less than 4 billion hectares. The loss has been concentrated in developing countries, driven by the growing demand for timber and agricultural land. Low-income countries lost about 8 percent of their forest in the 1990s. By contrast, high-income countries gained about 8 million hectares of forest in the same period (table 3.4).

Closely linked to changes in land use is biodiversity, another important dimension of environmental sustainability. Many countries have an informal goal of protecting about 10 percent of their land area, and crude measures of the extent of protected areas show how close to—or far from—this goal each country is (table 3.4). But even where protected areas are increased, losses of biologically diverse areas cannot be reversed. About 12 percent of the world's nearly 10,000 bird species are vulnerable or in immediate danger of extinction, as are 24 percent of the world's 4,800 mammal species and an estimated 30 percent of all fish species.

A thirsty planet

Water is crucial to economic growth and development—and to the survival of both terrestrial and aquatic systems. But more than 1 billion people lack access to safe water, and more than 430 million live in countries facing chronic and widespread water shortages—with water stress (less than 1,700 cubic meters of freshwater available per person a year) or water scarcity (less than 1,000 cubic meters; table 3.5).

Global per capita water supplies are declining, dropping by a third over the past 25 years. Further growth in population and economic activity will add to the demand for water, and by 2050 the share of the world's population facing water stress could increase by more than fivefold. These trends pose a significant challenge for meeting the Millennium Development Goal of halving the proportion of people without sustainable access to safe drinking water by 2015.

Energy use and its consequences

Economic growth and greater energy use have a direct and positive link, evident in the rapid growth of commercial energy use in low- and middle-income countries. At the highest income levels there are limited signs of declining per capita energy use. In Germany per capita energy use fell from 4,600 kilograms of oil equivalent in 1980 to 4,130 in 2000, and in the United States, despite strong economic growth, it increased by only 0.4 percent a year in the same period. Even so, high-income countries still use more than five times as much as developing countries on a per capita basis, and with only 15 percent of the world's population, they use more than half its commercial energy. The differences in per capita energy use can be striking: the United States uses 16 times as much energy as India, for example. High-income countries are net energy importers; middle-income countries have been their main suppliers (table 3.7).

The use of energy and, even more so, access to electricity are important in raising people's standard of living. But energy use and electricity generation also have significant environmental consequences. Generating energy produces emissions of carbon dioxide, the main greenhouse gas contributing to global warming. Anthropogenic (human caused) carbon dioxide emissions result primarily from fossil fuel combustion and cement manufacturing, with high-income countries contributing half (table 3.8). The extent of environmental damage depends largely on how energy is generated. For example, burning coal releases twice as much carbon dioxide as does burning an equivalent amount of natural gas (see *About the data* for table 3.9).

Urbanization and pollution

Urban areas are home to 47 percent of the world's population—two out of five people in low- and middle-income countries and almost four of five in high-income countries. Most of Latin

America is as urbanized as Europe, with 75 percent of its population living in urban areas. Asia is urbanizing rapidly. Even such traditionally rural countries as China, India, and Indonesia now have hundreds of millions of people living in urban areas, with both the number of people and the share of the population in cities growing rapidly (tables 3.10 and 3.11).

Urbanization can yield important social benefits, improving access to public services such as education, health care, and cultural facilities. But it can also lead to adverse environmental effects that require policy responses. Greater urbanization usually means greater pollution, which can overwhelm the natural capacities of air and water to absorb pollutants. The costs of controlling pollution can be enormous. And pollution exposes people to severe health hazards. Several major urban air pollutants—lead, sulfur dioxide, suspended particulate matter—are known to harm human health. A big source of urban air pollution is vehicles, whose numbers are strongly linked to rising income (tables 3.12 and 3.13).

This edition of *World Development Indicators* introduces a new indicator of air pollution—particulate matter. The print edition includes estimates for selected cities, while the CD-ROM version presents data for some 3,600 cities.

Government commitment to change

Working toward a cleaner environment and better management of environmental resources—whether at the national, regional, or global level—is central to meeting human needs and reducing poverty. But measuring governments' commitment to these goals is difficult. The indicators of government commitment in table 3.14 are imperfect, measuring the existence of policy instruments more than their effectiveness. Still, making a formal commitment is an essential first step toward taking action. The strength of environmental policies in any country reflects the priority its government gives to problems of environmental degradation—and that priority reflects the benefit expected from using scarce resources that have competing uses.

Beyond national environmental problems, governments are increasingly concerned about global environmental issues. To address these issues, countries have reached agreements and signed treaties on areas relating to the quality of life on earth. Many of these agreements resulted from the 1992 United Nations Conference on Environment and Development in Rio de Janeiro, which produced Agenda 21—an array of actions to address environmental challenges. But 10 years after Rio, the World Summit on Sustainable Development recognized that many of the proposed actions have yet to materialize.

Net adjusted savings—an indicator of sustainability

The question of an economy's sustainability can be reduced to whether welfare is expected to decline along the future development path as a result of decisions made today. Because flows of income and well-being are ultimately derived from the stocks of produced, natural, and human assets, a drop in the aggregate value of these stocks must lead eventually to a

3a

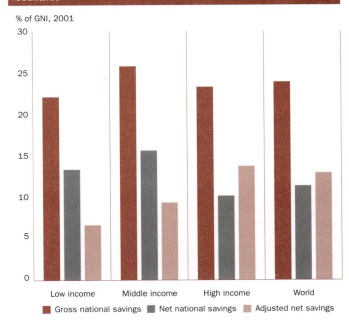

Adjusted net savings tend to be small in low- and middle-income countries

% of GNI, 2001

■ Gross national savings ■ Net national savings ■ Adjusted net savings

When estimates of national savings take into account spending on education, depletion of natural resources, and damage from carbon dioxide and particulate emissions, the results are lower than traditional estimates for low- and middle-income countries, where education spending is relatively low and depletion of natural resources is high. This adjusted net savings measure can serve as a proxy for the sustainability of economic activities.

Source: Table 3.15.

decline in welfare. One measure of change in total assets is provided by net adjusted savings—a measure of savings that accounts not only for a country's economic surplus but also for its depletion of natural resources, accumulation of pollutants, and investments in human capital.

The first estimates of such savings appeared in the World Bank's *Expanding the Measure of Wealth* (1997) and have been updated and refined since (table 3.15). The estimation in this edition of the *World Development Indicators* takes into account another source of loss: damage from particulates. Data limitations and the approximations used in calculating net adjusted savings mean that these estimates still must be used with caution (for more details, see *About the data* for table 3.15). But making progress on sustainability indicators is important enough to present these first steps toward a measure of sustainability.

Many developing countries have low or negative adjusted net savings (figure 3a). Broadly speaking, the lowest adjusted savings rates are recorded for countries that depend heavily on resource rents, particularly those endowed with minerals and fossil fuels. These rents account for a sizable share of GDP in many countries, suggesting that managing natural resources and resource revenues should receive even more attention as these countries strive to ensure the sustainability of their economies and the welfare of future generations.

3.1 Rural environment and land use

	Rural population			Rural population density	Land area	Land use					
	% of total		average annual % growth	people per sq. km of arable land	thousand sq. km	Arable land % of land area		Permanent cropland % of land area		Other % of land area	
	1980	2001	1980–2001	2000	2000	1980	2000	1980	2000	1980	2000
Afghanistan	84	78	2.2	262	652	12.1	12.1	0.2	0.2	87.7	87.6
Albania	66	57	0.1	313	27	21.4	21.1	4.3	4.4	74.4	74.5
Algeria	56	42	1.0	170	2,382	2.9	3.2	0.3	0.2	96.8	96.6
Angola	79	65	2.2	288	1,247	2.3	2.4	0.4	0.2	97.3	97.4
Argentina	17	12	–0.5	17	2,737	9.1	9.1	0.8	0.8	90.1	90.1
Armenia	34	33	0.8	252	28	..	17.6	..	2.3	..	80.1
Australia	14	9	–0.9	4	7,682	5.7	6.5	0.0	0.0	94.2	93.4
Austria	33	33	0.3	190	83	18.6	16.9	1.2	0.9	80.2	82.2
Azerbaijan	47	48	1.4	236	87	..	19.0	..	3.0	..	78.0
Bangladesh	85	74	1.5	1,208	130	68.3	62.5	2.0	2.7	29.6	34.8
Belarus	43	30	–1.5	50	207	..	29.6	..	0.6	..	69.8
Belgium	5	3	–2.5	34	33 [a]	23.2 [a]	24.8 [a]	0.4 [a]	0.7 [a]	76.4 [a]	74.5 [a]
Benin	73	57	1.8	186	111	13.6	17.6	0.8	2.4	85.7	80.0
Bolivia	55	37	0.4	161	1,084	1.7	1.8	0.2	0.2	98.1	98.0
Bosnia and Herzegovina	64	57	–0.7	454	51	..	9.8	..	2.9	..	87.3
Botswana	82	51	0.7	231	567	0.7	0.7	0.0	0.0	99.3	99.3
Brazil	33	18	–1.2	60	8,457	4.6	6.3	1.2	1.4	94.2	92.3
Bulgaria	39	33	–1.3	60	111	34.6	40.0	3.2	1.9	62.2	58.1
Burkina Faso	92	83	2.0	248	274	10.0	13.9	0.1	0.2	89.8	85.9
Burundi	96	91	2.2	689	26	36.2	35.0	12.5	14.0	51.3	50.9
Cambodia	88	83	2.5	270	177	11.3	21.0	0.4	0.6	88.3	78.4
Cameroon	69	50	1.2	128	465	12.7	12.8	2.2	2.6	85.1	84.6
Canada	24	21	0.4	14	9,221	4.9	4.9	0.0	0.0	95.0	95.0
Central African Republic	65	58	1.8	113	623	3.0	3.1	0.1	0.1	96.9	96.8
Chad	81	76	2.4	167	1,259	2.5	2.8	0.0	0.0	97.5	97.2
Chile	19	14	0.1	109	749	5.1	2.6	0.3	0.4	94.6	96.9
China [b]	80	63	0.1	653	9,327	10.4	13.3	0.4	1.2	89.3	85.5
Hong Kong, China	9	0	..	..	..	7.0	..	1.0	..	92.0	..
Colombia	37	25	0.0	376	1,039	3.6	2.7	1.4	1.7	95.0	95.6
Congo, Dem. Rep.	..	..	..	..	2,267	2.9	3.0	0.4	0.5	96.6	96.5
Congo, Rep.	58	34	0.4	597	342	0.4	0.5	0.1	0.1	99.5	99.4
Costa Rica	53	40	1.2	694	51	5.5	4.4	4.4	5.5	90.1	90.1
Côte d'Ivoire	65	56	2.6	306	318	6.1	9.3	7.2	13.8	86.6	76.9
Croatia	50	42	–1.1	127	56	..	26.1	..	2.3	..	71.6
Cuba	32	25	–0.6	76	110	23.9	33.1	6.4	7.6	69.7	59.3
Czech Republic	25	25	0.0	85	77	..	39.9	..	3.1	..	57.1
Denmark	16	15	–0.2	35	42	62.3	53.8	0.3	0.2	37.4	46.1
Dominican Republic	49	34	0.1	264	48	22.1	22.7	7.2	10.3	70.6	67.0
Ecuador	53	37	0.5	297	277	5.6	5.7	3.3	5.2	91.1	89.2
Egypt, Arab Rep.	56	57	2.3	1,298	995	2.3	2.8	0.2	0.5	97.5	96.7
El Salvador	56	39	–0.2	445	21	26.9	27.0	11.7	12.1	61.4	60.9
Eritrea	86	81	2.4	669	101	..	4.9	..	0.0	..	95.0
Estonia	30	31	–0.3	37	42	..	26.5	..	0.3	..	73.2
Ethiopia	90	84	2.4	543	1,000	..	10.0	..	0.7	..	89.3
Finland	40	41	0.5	97	305	7.8	7.2	0.0	0.0	92.2	92.8
France	27	24	0.0	79	550	31.8	33.5	2.5	2.1	65.7	64.4
Gabon	50	18	–2.1	70	258	1.1	1.3	0.6	0.7	98.2	98.1
Gambia, The	80	69	2.8	393	10	15.5	23.0	0.4	0.5	84.1	76.5
Georgia	48	44	–0.1	303	69	..	11.4	..	3.9	..	84.7
Germany	17	12	–1.4	87	357	33.7	33.1	1.4	0.6	64.9	66.3
Ghana	69	64	2.5	342	228	8.4	15.9	7.5	9.7	84.2	74.5
Greece	42	40	0.1	154	129	22.5	21.3	7.9	8.6	69.6	70.1
Guatemala	63	60	2.4	505	108	11.7	12.5	4.4	5.0	83.9	82.4
Guinea	81	72	2.0	607	246	2.9	3.6	1.8	2.4	95.4	94.0
Guinea-Bissau	83	68	1.3	274	28	9.1	10.7	1.1	1.8	89.9	87.6
Haiti	76	64	1.1	914	28	19.8	20.3	12.5	12.7	67.7	67.0

	Rural population			Rural population density	Land area	Land use					
	% of total		average annual % growth	people per sq. km of arable land	thousand sq. km	Arable land % of land area		Permanent cropland % of land area		Other % of land area	
	1980	2001	1980–2001	2000	2000	1980	2000	1980	2000	1980	2000
Honduras	65	46	1.3	284	112	13.3	9.5	2.4	3.2	84.3	87.2
Hungary	43	35	−1.2	78	92	54.4	49.8	3.3	2.2	42.2	48.0
India	77	72	1.6	454	2,973	54.8	54.4	1.8	2.7	43.4	42.9
Indonesia	78	58	0.2	594	1,812	9.9	11.3	4.4	7.2	85.6	81.5
Iran, Islamic Rep.	50	35	0.7	160	1,636	7.9	8.8	0.4	1.2	91.6	90.0
Iraq	34	32	2.6	145	437	12.0	11.9	0.4	0.8	87.6	87.3
Ireland	45	41	0.1	148	69	16.1	15.2	0.0	0.0	83.9	84.7
Israel	11	8	0.8	156	21	15.8	16.1	4.3	4.1	80.0	79.7
Italy	33	33	0.1	239	294	32.2	27.1	10.0	9.7	57.7	63.2
Jamaica	53	43	0.0	649	11	12.5	16.1	9.7	9.2	77.8	74.7
Japan	24	21	−0.2	603	365	13.3	12.3	1.6	1.0	85.1	86.7
Jordan	40	21	1.0	427	89	3.4	2.7	0.4	1.8	96.2	95.5
Kazakhstan	46	44	−0.2	31	2,700	..	8.0	..	0.1	..	92.0
Kenya	84	66	1.8	501	569	6.7	7.0	0.8	0.9	92.5	92.1
Korea, Dem. Rep.	43	39	0.8	521	120	13.4	14.1	2.4	2.5	84.2	83.4
Korea, Rep.	43	18	−3.2	496	99	20.9	17.4	1.4	2.0	77.8	80.6
Kuwait	9	4	−2.2	989	18	0.1	0.4	0.0	0.1	99.9	99.4
Kyrgyz Republic	62	66	1.8	236	192	..	7.1	..	0.3	..	92.5
Lao PDR	88	80	2.1	486	231	3.4	3.8	0.1	0.4	96.5	95.8
Latvia	32	40	0.7	51	62	..	29.7	..	0.5	..	69.8
Lebanon	26	10	−2.8	234	10	20.5	18.6	8.9	13.9	70.6	67.5
Lesotho	87	71	1.0	451	30	9.6	10.7	..	..	..	..
Liberia	65	55	1.7	454	96	3.9	3.9	2.1	2.2	94.0	93.8
Libya	31	12	−1.7	36	1,760	1.0	1.0	0.2	0.2	98.8	98.8
Lithuania	39	31	−0.9	38	65	..	45.3	..	0.9	..	53.8
Macedonia, FYR	47	41	−0.3	149	25	..	21.8	..	1.7	..	76.4
Madagascar	81	70	2.1	377	582	4.4	5.0	0.9	1.0	94.8	94.0
Malawi	91	85	2.2	419	94	16.1	22.3	0.9	1.5	83.0	76.2
Malaysia	58	42	1.1	544	329	3.0	5.5	11.6	17.6	85.4	76.9
Mali	82	69	1.7	163	1,220	1.6	3.8	0.0	0.0	98.3	96.2
Mauritania	72	41	0.0	231	1,025	0.2	0.5	0.0	0.0	99.8	99.5
Mauritius	58	58	1.1	697	2	49.3	49.3	3.4	3.0	47.3	47.8
Mexico	34	25	0.5	101	1,909	12.1	13.0	0.8	1.3	87.1	85.7
Moldova	60	58	0.2	137	33	..	55.3	..	11.2	..	33.5
Mongolia	48	43	1.3	89	1,567	0.8	0.8	0.0	0.0	99.2	99.2
Morocco	59	44	0.6	146	446	16.9	19.6	1.1	2.2	82.0	78.2
Mozambique	87	67	0.7	308	784	3.7	5.0	0.3	0.3	96.0	94.7
Myanmar	76	72	1.4	349	658	14.6	15.1	0.7	0.9	84.8	84.0
Namibia	77	69	2.3	149	823	0.8	1.0	0.0	0.0	99.2	99.0
Nepal	93	88	2.0	701	143	16.0	20.3	0.2	0.5	83.8	79.2
Netherlands	12	10	0.1	184	34	23.3	26.8	0.9	1.0	75.7	72.1
New Zealand	17	14	0.2	35	268	9.8	5.8	3.4	6.4	86.8	87.8
Nicaragua	50	43	2.1	91	121	9.5	20.2	1.5	2.4	89.1	77.4
Niger	87	79	2.8	192	1,267	2.8	3.5	0.0	0.0	97.2	96.4
Nigeria	73	55	1.5	252	911	30.6	31.0	2.8	2.9	66.6	66.1
Norway	29	25	−0.3	129	307	2.7	2.9	..	..	..	..
Oman	68	24	−1.2	3,049	310	0.0	0.1	0.1	0.2	99.9	99.7
Pakistan	72	67	2.2	434	771	25.9	27.6	0.4	0.9	73.7	71.5
Panama	50	43	1.3	250	74	5.8	6.7	1.6	2.1	92.5	91.2
Papua New Guinea	87	82	2.3	2,067	453	0.4	0.5	1.1	1.4	98.5	98.1
Paraguay	58	43	1.4	106	397	4.1	5.8	0.3	0.2	95.6	94.0
Peru	35	27	0.7	191	1,280	2.5	2.9	0.3	0.4	97.2	96.7
Philippines	63	41	0.3	572	298	17.5	18.6	14.8	15.1	67.7	66.3
Poland	42	37	−0.2	104	304	48.0	46.0	1.1	1.1	50.9	52.9
Portugal	71	34	−3.3	179	92	26.5	21.7	7.8	7.8	65.7	70.4
Puerto Rico	33	24	−0.6	2,701	9	8.3	3.9	7.3	5.2	84.3	90.9

	Rural population			Rural population density	Land area	Land use					
	% of total		average annual % growth	people per sq. km of arable land	thousand sq. km	Arable land % of land area		Permanent cropland % of land area		Other % of land area	
	1980	2001	1980–2001	2000	2000	1980	2000	1980	2000	1980	2000
Romania	51	45	−0.6	108	230	42.7	40.7	2.9	2.2	54.4	57.2
Russian Federation	30	27	−0.3	32	16,889	..	7.4	..	0.1	..	92.5
Rwanda	95	94	2.4	887	25	30.8	36.5	10.3	10.1	58.9	53.4
Saudi Arabia	34	13	−0.5	80	2,150	0.9	1.7	0.0	0.1	99.1	98.2
Senegal	64	52	1.7	212	193	12.2	12.3	0.0	0.2	87.8	87.5
Sierra Leone	76	63	1.3	651	72	6.3	6.8	0.7	0.8	93.0	92.3
Singapore	0	0	..	0	1	3.3	1.6	9.8	0.0	86.9	98.4
Slovak Republic	48	42	−0.2	158	48	..	30.4	..	2.8	..	66.8
Slovenia	52	51	0.1	584	20	..	8.6	..	1.5	..	89.9
Somalia	78	72	1.2	610	627	1.6	1.7	0.0	0.0	98.4	98.3
South Africa	52	42	1.2	125	1,221	10.2	12.1	0.7	0.8	89.1	87.1
Spain	27	22	−0.5	68	499	31.1	26.7	9.9	9.8	59.0	63.5
Sri Lanka	78	77	1.1	1,602	65	13.2	13.8	15.9	15.8	70.9	70.4
Sudan	80	63	1.2	122	2,376	5.2	6.8	0.0	0.1	94.8	93.1
Swaziland	82	73	2.5	432	17	10.8	10.3	0.2	0.7	89.0	89.0
Sweden	17	17	0.3	55	412	7.2	6.6	..	..	..	..
Switzerland	43	33	−0.7	567	40	9.9	10.4	0.5	0.6	89.6	89.0
Syrian Arab Republic	53	48	2.6	173	184	28.5	24.7	2.5	4.4	69.1	70.9
Tajikistan	66	72	2.6	614	141	..	5.2	..	0.9	..	93.9
Tanzania	85	67	1.8	571	884	3.5	4.5	1.0	1.1	95.5	94.4
Thailand	83	80	1.1	331	511	32.3	28.8	3.5	6.5	64.2	64.8
Togo	77	66	2.2	120	54	35.9	46.1	1.6	2.2	62.6	51.6
Trinidad and Tobago	37	26	−0.8	450	5	13.6	14.6	9.0	9.2	77.4	76.2
Tunisia	48	34	0.3	113	155	20.5	18.7	9.7	13.5	69.7	67.7
Turkey	56	34	−0.5	93	770	32.9	31.4	4.1	3.3	63.0	65.3
Turkmenistan	53	55	3.2	179	470	..	3.5	..	0.1	..	96.4
Uganda	91	85	2.4	377	197	20.7	25.7	8.1	9.6	71.2	64.7
Ukraine	38	32	−0.9	49	579	..	56.2	..	1.6	..	42.2
United Arab Emirates	29	13	1.2	644	84	0.2	0.7	0.1	2.2	99.7	97.0
United Kingdom	11	10	−0.1	105	241	28.7	24.4	0.3	0.2	71.0	75.4
United States	26	23	0.4	36	9,159	20.6	19.3	0.2	0.2	79.2	80.5
Uruguay	15	8	−2.3	21	175	8.0	7.4	0.3	0.2	91.7	92.3
Uzbekistan	59	63	2.5	350	414	..	10.8	..	0.9	..	88.3
Venezuela, RB	21	13	0.1	130	882	3.2	2.8	0.9	1.1	95.8	96.1
Vietnam	81	75	1.5	1,037	325	18.2	17.7	1.9	4.9	79.8	77.4
West Bank and Gaza	..	..	..	..	..	..	..	..	..	..	..
Yemen, Rep.	81	75	3.2	853	528	2.6	2.9	0.2	0.2	97.2	96.8
Yugoslavia, Fed. Rep.	54	48	−0.1	..	..	28.0	..	2.9	..	69.1	..
Zambia	60	60	2.8	116	743	6.9	7.1	0.0	0.0	93.1	92.9
Zimbabwe	78	64	1.9	254	387	6.5	8.3	0.3	0.3	93.3	91.3
World	**61 w**	**53 w**	**0.8 w**	**503 w**	**130,178 s**	**10.2 w**	**10.5 w**	**0.9 w**	**1.0 w**	**88.9 w**	**88.5 w**
Low income	76	69	1.6	510	33,031	11.7	13.1	1.0	1.5	87.3	85.4
Middle income	62	48	0.2	541	66,128	8.0	8.6	1.0	1.0	91.0	90.4
Lower middle income	68	54	0.3	575	44,993	9.8	9.4	1.0	0.9	89.2	89.7
Upper middle income	34	23	−0.3	185	21,135	5.8	6.9	1.0	1.2	93.2	91.8
Low & middle income	68	58	0.9	523	99,144	9.4	10.1	1.0	1.2	89.5	88.7
East Asia & Pacific	79	63	0.3	640	15,885	10.0	12.0	1.5	2.6	88.5	85.4
Europe & Central Asia	41	37	−0.2	127	23,722	37.1	11.2	3.1	0.4	59.8	88.4
Latin America & Carib.	35	24	0.0	235	20,062	5.8	6.7	1.1	1.3	93.1	92.1
Middle East & N. Africa	52	42	1.5	586	11,106	4.4	4.8	0.4	0.7	95.2	94.4
South Asia	78	72	1.7	549	4,781	42.5	42.5	1.5	2.1	56.1	55.4
Sub-Saharan Africa	79	68	1.8	359	23,603	5.5	6.6	0.7	0.9	93.8	92.5
High income	27	22	−0.3	193	31,018	12.0	11.6	0.5	0.5	87.5	87.9
Europe EMU	27	22	−0.5	143	2,537	26.2	24.7	4.6	4.4	69.2	70.9

a. Includes Luxembourg. b. Includes Taiwan, China.

About the data

Indicators of rural development are sparse, as few indicators are disaggregated between rural and urban areas (for some that are, see tables 2.6, 3.5, and 3.10). This table shows indicators of rural population and land use. Rural population is approximated as the midyear nonurban population.

The data in the table show that land use patterns are changing. They also indicate major differences in resource endowments and uses among countries. True comparability of the data is limited, however, by variations in definitions, statistical methods, and the quality of data collection. Countries use different definitions of rural population and land use, for example. The Food and Agriculture Organization (FAO), the primary compiler of these data, occasionally adjusts its definitions of land use categories and sometimes revises earlier data. (In 1985, for example, the FAO began to exclude from cropland the land used for shifting cultivation but currently lying fallow.) And following FAO practice, this year's edition of the *World Development Indicators*, like the previous four, breaks down the category cropland, used in earlier editions, into *arable land* and *permanent cropland*. Because the data reflect changes in data reporting procedures as well as actual changes in land use, apparent trends should be interpreted with caution.

Satellite images show land use that differs from that given by ground-based measures in both area under cultivation and type of land use. Moreover, land use data in countries such as India are based on reporting systems that were geared to the collection of tax revenue. Because taxes on land are no longer a major source of government revenue, the quality and coverage of land use data (except for cropland) have declined. Data on forest area, aggregated in the category *other*, may be particularly unreliable because of differences in definitions and irregular surveys (see *About the data* for table 3.4).

Definitions

- **Rural population** is calculated as the difference between the total population and the urban population (see *Definitions* for tables 2.1 and 3.10).
- **Rural population density** is the rural population divided by the arable land area. • **Land area** is a country's total area, excluding area under inland water bodies, national claims to continental shelf, and exclusive economic zones. In most cases the definition of inland water bodies includes major rivers and lakes. (See table 1.1 for the total surface area of countries.) • **Land use** is broken into three categories. • **Arable land** includes land defined by the FAO as land under temporary crops (double-cropped areas are counted once), temporary meadows for mowing or for pasture, land under market or kitchen gardens, and land temporarily fallow. Land abandoned as a result of shifting cultivation is excluded. • **Permanent cropland** is land cultivated with crops that occupy the land for long periods and need not be replanted after each harvest, such as cocoa, coffee, and rubber. This category includes land under flowering shrubs, fruit trees, nut trees, and vines, but excludes land under trees grown for wood or timber. • **Other land** includes forest and woodland as well as logged-over areas to be reforested in the near future. Also included are uncultivated land, grassland not used for pasture, wetlands, wastelands, and built-up areas—residential, recreational, and industrial lands and areas covered by roads and other fabricated infrastructure.

3.1a

The 10 countries with the largest shares of rural population in 2001— and the 10 with the smallest

% of total population

Country	Rural population	Country	Rural population
Rwanda	94	Belgium	3
Burundi	91	Kuwait	4
Nepal	88	Uruguay	8
Uganda	85	Israel	8
Malawi	85	Australia	9
Ethiopia	84	Lebanon	10
Burkina Faso	83	Netherlands	10
Cambodia	83	United Kingdom	10
Papua New Guinea	82	Argentina	12
Eritrea	81	Libya	12

Source: Table 3.1.

Data sources

The data on urban population shares used to estimate rural population come from the United Nations Population Division's *World Urbanization Prospects: The 2001 Revision*. The total population figures are World Bank estimates. The data on land area and land use are from the FAO's electronic files and are published in its *Production Yearbook*. The FAO gathers these data from national agencies through annual questionnaires and by analyzing the results of national agricultural censuses.

	Arable land		Irrigated land		Land under cereal production		Fertilizer consumption		Agricultural machinery			
	hectares per capita		% of cropland		thousand hectares		hundreds of grams per hectare of arable land		tractors per 1,000 agricultural workers		tractors per 100 sq. km of arable land	
	1979–81	1998–2000	1979–81	1998–2000	1979–81	1999–2001	1979–81	1998–2000	1979–81	1998–2000	1979–81	1998–2000
Afghanistan	0.50	0.31	31.1	29.6	3,037	2,400	62	7	0	0	1	1
Albania	0.22	0.19	53.0	48.6	367	213	1,556	261	15	11	173	142
Algeria	0.37	0.26	3.4	6.8	2,968	1,965	277	127	27	38	68	121
Angola	0.41	0.24	2.2	2.2	705	904	49	9	4	2	35	34
Argentina	0.89	0.68	5.7	5.7	11,154	11,004	46	323	132	191	73	112
Armenia	..	0.13	..	51.3	..	178	..	153	..	69	..	354
Australia	2.97	2.67	3.5	4.6	15,986	17,514	269	455	751	700	75	62
Austria	0.20	0.17	0.2	0.3	1,062	820	2,615	1,665	945	1,728	2,084	2,512
Azerbaijan	..	0.21	..	74.3		635	..	62	..	34	..	192
Bangladesh	0.10	0.06	17.1	47.6	10,823	11,736	459	1,593	0	0	5	7
Belarus	..	0.61	..	1.8	..	2,462	..	1,403	..	107	..	132
Belgium[a]	0.08	0.08	1.7	4.2	426	324	5,323	3,687	917	1,234	1,416	1,298
Benin	0.43	0.31	0.3	0.6	525	843	11	228	0	0	1	1
Bolivia	0.35	0.24	6.6	5.9	559	775	23	25	4	4	21	29
Bosnia and Herzegovina	..	0.13	..	0.4	..	367	..	872	..	284	..	580
Botswana	0.44	0.21	0.5	0.3	153	159	32	127	9	20	54	175
Brazil	0.32	0.32	3.3	4.4	20,612	17,629	915	1,200	31	59	139	152
Bulgaria	0.43	0.53	28.3	17.6	2,110	1,867	2,334	333	66	77	161	58
Burkina Faso	0.39	0.34	0.4	0.7	2,026	2,948	26	114	0	0	0	5
Burundi	0.23	0.13	4.2	5.9	203	202	11	41	0	0	1	2
Cambodia	0.29	0.31	5.8	7.1	1,241	2,050	45	7	0	0	6	5
Cameroon	0.68	0.41	0.2	0.5	1,021	734	56	76	0	0	1	1
Canada	1.86	1.49	1.3	1.6	19,561	18,016	416	572	827	1,761	144	156
Central African Republic	0.81	0.53	..	..	194	151	5	3	0	0	0	0
Chad	0.70	0.47	0.4	0.6	907	2,156	6	49	0	0	1	0
Chile	0.34	0.13	31.1	78.4	820	586	338	2,416	43	55	90	273
China	0.10	0.10	45.1	39.6	94,647	86,688	1,494	2,871	2	2	76	62
Hong Kong, China	0.00	..	37.5	..	0	0	..	..	0	..	10	..
Colombia	0.13	0.06	7.7	19.6	1,361	1,119	812	2,342	8	6	77	83
Congo, Dem. Rep.	0.25	0.14	0.1	0.1	1,115	2,066	12	2	0	0	3	4
Congo, Rep.	0.08	0.06	0.6	0.5	19	10	27	287	2	1	49	40
Costa Rica	0.12	0.06	12.1	21.2	136	79	2,650	8,572	22	21	210	311
Côte d'Ivoire	0.24	0.19	1.0	1.0	1,008	1,439	261	264	1	1	16	13
Croatia	..	0.33	..	0.2	..	665	..	1,354	..	12	..	17
Cuba	0.27	0.33	22.9	19.5	224	208	2,024	423	78	98	259	215
Czech Republic	..	0.30	..	0.7	..	1,624	..	936	..	173	..	273
Denmark	0.52	0.43	14.5	19.4	1,818	1,523	2,453	1,667	973	1,104	708	557
Dominican Republic	0.19	0.13	11.7	17.2	149	160	572	860	3	4	20	22
Ecuador	0.20	0.13	24.8	28.8	419	897	471	1,062	6	7	40	57
Egypt, Arab Rep.	0.06	0.05	100.0	100.0	2,007	2,716	2,864	4,284	4	10	158	303
El Salvador	0.12	0.09	4.3	4.9	422	380	1,376	1,497	5	4	61	61
Eritrea	..	0.12	..	4.3	..	333	..	189	..	0	..	12
Estonia	..	0.81	..	0.4	..	326	..	268	..	556	..	454
Ethiopia	..	0.16	..	1.8	..	7,562	..	163	..	0	..	3
Finland	0.50	0.42	2.5	2.9	1,190	1,154	2,024	1,419	721	1,268	893	893
France	0.32	0.31	4.6	10.8	9,804	8,963	3,260	2,491	737	1,326	836	692
Gabon	0.42	0.27	2.4	3.0	6	16	20	11	5	7	43	46
Gambia, The	0.26	0.17	0.6	0.9	54	133	136	70	0	0	3	2
Georgia	..	0.15	..	44.2	..	352	..	480	..	19	..	131
Germany	0.15	0.14	3.7	4.0	7,692	6,911	4,249	2,460	624	965	1,340	887
Ghana	0.18	0.19	0.2	0.2	902	1,304	104	39	1	1	19	10
Greece	0.30	0.26	24.2	37.2	1,600	1,254	1,927	1,688	120	302	485	877
Guatemala	0.19	0.12	5.0	6.8	716	655	726	1,511	3	2	32	32
Guinea	0.16	0.12	7.9	6.4	708	803	16	36	0	0	2	6
Guinea-Bissau	0.34	0.26	6.0	4.9	142	123	24	40	0	0	1	1
Haiti	0.10	0.07	7.9	8.2	416	460	62	203	0	0	3	3

	Arable land		Irrigated land		Land under cereal production		Fertilizer consumption		Agricultural machinery			
									tractors per 1,000 agricultural workers		tractors per 100 sq. km of arable land	
	hectares per capita		% of cropland		thousand hectares		hundreds of grams per hectare of arable land					
	1979–81	1998–2000	1979–81	1998–2000	1979–81	1999–2001	1979–81	1998–2000	1979–81	1998–2000	1979–81	1998–2000
Honduras	0.42	0.22	4.1	4.6	421	446	171	1,242	5	7	22	35
Hungary	0.47	0.47	3.6	4.2	2,878	2,758	2,906	897	59	171	111	192
India	0.24	0.16	22.8	32.2	104,350	100,967	345	1,063	2	6	24	93
Indonesia	0.12	0.10	16.2	14.7	11,825	15,270	645	1,326	0	1	5	36
Iran, Islamic Rep.	0.36	0.25	35.5	42.5	8,062	7,234	430	833	17	37	57	139
Iraq	0.40	0.23	32.1	63.6	2,159	2,646	172	732	23	76	44	95
Ireland	0.33	0.29	..	..	425	282	5,373	6,252	607	1,035	1,289	1,590
Israel	0.08	0.05	49.3	46.4	129	80	2,384	3,406	304	343	809	734
Italy	0.17	0.14	19.3	24.3	5,082	4,185	2,295	2,116	370	1,154	1,117	1,979
Jamaica	0.06	0.07	10.1	9.1	4	2	1,231	1,320	9	12	208	177
Japan	0.04	0.04	56.0	54.6	2,724	2,026	4,131	3,192	209	707	2,723	4,691
Jordan	0.14	0.05	11.0	19.1	158	34	404	882	47	28	153	197
Kazakhstan	..	1.47	..	10.4	..	12,121	..	12	..	44	..	28
Kenya	0.23	0.14	0.9	1.5	1,692	1,945	160	349	1	1	17	36
Korea, Dem. Rep.	0.09	0.08	58.9	73.0	1,625	1,287	4,688	1,530	12	21	275	441
Korea, Rep.	0.05	0.04	59.6	60.4	1,689	1,163	3,920	4,794	1	66	14	981
Kuwait	0.00	0.00	83.3	81.1	0	1	4,500	1,341	3	10	220	132
Kyrgyz Republic	..	0.28	..	74.8	..	607	..	210	..	47	..	190
Lao PDR	0.24	0.17	13.3	18.1	751	765	35	88	0	1	7	12
Latvia	..	0.77	..	1.1	..	422	..	278	..	324	..	293
Lebanon	0.07	0.04	28.3	32.3	34	39	1,663	3,416	28	113	141	298
Lesotho	0.22	0.16	..	..	203	233	150	170	6	6	47	62
Liberia	0.20	0.12	0.3	0.5	203	147	123	0	0	0	8	9
Libya	0.58	0.35	10.7	21.9	538	337	357	356	101	306	134	187
Lithuania	..	0.83	..	0.2	..	947	..	509	..	394	..	337
Macedonia, FYR	..	0.29	..	8.8	..	220	..	744	..	420	..	919
Madagascar	0.29	0.19	21.2	31.3	1,309	1,409	30	30	1	1	10	12
Malawi	0.25	0.20	1.1	1.3	1,155	1,622	203	217	0	0	8	7
Malaysia	0.07	0.08	6.7	4.8	729	719	4,273	7,843	4	24	77	238
Mali	0.31	0.44	4.5	3.0	1,346	2,411	61	107	0	1	5	6
Mauritania	0.14	0.19	22.8	9.8	125	246	57	29	1	1	13	8
Mauritius	0.10	0.09	15.0	18.9	0	0	2,547	3,463	4	6	33	37
Mexico	0.34	0.26	20.3	23.8	9,356	10,269	570	726	16	20	54	69
Moldova	..	0.42	..	14.1	..	854	..	28	..	82	..	239
Mongolia	0.71	0.52	3.0	6.8	559	222	83	28	32	22	82	56
Morocco	0.39	0.31	15.0	13.2	4,414	5,258	268	393	7	10	34	48
Mozambique	0.24	0.23	2.1	2.6	1,077	1,793	107	26	1	1	20	14
Myanmar	0.28	0.21	10.4	17.8	5,133	6,919	111	186	1	1	9	10
Namibia	0.66	0.47	0.6	0.9	195	308	0	3	11	11	39	39
Nepal	0.16	0.13	22.5	38.2	2,251	3,289	98	325	0	0	10	16
Netherlands	0.06	0.06	58.5	59.8	225	209	8,620	5,082	560	590	2,238	1,673
New Zealand	0.84	0.41	5.2	8.7	193	138	1,879	4,743	619	447	352	489
Nicaragua	0.39	0.50	6.0	3.2	266	398	392	141	6	7	19	11
Niger	0.62	0.43	0.7	1.5	3,872	7,569	10	7	0	0	0	0
Nigeria	0.39	0.23	0.7	0.8	6,048	18,995	59	63	1	2	3	11
Norway	0.20	0.20	..	..	311	328	3,146	2,230	824	1,266	1,603	1,549
Oman	0.01	0.01	92.7	77.2	2	2	840	3,586	1	1	76	77
Pakistan	0.24	0.16	72.7	82.1	10,693	12,443	525	1,312	5	13	50	151
Panama	0.22	0.18	5.0	5.3	166	129	692	716	27	20	122	100
Papua New Guinea	0.05	0.04	..	..	2	3	452	480	1	1	82	58
Paraguay	0.52	0.42	3.4	2.9	307	552	44	299	14	24	45	74
Peru	0.19	0.14	32.3	28.5	732	1,210	381	619	5	5	37	36
Philippines	0.11	0.07	12.8	15.4	6,790	6,581	636	1,269	1	1	20	21
Poland	0.41	0.36	0.7	0.7	7,875	8,778	2,393	1,092	112	293	425	930
Portugal	0.25	0.20	20.1	24.3	1,099	566	1,113	1,224	72	242	351	844
Puerto Rico	0.02	0.01	27.2	49.4	1	1	..	..	..	..	..	..

	Arable land		Irrigated land		Land under cereal production		Fertilizer consumption		Agricultural machinery			
	hectares per capita		% of cropland		thousand hectares		hundreds of grams per hectare of arable land		tractors per 1,000 agricultural workers		tractors per 100 sq. km of arable land	
	1979–81	1998–2000	1979–81	1998–2000	1979–81	1999–2001	1979–81	1998–2000	1979–81	1998–2000	1979–81	1998–2000
Romania	0.44	0.42	21.9	27.8	6,340	5,732	1,448	343	39	96	150	178
Russian Federation	..	0.86	..	3.6	..	37,953	..	108	..	96	..	65
Rwanda	0.15	0.10	0.4	0.4	239	266	3	3	0	0	1	1
Saudi Arabia	0.20	0.18	28.9	42.8	388	629	228	1,002	2	15	10	26
Senegal	0.42	0.25	2.6	3.0	1,216	1,247	104	162	0	0	2	2
Sierra Leone	0.14	0.10	4.1	5.4	434	220	58	4	0	0	6	2
Singapore	0.00	0.00	..	..	..	..	22,333	36,137	3	19	220	650
Slovak Republic	..	0.27	..	11.0	..	..	..	711	..	..	..	167
Slovenia	..	0.09	..	1.1	..	100	..	4,468	..	4,476	..	6,108
Somalia	0.15	0.12	13.3	18.7	638	507	9	5	1	1	17	18
South Africa	0.45	0.35	8.4	8.9	6,760	4,741	874	523	92	46	140	55
Spain	0.42	0.34	14.8	19.9	7,391	6,637	1,012	1,688	200	636	335	642
Sri Lanka	0.06	0.05	28.3	34.7	864	888	1,800	2,791	4	2	141	88
Sudan	0.64	0.54	14.4	11.8	4,447	6,764	51	23	2	1	8	6
Swaziland	0.30	0.17	34.0	36.7	70	58	1,050	320	29	26	173	164
Sweden	0.36	0.31	..	..	1,505	1,188	1,654	1,049	715	1,083	623	623
Switzerland	0.06	0.06	6.2	5.7	172	181	4,623	2,607	494	673	2,428	2,699
Syrian Arab Republic	0.60	0.29	9.6	22.1	2,642	3,060	250	766	29	68	54	201
Tajikistan	..	0.12	..	83.5	..	373	..	257	..	37	..	410
Tanzania	0.16	0.12	3.1	3.3	2,834	3,005	110	64	1	1	35	20
Thailand	0.35	0.25	16.4	27.1	10,625	11,154	177	1,113	1	10	11	148
Togo	0.77	0.56	0.3	0.3	416	680	14	73	0	0	0	0
Trinidad and Tobago	0.06	0.06	1.7	2.5	4	4	1,064	836	50	53	337	360
Tunisia	0.51	0.31	4.8	7.6	1,416	1,411	212	388	30	38	79	121
Turkey	0.57	0.38	9.6	16.7	13,499	13,174	529	890	38	63	169	372
Turkmenistan	..	0.32	..	..	..	779	..	558	..	75	..	307
Uganda	0.32	0.23	0.1	0.1	752	1,371	1	8	0	1	6	9
Ukraine	..	0.66	..	7.2	..	12,801	..	140	..	93	..	110
United Arab Emirates	0.01	0.02	..	47.2	0	1	2,250	8,034	6	4	106	70
United Kingdom	0.12	0.10	2.0	1.8	3,930	3,168	3,191	3,195	726	908	744	822
United States	0.83	0.64	10.8	12.5	72,639	57,456	1,092	1,090	1,230	1,542	253	271
Uruguay	0.48	0.39	5.4	13.5	614	542	564	974	171	174	236	257
Uzbekistan	..	0.18	..	88.3	..	1,520	..	1,733	..	57	..	380
Venezuela, RB	0.19	0.10	10.1	16.9	814	736	722	920	50	60	136	201
Vietnam	0.11	0.07	25.6	40.9	5,962	8,322	302	3,420	1	5	38	224
West Bank and Gaza	..	..	..	..	..	..	..	..	..	..	..	..
Yemen, Rep.	0.16	0.09	19.9	29.5	865	621	93	111	3	2	33	37
Yugoslavia, Fed. Rep.	0.73	..	1.9	..	4,310	..	1,261	..	140	..	616	..
Zambia	0.89	0.53	0.4	0.9	595	735	145	64	2	2	9	11
Zimbabwe	0.35	0.26	3.1	3.5	1,633	1,787	610	544	7	7	66	73
World	**0.25 w**	**0.23 w**	**17.7 w**	**19.8 w**	**588,602 s**	**668,229 s**	**870 w**	**1,013 w**	**19 w**	**20 w**	**175 w**	**190 w**
Low income	0.22	0.18	19.9	25.1	199,696	259,265	290	671	2	5	20	69
Middle income	0.18	0.22	23.2	20.7	232,195	274,711	969	1,125	8	11	114	127
Lower middle income	0.15	0.20	30.0	24.0	175,911	216,305	996	1,169	5	7	101	96
Upper middle income	0.33	0.30	9.6	11.4	56,284	58,406	914	999	42	89	139	217
Low & middle income	0.20	0.20	21.6	22.6	431,892	533,976	635	930	5	8	67	102
East Asia & Pacific	0.12	0.11	36.5	38.1	139,904	139,990	1,117	2,346	2	2	55	71
Europe & Central Asia	0.16	0.57	10.6	10.7	37,380	107,728	1,445	339	67	101	266	170
Latin America & Carib.	0.32	0.26	11.8	13.9	49,847	48,455	587	895	25	36	95	118
Middle East & N. Africa	0.29	0.19	25.8	37.3	25,655	25,954	422	787	12	24	61	123
South Asia	0.23	0.15	28.7	39.9	132,128	131,832	360	1,065	2	5	25	91
Sub-Saharan Africa	0.32	0.24	4.0	4.2	46,978	80,017	158	130	3	1	23	15
High income	0.45	0.38	10.1	11.9	156,710	134,253	1,328	1,249	429	851	385	438
Europe EMU	0.23	0.21	13.4	18.5	35,999	31,316	2,704	2,254	424	862	878	986

a. Includes Luxembourg.

About the data

Agricultural activities provide developing countries with food and revenue, but they also can degrade natural resources. Poor farming practices can cause soil erosion and loss of soil fertility. Efforts to increase productivity through the use of chemical fertilizers, pesticides, and intensive irrigation have environmental costs and health impacts. Excessive use of chemical fertilizers can alter the chemistry of soil. Pesticide poisoning is common in developing countries. And salinization of irrigated land diminishes soil fertility. Thus inappropriate use of inputs for agricultural production has far-reaching effects.

This table provides indicators of major inputs to agricultural production: land, fertilizers, and agricultural machinery. There is no single correct mix of inputs:

appropriate levels and application rates vary by country and over time, depending on the type of crops, the climate and soils, and the production process used.

The data shown here and in table 3.3 are collected by the Food and Agriculture Organization (FAO) through annual questionnaires. The FAO tries to impose standard definitions and reporting methods, but exact consistency across countries and over time is not possible. Data on agricultural employment in particular should be used with caution. In many countries much agricultural employment is informal and unrecorded, including substantial work performed by women and children.

Fertilizer consumption measures the quantity of plant nutrients in the form of nitrogen, potassium, and

phosphorous compounds available for direct application. Consumption is calculated as production plus imports minus exports. Traditional nutrients—animal and plant manures—are not included. Because some chemical compounds used for fertilizers have other industrial applications, the consumption data may overstate the quantity available for crops.

To smooth annual fluctuations in agricultural activity, the indicators in the table have been averaged over three years.

Definitions

• **Arable land** includes land defined by the FAO as land under temporary crops (double-cropped areas are counted once), temporary meadows for mowing or for pasture, land under market or kitchen gardens, and land temporarily fallow. Land abandoned as a result of shifting cultivation is excluded. • **Irrigated land** refers to areas purposely provided with water, including land irrigated by controlled flooding. Cropland refers to arable land and permanent cropland (see table 3.1). • **Land under cereal production** refers to harvested areas, although some countries report only sown or cultivated area. • **Fertilizer consumption** is the quantity of plant nutrients used per unit of arable land. Fertilizer products cover nitrogenous, potash, and phosphate fertilizers (including ground rock phosphate). The time reference for fertilizer consumption is the crop year (July through June). • **Agricultural machinery** refers to wheel and crawler tractors (excluding garden tractors) in use in agriculture at the end of the calendar year specified or during the first quarter of the following year.

3.2a

In low-income countries fertilizer consumption has more than doubled in the past two decades . . .

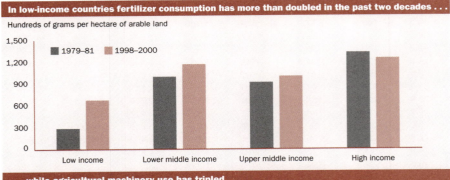

Hundreds of grams per hectare of arable land

. . . while agricultural machinery use has tripled . . .

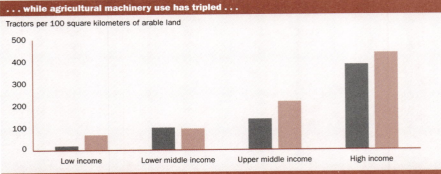

Tractors per 100 square kilometers of arable land

. . . but cereal yields remain less than a third of those in high-income countries

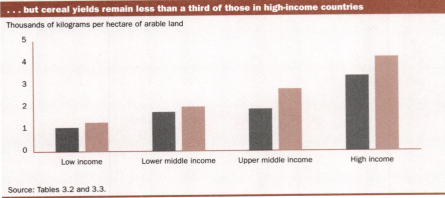

Thousands of kilograms per hectare of arable land

Source: Tables 3.2 and 3.3.

Data sources

The data are from electronic files that the FAO makes available to the World Bank. Data on arable land, irrigated land, and land under cereal production are published in the FAO's *Production Yearbook*.

3.3 | Agricultural output and productivity

	Crop production index		Food production index		Livestock production index		Cereal yield		Agricultural productivity	
									Agriculture value added per worker 1995 $	
	1989–91 = 100		1989–91 = 100		1989–91 = 100		kilograms per hectare			
	1979–81	**1999–2001**	**1979–81**	**1999–2001**	**1979–81**	**1999–2001**	**1979–81**	**1999–2001**	**1979–81**	**1999–2001**
Afghanistan	..	..	..	..	..	..	1,337	1,026	..	..
Albania	..	..	..	..	..	..	2,500	2,622	1,184	2,101
Algeria	77.5	127.9	67.3	133.1	54.6	128.3	656	929	1,357	1,939
Angola	101.9	151.2	90.0	146.3	83.8	136.8	526	630	..	131
Argentina	83.6	163.9	91.7	142.9	100.9	112.1	2,184	3,397	7,148	10,351
Armenia	..	98.5	..	73.9	..	60.2	..	1,675	..	5,435
Australia	79.9	171.2	91.3	145.7	85.6	114.8	1,321	2,038	20,872	33,225
Austria	92.8	102.6	92.2	107.6	94.5	106.3	4,131	5,629	11,082	31,091
Azerbaijan	..	57.4	..	78.0	..	79.6	..	2,373	..	768
Bangladesh	80.0	132.4	79.2	135.6	81.3	140.9	1,938	3,322	217	311
Belarus	..	86.7	..	59.5	..	56.8	..	1,722	..	2,180
Belgium[a]	84.9	146.1	88.5	113.6	88.8	109.7	4,861	7,679	21,861	29,098
Benin	53.8	181.9	63.0	157.6	69.0	110.8	698	1,047	311	608
Bolivia	71.9	163.0	71.5	144.8	75.5	126.8	1,183	1,577	..	748
Bosnia and Herzegovina	..	..	..	..	..	..	..	3,034	..	7,811
Botswana	86.4	80.4	87.2	95.5	87.5	97.4	203	146	657	575
Brazil	75.4	129.1	69.5	145.9	67.9	162.2	1,496	2,825	2,049	4,798
Bulgaria	107.7	59.8	105.5	66.0	96.3	60.7	3,853	2,696	2,754	8,277
Burkina Faso	59.3	137.8	62.7	135.4	59.9	141.4	575	880	136	183
Burundi	79.9	92.3	79.9	91.8	82.3	77.3	1,081	1,290	177	150
Cambodia	55.2	149.0	48.9	153.3	27.3	166.1	1,025	2,050	..	363
Cameroon	86.7	132.9	80.2	130.8	61.3	122.0	849	1,842	826	1,189
Canada	77.6	123.7	79.8	126.7	88.3	129.6	2,173	2,772	15,881	43,428
Central African Republic	102.8	133.3	79.7	139.4	48.9	137.3	529	1,217	380	490
Chad	66.9	144.5	79.9	138.0	89.2	119.9	587	555	160	213
Chile	70.7	131.2	71.5	137.8	75.8	147.4	2,124	4,453	3,488	6,040
China	67.1	146.1	60.8	175.9	45.4	217.9	3,027	4,869	161	334
Hong Kong, China	133.6	59.3	99.8	58.0	194.3	57.0	1,712	..	..	..
Colombia	84.1	104.1	75.5	120.2	72.6	122.9	2,452	3,236	3,034	3,590
Congo, Dem. Rep.	73.0	81.9	72.2	85.3	77.7	101.5	807	782	241	218
Congo, Rep.	86.4	126.0	83.5	128.3	80.1	133.4	838	782	385	471
Costa Rica	70.1	149.9	72.6	148.0	77.2	132.7	2,498	4,023	3,139	5,272
Côte d'Ivoire	73.7	135.8	70.7	138.0	74.7	122.9	867	1,307	1,026	1,057
Croatia	..	86.6	..	67.3	..	50.0	..	4,355	..	9,449
Cuba	84.1	58.4	90.1	62.2	96.0	68.3	2,458	2,601	..	..
Czech Republic	..	92.0	..	77.1	..	66.9	..	4,277	..	6,235
Denmark	65.2	91.9	83.3	104.2	95.0	116.8	4,040	6,032	19,350	57,896
Dominican Republic	96.5	87.3	85.2	110.1	68.8	141.0	3,024	4,105	2,020	3,179
Ecuador	78.2	157.6	77.4	156.1	73.0	153.1	1,633	2,212	1,206	1,716
Egypt, Arab Rep.	75.5	151.2	68.4	155.9	67.0	161.4	4,053	7,238	721	1,324
El Salvador	120.4	104.0	88.9	117.0	86.5	120.2	1,702	2,098	1,924	1,710
Eritrea	..	148.9	..	126.8	..	111.0	..	671	..	85
Estonia	..	69.5	..	43.4	..	37.2	..	1,704	..	4,265
Ethiopia	..	153.2	..	141.1	..	118.4	..	1,164	..	141
Finland	76.3	94.7	93.8	89.8	107.5	91.7	2,511	3,071	18,547	40,463
France	87.4	107.9	93.6	105.3	97.8	104.6	4,700	7,088	19,318	58,177
Gabon	76.2	119.9	79.0	115.9	86.5	119.0	1,718	1,638	1,814	2,047
Gambia, The	79.5	145.0	82.7	139.8	93.7	106.1	1,284	1,298	325	298
Georgia	..	52.5	..	78.7	..	94.9	..	1,576	..	..
Germany	90.0	119.4	91.4	98.2	98.7	87.8	4,166	6,749	9,061	32,814
Ghana	67.0	178.6	68.6	169.6	78.7	117.7	807	1,305	671	569
Greece	86.8	111.6	91.2	103.4	99.9	96.1	3,090	3,527	8,600	14,079
Guatemala	87.3	131.8	68.0	134.7	76.3	134.1	1,578	1,778	2,143	2,115
Guinea	89.7	153.8	95.8	155.3	112.0	174.4	958	1,311	..	274
Guinea-Bissau	64.9	144.7	68.3	140.0	78.0	126.2	711	1,271	237	322
Haiti	103.4	87.6	101.3	99.8	100.2	145.6	1,009	899	..	..

	Crop production index		Food production index		Livestock production index		Cereal yield		Agricultural productivity	
									Agriculture value added per worker	
							kilograms per hectare		1995 $	
	1989–91 = 100		1989–91 = 100		1989–91 = 100					
	1979–81	**1999–2001**	**1979–81**	**1999–2001**	**1979–81**	**1999–2001**	**1979–81**	**1999–2001**	**1979–81**	**1999–2001**
Honduras	90.4	105.1	88.2	112.1	80.8	149.5	1,170	1,327	696	990
Hungary	93.3	80.1	90.7	76.3	94.1	70.1	4,519	4,392	3,390	5,159
India	70.9	124.6	68.2	129.9	62.6	144.1	1,324	2,321	269	402
Indonesia	66.2	119.4	63.3	118.3	51.0	116.4	2,837	3,947	604	744
Iran, Islamic Rep.	57.5	135.9	61.2	139.0	68.0	145.1	1,108	1,806	2,165	3,698
Iraq	74.7	73.6	78.0	73.3	81.4	68.1	832	530	..	..
Ireland	93.9	111.0	83.3	113.5	83.3	115.2	4,733	7,241	..	..
Israel	99.8	100.3	85.0	115.0	78.4	122.5	1,840	2,411	..	..
Italy	106.1	104.7	101.4	104.9	93.0	106.6	3,548	4,920	11,090	26,690
Jamaica	98.6	118.1	86.0	118.8	73.9	122.3	1,667	1,183	965	1,540
Japan	108.3	88.0	94.1	92.5	85.1	94.1	5,252	6,147	17,378	30,828
Jordan	54.6	114.9	57.4	134.1	51.5	176.6	521	1,949	1,141	825
Kazakhstan	..	84.1	..	70.3	..	45.3	..	1,162	..	1,649
Kenya	74.5	110.4	67.5	107.7	60.1	106.5	1,364	1,477	265	216
Korea, Dem. Rep.	..	..	..	..	..	..	3,694	2,753	..	..
Korea, Rep.	87.8	113.0	77.4	131.0	52.3	161.6	4,986	6,500	3,765	13,782
Kuwait	37.1	166.2	91.4	208.1	106.6	210.0	3,124	2,260	..	..
Kyrgyz Republic	..	143.5	..	121.4	..	78.1	..	2,726	..	1,636
Lao PDR	73.5	153.7	70.3	163.4	56.0	185.7	1,402	2,978	..	614
Latvia	..	74.3	..	41.9	..	31.7	..	2,090	..	2,671
Lebanon	52.0	138.3	59.2	143.7	100.5	164.7	1,307	2,415	..	28,322
Lesotho	98.2	164.4	90.2	116.9	87.7	87.5	977	1,337	636	553
Liberia	..	..	..	..	..	..	1,251	1,278	..	525
Libya	76.3	133.8	78.7	157.5	68.4	162.1	430	637	..	..
Lithuania	..	74.6	..	59.8	..	49.4	..	2,480	..	3,131
Macedonia, FYR	..	105.2	..	94.6	..	86.1	..	2,711	..	4,155
Madagascar	83.1	103.3	83.8	109.5	87.7	110.0	1,664	1,831	158	155
Malawi	85.7	149.4	93.2	160.8	78.2	113.2	1,161	1,634	96	123
Malaysia	75.3	119.7	55.6	143.2	41.0	155.1	2,828	3,075	3,939	6,843
Mali	54.5	135.0	76.7	119.5	94.5	111.8	804	1,113	242	290
Mauritania	62.1	133.9	86.5	109.4	89.4	106.0	384	718	299	500
Mauritius	93.3	90.4	89.7	101.7	64.0	141.3	2,536	4,793	2,891	5,580
Mexico	86.5	121.9	83.8	133.6	83.5	145.1	2,164	2,765	1,482	1,801
Moldova	..	56.8	..	45.9	..	34.5	..	2,437	..	1,661
Mongolia	44.6	30.9	88.1	103.4	93.2	109.2	573	716	994	1,428
Morocco	54.8	93.1	55.8	103.8	59.8	121.9	811	670	1,146	1,512
Mozambique	109.6	140.8	100.9	128.5	85.8	103.2	603	929	..	138
Myanmar	89.0	167.9	88.2	163.6	89.1	157.9	2,521	3,082	..	..
Namibia	80.1	121.5	107.2	118.0	115.6	117.7	377	347	1,003	1,618
Nepal	62.6	127.8	65.9	127.6	77.3	125.5	1,615	2,089	156	200
Netherlands	79.8	115.4	86.5	102.9	88.3	100.5	5,696	7,701	24,343	58,280
New Zealand	74.4	142.7	90.7	128.0	95.5	117.9	4,089	6,303	16,636	28,791
Nicaragua	124.1	138.4	117.8	144.1	139.7	139.5	1,475	1,706	1,549	..
Niger	89.3	144.5	97.4	136.0	109.7	125.2	440	358	229	201
Nigeria	51.4	159.7	57.2	156.2	84.3	127.4	1,265	1,197	417	714
Norway	94.8	79.2	93.9	91.9	96.2	99.1	3,634	3,928	17,013	34,535
Oman	60.1	166.1	62.1	162.5	61.5	133.6	982	2,266	..	..
Pakistan	65.6	126.0	66.3	145.2	59.5	155.1	1,608	2,305	416	712
Panama	97.1	94.0	85.6	106.7	71.3	126.1	1,524	2,732	2,122	2,738
Papua New Guinea	86.5	122.2	86.2	122.8	85.0	140.9	2,087	4,079	694	815
Paraguay	58.7	114.6	60.7	137.5	62.1	132.6	1,535	2,092	2,641	3,389
Peru	82.1	173.0	77.3	171.8	78.0	160.0	1,946	2,977	1,273	1,834
Philippines	88.3	119.9	86.1	131.1	73.8	162.7	1,611	2,571	1,381	1,428
Poland	84.6	85.3	87.9	85.9	98.0	83.4	2,345	2,860	..	1,601
Portugal	85.0	93.8	72.2	102.9	71.8	119.9	1,102	2,729	3,796	7,552
Puerto Rico	131.3	67.9	99.8	83.8	90.3	89.2	7,970	1,870	..	..

	Crop production index		Food production index		Livestock production index		Cereal yield		Agricultural productivity	
									Agriculture value added per worker	
							kilograms per hectare		1995 $	
	1989–91 = 100		1989–91 = 100		1989–91 = 100					
	1979–81	1999–2001	1979–81	1999–2001	1979–81	1999–2001	1979–81	1999–2001	1979–81	1999–2001
Romania	114.1	92.4	113.0	96.3	110.0	88.2	2,854	2,569	1,277	3,193
Russian Federation	..	78.7	..	63.7	..	51.5	..	1,767	..	2,648
Rwanda	84.3	100.4	85.3	103.8	80.9	116.8	1,134	891	271	251
Saudi Arabia	27.2	88.1	26.7	83.3	32.7	144.6	820	3,649	..	..
Senegal	77.2	129.5	74.1	136.6	65.7	147.4	690	854	336	334
Sierra Leone	80.3	72.9	84.5	81.9	84.1	126.0	1,249	1,092	674	359
Singapore	595.0	48.2	154.3	39.5	173.7	39.5	..	..	15,938	44,907
Slovak Republic	..	..	..	..	..	..	..	..	..	..
Slovenia	..	94.4	..	108.9	..	104.7	..	4,912	..	34,697
Somalia	..	..	..	..	..	..	474	544	..	..
South Africa	95.0	106.9	91.0	107.7	86.8	103.0	2,105	2,334	2,857	3,837
Spain	83.0	112.3	82.0	114.8	84.2	128.4	1,986	3,047	7,556	22,088
Sri Lanka	99.3	120.3	98.3	122.2	93.2	135.0	2,462	3,270	642	734
Sudan	130.2	159.6	105.1	161.7	89.3	158.3	645	484	..	..
Swaziland	72.5	87.9	80.2	89.0	96.5	82.5	1,345	1,620	1,752	1,922
Sweden	93.1	89.2	100.6	97.1	103.8	102.5	3,595	4,557	18,020	36,365
Switzerland	95.5	90.1	95.8	94.1	98.8	93.5	4,883	6,204	..	..
Syrian Arab Republic	100.5	156.3	94.2	147.0	72.2	134.6	1,156	1,304	2,206	2,618
Tajikistan	..	51.6	..	51.5	..	39.5	..	1,025	..	1,332
Tanzania	81.8	97.2	76.7	103.8	69.3	121.8	1,063	1,273	..	185
Thailand	79.1	118.5	80.2	118.3	64.6	130.1	1,911	2,659	626	904
Togo	70.6	140.7	78.3	132.9	56.2	107.5	729	1,096	365	531
Trinidad and Tobago	119.9	108.2	101.9	114.7	84.3	100.8	3,167	2,928	3,536	3,036
Tunisia	68.1	122.1	66.3	132.4	60.3	162.8	828	1,109	1,743	3,168
Turkey	76.6	113.8	75.8	111.5	80.4	106.8	1,869	2,187	1,872	1,852
Turkmenistan	..	91.8	..	134.1	..	136.8	..	1,771	..	1,518
Uganda	67.5	135.5	69.9	131.8	81.9	127.3	1,555	1,605	..	342
Ukraine	..	63.9	..	49.5	..	46.4	..	2,226	..	1,521
United Arab Emirates	38.9	284.6	48.8	270.7	45.3	203.4	2,224	598	..	..
United Kingdom	80.1	97.9	92.2	95.5	98.1	95.7	4,792	6,836	20,326	33,520
United States	98.6	119.8	94.5	122.4	89.0	122.1	4,151	5,824	20,634	50,777
Uruguay	86.8	150.4	87.1	136.6	85.9	119.9	1,644	3,796	6,240	8,010
Uzbekistan	..	88.8	..	118.0	..	116.3	..	2,603	..	1,088
Venezuela, RB	76.3	118.2	80.2	123.2	84.9	118.6	1,904	3,341	3,935	5,304
Vietnam	66.6	166.8	63.0	153.9	49.5	154.9	2,049	4,075	..	253
West Bank and Gaza	..	..	..	..	..	..	..	..	..	..
Yemen, Rep.	82.3	129.6	75.0	134.1	68.9	145.9	1,038	1,094	..	406
Yugoslavia, Fed. Rep.	96.3	..	94.3	..	94.2	..	3,601	..	..	..
Zambia	64.5	100.7	72.9	106.0	86.2	117.5	1,676	1,437	186	195
Zimbabwe	77.8	121.3	83.3	110.0	89.7	114.5	1,359	1,221	310	361
World	**79.1 w**	**124.4 w**	**78.8 w**	**129.0 w**	**79.6 w**	**130.5 w**	**1,608 w**	**2,143 w**	**.. w**	**.. w**
Low income	71.7	125.8	70.7	127.8	68.4	132.1	1,090	1,309	..	415
Middle income	74.3	128.7	71.8	143.2	69.6	155.8	1,811	2,357	..	737
Lower middle income	72.5	131.9	68.8	150.8	60.8	176.0	1,771	2,004	..	558
Upper middle income	79.4	119.3	78.8	125.7	82.8	124.4	1,892	2,803	..	..
Low & middle income	73.3	127.6	71.5	137.9	69.3	149.7	1,422	1,818	..	583
East Asia & Pacific	68.5	136.9	63.4	159.7	47.9	202.7	2,034	2,978	..	..
Europe & Central Asia	..	..	..	..	..	..	2,854	2,388	..	2,049
Latin America & Carib.	80.3	125.9	78.3	133.0	79.8	133.4	1,842	2,545	2,209	3,680
Middle East & N. Africa	66.0	128.2	64.8	132.2	64.1	137.9	965	1,595	..	..
South Asia	71.9	122.8	69.6	127.1	64.0	137.1	1,510	2,182	284	568
Sub-Saharan Africa	75.4	129.4	78.3	125.8	84.1	114.9	895	1,188	421	675
High income	93.4	116.4	91.9	113.6	90.6	110.9	3,400	4,246	..	..
Europe EMU	90.7	109.6	91.4	104.0	93.9	101.1	4,035	5,629	..	..

a. Includes Luxembourg.

Agricultural output and productivity | 3.3

About the data

The agricultural production indexes in the table are prepared by the Food and Agriculture Organization (FAO). The FAO obtains data from official and semiofficial reports of crop yields, area under production, and livestock numbers. If data are not available, the FAO makes estimates. The indexes are calculated using the Laspeyres formula: production quantities of each commodity are weighted by average international commodity prices in the base period and summed for each year. Because the FAO's indexes are based on the concept of agriculture as a single enterprise, estimates of the amounts retained for seed and feed are subtracted from the production data to avoid double counting. The resulting aggregate represents production available for any use except as seed and feed. The FAO's indexes may differ from other sources because of differences in coverage, weights, concepts, time periods, calculation methods, and use of international prices.

To ease cross-country comparisons, the FAO uses international commodity prices to value production. These prices, expressed in international dollars (equivalent in purchasing power to the U.S. dollar), are derived using a Geary-Khamis formula applied to agricultural outputs (see Inter-Secretariat Working Group on National Accounts 1993, sections 16.93–96). This method assigns a single price to each commodity so that, for example, one metric ton of wheat has the same price regardless of where it was produced. The use of international prices eliminates fluctuations in the value of output due to transitory movements of nominal exchange rates unrelated to the purchasing power of the domestic currency.

Data on cereal yield may be affected by a variety of reporting and timing differences. The FAO allocates production data to the calendar year in which the bulk of the harvest took place. But most of a crop harvested near the end of a year will be used in the following year. Cereal crops harvested for hay or harvested green for food, feed, or silage, and those used for grazing, are generally excluded. But millet and sorghum, which are grown as feed for livestock and poultry in Europe and North America, are used as food in Africa, Asia, and countries of the former Soviet Union. So some cereal crops are excluded from the data for some countries and included elsewhere, depending on their use.

Agricultural productivity is measured by value added per unit of input. (For further discussion of the calculation of value added in national accounts, see *About the data* for tables 4.1 and 4.2.) Agricultural value added includes that from forestry and fishing. Thus interpretations of land productivity should be made with caution. To smooth annual fluctuations in agricultural activity, the indicators in the table have been averaged over three years.

Definitions

• **Crop production index** shows agricultural production for each period relative to the base period 1989–91. It includes all crops except fodder crops. The regional and income group aggregates for the FAO's production indexes are calculated from the underlying values in international dollars, normalized to the base period 1989–91. The data in this table are three-year averages. Missing observations have not been estimated or imputed.
• **Food production index** covers food crops that are considered edible and that contain nutrients. Coffee and tea are excluded because, although edible, they have no nutritive value. • **Livestock production index** includes meat and milk from all sources, dairy products such as cheese, and eggs, honey, raw silk, wool, and hides and skins. • **Cereal yield,** measured in kilograms per hectare of harvested land, includes wheat, rice, maize, barley, oats, rye, millet, sorghum, buckwheat, and mixed grains. Production data on cereals refer to crops harvested for dry grain only. Cereal crops harvested for hay or harvested green for food, feed, or silage, and those used for grazing, are excluded.
• **Agricultural productivity** refers to the ratio of agricultural value added, measured in constant 1995 U.S. dollars, to the number of workers in agriculture.

3.3a

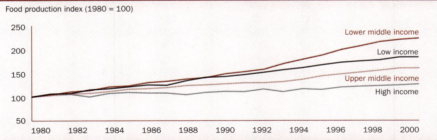

Food production has grown in all country income groups and regions in the past two decades . . .

Food production index (1980 = 100)

Lower middle income
Low income
Upper middle income
High income

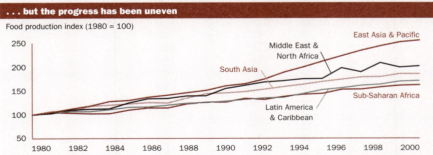

. . . but the progress has been uneven

Food production index (1980 = 100)

East Asia & Pacific
Middle East & North Africa
South Asia
Latin America & Caribbean
Sub-Saharan Africa

Food production has outpaced population growth in the past two decades, but the progress has been uneven. And despite the more than 80 percent increase in food production in low-income countries, hunger persists in parts of the world. Among developing regions, East Asia and Pacific has had the highest growth in food production, Sub-Saharan Africa the lowest.

Source: Table 3.3.

Data sources

The agricultural production indexes are prepared by the FAO and published annually in its *Production Yearbook*. The FAO makes these data and the data on cereal yield and agricultural employment available to the World Bank in electronic files that may contain more recent information than the published versions. For sources of data on agricultural value added, see *Data sources* for table 4.2.

3.4 Deforestation and biodiversity

	Forest area		Average annual deforestation		Mammals		Birds		Higher plants [a]		Nationally protected areas	
	thousand sq. km	% of total land area	sq. km	%	Species	Threatened species	Species	Threatened species	Species	Threatened species	thousand sq. km	% of total land area
	2000	2000	1990–2000	1990–2000	1996	2002 [b]	1996	2002 [b]	1997	1997	2002 [c]	2002 [c]
Afghanistan	14	2.1	0	0.0	123	13	235	11	4,000	4	2.2	0.3
Albania	10	36.2	78	0.8	68	3	230	3	3,031	79	1.0	3.8
Algeria	21	0.9	−266	−1.3	92	13	192	6	3,164	141	119.5	5.0
Angola	698	56.0	1,242	0.2	276	19	765	15	5,185	30	81.8	6.6
Argentina	346	12.7	2,851	0.8	320	34	897	39	9,372	247	181.6	6.6
Armenia	4	12.4	−42	−1.3	..	11	..	4	..	31	2.1	7.6
Australia	1,581	20.6	0	0.0	252	63	649	37	15,638	2,245	1,017.7	13.2
Austria	39	47.0	−77	−0.2	83	7	213	3	3,100	23	28.1	33.9
Azerbaijan	11	12.6	−130	−1.3	..	13	..	8	..	28	4.8	5.5
Bangladesh	13	10.2	−165	−1.3	109	23	295	23	5,000	24	1.0	0.8
Belarus	94	45.3	−2,562	−3.2	..	7	221	3	..	1	13.0	6.3
Belgium	..	..	..	..	58	11	180	2	1,550	2	0.9	2.6
Benin	27	24.0	699	2.3	188	8	307	2	2,201	4	12.6	11.4
Bolivia	531	48.9	1,611	0.3	316	24	..	28	17,367	227	151.0	13.9
Bosnia and Herzegovina	23	44.6	0	0.0	..	10	..	3	..	64	0.3	0.5
Botswana	124	21.9	1,184	0.9	164	6	386	7	2,151	7	105.0	18.5
Brazil	5,325	63.0	22,264	0.4	394	81	1,492	114	56,215	1,358	568.6	6.7
Bulgaria	37	33.4	−204	−0.6	81	14	240	10	3,572	106	5.0	4.5
Burkina Faso	71	25.9	152	0.2	147	7	335	2	1,100	0	28.6	10.4
Burundi	1	3.7	147	9.0	107	6	451	7	2,500	1	1.5	5.7
Cambodia	93	52.9	561	0.6	123	24	307	19	..	5	32.7	18.5
Cameroon	239	51.3	2,218	0.9	297	40	690	15	8,260	89	21.0	4.5
Canada	2,446	26.5	0	0.0	193	14	426	8	3,270	278	1,077.6	11.7
Central African Republic	229	36.8	300	0.1	209	14	537	3	3,602	1	55.2	8.9
Chad	127	10.1	817	0.6	134	17	370	5	1,600	12	114.9	9.1
Chile	155	20.7	203	0.1	91	21	296	22	5,284	329	141.4	18.9
China	1,589	17.0	−13,483	−0.9	499	94	1,258	183	32,200	312	730.4	7.8
Hong Kong, China	..	..	..	..	24	1	76	11	1,984	9	0.5	..
Colombia	496	47.8	1,905	0.4	359	41	1,695	78	51,220	712	94.7	9.1
Congo, Dem. Rep.	1,352	59.6	5,324	0.4	415	40	929	28	11,007	78	146.4	6.5
Congo, Rep.	221	64.6	175	0.1	200	15	449	3	6,000	3	17.0	5.0
Costa Rica	20	38.5	158	0.8	205	14	600	13	12,119	527	11.8	23.0
Côte d'Ivoire	71	22.4	2,649	3.1	230	19	535	12	3,660	94	20.5	6.4
Croatia	18	31.9	−20	−0.1	..	9	224	4	..	6	4.2	7.5
Cuba	23	21.4	−277	−1.3	31	11	137	18	6,522	888	74.1	67.5
Czech Republic	26	34.1	−5	0.0	..	8	199	2	..	81	12.5	16.1
Denmark	5	10.7	−10	−0.2	43	5	196	1	1,450	2	14.4	34.0
Dominican Republic	14	28.4	0	0.0	20	5	136	15	5,657	136	15.5	32.0
Ecuador	106	38.1	1,372	1.2	302	33	1,388	62	19,362	824	128.5	46.4
Egypt, Arab Rep.	1	0.1	−20	−3.4	98	13	153	7	2,076	82	10.1	1.0
El Salvador	1	5.8	72	4.6	135	2	251	0	2,911	42	0.1	0.4
Eritrea	16	15.7	54	0.3	112	12	319	7	..	0	5.0	5.0
Estonia	21	48.7	−125	−0.6	65	4	213	3	1,630	2	5.0	11.8
Ethiopia	46	4.6	403	0.8	255	35	626	16	6,603	163	227.7	22.8
Finland	219	72.0	−80	0.0	60	5	248	3	1,102	6	28.4	9.3
France	153	27.9	−616	−0.4	93	18	269	5	4,630	195	73.2	13.3
Gabon	218	84.7	101	0.0	190	15	466	5	6,651	91	7.2	2.8
Gambia, The	5	48.1	−45	−1.0	108	3	280	2	974	1	0.2	2.3
Georgia	30	43.0	0	0.0	..	13	..	3	..	29	2.0	2.8
Germany	107	30.1	0	0.0	76	11	239	5	2,682	14	111.6	31.3
Ghana	63	27.8	1,200	1.7	222	14	529	8	3,725	103	12.7	5.6
Greece	36	27.9	−300	−0.9	95	13	251	7	4,992	571	4.7	3.6
Guatemala	29	26.3	537	1.7	250	6	458	6	8,681	355	21.7	20.0
Guinea	69	28.2	347	0.5	190	12	409	10	3,000	39	1.6	0.7
Guinea-Bissau	22	77.8	216	0.9	108	3	243	0	1,000	0	..	..
Haiti	1	3.2	70	5.7	3	4	75	14	5,242	100	0.1	0.4

	Forest area		Average annual deforestation		Mammals		Birds		Higher plants [a]		Nationally protected areas	
	thousand sq. km	% of total land area	sq. km	%	Species	Threatened species	Species	Threatened species	Species	Threatened species	thousand sq. km	% of total land area
	2000	2000	1990–2000	1990–2000	1996	2002[b]	1996	2002[b]	1997	1997	2002[c]	2002[c]
Honduras	54	48.1	590	1.0	173	10	422	5	5,680	96	7.2	6.4
Hungary	18	19.9	−72	−0.4	72	9	205	8	2,214	30	6.5	7.0
India	641	21.6	−381	−0.1	316	88	923	72	16,000	1,236	154.7	5.2
Indonesia	1,050	58.0	13,124	1.2	436	147	1,519	114	29,375	264	357.4	19.7
Iran, Islamic Rep.	73	4.5	0	0.0	140	22	323	13	8,000	2	83.0	5.1
Iraq	8	1.8	0	0.0	81	11	172	11	..	2	0.0	0.0
Ireland	7	9.6	−170	−3.0	25	5	142	1	950	1	0.7	1.0
Israel	1	6.4	−50	−4.9	92	14	180	12	2,317	32	3.3	15.8
Italy	100	34.0	−295	−0.3	90	14	234	5	5,599	311	23.1	7.9
Jamaica	3	30.0	54	1.5	24	5	113	12	3,308	744	..	..
Japan	241	66.1	−34	0.0	132	37	250	34	5,565	707	25.6	7.0
Jordan	1	1.0	0	0.0	71	10	141	8	2,100	9	3.0	3.4
Kazakhstan	121	4.5	−2,390	−2.2	..	16	..	15	..	71	73.4	2.7
Kenya	171	30.0	931	0.5	359	51	844	24	6,506	240	45.5	8.0
Korea, Dem. Rep.	82	68.2	0	0.0	..	13	115	19	2,898	4	3.2	2.6
Korea, Rep.	63	63.3	49	0.1	49	13	112	25	2,898	66	6.8	6.9
Kuwait	0	0.3	−2	−5.2	21	1	20	7	*234*	*0*	0.3	1.5
Kyrgyz Republic	10	5.2	−228	−2.6	..	7	..	4	..	34	6.9	3.6
Lao PDR	126	54.4	527	0.4	172	31	487	20	..	2	30.3	13.1
Latvia	29	47.1	−127	−0.4	83	4	217	3	*1,153*	*0*	8.3	13.4
Lebanon	0	3.5	1	0.3	54	5	154	7	3,000	5	0.0	0.5
Lesotho	0	0.5	0	0.0	33	3	58	7	1,591	21	0.1	0.2
Liberia	35	36.1	760	2.0	193	17	372	11	2,200	25	2.5	2.6
Libya	4	0.2	−47	−1.4	76	8	91	1	1,825	57	1.7	0.1
Lithuania	20	30.8	−48	−0.2	68	5	202	4	1,796	1	6.5	10.0
Macedonia, FYR	9	35.6	0	0.0	..	11	..	3	..	*0*	1.8	7.1
Madagascar	117	20.2	1,174	0.9	105	50	202	27	9,505	306	12.3	2.1
Malawi	26	27.6	707	2.4	195	8	521	11	3,765	61	10.6	11.3
Malaysia	193	58.7	2,377	1.2	286	50	501	37	15,500	490	17.4	5.3
Mali	132	10.8	993	0.7	137	13	397	4	1,741	15	45.3	3.7
Mauritania	3	0.3	98	2.7	61	10	273	2	1,100	3	17.5	1.7
Mauritius	0	7.9	1	0.6	4	3	27	9	750	294	0.2	7.8
Mexico	552	28.9	6,306	1.1	450	70	769	39	26,071	1,593	195.2	10.2
Moldova	3	9.9	−7	−0.2	68	6	177	5	..	5	0.5	1.4
Mongolia	106	6.8	600	0.5	134	14	..	16	2,272	0	179.9	11.5
Morocco	30	6.8	12	0.0	105	16	210	9	3,675	186	3.2	0.7
Mozambique	306	39.0	637	0.2	179	14	498	16	5,692	89	66.0	8.4
Myanmar	344	52.3	5,169	1.4	251	39	867	35	7,000	32	5.6	0.9
Namibia	80	9.8	734	0.9	154	15	469	11	3,174	75	112.2	13.6
Nepal	39	27.3	783	1.8	167	31	611	25	6,973	20	12.7	8.9
Netherlands	4	11.1	−10	−0.3	55	10	191	4	1,221	1	4.8	14.2
New Zealand	79	29.7	−390	−0.5	10	8	150	63	2,382	211	63.4	23.7
Nicaragua	33	27.0	1,172	3.0	200	6	482	5	7,590	98	21.6	17.8
Niger	13	1.0	617	3.7	131	11	299	3	*1,170*	*0*	96.9	7.7
Nigeria	135	14.8	3,984	2.6	274	27	681	9	4,715	37	30.2	3.3
Norway	89	28.9	−310	−0.4	54	10	243	2	1,715	12	20.9	6.8
Oman	0	0.0	0	0.0	56	9	107	10	1,204	30	39.1	12.6
Pakistan	25	3.2	304	1.1	151	19	375	17	4,950	14	37.4	4.9
Panama	29	38.6	519	1.6	218	20	732	16	9,915	1,302	17.1	22.9
Papua New Guinea	306	67.6	1,129	0.4	214	58	644	32	11,544	92	10.5	2.3
Paraguay	234	58.8	1,230	0.5	305	10	556	26	7,851	129	14.0	3.5
Peru	652	50.9	2,688	0.4	344	49	1,538	76	18,245	906	78.3	6.1
Philippines	58	19.4	887	1.4	153	50	395	67	8,931	360	17.0	5.7
Poland	93	30.6	−110	−0.1	84	15	227	4	2,450	27	37.9	12.4
Portugal	37	40.1	−570	−1.7	63	17	207	7	5,050	269	6.0	6.6
Puerto Rico	2	25.8	5	0.2	16	2	105	8	2,493	223	0.3	3.5

	Forest area		Average annual deforestation		Mammals		Birds		Higher plants [a]		Nationally protected areas	
	thousand sq. km	% of total land area	sq. km	%	Species	Threatened species	Species	Threatened species	Species	Threatened species	thousand sq. km	% of total land area
	2000	**2000**	**1990–2000**	**1990–2000**	**1996**	**2002** [b]	**1996**	**2002** [b]	**1997**	**1997**	**2002** [c]	**2002** [c]
Romania	64	28.0	−147	−0.2	84	17	247	8	3,400	99	10.9	4.7
Russian Federation	8,514	50.4	−1,353	0.0	269	45	628	38	..	214	1,395.1	8.3
Rwanda	3	12.4	150	3.9	151	9	513	9	*2,288*	0	3.6	14.7
Saudi Arabia	15	0.7	0	0.0	77	8	155	15	2,028	7	825.7	38.4
Senegal	62	32.2	450	0.7	155	12	384	4	2,086	31	22.4	11.6
Sierra Leone	11	14.7	361	2.9	147	12	466	10	2,090	29	1.5	2.1
Singapore	0	3.3	0	0.0	45	3	118	7	2,168	29	0.0	4.9
Slovak Republic	20	42.5	−69	−0.3	..	9	209	4		65	11.0	..
Slovenia	11	55.0	−22	−0.2	69	9	207	1	..	13	1.2	6.0
Somalia	75	12.0	769	1.0	171	19	422	10	3,028	103	5.2	0.8
South Africa	89	7.3	80	0.1	247	42	596	28	23,420	2,215	67.3	5.5
Spain	144	28.8	−860	−0.6	82	24	278	7	5,050	985	42.4	8.5
Sri Lanka	19	30.0	348	1.6	88	22	250	14	3,314	455	8.7	13.5
Sudan	616	25.9	9,589	1.4	267	23	680	6	3,137	10	122.5	5.2
Swaziland	5	30.3	−58	−1.2	47	4	364	5	2,715	42	0.6	3.5
Sweden	271	65.9	−6	0.0	60	7	249	2	1,750	13	54.2	13.2
Switzerland	12	30.3	−43	−0.4	75	5	193	2	3,030	30	11.9	30.0
Syrian Arab Republic	5	2.5	0	0.0	63	4	204	8	3,000	8	..	..
Tajikistan	4	2.8	−20	−0.5	..	9	..	7	..	50	5.9	4.2
Tanzania	388	43.9	913	0.2	316	42	822	33	10,008	436	263.4	29.8
Thailand	148	28.9	1,124	0.7	265	37	616	37	11,625	385	70.8	13.9
Togo	5	9.4	209	3.4	196	9	391	0	2,201	4	4.3	7.9
Trinidad and Tobago	3	50.5	22	0.8	100	1	260	1	2,259	21	0.3	6.0
Tunisia	5	3.3	−11	−0.2	78	11	173	5	2,196	24	0.4	0.3
Turkey	102	13.3	−220	−0.2	116	17	302	11	8,650	1,876	12.0	1.6
Turkmenistan	38	8.0	0	0.0	..	13	..	6	..	17	19.8	4.2
Uganda	42	21.3	913	2.0	338	20	830	13	5,406	15	49.2	24.9
Ukraine	96	16.5	−310	−0.3	..	16	263	8	*2,927*	52	22.9	3.9
United Arab Emirates	3	3.8	−78	−2.8	25	3	67	8	..	0	0.0	0.0
United Kingdom	26	10.7	−200	−0.8	50	12	230	2	1,623	18	54.8	22.8
United States	2,260	24.7	−3,880	−0.2	428	37	650	55	19,473	4,669	2,373.9	25.9
Uruguay	13	7.4	−501	−5.0	81	6	237	11	2,278	15	0.5	0.3
Uzbekistan	20	4.8	−46	−0.2	..	9	..	9	..	41	8.2	2.0
Venezuela, RB	495	56.1	2,175	0.4	305	26	1,181	24	21,073	426	563.1	63.8
Vietnam	98	30.2	−516	−0.5	213	40	535	37	10,500	341	11.6	3.5
West Bank and Gaza	..	..	..	..	..	1	..	1	..	..	..	..
Yemen, Rep.	4	0.9	92	1.8	66	5	143	12	..	*149*	..	..
Yugoslavia, Fed. Rep.	29	..	14	0.0	..	12	..	5	5,351	155	..	..
Zambia	312	42.0	8,509	2.4	229	11	605	11	4,747	12	453.2	61.0
Zimbabwe	190	49.2	3,199	1.5	270	11	532	10	4,440	100	50.0	12.9
World	**38,607 s**	**29.7 w**	**90,419.0 s**	**0.2 w**							**15,177.0 s**	**11.7 w**
Low income	9,131	27.1	72,735.0	0.8							2,974.8	9.2
Middle income	21,442	32.7	25,646.0	0.1							6,141.4	9.3
Lower middle income	13,700	31.8	−11,406.0	−0.1							3,372.5	7.5
Upper middle income	7,742	34.5	37,052.0	0.5							2,768.9	13.0
Low & middle income	30,568	30.9	98,347.0	0.3							9,116.2	9.3
East Asia & Pacific	4,284	27.2	7,033.0	0.2							1,467.5	9.2
Europe & Central Asia	9,464	39.7	−8,143.0	−0.1							1,677.2	7.0
Latin America & Carib.	9,440	47.1	45,878.0	0.5							2,315.2	11.5
Middle East & N. Africa	168	1.5	−239.0	−0.1							1,086.0	10.4
South Asia	782	16.3	889.0	0.1							228.6	4.8
Sub-Saharan Africa	6,436	27.3	52,963.0	0.8							2,341.8	9.9
High income	8,034	26.1	−7,962.0	−0.1							6,060.8	19.5
Europe EMU	927	37.0	−2,988.0	−0.3							332.6	13.1

a. Flowering plants only. b. Data may be for earlier years. They are the most recent reported by the World Conservation Monitoring Centre in 2002. c. These are tentative data and are being finalized.

About the data

The estimates of forest area are from the Food and Agriculture Organization's (FAO) *State of the World's Forests 2001*, which provides information on forest cover in 2000 and a revised estimate of forest cover in 1990. The current survey is the latest global forest assessment and the first to use a uniform global definition of forest. According to this assessment, the global rate of net deforestation has slowed to 9 million hectares a year, a rate 20 percent lower than that previously reported.

No breakdown of forest cover between natural forest and plantation is shown in the table because of space limitations. (This breakdown is provided by the FAO only for developing countries.) For this reason the deforestation data in the table may underestimate the rate at which natural forest is disappearing in some countries.

Deforestation is a major cause of loss of biodiversity, and habitat conservation is vital for stemming this loss. Conservation efforts traditionally have focused on protected areas, which have grown substantially in recent decades. Measures of species richness are among the most straightforward ways to indicate the importance of an area for biodiversity. The number of small plants and animals is usually estimated by sampling plots. It is also important to know which aspects are under the most immediate threat. This, however, requires a large amount of data and time-consuming analysis. For this reason global analyses of the status of threatened species have been carried out for few groups of organisms. Only for birds has the status of all species been assessed. An estimated 45 percent of mammal species remain to be assessed. For plants the World Conservation Union's (IUCN) *1997 IUCN Red List of Threatened Plants* provides the first-ever comprehensive listing of threatened species on a global scale, the result of more than 20 years' work by botanists from around the world. Nearly 34,000 plant species, 12.5 percent of the total, are threatened with extinction.

The table shows information on protected areas, numbers of certain species, and numbers of those species under threat. The World Conservation Monitoring Centre (WCMC) compiles these data from a variety of sources. Because of differences in definitions and reporting practices, cross-country comparability is limited. Compounding these problems, available data cover different periods.

Nationally protected areas are areas of at least 1,000 hectares that fall into one of five management categories defined by the WCMC:

- Scientific reserves and strict nature reserves with limited public access.
- National parks of national or international significance (not materially affected by human activity).
- Natural monuments and natural landscapes with unique aspects.
- Managed nature reserves and wildlife sanctuaries.
- Protected landscapes and seascapes (which may include cultural landscapes).

Designating land as a protected area does not necessarily mean that protection is in force. For small countries that may only have protected areas smaller than 1,000 hectares, this size limit in the definition will result in an underestimate of the extent and number of protected areas.

Threatened species are defined according to the IUCN's classification categories: endangered (in danger of extinction and unlikely to survive if causal factors continue operating), vulnerable (likely to move into the endangered category in the near future if causal factors continue operating), rare (not endangered or vulnerable but at risk), indeterminate (known to be endangered, vulnerable, or rare but not enough information is available to say which), out of danger (formerly included in one of the above categories but now considered relatively secure because appropriate conservation measures are in effect), and insufficiently known (suspected but not definitely known to belong to one of the above categories).

Figures on species are not necessarily comparable across countries because taxonomic concepts and coverage vary. And while the number of birds and mammals is fairly well known, it is difficult to make an accurate count of plants. Although the data in the table should be interpreted with caution, especially for numbers of threatened species (where our knowledge is very incomplete), they do identify countries that are major sources of global biodiversity and show national commitments to habitat protection.

Definitions

• **Forest area** is land under natural or planted stands of trees, whether productive or not. • **Average annual deforestation** refers to the permanent conversion of natural forest area to other uses, including shifting cultivation, permanent agriculture, ranching, settlements, and infrastructure development. Deforested areas do not include areas logged but intended for regeneration or areas degraded by fuelwood gathering, acid precipitation, or forest fires. Negative numbers indicate an increase in forest area. • **Mammals** exclude whales and porpoises. • **Birds** are listed for countries included within their breeding or wintering ranges. • **Higher plants** refer to native vascular plant species. • **Threatened species** are the number of species classified by the IUCN as endangered, vulnerable, rare, indeterminate, out of danger, or insufficiently known. • **Nationally protected areas** are totally or partially protected areas of at least 1,000 hectares that are designated as national parks, natural monuments, nature reserves or wildlife sanctuaries, protected landscapes and seascapes, or scientific reserves with limited public access. The data do not include sites protected under local or provincial law. Total land area is used to calculate the percentage of total area protected (see table 3.1).

Data sources

The forestry data are from the FAO's *State of the World's Forests 2001*. The data on species are from the WCMC's electronic files and the IUCN's *2002 IUCN Red List of Threatened Animals* and *1997 IUCN Red List of Threatened Plants*. The data on protected areas are from the WCMC's Protected Areas Data Unit.

| | Freshwater resources | | | Annual freshwater withdrawals | | | | | Access to improved water source | | | |
| | Internal flows billion cu. m | Flows from other countries billion cu. m | Total renewable resources per capita cu. m[a] | billion cu. m[b] | % of total renewable resources[b] | % for agriculture[b] | % for industry[b] | % for domestic[b] | Urban % of population | | Rural % of population | |
	2000	2000	2000						1990	2000	1990	2000
Afghanistan	55	10.0	2,448	26.1	40.2	99	0	1	..	19	..	11
Albania	27	15.7	13,593	1.4	3.3	71	0	29	..	99	..	95
Algeria	14	0.4	471	5.0	35.0	52	14	34	..	94	..	82
Angola	184	..	14,009	0.5	0.3	76	10	14	..	34	..	40
Argentina	276	623.0	24,276	28.6	3.2	75	9	16	..	97	..	73
Armenia	9	1.5	2,787	2.9	27.4	66	4	30	..	..	..	..
Australia	492	0.0	25,649	14.6	3.0	33	2	65	100	100	100	100
Austria	55	29.0	10,357	2.4	2.9	9	58	33	100	100	100	100
Azerbaijan	8	21.0	3,615	16.5	56.7	70	25	5	..	93	..	58
Bangladesh	105	1,105.6	9,238	14.6	1.2	86	2	12	99	99	93	97
Belarus	37	20.8	5,797	2.7	4.7	35	43	22	..	100	..	100
Belgium	12	4.0	1,561	..	..	..	..	..	..	..	..	..
Benin	10	15.5	4,114	0.1	0.4	67	10	23	..	74	..	55
Bolivia	304	7.2	37,305	1.2	0.4	87	3	10	91	95	47	64
Bosnia and Herzegovina	36	2.0	9,429	1.0	2.7	60	10	30	..	..	..	..
Botswana	3	11.8	8,776	0.1	0.7	48	20	32	100	100	88	90
Brazil	5,418	1,900.0	43,022	54.9	0.8	61	18	21	93	95	54	53
Bulgaria	21	0.2	2,595	13.9	65.6	22	75	3	..	100	..	100
Burkina Faso	13	2.0	1,286	0.4	2.8	81	0	19	..	66	..	37
Burundi	4	..	529	0.1	2.8	64	0	36	96	91	67	77
Cambodia	121	355.6	39,613	0.5	0.1	94	1	5	..	54	..	26
Cameroon	273	0.0	18,352	0.4	0.1	35	19	46	78	78	32	39
Canada	2,850	52.0	94,314	45.1	1.6	12	70	18	100	100	99	99
Central African Republic	141	..	37,934	0.1	0.1	74	5	21	71	89	35	57
Chad	15	28.0	5,589	0.2	0.5	82	2	16	..	31	..	26
Chile	884	0.0	58,115	20.3	2.3	84	11	5	98	99	49	58
China	2,812	17.2	2,241	525.5	18.6	78	18	5	99	94	60	66
Hong Kong, China	..	..	..	..	..	..	..	..	..	..	..	..
Colombia	2,112	0.0	49,930	8.9	0.4	37	4	59	98	99	84	70
Congo, Dem. Rep.	900	313.0	23,809	0.4	0.0	23	16	61	..	89	..	26
Congo, Rep.	222	610.0	275,679	0.0	0.0	11	27	62	..	71	..	17
Costa Rica	112	..	29,501	5.8	5.2	80	7	13	..	99	..	92
Côte d'Ivoire	77	..	4,790	0.7	0.9	67	11	22	97	92	69	72
Croatia	38	33.7	16,301	0.8	1.1	0	50	50	..	..	..	..
Cuba	38	0.0	3,405	5.2	13.6	51	0	49	..	95	..	77
Czech Republic	13	1.0	1,382	2.7	19.0	2	57	41	..	..	..	..
Denmark	6	..	1,124	1.2	20.0	43	27	30	..	100	..	100
Dominican Republic	21	..	2,508	8.3	39.5	89	0	11	92	90	71	78
Ecuador	432	0.0	34,161	17.0	3.9	82	6	12	82	90	58	75
Egypt, Arab Rep.	2	66.7	1,071	66.0	96.4	82	11	7	97	99	92	96
El Salvador	18	..	2,836	0.7	3.9	46	20	34	88	91	48	64
Eritrea	3	6.0	2,148	..	..	..	..	..	..	63	..	42
Estonia	13	0.1	9,346	0.2	1.6	5	39	56	..	..	..	..
Ethiopia	110	0.0	1,711	2.2	2.0	86	3	11	80	81	17	12
Finland	107	3.0	21,268	2.2	2.0	3	85	12	100	100	100	100
France	179	11.0	3,218	32.3	17.0	10	72	18	..	..	..	..
Gabon	164	0.0	133,333	0.1	0.1	6	22	72	..	95	..	47
Gambia, The	3	5.0	6,140	0.0	0.0	91	2	7	..	80	..	53
Georgia	58	8.4	12,395	3.5	5.3	59	20	21	..	90	..	61
Germany	107	71.0	2,165	46.3	26.0	20	69	11	..	..	..	..
Ghana	30	22.9	2,756	0.3	0.6	52	13	35	85	91	36	62
Greece	58	15.0	6,913	8.7	11.9	87	3	10	..	..	..	..
Guatemala	109	0.0	9,591	1.2	1.1	74	17	9	88	98	69	88
Guinea	226	0.0	30,479	0.7	0.3	87	3	10	72	72	36	36
Guinea-Bissau	16	11.0	22,519	0.0	0.0	36	4	60	..	79	..	49
Haiti	13	..	1,633	1.0	7.7	94	1	5	59	49	50	45

	Freshwater resources			Annual freshwater withdrawals					Access to improved water source			
	Internal flows billion cu. m	Flows from other countries billion cu. m	Total renewable resources per capita cu. m[a]	billion cu. m[b]	% of total renewable resources[b]	% for agriculture[b]	% for industry[b]	% for domestic[b]	Urban % of population		Rural % of population	
	2000	2000	2000						1990	2000	1990	2000
Honduras	96	0.0	14,945	1.5	1.6	91	5	4	89	95	78	81
Hungary	6	114.0	11,855	6.8	5.7	36	55	9	100	100	98	98
India	1,261	647.2	1,878	500.0	26.2	92	3	5	88	95	61	79
Indonesia	2,838	..	13,759	74.3	2.6	93	1	6	92	90	62	69
Iran, Islamic Rep.	129	..	2,018	70.0	54.5	92	2	6	..	98	..	83
Iraq	35	75.9	4,776	42.8	38.5	92	5	3	..	96	..	48
Ireland	49	3.0	13,706	0.8	1.5	10	74	16	..	..	..	..
Israel	1	0.9	273	1.6	94.1	54	7	39	..	..	..	..
Italy	183	6.8	3,281	42.0	22.2	48	34	19	..	..	..	..
Jamaica	9	..	3,653	0.9	9.6	77	7	15	98	98	87	85
Japan	430	0.0	3,389	91.4	21.3	64	17	19	..	..	..	..
Jordan	1	0.9	143	1.0	..	75	3	22	99	100	92	84
Kazakhstan	75	34.2	7,278	33.7	30.7	81	17	2	..	98	..	82
Kenya	20	10.0	1,004	2.0	6.6	76	4	20	91	88	31	42
Korea, Dem. Rep.	67	10.1	3,462	14.2	18.4	73	16	11	..	100	..	100
Korea, Rep.	65	4.9	1,485	23.7	34.0	63	11	26	..	97	..	71
Kuwait	0	0.0	0	0.5	..	60	2	37	..	..	..	..
Kyrgyz Republic	47	0.0	9,461	10.1	21.7	94	3	3	..	98	..	66
Lao PDR	190	143.1	63,175	1.0	0.3	82	10	8	..	61	..	29
Latvia	17	18.7	14,924	0.3	0.8	13	32	55	..	..	..	..
Lebanon	5	0.0	1,109	1.3	27.1	68	6	27	..	100	..	100
Lesotho	5	0.0	2,555	0.1	1.9	56	22	22	..	88	..	74
Liberia	200	32.0	74,121	0.1	0.0	60	13	27	..	..	..	..
Libya	1	0.0	113	4.5	..	84	3	13	72	72	68	68
Lithuania	16	9.3	7,102	0.3	1.2	3	16	81	..	..	..	..
Macedonia, FYR	5	1.0	3,151	1.9	29.7	74	15	12	..	..	..	..
Madagascar	337	0.0	21,710	16.3	4.8	99	..	1	85	85	31	31
Malawi	16	1.1	1,668	0.9	5.2	86	3	10	90	95	43	44
Malaysia	580	..	24,925	12.7	2.2	77	13	11	..	..	..	94
Mali	60	40.0	9,225	1.4	1.4	97	1	2	65	74	52	61
Mauritania	0	11.0	4,278	1.6	14.0	92	2	6	34	34	40	40
Mauritius	2	0.0	1,853	..	..	77	7	16	100	100	100	100
Mexico	409	49.0	4,675	77.8	17.0	78	5	17	90	95	52	69
Moldova	1	10.7	2,735	3.0	25.6	26	65	9	..	97	..	88
Mongolia	35	..	14,512	0.4	1.1	53	27	20	..	77	..	30
Morocco	29	0.0	1,010	11.5	39.7	89	2	10	94	98	58	56
Mozambique	99	111.0	11,870	0.6	0.3	89	2	9	..	81	..	41
Myanmar	881	165.0	21,898	4.0	0.4	90	3	7	..	89	..	66
Namibia	6	39.3	25,896	0.2	0.4	68	3	29	98	100	63	67
Nepal	198	12.0	9,122	29.0	13.8	99	0	1	93	94	64	87
Netherlands	11	80.0	5,716	7.8	8.6	34	61	5	100	100	100	100
New Zealand	327	0.0	85,361	2.0	0.6	44	10	46	100	100	..	..
Nicaragua	190	0.0	37,409	1.3	0.7	84	2	14	93	91	44	59
Niger	4	29.0	3,000	0.5	1.5	82	2	16	65	70	51	56
Nigeria	221	59.0	2,206	3.6	1.3	54	15	31	83	78	37	49
Norway	382	11.0	87,508	2.0	0.5	8	72	20	100	100	100	100
Oman	1	..	415	1.2	..	94	2	5	41	41	30	30
Pakistan	52	170.3	1,610	155.6	70.0	97	2	2	96	95	77	87
Panama	147	..	51,647	1.6	1.1	70	2	28	..	99	..	79
Papua New Guinea	801	..	156,140	0.1	0.0	49	22	29	88	88	32	32
Paraguay	94	..	17,103	0.4	0.4	78	7	15	80	93	46	59
Peru	1,616	144.0	67,852	19.0	1.1	86	7	7	88	87	42	62
Philippines	479	0.0	6,251	55.4	11.6	88	4	8	93	91	82	79
Poland	54	8.0	1,594	12.3	20.0	11	76	13	..	..	..	..
Portugal	38	35.0	7,294	7.3	10.0	48	37	15	..	..	..	..
Puerto Rico	..	..	..	..	..	..	..	..	..	..	..	..

3.5 | Freshwater

	Freshwater resources			Annual freshwater withdrawals					Access to improved water source			
	Internal flows billion cu. m 2000	Flows from other countries billion cu. m 2000	Total renewable resources per capita cu. m [a] 2000	billion cu. m [b]	% of total renewable resources [b]	% for agriculture [b]	% for industry [b]	% for domestic [b]	Urban % of population 1990	2000	Rural % of population 1990	2000
Romania	42	170.0	9,463	26.0	12.2	59	33	8	..	91	..	16
Russian Federation	4,313	185.5	30,904	77.1	1.7	20	62	19	..	100	..	96
Rwanda	5	..	611	0.8	15.4	94	2	5	..	60	..	40
Saudi Arabia	2	..	116	17.0	..	90	1	9	..	100	..	64
Senegal	26	13.0	4,134	1.4	3.6	92	3	5	90	92	60	65
Sierra Leone	160	0.0	31,803	0.4	0.3	89	4	7	..	75	..	46
Singapore	..	..	..	..	..	4	51	45	100	100	100	..
Slovak Republic	13	70.0	15,293	1.8	2.2	..	..	..	..	100	..	100
Slovenia	19	0.0	9,402	1.3	7.0	1	80	20	100	100	100	100
Somalia	6	9.7	1,789	0.8	5.1	97	0	3	..	..	..	..
South Africa	45	5.2	1,168	13.3	26.6	72	11	17	99	99	73	73
Spain	111	0.3	2,753	35.2	31.6	68	19	13	..	..	..	..
Sri Lanka	50	0.0	2,708	9.8	19.6	96	2	2	91	98	62	70
Sudan	30	119.0	4,792	17.8	11.9	94	1	4	86	86	60	69
Swaziland	3	1.9	4,306	..	..	96	2	2	..	..	..	..
Sweden	171	12.2	20,656	2.9	1.6	9	55	36	100	100	100	100
Switzerland	40	13.0	7,437	1.2	2.2	4	73	23	100	100	100	100
Syrian Arab Republic	7	37.7	2,761	12.0	26.8	90	2	8	..	94	..	64
Tajikistan	66	13.3	12,853	11.9	14.9	92	4	3	..	93	..	47
Tanzania	82	9.0	2,701	1.2	1.3	89	2	9	76	90	28	57
Thailand	210	199.9	6,750	33.1	8.1	91	4	5	87	95	78	81
Togo	12	0.5	2,651	0.1	0.8	25	13	62	82	85	38	38
Trinidad and Tobago	4	..	2,921	0.3	7.9	6	26	68	..	..	..	..
Tunisia	4	0.4	481	2.8	60.9	86	1	13	91	92	54	58
Turkey	227	7.6	3,593	35.5	15.1	73	12	16	83	81	72	86
Turkmenistan	1	59.5	11,523	23.8	39.1	98	1	1	..	..	..	..
Uganda	39	27.0	2,972	0.2	0.3	60	8	32	81	80	40	47
Ukraine	53	86.5	2,820	26.0	18.6	30	52	18	..	100	..	94
United Arab Emirates	0	0.0	69	2.1	..	67	9	24	..	..	..	..
United Kingdom	145	2.0	2,503	11.8	8.0	3	77	20	100	100	100	100
United States	2,800	18.0	9,985	467.3	16.6	42	45	13	100	100	100	100
Uruguay	59	74.0	39,856	0.7	0.5	91	3	6	..	98	..	93
Uzbekistan	16	98.1	4,623	58.1	50.8	94	2	4	..	94	..	79
Venezuela, RB	723	..	29,892	4.1	0.6	46	10	44	..	85	..	70
Vietnam	367	524.7	11,350	54.3	6.1	87	10	4	86	95	48	72
West Bank and Gaza	..	..	..	..	..	..	..	..	..	..	..	..
Yemen, Rep.	4	..	234	2.9	70.7	92	1	7	..	74	..	68
Yugoslavia, Fed. Rep.	44	144.0	17,674	13.0	6.9	8	86	6	..	99	..	97
Zambia	80	35.8	11,498	1.7	1.5	77	7	16	88	88	28	48
Zimbabwe	14	..	1,117	1.2	8.5	79	7	14	99	100	69	73
World	**42,900 w**	**9,468.8 s**	**8,649 w**			**71 w**	**20 w**	**10 w**	**94 w**	**94 w**	**62 w**	**71 w**
Low income	11,247	4,903.6	6,559			90	5	5	88	90	59	70
Middle income	22,836	4,187.4	10,230			74	17	9	95	95	63	70
Lower middle income	13,877	1,274.8	7,066			75	18	8	96	95	63	70
Upper middle income	8,958	2,912.6	23,872			69	14	16	93	94	57	69
Low & middle income	34,082	9,091.0	8,460			81	12	7	93	93	61	70
East Asia & Pacific	9,454	1,415.6	6,020			81	14	5	97	93	61	67
Europe & Central Asia	5,255	1,134.8	13,465			57	33	10	..	96	..	83
Latin America & Carib.	13,429	2,833.8	31,530			74	9	18	92	94	58	65
Middle East & N. Africa	234	183.1	1,413			88	5	7	..	96	..	78
South Asia	1,816	1,945.1	2,777			94	3	4	90	94	66	80
Sub-Saharan Africa	3,895	1,578.7	8,306			85	6	10	86	83	40	46
High income	8,818	372.8	9,672			42	42	16	..	..	..	..
Europe EMU	910	258.8	3,832			38	47	15	..	..	..	..

a. River flows from other countries are included when available, but river outflows are not because of data unreliability. b. Most data are for years between 1980 and 2000. For specific year, please refer to the *Primary data documentation*.

The data on freshwater resources are based on estimates of runoff into rivers and recharge of groundwater. These estimates are based on different sources and refer to different years, so cross-country comparisons should be made with caution. Because the data are collected intermittently, they may hide significant variations in total renewable water resources from one year to the next. The data also fail to distinguish between seasonal and geographic variations in water availability within countries. Data for small countries and countries in arid and semiarid zones are less reliable than those for larger countries and countries with greater rainfall. Finally, caution is also needed in comparing data on annual freshwater withdrawals, which are subject to variations in collection and estimation methods.

3.5a

Agriculture accounts for most freshwater withdrawals in developing countries

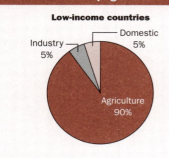

Low-income countries
Domestic 5%, Industry 5%, Agriculture 90%

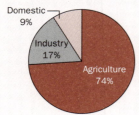

Middle-income countries
Domestic 9%, Industry 17%, Agriculture 74%

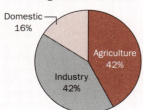

High-income countries
Domestic 16%, Industry 42%, Agriculture 42%

Note: Data are for the most recent year available (see table 3.5).
Source: Table 3.5.

The table shows both internal freshwater resources and river flows arising outside countries. However, river outflows are not shown because they are of different vintage and are deemed unreliable. Because the data on total freshwater resources include river flows entering a country without river flows out of the country being deducted, they overestimate the availability of water from international river ways. This can be important in water-short countries, notably in the Middle East.

The data on access to an improved water source measure the share of the population with reasonable and ready access to an adequate amount of safe water for domestic purposes. An improved source can be any form of collection or piping used to make water regularly available. While information on access to an improved water source is widely used, it is extremely subjective, and such terms as *safe*, *improved*, *adequate*, and *reasonable* may have very different meanings in different countries despite official World Health Organization definitions (see *Definitions*). Even in high-income countries treated water may not always be safe to drink. While access to an improved water source is equated with connection to a public supply system, this does not take into account variations in the quality and cost (broadly defined) of the service once connected. Thus cross-country comparisons must be made cautiously. Changes over time within countries may result from changes in definitions or measurements.

• **Freshwater resources** refer to total renewable resources, broken down between internal flows (internal river flows and groundwater from rainfall) in the country and river flows from other countries. Freshwater resources per capita are calculated using the World Bank's population estimates (see table 2.1). • **Annual freshwater withdrawals** refer to total water withdrawals, not counting evaporation losses from storage basins. Withdrawals also include water from desalination plants in countries where they are a significant source. Data on total withdrawals are for single years between 1980 and 2000 unless otherwise indicated. Withdrawals can exceed 100 percent of total renewable resources where extraction from nonrenewable aquifers or desalination plants is considerable or where there is significant water reuse. Withdrawals for agriculture and industry are total withdrawals for irrigation and livestock production and for direct industrial use (including withdrawals for cooling thermoelectric plants). Withdrawals for domestic uses include drinking water, municipal use or supply, and use for public services, commercial establishments, and homes. For most countries sectoral withdrawal data are estimated for 1987. • **Access to an improved water source** refers to the percentage of the population with reasonable access to an adequate amount of water from an improved source, such as a household connection, public standpipe, borehole, protected well or spring, or rainwater collection. Unimproved sources include vendors, tanker trucks, and unprotected wells and springs. Reasonable access is defined as the availability of at least 20 liters a person a day from a source within one kilometer of the dwelling.

The data on freshwater resources and withdrawals are compiled by the World Resources Institute from various sources and published in *World Resources 2000–01* and *World Resources 2002–03* (produced in collaboration with the United Nations Environment Programme, United Nations Development Programme, and World Bank). These are supplemented by the Food and Agriculture Organization's AQUASTAT data. The data on access to an improved water source come from the World Health Organization.

3.6 Water pollution

	Emissions of organic water pollutants				Industry shares of emissions of organic water pollutants							
	kilograms per day		kilograms per day per worker		Primary metals %	Paper and pulp %	Chemicals %	Food and beverages %	Stone, ceramics, and glass %	Textiles %	Wood %	Other %
	1980	2000[a]	1980	2000[a]	2000[a]	2000[a]	2000[a]	2000[a]	2000[a]	2000[a]	2000[a]	2000[a]
Afghanistan	6,680	..	0.17	..	..	..	..	..	0.2	..	..	..
Albania	..	6,512	..	0.29	14.3	0.9	6.0	73.5	0.3	4.6	0.7	1.5
Algeria	60,290	45,645	0.19	0.24	19.3	9.0	6.0	48.4	0.3	13.9	1.7	4.0
Angola	..	1,472	..	0.20	7.6	3.0	9.0	65.9	0.3	5.5	4.4	4.1
Argentina	244,711	177,882	0.18	0.21	7.1	11.6	8.0	59.0	0.2	8.4	1.8	3.9
Armenia	..	10,014	..	0.25	..	..	..	..	..	..	..	..
Australia	204,333	95,369	0.18	0.21	..	..	..	..	..	..	..	..
Austria	108,416	80,789	0.16	0.13	14.9	18.2	11.0	32.8	0.4	5.1	5.3	12.1
Azerbaijan	..	45,025	..	0.17	11.6	2.5	12.0	49.0	0.2	18.1	1.0	5.6
Bangladesh	66,713	273,082	0.16	0.14	4.5	8.2	3.0	30.3	0.1	48.6	0.3	1.5
Belarus	..	..	..	..	..	..	..	..	..	..	..	..
Belgium	136,452	113,460	0.16	0.16	16.2	16.9	12.0	34.5	0.2	9.9	1.9	9.9
Benin	1,646	..	0.28	..	..	2.9	..	82.6	0.2	12.2	0.5	..
Bolivia	9,343	12,759	0.22	0.25	0.9	20.5	7.0	61.4	0.3	7.1	2.4	0.9
Bosnia and Herzegovina	..	8,903	..	0.18	20.5	13.1	7.0	33.3	0.2	17.6	5.8	2.8
Botswana	1,307	4,635	0.24	0.20	1.7	5.2	5.0	80.1	0.2	10.7	1.8	1.8
Brazil	866,790	629,406	0.16	0.20	10.5	14.1	9.0	42.7	0.3	14.5	3.5	6.9
Bulgaria	152,125	107,945	0.13	0.17	10.6	6.9	7.0	46.7	0.4	15.7	2.3	9.3
Burkina Faso	2,385	2,598	0.29	0.22	1.6	2.8	5.0	81.5	0.0	6.5	0.6	1.3
Burundi	769	1,644	0.22	0.24	0.0	7.9	5.0	72.1	0.2	9.5	1.7	0.8
Cambodia	..	12,078	..	0.16	0.0	3.4	3.0	59.2	0.6	24.7	5.8	3.1
Cameroon	14,569	10,714	0.29	0.20	3.1	4.7	28.0	78.9	0.1	4.5	2.9	0.4
Canada	330,241	307,325	0.18	0.15	10.8	23.9	10.0	34.8	0.1	5.4	5.1	10.0
Central African Republic	861	670	0.26	0.17	0.0	..	4.0	62.0	0.0	13.8	19.6	..
Chad	..	..	..	..	..	..	..	..	..	..	..	..
Chile	44,371	72,850	0.21	0.24	6.9	11.3	9.0	62.7	0.1	5.0	2.6	2.5
China	3,377,105	6,519,911	0.14	0.14	20.5	10.9	15.0	28.7	0.5	14.7	0.8	8.7
Hong Kong, China	102,002	31,725	0.11	0.17	1.6	42.5	4.0	21.9	0.1	22.9	0.2	6.7
Colombia	96,055	100,752	0.19	0.21	3.9	16.2	10.0	51.1	0.2	14.8	0.7	2.7
Congo, Dem. Rep.	..	..	..	..	..	..	..	..	..	..	..	..
Congo, Rep.	1,039	..	0.21	..	..	..	..	..	..	..	..	..
Costa Rica	..	35,164	..	0.22	1.4	9.5	7.0	64.3	0.1	13.4	1.6	2.6
Côte d'Ivoire	15,414	12,401	0.23	0.24	0.5	3.9	7.0	73.5	0.1	10.3	5.2	1.6
Croatia	..	48,447	..	0.17	7.2	14.4	9.0	45.2	0.2	14.6	3.8	6.0
Cuba	120,703	..	0.24	..	..	..	..	..	..	..	..	..
Czech Republic	..	158,462	..	0.14	15.6	7.0	8.0	43.6	0.3	10.4	3.9	11.4
Denmark	65,465	83,591	0.17	0.17	3.6	20.1	8.0	53.4	0.2	5.0	2.2	8.5
Dominican Republic	54,935	..	0.38	..	0.6	2.8	..	92.1	0.1	1.9	0.2	0.3
Ecuador	25,297	32,266	0.23	0.27	2.0	10.8	6.0	65.5	0.2	9.6	2.2	2.5
Egypt, Arab Rep.	169,146	210,242	0.19	0.19	13.5	7.8	10.0	43.9	0.2	22.1	0.4	3.8
El Salvador	9,390	22,760	0.24	0.18	3.5	13.2	8.0	57.9	0.1	16.4	0.5	1.2
Eritrea	16,754	..	..	..	..	..	..	..	..	..	..	..
Estonia	..	..	..	..	..	..	..	..	..	..	..	..
Ethiopia	16,754	..	0.22	..	..	8.8	..	58.5	..	24.9	2.1	..
Finland	92,275	62,610	0.17	0.19	9.8	43.3	2.0	30.2	0.2	2.8	4.4	7.0
France	729,776	278,878	0.14	0.10	15.7	18.0	23.0	31.7	0.2	10.4	2.1	11.6
Gabon	2,661	1,886	0.15	0.26	5.1	5.8	5.0	54.5	0.2	3.4	22.3	3.7
Gambia, The	549	832	0.30	0.34	0.0	2.3	2.0	89.3	0.0	2.1	3.9	0.4
Georgia	..	..	..	..	..	..	..	..	..	..	..	..
Germany	..	792,194	..	0.13	11.2	22.3	10.0	34.4	0.2	3.2	2.3	16.5
Ghana	15,868	14,449	0.20	0.17	9.8	16.9	10.0	39.5	0.2	9.1	12.4	1.7
Greece	65,304	57,178	0.17	0.20	6.3	11.8	9.0	54.0	0.2	13.2	1.5	3.8
Guatemala	20,856	19,253	0.25	0.28	2.3	10.1	6.0	72.8	0.2	9.8	1.3	1.0
Guinea	..	..	..	..	..	..	..	..	..	..	..	..
Guinea-Bissau	..	..	..	..	..	..	..	..	..	..	..	..
Haiti	4,734	..	0.19	..	..	..	..	71.5	..	18.4	0.8	..

	Emissions of organic water pollutants				Industry shares of emissions of organic water pollutants							
	kilograms per day		kilograms per day per worker		Primary metals %	Paper and pulp %	Chemicals %	Food and beverages %	Stone, ceramics, and glass %	Textiles %	Wood %	Other %
	1980	2000[a]	1980	2000[a]	2000[a]	2000[a]	2000[a]	2000[a]	2000[a]	2000[a]	2000[a]	2000[a]
Honduras	13,067	34,036	0.23	0.20	1.1	7.8	4.0	55.5	0.1	26.8	4.0	0.8
Hungary	201,888	152,531	0.15	0.17	8.0	12.1	8.0	48.0	0.2	14.1	2.4	7.3
India	1,422,564	1,651,250	0.21	0.19	13.5	6.8	10.0	51.0	0.2	13.3	0.3	5.3
Indonesia	214,010	783,207	0.22	0.18	2.7	5.9	9.0	52.8	0.1	21.8	5.6	4.5
Iran, Islamic Rep.	72,334	101,900	0.15	0.17	20.6	8.0	8.0	39.7	0.5	17.3	0.7	5.4
Iraq	32,986	19,617	0.19	0.16	8.8	14.1	15.0	39.4	0.7	16.7	0.3	4.8
Ireland	43,544	49,144	0.19	0.15	1.3	14.2	11.0	56.4	0.2	3.1	1.6	11.8
Israel	39,113	54,149	0.15	0.16	3.7	19.7	9.0	43.9	0.2	12.1	1.8	9.3
Italy	442,712	495,411	0.13	0.13	9.5	16.9	11.0	30.3	0.3	16.0	3.7	12.5
Jamaica	11,123	17,507	0.25	0.29	6.9	7.2	4.0	70.8	0.1	9.8	1.3	0.0
Japan	1,456,016	1,369,931	0.14	0.15	7.9	21.8	9.0	41.0	0.2	5.6	1.7	12.9
Jordan	4,146	16,142	0.17	0.18	3.9	16.2	15.0	51.4	0.5	7.2	3.3	3.0
Kazakhstan	..	..	..	..	..	..	..	..	..	..	..	..
Kenya	26,834	52,945	0.19	0.25	4.1	11.8	6.0	69.9	0.1	8.5	1.8	2.7
Korea, Dem. Rep.	..	..	..	..	..	..	..	..	..	..	..	..
Korea, Rep.	281,900	303,091	0.14	0.12	12.2	17.0	12.0	26.0	0.2	15.7	1.3	15.3
Kuwait	6,921	11,050	0.16	0.17	2.6	16.6	11.0	47.7	0.4	13.7	2.8	5.4
Kyrgyz Republic	..	20,700	..	0.16	13.7	0.2	1.0	54.8	0.4	21.0	1.0	8.0
Lao PDR	..	..	..	..	..	..	..	..	..	..	..	..
Latvia	..	22,491	..	0.21	2.8	7.5	1.0	69.0	0.1	11.0	9.6	5.7
Lebanon	14,586	14,899	0.20	0.19	3.1	17.8	4.0	57.6	0.5	11.8	3.7	2.2
Lesotho	993	3,123	0.24	0.16	1.2	4.0	1.0	39.7	0.1	51.3	0.6	2.3
Liberia	..	..	..	..	..	..	..	..	..	..	..	..
Libya	3,532	..	0.21	..	..	1.4	..	77.0	0.7	9.6	..	..
Lithuania	..	37,125	..	0.18	1.4	12.5	5.0	54.6	0.2	17.8	4.1	4.4
Macedonia, FYR	..	23,490	..	0.18	11.7	9.6	6.0	45.0	0.1	20.9	1.7	4.9
Madagascar	9,131	..	0.23	..	..	7.1	..	73.4	..	15.4	0.6	..
Malawi	12,224	11,805	0.32	0.29	0.0	16.0	4.0	70.0	0.0	7.8	1.7	0.7
Malaysia	77,215	180,641	0.15	0.11	7.5	13.3	17.0	30.2	0.3	8.3	6.6	17.4
Mali	..	..	..	..	..	..	..	..	..	..	..	..
Mauritania	..	..	..	..	..	..	..	..	..	..	..	..
Mauritius	9,224	17,700	0.21	0.15	0.9	6.6	3.0	32.8	0.1	55.4	0.6	1.1
Mexico	130,993	296,093	0.22	0.20	7.8	12.5	10.0	55.6	0.2	7.5	0.9	5.1
Moldova	..	34,234	..	0.29	0.2	4.0	1.0	81.7	0.2	10.8	1.3	0.6
Mongolia	9,254	7,939	0.19	0.18	1.8	8.5	1.0	54.5	0.0	25.3	6.7	0.8
Morocco	26,598	89,200	0.15	0.17	2.0	12.1	7.0	39.3	0.4	30.1	1.9	4.5
Mozambique	..	495	..	0.16	3.1	41.4	4.0	10.9	0.1	30.3	17.4	1.1
Myanmar	..	3,356	..	0.13	14.0	9.0	40.0	27.0	0.5	4.9	2.9	1.2
Namibia	..	7,350	..	0.35	0.0	5.0	2.0	90.4	0.1	1.2	0.9	0.8
Nepal	18,692	26,550	0.25	0.14	1.5	8.1	4.0	43.3	1.2	39.3	1.7	1.0
Netherlands	165,416	124,182	0.18	0.18	7.3	26.7	11.0	43.0	0.2	2.3	1.2	8.2
New Zealand	59,012	50,706	0.21	0.22	4.0	19.1	5.0	58.6	0.1	4.9	3.1	4.2
Nicaragua	9,647	..	0.28	..	0.2	5.4	..	79.7	0.1	7.6	1.0	0.9
Niger	372	..	0.19	..	..	..	..	50.3	..	..	..	..
Nigeria	72,082	82,477	0.17	0.17	1.4	15.4	11.0	40.2	0.1	23.5	4.7	3.5
Norway	67,897	55,439	0.19	0.20	8.7	31.7	5.0	42.9	0.1	1.4	3.0	7.2
Oman	..	5,560	..	0.17	6.0	14.0	7.0	52.2	0.8	12.7	3.9	3.5
Pakistan	75,125	100,821	0.17	0.18	8.2	5.9	8.0	39.2	0.2	35.0	0.2	3.2
Panama	8,121	11,461	0.26	0.31	2.2	14.1	5.0	68.0	0.2	9.0	1.8	0.9
Papua New Guinea	4,365	..	0.22	..	2.7	9.5	..	73.3	0.1	0.7	8.7	4.0
Paraguay	..	3,250	..	0.28	2.3	9.9	6.0	73.6	0.3	6.7	0.3	0.9
Peru	50,367	52,644	0.18	0.21	7.9	14.0	9.0	47.2	0.2	14.1	2.2	3.8
Philippines	182,052	201,952	0.19	0.18	5.2	9.8	7.0	58.2	0.2	15.9	3.4	4.6
Poland	580,869	388,153	0.14	0.16	13.8	6.2	7.0	48.8	0.4	13.6	2.6	7.9
Portugal	105,441	121,013	0.15	0.14	4.0	17.4	5.0	33.6	0.4	27.4	5.4	7.1
Puerto Rico	24,034	16,207	0.16	0.14	1.0	13.5	19.0	37.6	0.2	17.3	1.6	9.4

	Emissions of organic water pollutants				Industry shares of emissions of organic water pollutants							
	kilograms per day		kilograms per worker		Primary metals %	Paper and pulp %	Chemicals %	Food and beverages %	Stone, ceramics, and glass %	Textiles %	Wood %	Other %
	1980	2000 [a]	1980	2000 [a]	2000 [a]	2000 [a]	2000 [a]	2000 [a]	2000 [a]	2000 [a]	2000 [a]	2000 [a]
Romania	343,145	333,168	0.12	0.14	23.9	5.5	9.0	25.5	0.3	20.2	5.4	10.9
Russian Federation	..	1,485,833	..	0.16	17.7	7.4	9.0	46.8	0.3	6.9	2.1	9.5
Rwanda	..	..	..	..	..	..	..	..	..	..	..	..
Saudi Arabia	18,181	24,436	0.12	0.14	4.7	17.2	21.0	41.3	1.4	14.4	4.3	10.8
Senegal	9,865	10,488	0.31	0.30	0.0	2.7	9.0	87.1	0.0	4.8	0.2	1.3
Sierra Leone	1,612	4,170	0.24	0.32	..	7.8	3.0	72.1	0.1	7.1	6.4	..
Singapore	28,558	33,331	0.10	0.09	1.3	26.8	16.0	20.9	0.1	4.0	1.3	29.5
Slovak Republic	..	57,970	..	0.15	17.2	12.7	8.0	37.5	0.3	11.9	2.7	9.9
Slovenia	..	38,213	..	0.17	30.1	15.8	8.0	25.6	0.2	11.9	2.0	5.8
Somalia	..	..	..	..	..	..	..	..	..	..	..	..
South Africa	237,599	234,012	0.17	0.17	13.7	16.3	9.0	40.3	0.2	10.2	3.4	6.8
Spain	376,253	374,589	0.16	0.15	6.7	19.8	9.0	42.5	0.3	9.3	4.0	8.6
Sri Lanka	30,086	83,885	0.18	0.18	3.5	13.9	7.0	50.1	0.5	33.2	1.6	1.2
Sudan	..	..	..	..	..	..	..	..	..	..	..	..
Swaziland	2,826	2,009	0.26	0.23	..	79.8	0.0	..	0.2	16.5	2.0	..
Sweden	130,439	103,913	0.15	0.14	11.3	35.0	8.0	26.6	0.1	1.3	3.0	14.9
Switzerland	..	123,752	..	0.17	24.9	23.6	10.0	25.0	0.2	3.2	4.2	8.7
Syrian Arab Republic	36,262	15,115	0.19	0.20	1.4	4.4	4.0	69.8	0.4	20.3	3.5	0.2
Tajikistan	..	..	..	..	..	..	..	..	..	..	..	..
Tanzania	21,084	35,155	0.21	0.25	2.1	8.1	3.0	58.6	0.1	22.7	1.7	1.8
Thailand	213,271	355,819	0.22	0.16	4.8	5.3	5.0	42.2	0.2	35.4	1.5	3.9
Togo	963	..	0.27	..	4.4	22.1	..	45.0	0.1	24.1	1.9	0.0
Trinidad and Tobago	7,835	11,787	0.18	0.28	4.4	14.6	7.0	51.6	0.3	8.8	2.2	1.2
Tunisia	20,294	46,025	0.16	0.16	5.9	8.0	6.0	45.8	0.4	22.7	1.9	3.4
Turkey	160,173	170,685	0.20	0.17	11.0	7.1	8.0	44.5	0.3	23.6	1.1	5.0
Turkmenistan	..	..	..	..	..	..	..	..	..	..	..	..
Uganda	..	..	..	..	..	..	..	..	..	..	..	..
Ukraine	..	499,886	..	0.18	22.8	3.4	7.0	51.6	0.3	5.8	1.6	7.9
United Arab Emirates	4,524	..	0.15	..	..	..	..	..	..	..	..	..
United Kingdom	964,510	569,736	0.15	0.15	7.2	30.4	10.0	32.1	0.2	5.6	2.5	12.0
United States	2,742,993	1,968,196	0.14	0.12	10.5	11.0	14.0	38.4	0.2	7.1	4.1	14.9
Uruguay	34,270	23,109	0.21	0.27	3.4	11.2	6.0	72.3	0.2	6.6	0.7	1.8
Uzbekistan	..	..	..	..	..	..	..	..	..	..	..	..
Venezuela, RB	84,797	94,175	0.20	0.21	13.7	13.9	10.0	46.9	0.2	9.9	1.7	3.9
Vietnam	..	..	..	..	..	..	..	..	..	..	..	..
West Bank and Gaza	..	..	..	..	..	..	..	..	..	..	..	..
Yemen, Rep.	..	7,823	..	0.25	5.4	9.1	13.0	71.1	0.3	4.9	1.0	0.0
Yugoslavia, Fed. Rep.	..	106,409	..	0.16	9.3	12.3	8.0	45.9	0.3	14.1	2.1	8.1
Zambia	13,605	11,433	0.23	0.22	3.1	7.8	7.0	68.0	0.2	9.8	1.7	2.5
Zimbabwe	32,681	29,617	0.20	0.20	15.9	9.2	6.0	50.5	0.2	13.3	2.9	3.5

Note: Industry shares may not sum to 100 percent because data may be for different years.
a. Data are for any year from 1993 to 2000.

About the data

Emissions of organic pollutants from industrial activities are a major cause of degradation of water quality. Water quality and pollution levels are generally measured in terms of concentration or load—the rate of occurrence of a substance in an aqueous solution. Polluting substances include organic matter, metals, minerals, sediment, bacteria, and toxic chemicals. This table focuses on organic water pollution resulting from industrial activities. Because water pollution tends to be sensitive to local conditions, the national-level data in the table may not reflect the quality of water in specific locations.

The data in the table come from an international study of industrial emissions that may be the first to include data from developing countries (Hettige, Mani, and Wheeler 1998). These data were updated through 2000 by the World Bank's Development Research Group. Unlike estimates from earlier studies based on engineering or economic models, these estimates are based on actual measurements of plant-level water pollution. The focus is on organic water pollution, measured in terms of biochemical oxygen demand (BOD), because the data for this indicator are the most plentiful and the most reliable for cross-country comparisons of emissions. BOD measures the strength of an organic waste in terms of the amount of oxygen consumed in breaking it down. A sewage overload in natural waters exhausts the water's dissolved oxygen content. Wastewater treatment, by contrast, reduces BOD.

Data on water pollution are more readily available than other emissions data because most industrial pollution control programs start by regulating emissions of organic water pollutants. Such data are fairly reliable because sampling techniques for measuring water pollution are more widely understood and much less expensive than those for air pollution.

Hettige, Mani, and Wheeler (1998) used plant- and sector-level information on emissions and employment from 13 national environmental protection agencies and sector-level information on output and employment from the United Nations Industrial Development Organization (UNIDO). Their econometric analysis found that the ratio of BOD to employment in each industrial sector is about the same across countries. This finding allowed the authors to estimate BOD loads across countries and over time. The estimated BOD intensities per unit of employ-

ment were multiplied by sectoral employment numbers from UNIDO's industry database for 1980–98. The estimates of sectoral emissions were then totaled to get daily emissions of organic water pollutants in kilograms per day for each country and year. The data in the table were derived by updating these estimates through 2000.

Definitions

• **Emissions of organic water pollutants** are measured in terms of biochemical oxygen demand, which refers to the amount of oxygen that bacteria in water will consume in breaking down waste. This is a standard water treatment test for the presence of organic pollutants. Emissions per worker are total emissions divided by the number of industrial workers.
• **Industry shares of emissions of organic water pollutants** refer to emissions from manufacturing activities as defined by two-digit divisions of the International Standard Industrial Classification (ISIC) revision 2: primary metals (ISIC division 37), paper and pulp (34), chemicals (35), food and beverages (31), stone, ceramics, and glass (36), textiles (32), wood (33), and other (38 and 39).

3.6a

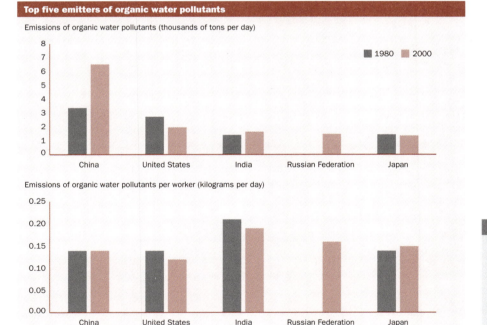

Top five emitters of organic water pollutants

Emissions of organic water pollutants (thousands of tons per day)

Emissions of organic water pollutants per worker (kilograms per day)

Total emissions of organic water pollutants have increased in most developing countries while they have fallen in several high-income countries. Relative to the number of industrial workers, emissions have generally declined.

Note: No data are available for the Russian Federation for 1980.
Source: Table 3.6.

Data sources

The data come from a 1998 study by Hemamala Hettige, Muthukumara Mani, and David Wheeler, "Industrial Pollution in Economic Development: Kuznets Revisited" (available on the Web at http://www.worldbank.org/nipr). These data were updated through 2000 by the World Bank's Development Research Group using the same methodology as the initial study. Sectoral employment numbers are from UNIDO's industry database.

3.7 Energy production and use

	Commercial energy production		Commercial energy use			Commercial energy use per capita			Net energy imports [a]	
	thousand metric tons of oil equivalent		thousand metric tons of oil equivalent		average annual % growth	kg of oil equivalent		average annual % growth	% of commercial energy use	
	1980	2000	1980	2000	1980–2000	1980	2000	1980–2000	1980	2000
Afghanistan	..	..	..	..	..	..	..	..	..	..
Albania	3,428	814	3,049	1,634	−5.6	1,142	521	−6.3	−12	50
Algeria	67,103	149,629	12,185	29,060	3.5	653	956	1.0	−451	−415
Angola	11,301	43,669	4,437	7,667	2.8	628	584	−0.3	−155	−470
Argentina	38,813	81,221	41,868	61,469	2.2	1,490	1,660	0.8	7	−32
Armenia	1,263	632	1,070	2,061	..	346	542	..	−18	69
Australia	86,096	232,552	70,372	110,174	2.4	4,790	5,744	1.0	−22	−111
Austria	7,561	9,686	22,823	28,582	1.6	3,022	3,524	1.1	67	66
Azerbaijan	14,821	18,951	15,001	11,703	..	2,433	1,454	..	1	−62
Bangladesh	6,745	15,053	8,441	18,666	4.1	99	142	1.9	20	19
Belarus	2,566	3,466	2,385	24,330	..	247	2,432	..	−8	86
Belgium	7,445	13,233	46,100	59,217	1.8	4,682	5,776	1.6	84	78
Benin	1,212	1,821	1,363	2,362	2.3	394	377	−0.8	11	23
Bolivia	4,372	5,901	2,436	4,929	3.8	455	592	1.5	−79	−20
Bosnia and Herzegovina	..	3,277	..	4,359	..	..	1,096	..	..	25
Botswana	..	..	..	..	..	..	..	..	..	..
Brazil	62,372	142,078	111,471	183,165	2.7	917	1,077	1.0	44	22
Bulgaria	7,737	10,005	28,673	18,784	−2.6	3,235	2,299	−2.2	73	47
Burkina Faso	..	..	..	..	..	..	..	..	..	..
Burundi	..	..	..	..	..	..	..	..	..	..
Cambodia	..	..	..	..	..	..	..	..	..	..
Cameroon	6,707	12,729	3,676	6,355	2.5	421	427	−0.2	−82	−100
Canada	207,417	374,864	193,000	250,967	1.6	7,848	8,156	0.4	−7	−49
Central African Republic	..	..	..	..	..	..	..	..	..	..
Chad	..	..	..	..	..	..	..	..	..	..
Chile	5,801	8,299	9,662	24,403	5.7	867	1,604	4.0	40	66
China	615,475	1,107,636	598,498	1,142,439	3.7	610	905	2.4	−3	3
Hong Kong, China	39	48	5,439	15,453	5.6	1,079	2,319	4.2	99	100
Colombia	18,040	74,584	19,348	28,786	2.5	680	681	0.5	7	−159
Congo, Dem. Rep.	8,697	15,446	8,706	14,888	2.7	324	292	−0.6	0	−4
Congo, Rep.	4,024	14,656	862	895	−1.1	516	296	−4.0	−367	−1,538
Costa Rica	767	1,591	1,527	3,281	4.2	669	861	1.5	50	52
Côte d'Ivoire	2,419	6,097	3,662	6,928	3.3	447	433	−0.1	34	12
Croatia	..	3,582	..	7,775	..	..	1,775	..	..	54
Cuba	4,227	6,051	14,910	13,203	−1.6	1,536	1,180	−2.4	72	54
Czech Republic	41,185	29,869	47,254	40,383	−1.2	4,618	3,931	−1.2	13	26
Denmark	952	27,831	19,783	19,456	0.6	3,862	3,643	0.4	95	−43
Dominican Republic	1,327	1,421	3,491	7,804	4.0	613	932	2.1	62	82
Ecuador	11,744	22,520	5,180	8,187	2.1	651	647	−0.3	−127	−175
Egypt, Arab Rep.	34,168	57,599	15,970	46,423	4.6	391	726	2.3	−114	−24
El Salvador	1,913	2,157	2,537	4,083	2.2	553	651	0.6	25	47
Eritrea	..	..	..	..	..	..	..	..	..	..
Estonia	6,951	2,917	6,275	4,523	..	4,248	3,303	..	−11	36
Ethiopia	10,575	17,583	11,145	18,732	2.6	295	291	−0.1	5	6
Finland	6,912	15,134	25,413	33,147	1.7	5,316	6,409	1.3	73	54
France	45,544	130,730	187,737	257,128	1.9	3,484	4,366	1.5	76	49
Gabon	9,441	16,800	1,493	1,563	−0.2	2,157	1,271	−3.1	−532	−975
Gambia, The	..	..	..	..	..	..	..	..	..	..
Georgia	1,504	737	4,474	2,860	..	882	533	..	66	74
Germany	185,628	134,317	360,385	339,640	−0.2	4,602	4,131	−0.5	48	60
Ghana	3,305	5,883	4,063	7,720	3.6	378	400	0.5	19	24
Greece	3,696	9,987	15,695	27,822	3.0	1,628	2,635	2.5	76	64
Guatemala	2,583	5,241	3,847	7,146	3.5	564	628	0.9	33	27
Guinea	..	..	..	..	..	..	..	..	..	..
Guinea-Bissau	..	..	..	..	..	..	..	..	..	..
Haiti	1,877	1,542	2,099	2,039	0.4	392	256	−1.6	11	24

	Commercial energy production		Commercial energy use			Commercial energy use per capita			Net energy imports [a]	
	thousand metric tons of oil equivalent		thousand metric tons of oil equivalent		average annual % growth	kg of oil equivalent		average annual % growth	% of commercial energy use	
	1980	2000	1980	2000	1980–2000	1980	2000	1980–2000	1980	2000
Honduras	1,315	1,522	1,892	3,012	2.8	530	469	–0.2	31	49
Hungary	14,935	11,090	28,940	24,783	–1.0	2,703	2,448	–0.7	48	55
India	221,322	421,565	241,016	501,894	3.8	351	494	1.8	8	16
Indonesia	128,996	229,478	59,933	145,575	4.8	404	706	3.1	–115	–58
Iran, Islamic Rep.	81,142	242,146	38,987	112,725	5.6	997	1,771	3.1	–108	–115
Iraq	136,643	134,089	12,030	27,678	4.3	925	1,190	1.3	–1,036	–384
Ireland	1,894	2,197	8,485	14,623	2.7	2,495	3,854	2.3	78	85
Israel	153	654	8,563	20,200	5.2	2,208	3,241	2.6	98	97
Italy	19,644	26,858	138,629	171,567	1.3	2,456	2,974	1.2	86	84
Jamaica	224	486	2,378	3,920	3.5	1,115	1,524	2.6	91	88
Japan	43,204	105,505	346,538	524,715	2.6	2,967	4,136	2.2	88	80
Jordan	1	286	1,714	5,185	4.9	786	1,061	0.5	100	94
Kazakhstan	76,799	78,102	76,799	39,063	..	5,163	2,594	..	0	–100
Kenya	7,891	12,260	9,791	15,482	2.2	589	515	–0.7	19	21
Korea, Dem. Rep.	29,669	42,576	32,631	46,112	1.9	1,898	2,071	0.5	9	8
Korea, Rep.	9,272	33,615	41,372	193,626	9.1	1,085	4,119	8.0	78	83
Kuwait	91,636	111,469	12,249	20,894	1.0	8,908	10,529	0.2	–648	–434
Kyrgyz Republic	2,190	1,443	1,717	2,445	..	473	497	..	–28	41
Lao PDR	..	..	..	..	..	..	..	..	..	..
Latvia	261	1,250	566	3,655	..	222	1,541	..	54	66
Lebanon	178	171	2,524	5,058	4.8	841	1,169	2.8	93	97
Lesotho	..	..	..	..	..	..	..	..	..	..
Liberia	..	..	..	..	..	..	..	..	..	..
Libya	96,550	73,904	7,193	16,438	3.6	2,364	3,107	1.0	–1,242	–350
Lithuania	..	3,212	..	7,124	..	..	2,032	..	..	55
Macedonia, FYR	..	..	..	..	..	..	..	..	..	..
Madagascar	..	..	..	..	..	..	..	..	..	..
Malawi	..	..	..	..	..	..	..	..	..	..
Malaysia	18,202	76,759	12,162	49,472	7.7	884	2,126	4.9	–50	–55
Mali	..	..	..	..	..	..	..	..	..	..
Mauritania	..	..	..	..	..	..	..	..	..	..
Mauritius	..	..	..	..	..	..	..	..	..	..
Mexico	149,359	229,653	98,898	153,513	2.1	1,464	1,567	0.2	–51	–50
Moldova	35	60	..	2,871	..	..	671	..	..	98
Mongolia	..	..	..	..	..	..	..	..	..	..
Morocco	877	572	4,778	10,293	4.3	247	359	2.2	82	94
Mozambique	7,413	7,219	8,074	7,126	–0.8	668	403	–2.6	8	–1
Myanmar	9,513	15,144	9,430	12,522	1.3	280	262	–0.4	–1	–21
Namibia	..	292	..	1,031	..	..	587	..	..	72
Nepal	4,403	6,872	4,576	7,900	2.7	314	343	0.4	4	13
Netherlands	71,821	57,239	64,984	75,799	1.4	4,593	4,762	0.8	–11	24
New Zealand	5,488	15,379	9,213	18,633	3.8	2,959	4,864	2.7	40	17
Nicaragua	907	1,553	1,553	2,746	2.7	531	542	0.0	42	43
Niger	..	..	..	..	..	..	..	..	..	..
Nigeria	148,479	197,726	52,846	90,169	2.6	743	710	–0.4	–181	–119
Norway	55,675	224,993	18,768	25,617	1.8	4,588	5,704	1.3	–197	–778
Oman	15,090	60,084	996	9,750	11.0	905	4,046	6.6	–1,415	–516
Pakistan	20,997	47,124	25,472	63,951	4.8	308	463	2.2	18	26
Panama	526	732	1,399	2,546	2.7	717	892	0.7	62	71
Papua New Guinea	..	..	..	..	..	..	..	..	..	..
Paraguay	1,605	6,886	2,089	3,930	4.2	671	715	1.2	23	–75
Peru	14,656	9,477	11,752	12,695	0.2	678	489	–1.8	–25	25
Philippines	10,670	20,922	21,212	42,424	3.9	442	554	1.5	50	51
Poland	122,222	78,960	123,031	89,975	–1.4	3,458	2,328	–1.8	1	12
Portugal	1,481	3,129	10,291	24,613	4.7	1,054	2,459	4.7	86	87
Puerto Rico	..	..	..	..	..	..	..	..	..	..

3.7 Energy production and use

	Commercial energy production		Commercial energy use			Commercial energy use per capita			Net energy imports [a]	
	thousand metric tons of oil equivalent		thousand metric tons of oil equivalent		average annual % growth	kg of oil equivalent		average annual % growth	% of commercial energy use	
	1980	2000	1980	2000	1980–2000	1980	2000	1980–2000	1980	2000
Romania	52,587	28,290	65,123	36,330	–3.1	2,933	1,619	–3.2	19	22
Russian Federation	748,647	966,512	763,707	613,969	..	5,494	4,218	..	2	–57
Rwanda	..	..	..	..	..	..	..	..	..	..
Saudi Arabia	533,071	487,889	31,108	105,303	5.0	3,319	5,081	1.0	–1,614	–363
Senegal	1,046	1,723	1,919	3,086	2.4	346	324	–0.3	45	44
Sierra Leone	..	..	..	..	..	..	..	..	..	..
Singapore	..	64	6,062	24,591	8.7	2,511	6,120	6.0	..	100
Slovak Republic	3,418	5,994	21,056	17,466	–1.4	4,224	3,234	–1.7	84	66
Slovenia	..	3,098	..	6,540	..	..	3,288	..	..	53
Somalia	..	..	..	..	..	..	..	..	..	..
South Africa	73,169	144,469	65,417	107,595	2.1	2,372	2,514	–0.2	–12	–34
Spain	15,636	31,865	68,576	124,881	3.2	1,834	3,084	2.9	77	74
Sri Lanka	3,209	4,530	4,536	8,063	2.5	311	437	1.4	29	44
Sudan	7,089	23,664	8,406	16,216	3.1	435	521	0.7	16	–46
Swaziland	..	..	..	..	..	..	..	..	..	..
Sweden	16,132	30,681	39,911	47,481	1.0	4,803	5,354	0.6	60	35
Switzerland	7,030	11,792	20,861	26,597	1.4	3,301	3,704	0.7	66	56
Syrian Arab Republic	9,502	32,890	5,348	18,407	5.4	614	1,137	2.2	–78	–79
Tajikistan	1,986	1,250	1,650	2,911	..	416	470	..	–20	57
Tanzania	9,502	14,601	10,280	15,386	2.0	553	457	–1.0	8	5
Thailand	11,182	41,118	22,808	73,618	7.4	488	1,212	6.0	51	44
Togo	562	1,036	715	1,530	3.8	284	338	0.8	21	32
Trinidad and Tobago	13,141	17,884	3,873	8,665	3.3	3,580	6,660	2.4	–239	–106
Tunisia	6,966	7,003	3,907	7,888	3.7	612	825	1.6	–78	11
Turkey	17,077	26,186	31,452	77,104	4.6	707	1,181	2.7	46	66
Turkmenistan	8,034	45,968	7,948	13,885	..	2,778	2,627	..	–1	–231
Uganda	..	..	..	..	..	..	..	..	..	..
Ukraine	109,708	82,330	97,893	139,592	..	1,956	2,820	..	–12	41
United Arab Emirates	89,716	143,589	6,273	29,559	8.2	6,014	10,175	2.8	–1,330	–386
United Kingdom	196,792	272,338	201,284	232,644	1.0	3,573	3,962	0.8	2	–17
United States	1,553,263	1,675,770	1,811,650	2,299,669	1.5	7,973	8,148	0.4	14	27
Uruguay	766	1,028	2,643	3,079	1.7	907	923	1.0	71	67
Uzbekistan	4,615	55,066	4,821	50,151	..	302	2,027	..	4	–10
Venezuela, RB	140,578	225,470	36,148	59,256	2.5	2,395	2,452	0.1	–289	–280
Vietnam	18,364	46,299	19,573	36,965	3.2	364	471	1.2	6	–25
West Bank and Gaza	..	..	..	..	..	..	..	..	..	..
Yemen, Rep.	60	22,046	1,424	3,526	4.2	167	201	0.3	96	–525
Yugoslavia, Fed. Rep.	..	10,122	..	13,706	..	..	1,289	..	..	26
Zambia	4,179	5,916	4,719	6,244	1.3	822	619	–1.6	11	5
Zimbabwe	5,793	8,708	6,570	10,219	2.6	921	809	–0.3	12	15
World	**6,912,364 t**	**10,010,145 t**	**6,930,291 t**	**9,886,146 t**	**2.9 w**	**1,623 w**	**1,694 w**	**0.9 w**	**0 w**	**0 w**
Low income	819,169	1,400,460	674,008	1,287,496	4.7	452	569	2.2	–22	–9
Middle income	3,302,613	4,812,604	2,446,876	3,457,150	4.1	1,252	1,318	2.1	–35	–39
Lower middle income	2,028,987	3,252,169	1,856,387	2,573,688	5.0	1,156	1,206	2.9	–9	–26
Upper middle income	1,273,626	1,560,436	590,489	883,462	2.1	1,694	1,805	0.3	–116	–77
Low & middle income	4,121,782	6,213,064	3,120,884	4,744,646	4.3	906	971	2.0	–32	–31
East Asia & Pacific	842,071	1,579,933	776,249	1,549,127	3.9	578	871	2.4	–8	–2
Europe & Central Asia	1,241,969	1,470,085	1,332,884	1,253,443	7.6	3,348	2,653	..	7	–17
Latin America & Carib.	476,911	847,298	381,002	601,859	2.4	1,074	1,181	0.6	–25	–41
Middle East & N. Africa	981,350	1,268,307	138,565	398,549	4.9	798	1,368	2.2	–610	–219
South Asia	256,676	495,144	284,041	600,474	3.9	321	453	1.8	10	18
Sub-Saharan Africa	322,805	552,297	208,143	341,194	2.3	714	669	–0.5	–55	–62
High income	2,790,581	3,797,081	3,809,407	5,141,500	1.8	4,623	5,430	1.1	27	26
Europe EMU	367,292	434,433	952,761	1,160,702	1.2	3,337	3,824	0.9	61	63

a. A negative value indicates that a country is a net exporter.

About the data

In developing countries growth in commercial energy use is closely related to growth in the modern sectors—industry, motorized transport, and urban areas—but commercial energy use also reflects climatic, geographic, and economic factors (such as the relative price of energy). Commercial energy use has been growing rapidly in low- and middle-income countries, but high-income countries still use more than five times as much on a per capita basis.

Because commercial energy is widely traded, it is necessary to distinguish between its production and its use. Net energy imports show the extent to which an economy's use exceeds its domestic production. High-income countries are net energy importers; middle-income countries have been their main suppliers.

Energy data are compiled by the International Energy Agency (IEA). IEA data for countries that are not members of the Organisation for Economic Co-operation and Development (OECD) are based on national energy data adjusted to conform to annual questionnaires completed by OECD member governments.

Commercial energy use refers to the use of domestic primary energy before transformation to other end-use fuels (such as electricity and refined petroleum products). It includes energy from combustible renewables and waste—solid biomass and animal products, gas and liquid from biomass, and industrial and municipal waste. Biomass is defined as any plant matter used directly as fuel or converted into fuel, heat, or electricity. (The data series published in *World Development Indicators 1998* and earlier editions did not include energy from combustible renewables and waste.) All forms of commercial energy—primary energy and primary electricity—are converted into oil equivalents. To convert nuclear electricity into oil equivalents, a notional thermal efficiency of 33 percent is assumed; for hydroelectric power 100 percent efficiency is assumed.

Definitions

- **Commercial energy production** refers to commercial forms of primary energy—petroleum (crude oil, natural gas liquids, and oil from nonconventional sources), natural gas, and solid fuels (coal, lignite, and other derived fuels)—and primary electricity, all converted into oil equivalents (see *About the data*).
- **Commercial energy use** refers to apparent consumption, which is equal to indigenous production plus imports and stock changes, minus exports and fuels supplied to ships and aircraft engaged in international transport (see *About the data*). • **Net energy imports** are calculated as energy use less production, both measured in oil equivalents. A negative value indicates that the country is a net exporter.

3.7a

High-income countries consume a disproportionate share of the world's energy

Commercial energy use, 2000

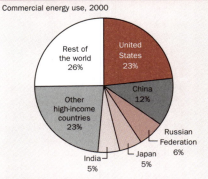

High-income countries, with 15 percent of the world's population, consume more than half its commercial energy.

Source: Table 3.7.

3.7b

People in high-income countries use almost 10 times as much commercial energy as do people in low-income countries

Energy use per capita (thousands of kg of oil equivalent)

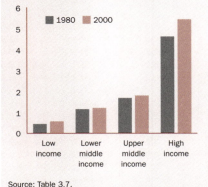

Source: Table 3.7.

Data sources

The data on commercial energy production and use come from IEA electronic files. The IEA's data are published in its annual publications, *Energy Statistics and Balances of Non-OECD Countries*, *Energy Statistics of OECD Countries*, and *Energy Balances of OECD Countries*.

3.8 Energy efficiency and emissions

	GDP per unit of energy use		Carbon dioxide emissions					
	PPP $ per kg oil equivalent		Total million metric tons		Per capita metric tons		kg per PPP $ of GDP	
	1980	2000	1980	1999	1980	1999	1980	1999
Afghanistan	..	..	1.7	1.0	0.1	0.0	..	..
Albania	..	6.7	4.8	1.5	1.8	0.5	..	0.2
Algeria	5.5	6.4	66.1	90.8	3.5	3.0	1.0	0.5
Angola	..	3.6	5.3	10.3	0.8	0.8	..	0.4
Argentina	4.4	7.2	107.5	137.8	3.8	3.8	0.6	0.3
Armenia	..	4.5	..	3.1	..	0.8	..	0.4
Australia	2.0	4.3	202.8	344.4	13.8	18.2	1.5	0.8
Austria	3.4	7.5	52.4	61.4	6.9	7.6	0.7	0.3
Azerbaijan	..	1.9	..	33.6	..	4.2	..	1.8
Bangladesh	5.4	10.8	7.6	25.4	0.1	0.2	0.2	0.1
Belarus	..	3.0	..	57.6	..	5.7	..	0.9
Belgium	2.2	4.4	131.3	104.4	13.3	10.2	1.3	0.4
Benin	1.2	2.5	0.5	1.3	0.1	0.2	0.3	0.2
Bolivia	3.0	3.9	4.5	11.2	0.8	1.4	0.6	0.6
Bosnia and Herzegovina	..	5.2	..	4.8	..	1.2	..	0.2
Botswana	..	..	1.0	3.9	1.1	2.4	0.7	0.4
Brazil	4.2	6.7	183.4	300.7	1.5	1.8	0.4	0.3
Bulgaria	1.0	2.8	75.3	42.1	8.5	5.1	2.7	0.9
Burkina Faso	..	..	0.4	1.0	0.1	0.1	0.1	0.1
Burundi	..	..	0.1	0.2	0.0	0.0	0.1	0.1
Cambodia	..	..	0.3	0.7	0.0	0.1	..	0.0
Cameroon	2.7	3.8	3.9	4.7	0.4	0.3	0.4	0.2
Canada	1.4	3.3	420.9	438.6	17.1	14.4	1.5	0.6
Central African Republic	..	..	0.1	0.3	0.0	0.1	0.1	0.1
Chad	..	..	0.2	0.1	0.0	0.0	0.1	0.1
Chile	3.0	5.6	27.5	62.5	2.5	4.2	1.0	0.5
China	0.7	4.1	1,476.8	2,825.0	1.5	2.3	3.5	0.7
Hong Kong, China	6.2	10.9	16.3	41.2	3.2	6.2	0.5	0.3
Colombia	4.7	10.3	39.8	63.6	1.4	1.5	0.4	0.2
Congo, Dem. Rep.	3.8	2.5	3.5	2.1	0.1	0.0	0.1	0.1
Congo, Rep.	0.8	3.2	0.4	2.4	0.2	0.8	0.6	0.9
Costa Rica	6.6	11.7	2.5	6.1	1.1	1.6	0.2	0.2
Côte d'Ivoire	2.7	3.6	4.6	12.1	0.6	0.8	0.5	0.5
Croatia	..	4.9	..	20.8	..	4.8	..	0.6
Cuba	..	..	30.8	25.4	3.2	2.3	..	..
Czech Republic	..	3.6	..	108.9	..	10.6	..	0.8
Denmark	3.0	7.9	62.9	49.7	12.3	9.3	1.1	0.3
Dominican Republic	4.1	7.4	6.4	23.3	1.1	2.8	0.4	0.4
Ecuador	2.8	4.9	13.4	23.3	1.7	1.9	0.9	0.6
Egypt, Arab Rep.	3.3	4.8	45.2	123.6	1.1	2.0	0.9	0.6
El Salvador	5.0	8.1	2.1	5.8	0.5	0.9	0.2	0.2
Eritrea	..	..	..	0.6	..	0.1	..	0.1
Estonia	..	2.9	..	16.2	..	11.7	..	1.4
Ethiopia	*1.6*	2.6	1.8	5.5	0.0	0.1	*0.1*	0.1
Finland	1.7	3.8	56.9	58.4	11.9	11.3	1.3	0.5
France	2.8	5.4	482.7	359.7	9.0	6.1	0.9	0.3
Gabon	1.8	4.7	6.2	3.6	8.9	3.0	2.3	0.5
Gambia, The	..	..	0.2	0.3	0.2	0.2	0.2	0.1
Georgia	4.6	4.5	..	5.4	..	1.0	..	0.5
Germany	2.2	6.1	..	792.2	..	9.7	..	0.4
Ghana	3.1	5.5	2.4	5.6	0.2	0.3	0.2	0.1
Greece	4.7	6.3	51.7	85.9	5.4	8.2	0.7	0.5
Guatemala	4.6	7.1	4.5	9.7	0.7	0.9	0.3	0.2
Guinea	..	..	0.9	1.3	0.2	0.2	..	0.1
Guinea-Bissau	..	..	0.5	0.3	0.7	0.2	1.4	0.3
Haiti	4.7	7.5	0.8	1.4	0.1	0.2	0.1	0.1

Energy efficiency and emissions

	GDP per unit of energy use		Carbon dioxide emissions					
	PPP $ per kg oil equivalent		Total million metric tons		Per capita metric tons		kg per PPP $ of GDP	
	1980	2000	1980	1999	1980	1999	1980	1999
Honduras	3.2	6.0	2.1	5.0	0.6	0.8	0.3	0.3
Hungary	2.0	4.9	82.5	56.9	7.7	5.6	1.5	0.5
India	2.2	5.5	347.3	1,077.0	0.5	1.1	0.7	0.4
Indonesia	2.0	4.2	94.6	235.6	0.6	1.2	0.8	0.4
Iran, Islamic Rep.	2.7	3.2	116.1	301.4	3.0	4.8	1.1	0.9
Iraq	..	..	44.0	74.2	3.4	3.3	..	..
Ireland	2.3	7.9	25.2	40.4	7.4	10.8	1.3	0.4
Israel	3.7	6.5	21.1	61.1	5.4	10.0	0.7	0.5
Italy	3.9	8.2	371.9	422.7	6.6	7.3	0.7	0.3
Jamaica	1.8	2.4	8.4	10.2	4.0	4.0	2.0	1.2
Japan	3.1	6.1	920.4	1,155.2	7.9	9.1	0.8	0.4
Jordan	3.1	3.6	4.7	14.6	2.2	3.1	0.9	0.8
Kazakhstan	..	2.2	..	112.8	..	7.4	..	1.5
Kenya	1.0	1.9	6.2	8.8	0.4	0.3	0.6	0.3
Korea, Dem. Rep.	..	..	124.9	208.7	7.3	9.4	..	..
Korea, Rep.	2.3	3.6	125.1	393.5	3.3	8.4	1.3	0.6
Kuwait	1.4	1.8	24.7	48.0	18.0	24.9	1.5	1.4
Kyrgyz Republic	..	5.4	..	4.7	..	1.0	..	0.4
Lao PDR	..	..	0.2	0.4	0.1	0.1	..	0.1
Latvia	19.8	4.6	..	6.6	..	2.8	..	0.4
Lebanon	..	3.5	6.2	16.9	2.1	4.0	..	1.0
Lesotho	..	..	..	..	..	..	..	..
Liberia	..	..	2.0	0.4	1.1	0.1	..	..
Libya	..	..	26.9	42.8	8.8	8.3	..	..
Lithuania	..	3.9	..	13.2	..	3.8	..	0.5
Macedonia, FYR	..	..	..	11.4	..	5.6	..	1.0
Madagascar	..	..	1.6	1.9	0.2	0.1	0.3	0.2
Malawi	..	..	0.7	0.8	0.1	0.1	0.3	0.1
Malaysia	2.6	4.3	28.0	123.7	2.0	5.4	0.9	0.7
Mali	..	..	0.4	0.5	0.1	0.0	0.1	0.1
Mauritania	..	..	0.6	3.0	0.4	1.2	0.3	0.6
Mauritius	..	..	0.6	2.5	0.6	2.1	0.3	0.2
Mexico	2.9	5.5	252.5	378.5	3.7	3.9	0.9	0.5
Moldova	..	3.1	..	6.5	..	1.5	..	0.8
Mongolia	..	..	6.8	7.5	4.1	3.2	3.7	1.9
Morocco	6.4	9.5	15.9	35.8	0.8	1.3	0.5	0.4
Mozambique	0.7	2.5	3.2	1.3	0.3	0.1	0.6	0.1
Myanmar	..	..	4.8	9.2	0.1	0.2	..	..
Namibia	..	12.0	..	0.1	..	0.1	..	0.0
Nepal	1.5	3.7	0.5	3.3	0.0	0.1	0.1	0.1
Netherlands	2.3	5.7	153.0	134.6	10.8	8.5	1.0	0.3
New Zealand	2.7	3.7	17.6	30.8	5.6	8.1	0.7	0.5
Nicaragua	4.0	4.6	2.0	3.8	0.7	0.8	0.3	0.3
Niger	..	..	0.6	1.1	0.1	0.1	0.1	0.1
Nigeria	0.8	1.2	68.1	40.4	1.0	0.3	1.7	0.4
Norway	2.3	5.1	38.7	38.7	9.5	8.7	0.9	0.3
Oman	4.5	3.0	5.9	19.9	5.3	8.5	1.3	0.7
Pakistan	2.1	4.0	31.6	98.9	0.4	0.7	0.6	0.4
Panama	4.1	6.5	3.5	8.3	1.8	2.9	0.6	0.5
Papua New Guinea	..	..	1.8	2.4	0.6	0.5	0.4	0.2
Paraguay	4.8	7.2	1.5	4.5	0.5	0.8	0.1	0.2
Peru	4.4	9.5	23.6	30.4	1.4	1.2	0.5	0.3
Philippines	5.3	6.8	36.5	73.2	0.8	1.0	0.3	0.3
Poland	..	4.0	456.2	314.4	12.8	8.1	..	0.9
Portugal	5.5	7.2	27.1	60.0	2.8	6.0	0.5	0.4
Puerto Rico	..	..	14.0	10.1	4.4	2.7	0.6	0.1

	GDP per unit of energy use		Carbon dioxide emissions					
	PPP $ per kg oil equivalent		Total million metric tons		Per capita metric tons		kg per PPP $ of GDP	
	1980	2000	1980	1999	1980	1999	1980	1999
Romania	..	3.4	191.8	81.2	8.6	3.6	..	0.7
Russian Federation	..	1.6	..	1,437.3	..	9.8	..	1.6
Rwanda	..	..	0.3	0.6	0.1	0.1	0.1	0.1
Saudi Arabia	4.0	2.6	130.7	235.4	14.0	11.7	1.1	0.9
Senegal	2.2	4.5	2.8	3.7	0.5	0.4	0.7	0.3
Sierra Leone	..	..	0.6	0.5	0.2	0.1	0.3	0.3
Singapore	2.2	3.9	30.1	54.3	12.5	13.7	2.3	0.7
Slovak Republic	..	3.6	..	38.6	..	7.2	..	0.7
Slovenia	..	5.0	..	14.4	..	7.3	..	0.5
Somalia	..	..	0.6	0.0	0.1	0.0	..	..
South Africa	3.1	4.4	211.3	334.6	7.7	7.9	1.0	0.8
Spain	3.8	6.4	200.0	273.7	5.3	6.8	0.8	0.4
Sri Lanka	3.1	7.8	3.4	8.6	0.2	0.5	0.2	0.2
Sudan	1.6	3.8	3.3	2.6	0.2	0.1	0.2	0.0
Swaziland	..	..	0.5	0.4	0.8	0.4	0.4	0.1
Sweden	2.0	4.4	71.4	46.6	8.6	5.3	0.9	0.2
Switzerland	4.4	7.5	40.9	40.6	6.5	5.7	0.4	0.2
Syrian Arab Republic	2.6	2.9	19.3	53.4	2.2	3.4	1.4	1.1
Tajikistan	..	2.3	..	5.1	..	0.8	..	0.8
Tanzania	..	1.1	1.9	2.5	0.1	0.1	..	0.2
Thailand	2.9	5.1	40.0	199.7	0.9	3.3	0.6	0.6
Togo	4.9	4.9	0.6	1.3	0.2	0.3	0.2	0.2
Trinidad and Tobago	1.2	1.3	16.7	25.1	15.4	19.4	3.6	2.4
Tunisia	3.8	7.4	9.4	17.5	1.5	1.8	0.6	0.3
Turkey	3.2	5.3	76.3	198.5	1.7	3.1	0.8	0.5
Turkmenistan	..	1.4	..	32.4	..	6.4	..	2.1
Uganda	..	..	0.6	1.4	0.1	0.1	0.1	0.0
Ukraine	..	1.4	..	374.3	..	7.5	..	2.1
United Arab Emirates	4.9	2.0	36.3	88.0	34.8	31.3	1.2	1.6
United Kingdom	2.5	6.0	580.3	539.3	10.3	9.2	1.2	0.4
United States	1.6	4.2	4,626.8	5,495.4	20.4	19.7	1.6	0.6
Uruguay	4.8	9.4	5.8	6.5	2.0	2.0	0.5	0.2
Uzbekistan	..	1.2	..	116.6	..	4.8	..	2.2
Venezuela, RB	1.6	2.3	90.1	125.8	6.0	5.3	1.6	1.0
Vietnam	..	4.2	16.8	46.6	0.3	0.6	..	0.3
West Bank and Gaza	..	..	..	..	..	..	..	..
Yemen, Rep.	..	4.0	..	18.3	..	1.1	..	1.4
Yugoslavia, Fed. Rep.	..	..	102.0	39.5	10.4	3.7	..	..
Zambia	0.8	1.2	3.5	1.8	0.6	0.2	0.9	0.3
Zimbabwe	1.5	3.1	9.6	17.6	1.3	1.4	1.0	0.5
World	**2.1 w**	**4.5 w**	**13,852.7 t**	**22,519.8 t**	**3.4 w**	**3.8 w**	**1.1 w**	**0.5 w**
Low income	2.1	4.0	774.3	2,429.2	0.5	1.0	0.6	0.5
Middle income	2.1	4.0	4,132.9	8,484.0	2.3	3.2	1.2	0.7
Lower middle income	1.6	3.7	2,682.6	6,391.3	1.8	3.0	1.6	0.7
Upper middle income	3.4	4.9	1,450.3	2,092.7	4.3	4.3	0.7	0.5
Low & middle income	2.1	4.0	4,907.1	10,913.2	1.5	2.2	1.0	0.6
East Asia & Pacific	..	..	1,833.3	3,734.4	1.3	2.1	2.2	0.6
Europe & Central Asia	..	2.3	989.0	3,144.1	..	6.6	1.3	1.2
Latin America & Carib.	3.6	6.1	848.8	1,286.7	2.4	2.5	0.6	0.4
Middle East & N. Africa	3.6	3.8	491.7	1,048.4	3.0	3.7	1.0	0.7
South Asia	2.3	5.5	392.3	1,215.1	0.4	0.9	0.6	0.4
Sub-Saharan Africa	2.0	2.9	352.0	484.6	0.9	0.8	0.8	0.4
High income	2.2	4.9	8,945.6	11,606.6	12.0	12.3	1.2	0.5
Europe EMU	2.8	6.2	1,565.2	2,408.4	7.5	7.9	0.8	0.4

About the data

The ratio of GDP to energy use provides a measure of energy efficiency. To produce comparable and consistent estimates of real GDP across countries relative to physical inputs to GDP—that is, units of energy use—GDP is converted to international dollars using purchasing power parity (PPP) rates. Differences in this ratio over time and across countries reflect in part structural changes in the economy, changes in the energy efficiency of particular sectors, and differences in fuel mixes.

Carbon dioxide emissions, largely a by-product of energy production and use (see table 3.7), account for the largest share of greenhouse gases, which are associated with global warming. Anthropogenic carbon dioxide emissions result primarily from fossil fuel combustion and cement manufacturing. In combustion, different fossil fuels release different amounts of carbon dioxide for the same level of energy use. Burning oil releases about 50 percent more carbon dioxide than burning natural gas, and burning coal releases about twice as much. Cement manufacturing releases about half a metric ton of carbon dioxide for each metric ton of cement produced.

The Carbon Dioxide Information Analysis Center (CDIAC), sponsored by the U.S. Department of Energy, calculates annual anthropogenic emissions of carbon dioxide. These calculations are based on data on fossil fuel consumption (from the World Energy Data Set maintained by the United Nations Statistics Division) and data on world cement manufacturing (from the Cement Manufacturing Data Set maintained by the U.S. Bureau of Mines). Emissions of carbon dioxide are often calculated and reported in terms of their content of elemental carbon. For this table these values were converted to the actual mass of carbon dioxide by multiplying the carbon mass by 3.664 (the ratio of the mass of carbon to that of carbon dioxide).

Although the estimates of global carbon dioxide emissions are probably within 10 percent of actual emissions (as calculated from global average fuel chemistry and use), country estimates may have larger error bounds. Trends estimated from a consistent time series tend to be more accurate than individual values. Each year the CDIAC recalculates the entire time series from 1950 to the present, incorporating its most recent findings and the latest corrections to its database. Estimates do not include fuels supplied to ships and aircraft engaged in international transport because of the difficulty of apportioning these fuels among the countries benefiting from that transport.

Definitions

• **GDP per unit of energy use** is the PPP GDP per kilogram of oil equivalent of commercial energy use. PPP GDP is gross domestic product converted to international dollars using purchasing power parity rates. An international dollar has the same purchasing power over GDP as a U.S. dollar has in the United States. • **Carbon dioxide emissions** are those stemming from the burning of fossil fuels and the manufacture of cement. They include carbon dioxide produced during consumption of solid, liquid, and gas fuels and gas flaring.

3.8a

Per capita emissions of carbon dioxide vary, even among the five largest producers of emissions

Carbon dioxide emissions (billions of metric tons)

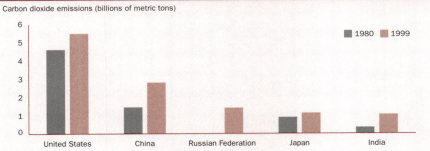

Per capita carbon dioxide emissions (kilograms)

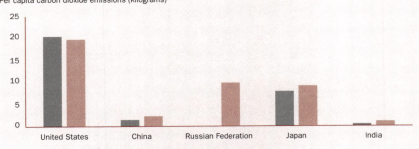

Note: No data are available for the Russian Federation for 1980.

Source: Table 3.8.

3.8b

. . . but emissions per unit of GDP have declined substantially across all income groups

Carbon dioxide emissions per unit of GDP (kilograms per PPP $ of GDP)

■ 1980 ■ 1999

Low income   Lower middle income   Upper middle income   High income

Carbon dioxide emissions rise initially with income but tend to decline in some countries at higher levels of income.

Source: Table 3.8.

Data sources

The underlying data on commercial energy production and use are from electronic files of the International Energy Agency. The data on carbon dioxide emissions are from the Carbon Dioxide Information Analysis Center, Environmental Sciences Division, Oak Ridge National Laboratory, in the U.S. state of Tennessee.

| | Electricity production | | Access to electricity | Sources of electricity [a] | | | | | | | | | |
| | billion kwh | | % of population | Hydropower % | | Coal % | | Oil % | | Gas % | | Nuclear power % | |
	1980	2000	2000	1980	2000	1980	2000	1980	2000	1980	2000	1980	2000
Afghanistan	..	..	2.0	..	..	..	..	..	..	..	..	..	..
Albania	3.7	4.9	..	79.4	98.7	..	..	20.6	1.3	..	..	..	..
Algeria	7.1	25.4	98.0	3.6	0.2	..	..	12.2	3.0	84.1	96.7	..	..
Angola	0.7	1.4	12.0	88.1	63.1	..	..	11.9	36.9	..	..	..	..
Argentina	39.7	89.0	94.6	38.1	32.4	2.1	1.8	31.6	3.5	22.0	55.1	5.9	6.9
Armenia	13.0	6.0	..	12.0	21.2	..	..	54.8	..	..	45.2	33.2	33.7
Australia	95.2	208.1	..	13.6	8.1	73.3	77.2	5.4	1.3	7.3	12.6	..	..
Austria	41.6	60.3	..	69.1	69.6	7.0	11.1	14.0	3.3	9.2	13.0	..	..
Azerbaijan	15.0	18.7	..	7.3	8.2	..	..	92.7	72.6	..	19.2	..	..
Bangladesh	2.4	15.8	20.4	24.8	6.0	..	..	26.6	7.8	48.6	86.2	..	..
Belarus	34.1	26.1	..	0.1	0.1	..	..	99.9	5.9	..	94.0	..	..
Belgium	53.1	82.7	..	0.5	0.6	29.4	19.4	34.7	1.0	11.2	19.3	23.6	58.3
Benin	0.0	0.1	22.0	..	..	..	..	100.0	100.0	..	..	..	..
Bolivia	1.6	4.0	60.4	68.2	49.9	..	..	10.3	2.5	20.0	46.0	..	..
Bosnia and Herzegovina	..	10.4	..	..	48.8	..	50.7	..	0.5	..	..	..	..
Botswana	..	..	22.0	..	..	..	..	..	..	..	..	..	..
Brazil	139.4	349.2	94.9	92.5	87.3	2.4	2.9	3.8	4.8	..	0.7	..	1.7
Bulgaria	34.8	40.6	..	10.7	6.6	49.2	42.3	22.5	1.6	..	4.7	17.7	44.7
Burkina Faso	..	..	13.0	..	..	..	..	..	..	..	..	..	..
Burundi	..	..	..	..	..	..	..	..	..	..	..	..	..
Cambodia	..	..	15.8	..	..	..	..	..	..	..	..	..	..
Cameroon	1.5	3.5	20.0	93.9	98.9	..	..	6.1	1.1	..	..	..	..
Canada	373.3	605.1	..	67.3	59.2	16.0	19.5	3.7	2.5	2.5	5.5	10.2	12.0
Central African Republic	..	..	..	..	..	..	..	..	..	..	..	..	..
Chad	..	..	..	..	..	..	..	..	..	..	..	..	..
Chile	11.8	41.3	99.0	67.0	46.2	16.1	27.0	14.7	2.9	1.3	21.9	..	..
China	300.6	1,355.6	98.6	19.4	16.4	54.6	78.3	25.8	3.4	0.2	0.5	..	1.2
Hong Kong, China	12.6	31.3	..	..	..	..	60.5	100.0	0.4	..	39.1	..	..
Colombia	20.4	44.0	81.0	70.0	73.0	7.9	6.7	1.8	0.2	19.3	18.8	..	..
Congo, Dem. Rep.	4.4	5.5	6.7	95.5	99.7	..	..	4.5	0.3	..	..	..	..
Congo, Rep.	0.2	0.3	20.9	64.5	99.7	..	..	35.5	0.3	..	..	..	..
Costa Rica	2.2	6.9	95.7	95.2	82.1	..	..	4.3	0.9	..	..	..	..
Côte d'Ivoire	1.7	4.8	50.0	77.3	36.6	..	..	22.7	11.0	..	52.4	..	..
Croatia	..	10.7	..	..	55.1	..	14.5	..	15.8	..	14.7	..	..
Cuba	9.9	15.0	97.0	1.0	0.6	..	..	89.7	94.0	..	0.3	..	..
Czech Republic	52.7	72.9	..	4.6	2.4	84.8	73.1	9.6	0.5	1.1	4.3	..	18.6
Denmark	26.8	36.2	..	0.1	0.1	81.8	46.0	18.0	12.2	..	24.3	..	..
Dominican Republic	3.3	9.5	66.8	17.1	8.0	..	2.6	80.5	89.0	..	..	..	..
Ecuador	3.4	10.6	80.0	25.9	71.7	..	..	74.1	28.3	..	..	..	..
Egypt, Arab Rep.	18.9	75.7	93.8	51.8	18.7	..	..	27.7	16.1	20.5	65.2	..	..
El Salvador	1.5	3.9	70.8	63.7	30.5	..	..	2.7	48.5	..	..	..	..
Eritrea	..	..	17.0	..	..	..	..	..	..	..	..	..	..
Estonia	18.9	8.5	..	..	0.1	..	90.2	100.0	0.7	..	8.9	..	..
Ethiopia	0.7	1.7	4.7	70.2	97.5	..	..	29.8	1.4	..	..	..	..
Finland	40.7	70.0	..	25.1	20.9	42.6	18.9	10.8	0.9	4.2	14.4	17.2	32.1
France	257.3	535.8	..	27.0	12.5	27.2	5.8	18.8	1.4	2.7	2.1	23.8	77.5
Gabon	0.5	1.0	31.0	49.1	71.3	..	..	50.9	18.1	..	10.7	..	..
Gambia, The	..	..	..	..	..	..	..	..	..	..	..	..	..
Georgia	14.7	7.4	..	43.8	79.2	..	0.4	56.2	3.4	..	17.0	..	..
Germany	466.3	567.1	..	4.1	3.8	62.9	52.7	5.7	0.8	14.2	9.3	11.9	29.9
Ghana	5.3	7.2	45.0	99.2	91.7	..	..	0.8	8.3	..	..	..	..
Greece	22.7	53.4	..	15.0	6.9	44.8	64.2	40.1	16.6	..	11.1	..	..
Guatemala	1.8	6.0	66.7	12.9	37.8	..	8.3	83.0	39.9	..	..	..	..
Guinea	..	..	..	..	..	..	..	..	..	..	..	..	..
Guinea-Bissau	..	..	..	..	..	..	..	..	..	..	..	..	..
Haiti	0.3	0.5	34.0	70.1	51.7	..	..	26.1	48.3	..	..	..	..

	Electricity production		Access to electricity	Sources of electricity [a]									
				Hydropower %		Coal %		Oil %		Gas %		Nuclear power %	
	billion kwh		% of population										
	1980	2000	2000	1980	2000	1980	2000	1980	2000	1980	2000	1980	2000
Honduras	0.9	3.7	54.5	86.3	61.9	..	..	13.7	38.1	..	..	..	..
Hungary	23.9	35.0	..	0.5	0.5	50.4	27.7	13.9	12.6	35.2	18.9	..	40.0
India	119.3	542.3	43.0	39.0	13.7	49.1	77.4	8.2	1.0	1.1	4.5	2.5	3.1
Indonesia	8.4	92.6	53.4	16.0	9.8	..	31.1	84.0	21.9	..	34.3	..	..
Iran, Islamic Rep.	22.4	121.4	97.9	25.1	3.0	..	..	50.1	20.4	24.8	76.6	..	..
Iraq	11.4	33.7	95.0	6.1	1.8	..	..	93.9	98.2	..	..	..	..
Ireland	10.6	23.7	..	7.9	3.6	16.4	36.3	60.4	19.6	15.2	39.1	..	..
Israel	12.4	43.0	100.0	0.0	0.1	..	69.0	100.0	30.9	..	0.0	..	..
Italy	183.5	269.9	..	24.7	16.4	9.9	11.3	57.0	31.8	5.0	37.5	1.2	..
Jamaica	1.7	6.6	90.0	7.2	1.7	..	..	76.0	96.7	..	..	..	..
Japan	572.5	1,081.9	..	15.4	8.1	9.6	23.5	46.2	14.7	14.2	22.1	14.4	29.8
Jordan	1.1	7.4	95.0	..	0.5	..	..	100.0	89.4	..	10.1	..	..
Kazakhstan	61.5	51.6	..	9.3	14.6	..	69.9	90.7	4.9	..	10.6	..	..
Kenya	1.5	3.9	7.9	71.1	34.1	..	..	28.9	54.8	..	..	..	..
Korea, Dem. Rep.	35.0	31.6	20.0	67.1	67.4	31.6	32.2	1.2	0.4	..	..	..	..
Korea, Rep.	37.2	292.5	..	5.3	1.4	6.7	43.2	78.7	8.4	..	9.6	9.3	37.3
Kuwait	9.0	32.5	100.0	..	..	..	..	20.1	75.6	79.9	24.4	..	..
Kyrgyz Republic	9.2	14.9	..	53.1	91.7	..	4.1	46.9	..	..	4.1	..	..
Lao PDR	..	..	..	..	..	..	..	..	..	..	..	..	..
Latvia	4.7	4.1	..	64.9	68.2	..	1.9	35.1	2.6	..	27.3	..	..
Lebanon	2.8	7.8	95.0	30.9	5.7	..	..	69.1	94.3	..	..	..	..
Lesotho	..	..	5.0	..	..	..	..	..	..	..	..	..	..
Liberia	..	..	..	..	..	..	..	..	..	..	..	..	..
Libya	4.8	20.7	99.8	..	..	..	..	100.0	100.0	..	..	..	..
Lithuania	11.7	11.1	..	4.0	3.0	..	..	96.0	5.9	..	15.3	..	75.7
Macedonia, FYR	..	..	..	..	..	..	..	..	..	..	..	..	..
Madagascar	..	..	8.0	..	..	..	..	..	..	..	..	..	..
Malawi	..	..	5.0	..	..	..	..	..	..	..	..	..	..
Malaysia	10.0	69.2	96.9	13.9	10.1	..	2.6	84.9	8.8	1.2	78.5	..	..
Mali	..	..	..	..	..	..	..	..	..	..	..	..	..
Mauritania	..	..	..	..	..	..	..	..	..	..	..	..	..
Mauritius	..	..	100.0	..	..	..	..	..	..	..	..	..	..
Mexico	67.0	204.4	..	25.2	16.2	0.0	9.3	57.9	47.5	15.5	19.8	..	4.0
Moldova	15.4	3.3	..	2.6	1.8	..	5.0	97.4	1.0	..	92.3	..	..
Mongolia	..	..	90.0	..	..	..	..	..	..	..	..	..	..
Morocco	5.2	14.1	71.1	28.9	5.1	19.5	58.1	51.6	36.4	..	..	..	..
Mozambique	0.5	7.0	7.2	65.2	99.6	17.5	..	17.3	0.4	..	0.0	..	..
Myanmar	1.5	5.1	5.0	53.5	36.9	2.0	..	31.3	6.1	13.2	57.0	..	..
Namibia	..	1.4	34.0	..	97.6	..	0.4	..	2.1	..	..	..	..
Nepal	0.2	1.7	15.4	93.5	98.4	..	..	6.5	1.6	..	..	..	..
Netherlands	64.8	89.6	..	..	0.2	13.7	28.4	38.4	3.5	39.8	57.7	6.5	4.4
New Zealand	22.6	39.0	..	83.6	63.1	1.9	2.6	0.2	..	7.5	23.8	..	..
Nicaragua	1.1	2.3	48.0	48.1	9.2	..	..	46.4	81.6	..	..	..	..
Niger	..	..	..	..	..	..	..	..	..	..	..	..	..
Nigeria	7.1	15.8	40.0	39.0	36.8	0.4	..	45.1	6.3	15.5	56.9	..	..
Norway	83.8	142.4	..	99.8	99.5	0.0	0.1	0.1	0.0	..	0.1	..	..
Oman	0.8	9.1	94.0	..	..	..	..	21.5	19.1	78.5	80.9	..	..
Pakistan	15.0	68.1	52.9	58.2	25.2	0.2	0.4	1.1	39.5	40.5	32.0	0.0	2.9
Panama	2.0	4.7	76.1	48.2	67.2	..	..	50.2	31.3	..	..	..	..
Papua New Guinea	..	..	..	..	..	..	..	..	..	..	..	..	..
Paraguay	0.8	53.5	74.7	80.0	99.9	..	..	11.1	0.0	..	..	..	..
Peru	10.0	19.9	73.0	69.9	81.2	..	1.0	27.4	13.4	1.9	3.6	..	..
Philippines	18.0	45.3	87.4	19.6	17.2	1.0	36.8	67.9	20.3	..	0.0	..	..
Poland	120.9	143.2	..	1.9	1.5	94.7	96.1	2.9	1.3	0.1	0.7	..	..
Portugal	15.2	43.4	..	52.7	26.1	2.3	33.9	42.9	19.4	..	16.5	..	..
Puerto Rico	..	..	..	..	..	..	..	..	..	..	..	..	..

| | Electricity production | | Access to electricity | Sources of electricity[a] | | | | | | | | | |
| | billion kwh | | % of population | Hydropower % | | Coal % | | Oil % | | Gas % | | Nuclear power % | |
	1980	2000	2000	1980	2000	1980	2000	1980	2000	1980	2000	1980	2000
Romania	67.5	51.9	..	18.7	28.5	31.4	37.2	9.6	6.5	40.2	17.3	..	10.5
Russian Federation	804.9	876.5	..	16.1	18.7	..	20.0	77.2	3.8	..	42.3	6.7	14.9
Rwanda	..	..	..	..	..	..	..	..	..	..	..	..	..
Saudi Arabia	20.5	128.4	97.7	..	..	..	..	58.5	63.4	41.5	36.6	..	..
Senegal	0.6	1.5	30.1	..	..	..	..	100.0	99.9	..	0.1	..	..
Sierra Leone	..	..	..	..	..	..	..	..	..	..	..	..	..
Singapore	7.0	31.3	100.0	..	..	..	..	100.0	82.3	..	15.4	..	..
Slovak Republic	20.0	30.4	..	11.3	15.5	37.9	18.5	17.9	0.7	10.2	11.1	22.7	54.2
Slovenia	..	13.6	..	..	28.1	..	33.7	..	0.5	..	2.2	..	34.9
Somalia	..	..	..	..	..	..	..	..	..	..	..	..	..
South Africa	99.0	207.8	66.1	1.0	0.6	99.0	93.1	0.0	..	..	..	..	6.3
Spain	109.2	221.7	..	27.1	12.8	30.0	36.5	35.2	10.2	2.7	9.1	4.7	28.1
Sri Lanka	1.7	6.8	62.0	88.7	46.7	..	..	11.3	53.3	..	..	..	..
Sudan	0.8	2.4	30.0	70.0	48.3	..	..	30.0	51.7	..	..	..	..
Swaziland	..	..	..	..	..	..	..	..	..	..	..	..	..
Sweden	96.3	145.9	..	61.1	54.1	0.2	2.1	10.4	1.2	..	0.3	27.5	39.3
Switzerland	48.2	66.0	..	68.1	55.8	0.1	..	1.0	0.1	0.6	1.5	29.8	40.1
Syrian Arab Republic	4.0	22.6	85.9	64.7	41.1	..	..	31.9	22.4	3.4	36.5	..	..
Tajikistan	13.6	14.2	..	93.4	97.7	..	..	6.6	..	..	2.3	..	..
Tanzania	0.8	2.3	10.5	86.4	96.5	..	..	13.6	3.5	..	..	..	..
Thailand	14.4	96.0	82.1	8.8	6.3	9.8	18.3	81.4	10.4	..	63.4	..	..
Togo	0.0	0.0	9.0	13.3	2.2	..	..	86.7	97.8	..	..	..	..
Trinidad and Tobago	2.0	5.5	99.0	..	..	..	..	2.3	..	96.5	99.7	..	..
Tunisia	2.9	10.6	94.6	0.8	0.6	..	..	64.5	12.1	34.7	87.1	..	..
Turkey	23.3	124.9	..	48.8	24.7	25.6	30.6	25.1	8.4	..	36.1	..	..
Turkmenistan	6.7	9.8	..	0.1	0.1	..	..	99.9	..	..	99.9	..	..
Uganda	..	..	3.7	..	..	..	..	..	..	..	..	..	..
Ukraine	236.0	171.4	..	5.7	6.7	..	26.8	88.3	4.0	..	17.4	6.0	45.1
United Arab Emirates	6.3	38.6	96.0	..	..	..	..	3.7	7.9	96.3	92.1	..	..
United Kingdom	284.1	372.2	..	1.4	1.4	73.2	33.4	11.7	1.5	0.7	39.4	13.0	22.9
United States	2,427.3	4,003.5	..	11.5	6.2	51.2	52.7	10.8	3.1	15.3	15.7	11.0	20.0
Uruguay	4.6	7.6	98.0	76.3	92.9	..	..	23.5	6.7	..	..	..	..
Uzbekistan	33.9	46.8	..	14.6	12.5	..	4.0	85.4	11.3	..	72.2	..	..
Venezuela, RB	35.8	85.2	94.0	40.7	73.7	..	..	32.4	9.8	26.9	16.5	..	..
Vietnam	3.6	26.6	75.8	41.8	54.7	39.9	11.8	18.3	17.1	..	16.4	..	..
West Bank and Gaza	..	..	..	..	..	..	..	..	..	..	..	..	..
Yemen, Rep.	0.5	3.0	50.0	..	..	..	..	100.0	100.0	..	..	..	..
Yugoslavia, Fed. Rep.	..	31.9	..	..	37.8	..	56.2	..	2.6	..	3.4	..	..
Zambia	9.3	7.8	12.0	98.9	99.4	0.7	0.2	0.5	0.4	..	..	..	..
Zimbabwe	4.5	7.0	39.7	88.3	46.6	11.7	52.5	..	0.9	..	..	..	..
World	**8,205.8 s**	**15,346.5 s**	**.. w**	**20.6 w**	**17.4 w**	**33.0 w**	**39.1 w**	**28.5 w**	**7.8 w**	**8.8 w**	**17.4 w**	**8.7 w**	**16.9 w**
Low income	577.7	1,144.7	37.4	28.0	21.4	12.4	45.0	54.2	8.5	1.7	16.2	3.7	8.6
Middle income	2,195.4	4,777.2	94.0	22.4	24.3	22.6	39.2	47.5	10.6	4.6	20.5	3.1	5.4
Lower middle income	1,598.4	3,429.3	93.8	17.4	18.4	19.4	47.0	56.1	7.3	3.1	21.3	3.8	5.4
Upper middle income	597.0	1,347.9	94.7	..	41.5	31.0	19.2	24.7	19.1	8.6	18.4	1.1	5.4
Low & middle income	2,773.1	5,921.9	65.0	23.6	23.7	20.5	40.3	48.9	10.2	4.0	19.7	3.2	6.0
East Asia & Pacific	391.6	1,722.1	87.3	..	..	45.5	66.2	30.3	5.6	0.3	9.3	..	1.0
Europe & Central Asia	1,640.1	1,827.5	..	13.7	17.1	13.6	31.4	65.4	4.8	2.3	30.7	5.1	15.7
Latin America & Carib.	360.9	973.2	86.6	60.5	60.2	2.1	4.7	25.8	17.6	9.8	13.5	0.6	2.1
Middle East & N. Africa	102.9	481.9	90.4	20.5	9.1	1.0	1.7	53.3	42.5	25.0	46.7	..	..
South Asia	138.5	634.8	40.8	41.6	15.3	42.3	66.2	7.8	5.8	6.2	9.4	2.2	3.0
Sub-Saharan Africa	139.2	282.4	24.6	..	..	70.9	69.8	4.4	2.9	0.8	4.1	..	4.6
High income	5,432.7	9,424.6	..	..	..	39.4	38.4	18.0	6.3	11.3	16.0	11.5	23.7
Europe EMU	1,265.9	2,018.0	..	17.9	11.6	37.3	27.8	23.2	7.4	9.8	14.5	11.7	35.8

a. Shares may not sum to 100 percent because some sources of generated electricity (such as wind, solar, and geothermal) are not shown.

About the data

Use of energy in general, and access to electricity in particular, are important in improving people's standard of living. But electricity generation also can damage the environment. Whether such damage occurs depends largely on how electricity is generated. For example, burning coal releases twice as much carbon dioxide—a major contributor to global warming—as does burning an equivalent amount of natural gas (see *About the data* for table 3.8). Nuclear energy does not generate carbon dioxide emissions, but it produces other dangerous waste products. The table provides information on electricity production by source. Shares may not sum to 100 percent because some sources of generated electricity (such as wind, solar, and geothermal) are not shown.

The International Energy Agency (IEA) compiles data on energy inputs used to generate electricity. IEA data for countries that are not members of the Organisation for Economic Co-operation and Development (OECD) are based on national energy data adjusted to conform to annual questionnaires completed by OECD member governments. In addition, estimates are sometimes made to complete major aggregates from which key data are missing, and adjustments are made to compensate for differences in definitions. The IEA makes these estimates in consultation with national statistical offices, oil companies, electricity utilities, and national energy experts.

The IEA occasionally revises its time series to reflect political changes. Since 1990, for example, it has constructed energy statistics for countries of the former Soviet Union. In addition, energy statistics for other countries have undergone continuous changes in coverage or methodology as more detailed energy accounts have become available in recent years. Breaks in series are therefore unavoidable.

There is no single internationally accepted definition for access to electricity. The definition used here covers access at the household level—that is, the number of people who have electricity in their home. It includes commercially sold electricity, both on-grid and off-grid. For countries where access to electricity has been assessed through surveys by government agencies, the definition also includes self-generated electricity. The data do not capture unauthorized connections.

Definitions

• **Electricity production** is measured at the terminals of all alternator sets in a station. In addition to hydropower, coal, oil, gas, and nuclear power generation, it covers generation by geothermal, solar, wind, and tide and wave energy as well as that from combustible renewables and waste. Production includes the output of electricity plants designed to produce electricity only as well as that of combined heat and power plants. • **Access to electricity** refers to the number of people with access to electricity as a percentage of the total population. • **Sources of electricity** refer to the inputs used to generate electricity: hydropower, coal, oil, gas, and nuclear power. Hydropower refers to electricity produced by hydroelectric power plants, oil refers to crude oil and petroleum products, gas refers to natural gas but not natural gas liquids, and nuclear power refers to electricity produced by nuclear power plants.

3.9a

Electricity sources have shifted over the past two decades, though coal still dominates

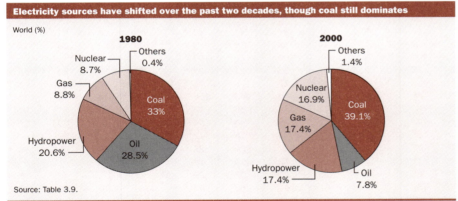

World (%)

Source: Table 3.9.

3.9b

The shift in electricity sources has been more profound in low-income countries

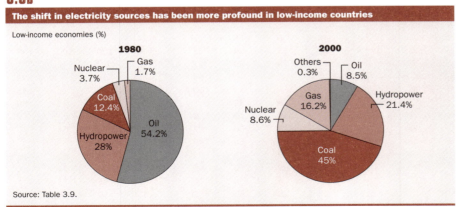

Low-income economies (%)

Source: Table 3.9.

Data sources

The data on electricity production are from the IEA's electronic files and its annual publications *Energy Statistics and Balances of Non-OECD Countries, Energy Statistics of OECD Countries,* and *Energy Balances of OECD Countries.* Data on access to electricity are from the IEA's *World Energy Outlook 2002: Energy and Poverty.*

3.10 | Urbanization

	Urban population				Population in urban agglomerations of more than one million			Population in largest city		Access to improved sanitation facilities			
										Urban		Rural	
	millions		% of total population			% of total population		% of urban population		% of population		% of population	
	1980	2001	1980	2001	1980	2000	2015	1980	2001	1990	2000	1990	2000
Afghanistan	2.5	6.1	16	22	6	10	14	39	45	..	25	..	8
Albania	0.9	1.4	34	43	..	..	..	..	22	..	99	..	85
Algeria	8.1	17.8	44	58	8	6	7	20	16	..	99	..	81
Angola	1.5	4.7	21	35	13	20	25	62	60	..	70	..	30
Argentina	23.3	33.1	83	88	42	41	40	43	37	..	87	..	47
Armenia	2.0	2.6	66	67	34	34	35	51	55	..	..	..	..
Australia	12.6	17.7	86	91	61	56	55	26	22	100	100	100	100
Austria	5.1	5.5	67	67	27	26	26	40	38	100	100	100	100
Azerbaijan	3.3	4.2	53	52	26	24	26	48	47	..	90	..	70
Bangladesh	12.7	34.1	15	26	6	13	18	26	38	81	71	31	41
Belarus	5.4	6.9	57	70	14	18	20	24	24	..	..	..	..
Belgium	9.4	10.0	95	97	12	11	11	13	11	..	..	..	..
Benin	0.9	2.8	27	43	..	..	..	..	8	46	46	6	6
Bolivia	2.4	5.4	45	63	14	18	20	33	28	73	86	26	42
Bosnia and Herzegovina	1.5	1.8	36	43	..	..	..	..	31	..	..	..	..
Botswana	0.2	0.8	18	49	..	..	..	..	27	87	88	41	43
Brazil	81.2	140.8	67	82	32	34	34	16	13	82	84	38	43
Bulgaria	5.4	5.4	61	67	12	15	16	20	22	..	100	..	100
Burkina Faso	0.6	1.9	8	17	..	..	..	45	45	..	39	..	27
Burundi	0.2	0.6	4	9	..	..	..	..	54	65	68	89	90
Cambodia	0.8	2.1	12	17	..	..	..	44	53	..	56	..	10
Cameroon	2.7	7.5	31	50	11	21	27	19	23	97	92	64	66
Canada	18.6	24.5	76	79	32	37	38	16	20	100	100	99	99
Central African Republic	0.8	1.6	35	42	..	..	..	..	42	38	38	16	16
Chad	0.8	1.9	19	24	..	..	..	..	38	70	81	4	13
Chile	9.1	13.3	81	86	33	36	37	41	42	98	96	92	97
China	192.8	466.7	20	37	13	14	17	6	3	57	68	18	24
Hong Kong, China	4.6	6.7	91	100	91	100	100	100	100	..	..	..	..
Colombia	17.8	32.5	63	75	26	32	35	21	21	96	96	55	56
Congo, Dem. Rep.	..	..	..	..	8	10	12	..	..	..	54	..	6
Congo, Rep.	0.7	2.0	42	66	27	41	44	263	158	..	14	..	..
Costa Rica	1.1	2.3	47	60	..	..	..	56	43	..	89	..	97
Côte d'Ivoire	2.8	7.2	35	44	15	21	25	44	54	70	71	29	35
Croatia	2.3	2.5	50	58	..	..	..	28	42	..	..	..	..
Cuba	6.6	8.5	68	75	20	20	20	29	27	..	99	..	95
Czech Republic	7.6	7.6	75	75	12	12	12	15	16	..	..	..	..
Denmark	4.3	4.6	84	85	27	26	26	32	29	..	..	..	..
Dominican Republic	2.9	5.6	51	66	34	61	67	50	47	70	70	60	60
Ecuador	3.7	8.2	47	63	23	32	37	29	27	88	92	49	74
Egypt, Arab Rep.	17.9	27.9	44	43	23	23	24	38	35	96	100	79	96
El Salvador	2.0	3.9	44	61	16	22	25	35	35	87	89	62	76
Eritrea	0.3	0.8	14	19	..	..	..	..	63	..	66	..	1
Estonia	1.0	0.9	70	69	..	..	..	..	42	..	93	..	..
Ethiopia	4.0	10.4	10	16	3	4	6	30	27	24	33	6	7
Finland	2.9	3.1	60	59	13	23	25	24	31	100	100	100	100
France	39.5	44.7	73	76	21	21	20	23	22	..	..	..	..
Gabon	0.3	1.0	50	82	..	..	..	..	55	..	55	..	43
Gambia, The	0.1	0.4	20	31	..	..	..	..	100	..	41	..	35
Georgia	2.6	3.1	52	57	22	24	29	42	..	..	100	..	99
Germany	64.7	72.2	83	88	39	41	43	10	9	..	..	..	..
Ghana	3.3	7.2	31	36	9	10	14	30	27	56	74	64	70
Greece	5.6	6.4	58	60	31	30	29	54	49	..	..	..	..
Guatemala	2.6	4.7	37	40	11	28	32	29	72	82	83	62	79
Guinea	0.9	2.1	19	28	12	25	32	75	60	94	94	41	41
Guinea-Bissau	0.1	0.4	17	32	..	..	..	..	74	87	95	33	44
Haiti	1.3	3.0	24	36	13	22	28	55	62	33	50	19	16

	Urban population				Population in urban agglomerations of more than one million			Population in largest city		Access to improved sanitation facilities			
										Urban % of population		Rural % of population	
	millions		% of total population		% of total population			% of urban population		% of population		% of population	
	1980	2001	1980	2001	1980	2000	2015	1980	2001	1990	2000	1990	2000
Honduras	1.2	3.5	35	54	..	..	..	33	28	88	93	41	55
Hungary	6.1	6.6	57	65	19	18	19	34	28	100	100	98	98
India	158.5	287.7	23	28	8	10	12	5	6	44	61	6	15
Indonesia	32.9	87.7	22	42	8	10	13	18	13	66	69	38	46
Iran, Islamic Rep.	19.4	41.7	50	65	21	23	24	26	17	..	86	..	79
Iraq	8.5	16.0	66	68	29	31	34	39	31	..	93	..	31
Ireland	1.9	2.3	55	59	..	..	..	48	44	..	..	..	..
Israel	3.4	5.8	89	92	37	35	33	41	35	..	..	..	..
Italy	37.6	38.9	67	67	24	19	20	14	11	..	..	..	..
Jamaica	1.0	1.5	47	57	..	..	..	..	46	99	99	99	99
Japan	89.0	100.2	76	79	34	38	39	25	26	..	..	..	..
Jordan	1.3	4.0	60	79	29	29	32	49	30	100	100	95	98
Kazakhstan	8.0	8.3	54	56	6	8	9	12	13	..	100	..	98
Kenya	2.7	10.5	16	34	5	8	10	32	22	91	96	77	82
Korea, Dem. Rep.	9.8	13.5	57	61	11	14	16	19	24	..	99	..	100
Korea, Rep.	21.7	39.0	57	82	40	47	45	38	26	..	76	..	4
Kuwait	1.2	2.0	91	96	60	60	55	67	46	..	..	..	..
Kyrgyz Republic	1.4	1.7	38	34	..	..	..	..	43	..	100	..	100
Lao PDR	0.4	1.1	12	20	..	..	..	..	62	..	67	..	19
Latvia	1.7	1.4	68	60	..	..	..	49	53	..	..	..	..
Lebanon	2.2	3.9	74	90	40	47	48	55	53	..	100	..	87
Lesotho	0.2	0.6	13	29	..	..	..	..	46	..	72	..	40
Liberia	0.7	1.5	35	45	..	..	..	..	34	..	..	..	..
Libya	2.1	4.8	69	88	26	34	34	38	37	97	97	96	96
Lithuania	2.1	2.4	61	69	..	..	..	..	24	..	..	..	..
Macedonia, FYR	1.0	1.2	53	59	..	..	..	..	36	..	..	..	..
Madagascar	1.6	4.8	19	30	6	10	13	33	35	70	70	25	30
Malawi	0.6	1.6	9	15	..	..	..	..	33	96	96	70	70
Malaysia	5.8	13.8	42	58	7	6	6	16	10	..	..	..	98
Mali	1.2	3.4	18	31	..	..	..	40	34	95	93	62	58
Mauritania	0.4	1.6	28	59	..	..	..	..	39	44	44	19	19
Mauritius	0.4	0.5	42	42	..	..	..	..	35	100	100	100	99
Mexico	44.8	74.2	66	75	28	28	25	29	25	87	88	26	34
Moldova	1.6	1.8	40	42	..	..	..	..	37	..	100	..	98
Mongolia	0.9	1.4	52	57	..	..	..	49	56	..	46	..	2
Morocco	8.0	16.4	41	56	15	18	20	26	21	88	86	31	44
Mozambique	1.6	6.0	13	33	6	17	21	35	19	..	68	..	26
Myanmar	8.1	13.6	24	28	7	9	11	27	33	..	84	..	57
Namibia	0.2	0.6	23	31	..	..	..	..	38	84	96	14	17
Nepal	1.0	2.9	7	12	..	..	..	..	26	69	73	15	22
Netherlands	12.5	14.4	88	90	14	14	14	8	8	100	100	100	100
New Zealand	2.6	3.3	83	86	..	..	..	30	34	..	..	..	..
Nicaragua	1.5	2.9	50	57	..	..	..	36	35	97	95	53	72
Niger	0.7	2.4	13	21	..	..	..	37	35	71	79	4	5
Nigeria	19.1	58.3	27	45	8	12	15	13	15	69	66	44	45
Norway	2.9	3.4	71	75	..	..	..	22	23	100	..	..	..
Oman	0.3	1.9	32	76	..	..	..	..	28	98	98	61	61
Pakistan	23.2	47.3	28	33	15	21	25	22	22	77	95	17	43
Panama	1.0	1.6	50	57	..	..	..	62	73	..	99	..	83
Papua New Guinea	0.4	0.9	13	18	..	..	..	..	28	92	92	80	80
Paraguay	1.3	3.2	42	57	22	23	26	52	41	96	94	91	93
Peru	11.2	19.3	65	73	25	29	30	39	39	77	79	21	49
Philippines	18.0	46.5	37	59	14	16	17	33	22	85	93	63	69
Poland	20.6	24.2	58	63	18	18	19	16	14	..	..	..	..
Portugal	2.9	6.6	29	66	19	57	68	46	60	..	..	..	..
Puerto Rico	2.1	2.9	67	76	34	36	37	51	48	..	..	..	..

	Urban population				Population in urban agglomerations of more than one million			Population in largest city		Access to improved sanitation facilities			
	millions		% of total population		% of total population			% of urban population		Urban % of population		Rural % of population	
	1980	2001	1980	2001	1980	2000	2015	1980	2001	1990	2000	1990	2000
Romania	10.9	12.4	49	55	9	9	10	18	16	..	86	..	10
Russian Federation	97.0	105.5	70	73	18	19	21	8	8	..	..	..	..
Rwanda	0.2	0.5	5	6	..	..	..	..	76	..	12	..	8
Saudi Arabia	6.2	18.5	66	87	19	25	24	17	25	..	100	..	100
Senegal	2.0	4.7	36	48	17	22	27	48	46	86	94	38	48
Sierra Leone	0.8	1.9	24	37	..	..	..	47	43	..	88	..	53
Singapore	2.4	4.1	100	100	100	89	83	100	100	..	100	..	..
Slovak Republic	2.6	3.1	52	58	..	..	..	..	15	..	100	..	100
Slovenia	0.9	1.0	48	49	..	..	..	..	26	100	..	..	..
Somalia	1.4	2.5	22	28	..	..	..	27	48	..	..	..	..
South Africa	13.3	24.9	48	58	27	32	36	13	12	93	93	80	80
Spain	27.2	32.0	73	78	20	17	17	16	13	..	..	..	..
Sri Lanka	3.1	4.3	22	23	..	..	..	..	16	94	97	82	93
Sudan	3.9	11.7	20	37	6	9	11	30	24	87	87	48	48
Swaziland	0.1	0.3	18	27	..	..	..	..	28	..	..	..	..
Sweden	6.9	7.4	83	83	17	18	18	20	22	100	100	100	100
Switzerland	3.6	4.9	57	67	..	..	..	20	19	100	100	100	100
Syrian Arab Republic	4.1	8.6	47	52	28	28	31	26	27	..	98	..	81
Tajikistan	1.4	1.7	34	28	..	..	..	..	30	..	97	..	88
Tanzania	2.7	11.4	15	33	5	12	18	30	19	84	99	84	86
Thailand	8.0	12.3	17	20	10	12	15	59	61	95	96	75	96
Togo	0.6	1.6	23	34	..	..	..	..	46	71	69	24	17
Trinidad and Tobago	0.7	1.0	63	74	..	..	..	..	6	..	..	..	..
Tunisia	3.3	6.4	52	66	18	20	21	35	30	96	96	48	62
Turkey	19.5	43.8	44	66	19	27	30	23	21	97	97	70	70
Turkmenistan	1.3	2.4	47	45	..	..	..	..	23	..	..	..	..
Uganda	1.1	3.3	9	15	..	..	..	42	39	..	93	..	77
Ukraine	30.9	33.4	62	68	14	15	17	7	7	..	100	..	98
United Arab Emirates	0.7	2.6	71	87	..	..	..	34	35	..	..	..	..
United Kingdom	50.0	52.7	89	90	25	23	23	15	15	100	100	100	100
United States	167.6	221.0	74	77	38	38	37	9	8	100	100	100	100
Uruguay	2.5	3.1	85	92	42	37	35	49	43	..	95	..	85
Uzbekistan	6.5	9.2	41	37	11	9	8	28	24	..	97	..	85
Venezuela, RB	12.0	21.5	79	87	28	29	30	21	15	..	71	..	48
Vietnam	10.3	19.5	19	25	14	13	14	33	24	52	82	23	38
West Bank and Gaza	..	..	..	..	..	..	..	..	..	..	..	..	..
Yemen, Rep.	1.6	4.5	19	25	..	..	..	15	31	69	89	21	21
Yugoslavia, Fed. Rep.	4.5	5.5	46	52	11	14	15	25	30	..	100	..	99
Zambia	2.3	4.1	40	40	9	16	22	23	41	86	99	48	64
Zimbabwe	1.6	4.6	22	36	9	14	19	39	40	70	71	50	57
World	**1,741.8 s**	**2,890.5 s**	**39 w**	**47 w**	**.. w**	**.. w**	**.. w**	**18 w**	**16 w**	**75 w**	**81 w**	**27 w**	**37 w**
Low income	381.0	772.5	24	31	..	..	..	16	17	58	72	20	31
Middle income	755.6	1,376.1	38	52	..	..	..	19	15	75	81	29	40
Lower middle income	515.6	987.4	32	46	15	17	20	16	13	70	80	28	39
Upper middle income	240.0	388.6	66	77	..	..	..	25	22	86	87	41	57
Low & middle income	1,136.6	2,148.5	32	42	..	..	..	18	16	68	78	24	35
East Asia & Pacific	288.6	679.9	21	37	..	..	..	13	9	61	72	24	34
Europe & Central Asia	249.2	298.1	59	63	16	18	20	15	15	..	..	..	..
Latin America & Carib.	234.1	396.9	65	76	29	32	32	27	24	85	86	41	52
Middle East & N. Africa	83.7	173.3	48	58	21	22	24	30	25	..	94	..	72
South Asia	201.1	382.5	22	28	8	12	14	9	11	52	66	11	21
Sub-Saharan Africa	80.0	217.8	21	32	..	..	..	27	26	75	76	45	45
High income	605.2	741.9	73	78	..	..	..	18	17	..	..	..	..
Europe EMU	210.3	237.7	73	78	26	27	27	17	16	..	..	..	..

The population of a city or metropolitan area depends on the boundaries chosen. For example, in 1990 Beijing, China, contained 2.3 million people in 87 square kilometers of "inner city" and 5.4 million in 158 square kilometers of "core city." The population of "inner city and inner suburban districts" was 6.3 million, and that of "inner city, inner and outer suburban districts, and inner and outer counties" was 10.8 million. (For most countries the last definition is used.)

Estimates of the world's urban population would change significantly if China, India, and a few other populous nations were to change their definition of urban centers. According to China's State Statistical Bureau, by the end of 1996 urban residents accounted for about 43 percent of China's population, while in 1994 only 20 percent of the population was considered urban. In addition to the continuous migration of people from rural to urban areas, one of the main reasons for this shift was the rapid growth in the hundreds of towns reclassified as cities in recent years. Because the estimates in the table are based on national definitions of what constitutes a city or metropolitan area, cross-country comparisons should be made with caution.

To estimate urban populations, the United Nations' ratios of urban to total population were applied to the World Bank's estimates of total population (see table 2.1).

The urban population with access to improved sanitation facilities is defined as those with access to at least adequate excreta disposal facilities that can effectively prevent human, animal, and insect contact with excreta. The rural population with access is included to allow comparison of rural and urban access. This definition and the definition of urban areas vary, however, so comparisons between countries can be misleading.

3.10a

The urban population in low-income countries has doubled in the past two decades . . .

Urban population (millions)

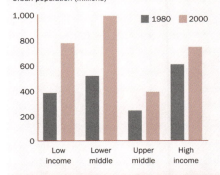

. . . surpassing the urban population in high-income countries

World urban population, 2001

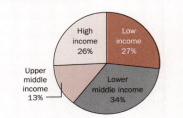

Low-income countries, with only 31 percent of their people in urban areas, still have a larger urban population than high-income countries.

Source: Table 3.10.

• **Urban population** is the midyear population of areas defined as urban in each country and reported to the United Nations (see *About the data*).
• **Population in urban agglomerations of more than one million** is the percentage of a country's population living in metropolitan areas that in 1990 had a population of more than one million. • **Population in largest city** is the percentage of a country's urban population living in that country's largest metropolitan area. • **Access to improved sanitation facilities** refers to the percentage of the urban or rural population with access to at least adequate excreta disposal facilities (private or shared but not public) that can effectively prevent human, animal, and insect contact with excreta. Improved facilities range from simple but protected pit latrines to flush toilets with a sewerage connection. To be effective, facilities must be correctly constructed and properly maintained.

Data sources

The data on urban population and the population in urban agglomerations and in the largest city come from the United Nations Population Division's *World Urbanization Prospects: The 2001 Revision*. The total population figures are World Bank estimates. The data on access to sanitation in urban and rural areas are from the World Health Organization.

3.11 Urban environment

Country	City	Urban population thousands 2000	Secure tenure % of population 1998[a]	House price to income ratio 1998[a]	Work trips by public transportation % 1998[a]	Travel time to work minutes 1998[a]	Households with access to services — Potable water % 1998[a]	Sewerage connection % 1998[a]	Electricity % 1998[a]	Telephone % 1998[a]	Wastewater treated % 1998[a]
Algeria	Algiers	2,562 [b]	93.2	..	..	75	..	..	..	..	80
Argentina	Buenos Aires	2,996 [b]	92.1	5.1	59	42	100	98	100	70	..
	Córdoba	1,322 [b]	85.0	6.8	44	32	99	40	99	80	49
	Rosario	1,248 [b]	..	5.7	..	22	98	67	93	76	1
Armenia	Yerevan	1,250 [b]	100.0	4.0	84	30	98	98	100	88	36
Bangladesh	Chittagong	2,301 [b]	..	8.1	27	45	44	..	95	..	..
	Dhaka	10,000 [b]	..	16.7	9	45	60	22	90	7	..
	Sylhet	242 [b]	..	6.0	10	50	29	0	93	40	..
	Tangail	152 [b]	85.7	13.9	..	30	12	0	90	12	..
Barbados	Bridgetown	..	99.7	4.4	..	..	98	5	99	78	7
Belize	Belize City	55 [b]	..	..	..	..	..	..	..	..	..
Bolivia	Santa Cruz de la Sierra	1,065 [c]	87.0	29.3	..	29	53	33	98	59	53
Bosnia and Herzegovina	Sarajevo	522 [c]	..	..	100	12	95	90	100	..	..
Brazil	Belém	1,638 [c]	..	..	..	..	..	..	..	..	..
	Icapui	..	91.7	4.5	..	30	88	..	90	33	..
	Maranguape	..	..	..	30	20	73	..	..	..	..
	Porto Alegre	3 [b]	..	..	..	..	99	87	100	..	..
	Recife	3,088 [b]	..	12.5	46	35	89	41	100	29	33
	Rio de Janeiro	10,192 [b]	..	..	..	..	88	80	10	..	..
	Santo André	1,658 [b]	80.3	23.4	43	40	98	95	100	79	..
Bulgaria	Bourgas	.. [b]	..	5.1	61	32	100	93	100	..	93
	Sofia	1,200 [b]	100.0	13.2	79	32	95	91	100	89	94
	Troyan	24 [b]	100.0	3.7	44	22	99	82	100	45	..
	Veliko Tarnovo	..	100.0	5.4	46	30	98	98	100	96	50
Burkina Faso	Bobo-Dioulasso	..	100.0	..	..	..	24	..	29	6	..
	Koudougou	..	..	..	..	..	30	..	26	7	..
	Ouagadougou	1,130 [c]	100.0	..	2	..	30	..	47	11	19
Burundi	Bujumbura	373 [b]	97.0	..	48	25	26	62	57	19	21
Cambodia	Phnom Penh	1,000 [b]	..	8.9	0	45	45	75	76	40	..
Cameroon	Douala	1,148 [b]	..	13.4	..	40	34	1	95	9	5
	Yaoundé	968 [b]	..	..	42	45	34	1	95	9	24
Canada	Hull	254 [b]	100.0	..	16	..	100	100	100	100	100
Central African Republic	Bangui	..	94.0	..	66	60	31	..	18	11	0
Chad	N'Djamena	998 [c]	..	..	35	..	42	0	13	6	21
Chile	Gran Concepción	..	..	..	57	35	100	91	95	69	6
	Santiago de Chile	5,737 [b]	..	..	60	38	100	99	99	73	3
	Tome	..	..	..	..	..	92	52	98	58	57
	Valparaiso	851 [b]	91.8	..	55	..	98	92	97	63	100
	Viña del Mar	851 [b]	92.7	..	..	..	97	97	98	65	93
Colombia	Armenia	..	94.1	5.0	42	60	90	50	99	97	..
	Marinilla	170 [b]	94.5	8.5	18	15	98	93	100	65	..
	Medellín	2,901 [b]	..	..	38	35	100	99	100	87	..
Congo, Rep	Brazzaville	989 [b]	87.9	..	55	20	56	0	52	18	..
Côte d'Ivoire	Abidjan	3,201 [b]	..	14.5	..	45	26	15	41	5	45
Croatia	Zagreb	2,497 [b]	96.5	7.8	56	31	98	100	94	..	..
Cuba	Baracoa	..	96.2	..	..	..	83	3	93	32	..
	Camagüey	..	84.7	..	2	60	72	47	97	..	..
	Cienfuegos	..	96.3	4.0	..	80	100	73	100	9	2
	Havana	..	..	8.5	58	83	100	85	100	14	..
	Pinar Del Rio	..	96.4	..	..	80	97	48	100	..	..
	Santa Clara	..	98.8	..	7	48	95	42	100	43	..
Czech Republic	Brno	..	..	..	50	25	100	96	100	69	100
	Prague	1,193 [b]	99.3	..	55	22	99	100	100	100	..
Congo, Dem. Rep.	Kinshasa	5,398 [b]	94.9	..	72	57	72	0	66	1	..
Dominican Republic	Santiago de los Caballeros	691 [b]	..	..	..	30	75	80	..	71	80

	City	Urban population	Secure tenure	House price to income ratio	Work trips by public trans-portation	Travel time to work	Households with access to services				Wastewater treated
							Potable water	Sewerage connection	Electricity	Telephone	
		thousands	% of population		%	minutes	%	%	%	%	%
		2000	1998[a]	1998[a]	1998[a]	1998[a]	1998[a]	1998[a]	1998[a]	1998[a]	1998[a]
Ecuador	Ambato	286[b]	..	..	..	..	90	81	91	87	..
	Cuenca	..	91.0	4.6	..	25	97	92	97	48	82
	Guayaquil	2,317[b]	45.8	3.4	89	45	70	42	..	44	9
	Manta	126[b]	..	..	..	30	70	52	98	40	..
	Puyo	40[b]	..	2.1	..	15	80	30	90	60	..
	Quito	1,531[b]	93.8	2.4	..	33	85	70	96	55	..
	Tena	..	..	6.3	..	5	80	60	..	..	..
El Salvador	San Salvador	1,863[b]	90.5	3.5	..	..	82	80	98	70	..
Estonia	Riik	..	99.5	..	..	..	92	90	98	55	..
	Tallin	397[c]	98.8	6.4	..	35	98	98	100	86	100
Gabon	Libreville	523[c]	..	..	80	30	55	0	95	45	44
Gambia, The	Banjul	50[b]	91.8	11.4	55	22	23	12	24	..	..
Georgia	Tbilisi	1,310[c]	100.0	9.4	..	..	..	98	100	58	..
Ghana	Accra	1,500[b]	..	14.0	54	21	..	..	..	..	..
	Kumasi	780[b]	77.7	13.7	51	21	65	..	95	51	..
Guatemala	Quezaltenango	333[b]	..	4.3	..	15	60	55	80	40	..
Guinea	Conakry	1,824[c]	..	..	26	45	30	32	54	6	..
Indonesia	Jakarta	9,489[b]	95.5	14.6	..	..	50	65	99	..	16
	Semarang	1,076[b]	80.2	..	..	..	34	..	85	..	..
	Surabaya	2,373[b]	97.6	3.4	18	35	41	56	89	71	..
Iraq	Baghdad	4,797[c]	..	..	..	..	..	..	..	..	..
Italy	Aversa	..	..	..	..	..	..	..	..	..	90
Jamaica	Kingston	655[c]	..	..	..	..	97	..	88	..	20
	Montego Bay	..	..	..	..	..	78	..	86	..	15
Jordan	Amman	1,621[b]	97.3	6.1	21	25	98	81	99	62	54
Kenya	Kisumu	134[b]	97.3	8.5	43	24	38	31	49	..	65
	Mombasa	..	..	..	47	20	..	..	..	..	50
	Nairobi	2,310[c]	..	..	71	57	89	..	..	..	52
Korea, Rep	Hanam	124[b]	..	3.7	..	..	81	68	100	100	81
	Pusan	3,843[b]	100.0	4.0	39	42	98	69	100	100	69
	Seoul	10,389[b]	98.6	5.7	71	60	100	99	100	..	99
Kuwait	Kuwait City	1,165[c]	..	6.5	21	10	100	98	100	98	..
Kyrgyz Republic	Bishkek	60[b]	94.8	..	95	35	30	23	100	20	15
Lao	Vientiane	562[b]	92.2	23.2	2	27	87	..	100	87	20
Latvia	Riga	775[c]	97.4	15.6	..	..	95	93	100	70	..
Lebanon	Sin El Fil	..[b]	..	8.3	50	10	80	30	98	80	..
Liberia	Monrovia	651[b]	57.6	28.0	80	60	..	..	..	..	..
Libya	Tripoli	1,773[b]	..	0.8	18	20	97	90	99	6	40
Lithuania	Vilnius	578[b]	100.0	20.0	52	37	89	89	100	77	54
Madagascar	Antananarivo	1,507[c]	..	..	..	..	..	..	..	..	..
Malawi	Lilongwe	765[c]	..	..	27	5	65	12	50	10	..
Malaysia	Penang	..	..	7.2	55	40	99	..	100	98	20
Mauritania	Nouakchott	881[c]	89.9	5.4	45	50	..	..	..	..	..
Mexico	Ciudad Juarez	1,018[b]	..	..	24	23	89	77	96	45	..
Moldova	Chisinau	..	..	..	80	23	100	95	100	83	71
Mongolia	Ulaanbaatar	627[b]	51.6	7.8	80	30	60	60	100	90	96
Morocco	Casablanca	3,292[b]	..	..	..	30	83	93	91	..	..
	Rabat	646[b]	..	..	40	20	93	97	52	..	..
Myanmar	Yangon	3,692[b]	..	8.3	69	45	78	81	85	17	..
Nicaragua	Leon	..	98.8	..	..	15	78	..	84	21	..
Niger	Niamey	731[c]	87.4	..	..	30	33	0	51	4	..
Nigeria	Ibadan	1,731[c]	85.8	..	46	45	26	12	41	..	..
	Lagos	13,427[c]	93.0	..	48	60	..	..	41	..	..
Oman	Muscat	887[b]	..	..	..	20	80	90	89	53	..
Panama	Colón	132[b]	..	14.2	..	15	..	..	..	..	..
Paraguay	Asunción	1,262[c]	90.2	10.7	..	25	46	8	86	17	..

3.11 Urban environment

City		Urban population	Secure tenure	House price to income ratio	Work trips by public trans-portation	Travel time to work	Households with access to services				Wastewater treated
							Potable water	Sewerage connection	Electricity	Telephone	
			% of population				%	%	%	%	%
		thousands 2000	1998[a]	1998[a]	1998[a]	minutes 1998[a]	1998[a]	1998[a]	1998[a]	1998[a]	1998[a]
Peru	Cajamarca	..	90.0	3.9	..	20	86	69	81	38	62
	Huanuco	747[b]	..	30.0	..	20	57	28	80	32	..
	Huaras	54[b]	..	6.7	..	15	..	..	71	..	..
	Iquitos	347[b]	97.3	5.6	25	10	73	60	82	62	..
	Lima	7,431[b]	80.6	10.4	82	..	75	71	99	..	4
	Tacna	..	..	4.0	..	25	65	58	74	16	64
	Tumbes	..	..	..	..	20	60	35	80	25	..
Philippines	Cebu	2,189[b]	95.0	13.3	..	35	41	92	80	25	..
Poland	Bydgoszcz	..	60.5	4.3	35	18	95	87	100	85	28
	Gdansk	893[c]	..	4.4	56	20	99	94	100	56	100
	Katowice	3,487[c]	27.8	1.7	29	36	99	94	100	75	67
	Poznan	..	65.5	5.8	51	25	95	96	100	86	78
Qatar	Doha	391[c]	..	..	..	..	..	..	..	..	..
Russian Federation	Astrakhan	..	100.0	5.0	66	35	81	79	100	51	92
	Belgorod	..	100.0	4.0	..	25	90	89	100	51	96
	Kostroma	..	100.0	6.9	68	20	88	84	100	46	96
	Moscow	9,321[c]	100.0	5.1	85	62	100	100	100	100	98
	Nizhny Novgorod	1,458[c]	100.0	6.9	79	35	98	98	100	64	98
	Novomoscowsk	..	100.0	4.2	61	25	99	93	100	62	97
	Omsk	1,216[c]	99.7	3.9	86	43	87	87	100	41	89
	Pushkin	..	100.0	9.6	60	15	99	99	100	89	100
	Surgut	..	100.0	4.5	81	57	98	98	100	50	93
	Veliky Novgorod	..	100.0	3.4	75	30	97	97	100	51	95
Rwanda	Kigali	358[b]	..	11.4	32	45	36	20	57	6	20
Samoa	Apia	34[b]	..	10.0	..	..	60	0	98	96	..
Singapore	Singapore	3,164[b]	100.0	3.1	53	30	100	100	100	100	100
Slovenia	Ljubljana	273[b]	98.9	7.8	20	30	100	100	100	97	98
Spain	Madrid	4,577[b]	..	..	16	32	..	..	..	..	100
	Pamplona	..	..	..	..	..	100	..	100	..	79
Sweden	Amal	13[b]	..	2.9	..	..	100	100	100	..	100
	Stockholm	736[b]	..	6.0	48	28	100	100	100	..	100
	Umea	104[b]	..	5.3	..	16	100	100	100	..	100
Switzerland	Basel	170[b]	..	12.3	..	..	100	100	100	99	100
Syrian Arab Republic	Damascus	2,335[b]	..	10.3	33	40	98	71	95	10	3
Thailand	Bangkok	5,647[b]	77.2	8.8	28	60	99	100	100	60	..
	Chiang Mai	499[b]	96.5	6.8	5	30	95	60	100	75	70
Togo	Lomé	663[b]	64.0	..	40	30	..	70	51	18	..
Trinidad and Tobago	Port of Spain	..	78.6	..	44	..	..	..	..	..	..
Tunisia	Tunis	2,023[b]	..	5.0	..	..	75	47	95	27	83
Turkey	Ankara	2,837[b]	91.3	4.5	..	32	97	98	100	..	80
Uganda	Entebbe	65[b]	74.0	10.4	65	20	48	13	42	0	30
	Jinja	92[b]	82.0	15.4	49	12	65	43	55	5	30
Uruguay	Montevideo	1,670[b]	88.0	5.6	60	45	98	79	100	75	34
West Bank and Gaza	Gaza	367[b]	87.3	5.4	..	..	85	38	99	38	..
Yemen, Rep.	Aden	1,200[b]	..	..	78	20	..	..	96	..	30
	Sana'a	1,200[b]	..	..	78	20	30	9	96	..	30
Yugoslavia, Fed. Rep.	Belgrade	1,182[b]	96.5	13.5	72	40	95	86	100	86	20
Zimbabwe	Bulawayo	900[b]	99.4	..	75	15	100	100	98	..	80
	Chegutu	..	51.5	3.4	20	22	100	68	9	3	69
	Gweru	..	94.0	..	..	15	100	100	90	61	95
	Harare	1,634[b]	99.9	..	32	45	100	100	88	42	..
	Mutare	149[b]	..	..	70	20	88	88	74	4	100

a. Data are preliminary. b. Data are for 1998 and are from the United Nations Centre for Human Settlements. c. Data are for 2000 and are from the United Nations Population Division's *World Urbanization Prospects: The 2001 Revision.*

About the data

Despite the importance of cities and urban agglomerations as home to almost half the world's people, data on many aspects of urban life are sparse. The available data have been scattered among international agencies with different mandates, and compiling comparable data has been difficult. Even within cities it is difficult to assemble an integrated data set. Urban areas are often spread across many jurisdictions with no single agency responsible for collecting and reporting data for the entire area. Adding to the difficulties of data collection are gaps and overlaps in the data collection and reporting responsibilities of different administrative units. Creating a comprehensive, comparable international data set is further complicated by differences in the definition of an urban area and by uneven data quality.

The United Nations Global Plan of Action calls for monitoring the changing role of the world's cities and human settlements. The international agency with the mandate to assemble information on urban areas is the United Nations Centre for Human Settlements (UNCHS, or Habitat). Its Urban Indicators Programme is intended to provide data for monitoring and evaluating the performance of urban areas and for developing government policies and strategies. These data are collected through questionnaires completed by city officials in more than a hundred countries.

The table shows selected indicators for more than 160 cities from the UNCHS data set. A few more indicators are included on the *World Development Indicators* CD-ROM. These data are still preliminary and are undergoing further validation.

The selection of cities in the UNCHS database does not reflect population weights or the economic importance of cities and is therefore biased toward smaller cities. Moreover, it is based on demand for participation in the Urban Indicators Programme. As a result, the database excludes a large number of major cities. The table reflects this bias as well as the criterion of data availability for the indicators shown.

The data should be used with care. Because different data collection methods and definitions may have been used, comparisons can be misleading. In addition, the definitions used here for urban population and access to potable water are more stringent than those used for tables 3.5 and 3.10 (see *Definitions*).

Definitions

• **Urban population** refers to the population of the urban agglomeration, a contiguous inhabited territory without regard to administrative boundaries. • **Secure tenure** refers to the percentage of the population protected from involuntary removal from land or residence—including subtenancy, residence in social housing, and residences owned, purchased, or privately rented—except through due legal process. • **House price to income ratio** is the average house price divided by the average household income. • **Work trips by public transportation** are the percentage of trips to work made by bus or minibus, tram, or train. Buses or minibuses are road vehicles other than cars taking passengers on a fare-paying basis. Other means of transport commonly used in developing countries, such as taxi, ferry, rickshaw, or animal, are not included. • **Travel time to work** is the average time in minutes, for all modes, for a one-way trip to work. Train and bus times include average walking and waiting times, and car times include parking and walking to the workplace. • **Households with access to services** are the percentage of households in formal settlements with access to potable water and connections to sewerage, electricity, and telephone service. Households with access to potable water are those having access to safe or potable drinking water within 200 meters of the dwelling. Potable water is water that is free from contamination and safe to drink without further treatment. • **Wastewater treated** is the percentage of all wastewater undergoing some form of treatment.

3.11a

The use of public transportation for work trips varied widely across cities in 1998

%

Country	City	Share of total work trips	Country	City	Share of total work trips
Lao PDR	Vientiane	2	Kyrgyz Republic	Bishkek	95
Spain	Madrid	16	Russian Federation	Moscow	85
Canada	Hull	16	Armenia	Yerevan	84
Libya	Tripoli	18	Peru	Lima	82
Slovenia	Ljubljana	20	Gabon	Libreville	80
Kuwait	Kuwait City	21	Liberia	Monrovia	80
Jordan	Amman	21	Mongolia	Ulaanbaatar	80
Mexico	Ciudad Juarez	24	Moldova	Chisinau	80
Guinea	Conakry	26	Bulgaria	Sofia	79
Malawi	Lilongwe	27	Yemen, Rep.	Aden	78

Source: Table 3.11.

Data sources

The data are from the Global Urban Indicators database of the UNCHS.

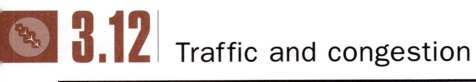

Traffic and congestion

	Motor vehicles				Passenger cars		Two-wheelers		Road traffic		Fuel prices	
	per 1,000 people		per kilometer of road		per 1,000 people		per 1,000 people		million vehicle kilometers		Super $ per liter	Diesel $ per liter
	1990	2000	1990	2000	1990	2000	1990	2000	1990	2000	2002	2002
Afghanistan	..	..	..	..	..	..	..	..	..	..	0.34	0.27
Albania	11	47	3	10	2	37	3	1	..	..	0.80	0.51
Algeria	..	..	..	..	..	..	..	..	..	..	0.22	0.10
Angola	18	..	..	..	14	..	..	..	..	..	0.19	0.13
Argentina	181	181	27	30	134	140	1	..	43,119	27,458	0.30	0.15
Armenia	5	..	2	..	1	..	..	..	..	..	0.42	0.29
Australia	530	..	11	13	450	510	18	18	138,501	..	0.50	0.48
Austria	421	536	30	22	387	495	71	77	..	..	0.84	0.73
Azerbaijan	52	49	7	16	36	41	5	1	..	..	0.37	0.16
Bangladesh	1	1	0	1	0	0	1	1	..	..	0.52	0.29
Belarus	61	135	13	20	59	145	..	52	10,026	4,964	0.50	0.36
Belgium	423	497	30	35	385	448	14	25	..	158,759	1.04	0.80
Benin	3	..	2	..	2	..	34	..	..	..	0.54	0.41
Bolivia	41	..	6	8	25	22	9	3	1,139	..	0.69	0.42
Bosnia and Herzegovina	114	..	24	..	101	..	..	..	..	..	0.74	0.74
Botswana	18	68	3	11	10	29	..	1	..	..	0.41	0.38
Brazil	88	..	8	17	..	137	..	28	..	..	0.55	0.31
Bulgaria	163	266	39	60	146	234	55	64	..	..	0.68	0.59
Burkina Faso	4	..	3	..	2	..	9	..	..	..	0.58	0.54
Burundi	..	..	..	..	..	..	..	..	..	..	0.58	0.54
Cambodia	1	6	0	31	0	26	9	134	314	7,210	0.63	0.44
Cameroon	10	..	3	..	6	..	..	..	..	..	0.68	0.57
Canada	605	581	20	19	468	459	12	11	..	..	0.51	0.43
Central African Republic	1	0	0	0	1	0	0	..	1,494	..	0.81	0.65
Chad	2	..	0	..	1	..	0	..	..	..	0.79	0.77
Chile	81	135	13	25	52	87	2	2	..	..	0.58	0.39
China	5	..	4	11	1	7	3	26	..	..	0.42	0.37
Hong Kong, China	66	79	253	287	42	59	4	5	8,192	10,781	1.47	0.77
Colombia	..	51	..	19	..	43	8	12	50,945	41,587	0.44	0.24
Congo, Dem. Rep.	..	..	..	..	..	..	..	..	..	..	0.70	0.69
Congo, Rep.	18	..	3	..	12	..	..	..	..	..	0.69	0.48
Costa Rica	87	133	7	14	55	88	14	22	..	507,796	0.64	0.44
Côte d'Ivoire	24	..	6	..	15	..	..	..	..	..	0.85	0.60
Croatia	..	..	..	44	..	257	..	15	..	13,764	0.89	0.74
Cuba	37	32	16	6	18	16	19	16	..	..	0.50	0.27
Czech Republic	246	362	46	67	228	335	113	73	..	..	0.81	0.71
Denmark	368	411	27	31	320	357	9	13	36,304	45,165	1.09	0.94
Dominican Republic	75	..	48	..	21	..	..	..	..	..	0.49	0.27
Ecuador	35	46	8	14	31	43	2	2	10,306	14,449	1.30	0.90
Egypt, Arab Rep.	29	..	33	..	21	..	6	..	..	..	0.19	0.08
El Salvador	33	61	14	36	17	30	0	5	2,002	3,646	0.46	0.33
Eritrea	1	..	1	..	1	..	..	..	..	..	0.36	0.25
Estonia	211	397	22	11	154	339	66	5	..	6,412	0.58	0.56
Ethiopia	1	1	2	3	1	1	0	0	..	1,642	0.52	0.32
Finland	441	462	29	31	386	403	12	35	39,750	46,010	1.12	0.80
France	494	564	32	38	405	476	55	0	422,000	519,400	1.05	0.80
Gabon	32	..	4	..	19	..	..	..	..	..	0.53	0.37
Gambia, The	13	..	5	..	6	..	..	..	..	..	0.46	0.40
Georgia	107	58	27	15	89	46	5	1	4,620	..	0.48	0.41
Germany	405	..	53	..	386	516	18	56	446,000	589,500	1.03	0.82
Ghana	..	..	..	..	..	..	..	..	..	..	0.28	0.23
Greece	248	348	22	31	171	254	120	203	..	77,954	0.78	0.68
Guatemala	..	57	..	45	..	52	..	12	..	3,455	1.23	0.92
Guinea	4	..	1	..	2	..	..	..	..	..	0.66	0.56
Guinea-Bissau	7	..	2	..	4	..	..	..	..	..	..	..
Haiti	..	..	..	..	..	..	..	..	..	..	0.54	0.30

Traffic and congestion

	Motor vehicles				Passenger cars		Two-wheelers		Road traffic		Fuel prices	
	per 1,000 people		per kilometer of road		per 1,000 people		per 1,000 people		million vehicle kilometers		Super $ per liter	Diesel $ per liter
	1990	2000	1990	2000	1990	2000	1990	2000	1990	2000	2002	2002
Honduras	22	62	9	28	..	52	..	15	3,288	..	0.63	0.46
Hungary	212	272	21	15	188	238	16	14	22,898	..	0.94	0.85
India	4	8	2	3	2	5	15	29	..	..	0.66	0.41
Indonesia	16	25	10	14	7	14	34	63	..	..	0.27	0.19
Iran, Islamic Rep.	34	..	14	..	25	..	36	..	..	..	0.07	0.02
Iraq	14	..	6	..	1	..	..	..	..	..	0.02	0.01
Ireland	270	..	10	14	227	296	6	11	24,205	..	0.90	0.80
Israel	210	270	74	107	174	228	8	12	18,212	35,863	0.90	0.62
Italy	529	591	99	73	476	545	45	125	344,726	..	1.05	0.86
Jamaica	..	..	..	..	..	..	..	..	..	..	0.52	0.44
Japan	469	560	52	62	283	492	146	110	628,581	765,056	0.91	0.66
Jordan	60	..	26	..	..	..	0	..	1,098	..	0.52	0.17
Kazakhstan	76	84	8	12	50	65	..	10	18,248	3,215	0.35	0.29
Kenya	12	..	5	..	10	..	1	..	5,170	..	0.70	0.56
Korea, Dem. Rep.	..	..	..	..	..	..	..	..	..	..	0.55	0.41
Korea, Rep.	79	239	60	128	48	168	32	59	30,464	67,266	0.92	0.51
Kuwait	..	..	..	..	..	..	..	..	..	..	0.20	0.18
Kyrgyz Republic	44	39	10	10	44	39	..	4	5,220	..	0.39	0.25
Lao PDR	9	..	3	..	6	..	18	..	..	..	0.36	0.30
Latvia	135	262	6	9	106	235	76	9	3,932	..	0.70	0.65
Lebanon	321	336	183	..	300	313	13	15	..	..	0.65	0.25
Lesotho	11	..	4	..	3	..	..	..	..	..	0.50	0.47
Liberia	14	..	4	..	7	..	..	..	..	..	..	..
Libya	..	..	..	..	..	..	..	..	..	..	0.10	0.08
Lithuania	160	338	12	17	133	334	52	6	..	..	0.69	0.59
Macedonia, FYR	132	..	30	..	121	..	1	..	3,102	..	0.85	0.63
Madagascar	6	..	2	..	4	..	..	..	41,500	..	1.08	0.65
Malawi	4	..	4	..	2	..	..	..	..	..	0.66	0.62
Malaysia	124	200	26	69	101	181	167	230	..	..	0.35	0.19
Mali	3	..	2	..	2	..	..	..	..	..	0.69	0.55
Mauritania	10	..	3	..	7	..	..	..	..	..	0.63	0.39
Mauritius	59	98	35	49	44	73	54	96	..	..	..	..
Mexico	119	151	41	44	82	107	3	..	55,095	..	0.62	0.47
Moldova	53	70	17	24	48	54	45	..	..	538	0.45	0.31
Mongolia	21	30	1	2	6	18	22	10	340	40	0.38	0.37
Morocco	37	52	15	21	28	41	1	1	..	..	0.87	0.55
Mozambique	4	..	2	0	3	..	..	..	1,889	..	0.46	0.43
Myanmar	..	..	..	..	..	..	..	..	..	..	0.33	0.12
Namibia	71	..	1	2	39	..	1	..	1,896	2,706	0.45	0.43
Nepal	..	..	..	..	..	..	..	..	..	..	0.66	0.34
Netherlands	405	427	58	58	368	383	44	25	90,150	109,955	1.12	0.81
New Zealand	524	540	19	29	436	580	24	21	..	..	0.55	0.33
Nicaragua	19	10	5	8	10	12	3	5	108	523	0.58	0.53
Niger	6	..	4	5	5	..	..	..	178	240	0.77	0.55
Nigeria	30	..	21	14	12	..	5	..	2,927,931	2,701,208	0.20	0.19
Norway	458	505	22	25	380	412	48	56	..	30,148	1.23	1.18
Oman	130	..	9	..	83	..	3	..	..	..	0.31	0.29
Pakistan	6	8	4	4	4	5	8	15	18,933	218,779	0.52	0.35
Panama	75	113	18	27	60	83	2	3	..	..	0.51	0.36
Papua New Guinea	..	..	..	..	..	..	..	..	..	..	0.53	0.34
Paraguay	..	..	..	..	..	..	..	..	..	..	0.56	0.34
Peru	..	43	..	15	..	27	..	..	..	..	0.21	0.14
Philippines	10	31	4	11	7	10	6	14	6,189	9,548	0.35	0.27
Poland	168	286	18	33	138	259	36	21	59,608	138,100	0.83	0.68
Portugal	222	348	34	..	162	321	5	77	28,623	93,020	0.97	0.71
Puerto Rico	..	..	..	..	..	..	..	..	..	..	0.34	0.32

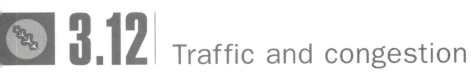

	Motor vehicles				Passenger cars		Two-wheelers		Road traffic		Fuel prices	
	per 1,000 people		per kilometer of road		per 1,000 people		per 1,000 people		million vehicle kilometers		Super $ per liter	Diesel $ per liter
	1990	2000	1990	2000	1990	2000	1990	2000	1990	2000	2002	2002
Romania	72	154	11	17	56	133	13	14	23,907	36,884	0.64	0.57
Russian Federation	87	153	14	48	65	140	..	43	..	60,950	0.35	0.25
Rwanda	2	..	1	2	1	..	..	..	..	..	0.84	0.84
Saudi Arabia	165	..	19	..	98	..	0	..	..	..	0.24	0.10
Senegal	11	..	6	8	8	..	0	..	..	..	0.75	0.53
Sierra Leone	10	..	4	2	7	2	2	0	996	529	0.51	0.50
Singapore	130	132	142	170	89	97	40	34	..	..	0.85	0.38
Slovak Republic	194	260	57	33	163	229	61	8	..	0	0.74	0.70
Slovenia	306	455	42	46	289	426	8	6	5,620	9,245	0.76	0.67
Somalia	2	..	1	0	1	..	..	..	..	..	..	..
South Africa	139	143	26	11	97	94	8	4	..	..	0.43	0.40
Spain	360	467	43	53	309	404	79	90	100,981	201,896	0.83	0.72
Sri Lanka	21	36	4	7	7	12	24	44	3,468	15,630	0.54	0.31
Sudan	9	..	21	28	8	..	..	..	..	..	0.30	0.24
Swaziland	66	70	18	17	35	34	3	3	..	..	0.47	0.44
Sweden	464	478	29	21	426	451	11	31	61,040	69,200	1.06	0.96
Switzerland	491	526	46	54	449	494	114	102	48,660	53,506	0.89	0.93
Syrian Arab Republic	26	30	10	11	10	9	..	..	..	..	0.53	0.18
Tajikistan	3	..	1	..	0	..	..	..	..	..	0.36	0.24
Tanzania	5	..	2	2	1	..	..	..	..	..	0.67	0.61
Thailand	46	..	36	..	14	..	86	..	45,769	..	0.36	0.32
Togo	24	..	11	..	16	..	8	..	..	..	0.56	0.46
Trinidad and Tobago	..	..	..	..	..	..	..	..	..	..	0.40	0.21
Tunisia	48	..	19	40	23	54	..	1	..	1,092,675	0.29	0.19
Turkey	50	85	8	14	34	63	10	15	27,041	49,846	1.02	0.78
Turkmenistan	..	..	..	..	..	..	..	..	..	..	0.02	0.01
Uganda	2	5	..	4	1	2	0	3	..	..	0.83	0.70
Ukraine	63	..	19	..	63	104	..	49	59,500	61,200	0.47	0.34
United Arab Emirates	121	..	52	..	97	..	..	..	..	..	0.29	0.30
United Kingdom	400	424	64	62	341	389	14	3	399,000	462,400	1.18	1.20
United States	758	759	30	34	573	475	17	15	2,527,441	2,653,043	0.40	0.39
Uruguay	138	174	45	63	122	158	74	110	..	..	0.46	0.20
Uzbekistan	..	..	..	..	..	..	..	..	..	..	0.38	0.26
Venezuela, RB	..	..	..	..	..	..	..	..	..	563	0.05	0.05
Vietnam	..	..	..	..	..	..	45	..	..	..	0.34	0.27
West Bank and Gaza	..	..	..	..	..	..	..	..	..	..	0.99	0.52
Yemen, Rep.	34	..	8	..	14	..	..	..	8,681	11,476	0.21	0.10
Yugoslavia, Fed. Rep.	137	190	31	36	133	150	3	3	..	..	0.74	0.66
Zambia	14	..	3	..	8	..	..	..	..	..	0.72	0.60
Zimbabwe	..	..	..	..	..	..	..	..	..	..	..	..
World	**120 w**	**176 w**	**.. w**	**.. w**	**91 w**	**141 w**	**.. w**	**.. w**	**.. w**	**.. w**	**0.56 m**	**0.43 m**
Low income	9	10	..	..	6	9	..	..	..	..	0.54	0.41
Middle income	39	65	..	..	25	49	..	..	..	..	0.54	0.38
Lower middle income	19	32	..	..	11	23	..	..	..	..	0.51	0.37
Upper middle income	127	193	..	..	114	153	..	..	..	..	0.57	0.40
Low & middle income	25	57	..	..	16	45	..	..	..	..	0.54	0.39
East Asia & Pacific	9	16	..	..	4	10	..	..	..	..	0.36	0.31
Europe & Central Asia	98	204	..	..	82	171	..	..	..	..	0.64	0.56
Latin America & Carib.	92	158	..	..	..	119	..	..	..	..	0.54	0.36
Middle East & N. Africa	57	..	..	..	31	..	..	..	..	..	0.30	0.17
South Asia	4	8	..	..	2	5	..	..	..	..	0.54	0.34
Sub-Saharan Africa	24	..	..	..	14	..	..	..	..	..	0.59	0.48
High income	514	586	..	..	396	443	..	..	..	..	0.89	0.68
Europe EMU	453	558	..	..	379	496	..	..	..	..	1.00	0.80

Traffic congestion in urban areas constrains economic productivity, damages people's health, and degrades the quality of their lives. The particulate air pollution emitted by motor vehicles—the dust and soot in exhaust—is proving to be far more damaging to human health than was once believed. (For information on suspended particulates and other air pollutants, see table 3.13.)

In recent years ownership of passenger cars has increased, and the expansion of economic activity has led to the transport by road of more goods and services over greater distances (see table 5.9). These developments have increased demand for roads and vehicles, adding to urban congestion, air pollution, health hazards, traffic accidents, and injuries.

Congestion, the most visible cost of expanding vehicle ownership, is reflected in the indicators in the table. Other relevant indicators—such as average vehicle speed in major cities or the cost of traffic congestion, which takes a heavy toll on economic productivity—are not included here because data are incomplete or difficult to compare.

The data in the table—except for those on fuel prices—are compiled by the International Road Federation (IRF) through questionnaires sent to national organizations. The IRF uses a hierarchy of sources to gather as much information as possible. The primary sources are national road associations. Where such an association lacks data or does not respond, other agencies are contacted, including road directorates, ministries of transport or public works, and central statistical offices. As a result, the compiled data are of uneven quality. The coverage of each indicator may differ across countries because of differences in definitions. Comparability also is limited when time-series data are reported. Moreover, the data do not capture the quality or age of vehicles or the condition or width of roads. Thus comparisons over time and between countries should be made with caution.

The data on fuel prices are compiled by the German Agency for Technical Cooperation (GTZ) from its global network of regional offices and representatives as well as other sources, including the Allgemeiner Deutscher Automobil Club (for Europe) and a project of the Latin American Energy Organization (OLADE, for Latin America). Local prices have been converted to U.S. dollars using the exchange rate on the survey date as listed in the international monetary table of the *Financial Times*. For countries with multiple exchange rates, the market, parallel, or black market rate was used rather than the official exchange rate.

• **Motor vehicles** include cars, buses, and freight vehicles but not two-wheelers. Population figures refer to the midyear population in the year for which data are available. Roads refer to motorways, highways, main or national roads, and secondary or regional roads. A motorway is a road specially designed and built for motor traffic that separates the traffic flowing in opposite directions. • **Passenger cars** refer to road motor vehicles, other than two-wheelers, intended for the carriage of passengers and designed to seat no more than nine people (including the driver). • **Two-wheelers** refer to mopeds and motorcycles. • **Road traffic** is the number of vehicles multiplied by the average distances they travel. • **Fuel prices** refer to the pump prices of the most widely sold grade of gasoline and of diesel fuel. Prices have been converted from the local currency to U.S. dollars (see *About the data*).

3.12a

The 10 countries with the fewest passenger cars per 1,000 people in 2002—and the 10 with the most

Per 1,000 people

Country	Passenger cars	Country	Passenger cars
Central African Republic	0 [a]	New Zealand	580
Bangladesh	1 [b]	Italy	545
Ethiopia	1	Germany	516
Sierra Leone	2	Australia	510
Uganda	2	Austria	495
Pakistan	5	Switzerland	494
India	5	Japan	492
China	7	France	476
Syrian Arab Republic	9	United States	475
Philippines	10	Canada	459
Sri Lanka	12	Sweden	451
World (average)	141		

a. One for every 4,000 people.
b. One for every 2,000 people.

Source: Table 3.12.

3.13 Air pollution

City		City population	Particulate matter	Sulfur dioxide	Nitrogen dioxide
		thousands	micrograms per cubic meter	micrograms per cubic meter	micrograms per cubic meter
		2000	**1999**	**1990–98**[a]	**1990–98**[a]
Argentina	Cordoba City	1,370	52	..	97
Australia	Melbourne	3,293	15	..	30
	Perth	1,245	15	5	19
	Sydney	3,855	22	28	81
Austria	Vienna	1,904	39	14	42
Belgium	Brussels	983	31	20	48
Brazil	Rio de Janeiro	5,902	40	129	..
	São Paulo	9,984	46	43	83
Bulgaria	Sofia	1,177	83	39	122
Canada	Montreal	3,519	22	10	42
	Toronto	4,535	26	17	43
	Vancouver	1,880	15	14	37
Chile	Santiago	4,522	73	29	81
China	Anshan	3,132	99	115	88
	Beijing	9,302	106	90	122
	Changchun	3,766	88	21	64
	Chengdu	4,401	103	77	74
	Chongqing	3,945	147	340	70
	Dalian	4,389	60	61	100
	Guangzhu	495	74	57	136
	Guiyang	2,103	84	424	53
	Harbin	4,545	91	23	30
	Jinan	3,037	112	132	45
	Kunming	2,037	84	19	33
	Lanzhou	2,044	109	102	104
	Liupanshui	2,330	70	102	..
	Nanchang	1,594	94	69	29
	Pinxiang	1,754	80	75	..
	Quingdao	2,316	..	190	64
	Shanghai	10,367	87	53	73
	Shenyang	5,881	120	99	73
	Taiyuan	2,811	105	211	55
	Tianjin	7,333	149	82	50
	Urumqi	1,467	61	60	70
	Wuhan	4,842	94	40	43
	Zhengzhou	2,214	116	63	95
	Zibo	3,139	88	198	43
Colombia	Bogota	5,442	33	..	..
Croatia	Zagreb	908	39	31	..
Cuba	Havana	2,270	28	1	5
Czech Republic	Prague	1,211	27	14	33
Denmark	Copenhagen	1,371	24	7	54
Ecuador	Guayaquil	2,120	26	15	..
	Quito	1,598	34	22	..
Egypt, Arab Rep.	Cairo	7,941	178	69	..
Finland	Helsinki	1,095	22	4	35
France	Paris	9,851	15	14	57
Germany	Berlin	3,555	25	18	26
	Frankfurt	668	22	11	45
	Munich	1,275	22	8	53
Ghana	Accra	1,938	31	..	..
Greece	Athens	3,229	50	34	64
Hungary	Budapest	1,958	26	39	51
Iceland	Reykjavik	164	21	5	42

About the data

In many towns and cities exposure to air pollution is the main environmental threat to human health. Long-term exposure to high levels of soot and small particles in the air contributes to a wide range of health effects, including respiratory diseases, lung cancer, and heart disease. Particulate pollution, on its own or in combination with sulfur dioxide, leads to an enormous burden of ill health.

Emissions of sulfur dioxide and nitrogen oxides lead to the deposition of acid rain and other acidic compounds over long distances. Acid deposition changes the chemical balance of soils and can lead to the leaching of trace minerals and nutrients critical to trees and plants.

Where coal is the primary fuel for power plants, steel mills, industrial boilers, and domestic heating, the result is usually high levels of urban air pollution—especially particulates and sometimes sulfur dioxide—and, if the sulfur content of the coal is high, widespread acid deposition. Where coal is not an important primary fuel or is used by plants with effective dust control, the worst emissions of air pollutants stem from the combustion of petroleum products.

The data on sulfur dioxide and nitrogen dioxide concentrations are based on reports from urban monitoring sites. Annual means (measured in micrograms per cubic meter) are average concentrations observed at these sites. Coverage is not comprehensive because not all cities have monitoring systems.

The data on particulate matter concentrations are new estimates, for selected cities, of average annual concentrations in residential areas away from air pollution "hotspots," such as industrial districts and transport corridors. The data have been extracted from a complete set of estimates developed by the World Bank's Development Research Group and Environment Department in a study of annual ambient concentrations of particulate matter in world cities with populations exceeding 100,000 (Pandey and others 2003).

Pollutant concentrations are sensitive to local conditions, and even in the same city different monitoring sites may register different concentrations. Thus these data should be considered only a general indication of air quality in each city, and cross-country comparisons should be made with caution. The current World Health Organization (WHO) air quality guidelines for annual mean concentrations are 50 micrograms per cubic meter for sulfur dioxide and 40 for nitrogen dioxide. The WHO has set no guidelines for particulate matter concentrations below which there are no appreciable health effects.

City		City population	Particulate matter	Sulfur dioxide	Nitrogen dioxide
		thousands **2000**	micrograms per cubic meter **1999**	micrograms per cubic meter **1998** [a]	micrograms per cubic meter **1998** [a]
India	Ahmedabad	4,154	104	30	21
	Bangalore	5,180	56	..	..
	Calcutta	13,822	153	49	34
	Chennai	6,002	..	15	17
	Delhi	10,558	187	24	41
	Hyderabad	5,448	51	12	17
	Kanpur	2,546	136	15	14
	Lucknow	2,093	136	26	25
	Mumbai	15,797	79	33	39
	Nagpur	2,087	69	6	13
	Pune	3,128	58		
Indonesia	Jakarta	10,845	103	..	..
Iran, Islamic Rep.	Tehran	7,689	71	209	..
Ireland	Dublin	991	23	20	..
Italy	Milan	1,381	36	31	248
	Rome	2,713	35	..	..
	Torino	969	53	..	..
Japan	Osaka	2,626	39	19	63
	Tokyo	12,483	43	18	68
	Yokohama	3,366	32	100	13
Kenya	Nairobi	2,383	49	..	..
Korea, Rep	Pusan	4,075	43	60	51
	Seoul	11,548	45	44	60
	Taegu	2,417	49	81	62
Malaysia	Kuala Lumpur	1,530	24	24	..
Mexico	Mexico City	18,017	69	74	130
Netherlands	Amsterdam	1,131	37	10	58
New Zealand	Auckland	989	15	3	20
Norway	Oslo	805	23	8	43
Philippines	Manila	10,432	60	33	..
Poland	Lodz	873	45	21	43
	Warsaw	1,716	49	16	32
Portugal	Lisbon	3,318	30	8	52
Romania	Bucharest	2,070	25	10	71
Russian Federation	Moscow	8,811	27	109	..
	Omsk	1,206	28	20	34
Singapore	Singapore	3,163	41	20	30
Slovak Republic	Bratislava	456	22	21	27
South Africa	Cape Town	2,942	15	21	72
	Durban	1,364	29	31	..
	Johannesburg	2,344	30	19	31
Spain	Barcelona	1,645	43	11	43
	Madrid	3,068	37	24	66
Sweden	Stockholm	916	15	3	20
Switzerland	Zurich	980	24	11	39
Thailand	Bangkok	7,296	82	11	23
Turkey	Ankara	3,702	53	55	46
	Istanbul	9,286	62	120	..
Ukraine	Kiev	2,622	45	14	51
United Kingdom	Birmingham	2,344	17	9	45
	London	7,812	23	25	77
	Manchester	2,325	19	26	49
United States	Chicago	9,024	27	14	57
	Los Angeles	16,195	38	9	74
	New York	20,951	23	26	79
Venezuela, RB	Caracas	3,488	18	33	57

a. Data are for the most recent year available.

Definitions

• **City population** is the number of residents of the city or metropolitan area as defined by national authorities and reported to the United Nations.
• **Particulate matter** refers to fine suspended particulates less than 10 microns in diameter that are capable of penetrating deep into the respiratory tract and causing significant health damage. The state of a country's technology and pollution controls is an important determinant of particulate matter concentrations. • **Sulfur dioxide** is an air pollutant produced when fossil fuels containing sulfur are burned. It contributes to acid rain and can damage human health, particularly that of the young and the elderly.
• **Nitrogen dioxide** is a poisonous, pungent gas formed when nitric oxide combines with hydrocarbons and sunlight, producing a photochemical reaction. These conditions occur in both natural and anthropogenic activities. Nitrogen dioxide is emitted by bacteria, motor vehicles, industrial activities, nitrogenous fertilizers, combustion of fuels and biomass, and aerobic decomposition of organic matter in soils and oceans.

Data sources

City population data are from United Nations Population Division. The data on sulfur dioxide and nitrogen dioxide concentrations are from the WHO's Healthy Cities Air Management Information System and the World Resources Institute, which relies on various national sources as well as, among others, the United Nations Environment Programme (UNEP) and WHO's *Urban Air Pollution in Megacities of the World* (1992), the Organisation for Economic Co-operation and Development's (OECD) *OECD Environmental Data: Compendium 1999,* the U.S. Environmental Protection Agency's *National Air Quality and Emissions Trends Report 1995,* AIRS Executive International database, and the United Nations Centre for Human Settlements' (UNCHS) Urban Indicators database. The data on particulate matter concentrations are from a recent World Bank study by Kiran D. Pandey, Katharine Bolt, Uwe Deichman, Kirk Hamilton, Bart Ostro, and David Wheeler, "The Human Cost of Air Pollution: New Estimates for Developing Countries" (2003).

	Environmental strategy or action plan	Country environmental profile	Biodiversity assessment, strategy, or action plan	Participation in treaties [a]				
				Climate change	Ozone layer	CFC control	Law of the Sea [b]	Biological diversity
Afghanistan	..	..	..	2002	..	..	..	2002
Albania	1993	..	..	1995	1999	1999	..	1994
Algeria	2001	..	..	1994	1992	1992	1996	1995
Angola	..	..	..	2000	2000	2000	1994	1998
Argentina	1992	..	..	1994	1990	1990	1996	1995
Armenia	..	..	..	1994	1999	1999	2002	1993
Australia	1992	..	1994	1994	1987	1989	1995	1993
Austria	..	..	..	1994	1987	1989	1995	1994
Azerbaijan	1998	..	..	1995	1996	1996	..	2000 c
Bangladesh	1991	1989	1990	1994	1990	1990	2001	1994
Belarus	..	..	..	2000	1986	1988	..	1993
Belgium	..	..	..	1996	1988	1988	1998	1997
Benin	1993	..	..	1994	1993	1993	1997	1994
Bolivia	1994	1986	1988	1995	1994	1994	1995	1995
Bosnia and Herzegovina	..	..	..	2000	1992	1992	1994	2002
Botswana	1990	1986	1991	1994	1991	1991	1994	1996
Brazil	..	..	1988	1994	1990	1990	1994	1994
Bulgaria	..	..	1994	1995	1990	1990	1996	1996
Burkina Faso	1993	1994	..	1994	1989	1989	..	1993
Burundi	1994	1981	1989	1997	1997	1997	..	1997
Cambodia	1999	..	..	1996	2001	2001	..	1995
Cameroon	..	1989	1989	1995	1989	1989	1994	1995
Canada	1990	..	1994	1994	1986	1988	..	1993
Central African Republic	..	..	..	1995	1993	1993	..	1995
Chad	1990	1982	..	1994	1989	1994	..	1994
Chile	..	1987	1993	1995	1990	1990	1997	1994
China	1994	..	1994	1994	1989	1991	1996	1993
Hong Kong, China	..	..	..	..	..	..	..	..
Colombia	1998	1990	1988	1995	1990	1993	..	1995
Congo, Dem. Rep.	..	1986	1990	1995	1994	1994	1994	1995
Congo, Rep.	..	..	1990	1997	1994	1994	..	1996
Costa Rica	1990	1987	1992	1994	1991	1991	1994	1994
Côte d'Ivoire	1994	..	1991	1995	1993	1993	1994	1995
Croatia	2001	1998	2000	1996	1991	1991	1994	1997
Cuba	..	..	..	1994	1992	1992	1994	1994
Czech Republic	1994	..	..	1994	1993	1993	1996	1994
Denmark	1994	..	..	1994	1988	1998	..	1994
Dominican Republic	..	1984	1995	1999	1993	1993	..	1996
Ecuador	1993	1987	1995	1994	1990	1990	..	1993
Egypt, Arab Rep.	1992	1992	1988	1995	1988	1988	1994	1994
El Salvador	1994	1985	1988	1996	1992	1992	..	1994
Eritrea	1995	..	..	1995	..	..	..	1996
Estonia	1998	..	..	1994	1996	1996	..	1994
Ethiopia	1994	..	1991	1994	1994	1994	..	1994
Finland	1995	..	..	1994	1986	1988	1996	1994
France	1990	..	..	1994	1987	1988	1996	1994
Gabon	..	..	1990	1998	1994	1994	..	2000
Gambia, The	1992	1981	1989	1994	1990	1990	1998	1994
Georgia	1998	..	..	1994	1996	1996	1996	1994
Germany	..	..	..	1994	1988	1988	1994	1994
Ghana	1992	1985	1988	1995	1989	1989	1994	1994
Greece	..	..	..	1994	1988	1988	1995	1994
Guatemala	1994	1984	1988	1996	1987	1989	1997	1995
Guinea	1994	1983	1988	1994	1992	1992	1994	1993
Guinea-Bissau	1993	..	1991	1996	2002	2002	1994	1996
Haiti	1999	1985	..	1996	2000	2000	1996	1996

3.14a

Status of national environmental action plans

Completed

Albania	Ghana	Niger
Algeria	Grenada	Nigeria
Armenia	Guinea	Pakistan
Azerbaijan	Guinea-Bissau	Papua New Guinea
Bangladesh	Guyana	Poland
Belarus	Haiti	Romania
Benin	Honduras	Russian Federation
Bhutan	India	Rwanda
Bolivia	Indonesia	São Tomé and Principe
Botswana	Iran, Islamic Rep.	Senegal
Bulgaria	Kazakhstan	Seychelles
Burkina Faso	Kenya	Sierra Leone
Burundi	Kiribati	Slovak Republic
Cambodia	Kyrgyz Republic	Slovenia
Cameroon	Lao PDR	Solomon Islands
Cape Verde	Latvia	South Africa
China	Lebanon	Sri Lanka
Colombia	Lesotho	St. Kitts and Nevis
Comoros	Lithuania	Swaziland
Congo, Dem. Rep.	Macedonia, FYR	Syrian Arab Rep.
Congo, Rep.	Madagascar	Tanzania
Costa Rica	Malawi	Togo
Côte d'Ivoire	Maldives	Tonga
Croatia	Mali	Tunisia
Czech Republic	Mauritania	Turkey
Djibouti	Mauritius	Uganda
Egypt, Arab Rep.	Mexico	Ukraine
El Salvador	Moldova	Uruguay
Equatorial Guinea	Mongolia	Uzbekistan
Eritrea	Montserrat	Vanuatu
Estonia	Morocco	West Bank and Gaza
Ethiopia	Mozambique	Vietnam
Gabon	Namibia	Yemen, Rep.
Gambia, The	Nepal	Zambia
Georgia	Nicaragua	

Under preparation

Argentina	Ecuador	Tajikistan
Belize	Korea, Rep.	Turkmenistan
Central African Republic	Malaysia	Zimbabwe
Dominican Republic	Paraguay	

Note: Status is as of February 2003.
Source: World Bank Environmentally and Socially Sustainable Development Network Advisory Service, World Resources Institute, and International Institute for Environment and Development.

	Environmental strategies or action plans	Country environmental profile	Biodiversity assessments, strategies or action plans	Participation in treaties [a]				
				Climate change	Ozone layer	CFC control	Law of the Sea [b]	Biological diversity
Honduras	1993	1989	..	1996	1993	1993	1994	1995
Hungary	1995	..	..	1994	1988	1989	2002	1994
India	1993	1989	1994	1994	1991	1992	1995	1994
Indonesia	1993	1994	1993	1994	1992	1992	1994	1994
Iran, Islamic Rep.	..	..	..	1996	1990	1990	..	1996
Iraq	..	..	..	..	..	..	1994	..
Ireland	..	..	..	1994	1988	1988	..	1996
Israel	..	..	..	1996	1992	1992	..	1995
Italy	..	..	..	1994	1988	1988	1995	1994
Jamaica	1994	1987	..	1995	1993	1993	1994	1995
Japan	..	..	..	1994	1988	1988	1996	1993
Jordan	1991	1979	..	1994	1989	1989	1995	1994
Kazakhstan	..	..	..	1995	1998	1998	..	1994
Kenya	1994	1989	1992	1994	1988	1988	1994	1994
Korea, Dem. Rep.	..	..	..	1995	1995	1995	..	1995
Korea, Rep.	..	..	..	1994	1992	1992	1996	1995
Kuwait	..	..	..	1995	1992	1992	1994	2002
Kyrgyz Republic	1995	..	..	2000	2000	2000	..	1996
Lao PDR	1995	..	..	1995	1998	1998	1998	1996
Latvia	..	..	..	1995	1995	1995	..	1996
Lebanon	..	..	..	1995	1993	1993	1995	1995
Lesotho	1989	1982	..	1995	1994	1994	..	1995
Liberia	..	..	..	2002	1996	1996	..	2000
Libya	..	..	..	1999	1990	1990	..	2001
Lithuania	..	..	..	1995	1995	1995	..	1996
Macedonia, FYR	..	..	..	1998	1994	1994	1994	1997 [c]
Madagascar	1988	..	1991	1996	1996	1996	2001	1996
Malawi	1994	1982	..	1994	1991	1991	..	1994
Malaysia	1991	1979	1988	1994	1989	1989	1997	1994
Mali	..	1991	1989	1995	1994	1994	1994	1995
Mauritania	1988	1984	..	1994	1994	1994	1996	1996
Mauritius	1990	..	..	1994	1992	1992	1994	1993
Mexico	..	..	1988	1994	1987	1988	1994	1993
Moldova	2002	..	..	1995	1996	1996	..	1996
Mongolia	1995	..	..	1994	1996	1996	1997	1993
Morocco	..	1980	1988	1996	1995	1995	..	1995
Mozambique	1994	..	..	1995	1994	1994	1997	1995
Myanmar	..	1982	1989	1995	1993	1993	1996	1995
Namibia	1992	..	..	1995	1993	1993	1994	1997
Nepal	1993	1983	..	1994	1994	1994	1998	1994
Netherlands	1994	..	..	1994	1988	1988	1996	1994
New Zealand	1994	..	..	1994	1987	1988	1996	1993
Nicaragua	1994	1981	..	1996	1993	1993	2000	1996
Niger	..	1985	1991	1995	1992	1992	..	1995
Nigeria	1990	..	1992	1994	1988	1988	1994	1994
Norway	..	..	1994	1994	1986	1988	1996	1993
Oman	..	1981	..	1995	1999	1999	1994	1995
Pakistan	1994	1994	1991	1994	1992	1992	1997	1994
Panama	1990	1980	..	1995	1989	1989	1996	1995
Papua New Guinea	1992	1994	1993	1994	1992	1992	1997	1993
Paraguay	..	1985	..	1994	1992	1992	1994	1994
Peru	..	1988	1988	1994	1989	1993	..	1993
Philippines	1989	1992	1989	1994	1991	1991	1994	1994
Poland	1993	..	1991	1994	1990	1990	1998	1996
Portugal	1995	..	..	1994	1988	1988	1997	1994
Puerto Rico	..	..	..	..	..	..	..	..

3.14b

States that have signed the Kyoto Protocol of the Convention on Climate Change

Completed

Antigua and Barbuda [a]	Greece [a]	Niue [a]
Argentina [a]	Grenada [a]	Norway [a]
Australia	Guatemala [a]	Palau [a]
Austria [a]	Guinea [a]	Panama [a]
Azerbaijan [a]	Honduras [a]	Papua New Guinea [a]
Bahamas, The [a]	Hungary [a]	Paraguay [a]
Bangladesh [a]	Iceland [a]	Peru [a]
Barbados [a]	India [a]	Philippines
Belgium [a]	Indonesia	Poland [a]
Benin [a]	Ireland [a]	Portugal
Bhutan [a]	Israel	Romania [a]
Bolivia [a]	Italy [a]	Russian Federation
Brazil [a]	Jamaica [a]	Samoa [a]
Bulgaria [a]	Japan	Senegal [a]
Burundi [a]	Jordan [a]	Seychelles [a]
Cambodia [a]	Kazakhstan	Slovak Republic [a]
Canada [a]	Kiribati [a]	Slovenia [a]
Chile [a]	Korea, Rep. [a]	Solomon Islands
China	Latvia [a]	South Africa [a]
Colombia [a]	Lesotho [a]	Spain [a]
Cook Islands [a]	Liechtenstein	Sri Lanka [a]
Costa Rica [a]	Lithuania [a]	St. Lucia
Croatia	Luxembourg [a]	St. Vincent and the Grenadines
Cuba [a]	Malawi [a]	Sweden [a]
Cyprus [a]	Malaysia [a]	Switzerland
Czech Republic	Maldives [a]	Thailand [a]
Denmark [a]	Mali [a]	Trinidad and Tobago [a]
Djibouti [a]	Malta [a]	Tunisia [a]
Dominican Republic [a]	Marshall Islands	Turkmenistan [a]
Ecuador [a]	Mauritius [a]	Tuvalu [a]
Egypt, Arab Rep. [a]	Mexico [a]	Uganda [a]
El Salvador [a]	Micronesia [a]	Ukraine
Equatorial Guinea [a]	Monaco	United Kingdom [a]
Estonia [a]	Mongolia [a]	United States
Fiji [a]	Morocco [a]	Uruguay [a]
Finland [a]	Nauru [a]	Uzbekistan [a]
France	Netherlands [a]	Vanuatu [a]
Gambia, The [a]	New Zealand [a]	Vietnam [a]
Georgia [a]	Nicaragua [a]	Zambia
Germany [a]	Niger	

Note: Status is as of January 2003.
a. Ratification or accession signed.
Source: Secretariat of the United Nations Framework Convention on Climate Change.

3.14 Government commitment

	Environ-mental strategies or action plans	Country environ-mental profile	Biodiversity assessments, strategies or action plans	Participation in treaties [a]				
				Climate change	Ozone layer	CFC control	Law of the Sea [b]	Biological diversity
Romania	1995	..	..	1994	1993	1993	1997	1994
Russian Federation	1999	..	1994	1995	1986	1988	1997	1995
Rwanda	1991	1987	..	1998	2001	2001	..	1996
Saudi Arabia	..	..	..	1995	1993	1993	..	2001
Senegal	1984	1990	1991	1995	1993	1993	1994	1995
Sierra Leone	1994	..	..	1995	2001	2001	1995	1995
Singapore	1993	1988	1995	1997	1989	1989	1994	1996
Slovak Republic	..	..	..	1994	1993	1993	1996	1994
Slovenia	1994	..	..	1996	1992	1992	1994	1996
Somalia	..	..	..	..	2001	2001	1994	..
South Africa	1993	..	..	1997	1990	1990	1997	2000
Spain	..	..	..	1994	1988	1989	1997	1994
Sri Lanka	1994	1983	1991	1994	1989	1989	1994	1994
Sudan	..	1989	..	1994	1993	1993	1994	1996
Swaziland	..	..	..	1997	1992	1992	..	1995
Sweden	..	..	..	1994	1986	1988	1996	1994
Switzerland	..	..	..	1994	1987	1988	..	1995
Syrian Arab Republic	1999	1981	..	1996	1989	1989	..	1996
Tajikistan	..	..	..	1998	1996	1998	..	1997
Tanzania	1994	1989	1988	1996	1993	1993	1994	1996
Thailand	..	1992	..	1995	1989	1989	..	..
Togo	1991	..	..	1995	1991	1991	1994	1996
Trinidad and Tobago	..	..	..	1994	1989	1989	1994	1996
Tunisia	1994	1980	1988	1994	1989	1989	1994	1993
Turkey	1998	1982	..	..	1991	1991	..	1997
Turkmenistan	..	..	..	1995	1993	1993	..	1996
Uganda	1994	1982	1988	1994	1988	1988	1994	1993
Ukraine	1999	..	..	1997	1986	1988	1999	1995
United Arab Emirates	..	..	..	1996	1989	1989	..	2000
United Kingdom	1995	..	1994	1994	1987	1988	1997	1994
United States	1995	..	1995	1994	1986	1988	..	..
Uruguay	..	..	..	1994	1989	1991	1994	1994
Uzbekistan	..	..	..	1994	1993	1993	..	1995
Venezuela	..	..	..	1995	1988	1989	..	1994
Vietnam	..	..	1993	1995	1994	1994	1994	1995
West Bank and Gaza	..	..	..	..	..	..	..	..
Yemen, Rep.	1996	1990	1992	1996	1996	1996	1994	1996
Yugoslavia, Fed. Rep.	..	..	..	2001	1992	1992	2001	..
Zambia	1994	1988	..	1994	1990	1990	1994	1993
Zimbabwe	1987	1982	..	1994	1992	1992	1994	1995

a. The year shown for a country refers to the year in which a treaty entered into force in that country. b. Convention became effective November 16, 1994. c. Ratification of the treaty.

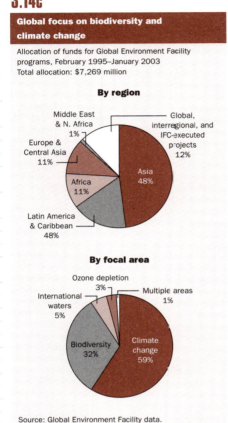

3.14c

Global focus on biodiversity and climate change

Allocation of funds for Global Environment Facility programs, February 1995–January 2003
Total allocation: $7,269 million

By region

Middle East & N. Africa 1%
Europe & Central Asia 11%
Africa 11%
Latin America & Caribbean 48%
Asia 48%
Global, interregional, and IFC-executed projects 12%

By focal area

Ozone depletion 3%
International waters 5%
Multiple areas 1%
Biodiversity 32%
Climate change 59%

Source: Global Environment Facility data.

National environmental strategies and participation in international treaties on environmental issues provide some evidence of government commitment to sound environmental management. But the signing of these treaties does not always imply ratification, nor does it guarantee that governments will comply with treaty obligations.

In many countries efforts to halt environmental degradation have failed, primarily because governments have neglected to make this issue a priority, a reflection of competing claims on scarce resources. To address this problem, many countries are preparing national environmental strategies—some focusing narrowly on environmental issues, and others integrating environmental, economic, and social concerns. Among such initiatives are conservation strategies and environmental action plans. Some countries have also prepared country environmental profiles and biodiversity strategies and profiles.

National conservation strategies—promoted by the World Conservation Union (IUCN)—provide a comprehensive, cross-sectoral analysis of conservation and resource management issues to help integrate environmental concerns with the development process. Such strategies discuss current and future needs, institutional capabilities, prevailing technical conditions, and the status of natural resources in a country.

National environmental action plans, supported by the World Bank and other development agencies, describe a country's main environmental concerns, identify the principal causes of environmental problems, and formulate policies and actions to deal with them (table 3.14a). These plans are a continuing process in which governments develop comprehensive environmental policies, recommend specific actions, and outline the investment strategies, legislation, and institutional arrangements required to implement them.

Country environmental profiles identify how national economic and other activities can stay within the constraints imposed by the need to conserve natural resources. Some profiles consider issues of equity, justice, and fairness. Biodiversity profiles—prepared by the World Conservation Monitoring Centre and the IUCN—provide basic background on species diversity, protected areas, major ecosystems and habitat types, and legislative and administrative support. In an effort to establish a scientific baseline for measuring progress in biodiversity conservation, the United Nations Environment Programme (UNEP) coordinates global biodiversity assessments.

To address global issues, many governments have also signed international treaties and agreements launched in the wake of the 1972 United Nations Conference on Human Environment in Stockholm and the 1992 United Nations Conference on Environment and Development (the Earth Summit) in Rio de Janeiro:

- The Framework Convention on Climate Change aims to stabilize atmospheric concentrations of greenhouse gases at levels that will prevent human activities from interfering dangerously with the global climate.

- The Vienna Convention for the Protection of the Ozone Layer aims to protect human health and the environment by promoting research on the effects of changes in the ozone layer and on alternative substances (such as substitutes for chlorofluorocarbons) and technologies, monitoring the ozone layer, and taking measures to control the activities that produce adverse effects.

- The Montreal Protocol for CFC Control requires that countries help protect the earth from excessive ultraviolet radiation by cutting chlorofluorocarbon consumption by 20 percent over their 1986 level by 1994 and by 50 percent over their 1986 level by 1999, with allowances for increases in consumption by developing countries.

- The United Nations Convention on the Law of the Sea, which became effective in November 1994, establishes a comprehensive legal regime for seas and oceans, establishes rules for environmental standards and enforcement provisions, and develops international rules and national legislation to prevent and control marine pollution.

- The Convention on Biological Diversity promotes conservation of biodiversity among nations through scientific and technological cooperation, access to financial and genetic resources, and transfer of ecologically sound technologies.

To help developing countries comply with their obligations under these agreements, the Global Environment Facility (GEF) was created to focus on global improvement in biodiversity, climate change, international waters, and ozone layer depletion. The UNEP, United Nations Development Programme (UNDP), and the World Bank manage the GEF according to the policies of its governing body of country representatives. The World Bank is responsible for the GEF Trust Fund and is chair of the GEF.

- **Environmental strategies and action plans** provide a comprehensive, cross-sectoral analysis of conservation and resource management issues to help integrate environmental concerns with the development process. They include national conservation strategies, national environmental action plans, national environmental management strategies, and national sustainable development strategies. The year shown for a country refers to the year in which a strategy or action plan was adopted. • **Country environmental profiles** identify how national economic and other activities can stay within the constraints imposed by the need to conserve natural resources. The year shown for a country refers to the year in which a profile was completed. • **Biodiversity assessments, strategies, and action plans** include biodiversity profiles (see *About the data*). • **Participation in treaties** covers five international treaties (see *About the data*). • **Climate change** refers to the Framework Convention on Climate Change (signed in New York in 1992). • **Ozone layer** refers to the Vienna Convention for the Protection of the Ozone Layer (signed in 1985). • **CFC control** refers to the Montreal Protocol for CFC Control (formally, the Protocol on Substances That Deplete the Ozone Layer, signed in 1987). • **Law of the Sea** refers to the United Nations Convention on the Law of the Sea (signed in Montego Bay, Jamaica, in 1982). • **Biological diversity** refers to the Convention on Biological Diversity (signed at the Earth Summit in Rio de Janeiro in 1992). The year shown for a country refers to the year in which a treaty entered into force in that country.

Data sources

The data are from the Secretariat of the United Nations Framework Convention on Climate Change; the Ozone Secretariat of the UNEP; the World Resources Institute; the UNEP; the U.S. National Aeronautics and Space Administration's Socioeconomic Data and Applications Center, Center for International Earth Science Information Network; and the World Resources Institute, International Institute for Environment and Development, and IUCN's *1996 World Directory of Country Environmental Studies*.

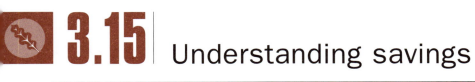
	Gross national savings	Consumption of fixed capital	Net national savings	Education expenditure	Energy depletion	Mineral depletion	Net forest depletion	Carbon dioxide emissions damage	Particulate emissions damage	Adjusted net savings
	% of GNI 2001	% of GNI 2001	% of GNI 2001	% of GNI 2001	% of GNI 2001	% of GNI 2001	% of GNI 2001	% of GNI 2001	% of GNI 2001	% of GNI 2001
Afghanistan	..	..	..	..	..	..	..	..	..	..
Albania	13.9	9.2	4.7	2.8	1.0	0.0	0.0	0.3	0.1	6.1
Algeria	..	11.0	..	4.5	33.6	0.0	0.1	1.3	0.7	..
Angola	35.0	10.5	24.5	4.4	35.0	0.0	0.0	0.7	..	−6.8 [a]
Argentina	12.8	12.0	0.8	3.2	2.6	0.1	0.0	0.3	1.6	−0.6
Armenia	9.2	8.2	1.0	1.8	0.0	0.1	0.0	1.2	2.0	−0.5
Australia	18.9	16.1	2.8	5.4	1.6	1.6	0.0	0.6	0.1	4.3
Austria	21.2	14.5	6.7	5.0	0.1	0.0	0.0	0.2	0.2	11.2
Azerbaijan	21.5	15.0	6.5	3.0	41.7	0.0	0.0	5.3	1.0	−38.5
Bangladesh	20.8	6.1	14.7	1.7	1.6	0.0	0.8	0.4	0.3	13.3
Belarus	20.0	9.2	10.8	5.5	2.5	0.0	0.0	3.7	0.0	10.1
Belgium	24.9	14.3	10.6	3.1	0.0	0.0	0.0	0.3	0.2	13.2
Benin	11.6	8.0	3.6	2.7	0.1	0.0	1.3	0.4	0.3	4.2
Bolivia	9.4	9.3	0.1	5.5	7.3	0.7	0.0	1.0	0.7	−4.1
Bosnia and Herzegovina	..	8.9	..	..	0.1	0.0	0.0	0.8	0.4	..
Botswana	34.7	12.0	22.7	5.6	0.0	0.3	0.0	0.6	..	27.4 [a]
Brazil	17.0	10.9	6.1	4.8	2.3	1.0	0.0	0.4	0.2	7.0
Bulgaria	14.6	10.0	4.6	3.1	0.3	0.4	0.0	2.4	2.1	2.5
Burkina Faso	11.5	7.2	4.3	2.4	0.0	0.0	1.3	0.3	0.5	4.6
Burundi	5.4	6.4	−1.0	3.1	0.0	0.1	11.4	0.2	0.1	−9.7
Cambodia	14.8	7.8	7.0	1.8	0.0	0.0	1.7	0.1	0.1	6.9
Cameroon	17.0	9.0	8.0	2.3	7.3	0.0	0.0	0.4	0.7	1.9
Canada	23.2	13.0	10.2	7.0	5.0	0.1	0.0	0.5	0.2	11.4
Central African Republic	17.1	7.5	9.6	1.6	0.0	0.0	0.0	0.2	0.4	10.6
Chad	4.5	7.2	−2.7	2.0	0.0	0.0	0.0	0.1	..	−0.8 [a]
Chile	20.3	10.0	10.3	3.4	0.3	4.8	0.0	0.6	1.0	7.0
China	40.1	9.2	30.9	2.0	2.8	0.2	0.1	2.2	1.0	26.6
Hong Kong, China	32.0	12.8	19.2	2.8	0.0	0.0	0.0	0.1	0.0	21.9
Colombia	14.8	10.3	4.5	3.1	6.6	0.1	0.0	0.5	0.1	0.3
Congo, Dem. Rep.	..	8.4	..	0.9	2.0	0.1	0.0	0.3	0.0	..
Congo, Rep.	44.4	12.9	31.5	6.0	54.6	0.0	0.0	0.8	..	−17.9 [a]
Costa Rica	15.1	5.8	9.3	5.1	0.0	0.0	0.4	0.3	0.3	13.4
Côte d'Ivoire	8.8	9.1	−0.3	4.5	0.0	0.0	0.6	0.7	0.6	2.3
Croatia	20.4	11.4	9.0	..	1.1	0.0	0.0	0.7	0.3	..
Cuba	..	..	..	6.1	..	..	..	..	..	..
Czech Republic	26.0	11.6	14.4	4.6	0.1	0.0	0.0	1.4	0.1	17.4
Denmark	24.6	15.3	9.3	8.2	0.5	0.0	0.0	0.2	0.1	16.7
Dominican Republic	20.6	5.4	15.2	1.7	0.0	0.1	0.8	0.8	0.2	15.8
Ecuador	23.1	10.6	12.5	3.2	19.0	0.0	0.0	0.9	0.1	−4.3
Egypt, Arab Rep.	15.4	9.6	5.8	4.4	4.5	0.0	0.2	0.8	1.4	3.3
El Salvador	15.0	10.3	4.7	2.2	0.0	0.0	0.6	0.3	0.2	5.8
Eritrea	..	6.9	..	1.4	0.0	0.0	0.0	0.5	0.5	..
Estonia	22.8	14.4	8.4	6.3	0.6	0.0	0.0	2.4	0.2	11.5
Ethiopia	14.0	6.3	7.7	4.0	0.0	0.1	13.0	0.6	0.3	−2.3
Finland	27.0	16.4	10.6	7.1	0.0	0.0	0.0	0.3	0.1	17.3
France	21.3	12.6	8.7	5.6	0.0	0.0	0.0	0.2	0.2	14.1
Gabon	40.7	12.4	28.3	2.2	30.2	0.0	0.0	0.6	0.1	−0.4
Gambia, The	5.7	7.8	−2.1	3.6	0.0	0.0	0.5	0.5	0.7	−0.2
Georgia	6.6	16.1	−9.5	2.5	0.6	0.0	0.0	1.1	2.5	−11.2
Germany	20.6	14.9	5.7	4.4	0.1	0.0	0.0	0.3	0.1	9.6
Ghana	17.2	7.3	9.9	4.0	0.0	1.2	3.0	0.8	0.2	8.7
Greece	17.9	8.7	9.2	3.0	0.1	0.0	0.0	0.5	0.7	10.9
Guatemala	10.5	9.9	0.6	1.6	0.8	0.0	1.0	0.3	0.2	−0.1
Guinea	21.0	8.2	12.8	2.0	0.0	4.1	1.9	0.3	0.6	7.9
Guinea-Bissau	−3.5	7.5	−11.0	..	0.0	0.0	0.0	0.8	..	..
Haiti	26.0	1.8	24.2	1.5	0.0	0.0	0.9	0.2	0.2	24.4

	Gross national savings	Consumption of fixed capital	Net national savings	Education expenditure	Energy depletion	Mineral depletion	Net forest depletion	Carbon dioxide emissions damage	Particulate emissions damage	Adjusted net savings
	% of GNI 2001	% of GNI 2001	% of GNI 2001	% of GNI 2001	% of GNI 2001	% of GNI 2001	% of GNI 2001	% of GNI 2001	% of GNI 2001	% of GNI 2001
Honduras	25.9	5.6	20.3	3.5	0.0	0.1	0.0	0.5	0.2	23.0
Hungary	23.4	11.5	11.9	4.3	0.6	0.0	0.0	0.8	0.4	14.4
India	22.9	9.6	13.3	3.2	1.9	0.4	0.0	1.7	0.7	11.8
Indonesia	23.6	5.4	18.2	0.6	12.0	1.2	0.0	1.1	0.5	4.0
Iran, Islamic Rep.	35.3	10.0	25.3	3.2	31.4	0.2	0.0	1.8	0.7	−5.6
Iraq	..	..	..	..	..	..	..	..	..	..
Ireland	27.4	12.3	15.1	5.5	0.0	0.1	0.0	0.4	0.1	20.0
Israel	14.9	13.2	1.7	6.6	0.0	0.0	0.0	0.4	0.0	7.9
Italy	20.5	13.6	6.9	4.7	0.1	0.0	0.0	0.3	0.2	11.0
Jamaica	22.2	11.2	11.0	5.8	0.0	1.9	0.0	0.9	0.3	13.7
Japan	27.1	15.9	11.2	3.6	0.0	0.0	0.0	0.2	0.4	14.2
Jordan	24.4	10.5	13.9	5.6	0.0	0.0	0.0	1.1	0.7	17.7
Kazakhstan	20.1	10.2	9.9	4.4	30.2	0.0	0.0	4.5	0.4	−20.8
Kenya	10.5	8.0	2.5	6.3	0.0	0.0	0.1	0.5	0.2	8.0
Korea, Dem. Rep.	..	..	..	..	..	..	..	..	..	..
Korea, Rep.	28.8	11.9	16.9	3.7	0.0	0.0	0.0	0.7	0.8	19.1
Kuwait	30.2	6.7	23.5	5.0	48.4	0.0	0.0	0.8	2.0	−22.7
Kyrgyz Republic	16.0	8.0	8.0	5.5	1.0	0.0	0.0	2.7	0.2	9.6
Lao PDR	..	8.2	..	1.8	0.0	0.0	0.0	0.2	0.2	..
Latvia	20.4	10.7	9.7	6.2	0.0	0.0	0.0	0.7	0.3	14.9
Lebanon	−4.9	10.3	−15.2	2.5	0.0	0.0	0.0	0.6	0.6	−13.9
Lesotho	20.5	6.5	14.0	6.6	0.0	0.0	2.3	0.0	0.4	17.9
Liberia	..	8.1	..	..	0.0	0.2	2.7	1.1	0.0	..
Libya	..	..	..	..	..	..	..	..	..	..
Lithuania	17.0	10.1	6.9	5.3	0.4	0.0	0.0	0.9	0.7	10.2
Macedonia, FYR	7.2	9.9	−2.7	4.4	0.0	0.0	0.0	2.2	0.3	−0.8
Madagascar	11.5	7.7	3.8	1.9	0.0	0.0	0.0	0.3	0.2	5.2
Malawi	−2.0	7.0	−9.0	4.5	0.0	0.0	1.6	0.3	0.2	−6.6
Malaysia	39.0	11.9	27.1	4.1	11.2	0.0	0.3	1.1	0.1	18.5
Mali	9.4	7.8	1.6	2.1	0.0	0.0	0.0	0.1	0.5	3.1
Mauritania	25.9	8.1	17.8	3.7	0.0	19.2	0.8	2.2	..	−0.7 [a]
Mauritius	27.0	10.8	16.2	3.3	0.0	0.0	0.0	0.4	..	19.1 [a]
Mexico	18.1	10.6	7.5	4.6	5.2	0.1	0.0	0.4	0.5	5.9
Moldova	12.0	7.3	4.7	9.4	0.0	0.0	0.0	3.5	0.5	10.1
Mongolia	21.7	10.9	10.8	5.7	0.0	4.3	0.0	5.0	0.5	6.7
Morocco	27.7	9.6	18.1	4.9	0.0	0.3	0.2	0.7	0.2	21.6
Mozambique	29.5	7.7	21.8	3.8	0.0	0.0	0.0	0.3	0.4	24.9
Myanmar	..	..	..	0.9	0.0	..	..	..	..	..
Namibia	27.8	12.7	15.1	8.5	0.0	0.3	0.0	0.0	0.2	23.1
Nepal	31.7	2.3	29.4	3.2	0.0	0.0	2.6	0.4	0.1	29.5
Netherlands	27.3	14.6	12.7	4.9	0.7	0.0	0.0	0.3	0.4	16.2
New Zealand	21.4	10.7	10.7	6.9	1.6	0.0	0.0	0.4	0.0	15.6
Nicaragua	..	..	..	3.6	0.0	..	..	..	0.0	..
Niger	2.7	7.0	−4.3	2.3	0.0	0.0	3.7	0.4	0.4	−6.5
Nigeria	25.5	8.4	17.1	0.5	43.0	0.0	0.0	0.7	0.8	−26.9
Norway	36.8	16.2	20.6	6.8	5.6	0.0	0.0	0.1	0.1	21.6
Oman	..	9.8	..	4.1	51.8	0.0	0.0	0.7	..	..
Pakistan	19.4	7.7	11.7	2.3	5.0	0.0	0.8	1.1	1.0	6.1
Panama	24.4	7.9	16.5	4.8	0.0	0.0	0.0	0.6	0.3	20.4
Papua New Guinea	18.4	8.9	9.5	..	11.6	11.1	0.0	0.5	0.0	..
Paraguay	10.6	9.5	1.1	3.9	0.0	0.0	0.0	0.4	0.4	4.2
Peru	16.9	10.3	6.6	2.6	1.0	1.2	0.0	0.3	0.6	6.1
Philippines	24.9	8.1	16.8	2.9	0.0	0.1	0.8	0.7	0.4	17.7
Poland	18.7	11.2	7.5	7.5	0.4	0.1	0.0	1.3	0.7	12.5
Portugal	19.4	15.3	4.1	5.6	0.0	0.0	0.0	0.4	0.4	8.9
Puerto Rico	..	7.4	..	..	0.0	0.0	0.0	0.2	..	..

	Gross national savings	Consumption of fixed capital	Net national savings	Education expenditure	Energy depletion	Mineral depletion	Net forest depletion	Carbon dioxide emissions damage	Particulate emissions damage	Adjusted net savings
	% of GNI	% of GNI	% of GNI	% of GNI	% of GNI	% of GNI	% of GNI	% of GNI	% of GNI	% of GNI
	2001	2001	2001	2001	2001	2001	2001	2001	2001	2001
Romania	16.0	9.9	6.1	3.6	3.9	0.1	0.0	1.5	0.2	4.0
Russian Federation	32.3	10.4	21.9	3.6	31.0	0.3	0.0	3.4	0.6	−9.8
Rwanda	12.2	7.2	5.0	3.5	0.0	0.0	4.2	0.3	0.0	4.0
Saudi Arabia	28.0	10.0	18.0	7.2	42.5	0.0	0.0	0.8	1.0	−19.1
Senegal	14.5	8.4	6.1	3.4	0.0	0.0	0.3	0.6	..	8.6 [a]
Sierra Leone	−9.9	6.9	−16.8	0.9	0.0	0.0	5.3	0.4	0.4	−22.0
Singapore	44.8	14.1	30.7	2.3	0.0	0.0	0.0	0.5	0.4	32.1
Slovak Republic	23.3	11.0	12.3	4.6	0.1	0.0	0.0	1.3	0.1	15.4
Slovenia	*24.8*	12.0	12.8	5.4	0.1	0.0	0.0	0.6	0.2	17.3
Somalia	..	..	..	..	..	..	..	..	..	..
South Africa	13.9	13.3	0.6	7.5	1.3	1.0	0.3	2.0	0.2	3.3
Spain	22.8	12.9	9.9	4.6	0.0	0.0	0.0	0.3	0.4	13.8
Sri Lanka	23.2	5.0	18.2	2.9	0.0	0.0	0.5	0.3	0.3	20.0
Sudan	7.6	9.0	−1.4	0.9	0.0	0.0	0.0	0.2	0.6	−1.3
Swaziland	14.6	9.2	5.4	6.5	0.0	0.0	0.0	0.2	0.1	11.6
Sweden	20.7	14.1	6.6	8.3	0.1	0.1	0.0	0.2	0.0	14.5
Switzerland	31.3	14.3	17.0	4.9	0.0	0.0	0.0	0.1	0.2	21.6
Syrian Arab Republic	28.5	9.7	18.8	2.6	28.8	0.0	0.0	1.7	0.8	−9.9
Tajikistan	*1.7*	7.1	−5.4	2.0	..	0.0	0.0	3.9	0.2	..
Tanzania	8.6	7.6	1.0	2.4	0.0	0.3	0.0	0.2	0.2	2.7
Thailand	28.7	15.1	13.6	3.5	1.4	0.0	0.2	1.1	0.4	14.0
Togo	4.9	7.7	−2.8	4.3	0.0	0.0	4.4	0.6	0.3	−3.8
Trinidad and Tobago	27.4	12.2	15.2	3.4	23.4	0.0	0.0	2.1	0.0	−6.9
Tunisia	24.6	10.0	14.6	6.6	4.1	0.0	0.1	0.7	0.3	16.0
Turkey	16.7	7.0	9.7	2.2	0.4	0.1	0.0	0.8	1.2	9.4
Turkmenistan	36.3	9.5	26.8	..	..	0.0	0.0	5.1	0.3	..
Uganda	13.8	7.6	6.2	1.9	0.0	0.0	6.2	0.2	0.0	1.7
Ukraine	24.7	19.1	5.6	6.3	8.0	0.0	0.0	6.8	1.0	−3.9
United Arab Emirates	..	..	..	..	..	..	..	..	..	..
United Kingdom	14.9	11.5	3.4	5.4	1.0	0.0	0.0	0.3	0.1	7.4
United States	17.5	11.9	5.6	5.4	1.1	0.0	0.0	0.4	0.3	9.2
Uruguay	10.9	11.5	−0.6	3.0	0.0	0.0	0.2	0.2	1.9	0.1
Uzbekistan	18.8	8.3	10.5	9.4	49.8	0.0	0.0	7.3	0.6	−37.8
Venezuela, RB	22.4	7.2	15.2	4.4	23.1	0.3	0.0	0.6	0.0	−4.4
Vietnam	32.6	8.0	24.6	2.8	7.0	0.0	0.9	1.0	0.4	18.1
West Bank and Gaza	..	8.5	..	..	0.0	0.0	..	0.0	..	..
Yemen, Rep.	32.3	9.0	23.3	..	36.4	0.0	0.0	1.3	0.5	..
Yugoslavia, Fed. Rep.	8.0	9.2	−1.2	..	0.6	0.2	0.0	2.7	0.2	..
Zambia	5.6	8.2	−2.6	2.1	0.0	1.3	0.0	0.4	..	−2.2 [a]
Zimbabwe	6.8	9.0	−2.2	7.8	0.3	0.3	0.0	1.1	0.5	3.4
World	**23.9 w**	**12.6 w**	**11.3 w**	**4.7 w**	**2.1 w**	**0.1 w**	**0.0 w**	**0.5 w**	**0.3 w**	**12.9 w**
Low income	22.1	8.8	13.3	2.8	6.6	0.4	0.3	1.6	0.6	6.6
Middle income	25.8	10.2	15.6	3.8	7.8	0.3	0.1	1.3	0.7	9.3
Lower middle income	31.2	9.8	21.4	3.0	8.1	0.2	0.1	1.9	0.8	13.3
Upper middle income	19.6	10.6	8.9	4.8	7.5	0.4	0.0	0.6	0.6	4.7
Low & middle income	25.2	9.9	15.2	3.7	7.6	0.3	0.1	1.3	0.7	8.9
East Asia & Pacific	36.8	9.3	27.5	2.2	3.9	0.3	0.2	1.9	0.8	22.6
Europe & Central Asia	24.4	10.5	13.9	4.5	11.9	0.1	..	2.3	0.7	3.5
Latin America & Carib.	17.1	10.4	6.7	4.2	4.8	0.5	0.0	0.4	0.5	4.6
Middle East & N. Africa	26.9	10.0	16.9	5.1	25.8	0.1	0.1	1.1	0.9	−5.9
South Asia	22.5	9.0	13.5	3.0	2.1	0.3	0.2	1.5	0.7	11.8
Sub-Saharan Africa	15.0	10.4	4.6	4.7	7.9	0.5	0.7	1.1	0.4	−1.3
High income	23.3	13.2	10.1	5.0	0.8	0.0	..	0.3	0.3	13.7
Europe EMU	21.4	*13.8*	7.6	*4.7*	*0.1*	*0.0*	..	*0.3*	..	11.8

a. Adjusted net savings do not include particulate emissions damage.

About the data

Adjusted net savings measure the change in value of a specified set of assets, excluding capital gains. If a country's net savings are positive and the accounting includes a sufficiently broad range of assets, economic theory suggests that the present value of social welfare is increasing. Conversely, persistently negative adjusted net savings indicate that an economy is on an unsustainable path.

Adjusted net savings are derived from standard national accounting measures of gross national savings by making four adjustments. First, estimates of capital consumption of produced assets are deducted to obtain net national savings. Second, current expenditures on education are added to net national savings (in standard national accounting these expenditures are treated as consumption). Third, estimates of the depletion of a variety of natural resources are deducted to reflect the decline in asset values associated with their extraction and harvest. And fourth, deductions are made for damage from carbon dioxide and particulate emissions. (In earlier editions of the *World Development Indicators* these adjustments were made to gross domestic savings and adjusted net savings were referred to as genuine savings.)

The exercise treats education expenditures as an addition to savings effort. But because of the wide variability in the effectiveness of government education expenditures, these figures cannot be construed as the value of investments in human capital. The accounting for human capital is also incomplete because depreciation of human capital is not estimated.

There are also gaps in the accounting of natural resource depletion and pollution costs. Key estimates missing on the resource side include the value of fossil water extracted from aquifers, net depletion of fish stocks, and depletion and degradation of soils. Important pollutants affecting human health and economic assets are excluded because no internationally comparable data are widely available on damage from ground-level ozone or from sulfur oxides. For the first time, however, the table includes values for damage from particulate emissions, based on new estimates developed by the World Bank (Pandey and others 2003).

Estimates of resource depletion are based on the calculation of unit resource rents. An economic rent represents an excess return to a given factor of production—that is, in this case the returns from resource extraction or harvest are higher than the normal rate of return on capital. Natural resources

give rise to rents because they are not produced; in contrast, for produced goods and services competitive forces will expand supply until economic profits are driven to zero. For each type of resource and each country, unit resource rents are derived by taking the difference between world prices and the average unit extraction or harvest costs (including a "normal" return on capital). Unit rents are then multiplied by the physical quantity extracted or harvested in order to arrive at a depletion figure. This figure is one of a range of depletion estimates that are possible, depending on the assumptions made about future quantities, prices, and costs, and there is reason to believe that it is at the high end of the range. Some of the largest depletion estimates in the table should therefore be viewed with caution.

A positive net depletion figure for forest resources implies that the harvest rate exceeds the rate of natural growth; this is not the same as deforestation, which represents a change in land use (see *Definitions* for table 3.4). In principle, there should be an addition to savings in countries where growth exceeds harvest, but empirical estimates suggest that most of this net growth is in forested areas that cannot be exploited economically at present. Because the depletion estimates reflect only timber values, they ignore all the external and nontimber benefits associated with standing forests.

Pollution damage from emissions of carbon dioxide is calculated as the marginal social cost per unit multiplied by the increase in the stock of carbon dioxide. The unit damage figure represents the present value of global damage to economic assets and to human welfare over the time the unit of pollution remains in the atmosphere.

Pollution damage from particulate emissions was estimated by valuing the human health effects from exposure to particulate matter less than 10 microns in diameter. The estimates were calculated as willingness to pay to avoid mortality attributable to particulate emissions (in particular, mortality relating to cardiopulmonary disease in adults, lung cancer in adults, and acute respiratory infections in children).

Definitions

• **Gross national savings** are calculated as the difference between gross national income and public and private consumption, plus net current transfers. • **Consumption of fixed capital** represents the replacement value of capital used up in the process of production. • **Net national savings** are equal to gross national savings less the value of consumption of fixed capital. • **Education expenditure** refers to current operating expenditures in education, including wages and salaries and excluding capital investments in buildings and equipment. • **Energy depletion** is equal to the product of unit resource rents and the physical quantities of energy extracted. It covers coal, crude oil, and natural gas. • **Mineral depletion** is equal to the product of unit resource rents and the physical quantities of minerals extracted. It refers to tin, gold, lead, zinc, iron, copper, nickel, silver, bauxite, and phosphate. • **Net forest depletion** is calculated as the product of unit resource rents and the excess of roundwood harvest over natural growth. • **Carbon dioxide emissions damage** is estimated to be $20 per ton of carbon (the unit damage in 1995 U.S. dollars) times the number of tons of carbon emitted. • **Particulate emissions damage** is calculated as the willingness to pay to avoid mortality attributable to particulate emissions. • **Adjusted net savings** are equal to net national savings plus education expenditure and minus energy depletion, mineral depletion, net forest depletion, and carbon dioxide and particulate emissions damage.

Data sources

Gross national savings are derived from the World Bank's national accounts data files, described in the *Economy* section. Consumption of fixed capital is from the United Nations Statistics Division's *National Accounts Statistics: Main Aggregates and Detailed Tables, 1997*, extrapolated to 2001. The education expenditure data are from the United Nations Statistics Division's *Statistical Yearbook 1997*, extrapolated to 2001. The wide range of data sources and estimation methods used to arrive at resource depletion estimates are described in a World Bank working paper, "Estimating National Wealth" (Kunte and others 1998). The unit damage figure for carbon dioxide emissions is from Fankhauser (1995). The estimates of damage from particulate emissions are from Pandey and others (2003). The conceptual underpinnings of the savings measure appear in Hamilton and Clemens (1999).

4 ECONOMY

The economy supplies the goods and services that individuals, firms, and governments demand and pay for with the income they earn by supplying labor, capital, and other resources—which in turn are used to produce goods and services. The systematic analysis of this circular flow of economic activity and its codification in a system of national accounts were among the important accomplishments of 20th-century economics. National accounting, along with the complementary analysis of the flow of exports, imports, and financing between countries through the balance of payments, allows comprehensive, consistent measurement of world economic activity such as that presented in this section.

While no person on earth is completely isolated from the global economy, some economic transactions are not measured in the national accounts. Some exclusions from the national accounts are deliberate—the goods and services produced by women working at home are a famous example. But other types of production are left out also because they are unpriced, unmarketed, and therefore unrecorded. Often these are the activities of greatest importance to the poorest people. Other omissions occur because the producers or consumers have reason to hide their activities or because national statistical systems are inadequate for the task of measuring them. And measurement errors affect the reliability of all economic statistics.

These gaps in the statistical record, along with inevitable errors in collecting and tabulating data, limit the ability to monitor economic activity and to shape policies based on timely and accurate statistics. And difficult conceptual issues remain relating to the measurement of prices and product quality across countries and over time that further limit the reliability of comparisons along those dimensions (box 4a).

Even so, the measurement and analysis of economic activity remains a fundamental source of information about development. The indicators in this section measure changes in the size and structure of the global economy and the varying effects of these changes on national economies. They include measures of macroeconomic performance (gross domestic product (GDP), consumption, demand, and international trade) and of stability (central government budgets, prices, the money supply, the balance of payments, and external debt). Other important economic indicators appear throughout the book, but especially in the *States and markets* section (credit, investment, financial markets, tax policies, exchange rates) and the *Global links* section (trade and tariffs, foreign investment, and aid flows).

Slower economic growth

In 2001 the world economy grew by 1.1 percent, a sharp drop from the 3.9 percent growth in 2000 and well below the average annual growth of 2.7 percent in the 1990s. Still, the world's recorded output—and income—grew by more than $300 billion.

Low-income economies saw the fastest growth, almost twice the rate of middle-income economies. Upper-middle-income and high-income economies, affected by slowing investment and widespread uncertainty in financial markets, had the slowest growth.

Over the past decade economic growth was fastest in East Asia and Pacific (averaging 7.5 percent a year) and South Asia (5.5 percent). Leading this growth were China and India, each accounting for more than 70 percent of its region's output. Even in 2001 these two regions did comparatively well, with East Asia registering 5.5 percent growth—demonstrating its recovery from the financial crisis in 1998, when annual growth fell to 0.7 percent—and South Asia recording 4.9 percent growth.

Since 1990 growth has been slowest in the transition economies of Europe and Central Asia, which experienced sharp declines in the early part of the decade and a big setback after the Russian ruble crisis in 1998. In 2000 growth resumed, reaching 6.6 percent before falling to 2.3 percent in 2001. But Kazakhstan and Turkmenistan continued to register extraordinarily high growth (13.2 percent and 20.5 percent), buoyed by higher prices for their petroleum exports.

In Sub-Saharan Africa, Latin America and the Caribbean, and the Middle East and North Africa growth in 1990–2000 exceeded that in the previous decade but declined in 2001. The downturn was most severe in Latin America, where the large economies of Argentina and Mexico shrank and Brazil grew by only 1.5 percent.

4a

Measuring national income

Reliable statistics on income, output, consumption, savings, and investment are critical for assessing the health of a national economy and, in aggregate, the world economy.

The modern system of national accounts has its origins in the work of Richard Stone and a report prepared in the 1940s for the United Nations, *Measurement of National Income and the Construction of Social Accounts* (United Nations 1947). Standards for preparing national accounts have continued to evolve, and most countries now use the United Nations System of National Accounts, series F, no. 2, version 3 (universally referred to as the 1968 SNA), though version 4 of the SNA was completed in 1993. As more countries switched to the new version, the 2001 edition of the *World Development Indicators* introduced the 1993 SNA terminology (see *Primary data documentation*).

National income may be compiled as the sum of incomes received by factors of production, or the sum of spending from income, or the sum of value added in each stage of production. Each approach uses different data from different sources, but ideally each should arrive at the same total. Because these measures do not allow for the depreciation of physical capital, they are gross measures. When the sum is the total value of production by residents and domestic businesses, it is gross domestic product (GDP). When it also includes net income from abroad, it is gross national income (GNI).

Defining national income is easy, but compiling consistent, timely, and accurate national accounts is difficult and costly. Three broad problems face compilers of national accounts: identifying and correctly accounting for all sources of income (or output) in the economy; adjusting data for price changes to allow comparisons of real values over time; and, when international comparisons are to be made, selecting the appropriate conversion factor to transform values in

national currencies into a common unit of value. Each has conceptual and practical difficulties.

Measuring income requires regular surveys of producers and households, supplemented by records of the tax system, customs service, and monetary and banking authorities. In all economies, but particularly in developing economies with many small, unincorporated businesses, it may be difficult to identify the population to be surveyed and to distinguish business spending (investment or purchases of intermediate inputs) from household spending (consumption).

Measuring real output is especially vexing. As an economy grows, relative prices change, as do the underlying qualities of goods. New products appear and others disappear. And the value of the output of the increasingly important service sector is often measured only by the cost of inputs, mainly labor. The result of all these factors? Real growth and price change are difficult to measure.

Comparisons across countries are complicated by multiple exchange rates, some of which may be used only for official transactions, while others may not be officially reported. Moreover, relative prices of goods and services not traded on the international market may vary substantially from one economy to another, leading to big differences in the purchasing power of one currency compared with that of another and thus to differences in welfare as measured by GNI per capita.

Although the *World Development Indicators* points out the most obvious and serious deficiencies in international statistics, it can neither list nor correct for the many sources of error and noncomparability. The solution lies with the national statistical offices that collect and report the data and with the international agencies that assist their efforts and try to ensure comparability.

Source: Adapted from World Bank, *World Development Indicators 1997*.

Patterns of change

Most developing economies are following familiar patterns of growth, with agriculture giving way first to manufacturing and later to services as the main source of income. But some, such as Jordan and Panama, have moved directly from agriculture to service-based economies. For most economies services have been the most rapidly growing sector. In 1990–2001 the service sector grew by 3.9 percent a year in developing and transition economies and by 3 percent in high-income economies. Among developing regions, South Asia had the fastest growth in services in the 1990s (7 percent a year), and Europe and Central Asia the slowest (1.8 percent) (table 4.1).

In developing economies services generated more than half of GDP in 2001, compared with 70 percent in high-income economies (table 4.2). But in East Asia and Pacific services produced only 36 percent of GDP in 2001, and growth in manufacturing (10 percent a year) outpaced growth in services (6.5percent) in 1990–2001. This trend reflects the rapid growth of manufacturing in China (12.1 percent annually), which also had rapid expansion in services (8.9 percent a year).

The contribution of trade

After expanding by 6.8 percent a year in 1990–2000, global trade (exports plus imports) grew by only 1.2 percent in 2001. High-income economies, which account for more than 75 percent of global trade, experienced the greatest slowdown, with trade growing by only 0.3 percent in 2001. But trade by low-income economies grew by 6.4 percent, compared to the 4.4 percent average rate in 1990–2000.

Trade in services has grown rapidly, but trade in merchandise—primary commodities and manufactured goods—continues to dominate. In 2001 merchandise accounted for 81 percent of all exports of goods and commercial services, and manufactured goods for 78 percent of merchandise exports (tables 4.5 and 4.7). Exporters of primary nonfuel commodities saw their trade volumes increase, but a continuing decline in their terms of trade left them with less income (table 4.4). The economies of Sub-Saharan Africa were hit particularly hard.

Steady trends in consumption, investment, and saving

Most of the world's output goes to final consumption by households (including individuals) and governments. The share of final consumption in world output has remained fairly constant over time, averaging about 76 percent in 1990–2001 (table 4.9). The growth of per capita household consumption expenditure provides an important indicator of the potential for reducing poverty. In 1990–2001 per capita consumption grew by 5.6 percent a year in East Asia and Pacific but fell by an additional 0.1 percent in Sub-Saharan Africa and rose by only 0.8 percent in Europe and Central Asia (table 4.10).

Output that is not consumed goes to exports (less imports) and gross capital formation (investment). Investment is financed out of domestic and foreign savings. In recent years the global savings rate has averaged 24 percent of total output. But global averages disguise large differences between countries. Savings rates are consistently lower in Sub-Saharan Africa. And they tend to be volatile in countries dependent on commodity exports. Gross domestic savings in the Middle East and North Africa rose from 23 percent of GDP in 1999 to 30 percent in 2000 and 29 percent in 2001, buoyed by higher oil prices. The highest savings rate was in East Asia and Pacific, where gross domestic savings have averaged about 36 percent over most of the past decade (table 4.9).

In 1990–2001 gross capital formation increased by about 6.8 percent a year in East Asia and Pacific and 7.1 percent in South Asia, but declined by 7 percent in Europe and Central Asia. East Asia and Pacific continued to have the highest investment rate in the world, at 31 percent of GDP in 2001. By contrast, investment averaged only 18 percent of GDP in Sub-Saharan Africa (tables 4.9 and 4.10).

Fiscal affairs

Central governments had expenditures averaging 26 percent of GDP in 1999 while raising revenues (mainly through taxes) equal to 25 percent of GDP, leaving a global fiscal deficit of about 1 percent of GDP (table 4.11). Government expenditures go mostly to the purchase of goods and services (including the wages and salaries of public employees) and to subsidies and current transfers to private and public enterprises and local governments. The rest goes to interest payments and capital expenditures. In 1999 subsidies accounted for 59 percent of government spending in high-income economies and 49 percent in Europe and Central Asia, but only 14 percent in the Middle East and North Africa (table 4.12).

The sources of government revenue have been changing. Taxes on income, profits, and capital gains generated 23 percent of current revenues in 1990, but their share fell to 18 percent in 1999. High-income economies depended more on income taxes than did low- and middle-income economies, which derived 35 percent of their revenue from taxes on goods and services and 9 percent from taxes on trade (table 4.13).

Governments, because of their size, have a large effect on the performance of economies. High taxes and subsidies can distort economic behavior, and large fiscal deficits make it harder to manage the growth of the money supply and thus increase the likelihood of inflation. As governments have adopted policies leading to greater fiscal stability, inflation rates and interest rates have tended to decline (table 4.14).

Declining external debt

In 2001 the external debt of low- and middle-income economies declined by $30 billion, or about 1 percent of their total stock of debt. The decline extended to all developing regions except East Asia and Pacific, where total debt increased by $7 billion. Debt stocks fell by $18 billion in Latin America and the Caribbean and by $8 billion in Sub-Saharan African, where heavily indebted poor countries (HIPCs) have received significant debt relief. The debt relief appears to have boosted the economic outlook for HIPCs, which had GDP growth of about 4.3 percent and GDP per capita growth of 2.1 percent in 2001.

4.a

	Gross domestic product		Exports of goods and services		Imports of goods and services		GDP deflator		Current account balance		Gross international reserves	
	annual % growth		annual % growth		annual % growth		% growth		% of GDP		$ millions	months of import coverage
	2001	2002	2001	2002	2001	2002	2001	2002	2001	2002	2002	2002
Algeria	1.9	2.9	−1.1	1.8	17.2	2.2	0.1	−2.1	..	7.7	20,941	16.6
Argentina	−4.5	−15.0	2.9	−6.5	−14.0	−50.9	−1.1	74.5	−1.7	7.9	13,482	6.5
Armenia	9.6	12.9	22.9	25.0	2.1	9.4	4.0	2.3	−9.5	−6.6	352	4.1
Azerbaijan	9.9	7.9	24.4	−3.0	12.3	47.6	2.2	2.6	−0.9	−18.9	686	2.3
Bangladesh	5.3	4.4	22.8	−8.7	23.5	−3.1	1.6	2.7	−1.7	0.5	1,661	2.1
Bolivia	1.2	2.5	4.9	7.5	−7.4	6.6	0.7	2.0	−3.7	−4.0	858	4.5
Bosnia and Herzegovina	6.0	2.3	0.8	5.0	−0.6	5.5	4.0	2.3	−20.0	−20.5	1,540	6.1
Botswana	6.3	3.5	7.8	−0.9	7.8	1.7	4.4	4.5	8.4	7.9	7,648	30.8
Brazil	1.5	1.4	12.1	−4.0	0.7	−12.5	7.4	7.5	−4.6	−4.0	25,569	3.5
Bulgaria	4.0	4.0	8.5	4.0	13.0	7.9	6.5	5.3	−6.6	−6.2	4,327	5.3
Cameroon	5.3	5.2	1.9	5.7	11.7	3.4	3.0	1.9	−1.7	−3.9	11	0.0
Chile	2.8	2.7	9.7	1.8	−1.3	−3.1	1.5	3.0	−1.9	−1.4	17,495	8.9
China	7.3	8.0	9.6	10.2	10.8	16.1	0.0	1.0	1.5	1.8	286,407	9.8
Colombia	1.4	1.5	4.1	−3.3	11.2	1.5	7.6	6.9	−2.2	−2.5	10,649	6.6
Congo, Dem. Rep.	−4.5	3.0	2.0	−31.6	10.0	−25.0	386.6	23.3	0.0	−3.7	..	..
Congo, Rep.	2.9	2.5	5.0	−2.3	0.7	9.2	−14.5	−4.4	..	−4.3	173	1.0
Costa Rica	0.9	2.0	−6.4	−2.2	0.2	0.3	7.1	8.6	−4.4	−5.4	1,015	1.5
Côte d'Ivoire	−0.9	2.9	−1.2	1.1	−4.0	2.6	2.1	2.3	−0.6	−2.6	..	..
Croatia	4.1	4.3	9.0	0.3	9.3	3.9	3.1	2.9	−3.0	−5.0	4,973	..
Dominican Republic	2.7	4.0	−7.9	6.6	−4.9	5.0	8.9	4.8	−4.0	−3.8	1,235	1.6
Ecuador	5.6	3.5	5.0	0.6	33.7	22.6	25.1	12.8	−4.4	−5.0	1,247	1.6
Egypt, Arab Rep.	2.9	2.0	8.2	−10.4	10.7	−10.8	3.8	4.5	0.0	−0.6	14,592	8.6
El Salvador	1.8	3.0	11.9	1.6	3.3	8.9	2.7	3.3	−1.3	−4.5	1,890	3.3
Estonia	5.0	4.5	−0.2	8.0	2.1	9.3	5.4	4.4	−6.1	−5.6	1,217	2.4
Gabon	2.5	3.0	1.7	3.1	2.3	2.8	−11.7	2.0	10.0	4.6	..	..
Ghana	4.0	5.0	0.3	4.2	2.0	6.6	34.6	20.5	−5.9	−10.0	679	2.1
Guatemala	2.1	2.3	0.0	2.8	0.2	9.4	6.5	8.5	−6.0	−5.3	2,094	3.6
Honduras	2.6	2.5	4.6	4.6	3.6	2.1	9.6	9.0	−5.1	−8.4	1,132	3.6
India	5.4	4.4	9.0	5.8	4.9	7.7	3.5	4.5	0.3	0.0	63,814	8.9
Indonesia	3.3	3.7	1.9	−1.2	8.1	−8.3	12.6	11.8	4.7	4.4	31,571	6.4
Iran, Islamic Rep.	4.8	5.3	9.7	4.3	4.5	3.8	8.8	14.5	4.2	2.7	8,628	3.9
Jamaica	1.7	1.5	1.6	−0.2	8.1	5.5	6.9	9.0	−10.1	−7.2	1,845	4.1
Jordan	4.2	5.1	7.9	5.2	3.4	10.6	0.3	3.1	0.0	−0.3	2,220	3.7
Kazakhstan	13.2	8.0	−3.3	7.2	10.5	6.7	11.6	5.6	−5.5	−7.5	2,778	2.5
Kenya	1.1	1.2	6.8	5.0	−1.2	0.1	11.3	6.2	−2.8	−4.2	1,160	3.7
Latvia	7.6	5.0	6.5	8.2	6.1	10.6	1.6	3.0	−9.7	−8.5	..	..
Lebanon	1.3	1.0	−10.3	11.5	12.8	−3.6	0.0	5.0	−23.8	−19.0	7,315	11.4
Lesotho	4.0	2.6	40.4	33.3	4.9	7.2	5.7	7.9	−11.9	−8.4	372	6.6
Lithuania	5.9	5.0	20.8	3.5	17.7	8.7	0.4	1.0	−4.8	−6.2	..	..
Macedonia, FYR	−4.1	2.5	−12.4	2.2	−13.0	3.2	2.8	2.5	−9.5	−6.5	833	4.8

continues on page 184

4.b

	Nominal exchange rate			Real effective exchange rate		Money and quasi money		Gross domestic credit		Real interest rate		Short-term debt[a]
	local currency units per $	% change		1995 = 100		annual % growth		annual % growth		%		% of exports
	2002	2001	2002	2001	2002	2001	2002	2001	2002	2001	2002	2001
Algeria	79.7	3.3	2.4	110.5	93.8	48.9	..	28.5	..	6.5	5.3	0.9
Argentina	3.3	0.0	232.2	..	..	−19.4	..	2.5	..	29.1	21.0	54.7
Armenia	585.8	1.7	3.4	105.3	85.6	4.3	11.0	−9.8	−15.3	21.8	17.4	6.4
Azerbaijan	4,893.0	4.6	2.5	..	..	−10.5	14.6	−38.1	83.9	16.5	15.0	4.1
Bangladesh	57.9	5.6	1.6	..	..	14.7	14.1	17.2	10.0	14.0	10.5	3.2
Bolivia	7.5	6.7	9.8	117.8	114.7	2.2	−8.3	−3.3	3.6	19.3	16.6	21.7
Bosnia and Herzegovina	..	..	..	..	..	..	..	..	..	..	..	3.7
Botswana	5.5	30.2	−21.7	..	..	31.2	14.4	16.2	−43.0	10.9	11.8	0.7
Brazil	3.5	18.7	52.3	..	..	12.1	33.0	31.3	23.2	46.7	55.8	39.3
Bulgaria	1.9	5.6	−15.1	130.3	138.3	26.7	15.8	25.5	20.0	4.4	5.1	4.4
Cameroon	625.5	5.6	−16.0	98.7	105.1	15.1	16.8	8.6	9.0	17.2	16.7	35.1
Chile	712.4	14.6	8.6	96.6	87.9	4.5	0.5	10.1	6.0	10.2	4.6	10.8
China	8.3	0.0	0.0	110.5	106.2	15.0	20.6	13.6	29.0	5.8	..	14.2
Colombia	2,854.3	5.2	24.0	98.0	90.3	16.0	17.0	11.1	21.8	12.2	8.9	21.5
Congo, Dem. Rep.	..	..	..	249.6	93.5	..	..	..	..	..	..	332.8
Congo, Rep.	625.5	5.6	−16.0	..	..	−22.8	9.8	37.4	−11.2	41.2	21.4	33.1
Costa Rica	378.7	7.4	10.8	111.9	109.2	10.4	17.9	10.6	31.2	15.6	16.0	15.1
Côte d'Ivoire	625.5	5.6	−16.0	99.9	105.2	12.0	34.2	−2.3	7.1	..	..	25.2
Croatia	7.1	2.5	−14.5	103.2	103.3	45.7	20.7	21.6	25.2	6.3	..	2.7
Dominican Republic	21.2	2.8	23.6	117.0	101.4	26.9	12.9	23.6	21.1	14.1	23.0	12.4
Ecuador	25,000.0	0.0	0.0	102.3	119.0	21.4	..	23.0	..	−7.7	10.8	20.7
Egypt, Arab Rep.	4.5	21.7	0.2	..	..	13.2	7.9	10.8	14.1	9.1	9.5	15.5
El Salvador	8.8	−0.1	0.0	..	..	..	..	..	..	..	..	21.0
Estonia	14.9	5.2	−15.6	..	..	23.0	11.2	24.4	27.6	2.3	3.1	20.0
Gabon	625.5	5.6	−16.0	91.0	91.9	7.5	4.0	46.1	−3.4	36.7	15.7	9.3
Ghana	8,275.4	3.9	15.0	81.6	79.5	31.7	..	19.0	..	..	..	22.9
Guatemala	7.8	3.5	−2.4	..	..	18.1	9.7	1.5	22.5	11.7	9.7	30.3
Honduras	16.9	5.1	6.3	..	..	17.5	15.0	21.0	9.6	13.0	15.1	10.9
India	48.0	3.1	−0.3	..	..	14.3	16.8	11.8	14.8	8.3	7.0	3.7
Indonesia	8,940.0	8.4	−14.0	..	..	12.8	5.8	6.6	6.6	5.3	12.8	33.1
Iran, Islamic Rep.	7,952.0	−22.6	354.2	181.1	209.3	27.6	28.0	16.9	18.2	..	..	7.7
Jamaica	50.8	4.1	7.4	..	..	8.6	9.6	−35.3	..	12.8	..	19.4
Jordan	0.7	0.0	0.0	..	..	8.1	11.0	11.9	5.4	10.6	8.1	7.2
Kazakhstan	154.6	3.9	2.9	..	..	40.2	30.0	17.1	29.6	..	..	7.8
Kenya	77.1	0.7	−1.9	..	..	2.5	9.7	3.2	4.7	7.6	11.8	23.0
Latvia	0.6	4.1	−6.9	..	..	19.8	17.4	34.4	49.9	9.4	4.8	80.4
Lebanon	1,507.5	0.0	0.0	..	..	7.5	6.0	11.6	5.6	17.1	14.4	138.3
Lesotho	8.6	60.2	−28.8	69.6	64.6	17.2	9.5	59.2	150.4	10.2	14.0	0.7
Lithuania	3.3	0.0	−17.2	..	..	21.4	20.3	9.3	23.5	9.2	4.3	24.9
Macedonia, FYR	..	4.3	..	73.2	73.4	32.1	..	33.8	..	16.1	..	4.5

continues on page 185

4.a

	Gross domestic product		Exports of goods and services		Imports of goods and services		GDP deflator		Current account balance		Gross international reserves	
	annual % growth		annual % growth		annual % growth		% growth		% of GDP		$ millions	months of import coverage
	2001	2002	2001	2002	2001	2002	2001	2002	2001	2002	2002	2002
Malawi	−1.5	3.0	3.7	7.8	4.7	16.7	26.1	12.0	−30.4	−14.0	..	..
Malaysia	0.4	4.0	−7.5	2.5	−8.6	7.2	−2.6	2.0	8.3	6.5	..	..
Mauritius	7.2	5.3	5.5	2.7	1.4	3.8	2.6	5.6	5.5	1.7	912	3.8
Mexico	−0.3	1.5	−5.1	0.2	−2.9	0.0	5.5	5.4	−2.9	−2.7	47,232	2.8
Moldova	6.1	5.5	14.7	6.0	10.9	9.7	11.9	5.5	−6.7	−6.0	273	2.6
Morocco	6.5	4.4	1.4	−7.5	2.3	5.2	2.5	3.0	4.7	0.0	9,128	7.9
Nicaragua	..	1.5	..	6.3	..	−3.5	..	5.8	..	−28.2	405	2.3
Nigeria	3.9	1.8	5.6	−7.3	18.9	−17.7	6.0	3.6	11.9	−10.6	..	..
Pakistan	2.7	4.4	11.8	12.5	1.5	−10.7	5.7	4.5	−1.9	0.3	4,818	4.1
Panama	0.3	1.0	−1.1	4.5	−9.9	2.3	1.2	0.8	−4.9	−4.5	1,163	2.4
Paraguay	2.7	−3.5	−0.4	−9.3	−1.6	−15.0	7.0	10.2	−2.9	−0.9	758	2.9
Peru	0.2	4.6	6.9	6.0	1.6	2.5	1.3	4.0	−2.0	−1.9	7,088	..
Philippines	3.4	4.6	−3.2	3.3	0.5	4.9	6.7	4.5	6.3	1.8	16,180	5.8
Poland	1.0	1.2	11.8	4.1	3.2	1.5	4.3	3.5	−3.0	−3.6	27,933	6.5
Romania	5.3	4.3	10.6	9.6	17.5	7.9	37.0	22.0	−6.0	−5.4	5,123	3.3
Russian Federation	5.0	4.0	2.6	2.6	16.5	12.0	17.9	17.0	11.2	7.0	45,810	6.1
Senegal	5.7	5.0	6.6	5.4	5.2	4.5	2.9	2.7	−6.4	−5.0	660	4.0
Slovak Republic	3.3	4.0	6.5	5.9	11.7	5.3	5.4	3.6	..	−8.9	..	..
South Africa	2.2	2.2	3.1	4.1	9.2	8.1	7.5	3.8	−0.1	−1.3	17,387	5.1
Sri Lanka	−1.4	3.0	−6.5	−8.7	−10.1	21.3	13.2	8.6	−1.7	−2.2	1,214	2.0
Sudan	6.9	10.6	−9.8	..	37.5	..	4.8	0.9	−4.2	−14.5	323	0.9
Swaziland	1.6	5.6	−4.3	4.6	2.8	6.3	8.4	−4.0	−4.2	..	..	..
Syrian Arab Republic	2.8	3.1	6.7	4.5	9.1	6.8	6.0	2.5	..	4.4	3,810	5.9
Thailand	1.8	5.0	−4.2	10.7	−8.3	10.5	2.2	1.2	5.4	6.0	38,924	5.8
Trinidad and Tobago	5.0	3.0	7.0	−5.2	0.0	5.0	3.3	−2.1	..	2.7	2,385	6.5
Tunisia	4.9	1.9	14.4	−2.5	13.6	−1.5	2.8	2.7	−4.3	−4.3	2,630	2.8
Turkey	−7.4	3.5	7.4	1.3	−24.8	7.3	57.2	48.6	2.3	−0.8	33,412	6.9
Ukraine	9.1	4.5	2.9	5.8	2.2	6.3	8.8	3.2	3.7	4.8	4,370	2.3
Uruguay	−3.1	−10.0	−8.8	−10.0	−7.7	−25.0	5.6	18.3	−2.7	0.3	2,259	7.0
Uzbekistan	4.5	3.2	−5.4	−0.5	6.4	0.5	43.1	39.1	−1.0	−0.9	1,190	4.2
Venezuela, RB	2.7	−6.1	2.2	0.2	9.4	−0.5	6.8	33.7	3.1	5.8	11,829	5.5
Yugoslavia, Fed. Rep.	5.5	4.0	9.4	18.2	30.0	32.9	91.7	25.5	−5.5	−8.9	2,280	3.4
Zambia	4.9	4.3	29.0	1.6	27.2	−3.5	24.3	16.4	..	−17.2	..	..
Zimbabwe	−8.4	−5.6	−3.6	−0.8	−0.7	−4.8	70.1	107.5	..	−0.7	..	..

Note: Data for 2002 are the latest preliminary estimates and may differ from those in earlier World Bank publications.
Source: World Bank staff estimates.

4.b

Key macroeconomic indicators

	Nominal exchange rate			Real effective exchange rate		Money and quasi money		Gross domestic credit		Real interest rate		Short-term debt [a]
	local currency units per $	% change		1995 = 100		annual % growth		annual % growth		%		% of exports
	2002	2001	2002	2001	2002	2001	2002	2001	2002	2001	2002	2001
Malawi	87.1	−16.0	29.5	116.8	112.4	14.8	15.9	74.0	33.9	23.9	45.2	9.2
Malaysia	3.8	0.0	0.0	91.4	89.8	2.5	3.2	2.2	7.2	9.5	2.8	4.9
Mauritius	29.2	9.0	−3.9	..	..	10.9	12.3	14.8	8.3	18.0	15.5	30.0
Mexico	10.3	−4.5	12.8	..	..	14.1	2.3	2.6	14.0	7.9	5.7	9.7
Moldova	13.8	5.7	5.6	107.0	97.3	35.8	38.6	29.6	25.8	15.0	16.0	2.2
Morocco	10.2	8.9	−12.1	103.7	101.8	14.1	6.4	−1.2	4.6	10.5	..	1.7
Nicaragua	14.7	6.0	6.0	116.5	107.3	41.0	..	9.6	..	..	17.2	52.5
Nigeria	126.4	3.1	12.8	89.8	82.0	27.0	25.5	75.8	26.5	16.4	13.3	8.0
Pakistan	58.5	4.9	−3.8	87.2	87.8	11.7	18.1	−0.4	1.5	..	..	11.4
Panama	1.0	0.0	0.0	..	..	9.6	..	6.7	..	9.6	..	5.1
Paraguay	7,103.6	32.8	51.7	93.1	68.9	16.4	2.8	15.6	12.6	19.9	27.9	13.8
Peru	3.5	−2.4	2.0	..	..	2.1	6.1	1.2	1.6	18.9	11.6	30.5
Philippines	53.1	2.8	3.3	85.4	81.3	3.6	9.1	2.0	1.3	5.4	3.3	14.4
Poland	4.0	−3.8	−1.9	138.3	131.4	15.0	−1.3	11.8	..	13.5	6.6	12.7
Romania	33,500.0	21.9	6.0	108.8	110.8	46.2	36.7	26.9	36.8	..	..	3.8
Russian Federation	31.8	7.0	5.5	105.5	107.6	36.1	31.1	30.0	34.1	0.0	2.9	17.6
Senegal	625.5	5.6	−16.0	..	..	13.6	11.5	6.8	−6.1	..	..	12.5
Slovak Republic	40.0	2.3	−17.4	107.8	112.9	11.9	7.0	14.8	−4.3	5.5	4.3	19.9
South Africa	8.6	60.2	−28.8	73.2	67.5	16.7	17.1	20.2	13.2	5.9	9.2	22.3
Sri Lanka	96.7	12.8	3.8	..	..	14.4	..	18.2	..	5.5	..	6.1
Sudan	261.7	1.6	0.1	..	..	24.7	30.5	22.6	32.7	..	..	236.1
Swaziland	8.6	60.2	−28.8	..	..	10.7	17.9	71.4	−185.5	4.5	9.7	7.1
Syrian Arab Republic	11.2	0.0	0.0	..	..	23.5	..	18.6	..	2.9	3.2	70.2
Thailand	43.2	2.2	−2.4	..	..	2.2	0.6	−5.9	4.2	5.0	3.4	16.5
Trinidad and Tobago	6.3	−0.1	−0.1	124.1	126.6	6.9	..	−1.2	..	12.0	..	17.4
Tunisia	1.3	6.0	−9.1	97.3	97.5	10.7	7.8	8.9	6.2	..	..	6.5
Turkey	1,643,699.0	115.3	13.3	..	..	86.3	..	93.7	..	..	..	29.2
Ukraine	5.3	−2.5	0.6	119.6	110.1	43.0	42.3	18.7	28.9	21.5	16.5	3.5
Uruguay	27.2	18.0	84.2	112.0	75.1	19.0	40.7	7.7	50.0	43.6	..	71.4
Uzbekistan	..	..	..	..	..	..	..	..	..	..	..	15.7
Venezuela, RB	1,398.8	9.0	83.3	173.1	121.4	15.3	16.3	27.5	15.4	14.6	16.7	12.2
Yugoslavia, Fed. Rep.	..	..	..	..	..	..	..	..	..	..	..	107.3
Zambia	4,334.4	−7.9	13.2	122.4	97.7	13.6	34.6	−5.4	18.3	17.6	36.6	15.8
Zimbabwe	..	−0.1	..	..	..	128.5	170.2	83.9	126.9	−18.9	15.5	24.9

Note: Data for 2002 are preliminary and may not cover the entire year.
a. More recent data on short-term debt are available on a Web site maintained by the Bank for International Settlements, the International Monetary Fund, the Organisation for Economic Co-operation and Development, and the World Bank: http://www.oecd.org/dac/debt.
Source: International Monetary Fund, *International Financial Statistics*; World Bank, Debtor Reporting System.

	Gross domestic product average annual % growth		Agriculture average annual % growth		Industry average annual % growth		Manufacturing average annual % growth		Services average annual % growth	
	1980–90	1990–2001	1980–90	1990–2001	1980–90	1990–2001	1980–90	1990–2001	1980–90	1990–2001
Afghanistan	..	..	..	..	..	..	..	..	..	..
Albania	1.5	3.7	1.9	5.7	2.1	1.0	..	–5.0	–0.4	4.5
Algeria	2.7	2.0	4.1	3.7	2.6	1.9	4.1	–1.6	3.0	1.9
Angola	3.6	2.0	0.5	0.1	6.4	4.0	–11.1	0.6	1.3	–1.0
Argentina	–0.7	3.6	0.7	3.2	–1.3	2.9	–0.8	1.9	0.0	3.9
Armenia	..	–0.7	..	1.0	..	–6.1	..	–3.2	..	6.7
Australia	3.5	3.9	3.2	2.9	3.0	3.0	1.9	2.5	3.8	4.3
Austria	2.3	2.2	1.4	3.7	1.8	2.8	2.5	2.7	2.8	1.9
Azerbaijan	..	–0.3	..	–0.5	..	–4.0	..	–11.8	..	10.3
Bangladesh	4.3	4.9	2.7	3.1	4.9	7.2	3.0	7.0	4.4	4.6
Belarus	..	–0.8	..	–3.5	..	–0.7	..	0.4	..	0.5
Belgium	2.1	2.2	2.2	2.3	2.4	2.0	..	..	1.8	2.0
Benin	2.5	4.8	5.1	5.7	3.4	4.4	5.1	5.9	0.7	4.2
Bolivia	–0.2	3.8	..	2.8	..	3.7	..	3.6	..	4.1
Bosnia and Herzegovina	..	..	..	..	..	..	..	..	..	..
Botswana	11.0	5.2	2.5	–1.3	11.4	4.2	11.4	4.4	15.9	8.1
Brazil	2.7	2.8	2.8	3.3	2.0	2.4	1.6	1.5	3.3	2.9
Bulgaria	3.4	–1.2	–2.1	3.0	5.2	–4.0	..	..	4.7	–3.9
Burkina Faso	3.6	4.5	3.1	3.7	3.8	4.4	2.0	5.4	4.6	4.6
Burundi	4.4	–2.2	3.1	–1.1	4.5	–4.3	5.7	–8.0	5.6	–1.5
Cambodia	..	5.0	..	1.8	..	10.2	..	8.2	..	6.2
Cameroon	3.4	2.1	2.2	5.5	5.9	0.0	5.0	2.0	2.1	0.5
Canada	3.2	3.1	2.3	1.1	2.9	3.1	3.8	4.3	3.2	2.9
Central African Republic	1.4	2.1	1.6	3.9	1.4	1.0	5.0	0.3	1.0	–0.5
Chad	6.1	2.5	2.3	4.0	8.1	2.8	..	..	6.7	1.7
Chile	4.2	6.3	5.9	1.9	3.5	5.7	3.4	4.1	2.9	4.9
China	10.3	10.0	5.9	4.0	11.1	13.1	10.8	12.1	13.5	8.9
Hong Kong, China	6.9	3.8	..	..	..	..	..	..	..	..
Colombia	3.6	2.7	2.9	–1.8	5.0	1.4	3.5	–1.9	3.1	3.9
Congo, Dem. Rep.	1.6	–4.8	2.5	0.6	0.9	–7.8	1.6	..	1.3	–10.9
Congo, Rep.	3.3	1.4	3.4	1.4	5.2	3.0	6.8	–1.8	2.2	–0.2
Costa Rica	3.0	5.1	3.1	3.9	2.8	5.8	3.0	6.2	3.3	4.6
Côte d'Ivoire	0.7	3.1	0.3	3.2	4.4	4.0	3.0	2.9	–0.3	2.7
Croatia	..	1.1	..	–1.6	..	–1.7	..	–2.2	..	2.5
Cuba	..	4.2	..	5.2	..	6.6	..	6.3	..	2.5
Czech Republic	..	1.2	..	3.5	..	–0.3	..	..	..	2.0
Denmark	2.0	2.4	2.6	2.7	2.0	2.2	1.3	2.2	1.9	2.5
Dominican Republic	3.1	6.0	–1.0	3.9	3.0	6.9	2.3	4.7	4.2	6.0
Ecuador	2.0	1.8	4.4	1.5	1.2	2.6	0.0	2.1	1.7	1.2
Egypt, Arab Rep.	5.4	4.5	2.7	3.4	3.3	4.6	..	6.5	7.8	4.6
El Salvador	0.2	4.5	–1.1	1.1	0.1	5.1	–0.2	5.2	0.7	5.1
Eritrea	..	5.3	..	1.2	..	12.8	..	8.8	..	5.0
Estonia	2.2	0.2	..	–2.8	..	–1.9	..	3.4	..	2.2
Ethiopia	1.1	4.7	0.2	2.3	0.4	5.4	–0.9	5.4	3.1	7.2
Finland	3.3	2.9	–0.4	1.2	3.3	4.8	3.4	6.4	3.6	2.5
France	2.4	1.9	1.3	1.9	1.4	1.5	..	2.1	3.0	2.0
Gabon	0.9	2.6	1.2	–1.0	1.5	2.4	1.8	0.6	0.1	3.4
Gambia, The	3.6	3.4	0.9	5.2	4.7	2.5	7.8	1.3	2.7	3.7
Georgia	0.4	–5.6	..	..	..	..	..	..	..	..
Germany	2.3	1.5	1.7	1.7	1.1	0.0	..	–0.1	3.1	2.4
Ghana	3.0	4.2	1.0	3.4	3.3	2.8	3.9	–2.2	5.7	5.5
Greece	0.9	2.4	–0.1	0.7	1.3	1.0	..	..	0.9	2.8
Guatemala	0.8	4.1	1.2	2.8	–0.2	4.1	0.0	2.7	0.9	4.6
Guinea	..	4.2	..	4.2	..	4.7	..	4.3	..	3.4
Guinea-Bissau	4.0	1.0	4.7	3.6	2.2	–3.1	..	–2.2	3.5	–0.2
Haiti	–0.2	–0.4	–0.1	–2.8	–1.7	1.6	–1.7	–9.3	0.9	0.2

	Gross domestic product		Agriculture		Industry		Manufacturing		Services	
	average annual % growth		average annual % growth		average annual % growth		average annual % growth		average annual % growth	
	1980–90	1990–2001	1980–90	1990–2001	1980–90	1990–2001	1980–90	1990–2001	1980–90	1990–2001
Honduras	2.7	3.1	2.7	1.9	3.3	3.6	3.7	4.1	2.5	3.7
Hungary	1.3	1.9	1.7	–2.2	0.2	3.8	..	7.9	2.1	1.4
India	5.7	5.9	3.1	3.0	6.9	6.1	7.4	6.7	6.9	7.9
Indonesia	6.1	3.8	3.6	1.9	7.3	4.8	12.8	6.3	6.5	3.6
Iran, Islamic Rep.	1.7	3.6	4.5	4.0	3.3	–2.8	4.5	5.1	–1.0	8.5
Iraq	–6.8	..	..	..	..	..	..	..	..	..
Ireland	3.2	7.7	..	..	..	..	..	..	..	..
Israel	3.5	4.7	..	..	..	..	..	..	..	..
Italy	2.5	1.6	–0.5	1.4	1.8	1.2	2.1	1.5	3.0	1.8
Jamaica	2.0	0.2	2.8	0.6	2.4	–0.4	2.7	–1.7	1.6	0.6
Japan	4.1	1.3	1.3	–3.1	4.1	–0.2	..	0.7	4.2	2.3
Jordan	2.5	4.8	6.8	–2.0	1.7	4.7	0.5	5.4	2.3	5.0
Kazakhstan	..	–2.8	..	–6.5	..	–6.9	..	..	..	3.1
Kenya	4.2	2.0	3.3	1.2	3.9	1.6	4.9	2.0	4.9	3.1
Korea, Dem. Rep.	..	..	..	..	..	..	..	..	..	..
Korea, Rep.	8.9	5.7	3.0	2.0	11.4	6.3	12.1	7.6	8.4	5.6
Kuwait	1.3	3.4	14.7	..	1.0	..	2.3	..	2.1	..
Kyrgyz Republic	..	–2.9	..	2.1	..	–8.5	..	–14.1	..	–3.9
Lao PDR	3.7	6.4	3.5	4.9	6.1	10.9	8.9	12.6	3.3	6.5
Latvia	3.5	–2.2	2.3	–5.9	4.3	–6.7	4.4	–6.2	3.3	3.1
Lebanon	..	5.4	..	1.8	..	–1.6	..	–4.3	..	4.1
Lesotho	4.6	4.0	2.8	1.7	3.9	7.8	8.5	6.2	5.1	3.0
Liberia	–7.0	6.2	..	6.5	..	–11.2	..	..	..	–12.5
Libya	–7.0	..	..	..	..	..	..	..	..	..
Lithuania	..	–2.2	..	–0.3	..	2.8	..	4.4	..	4.3
Macedonia, FYR	..	–0.2	..	–0.3	..	–2.3	..	–4.5	..	1.1
Madagascar	1.1	2.4	2.5	1.9	0.9	2.8	2.1	2.6	0.3	2.8
Malawi	2.5	3.6	2.0	7.2	2.9	1.8	3.6	0.4	3.3	2.3
Malaysia	5.3	6.5	3.4	0.3	6.8	8.0	9.3	8.8	4.9	6.7
Mali	0.8	4.1	3.3	2.9	4.3	7.5	6.8	2.8	1.9	3.1
Mauritania	1.8	4.2	1.7	4.8	4.9	2.3	–2.1	0.0	0.4	5.2
Mauritius	6.0	5.2	2.6	–0.2	9.2	5.5	10.4	5.3	5.1	6.3
Mexico	1.1	3.1	0.8	1.6	1.1	3.7	1.5	4.2	1.4	3.0
Moldova	2.8	–8.4	..	–9.5	..	–11.5	..	–3.4	..	0.3
Mongolia	5.4	1.2	1.4	3.2	6.6	–0.1	..	..	8.4	0.4
Morocco	4.2	2.5	6.7	–0.6	3.0	3.2	4.1	2.8	4.2	3.0
Mozambique	–0.1	6.7	6.6	4.9	–4.5	15.2	..	18.0	9.1	1.9
Myanmar	0.6	7.4	0.5	5.7	0.5	10.5	–0.2	7.9	0.8	7.2
Namibia	1.0	4.6	2.5	4.1	–0.2	2.1	3.1	2.6	2.2	4.3
Nepal	4.6	4.9	4.0	2.6	8.8	6.9	9.3	8.4	3.9	6.2
Netherlands	2.4	2.9	3.6	2.0	1.6	1.7	..	..	2.6	3.2
New Zealand	1.9	3.1	4.0	3.4	1.0	2.3	..	2.4	2.1	3.5
Nicaragua	–1.9	2.8	–2.2	5.2	–2.3	3.2	–3.2	1.3	–1.5	1.2
Niger	–0.1	2.5	1.7	3.2	–1.7	2.1	–2.7	2.7	–0.7	2.2
Nigeria	1.6	2.5	3.3	3.5	–1.1	1.0	0.7	1.2	3.7	2.9
Norway	2.8	3.5	0.1	2.4	4.0	3.9	0.2	2.3	2.9	3.4
Oman	8.4	4.3	7.9	..	10.3	..	20.6	..	5.9	..
Pakistan	6.3	3.7	4.0	4.1	7.7	4.0	8.1	3.9	6.8	4.4
Panama	0.5	3.8	2.5	2.2	–1.3	4.7	0.4	1.8	0.7	3.8
Papua New Guinea	1.9	3.6	1.8	3.5	1.9	4.6	0.1	4.4	2.0	3.0
Paraguay	2.5	2.1	3.6	2.3	0.3	3.1	4.0	0.8	3.1	1.4
Peru	–0.1	4.3	3.0	5.6	0.1	5.0	–0.2	3.5	–0.4	3.7
Philippines	1.0	3.3	1.0	1.8	–0.9	3.2	0.2	3.0	2.8	4.1
Poland	..	4.5	..	–0.2	..	4.2	..	7.1	..	4.2
Portugal	3.2	2.7	1.5	–0.2	3.4	3.0	..	2.6	2.5	2.2
Puerto Rico	4.0	4.3	1.8	..	3.6	..	3.6	..	4.6	..

	Gross domestic product		Agriculture		Industry		Manufacturing		Services	
	average annual % growth		average annual % growth		average annual % growth		average annual % growth		average annual % growth	
	1980–90	1990–2001	1980–90	1990–2001	1980–90	1990–2001	1980–90	1990–2001	1980–90	1990–2001
Romania	1.0	−0.4	..	..	..	..	..	..	..	..
Russian Federation	..	−3.7	..	−4.5	..	−6.1	..	..	..	−0.3
Rwanda	2.2	0.8	0.5	3.4	2.5	−2.3	2.6	−4.8	3.6	−0.2
Saudi Arabia	0.0	1.5	13.4	..	−2.3	..	7.5	..	1.3	..
Senegal	3.1	3.9	2.8	2.3	4.3	5.1	4.6	4.2	2.8	4.0
Sierra Leone	0.5	−4.4	3.1	−4.5	1.7	−4.6	..	5.0	−0.9	−3.4
Singapore	6.7	7.4	−5.3	−2.1	5.2	7.2	6.6	6.5	7.6	7.6
Slovak Republic	2.0	2.1	1.6	1.6	2.0	−2.1	..	4.3	0.9	5.6
Slovenia	..	2.9	..	−0.1	..	2.9	..	4.0	..	3.9
Somalia	2.1	..	3.3	..	1.0	..	−1.7	..	0.9	..
South Africa	1.0	2.1	2.9	0.8	0.7	1.0	1.1	1.2	2.4	2.7
Spain	3.1	2.7	3.1	1.0	2.7	2.3	..	..	3.3	2.9
Sri Lanka	4.0	5.0	2.2	1.7	4.6	6.5	6.3	7.5	4.7	5.7
Sudan	2.3	5.6	1.8	9.0	1.6	6.8	4.8	4.6	4.5	2.7
Swaziland	6.7	3.2	2.3	1.5	12.0	3.6	15.7	2.7	4.8	3.4
Sweden	2.5	2.1	1.4	0.0	2.8	3.6	..	..	2.4	1.8
Switzerland	2.0	1.0	..	..	..	..	..	..	..	..
Syrian Arab Republic	1.5	4.8	−0.6	4.9	6.6	9.3	..	10.2	1.6	3.0
Tajikistan	2.0	−8.5	−2.8	−5.8	5.5	−13.2	5.6	−12.6	3.4	−1.1
Tanzania [a]	..	3.2	..	3.3	..	3.6	..	3.0	..	3.0
Thailand	7.6	3.8	3.9	1.7	9.8	5.4	9.5	6.5	7.3	3.8
Togo	1.7	2.2	5.6	3.8	1.1	2.7	1.7	3.9	−0.3	0.4
Trinidad and Tobago	−0.8	3.6	−5.9	3.4	−5.5	4.2	−10.1	6.7	6.7	3.1
Tunisia	3.3	4.7	2.8	2.4	3.1	4.7	3.7	5.6	3.5	5.4
Turkey	5.3	3.3	1.2	1.1	7.7	3.4	7.9	4.1	4.5	3.5
Turkmenistan	..	−2.8	..	−3.2	..	−6.7	..	..	..	−3.2
Uganda	2.9	6.8	2.1	3.8	5.0	11.9	3.7	12.8	2.8	7.7
Ukraine	..	−7.9	..	−4.9	..	−9.5	..	−9.0	..	−0.9
United Arab Emirates	−2.1	2.9	9.6	..	−4.2	..	3.1	..	3.6	..
United Kingdom	3.2	2.7	2.4	−1.0	3.3	1.3	..	..	3.1	3.4
United States	3.5	3.4	3.2	3.5	3.0	3.7	..	4.3	3.4	3.7
Uruguay	0.5	2.8	0.1	2.0	−0.2	0.7	0.4	−0.5	1.0	4.0
Uzbekistan	..	0.4	..	0.9	..	−2.6	..	..	..	1.6
Venezuela, RB	1.1	1.5	3.1	1.4	1.7	2.6	4.4	0.8	0.5	0.5
Vietnam	4.6	7.7	2.8	4.2	4.4	11.6	1.9	11.2	7.1	7.3
West Bank and Gaza	..	1.2	..	−4.2	..	0.8	..	3.6	..	2.8
Yemen, Rep.	..	5.8	..	5.6	..	7.5	..	4.1	..	5.0
Yugoslavia, Fed. Rep.	..	..	..	..	..	..	..	..	..	..
Zambia	1.0	0.8	3.6	3.9	1.0	−3.6	4.1	1.1	−0.2	2.8
Zimbabwe	3.6	1.8	3.1	3.7	3.2	−0.4	2.8	−0.8	3.0	2.5
World	**3.3 w**	**2.7 w**	**2.6 w**	**1.8 w**	**3.1 w**	**2.1 w**	**.. w**	**2.9 w**	**3.5 w**	**3.1 w**
Low income	4.5	3.4	3.0	2.6	5.5	2.9	7.7	3.0	5.5	5.1
Middle income	2.9	3.4	3.4	2.1	3.2	3.7	3.7	5.7	3.2	3.7
Lower middle income	4.0	3.7	3.9	2.1	5.2	4.2	6.3	7.9	5.0	4.1
Upper middle income	1.7	3.1	2.3	2.2	1.5	3.0	1.6	2.9	2.0	3.3
Low & middle income	3.2	3.4	3.3	2.2	3.6	3.6	4.2	5.2	3.6	3.9
East Asia & Pacific	7.5	7.5	4.6	3.2	8.4	10.1	9.5	10.0	8.6	6.5
Europe & Central Asia	2.1	−1.0	..	−1.9	..	−3.0	..	..	..	1.8
Latin America & Carib.	1.7	3.2	2.3	2.4	1.4	2.9	1.4	2.1	1.9	3.2
Middle East & N. Africa	2.0	3.0	4.0	3.0	..	..	..	4.2	..	..
South Asia	5.6	5.5	3.2	3.1	6.8	6.0	7.1	6.4	6.5	7.0
Sub-Saharan Africa	1.6	2.6	2.2	2.8	1.2	1.7	1.7	1.6	2.4	2.8
High income	3.3	2.5	1.9	1.1	3.0	1.8	..	2.4	3.5	3.0
Europe EMU	2.4	2.0	1.3	1.6	1.6	1.1	..	1.2	2.9	2.3

a. Data cover mainland Tanzania only.

Growth of output | 4.1

An economy's growth is measured by the change in the volume of its output or in the real incomes of persons resident in the economy. The 1993 United Nations System of National Accounts (1993 SNA) offers three plausible indicators from which to calculate growth: the volume of gross domestic product (GDP), real gross domestic income, and real gross national income. The volume of GDP is the sum of value added, measured at constant prices, by households, government, and the industries operating in the economy. This year's edition of the *World Development Indicators* continues to follow the practice of past editions, measuring the growth of the economy by the change in GDP measured at constant prices.

Each industry's contribution to the growth in the economy's output is measured by the growth in value added by the industry. In principle, value added in constant prices can be estimated by measuring the quantity of goods and services produced in a period, valuing them at an agreed set of base year prices, and subtracting the cost of intermediate inputs, also in constant prices. This double deflation method, recommended by the 1993 SNA and its predecessors, requires detailed information on the structure of prices of inputs and outputs.

In many industries, however, value added is extrapolated from the base year using single volume indexes of outputs or, more rarely, inputs. Particularly in the service industries, including most of government, value added in constant prices is often imputed from labor inputs, such as real wages or the number of employees. In the absence of well-defined measures of output, measuring the growth of services remains difficult.

Moreover, technical progress can lead to improvements in production processes and in the quality of goods and services that, if not properly accounted for, can distort measures of value added and thus of growth. When inputs are used to estimate output, as is the case for nonmarket services, unmeasured technical progress leads to underestimates of the volume of output. Similarly, unmeasured changes in the quality of goods and services produced lead to underestimates of the value of output and value added. The result can be underestimates of growth and productivity improvement, and overestimates of inflation. These issues are highly complex, and only a few high-income countries have attempted to introduce any GDP adjustments for these factors.

Informal economic activities pose a particular measurement problem, especially in developing countries, where much economic activity may go unrecorded.

Obtaining a complete picture of the economy requires estimating household outputs produced for home use, sales in informal markets, and barter exchanges, and illicit or deliberately unreported activities. The consistency and completeness of such estimates depend on the skill and methods of the compiling statisticians and the resources available to them.

Rebasing national accounts

When countries rebase their national accounts, they update the weights assigned to various components to better reflect the current pattern of production or uses of output. The new base year should represent normal operation of the economy—that is, it should be a year without major shocks or distortions—but the choice of base year is often constrained by lack of data. Some developing countries have not rebased their national accounts for many years. Using an old base year can be misleading because implicit price and volume weights become progressively less relevant and useful.

To obtain comparable series of constant price data, the World Bank rescales GDP and value added by industrial origin to a common reference year, currently 1995. This process gives rise to a discrepancy between the rescaled GDP and the sum of the rescaled components. Because allocating the discrepancy would give rise to distortions in the growth rates, the discrepancy is left unallocated. As a result, the weighted average of the growth rates of the components generally will not equal the GDP growth rate.

Growth rates of GDP and its components are calculated using constant price data in the local currency. Regional and income group growth rates are calculated after converting local currencies to constant price U.S. dollars using an exchange rate in the common reference year. The growth rates in the table are annual average compound growth rates. Methods of computing growth rates and the alternative conversion factor are described in *Statistical methods*.

Changes in the System of National Accounts

The *World Development Indicators* adopted the terminology of the 1993 SNA in 2001. Although most countries continue to compile their national accounts according to the SNA version 3 (referred to as the 1968 SNA), more and more are adopting the 1993 SNA. Some low-income countries still use concepts from the even older 1953 SNA guidelines, including valuations such as factor cost, in describing major economic aggregates. Countries that use the 1993 SNA are identified in *Primary data documentation*.

- **Gross domestic product** (GDP) at purchaser prices is the sum of gross value added by all resident producers in the economy plus any product taxes (less subsidies) not included in the valuation of output. It is calculated without making deductions for depreciation of fabricated capital assets or for depletion and degradation of natural resources. Value added is the net output of an industry after adding up all outputs and subtracting intermediate inputs. The industrial origin of value added is determined by the International Standard Industrial Classification (ISIC) revision 3. • **Agriculture** corresponds to ISIC divisions 1–5 and includes forestry and fishing. • **Industry** comprises mining, manufacturing (also reported as a separate subgroup), construction, electricity, water, and gas (ISIC divisions 10–45). • **Manufacturing** refers to industries belonging to divisions 15–37. • **Services** correspond to ISIC divisions 50–99. This sector is derived as a residual (from GDP less agriculture and industry) and may not properly reflect the sum of service output, including banking and financial services. For some countries it includes product taxes (minus subsidies) and may also include statistical discrepancies.

The national accounts data for most developing countries are collected from national statistical organizations and central banks by visiting and resident World Bank missions. The data for high-income economies come from data files of the Organisation for Economic Co-operation and Development (for information on the OECD's national accounts series, see its monthly *Main Economic Indicators*). The World Bank rescales constant price data to a common reference year. The complete national accounts time series is available on the *World Development Indicators 2003* CD-ROM. The United Nations Statistics Division publishes detailed national accounts for United Nations member countries in *National Accounts Statistics: Main Aggregates and Detailed Tables* and publishes updates in the *Monthly Bulletin of Statistics*.

4.2 | Structure of output

	Gross domestic product		Agriculture value added		Industry value added		Manufacturing value added		Services value added	
	$ millions		% of GDP		% of GDP		% of GDP		% of GDP	
	1990	2001	1990	2001	1990	2001	1990	2001	1990	2001
Afghanistan	..	..	..	..	..	..	..	..	..	..
Albania	2,102	4,114	36	50	48	23	42	13	16	26
Algeria	62,045	54,680	11	10	48	55	11	8	40	36
Angola	10,260	9,471	18	8	41	67	5	4	41	25
Argentina	141,352	268,638	8	5	36	27	27	17	56	69
Armenia	4,124	2,118	17	28	52	34	33	22	31	38
Australia	310,202	368,726	4	4	29	26	14	13	67	70
Austria	161,692	188,546	4	2	34	33	23	22	62	65
Azerbaijan	..	5,585	..	17	..	46	..	6	..	36
Bangladesh	30,129	46,706	29	23	21	25	13	15	50	52
Belarus	35,203	12,219	24	11	47	39	39	33	29	50
Belgium	197,174	229,610	2	2	33	27	..	20	65	71
Benin	1,845	2,372	36	36	13	14	8	9	51	50
Bolivia	4,868	7,969	17	16	35	29	18	15	48	56
Bosnia and Herzegovina	..	4,769	..	15	..	31	..	16	..	55
Botswana	3,791	5,196	5	2	57	47	5	4	39	51
Brazil	464,989	502,509	8	9	39	34	25	21	53	57
Bulgaria	20,726	13,553	17	14	49	29	..	18	34	57
Burkina Faso	2,765	2,486	32	38	22	21	16	15	45	41
Burundi	1,132	689	56	50	19	19	13	9	25	31
Cambodia	1,115	3,404	56	37	11	22	5	..	33	41
Cameroon	11,152	8,501	25	43	29	20	15	11	46	38
Canada	574,204	694,475	3	..	32	..	17	..	65	..
Central African Republic	1,488	967	48	55	20	21	11	9	33	24
Chad	1,739	1,600	29	39	18	14	14	10	53	48
Chile	30,323	66,450	9	9	41	34	20	16	50	57
China	354,644	1,159,031	27	15	42	51	33	35	31	34
Hong Kong, China	74,782	161,896	0	0	25	14	18	6	74	86
Colombia	40,274	82,411	17	13	38	30	21	16	45	57
Congo, Dem. Rep.	9,348	5,187	30	56	28	19	11	4	42	25
Congo, Rep.	2,799	2,751	13	6	41	66	8	4	46	28
Costa Rica	5,713	16,108	18	9	29	29	22	21	53	62
Côte d'Ivoire	10,796	10,411	32	24	23	22	21	19	44	54
Croatia	18,156	20,260	10	9	34	33	28	23	56	58
Cuba	..	..	..	7	..	46	..	37	..	47
Czech Republic	34,880	56,784	6	4	49	41	..	..	45	55
Denmark	133,361	161,542	4	3	27	26	18	17	69	71
Dominican Republic	7,074	21,211	13	11	31	33	18	16	55	55
Ecuador	10,686	17,982	13	11	38	33	19	18	49	56
Egypt, Arab Rep.	43,130	98,476	19	17	29	33	18	19	52	50
El Salvador	4,807	13,739	17	9	26	30	22	23	57	61
Eritrea	451	688	31	19	12	22	8	11	57	59
Estonia	6,760	5,525	17	6	50	29	42	19	34	65
Ethiopia	6,842	6,233	49	52	13	11	8	7	38	37
Finland	136,794	120,855	7	3	34	33	23	26	60	63
France	1,215,893	1,309,807	4	3	30	26	21	18	66	72
Gabon	5,952	4,334	7	8	43	51	6	5	50	42
Gambia, The	317	390	29	40	13	14	7	5	58	46
Georgia	12,171	3,138	32	21	33	23	24	..	35	57
Germany	1,688,568	1,846,069	2	1	38	31	28	24	60	68
Ghana	5,886	5,301	45	36	17	25	10	9	38	39
Greece	84,075	117,169	11	8	28	21	..	12	61	71
Guatemala	7,650	20,496	26	23	20	19	15	13	54	58
Guinea	2,818	2,989	24	24	33	38	5	4	43	38
Guinea-Bissau	244	199	61	56	19	13	8	10	21	31
Haiti	2,864	3,737	..	..	..	..	..	..	..	..

Structure of output 4.2

	Gross domestic product		Agriculture value added		Industry value added		Manufacturing value added		Services value added	
	$ millions		% of GDP		% of GDP		% of GDP		% of GDP	
	1990	2001	1990	2001	1990	2001	1990	2001	1990	2001
Honduras	3,049	6,386	22	14	26	32	16	20	51	55
Hungary	33,056	51,926	15	..	39	..	23	..	46	..
India	316,937	477,342	31	25	28	26	17	16	41	48
Indonesia	114,426	145,306	20	16	38	47	18	26	42	37
Iran, Islamic Rep.	120,404	114,052	24	19	29	33	12	16	48	48
Iraq	48,657	..	..	..	..	..	..	..	..	..
Ireland	47,301	103,298	9	4	35	42	28	33	56	55
Israel	52,490	108,325	..	..	..	..	..	..	..	..
Italy	1,102,437	1,088,754	4	3	34	29	25	21	63	68
Jamaica	4,592	7,784	7	6	40	31	19	13	52	63
Japan	3,052,058	4,141,431	2	1	39	32	27	22	58	67
Jordan	4,020	8,829	8	2	28	25	15	15	64	73
Kazakhstan	40,304	22,389	27	9	45	39	9	16	29	52
Kenya	8,533	11,396	29	19	19	18	12	13	52	63
Korea, Dem. Rep.	..	..	..	..	..	..	..	..	..	..
Korea, Rep.	252,622	422,167	9	4	43	41	29	30	48	54
Kuwait	18,428	32,806	1	..	52	..	12	..	47	..
Kyrgyz Republic	2,389	1,525	34	38	36	27	28	8	30	35
Lao PDR	865	1,761	61	51	15	23	10	18	24	26
Latvia	12,490	7,549	22	5	46	26	34	15	32	69
Lebanon	2,838	16,709	..	12	..	22	..	10	..	66
Lesotho	622	797	23	16	26	42	6	14	50	42
Liberia	384	523	..	..	..	..	..	..	..	..
Libya	28,905	34,137	..	..	..	..	..	..	..	..
Lithuania	14,821	11,992	27	7	31	35	21	23	42	58
Macedonia, FYR	4,472	3,426	9	11	46	31	36	20	46	58
Madagascar	3,081	4,604	29	30	13	14	11	12	59	56
Malawi	1,881	1,749	45	34	29	18	19	13	26	48
Malaysia	44,024	88,041	15	9	42	49	24	31	43	42
Mali	2,421	2,647	46	38	16	26	9	4	39	36
Mauritania	1,020	1,007	30	21	29	29	10	8	42	50
Mauritius	2,383	4,500	13	6	33	31	25	23	54	62
Mexico	262,710	617,820	8	4	28	27	21	19	64	69
Moldova	10,583	1,479	51	26	31	24	..	18	18	50
Mongolia	..	1,049	17	30	30	17	..	5	52	53
Morocco	25,821	34,219	18	16	32	31	18	17	50	53
Mozambique	2,463	3,607	37	22	18	26	10	12	44	52
Myanmar	..	..	57	57	11	10	8	7	32	33
Namibia	2,786	3,100	11	11	31	33	15	11	58	56
Nepal	3,628	5,562	52	39	16	22	6	9	32	39
Netherlands	294,401	380,137	4	3	30	27	..	17	65	70
New Zealand	43,618	50,425	7	..	28	..	19	..	65	..
Nicaragua	1,009	..	31	..	21	..	17	..	48	..
Niger	2,481	1,954	35	40	16	17	7	7	49	43
Nigeria	28,472	41,373	33	30	41	46	6	4	26	25
Norway	115,453	166,145	4	2	35	43	13	..	61	55
Oman	10,535	19,826	3	..	58	..	4	..	39	..
Pakistan	40,010	58,668	26	25	25	23	17	16	49	52
Panama	5,313	10,171	9	7	15	16	9	7	76	77
Papua New Guinea	3,221	2,959	29	26	30	42	9	8	41	32
Paraguay	5,265	7,206	28	20	25	26	17	13	47	54
Peru	26,294	54,047	9	9	27	30	18	15	64	62
Philippines	44,331	71,438	22	15	34	31	25	22	44	54
Poland	58,976	176,256	8	4	50	37	..	20	42	59
Portugal	71,466	109,803	9	4	32	30	22	19	60	66
Puerto Rico	30,604	67,897	1	1	42	43	40	40	57	56

	Gross domestic product ($ millions)		Agriculture value added (% of GDP)		Industry value added (% of GDP)		Manufacturing value added (% of GDP)		Services value added (% of GDP)	
	1990	2001	1990	2001	1990	2001	1990	2001	1990	2001
Romania	38,299	38,718	24	15	50	35	..	..	26	50
Russian Federation	579,068	309,951	17	7	48	37	..	..	35	56
Rwanda	2,584	1,703	33	40	25	22	18	10	43	38
Saudi Arabia	104,670	186,489	6	..	50	..	8	..	43	..
Senegal	5,699	4,645	20	18	19	27	13	18	61	55
Sierra Leone	650	749	32	50	13	30	5	5	55	20
Singapore	36,670	85,648	0	0	34	32	27	23	65	68
Slovak Republic	15,485	20,459	7	4	59	29	..	21	33	67
Slovenia	12,673	18,810	6	3	46	38	35	28	49	58
Somalia	917	..	65	..	..	..	5	..	..	..
South Africa	111,997	113,274	5	3	40	31	24	19	55	66
Spain	509,968	581,823	6	4	35	30	..	19	59	66
Sri Lanka	8,032	15,911	26	19	26	27	15	16	48	54
Sudan	13,167	12,525	..	39	..	19	..	10	..	42
Swaziland	882	1,255	13	17	42	44	35	36	45	39
Sweden	238,327	209,814	3	2	32	27	..	..	64	71
Switzerland	228,415	247,091	..	..	..	..	..	..	..	..
Syrian Arab Republic	12,309	19,495	28	22	24	28	20	25	48	50
Tajikistan	4,339	1,056	33	29	38	29	25	25	29	41
Tanzania[a]	4,259	9,341	46	45	18	16	9	7	36	39
Thailand	85,345	114,681	12	10	37	40	27	32	50	49
Togo	1,628	1,259	34	39	23	21	10	10	44	39
Trinidad and Tobago	5,068	8,842	3	2	46	44	9	8	51	55
Tunisia	12,291	19,990	16	12	30	29	17	18	54	60
Turkey	150,642	147,683	18	14	30	26	20	15	52	61
Turkmenistan	..	5,962	32	29	30	51	..	..	38	20
Uganda	4,304	5,675	57	36	11	21	6	10	32	43
Ukraine	91,327	37,588	26	17	45	39	44	23	30	44
United Arab Emirates	34,132	..	2	..	64	..	8	..	35	..
United Kingdom	989,564	1,424,094	2	1	35	27	23	19	63	72
United States	5,750,800	10,065,265	2	2	28	25	20	17	70	73
Uruguay	9,287	18,666	9	6	35	26	28	16	56	67
Uzbekistan	23,673	11,270	33	34	33	23	..	9	34	43
Venezuela, RB	48,593	124,948	5	5	50	50	20	20	44	45
Vietnam	6,472	32,723	39	24	23	38	12	20	39	39
West Bank and Gaza	..	3,972	..	8	..	27	..	15	..	66
Yemen, Rep.	4,828	9,276	24	16	27	50	9	7	49	35
Yugoslavia, Fed. Rep.	..	10,861	..	15	..	32	..	..	..	53
Zambia	3,288	3,639	21	22	51	26	36	11	28	52
Zimbabwe	8,784	9,057	16	18	33	24	23	14	50	58
World	**21,814,741 t**	**31,121,436 t**	**5 w**	**4 w**	**34 w**	**30 w**	**22 w**	**20 w**	**60 w**	**66 w**
Low income	872,667	1,082,138	29	24	30	32	16	18	40	45
Middle income	3,283,362	5,156,519	14	10	39	36	24	23	47	54
Lower middle income	1,890,857	2,739,311	20	12	39	40	26	26	41	48
Upper middle income	1,406,681	2,422,397	8	7	39	33	23	20	53	60
Low & middle income	4,151,747	6,237,602	16	12	38	36	23	22	46	52
East Asia & Pacific	674,031	1,664,945	24	15	39	49	28	32	37	36
Europe & Central Asia	1,240,117	993,753	17	10	44	34	..	..	39	55
Latin America & Carib.	1,134,854	1,968,782	9	8	36	32	24	20	55	60
Middle East & N. Africa	413,007	698,444	15	..	39	..	12	..	47	..
South Asia	404,808	613,755	30	25	27	26	17	15	43	49
Sub-Saharan Africa	296,694	315,705	18	16	34	28	17	15	48	56
High income	17,666,811	24,886,672	3	2	33	29	22	20	64	70
Europe EMU	5,534,967	6,110,901	3	2	34	29	25	22	62	69

a. Data cover mainland Tanzania only.

Structure of output | 4.2

About the data

An economy's gross domestic product (GDP) represents the sum of value added by all producers in that economy. Value added is the value of the gross output of producers less the value of intermediate goods and services consumed in production, before taking account of the consumption of fixed capital in the production process. Since 1968 the System of National Accounts has called for estimates of value added to be valued at either basic prices (excluding net taxes on products) or producer prices (including net taxes on products paid by the producers but excluding sales or value added taxes). Both valuations exclude transport charges that are invoiced separately by the producers. Some countries, however, report such data at purchaser prices—the prices at which final sales are made (including transport charges)—which may affect estimates of the distribution of output. Total GDP as shown in the table and elsewhere in this book is measured at purchaser prices. Value added by industry is normally measured at basic prices. When value added is measured at producer prices, this is noted in *Primary data documentation*.

While GDP estimates based on the production approach are generally more reliable than estimates compiled from the income or expenditure side, different countries use different definitions, methods, and reporting standards. World Bank staff review the quality of national accounts data and sometimes make adjustments to increase consistency with international guidelines. Nevertheless, significant discrepancies remain between international standards and actual practice. Many statistical offices, especially those in developing countries, face severe limitations in the resources, time, training, and budgets required to produce reliable and comprehensive series of national accounts statistics.

Data problems in measuring output

Among the difficulties faced by compilers of national accounts is the extent of unreported economic activity in the informal or secondary economy. In developing countries a large share of agricultural output is either not exchanged (because it is consumed within the household) or not exchanged for money.

Agricultural production often must be estimated indirectly, using a combination of methods involving estimates of inputs, yields, and area under cultivation. This approach sometimes leads to crude approximations that can differ from the true values over time and across crops for reasons other than climatic conditions or farming techniques. Similarly, agricultural inputs that cannot easily be allocated to specific outputs are frequently "netted out" using equally crude and ad hoc approximations. For further discussion of the measure-

ment of agricultural production, see *About the data* for table 3.3.

Ideally, industrial output should be measured through regular censuses and surveys of firms. But in most developing countries such surveys are infrequent, so earlier survey results must be extrapolated using an appropriate indicator. The choice of sampling unit, which may be the enterprise (where responses may be based on financial records) or the establishment (where production units may be recorded separately), also affects the quality of the data. Moreover, much industrial production is organized in unincorporated or owner-operated ventures that are not captured by surveys aimed at the formal sector. Even in large industries, where regular surveys are more likely, evasion of excise and other taxes and nondisclosure of income lower the estimates of value added. Such problems become more acute as countries move from state control of industry to private enterprise, because new firms enter business and growing numbers of established firms fail to report. In accordance with the System of National Accounts, output should include all such unreported activity as well as the value of illegal activities and other unrecorded, informal, or small-scale operations. Data on these activities need to be collected using techniques other than conventional surveys of firms.

In industries dominated by large organizations and enterprises, such as public utilities, data on output, employment, and wages are usually readily available and reasonably reliable. But in the service industry the many self-employed workers and one-person businesses are sometimes difficult to locate, and they have little incentive to respond to surveys, let alone report their full earnings. Compounding these problems are the many forms of economic activity that go unrecorded, including the work that women and children do for little or no pay. For further discussion of the problems of using national accounts data, see Srinivasan (1994) and Heston (1994).

Dollar conversion

To produce national accounts aggregates that are measured in the same standard monetary units, the value of output must be converted to a single common currency. The World Bank conventionally uses the U.S. dollar and applies the average official exchange rate reported by the International Monetary Fund for the year shown. An alternative conversion factor is applied if the official exchange rate is judged to diverge by an exceptionally large margin from the rate effectively applied to transactions in foreign currencies and traded products.

Definitions

- **Gross domestic product** (GDP) at purchaser prices is the sum of gross value added by all resident producers in the economy plus any product taxes (less subsidies) not included in the valuation of output. It is calculated without making deductions for depreciation of fabricated assets or for depletion and degradation of natural resources. • **Value added** is the net output of an industry after adding up all outputs and subtracting intermediate inputs. The industrial origin of value added is determined by the International Standard Industrial Classification (ISIC) revision 3. • **Agriculture** corresponds to ISIC divisions 1–5 and includes forestry and fishing. • **Industry** comprises mining, manufacturing (also reported as a separate subgroup), construction, electricity, water, and gas (ISIC divisions 10–45). • **Manufacturing** refers to industries belonging to divisions 15–37. • **Services** correspond to ISIC divisions 50–99. This sector is derived as a residual (from GDP less agriculture and industry) and may not properly reflect the sum of service output, including banking and financial services. For some countries it includes product taxes (minus subsidies) and may also include statistical discrepancies.

Data sources

The national accounts data for most developing countries are collected from national statistical organizations and central banks by visiting and resident World Bank missions. The data for high-income economies come from data files of the Organisation for Economic Co-operation and Development (for information on the OECD's national accounts series, see its monthly *Main Economic Indicators*). The United Nations Statistics Division publishes detailed national accounts for United Nations member countries in *National Accounts Statistics: Main Aggregates and Detailed Tables* and publishes updates in the *Monthly Bulletin of Statistics*.

4.3 Structure of manufacturing

	Value added in manufacturing		Food, beverages, and tobacco		Textiles and clothing		Machinery and transport equipment		Chemicals		Other manufacturing [a]	
	$ millions		% of total		% of total		% of total		% of total		% of total	
	1990	2000	1990	2000	1990	2000	1990	2000	1990	2000	1990	2000
Afghanistan	..	..	..	..	..	..	..	..	..	..	..	..
Albania	878	495	24	..	33	..	..	..	..	..	44	..
Algeria	6,452	3,897	13	..	17	..	..	..	..	..	70	..
Angola	513	264	..	..	..	..	..	..	..	..	..	..
Argentina	37,868	46,877	20	..	10	..	13	..	12	..	46	..
Armenia	1,243	418	..	..	..	..	..	..	..	..	..	..
Australia	38,868	45,376	18	..	6	..	20	..	7	..	48	..
Austria	33,386	37,384	15	12	7	3	28	41	7	6	43	38
Azerbaijan	..	279	..	..	..	..	..	..	..	..	..	..
Bangladesh	3,839	6,922	24	22	38	33	7	16	17	10	15	19
Belarus	13,437	3,432	..	..	..	..	..	..	..	..	..	..
Belgium	..	39,904	17	18	7	15	..	24	13	7	62	37
Benin	145	198	..	61	..	17	..	..	..	7	..	16
Bolivia	826	1,121	28	31	5	4	1	1	3	3	63	60
Bosnia and Herzegovina	..	692	12	..	15	..	18	..	7	..	49	..
Botswana	181	255	51	..	12	..	..	..	..	..	36	..
Brazil	90,052	79,984	14	..	12	..	27	..	..	..	48	..
Bulgaria	..	1,985	22	..	9	..	19	..	5	..	45	..
Burkina Faso	423	301	69	62	2	4	2	3	0	0	27	31
Burundi	134	60	83	..	9	..	..	..	2	..	7	..
Cambodia	58	178	..	..	..	..	..	..	..	..	..	..
Cameroon	1,581	937	61	47	−13	15	1	1	5	4	46	32
Canada	91,243	104,987	15	13	6	3	26	36	10	8	44	39
Central African Republic	154	81	57	..	6	..	2	..	6	..	28	..
Chad	239	152	..	42	..	40	..	..	..	..	..	18
Chile	5,613	10,663	25	32	7	4	5	5	10	14	52	45
China	116,573	372,836	15	16	15	11	24	29	13	12	34	32
Hong Kong, China	12,625	8,953	8	8	36	22	21	29	2	3	33	37
Colombia	8,034	12,242	31	31	15	10	9	6	14	17	31	36
Congo, Dem. Rep.	1,029	205	..	..	..	..	..	..	..	..	..	..
Congo, Rep.	234	112	..	..	..	..	..	..	..	..	..	..
Costa Rica	1,107	3,571	47	58	8	13	7	2	9	5	30	22
Côte d'Ivoire	2,257	2,024	..	27	..	17	..	10	..	..	..	46
Croatia	4,770	3,658	22	..	15	..	20	..	8	..	36	..
Cuba	..	..	..	..	..	..	..	..	..	..	..	..
Czech Republic	..	..	..	..	..	..	..	..	..	..	..	..
Denmark	20,757	23,156	22	21	4	8	24	25	12	7	39	40
Dominican Republic	1,270	3,300	64	67	2	3	0	0	5	6	29	24
Ecuador	2,068	2,302	22	50	10	17	5	0	8	8	56	26
Egypt, Arab Rep.	7,296	17,969	19	12	15	39	9	6	14	..	43	43
El Salvador	1,044	3,029	36	45	14	34	4	1	24	7	23	12
Eritrea	35	67	..	..	..	..	..	..	..	..	..	..
Estonia	2,679	830	..	..	..	..	..	..	..	..	..	..
Ethiopia	497	409	62	..	21	..	1	..	2	..	14	..
Finland	27,533	27,672	13	7	4	2	24	24	8	2	52	64
France	228,105	214,034	13	13	6	12	31	22	9	7	41	46
Gabon	332	205	45	..	2	..	1	..	7	..	45	..
Gambia, The	18	18	..	..	..	..	..	..	..	..	..	..
Georgia	2,789	..	..	..	..	..	..	..	..	..	..	..
Germany	456,313	402,886	..	..	..	..	..	..	..	..	..	..
Ghana	575	449	..	37	..	5	..	1	..	7	..	50
Greece	..	11,337	22	28	20	11	12	11	10	11	36	38
Guatemala	1,151	2,518	..	..	..	..	..	..	..	..	..	..
Guinea	126	121	..	..	..	..	..	..	..	..	..	..
Guinea-Bissau	19	21	..	..	..	..	..	..	..	..	..	..
Haiti	..	..	51	..	9	..	..	..	..	..	40	..

Structure of manufacturing | 4.3

	Value added in manufacturing		Food, beverages, and tobacco		Textiles and clothing		Machinery and transport equipment		Chemicals		Other manufacturing [a]	
	$ millions		% of total		% of total		% of total		% of total		% of total	
	1990	2000	1990	2000	1990	2000	1990	2000	1990	2000	1990	2000
Honduras	443	1,025	45	59	10	8	3	0	5	3	36	30
Hungary	6,613	9,958	14	19	9	8	26	26	12	7	39	40
India	48,808	65,614	12	13	15	11	25	22	14	25	34	29
Indonesia	20,947	39,818	27	20	15	20	12	17	9	11	37	32
Iran, Islamic Rep.	14,503	15,456	12	15	20	22	20	17	8	4	40	42
Iraq	..	..	20	38	16	22	4	11	11	4	49	25
Ireland	11,982	27,838	27	16	4	1	29	31	16	36	24	16
Israel	..	..	14	19	9	15	32	18	9	7	37	41
Italy	247,930	204,542	8	10	13	12	34	26	7	8	37	44
Jamaica	853	1,012	41	56	5	7	..	6	..	3	54	29
Japan	810,232	1,029,336	9	11	5	3	40	39	10	10	37	36
Jordan	520	1,122	28	2	7	9	4	2	15	3	47	85
Kazakhstan	2,136	3,139	..	..	..	..	..	..	..	..	..	..
Kenya	862	1,165	38	48	10	8	10	9	9	7	33	28
Korea, Dem. Rep.	..	..	..	..	..	..	..	..	..	..	..	..
Korea, Rep.	72,837	144,376	11	8	12	8	32	45	9	9	36	30
Kuwait	2,142	..	4	8	3	5	2	4	3	3	88	81
Kyrgyz Republic	631	105	..	..	..	..	..	..	..	..	..	..
Lao PDR	85	292	..	..	..	..	..	..	..	..	..	..
Latvia	4,150	913	..	..	..	..	..	..	..	..	..	..
Lebanon	..	1,560	..	..	..	..	..	..	..	..	..	..
Lesotho	33	99	..	..	..	..	..	..	..	..	..	..
Liberia	..	..	..	..	..	..	..	..	..	..	..	..
Libya	..	..	24	40	2	6	0	10	7	7	67	36
Lithuania	6,218	2,127	..	..	..	..	..	..	..	..	..	..
Macedonia, FYR	1,411	621	20	..	26	..	14	..	9	..	31	..
Madagascar	314	430	..	..	..	..	..	..	..	..	..	..
Malawi	313	197	38	30	10	5	1	0	18	9	33	55
Malaysia	10,665	29,672	13	8	6	4	31	47	11	7	39	33
Mali	200	83	..	..	..	..	..	..	..	..	..	..
Mauritania	94	75	..	..	..	..	..	..	..	..	..	..
Mauritius	491	918	30	31	46	48	2	2	4	5	17	15
Mexico	49,992	107,166	22	25	5	4	24	28	18	15	32	28
Moldova	..	183	..	..	..	..	..	..	..	..	..	..
Mongolia	..	58	33	..	37	..	1	..	1	..	27	..
Morocco	4,753	5,857	22	33	17	17	8	12	12	15	41	23
Mozambique	230	432	..	43	..	2	..	8	..	1	..	47
Myanmar	..	..	..	..	..	..	..	..	..	..	..	..
Namibia	374	350	..	..	..	..	..	..	..	..	..	..
Nepal	209	484	37	..	31	..	1	..	5	..	25	..
Netherlands	..	60,707	21	23	3	2	25	25	16	14	35	35
New Zealand	7,574	..	28	22	8	13	13	14	7	4	44	47
Nicaragua	170	322	..	..	..	..	..	..	..	..	..	..
Niger	163	122	37	20	29	9	..	..	..	..	34	71
Nigeria	1,562	1,635	15	..	46	..	13	..	4	..	22	..
Norway	13,450	17,076	18	16	2	2	25	29	9	8	46	46
Oman	396	..	..	19	..	8	..	5	..	7	..	62
Pakistan	6,184	8,637	24	16	27	33	9	6	15	7	25	38
Panama	502	713	51	45	8	7	2	2	8	4	31	42
Papua New Guinea	289	288	..	23	..	..	..	8	..	..	..	70
Paraguay	883	1,033	55	61	16	9	..	1	..	4	29	25
Peru	3,926	7,621	23	..	11	..	8	..	9	..	49	..
Philippines	11,008	16,878	39	38	11	9	13	9	12	11	26	33
Poland	..	28,514	21	26	9	6	26	23	7	6	37	38
Portugal	13,631	19,096	15	..	21	..	13	..	6	..	45	..
Puerto Rico	12,126	23,375	16	8	5	3	18	14	44	63	17	12

	Value added in manufacturing		Food, beverages, and tobacco		Textiles and clothing		Machinery and transport equipment		Chemicals		Other manufacturing[a]	
	$ millions		% of total		% of total		% of total		% of total		% of total	
	1990	2000	1990	2000	1990	2000	1990	2000	1990	2000	1990	2000
Romania	..	..	19	..	18	..	14	..	4	..	45	..
Russian Federation	..	..	..	18	..	3	..	18	..	11	..	50
Rwanda	473	176	..	..	..	..	..	..	..	..	..	..
Saudi Arabia	7,962	..	..	..	..	..	..	..	..	..	..	..
Senegal	747	779	60	44	3	5	5	3	9	26	23	21
Sierra Leone	31	28	..	..	..	..	..	..	..	..	..	..
Singapore	9,937	24,896	4	3	3	1	53	62	10	15	29	20
Slovak Republic	..	4,197	..	..	..	..	..	..	..	..	..	..
Slovenia	4,008	4,358	12	11	15	10	16	16	9	12	48	51
Somalia	41	..	..	..	..	..	..	..	..	..	..	..
South Africa	24,040	21,452	14	14	8	7	18	20	9	9	50	50
Spain	..	103,128	18	14	8	7	25	23	10	10	39	47
Sri Lanka	1,077	2,459	51	39	24	30	4	6	4	7	17	19
Sudan	..	1,059	..	21	..	29	..	1	..	1	..	49
Swaziland	250	346	69	..	8	..	1	..	0	..	22	..
Sweden	..	..	10	7	2	1	32	39	9	11	47	42
Switzerland	..	..	10	9	4	3	34	27	..	..	53	60
Syrian Arab Republic	2,508	4,579	35	33	29	43	..	1	..	1	36	21
Tajikistan	1,078	237	..	..	..	..	..	..	..	..	..	..
Tanzania[b]	361	624	51	45	3	0	6	5	11	7	28	43
Thailand	23,217	38,650	24	26	30	17	19	10	2	8	26	40
Togo	162	118	..	..	..	..	..	..	..	..	..	..
Trinidad and Tobago	438	620	30	17	3	3	3	0	19	2	44	79
Tunisia	2,075	3,545	19	35	20	9	5	3	4	7	52	46
Turkey	26,882	26,994	16	13	15	18	16	17	10	11	43	41
Turkmenistan	..	838	..	..	..	..	..	..	..	..	..	..
Uganda	230	527	..	35	..	33	..	1	..	2	..	29
Ukraine	40,810	5,099	..	..	..	..	..	..	..	..	..	..
United Arab Emirates	2,643	..	..	3	..	3	..	3	..	1	..	90
United Kingdom	206,727	234,857	13	..	5	..	32	..	11	..	38	..
United States	1,040,600	1,566,600	12	..	5	..	31	..	12	..	40	..
Uruguay	2,597	3,490	31	43	18	9	9	4	10	8	32	36
Uzbekistan	..	1,136	..	..	..	..	..	..	..	..	..	..
Venezuela, RB	9,809	23,430	17	21	5	10	5	21	9	9	64	39
Vietnam	793	5,785	..	..	..	..	..	..	..	..	..	..
West Bank and Gaza	..	562	..	..	..	..	..	..	..	..	..	..
Yemen, Rep.	449	593	..	..	..	..	..	..	..	..	..	..
Yugoslavia, Fed. Rep.	..	..	..	30	..	9	..	16	..	10	..	36
Zambia	1,048	330	44	31	11	12	7	17	9	21	29	19
Zimbabwe	1,799	1,003	28	32	19	15	9	7	6	10	38	36
World	**4,509,877 t**	**5,909,932 t**										
Low income	161,474	157,379										
Middle income	683,113	1,141,321										
Lower middle income	349,698	742,365										
Upper middle income	307,763	405,113										
Low & middle income	793,290	1,295,650										
East Asia & Pacific	186,119	511,101										
Europe & Central Asia	..	..										
Latin America & Carib.	255,228	338,774										
Middle East & N. Africa	..	75,539										
South Asia	61,086	85,492										
Sub-Saharan Africa	42,925	38,043										
High income	3,706,881	4,624,819										
Europe EMU	1,230,758	1,137,809										

a. Includes unallocated data. b. Data cover mainland Tanzania only.

Structure of manufacturing | 4.3

The data on the distribution of manufacturing value added by industry are provided by the United Nations Industrial Development Organization (UNIDO). UNIDO obtains data on manufacturing value added from a variety of national and international sources, including the United Nations Statistics Division, the World Bank, the Organisation for Economic Co-operation and Development, and the International Monetary Fund. To improve comparability over time and across countries, UNIDO supplements these data with information from industrial censuses, statistics supplied by national and international organizations, unpublished data that it collects in the field, and estimates by the UNIDO Secretariat. Nevertheless, coverage may be less than complete, particularly for the informal sector. To the extent that direct information on inputs and outputs is not available, estimates may be used that may result in errors in industry totals. Moreover, countries use different reference periods (calendar or fiscal year) and valuation methods (basic, producer, or purchaser prices) to estimate value added. (See also *About the data* for table 4.2.)

The data on manufacturing value added in U.S. dollars are from the World Bank's national accounts files. These figures may differ from those used by UNIDO to calculate the shares of value added by industry, in part because of differences in exchange rates. Thus estimates of value added in a particular industry group calculated by applying the shares to total manufacturing value added will not match those from UNIDO sources.

The classification of manufacturing industries in the table accords with the United Nations International Standard Industrial Classification (ISIC) revision 2. First published in 1948, the ISIC has its roots in the work of the League of Nations Committee of Statistical Experts. The committee's efforts, interrupted by the Second World War, were taken up by the United Nations Statistical Commission, which at its first session appointed a committee on industrial classification. The latest revision, ISIC revision 3, was completed in 1989, and many countries have now switched to it. But revision 2 is still widely used for compiling cross-country data. Concordances matching ISIC categories to national systems of classification and to related systems such as the Standard International Trade Classification (SITC) are readily available.

In establishing a classification system, compilers must define both the types of activities to be described and the organizational units whose activities are to be reported. There are many possibilities, and the choices made affect how the resulting statistics can be interpreted and how useful they are in analyzing economic behavior. The ISIC emphasizes commonalities in the production process and is explicitly not intended to measure outputs (for which there is a newly developed Central Product Classification). Nevertheless, the ISIC views an activity as defined by "a process resulting in a homogeneous set of products" (United Nations 1990 [ISIC, series M, no. 4, rev. 3], p. 9). Firms typically use a multitude of processes to produce a final product. For example, an automobile manufacturer engages in forg-

ing, welding, and painting as well as advertising, accounting, and many other service activities. In some cases the processes may be carried out by different technical units within the larger enterprise, but collecting data at such a detailed level is not practical. Nor would it be useful to record production data at the very highest level of a large, multiplant, multiproduct firm. The ISIC has therefore adopted as the definition of an establishment "an enterprise or part of an enterprise which independently engages in one, or predominantly one, kind of economic activity at or from one location …for which data are available…" (United Nations 1990, p. 25). By design, this definition matches the reporting unit required for the production accounts of the United Nations System of National Accounts.

• **Value added in manufacturing** is the sum of gross output less the value of intermediate inputs used in production for industries classified in ISIC major division 3. • **Food, beverages, and tobacco** comprise ISIC division 31. • **Textiles and clothing** comprise ISIC division 32. • **Machinery and transport equipment** comprise ISIC groups 382–84. • **Chemicals** comprise ISIC groups 351 and 352. • **Other manufacturing** includes wood and related products (ISIC division 33), paper and related products (ISIC division 34), petroleum and related products (ISIC groups 353–56), basic metals and mineral products (ISIC divisions 36 and 37), fabricated metal products and professional goods (ISIC groups 381 and 385), and other industries (ISIC group 390). When data for textiles and clothing, machinery and transport equipment, or chemicals are shown in the table as not available, they are included in other manufacturing.

Data sources

The data on value added in manufacturing in U.S. dollars are from the World Bank's national accounts files. The data used to calculate shares of value added by industry are provided to the World Bank in electronic files by UNIDO. The most recent published source is UNIDO's *International Yearbook of Industrial Statistics 2002*. The ISIC system is described in the United Nations' *International Standard Industrial Classification of All Economic Activities, Third Revision* (1990). The discussion of the ISIC draws on Jacob Ryten's paper "Fifty Years of ISIC: Historical Origins and Future Perspectives" (1998).

4.3a

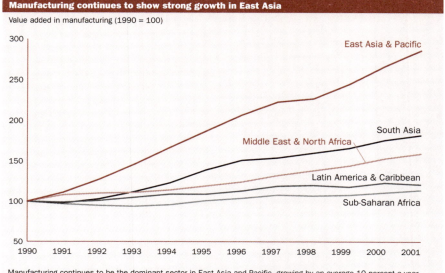

Manufacturing continues to show strong growth in East Asia

Value added in manufacturing (1990 = 100)

Manufacturing continues to be the dominant sector in East Asia and Pacific, growing by an average 10 percent a year in 1990–2001.

Source: World Bank data files.

	Export volume		Import volume		Export value		Import value		Net barter terms of trade	
	average annual % growth		average annual % growth		average annual % growth		average annual % growth		1995 = 100	
	1980–90	1990–2000	1980–90	1990–2000	1980–90	1990–2000	1980–90	1990–2000	1990	2000
Afghanistan	−9.7	−3.9	−1.8	−0.2	−10.5	−4.7	−0.1	−1.1	99	100
Albania [a]	..	..	..	..	..	13.6	..	18.0	..	..
Algeria	3.4	3.7	−8.1	1.6	−4.4	3.0	−2.7	1.1	128	172
Angola	6.0	0.7	2.7	3.1	6.4	4.9	0.7	4.9	136	215
Argentina	5.0	9.3	−6.8	16.8	2.1	10.1	−6.5	16.9	97	109
Armenia [a]	..	..	..	..	..	−9.5	..	−0.3	..	..
Australia [a]	6.3	7.3	6.0	9.2	6.6	5.0	6.4	6.4	85	99
Austria [a]	6.6		..		10.2	5.6	8.7	4.1		
Azerbaijan [a]	..	..	..	..	..	−6.4	..	4.0	..	..
Bangladesh	0.4	15.6	−4.5	18.5	7.8	11.1	3.6	10.3	80	89
Belarus [a]	..	..	..	..	..	15.6	..	16.2	..	..
Belgium [a, b]	4.5	6.2	4.0	5.4	7.8	6.3	6.4	4.5	100	..
Benin	3.5	6.3	−10.0	8.5	10.0	7.5	−4.9	9.5	100	82
Bolivia	3.1	2.8	−1.2	9.0	−1.9	4.3	−0.3	9.7	115	112
Bosnia and Herzegovina	..	..	..	..	..	..	..	..	..	..
Botswana	11.4	10.5	9.1	3.7	18.8	4.9	9.0	2.7	110	75
Brazil	6.3	5.1	0.7	16.7	5.1	5.9	−1.9	12.6	60	91
Bulgaria [a]	..	..	..	..	−12.3	2.2	−14.0	5.3	..	..
Burkina Faso	−0.3	13.3	3.7	2.5	7.9	12.8	4.3	2.5	91	76
Burundi	3.5	8.6	1.0	4.0	2.5	−4.3	2.2	−6.9	78	61
Cambodia	..	..	..	..	..	..	..	..	..	..
Cameroon	7.3	1.8	4.8	4.8	1.4	−0.5	0.1	1.9	90	110
Canada [a]	6.4	9.1	7.4	9.0	6.8	8.3	7.9	7.5	100	97
Central African Republic	0.1	19.1	4.2	6.0	3.6	2.8	7.9	1.9	124	52
Chad	8.7	1.9	10.8	−0.4	9.4	2.8	12.6	4.0	116	80
Chile	9.1	10.0	−3.0	10.0	8.1	8.3	2.8	9.6	84	74
China [†]	13.7	10.6	15.6	9.2	12.8	14.5	13.5	12.6	101	102
Hong Kong, China	10.8	8.4	9.3	9.0	16.8	8.3	15.0	8.8	101	101
Colombia	7.9	4.5	−2.1	8.5	7.7	7.3	0.0	9.7	95	116
Congo, Dem. Rep.	10.6	−4.2	29.6	−10.4	3.6	−4.5	19.1	−6.7	108	81
Congo, Rep.	7.4	8.5	−2.2	9.8	2.1	7.9	−0.7	5.7	83	144
Costa Rica	3.7	13.9	5.2	14.8	4.6	16.9	4.4	13.9	72	96
Côte d'Ivoire	2.6	5.4	−2.1	4.4	1.7	6.0	−1.5	4.1	82	96
Croatia [a]	..	..	..	..	..	1.0	..	7.6	..	..
Cuba	−1.1	−1.0	−0.5	3.1	−0.9	−1.5	1.5	2.3	96	92
Czech Republic [a]	..	..	..	..	..	9.9	..	10.3	..	..
Denmark [a]	4.1	5.2	3.1	6.0	8.4	3.7	6.3	4.2	100	98
Dominican Republic	−0.9	3.9	0.8	13.9	−2.1	4.9	3.3	14.4	97	102
Ecuador	7.1	6.3	−1.8	5.8	−0.4	6.8	−1.3	7.8	141	124
Egypt, Arab Rep.	2.1	2.7	8.1	1.7	−3.4	3.7	12.6	4.7	86	86
El Salvador	−4.6	2.9	4.6	7.6	−4.6	10.1	2.4	11.1	69	83
Eritrea	..	..	..	..	..	..	..	..	..	..
Estonia [a]	..	..	..	..	..	20.3	..	23.2	..	..
Ethiopia	−0.5	8.0	3.6	2.6	−1.1	11.5	4.3	7.9	90	81
Finland [a]	2.3	9.3	4.4	4.3	7.4	7.6	6.9	4.8	100	111
France [a]	3.6	6.3	3.7	5.4	7.5	4.2	6.5	3.4	103	105
Gabon	2.5	7.4	−3.5	3.7	−3.9	3.3	1.1	3.3	126	80
Gambia, The	−4.1	−7.7	−6.0	1.1	0.0	−7.4	2.5	1.4	100	100
Georgia	..	..	..	..	..	..	..	..	..	..
Germany [a, c]	4.5	5.9	4.9	4.3	9.2	3.9	7.1	3.4	98	107
Ghana	−17.2	8.3	−20.1	10.5	−2.7	8.8	−0.4	9.6	94	94
Greece [a]	5.0	8.9	6.4	8.9	5.8	3.0	6.6	4.5	93	94
Guatemala	−1.1	8.5	0.1	10.0	−2.2	10.0	0.6	11.0	98	85
Guinea	..	6.9	..	−0.5	4.0	2.8	9.7	−0.2	135	87
Guinea-Bissau	−2.0	17.7	−0.3	−3.4	4.2	13.6	5.2	−2.6	143	90
Haiti	−0.4	4.3	−4.6	13.3	−1.2	3.9	−2.9	14.4	116	88
[†] Data for Taiwan, China	16.6	3.0	17.6	4.7	14.9	7.2	12.4	8.5	102	105

Growth of merchandise trade | 4.4

	Export volume		Import volume		Export value		Import value		Net barter terms of trade	
	average annual % growth		average annual % growth		average annual % growth		average annual % growth		1995 = 100	
	1980–90	1990–2000	1980–90	1990–2000	1980–90	1990–2000	1980–90	1990–2000	1990	2000
Honduras	4.0	2.7	1.6	12.8	1.6	7.3	0.6	13.9	81	104
Hungary [a]	3.4	10.1	1.3	11.6	1.4	12.7	0.1	13.5	94	105
India	–3.0	2.6	–2.8	4.7	7.3	9.5	4.2	10.1	79	93
Indonesia	8.1	8.2	1.8	4.0	–0.9	8.1	2.6	2.7	102	106
Iran, Islamic Rep.	17.1	–0.9	–2.4	–7.5	7.2	1.2	0.2	–6.5	170	225
Iraq	2.3	29.5	–4.5	9.8	–4.0	29.4	–2.2	10.3	132	162
Ireland [a]	9.3	15.2	4.8	11.4	12.8	13.5	7.0	11.0	94	99
Israel [a]	..	..	..	..	..	..	..	..	..	..
Italy [a]	4.3	5.6	5.3	4.6	8.7	4.6	6.9	3.2	102	100
Jamaica	1.6	4.6	3.0	7.3	1.1	2.2	2.8	6.8	105	87
Japan [a]	5.1	2.3	6.6	5.2	8.9	4.1	5.1	4.6	137	104
Jordan	7.7	5.3	1.1	3.7	6.2	6.6	–1.9	5.0	85	86
Kazakhstan [a]	..	..	..	..	..	12.8	..	2.9	..	..
Kenya	1.7	4.1	2.5	7.6	–1.1	6.3	1.7	6.0	68	94
Korea, Dem. Rep.	..	..	..	..	..	..	..	..	..	..
Korea, Rep.	11.5	15.6	10.9	9.5	15.0	10.1	11.9	7.1	98	72
Kuwait	–2.2	13.6	–6.3	6.5	–7.7	16.1	–4.1	5.5	95	158
Kyrgyz Republic [a]	..	..	..	..	..	6.5	..	7.8	..	..
Lao PDR [a]	..	..	..	..	11.0	15.4	6.6	12.7	..	..
Latvia [a]	..	7.2	..	..	..	11.6	..	19.8	..	..
Lebanon	–5.6	2.4	–7.5	8.6	–5.6	4.1	–5.5	8.9	105	112
Lesotho	6.2	14.2	3.5	1.0	3.7	12.5	3.5	0.6	97	77
Liberia	–3.5	7.4	–7.6	9.7	–3.1	4.6	–7.2	8.8	112	89
Libya	0.1	–4.1	–6.6	0.3	–7.3	–2.2	–4.4	1.8	145	200
Lithuania [a]	..	..	..	..	..	9.3	..	14.4	..	..
Macedonia, FYR [a]	..	..	..	..	..	2.8	..	6.4	..	..
Madagascar	–3.0	–5.9	–3.7	–0.9	–0.9	–2.9	–1.7	0.2	92	100
Malawi	2.4	2.8	–0.1	–1.7	2.0	1.0	3.3	0.1	141	94
Malaysia	14.6	15.2	6.0	10.4	8.6	12.2	7.7	9.5	102	90
Mali	4.4	11.3	4.6	3.2	6.0	6.9	4.3	1.7	122	88
Mauritania	3.9	6.3	–2.9	1.9	8.0	2.5	–1.8	–1.6	96	104
Mauritius	10.4	4.1	11.2	3.6	14.4	3.5	12.9	3.8	108	96
Mexico	15.3	15.5	0.9	13.2	5.9	16.1	6.4	14.2	109	107
Moldova [a]	..	..	..	..	..	9.1	..	11.8	..	..
Mongolia	3.1	..	..	..	5.0	–1.7	5.0	0.8	..	..
Morocco	5.7	7.1	3.2	7.2	6.2	7.4	3.6	5.5	95	112
Mozambique	–9.5	14.5	–2.7	1.7	–9.6	9.6	0.1	1.2	115	91
Myanmar	–3.0	14.8	–6.5	13.7	–7.6	14.4	–4.7	22.6	116	52
Namibia [a]	..	..	..	..	..	0.9	..	4.0	..	..
Nepal [a]	..	..	..	..	8.1	10.7	6.9	9.3	..	..
Netherlands [a]	4.5	7.1	4.5	6.9	4.6	5.5	4.4	5.4	102	102
New Zealand [a]	3.5	4.4	4.3	5.9	6.2	3.8	5.4	5.6	97	101
Nicaragua	–4.8	10.3	–3.5	9.2	–5.8	10.2	–3.1	11.5	119	77
Niger	–5.2	3.8	–5.2	–2.7	–5.4	0.0	–3.5	0.0	136	72
Nigeria	–4.4	3.3	–21.4	2.1	–8.4	3.2	–15.6	2.8	162	180
Norway [a]	4.1	7.1	3.4	7.4	5.3	4.9	6.2	3.8	89	66
Oman	7.1	4.3	–1.7	4.4	3.3	5.3	0.7	6.1	167	212
Pakistan	–0.3	–6.3	–5.3	–5.7	8.1	4.3	3.0	3.3	97	95
Panama	–0.6	5.9	–6.7	7.8	–0.5	9.4	–3.6	8.7	69	100
Papua New Guinea	1.3	–8.1	..	..	4.9	3.1	1.3	–1.0	..	..
Paraguay	12.8	–0.2	10.4	4.0	11.6	1.7	4.2	5.5	87	84
Peru	2.7	9.3	–2.0	10.5	–1.5	8.9	1.3	10.8	93	81
Philippines	–7.5	17.1	–7.8	12.4	3.9	18.8	2.9	12.0	90	111
Poland [a]	4.8	9.3	1.5	18.5	1.4	9.9	–3.2	18.3	117	108
Portugal [a]	11.9	..	..	..	15.1	5.2	10.3	5.1	..	..
Puerto Rico	..	..	..	..	..	..	..	..	..	..

4.4 Growth of merchandise trade

	Export volume		Import volume		Export value		Import value		Net barter terms of trade	
	average annual % growth		average annual % growth		average annual % growth		average annual % growth		1995 = 100	
	1980–90	1990–2000	1980–90	1990–2000	1980–90	1990–2000	1980–90	1990–2000	1990	2000
Romania [a]	..	..	..	..	–4.0	8.5	–3.8	6.8	..	..
Russian Federation [a]	..	..	..	..	..	9.7	..	4.1	..	..
Rwanda	3.3	–7.0	2.4	1.8	–0.3	–3.5	3.3	–1.2	38	96
Saudi Arabia	–6.3	1.9	–8.4	–0.8	–13.4	3.1	–6.1	0.8	168	194
Senegal	1.2	6.3	0.4	5.2	3.5	4.0	1.4	3.6	109	90
Sierra Leone	–1.0	–31.1	–6.3	–4.5	–2.4	–29.5	–8.7	–4.2	71	72
Singapore	13.5	13.3	9.9	9.3	9.9	9.9	8.0	7.8	111	93
Slovak Republic [a]	..	..	..	..	..	10.2	..	11.1	..	..
Slovenia [a]	..	..	..	..	..	8.2	..	9.3	..	..
Somalia	–1.5	–0.5	–11.1	2.3	–1.1	–2.4	–9.2	1.7	99	82
South Africa [a, d]	3.3	7.4	–0.8	7.9	0.7	2.5	–1.3	5.8	102	100
Spain [a]	3.0	..	..	..	10.8	8.6	10.6	6.1	104	104
Sri Lanka	–4.4	0.6	–6.8	1.9	5.4	11.3	2.2	9.6	80	107
Sudan	–3.0	17.1	–7.7	11.2	–2.5	14.0	–6.4	9.9	123	141
Swaziland	8.7	3.8	4.1	2.3	4.7	5.8	–0.5	4.3	100	100
Sweden [a]	4.4	0.7	5.0	1.2	8.0	6.0	6.7	4.5	101	109
Switzerland [a]	3.7	..	..	..	9.5	2.6	8.8	1.9	..	..
Syrian Arab Republic	6.6	–1.2	–11.7	3.9	2.4	1.3	–8.5	4.2	131	170
Tajikistan	..	..	..	..	..	..	..	..	..	..
Tanzania	–1.6	5.0	–0.8	–5.3	–4.2	6.3	–0.5	0.1	110	74
Thailand	11.2	4.0	8.8	–2.5	14.0	10.5	12.7	5.0	102	86
Togo	–1.2	8.7	0.6	5.8	1.1	6.6	2.0	5.5	133	104
Trinidad and Tobago	–10.9	3.6	–20.4	10.2	–9.4	7.3	–12.3	11.3	117	172
Tunisia	4.9	5.3	1.7	4.2	3.5	6.0	2.7	5.2	103	100
Turkey	..	10.6	..	11.0	14.0	8.9	9.3	10.2	104	95
Turkmenistan	..	..	..	..	..	..	..	..	..	..
Uganda	–5.4	17.1	–6.1	25.4	–4.0	15.4	4.5	21.3	74	71
Ukraine [a]	..	..	..	..	..	7.4	..	9.1	..	..
United Arab Emirates	8.9	2.1	–1.3	9.2	–0.8	4.0	0.7	11.2	174	213
United Kingdom [a]	4.5	6.4	6.7	6.6	5.9	5.4	8.5	5.4	99	97
United States [a]	3.6	6.7	7.2	9.1	5.7	7.3	8.2	9.5	102	103
Uruguay	4.4	6.1	1.2	10.5	4.5	5.2	–1.2	10.1	100	86
Uzbekistan	..	..	..	..	..	..	..	..	..	..
Venezuela, RB	3.4	5.3	–4.0	4.7	–4.4	5.5	–3.2	5.3	142	157
Vietnam	..	..	..	..	..	..	..	..	..	..
West Bank and Gaza	..	..	..	..	..	..	..	..	..	..
Yemen, Rep. [a]	..	..	..	..	..	22.7	..	–1.0	..	..
Yugoslavia, Fed. Rep.	..	..	..	..	..	..	..	..	..	..
Zambia	–0.5	5.9	2.1	1.1	0.9	–2.0	0.0	–1.6	109	57
Zimbabwe	4.0	8.2	3.4	4.9	2.9	2.7	–0.5	0.0	100	94

a. Data are from the International Monetary Fund's International Financial Statistics database. b. Includes Luxembourg. c. Data prior to 1990 refer to the Federal Republic of Germany before unification. d. Data prior to 1998 refer to the South African Customs Union (Botswana, Lesotho, Namibia, South Africa, and Swaziland); those after January 1998 refer to South Africa only.

Growth of merchandise trade | 4.4

Data on international trade in goods are available from each country's balance of payments and customs records. While the balance of payments focuses on the financial transactions that accompany trade, customs data record the direction of trade and the physical quantities and value of goods entering or leaving the customs area. Customs data may differ from those recorded in the balance of payments because of differences in valuation and the time of recording. The 1993 System of National Accounts and the fifth edition of the International Monetary Fund's (IMF) *Balance of Payments Manual* (1993) attempted to reconcile the definitions and reporting standards for international trade statistics, but differences in sources, timing, and national practices limit comparability. Real growth rates derived from trade volume indexes and terms of trade based on unit price indexes may therefore differ from those derived from national accounts aggregates.

Trade in goods, or merchandise trade, includes all goods that add to or subtract from an economy's material resources. Thus the total supply of goods in an economy is made up of gross output plus imports less exports (currency in circulation, titles of ownership, and securities are excluded, but nonmonetary gold is included). Trade data are collected on the basis of a country's customs area, which in most cases is the same as its geographic area. Goods provided as part of foreign aid are included, but goods destined for extraterritorial agencies (such as embassies) are not.

Collecting and tabulating trade statistics is difficult. Some developing countries lack the capacity to report timely data; this is a problem especially for countries that are landlocked and those whose territorial boundaries are porous. As a result, it is necessary to estimate their trade from the data reported by their partners. (For further discussion of the use of partner country reports, see *About the data* for table 6.2.) Countries that belong to common customs unions may need to collect data through direct inquiry of companies. In some cases economic or political concerns may lead national authorities to suppress or misrepresent data on certain trade flows, such as oil, military equipment, or the exports of a dominant producer. In other cases reported trade data may be distorted by deliberate under- or overinvoicing to effect capital transfers or avoid taxes. And in some regions smuggling and black market trading result in unreported trade flows.

By international agreement customs data are reported to the United Nations Statistics Division, which maintains the Commodity Trade (COMTRADE)

database. The United Nations Conference on Trade and Development (UNCTAD) compiles a variety of international trade statistics, including price and volume indexes, based on the COMTRADE data. The IMF and the World Trade Organization also compile data on trade prices and volumes. The growth rates and terms of trade for low- and middle-income economies shown in this table were calculated from index numbers compiled by UNCTAD. Volume measures for high-income economies were derived by deflating the value of trade using deflators from the IMF's *International Financial Statistics*. In some cases price and volume indexes from different sources may vary significantly as a result of differences in estimation procedures. All indexes are rescaled to a 1995 base year. Terms of trade were computed from the same indicators.

The terms of trade measure the relative prices of a country's exports and imports. There are a number of ways to calculate terms of trade. The most common is the net barter (or commodity) terms of trade, constructed as the ratio of the export price index to the import price index. When a country's net barter terms of trade increase, its exports are becoming more valuable or its imports cheaper.

• **Growth rates of export and import volumes** are average annual growth rates calculated for low- and middle-income economies from UNCTAD's quantum index series and for high-income economies from export and import data deflated by the IMF's trade price deflators. • **Growth rates of export and import values** are average annual growth rates calculated from UNCTAD's value indexes or from current values of merchandise exports and imports. • **Net barter terms of trade** are calculated as the ratio of the export price index to the corresponding import price index measured relative to the base year 1995.

Data sources

The main source of trade data for developing countries is UNCTAD's annual *Handbook of International Trade and Development Statistics*. The IMF's *International Financial Statistics* includes data on the export and import values and deflators for high-income and selected developing economies.

Structure of merchandise exports

	Merchandise exports ($ millions)		Food (% of total)		Agricultural raw materials (% of total)		Fuels (% of total)		Ores and metals (% of total)		Manufactures (% of total)	
	1990	2001	1990	2001	1990	2001	1990	2001	1990	2001	1990	2001
Afghanistan	235	81	..	..	..	..	..	..	..	..	..	..
Albania	230	305	..	6	..	6	..	1	..	3	..	84
Algeria	12,930	20,050	0	0	0	0	96	97	0	0	3	2
Angola	3,910	6,695	0	..	0	..	93	..	6	..	0	..
Argentina	12,353	26,655	56	44	4	2	8	17	2	3	29	33
Armenia	..	340	..	14	..	5	..	11	..	22	..	43
Australia	39,752	63,387	22	21	10	6	21	22	20	17	24	28
Austria	41,265	70,327	3	5	4	2	1	2	3	3	88	82
Azerbaijan	..	2,315	..	2	..	1	..	91	..	1	..	4
Bangladesh	1,671	6,530	14	..	7	..	1	..	..	..	77	..
Belarus	..	7,525	..	8	..	3	..	18	..	1	..	69
Belgium [a]	117,703	189,624	9	9	2	1	3	4	4	3	77	79
Benin	288	380	15	23	56	71	15	0	0	0	13	6
Bolivia	926	1,285	19	31	8	3	25	24	44	20	5	22
Bosnia and Herzegovina	276	1,100	..	..	..	..	..	..	..	..	..	..
Botswana	1,784	2,310	..	..	..	..	..	..	..	..	..	..
Brazil	31,414	58,223	28	28	3	4	2	4	14	8	52	54
Bulgaria	5,030	5,105	..	10	..	3	..	12	..	13	..	57
Burkina Faso	152	174	..	..	..	..	..	..	..	..	..	..
Burundi	75	40	..	91	..	8	..	..	..	1	..	0
Cambodia	86	1,552	..	..	..	..	..	..	..	..	..	..
Cameroon	2,002	1,749	20	17	14	21	50	52	7	5	9	5
Canada	127,629	259,858	9	7	9	6	10	14	9	4	59	62
Central African Republic	120	131	..	..	..	..	..	..	..	..	..	..
Chad	188	165	..	..	..	..	..	..	..	..	..	..
Chile	8,372	17,440	24	26	9	10	1	1	55	41	11	18
China †	62,091	266,155	13	5	3	1	8	3	2	2	72	89
Hong Kong, China [b]	82,390	191,066	3	2	0	0	0	1	1	2	95	95
Colombia	6,766	12,257	33	18	4	5	37	36	0	1	25	39
Congo, Dem. Rep.	2,326	750	..	..	..	..	..	..	..	..	..	..
Congo, Rep.	981	2,080	..	..	..	..	..	..	..	..	..	..
Costa Rica	1,448	5,010	58	32	5	3	1	1	1	1	27	62
Côte d'Ivoire	3,072	3,715	..	50	..	14	..	21	..	0	..	14
Croatia	4,597	4,659	13	10	6	4	9	10	5	3	68	73
Cuba	5,100	1,708	..	..	..	..	..	..	..	..	..	..
Czech Republic	12,170	33,405	..	4	..	2	..	3	..	2	..	89
Denmark	36,870	51,873	27	20	3	3	3	6	1	1	60	65
Dominican Republic	2,170	5,333	21	..	0	..	0	..	0	..	78	..
Ecuador	2,714	4,495	44	42	1	6	52	40	0	0	2	12
Egypt, Arab Rep.	3,477	4,128	10	10	10	5	29	40	9	5	42	33
El Salvador	582	2,865	57	35	1	1	2	6	3	3	38	55
Eritrea	15	30	..	..	..	..	..	..	..	..	..	..
Estonia	..	3,310	..	10	..	8	..	4	..	3	..	75
Ethiopia	298	420	..	71	..	19	..	..	..	1	..	10
Finland	26,571	42,929	2	2	10	6	1	3	4	3	83	86
France	216,588	321,843	16	11	2	1	2	3	3	2	77	82
Gabon	2,204	2,626	..	1	..	12	..	83	..	2	..	2
Gambia, The	31	9	..	81	..	1	..	0	..	0	..	17
Georgia	..	345	..	..	..	..	..	..	..	..	..	..
Germany	421,100	570,791	5	4	1	1	1	1	3	2	89	86
Ghana	897	1,700	51	49	15	8	9	12	17	16	8	16
Greece	8,105	8,670	30	24	3	3	7	11	7	8	54	52
Guatemala	1,163	2,466	67	51	6	4	2	5	0	1	24	38
Guinea	671	825	..	2	..	0	..	1	..	68	..	28
Guinea-Bissau	19	55	..	..	..	..	..	..	..	..	..	..
Haiti	160	278	14	..	1	..	0	..	0	..	85	..
† Data for Taiwan, China	67,079	122,505	4	1	2	1	1	1	1	1	93	94

Structure of merchandise exports

	Merchandise exports		Food		Agricultural raw materials		Fuels		Ores and metals		Manufactures	
	$ millions		% of total		% of total		% of total		% of total		% of total	
	1990	2001	1990	2001	1990	2001	1990	2001	1990	2001	1990	2001
Honduras	831	1,318	82	64	4	4	1	0	4	4	9	27
Hungary	10,000	30,500	23	8	3	1	3	2	6	2	63	85
India	17,969	43,611	16	13	4	1	3	4	5	3	71	77
Indonesia	25,675	56,321	11	9	5	4	44	26	4	5	35	56
Iran, Islamic Rep.	19,305	25,270	..	4	..	1	..	84	..	1	..	10
Iraq	12,380	15,905	..	..	..	..	..	..	..	..	..	..
Ireland	23,743	82,826	22	7	2	0	1	0	1	0	70	88
Israel	12,080	29,019	8	3	3	1	1	1	2	1	87	94
Italy	170,304	241,134	6	6	1	1	2	2	1	1	88	88
Jamaica	1,158	1,225	19	23	0	0	1	0	10	4	69	73
Japan	287,581	403,496	1	1	1	1	0	0	1	1	96	93
Jordan	1,064	2,293	11	15	0	0	0	0	38	19	51	66
Kazakhstan	..	8,645	..	7	..	1	..	54	..	18	..	20
Kenya	1,031	1,945	49	59	6	9	13	8	3	3	29	21
Korea, Dem. Rep.	1,857	661	..	..	..	..	..	..	..	..	..	..
Korea, Rep.	65,016	150,439	3	2	1	1	1	5	1	1	94	91
Kuwait	7,042	16,142	1	0	0	0	93	79	0	0	6	20
Kyrgyz Republic	..	475	..	16	..	6	..	12	..	6	..	20
Lao PDR	79	336	..	..	..	..	..	..	..	..	..	..
Latvia	..	2,000	..	9	..	25	..	1	..	5	..	59
Lebanon	494	871	..	19	..	6	..	0	..	6	..	69
Lesotho	62	282	..	..	..	..	..	..	..	..	..	..
Liberia	330	615	..	..	..	..	..	..	..	..	..	..
Libya	13,225	11,650	0	..	0	..	94	..	0	..	5	..
Lithuania	..	4,585	..	12	..	4	..	23	..	2	..	58
Macedonia, FYR	1,199	1,170	..	16	..	1	..	4	..	8	..	70
Madagascar	319	940	73	36	4	6	1	2	8	4	14	50
Malawi	417	310	93	..	2	..	0	..	0	..	5	..
Malaysia	29,452	87,921	12	6	14	2	18	10	2	1	54	80
Mali	359	740	36	..	62	..	..	..	0	..	2	..
Mauritania	469	280	..	..	..	..	..	..	..	..	..	..
Mauritius	1,194	1,521	32	24	1	1	1	0	0	0	66	74
Mexico	40,711	158,547	12	5	2	1	38	8	6	1	43	85
Moldova	..	570	..	63	..	2	..	0	..	1	..	34
Mongolia	661	250	..	4	..	28	..	1	..	41	..	26
Morocco	4,265	7,116	26	21	3	2	4	4	15	9	52	64
Mozambique	126	703	..	23	..	4	..	10	..	55	..	8
Myanmar	325	2,269	51	..	36	..	0	..	2	..	10	..
Namibia	1,085	1,500	..	..	..	..	..	..	..	..	..	..
Nepal	204	737	13	10	3	0	..	0	0	0	83	67
Netherlands	131,775	229,464	20	16	4	3	10	8	3	2	59	70
New Zealand	9,394	13,726	47	47	18	13	4	2	6	4	23	29
Nicaragua	330	606	77	82	14	3	0	2	1	0	8	13
Niger	282	275	..	38	..	1	..	0	..	56	..	3
Nigeria	13,596	19,150	1	0	1	0	97	100	0	0	1	0
Norway	34,047	57,856	7	6	2	1	48	62	10	6	33	21
Oman	5,508	11,074	1	6	0	0	92	81	1	1	5	12
Pakistan	5,615	9,242	9	11	10	2	1	2	0	0	79	85
Panama	340	911	75	77	1	1	0	7	1	2	21	13
Papua New Guinea	1,177	1,805	22	15	9	2	0	29	58	51	10	2
Paraguay	959	989	52	69	38	14	0	0	0	0	10	16
Peru	3,230	7,092	21	31	3	2	10	7	47	37	18	22
Philippines	8,117	32,128	19	6	2	1	2	1	8	2	38	91
Poland	14,320	36,090	13	8	3	1	11	5	9	4	59	79
Portugal	16,417	23,923	7	7	6	3	3	2	3	2	80	85
Puerto Rico	..	..	..	..	..	..	..	..	..	..	..	..

4.5 Structure of merchandise exports

	Merchandise exports		Food		Agricultural raw materials		Fuels		Ores and metals		Manufactures	
	$ millions		% of total		% of total		% of total		% of total		% of total	
	1990	2001	1990	2001	1990	2001	1990	2001	1990	2001	1990	2001
Romania	4,960	11,385	1	4	3	4	18	6	4	5	73	81
Russian Federation	..	103,100	..	1	..	3	..	54	..	8	..	22
Rwanda	110	85	..	..	..	..	..	..	..	..	..	..
Saudi Arabia	44,417	68,200	1	1	0	0	92	90	0	0	7	9
Senegal	761	1,080	53	46	3	2	12	18	9	4	23	29
Sierra Leone	138	28	..	..	..	..	..	..	..	..	..	..
Singapore [b]	52,730	121,751	5	2	3	0	18	8	2	1	72	85
Slovak Republic	6,355	12,630	..	4	..	2	..	7	..	3	..	84
Slovenia	6,681	9,251	7	4	2	1	3	1	3	4	86	90
Somalia	150	110	..	..	..	..	..	..	..	..	..	..
South Africa [c]	23,549	29,284	8	8	4	2	7	8	11	9	22	59
Spain	55,642	109,681	15	15	2	1	5	3	2	2	75	78
Sri Lanka	1,912	4,817	34	21	6	2	1	0	2	0	54	77
Sudan	374	1,630	61	..	38	..	..	..	0	..	1	..
Swaziland	556	810	..	..	..	..	..	..	..	..	..	..
Sweden	57,540	75,259	2	3	7	1	3	3	3	3	83	84
Switzerland	63,784	82,064	3	3	1	1	0	0	3	4	94	92
Syrian Arab Republic	4,212	4,490	14	9	4	5	45	76	1	1	36	8
Tajikistan	..	650	..	..	..	..	..	..	..	..	..	..
Tanzania	331	780	..	70	..	13	..	0	..	1	..	15
Thailand	23,068	65,113	29	15	5	3	1	3	1	1	63	74
Togo	268	432	23	18	21	11	0	0	45	21	9	50
Trinidad and Tobago	2,080	4,690	5	5	0	0	67	49	1	0	27	46
Tunisia	3,526	6,606	11	9	1	1	17	12	2	2	69	77
Turkey	12,959	31,197	22	13	3	1	2	1	4	2	68	82
Turkmenistan	..	2,620	..	0	..	10	..	81	..	0	..	7
Uganda	152	457	..	69	..	15	..	6	..	3	..	7
Ukraine	..	16,265	..	..	..	..	..	..	..	..	..	..
United Arab Emirates	23,544	42,900	8	..	1	..	5	..	39	..	46	..
United Kingdom	185,172	273,086	7	5	1	1	8	9	3	2	79	80
United States	393,592	730,803	11	8	4	2	3	2	3	2	74	82
Uruguay	1,693	2,060	40	45	21	11	0	2	0	1	39	42
Uzbekistan	..	3,450	..	..	..	..	..	..	..	..	..	..
Venezuela, RB	17,497	27,409	2	2	0	0	80	83	7	4	10	11
Vietnam	2,404	15,093	..	..	..	..	..	..	..	..	..	..
West Bank and Gaza	..	..	..	..	..	..	..	..	..	..	..	..
Yemen, Rep.	692	3,205	75	..	10	..	8	..	7	..	1	..
Yugoslavia, Fed. Rep.	2,929	1,903	19	17	3	6	6	0	10	16	62	59
Zambia	1,309	870	..	10	..	3	..	1	..	73	..	13
Zimbabwe	1,726	1,770	44	47	7	13	1	1	16	11	31	28
World	**3,444,192 t**	**6,155,800 t**	**10 w**	**7 w**	**3 w**	**2 w**	**8 w**	**7 w**	**4 w**	**3 w**	**74 w**	**78 w**
Low income	101,915	220,569	15	15	5	4	27	24	5	6	47	52
Middle income	540,593	1,319,759	17	10	4	2	22	21	6	4	47	61
Lower middle income	276,215	702,607	18	8	4	2	11	18	4	4	57	63
Upper middle income	263,168	617,152	16	12	5	2	34	24	7	4	37	58
Low & middle income	642,652	1,540,328	17	10	5	2	22	21	6	4	47	60
East Asia & Pacific	155,919	530,693	15	8	6	2	14	7	3	2	59	80
Europe & Central Asia [d]	..	325,644	..	5	..	3	..	26	..	5	..	56
Latin America & Carib.	143,391	344,370	26	22	4	3	24	17	12	8	34	49
Middle East & N. Africa	126,653	182,788	4	3	1	0	78	81	2	1	17	14
South Asia	27,728	65,208	16	12	5	2	2	4	4	2	71	78
Sub-Saharan Africa	67,877	91,624	13	16	3	6	28	31	7	8	20	33
High income	2,799,783	4,615,416	8	6	3	2	5	4	3	2	79	82
Europe EMU	1,229,887	1,892,062	10	8	2	1	3	3	2	2	81	83

Note: Components may not sum to 100 percent because of unclassified trade.
a. Includes Luxembourg. b. Includes re-exports. c. Data on total merchandise exports for 1990 refer to the South African Customs Union (Botswana, Lesotho, Namibia, South Africa, and Swaziland); those for 2001 refer to South Africa only. d. Data for 2001 include the intratrade of the Baltic states and the Commonwealth of Independent States.

About the data

Data on merchandise trade come from customs reports of goods entering an economy or from reports of the financial transactions related to merchandise trade recorded in the balance of payments. Because of differences in timing and definitions, estimates of trade flows from customs reports are likely to differ from those based on the balance of payments. Moreover, several international agencies process trade data, each making estimates to correct for unreported or misreported data, and this leads to other differences in the available data.

The most detailed source of data on international trade in goods is the Commodity Trade (COMTRADE) database maintained by the United Nations Statistics Division. In addition, the International Monetary Fund (IMF) collects customs-based data on exports and imports of goods. The value of exports is recorded as the cost of the goods delivered to the frontier of the exporting country for shipment—the f.o.b. (free on board) value. Many countries report trade data in U.S. dollars. When countries report in local currency, the United Nations Statistics Division applies the average official exchange rate for the period shown.

Countries may report trade according to the general or special system of trade (see *Primary data documentation*). Under the general system exports comprise outward-moving goods that are (a) goods wholly or partly produced in the country; (b) foreign goods, neither transformed nor declared for domestic consumption in the country, that move outward from customs storage; and (c) goods previously included as imports for domestic consumption but subsequently exported without transformation.

Under the special system exports comprise categories a and c. In some compilations categories b and c are classified as re-exports. Because of differences in reporting practices, data on exports may not be fully comparable across economies.

The data on total exports of goods (merchandise) in this table come from the World Trade Organization (WTO). The WTO uses two main sources, national statistical offices and the IMF's *International Financial Statistics*. It supplements these with the COMTRADE database and publications or databases of regional organizations, specialized agencies, and economic groups (such as the Commonwealth of Independent States, the Economic Commission for Latin America and the Caribbean, Eurostat, the Food and Agriculture Organization, the Organisation for Economic Co-operation and Development, and the Organization of Petroleum Exporting Countries). It also consults private sources, such as country reports of the Economist Intelligence Unit and press clippings. In recent years country Web sites and direct contacts through email have helped to improve the collection of up-to-date statistics for many countries, reducing the proportion of estimated figures. The WTO database now covers most of the major traders in Africa, Asia, and Latin America, which together with the high-income countries account for nearly 90 percent of total world trade. There has also been a remarkable improvement in the availability of recent, reliable, and standardized figures for countries in Europe and Central Asia.

The shares of exports by major commodity group were estimated by World Bank staff from the COMTRADE database. The values of total exports reported here have not been fully reconciled with the estimates of exports of goods and services from the national accounts (shown in table 4.9) or those from the balance of payments (table 4.15).

The classification of commodity groups is based on the Standard International Trade Classification (SITC) revision 1. Most countries now report using later revisions of the SITC or the Harmonized System. Concordance tables are used to convert data reported in one system of nomenclature to another. The conversion process may introduce some errors of classification, but conversions from later to early systems are generally reliable. Shares may not sum to 100 percent because of unclassified trade.

Definitions

• **Merchandise exports** show the f.o.b. value of goods provided to the rest of the world valued in U.S. dollars. • **Food** comprises the commodities in SITC sections 0 (food and live animals), 1 (beverages and tobacco), and 4 (animal and vegetable oils and fats) and SITC division 22 (oil seeds, oil nuts, and oil kernels). • **Agricultural raw materials** comprise SITC section 2 (crude materials except fuels) excluding divisions 22, 27 (crude fertilizers and minerals excluding coal, petroleum, and precious stones), and 28 (metalliferous ores and scrap). • **Fuels** comprise SITC section 3 (mineral fuels). • **Ores and metals** comprise the commodities in SITC divisions 27, 28, and 68 (nonferrous metals). • **Manufactures** comprise the commodities in SITC sections 5 (chemicals), 6 (basic manufactures), 7 (machinery and transport equipment), and 8 (miscellaneous manufactured goods), excluding division 68.

4.5a

Top 10 developing country exporters in 2001

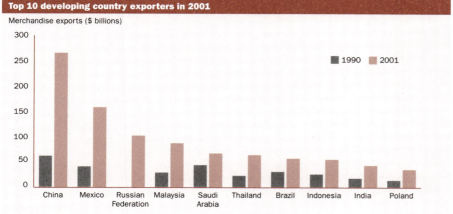

Merchandise exports ($ billions)

China led developing countries in merchandise exports in 2001, followed by Mexico.

Note: No data are available for the Russian Federation for 1990.
Source: World Trade Organization data files.

Data sources

The WTO publishes data on world trade in its *Annual Report*. The IMF publishes estimates of total exports of goods in its *International Financial Statistics* and *Direction of Trade Statistics*, as does the United Nations Statistics Division in its *Monthly Bulletin of Statistics*. And the United Nations Conference on Trade and Development (UNCTAD) publishes data on the structure of exports and imports in its *Handbook of International Trade and Development Statistics*. Tariff line records of exports and imports are compiled in the United Nations Statistics Division's COMTRADE database.

4.6 Structure of merchandise imports

	Merchandise imports		Food		Agricultural raw materials		Fuels		Ores and metals		Manufactures	
	$ millions		% of total		% of total		% of total		% of total		% of total	
	1990	2001	1990	2001	1990	2001	1990	2001	1990	2001	1990	2001
Afghanistan	936	554	..	..	..	..	..	..	..	..	..	..
Albania	380	1,315	..	19	..	1	..	10	..	2	..	68
Algeria	9,780	9,700	24	28	5	3	1	1	2	1	68	67
Angola	1,578	3,351	..	..	..	..	..	..	..	..	..	..
Argentina	4,076	20,311	4	6	4	2	8	4	6	2	78	86
Armenia	..	870	..	25	..	1	..	21	..	1	..	52
Australia	41,985	63,886	5	5	2	1	6	9	1	1	84	84
Austria	49,146	74,428	5	6	3	3	6	6	4	3	81	82
Azerbaijan	..	1,675	..	16	..	1	..	15	..	2	..	65
Bangladesh	3,618	8,397	19	..	5	..	16	..	3	..	56	..
Belarus	..	8,045	..	12	..	2	..	27	..	3	..	54
Belgium a	119,702	180,660	10	9	2	2	8	9	6	3	68	77
Benin	265	651	38	20	4	5	1	17	1	1	56	56
Bolivia	687	1,724	12	15	2	2	1	7	1	1	85	76
Bosnia and Herzegovina	360	2,790	..	..	..	..	..	..	..	..	..	..
Botswana	1,946	2,450	..	..	..	..	..	..	..	..	..	..
Brazil	22,524	58,265	9	6	3	1	27	14	5	3	56	75
Bulgaria	5,100	7,240	8	5	3	1	36	26	4	6	49	59
Burkina Faso	536	656	..	..	..	..	..	..	..	..	..	..
Burundi	231	139	..	23	..	2	..	12	..	2	..	60
Cambodia	164	1,570	..	..	..	..	..	..	..	..	..	..
Cameroon	1,400	1,852	19	15	0	1	2	18	1	1	78	64
Canada	123,244	227,165	6	6	2	1	6	6	3	2	81	83
Central African Republic	154	130	..	..	..	..	..	..	..	..	..	..
Chad	285	632	..	..	..	..	..	..	..	..	..	..
Chile	7,742	17,243	4	7	2	1	16	17	1	1	75	73
China †	53,345	243,613	9	4	6	4	2	7	3	6	80	78
Hong Kong, China	84,725	202,008	8	4	2	1	2	2	2	2	85	91
Colombia	5,590	12,834	7	12	4	2	6	2	3	2	77	81
Congo, Dem. Rep.	1,739	1,024	..	..	..	..	..	..	..	..	..	..
Congo, Rep.	621	940	..	..	..	..	..	..	..	..	..	..
Costa Rica	1,990	6,564	8	8	2	1	10	7	2	1	66	83
Côte d'Ivoire	2,097	2,560	..	17	..	1	..	34	..	1	..	46
Croatia	4,500	8,044	12	9	4	2	10	13	4	2	64	74
Cuba	4,600	4,930	..	..	..	..	..	..	..	..	..	..
Czech Republic	12,880	36,490	..	5	..	2	..	9	..	3	..	81
Denmark	33,333	45,398	12	12	3	3	7	4	2	2	73	76
Dominican Republic	3,006	8,784	..	..	..	..	..	..	..	..	..	..
Ecuador	1,861	5,299	9	8	3	2	2	4	2	1	84	81
Egypt, Arab Rep.	12,412	12,756	32	26	7	5	3	5	2	2	56	55
El Salvador	1,263	5,027	14	17	3	3	15	13	4	1	63	66
Eritrea	278	470	..	..	..	..	..	..	..	..	..	..
Estonia	..	4,300	..	11	..	3	..	7	..	2	..	78
Ethiopia	1,081	1,040	..	7	..	1	..	20	..	1	..	71
Finland	27,001	32,008	5	6	2	3	12	12	4	5	76	73
France	234,436	325,752	10	8	3	2	10	10	4	3	74	78
Gabon	918	940	..	18	..	1	..	4	..	1	..	75
Gambia, The	188	200	..	35	..	1	..	12	..	1	..	51
Georgia	..	685	..	..	..	..	..	..	..	..	..	..
Germany	355,686	492,825	10	7	3	2	8	8	4	3	72	70
Ghana	1,205	3,030	11	18	1	2	17	23	0	1	70	56
Greece	19,777	25,416	15	12	3	1	8	15	3	3	70	68
Guatemala	1,649	5,607	10	14	2	1	17	14	2	1	69	69
Guinea	723	601	..	23	..	1	..	19	..	0	..	56
Guinea-Bissau	86	65	..	..	..	..	..	..	..	..	..	..
Haiti	332	1,013	..	..	..	..	..	..	..	..	..	..
† Data for Taiwan, China	54,831	107,274	7	4	5	2	11	11	6	5	69	76

Structure of merchandise imports

	Merchandise imports		Food		Agricultural raw materials		Fuels		Ores and metals		Manufactures	
	$ millions		% of total		% of total		% of total		% of total		% of total	
	1990	2001	1990	2001	1990	2001	1990	2001	1990	2001	1990	2001
Honduras	935	2,918	10	18	1	1	16	13	1	1	71	67
Hungary	10,340	33,680	8	3	4	1	14	5	4	2	70	84
India	23,580	49,618	3	5	4	3	27	37	8	5	51	48
Indonesia	21,837	30,962	5	10	5	7	9	18	4	3	77	61
Iran, Islamic Rep.	20,322	17,500	..	16	..	2	..	4	..	2	..	76
Iraq	7,660	11,000	..	..	..	..	..	..	..	..	..	..
Ireland	20,669	50,691	11	7	2	1	6	4	2	1	76	82
Israel	16,793	35,123	8	5	2	1	9	10	3	2	77	81
Italy	181,968	232,910	12	9	6	4	11	9	5	4	64	70
Jamaica	1,928	3,331	15	15	1	1	20	18	1	1	61	61
Japan	235,368	349,089	15	13	7	3	25	20	9	5	44	57
Jordan	2,600	4,844	26	18	2	2	18	14	1	2	51	62
Kazakhstan	..	6,365	..	9	..	1	..	12	..	3	..	75
Kenya	2,223	2,890	9	14	3	2	20	22	2	1	66	60
Korea, Dem. Rep.	2,930	2,400	..	..	..	..	..	..	..	..	..	..
Korea, Rep.	69,844	141,098	6	6	8	3	16	24	7	6	63	61
Kuwait	3,972	7,734	17	17	1	1	1	1	2	2	79	79
Kyrgyz Republic	..	465	..	14	..	1	..	20	..	2	..	64
Lao PDR	185	551	..	..	..	..	..	..	..	..	..	..
Latvia	..	3,505	..	12	..	2	..	11	..	2	..	73
Lebanon	2,529	7,291	..	18	..	2	..	18	..	2	..	60
Lesotho	672	681	..	..	..	..	..	..	..	..	..	..
Liberia	220	290	..	..	..	..	..	..	..	..	..	..
Libya	5,336	8,700	23	..	2	..	0	..	1	..	74	..
Lithuania	..	6,280	..	9	..	3	..	20	..	1	..	64
Macedonia, FYR	1,206	1,630	..	14	..	2	..	14	..	2	..	44
Madagascar	651	1,164	11	14	1	1	17	24	1	0	69	60
Malawi	575	550	9	..	1	..	11	..	1	..	78	..
Malaysia	29,258	74,079	7	5	1	1	5	5	4	3	82	83
Mali	602	657	26	..	1	..	19	..	1	..	53	..
Mauritania	388	335	..	..	..	..	..	..	..	..	..	..
Mauritius	1,618	1,992	12	16	3	2	8	11	1	1	76	69
Mexico	43,548	176,162	15	5	4	1	4	3	3	2	75	88
Moldova	..	895	..	14	..	2	..	26	..	1	..	56
Mongolia	924	461	..	17	..	1	..	19	..	0	..	63
Morocco	6,922	10,960	10	14	6	3	17	18	6	3	61	63
Mozambique	878	1,063	..	14	..	1	..	16	..	0	..	47
Myanmar	270	2,767	13	..	1	..	5	..	0	..	81	..
Namibia	1,163	1,440	..	..	..	..	..	..	..	..	..	..
Nepal	672	1,473	15	13	7	4	9	16	2	3	67	49
Netherlands	126,098	207,284	13	10	2	2	10	11	3	2	71	74
New Zealand	9,501	13,347	7	9	1	1	8	8	3	2	81	80
Nicaragua	638	1,776	19	16	1	1	19	17	1	1	59	64
Niger	388	415	..	44	..	1	..	13	..	2	..	40
Nigeria	5,627	11,150	6	20	1	1	0	1	2	2	67	76
Norway	27,231	32,361	6	7	2	2	4	4	6	6	82	80
Oman	2,681	5,798	19	22	1	1	4	3	1	3	69	68
Pakistan	7,411	10,617	17	12	4	4	21	29	4	3	54	50
Panama	1,539	2,964	12	12	1	1	16	21	1	1	70	66
Papua New Guinea	1,193	1,073	18	18	0	1	7	22	1	1	73	58
Paraguay	1,352	2,145	8	14	0	1	14	16	1	1	77	68
Peru	3,470	8,620	24	13	2	2	12	13	1	1	61	71
Philippines	13,042	31,358	10	9	2	1	15	11	3	3	53	76
Poland	11,570	50,275	8	6	3	2	22	10	4	3	63	77
Portugal	25,263	37,955	12	11	4	3	11	10	2	2	71	73
Puerto Rico	..	..	..	..	..	..	..	..	..	..	..	..

4.6 Structure of merchandise imports

	Merchandise imports ($ millions)		Food (% of total)		Agricultural raw materials (% of total)		Fuels (% of total)		Ores and metals (% of total)		Manufactures (% of total)	
	1990	2001	1990	2001	1990	2001	1990	2001	1990	2001	1990	2001
Romania	7,600	15,550	12	8	4	1	38	13	6	3	39	75
Russian Federation	33,100	53,860	..	20	..	2	..	2	..	3	..	63
Rwanda	288	250	..	..	..	..	..	..	..	..	..	..
Saudi Arabia	24,069	31,223	15	16	1	1	0	0	3	3	81	79
Senegal	1,219	1,510	29	27	2	2	16	17	2	2	51	53
Sierra Leone	149	166	..	..	..	..	..	..	..	..	..	..
Singapore	60,774	116,000	6	4	2	0	16	13	2	2	73	81
Slovak Republic	6,670	14,765	..	6	..	2	..	15	..	3	..	74
Slovenia	6,142	10,144	9	6	4	3	11	8	4	5	67	77
Somalia	95	220	..	..	..	..	..	..	..	..	..	..
South Africa[b]	18,399	28,405	5	5	2	1	1	16	2	1	77	68
Spain	87,715	142,740	11	10	3	2	12	11	4	3	71	73
Sri Lanka	2,688	5,925	19	14	2	1	13	9	1	1	65	74
Sudan	618	1,575	13	..	1	..	20	..	0	..	66	..
Swaziland	663	832	..	..	..	..	..	..	..	..	..	..
Sweden	54,264	62,562	6	7	2	1	9	8	3	3	79	76
Switzerland	69,681	84,077	6	5	2	1	5	5	3	6	84	82
Syrian Arab Republic	2,400	4,300	31	19	2	3	3	4	1	2	62	65
Tajikistan	..	690	..	..	..	..	..	..	..	..	..	..
Tanzania	1,027	1,660	..	16	..	2	..	8	..	1	..	72
Thailand	33,045	62,058	5	5	5	3	9	12	4	3	75	76
Togo	581	620	22	23	1	1	8	16	1	2	67	58
Trinidad and Tobago	1,262	3,560	19	9	1	1	11	23	6	1	62	65
Tunisia	5,513	9,552	11	8	4	3	9	11	4	2	72	76
Turkey	22,302	40,573	8	4	4	4	21	15	5	4	61	67
Turkmenistan	..	2,105	..	12	..	0	..	1	..	1	..	80
Uganda	288	1,594	..	12	..	2	..	16	..	2	..	67
Ukraine	..	15,775	..	..	..	..	..	..	..	..	..	..
United Arab Emirates	11,199	41,700	14	..	1	..	3	..	4	..	77	..
United Kingdom	222,977	331,793	10	8	3	1	6	4	4	3	75	79
United States	516,987	1,180,154	6	4	2	1	13	11	3	2	73	77
Uruguay	1,343	3,061	7	11	4	3	18	12	2	1	69	72
Uzbekistan	..	2,630	..	..	..	..	..	..	..	..	..	..
Venezuela, RB	7,335	18,022	11	11	4	1	3	4	4	2	77	82
Vietnam	2,752	15,550	..	..	..	..	..	..	..	..	..	..
West Bank and Gaza	..	..	..	..	..	..	..	..	..	..	..	..
Yemen, Rep.	1,571	2,260	27	..	1	..	40	..	1	..	31	..
Yugoslavia, Fed. Rep.	4,634	4,837	9	9	3	3	23	20	3	4	62	58
Zambia	1,220	960	..	8	..	2	..	9	..	2	..	80
Zimbabwe	1,847	1,540	4	9	3	2	16	12	2	3	73	75
World	**3,524,806 t**	**6,357,673 t**	**9 w**	**7 w**	**3 w**	**2 w**	**11 w**	**10 w**	**4 w**	**3 w**	**71 w**	**75 w**
Low income	105,606	202,458	7	11	3	4	17	24	4	3	64	56
Middle income	494,625	1,265,184	10	8	4	2	10	9	3	3	72	76
Lower middle income	290,853	663,596	10	9	4	3	8	9	3	3	71	72
Upper middle income	204,672	601,580	10	7	2	1	11	8	4	3	73	80
Low & middle income	600,718	1,467,639	10	8	4	2	11	10	4	3	71	75
East Asia & Pacific	160,449	468,386	7	6	4	4	6	9	3	4	77	77
Europe & Central Asia[c]	136,692	325,334	..	10	..	2	..	9	..	3	..	71
Latin America & Carib.	121,363	373,978	11	8	3	1	13	9	3	2	69	79
Middle East & N. Africa	105,974	138,636	19	18	3	2	4	5	3	2	70	71
South Asia	39,124	77,158	9	7	4	3	23	35	6	4	54	48
Sub-Saharan Africa	57,164	84,141	9	11	..	2	..	14	..	2	..	67
High income	2,916,941	4,889,755	9	7	3	2	11	10	4	3	71	75
Europe EMU	1,253,828	1,810,883	11	8	3	2	9	9	4	3	72	73

Note: Components may not sum to 100 percent because of unclassified trade.

a. Includes Luxembourg. b. Data on total merchandise imports for 1990 refer to the South African Customs Union (Botswana, Lesotho, Namibia, South Africa, and Swaziland); those for 2001 refer to South Africa only. c. Data for 2001 include the intratrade of the Baltic states and the Commonwealth of Independent States.

Structure of merchandise imports | 4.6

Data on imports of goods are derived from the same sources as data on exports. In principle, world exports and imports should be identical. Similarly, exports from an economy should equal the sum of imports by the rest of the world from that economy. But differences in timing and definitions result in discrepancies in reported values at all levels. For further discussion of indicators of merchandise trade, see *About the data* for tables 4.4 and 4.5.

The value of imports is generally recorded as the cost of the goods when purchased by the importer plus the cost of transport and insurance to the frontier of the importing country—the c.i.f. (cost, insurance, and freight) value, corresponding to the landed cost at the point of entry of foreign goods into the country. A few countries, including Australia, Canada, and the United States, collect import data on an f.o.b. (free on board) basis and adjust them for freight and insurance costs. Many countries collect and report trade data in U.S. dollars. When countries report in local currency, the United Nations Statistics Division applies the average official exchange rate for the period shown.

Countries may report trade according to the general or special system of trade (see *Primary data documentation*). Under the general system imports include goods imported for domestic consumption and imports into bonded warehouses and free trade zones. Under the special system imports comprise goods imported for domestic consumption (including transformation and repair) and withdrawals for domestic consumption from bonded warehouses and free trade zones. Goods transported through a country en route to another are excluded.

The data on total imports of goods (merchandise) in this table come from the World Trade Organization

(WTO). For further discussion of the WTO's sources and methodology, see *About the data* for table 4.5.

The shares of imports by major commodity group were estimated by World Bank staff from the United Nations Statistics Division's Commodity Trade (COMTRADE) database. The values of total imports reported here have not been fully reconciled with the estimates of imports of goods and services from the national accounts (shown in table 4.9) or those from the balance of payments (table 4.15).

The classification of commodity groups is based on the Standard International Trade Classification (SITC) revision 1. Most countries now report using later revisions of the SITC or the Harmonized System. Concordance tables are used to convert data reported in one system of nomenclature to another. The conversion process may introduce some errors of classification, but conversions from later to early systems are generally reliable. Shares may not sum to 100 percent because of unclassified trade.

• **Merchandise imports** show the c.i.f. value of goods purchased from the rest of the world valued in U.S. dollars. • **Food** comprises the commodities in SITC sections 0 (food and live animals), 1 (beverages and tobacco), and 4 (animal and vegetable oils and fats) and SITC division 22 (oil seeds, oil nuts, and oil kernels). • **Agricultural raw materials** comprise SITC section 2 (crude materials except fuels) excluding divisions 22, 27 (crude fertilizers and minerals excluding coal, petroleum, and precious stones), and 28 (metalliferous ores and scrap). • **Fuels** comprise SITC section 3 (mineral fuels). • **Ores and metals** comprise the commodities in SITC divisions 27, 28, and 68 (nonferrous metals). • **Manufactures** comprise the commodities in SITC sections 5 (chemicals), 6 (basic manufactures), 7 (machinery and transport equipment), and 8 (miscellaneous manufactured goods), excluding division 68.

4.6a

Manufactures account for the biggest share of merchandise imports

% of merchandise imports, 2001

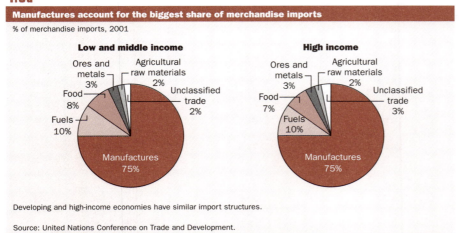

Developing and high-income economies have similar import structures.

Source: United Nations Conference on Trade and Development.

The WTO publishes data on world trade in its *Annual Report*. The International Monetary Fund (IMF) publishes estimates of total imports of goods in its *International Financial Statistics* and *Direction of Trade Statistics*, as does the United Nations Statistics Division in its *Monthly Bulletin of Statistics*. And the United Nations Conference on Trade and Development (UNCTAD) publishes data on the structure of exports and imports in its *Handbook of International Trade and Development Statistics*. Tariff line records of exports and imports are compiled in the United Nations Statistics Division's COMTRADE database.

4.7 Structure of service exports

	Commercial service exports $ millions		Transport % of total services		Travel % of total services		Other % of total services	
	1990	2001	1990	2001	1990	2001	1990	2001
Afghanistan	..	..	..	..	..	..	..	..
Albania	32	495	20.0	3.1	11.1	90.2	68.9	6.7
Algeria	479	..	41.7	..	13.4	..	44.9	..
Angola	65	*267*	48.8	*6.0*	20.6	*0.0*	30.7	*94.0*
Argentina	2,264	4,152	51.1	20.5	39.9	63.0	9.1	16.5
Armenia	..	179	..	39.7	..	36.2	..	24.2
Australia	9,833	15,837	35.5	26.0	43.2	48.6	21.4	25.4
Austria	22,755	32,535	6.4	15.3	59.0	31.5	34.6	53.2
Azerbaijan	..	256	..	63.2	..	16.6	..	20.2
Bangladesh	296	242	12.9	29.5	6.4	19.6	80.6	50.8
Belarus	..	994	..	63.1	..	8.3	..	28.6
Belgium[a]	26,646	48,970	27.5	20.8	14.0	15.5	58.5	63.7
Benin	109	*126*	33.4	*14.3*	50.2	*60.8*	16.4	*24.8*
Bolivia	133	221	35.8	30.4	43.6	34.2	20.6	35.4
Bosnia and Herzegovina	..	..	..	..	..	..	..	..
Botswana	183	*346*	20.4	*27.7*	64.1	*67.7*	15.5	*4.7*
Brazil	3,706	8,719	36.4	16.3	37.3	19.9	26.3	63.8
Bulgaria	837	2,377	27.5	29.3	38.2	50.4	34.2	20.3
Burkina Faso	34	..	37.1	..	34.1	..	28.9	..
Burundi	7	*2*	38.7	*42.8*	51.4	*36.6*	9.9	*20.6*
Cambodia	*50*	253	..	34.4	*100.0*	58.7	*0.0*	6.9
Cameroon	369	..	42.6	..	14.4	..	43.0	..
Canada	18,350	35,643	23.0	19.1	34.7	30.3	42.3	50.7
Central African Republic	17	..	50.9	..	16.0	..	33.1	..
Chad	23	..	18.4	..	34.1	..	47.5	..
Chile	1,786	3,730	40.0	44.4	29.8	22.9	30.3	32.6
China	5,748	32,901	47.1	14.1	30.2	54.1	22.7	31.8
Hong Kong, China	..	41,428	..	*31.4*	..	*19.5*	..	*49.1*
Colombia	1,548	2,089	31.3	25.4	26.2	57.9	42.5	16.8
Congo, Dem. Rep.	..	..	..	..	..	..	..	..
Congo, Rep.	65	..	53.9	..	12.9	..	33.1	..
Costa Rica	583	2,025	16.3	10.5	48.9	67.1	34.8	22.4
Côte d'Ivoire	425	420	62.4	20.4	12.1	11.5	25.5	68.0
Croatia	..	4,871	..	12.1	..	68.5	..	19.5
Cuba	..	..	..	..	..	..	..	..
Czech Republic	..	7,034	..	21.5	..	44.1	..	34.4
Denmark	12,731	26,913	32.5	60.0	26.2	17.2	41.3	22.8
Dominican Republic	1,086	2,912	5.6	2.3	66.8	92.4	27.5	5.3
Ecuador	508	848	47.6	35.1	37.0	50.7	15.4	14.2
Egypt, Arab Rep.	4,812	8,815	50.1	31.1	22.9	43.1	27.1	25.8
El Salvador	301	1,052	26.2	26.8	25.2	19.1	48.6	54.1
Eritrea	..	..	..	..	..	..	..	..
Estonia	*200*	1,634	*74.7*	48.3	*13.7*	30.9	*11.6*	20.7
Ethiopia	261	391	80.6	60.0	2.1	13.0	17.3	27.0
Finland	4,562	5,775	38.4	27.1	25.8	24.9	35.7	48.0
France	74,948	79,848	21.7	22.6	27.0	38.1	51.3	39.2
Gabon	214	*249*	33.4	*60.9*	1.4	*6.0*	65.2	*33.2*
Gambia, The	53	..	8.8	..	87.9	..	3.3	..
Georgia	..	206	..	49.7	..	46.9	..	3.5
Germany	51,605	83,225	28.6	24.7	27.9	20.7	43.5	54.7
Ghana	79	*490*	49.2	*20.1*	5.6	*68.3*	45.2	*11.6*
Greece	6,514	19,384	4.9	42.1	39.7	47.2	55.4	10.6
Guatemala	313	934	7.4	10.7	37.6	60.1	55.0	29.2
Guinea	91	72	14.2	43.9	32.6	0.1	53.3	56.0
Guinea-Bissau	4	..	5.4	..	0.0	..	94.6	..
Haiti	43	..	19.8	..	78.9	..	1.3	..

	Commercial service exports		Transport		Travel		Other	
	$ millions		% of total services		% of total services		% of total services	
	1990	2001	1990	2001	1990	2001	1990	2001
Honduras	121	426	35.1	11.9	24.0	60.2	40.9	27.9
Hungary	2,677	7,627	1.6	8.5	36.8	51.4	61.6	40.1
India	4,610	20,390 [b]	20.8	*10.6*	33.8	*17.9*	45.4	*71.4*
Indonesia	2,488	5,361	2.8	*0.0*	86.5	98.4	10.7	1.6
Iran, Islamic Rep.	343	*1,357*	10.5	*49.4*	8.2	*36.9*	81.3	*13.6*
Iraq	..	..	..	..	..	..	..	..
Ireland	3,286	20,032	31.1	7.4	44.4	13.7	24.5	78.8
Israel	4,546	11,949	30.8	17.8	30.7	20.6	38.5	61.7
Italy	48,579	56,970	21.0	14.4	33.9	45.3	45.2	40.3
Jamaica	976	1,871	18.0	18.7	77.0	65.9	5.0	15.4
Japan	41,384	63,670	*40.4*	37.7	*7.9*	5.2	*51.7*	57.1
Jordan	1,430	1,391	26.0	18.5	35.7	50.3	38.3	31.2
Kazakhstan	..	1,119	..	55.7	..	35.9	..	8.3
Kenya	774	791	32.0	54.1	60.2	39.0	7.8	6.9
Korea, Dem. Rep.	..	..	..	..	..	..	..	..
Korea, Rep.	9,155	29,602	34.7	45.6	34.5	21.3	30.7	33.1
Kuwait	1,054	1,523	87.5	87.2	12.5	6.9	0.0	6.0
Kyrgyz Republic	..	72	..	25.9	..	33.8	..	40.3
Lao PDR	11	127	74.8	18.0	24.3	82.0	0.9	0.0
Latvia	*290*	1,169	*94.9*	65.8	*2.5*	10.2	*2.6*	23.9
Lebanon	..	..	..	..	..	..	..	..
Lesotho	34	35	14.1	1.2	51.2	65.6	34.7	33.2
Liberia	..	..	..	..	..	..	..	..
Libya	83	*46*	83.8	*37.9*	7.7	*53.9*	8.5	*8.2*
Lithuania	..	1,147	..	46.4	..	33.4	..	20.2
Macedonia, FYR	..	189	..	39.6	..	13.3	..	47.1
Madagascar	129	33	32.1	20.6	31.3	42.0	36.6	37.4
Malawi	37	..	46.1	..	42.6	..	11.3	..
Malaysia	3,769	14,331	31.8	19.2	44.7	47.9	23.5	32.9
Mali	71	..	31.0	..	54.3	..	14.7	..
Mauritania	14	..	35.3	..	64.7	..	0.0	..
Mauritius	478	1,218	32.9	19.3	51.1	51.1	15.9	29.5
Mexico	7,222	12,547	12.4	10.2	76.5	66.9	11.1	22.8
Moldova	..	164	..	47.0	..	28.1	..	24.9
Mongolia	48	82	41.8	43.1	10.4	47.8	47.8	9.1
Morocco	1,871	3,787	9.6	17.4	68.4	68.2	22.0	14.4
Mozambique	103	587	61.3	25.1	0.0	23.2	38.7	51.7
Myanmar	93	401	10.3	19.8	20.9	31.0	68.8	49.2
Namibia	106	..	0.0	..	81.0	..	19.0	..
Nepal	166	303	3.6	15.6	65.6	47.5	30.8	36.9
Netherlands	28,478	51,973	45.4	37.8	14.6	12.9	40.0	49.3
New Zealand	2,415	4,286	43.4	26.7	42.7	54.7	13.9	18.6
Nicaragua	34	296	19.2	8.7	35.5	45.7	45.3	45.6
Niger	22	..	5.2	..	59.5	..	35.3	..
Nigeria	965	*980*	3.9	*12.0*	2.5	*5.5*	93.6	*82.5*
Norway	12,452	17,805	68.7	60.6	12.6	10.8	18.7	28.6
Oman	68	349	15.3	45.5	84.7	41.0	0.0	13.4
Pakistan	1,218	1,302	59.3	62.8	12.0	6.8	28.7	30.4
Panama	907	1,791	64.9	53.7	18.9	27.1	16.2	19.1
Papua New Guinea	198	285	11.2	7.5	12.0	1.8	76.8	90.7
Paraguay	404	550	18.3	15.8	21.1	14.0	60.5	70.1
Peru	714	1,378	43.4	18.7	30.4	59.3	26.2	22.1
Philippines	2,897	3,115	8.5	21.2	16.1	55.3	75.4	23.5
Poland	3,200	9,747	57.3	27.5	11.2	47.7	31.5	24.8
Portugal	5,054	8,674	15.6	18.2	70.4	63.0	14.0	18.8
Puerto Rico	..	..	..	..	..	..	..	..

	Commercial service exports		Transport		Travel		Other	
	$ millions		% of total services		% of total services		% of total services	
	1990	2001	1990	2001	1990	2001	1990	2001
Romania	610	1,969	50.5	40.1	17.4	18.4	32.2	41.5
Russian Federation	..	10,677	..	43.6	..	35.1	..	21.3
Rwanda	31	29	56.1	55.3	32.8	30.6	11.0	14.1
Saudi Arabia	3,031	5,182	..	..	..	..	..	..
Senegal	356	351	19.1	10.1	42.7	49.4	38.1	40.4
Sierra Leone	45	..	9.7	..	76.2	..	14.1	..
Singapore	12,719	26,092	17.5	18.1	36.6	19.6	45.9	62.3
Slovak Republic	..	2,218	..	44.9	..	19.5	..	35.6
Slovenia	1,219	1,956	22.6	25.6	55.0	51.2	22.4	23.3
Somalia	..	..	..	..	..	..	..	..
South Africa	3,290	4,544	21.6	26.1	55.8	55.0	22.7	18.9
Spain	27,649	57,416	17.2	14.4	67.2	57.0	15.6	28.6
Sri Lanka	425	1,344	39.7	29.7	30.2	15.8	30.1	54.5
Sudan	134	14	14.1	44.4	15.7	23.0	70.2	32.6
Swaziland	102	83	24.5	16.3	29.2	34.2	46.3	49.6
Sweden	13,453	21,758	35.8	24.2	21.7	19.5	42.6	56.3
Switzerland	18,234	26,100	16.3	17.0	40.6	28.8	43.0	54.2
Syrian Arab Republic	740	1,481	29.7	16.6	43.3	73.1	27.0	10.3
Tajikistan	..	..	..	..	..	..	..	..
Tanzania	131	615	19.9	9.2	36.4	61.3	43.6	29.5
Thailand	6,292	12,932	21.1	23.6	68.7	54.7	10.2	21.6
Togo	114	46	26.9	23.0	50.7	17.6	22.3	59.4
Trinidad and Tobago	322	..	50.7	..	29.4	..	19.9	..
Tunisia	1,575	2,829	23.0	22.6	64.8	61.9	12.2	15.6
Turkey	7,882	15,913	11.7	17.9	40.9	50.8	47.4	31.2
Turkmenistan	..	..	..	..	..	..	..	..
Uganda	..	174	..	3.0	..	90.5	..	6.5
Ukraine	..	3,897	..	76.0	..	14.7	..	9.3
United Arab Emirates	..	..	..	..	..	..	..	..
United Kingdom	53,830	107,529	25.2	16.4	29.0	16.9	45.8	66.7
United States	132,880	259,380	28.1	17.9	37.9	34.7	34.0	47.4
Uruguay	460	1,112	36.9	30.3	51.8	54.9	11.3	14.8
Uzbekistan	..	..	..	..	..	..	..	..
Venezuela, RB	1,121	1,100	40.9	31.9	44.2	62.0	14.9	6.1
Vietnam	..	2,810	..	..	..	..	..	..
West Bank and Gaza	..	..	..	..	..	..	..	..
Yemen, Rep.	82	174	27.2	12.3	48.8	41.7	24.0	46.0
Yugoslavia, Fed. Rep.	..	..	..	..	..	..	..	..
Zambia	94	114	68.9	37.2	13.5	58.3	17.5	4.5
Zimbabwe	253	..	44.3	..	25.3	..	30.4	..
World	**750,362 s**	**1,452,403 s**	**28.1 w**	**23.2 w**	**34.1 w**	**32.1 w**	**37.8 w**	**44.7 w**
Low income	14,230	38,980	24.8	18.8	37.8	32.6	37.4	48.6
Middle income	80,533	209,600	28.4	20.6	44.3	48.0	27.3	31.4
Lower middle income	46,342	118,290	27.5	18.9	42.7	51.6	29.8	29.5
Upper middle income	34,191	91,310	29.8	22.8	47.1	43.5	23.1	33.7
Low & middle income	94,763	248,580	27.8	20.4	43.3	46.1	28.8	33.4
East Asia & Pacific	22,049	72,725	26.1	14.8	48.5	54.1	25.4	31.0
Europe & Central Asia	15,237	71,531	25.0	26.5	35.8	40.7	39.3	32.8
Latin America & Carib.	25,940	48,279	27.7	20.2	52.0	49.9	20.3	29.9
Middle East & N. Africa	15,235	23,439	33.2	24.8	40.3	53.1	26.5	22.1
South Asia	6,816	23,932	27.9	11.0	30.1	19.0	42.0	70.0
Sub-Saharan Africa	9,487	12,427	32.1	24.1	38.6	54.8	29.3	21.1
High income	655,599	1,203,824	28.1	23.7	32.8	29.5	39.1	46.8
Europe EMU	300,074	484,536	24.7	22.5	34.5	33.7	40.8	43.8

a. Includes Luxembourg. b. Data are an estimate from the World Trade Organization.

Structure of service exports | **4.7**

Balance of payments statistics, the main source of information on international trade in services, have many weaknesses. Some large economies—such as the former Soviet Union—did not report data on trade in services until recently. Disaggregation of important components may be limited, and it varies significantly across countries. There are inconsistencies in the methods used to report items. And the recording of major flows as net items is common (for example, insurance transactions are often recorded as premiums less claims). These factors contribute to a downward bias in the value of the service trade reported in the balance of payments.

Efforts are being made to improve the coverage, quality, and consistency of these data. Eurostat and the Organisation for Economic Co-operation and Development, for example, are working together to improve the collection of statistics on trade in services in member countries. In addition, the International Monetary Fund (IMF) has implemented the new classification of trade in services introduced in the fifth edition of its *Balance of Payments Manual* (1993).

Still, difficulties in capturing all the dimensions of international trade in services mean that the record is likely to remain incomplete. Cross-border intrafirm service transactions, which are usually not captured in the balance of payments, have increased in recent years. One example of such transactions is transnational corporations' use of mainframe computers around the clock for data processing, exploiting time zone differences between their home country and the host countries of their affiliates. Another important

dimension of service trade not captured by conventional balance of payments statistics is establishment trade—sales in the host country by foreign affiliates. By contrast, cross-border intrafirm transactions in merchandise may be reported as exports or imports in the balance of payments.

The data on exports of services in this table and on imports of services in table 4.8, unlike those in editions before 2000, include only commercial services and exclude the category *government services not included elsewhere*. The data are compiled by the IMF based on returns from national sources.

Data on total trade in goods and services from the IMF's Balance of Payments database are shown in table 4.15.

• **Commercial service exports** are total service exports minus exports of government services not included elsewhere. International transactions in services are defined by the IMF's *Balance of Payments Manual* (1993) as the economic output of intangible commodities that may be produced, transferred, and consumed at the same time. Definitions may vary among reporting economies. • **Transport** covers all transport services (sea, air, land, internal waterway, space, and pipeline) performed by residents of one economy for those of another and involving the carriage of passengers, movement of goods (freight), rental of carriers with crew, and related support and auxiliary services. Excluded are freight insurance, which is included in insurance services; goods procured in ports by nonresident carriers and repairs of transport equipment, which are included in goods; repairs of harbors, railway facilities, and airfield facilities, which are included in construction services; and rental of carriers without crew, which is included in other services. • **Travel** covers goods and services acquired from an economy by travelers in that economy for their own use during visits of less than one year for business or personal purposes. Travel services include the goods and services consumed by travelers, such as meals, lodging, and transport (within the economy visited), including car rental. • **Other commercial services** include such activities as insurance and financial services, international telecommunications, and postal and courier services; computer data; news-related service transactions between residents and nonresidents; construction services; royalties and license fees; miscellaneous business, professional, and technical services; and personal, cultural, and recreational services.

4.7a

Top 10 developing country exporters of commercial services

Commercial service exports ($ billions)

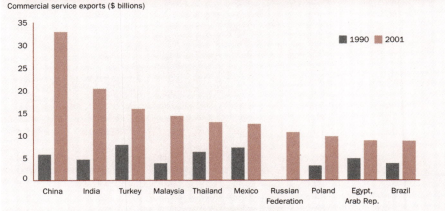

Major exporters of merchandise also tend to be major exporters of commercial services. The exceptions are fuel exporters—Saudi Arabia and Indonesia.

Source: International Monetary Fund and World Trade Organization data files.

The data on exports of commercial services are from the IMF. The IMF publishes balance of payments data in its *International Financial Statistics* and *Balance of Payments Statistics Yearbook*.

	Commercial service imports $ millions		Transport % of total		Travel % of total		Other % of total	
	1990	**2001**	**1990**	**2001**	**1990**	**2001**	**1990**	**2001**
Afghanistan	..	..	..	..	..	..	..	..
Albania	29	422	26.3	25.4	0.0	61.0	73.7	13.6
Algeria	1,155	..	58.1	..	12.9	..	29.0	..
Angola	1,288	*2,271*	38.3	*13.7*	3.0	*6.0*	58.7	*80.3*
Argentina	2,876	8,175	32.6	26.0	40.7	48.5	26.7	25.5
Armenia	..	192	..	62.8	..	20.7	..	16.5
Australia	13,388	16,421	33.9	35.0	31.5	35.4	34.7	29.6
Austria	14,104	31,471	8.4	10.6	54.9	28.2	36.7	61.1
Azerbaijan	..	650	..	24.1	..	16.7	..	59.2
Bangladesh	554	1,375	71.1	75.0	14.1	12.0	14.9	12.9
Belarus	..	591	..	21.1	..	44.4	..	34.4
Belgium[a]	25,924	42,856	23.3	19.5	21.1	24.7	55.6	55.8
Benin	113	*186*	46.9	*67.4*	12.8	*6.6*	40.3	*26.0*
Bolivia	291	485	61.7	58.2	20.6	17.1	17.7	24.7
Bosnia and Herzegovina	..	..	..	..	..	..	..	..
Botswana	371	*511*	57.5	*42.4*	15.0	*28.0*	27.5	*29.7*
Brazil	6,733	15,816	44.4	27.7	22.4	20.2	33.2	52.1
Bulgaria	600	1,863	40.5	43.2	31.5	30.5	28.0	26.3
Burkina Faso	196	..	64.7	..	16.6	..	18.7	..
Burundi	59	*34*	62.6	*55.7*	29.0	*39.7*	8.4	*4.5*
Cambodia	*64*	244	*24.5*	63.5	..	14.2	*75.5*	22.3
Cameroon	1,018	..	45.3	..	27.5	..	27.3	..
Canada	27,479	41,492	21.1	22.1	39.8	28.1	39.2	49.8
Central African Republic	166	..	49.7	..	30.6	..	19.6	..
Chad	223	..	45.1	..	31.2	..	23.7	..
Chile	1,982	4,673	47.4	37.0	21.5	12.4	31.1	50.5
China	4,113	39,032	78.9	29.0	11.4	35.6	9.7	35.4
Hong Kong, China	..	24,314	..	25.5	..	51.1	..	23.4
Colombia	1,683	3,511	34.9	39.9	27.0	33.0	38.1	27.1
Congo, Dem. Rep.	..	..	..	..	..	..	..	..
Congo, Rep.	748	..	18.4	..	15.2	..	66.5	..
Costa Rica	540	1,262	41.2	33.6	28.8	37.3	30.0	29.1
Côte d'Ivoire	1,518	1,149	32.1	45.4	11.1	16.7	56.8	37.9
Croatia	..	1,909	..	22.0	..	31.8	..	46.3
Cuba	..	..	..	..	..	..	..	..
Czech Republic	..	5,487	..	14.7	..	25.3	..	60.1
Denmark	10,106	23,506	38.3	52.2	36.5	23.5	25.2	24.3
Dominican Republic	435	1,260	40.0	60.6	33.1	22.8	26.9	16.6
Ecuador	755	1,390	41.6	39.8	23.2	24.5	35.2	35.8
Egypt, Arab Rep.	3,327	6,356	44.0	32.1	3.9	17.8	52.1	50.1
El Salvador	296	1,062	45.9	36.4	20.5	18.4	33.5	45.2
Eritrea	..	..	..	..	..	..	..	..
Estonia	*123*	972	*76.3*	50.0	*15.4*	19.6	*8.3*	30.3
Ethiopia	348	517	76.5	63.3	3.3	8.5	20.3	28.3
Finland	7,432	7,994	26.1	32.2	37.2	23.2	36.6	44.6
France	59,560	61,580	29.4	28.2	20.7	29.3	49.9	42.5
Gabon	984	*854*	23.2	*33.7*	13.9	*10.7*	62.9	*55.6*
Gambia, The	35	..	65.1	..	23.1	..	11.8	..
Georgia	..	*216*	..	*41.2*	..	*51.0*	..	*7.8*
Germany	79,214	137,156	21.6	18.3	42.8	33.6	35.6	48.0
Ghana	226	*527*	55.1	*53.7*	5.9	*19.0*	39.0	*27.3*
Greece	2,756	11,189	34.0	42.8	39.5	37.3	26.5	19.8
Guatemala	363	861	41.0	54.1	27.4	22.7	31.6	23.2
Guinea	243	220	57.5	51.0	12.2	8.1	30.3	40.8
Guinea-Bissau	17	..	54.5	..	19.8	..	25.6	..
Haiti	71	..	47.9	..	52.1	..	0.0	..

	Commercial service imports		Transport		Travel		Other	
	$ millions		% of total		% of total		% of total	
	1990	2001	1990	2001	1990	2001	1990	2001
Honduras	213	639	45.4	48.6	17.6	20.0	37.0	31.4
Hungary	2,264	5,464	8.8	10.3	25.9	23.9	65.3	65.8
India	5,943	23,419 [b]	57.5	*41.1*	6.6	*13.1*	35.9	*45.8*
Indonesia	5,898	15,595	47.4	24.9	14.2	21.8	38.4	53.3
Iran, Islamic Rep.	3,703	*1,577*	47.3	*72.4*	9.2	*13.0*	43.5	*14.6*
Iraq	..	..	..	..	..	..	..	..
Ireland	5,145	34,764	24.3	7.4	22.6	8.3	53.1	84.4
Israel	4,825	12,361	39.6	36.2	29.7	23.8	30.7	40.0
Italy	46,602	55,679	23.7	21.4	22.1	25.5	54.2	53.0
Jamaica	667	1,485	47.9	40.8	17.0	13.9	35.1	45.3
Japan	84,281	107,027	*30.8*	30.3	*27.9*	24.8	*41.4*	45.0
Jordan	1,118	1,519	52.0	45.9	30.1	27.6	17.9	26.5
Kazakhstan	..	2,785	..	22.5	..	24.1	..	53.4
Kenya	598	764	66.2	48.8	6.4	18.7	27.4	32.4
Korea, Dem. Rep.	..	..	..	..	..	..	..	..
Korea, Rep.	10,050	33,128	39.8	32.4	27.5	22.9	32.7	44.7
Kuwait	2,805	4,503	31.9	34.5	65.5	63.1	2.6	2.3
Kyrgyz Republic	..	122	..	41.2	..	9.8	..	49.0
Lao PDR	25	5	73.0	99.0	0.0	1.0	27.0	0.0
Latvia	*120*	683	*82.3*	30.4	*10.9*	32.8	*6.8*	36.8
Lebanon	..	..	..	..	..	..	..	..
Lesotho	48	38	67.9	74.5	24.7	23.8	7.3	1.7
Liberia	..	..	..	..	..	..	..	..
Libya	926	*824*	41.9	*45.7*	45.7	*45.3*	12.4	*9.0*
Lithuania	..	669	..	35.4	..	32.7	..	31.9
Macedonia, FYR	..	331	..	42.6	..	11.6	..	45.8
Madagascar	172	51	43.5	49.8	23.4	30.6	33.0	19.6
Malawi	268	..	81.8	..	5.9	..	12.3	..
Malaysia	5,394	16,539	46.9	34.7	26.9	15.8	26.2	49.5
Mali	352	..	57.4	..	15.8	..	26.8	..
Mauritania	126	..	76.9	..	18.3	..	4.8	..
Mauritius	407	794	51.6	32.3	23.0	24.9	25.4	42.8
Mexico	10,063	16,520	25.0	12.7	54.9	34.5	20.2	52.7
Moldova	..	209	..	29.6	..	42.2	..	28.1
Mongolia	155	169	56.2	54.3	0.8	32.8	43.0	12.9
Morocco	940	1,705	58.3	45.9	19.9	22.8	21.9	31.3
Mozambique	206	1,439	57.7	29.2	0.0	19.7	42.3	51.1
Myanmar	72	361	35.4	82.1	22.6	7.6	42.0	10.3
Namibia	341	..	46.9	..	17.9	..	35.2	..
Nepal	159	205	40.8	34.9	28.5	38.8	30.7	26.3
Netherlands	28,995	53,313	37.7	26.4	25.4	22.5	36.9	51.1
New Zealand	3,251	4,156	40.6	34.6	29.5	32.1	30.0	33.3
Nicaragua	73	336	70.7	49.8	20.1	22.6	9.3	27.6
Niger	209	..	68.3	..	10.4	..	21.4	..
Nigeria	1,901	*3,311*	33.6	*19.8*	30.3	*18.7*	36.1	*61.4*
Norway	12,247	15,261	44.6	37.6	30.0	28.0	25.3	34.4
Oman	719	1,678	36.6	37.1	6.5	21.9	56.9	41.1
Pakistan	1,863	2,216	67.0	70.1	23.1	11.4	9.9	18.5
Panama	666	1,098	66.6	56.0	14.8	16.0	18.6	28.0
Papua New Guinea	393	662	35.6	26.1	12.8	5.8	51.5	68.1
Paraguay	361	382	61.6	56.1	19.8	23.8	18.6	20.1
Peru	1,070	2,168	43.5	42.2	27.6	27.3	29.0	30.5
Philippines	1,721	5,088	56.9	45.7	6.4	24.1	36.6	30.2
Poland	2,847	8,842	52.4	17.9	14.9	39.5	32.8	42.6
Portugal	3,772	6,011	48.4	33.0	23.0	35.0	28.6	32.1
Puerto Rico	..	..	..	..	..	..	..	..

	Commercial service imports		Transport		Travel		Other	
	$ millions		% of total		% of total		% of total	
	1990	**2001**	**1990**	**2001**	**1990**	**2001**	**1990**	**2001**
Romania	787	2,163	65.5	36.4	13.1	20.8	21.4	42.8
Russian Federation	..	18,651	..	16.0	..	55.5	..	28.5
Rwanda	96	113	69.0	71.9	23.7	17.8	7.3	10.3
Saudi Arabia	12,694	7,165	18.1	32.4	0.0	0.0	81.9	67.6
Senegal	368	*419*	60.1	*60.4*	12.4	*12.9*	27.5	*26.8*
Sierra Leone	67	..	29.5	..	32.7	..	37.8	..
Singapore	8,575	20,308	41.0	34.6	21.0	25.5	38.0	39.9
Slovak Republic	..	*1,779*	..	*24.4*	..	*16.6*	..	*59.0*
Slovenia	*1,034*	1,442	*42.5*	22.1	*27.3*	36.6	*30.3*	41.3
Somalia	..	..	..	..	..	..	..	..
South Africa	3,593	5,085	40.2	44.4	31.5	37.7	28.3	17.9
Spain	15,197	33,237	30.8	24.6	28.0	17.9	41.2	57.4
Sri Lanka	620	1,729	64.2	48.9	11.9	14.2	23.9	36.9
Sudan	202	638	31.9	87.6	25.4	11.6	42.7	0.8
Swaziland	171	177	6.1	15.9	20.6	24.7	73.4	59.5
Sweden	16,959	22,920	23.2	15.7	37.1	30.2	39.7	54.1
Switzerland	11,093	15,159	33.7	32.9	52.9	41.9	13.4	25.2
Syrian Arab Republic	702	*1,468*	54.5	*47.5*	35.5	*45.6*	10.1	*6.9*
Tajikistan	..	..	..	..	..	..	..	..
Tanzania	288	*670*	58.0	*33.5*	7.9	*50.3*	34.1	*16.2*
Thailand	6,160	14,484	58.0	47.2	23.3	20.2	18.7	32.6
Togo	217	*116*	56.9	*72.2*	18.4	*1.7*	24.7	*26.1*
Trinidad and Tobago	460	..	51.7	..	26.6	..	21.8	..
Tunisia	682	1,332	51.4	49.1	26.2	20.5	22.4	30.4
Turkey	2,794	6,464	32.2	31.3	18.6	26.9	49.2	41.8
Turkmenistan	..	..	..	..	..	..	..	..
Uganda	195	492	58.3	32.5	0.0	*0.0*	41.7	67.5
Ukraine	..	3,167	..	12.9	..	17.9	..	69.2
United Arab Emirates	..	..	..	..	..	..	..	..
United Kingdom	44,713	91,781	33.2	24.8	41.0	41.3	25.8	33.9
United States	97,950	192,690	36.3	31.8	38.9	32.5	24.8	35.7
Uruguay	363	764	48.2	47.0	30.7	33.0	21.1	20.0
Uzbekistan	..	..	..	..	..	..	..	..
Venezuela, RB	2,390	4,442	33.5	41.9	42.8	40.5	23.7	17.6
Vietnam	..	3,382	..	..	..	..	..	..
West Bank and Gaza	..	..	..	..	..	..	..	..
Yemen, Rep.	639	*757*	27.6	*44.9*	9.9	*9.2*	62.5	*45.9*
Yugoslavia, Fed. Rep.	..	..	..	..	..	..	..	..
Zambia	370	*328*	76.8	*67.7*	14.6	*13.3*	8.6	*19.0*
Zimbabwe	460	..	51.8	..	14.4	..	33.8	..
World	**774,558 s**	**1,427,871 s**	**32.5 w**	**28.0 w**	**31.7 w**	**30.9 w**	**35.8 w**	**41.2 w**
Low income	28,314	57,743	50.4	*35.0*	13.9	*17.4*	35.6	*47.6*
Middle income	93,074	227,482	41.7	*32.5*	21.5	*30.7*	36.8	*36.8*
Lower middle income	39,304	123,383	42.7	*31.6*	13.6	*34.2*	43.7	*34.2*
Upper middle income	53,770	104,099	40.5	*33.5*	31.4	*27.0*	28.1	*39.6*
Low & middle income	121,387	285,225	43.7	*32.9*	19.7	*28.7*	36.6	*38.4*
East Asia & Pacific	24,308	95,651	56.0	*33.1*	18.2	*25.9*	25.8	*41.0*
Europe & Central Asia	9,321	61,636	24.8	*20.1*	8.6	*34.6*	66.6	*45.3*
Latin America & Carib.	33,098	66,686	37.3	*38.1*	35.7	*33.0*	27.0	*28.9*
Middle East & N. Africa	27,105	20,522	55.3	*38.2*	13.5	*19.5*	31.2	*42.3*
South Asia	9,176	29,052	60.7	*44.2*	11.2	*13.5*	28.2	*42.2*
Sub-Saharan Africa	18,380	*20,160*	45.8	*45.0*	18.0	*35.4*	36.1	*19.6*
High income	653,171	1,142,646	30.2	*26.9*	34.1	*31.3*	35.7	*41.7*
Europe EMU	288,701	488,916	26.8	*22.0*	31.4	*28.2*	41.8	*49.8*

a. Includes Luxembourg.   b. Data are an estimate from the World Trade Organization.

About the data

Trade in services differs from trade in goods because services are produced and consumed at the same time. Thus services to a traveler may be consumed in the producing country (for example, use of a hotel room) but are classified as imports of the traveler's country. In other cases services may be supplied from a remote location; for example, insurance services may be supplied from one location and consumed in another. For further discussion of the problems of measuring trade in services, see *About the data* for table 4.7.

The data on exports of services in table 4.7 and on imports of services in this table, unlike those in editions before 2000, include only commercial services and exclude the category *government services not included elsewhere*. The data are compiled by the International Monetary Fund (IMF) based on returns from national sources.

Definitions

• **Commercial service imports** are total service imports minus imports of government services not included elsewhere. International transactions in services are defined by the IMF's *Balance of Payments Manual* (1993) as the economic output of intangible commodities that may be produced, transferred, and consumed at the same time. Definitions may vary among reporting economies. • **Transport** covers all transport services (sea, air, land, internal waterway, space, and pipeline) performed by residents of one economy for those of another and involving the carriage of passengers, movement of goods (freight), rental of carriers with crew, and related support and auxiliary services. Excluded are freight insurance, which is included in insurance services; goods procured in ports by nonresident carriers and repairs of transport equipment, which are included in goods; repairs of harbors, railway facilities, and airfield facilities, which are included in construction services; and rental of carriers without crew, which is included in other services. • **Travel** covers goods and services acquired from an economy by travelers in that economy for their own use during visits of less than one year for business or personal purposes. Travel services include the goods and services consumed by travelers, such as meals, lodging, and transport (within the economy visited), including car rental. • **Other commercial services** include such activities as insurance and financial services, international telecommunications, and postal and courier services; computer data; news-related service transactions between residents and nonresidents; construction services; royalties and license fees; miscellaneous business, professional, and technical services; and personal, cultural, and recreational services.

4.8a

Developing economies are consuming more international travel services

% of commercial service imports

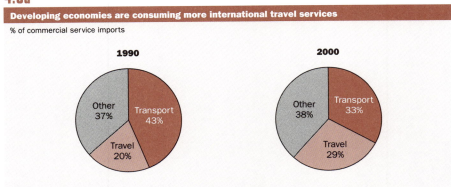

Between 1990 and 2000 travel and other commercial services displaced transport as the most important category of service imports for developing economies.

Source: International Monetary Fund and World Trade Organization data files.

Data sources

The data on imports of commercial services are from the IMF. The IMF publishes balance of payments data in its *International Financial Statistics* and *Balance of Payments Statistics Yearbook*.

4.9 | Structure of demand

	Household final consumption expenditure		General government final consumption expenditure		Gross capital formation		Exports of goods and services		Imports of goods and services		Gross domestic savings	
	% of GDP		% of GDP		% of GDP		% of GDP		% of GDP		% of GDP	
	1990	2001	1990	2001	1990	2001	1990	2001	1990	2001	1990	2001
Afghanistan	..	..	..	..	..	..	..	..	..	..	..	..
Albania	61	92	19	11	29	19	15	19	23	42	21	−3
Algeria	57	44	16	15	29	26	23	37	25	21	27	41
Angola	36	54	34	..ᵃ	12	34	39	74	21	62	30	46
Argentina	77	74	3	11	14	14	10	11	5	10	20	15
Armenia	46	91	18	11	47	19	35	26	46	46	36	−2
Australia	59	60	19	19	22	21	17	23	17	23	22	21
Austria	55	58	19	19	25	23	40	52	38	53	26	23
Azerbaijan	51	65	18	10	27	21	44	42	39	38	31	25
Bangladesh	86	79	4	5	17	23	6	15	14	22	10	16
Belarus	47	61	24	21	27	22	46	68	44	71	29	19
Belgium	55	54	20	22	22	21	71	84	69	81	24	24
Benin	87	82	11	12	14	19	14	15	26	28	2	6
Bolivia	77	78	12	15	13	13	23	18	24	24	11	7
Bosnia and Herzegovina	..	113	..	..ᵃ	..	21	..	27	..	60	..	−13
Botswana	33	35	24	27	37	22	55	51	50	35	43	38
Brazil	59	60	19	20	20	21	8	13	7	14	21	20
Bulgaria	60	71	18	16	26	20	33	56	37	63	22	13
Burkina Faso	77	77	15	14	21	25	13	10	26	26	8	10
Burundi	95	91	11	14	15	7	8	6	28	18	−5	−5
Cambodia	91	84	7	6	8	18	6	53	13	61	2	10
Cameroon	67	68	13	11	18	18	20	32	17	29	21	20
Canada	56	56	23	19	21	20	26	44	26	39	21	25
Central African Republic	86	77	15	11	12	14	15	12	28	15	−1	11
Chad	88	89	10	8	16	42	13	14	28	53	2	3
Chile	62	65	10	12	25	21	35	35	31	33	28	23
China	50	46	12	14	35	38	18	26	14	23	38	40
Hong Kong, China	57	59	7	10	27	26	134	144	126	139	36	31
Colombia	66	64	9	21	19	15	21	19	15	19	24	15
Congo, Dem. Rep.	79	92	12	1	9	5	30	18	29	17	9	6
Congo, Rep.	62	28	14	11	16	27	54	84	46	50	24	61
Costa Rica	61	70	18	14	27	18	35	43	41	45	21	16
Côte d'Ivoire	72	74	17	9	7	10	32	39	27	32	11	17
Croatia	74	58	24	24	11	24	78	47	86	53	2	18
Cuba	..	70	..	23	..	10	..	16	..	18	..	7
Czech Republic	49	53	23	20	25	30	45	71	43	74	28	27
Denmark	49	47	26	26	20	21	36	46	31	39	25	28
Dominican Republic	80	76	5	9	25	23	34	24	44	32	15	15
Ecuador	69	68	9	10	17	25	33	31	27	34	23	22
Egypt, Arab Rep.	73	78	11	12	29	15	20	18	33	23	16	10
El Salvador	89	88	10	10	14	16	19	29	31	43	1	2
Eritrea	..	79	..	40	..	35	..	21	..	76	..	−19
Estonia	62	56	16	20	30	28	60	91	54	94	22	24
Ethiopia	74	80	19	18	12	18	8	15	12	31	7	2
Finland	51	50	22	21	29	20	23	40	24	32	27	29
France	55	55	22	23	23	20	21	28	22	26	22	22
Gabon	50	50	13	..ᵃ	22	31	46	60	31	41	37	50
Gambia, The	76	84	14	15	22	18	60	54	72	71	11	1
Georgia	65	89	10	9	31	19	40	22	46	38	25	3
Germany	55	59	19	19	22	20	29	35	25	33	26	22
Ghana	85	79	9	16	14	24	17	52	26	70	5	6
Greece	72	70	15	15	23	23	18	25	28	33	13	15
Guatemala	84	86	7	8	14	15	21	19	25	28	10	6
Guinea	73	75	9	5	18	22	31	28	31	29	18	20
Guinea-Bissau	87	99	10	12	30	22	10	41	37	74	3	−11
Haiti	81	86	8	7	13	31	18	13	20	33	11	10

Structure of demand | **4.9**

	Household final consumption expenditure		General government final consumption expenditure		Gross capital formation		Exports of goods and services		Imports of goods and services		Gross domestic savings	
	% of GDP		% of GDP		% of GDP		% of GDP		% of GDP		% of GDP	
	1990	2001	1990	2001	1990	2001	1990	2001	1990	2001	1990	2001
Honduras	66	72	14	14	23	31	36	38	40	55	20	14
Hungary	61	64	11	11	25	27	31	60	29	63	28	25
India	67	66	12	13	24	23	7	14	10	15	21	21
Indonesia	59	67	9	7	31	17	25	41	24	33	32	26
Iran, Islamic Rep.	62	51	11	13	29	29	22	28	24	21	27	36
Iraq	..	..	..	..	..	..	..	..	..	..	..	..
Ireland	58	*48*	16	*13*	21	*24*	57	95	52	80	26	*38*
Israel	56	*59*	30	*29*	25	*19*	35	*40*	45	*47*	14	*12*
Italy	58	60	20	18	22	20	20	28	20	27	22	21
Jamaica	65	69	13	16	26	30	48	41	52	56	22	16
Japan	53	56	13	18	33	25	10	10	9	10	34	26
Jordan	74	76	25	23	32	26	62	44	93	69	1	1
Kazakhstan	52	60	*18*	16	*32*	26	*74*	46	*75*	49	*30*	23
Kenya	67	79	19	17	20	13	26	26	31	35	14	4
Korea, Dem. Rep.	..	..	..	..	..	..	..	..	..	..	..	..
Korea, Rep.	53	61	10	10	38	27	29	43	30	41	37	29
Kuwait	57	48	39	26	18	9	45	55	58	37	4	26
Kyrgyz Republic	71	66	25	17	24	16	29	37	50	37	4	16
Lao PDR	..	..	..	..	..	..	..	..	..	..	..	..
Latvia	53	59	9	22	40	28	48	46	49	54	39	19
Lebanon	140	94	25	18	18	19	18	12	100	42	−64	−12
Lesotho	132	90	20	24	52	37	17	34	121	86	−52	−15
Liberia	..	..	..	..	..	..	..	..	..	..	..	..
Libya	48	*46*	24	*21*	19	*13*	40	*36*	31	*15*	27	*33*
Lithuania	57	68	19	16	33	22	52	50	61	56	24	16
Macedonia, FYR	72	74	19	25	19	17	26	40	36	56	9	1
Madagascar	86	80	8	8	17	16	17	29	28	32	6	12
Malawi	72	83	15	18	23	11	24	26	33	38	13	−1
Malaysia	52	41	14	12	32	29	75	116	72	98	34	47
Mali	80	77	14	13	23	21	17	31	34	42	6	10
Mauritania	69	70	26	16	20	27	46	38	61	51	5	14
Mauritius	64	62	13	13	31	24	64	64	71	63	23	25
Mexico	70	70	8	12	23	21	19	28	20	30	22	18
Moldova	*77*	92	..[a]	12	25	20	49	50	51	74	23	−4
Mongolia	58	67	32	19	38	30	24	64	53	80	9	14
Morocco	65	63	15	18	25	25	26	30	32	36	19	19
Mozambique	101	70	12	10	16	42	8	22	36	44	−12	19
Myanmar	89	*87*	..[a]	..[a]	13	*13*	3	*0*	5	*0*	11	*13*
Namibia	59	60	26	29	28	24	44	54	57	66	15	12
Nepal	83	75	9	10	18	24	11	22	21	32	8	15
Netherlands	50	50	24	23	23	22	54	65	51	60	27	27
New Zealand	61	*60*	19	*18*	20	*20*	27	*37*	27	*35*	20	*22*
Nicaragua	59	..	43	..	19	..	25	..	46	..	−2	..
Niger	84	84	15	12	8	11	15	17	22	25	1	3
Nigeria	56	48	15	25	15	28	43	48	29	49	29	27
Norway	49	*43*	21	*19*	23	*22*	41	*47*	34	*30*	30	*38*
Oman	27	..	38	..	13	..	53	..	31	..	35	..
Pakistan	74	75	15	10	19	16	16	18	23	19	11	15
Panama	60	58	18	15	17	28	38	33	34	35	21	26
Papua New Guinea	59	*64*	25	*14*	24	*19*	41	*47*	49	*43*	16	*22*
Paraguay	77	82	6	9	23	24	33	23	39	38	17	9
Peru	74	72	8	11	16	18	16	16	14	17	18	17
Philippines	72	68	10	12	24	18	28	49	33	47	18	20
Poland	48	66	19	17	26	22	29	29	22	33	33	18
Portugal	63	61	16	21	28	28	33	32	39	41	21	19
Puerto Rico	65	..	14	..	17	..	*77*	..	*101*	..	21	..

4.9 | Structure of demand

	Household final consumption expenditure		General government final consumption expenditure		Gross capital formation		Exports of goods and services		Imports of goods and services		Gross domestic savings	
	% of GDP		% of GDP		% of GDP		% of GDP		% of GDP		% of GDP	
	1990	2001	1990	2001	1990	2001	1990	2001	1990	2001	1990	2001
Romania	66	80	13	6	30	22	17	34	26	42	21	14
Russian Federation	49	51	21	14	30	22	18	37	18	24	30	35
Rwanda	84	86	10	12	15	18	6	9	14	26	6	2
Saudi Arabia	40	37	31	27	20	19	46	42	36	24	30	36
Senegal	76	78	15	10	14	20	25	30	30	38	9	12
Sierra Leone	83	95	8	17	10	8	22	17	24	37	9	–12
Singapore	46	42	10	12	37	24	184	174	177	152	44	46
Slovak Republic	54	56	22	21	33	32	27	74	36	82	24	23
Slovenia	55	55	19	21	17	28	84	59	74	63	26	24
Somalia	113	..	..a	..	16	..	10	..	38	..	–12	..
South Africa	63	63	20	19	12	15	24	28	19	25	18	18
Spain	60	59	17	17	27	25	16	30	20	31	23	24
Sri Lanka	76	75	10	10	23	22	29	37	38	44	14	15
Sudan	..	76	..	6	..	18	..	13	..	16	..	15
Swaziland	62	74	18	20	19	19	75	69	74	81	20	6
Sweden	49	50	28	27	23	18	30	46	29	41	24	24
Switzerland	57	61	14	13	28	22	36	45	36	41	29	26
Syrian Arab Republic	69	61	14	11	17	21	28	38	28	31	17	29
Tajikistan	74	84	9	8	25	12	28	83	35	87	17	7
Tanzania b	81	85	18	6	26	17	13	16	37	24	1	8
Thailand	57	58	9	12	41	24	34	66	42	60	34	30
Togo	71	87	14	9	27	21	33	33	45	50	15	4
Trinidad and Tobago	59	58	12	11	13	19	45	55	29	43	29	31
Tunisia	58	61	16	16	32	28	44	48	51	52	25	23
Turkey	69	67	11	14	24	16	13	34	18	31	20	19
Turkmenistan	49	49	23	15	40	37	..	47	..	47	28	36
Uganda	92	81	8	12	13	20	7	12	19	26	1	6
Ukraine	57	55	17	23	27	20	28	56	29	54	26	22
United Arab Emirates	39	..	16	..	20	..	65	..	40	..	45	..
United Kingdom	63	66	20	19	20	17	24	27	27	29	18	15
United States	67	69	17	14	18	21	10	11	11	15	16	17
Uruguay	70	74	12	13	12	13	24	19	18	20	18	12
Uzbekistan	61	62	25	18	32	19	29	28	48	28	13	20
Venezuela, RB	62	68	8	8	10	19	39	23	20	18	29	24
Vietnam	84	65	12	6	13	31	36	55	45	57	3	29
West Bank and Gaza	..	92	..	32	..	33	..	14	..	71	..	–24
Yemen, Rep.	74	65	17	14	15	20	14	38	20	37	9	21
Yugoslavia, Fed. Rep.	..	90	..	18	..	13	..	25	..	48	..	–9
Zambia	64	77	19	13	17	20	36	27	37	37	17	10
Zimbabwe	63	72	19	19	17	8	23	22	23	21	17	9
World	**59 w**	**58 w**	**17 w**	**18 w**	**24 w**	**22 w**	**20 w**	**30 w**	**20 w**	**28 w**	**24 w**	**24 w**
Low income	66	68	12	12	24	20	18	28	21	28	21	20
Middle income	59	59	15	15	25	24	21	30	19	28	26	25
Lower middle income	58	56	14	14	29	26	21	33	22	30	29	30
Upper middle income	61	62	15	17	21	21	20	27	17	26	23	21
Low & middle income	61	61	14	15	25	23	20	29	20	28	25	25
East Asia & Pacific	54	52	11	12	34	31	25	41	24	36	34	36
Europe & Central Asia	55	60	18	16	28	22	23	41	24	38	26	25
Latin America & Carib.	65	65	13	16	19	20	14	19	12	20	21	19
Middle East & N. Africa	57	53	20	18	24	22	33	34	34	27	23	29
South Asia	70	69	12	12	23	22	9	15	13	17	19	19
Sub-Saharan Africa	66	67	18	17	15	18	27	31	26	32	16	17
High income	59	61	17	17	24	22	20	25	20	25	24	22
Europe EMU	56	57	20	20	23	21	28	37	28	35	24	22

a. Data on general government final consumption expenditure are not available separately; they are included in household final consumption expenditure. b. Data cover mainland Tanzania only.

Gross domestic product (GDP) from the expenditure side is made up of household final consumption expenditure, general government final consumption expenditure, gross capital formation (private and public investment in fixed assets, changes in inventories, and net acquisitions of valuables), and net exports (exports minus imports) of goods and services. Such expenditures are recorded in purchaser prices and include net taxes on products.

Because policymakers have tended to focus on fostering the growth of output, and because data on production are easier to collect than data on spending, many countries generate their primary estimate of GDP using the production approach. Moreover, many countries do not estimate all the separate components of national expenditures but instead derive some of the main aggregates indirectly using GDP (based on the production approach) as the control total.

Household final consumption expenditure (private consumption in the 1968 System of National Accounts, or SNA) is often estimated as a residual, by subtracting from GDP all other known expenditures. The resulting aggregate may incorporate fairly large discrepancies. When household consumption is calculated separately, the household surveys on which many of the estimates are based tend to be one-year studies with limited coverage. Thus the estimates quickly become outdated and must be supplemented by price- and quantity-based statistical estimating procedures. Complicating the issue, in many developing countries the distinction between cash outlays for personal business and those for household use may be blurred. The *World Development Indicators* includes in household consumption the expenditures of nonprofit institutions serving households.

General government final consumption expenditure (general government consumption in the 1968 SNA) includes expenditures on goods and services for individual consumption as well as those on services for collective consumption. Defense expenditures, including those on capital outlays (with certain exceptions), are treated as current spending.

Gross capital formation (gross domestic investment in the 1968 SNA) consists of outlays on additions to the economy's fixed assets plus net changes in the level of inventories. It is generally obtained from reports by industry of acquisition and distinguishes only the broad categories of capital formation. The 1993 SNA recognizes a third category of capital formation: net acquisitions of valuables. Included in gross capital formation under the 1993 SNA guidelines are capital outlays on defense establishments

that may be used by the general public, such as schools, airfields, and hospitals. These expenses were treated as consumption in the earlier version of the SNA. Data on capital formation may be estimated from direct surveys of enterprises and administrative records or based on the commodity flow method using data from production, trade, and construction activities. The quality of data on fixed capital formation by government depends on the quality of government accounting systems (which tend to be weak in developing countries). Measures of fixed capital formation by households and corporations—particularly capital outlays by small, unincorporated enterprises—are usually very unreliable.

Estimates of changes in inventories are rarely complete but usually include the most important activities or commodities. In some countries these estimates are derived as a composite residual along with household final consumption expenditure. According to national accounts conventions, adjustments should be made for appreciation of the value of inventory holdings due to price changes, but this is not always done. In highly inflationary economies this element can be substantial.

Data on exports and imports are compiled from customs reports and balance of payments data. Although the data on exports and imports from the payments side provide reasonably reliable records of cross-border transactions, they may not adhere strictly to the appropriate definitions of valuation and timing used in the balance of payments or correspond with the change-of-ownership criterion. This issue has assumed greater significance with the increasing globalization of international business. Neither customs nor balance of payments data usually capture the illegal transactions that occur in many countries. Goods carried by travelers across borders in legal but unreported shuttle trade may further distort trade statistics.

Domestic savings, a concept used by the World Bank, represent the difference between GDP and total consumption. Domestic savings also satisfy the fundamental identity: exports minus imports equal domestic savings minus capital formation. Domestic savings differ from savings as defined in the national accounts; this SNA concept represents the difference between disposable income and consumption.

For further discussion of the problems in compiling national accounts, see Srinivasan (1994), Heston (1994), and Ruggles (1994). For a classic analysis of the reliability of foreign trade and national income statistics, see Morgenstern (1963).

• **Household final consumption expenditure** is the market value of all goods and services, including durable products (such as cars, washing machines, and home computers), purchased by households. It excludes purchases of dwellings but includes imputed rent for owner-occupied dwellings. It also includes payments and fees to governments to obtain permits and licenses. The *World Development Indicators* includes in household consumption expenditure the expenditures of nonprofit institutions serving households, even when reported separately by the country. In practice, household consumption expenditure may include any statistical discrepancy in the use of resources relative to the supply of resources. • **General government final consumption expenditure** includes all government current expenditures for purchases of goods and services (including compensation of employees). It also includes most expenditures on national defense and security but excludes government military expenditures that potentially have wider public use and are part of government capital formation. • **Gross capital formation** consists of outlays on additions to the fixed assets of the economy, net changes in the level of inventories, and net acquisitions of valuables. Fixed assets include land improvements (fences, ditches, drains, and so on); plant, machinery, and equipment purchases; and the construction of roads, railways, and the like, including schools, offices, hospitals, private residential dwellings, and commercial and industrial buildings. Inventories are stocks of goods held by firms to meet temporary or unexpected fluctuations in production or sales, and "work in progress." • **Exports and imports of goods and services** represent the value of all goods and other market services provided to, or received from, the rest of the world. They include the value of merchandise, freight, insurance, transport, travel, royalties, license fees, and other services, such as communication, construction, financial, information, business, personal, and government services. They exclude labor and property income (factor services in the 1968 SNA) as well as transfer payments. • **Gross domestic savings** are calculated as GDP less total consumption.

The national accounts indicators for most developing countries are collected from national statistical organizations and central banks by visiting and resident World Bank missions. The data for high-income economies come from OECD data files (see the OECD's *National Accounts, 1989–2000*, volumes 1 and 2). The United Nations Statistics Division publishes detailed national accounts for United Nations member countries in *National Accounts Statistics: Main Aggregates and Detailed Tables* and updates in the *Monthly Bulletin of Statistics*.

4.10 Growth of consumption and investment

	Household final consumption expenditure				Household final consumption expenditure per capita		General government final consumption expenditure		Gross capital formation	
	$ millions		average annual % growth		average annual % growth		average annual % growth		average annual % growth	
	1990	2001	1980–90	1990–2001	1980–90	1990–2001	1980–90	1990–2001	1980–90	1990–2001
Afghanistan	..	..	..	..	..	..	..	..	..	..
Albania	1,271	3,793	..	4.6	..	5.1	..	–0.1	–0.3	20.5
Algeria	35,265	23,855	1.5	0.2	–1.4	–1.7	0.7	3.5	–1.8	–0.6
Angola	3,674	..	–3.6	..	..	..	8.4	..	–5.6	..
Argentina	109,038	198,798	..	1.9	..	0.6	..	1.9	–5.2	5.4
Armenia	2,005	1,995	..	0.4	..	–0.1	..	–1.4	..	–12.0
Australia	182,448	233,464	2.9	3.7	1.4	2.5	3.8	3.0	3.7	6.6
Austria	89,789	108,354	2.4	2.4	2.2	2.0	1.4	1.7	2.4	2.2
Azerbaijan	..	3,631	..	..	..	..	..	..	..	15.0
Bangladesh	25,952	36,472	4.5	3.7	1.8	2.0	5.0	4.6	1.4	9.1
Belarus	16,667	7,146	..	0.9	..	1.2	..	–1.1	..	–6.6
Belgium	109,154	124,908	2.0	1.9	1.9	1.7	1.1	1.6	2.9	1.9
Benin	1,602	1,942	1.9	4.4	–1.2	1.5	0.5	3.9	–5.3	5.9
Bolivia	3,741	6,250	1.2	3.5	–0.9	1.1	–3.8	3.4	1.0	6.0
Bosnia and Herzegovina	..	..	..	..	..	..	..	..	..	..
Botswana	1,260	1,799	6.3	4.7	2.7	1.9	14.9	7.1	7.6	4.9
Brazil	275,753	302,105	1.2	5.1	–0.7	3.6	7.3	–1.1	3.3	3.5
Bulgaria	12,401	9,642	3.1	–1.7	3.2	–1.0	5.1	–7.0	2.3	0.6
Burkina Faso	2,141	1,905	2.6	3.7	0.1	1.2	6.2	–0.2	8.6	7.7
Burundi	1,070	652	3.4	–2.0	0.5	–4.1	3.2	–1.8	6.9	0.8
Cambodia	1,016	2,812	..	1.7	..	–0.7	..	3.1	..	10.5
Cameroon	7,423	5,810	3.5	3.3	0.6	0.8	6.8	1.9	–2.6	1.4
Canada	322,564	391,155	3.2	2.7	2.0	1.7	2.4	0.5	5.0	4.6
Central African Republic	1,274	748	1.5	..	..	..	–1.7	..	10.0	..
Chad	1,482	1,427	5.3	1.9	2.8	–1.1	14.5	0.0	..	6.8
Chile	18,759	43,366	2.0	6.8	0.3	5.3	0.4	3.7	6.4	7.4
China	174,249	554,407	8.8	8.9	7.2	7.8	9.8	9.0	10.8	10.8
Hong Kong, China	42,421	94,764	6.7	3.5	5.3	1.7	5.0	3.8	4.0	4.6
Colombia	26,357	52,430	2.6	2.2	0.5	0.3	4.2	9.3	1.4	1.1
Congo, Dem. Rep.	7,398	4,792	3.4	–5.6	0.1	–8.5	0.0	–17.1	–5.1	–0.2
Congo, Rep.	1,746	776	2.3	–0.1	–0.6	–3.1	4.3	–1.5	–11.6	1.9
Costa Rica	3,502	11,205	3.6	4.8	0.6	2.5	1.1	1.9	4.6	4.8
Côte d'Ivoire	7,766	7,702	1.5	3.6	–2.1	0.5	–0.1	0.4	–10.4	6.7
Croatia	13,527	11,786	..	2.7	..	3.6	..	0.4	..	7.6
Cuba	..	..	..	2.6	..	..	..	1.9	..	16.9
Czech Republic	17,195	30,032	..	2.7	..	2.7	..	–1.2	..	5.3
Denmark	65,430	75,850	1.4	2.0	1.4	1.6	0.9	2.2	4.7	5.4
Dominican Republic	5,633	16,069	3.9	5.4	1.7	3.7	–3.2	13.8	4.5	5.7
Ecuador	7,323	12,235	1.9	1.2	–0.7	–0.9	–1.4	–2.0	–3.8	1.1
Egypt, Arab Rep.	30,933	76,538	4.6	4.8	2.0	2.7	3.1	3.1	0.0	3.5
El Salvador	4,273	12,080	0.8	4.9	–0.2	2.8	0.1	2.7	2.2	6.1
Eritrea	..	546	..	1.0	..	–1.7	..	16.7	..	5.0
Estonia	4,074	3,116	..	0.5	..	1.9	..	4.3	..	0.3
Ethiopia	5,081	5,003	0.2	2.9	–2.8	0.6	4.5	9.2	2.1	9.9
Finland	68,939	60,487	3.9	2.1	3.4	1.8	3.2	1.0	3.4	2.0
France	672,960	721,076	2.2	1.5	1.7	1.1	2.6	1.8	3.3	2.0
Gabon	2,961	3,040	1.5	1.7	–1.5	–1.0	–0.6	4.6	–5.7	3.5
Gambia, The	240	327	–2.4	4.5	–5.9	1.1	1.7	–0.5	0.0	2.2
Georgia	8,228	2,497	..	2.4	..	2.7	..	6.8	..	–10.3
Germany	941,915	1,090,022	2.2	1.6	2.1	1.3	1.5	1.5	2.0	1.1
Ghana	5,016	4,171	2.8	3.9	–0.8	1.6	2.4	5.9	3.3	1.5
Greece	60,164	78,122	2.0	2.2	1.5	1.9	1.1	1.4	–0.7	3.6
Guatemala	6,398	17,677	1.1	4.1	–1.4	1.4	2.6	5.4	–1.8	5.9
Guinea	2,068	2,236	..	3.5	..	0.9	..	4.6	..	3.1
Guinea-Bissau	212	197	0.8	2.7	–1.5	0.4	7.2	2.3	12.9	–9.2
Haiti	2,332	3,418	0.9	..	..	..	–4.4	..	–0.6	3.4

	Household final consumption expenditure				Household final consumption expenditure per capita		General government final consumption expenditure		Gross capital formation	
	$ millions		average annual % growth		average annual % growth		average annual % growth		average annual % growth	
	1990	2001	1980–90	1990–2001	1980–90	1990–2001	1980–90	1990–2001	1980–90	1990–2001
Honduras	2,026	4,613	2.7	2.9	−0.5	0.1	3.3	3.1	2.9	6.2
Hungary	20,290	33,169	1.3	−0.3	1.7	0.0	1.9	0.9	−0.9	9.5
India	212,322	315,787	5.8	4.4	3.6	2.6	4.2	7.0	6.2	7.7
Indonesia	67,388	97,386	5.6	6.2	3.7	4.7	4.6	0.3	7.2	−2.2
Iran, Islamic Rep.	74,476	58,179	2.8	3.1	−0.6	1.5	−5.0	4.9	−2.5	3.2
Iraq	..	..	..	..	..	..	..	..	..	..
Ireland	27,957	45,494	2.2	5.5	1.9	4.7	−0.3	4.1	−0.4	9.6
Israel	32,112	65,189	5.4	6.3	3.6	3.4	0.5	2.9	2.2	4.9
Italy	634,194	655,259	2.9	1.6	2.8	1.4	2.9	0.2	2.1	1.5
Jamaica	2,980	5,348	2.8	1.9	1.7	1.1	6.2	0.7	0.0	0.3
Japan	1,617,071	2,334,025	3.6	1.5	3.0	1.2	3.4	3.0	5.5	−0.2
Jordan	2,978	6,582	1.9	4.4	−1.9	0.5	1.9	4.6	−1.9	1.4
Kazakhstan	14,148	13,126	..	−6.8	..	−5.9	..	−4.5	..	−12.8
Kenya	5,309	8,805	4.6	2.6	1.1	0.0	2.6	7.9	0.4	3.4
Korea, Dem. Rep.	..	..	..	..	..	..	..	..	..	..
Korea, Rep.	132,113	251,145	7.9	4.9	6.7	3.9	5.2	2.7	12.0	1.4
Kuwait	10,459	15,661	−1.4	..	..	..	2.2	..	−4.5	..
Kyrgyz Republic	1,703	1,012	..	−5.5	..	−6.4	..	−7.8	..	−3.2
Lao PDR	..	..	..	..	..	..	..	..	..	..
Latvia	6,578	4,450	2.3	−1.1	1.8	0.1	5.0	3.4	3.4	−7.1
Lebanon	3,961	15,635	..	2.8	..	1.1	..	5.3	..	6.5
Lesotho	821	721	3.9	1.4	1.7	−0.5	2.8	4.8	5.0	−0.2
Liberia	..	..	..	..	..	..	..	..	..	..
Libya	13,999	15,625	..	..	..	..	..	..	..	..
Lithuania	8,343	7,654	..	5.2	..	5.9	..	0.5	..	6.4
Macedonia, FYR	3,021	2,535	..	2.2	..	1.5	..	1.2	..	0.8
Madagascar	2,663	3,666	−0.7	2.5	−3.4	−0.5	0.5	0.7	4.9	4.7
Malawi	1,345	1,458	1.5	4.9	−1.7	2.8	6.3	−1.9	−2.8	−8.4
Malaysia	22,806	35,707	3.3	5.0	0.4	2.5	2.7	5.3	3.1	4.0
Mali	1,943	2,031	0.6	3.7	−1.9	1.2	7.9	5.5	3.6	2.1
Mauritania	705	709	1.4	2.6	−1.1	−0.3	−3.8	1.0	6.9	9.5
Mauritius	1,519	2,816	6.2	5.0	5.3	3.8	3.3	4.8	10.3	4.5
Mexico	182,791	432,958	1.1	2.7	−1.0	1.0	2.4	1.8	−3.3	4.6
Moldova	730	1,362	..	9.1	..	9.4	..	−11.4	..	−14.1
Mongolia	..	698	..	..	..	..	..	..	..	..
Morocco	16,833	21,491	4.3	2.9	2.0	1.1	2.1	3.7	1.2	2.8
Mozambique	2,481	2,538	−1.4	3.5	−2.9	1.2	−2.6	2.8	3.8	15.1
Myanmar	..	..	0.6	3.9	..	..	..	..	−4.1	15.3
Namibia	1,640	1,845	..	1.3	..	−1.0	..	7.8	..	7.5
Nepal	3,028	4,194	..	..	..	..	..	..	..	..
Netherlands	145,871	188,587	1.7	2.8	1.1	2.2	2.2	2.1	3.3	3.1
New Zealand	26,632	30,010	2.1	2.9	1.2	1.8	1.6	2.4	3.0	5.5
Nicaragua	592	..	−3.6	6.0	−6.2	3.0	3.4	−4.2	−4.8	10.0
Niger	2,079	1,650	0.0	1.8	−3.1	−1.7	4.4	0.8	−7.1	4.0
Nigeria	15,816	19,828	−2.6	0.2	−5.5	−2.7	−3.5	−1.8	−8.5	5.4
Norway	57,047	69,082	2.2	3.3	1.9	2.7	2.3	2.4	0.7	5.2
Oman	2,810	..	..	..	..	..	..	..	25.5	..
Pakistan	29,512	44,089	4.3	4.7	1.6	2.1	10.3	0.5	5.8	1.6
Panama	3,022	5,673	2.1	3.4	0.0	1.6	1.2	2.6	−8.9	9.5
Papua New Guinea	1,902	2,231	0.4	5.2	−2.1	2.6	−0.1	2.2	−0.9	1.3
Paraguay	4,063	5,916	2.4	3.5	−0.7	0.8	1.5	5.5	−0.8	−0.8
Peru	19,376	38,857	0.7	3.8	−1.5	1.9	−0.9	5.0	−3.8	5.8
Philippines	31,566	50,227	2.6	3.7	0.2	1.4	0.6	3.1	−2.1	2.8
Poland	28,281	115,720	..	5.0	..	4.9	..	3.0	..	9.6
Portugal	44,679	66,823	2.6	2.8	2.4	2.6	5.0	2.8	3.0	5.5
Puerto Rico	19,827	..	3.5	..	..	..	5.1	..	6.9	..

	Household final consumption expenditure				Household final consumption expenditure per capita		General government final consumption expenditure		Gross capital formation	
	$ millions		average annual % growth		average annual % growth		average annual % growth		average annual % growth	
	1990	2001	1980–90	1990–2001	1980–90	1990–2001	1980–90	1990–2001	1980–90	1990–2001
Romania	25,232	30,924	..	1.7	..	2.0	..	0.9	..	−4.7
Russian Federation	282,978	157,940	..	0.2	..	0.4	..	−2.4	..	−15.7
Rwanda	2,162	1,471	1.2	1.6	−1.8	−0.5	5.2	−0.4	4.3	2.2
Saudi Arabia	41,621	68,299	..	..	..	..	..	..	..	..
Senegal	4,353	3,620	2.1	3.9	−0.8	1.1	3.3	0.1	5.2	5.2
Sierra Leone	546	712	−2.7	−1.3	−4.7	−3.5	−4.7	1.2	44.9	2.8
Singapore	17,019	36,165	5.8	5.5	3.9	2.5	6.6	8.8	3.1	6.3
Slovak Republic	8,350	11,416	3.8	1.4	3.5	1.2	4.8	1.2	0.0	6.2
Slovenia	6,917	9,956	..	3.8	..	3.9	..	3.2	..	10.7
Somalia	..	..	1.3	..	..	..	7.0	..	−2.6	..
South Africa	70,283	71,899	2.4	2.6	−0.2	0.7	3.5	0.7	−5.3	2.6
Spain	306,953	341,728	2.6	2.4	2.3	1.9	4.9	2.8	5.9	3.1
Sri Lanka	6,143	11,864	4.0	5.7	2.9	4.5	7.3	7.5	0.6	5.7
Sudan	..	8,706	0.0	..	..	..	−0.5	..	−1.8	10.7
Swaziland	547	930	5.3	3.4	2.1	0.3	1.4	4.7	−0.4	2.4
Sweden	116,247	104,533	2.2	1.3	1.9	1.0	1.6	0.4	4.7	2.1
Switzerland	130,900	150,092	1.6	1.1	1.1	0.5	3.1	0.7	3.9	1.5
Syrian Arab Republic	8,458	11,797	3.6	2.0	0.2	−0.8	−3.6	0.5	−5.3	3.0
Tajikistan	3,202	837	4.0	−6.6	0.9	−8.1	4.1	−12.8	−6.8	−18.8
Tanzania [a]	3,526	7,967	..	2.2	..	−0.6	..	3.1	..	−0.9
Thailand	48,270	65,281	5.9	3.4	4.1	2.6	4.2	4.8	9.5	−4.3
Togo	1,158	1,096	4.7	3.7	1.3	0.9	−1.2	−2.2	2.7	0.6
Trinidad and Tobago	2,975	4,702	−1.3	1.7	−2.5	1.0	−1.7	1.5	−10.1	11.3
Tunisia	7,152	12,147	2.9	4.4	0.3	2.8	3.8	4.1	−1.8	3.8
Turkey	103,324	106,843	..	3.0	..	1.5	..	4.5	..	2.7
Turkmenistan	..	2,918	..	..	..	..	..	..	..	3.3
Uganda	4,002	3,416	2.6	7.5	0.0	4.2	2.0	6.4	8.0	9.1
Ukraine	52,131	20,835	..	−5.8	..	−5.3	..	−3.6	..	−15.9
United Arab Emirates	12,726	..	4.6	..	..	..	−3.9	..	−8.7	..
United Kingdom	619,782	937,655	4.0	3.1	3.8	2.9	0.8	1.3	6.4	4.2
United States	3,831,500	6,728,400	3.8	3.5	2.9	2.2	3.3	0.6	4.0	7.6
Uruguay	6,525	13,883	0.7	4.3	0.1	3.6	1.8	2.1	−6.6	4.7
Uzbekistan	13,321	6,947	..	..	..	..	..	..	..	−0.6
Venezuela, RB	30,171	85,209	1.3	0.5	−1.2	−1.6	2.0	0.2	−5.3	4.1
Vietnam	5,485	21,255	..	..	..	..	..	..	..	18.5
West Bank and Gaza	..	4,019	..	2.5	..	−1.7	..	12.6	..	3.8
Yemen, Rep.	3,561	6,432	..	3.3	..	−0.1	..	1.8	..	10.0
Yugoslavia, Fed. Rep.	..	9,793	..	..	..	..	..	..	..	..
Zambia	2,078	2,815	1.8	−2.2	−1.3	−4.6	−3.4	−7.0	−4.3	6.3
Zimbabwe	5,543	6,501	3.7	−0.2	0.0	−2.2	4.7	−2.3	3.6	−5.2
World	**12,914,929 t**	**18,877,392 t**	**3.3 w**	**2.8 w**	**1.6 w**	**1.3 w**	**2.9 w**	**1.7 w**	**3.9 w**	**2.9 w**
Low income	572,667	727,717	4.2	3.7	1.9	1.6	3.9	2.8	4.3	1.5
Middle income	1,890,669	3,030,497	2.8	3.7	1.1	2.5	4.9	2.0	1.6	2.1
Lower middle income	1,054,957	1,540,572	4.3	3.8	2.6	2.7	3.7	3.9	3.4	0.7
Upper middle income	844,108	1,490,652	1.1	3.7	−0.6	2.3	7.2	0.3	−0.1	4.7
Low & middle income	2,459,296	3,756,453	3.1	3.7	1.1	2.1	4.8	2.2	2.0	2.0
East Asia & Pacific	363,883	854,343	6.5	6.9	4.8	5.6	6.3	6.7	8.4	6.8
Europe & Central Asia	667,012	604,551	..	0.9	..	0.8	..	−0.4	..	−7.0
Latin America & Carib.	737,426	1,307,727	1.3	3.7	−0.6	2.0	5.6	0.4	−0.3	4.2
Middle East & N. Africa	225,422	371,112	..	..	..	..	..	..	..	..
South Asia	281,101	418,649	5.4	4.4	3.1	2.4	5.2	6.1	5.5	7.1
Sub-Saharan Africa	191,901	203,255	1.6	2.5	−1.3	−0.1	2.7	1.4	−3.8	3.1
High income	10,456,766	15,611,354	3.3	2.6	2.7	1.9	2.7	1.7	4.3	3.0
Europe EMU	3,116,941	3,499,161	2.3	1.8	2.1	1.5	2.3	1.6	2.7	1.9

a. Data cover mainland Tanzania only.

Growth of consumption and investment

Measures of growth in consumption and capital formation are subject to two kinds of inaccuracy. The first stems from the difficulty of measuring expenditures at current price levels, as described in *About the data* for table 4.9. The second arises in deflating current price data to measure volume growth, where results depend on the relevance and reliability of the price indexes and weights used. Measuring price changes is more difficult for investment goods than for consumption goods because of the one-time nature of many investments and because the rate of technological progress in capital goods makes capturing change in quality difficult. (An example is computers—prices have fallen as quality has improved.) Several countries estimate capital formation from the supply side, identifying capital goods entering an economy directly from detailed production and international trade statistics. This means that the price indexes used in deflating production and international trade, reflecting delivered or offered prices, will determine the deflator for capital formation expenditures on the demand side.

The data in the table on household final consumption expenditure (private consumption in the 1968 System of National Accounts), in current U.S. dollars, are converted from national currencies using official exchange rates or an alternative conversion factor as noted in *Primary data documentation*. (For a discussion of alternative conversion factors, see *Statistical methods*.)

Growth rates of household final consumption expenditure, household final consumption expenditure per capita, general government final consumption expenditure, and gross capital formation are estimated using constant price data. (Consumption and capital formation as shares of GDP are shown in table 4.9.)

To obtain government consumption in constant prices, countries may deflate current values by applying a wage (price) index or extrapolate from the change in government employment. Neither technique captures improvements in productivity or changes in the quality of government services. Deflators for household consumption are usually calculated on the basis of the consumer price index. Many countries estimate household consumption as a residual that includes statistical discrepancies associated with the estimation of other expenditure items, including changes in inventories; thus these estimates lack detailed breakdowns of household consumption expenditures.

Definitions

• **Household final consumption expenditure** is the market value of all goods and services, including durable products (such as cars, washing machines, and home computers), purchased by households. It excludes purchases of dwellings but includes imputed rent for owner-occupied dwellings. It also includes payments and fees to governments to obtain permits and licenses. The *World Development Indicators* includes in household consumption expenditure the expenditures of nonprofit institutions serving households, even when reported separately by the country. In practice, household consumption expenditure may include any statistical discrepancy in the use of resources relative to the supply of resources.
• **General government final consumption expenditure** includes all government current expenditures for purchases of goods and services (including compensation of employees). It also includes most expenditures on national defense and security but excludes government military expenditures that potentially have wider public use and are part of government capital formation. • **Gross capital formation** consists of outlays on additions to the fixed assets of the economy, net changes in the level of inventories, and net acquisitions of valuables. Fixed assets include land improvements (fences, ditches, drains, and so on); plant, machinery, and equipment purchases; and the construction of roads, railways, and the like, including schools, offices, hospitals, private residential dwellings, and commercial and industrial buildings. Inventories are stocks of goods held by firms to meet temporary or unexpected fluctuations in production or sales, and "work in progress."

4.10a

Per capita consumption has risen in Asia, fallen in Africa

Per capita household consumption (1995 $)

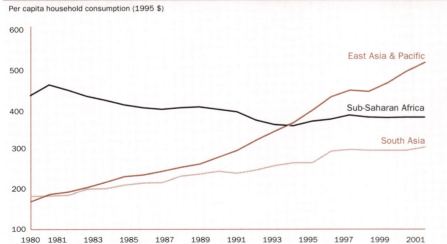

In East Asia and Pacific per capita household consumption has risen more rapidly, and poverty fallen faster, than in South Asia, though the two regions started from similar levels in 1980. In stark contrast, in Sub-Saharan Africa per capita household consumption started out much higher in 1980 and has since fallen below the level in East Asia.

Source: World Bank data files.

Data sources

The national accounts indicators for most developing countries are collected from national statistical organizations and central banks by visiting and resident World Bank missions. Data for high-income economies come from data files of the Organisation for Economic Co-operation and Development (see the OECD's *National Accounts, 1989–2000*, volumes 1 and 2). The United Nations Statistics Division publishes detailed national accounts for United Nations member countries in *National Accounts Statistics: Main Aggregates and Detailed Tables* and updates in the *Monthly Bulletin of Statistics*.

4.11 Central government finances

	Current revenue [a]		Total expenditure		Overall budget balance (including grants)		Financing from abroad		Domestic financing		Debt and interest payments	
	% of GDP		% of GDP		% of GDP		% of GDP		% of GDP		Total debt % of GDP	Interest % of current revenue
	1990	2000	1990	2000	1990	2000	1990	2000	1990	2000	2000	2000
Afghanistan	..	..	..	..	..	..	..	..	..	..	..	..
Albania	..	19.3	..	29.8	..	−8.5	..	2.5	..	6.0	46.4	40.3
Algeria	..	39.2	..	29.3	..	9.9	..	−2.4	..	−7.5	56.1	10.3
Angola	..	..	..	..	..	..	..	..	..	..	..	..
Argentina	10.4	14.2	10.6	17.0	−0.4	−2.3	0.2	2.7	0.2	−0.5	..	23.9
Armenia	..	..	..	..	..	..	..	..	..	..	..	..
Australia	24.9	23.9	23.3	23.5	2.0	1.4	0.2	−0.5	−2.2	−0.9	15.4	5.3
Austria	34.0	37.3	37.6	40.4	−4.4	..	0.5	..	3.9	..	62.5	8.9
Azerbaijan	..	17.6	..	22.6	..	−2.5	..	..	..	..	..	2.5
Bangladesh	..	9.3	..	12.7	..	−2.8	..	0.1	..	2.7	40.1	15.7
Belarus	30.9	28.7	37.3	28.9	−4.8	0.1	2.7	−0.5	2.4	0.5	15.0	2.9
Belgium	42.7	43.6	47.9	45.6	−5.5	−1.8	−0.3	−0.9	5.8	2.7	114.4	16.7
Benin	..	..	..	..	..	..	..	..	..	..	..	..
Bolivia	13.7	17.5	16.4	23.8	−1.7	−3.3	0.7	1.2	1.0	2.1	60.4	9.9
Bosnia and Herzegovina	..	..	..	..	..	..	..	..	..	..	..	..
Botswana	50.8	..	33.6	..	11.2	..	0.0	..	−11.3	..	..	..
Brazil	22.8	24.9	34.9	26.8	−5.8	−7.8	..	..	..	..	..	15.4
Bulgaria	47.1	33.7	55.1	35.3	−8.3	0.6	−0.8	−1.6	9.1	1.0	..	11.8
Burkina Faso	11.0	..	15.0	..	−1.3	..	..	..	..	..	..	..
Burundi	18.2	17.9	28.7	26.1	−3.3	−4.7	4.9	3.3	−1.6	1.5	183.9	13.2
Cambodia	..	..	..	..	..	..	..	..	..	..	..	..
Cameroon	15.4	15.7	21.2	15.5	−5.9	0.1	5.2	0.2	1.2	−0.3	102.3	19.2
Canada	21.5	21.8	26.1	20.3	−4.8	1.3	0.2	−0.1	4.6	−1.2	61.5	14.2
Central African Republic	..	..	..	..	..	..	..	..	..	..	..	..
Chad	6.7	..	21.8	..	−4.7	..	5.0	..	−0.3	..	..	..
Chile	20.6	22.2	20.4	21.9	0.8	0.1	0.9	−0.3	−2.5	0.1	13.9	2.0
China	6.3	7.2	10.1	10.9	−1.9	−2.9	0.8	−0.1	1.1	3.0	12.7	..
Hong Kong, China	..	..	..	..	..	..	..	..	..	..	..	..
Colombia	12.6	12.6	11.6	19.1	3.9	−7.1	..	2.2	..	5.0	29.8	26.8
Congo, Dem. Rep.	10.1	0.0	18.8	0.1	−6.5	0.0	0.0	0.0	6.5	0.0	..	0.0
Congo, Rep.	22.5	26.4	35.6	25.5	−14.1	1.2	..	2.0	..	−3.1	160.6	26.5
Costa Rica	23.0	20.9	25.6	22.3	−3.1	−1.3	0.3	0.1	2.8	1.2	36.2	17.2
Côte d'Ivoire	22.0	16.4	24.5	17.9	−2.9	−1.1	4.0	1.7	0.4	−0.6	103.5	23.8
Croatia	33.0	40.4	37.6	46.5	−4.6	−4.9	0.0	4.4	4.7	0.5	..	4.3
Cuba	..	..	..	..	..	..	..	..	..	..	..	..
Czech Republic	..	32.7	..	36.8	..	−3.0	..	0.0	..	2.9	15.1	3.0
Denmark	37.8	36.2	39.0	34.9	−0.7	1.6	..	..	..	..	64.5	10.8
Dominican Republic	12.0	16.9	11.7	16.0	0.6	1.0	0.0	−1.0	−0.6	0.0	20.7	4.5
Ecuador	18.2	..	14.5	..	3.7	..	..	..	..	..	..	..
Egypt, Arab Rep.	23.0	..	27.8	..	−5.7	..	−0.7	..	6.4	..	..	..
El Salvador	..	15.9	..	17.0	..	1.7	..	−0.2	..	−1.5	28.1	8.6
Eritrea	..	..	..	..	..	..	..	..	..	..	..	..
Estonia	26.2	30.1	23.7	31.4	0.4	0.2	0.0	−0.1	−0.4	−0.1	3.1	0.6
Ethiopia	17.4	19.2	27.2	26.8	−9.8	−5.0	2.8	2.8	7.0	2.2	102.2	10.8
Finland	30.6	32.0	30.3	33.4	0.2	−0.3	0.7	−1.1	−0.8	1.4	61.1	14.3
France	39.7	..	41.8	..	−2.1	..	1.1	..	1.0	..	..	..
Gabon	20.6	..	20.2	..	3.2	..	2.7	..	−5.8	..	..	..
Gambia, The	19.4	..	23.6	..	−0.8	..	..	..	..	..	..	..
Georgia	..	10.5	..	12.4	..	−1.6	..	−0.9	..	2.5	70.8	27.1
Germany	25.6	31.3	26.3	32.7	−1.4	−0.9	0.5	0.6	1.0	−0.1	20.0	7.3
Ghana	12.5	..	13.2	..	0.2	..	1.3	..	−1.5	..	..	..
Greece	27.8	23.4	52.2	30.7	−22.9	−4.4	1.6	2.4	21.3	2.0	112.7	38.4
Guatemala	..	..	..	..	..	..	..	..	..	..	..	..
Guinea	16.0	11.7	22.9	21.0	−3.3	−2.4	4.1	2.3	−0.8	0.2	..	37.1
Guinea-Bissau	..	..	..	..	..	..	..	..	..	..	..	..
Haiti	..	7.9	..	10.5	..	−2.3	..	−0.2	..	2.5	..	6.1

Central government finances

	Current revenue [a]		Total expenditure		Overall budget balance (including grants)		Financing from abroad		Domestic financing		Debt and interest payments	
	% of GDP		% of GDP		% of GDP		% of GDP		% of GDP		Total debt % of GDP	Interest % of current revenue
	1990	2000	1990	2000	1990	2000	1990	2000	1990	2000	2000	2000
Honduras	..	..	..	..	..	..	..	..	..	..	..	..
Hungary	52.9	36.0	52.1	40.2	0.8	−3.5	−0.5	1.5	−0.3	2.0	54.9	16.6
India	12.6	12.8	16.3	16.7	−7.6	−5.2	0.6	0.0	7.1	5.2	55.7	37.0
Indonesia	18.8	18.1	18.4	20.5	0.4	−1.1	0.7	1.4	−1.1	−0.3	45.2	21.6
Iran, Islamic Rep.	18.1	21.0	19.9	21.9	−1.8	−0.6	0.0	0.1	1.8	0.5	..	0.7
Iraq	..	..	..	..	..	..	..	..	..	..	..	..
Ireland	33.6	..	37.7	..	−2.4	..	..	..	..	..	..	..
Israel	39.4	43.3	50.7	46.3	−5.3	0.9	0.8	−0.5	4.6	−0.4	97.8	12.9
Italy	38.2	41.3	47.4	41.9	−10.2	−1.6	0.0	..	9.9	..	..	15.5
Jamaica	25.4	34.6	23.2	37.3	3.5	−1.2	..	..	..	..	115.6	38.0
Japan	14.0	..	15.3	..	−1.5	..	0.0	..	−1.7	..	..	..
Jordan	26.1	25.1	35.8	31.2	−3.5	−2.0	3.0	0.2	0.5	1.8	93.8	13.9
Kazakhstan	..	11.3	..	14.3	..	−0.6	..	1.2	..	−0.7	21.5	11.9
Kenya	22.4	25.8	27.5	26.0	−3.8	0.6	1.3	−2.4	4.5	1.8	69.1	22.3
Korea, Dem. Rep.	..	..	..	..	..	..	..	..	..	..	..	..
Korea, Rep.	17.5	..	16.2	..	−0.7	..	−0.2	..	0.9	..	..	..
Kuwait	58.7	34.5	55.3	44.2	..	−9.7	..	..	..	..	..	4.0
Kyrgyz Republic	..	14.2	..	18.0	..	−2.2	..	..	..	..	114.5	10.2
Lao PDR	..	..	..	..	..	..	..	..	..	..	..	..
Latvia	..	28.6	..	31.6	..	−2.7	..	−0.3	..	3.0	13.2	3.6
Lebanon	..	19.5	..	35.7	..	−16.2	..	8.1	..	8.1	135.2	74.4
Lesotho	39.0	44.1	51.2	49.7	−1.0	−3.6	7.9	0.7	−6.9	2.9	67.8	4.9
Liberia	..	..	..	..	..	..	..	..	..	..	..	..
Libya	..	..	..	..	..	..	..	..	..	..	..	..
Lithuania	31.9	24.6	28.9	27.6	1.4	−1.3	..	2.0	..	−0.7	23.3	7.0
Macedonia, FYR	..	..	..	..	..	..	..	..	..	..	..	..
Madagascar	11.6	11.7	16.0	17.1	−1.1	−2.4	2.1	1.7	−1.2	0.5	..	12.1
Malawi	19.8	..	25.4	..	−1.6	..	..	..	..	..	..	..
Malaysia	26.4	..	29.3	..	−2.0	..	−0.7	..	2.8	..	..	..
Mali	..	..	..	..	..	..	..	..	..	..	..	..
Mauritania	..	..	..	..	..	..	..	..	..	..	..	..
Mauritius	24.3	22.2	24.3	24.0	−0.4	−1.3	−0.5	−0.4	0.9	1.7	34.8	12.0
Mexico	15.3	14.8	17.9	16.0	−2.5	−1.3	0.3	−0.9	2.3	2.1	23.3	14.0
Moldova	..	24.5	..	29.6	..	−1.3	..	−0.2	..	1.5	73.0	26.0
Mongolia	19.6	28.5	23.1	29.3	−6.4	−6.1	7.5	6.4	−1.1	−0.3	91.9	6.1
Morocco	26.4	29.6	28.8	32.5	−2.2	−2.5	3.9	−1.5	−1.6	4.0	72.7	16.5
Mozambique	..	..	..	..	..	..	..	..	..	..	..	..
Myanmar	10.5	5.3	16.0	8.7	−5.1	−3.4	0.0	0.0	5.1	3.4	..	..
Namibia	26.4	32.6	28.1	36.2	−1.0	−3.6	..	..	..	..	..	7.0
Nepal	8.4	10.6	17.2	16.0	−6.8	−3.3	5.4	2.1	1.4	1.1	64.6	12.0
Netherlands	45.3	..	49.7	..	−4.3	..	−0.3	1.9	4.6	−1.8	55.3	..
New Zealand	42.1	30.6	43.4	30.8	4.0	−0.3	..	..	..	..	32.6	7.3
Nicaragua	33.5	31.8	72.0	35.9	−35.6	−1.0	12.7	7.7	22.9	−6.7	..	11.5
Niger	..	..	..	..	..	..	..	..	..	..	..	..
Nigeria	..	..	..	..	..	..	..	..	..	..	..	..
Norway	42.4	41.3	41.3	36.5	0.5	−3.9	−0.6	3.8	0.0	0.1	20.5	3.8
Oman	38.9	23.9	39.5	28.6	−0.8	−4.8	−3.9	3.8	4.7	1.0	19.1	5.9
Pakistan	19.1	16.9	22.4	23.1	−5.4	−5.5	2.3	0.9	3.1	4.6	90.0	44.5
Panama	25.6	26.8	23.7	28.0	3.0	0.3	−3.4	1.7	0.4	−2.0	..	20.7
Papua New Guinea	25.2	23.0	34.7	31.4	−3.5	−2.8	0.4	1.7	3.0	1.0	63.9	19.0
Paraguay	12.3	15.6	9.4	19.4	2.9	−4.0	−0.9	..	−2.1	..	..	7.2
Peru	12.5	16.5	20.6	19.3	−8.1	−1.8	5.4	1.1	2.7	0.7	44.9	13.2
Philippines	16.2	15.4	19.6	19.6	−3.5	−4.1	0.4	2.6	3.1	1.5	65.6	27.7
Poland	..	31.1	..	34.6	..	0.3	..	0.0	..	−0.3	39.6	8.5
Portugal	31.3	34.2	37.6	38.5	−4.4	−1.2	−1.3	−2.1	5.7	3.3	0.8	8.4
Puerto Rico	..	..	..	..	..	..	..	..	..	..	..	..

	Current revenue [a]		Total expenditure		Overall budget balance (including grants)		Financing from abroad		Domestic financing		Debt and interest payments	
											Total debt % of GDP	Interest % of current revenue
	% of GDP		% of GDP		% of GDP		% of GDP		% of GDP			
	1990	2000	1990	2000	1990	2000	1990	2000	1990	2000	2000	2000
Romania	34.4	29.6	33.8	34.2	0.9	–4.0	0.0	1.0	–0.9	3.0	..	13.7
Russian Federation	..	24.6	..	22.9	..	3.9	..	–0.3	..	–3.7	62.2	14.4
Rwanda	10.8	..	18.9	..	–5.3	..	2.5	..	2.8	..	..	..
Saudi Arabia	..	..	..	..	..	..	..	..	..	..	..	..
Senegal	..	18.1	..	20.6	..	–1.2	..	0.6	..	0.6	78.9	8.1
Sierra Leone	5.6	7.1	8.3	20.9	–2.5	–8.5	0.5	1.1	2.0	7.4	247.4	81.8
Singapore	26.9	26.1	21.4	18.8	10.8	10.0	–0.1	0.0	–10.7	–10.0	86.9	1.3
Slovak Republic	..	35.6	..	40.5	..	–3.0	..	3.1	..	–0.1	30.2	7.7
Slovenia	39.8	38.6	38.6	40.2	0.3	–1.3	0.1	1.7	–0.4	–0.5	25.7	3.9
Somalia	..	..	..	..	..	..	..	..	..	..	..	..
South Africa	26.3	26.7	30.1	29.1	–4.1	–2.2	0.0	0.3	4.1	1.9	47.0	19.6
Spain	29.3	..	32.6	..	–3.1	..	0.7	..	2.4	..	..	..
Sri Lanka	21.0	16.8	28.4	25.7	–7.8	–9.5	3.6	0.0	4.2	9.4	97.1	33.7
Sudan	..	8.3	..	8.7	..	–0.9	..	0.2	..	0.8	9.0	9.4
Swaziland	32.7	28.0	25.5	30.0	0.0	–0.9	–0.2	–0.6	0.2	1.5	28.6	2.0
Sweden	42.6	39.4	39.3	39.3	1.0	0.1	–0.3	–5.5	–0.7	5.4	..	11.4
Switzerland	20.8	25.4	23.3	26.7	–0.9	3.0	0.0	0.0	0.9	–3.0	26.7	3.6
Syrian Arab Republic	21.9	23.9	21.8	23.2	0.3	0.7	..	2.1	..	–2.8	..	..
Tajikistan	..	10.5	..	11.3	..	–0.2	..	0.5	..	–0.3	112.8	3.7
Tanzania	..	..	..	..	..	..	..	..	..	..	..	..
Thailand	18.5	16.0	14.1	18.0	4.6	–3.0	–1.5	1.4	–3.1	1.7	22.7	7.4
Togo	..	..	..	..	..	..	..	..	..	..	..	..
Trinidad and Tobago	..	..	..	..	..	..	..	..	..	..	..	..
Tunisia	30.7	28.6	34.6	32.0	–5.4	–2.6	1.8	0.7	3.6	1.8	62.6	11.4
Turkey	13.7	28.1	17.4	39.4	–3.0	–11.4	0.0	2.8	3.0	8.6	51.2	58.7
Turkmenistan	..	..	..	..	..	..	..	..	..	..	..	..
Uganda	..	11.3	..	20.4	..	–7.2	..	2.9	..	4.8	45.1	7.5
Ukraine	..	26.8	..	28.3	..	–0.6	..	–0.3	..	1.0	45.3	9.5
United Arab Emirates	1.6	3.5	11.5	11.2	0.4	–0.3	0.0	0.0	–0.4	0.3	..	0.0
United Kingdom	36.0	36.0	37.5	36.0	0.6	0.0	0.2	–0.4	–0.8	0.3	..	7.7
United States	18.9	21.5	22.7	19.2	–3.8	2.4	0.2	–2.2	3.6	–0.1	34.8	11.2
Uruguay	23.8	28.0	23.3	31.5	0.3	–3.4	1.4	2.6	–1.7	1.2	..	7.8
Uzbekistan	..	..	..	..	..	..	..	..	..	..	..	..
Venezuela, RB	23.7	20.5	20.7	21.7	0.0	–1.7	1.0	–2.2	–1.0	3.9	..	12.0
Vietnam	..	19.9	..	23.4	..	–2.8	..	1.4	..	1.4	..	4.0
West Bank and Gaza	..	..	..	..	..	..	..	..	..	..	..	..
Yemen, Rep.	18.9	23.9	27.8	26.7	–8.8	–3.5	3.2	1.3	5.6	2.2	..	9.8
Yugoslavia, Fed. Rep.	..	..	..	..	..	..	..	..	..	..	..	..
Zambia	..	..	..	..	..	..	..	..	..	..	..	..
Zimbabwe	24.1	..	27.3	..	–5.3	..	0.9	..	4.4	..	..	..
World	**22.7 w**	**24.7 w**	**25.8 w**	**25.8 w**	**–2.8 w**	**–1.0 w**	**0.6 m**	**1.1 m**	**1.1 m**	**0.8 m**	**.. m**	**11.3 m**
Low income	15.5	15.0	18.4	18.3	–4.8	–3.6	..	..	..	..	..	..
Middle income	17.3	17.7	22.1	21.3	–2.7	–3.3	0.3	0.1	0.2	1.0	33.2	10.3
Lower middle income	13.7	16.6	16.3	20.7	–1.7	–3.8	..	0.2	..	1.5	51.3	11.6
Upper middle income	20.6	22.3	27.3	24.4	–3.5	–4.7	.0.2	0.1	–0.4	0.8	26.7	7.8
Low & middle income	17.1	17.1	21.6	20.7	–3.0	–3.3	..	1.3	..	1.0	..	11.8
East Asia & Pacific	11.7	10.9	13.8	15.0	–0.9	–3.7	0.4	1.3	2.8	1.0	52.3	13.9
Europe & Central Asia	..	27.6	..	30.5	..	–1.3	..	0.0	..	0.7	42.4	9.5
Latin America & Carib.	18.8	20.0	25.6	21.9	–3.5	–4.8	0.3	1.4	–1.3	0.9	..	11.5
Middle East & N. Africa	..	..	..	..	..	..	1.8	1.3	3.6	1.7	..	12.2
South Asia	13.8	13.5	17.6	17.9	–7.3	–5.4	3.0	0.5	3.6	4.9	77.3	35.4
Sub-Saharan Africa	24.0	23.5	27.6	25.9	–3.5	–1.6	..	..	..	..	..	..
High income	23.8	..	26.6	..	–2.8	..	0.2	0.0	1.0	0.1	55.3	7.5
Europe EMU	33.5	..	37.1	..	–4.0	..	0.5	0.5	3.9	1.7	60.2	14.3

a. Excluding grants.

Central government finances | 4.11

Tables 4.11–4.13 present an overview of the size and role of central governments relative to national economies. The International Monetary Fund's (IMF) *Manual on Government Finance Statistics* describes the government as the sector of the economy responsible for "implementation of public policy through the provision of primarily nonmarket services and the transfer of income, supported mainly by compulsory levies on other sectors" (1986, p. 3). The definition of government generally excludes nonfinancial public enterprises and public financial institutions (such as the central bank).

Units of government meeting this definition exist at many levels, from local administrative units to the highest level of national government. Inadequate statistical coverage precludes the presentation of subnational data, however, making cross-country comparisons potentially misleading.

Central government can refer to one of two accounting concepts: consolidated or budgetary. For most countries central government finance data have been consolidated into one account, but for others only budgetary central government accounts are available. Countries reporting budgetary data are noted in *Primary data documentation*. Because budgetary accounts do not necessarily include all central government units, the picture they provide of central government activities is usually incomplete. A key issue is the failure to include the quasi-fiscal operations of the central bank. Central bank losses arising from monetary operations and subsidized financing can result in sizable quasi-fiscal deficits. Such deficits may also result from the operations of other financial intermediaries, such as public development

finance institutions. Also missing from the data are governments' contingent liabilities for unfunded pension and national insurance plans.

Data on government revenues and expenditures are collected by the IMF through questionnaires distributed to member governments and by the Organisation for Economic Co-operation and Development. Despite the IMF's efforts to systematize and standardize the collection of public finance data, statistics on public finance are often incomplete, untimely, and not comparable across countries.

Government finance statistics are reported in local currency. The indicators here are shown as percentages of GDP. Many countries report government finance data according to fiscal years; see *Primary data documentation* for the timing of these years. For further discussion of government finance statistics, see *About the data* for tables 4.12 and 4.13.

• **Current revenue** includes all revenue from taxes and current nontax revenues (other than grants), such as fines, fees, recoveries, and income from property or sales. • **Total expenditure** includes nonrepayable current and capital expenditures. It does not include government lending or repayments to the government or government acquisition of equity for public policy purposes. • **Overall budget balance** is current and capital revenue and official grants received, less total expenditure and lending minus repayments. • **Financing from abroad** (obtained from nonresidents) and **domestic financing** (obtained from residents) refer to the means by which a government provides financial resources to cover a budget deficit or allocates financial resources arising from a budget surplus. The data include all government liabilities—other than those for currency issues or demand, time, or savings deposits with government—or claims on others held by government, and changes in government holdings of cash and deposits. They exclude government guarantees of the debt of others. • **Debt** is the entire stock of direct government fixed term contractual obligations to others outstanding on a particular date. It includes domestic debt (such as debt held by monetary authorities, deposit money banks, nonfinancial public enterprises, and households) and foreign debt (such as debt to international development institutions and foreign governments). It is the gross amount of government liabilities not reduced by the amount of government claims against others. Because debt is a stock rather than a flow, it is measured as of a given date, usually the last day of the fiscal year. • **Interest payments** include interest payments on government debt—including long-term bonds, long-term loans, and other debt instruments—to both domestic and foreign residents.

Data sources

The data on central government finances are from the IMF's *Government Finance Statistics Yearbook, 2002* and IMF data files. Each country's accounts are reported using the system of common definitions and classifications in the IMF's *Manual on Government Finance Statistics* (1986). See these sources for complete and authoritative explanations of concepts, definitions, and data sources.

Central government expenditures

	Goods and services		Wages and salaries [a]		Interest payments		Subsidies and other current transfers		Capital expenditure	
	% of total expenditure		% of total expenditure		% of total expenditure		% of total expenditure		% of total expenditure	
	1990	2000	1990	2000	1990	2000	1990	2000	1990	2000
Afghanistan	..	..	..	..	..	..	..	..	..	..
Albania	..	17	..	9	..	26	..	42	..	16
Algeria	..	29	..	20	..	14	..	30	..	27
Angola	..	..	..	..	..	..	..	..	..	..
Argentina	30	19	23	15	8	20	57	55	5	6
Armenia	..	..	..	..	..	..	..	..	..	..
Australia	27	27	2	3	8	5	56	61	9	5
Austria	25	25	10	10	9	8	57	61	9	5
Azerbaijan	..	31	..	11	..	2	..	50	..	17
Bangladesh	..	27	..	18	..	11	..	25	..	23
Belarus	37	22	2	9	2	3	46	59	16	17
Belgium	19	19	14	13	21	16	56	60	5	5
Benin	..	..	..	..	..	..	..	..	..	..
Bolivia	63	39	36	24	6	7	16	37	15	17
Bosnia and Herzegovina	..	..	..	..	..	..	..	..	..	..
Botswana	51	..	23	..	2	..	25	..	21	..
Brazil	16	22	9	12	78	14	39	62	2	2
Bulgaria	35	30	3	8	10	11	52	48	3	11
Burkina Faso	60	..	51	..	6	..	11	..	23	..
Burundi	34	50	22	30	5	9	10	11	51	23
Cambodia	..	..	..	..	..	..	..	..	..	..
Cameroon	51	52	39	32	5	19	13	15	26	14
Canada	21	18	9	9	20	15	57	65	2	2
Central African Republic	..	..	..	..	..	..	..	..	..	..
Chad	41	..	28	..	2	..	3	..	56	..
Chile	28	28	18	20	10	2	51	55	11	15
China	..	..	..	..	..	..	..	..	..	..
Hong Kong, China	..	..	..	..	..	..	..	..	..	..
Colombia	26	19	18	14	10	18	42	41	22	22
Congo, Dem. Rep.	73	80	23	25	7	0	4	12	16	7
Congo, Rep.	56	37	49	18	22	27	20	8	2	27
Costa Rica	57	48	43	37	12	16	20	25	11	11
Côte d'Ivoire	69	49	38	32	1	22	30	13	0	16
Croatia	54	47	22	25	0	4	42	41	3	8
Cuba	..	..	..	..	..	..	..	..	..	..
Czech Republic	..	13	..	7	..	3	..	74	..	10
Denmark	20	22	12	13	15	11	61	64	3	3
Dominican Republic	39	53	29	41	4	5	13	16	44	22
Ecuador	42	..	38	..	23	..	16	..	18	..
Egypt, Arab Rep.	42	..	23	..	14	..	26	..	17	..
El Salvador	..	76	..	45	..	8	..	2	..	19
Eritrea	..	..	..	..	..	..	..	..	..	..
Estonia	25	45	8	13	0	1	73	49	8	6
Ethiopia	77	52	40	18	5	8	9	31	16	19
Finland	20	18	10	7	3	14	70	63	7	5
France	26	..	17	..	5	..	63	..	6	..
Gabon	63	..	37	..	0	..	6	..	32	..
Gambia, The	41	..	21	..	16	..	9	..	34	..
Georgia	..	26	..	9	..	23	..	45	..	5
Germany	32	31	8	8	5	7	58	57	5	4
Ghana	50	..	32	..	11	..	20	..	19	..
Greece	31	34	21	28	20	29	41	20	8	17
Guatemala	..	..	..	..	..	..	..	..	..	..
Guinea	37	29	18	19	7	21	4	8	53	36
Guinea-Bissau	..	..	..	..	..	..	..	..	..	..
Haiti	..	65	..	42	..	5	..	8	..	22

Central government expenditures

	Goods and services		Wages and salaries [a]		Interest payments		Subsidies and other current transfers		Capital expenditure	
	% of total expenditure		% of total expenditure		% of total expenditure		% of total expenditure		% of total expenditure	
	1990	2000	1990	2000	1990	2000	1990	2000	1990	2000
Honduras	..	..	..	..	..	..	..	..	..	..
Hungary	27	18	6	9	6	15	64	51	4	12
India	24	23	11	10	22	28	43	41	11	8
Indonesia	23	18	16	8	13	19	21	39	43	24
Iran, Islamic Rep.	53	68	40	52	0	1	22	10	25	21
Iraq	..	..	..	..	..	..	..	..	..	..
Ireland	19	..	14	..	21	..	54	..	7	..
Israel	38	33	14	14	18	12	37	49	6	5
Italy	17	20	13	16	21	15	54	59	8	6
Jamaica	47	51	21	29	29	35	1	0	23	14
Japan	14	..	..	..	19	..	54	..	13	..
Jordan	55	66	44	48	18	11	11	7	16	15
Kazakhstan	..	33	..	8	..	9	..	49	..	8
Kenya	51	..	31	..	19	22	10	..	20	7
Korea, Dem. Rep.	..	..	..	..	..	..	..	..	..	..
Korea, Rep.	35	..	13	..	4	..	46	..	15	..
Kuwait	62	58	31	35	0	3	20	26	18	13
Kyrgyz Republic	..	67	..	26	..	8	..	13	..	12
Lao PDR	..	..	..	..	..	..	..	..	..	..
Latvia	..	25	..	12	..	3	..	65	..	7
Lebanon	..	30	..	23	..	41	..	12	..	17
Lesotho	40	76	22	35	11	4	5	0	45	19
Liberia	..	..	..	..	..	..	..	..	..	..
Libya	..	..	..	..	..	..	..	..	..	..
Lithuania	12	46	6	16	..	6	67	41	20	7
Macedonia, FYR	..	..	..	..	..	..	..	..	..	..
Madagascar	37	36	25	23	9	8	9	6	43	38
Malawi	54	..	23	..	14	..	8	..	24	..
Malaysia	41	..	26	..	20	..	16	..	24	..
Mali	..	..	..	..	..	..	..	..	..	..
Mauritania	..	..	..	..	..	..	..	..	..	..
Mauritius	47	45	37	34	15	11	22	29	17	14
Mexico	25	24	18	17	45	13	17	52	14	10
Moldova	..	20	..	8	..	22	..	53	..	6
Mongolia	30	32	7	11	1	6	56	47	13	15
Morocco	48	46	35	36	16	15	8	16	28	22
Mozambique	..	..	..	..	..	..	..	..	..	..
Myanmar	..	..	..	..	..	..	..	..	29	39
Namibia	73	63	46	44	1	6	10	17	15	14
Nepal	..	..	..	..	..	8	..	..	..	..
Netherlands	15	..	9	..	9	..	70	..	6	..
New Zealand	19	52	12	..	15	7	64	38	2	3
Nicaragua	43	30	23	16	0	8	14	21	4	40
Niger	..	..	..	..	..	..	..	..	..	..
Nigeria	..	..	..	..	..	..	..	..	..	..
Norway	19	21	8	8	6	4	69	70	5	5
Oman	76	77	22	28	6	5	7	6	11	12
Pakistan	44	47	..	4	25	33	20	11	12	9
Panama	64	47	49	34	8	20	26	24	2	9
Papua New Guinea	61	56	34	29	11	14	18	24	11	6
Paraguay	54	51	36	45	10	6	19	23	17	20
Peru	30	39	17	18	37	11	25	36	8	14
Philippines	44	51	29	28	34	22	7	17	16	9
Poland	..	15	..	7	..	8	..	73	..	4
Portugal	38	41	27	32	18	7	33	38	12	13
Puerto Rico	..	..	..	..	..	..	..	..	..	..

4.12 | Central government expenditures

	Goods and services		Wages and salaries[a]		Interest payments		Subsidies and other current transfers		Capital expenditure	
	% of total expenditure		% of total expenditure		% of total expenditure		% of total expenditure		% of total expenditure	
	1990	2000	1990	2000	1990	2000	1990	2000	1990	2000
Romania	26	36	12	16	0	12	57	42	17	11
Russian Federation	..	39	..	13	..	15	..	38	..	8
Rwanda	53	..	29	..	5	..	16	..	33	..
Saudi Arabia	..	..	..	..	..	..	..	..	..	..
Senegal	..	45	..	27	..	7	..	12	..	34
Sierra Leone	77	60	35	46	18	28	1	6	8	11
Singapore	51	54	27	25	14	2	12	18	24	27
Slovak Republic	..	23	..	14	..	7	..	57	..	13
Slovenia	40	40	20	22	1	4	52	50	7	7
Somalia	..	..	..	..	..	..	..	..	..	..
South Africa	53	27	23	13	14	18	23	51	10	4
Spain	19	..	13	..	9	..	63	..	9	..
Sri Lanka	33	41	17	21	23	22	23	16	21	21
Sudan	..	74	..	34	..	9	..	7	..	10
Swaziland	62	57	42	32	3	2	11	22	24	19
Sweden	15	18	6	6	11	11	72	69	2	2
Switzerland	31	28	5	4	3	3	61	64	5	5
Syrian Arab Republic	..	..	..	..	..	..	..	..	27	36
Tajikistan	..	41	..	15	..	3	..	34	..	22
Tanzania	..	..	..	..	..	..	..	..	..	..
Thailand	60	55	35	33	13	7	9	12	18	26
Togo	..	..	..	..	..	..	..	..	..	..
Trinidad and Tobago	..	..	..	..	..	..	..	..	..	..
Tunisia	34	41	28	34	10	10	35	25	22	23
Turkey	52	28	38	21	18	42	16	22	13	8
Turkmenistan	..	..	..	..	..	..	..	..	..	..
Uganda	..	34	..	10	..	4	..	17	..	45
Ukraine	..	32	..	12	..	9	..	53	..	6
United Arab Emirates	88	78	33	35	0	0	10	18	1	4
United Kingdom	30	29	13	6	9	8	52	59	10	4
United States	28	21	10	8	15	13	49	61	8	5
Uruguay	35	26	20	14	8	7	50	63	7	4
Uzbekistan	..	..	..	..	..	..	..	..	..	..
Venezuela, RB	31	26	23	18	16	11	37	45	16	17
Vietnam	..	..	..	..	..	3	..	..	..	32
West Bank and Gaza	..	..	..	..	..	..	..	..	..	..
Yemen, Rep.	64	54	55	39	8	9	6	18	33	17
Yugoslavia, Fed. Rep.	..	..	..	..	..	..	..	..	..	..
Zambia	..	..	..	..	..	..	..	..	..	..
Zimbabwe	56	..	37	..	16	..	18	..	10	..
World	**39 m**	**37 m**	**23 m**	**18 m**	**10 m**	**9 m**	**23 m**	**31 m**	**13 m**	**13 m**
Low income	..	..	..	..	..	..	..	..	..	..
Middle income	42	39	25	20	11	9	23	37	16	12
Lower middle income	44	41	29	26	13	11	19	23	17	16
Upper middle income	35	26	23	16	10	7	26	51	11	10
Low & middle income	..	39	..	21	..	9	..	26	..	16
East Asia & Pacific	42	..	27	..	10	11	16	..	21	24
Europe & Central Asia	..	30	..	12	..	8	..	49	..	8
Latin America & Carib.	35	39	23	24	10	8	25	25	11	15
Middle East & N. Africa	53	50	35	35	10	11	11	14	23	19
South Asia	33	41	..	10	23	25	23	16	12	9
Sub-Saharan Africa	53	..	31	..	7	..	10	..	20	..
High income	25	29	13	11	11	7	56	59	7	5
Europe EMU	20	25	13	13	9	14	57	58	7	5

Note: Components include expenditures financed by grants in kind and other cash adjustments to total expenditure.
a. Part of goods and services.

About the data

Government expenditures include all nonrepayable payments, whether current or capital, requited or unrequited. Total central government expenditure as presented in the International Monetary Fund's (IMF) *Government Finance Statistics Yearbook* is a more limited measure of general government consumption than that shown in the national accounts (see table 4.10) because it excludes consumption expenditures by state and local governments. At the same time, the IMF's concept of central government expenditure is broader than the national accounts definition because it includes government gross capital formation and transfer payments.

Expenditures can be measured either by function (health, defense, education) or by economic type (interest payments, wages and salaries, purchases of goods and services). Functional data are often incomplete, and coverage varies by country because functional responsibilities stretch across levels of government for which no data are available. Defense expenditures, usually the central government's responsibility, are shown in table 5.8. For more information on education expenditures, see table 2.11; for more on health expenditures, see table 2.15.

The classification of expenditures by economic type can also be problematic. For example, the distinction between current and capital expenditure may be arbitrary, and subsidies to state-owned enterprises or banks may be disguised as capital financing. Subsidies may also be hidden in special contractual pricing for goods and services.

Expenditure shares may not sum to 100 percent because adjustments to total expenditures financed by grants in kind and other cash adjustments (which may be positive or negative) are not shown separately.

For further discussion of government finance statistics, see *About the data* for tables 4.11 and 4.13.

Definitions

- **Total expenditure of the central government** includes both current and capital (development) expenditures and excludes lending minus repayments.
- **Goods and services** include all government payments in exchange for goods and services, whether in the form of wages and salaries to employees or other purchases of goods and services. • **Wages and salaries** consist of all payments in cash, but not in kind (such as food and housing), to employees in return for services rendered, before deduction of withholding taxes and employee contributions to social security and pension funds. • **Interest payments** are payments made to domestic sectors and to nonresidents for the use of borrowed money. (Repayment of principal is shown as a financing item, and commission charges are shown as purchases of services.) Interest payments do not include payments by government as guarantor or surety of interest on the defaulted debts of others, which are classified as government lending.
- **Subsidies and other current transfers** include all unrequited, nonrepayable transfers on current account to private and public enterprises and the cost to the public of covering the cash operating deficits on sales to the public by departmental enterprises. • **Capital expenditure** is spending to acquire fixed capital assets, land, intangible assets, government stocks, and nonmilitary, nonfinancial assets. Also included are capital grants.

4.12a

Some developing and high-income economies direct more than half their central government spending to subsidies and other current transfers

Subsidies and other current transfers as % of central government expenditure

Developing economies

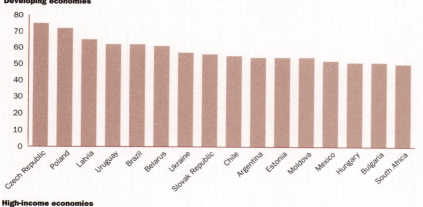

High-income economies

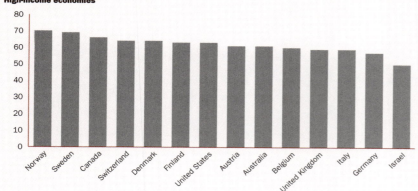

Note: Data refer to the most recent year available in 1998–2001.
Source: International Monetary Fund, Government Finance Statistics data files.

Data sources

The data on central government expenditures are from the IMF's *Government Finance Statistics Yearbook, 2002* and IMF data files. Each country's accounts are reported using the system of common definitions and classifications in the IMF's *Manual on Government Finance Statistics* (1986). See these sources for complete and authoritative explanations of concepts, definitions, and data sources.

	Taxes on income, profits, and capital gains		Social security taxes		Taxes on goods and services		Taxes on international trade		Other taxes		Nontax revenue	
	% of total current revenue		% of total current revenue		% of total current revenue		% of total current revenue		% of total current revenue		% of total current revenue	
	1990	2000	1990	2000	1990	2000	1990	2000	1990	2000	1990	2000
Afghanistan	..	..	..	..	..	..	..	..	..	..	..	..
Albania	..	7	..	14	..	40	..	15	..	1	..	23
Algeria	..	80	..	0	..	7	..	9	..	1	..	4
Angola	..	..	..	..	..	..	..	..	..	..	..	..
Argentina	2	17	44	23	20	43	14	5	10	3	10	9
Armenia	..	..	..	..	..	..	..	..	..	..	..	..
Australia	65	68	0	0	21	21	4	3	2	2	8	8
Austria	19	25	37	40	25	25	1	0	9	4	9	6
Azerbaijan	..	22	..	22	..	40	..	9	..	2	..	5
Bangladesh	..	11	..	0	..	40	..	23	..	1	..	25
Belarus	12	11	32	35	40	39	5	5	9	3	2	7
Belgium	35	37	35	33	24	25	0	0	3	3	3	2
Benin	..	..	..	..	..	..	..	..	..	..	..	..
Bolivia	5	8	9	10	31	49	7	6	11	8	38	19
Bosnia and Herzegovina	..	..	..	..	..	..	..	..	..	..	..	..
Botswana	39	..	0	..	2	..	13	..	0	..	46	..
Brazil	20	20	31	34	24	21	2	3	6	4	16	17
Bulgaria	30	12	23	25	18	39	2	2	1	1	27	21
Burkina Faso	23	..	0	..	30	..	33	..	7	..	8	..
Burundi	21	21	6	7	37	44	24	20	1	1	10	6
Cambodia	..	..	..	..	..	..	..	..	..	..	..	..
Cameroon	18	21	6	0	21	26	14	28	4	4	28	20
Canada	51	53	16	20	17	16	3	1	0	0	13	9
Central African Republic	..	..	..	..	..	..	..	..	..	..	..	..
Chad	19	..	0	..	39	..	24	..	10	..	8	..
Chile	12	18	8	6	43	46	12	6	3	3	21	20
China	31	6	0	0	18	75	14	10	0	4	37	6
Hong Kong, China	..	..	..	..	..	..	..	..	..	..	..	..
Colombia	29	34	0	0	30	39	20	7	1	5	19	14
Congo, Dem. Rep.	27	12	1	0	18	22	46	23	1	36	7	7
Congo, Rep.	26	3	0	0	16	15	21	5	2	0	35	77
Costa Rica	10	13	29	32	27	40	23	5	1	0	14	10
Côte d'Ivoire	16	24	7	8	27	20	29	40	11	4	9	4
Croatia	17	9	52	32	24	46	3	6	0	1	3	5
Cuba	..	..	..	..	..	..	..	..	..	..	..	..
Czech Republic	..	13	..	45	..	35	..	2	..	1	..	3
Denmark	37	35	4	4	41	45	0	0	3	4	15	12
Dominican Republic	21	18	4	4	23	25	40	43	1	2	10	8
Ecuador	62	..	0	..	22	..	13	..	1	..	2	..
Egypt, Arab Rep.	19	..	15	..	14	..	14	..	11	..	27	..
El Salvador	..	20	..	15	..	41	..	7	..	1	..	17
Eritrea	..	..	..	..	..	..	..	..	..	..	..	..
Estonia	27	14	28	34	41	42	1	0	1	0	2	9
Ethiopia	29	22	0	0	25	17	15	26	2	3	30	32
Finland	31	29	9	10	47	44	1	0	3	2	9	13
France	17	..	44	..	28	..	0	..	3	..	7	..
Gabon	24	..	1	..	23	..	18	..	2	..	32	..
Gambia, The	13	..	0	..	37	..	43	..	1	..	6	..
Georgia	..	8	..	21	..	58	..	7	..	0	..	5
Germany	16	15	53	48	24	20	0	0	0	0	6	16
Ghana	23	..	0	..	30	..	39	..	0	..	8	..
Greece	22	39	29	2	43	55	0	0	8	8	8	7
Guatemala	..	..	..	..	..	..	..	..	..	..	..	..
Guinea	9	10	0	1	15	5	47	77	0	4	28	4
Guinea-Bissau	..	..	..	..	..	..	..	..	..	..	..	..
Haiti	..	..	..	..	..	..	..	..	..	..	..	..

Central government revenues

	Taxes on income, profits, and capital gains		Social security taxes		Taxes on goods and services		Taxes on international trade		Other taxes		Nontax revenue	
	% of total current revenue		% of total current revenue		% of total current revenue		% of total current revenue		% of total current revenue		% of total current revenue	
	1990	2000	1990	2000	1990	2000	1990	2000	1990	2000	1990	2000
Honduras	..	..	..	..	..	..	..	..	..	..	..	..
Hungary	18	21	29	27	31	36	6	3	0	2	16	11
India	15	28	0	0	36	28	29	19	0	0	20	26
Indonesia	62	59	0	2	24	28	6	3	3	0	5	8
Iran, Islamic Rep.	10	17	8	9	4	6	13	7	4	1	60	60
Iraq	..	..	..	..	..	..	..	..	..	..	..	..
Ireland	37	..	15	..	38	..	0	..	3	..	7	..
Israel	36	40	9	14	33	30	2	1	4	3	14	13
Italy	37	36	29	30	29	24	0	0	2	3	3	7
Jamaica	36	31	0	0	30	30	12	7	9	7	13	26
Japan	69	..	0	..	17	..	1	..	7	..	5	..
Jordan	16	11	0	0	21	36	27	20	7	10	29	24
Kazakhstan	..	28	..	0	..	48	..	6	..	8	..	10
Kenya	30	31	0	0	43	37	16	14	1	0	10	18
Korea, Dem. Rep.	..	..	..	..	..	..	..	..	..	..	..	..
Korea, Rep.	34	..	5	..	35	..	12	..	5	..	9	..
Kuwait	1	1	0	6	0	0	2	3	0	0	97	90
Kyrgyz Republic	..	15	..	0	..	65	..	3	..	0	..	17
Lao PDR	..	..	..	..	..	..	..	..	..	..	..	..
Latvia	..	12	..	34	..	41	..	1	..	0	..	11
Lebanon	..	11	..	0	..	20	..	28	..	13	..	28
Lesotho	11	18	0	0	21	12	57	48	0	0	11	22
Liberia	..	..	..	..	..	..	..	..	..	..	..	..
Libya	..	..	..	..	..	..	..	..	..	..	..	..
Lithuania	20	12	28	32	40	47	1	1	3	0	8	7
Macedonia, FYR	..	..	..	..	..	..	..	..	..	..	..	..
Madagascar	13	15	0	0	19	28	48	52	2	2	18	3
Malawi	37	..	0	..	33	..	16	..	1	..	13	..
Malaysia	31	..	1	..	20	..	18	..	3	..	28	..
Mali	..	..	..	..	..	..	..	..	..	..	..	..
Mauritania	..	..	..	..	..	..	..	..	..	..	..	..
Mauritius	14	11	4	5	21	38	46	28	6	5	9	12
Mexico	31	34	13	10	56	62	6	4	2	1	11	10
Moldova	..	3	..	26	..	51	..	6	..	0	..	14
Mongolia	24	12	14	18	31	37	17	7	0	1	15	25
Morocco	24	24	4	5	38	36	18	16	4	3	13	16
Mozambique	..	..	..	..	..	..	..	..	..	..	..	..
Myanmar	18	20	0	0	28	33	14	4	0	0	41	44
Namibia	34	32	0	0	25	21	27	37	1	1	13	8
Nepal	11	17	0	0	36	34	31	27	5	4	17	18
Netherlands	31	..	35	..	22	..	0	..	3	..	9	..
New Zealand	53	62	0	0	27	29	2	2	3	1	15	7
Nicaragua	17	13	9	16	35	55	19	7	8	..	13	9
Niger	..	..	..	..	..	..	..	..	..	..	..	..
Nigeria	..	..	..	..	..	..	..	..	..	..	..	..
Norway	16	20	24	23	34	36	1	0	1	1	24	20
Oman	23	24	0	0	1	1	2	3	1	2	73	70
Pakistan	9	20	0	0	30	32	31	12	0	8	30	27
Panama	17	18	20	19	17	..	12	..	3	4	31	37
Papua New Guinea	37	54	0	0	14	11	25	27	3	4	20	5
Paraguay	9	11	0	0	21	38	20	12	24	3	25	36
Peru	5	20	7	8	50	50	17	9	19	2	7	20
Philippines	28	40	0	0	31	27	25	19	3	4	13	10
Poland	..	19	..	30	..	38	..	2	..	1	..	10
Portugal	23	27	25	25	34	36	2	0	4	2	12	10
Puerto Rico	..	..	..	..	..	..	..	..	..	..	..	..

	Taxes on income, profits, and capital gains		Social security taxes		Taxes on goods and services		Taxes on international trade		Other taxes		Nontax revenue	
	% of total current revenue		% of total current revenue		% of total current revenue		% of total current revenue		% of total current revenue		% of total current revenue	
	1990	2000	1990	2000	1990	2000	1990	2000	1990	2000	1990	2000
Romania	19	13	23	37	33	33	1	4	15	1	10	11
Russian Federation	..	12	..	29	..	31	..	13	..	0	..	15
Rwanda	18	..	7	..	34	..	26	..	4	..	12	..
Saudi Arabia	..	..	..	..	..	..	..	..	..	..	..	..
Senegal	..	23	..	0	..	37	..	32	..	4	..	4
Sierra Leone	31	26	0	0	23	22	40	49	0	0	5	4
Singapore	26	30	0	0	16	18	2	1	14	10	43	41
Slovak Republic	..	19	..	35	..	31	..	4	..	1	..	10
Slovenia	12	14	47	36	27	38	8	2	0	4	5	5
Somalia	..	..	..	..	..	..	..	..	..	..	..	..
South Africa	51	53	2	2	34	34	4	3	2	3	8	5
Spain	32	..	38	..	22	..	2	..	0	..	5	..
Sri Lanka	11	13	0	0	46	58	29	11	5	4	10	14
Sudan	..	15	..	0	..	35	..	29	..	1	..	20
Swaziland	30	25	0	0	11	14	47	52	2	4	10	5
Sweden	18	14	31	33	29	27	1	0	9	15	13	11
Switzerland	15	16	51	47	23	25	1	1	3	4	7	7
Syrian Arab Republic	31	38	0	0	31	19	7	10	7	6	24	27
Tajikistan	..	3	..	20	..	55	..	14	..	1	..	7
Tanzania	..	..	..	..	..	..	..	..	..	..	..	..
Thailand	24	30	0	3	41	43	22	11	4	1	8	11
Togo	..	..	..	..	..	..	..	..	..	..	..	..
Trinidad and Tobago	..	..	..	..	..	..	..	..	..	..	..	..
Tunisia	13	20	13	17	19	38	28	11	5	4	22	9
Turkey	43	29	0	0	32	41	6	1	3	7	15	21
Turkmenistan	..	..	..	..	..	..	..	..	..	..	..	..
Uganda	..	17	..	0	..	31	..	48	..	1	..	3
Ukraine	..	13	..	31	..	34	..	4	..	2	..	16
United Arab Emirates	0	0	2	1	36	51	0	0	0	0	62	48
United Kingdom	39	40	17	17	28	31	0	0	7	7	9	5
United States	52	57	35	31	3	3	2	1	1	1	8	6
Uruguay	7	15	27	29	36	34	10	3	12	8	5	12
Uzbekistan	..	..	..	..	..	..	..	..	..	..	..	..
Venezuela, RB	64	27	4	4	3	25	7	7	0	4	22	34
Vietnam	..	27	..	0	..	34	..	15	..	6	..	17
West Bank and Gaza	..	..	..	..	..	..	..	..	..	..	..	..
Yemen, Rep.	26	18	0	0	10	9	17	10	5	2	43	61
Yugoslavia, Fed. Rep.	..	..	..	..	..	..	..	..	..	..	..	..
Zambia	..	..	..	..	..	..	..	..	..	..	..	..
Zimbabwe	45	..	0	..	26	..	17	..	1	..	10	..
World	**23 m**	**18 m**	**4 m**	**5 m**	**27 m**	**34 m**	**13 m**	**7 m**	**3 m**	**2 m**	**13 m**	**12 m**
Low income	..	..	..	..	..	..	..	..	..	..	..	..
Middle income	21	18	4	10	25	38	14	6	3	2	16	11
Lower middle income	24	20	0	3	30	37	17	9	4	3	15	13
Upper middle income	18	17	13	29	21	39	12	3	3	1	16	10
Low & middle income	19	17	0	2	28	35	17	9	3	2	14	12
East Asia & Pacific	31	25	0	0	24	32	18	9	3	2	20	11
Europe & Central Asia	..	13	..	30	..	41	..	4	..	1	..	10
Latin America & Carib.	17	18	9	10	27	41	13	7	3	3	14	18
Middle East & N. Africa	21	19	2	0	17	19	15	14	5	3	28	28
South Asia	11	19	0	0	36	33	30	15	3	4	18	22
Sub-Saharan Africa	23	..	0	..	25	..	27	..	1	..	10	..
High income	32	26	17	19	28	27	1	1	3	3	9	9
Europe EMU	31	29	35	31	28	26	0	0	3	3	7	7

Note: Components may not sum to 100 percent as a result of adjustments to tax revenue.

About the data

The International Monetary Fund (IMF) classifies government transactions as receipts or payments and according to whether they are repayable or nonrepayable. If nonrepayable, they are classified as capital (meant to be used in production for more than a year) or current and as requited (involving payment in return for a benefit or service) or unrequited. Revenues include all nonrepayable receipts (other than grants), the most important of which are taxes. Grants are unrequited, nonrepayable, noncompulsory receipts from other governments or from international organizations. Transactions are generally recorded on a cash rather than an accrual basis. Measuring the accumulation of arrears on revenues or payments on an accrual basis would typically result in a higher deficit. Transactions within a level of government are not included, but transactions between levels are included. In some cases the government budget may include transfers used to finance the deficits of autonomous, extrabudgetary agencies.

The IMF's *Manual on Government Finance Statistics* (1986) describes taxes as compulsory, unrequited payments made to governments by individuals, businesses, or institutions. Taxes traditionally have been classified as either direct (those levied directly on the income or profits of individuals and corporations) or indirect (sales and excise taxes and duties levied on goods and services). This distinction may be a useful simplification, but it has no particular analytical significance except with respect to the capacity to fix tax rates.

Social security taxes do not reflect compulsory payments made by employers to provident funds or other agencies with a similar purpose. Similarly, expenditures from such funds are not reflected in government expenditure (see table 4.12). The revenue shares shown in this table may not sum to 100 percent because adjustments to tax revenues are not shown.

For further discussion of taxes and tax policies, see *About the data* for table 5.6. For further discussion of government revenues and expenditures, see *About the data* for tables 4.11 and 4.12.

Definitions

- **Taxes on income, profits, and capital gains** are levied on the actual or presumptive net income of individuals, on the profits of enterprises, and on capital gains, whether realized or not, on land, securities, or other assets. Intragovernmental payments are eliminated in consolidation. • **Social security taxes** include employer and employee social security contributions and those of self-employed and unemployed people. • **Taxes on goods and services** include general sales and turnover or value added taxes, selective excises on goods, selective taxes on services, taxes on the use of goods or property, and profits of fiscal monopolies. • **Taxes on international trade** include import duties, export duties, profits of export or import monopolies, exchange profits, and exchange taxes. • **Other taxes** include employer payroll or labor taxes, taxes on property, and taxes not allocable to other categories. They may include negative values that are adjustments (for example, for taxes collected on behalf of state and local governments and not allocable to individual tax categories). • **Nontax revenue** includes requited, nonrepayable receipts for public purposes—such as fines, administrative fees, or entrepreneurial income from government ownership of property—and voluntary, unrequited, nonrepayable receipts other than from government sources. It does not include proceeds of grants and borrowing, funds arising from the repayment of previous lending by governments, incurrence of liabilities, and proceeds from the sale of capital assets.

4.13a

The level of a country's income tends to determine its method of taxation

Direct taxes as % of current revenue, 1999–2000

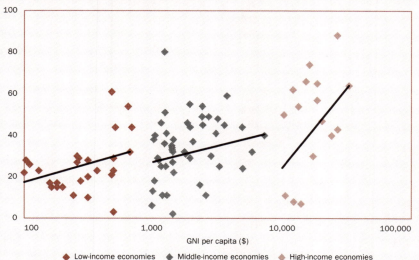

GNI per capita ($)

◆ Low-income economies   ◆ Middle-income economies   ◆ High-income economies

High-income countries generally rely on direct taxes (such as income and property taxes) and social security contributions, while low- and middle-income countries tend to rely on indirect taxes on goods and services and on international trade. But in all groups there are many exceptions to the rule.

Note: Data are for the most recent year available in 1999–2000.
Source: International Monetary Fund Government Finance Statistics data files.

Data sources

The data on central government revenues are from the IMF's *Government Finance Statistics Yearbook, 2002* and IMF data files. Each country's accounts are reported using the system of common definitions and classifications in the IMF's *Manual on Government Finance Statistics* (1986). The IMF receives additional information from the Organisation for Economic Co-operation and Development on the tax revenues of some of its members. See the IMF sources for complete and authoritative explanations of concepts, definitions, and data sources.

Monetary indicators and prices

	Money and quasi money		Claims on private sector		Claims on governments and other public entities		GDP implicit deflator		Consumer price index		Food price index	
	annual % growth of M2		annual growth as % of M2		annual growth as % of M2		average annual % growth		average annual % growth		average annual % growth	
	1990	2001	1990	2001	1990	2001	1980–90	1990–2001	1980–90	1990–2001	1980–90	1990–2001
Afghanistan	..	..	..	..	..	..	..	..	..	..	..	..
Albania	..	19.9	..	3.2	..	2.6	–0.4	34.4	..	24.2	..	31.2
Algeria	11.4	48.9	12.2	5.5	3.2	16.4	8.3	17.0	9.1	15.5	9.7	16.4
Angola	..	160.6	..	34.2	..	42.3	5.9	658.8	..	633.2	..	223.1
Argentina	1,113.3	–19.4	1,444.7	–12.9	1,573.2	15.1	391.1	4.3	390.6	7.4	486.5	6.6
Armenia	..	4.3	..	–7.8	..	0.1	..	172.0	..	55.8	..	145.8
Australia	12.8	13.2	15.3	10.8	–2.2	1.0	7.2	1.7	7.9	2.2	7.4	2.8
Austria [a]	..	..	..	..	..	..	3.3	1.8	3.2	2.2	2.7	1.5
Azerbaijan	..	–10.5	..	–1.7	..	–20.8	..	96.9	..	134.5	..	135.5
Bangladesh	10.4	14.7	9.2	11.2	–0.2	5.8	9.5	3.9	..	5.1	10.8	5.3
Belarus	..	58.9	..	37.4	..	32.7	..	318.1	..	294.7	2.4	176.5
Belgium [a]	..	..	..	..	..	..	4.1	1.9	4.2	1.9	4.0	1.1
Benin	28.6	12.2	–1.3	–0.2	12.4	–11.5	1.7	8.2	..	7.9	–3.5	10.5
Bolivia	52.8	2.2	40.8	–9.4	18.0	4.7	326.9	8.0	322.5	8.1	321.8	7.6
Bosnia and Herzegovina	..	..	..	..	..	..	..	2.7	..	..	..	..
Botswana	–14.0	31.2	12.6	7.8	–51.9	–49.5	13.6	9.0	10.0	10.0	10.1	10.0
Brazil	1,289.2	12.1	1,566.4	9.3	3,093.6	38.4	284.0	168.2	285.6	161.6	314.0	–17.6
Bulgaria	53.8	26.7	1.9	11.1	83.1	1.8	1.8	93.4	6.3	105.3	1.8	101.1
Burkina Faso	–0.5	1.6	3.6	7.9	–1.5	–4.2	3.3	4.5	1.0	5.2	0.7	5.3
Burundi	9.6	15.7	15.4	9.5	–6.9	25.2	4.4	12.6	7.1	15.9	6.1	..
Cambodia	..	20.4	..	2.1	..	–4.1	..	21.7	..	5.3	..	..
Cameroon	–1.7	15.1	0.9	6.1	–3.0	1.8	5.6	4.9	8.7	5.9	..	4.1
Canada	7.8	6.5	9.2	6.3	0.6	2.1	4.6	1.5	5.3	1.7	4.6	1.6
Central African Republic	–3.7	–1.1	–1.6	3.3	2.3	4.4	7.9	4.2	3.2	4.9	2.0	5.5
Chad	–2.4	22.0	1.3	7.4	–17.3	14.0	1.4	6.7	0.6	7.9	–5.3	7.1
Chile	23.5	4.5	21.4	11.8	16.4	3.3	20.7	7.5	20.6	8.3	20.7	7.4
China	28.9	15.0	26.5	7.8	1.5	4.1	5.7	6.2	..	7.6	8.8	11.3
Hong Kong, China	8.5	–0.3	7.9	–1.4	–1.0	1.7	7.7	3.3	..	4.9	6.3	4.1
Colombia	33.0	16.0	8.7	8.0	–5.1	6.9	24.8	20.0	22.7	19.5	24.6	18.2
Congo, Dem. Rep.	195.4	..	18.0	..	429.7	..	62.9	846.2	57.1	813.4	..	..
Congo, Rep.	18.5	–22.8	5.1	–2.6	–12.6	24.5	0.5	8.8	0.9	8.5	4.3	8.8
Costa Rica	27.5	10.4	7.3	17.3	8.2	–7.9	23.6	16.3	23.0	15.1	16.0	3.1
Côte d'Ivoire	–2.6	12.0	–3.9	3.9	–3.0	–6.1	2.8	8.4	5.4	6.7	..	..
Croatia	..	45.7	..	17.9	..	3.5	..	72.2	304.1	72.1	124.6	69.5
Cuba	..	..	..	..	..	..	..	1.1	..	..	..	..
Czech Republic	..	11.2	..	–8.0	..	7.5	..	10.6	..	7.3	..	2.5
Denmark	6.5	3.6	3.0	23.8	–3.1	2.1	5.8	2.2	5.6	2.1	4.8	2.0
Dominican Republic	42.5	26.9	19.1	18.7	0.7	1.8	21.6	9.1	22.4	8.5	25.4	7.8
Ecuador	48.9	21.4	17.2	29.8	–27.4	–0.1	–4.9	1.7	35.8	38.7	40.7	36.5
Egypt, Arab Rep.	28.7	13.2	6.3	7.8	25.3	4.4	13.7	7.8	17.4	8.1	22.0	6.9
El Salvador	32.4	1.0	8.8	–0.3	9.6	2.8	16.3	6.8	19.6	7.8	21.5	8.8
Eritrea	..	..	..	..	..	..	..	9.0	..	..	..	..
Estonia	76.5	23.0	27.6	12.4	–6.8	2.6	2.3	46.1	..	18.9	..	–19.2
Ethiopia	18.5	9.8	0.3	1.6	21.7	–5.0	4.6	6.1	4.0	4.7	3.8	–3.3
Finland [a]	..	..	..	..	..	..	6.7	1.9	6.2	1.6	5.8	–0.5
France [a]	..	..	..	..	..	..	5.8	1.5	5.8	1.6	5.7	1.3
Gabon	3.3	7.5	0.7	11.6	–20.6	28.5	1.8	5.6	5.1	4.6	4.9	4.3
Gambia, The	8.4	19.4	7.8	11.2	–35.4	28.6	17.9	4.1	20.0	4.0	20.3	3.7
Georgia	..	18.5	..	–4.4	..	9.1	1.9	279.0	..	20.6	..	21.5
Germany [a]	..	..	..	..	..	..	2.4	1.8	2.2 [b]	2.2	..	0.3
Ghana	13.3	–9.0	4.9	28.4	–0.8	65.2	42.1	26.6	39.1	28.1	33.1	25.0
Greece [a]	..	..	..	..	..	..	19.3	8.5	18.7	8.3	18.0	7.1
Guatemala	25.8	18.1	15.0	8.9	0.5	–8.1	14.6	9.9	14.0	9.7	22.1	10.0
Guinea	–17.4	12.9	13.1	2.3	2.9	8.0	..	5.1	..	..	..	9.2
Guinea-Bissau	574.6	7.3	90.5	–11.7	460.7	–0.5	57.4	28.7	..	30.6	..	..
Haiti	2.5	14.1	–0.6	3.2	0.4	7.8	7.3	20.3	5.2	20.8	4.1	..

Monetary indicators and prices

	Money and quasi money		Claims on private sector		Claims on governments and other public entities		GDP implicit deflator		Consumer price index		Food price index	
	annual % growth of M2		annual growth as % of M2		annual growth as % of M2		average annual % growth		average annual % growth		average annual % growth	
								1990–		1990–		1990–
	1990	2001	1990	2001	1990	2001	1980–90	2001	1980–90	2001	1980–90	2001
Honduras	21.4	17.5	13.0	8.1	−10.5	3.9	5.7	18.0	6.3	18.0	5.2	17.8
Hungary	29.2	16.6	23.0	13.0	69.7	−8.9	8.9	18.3	9.6	19.2	9.5	18.5
India	15.1	14.3	5.9	4.8	10.5	6.5	8.2	7.6	8.6	8.7	8.8	8.5
Indonesia	44.6	12.8	66.9	3.8	−8.2	3.5	8.6	15.8	8.3	13.9	8.7	17.0
Iran, Islamic Rep.	18.0	27.6	14.7	20.0	5.8	−3.1	14.4	25.7	18.2	24.7	16.2	25.5
Iraq	..	..	..	..	..	..	10.3	..	..	..	..	..
Ireland [a]	..	..	..	..	..	..	6.6	3.7	6.8	2.4	6.0	2.7
Israel	19.4	9.5	18.5	11.0	4.9	−0.9	101.1	9.3	101.7	8.9	102.4	8.4
Italy [a]	..	..	..	..	..	..	10.0	3.6	9.1	3.5	8.2	2.9
Jamaica	21.5	8.6	12.5	−40.7	−16.0	13.3	19.9	22.1	15.1	21.4	16.1	20.5
Japan	8.2	2.2	9.7	−3.2	1.5	4.4	1.8	−0.1	1.7	0.6	1.5	0.4
Jordan	8.3	8.1	4.7	7.1	1.0	1.8	4.3	2.9	5.7	3.3	4.7	3.7
Kazakhstan	..	40.2	..	57.5	..	−46.1	..	168.5	..	54.8	..	127.9
Kenya	20.1	2.5	8.0	−2.4	21.5	5.4	9.1	13.4	11.2	14.5	10.0	15.2
Korea, Dem. Rep.	..	..	..	..	..	..	..	..	..	..	..	..
Korea, Rep.	17.2	13.2	36.1	15.5	−1.2	0.5	6.5	4.5	4.9	4.9	5.0	5.1
Kuwait	0.7	12.8	3.3	10.7	−3.1	−2.7	−2.8	1.9	2.9	2.0	1.6	1.5
Kyrgyz Republic	..	11.3	..	1.5	..	−10.1	..	95.2	..	21.2	..	53.2
Lao PDR	7.8	13.7	3.6	12.7	7.0	30.0	37.6	28.5	..	29.8	..	..
Latvia	..	19.8	..	22.4	..	−2.6	0.0	42.0	..	25.0	..	21.1
Lebanon	55.1	7.5	27.6	0.0	18.5	10.7	..	15.1	..	..	..	19.8
Lesotho	8.4	17.2	6.8	3.4	−14.9	4.5	12.1	9.5	13.6	8.8	13.5	13.0
Liberia	19.6	12.7	16.1	7.2	29.5	206.4	2.9	53.3	..	..	..	..
Libya	19.0	4.3	2.0	0.4	15.0	14.7	1.2	..	..	..	..	..
Lithuania	..	21.4	..	3.2	..	0.4	..	63.3	..	27.0	2.7	46.6
Macedonia, FYR	..	32.1	..	−2.2	..	27.4	..	66.0	..	8.0	..	..
Madagascar	4.5	23.8	23.8	6.7	−14.8	8.8	17.1	17.9	16.6	17.5	15.7	19.1
Malawi	11.1	14.8	15.5	1.4	−12.9	28.8	15.1	33.0	16.9	33.5	16.4	34.5
Malaysia	10.6	2.5	20.8	3.6	−1.2	−2.0	1.7	3.6	2.6	3.4	2.2	4.9
Mali	−4.9	19.6	0.1	14.0	−13.4	6.5	4.5	6.9	..	4.8	..	..
Mauritania	11.5	17.3	20.2	30.8	1.5	−8.8	8.4	6.2	7.1	5.9	..	6.3
Mauritius	21.2	10.9	10.8	7.7	0.8	6.2	9.4	6.2	6.9	6.7	7.8	5.9
Mexico	81.9	14.1	48.5	−5.6	13.6	4.5	71.5	18.2	73.8	18.6	73.1	18.4
Moldova	358.0	35.8	53.3	21.8	469.1	12.5	..	103.1	..	19.3	..	110.5
Mongolia	31.6	27.9	40.2	21.7	38.5	−8.4	−1.6	51.4	..	39.0	..	..
Morocco	21.5	14.1	12.4	0.3	−4.9	1.1	7.1	2.7	7.0	3.5	6.7	3.4
Mozambique	37.2	28.2	22.0	−50.8	−5.1	70.2	38.3	29.6	..	28.8	..	..
Myanmar	37.7	43.9	12.8	18.7	24.2	29.4	12.2	24.6	11.5	25.0	11.9	27.5
Namibia	30.3	4.5	15.4	14.8	−4.2	−0.7	14.1	8.5	12.6	9.5	13.9	8.6
Nepal	18.5	11.5	5.7	7.1	7.3	5.6	11.1	7.8	10.2	8.1	10.5	8.4
Netherlands [a]	..	..	..	..	..	..	1.5	2.1	2.0	2.4	1.3	1.3
New Zealand	12.5	6.8	4.2	9.7	−1.7	−1.1	10.5	1.6	11.0	1.8	9.8	1.5
Nicaragua	7,677.8	41.0	4,932.9	−10.2	12,679.2	30.7	422.3	45.2	535.7	35.1	69.2	25.4
Niger	−4.1	31.4	−5.1	4.4	1.4	−7.3	1.9	5.8	0.7	5.7	−1.5	6.8
Nigeria	32.7	27.0	7.8	23.0	27.1	13.3	16.7	26.5	21.5	30.0	22.5	27.9
Norway	5.6	8.7	5.0	14.6	−0.6	−31.8	5.6	3.2	7.4	2.2	7.8	1.9
Oman	10.0	9.2	9.6	8.0	−10.9	9.0	−3.6	1.8	..	0.0	0.9	0.2
Pakistan	11.6	11.7	5.9	2.3	7.7	−2.7	6.7	9.6	6.3	9.1	6.6	9.4
Panama	36.6	9.6	0.8	11.4	−25.7	−2.9	1.9	1.9	1.4	1.1	1.5	0.8
Papua New Guinea	4.3	1.6	−0.9	−2.1	8.8	−8.2	5.3	7.3	5.6	9.7	4.6	9.6
Paraguay	54.4	16.4	32.0	9.0	−9.2	1.6	24.4	12.0	21.9	12.5	24.9	10.9
Peru	6,384.9	2.1	2,123.7	−3.5	2,129.5	4.3	220.2	23.3	246.1	23.8	221.8	21.5
Philippines	22.4	3.6	15.6	−1.1	3.4	2.8	14.9	8.2	13.4	8.0	14.1	7.1
Poland	160.1	15.0	20.8	5.6	75.6	4.1	..	21.3	50.9	23.1	52.4	19.8
Portugal [a]	..	..	..	..	..	..	17.9	5.1	17.1	4.3	16.7	3.5
Puerto Rico	..	..	..	..	..	..	3.5	3.1	..	..	2.7	9.6

	Money and quasi money		Claims on private sector		Claims on governments and other public entities		GDP implicit deflator		Consumer price index		Food price index	
	annual % growth of M2		annual growth as % of M2		annual growth as % of M2		average annual % growth		average annual % growth		average annual % growth	
	1990	2001	1990	2001	1990	2001	1980–90	1990–2001	1980–90	1990–2001	1980–90	1990–2001
Romania	26.4	46.2	..	17.6	0.0	–3.9	..	91.0	..	92.8	4.3	74.1
Russian Federation	..	36.1	..	33.4	..	–1.4	..	139.6	..	85.9	..	52.4
Rwanda	5.6	11.0	–10.0	5.8	26.8	–0.5	4.0	13.1	3.9	14.7	6.4	14.1
Saudi Arabia	4.6	5.1	–4.5	4.7	4.2	3.1	–4.9	3.7	–0.8	0.8	–0.2	0.8
Senegal	–4.8	13.6	–8.4	4.3	–5.3	2.4	6.5	4.2	6.2	5.0	5.3	5.4
Sierra Leone	74.0	33.7	4.9	3.2	228.7	19.9	60.3	29.2	72.4	27.0	..	..
Singapore	20.0	5.9	13.7	15.2	–4.9	–4.7	1.9	0.9	1.6	1.6	1.0	1.6
Slovak Republic	..	11.9	..	–3.7	..	16.8	1.8	10.4	..	8.5	1.6	14.6
Slovenia	123.0	30.4	96.1	14.4	–10.4	3.1	..	18.3	..	22.0	129.5	23.5
Somalia	..	..	..	..	..	..	49.7	..	..	..	..	..
South Africa	11.4	16.7	13.7	28.6	1.8	–1.6	15.5	9.3	14.8	8.3	15.2	9.5
Spain [a]	..	..	..	..	..	..	9.3	3.9	9.0	3.7	9.3	3.0
Sri Lanka	19.9	14.4	16.2	6.9	6.8	13.6	11.0	9.1	10.9	9.9	11.0	10.3
Sudan	48.8	24.7	12.6	8.6	29.4	8.6	38.4	58.2	37.6	66.8	..	..
Swaziland	0.6	10.7	20.5	3.6	–13.1	–16.7	10.7	12.3	14.6	9.3	13.3	12.2
Sweden	0.8	1.9	13.4	12.4	–12.1	2.1	7.3	2.0	7.0	1.8	8.2	–0.3
Switzerland	0.8	3.9	11.7	–1.5	1.0	1.1	3.4	1.2	2.9	1.5	3.1	0.7
Syrian Arab Republic	26.4	23.5	3.4	0.4	11.6	7.4	15.3	7.4	23.2	5.9	25.0	4.5
Tajikistan	..	35.0	..	223.1	..	–17.2	2.5	202.4	..	..	..	477.3
Tanzania	41.9	17.1	22.6	5.0	80.6	–9.9	..	20.1	31.0	19.3	32.0	20.1
Thailand	26.7	2.2	30.0	–8.4	–4.0	1.1	3.9	3.9	3.5	4.6	2.7	5.4
Togo	9.5	–2.6	1.8	–4.2	6.9	–2.9	4.8	6.6	2.5	7.8	1.1	2.5
Trinidad and Tobago	6.2	6.9	2.7	2.4	–1.9	–6.0	2.4	5.4	10.7	5.7	14.6	12.7
Tunisia	7.6	10.7	5.9	11.6	1.8	–1.0	7.4	4.3	7.4	4.2	8.3	4.3
Turkey	53.2	86.2	42.9	12.0	2.2	96.5	45.3	74.2	44.9	77.9	18.3	31.8
Turkmenistan	..	83.3	..	10.8	..	59.0	..	328.0	..	..	..	..
Uganda	60.2	9.2	..	0.4	–0.9	–8.7	113.8	10.9	102.5	9.5	..	9.7
Ukraine	..	43.0	..	24.1	..	–0.1	..	220.9	..	200.4	2.0	120.7
United Arab Emirates	–8.2	23.2	1.3	8.4	–4.8	–8.3	0.8	2.3	..	..	..	..
United Kingdom	10.5	8.6	13.1	10.7	1.0	0.8	5.8	2.8	5.8	2.8	4.5	1.8
United States	4.9	14.0	1.1	7.8	0.6	2.0	3.8	2.0	4.2	2.7	3.9	2.5
Uruguay	118.5	19.0	56.2	7.5	25.8	0.8	62.7	27.8	61.1	30.2	62.0	27.5
Uzbekistan	..	..	..	..	..	..	..	210.7	..	..	..	..
Venezuela, RB	64.9	15.3	17.6	13.6	45.3	10.3	19.3	42.8	20.9	45.9	35.1	48.0
Vietnam	..	27.3	..	16.9	..	1.3	222.2	13.8	..	3.2	..	..
West Bank and Gaza	..	..	..	..	..	..	..	8.4	..	..	..	..
Yemen, Rep.	11.3	20.9	1.4	4.2	10.2	–10.0	..	21.1	..	32.6	..	..
Yugoslavia, Fed. Rep.	..	..	..	..	..	..	..	..	..	..	..	–0.6
Zambia	47.9	13.6	22.8	3.5	195.2	–19.5	42.2	48.1	72.5	80.8	42.8	58.1
Zimbabwe	15.1	128.5	13.5	49.6	5.0	69.9	11.6	28.4	13.8	31.8	15.1	36.5

a. As members of the European Monetary Union, these countries share a single currency, the euro. b. Data prior to 1990 refer to the Federal Republic of Germany before unification.

About the data

Money and the financial accounts that record the supply of money lie at the heart of a country's financial system. There are several commonly used definitions of the money supply. The narrowest, M1, encompasses currency held by the public and demand deposits with banks. M2 includes M1 plus time and savings deposits with banks that require a notice for withdrawal. M3 includes M2 as well as various money market instruments, such as certificates of deposit issued by banks, bank deposits denominated in foreign currency, and deposits with financial institutions other than banks. However defined, money is a liability of the banking system, distinguished from other bank liabilities by the special role it plays as a medium of exchange, a unit of account, and a store of value.

The banking system's assets include its net foreign assets and net domestic credit. Net domestic credit includes credit to the private sector and general government, and credit extended to the nonfinancial public sector in the form of investments in short- and long-term government securities and loans to state enterprises; liabilities to the public and private sectors in the form of deposits with the banking system are netted out. Net domestic credit also includes credit to banking and nonbank financial institutions.

Domestic credit is the main vehicle through which changes in the money supply are regulated, with central bank lending to the government often playing the most important role. The central bank can regulate lending to the private sector in several ways—for example, by adjusting the cost of the refinancing facilities it provides to banks, by changing market interest rates through open market operations, or by controlling the availability of credit through changes in the reserve requirements imposed on banks and ceilings on the credit provided by banks to the private sector.

Monetary accounts are derived from the balance sheets of financial institutions—the central bank, commercial banks, and nonbank financial intermediaries. Although these balance sheets are usually reliable, they are subject to errors of classification, valuation, and timing and to differences in accounting practices. For example, whether interest income is recorded on an accrual or a cash basis can make a substantial difference, as can the treatment of nonperforming assets. Valuation errors typically arise with respect to foreign exchange transactions, particularly in countries with flexible exchange rates or in those that have undergone a currency devaluation during the reporting period. The valuation of

financial derivatives and the net liabilities of the banking system can also be difficult.

The quality of commercial bank reporting also may be adversely affected by delays in reports from bank branches, especially in countries where branch accounts are not computerized. Thus the data in the balance sheets of commercial banks may be based on preliminary estimates subject to constant revision. This problem is likely to be even more serious for nonbank financial intermediaries.

Controlling inflation is one of the primary goals of monetary policy and is intimately linked to the growth in money supply. Inflation is measured by the rate of increase in a price index, but actual price change can also be negative. Which index is used depends on which set of prices in the economy is being examined. The GDP deflator reflects changes in prices for total gross domestic product. The most general measure of the overall price level, it takes into account changes in government consumption, capital formation (including inventory appreciation), international trade, and the main component, household final consumption expenditure. The GDP deflator is usually derived implicitly as the ratio of current to constant price GDP, resulting in a Paasche index. It is defective as a general measure of inflation for use in policy because of the long lags in deriving estimates and because it is often only an annual measure.

Consumer price indexes are more current and produced more frequently. They are also constructed explicitly, based on surveys of the cost of a defined basket of consumer goods and services. Nevertheless, consumer price indexes should be interpreted with caution. The definition of a household, the basket of goods chosen, and the geographic (urban or rural) and income group coverage of consumer price surveys can all vary widely across countries. In addition, the weights are derived from household expenditure surveys, which, for budgetary reasons, tend to be conducted infrequently in developing countries, leading to poor comparability over time. Although useful for measuring consumer price inflation within a country, consumer price indexes are of less value in making comparisons across countries. Like consumer price indexes, food price indexes should be interpreted with caution because of the high variability across countries in the items covered.

The least-squares method is used to calculate the growth rates of the GDP implicit deflator, consumer price index, and food price index.

Definitions

• **Money and quasi money** comprise the sum of currency outside banks, demand deposits other than those of the central government, and the time, savings, and foreign currency deposits of resident sectors other than the central government. This definition of the money supply, often called M2, corresponds to lines 34 and 35 in the International Monetary Fund's (IMF) *International Financial Statistics* (IFS). The change in money supply is measured as the difference in end-of-year totals relative to M2 in the preceding year. • **Claims on private sector** (IFS line 32d) include gross credit from the financial system to individuals, enterprises, nonfinancial public entities not included under net domestic credit, and financial institutions not included elsewhere. • **Claims on governments and other public entities** (IFS line 32an + 32b + 32bx + 32c) usually comprise direct credit for specific purposes, such as financing the government budget deficit, loans to state enterprises, advances against future credit authorizations, and purchases of treasury bills and bonds, net of deposits by the public sector. Public sector deposits with the banking system also include sinking funds for the service of debt and temporary deposits of government revenues. • **GDP implicit deflator** measures the average annual rate of price change in the economy as a whole for the periods shown. • **Consumer price index** reflects changes in the cost to the average consumer of acquiring a basket of goods and services that may be fixed or may change at specified intervals, such as yearly. The Laspeyres formula is generally used. • **Food price index** is a subindex of the consumer price index.

Data sources

The monetary, financial, and consumer price index data are published by the IMF in its monthly *International Financial Statistics* and annual *International Financial Statistics Yearbook*. The IMF collects data on the financial systems of its member countries. The World Bank receives data from the IMF in electronic files that may contain more recent revisions than the published sources. The GDP deflator data are from the World Bank's national accounts files. The food price index data are from the United Nations Statistics Division's *Statistical Yearbook* and *Monthly Bulletin of Statistics*. The discussion of monetary indicators draws from an IMF publication by Marcello Caiola, *A Manual for Country Economists* (1995).

	Goods and services				Net income		Net current transfers		Current account balance		Gross international reserves	
	Exports		Imports									
	$ millions		$ millions		$ millions		$ millions		$ millions		$ millions	
	1990	2001	1990	2001	1990	2001	1990	2001	1990	2001	1990	2001
Afghanistan	..	..	..	..	..	..	..	..	..	..	638	..
Albania	354	839	485	1,776	–2	146	15	571	–118	–220	..	393
Algeria	13,462	21,829	10,106	11,270	–2,268	–2,877	333	..	1,420	..	2,703	19,625
Angola	3,992	7,011	3,385	5,908	–765	–1,491	–77	33	–236	–355	..	732
Argentina	14,800	30,920	6,846	27,563	–4,400	–8,095	998	183	4,552	–4,554	6,222	14,556
Armenia	..	540	..	978	..	64	..	174	..	–201	1	333
Australia	49,843	79,909	53,056	78,512	–13,176	–10,293	439	21	–15,950	–8,876	19,319	18,664
Austria	63,694	99,795	61,580	99,762	–942	–2,995	–6	–1,141	1,166	–4,103	17,228	15,599
Azerbaijan	..	2,369	..	2,130	..	–367	..	77	..	–52	..	897
Bangladesh	1,903	7,235	4,156	10,103	–122	–264	802	2,316	–1,573	–816	660	1,306
Belarus	..	8,269		8,666	..	–43	..	154	..	–285	..	391
Belgium[a]	138,605	213,811	135,098	203,106	2,316	2,907	–2,197	–4,220	3,627	9,392	23,789[b]	13,560[b]
Benin	364	554	454	736	–25	–32	97	139	–18	–74	69	578
Bolivia	977	1,521	1,086	1,996	–249	–210	159	393	–199	–293	511	1,146
Bosnia and Herzegovina	..	1,274	..	2,617	..	223	..	168	..	–952	..	..
Botswana	2,005	2,655	1,987	2,145	–106	–275	130	204	42	438	3,331	5,897
Brazil	35,170	67,547	28,184	72,652	–11,608	–19,745	799	1,639	–3,823	–23,211	9,200	35,867
Bulgaria	6,950	7,526	8,027	8,562	–758	–342	125	488	–1,710	–889	670	3,646
Burkina Faso	349	275	758	641	0	–24	332	53	–77	–338	305	261
Burundi	89	52	318	148	–15	–9	174	80	–69	–24	112	18
Cambodia	314	1,634	507	1,969	–21	–43	120	273	–93	–105	..	587
Cameroon	2,251	2,708	1,931	2,479	–478	–494	–39	119	–196	–147	37	340
Canada	149,538	304,491	149,118	268,490	–19,388	–17,778	–796	1,255	–19,764	19,479	23,530	34,253
Central African Republic	220	106	410	144	–22	–4	123	59	–89	16	123	122
Chad	271	290	488	974	–21	–8	192	31	–46	–660	132	125
Chile	10,221	22,317	9,166	21,226	–1,737	–2,757	198	423	–485	–1,243	6,784	14,399
China[†]	57,374	299,409	46,706	271,325	1,055	–19,175	274	8,492	11,997	17,401	34,476	220,057
Hong Kong, China	100,413	232,356	94,084	223,573	0	4,633	..	–1,682	6,329	11,736	24,656	111,174
Colombia	8,679	14,932	6,858	15,840	–2,305	–2,975	1,026	2,094	542	–1,788	4,869	10,244
Congo, Dem. Rep.	2,557	1,015	2,497	953	–770	–416	..	..	..	..	261	..
Congo, Rep.	1,488	2,497	1,282	1,373	–460	–733	3	..	–251	..	10	72
Costa Rica	1,963	6,959	2,346	7,393	–233	–415	192	148	–424	–702	525	1,330
Côte d'Ivoire	3,503	4,435	3,445	3,640	–1,091	–577	–181	–275	–1,214	–58	21	1,019
Croatia	..	9,631	..	10,677	..	–537	..	966	..	–617	167	4,703
Cuba	..	..	..	..	..	..	..	..	..	..	..	..
Czech Republic	..	40,495	..	42,049	..	–1,540	..	470	..	–2,624	..	14,464
Denmark	48,902	77,856	41,415	67,489	–5,708	–3,598	–408	–2,627	1,372	4,142	11,226	17,702
Dominican Republic	1,832	8,332	2,233	10,079	–249	–1,119	371	2,028	–280	–839	69	1,105
Ecuador	3,262	5,774	2,519	6,754	–1,210	–1,364	107	1,544	–360	–800	1,009	1,073
Egypt, Arab Rep.	9,151	16,925	13,710	21,772	–912	1,072	4,836	3,742	–634	–33	3,620	13,598
El Salvador	973	3,977	1,624	5,892	–132	–266	631	2,004	–152	–177	595	1,871
Eritrea	88	147	278	523	0	–4	171	173	–19	–206	..	..
Estonia	664	4,981	711	5,190	–13	–281	97	151	36	–339	198	822
Ethiopia	672	957	1,069	1,944	–67	–59	220	774	–244	–272	55	490
Finland	31,180	48,812	33,456	38,427	–3,735	–1,070	–952	–684	–6,962	8,631	10,415	8,420
France	285,389	371,795	283,238	351,033	–3,896	15,384	–8,199	–14,788	–9,944	21,359	68,291	58,637
Gabon	2,730	3,180	1,812	1,961	–617	–711	–134	–73	168	435	279	13
Gambia, The	168	277	192	349	–11	–7	59	26	23	–53	55	106
Georgia	..	676	..	1,254	..	125	..	135	..	–269	..	159
Germany	474,713	657,453	423,497	619,920	20,832	–11,268	–23,745	–23,823	48,303	2,442	104,547	82,037
Ghana	983	2,380	1,506	3,247	–111	–138	411	753	–223	–251	309	376
Greece	13,018	30,071	19,564	41,291	–1,709	–1,767	4,718	3,587	–3,537	–9,400	4,721	6,244
Guatemala	1,568	3,896	1,812	6,040	–196	–90	227	997	–213	–1,238	362	2,352
Guinea	829	834	953	881	–149	–102	70	90	–203	–60	80	200
Guinea-Bissau	26	55	88	96	–22	–16	39	..	–45	..	18	69
Haiti	303	463	655	1,230	–5	9	70	582	–288	–177	10	142
[†] Data for Taiwan, China	74,175	142,514	67,015	126,598	4,361	5,679	–601	–2,734	10,920	18,861	77,653	125,960

	Goods and services				Net income		Net current transfers		Current account balance		Gross international reserves	
	Exports $ millions		Imports $ millions		$ millions		$ millions		$ millions		$ millions	
	1990	2001	1990	2001	1990	2001	1990	2001	1990	2001	1990	2001
Honduras	1,032	2,412	1,127	3,461	−237	−147	280	871	−51	−325	47	1,421
Hungary	12,035	35,778	11,017	35,633	−1,427	−1,488	787	246	379	−1,097	1,185	10,755
India	23,028	65,200	31,485	73,700	−3,753	−2,700	2,068	12,500	−10,142	1,300	5,637	49,051
Indonesia	29,295	62,864	27,511	50,549	−5,190	−6,936	418	1,520	−2,988	6,899	8,657	28,104
Iran, Islamic Rep.	19,741	23,716	22,292	18,138	378	−1,144	−582	320	−2,755	4,754	..	..
Iraq	..	..	..	..	..	..	..	..	..	..	..	..
Ireland	26,786	98,566	24,576	83,221	−4,955	−16,864	2,384	477	−361	−1,043	5,362	5,636
Israel	17,312	39,669	20,228	43,505	−1,981	−4,415	5,060	6,399	163	−1,852	6,598	23,379
Italy	219,971	299,978	218,573	283,912	−14,712	−10,281	−3,164	−5,948	−16,479	−163	88,595	46,215
Jamaica	2,217	3,355	2,390	4,592	−430	−438	291	886	−312	−788	168	1,901
Japan	323,692	448,107	297,306	421,627	22,492	69,221	−4,800	−7,904	44,078	87,797	87,828	401,958
Jordan	2,511	3,776	3,569	6,026	−214	187	1,045	2,059	−227	−4	1,139	3,174
Kazakhstan	..	10,304	..	10,660	..	−1,115	..	230	..	−1,240	..	2,506
Kenya	2,228	2,981	2,705	4,002	−418	−147	368	850	−527	−318	236	1,065
Korea, Dem. Rep.	..	..	..	..	..	..	..	..	..	..	..	..
Korea, Rep.	73,295	180,973	76,360	171,107	−87	−886	1,150	−363	−2,003	8,617	14,916	102,875
Kuwait	8,268	17,953	7,169	12,267	7,738	4,956	−4,951	−2,080	3,886	8,562	2,929	10,599
Kyrgyz Republic	..	561	..	566	..	−66	..	51	..	−20	..	287
Lao PDR	102	477	212	560	−1	−34	56	34	−55	−82	8	151
Latvia	1,090	3,403	997	4,259	2	44	96	78	191	−734	..	1,217
Lebanon	511	1,922	2,836	7,031	622	942	1,818	183	115	−3,984	4,210	7,564
Lesotho	100	319	754	728	433	179	286	135	65	−95	72	386
Liberia	..	146	..	181	..	−80	..	..	..	..	1	0
Libya	11,469	6,813	8,960	4,914	174	289	−481	−204	2,201	1,984	7,225	16,079
Lithuania	..	6,046	..	6,697	..	−180	..	258	..	−574	107	1,669
Macedonia, FYR	..	1,387	..	1,912	..	−41	..	241	..	−324	..	799
Madagascar	471	152	809	175	−161	−10	234	15	−265	−17	92	398
Malawi	443	495	549	966	−80	−74	99	15	−86	−531	142	210
Malaysia	32,665	102,435	31,765	86,254	−1,872	−6,743	102	−2,152	−870	7,287	10,659	30,798
Mali	420	825	830	1,085	−37	−129	225	..	−221	..	198	349
Mauritania	471	377	520	434	−46	−16	86	137	−10	65	59	228
Mauritius	1,722	2,837	1,916	2,675	−23	14	97	70	−119	247	761	853
Mexico	48,805	171,142	51,915	185,592	−8,316	−12,574	3,975	9,341	−7,451	−17,683	10,217	44,805
Moldova	..	740	..	1,101	..	109	..	153	..	−99	..	229
Mongolia	493	546	1,096	723	−44	4	7	94	−640	−79	23	257
Morocco	6,239	11,171	7,783	12,282	−988	−833	2,336	3,555	−196	1,611	2,338	8,669
Mozambique	229	2,304	996	3,905	−97	−574	448	571	−415	−1,604	233	729
Myanmar	641	2,646	1,182	3,016	−61	−57	77	209	−526	−218	410	464
Namibia	1,220	1,747	1,584	1,985	37	109	354	..	28	..	50	234
Nepal	379	1,358	761	1,983	71	9	60	788	−251	172	354	1,080
Netherlands	159,304	255,875	147,652	237,984	−620	−7,522	−2,943	−6,626	8,089	3,743	34,401	16,897
New Zealand	11,683	18,264	11,699	16,663	−1,576	−3,146	138	141	−1,453	−1,403	4,129	3,008
Nicaragua	392	934	682	1,983	−217	−249	202	740	−305	−557	166	380
Niger	533	324	728	486	−54	−11	14	4	−236	−170	226	107
Nigeria	14,550	21,201	6,909	15,418	−2,738	−2,274	85	1,292	4,988	506	4,129	10,647
Norway	47,078	77,657	38,911	49,073	−2,700	−940	−1,476	−1,684	3,992	25,960	15,788	15,815
Oman	5,577	11,423	3,342	6,988	−254	−588	−874	−1,532	1,106	2,315	1,784	2,445
Pakistan	6,217	10,284	9,351	12,535	−966	−2,160	2,748	3,299	−1,352	−1,112	1,046	4,218
Panama	4,438	7,701	4,193	7,853	−255	−545	219	199	209	−500	344	1,092
Papua New Guinea	1,381	2,098	1,509	1,594	−103	−230	156	13	−76	286	427	440
Paraguay	2,514	2,989	2,169	3,364	2	2	43	166	390	−207	675	723
Peru	4,120	8,597	4,087	9,489	−1,733	−1,203	281	997	−1,419	−1,098	1,891	8,980
Philippines	11,430	34,393	13,967	33,586	−872	3,252	714	444	−2,695	4,503	2,036	15,649
Poland	19,037	51,419	15,095	58,275	−3,386	−1,390	2,511	2,889	3,067	−5,357	4,674	26,563
Portugal	21,554	34,582	27,146	44,967	−96	−3,054	5,507	3,480	−181	−9,959	20,579	15,060
Puerto Rico	..	..	..	..	..	..	..	..	..	..	..	..

	Goods and services				Net income		Net current transfers		Current account balance		Gross international reserves	
	Exports		Imports									
	$ millions		$ millions		$ millions		$ millions		$ millions		$ millions	
	1990	2001	1990	2001	1990	2001	1990	2001	1990	2001	1990	2001
Romania	6,380	13,379	9,901	16,557	161	−282	106	1,143	−3,254	−2,317	1,374	6,377
Russian Federation	..	112,507	..	73,168	..	−3,959	..	−759	..	34,621	..	36,303
Rwanda	145	143	359	434	−17	−20	145	193	−86	−118	44	212
Saudi Arabia	47,445	78,214	43,939	47,952	7,979	−520	−15,637	−15,240	−4,152	14,502	13,437	18,867
Senegal	1,453	1,373	1,840	1,745	−129	−106	153	180	−363	−297	22	447
Sierra Leone	210	91	215	284	−71	−16	7	..	−69	..	5	51
Singapore	67,489	148,646	64,953	130,048	1,006	664	−421	−1,377	3,122	17,884	27,748	75,375
Slovak Republic	..	15,096	..	16,750	..	−315	..	120	..	−694	..	4,453
Slovenia	7,900	11,302	6,930	11,420	−38	19	46	129	978	31	112	4,397
Somalia	70	..	322	..	..	..	..	..	..	..	..	..
South Africa	27,742	35,304	21,016	30,885	−4,271	−3,846	−321	−738	2,134	−166	2,583	7,627
Spain	83,595	175,336	100,870	182,577	−3,533	−9,545	2,799	1,705	−18,009	−15,082	57,238	34,235
Sri Lanka	2,293	6,187	2,965	7,130	−167	−280	541	959	−298	−265	447	1,304
Sudan	499	1,713	877	2,055	−136	−554	141	374	−372	−522	11	118
Swaziland	658	894	768	1,061	59	34	102	80	51	−53	216	272
Sweden	70,560	98,197	70,490	85,388	−4,473	−2,852	−1,936	−3,261	−6,339	6,696	20,324	15,625
Switzerland	96,928	123,552	96,389	109,531	8,746	12,677	−2,329	−4,073	6,957	22,624	61,284	51,543
Syrian Arab Republic	5,030	7,448	2,955	5,994	−401	−783	88	485	1,762	1,062	..	..
Tajikistan	185	673	238	801	0	−30	..	84	−53	−74	..	94
Tanzania	538	1,402	1,474	2,179	−185	−46	562	86	−559	−738	193	1,157
Thailand	29,229	76,226	35,870	69,239	−853	−1,361	213	601	−7,281	6,227	14,258	33,041
Togo	663	436	847	624	−32	−24	132	68	−84	−140	358	126
Trinidad and Tobago	2,289	4,827	1,427	3,788	−397	−471	−6	..	459	..	513	1,924
Tunisia	5,203	9,518	6,039	10,422	−455	−940	828	935	−463	−910	867	2,050
Turkey	21,042	50,438	25,652	45,845	−2,508	−5,000	4,493	3,803	−2,625	3,396	7,626	19,911
Turkmenistan	1,238	2,777	857	2,807	0	−111	66	68	447	−74	..	1,513
Uganda	246	664	676	1,454	−77	−119	78	540	−429	−369	44	983
Ukraine	..	21,086	..	20,473	..	−667	..	1,456	..	1,402	469	3,089
United Arab Emirates	..	..	..	..	..	..	..	..	..	..	4,891	14,256
United Kingdom	239,226	385,830	264,090	418,989	−5,154	13,166	−8,794	−10,283	−38,811	−30,277	43,146	40,442
United States	535,260	998,030	616,120	1,356,320	28,560	14,370	−26,660	−49,470	−78,960	−393,390	173,094	130,077
Uruguay	2,158	3,276	1,659	3,718	−321	−114	8	43	186	−513	1,446	3,099
Uzbekistan	..	3,201	..	3,152	−11	−205	2	43	−236	−113	..	1,242
Venezuela, RB	18,806	28,006	9,451	22,005	−774	−1,453	−302	−617	8,279	3,931	12,733	12,264
Vietnam	..	17,837	..	17,928	..	−477	..	1,250	..	682	..	3,675
West Bank and Gaza	..	..	..	..	..	..	..	..	..	..	..	..
Yemen, Rep.	1,490	4,125	2,170	3,265	−372	−1,254	1,790	1,501	739	1,107	441	3,672
Yugoslavia, Fed. Rep.	..	2,762	..	5,160	..	−26	..	1,828	..	−596	..	..
Zambia	1,360	1,053	1,897	1,626	−437	−108	380	32	−594	−553	201	183
Zimbabwe	2,012	1,961	2,001	1,905	−263	−245	112	..	−140	..	295	119
World	**4,253,268 t**	**7,555,367 t**	**4,257,473 t**	**7,580,229 t**								
Low income	134,108	274,876	153,830	280,252								
Middle income	629,670	1,547,335	585,956	1,454,555								
Lower middle income	317,372	819,932	318,412	754,424								
Upper middle income	310,090	727,315	268,056	699,645								
Low & middle income	762,775	1,822,224	737,971	1,734,704								
East Asia & Pacific	166,961	604,321	165,987	541,844								
Europe & Central Asia	..	407,735	..	386,921								
Latin America & Carib.	169,974	404,153	147,208	431,219								
Middle East & N. Africa	129,973	202,257	130,645	160,598								
South Asia	34,113	90,957	49,041	106,305								
Sub-Saharan Africa	81,250	113,199	74,104	107,805								
High income	3,481,648	5,732,565	3,497,811	5,846,561								
Europe EMU	1,518,561	2,277,557	1,482,825	2,189,310								

a. Includes Luxembourg. b. Excludes Luxembourg.

About the data

The balance of payments records an economy's transactions with the rest of the world. Balance of payments accounts are divided into two groups: the current account, which records transactions in goods, services, income, and current transfers; and the capital and financial account, which records capital transfers, acquisition or disposal of nonproduced, nonfinancial assets, and transactions in financial assets and liabilities. The table presents data from the current account with the addition of gross international reserves.

The balance of payments is a double-entry accounting system that shows all flows of goods and services into and out of an economy; all transfers that are the counterpart of real resources or financial claims provided to or by the rest of the world without a quid pro quo, such as donations and grants; and all changes in residents' claims on, and liabilities to, nonresidents that arise from economic transactions. All transactions are recorded twice—once as a credit and once as a debit. In principle the net balance should be zero, but in practice the accounts often do not balance. In these cases a balancing item, net errors and omissions, is included.

Discrepancies may arise in the balance of payments because there is no single source for balance of payments data and therefore no way to ensure that the data are fully consistent. Sources include customs data, monetary accounts of the banking system, external debt records, information provided by enterprises, surveys to estimate service transactions, and foreign exchange records. Differences in collection methods—such as in timing, definitions of residence and ownership, and the exchange rate used to value transactions—contribute to net errors and omissions. In addition, smuggling and other illegal or quasi-legal transactions may be unrecorded or misrecorded. For further discussion of issues relating to the recording of data on trade in goods and services, see *About the data* for tables 4.4–4.8.

The concepts and definitions underlying the data in the table are based on the fifth edition of the International Monetary Fund's (IMF) *Balance of Payments Manual* (1993). The fifth edition redefined as capital transfers some transactions previously included in the current account, such as debt forgiveness, migrants' capital transfers, and foreign aid to acquire capital goods. Thus the current account balance now reflects more accurately net current transfer receipts in addition to transactions in goods, services (previously nonfactor services), and income (previously factor income). Many countries maintain their data collection systems according to the fourth edition. Where necessary, the IMF converts data reported in such systems to conform to the fifth edition (see *Primary data documentation*). Values are in U.S. dollars converted at market exchange rates.

The data in this table come from the IMF's Balance of Payments and International Financial Statistics databases, supplemented by estimates by World Bank staff for countries whose national accounts are recorded in fiscal years (see *Primary data documentation*) and countries for which the IMF does not collect balance of payments statistics. In addition, World Bank staff make estimates of missing data for the most recent year.

Definitions

• **Exports and imports of goods and services** comprise all transactions between residents of an economy and the rest of the world involving a change in ownership of general merchandise, goods sent for processing and repairs, nonmonetary gold, and services. • **Net income** refers to receipts and payments of employee compensation for nonresident workers, and investment income (receipts and payments on direct investment, portfolio investment, and other investments and receipts on reserve assets). Income derived from the use of intangible assets is recorded under business services. • **Net current transfers** are recorded in the balance of payments whenever an economy provides or receives goods, services, income, or financial items without a quid pro quo. All transfers not considered to be capital are current. • **Current account balance** is the sum of net exports of goods and services, net income, and net current transfers. • **Gross international reserves** comprise holdings of monetary gold, special drawing rights, reserves of IMF members held by the IMF, and holdings of foreign exchange under the control of monetary authorities. The gold component of these reserves is valued at year-end (31 December) London prices ($385 an ounce in 1990 and $276.50 an ounce in 2001).

4.15a

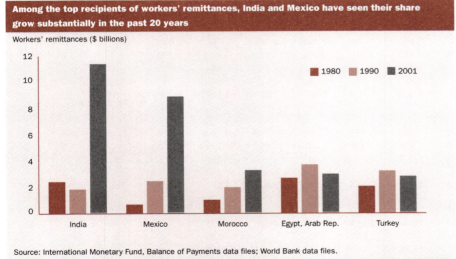

Among the top recipients of workers' remittances, India and Mexico have seen their share grow substantially in the past 20 years

Workers' remittances ($ billions)

Legend: 1980 | 1990 | 2001

Categories: India, Mexico, Morocco, Egypt, Arab Rep., Turkey

Source: International Monetary Fund, Balance of Payments data files; World Bank data files.

Data sources

More information about the design and compilation of the balance of payments can be found in the IMF's *Balance of Payments Manual*, fifth edition (1993), *Balance of Payments Textbook* (1996a), and *Balance of Payments Compilation Guide* (1995). The balance of payments data are published in the IMF's *Balance of Payments Statistics Yearbook* and *International Financial Statistics*. The World Bank exchanges data with the IMF through electronic files that in most cases are more timely and cover a longer period than the published sources. The IMF's *International Financial Statistics* and *Balance of Payments* databases are available on CD-ROM.

	Total external debt $ millions		Long-term debt $ millions		Public and publicly guaranteed debt				Private nonguaranteed external debt $ millions		Use of IMF credit $ millions	
					Total $ millions		IBRD loans and IDA credits $ millions					
	1990	2001	1990	2001	1990	2001	1990	2001	1990	2001	1990	2001
Afghanistan	..	..	..	..	..	..	..	..	..	..	..	..
Albania	349	1,094	36	980	36	970	0	366	0	11	0	83
Algeria	28,149	22,503	26,688	20,786	26,688	20,786	1,208	1,328	0	0	670	1,518
Angola	8,594	9,600	7,605	7,443	7,605	7,443	0	228	0	0	0	0
Argentina	62,233	136,709	48,676	102,733	46,876	85,337	2,609	9,440	1,800	17,396	3,083	13,976
Armenia	..	1,001	..	786	..	766	..	435	..	20	..	173
Australia	..	..	..	..	..	..	..	..	..	..	..	..
Austria	..	..	..	..	..	..	..	..	..	..	..	..
Azerbaijan	..	1,219	..	821	..	726	..	235	..	95	..	295
Bangladesh	12,439	15,216	11,657	14,773	11,657	14,773	4,159	6,456	0	0	626	149
Belarus	..	869	..	642	..	641	..	91	..	2	..	81
Belgium	..	..	..	..	..	..	..	..	..	..	..	..
Benin	1,292	1,665	1,218	1,503	1,218	1,503	326	598	0	0	18	77
Bolivia	4,275	4,682	3,864	4,095	3,687	3,116	587	1,146	177	979	257	207
Bosnia and Herzegovina	..	2,226	..	2,057	..	2,045	..	983	..	12	..	111
Botswana	563	370	557	349	557	349	169	19	0	0	0	0
Brazil	119,964	226,362	94,427	189,748	87,756	93,467	8,427	7,963	6,671	96,280	1,821	8,337
Bulgaria	10,890	9,615	9,834	8,159	9,834	7,378	0	844	0	782	0	1,110
Burkina Faso	834	1,490	750	1,310	750	1,310	282	636	0	0	0	117
Burundi	907	1,065	851	974	851	974	398	582	0	0	43	2
Cambodia	1,845	2,704	1,683	2,401	1,683	2,401	0	238	0	0	27	80
Cameroon	6,676	8,338	5,595	7,138	5,365	6,913	889	936	230	225	121	244
Canada	..	..	..	..	..	..	..	..	..	..	..	..
Central African Republic	698	822	624	757	624	757	265	372	0	0	37	31
Chad	524	1,104	464	992	464	992	186	525	0	0	31	89
Chile	19,226	38,360	14,687	35,803	10,425	5,544	1,874	734	4,263	30,259	1,156	0
China	55,301	170,110	45,515	126,190	45,515	91,706	5,881	20,203	0	34,484	469	0
Hong Kong, China	..	..	..	..	..	..	..	..	..	..	..	..
Colombia	17,222	36,699	15,784	32,960	14,671	21,777	3,874	2,012	1,113	11,184	0	0
Congo, Dem. Rep.	10,259	11,392	8,994	7,584	8,994	7,584	1,161	1,232	0	0	521	377
Congo, Rep.	4,947	4,496	4,200	3,631	4,200	3,631	239	203	0	0	11	39
Costa Rica	3,756	4,586	3,367	3,424	3,063	3,208	412	104	304	216	11	0
Côte d'Ivoire	17,251	11,582	13,223	9,963	10,665	8,590	1,920	1,817	2,558	1,372	431	464
Croatia	..	10,742	..	10,335	..	6,400	..	427	..	3,935	..	122
Cuba	..	..	..	..	..	..	..	..	..	..	..	..
Czech Republic	6,383	21,691	3,983	12,735	3,983	5,915	0	205	0	6,820	0	0
Denmark	..	..	..	..	..	..	..	..	..	..	..	..
Dominican Republic	4,372	5,093	3,518	3,749	3,419	3,749	258	330	99	0	72	50
Ecuador	12,107	13,910	10,029	12,220	9,865	11,149	848	908	164	1,071	265	190
Egypt, Arab Rep.	33,017	29,234	28,438	25,861	27,438	25,243	2,401	1,792	1,000	618	125	0
El Salvador	2,149	4,683	1,938	3,413	1,913	3,257	164	349	26	156	0	0
Eritrea	..	410	..	398	..	398	..	158	..	0	..	0
Estonia	..	2,852	..	1,810	..	187	..	65	..	1,623	..	13
Ethiopia	8,630	5,697	8,479	5,532	8,479	5,532	851	2,151	0	0	6	106
Finland	..	..	..	..	..	..	..	..	..	..	..	..
France	..	..	..	..	..	..	..	..	..	..	..	..
Gabon	3,983	3,409	3,150	3,030	3,150	3,030	69	55	0	0	140	75
Gambia, The	369	489	308	438	308	438	102	170	0	0	45	26
Georgia	..	1,714	..	1,366	..	1,314	..	396	..	53	..	287
Germany	..	..	..	..	..	..	..	..	..	..	..	..
Ghana	3,881	6,759	2,816	5,921	2,783	5,666	1,423	3,178	33	255	745	284
Greece	..	..	..	..	..	..	..	..	..	..	..	..
Guatemala	3,080	5,037	2,605	3,577	2,478	3,456	293	330	127	121	67	0
Guinea	2,476	3,254	2,253	2,844	2,253	2,844	420	1,003	0	0	52	123
Guinea-Bissau	692	668	630	627	630	627	146	220	0	0	5	23
Haiti	910	1,250	772	1,028	772	1,028	324	467	0	0	38	39

External debt

	Total external debt $ millions		Long-term debt $ millions		Public and publicly guaranteed debt				Private nonguaranteed external debt $ millions		Use of IMF credit $ millions	
					Total $ millions		IBRD loans and IDA credits $ millions					
	1990	2001	1990	2001	1990	2001	1990	2001	1990	2001	1990	2001
Honduras	3,718	5,051	3,487	4,501	3,420	3,995	635	1,028	66	506	32	220
Hungary	21,202	30,289	17,931	25,666	17,931	12,681	1,512	564	0	12,985	330	0
India	83,628	97,071	72,462	94,120	70,974	82,446	20,996	26,105	1,488	11,674	2,623	0
Indonesia	69,872	135,704	58,242	104,783	47,982	68,378	10,385	12,157	10,261	36,405	494	9,113
Iran, Islamic Rep.	9,020	7,483	1,797	5,465	1,797	5,295	86	456	0	170	0	0
Iraq	..	..	..	..	..	..	..	..	..	..	..	..
Ireland	..	..	..	..	..	..	..	..	..	..	..	..
Israel	..	..	..	..	..	..	..	..	..	..	..	..
Italy	..	..	..	..	..	..	..	..	..	..	..	..
Jamaica	4,667	4,956	3,964	4,041	3,930	3,947	672	443	34	94	357	40
Japan	..	..	..	..	..	..	..	..	..	..	..	..
Jordan	8,333	7,479	7,202	6,599	7,202	6,599	593	941	0	0	94	433
Kazakhstan	..	14,372	..	13,541	..	3,446	..	1,070	..	10,095	..	0
Kenya	7,058	5,833	5,642	5,039	4,762	4,930	2,056	2,287	880	109	482	99
Korea, Dem. Rep.	..	..	..	..	..	..	..	..	..	..	..	..
Korea, Rep.	34,968	110,109	24,168	74,994	18,768	33,742	3,337	7,900	5,400	41,252	0	0
Kuwait	..	..	..	..	..	..	..	..	..	..	..	..
Kyrgyz Republic	..	1,717	..	1,490	..	1,256	..	389	..	234	..	179
Lao PDR	1,768	2,495	1,758	2,456	1,758	2,456	131	415	0	0	8	37
Latvia	..	5,710	..	2,651	..	978	..	243	..	1,673	..	24
Lebanon	1,779	12,450	358	9,792	358	8,956	34	259	0	836	0	0
Lesotho	396	592	378	573	378	573	112	242	0	0	15	15
Liberia	1,849	1,987	1,116	1,012	1,116	1,012	248	221	0	0	322	281
Libya	..	..	..	..	..	..	..	..	..	..	..	..
Lithuania	..	5,248	..	3,539	..	2,359	..	273	..	1,180	..	151
Macedonia, FYR	..	1,423	..	1,284	..	1,136	..	372	..	149	..	71
Madagascar	3,704	4,160	3,335	3,793	3,335	3,793	797	1,408	0	0	144	127
Malawi	1,558	2,602	1,385	2,483	1,382	2,483	854	1,627	3	0	115	73
Malaysia	15,328	43,351	13,422	38,249	11,592	24,068	1,102	788	1,830	14,181	0	0
Mali	2,468	2,890	2,337	2,616	2,337	2,616	498	981	0	0	69	171
Mauritania	2,096	2,164	1,789	1,865	1,789	1,865	264	475	0	0	70	105
Mauritius	984	1,724	910	852	762	765	195	84	148	87	22	0
Mexico	104,442	158,290	81,809	140,290	75,974	86,199	11,030	10,883	5,835	54,091	6,551	0
Moldova	..	1,214	..	1,046	..	779	..	294	..	267	..	146
Mongolia	..	885	..	824	..	824	0	155	..	0	0	47
Morocco	24,458	16,962	23,301	16,715	23,101	14,325	3,138	2,525	200	2,390	750	0
Mozambique	4,650	4,466	4,231	3,772	4,211	2,222	268	777	19	1,550	74	196
Myanmar	4,695	5,670	4,466	5,006	4,466	5,006	716	693	0	0	0	0
Namibia	..	..	..	..	..	..	..	..	..	..	..	..
Nepal	1,640	2,700	1,572	2,643	1,572	2,643	668	1,127	0	0	44	8
Netherlands	..	..	..	..	..	..	..	..	..	..	..	..
New Zealand	..	..	..	..	..	..	..	..	..	..	..	..
Nicaragua	10,745	6,391	8,313	5,560	8,313	5,437	299	691	0	123	0	158
Niger	1,726	1,555	1,487	1,432	1,226	1,371	461	753	261	62	85	81
Nigeria	33,439	31,119	31,935	29,396	31,545	29,215	3,321	1,958	391	181	0	0
Norway	..	..	..	..	..	..	..	..	..	..	..	..
Oman	2,736	6,025	2,400	4,759	2,400	2,691	52	1	0	2,068	0	0
Pakistan	20,663	32,019	16,643	28,899	16,506	26,801	3,922	7,041	138	2,098	836	1,807
Panama	6,507	8,245	3,856	7,727	3,856	6,332	462	282	0	1,395	272	54
Papua New Guinea	2,594	2,521	2,461	2,345	1,523	1,413	349	363	938	932	61	108
Paraguay	2,105	2,817	1,732	2,355	1,713	2,120	320	231	19	235	0	0
Peru	20,064	27,512	13,959	24,087	13,629	18,831	1,188	2,625	330	5,256	755	387
Philippines	30,580	52,356	25,241	44,355	24,040	34,190	4,044	3,454	1,201	10,165	912	1,952
Poland	49,364	62,393	39,261	55,427	39,261	24,828	55	2,211	0	30,599	509	0
Portugal	..	..	..	..	..	..	..	..	..	..	..	..
Puerto Rico	..	..	..	..	..	..	..	..	..	..	..	..

	Total external debt		Long-term debt		Public and publicly guaranteed debt				Private nonguaranteed external debt		Use of IMF credit	
					Total		IBRD loans and IDA credits					
	$ millions		$ millions		$ millions		$ millions		$ millions		$ millions	
	1990	2001	1990	2001	1990	2001	1990	2001	1990	2001	1990	2001
Romania	1,140	11,653	230	10,744	223	6,682	0	1,876	7	4,061	0	387
Russian Federation [a]	59,340	152,649	47,540	124,244	47,540	101,918	0	6,746	0	22,326	0	7,433
Rwanda	712	1,283	664	1,163	664	1,163	340	713	0	0	0	84
Saudi Arabia	..	..	..	..	..	..	..	..	..	..	..	..
Senegal	3,736	3,461	3,000	3,012	2,940	2,961	835	1,384	60	51	314	248
Sierra Leone	1,196	1,188	940	1,014	940	1,014	92	407	0	0	108	152
Singapore	..	..	..	..	..	..	..	..	..	..	..	..
Slovak Republic	2,008	11,121	1,505	8,048	1,505	5,498	0	205	0	2,550	0	0
Slovenia	..	..	..	..	..	..	..	..	..	..	..	..
Somalia	2,370	2,532	1,926	1,795	1,926	1,795	419	386	0	0	159	141
South Africa	..	24,050	..	15,695	..	7,941	0	7	..	7,754	0	0
Spain	..	..	..	..	..	..	..	..	..	..	..	..
Sri Lanka	5,863	8,529	5,049	7,862	4,947	7,472	946	1,578	102	389	410	214
Sudan	14,762	15,348	9,651	8,985	9,155	8,489	1,048	1,138	496	496	956	551
Swaziland	243	308	238	236	238	236	44	13	0	0	0	0
Sweden	..	..	..	..	..	..	..	..	..	..	..	..
Switzerland	..	..	..	..	..	..	..	..	..	..	..	..
Syrian Arab Republic	17,259	21,305	15,108	15,811	15,108	15,811	523	44	0	0	0	0
Tajikistan	..	1,086	..	896	..	789	..	172	..	107	..	110
Tanzania	6,456	6,676	5,796	5,781	5,785	5,758	1,493	2,596	12	24	140	341
Thailand	28,095	67,384	19,771	52,480	12,460	26,411	2,530	3,084	7,311	26,069	1	1,681
Togo	1,281	1,406	1,081	1,203	1,081	1,203	398	585	0	0	87	57
Trinidad and Tobago	2,512	2,422	2,055	1,562	1,782	1,452	41	90	273	110	329	0
Tunisia	7,690	10,884	6,880	10,203	6,662	9,084	1,406	1,333	218	1,118	176	0
Turkey	49,424	115,118	39,924	84,656	38,870	56,004	6,429	4,802	1,054	28,652	0	14,117
Turkmenistan	..	..	..	..	..	..	..	30	..	..	..	0
Uganda	2,583	3,733	2,160	3,306	2,160	3,306	969	2,310	0	0	282	275
Ukraine	..	12,811	..	10,159	..	8,197	..	2,248	..	1,961	..	1,911
United Arab Emirates	..	..	..	..	..	..	..	..	..	..	..	..
United Kingdom	..	..	..	..	..	..	..	..	..	..	..	..
United States	..	..	..	..	..	..	..	..	..	..	..	..
Uruguay	4,415	9,706	3,114	6,634	3,045	6,110	359	544	69	524	101	144
Uzbekistan	..	4,627	..	4,046	..	3,759	..	237	..	286	..	78
Venezuela, RB	33,171	34,660	28,159	30,931	24,509	24,916	974	838	3,650	6,015	3,012	0
Vietnam	23,270	12,578	21,378	11,428	21,378	11,428	59	1,344	0	0	112	366
West Bank and Gaza	..	..	..	..	..	..	..	..	..	..	..	..
Yemen, Rep.	6,352	4,954	5,160	4,062	5,160	4,062	602	1,237	0	0	0	374
Yugoslavia, Fed. Rep. [b]	17,792	11,740	16,802	6,629	12,942	6,002	2,433	1,085	3,860	627	467	273
Zambia	6,916	5,671	4,554	4,513	4,552	4,394	813	1,886	2	119	949	982
Zimbabwe	3,247	3,780	2,649	3,023	2,464	2,847	449	810	185	175	7	262
World	.. s	.. s	.. s	.. s	.. s	.. s	.. s	.. s	.. s	.. s	.. s	.. s
Low income	421,446	533,346	360,309	457,309	342,356	398,406	67,080	100,459	17,953	58,903	11,317	21,712
Middle income [c]	1,000,132	1,799,275	794,285	1,450,505	752,125	995,967	70,258	101,295	42,160	454,538	23,334	53,569
Lower middle income	517,056	917,706	424,075	729,903	406,864	560,385	40,825	64,951	17,212	169,518	5,991	30,670
Upper middle income [c]	483,076	881,570	370,209	720,601	345,261	435,582	29,433	36,344	24,948	285,020	17,344	22,898
Low & middle income [c]	1,421,578	2,332,621	1,154,594	1,907,814	1,094,481	1,394,373	137,338	201,755	60,113	513,441	34,652	75,281
East Asia & Pacific	239,005	504,125	198,549	397,922	176,913	275,645	25,306	43,011	21,635	122,277	2,085	13,384
Europe & Central Asia	217,913	497,827	177,054	394,989	172,133	263,858	10,429	26,863	4,921	131,130	1,305	27,156
Latin America & Carib.	475,374	765,395	379,681	645,027	354,630	419,010	35,877	41,739	25,051	226,017	18,298	23,901
Middle East & N. Africa	182,898	200,641	137,048	150,936	135,547	143,540	10,074	9,972	1,502	7,396	1,815	2,340
South Asia	129,481	161,657	112,573	154,354	110,845	140,192	30,717	42,743	1,727	14,161	4,537	2,178
Sub-Saharan Africa	176,906	202,976	149,689	164,587	144,413	152,128	24,935	37,426	5,276	12,459	6,612	6,323
High income												
Europe EMU												

a. Data for 1990 refer to the debt of the former Soviet Union on the assumption that 100 percent of all outstanding external debt as of December 1991 has become a liability of the Russian Federation. b. Data for 1990 refer to the former Socialist Federal Republic of Yugoslavia. Data for 2001 are estimates and reflect borrowings by the former Socialist Federal Republic of Yugoslavia that are not yet allocated to the successor republics. c. Includes data for Gibraltar not included in other tables.

About the data

Data on the external debt of developing countries are gathered by the World Bank through its Debtor Reporting System. World Bank staff calculate the indebtedness of these countries using loan-by-loan reports submitted by them on long-term public and publicly guaranteed borrowing, along with information on short-term debt collected by the countries or collected from creditors through the reporting systems of the Bank for International Settlements and the Organisation for Economic Co-operation and Development. These data are supplemented by information on loans and credits from major multilateral banks, loan statements from official lending agencies in major creditor countries, and estimates by World Bank and International Monetary Fund (IMF) staff. In addition, the table includes data on private nonguaranteed debt for 78 countries either reported to the World Bank or estimated by its staff.

The coverage, quality, and timeliness of debt data vary across countries. Coverage varies for both debt instruments and borrowers. With the widening spectrum of debt instruments and investors and the expansion of private nonguaranteed borrowing, comprehensive coverage of long-term external debt becomes more complex. Reporting countries differ in their capacity to monitor debt, especially private nonguaranteed debt. Even data on public and publicly guaranteed debt are affected by coverage and accuracy in reporting—again because of monitoring capacity and sometimes because of unwillingness to provide information. A key part often underreported is military debt.

Because debt data are normally reported in the currency of repayment, they have to be converted into U.S. dollars to produce summary tables. Stock figures (amount of debt outstanding) are converted using end-of-period exchange rates, as published in the IMF's *International Financial Statistics* (line ae). Flow figures are converted at annual average exchange rates (line rf). Projected debt service is converted using end-of-period exchange rates. Debt repayable in multiple currencies, goods, or services and debt with a provision for maintenance of the value of the currency of repayment are shown at book value.

Because flow data are converted at annual average exchange rates and stock data at end-of-period exchange rates, year-to-year changes in debt outstanding and disbursed are sometimes not equal to net flows (disbursements less principal repayments); similarly, changes in debt outstanding, including undisbursed debt, differ from commitments less repayments. Discrepancies are particularly significant when exchange rates have moved sharply during the year. Cancellations and reschedulings of other liabilities into long-term public debt also contribute to the differences.

Variations in reporting rescheduled debt also affect cross-country comparability. For example, rescheduling under the auspices of the Paris Club of official creditors may be subject to lags between the completion of the general rescheduling agreement and the completion of the specific, bilateral agreements that define the terms of the rescheduled debt. Other areas of inconsistency include country treatment of arrears and of nonresident national deposits denominated in foreign currency.

Definitions

• **Total external debt** is debt owed to nonresidents repayable in foreign currency, goods, or services. It is the sum of public, publicly guaranteed, and private nonguaranteed long-term debt, use of IMF credit, and short-term debt. Short-term debt includes all debt having an original maturity of one year or less and interest in arrears on long-term debt. • **Long-term debt** is debt that has an original or extended maturity of more than one year. It has three components: public, publicly guaranteed, and private nonguaranteed debt. • **Public and publicly guaranteed debt** comprises long-term external obligations of public debtors, including the national government and political subdivisions (or an agency of either) and autonomous public bodies, and external obligations of private debtors that are guaranteed for repayment by a public entity. • **IBRD loans and IDA credits** are extended by the World Bank. The International Bank for Reconstruction and Development (IBRD) lends at market rates. The International Development Association (IDA) provides credits at concessional rates. • **Private nonguaranteed external debt** comprises long-term external obligations of private debtors that are not guaranteed for repayment by a public entity. • **Use of IMF credit** denotes repurchase obligations to the IMF for all uses of IMF resources (excluding those resulting from drawings on the reserve tranche). These obligations, shown for the end of the year specified, comprise purchases outstanding under the credit tranches (including enlarged access resources) and all special facilities (the buffer stock, compensatory financing, extended fund, and oil facilities), trust fund loans, and operations under the structural adjustment and enhanced structural adjustment facilities.

4.16a

Thanks to traditional debt relief and the HIPC Debt Initiative, the total debt burden of heavily indebted poor countries, most in Sub-Saharan Africa, has declined since 1999

Total external debt ($ billions)

Heavily indebted poor countries (HIPCs)

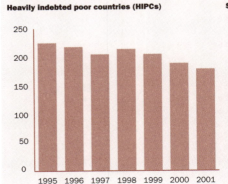

Sub-Saharan Africa

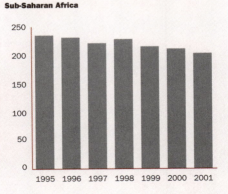

Source: World Bank data files.

Data sources

The main sources of external debt information are reports to the World Bank through its Debtor Reporting System from member countries that have received IBRD loans or IDA credits. Additional information has been drawn from the files of the World Bank and the IMF. Summary tables of the external debt of developing countries are published annually in the World Bank's *Global Development Finance* and on its *Global Development Finance* CD-ROM.

	Indebtedness classification [a]	Present value of debt		Total debt service				Public and publicly guaranteed debt service		Short-term debt	
		% of GNI	% of exports of goods and services	% of GNI		% of exports of goods and services		% of central government current revenue		% of total debt	
	2001	2001	2001	1990	2001	1990	2001	1990	2001	1990	2001
Afghanistan	..	..	..	..	..	..	..	..	..	..	..
Albania	L	18	47	0.1	0.8	0.9	3.1	..	..	89.8	2.8
Algeria	L	41	97	14.7	8.3	63.7	19.5	..	21.3	2.8	0.9
Angola	S	119	133	4.0	23.7	7.1	26.0	..	..	11.5	22.5
Argentina	S	57	407	4.6	9.3	34.7	48.6	32.5	43.6	16.8	14.6
Armenia	L	30	100	..	2.5	..	8.1	..	..	..	4.2
Australia	..	..	..	..	..	..	..	..	..	..	..
Austria	..	..	..	..	..	..	..	..	..	..	..
Azerbaijan	L	19	40	..	2.5	..	4.7	..	..	..	8.4
Bangladesh	L	21	105	2.5	1.4	37.5	9.0	..	..	1.3	1.9
Belarus	L	7	10	..	1.9	..	2.7	..	5.4	..	16.8
Belgium	..	..	..	..	..	..	..	..	..	..	..
Benin	S	36 [b]	134 [b]	2.1	2.1	9.2 [b]	10.0 [b]	..	..	4.3	5.1
Bolivia	M	26 [b]	114 [b]	8.3	7.0	33.5 [b]	16.1 [b]	41.3	17.4	3.6	8.1
Bosnia and Herzegovina	L	32	101	..	6.0	..	18.3	..	..	..	2.6
Botswana	L	6	10	2.9	1.1	4.4	1.7	5.5	..	1.0	5.6
Brazil	S	49	330	1.8	11.3	18.5	28.6	3.9	..	19.8	12.5
Bulgaria	M	63	106	7.2	10.3	18.6	15.5	12.9	19.1	9.7	3.6
Burkina Faso	S	29 [b, c]	224 [b, c]	1.2	1.5	7.8 [b, c]	11.0 [b, c]	9.1	..	10.1	4.3
Burundi	S	96	1,122	3.8	3.4	41.7	36.3	..	..	1.5	8.3
Cambodia	M	70	138	2.7	0.6	..	1.1	..	..	7.3	8.3
Cameroon	M	62 [b]	181 [b]	4.9	4.3	14.7 [b]	9.9 [b]	16.8	..	14.4	11.5
Canada	..	..	..	..	..	..	..	..	..	..	..
Central African Republic	S	56	482	2.0	1.4	12.5	11.5	..	..	5.4	4.2
Chad	S	39 [b]	213 [b]	0.7	1.5	3.8 [b]	10.0 [b]	5.6	..	5.7	2.1
Chile	M	59	160	9.7	10.4	18.1	5.2	25.6	8.0	17.6	6.7
China	L	14	53	2.0	2.1	10.6	4.2	23.9	..	16.8	25.8
Hong Kong, China	..	..	..	..	..	..	..	..	..	..	..
Colombia	M	47	215	10.2	7.9	34.5	28.1	61.2	..	8.4	10.2
Congo, Dem. Rep.	S	222	1,029	4.1	0.4	12.7	0.0	14.5	..	7.2	30.1
Congo, Rep.	S	221	170	22.9	4.8	32.2	3.3	..	9.2	14.9	18.4
Costa Rica	L	30	62	9.2	4.4	22.0	8.2	32.8	16.9	10.0	25.3
Côte d'Ivoire	S	109	233	13.7	6.3	19.1	8.1	22.1	16.6	20.8	10.0
Croatia	M	54	101	..	15.0	..	13.7	..	16.9	..	2.7
Cuba	..	..	..	..	..	..	..	..	..	..	..
Czech Republic	L	39	50	..	8.7	..	4.4	..	9.7	37.6	41.3
Denmark	..	..	..	..	..	..	..	..	..	..	..
Dominican Republic	L	24	46	3.4	3.1	10.7	6.6	16.1	..	17.9	25.4
Ecuador	S	89	200	11.4	9.6	31.0	22.0	45.0	..	15.0	10.8
Egypt, Arab Rep.	L	25	115	7.3	1.9	25.7	8.8	16.5	..	13.5	11.5
El Salvador	L	34	76	4.4	2.9	18.2	7.4	..	110.9	9.8	27.1
Eritrea	L	34	57	..	1.0	..	4.5	..	..	..	2.9
Estonia	M	56	57	..	7.3	..	0.9	..	2.3	..	36.1
Ethiopia	S	47 [b]	301 [b]	3.5	3.0	33.7 [b]	20.6 [b]	13.4	..	1.7	1.0
Finland	..	..	..	..	..	..	..	..	..	..	..
France	..	..	..	..	..	..	..	..	..	..	..
Gabon	S	89	102	3.3	12.1	4.8	13.6	7.6	..	17.4	8.9
Gambia, The	S	69 [b]	94 [b]	12.9	2.8	21.8 [b]	13.8 [b]	49.1	..	4.3	5.3
Georgia	L	34	124	..	2.5	..	8.1	..	15.2	..	3.5
Germany	..	..	..	..	..	..	..	..	..	..	..
Ghana	M	77 [b]	163 [b]	6.4	6.2	34.9 [b]	8.9 [b]	26.2	..	8.2	8.2
Greece	..	..	..	..	..	..	..	..	..	..	..
Guatemala	L	24	101	2.9	2.2	11.6	8.5	..	..	13.3	29.0
Guinea	S	60 [b]	203 [b]	6.3	3.6	19.6 [b]	9.2 [b]	33.0	..	6.9	8.8
Guinea-Bissau	S	231 [b]	747 [b]	3.6	12.7	22.1 [b]	0.7 [b]	..	..	8.2	2.7
Haiti	M	22	165	1.3	0.7	..	4.5	..	..	11.1	14.6

	Indebtedness classification[a]	Present value of debt		Total debt service				Public and publicly guaranteed debt service		Short-term debt	
		% of GNI	% of exports of goods and services	% of GNI		% of exports of goods and services		% of central government current revenue		% of total debt	
	2001	2001	2001	1990	2001	1990	2001	1990	2001	1990	2001
Honduras	M	51[b]	104[b]	13.7	5.4	33.0[b]	5.7[b]	..	..	5.4	6.5
Hungary	M	56	77	13.4	27.2	33.4	8.5	21.4	..	13.9	15.3
India	L	14	85	2.6	2.0	29.2	12.6	14.5	13.0	10.2	3.0
Indonesia	S	94	199	9.1	11.1	25.6	13.8	34.4	22.4	15.9	16.1
Iran, Islamic Rep.	L	6	26	0.5	1.1	1.3	4.1	0.3	..	80.1	27.0
Iraq	..	..	..	..	..	..	..	..	..	..	..
Ireland	..	..	..	..	..	..	..	..	..	..	..
Israel	..	..	..	..	..	..	..	..	..	..	..
Italy	..	..	..	..	..	..	..	..	..	..	..
Jamaica	M	73	119	15.9	8.8	27.0	16.8	..	21.6	7.4	17.7
Japan	..	..	..	..	..	..	..	..	..	..	..
Jordan	S	78	111	16.5	7.6	22.1	14.7	52.5	26.0	12.4	6.0
Kazakhstan	M	67	134	..	15.7	..	4.7	..	18.6	..	5.8
Kenya	M	39	146	9.8	4.1	28.6	11.4	26.6	..	13.2	11.9
Korea, Dem. Rep.	..	..	..	..	..	..	..	..	..	..	..
Korea, Rep.	..	..	..	3.3	6.2	6.3	7.1	10.5	..	30.9	31.9
Kuwait	..	..	..	..	..	..	..	..	..	..	..
Kyrgyz Republic	S	91	223	..	12.1	..	12.0	..	..	..	2.8
Lao PDR	S	77	268	1.1	2.6	8.5	9.0	..	..	0.1	0.1
Latvia	M	73	147	..	6.8	..	2.9	..	4.9	..	53.2
Lebanon	S	76	470	2.9	8.3	3.2	40.5	..	..	79.9	21.3
Lesotho	L	41	73	2.3	7.0	4.2	12.4	9.4	..	0.7	0.7
Liberia	S	436	1,321	..	0.2	..	0.6	..	..	22.2	34.9
Libya	..	..	..	..	..	..	..	..	..	..	..
Lithuania	L	44	83	..	16.4	..	5.9	..	11.1	..	29.7
Macedonia, FYR	L	35	78	..	5.7	..	10.3	..	..	..	4.8
Madagascar	S	45[b]	1,317[b]	7.5	1.5	44.4[b]	3.4[b]	42.9	..	6.1	5.7
Malawi	S	87[b]	296[b]	7.2	2.3	28.0[b]	15.5[b]	27.2	..	3.7	1.8
Malaysia	M	58	44	10.3	7.8	10.6	3.6	31.4	..	12.4	11.8
Mali	M	56[b]	154[b]	2.8	3.2	14.7[b]	4.5[b]	..	..	2.5	3.6
Mauritania	S	143[b,c]	359[b,c]	13.6	9.1	28.8[b,c]	16.5[b,c]	..	..	11.3	9.0
Mauritius	L	37	57	6.6	4.5	7.3	4.7	13.5	15.8	5.3	50.6
Mexico	L	29	93	4.5	8.1	18.3	14.1	19.5	..	15.4	11.4
Moldova	S	71	116	..	12.0	..	15.3	..	40.6	..	1.8
Mongolia	M	59	103	..	4.4	0.3	7.9	..	11.6	..	1.6
Morocco	L	44	100	7.2	7.9	27.9	21.9	21.3	..	1.7	1.5
Mozambique	L	28[b]	36[b]	3.4	2.6	17.3[b]	2.7[b]	..	..	7.4	11.2
Myanmar	S	..	150	..	..	8.8	2.8	2.2	..	4.9	11.7
Namibia	..	..	..	..	..	..	..	..	..	..	..
Nepal	L	27	86	1.9	1.5	14.7	6.2	18.2	13.5	1.5	1.8
Netherlands	..	..	..	..	..	..	..	..	..	..	..
New Zealand	..	..	..	..	..	..	..	..	..	..	..
Nicaragua	S	..	336[b]	1.6	..	2.3[b]	22.2[b]	2.6	..	22.6	10.5
Niger	S	53[b]	282[b]	4.1	1.3	6.6[b]	6.6[b]	..	..	8.9	2.7
Nigeria	S	81	144	13.0	6.7	22.3	11.5	..	..	4.5	5.5
Norway	..	..	..	..	..	..	..	..	..	..	..
Oman	L	..	50	7.8	..	12.0	6.8	17.4	14.7	12.3	21.0
Pakistan	S	44	222	4.9	5.1	25.1	21.3	18.1	23.1	15.4	4.1
Panama	S	94	99	6.8	12.2	4.1	11.2	10.4	..	36.6	5.6
Papua New Guinea	M	78	103	17.9	9.5	18.4	7.1	33.2	..	2.8	2.7
Paraguay	L	37	80	6.0	5.0	11.5	8.3	46.8	22.7	17.7	16.4
Peru	S	53	283	1.9	4.1	7.3	20.8	4.9	20.5	26.7	11.0
Philippines	M	73	132	8.1	10.3	25.6	13.3	39.5	49.4	14.5	11.6
Poland	L	34	108	1.7	8.8	4.4	11.5	..	11.4	19.4	11.2
Portugal	..	..	..	..	..	..	..	..	..	..	..
Puerto Rico	..	..	..	..	..	..	..	..	..	..	..

	Indebtedness classification [a]	Present value of debt % of GNI 2001	Present value of debt % of exports of goods and services 2001	Total debt service % of GNI 1990	Total debt service % of GNI 2001	Total debt service % of exports of goods and services 1990	Total debt service % of exports of goods and services 2001	Public and publicly guaranteed debt service % of central government current revenue 1990	Public and publicly guaranteed debt service % of central government current revenue 2001	Short-term debt % of total debt 1990	Short-term debt % of total debt 2001
Romania	L	29	80	0.0	6.8	0.0	13.7	0.0	16.4	79.8	4.5
Russian Federation [d]	M	49	123	2.0	5.8	..	12.0	..	12.0	19.9	13.7
Rwanda	S	40 [b]	411 [b]	0.8	1.1	10.6 [b]	7.6 [b]	5.4	..	6.6	2.8
Saudi Arabia	..	..	..	..	..	..	..	..	..	..	..
Senegal	M	53 [b]	150 [b]	5.9	4.7	18.3 [b]	9.3 [b]	..	20.0	11.3	5.8
Sierra Leone	S	114 [b]	888 [b]	3.7	13.1	10.1 [b]	74.3 [b]	45.4	..	12.4	1.9
Singapore	..	..	..	..	..	..	..	..	..	..	..
Slovak Republic	M	54	71	2.1	13.0	..	6.2	..	14.0	25.0	27.6
Slovenia	..	..	..	..	..	..	..	..	..	..	..
Somalia	S	..	..	1.3	..	14.6	..	..	..	12.0	23.5
South Africa	L	21	62	..	4.0	0.0	6.8	..	8.1	..	34.7
Spain	..	..	..	..	..	..	..	..	..	..	..
Sri Lanka	L	42	93	4.9	4.4	14.8	9.2	16.8	19.5	6.9	5.3
Sudan	S	130	591	0.4	0.5	4.8	3.2	..	..	28.1	37.9
Swaziland	L	23	29	4.9	2.2	5.6	2.5	15.8	..	1.9	23.5
Sweden	..	..	..	..	..	..	..	..	..	..	..
Switzerland	..	..	..	..	..	..	..	..	..	..	..
Syrian Arab Republic	S	111	266	9.9	1.4	20.3	2.1	21.2	..	12.5	25.8
Tajikistan	S	83	120	..	7.8	..	6.3	..	25.5	..	7.3
Tanzania [e]	L	14 [b]	91 [b]	4.4	1.6	31.3 [b]	7.3 [b]	..	..	8.1	8.3
Thailand	M	60	83	6.3	18.0	11.4	7.9	20.7	24.3	29.6	19.6
Togo	M	81	206	5.4	2.6	11.5	5.9	..	..	8.8	10.4
Trinidad and Tobago	L	31	53	9.7	2.8	15.6	3.8	..	..	5.1	35.5
Tunisia	M	57	103	12.0	7.1	25.6	13.4	32.2	..	8.2	6.3
Turkey	M	80	208	4.9	15.3	29.9	24.6	30.9	26.0	19.2	14.2
Turkmenistan	M	..	..	..	..	..	14.4	..	..	..	..
Uganda	M	21 [b]	162 [b]	3.4	0.9	56.9 [b]	9.7 [b]	..	4.9	5.4	4.1
Ukraine	L	31	54	..	6.1	..	6.5	..	8.2	..	5.8
United Arab Emirates	..	..	..	..	..	..	..	..	..	..	..
United Kingdom	..	..	..	..	..	..	..	..	..	..	..
United States	..	..	..	..	..	..	..	..	..	..	..
Uruguay	S	54	241	11.0	8.1	35.2	30.3	32.0	26.3	27.2	30.2
Uzbekistan	M	40	138	..	7.5	..	20.6	..	..	..	10.9
Venezuela, RB	L	30	122	10.6	6.1	19.6	20.9	36.2	23.1	6.0	10.8
Vietnam	L	33	60	2.9	3.7	..	6.5	..	17.2	7.7	6.2
West Bank and Gaza	..	..	..	..	..	..	..	..	..	..	..
Yemen, Rep.	L	41	61	3.5	3.4	7.1	6.3	..	..	18.8	10.5
Yugoslavia, Fed. Rep. [f]	S	108	260	..	1.0	..	2.0	..	..	2.9	41.2
Zambia	S	115 [b]	365 [b]	6.7	3.7	14.6 [b]	13.4 [b]	..	..	20.4	3.1
Zimbabwe	M	40	175	5.5	1.5	19.4	3.4	17.4	..	18.2	13.1
World				.. w	.. w	.. w	.. w			.. w	.. w
Low income				4.8	4.2	23.5	11.4			11.8	10.2
Middle income				3.9	6.9	17.0	11.3			18.2	16.4
Lower middle income				3.8	5.1	16.8	9.5			16.8	17.1
Upper middle income				4.0	8.9	17.1	13.7			19.8	15.7
Low & middle income				4.1	6.4	18.2	11.4			16.3	15.0
East Asia & Pacific				4.8	4.7	14.5	6.1			16.1	18.4
Europe & Central Asia				2.9	9.8	18.9	11.4			18.2	15.2
Latin America & Carib.				4.2	8.7	20.5	19.4			16.3	12.6
Middle East & N. Africa				5.1	3.2	23.5	11.3			24.1	23.6
South Asia				2.9	2.3	27.6	12.9			9.6	3.2
Sub-Saharan Africa				..	4.5	11.6	9.0			11.6	15.8
High income											
Europe EMU											

a. S = severely indebted, M = moderately indebted, L = less indebted. b. Data are from debt sustainability analyses undertaken as part of the Debt Initiative for Heavily Indebted Poor Countries (HIPCs). Present value estimates for these countries are for public and publicly guaranteed debt only, and export figures exclude workers' remittances. c. Enhanced HIPC assistance will be accounted for in the World Bank's *Global Development Finance 2004*. d. Data for 1990 are for the debt of the former Soviet Union on the assumption that 100 percent of all outstanding external debt as of December 1991 has become a liability of the Russian Federation. e. Data refer to mainland Tanzania only. f. Data for 1990 are for the former Socialist Federal Republic of Yugoslavia. Data for 2001 are estimates and reflect borrowings by the former socialist Federal Republic of Yugoslavia that are not yet allocated to the successor republics.

About the data

The indicators in the table measure the relative burden on developing countries of servicing external debt. The present value of external debt provides a measure of future debt service obligations that can be compared with the current value of such indicators as gross national income (GNI), and exports of goods and services. The table shows the present value of total debt service both as a percentage of GNI in 2001 and as a percentage of exports in 2001. The ratios compare total debt service obligations with the size of the economy and its ability to obtain foreign exchange through exports. The ratios shown here may differ from those published elsewhere because estimates of exports and GNI have been revised to incorporate data available as of February 1, 2003. The ratio of total debt service to exports reflects adjustments made to countries receiving debt relief under the Debt Initiative for Heavily Indebted Poor Countries (HIPCs).

The present value of external debt is calculated by discounting the debt service (interest plus amortization) due on long-term external debt over the life of existing loans. Short-term debt is included at its face value. The data on debt are in U.S. dollars converted at official exchange rates (see *About the data* for table 4.16). The discount rate applied to long-term debt is determined by the currency of repayment of the loan and is based on reference rates for commercial interest established by the Organisation for Economic Co-operation and Development. Loans from the International Bank for Reconstruction and Development (IBRD) and credits from the International Development Association (IDA) are discounted using an SDR (special drawing rights) reference rate, as are obligations to the International Monetary Fund (IMF). When the discount rate is greater than the interest rate of the loan, the present value is less than the nominal sum of future debt service obligations.

The ratios in the table are used to assess the sustainability of a country's debt service obligations, but there are no absolute rules that determine what values are too high. Empirical analysis of the experience of developing countries and their debt service performance has shown that debt service difficulties become increasingly likely when the ratio of the present value of debt to exports reaches 200 percent. Still, what constitutes a sustainable debt burden varies from one country to another. Countries with fast-growing economies and exports are likely to be able to sustain higher debt levels.

The World Bank classifies countries by their level of indebtedness for the purpose of developing debt management strategies. The most severely indebted countries may be eligible for debt relief under special programs, such as the HIPC Debt Initiative. Indebted countries may also apply to the Paris and London Clubs for renegotiation of obligations to public and private creditors. In 2001 countries with a present value of debt service greater than 220 percent of exports or 80 percent of GNI were classified as severely indebted; countries that were not severely indebted but whose present value of debt service exceeded 132 percent of exports or 48 percent of GNI were classified as moderately indebted; and countries that did not fall into the above two groups were classified as less indebted.

Definitions

• **Indebtedness** is assessed on a three-point scale: severely indebted (S), moderately indebted (M), and less indebted (L). • **Present value of debt** is the sum of short-term external debt plus the discounted sum of total debt service payments due on public, publicly guaranteed, and private nonguaranteed long-term external debt over the life of existing loans. • **Total debt service** is the sum of principal repayments and interest actually paid in foreign currency, goods, or services on long-term debt; interest paid on short-term debt; and repayments (repurchases and charges) to the IMF. • **Public and publicly guaranteed debt service** is the sum of principal repayments and interest actually paid on long-term obligations of public debtors and long-term private obligations guaranteed by a public entity. • **Short-term debt** includes all debt having an original maturity of one year or less and interest in arrears on long-term debt.

Data sources

The main sources of external debt information are reports to the World Bank through its Debtor Reporting System from member countries that have received IBRD loans or IDA credits. Additional information has been drawn from the files of the World Bank and the IMF. The data on GNI and exports of goods and services are from the World Bank's national accounts files and the IMF's Balance of Payments database. Summary tables of the external debt of developing countries are published annually in the World Bank's *Global Development Finance* and on its *Global Development Finance* CD-ROM.

5 | STATES AND MARKETS

States and markets have intertwining roles—and both are needed for a healthy economy. In countries whose public and private sectors have balanced and complementary roles, the economy has grown, poverty has declined, and the quality of life has improved. There is no "right" size for government, because each country has a unique history and culture and different starting points and objectives. More important than the size of government is its effectiveness. If public institutions function poorly and governance is weak, the private sector will be stifled, investment will be deterred, and growth and equitable development will falter.

This section covers a broad range of indicators showing how effective and accountable government—combined with energetic private initiative—produces employment opportunities and services that empower the poor. Its 12 tables cover three cross-cutting development themes: private sector development, public sector policies, and infrastructure, information, and telecommunications.

Creating the conditions for private sector development

Private firms generate jobs and bring growth to the entire economy, the biggest factor in reducing poverty. But to do so they need a sound investment climate—with good macroeconomic management, trade and investment policies that promote openness, and good-quality infrastructure and services. They also need a legal and regulatory system that supports the day-to-day operations of firms by protecting property rights, promoting access to credit, and ensuring efficient tax, customs, and judicial services.

Investment in infrastructure—whether in power, transport, housing, telecommunications, or water and sanitation—enables businesses to grow. And when private firms participate in infrastructure, bringing with them capital and know-how, they can improve access to basic infrastructure services, a key to reducing poverty. In developing countries private firms participate mainly in telecommunications and energy. From 1996 to 2001 investment in telecommunications projects with private participation totaled about $60 billion in Brazil and more than $17 billion in the Republic of Korea. Investment in energy projects with private participation in the 1990s increased dramatically in Brazil (from $0.6 billion in 1990–95 to $42 billion in 1996–2001), Peru (from $1.2 billion to $2.8 billion), and in Turkey ($2.5 billion to $4.8 billion; table 5.1).

Telecommunications has received the largest share of investment in projects with private participation (44 percent of the total in 1990–2001), with water and sanitation, considered a "basic needs" sector, receiving only a small fraction (5 percent). Private participation in infrastructure was initially concentrated in a few countries, with the top 10 accounting for 98 percent of investment in 1990, but by 2001 their share had fallen to 67 percent. Private participation in infrastructure has many of the same advantages and risks as public investment financed though foreign borrowing (see tables 5.9–5.11).

Part of what determines the business environment in a country is the regulation of new entry. Countries differ significantly in the obstacles they impose on the entry of new businesses. To meet government requirements for starting a business in Mozambique, for instance, entrepreneurs must complete 16 procedures, a process that takes an average of 214 business days and costs the equivalent of 74 percent of gross national income (GNI) per capita. In Italy they must complete 13 procedures, wait 62 business days on average, and pay 23 percent of GNI per capita. But Canada requires only 2 procedures, and the process takes only two days and costs about 1 percent of GNI per capita (table 5.3).

The case for creating a good investment climate is simple: an economy needs a predictable environment in which people, ideas, and money can work together productively and efficiently. Countries should focus on improving the investment climate for domestic entrepreneurs, but a better investment climate will also attract foreign investors. And countries that receive more foreign investment—an important conduit for new technologies, management experience, and access to markets—enjoy faster growth and greater poverty reduction.

External perceptions of the investment climate are reflected in risk ratings. While risk ratings do not always capture the actual situation or specific investment opportunities in a country, they are a reality that policymakers face. Among such ratings are the Euromoney creditworthiness ratings, which rank the risk of investing in an economy from 0 (high risk) to 100 (low risk). Countries with high risk, such as Kenya (36) and Haiti (24), have very low foreign direct investment (0.4 percent of gross capital formation for Kenya and 0.3 percent for Haiti). By contrast, countries with low perceived risk, such as Chile (65) and the Czech Republic (66), have much higher levels of foreign direct investment (about 33 percent for Chile and 29 percent for the Czech Republic; table 5.2). Countries with low risk ratings also have large stock markets relative to gross domestic product (GDP). Market capitalization is about 85 percent of GDP in Chile, 102 percent in Australia, 135 percent in Malaysia, 137 percent in Singapore, and 158 percent in Finland (table 5.4).

Designing public sector policies to enhance private activity

The public sector's main economic functions fit into three broad categories: making policy, delivering services, and providing oversight and accountability. As global competition has increased in the past two decades, the governments of many developing countries have shifted their focus from trying to preserve jobs in a stagnant public sector to creating jobs in a vibrant private sector. Governments are now in the business of designing and implementing good policies and strong institutions that enhance the business and investment climate.

Government functions and policies affect many areas of social and economic life: health and education, natural resources and environmental protection, fiscal and monetary stability, and flows of trade. Data related to these topics are presented in the respective sections. This section provides data on key public sector activities: tax policy, exchange rates, and defense expenditures (tables 5.6–5.8).

Taxes are the main source of revenue for many governments. They are levied mainly on income, profits, capital gains, goods and services, and exports and imports. (Nontax revenue is also important in some economies; see table 4.13.) A comparison of taxation levels across countries provides an overview of the fiscal obligations and incentives facing the private sector. Central government tax revenues (excluding state and local taxes) range from about 3 percent of GDP in Kuwait and 7 percent in Bangladesh to 35 percent in Austria and 36 percent in Slovenia (table 5.6).

Investment in infrastructure projects with private participation grew dramatically in developing countries in the 1990s

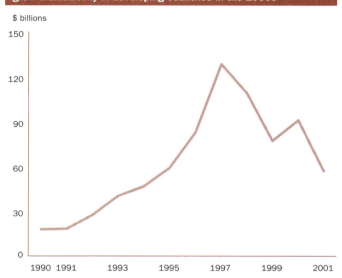

$ billions

In 1990–2001 the private sector took over the operating or construction risk, or both, for almost 2,500 infrastructure projects in developing countries. Latin America and the Caribbean led the developing regions in private participation in infrastructure, capturing almost 50 percent of the total investment in 1990–2001.

Source: World Bank, Private Participation in Infrastructure (PPI) Project Database.

The level and progressivity of taxes on personal and corporate income influence incentives to work and invest. Marginal tax rates on individual income range from 0 percent (in countries such as Kuwait, Oman, Paraguay, the United Arab Emirates, and Uruguay) to 50 percent or more (in such countries as Austria, Belgium, the Democratic Republic of Congo, Denmark, the Islamic Republic of Iran, and Senegal). Most marginal tax rates on corporate income are in the 20–30 percent range (table 5.6).

Tapping the benefits of infrastructure, information, and telecommunications

High-quality infrastructure and other business services help determine the success of manufacturing and agricultural businesses. Investments in water, sanitation, energy, housing, and transport improve health and education and help reduce poverty. And new information and communications technologies offer vast opportunities for economic growth, improved health, better service delivery, learning through distance education, and social and cultural advances.

Until the 1990s public sector monopolies in most developing countries financed and operated the infrastructure, often with poor results. Technical inefficiencies in roads, power, water, and railways caused losses of $55 billion a year in the

early 1990s—about 1 percent of all developing countries' GDP. But beginning in the late 1980s countries around the world had begun turning to the private sector, both to take over the operation of existing infrastructure and to finance new infrastructure. In 1990–2001 infrastructure projects with private participation in developing countries attracted more than $750 billion in investment (figure 5a).

Efficient transport is critical to the development of competitive economies, but measuring progress in transport is difficult. Data for most transport sectors are often not strictly comparable across countries that do not consistently follow common definitions and specifications. Moreover, the data do not indicate the quality and level of service, which depend on such factors as maintenance budgets, the availability of trained personnel, geographic and climatic conditions, and incentives and competition to provide the best service at the lowest cost.

About 43 percent of the world's roads are paved, but the share ranges from only about 16 percent in low-income economies to 92 percent in high-income economies. Sub-Saharan Africa scores the lowest among regions, with only about 13 percent of roads paved, while developing countries in Europe and Central Asia, with 91 percent, are almost on a par with high-income economies (table 5.9).

Telecommunications services are improving in quality, accessibility, and affordability around the world, thanks to competition in the marketplace accompanied by sound regulation. Globally, there are 172 fixed telephone mainlines for every 1,000 people, but large differences remain between low-income economies (around 30 per 1,000) and high-income economies (around 600 per 1,000). And within countries there are often stark differences in access between the largest city and the average for the country. In Sri Lanka, for example, there are about 300 telephone mainlines for every 1,000 residents in Colombo, while the average for the country is only 44 per 1,000. In many countries people are turning to mobile phones. In Latin America, at 161 per 1,000 people, mobile phones are almost as numerous as fixed line telephones (165 per 1,000 people; table 5.10).

Essential to building a knowledge economy is ensuring access for all to computers and the Internet. The digital divide between rich and poor economies—the gap in access to information and communications technology—remains wide, with high-income economies having 416 personal computers per 1,000 people and low-income economies only 6 per 1,000. Even so, ownership of personal computers is growing twice as fast in developing as in high-income economies. Large gaps also exist among developing regions, with developing countries in Europe and Central Asia having about 52 personal computers per 1,000 people, but South Asia only about 5 (table 5.11).

5.1 Private sector development

	Domestic credit to private sector		Investment in infrastructure projects with private participation [a]							
	% of GDP		Telecommunications $ millions		Energy $ millions		Transport $ millions		Water and sanitation $ millions	
	1990	2001	1990–95	1996–2001	1990–95	1996–2001	1990–95	1996–2001	1990–95	1996–2001
Afghanistan	..	..	..	..	..	..	..	..	..	..
Albania	..	5.9	..	165.2	..	..	..	..	..	..
Algeria	44.4	8.0	..	..	..	..	..	..	..	..
Angola	..	3.5	..	68.0	..	..	..	..	..	..
Argentina	15.6	20.8	11,907.0	11,841.3	12,035.1	12,048.2	5,989.1	8,363.8	5,166.0	3,071.5
Armenia	40.4	8.3	..	442.0	..	..	..	50.0	..	..
Australia	64.3	89.8	..	..	..	..	..	..	..	..
Austria	91.6	106.9	..	..	..	..	..	..	..	..
Azerbaijan	10.8	5.0	14.0	144.6	..	230.0	..	..	..	..
Bangladesh	16.7	26.7	146.0	533.5	..	1,040.2	..	..	..	..
Belarus	..	8.4	10.0	40.0	..	500.0	..	..	..	..
Belgium	37.0	77.1	..	..	..	..	..	..	..	..
Benin	20.3	11.1	..	90.4	..	..	..	..	..	..
Bolivia	24.0	54.5	38.0	692.4	252.4	518.2	..	163.2	..	682.0
Bosnia and Herzegovina	..	..	..	..	..	..	..	..	..	..
Botswana	9.4	16.2	..	80.0	..	..	..	..	..	..
Brazil	38.9	34.7	..	60,485.5	614.6	42,036.2	1,230.8	18,515.7	155.3	2,750.0
Bulgaria	7.2	14.3	64.0	396.4	..	..	..	..	..	152.0
Burkina Faso	19.0	13.6	..	35.6	..	5.6	..	..	..	..
Burundi	13.7	22.4	0.5	15.6	..	..	..	..	..	..
Cambodia	..	7.0	31.6	115.3	..	123.0	120.0	65.0	..	..
Cameroon	26.7	9.6	..	266.1	..	70.4	30.8	95.0	..	..
Canada	75.9	80.8	..	..	..	..	..	..	..	..
Central African Republic	7.2	4.9	1.1	..	..	..	..	..	0.7	..
Chad	7.3	3.7	..	11.6	..	..	..	..	..	..
Chile	47.2	65.9	148.9	1,190.9	2,260.0	4,857.3	539.9	4,639.0	67.5	3,886.7
China	87.7	127.2	..	5,970.0	6,113.5	14,110.2	6,219.8	14,666.8	104.0	613.4
Hong Kong, China	165.1	155.9	..	..	..	..	..	..	..	..
Colombia	30.8	25.1	1,551.2	1,298.3	1,813.2	5,762.2	1,008.8	1,556.9	..	272.0
Congo, Dem. Rep.	1.8	..	..	228.7	..	..	..	..	..	..
Congo, Rep.	15.7	5.0	4.6	104.9	..	325.0	..	..	..	..
Costa Rica	15.8	28.1	10.0	274.5	76.3	243.1	..	161.0	..	..
Côte d'Ivoire	36.5	15.9	..	827.4	147.2	223.0	..	178.0	..	..
Croatia	..	41.5	..	1,425.5	..	368.5	..	672.2	..	298.7
Cuba	..	..	371.0	..	..	165.0	..	..	..	600.0
Czech Republic	..	44.4	876.0	7,427.3	356.0	944.1	263.7	126.7	36.5	261.3
Denmark	52.2	141.8	..	..	..	..	..	..	..	..
Dominican Republic	27.5	38.0	10.0	274.5	372.5	1,536.3	..	833.9	..	..
Ecuador	13.2	32.7	51.2	692.8	..	310.0	12.5	686.8	..	550.0
Egypt, Arab Rep.	30.6	61.6	..	2,550.0	..	1,378.0	..	1,057.2	..	..
El Salvador	20.1	41.6	..	701.5	106.0	879.2	..	..	..	..
Eritrea	..	..	..	..	..	..	..	..	..	..
Estonia	20.2	27.3	211.7	629.0	..	26.5	..	299.4	..	81.0
Ethiopia	19.5	27.5	..	..	..	..	..	..	..	..
Finland	86.7	57.7	..	..	..	..	..	..	..	..
France	96.1	89.8	..	..	..	..	..	..	..	..
Gabon	13.0	11.8	..	26.0	..	624.8	..	46.7	..	..
Gambia, The	11.0	14.7	..	..	..	..	..	..	..	..
Georgia	..	7.6	21.6	43.8	..	36.0	..	..	..	..
Germany	89.7	121.0	..	..	..	..	..	..	..	..
Ghana	4.9	14.1	25.0	436.1	..	60.0	..	10.0	..	..
Greece	36.3	63.6	..	..	..	..	..	..	..	..
Guatemala	14.2	20.4	20.0	1,443.3	134.8	1,238.4	..	33.8	..	..
Guinea	3.5	3.8	45.0	75.3	36.4	..	..	..	..	..
Guinea-Bissau	22.0	3.0	..	..	23.2	..	..	..	..	..
Haiti	12.6	15.0	..	1.5	..	..	..	..	..	..

Private sector development

5.1

	Domestic credit to private sector		Investment in infrastructure projects with private participation [a]							
			Telecommunications $ millions		Energy $ millions		Transport $ millions		Water and sanitation $ millions	
	% of GDP									
	1990	2001	1990–95	1996–2001	1990–95	1996–2001	1990–95	1996–2001	1990–95	1996–2001
Honduras	31.1	41.3	..	38.1	95.3	86.8	..	130.5	..	220.0
Hungary	46.6	33.8	3,510.9	5,298.9	2,156.7	1,906.1	1,004.0	135.0	2.9	167.6
India	25.2	29.1	722.9	10,511.2	2,888.5	9,582.0	126.9	1,448.8	..	216.0
Indonesia	46.9	20.5	3,549.0	7,780.0	3,202.5	7,347.1	1,204.9	1,728.0	3.8	882.8
Iran, Islamic Rep.	32.5	33.4	5.0	23.0	..	..	..	..	..	..
Iraq	..	..	..	..	..	..	..	..	..	..
Ireland	47.6	111.8	..	..	..	..	..	..	..	..
Israel	57.6	96.4	..	..	..	..	..	..	..	..
Italy	56.5	80.0	..	..	..	..	..	..	..	..
Jamaica	36.1	12.8	..	389.0	289.0	201.0	30.0	..	..	..
Japan	195.2	186.7	..	..	..	..	..	..	..	..
Jordan	72.3	75.5	43.0	732.9	..	..	..	182.0	..	55.0
Kazakhstan	..	15.8	30.0	1,849.5	..	2,125.0	..	..	..	40.0
Kenya	32.8	24.6	..	107.0	..	171.5	..	53.4	..	..
Korea, Dem. Rep.	..	..	..	..	..	..	..	..	..	..
Korea, Rep.	65.5	108.0	2,649.0	17,559.3	..	2,688.2	2,276.0	5,945.7		
Kuwait	52.1	69.4	..	..	..	..	..	..		
Kyrgyz Republic	..	3.8	..	94.0	..	..	..	..	..	..
Lao PDR	1.0	9.6	..	175.1	..	535.5	..	..	..	..
Latvia	..	23.2	230.0	817.8	..	177.1	..	75.0	..	..
Lebanon	79.4	90.9	100.0	273.0	..	..	..	200.0	..	..
Lesotho	15.6	13.7	..	33.5	..	..	..	..	..	..
Liberia	30.9	3.5	..	..	..	..	..	..	..	..
Libya	31.0	23.7	..	..	..	..	..	..	..	..
Lithuania	..	11.5	76.0	1,294.8	..	20.0	..	..	..	..
Macedonia, FYR	..	17.7	..	607.3	..	..	..	..	..	..
Madagascar	16.9	9.2	5.0	10.1	..	..	..	20.3	..	..
Malawi	10.9	6.8	8.0	24.5	..	..	..	6.0	..	..
Malaysia	69.4	149.2	2,630.0	2,603.3	6,909.5	2,121.1	4,657.6	7,603.2	3,986.7	1,105.5
Mali	12.8	17.8	..	..	0.1	697.3	..	..	..	..
Mauritania	43.5	27.1	..	99.6	..	..	..	..	..	..
Mauritius	35.6	62.7	..	261.0	..	109.3	..	42.6	..	..
Mexico	17.5	11.5	18,031.0	14,774.7	1.0	4,575.1	7,906.3	5,431.5	312.1	331.5
Moldova	5.9	14.8	..	84.6	..	85.3	..	..	..	..
Mongolia	19.0	12.2	8.6	20.2	..	..	..	..	..	..
Morocco	34.0	54.0	..	3,643.0	2,300.0	5,819.9	..	..	..	..
Mozambique	17.6	2.5	..	29.0	..	..	..	432.0	..	0.6
Myanmar	4.7	12.1	4.0	..	..	..	..	50.0	..	..
Namibia	19.0	47.3	18.0	4.0	..	5.0	..	..	..	..
Nepal	12.8	31.8	..	35.2	131.4	137.2	..	..	..	..
Netherlands	80.0	142.6	..	..	..	..	..	..	..	..
New Zealand	76.0	115.7	..	..	..	..	..	..	..	..
Nicaragua	112.6	..	9.9	54.2	..	347.4	..	104.0	..	..
Niger	12.3	4.6	..	18.0	..	..	..	..	..	..
Nigeria	9.4	17.8	..	968.7	..	225.0	..	..	..	..
Norway	82.2	82.8	..	..	..	..	..	..	..	..
Oman	22.9	36.9	..	..	204.5	728.3	..	106.1	..	..
Pakistan	27.7	28.4	602.0	173.0	3,417.3	2,519.7	299.6	118.7	..	..
Panama	46.7	126.0	..	1,429.2	..	1,064.9	409.9	806.0	..	25.0
Papua New Guinea	28.6	16.0	..	..	..	65.0	..	..	..	175.0
Paraguay	15.8	25.9	48.1	204.4	..	..	..	58.0	..	..
Peru	11.8	24.3	2,568.7	5,224.5	1,207.7	2,817.4	6.6	240.8	..	56.0
Philippines	22.3	40.1	1,279.0	5,528.6	6,831.3	6,943.1	300.0	1,966.8	..	5,846.1
Poland	3.1	25.5	479.0	10,806.5	145.0	1,503.6	3.1	705.9	..	22.1
Portugal	49.1	146.2	..	..	..	..	..	..	..	..
Puerto Rico	..	..	..	..	..	..	..	..	..	..

5.1 Private sector development

| | Domestic credit to private sector | | Investment in infrastructure projects with private participation [a] | | | | | | | |
| | % of GDP | | Telecommunications $ millions | | Energy $ millions | | Transport $ millions | | Water and sanitation $ millions | |
	1990	2001	1990–95	1996–2001	1990–95	1996–2001	1990–95	1996–2001	1990–95	1996–2001
Romania	..	7.8	5.0	2,326.3	..	100.0	..	23.4	..	1,025.0
Russian Federation	..	15.4	918.0	6,216.8	1,100.0	2,281.3	..	515.4	..	108.0
Rwanda	6.9	10.2	..	15.6	..	..	..	..	..	..
Saudi Arabia	61.0	55.0	..	..	..	..	..	..	..	..
Senegal	26.5	19.4	..	406.8	..	124.0	..	..	..	3.7
Sierra Leone	3.2	2.3	..	20.5	..	..	..	..	..	..
Singapore	97.4	128.4	..	..	..	..	..	..	..	..
Slovak Republic	..	25.5	118.6	1,656.0	..	..	..	..	..	..
Slovenia	34.9	40.0	..	..	..	..	..	..	..	..
Somalia	..	..	..	..	..	..	..	..	..	..
South Africa	81.0	148.5	1,072.8	8,537.7	3.0	44.3	..	1,874.1	..	212.5
Spain	80.1	105.9	..	..	..	..	..	..	..	..
Sri Lanka	19.6	28.3	43.6	727.9	21.7	286.6	..	240.0	..	..
Sudan	4.8	3.1	..	6.0	..	..	..	..	..	..
Swaziland	20.7	13.1	..	12.0	..	..	..	..	..	..
Sweden	128.4	45.7	..	..	..	..	..	..	..	..
Switzerland	167.9	158.5	..	..	..	..	..	..	..	..
Syrian Arab Republic	7.5	8.1	..	130.0	..	..	..	..	..	..
Tajikistan	..	22.9	..	1.0	..	..	..	..	..	..
Tanzania	13.9	4.9	30.1	321.0	6.0	490.0	..	23.0	..	..
Thailand	83.4	97.5	4,814.0	3,679.1	2,059.6	6,445.5	2,395.9	499.4	153.0	347.5
Togo	22.6	14.9	..	5.0	..	..	..	..	..	..
Trinidad and Tobago	44.7	41.8	47.0	146.7	..	207.0	..	..	..	120.0
Tunisia	55.1	67.9	..	..	627.0	265.0	..	..	..	..
Turkey	16.7	20.6	190.3	7,875.4	2,478.0	4,807.2	..	724.8	..	942.0
Turkmenistan	..	2.3	..	..	..	..	..	..	..	..
Uganda	4.0	5.9	8.8	200.1	..	..	..	..	..	..
Ukraine	2.6	13.2	100.6	1,299.9	..	160.0	..	..	..	..
United Arab Emirates	37.4	..	..	..	..	..	..	..	..	..
United Kingdom	115.8	138.8	..	..	..	..	..	..	..	..
United States	93.5	145.8	..	..	..	..	..	..	..	..
Uruguay	32.4	53.9	19.0	57.7	86.0	160.0	96.0	154.1	10.0	351.0
Uzbekistan	..	..	2.5	357.4	..	..	..	..	..	..
Venezuela, RB	25.4	12.0	4,603.3	5,956.7	..	133.0	100.0	268.0	..	40.0
Vietnam	2.5	39.0	..	..	..	435.5	10.0	85.0	..	212.8
West Bank and Gaza	..	..	65.0	90.0	..	150.0	..	..	..	..
Yemen, Rep.	6.1	6.1	25.0	..	..	..	..	190.0	..	..
Yugoslavia, Fed. Rep.	..	..	..	1,929.5	..	..	..	..	..	..
Zambia	8.9	7.2	..	48.4	..	289.4	..	..	..	..
Zimbabwe	23.0	25.8	..	46.0	..	600.0	18.0	70.0	..	..
World	**97.4 w**	**120.7 w**	.. s	.. s	.. s	.. s	.. s	.. s	.. s	.. s
Low income	26.6	24.1	..	26,396.0	..	..	..	..	..	..
Middle income	43.2	57.9	..	192,659.4	..	132,926.4	..	..	..	..
Lower middle income	61.1	79.8	13,327.0	64,152.6	..	59,045.9	..	..	..	..
Upper middle income	32.5	32.9	..	128,506.8	..	73,880.4	..	..	..	..
Low & middle income	39.6	52.1	..	219,055.4	..	..	..	..	..	..
East Asia & Pacific	73.6	110.3	..	..	..	..	..	..	..	..
Europe & Central Asia	..	21.0	6,858.2	53,229.5	..	15,270.7	..	..	..	..
Latin America & Carib.	28.6	24.4	39,489.4	106,928.4	..	79,288.0	..	42,147.0	..	..
Middle East & N. Africa	41.2	47.1	..	..	..	..	..	..	..	..
South Asia	24.6	28.8	..	11,980.8	..	13,565.7	..	..	..	..
Sub-Saharan Africa	42.5	65.2	..	13,465.2	..	..	..	..	..	..
High income	107.7	137.4	..	..	..	..	..	..	..	..
Europe EMU	79.5	102.8	..	..	..	..	..	..	..	..

a. Data refer to total for the period shown.

Private sector development—that is, tapping private sector initiative for socially useful purposes—is critical for poverty reduction. In parallel with public sector efforts, private initiative, especially in competitive markets, has tremendous potential to contribute to growth. Private markets serve as the engine of productivity growth, creating productive jobs and higher incomes. And with government playing a complementary role of regulation, funding, and provision of services, private initiative can help provide the basic services and conditions that empower the poor—by improving health, education, and infrastructure.

Credit is an important link in the money transmission process; it finances production, consumption, and capital formation, which in turn affects the level of economic activity. The data on domestic credit to the private sector are taken from the banking survey of the International Monetary Fund's (IMF) *International Financial Statistics* or, when data are unavailable, from its monetary survey. The monetary survey includes monetary authorities (the central bank) and deposit money banks. In addition to these, the banking survey includes other banking institutions, such as finance companies, development banks, and savings and loan institutions. In some cases credit to the private sector may include credit to state-owned or partially state-owned enterprises.

Private participation in infrastructure has made important contributions to easing fiscal constraints, improving the efficiency of infrastructure services, and extending their delivery to poor people. The privatization trend in infrastructure that began in the 1970s and 1980s took off in the 1990s. Developing countries have been at the head of this wave, pioneering better approaches to providing infrastructure

services and reaping the benefits of greater competition and customer focus. In 1990–2001 more than 130 developing countries introduced private participation in at least one infrastructure sector, awarding almost 2,500 projects attracting investment commitments of $750 billion.

The data on investment in infrastructure projects with private participation refer to all investment (public and private) in projects in which a private company assumes operating risk during the operating period or assumes development and operating risk during the contract period. Foreign state-owned companies are considered private entities for the purposes of this measure. The data are from the World Bank's Private Participation in Infrastructure (PPI) Project Database, which tracks almost 2,500 projects, newly owned or managed by private companies, that reached financial closure in low- and middle-income economies in 1990–2001. For more information, go to http://www.worldbank.org/privatesector/ppi/ppi_database.htm.

• **Domestic credit to private sector** refers to financial resources provided to the private sector—such as through loans, purchases of nonequity securities, and trade credits and other accounts receivable—that establish a claim for repayment. For some countries these claims include credit to public enterprises. • **Investment in infrastructure projects with private participation** covers infrastructure projects in telecommunications, energy (electricity and natural gas transmission and distribution), transport, and water and sanitation that have reached financial closure and directly or indirectly serve the public. Incinerators, movable assets, stand-alone solid waste projects, and small projects such as windmills are excluded. The types of projects included are operation and management contracts, operation and management contracts with major capital expenditure, greenfield projects (in which a private entity or a public-private joint venture builds and operates a new facility), and divestiture.

5.1a

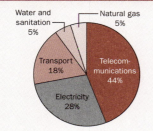

Source: World Bank, Private Participation in Infrastructure (PPI) Project Database.

The data on domestic credit are from the IMF's *International Financial Statistics*. The data on investment in infrastructure projects with private participation are from the World Bank's Private Participation in Infrastructure (PPI) Project Database (http://www.worldbank.org/privatesector/ppi/ppi_database.htm).

5.2 Investment climate

	Foreign direct investment		Entry and exit regulations [a]			Composite ICRG risk rating [b]	Institutional Investor credit rating [b]	Euromoney country credit-worthiness rating [b]	Moody's sovereign long-term debt rating [b]		Standard & Poor's sovereign long-term debt rating [b]	
	% of gross capital formation		Entry	Repatriation of					Foreign currency	Domestic currency	Foreign currency	Domestic currency
				income	capital	December	September	September	January	January	January	January
	1990	2001	2001	2001	2001	2002	2002	2002	2003	2003	2003	2003
Afghanistan	..	..	..	..	..	..	6.9	1.6	..	..	..	..
Albania	0.0	25.9	..	..	..	67.3	15.9	32.1	..	..	..	..
Algeria	0.0	8.2	..	..	..	63.8	31.5	40.8	..	..	..	..
Angola	−27.9	34.8	..	..	..	53.8	14.0	23.6	..	..	..	..
Argentina	9.3	8.5	F	F	F	48.0	15.8	27.1	Ca	Ca	SD	SD
Armenia	..	17.7	..	..	..	60.3	..	32.8	..	..	..	..
Australia	11.7	14.0	..	..	..	82.5	84.5	90.4	Aaa	Aaa	AA+	AAA
Austria	1.6	13.6	..	..	..	86.8	90.7	93.0	Aaa	Aaa	AAA	AAA
Azerbaijan	..	19.4	..	..	..	67.3	26.8	42.7	..	..	..	..
Bangladesh	0.1	0.7	F	F	F	61.3	27.3	38.5	..	..	..	..
Belarus	..	3.5	..	..	..	61.5	13.8	29.8	..	..	..	..
Belgium	13.5	18.2	..	..	..	84.3	89.5	91.0	Aa1	Aa1	AA+	AA+
Benin	23.8	28.8	..	..	..	..	20.1	28.1	..	..	..	..
Bolivia	4.5	64.1	..	..	..	65.8	30.9	44.0	B1	B1	B+	B+
Bosnia and Herzegovina	..	18.9	..	..	..	..	..	24.4	..	..	..	..
Botswana	6.8	5.0	F	F	F	79.3	59.0	64.7	A2	A1	A	A+
Brazil	1.1	21.5	F	F	F	62.3	39.0	42.6	B2	B2	B+	BB
Bulgaria	0.1	25.1	F	F	F	70.8	40.7	49.3	B1	B1	BB	BB+
Burkina Faso	0.0	4.0	..	..	..	58.3	18.8	30.2	..	..	..	..
Burundi	0.8	0.0	..	..	..	..	11.3	20.5	..	..	..	..
Cambodia	0.0	18.6	..	..	..	..	19.6	28.1	..	..	..	..
Cameroon	−5.7	5.0	..	..	..	62.0	19.7	29.6	..	..	..	..
Canada	6.2	20.2	..	..	..	84.8	89.4	91.9	Aaa	Aaa	AAA	AAA
Central African Republic	0.4	5.7	..	..	..	..	..	23.0	..	..	..	..
Chad	3.2	12.0	..	..	..	..	14.8	23.5	..	..	..	..
Chile	8.7	32.6	F	F	F	76.8	66.1	64.5	Baa1	A1	A−	AA
China	2.8	10.1	S	F	F	75.0	58.9	56.4	A3	..	BBB	..
Hong Kong, China	..	54.7	..	..	..	84.3	67.7	81.6	A3	Aa3	A+	AA−
Colombia	6.7	18.9	A	F	F	60.8	38.7	47.4	Ba2	Baa2	BB	BBB
Congo, Dem. Rep.	−1.7	12.1	..	..	..	47.3	8.7	14.1	..	..	..	..
Congo, Rep.	1.5	7.9	..	..	..	60.8	10.5	26.0	..	..	..	..
Costa Rica	10.4	15.5	..	..	..	73.5	46.2	51.7	Ba1	Ba1	BB	BB+
Côte d'Ivoire	6.7	23.9	F	F	F	51.8	18.5	30.0	..	..	..	..
Croatia	..	31.4	F	F	F	72.3	48.3	59.7	Baa3	Baa1	BBB−	BBB+
Cuba	..	..	..	..	..	62.5	15.7	13.3	Caa1	..	..	..
Czech Republic	0.8	28.9	F	F	F	76.3	64.0	65.6	A1	A1	A−	A+
Denmark	4.2	21.2	..	..	..	87.8	90.5	96.0	Aaa	Aaa	AAA	AAA
Dominican Republic	7.5	24.2	..	..	..	67.3	38.1	47.3	Ba2	Ba2	BB−	BB−
Ecuador	6.7	29.6	F	F	F	60.8	22.5	30.3	Caa2	Caa1	CCC+	CCC+
Egypt, Arab Rep.	5.9	3.3	F	F	F	67.5	45.5	50.3	Ba1	Baa1	BB+	BBB
El Salvador	0.3	12.2	..	..	..	71.8	46.0	52.1	Baa3	Baa2	BB+	BB+
Eritrea	..	14.1	..	..	..	..	..	22.3	..	..	..	..
Estonia	7.3	35.2	F	F	F	74.8	59.5	64.0	A1	A1	A−	A−
Ethiopia	1.5	1.7	..	..	..	57.0	16.0	29.6	..	..	..	..
Finland	2.0	15.4	..	..	..	89.0	91.1	93.8	Aaa	Aaa	AAA	AAA
France	4.6	19.9	..	..	..	81.3	92.9	92.4	Aaa	Aaa	AAA	AAA
Gabon	5.7	15.1	..	..	..	66.3	21.8	32.1	..	..	..	..
Gambia, The	0.0	50.8	..	..	..	66.3	..	31.9	..	..	..	..
Georgia	0.0	27.1	..	..	..	..	15.4	33.2	..	..	..	..
Germany	0.7	8.5	..	..	..	82.8	94.0	91.9	Aaa	Aaa	AAA	AAA
Ghana	1.7	7.0	F	F	F	59.8	25.7	36.8	..	..	..	..
Greece	5.2	4.3	..	..	..	74.5	75.3	81.9	A1	A1	A	A
Guatemala	4.6	14.4	..	..	..	67.0	33.0	45.0	Ba2	Ba1	BB	BB+
Guinea	3.6	0.2	..	..	..	63.0	15.1	28.2	..	..	..	..
Guinea-Bissau	2.7	69.7	..	..	..	47.3	..	22.5	..	..	..	..
Haiti	0.0	0.3	..	..	..	51.5	14.8	23.6	..	..	..	..

	Foreign direct investment % of gross capital formation		Entry and exit regulations[a]			Composite ICRG risk rating[b]	Institutional Investor credit rating[b]	Euromoney country credit-worthiness rating[b]	Moody's sovereign long-term debt rating[b]		Standard & Poor's sovereign long-term debt rating[b]	
			Entry	Repatriation of income	Repatriation of capital				Foreign currency	Domestic currency	Foreign currency	Domestic currency
	1990	2001	2001	2001	2001	December 2002	September 2002	September 2002	January 2003	January 2003	January 2003	January 2003
Honduras	6.2	10.0	..	..	..	63.5	26.1	39.0	B2	B2	..	..
Hungary	3.7	17.2	F	F	F	78.0	66.1	69.3	A1	A1	A–	A
India	0.3	3.2	A	F	F	66.3	47.3	55.1	Ba2	Ba2	BB	BB+
Indonesia	3.1	–13.2	R	RS	RS	58.3	23.8	37.5	B3	B3	CCC+	B–
Iran, Islamic Rep.	–1.1	0.1	..	..	..	63.3	34.1	46.4	..	..	..	..
Iraq	..	..	..	..	..	44.0	10.2	3.6	..	..	..	..
Ireland	6.3	99.9	..	..	..	88.8	88.5	93.2	Aaa	Aaa	AAA	AAA
Israel	1.1	21.2	F	F	F	65.3	58.6	68.7	A2	A2	A–	A+
Italy	2.6	6.9	..	..	..	79.3	86.2	88.5	Aa2	Aa2	AA	AA
Jamaica	11.6	26.2	R	F	F	69.8	28.9	41.5	Ba3	Baa3	B+	BB–
Japan	0.2	0.6	..	..	..	85.3	82.7	88.7	Aa1	A2	AA–	AA–
Jordan	2.9	4.4	F	F	F	70.5	38.7	45.4	Ba3	Ba3	BB–	BBB–
Kazakhstan	1.2	47.9	..	..	..	71.8	38.8	48.4	Baa3	Baa1	BB	BB+
Kenya	3.4	0.4	R	F	F	57.5	22.9	36.0	..	..	..	..
Korea, Dem. Rep.	..	..	..	..	..	46.0	7.3	1.4	..	..	..	..
Korea, Rep.	0.8	2.8	R	F	F	79.8	65.6	69.5	A3	A3	A–	A+
Kuwait	..	–1.4	..	..	..	81.0	62.9	76.2	A2	A2	A+	A+
Kyrgyz Republic	0.0	2.0	..	..	..	..	16.9	25.2	..	..	..	..
Lao PDR	..	6.1	..	..	..	..	15.2	24.3	..	..	..	..
Latvia	1.1	8.4	F	F	F	76.5	52.0	58.8	A2	A2	BBB+	A–
Lebanon	1.3	8.0	F	F	F	55.5	26.8	39.1	B2	B3	B–	B–
Lesotho	5.3	39.9	..	..	..	..	26.8	33.5	..	..	..	..
Liberia	..	..	..	..	..	45.3	9.6	14.2	..	..	..	..
Libya	..	..	..	..	..	70.0	33.5	24.0	..	..	..	..
Lithuania	0.0	17.3	F	F	F	74.0	50.8	56.0	Baa1	Baa1	BBB	BBB+
Macedonia, FYR	..	77.5	..	..	..	..	20.6	35.3	..	..	..	..
Madagascar	4.3	1.6	..	..	..	58.8	..	28.5	..	..	..	..
Malawi	5.4	30.6	..	..	..	53.5	19.6	28.8	..	..	..	..
Malaysia	16.4	2.2	R	F	D	77.5	57.7	63.0	Baa1	A3	BBB+	A+
Mali	1.0	18.4	..	..	..	58.3	19.1	28.3	..	..	..	..
Mauritania	3.3	11.2	..	..	..	..	..	24.5	..	..	..	..
Mauritius	5.6	–4.3	R	F	F	..	53.5	58.8	Baa2	A2	..	..
Mexico	4.2	19.3	F	F	F	70.8	59.0	60.8	Baa2	Baa1	BBB–	A–
Moldova	0.0	31.5	..	..	..	64.0	15.7	26.2	Ca	Caa2	..	..
Mongolia	..	20.0	..	..	..	64.0	21.7	27.1	..	..	B	B
Morocco	2.5	31.6	F	F	F	72.8	48.2	53.6	Ba1	Ba1	BB	BBB
Mozambique	2.4	32.0	..	..	..	61.3	19.1	32.7	..	..	..	..
Myanmar	..	..	..	..	..	62.3	13.8	21.8	..	..	..	..
Namibia	..	..	F	F	F	76.5	40.8	26.6	..	..	..	..
Nepal	0.9	1.4	..	..	..	..	24.4	28.3	..	..	..	..
Netherlands	15.4	61.8	..	..	..	83.5	94.6	93.6	Aaa	Aaa	AAA	AAA
New Zealand	20.4	32.7	..	..	..	80.8	81.2	86.7	Aaa	Aaa	AA+	AAA
Nicaragua	0.0	..	..	..	..	53.8	17.6	30.8	B2	B2	..	..
Niger	20.3	5.9	..	..	..	57.5	13.6	30.6	..	..	..	..
Nigeria	14.0	9.7	R	F	F	51.0	17.6	24.5	..	..	..	..
Norway	3.7	16.2	..	..	..	91.3	93.1	97.7	Aaa	Aaa	AAA	AAA
Oman	10.3	..	F	F	F	79.8	57.8	62.7	Baa2	Baa2	BBB	BBB+
Pakistan	3.2	4.1	F	F	F	58.5	20.0	38.9	B3	B3	B	BB–
Panama	15.2	18.0	..	..	..	71.0	47.2	51.3	Ba1	..	BB	BB
Papua New Guinea	19.7	46.3	..	..	..	63.0	30.4	37.6	B1	B1	B	BB–
Paraguay	6.4	4.6	..	..	..	56.5	29.7	36.8	B2	B1	B–	B
Peru	0.9	10.7	F	F	F	68.8	38.3	46.6	Ba3	Baa3	BB–	BB+
Philippines	5.0	13.9	S	F	F	71.0	44.9	51.0	Ba1	Baa3	BB+	BBB+
Poland	0.6	15.0	F	F	F	76.3	60.1	64.6	A2	A2	BBB+	A
Portugal	13.1	19.2	..	..	..	78.3	84.2	84.9	Aa2	Aa2	AA	AA
Puerto Rico	..	..	..	..	..	..	..	..	..	..	..	..

	Foreign direct investment		Entry and exit regulations[a]			Composite ICRG risk rating[b]	Institutional Investor credit rating[b]	Euromoney country credit-worthiness rating[b]	Moody's sovereign long-term debt rating[b]		Standard & Poor's sovereign long-term debt rating[b]	
	% of gross capital formation		Entry	Repatriation of income	capital	December	September	September	Foreign currency January	Domestic currency January	Foreign currency January	Domestic currency January
	1990	2001	2001	2001	2001	2002	2002	2002	2003	2003	2003	2003
Romania	0.0	13.7	F	F	F	69.5	33.8	46.5	B1	B1	B+	BB–
Russian Federation	0.0	3.6	F	F	F	70.0	39.0	45.0	Ba2	Ba2	BB	BB+
Rwanda	2.0	1.5	..	..	..	..	..	20.1	..	..	..	..
Saudi Arabia[c]	..	..	C	RS	RS	72.5	58.0	65.8	Baa3	Ba1	..	..
Senegal	7.2	13.5	..	..	..	65.5	27.8	38.5	..	..	B+	B+
Sierra Leone	49.7	6.8	..	..	..	52.3	9.6	21.8	..	..	..	..
Singapore	41.5	41.4	..	..	..	90.0	86.1	90.2	Aaa	Aaa	AAA	AAA
Slovak Republic	0.0	22.6	F	F	F	75.8	51.4	58.1	A3	A3	BBB	A–
Slovenia	5.0	2.7	R	F	RS	80.3	65.8	75.4	Aa3	Aa3	A	AA
Somalia	3.9	..	..	..	..	44.5	..	14.5	..	..	..	..
South Africa	..	42.2	F	F	F	68.8	52.7	59.1	Baa2	A2	BBB–	A–
Spain	10.3	14.5	..	..	..	80.8	87.0	88.6	Aaa	Aaa	AA+	AA+
Sri Lanka	2.4	4.9	R	RS	F	63.3	33.6	40.5	..	..	..	..
Sudan	..	25.9	..	..	..	54.3	9.7	25.3	..	..	..	..
Swaziland	17.9	8.9	..	..	..	..	28.2	33.6	..	..	..	..
Sweden	3.6	35.4	..	..	..	84.5	89.3	94.1	Aaa	Aaa	AA+	AAA
Switzerland	9.3	16.2	..	..	..	91.5	96.2	98.5	Aaa	Aaa	AAA	AAA
Syrian Arab Republic	3.5	5.0	..	..	..	69.8	23.1	36.5	..	..	..	..
Tajikistan	1.0	19.2	..	..	..	..	12.7	32.0	..	..	..	..
Tanzania	0.0	14.1	..	..	..	58.0	21.3	34.2	..	..	..	..
Thailand	6.9	13.9	R	F	F	76.3	51.9	56.3	Baa3	Baa1	BBB–	A–
Togo	4.2	25.7	..	..	..	59.3	15.5	28.6	..	..	..	..
Trinidad and Tobago	17.1	49.4	R	F	F	73.3	53.3	58.4	Baa3	Baa1	BBB–	BBB+
Tunisia	1.9	8.3	F	F	F	72.0	53.7	57.2	Baa3	Baa2	BBB	A
Turkey	1.9	13.4	F	F	F	59.8	33.8	43.8	B1	B3	B–	B–
Turkmenistan	..	6.8	..	..	..	..	19.2	33.8	B2	..	..	..
Uganda	0.0	12.7	..	..	..	62.5	20.0	38.3	..	..	..	..
Ukraine	0.6	10.3	F	F	F	67.5	25.3	34.5	B2	B2	B	B
United Arab Emirates	..	..	..	..	..	81.8	68.2	76.3	A2	..	..	..
United Kingdom	16.8	25.8	..	..	..	82.0	94.1	92.7	Aaa	Aaa	AAA	AAA
United States	4.8	15.1	..	..	..	77.5	93.1	95.2	Aaa	Aaa	AAA	AAA
Uruguay	0.0	12.7	..	..	..	61.5	41.9	43.1	B3	B3	B–	B–
Uzbekistan	0.3	3.2	..	..	..	..	18.6	32.3	..	..	..	..
Venezuela, RB	9.1	14.7	F	F	F	53.8	30.6	39.9	B3	Caa1	CCC+	..
Vietnam	2.0	12.9	..	..	..	70.3	32.3	46.1	B1	..	BB–	BB
West Bank and Gaza	..	..	..	..	..	..	..	..	..	..	..	..
Yemen, Rep.	–18.6	–10.8	..	..	..	66.0	..	33.8	..	..	..	..
Yugoslavia, Fed. Rep.	..	0.0	..	..	..	50.0	16.5	29.6	..	..	..	..
Zambia	35.7	9.9	..	..	..	48.0	15.8	26.0	..	..	..	..
Zimbabwe	–0.8	0.8	R	F	F	37.0	11.9	22.3	..	..	..	..
World	**4.0 w**	**17.6 w**				**67.4 m**	**33.5 m**	**39.9 m**				
Low income	1.6	3.9				58.4	18.0	28.4				
Middle income	2.6	13.2				70.0	39.0	46.5				
Lower middle income	1.8	11.0				67.5	33.8	44.0				
Upper middle income	4.5	16.7				73.4	52.0	58.8				
Low & middle income	2.6	11.8				63.5	26.8	34.3				
East Asia & Pacific	4.6	9.0				67.2	27.1	37.5				
Europe & Central Asia	0.4	13.8				70.4	33.8	42.7				
Latin America & Carib.	3.8	18.9				64.7	35.5	43.5				
Middle East & N. Africa	..	4.5				69.8	36.4	45.4				
South Asia	0.6	3.1				62.3	25.9	38.7				
Sub-Saharan Africa	..	21.7				58.2	19.0	28.4				
High income	4.4	19.2				82.5	87.0	90.4				
Europe EMU	4.5	16.0				82.8	89.5	91.9				

a. Entry and exit regulations are classified as free (F), relatively free (R), delayed (D), special classes of shares (S), authorized investors only (A), restricted (RS), and closed (C). For explanations of the terms, see *About the data*. b. This copyrighted material is reprinted with permission from the following data providers: PRS Group, Inc., 6320 Fly Road, Suite 102, PO Box 248, East Syracuse, NY 13057; Institutional Investor Inc., 488 Madison Avenue, New York, NY 13057; Euromoney Publications PLC, Nestor House, Playhouse Yard, London EC4V 5EX, UK; Moody's Investors Service, 99 Church Street, New York, NY 10007; and Standard & Poor's Rating Services, The McGraw-Hill Companies, Inc., 1221 Avenue of the Americas, New York, NY 10020. Prior written consent from the original data providers cited must be obtained for third-party use of these data. c. Foreigners are barred from investing directly in the Saudi stock market, but they may invest indirectly through mutual funds.

As investment portfolios become increasingly global, investors as well as governments seeking to attract investment must have a good understanding of trends in foreign direct investment and country risk. This table presents data on foreign direct investment, information on the regulation of entry to and exit from emerging stock markets reported by Standard & Poor's, and country risk and creditworthiness ratings from several major international rating services.

The statistics on foreign direct investment are based on balance of payments data reported by the International Monetary Fund (IMF), supplemented by data on net foreign direct investment reported by the Organisation for Economic Co-operation and Development and official national sources. (For a detailed discussion of data on foreign direct investment, see *About the data* for table 6.7.)

Entry and exit restrictions on investments are among the mechanisms by which countries attempt to reduce the risk to their economies associated with foreign investment. Yet such restrictions may increase the risk or uncertainty perceived by investors. Many countries close industries considered strategic to foreign or nonresident investors. And national law or corporate policy may limit foreign investment in a company or in certain classes of stocks.

The entry and exit regulations summarized in the table refer to "new money" investment by foreign institutions; other regulations may apply to capital invested through debt conversion schemes or to capital from other sources. The regulations reflected here are formal ones. But even formal regulations may have very different effects in different countries because of differences in the bureaucratic culture, the speed with which applications are processed, and the extent of red tape. The regulations on entry are evaluated using the terms *free* (no significant restrictions), *relatively free* (some registration procedures required to ensure repatriation rights), *special classes* (foreigners restricted to certain classes of stocks designated for foreign investors), *authorized investors only* (only approved foreign investors may buy stocks), and *closed* (closed or access severely restricted, as for nonresident nationals only). Regulations on repatriation of income and capital are evaluated as *free* (repatriation done routinely), *delayed* (repatriation of capital after one year), or *restricted* (repatriation requires registration with or permission of a government agency that may restrict the timing of exchange release).

Most risk ratings are numerical or alphabetical indexes, with a higher number or a letter closer to the beginning of the alphabet meaning lower risk (a good

prospect). (For more on the rating processes of the rating agencies, see the data sources.) Risk ratings may be highly subjective, reflecting external perceptions that do not always capture the actual situation in a country. But these subjective perceptions are the reality that policymakers face. Countries not rated by credit risk rating agencies typically do not attract registered flows of private capital. The risk ratings presented here are included for their analytical usefulness and are not endorsed by the World Bank.

The PRS Group's *International Country Risk Guide* (ICRG) collects information on 22 components of risk, groups it into three major categories (political, financial, and economic), and converts it into a single numerical risk assessment ranging from 0 to 100. Ratings below 50 indicate very high risk, and those above 80 very low risk. Ratings are updated monthly.

Institutional Investor country credit ratings are based on information provided by leading international banks. Responses are weighted using a formula that gives more importance to responses from banks with greater worldwide exposure and more sophisticated country analysis systems. Countries are rated on a scale of 0 to 100 (highest risk to lowest), and ratings are updated every six months.

Euromoney country creditworthiness ratings are based on nine weighted categories (covering debt, economic performance, political risk, and access to financial and capital markets) that assess country risk. The ratings, also on a scale of 0 to 100 (highest risk to lowest), are based on polls of economists and political analysts supplemented by quantitative data such as debt ratios and access to capital markets.

Moody's sovereign long-term debt ratings are opinions of the capacity of entities to honor senior unsecured financial obligations and contracts denominated in foreign currency (foreign currency issuer ratings) or in their domestic currency (domestic currency issuer ratings).

Standard & Poor's ratings of sovereign long-term foreign and domestic currency debt are based on current information furnished by obligors or obtained by Standard & Poor's from other sources it considers reliable. A Standard & Poor's issuer credit rating (one form of which is a sovereign credit rating) is a current opinion of an obligor's capacity and willingness to pay its financial obligations as they come due (its creditworthiness). This opinion does not apply to any specific financial obligation, as it does not take into account the nature and provisions of obligations, their standing in bankruptcy or liquidation, statutory preferences, or the legality and enforceability of obligations.

• **Foreign direct investment** is net inflows of investment to acquire a lasting management interest (10 percent or more of voting stock) in an enterprise operating in an economy other than that of the investor. It is the sum of equity capital, reinvestment of earnings, other long-term capital, and short-term capital as shown in the balance of payments. Gross capital formation is the sum of gross fixed capital formation, changes in inventories, and acquisitions less disposals of valuables. • **Regulations on entry to emerging stock markets** are assessed on a scale from free to closed (see *About the data*). • **Regulations on repatriation of income** (dividends, interest, and realized capital gains) and **repatriation of capital from emerging stock markets** are evaluated as free, delayed, or restricted (see *About the data*). • **Composite International Country Risk Guide (ICRG) risk rating** is an overall index, ranging from 0 to 100, based on 22 components of risk. • **Institutional Investor credit rating** ranks, from 0 to 100, the chances of a country's default. • **Euromoney country creditworthiness rating** ranks, from 0 to 100, the risk of investing in an economy. • **Moody's sovereign foreign or domestic currency long-term debt rating** assesses the risk of lending to governments. An entity's capacity to meet its senior financial obligations is rated from AAA (offering exceptional financial security) to C (usually in default, with potential recovery values low). Modifiers 1–3 are applied to ratings from AA to B, with 1 indicating a high ranking in the rating category. • **Standard & Poor's sovereign foreign or domestic currency long-term debt rating** ranges from AAA (extremely strong capacity to meet financial commitments) to CC (currently highly vulnerable). Ratings from AA to CCC may be modified by a plus or minus sign to show relative standing in the category. An obligor rated SD (selective default) has failed to pay one or more financial obligations when due.

The data on foreign direct investment are based on estimates compiled by the IMF in its *Balance of Payments Statistics Yearbook*, supplemented by World Bank staff estimates. The data on entry and exit regulations are from Standard & Poor's *Emerging Stock Markets Factbook 2002*. The country risk and creditworthiness ratings are from the PRS Group's monthly *International Country Risk Guide* (http://www.ICRGonline.com), the monthly *Institutional Investor*, the monthly *Euromoney*, Moody's Investors Service's *Sovereign, Subnational and Sovereign-Guaranteed Issuers*, and Standard & Poor's Sovereign List in *Credit Week*.

5.3 Business environment

	Entry regulations				Contract enforcement			Insolvency	
	Start-up procedures January 2002	Time to start up a business days January 2002	Costs to register a business % of GNI per capita January 2002	Minimum capital requirement % of GNI per capita January 2002	Procedures to enforce a contract January 2002	Time to enforce a contract days January 2002	Costs to enforce a contract % of GNI per capita January 2002	Time to resolve insolvency days January 2002	Costs to resolve insolvency % of insolvency estate January 2002
Afghanistan	..	..	..	..	..	..	..	..	..
Albania	11	62	63	67	37	220	73	733	38
Algeria	18	29	36	81	20	387	13	1,292	4
Angola	..	..	..	..	..	..	..	..	..
Argentina	14	63	11	20	32	300	9	730	18
Armenia	11	79	12	17	22	65	15	709	4
Australia	2	6	2	0	11	320	8	381	18
Austria	9	30	18	125	20	434	1	482	18
Azerbaijan	15	104	21	0	25	115	3	972	8
Bangladesh	7	30	78	0	15	270	48	..	..
Belarus	20	143	39	0	19	135	44	795	1
Belgium	7	34	15	69	22	365	9	323	4
Benin	9	63	168	370	44	248	31	1,150	18
Bolivia	18	77	164	0	44	464	2	736	18
Bosnia and Herzegovina	12	74	56	372	31	630	21	677	8
Botswana	8	70	16	0	20	77	21	..	..
Brazil	16	86	12	0	16	180	2	3,650	8
Bulgaria	10	30	9	154	26	410	6	1,385	18
Burkina Faso	15	39	328	627	24	376	173	..	..
Burundi	..	..	..	..	..	..	..	..	..
Cambodia	..	..	..	..	..	..	..	..	..
Cameroon	13	56	197	116	46	548	63	328	18
Canada	2	2	1	0	17	421	1	290	4
Central African Republic	..	..	..	..	..	..	..	..	..
Chad	..	..	..	..	..	..	..	..	..
Chile	10	34	14	0	21	200	15	1,454	18
China	12	55	13	4,338	20	180	32	955	18
Hong Kong, China	5	20	3	0	17	180	7	381	18
Colombia	18	60	15	0	37	527	6	1,106	1
Congo, Dem. Rep.	..	..	..	..	..	..	..	..	..
Congo, Rep.	..	..	..	..	..	..	..	..	..
Costa Rica	11	80	21	0	21	370	23	915	18
Côte d'Ivoire	10	91	136	99	18	150	83	800	18
Croatia	13	50	17	50	20	330	7	1,130	18
Cuba	..	..	..	..	..	..	..	..	..
Czech Republic	10	89	5	53	16	270	19	3,350	38
Denmark	3	3	..	47	14	83	4	1,517	8
Dominican Republic	20	86	41	28	19	215	441	..	..
Ecuador	14	90	65	6	33	333	11	..	..
Egypt, Arab Rep.	13	52	76	748	17	202	31	1,560	18
El Salvador	..	..	..	..	..	..	..	..	..
Eritrea	..	..	..	..	..	..	..	..	..
Estonia	..	..	..	..	..	..	..	..	..
Ethiopia	8	44	429	1,752	24	895	35	..	..
Finland	7	36	1	29	19	240	16	330	1
France	10	53	3	29	21	210	4	624	..
Gabon	..	..	..	..	..	..	..	..	..
Gambia, The	..	..	..	..	..	..	..	..	..
Georgia	12	62	38	149	17	180	63	..	..
Germany	9	45	6	90	14	154	6	430	8
Ghana	10	126	98	1	21	90	24	591	18
Greece	16	45	50	131	15	315	8	795	8
Guatemala	13	41	69	37	19	1460	20	1,460	18
Guinea	..	..	..	..	..	..	..	..	..
Guinea-Bissau	..	..	..	..	..	..	..	..	..
Haiti	..	..	..	..	..	..	..	..	..

	Entry regulations				Contract enforcement			Insolvency	
	Start-up procedures	Time to start up a business days	Costs to register a business % of GNI per capita	Minimum capital requirement % of GNI per capita	Procedures to enforce a contract	Time to enforce a contract days	Costs to enforce a contract % of GNI per capita	Time to resolve insolvency days	Costs to resolve insolvency % of insolvency estate
	January 2002	January 2002	January 2002	January 2002	January 2002	January 2002	January 2002	January 2002	January 2002
Honduras	15	146	67	186	32	225	7	..	..
Hungary	5	65	65	232	17	365	2	..	..
India	10	88	51	0	22	106	222	4,115	8
Indonesia	11	168	15	326	29	225	386	..	..
Iran, Islamic Rep.	9	69	11	34	23	150	6	655	8
Iraq	..	..	..	..	..	..	..	..	..
Ireland	3	16	10	0	16	183	7	161	8
Israel	5	44	21	0	19	315	34	..	..
Italy	13	62	23	46	16	645	4	226	18
Jamaica	7	37	16	0	11	202	42	400	18
Japan	11	30	12	544	16	60	1	211	4
Jordan	14	89	48	4,154	32	147	0	1,572	8
Kazakhstan	12	54	39	51	41	120	8	..	..
Kenya	11	68	44	0	25	255	26	1,667	18
Korea, Dem. Rep.	..	..	..	..	..	..	..	..	..
Korea, Rep.	13	36	19	429	23	75	5	535	4
Kuwait	..	..	..	..	..	..	..	..	..
Kyrgyz Republic	9	26	13	73	44	365	255	..	..
Lao PDR	..	..	0	..	..	..	..	..	..
Latvia	7	11	17	110	19	189	8	419	4
Lebanon	6	46	116	83	27	721	54	1,460	18
Lesotho	9	92	68	20	..	..	..	..	..
Liberia	..	..	..	..	..	..	..	..	..
Libya	..	..	..	..	..	..	..	..	..
Lithuania	11	62	5	85	30	150	6	437	18
Macedonia, FYR	..	..	..	..	27	509	42	..	..
Madagascar	15	68	58	0	29	166	120	800	18
Malawi	11	56	94	0	12	108	521	..	..
Malaysia	7	56	27	0	22	270	2	..	..
Mali	13	61	230	886	27	150	7	1,278	18
Mauritania	..	..	..	..	..	..	..	..	..
Mauritius	..	..	..	..	..	..	..	..	..
Mexico	7	51	21	109	47	283	10	714	18
Moldova	11	41	31	106	36	210	14	545	8
Mongolia	8	31	14	2,307	26	224	2	450	8
Morocco	13	62	19	731	17	192	9	665	18
Mozambique	16	214	74	30	18	540	10	..	..
Myanmar	..	..	..	..	..	..	..	..	..
Namibia	..	..	..	..	..	..	..	..	..
Nepal	8	25	189	0	24	350	44	1,832	..
Netherlands	8	42	17	65	21	39	1	861	1
New Zealand	2	2	0	0	19	50	12	704	18
Nicaragua	12	69	309	0	17	65	18	827	8
Niger	11	27	390	755	29	365	57	..	18
Nigeria	9	50	92	32	25	241	4	573	18
Norway	4	24	4	32	12	87	10	336	1
Oman	..	..	..	..	..	..	..	..	..
Pakistan	10	53	44	0	30	365	46	1,010	4
Panama	7	19	30	0	44	197	20	2,373	38
Papua New Guinea	..	..	..	..	..	..	..	..	..
Paraguay	..	..	..	..	..	..	..	..	..
Peru	8	114	23	0	35	441	30	763	8
Philippines	14	62	15	9	28	164	104	2,083	38
Poland	11	58	23	24	18	1000	11	558	18
Portugal	12	104	22	16	22	420	5	931	8
Puerto Rico	..	..	..	..	..	..	..	..	..

5.3 Business environment

	Entry regulations				Contract enforcement			Insolvency	
	Start-up procedures	Time to start up a business days	Costs to register a business % of GNI per capita	Minimum capital requirement % of GNI per capita	Procedures to enforce a contract	Time to enforce a contract days	Costs to enforce a contract % of GNI per capita	Time to resolve insolvency days	Costs to resolve insolvency % of insolvency estate
	January 2002	January 2002	January 2002	January 2002	January 2002	January 2002	January 2002	January 2002	January 2002
Romania	9	46	36	380	28	225	13	1,171	8
Russian Federation	19	50	7	38	16	160	20	558	4
Rwanda	..	..	..	..	..	..	..	..	..
Saudi Arabia	13	99	153	1,887	19	195	0	..	..
Senegal	9	58	116	277	30	335	49	..	..
Sierra Leone	..	..	..	..	..	..	..	..	..
Singapore	7	8	6	0	20	47	2	258	1
Slovak Republic	11	119	13	112	26	420	13	1,734	18
Slovenia	9	62	13	64	22	1,003	4	520	1
Somalia	..	..	..	..	..	..	..	..	..
South Africa	9	32	7	0	18	207	55	730	18
Spain	11	100	16	18	20	147	11	558	8
Sri Lanka	8	73	16	323	17	440	8	..	..
Sudan	..	..	..	..	..	..	..	..	..
Swaziland	..	..	..	..	..	..	..	..	..
Sweden	5	18	1	36	21	190	8	730	8
Switzerland	6	20	18	32	14	224	4	1,681	4
Syrian Arab Republic	10	42	17	6,793	36	596	31	1,513	8
Tajikistan	..	..	..	..	..	..	..	..	..
Tanzania	13	37	229	0	14	127	4	1,095	8
Thailand	8	45	7	0	19	210	1	960	38
Togo	..	..	..	..	..	..	..	..	..
Trinidad and Tobago	..	..	..	..	..	..	..	..	..
Tunisia	9	47	21	33	14	7	4	906	8
Turkey	13	53	43	12	18	105	5	655	8
Turkmenistan	..	..	..	..	..	..	..	..	..
Uganda	17	36	114	0	16	99	10	730	38
Ukraine	13	42	22	434	20	224	11	1,085	18
United Arab Emirates	10	29	24	404	27	559	11	..	..
United Kingdom	5	4	1	0	12	101	1	378	8
United States	5	4	1	0	17	270	0	1,095	4
Uruguay	10	27	49	831	38	360	14	1,460	8
Uzbekistan	9	33	17	33	34	258	2	774	4
Venezuela, RB	14	119	24	0	41	360	47	1,476	38
Vietnam	10	68	36	0	28	120	9	730	18
West Bank and Gaza	..	..	..	..	..	..	..	..	..
Yemen, Rep.	13	95	317	2,731	27	240	1	891	4
Yugoslavia, Fed. Rep.	16	71	20	500	40	1,028	20	2,665	38
Zambia	6	40	43	151	16	188	16	1,365	8
Zimbabwe	10	122	27	0	13	197	40	..	..

Business environment | **5.3**

About the data

This new table presents key indicators on the environment for doing business. The indicators, covering entry regulations, contract enforcement, and access to finance, identify regulations that enhance or constrain business investment, productivity, and growth. The data are from a new World Bank database, Doing Business.

A vibrant private sector is central to promoting growth and expanding opportunities for poor people. But encouraging firms to invest, improve productivity, and create jobs requires a legal and regulatory environment that fosters access to credit, protection of property rights, and efficient judicial, taxation, and customs systems. The indicators in the table point to the administrative and regulatory reforms and institutions needed to create a favorable environment for doing business.

When entrepreneurs start a business, the first obstacles they face are the administrative and legal procedures required to register the new firm. Countries differ widely in how they regulate the entry of new businesses. In some countries the process is straightforward and affordable. But in others the procedures are so burdensome that entrepreneurs may opt to run their business informally.

The data on entry regulations are derived from a survey of the procedures that a typical domestic limited-liability company must complete before legally starting operation. The data cover the number and duration of start-up procedures, the cost to register a business, and the minimum capital requirement.

Contract enforcement is critical to enable businesses to engage with new borrowers or customers. Without good contract enforcement, trade and credit will be restricted to a small community of people who have developed relationships through repeated dealings or through the security of assets. The institution that enforces contracts between debtors and creditors, and suppliers and customers, is the court.

The efficiency of contract enforcement is reflected in three indicators: the number of judicial procedures to resolve a dispute, the time it takes to enforce a commercial contract, and the associated costs. The data are derived from structured surveys answered by attorneys at private law firms. The questionnaires cover the step-by-step evolution of a commercial case before local courts in the country's largest city.

The continuing existence of unviable competitors is consistently rated by firms as one of the greatest potential barriers to operation and growth. The institution that deals with the exit of unviable companies and the rehabilitation of viable but financially dis-

tressed companies is the insolvency system. Two indicators measure the time it takes to resolve insolvency and the associated costs. With effective insolvency systems, one may expect greater access and better allocation of credit.

To ensure cross-country comparability, several standard characteristics of a company are defined in all surveys, such as size, ownership, location, legal status, and type of activities undertaken. The data were collected through a study of laws and regulations in each country, surveys of regulators or private sector professionals on each topic, and cooperative arrangements with private consulting firms and business and law associations.

Definitions

• **Start-up procedures** include those that are always required to start a business. The procedures are interactions of the company with external parties (government agencies, lawyers, auditors, notaries, and the like), including interactions required to obtain all necessary permits and licenses and to complete all inscriptions, verifications, and notifications needed to start operation. • **Time to start up a business** refers to the time, measured in calendar days, needed to complete all the required procedures for legally operating a business. If a procedure can be speeded up at additional cost, the fastest procedure, independent of cost, is chosen. Time spent gathering information about the registration process is excluded. • **Costs to register a business** is normalized by presenting it as a percentage of gross national income (GNI) per capita. • **Minimum capital requirement** is the amount that the entrepreneur needs to deposit in a bank account to obtain a company registration number. This amount is typically specified in the commercial code or the company law and is often returned to the entrepreneur only when the company is dissolved. • **Procedures to enforce a contract** are independent actions, with each action defined as a procedure—mandated by law or court regulation—that demands interaction between the parties or between them and the judge or court officer. • **Time to enforce a contract** refers to the number of calendar days from the moment the plaintiff files the lawsuit in court until the moment of final determination and, in appropriate cases, payment. • **Costs to enforce a contract** include filing fees, court costs, and estimated attorney fees. • **Time to resolve insolvency** refers to the number of calendar days from the moment of filing for insolvency in court until the moment of actual resolution of distressed assets. • **Costs to resolve insolvency** include filing fees and court costs, and attorney fees and payments to other professionals (accountants, assessors), out of the insolvency estate. The cost figures are averages of the estimates of survey respondents, who chose among six options: 0–2 percent, 3–5 percent, 6–10 percent, 11–25 percent, 26–50 percent, and more than 50 percent.

Data sources

All data are from the World Bank's Doing Business project (http://rru.worldbank.org/DoingBusiness/).

5.4 Stock markets

	Market capitalization				Value traded		Turnover ratio		Listed domestic companies		S&P/IFC Investable Index	
	$ millions		% of GDP		% of GDP		value of shares traded as % of capitalization				% change in price index	
	1990	2002	1990	2001	1990	2001	1990	2002	1990	2002	2001	2002
Afghanistan	..	..	..	..	..	..	..	..	..	..	..	..
Albania	..	..	..	..	..	..	..	..	..	..	..	..
Algeria	..	..	..	..	..	..	..	..	..	..	..	..
Angola	..	..	..	..	..	..	..	..	..	..	..	..
Argentina	3,268	103,434	2.3	71.7	0.6	1.6	33.6	2.2	179	83	–31.7	–51.4
Armenia	..	..	..	1.4	..	..	..	..	..	..	..	..
Australia	108,879	*374,269*	35.1	101.5	12.9	65.3	31.6	64.3	1,089	*1,334*	..	..
Austria	11,476	25,204	7.1	13.4	11.5	3.8	110.3	28.8	97	114	..	..
Azerbaijan	..	..	..	0.1	..	..	..	..	..	..	..	..
Bangladesh	321	1,193	1.1	2.5	0.0	1.6	1.5	64.7	134	239	–20.7[a]	–4.2[a]
Belarus	..	..	..	..	..	..	..	..	..	..	..	..
Belgium	65,449	*16,584*	33.2	7.2	3.3	17.9	..	247.9	182	*156*	..	..
Benin	..	..	..	..	..	..	..	..	..	..	..	..
Bolivia	..	1,555	..	19.5	..	0.0	..	0.1	..	29	..	..
Bosnia and Herzegovina	..	..	..	..	..	..	..	..	..	..	..	..
Botswana	*261*	1,723	*6.6*	24.8	*0.2*	1.3	6.1	5.0	*9*	18	43.9[a]	31.1[a]
Brazil	16,354	123,807	3.5	37.1	1.2	13.0	23.6	35.0	581	399	–22.5	–33.0
Bulgaria	..	733	..	3.7	..	0.5	..	13.9	..	354	–7.5[a]	62.5[a]
Burkina Faso	..	..	..	..	..	..	..	..	..	..	..	..
Burundi	..	..	..	..	..	..	..	..	..	..	..	..
Cambodia	..	..	..	..	..	..	..	..	..	..	..	..
Cameroon	..	..	..	..	..	..	..	..	..	..	..	..
Canada	241,920	*700,751*	42.1	100.9	12.4	66.5	26.7	65.9	1,144	*4,004*	..	..
Central African Republic	..	..	..	..	..	..	..	..	..	..	..	..
Chad	..	..	..	..	..	..	..	..	..	..	..	..
Chile	13,645	47,584	45.0	85.4	2.6	6.4	6.3	7.4	215	254	–8.3	–14.8
China	*2,028*	463,080	*0.5*	45.2	*0.2*	38.7	*158.9*	85.7	*14*	1,235	–19.5	–14.5
Hong Kong, China	83,397	*506,131*	111.5	312.6	46.3	121.3	43.1	38.8	284	*857*	..	..
Colombia	1,416	9,664	3.5	16.0	0.2	0.4	5.6	2.7	80	114	25.2[a]	9.7[a]
Congo, Dem. Rep.	..	..	..	..	..	..	..	..	..	..	..	..
Congo, Rep.	..	..	..	..	..	..	..	..	..	..	..	..
Costa Rica	*475*	..	5.5	14.6	..	..	5.8	..	82	..	..	..
Côte d'Ivoire	549	1,328	5.1	11.2	0.2	0.1	3.4	0.7	23	38	–2.4[a]	17.4[a]
Croatia	..	3,976	..	15.2	..	0.6	..	3.8	2	66	–3.5[a]	44.2[a]
Cuba	..	..	..	..	..	..	..	..	..	..	..	..
Czech Republic	..	15,893	..	16.1	..	5.9	..	36.6	..	78	–13.7	38.9
Denmark	39,063	*94,958*	29.3	58.8	8.3	43.7	28.0	74.3	258	*208*	..	..
Dominican Republic	..	..	..	0.8	..	..	..	..	..	..	..	..
Ecuador	*69*	1,750	*0.5*	7.9	..	0.1	..	0.7	*65*	31	85.4[a]	23.3[a]
Egypt, Arab Rep.	1,765	26,094	4.1	24.5	0.3	4.0	..	16.1	573	1,148	–45.5	–5.8
El Salvador	..	*1,522*	..	11.1	..	0.2	..	1.5	..	*32*	..	..
Eritrea	..	..	..	..	..	..	..	..	..	..	..	..
Estonia	..	2,430	..	26.7	..	4.0	..	14.9	..	14	–3.7[a]	66.3[a]
Ethiopia	..	..	..	..	..	..	..	..	..	..	..	..
Finland	22,721	*190,456*	16.6	157.6	2.9	148.2	..	94.0	73	*152*	..	..
France	314,384	*1,174,428*	25.9	89.7	9.6	82.3	..	91.7	578	*791*	..	..
Gabon	..	..	..	..	..	..	..	..	..	..	..	..
Gambia, The	..	..	..	..	..	..	..	..	..	..	..	..
Georgia	..	..	..	..	..	..	..	..	..	..	..	..
Germany	355,073	*1,071,749*	21.0	58.1	29.7	76.9	139.3	132.4	413	*988*	..	..
Ghana	*76*	740	*1.2*	10.1	..	0.2	..	2.5	*13*	24	4.5[a]	27.6[a]
Greece	15,228	*86,538*	18.1	73.9	4.7	31.9	36.3	43.2	145	*338*	–31.2	..
Guatemala	..	*232*	..	1.1	..	0.0	..	3.1	..	10	..	..
Guinea	..	..	..	..	..	..	..	..	..	..	..	..
Guinea-Bissau	..	..	..	..	..	..	..	..	..	..	..	..
Haiti	..	..	..	..	..	..	..	..	..	..	..	..

	Market capitalization				Value traded		Turnover ratio		Listed domestic companies		S&P/IFC Investable Index	
	$ millions		% of GDP		% of GDP		value of shares traded as % of capitalization				% change in price index	
	1990	2002	1990	2001	1990	2001	1990	2002	1990	2002	2001	2002
Honduras	40	..	1.3	..	..	..	..	..	26	46	..	..
Hungary	505	13,110	1.5	20.0	0.3	9.3	6.3	46.5	21	48	–10.3	34.6
India	38,567	131,011	12.2	23.1	6.9	2.0	65.9	225.8	2,435	5,650	–19.9	6.8
Indonesia	8,081	29,991	7.1	15.8	3.5	171.6	75.8	42.0	125	331	–18.5	33.3
Iran, Islamic Rep.	34,282	9,704	..	8.5	..	1.0	30.4	11.3	97	316	..	..
Iraq	..	..	..	..	..	..	..	..	..	..	..	..
Ireland	..	75,298	..	72.9	..	21.8	..	29.9	..	68	..	..
Israel	3,324	45,371	6.3	53.2	10.5	27.5	95.8	51.7	216	615	–16.4	–26.6
Italy	148,766	527,396	13.5	48.4	3.9	50.7	26.8	104.7	220	288	..	..
Jamaica	911	5,838	19.8	59.6	0.7	1.0	3.4	1.6	44	42	4.3[a]	40.0[a]
Japan	2,917,679	2,251,814	95.6	54.4	52.5	44.1	43.8	81.1	2,071	2,471	–33.4[b]	–8.7[b]
Jordan	2,001	7,087	49.8	71.5	10.1	10.6	20.0	14.8	105	158	31.4[a]	–2.1[a]
Kazakhstan	..	1,204	..	5.4	..	1.4	..	26.5	..	31	..	..
Kenya	453	1,423	5.3	9.2	0.1	0.4	2.2	3.8	54	57	–22.7[a]	42.2[a]
Korea, Dem. Rep.	..	..	..	..	..	..	..	..	..	..	..	..
Korea, Rep.	110,594	248,533	43.8	55.0	30.1	166.7	61.3	303.3	669	1,518	51.2	5.8
Kuwait	..	20,772	..	58.0	..	11.7	..	21.3	..	77	..	..
Kyrgyz Republic	..	..	..	..	..	..	..	..	..	..	..	..
Lao PDR	..	..	..	..	..	..	..	..	..	..	..	..
Latvia	..	714	..	9.1	..	2.2	..	24.0	..	62	60.1[a]	–14.1[a]
Lebanon	..	1,401	..	7.3	..	0.3	..	4.7	..	13	–29.2[a]	5.7[a]
Lesotho	..	..	..	..	..	..	..	..	..	..	..	..
Liberia	..	..	..	..	..	..	..	..	..	..	..	..
Libya	..	..	..	..	..	..	..	..	..	..	..	..
Lithuania	..	1,463	..	10.0	..	1.8	..	17.5	..	51	–23.6[a]	25.7[a]
Macedonia, FYR	..	46	..	1.3	..	0.1	..	4.3	..	2	..	..
Madagascar	..	..	..	..	..	..	..	..	..	..	..	..
Malawi	..	156	..	8.9	..	1.3	..	13.8	..	8	..	..
Malaysia	48,611	123,872	110.4	135.1	24.7	23.6	24.6	17.5	282	865	4.2	–2.6
Mali	..	..	..	..	..	..	..	..	..	..	..	..
Mauritania	..	1,091	..	108.4	..	..	..	..	..	40	..	..
Mauritius	268	1,328	11.2	21.6	0.3	2.5	1.9	11.5	13	40	–21.8[a]	22.9[a]
Mexico	32,725	103,137	12.5	20.5	4.6	6.5	44.0	31.6	199	166	12.8	–16.4
Moldova	..	350	..	23.7	..	14.2	..	60.1	..	22	..	..
Mongolia	..	..	..	3.5	..	..	..	..	..	..	..	..
Morocco	966	8,591	3.7	26.7	0.2	2.8	..	10.6	71	55	–17.3	–8.1
Mozambique	..	..	..	..	..	..	..	..	..	..	..	..
Myanmar	..	..	..	..	..	..	..	..	..	..	..	..
Namibia	21	171	0.7	4.8	..	0.3	..	5.2	3	13	–31.0[a]	22.5[a]
Nepal	..	800	..	14.6	..	0.6	..	..	..	110	..	..
Netherlands	119,825	458,221	40.7	120.5	13.7	271.9	29.0	225.5	260	180	..	..
New Zealand	8,835	17,779	20.3	35.3	4.4	16.7	17.3	47.4	171	145	..	..
Nicaragua	..	..	..	..	..	..	..	..	..	..	..	..
Niger	..	..	..	..	..	..	..	..	..	..	..	..
Nigeria	1,372	5,740	4.8	11.3	0.0	1.2	0.9	10.6	131	195	25.1[a]	–0.3[a]
Norway	26,130	69,054	22.6	41.6	12.1	31.5	54.4	75.8	112	186	..	..
Oman	1,061	3,997	9.4	17.5	0.9	2.8	12.3	13.0	55	96	–27.0[a]	31.8[a]
Pakistan	2,850	10,200	7.1	8.4	0.6	21.2	8.7	251.9	487	712	–32.8[a]	112.0[a]
Panama	226	2,602	3.4	25.6	0.0	0.4	0.9	1.7	13	29	..	..
Papua New Guinea	..	..	..	..	..	..	..	..	..	..	..	..
Paraguay	..	..	..	5.5	..	..	..	..	..	..	..	..
Peru	812	13,363	3.1	18.1	0.4	1.6	19.3	8.7	294	202	14.2	33.5
Philippines	5,927	39,021	13.4	29.9	2.7	4.4	13.6	14.8	153	235	–29.9	–19.7
Poland	144	28,750	0.2	14.7	0.0	4.2	89.7	28.7	9	216	–24.9	2.2
Portugal	9,201	46,338	12.9	42.2	2.4	24.8	16.9	58.9	181	97	..	..
Puerto Rico	..	..	..	..	..	..	..	..	..	..	..	..

	Market capitalization				Value traded		Turnover ratio		Listed domestic companies		S&P/IFC Investable Index	
	$ millions		% of GDP		% of GDP		value of shares traded as % of capitalization				% change in price index	
	1990	2002	1990	2001	1990	2001	1990	2002	1990	2002	2001	2002
Romania	..	4,561	..	2.9	..	0.7	..	23.0	..	4,870	−25.3[a]	96.7[a]
Russian Federation	244	124,198	0.0	24.6	..	7.4	..	30.1	13	196	52.4	34.8
Rwanda	..	..	..	..	..	..	..	..	..	..	..	..
Saudi Arabia	48,213	74,855	40.8	39.3	1.9	11.9	..	30.4	59	68	3.7[a]	3.8[a]
Senegal	..	..	..	..	..	..	..	..	..	..	..	..
Sierra Leone	..	..	..	..	..	..	..	..	..	..	..	..
Singapore	34,308	117,338	93.6	137.0	55.3	74.0	..	54.0	150	386	..	..
Slovak Republic	..	1,904	..	2.6	..	4.7	..	179.5	..	354	21.3[a]	23.6[a]
Slovenia	..	4,606	..	14.8	..	..	..	30.5	24	35	2.0[a]	78.3[a]
Somalia	..	..	..	..	..	..	..	..	..	..	..	..
South Africa	137,540	184,622	122.8	78.0	7.3	61.5	..	78.9	732	450	−22.1	44.9
Spain	111,404	468,203	21.8	80.5	8.0	144.1	..	179.1	427	1,458	..	..
Sri Lanka	917	1,681	11.4	8.4	0.5	1.0	5.8	11.5	175	238	36.5[a]	28.4[a]
Sudan	..	..	..	..	..	..	..	..	..	..	..	..
Swaziland	17	127	1.9	10.1	..	0.6	..	6.7	1	5	..	..
Sweden	97,929	232,561	41.1	110.8	7.4	143.7	14.9	129.7	258	285	..	..
Switzerland	160,044	521,190	70.1	210.9	29.6	121.8	..	57.7	182	263	..	..
Syrian Arab Republic	..	..	..	..	..	..	..	..	..	..	..	..
Tajikistan	..	..	..	..	..	..	..	..	..	..	..	..
Tanzania	..	398	..	4.3	..	0.1	..	1.9	..	4	..	..
Thailand	23,896	46,084	28.0	31.7	26.8	31.1	92.6	98.3	214	466	3.0	18.3
Togo	..	..	..	..	..	..	..	..	..	..	..	..
Trinidad and Tobago	696	6,506	13.7	44.0	1.1	2.0	10.0	4.5	30	31	1.6[a]	33.2[a]
Tunisia	533	2,131	4.3	11.5	0.2	1.6	3.3	13.7	13	47	−29.0[a]	−2.5[a]
Turkey	19,065	33,958	12.7	32.3	3.9	52.8	42.5	163.4	110	288	−30.2	−33.5
Turkmenistan	..	..	..	..	..	..	..	..	..	..	..	..
Uganda	..	36	..	0.6	..	..	..	..	..	2	..	..
Ukraine	..	3,119	..	4.0	..	0.6	..	14.8	..	184	−36.3[a]	26.7[a]
United Arab Emirates	..	7,881	..	..	..	..	..	3.4	..	12	..	..
United Kingdom	848,866	2,217,324	85.8	155.7	28.2	131.4	33.4	84.4	1,701	1,923	−18.3[c]	−16.5[c]
United States	3,059,434	13,810,429	53.2	137.2	30.5	288.5	53.4	210.3	6,599	6,355	−13.0[d]	−23.4[d]
Uruguay	..	153	..	0.8	..	0.0	..	0.5	36	15	..	..
Uzbekistan	..	50	..	0.4	..	0.1	..	..	..	5	..	..
Venezuela, RB	8,361	3,962	17.2	4.9	4.6	0.3	43.0	6.4	76	59	−20.1[a]	−35.1[a]
Vietnam	..	..	..	..	..	..	..	..	..	..	..	..
West Bank and Gaza	..	723	..	18.2	..	1.9	..	10.3	..	24	..	..
Yemen, Rep.	..	..	..	..	..	..	..	..	..	..	..	..
Yugoslavia, Fed. Rep.	..	0	..	0.0	..	0.0	..	..	..	0	..	..
Zambia	..	217	..	6.0	..	1.3	..	22.5	..	9	..	..
Zimbabwe	2,395	15,632	27.3	88.0	0.6	16.9	2.9	19.2	57	76	134.3[a]	97.9[a]
World	9,399,659 s	27,561,743 s	47.9 w	90.7 w	28.5 w	138.6 w	57.2 w	123.6 w	25,424 s	43,319 s		
Low income	54,588	158,646	9.8	18.3	4.7	32.0	53.8	133.8	3,446	7,842		
Middle income	319,976	1,712,619	20.0	35.7	5.3	17.6	..	44.4	4,245	9,442		
Lower middle income	195,766	833,032	16.6	35.2	..	26.6	..	61.4	2,565	5,756		
Upper middle income	124,210	829,587	12.4	36.3	3.3	7.7	30.3	25.7	1,680	3,686		
Low & middle income	374,564	1,871,265	18.8	33.1	5.2	19.8	..	58.0	7,691	17,284		
East Asia & Pacific	86,515	723,605	16.4	45.8	6.6	48.0	118.1	72.5	774	2,886		
Europe & Central Asia	19,065	181,064	2.1	19.3	..	12.7	..	54.2	110	2,759		
Latin America & Carib.	78,470	609,072	7.6	33.4	2.1	6.3	29.8	21.6	1,748	1,570		
Middle East & N. Africa	5,265	131,528	29.0	26.3	2.4	6.1	..	19.8	817	2,020		
South Asia	42,655	117,817	10.8	19.7	5.6	3.8	54.0	180.3	3,231	7,010		
Sub-Saharan Africa	142,594	108,179	52.0	47.8	..	32.8	..	23.8	1,011	1,039		
High income	9,025,095	25,690,523	51.6	103.9	31.4	165.8	59.5	138.5	17,733	26,035		
Europe EMU	1,183,983	4,164,198	21.6	68.3	14.2	85.9	..	106.0	2,630	4,682		

Note: Aggregates for market capitalization are unavailable for 2002; those shown are for 2001.
a. Data refer to the S&P/IFC Global index. b. Data refer to the Nikkei 225 index. c. Data refer to the FT 100 index. d. Data refer to the S&P 500 index.

About the data

The development of an economy's financial markets is closely related to its overall development. Well-functioning financial systems provide good and easily accessible information. That lowers transaction costs, which in turn improves resource allocation and boosts economic growth. Both banking systems and stock markets enhance growth, the main factor in poverty reduction. At low levels of economic development commercial banks tend to dominate the financial system, while at higher levels domestic stock markets tend to become more active and efficient relative to domestic banks. The structure and development of a country's financial system are also influenced by the legal, regulatory, tax, and macroeconomic environment.

The stock market indicators in the table include measures of size (market capitalization, number of listed domestic companies) and liquidity (value traded as a percentage of gross domestic product, turnover ratio). The comparability of such indicators between countries may be limited by conceptual and statistical weaknesses, such as inaccurate reporting and differences in accounting standards. The percentage change in stock market prices in U.S. dollars, from the Standard & Poor's Investable (S&P/IFCI) and Global (S&P/IFCG) country indexes, is an important measure of overall performance. Regulatory and institutional factors that can affect investor confidence, such as the existence of a securities and exchange commission and the quality of laws to protect investors, may influence the functioning of stock markets but are not included in this table.

Stock market size can be measured in a number of ways, each of which may produce a different ranking among countries. Market capitalization shows the overall size of the stock market in U.S. dollars and as a percentage of GDP. The number of listed domestic companies is another measure of market size. Market size is positively correlated with the ability to mobilize capital and diversify risk.

Market liquidity, the ability to easily buy and sell securities, is measured by dividing the total value traded by GDP. This indicator complements the market capitalization ratio by showing whether market size is matched by trading. The turnover ratio—the value of shares traded as a percentage of market capitalization—is also a measure of liquidity as well as of transaction costs. (High turnover indicates low transaction costs.) The turnover ratio complements the ratio of value traded to GDP, because the turnover ratio is related to the size of the market and the value traded ratio to the size of the economy. A small, liquid market will have a high turnover ratio but a low value traded ratio. Liquidity is an important attribute of stock markets because, in theory, liquid markets improve the allocation of capital and enhance prospects for long-term economic growth. A more comprehensive measure of liquidity would include trading costs and the time and uncertainty in finding a counterpart in settling trades.

Standard & Poor's maintains a series of indexes for investors interested in investing in stock markets in developing countries. At the core of the Standard & Poor's family of emerging market indexes, the S&P/IFCG index is intended to represent the most active stocks in the markets it covers and to be the broadest possible indicator of market movements. The S&P/IFCI index, which applies the same calculation methodology as the S&P/IFCG index, is designed to measure the returns foreign portfolio investors might receive from investing in emerging market stocks that are legally and practically open to foreign portfolio investment.

Standard & Poor's Emerging Markets Data Base, the source for all the data in the table, provides regular updates on 54 emerging stock markets encompassing more than 2,200 stocks. The S&P/IFCG index includes 34 markets and more than 1,900 stocks, and the S&P/IFCI index covers 30 markets and close to 1,200 stocks. These indexes are widely used benchmarks for international portfolio management. See Standard & Poor's (2001b) for further information on the indexes.

Because markets included in Standard & Poor's emerging markets category vary widely in level of development, it is best to look at the entire category to identify the most significant market trends. And it is useful to remember that stock market trends may be distorted by currency conversions, especially when a currency has registered a significant devaluation.

Definitions

- **Market capitalization** (also known as market value) is the share price times the number of shares outstanding. • **Value traded** refers to the total value of shares traded during the period. • **Turnover ratio** is the total value of shares traded during the period divided by the average market capitalization for the period. Average market capitalization is calculated as the average of the end-of-period values for the current period and the previous period. • **Listed domestic companies** are the domestically incorporated companies listed on the country's stock exchanges at the end of the year. This indicator does not include investment companies, mutual funds, or other collective investment vehicles. • **S&P/IFC Investable Index price change** is the U.S. dollar price change in the stock markets covered by the S&P/IFCI country index, supplemented by the S&P/IFCG country index.

5.4a

Top five emerging stock markets in 2002

Market capitalization ($ billions)

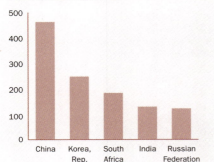

Market capitalization in China fell from $524 billion in 2001 to $463 billion in 2002, yet it remains almost twice that in the Republic of Korea, with the second highest market capitalization.

Source: Table 5.4.

Data sources

The data on stock markets are from Standard & Poor's *Emerging Stock Markets Factbook 2002*, which draws on the Emerging Markets Data Base, supplemented by other data from Standard & Poor's. The firm collects data through an annual survey of the world's stock exchanges, supplemented by information provided by its network of correspondents and by Reuters. The GDP data are from the World Bank's national accounts data files. *About the data* is based on Demirgüç-Kunt and Levine (1996a) and Beck and Levine (2001).

5.5 Financial depth and efficiency

	Domestic credit provided by banking sector		Liquid liabilities		Quasi-liquid liabilities		Ratio of bank liquid reserves to bank assets		Interest rate spread		Risk premium on lending	
									Lending minus deposit rate percentage		Prime lending rate minus	
	% of GDP		% of GDP		% of GDP		%		points		Treasury bill rate	
	1990	2001	1990	2001	1990	2001	1990	2001	1990	2001	1990	2001
Afghanistan	..	..	..	..	..	..	..	..	..	..	..	..
Albania	..	46.5	..	66.7	..	42.4	..	11.6	2.1	11.9	..	11.9
Algeria	74.5	39.0	73.5	58.6	24.8	29.3	1.3	10.6	..	3.3	..	3.8
Angola	..	−0.6	..	20.1	..	13.3	..	16.6	..	48.1	..	..
Argentina	32.4	37.3	11.5	27.2	7.1	21.3	7.4	9.3	..	11.5	..	..
Armenia	58.7	9.1	79.9	13.5	42.9	6.9	13.6	8.5	..	11.8	..	6.8
Australia	71.5	94.0	55.1	71.1	43.3	47.6	1.5	1.2	4.5	4.9	4.0	3.3
Austria	121.4	126.3	..	..	..	..	2.1	..	..	3.4	..	..
Azerbaijan	65.9	5.3	38.6	12.9	13.4	6.6	4.5	10.4	..	11.2	..	3.2
Bangladesh	23.9	38.7	23.4	37.2	16.8	27.7	12.8	10.3	4.0	7.3	..	..
Belarus	..	17.1	..	15.2	..	9.9	..	9.8	..	12.8	..	..
Belgium	73.1	120.4	..	..	..	..	0.2	..	6.9	5.1	3.4	4.3
Benin	22.4	4.6	26.7	31.0	5.9	7.9	29.3	19.5	9.0	..	..	..
Bolivia	30.7	63.0	24.5	55.9	18.0	46.9	18.8	6.0	18.0	10.2	..	8.6
Bosnia and Herzegovina	..	..	..	..	..	..	..	..	..	..	..	..
Botswana	−46.0	−73.5	21.9	31.7	13.6	23.9	11.0	3.4	1.8	5.6	..	..
Brazil	89.8	59.2	26.4	30.0	18.5	23.0	6.7	7.8	..	39.8	..	37.6
Bulgaria	118.5	20.4	71.9	40.9	53.6	24.4	10.2	8.2	8.9	8.2	8.6	6.5
Burkina Faso	13.7	15.3	21.3	21.6	7.5	7.2	12.7	8.8	9.0	..	..	..
Burundi	23.2	32.7	18.2	20.1	6.5	6.1	2.8	4.8	..	..	..	..
Cambodia	..	6.5	..	16.5	..	11.9	..	48.5	..	12.1	..	..
Cameroon	31.2	16.4	22.6	18.3	10.1	7.1	3.4	20.8	11.0	15.7	..	..
Canada	82.3	91.0	74.3	77.1	59.8	53.6	1.6	0.6	1.3	2.0	1.3	2.0
Central African Republic	12.9	12.2	15.3	15.5	1.8	1.5	2.8	2.5	11.0	15.7	..	..
Chad	11.5	12.5	14.6	12.7	0.6	0.8	3.3	12.4	11.0	15.7	..	..
Chile	73.0	73.4	40.7	46.9	32.8	37.1	3.8	3.1	8.5	5.7	..	..
China	90.0	140.6	79.2	163.0	41.4	98.7	15.7	12.7	0.7	3.6	..	..
Hong Kong, China	156.3	142.5	181.7	237.0	166.8	220.3	0.1	0.2	3.3	2.7	2.7	3.4
Colombia	35.9	34.7	29.8	31.7	19.3	22.0	26.3	5.5	8.8	8.3	..	..
Congo, Dem. Rep.	25.3	..	12.9	..	2.1	..	49.0	..	..	..	..	..
Congo, Rep.	29.1	13.5	22.0	12.8	6.1	1.0	2.0	21.6	11.0	15.7	..	..
Costa Rica	29.9	33.3	42.7	37.5	30.0	23.9	68.5	14.7	11.4	12.1	..	..
Côte d'Ivoire	44.5	21.9	28.8	24.1	10.9	6.8	2.1	5.8	9.0	..	..	..
Croatia	..	51.9	..	62.6	..	48.6	..	11.8	499.3	6.3	..	..
Cuba	..	..	..	..	..	..	..	..	..	..	..	..
Czech Republic	..	49.8	..	74.5	..	47.4	..	19.0	..	4.1	..	2.0
Denmark	63.0	151.6	59.0	49.7	29.4	18.8	1.1	0.7	6.2	4.9	..	..
Dominican Republic	31.5	41.7	28.6	39.7	13.3	28.2	31.1	24.1	15.2	8.7	..	..
Ecuador	15.0	37.1	20.4	28.9	11.3	18.2	22.6	3.3	−6.0	8.9	..	..
Egypt, Arab Rep.	106.8	103.6	87.9	88.8	60.7	70.2	17.1	18.8	7.0	3.8	..	6.1
El Salvador	32.0	42.5	30.6	46.5	19.6	38.1	33.4	29.8	3.2	4.6	..	..
Eritrea	..	..	..	..	..	..	..	..	..	..	..	..
Estonia	66.7	43.5	136.0	42.3	95.2	16.4	43.1	11.2	..	3.7	..	..
Ethiopia	67.0	58.2	42.2	46.5	12.6	23.6	24.0	8.4	3.6	3.9	3.0	7.8
Finland	83.1	63.7	54.4	..	..	..	4.1	..	4.1	3.8	..	..
France	104.4	108.0	..	..	..	..	1.0	..	6.1	4.0	0.4	2.7
Gabon	20.0	20.8	17.8	17.8	6.6	7.4	2.0	9.6	11.0	15.7	..	..
Gambia, The	3.4	25.0	20.7	38.7	8.8	20.3	8.8	12.7	15.2	11.5	..	..
Georgia	..	20.5	..	11.3	..	5.3	..	11.6	..	19.5	..	..
Germany	103.4	147.5	68.9	..	..	..	3.2	..	4.5	6.5	3.5	6.4
Ghana	13.2	0.8	14.1	17.4	3.4	17.4	20.2	8.3	..	..	..	..
Greece	99.3	110.4	..	..	..	..	13.9	17.2	8.1	5.3	3.6	4.5
Guatemala	17.4	15.5	21.2	30.9	11.8	17.8	31.8	15.8	5.1	10.2	..	..
Guinea	6.0	9.0	0.8	11.8	0.8	2.2	6.2	25.7	0.2	11.9	..	4.7
Guinea-Bissau	77.5	13.6	68.9	48.2	4.4	0.5	10.8	32.9	13.1	..	..	..
Haiti	34.3	31.5	32.6	37.7	16.6	25.8	74.9	43.6	..	15.0	..	15.1

	Domestic credit provided by banking sector		Liquid liabilities		Quasi-liquid liabilities		Ratio of bank liquid reserves to bank assets		Interest rate spread		Risk premium on lending	
									Lending minus deposit rate percentage points		Prime lending rate minus Treasury bill rate	
	% of GDP		% of GDP		% of GDP		%					
	1990	2001	1990	2001	1990	2001	1990	2001	1990	2001	1990	2001
Honduras	40.9	34.7	33.6	54.8	18.8	42.3	6.6	18.2	8.3	9.3	..	..
Hungary	105.5	50.0	43.8	46.9	19.0	28.2	11.0	6.7	4.1	2.9	–1.4	1.3
India	51.5	54.7	43.1	58.7	28.1	41.8	14.8	7.2	..	..	..	..
Indonesia	45.5	60.6	40.4	56.7	29.1	44.9	4.2	6.7	3.3	3.1	..	..
Iran, Islamic Rep.	70.8	47.4	57.6	44.8	31.1	25.9	66.0	34.1	..	..	..	..
Iraq	..	..	..	..	..	..	..	..	..	..	..	..
Ireland	55.2	110.8	44.5	..	..	..	4.8	..	5.0	4.7	0.4	..
Israel	106.2	95.2	70.2	105.4	63.6	97.1	11.9	11.9	12.0	3.9	11.4	3.5
Italy	89.4	99.8	70.5	..	..	..	12.0	..	7.3	4.6	1.7	2.5
Jamaica	32.2	23.4	47.2	46.7	35.0	31.6	37.4	22.4	6.6	11.0	4.3	3.9
Japan	259.7	317.5	182.4	199.5	155.3	143.5	1.5	2.5	3.4	1.9	..	..
Jordan	117.9	89.7	131.2	116.6	77.8	83.1	20.5	24.0	2.2	5.1	..	..
Kazakhstan	..	11.4	..	16.9	..	8.7	..	6.1	..	..	..	..
Kenya	52.9	42.8	43.3	41.5	29.3	27.4	9.9	9.7	5.1	13.0	4.0	7.1
Korea, Dem. Rep.	..	..	..	..	..	..	..	..	..	..	..	..
Korea, Rep.	65.7	110.4	54.6	104.3	45.7	94.5	6.3	2.4	0.0	1.9	..	..
Kuwait	243.0	102.1	192.2	91.6	153.9	75.2	1.2	1.0	0.4	3.4	..	..
Kyrgyz Republic	..	9.7	..	11.1	..	3.6	..	7.1	..	24.8	..	18.3
Lao PDR	5.1	15.3	7.2	16.4	3.1	14.0	3.4	25.7	2.5	19.7	..	3.5
Latvia	..	31.4	..	33.3	..	15.1	..	5.4	..	5.9	..	6.0
Lebanon	132.6	201.9	193.7	210.1	170.9	200.7	3.9	18.3	23.1	6.3	21.1	6.0
Lesotho	32.5	5.3	38.8	29.1	22.4	10.2	23.0	5.2	7.4	11.7	4.1	7.1
Liberia	319.5	170.3	101.9	11.2	20.8	4.5	67.3	67.8	..	16.2	..	..
Libya	104.1	57.8	68.1	54.7	13.7	12.6	26.4	24.3	1.5	4.0	1.5	1.5
Lithuania	..	15.8	..	26.5	..	12.4	..	11.5	..	6.6	..	1.9
Macedonia, FYR	..	19.5	..	25.9	..	21.1	..	6.6	..	9.4	..	..
Madagascar	26.2	15.9	17.8	22.3	5.3	5.0	8.5	25.9	5.3	13.3	..	15.0
Malawi	19.7	13.4	20.2	19.4	10.8	11.5	32.9	28.5	8.9	21.2	8.1	13.8
Malaysia	75.7	155.3	64.4	134.2	43.0	109.2	5.9	10.6	1.3	3.3	1.1	3.9
Mali	13.7	17.1	20.5	25.3	5.5	5.7	50.8	11.5	9.0	..	..	..
Mauritania	54.7	0.5	28.5	15.0	7.0	4.2	6.1	3.9	5.0	..	..	..
Mauritius	48.4	79.5	67.9	85.4	52.7	72.9	8.8	5.0	5.4	11.3	..	..
Mexico	36.6	24.7	22.8	24.8	16.4	15.6	4.2	8.2	..	9.1	..	2.6
Moldova	62.8	27.5	70.3	25.5	35.4	12.4	8.3	14.4	..	7.8	..	14.5
Mongolia	73.4	12.5	56.2	28.7	14.7	15.2	2.0	14.8	..	15.9	..	..
Morocco	60.1	85.9	61.0	86.4	18.4	21.8	11.3	8.5	0.5	8.2	..	..
Mozambique	15.6	13.1	26.5	30.7	5.2	17.3	61.5	13.7	..	7.7	..	–2.0
Myanmar	32.8	35.1	27.9	33.5	7.8	13.1	271.8	22.1	2.1	5.5	..	..
Namibia	17.1	49.7	20.5	43.2	12.0	19.6	4.4	3.3	10.6	7.7	6.3	5.2
Nepal	28.9	46.2	32.2	53.2	18.5	35.6	12.7	9.7	2.5	2.9	6.5	2.7
Netherlands	103.5	155.4	..	..	..	..	0.3	..	8.4	1.9	..	..
New Zealand	80.6	114.9	77.0	87.1	64.0	72.3	0.8	0.5	4.4	4.5	2.2	4.3
Nicaragua	206.6	..	56.9	..	23.1	..	20.2	27.7	12.5	13.8	..	..
Niger	16.2	8.0	19.8	9.5	8.3	2.3	42.9	13.1	9.0	..	..	..
Nigeria	23.7	18.0	23.6	28.6	10.3	10.8	11.6	24.0	5.5	8.2	6.9	5.9
Norway	89.5	46.3	59.9	52.7	27.0	8.6	0.5	2.2	4.6	1.5	..	..
Oman	16.6	37.0	28.9	31.5	19.3	24.3	6.9	3.5	1.4	4.7	..	..
Pakistan	50.9	45.5	39.8	49.5	10.0	21.2	8.9	12.4	..	..	..	..
Panama	52.7	114.9	41.1	92.7	33.0	79.9	..	..	3.6	4.1	..	..
Papua New Guinea	35.7	24.2	35.2	31.9	24.0	17.7	3.2	8.6	6.9	7.3	4.1	3.9
Paraguay	14.9	27.9	22.3	38.0	13.7	28.7	31.0	23.0	8.1	12.0	..	..
Peru	20.2	25.8	24.8	32.3	11.8	21.0	22.0	23.2	2,335.0	10.5	..	..
Philippines	26.9	63.1	37.0	62.9	28.4	52.1	20.9	7.3	4.6	3.7	0.4	2.7
Poland	19.5	37.7	34.0	47.0	17.2	33.9	20.6	6.3	462.5	6.6	–5.0	3.4
Portugal	69.4	150.1	..	..	..	..	29.0	..	7.8	2.8	8.3	..
Puerto Rico	..	..	..	..	..	..	..	..	..	..	..	..

5.5 Financial depth and efficiency

	Domestic credit provided by banking sector		Liquid liabilities		Quasi-liquid liabilities		Ratio of bank liquid reserves to bank assets		Interest rate spread Lending minus deposit rate percentage points		Risk premium on lending Prime lending rate minus Treasury bill rate	
	% of GDP		% of GDP		% of GDP		%					
	1990	2001	1990	2001	1990	2001	1990	2001	1990	2001	1990	2001
Romania	79.7	12.4	60.4	23.4	32.7	18.1	1.2	44.5	..	..	..	..
Russian Federation	..	24.3	..	23.5	..	10.3	..	13.1	..	13.1	..	5.5
Rwanda	17.1	12.5	14.9	16.8	7.0	8.4	4.3	2.5	6.3	..	..	..
Saudi Arabia	58.7	66.9	47.9	47.4	21.9	21.7	5.6	4.5	..	..	..	..
Senegal	33.8	24.7	22.9	26.5	9.7	10.7	14.1	10.0	9.0	..	..	..
Sierra Leone	36.3	52.1	18.1	19.5	3.6	6.8	64.1	9.4	12.0	16.6	5.0	10.5
Singapore	75.6	102.0	123.4	117.9	100.5	94.4	3.7	2.5	2.7	4.1	3.7	4.0
Slovak Republic	..	61.6	..	68.0	..	45.2	..	9.3	..	4.8	..	..
Slovenia	36.8	49.5	34.2	57.3	25.8	47.1	2.7	4.3	142.0	5.2	..	4.2
Somalia	..	..	..	..	..	..	..	..	..	..	..	..
South Africa	97.8	166.9	44.6	48.7	27.2	16.7	3.3	2.6	2.1	4.4	3.2	4.1
Spain	106.9	125.3	..	..	..	..	8.7	..	5.4	2.1	1.8	1.2
Sri Lanka	43.1	47.1	34.9	47.7	22.6	39.0	9.9	8.0	−6.4	8.4	−1.1	1.8
Sudan	20.4	9.6	20.1	13.3	2.9	5.0	79.5	27.5	..	..	..	..
Swaziland	7.5	−6.1	28.3	21.6	19.8	14.5	21.5	5.7	5.8	7.1	3.4	6.1
Sweden	140.3	78.7	52.3	44.6	..	..	1.8	0.4	6.8	3.7	3.0	1.9
Switzerland	179.0	173.5	145.2	132.1	118.6	90.4	1.1	0.9	−0.9	2.6	−0.9	1.6
Syrian Arab Republic	56.6	28.5	54.1	71.3	9.8	28.3	46.0	6.2	5.0	5.0	..	..
Tajikistan	..	24.8	..	7.9	..	2.8	..	13.5	..	−15.9	..	..
Tanzania	34.6	9.8	19.9	20.4	6.3	11.1	5.3	14.3	..	15.5	..	16.1
Thailand	91.1	112.0	74.9	117.2	66.0	104.7	3.1	3.3	2.2	4.7	..	..
Togo	21.3	20.5	36.1	26.0	19.1	8.5	59.0	6.1	9.0	..	..	..
Trinidad and Tobago	58.5	40.3	54.6	55.4	42.7	43.1	13.5	15.6	6.9	8.0	5.4	7.1
Tunisia	62.5	73.9	51.5	59.5	26.7	35.1	1.6	3.8	..	..	..	..
Turkey	19.4	72.5	24.1	59.0	16.4	53.0	16.3	8.9	..	..	..	..
Turkmenistan	..	30.7	..	20.4	..	8.9	..	6.7	..	..	..	..
Uganda	17.8	10.2	7.6	16.5	1.4	7.4	15.2	14.1	7.4	14.2	−2.3	11.7
Ukraine	83.2	23.8	50.1	22.4	9.0	7.6	49.0	15.9	..	21.3	..	..
United Arab Emirates	34.7	..	46.3	..	37.7	..	4.4	11.4	..	..	..	..
United Kingdom	121.2	140.5	..	..	..	..	0.5	0.3	2.2	..	0.7	0.3
United States	110.9	163.9	65.5	69.2	49.4	53.3	2.3	1.1	..	..	2.5	3.5
Uruguay	46.7	57.1	58.1	59.6	51.5	54.1	31.1	14.7	76.6	37.4	..	..
Uzbekistan	..	..	..	..	..	..	..	..	..	..	..	..
Venezuela, RB	37.4	15.5	38.8	18.6	29.4	8.3	21.9	28.7	7.7	6.9	..	..
Vietnam	4.7	39.5	22.7	51.8	9.3	28.6	25.3	6.6	..	4.1	..	3.9
West Bank and Gaza	..	..	..	..	..	..	..	..	..	..	..	..
Yemen, Rep.	60.6	2.8	55.1	36.3	10.4	18.2	121.2	18.7	..	4.5	..	4.2
Yugoslavia, Fed. Rep.	..	..	..	..	..	..	..	..	..	..	..	..
Zambia	67.8	51.6	21.8	21.0	10.6	13.1	33.7	16.9	9.4	22.8	9.2	2.0
Zimbabwe	41.7	52.9	41.8	43.6	30.3	17.1	12.2	16.5	2.9	24.1	3.3	20.4
World	**121.3 w**	**152.4 w**	**83.7 w**	**95.7 w**	**.. w**	**69.6 w**	**9.9 m**	**9.8 m**	**5.5 m**	**7.3 m**	**.. m**	**.. m**
Low income	44.6	45.1	37.1	48.3	22.2	32.4	12.8	12.9	8.2	13.5	..	..
Middle income	65.7	73.6	44.0	72.1	26.1	46.6	14.6	9.3	5.0	7.4	..	..
Lower middle income	71.7	96.0	61.7	100.8	36.4	63.2	18.8	8.9	6.2	8.3	..	..
Upper middle income	62.2	48.1	30.8	39.4	19.5	27.7	8.8	9.5	6.2	6.3	..	..
Low & middle income	61.2	68.7	42.6	68.0	25.3	44.1	13.5	11.2	6.7	8.8	..	..
East Asia & Pacific	76.4	125.9	67.5	141.1	41.5	90.9	5.1	10.6	2.2	4.7	..	..
Europe & Central Asia	..	37.5	..	39.6	..	26.6	..	10.4	..	8.0	..	..
Latin America & Carib.	59.3	38.9	25.4	29.3	17.8	20.8	22.3	15.6	8.2	10.2	..	..
Middle East & N. Africa	72.4	70.5	62.5	65.2	29.4	39.3	14.2	14.5	2.2	4.7	..	..
South Asia	48.9	52.2	41.0	55.8	25.2	38.6	12.7	9.7	2.5	7.3	..	..
Sub-Saharan Africa	56.8	74.2	32.4	35.2	17.2	14.5	11.9	11.5	8.9	14.2	..	..
High income	132.1	172.9	93.0	105.5	..	78.6	1.9	1.1	4.6	4.0	2.5	3.5
Europe EMU	99.2	124.2	..	..	..	..	4.1	..	6.5	4.6	2.6	3.5

About the data

The organization and performance of financial activities in a country affect economic growth through their impact on how businesses raise and manage funds. These funds come from savings: savers accumulate claims on financial institutions, which pass the funds to their final users. But even if a country has savings, growth may not materialize—because the financial system may fail to direct the savings to where they can be invested most efficiently. Enabling it to do so requires established payments systems, the availability of price information, a way to manage uncertainty and control risk, and mechanisms to deal with problems of asymmetric information between parties to a financial transaction.

As an economy develops, the indirect lending by savers to investors becomes more efficient and gradually increases financial assets relative to gross domestic product (GDP). More specialized savings and financial institutions emerge and more financing instruments become available, spreading risks and reducing costs to liability holders. Securities markets mature, allowing savers to invest their resources directly in financial assets issued by firms. Financial systems vary widely across countries: banks, nonbank financial institutions, and stock markets are larger, more active, and more efficient in richer countries.

The ratio of domestic credit provided by the banking sector to GDP is used to measure the growth of the banking system because it reflects the extent to which savings are financial. In a few countries governments may hold international reserves as deposits in the banking system rather than in the central bank. Since the claims on the central government are a net item (claims on the central government minus central government deposits), this net figure may be negative, resulting in a negative figure for domestic credit provided by the banking sector.

Liquid liabilities are a general indicator of the size of financial intermediaries relative to the size of the economy, or an overall measure of financial sector development. Quasi-liquid liabilities are long-term deposits and assets—such as bonds, commercial paper, and certificates of deposit—that can be converted into currency or demand deposits, but at a cost. The ratio of bank liquid reserves to bank assets captures the banking system's liquidity. In countries whose banking system is liquid, adverse macroeconomic conditions should be less likely to lead to banking and financial crises. Data on domestic credit and liquid and quasi-liquid liabilities are cited on an end-of-year basis.

No less important than the size and structure of the financial sector is its efficiency, as indicated by the margin between the cost of mobilizing liabilities and the earnings on assets—or the interest rate spread. A narrowing of the interest rate spread reduces transaction costs, which lowers the overall cost of investment and is therefore crucial to economic growth. Interest rates reflect the responsiveness of financial institutions to competition and price incentives. The interest rate spread, also known as the intermediation margin, is a summary measure of a banking system's efficiency (although if governments set interest rates, the spreads become less reliable measures of efficiency). The risk premium on lending can be approximated by the spread between the lending rate to the private sector (line 60p in the International Monetary Fund's *International Financial Statistics*, or IFS) and the "risk free" treasury bill interest rate (IFS line 60c). A small spread indicates that the market considers its best corporate customers to be low risk. Interest rates are expressed as annual averages.

In some countries financial markets are distorted by restrictions on foreign investment, selective credit controls, and controls on deposit and lending rates. Interest rates may reflect the diversion of resources to finance the public sector deficit through statutory reserve requirements and direct borrowing from the banking system. And where state-owned banks dominate the financial sector, noncommercial considerations may unduly influence credit allocation. The indicators in the table provide quantitative assessments of each country's financial sector, but qualitative assessments of policies, laws, and regulations are needed to analyze overall financial conditions. Recent international financial crises highlight the risks of weak financial intermediation, poor corporate governance, and deficient government policies.

The accuracy of financial data depends on the quality of accounting systems, which are weak in some developing countries. Some of the indicators in the table are highly correlated, particularly the ratios of domestic credit, liquid liabilities, and quasi-liquid liabilities to GDP, because changes in liquid and quasi-liquid liabilities flow directly from changes in domestic credit. Moreover, the precise definition of the financial aggregates presented varies by country.

The indicators reported here do not capture the activities of the informal sector, which remains an important source of finance in developing economies. Personal credit or credit extended through community-based pooling of assets may be the only source of credit for small farmers, small businesses, and home-based producers. And in financially repressed economies the rationing of formal credit forces many borrowers and lenders to turn to the informal market, which is very expensive, or to self-financing and family savings.

Definitions

• **Domestic credit provided by banking sector** includes all credit to various sectors on a gross basis, with the exception of credit to the central government, which is net. The banking sector includes monetary authorities, deposit money banks, and other banking institutions for which data are available (including institutions that do not accept transferable deposits but do incur such liabilities as time and savings deposits). Examples of other banking institutions include savings and mortgage loan institutions and building and loan associations. • **Liquid liabilities** are also known as broad money, or M3. They include bank deposits of generally less than one year plus currency. Liquid liabilities are the sum of currency and deposits in the central bank (M0), plus transferable deposits and electronic currency (M1), plus time and savings deposits, foreign currency transferable deposits, certificates of deposit, and securities repurchase agreements (M2), plus travelers' checks, foreign currency time deposits, commercial paper, and shares of mutual funds or market funds held by residents. The ratio of liquid liabilities to GDP indicates the relative size of these readily available forms of money—money that the owners can use to buy goods and services without incurring any cost. • **Quasi-liquid liabilities** are the M3 money supply less M1. • **Ratio of bank liquid reserves to bank assets** is the ratio of domestic currency holdings and deposits with the monetary authorities to claims on other governments, nonfinancial public enterprises, the private sector, and other banking institutions. • **Interest rate spread** is the interest rate charged by banks on loans to prime customers minus the interest rate paid by commercial or similar banks for demand, time, or savings deposits. • **Risk premium on lending** is the interest rate charged by banks on loans to prime private sector customers minus the "risk free" treasury bill interest rate at which short-term government securities are issued or traded in the market. In some countries this spread may be negative, indicating that the market considers its best corporate clients to be lower risk than the government.

Data sources

The data on credit, liabilities, bank reserves, and interest rates are collected from central banks and finance ministries and reported in the print and electronic editions of the International Monetary Fund's *International Financial Statistics*.

5.6 Tax policies

	Tax revenue	Taxes on income, profits, and capital gains		Domestic taxes on goods and services		Export duties		Import duties		Highest marginal tax rate [a]		
	% of GDP	% of total taxes		% of value added in industry and services		% of tax revenue		% of tax revenue		Individual rate %	on income over $	Corporate rate %
	2001	1990	2001	1990	2001	1990	2001	1990	2001	2002	2002	2002
Afghanistan	..	..	..	..	..	..	..	..	..	..	..	..
Albania	..	..	..	..	..	..	..	..	..	..	..	..
Algeria	32.1	..	77.9	..	3.3	..	0.0	..	12.1	..	..	..
Angola	..	..	..	..	..	..	..	..	..	..	..	..
Argentina	12.5	2.7	19.9	2.2	5.5	9.3	0.2	2.6	4.5	35	120,000	35
Armenia	..	..	..	..	..	..	..	..	..	..	..	..
Australia	22.0	70.9	..	5.9	..	0.1	..	4.4	..	47	30,451	30
Austria	35.1	20.8	27.0	10.0	10.6	0.0	..	1.6	..	50	52,324	34
Azerbaijan	16.6	..	23.1	..	9.0	..	0.0	..	9.0	35	12,428	27
Bangladesh	7.0	..	14.5	..	5.0	..	0.0	..	30.0	..	..	..
Belarus	27.0	12.1	10.3	17.1	13.6	3.6	..	0.4	..	..	..	..
Belgium	..	36.1	..	11.5	..	0.0	..	0.0	..	52	39,665	39
Benin	..	..	..	..	..	..	..	..	..	..	..	..
Bolivia	13.9	7.9	8.7	5.6	11.3	0.0	0.0	11.1	6.4	13	..	25
Bosnia and Herzegovina	..	..	..	..	..	..	..	..	..	..	..	..
Botswana	..	71.7	..	1.0	..	0.0	..	24.7	..	25	14,085	15
Brazil	..	24.5	..	7.1	..	0.0	..	2.5	..	28	10,575	15
Bulgaria	25.3	40.6	17.0	9.9	16.3	0.0	0.0	2.5	2.6	29	5,545	15
Burkina Faso	..	24.7	..	4.9	..	1.1	..	33.1	..	..	..	..
Burundi	16.7	23.4	22.5	16.6	17.0	3.1	0.0	23.2	16.4	..	..	..
Cambodia	..	..	..	..	..	..	..	..	..	20	38,462	20
Cameroon	12.5	25.1	26.0	4.3	7.2	1.7	3.9	18.9	31.6	60	10,726	39
Canada	19.3	59.1	57.3	4.0	..	0.0	0.0	3.2	1.4	29	62,783	38
Central African Republic	..	..	..	..	..	..	..	..	..	..	..	..
Chad	..	20.3	..	3.9	..	..	..	..	..	..	..	..
Chile	18.7	15.8	24.7	10.4	13.0	..	..	..	..	43	6,534	16
China	6.8	49.8	6.8	1.5	6.5	0.0	..	22.1	..	45	12,048	30
Hong Kong, China	..	..	..	..	..	..	..	..	..	17	13,462	16
Colombia	10.8	36.4	39.9	4.8	6.2	2.0	0.0	22.5	8.5	35	35,073	35
Congo, Dem. Rep.	0.0	28.5	16.7	2.6	0.0	4.1	1.0	45.1	33.7	60	1,500	40
Congo, Rep.	10.7	40.2	16.0	4.1	6.6	0.0	0.0	32.3	23.2	50	14,210	45
Costa Rica	20.3	11.5	15.1	8.7	10.9	8.0	0.2	18.2	4.2	25	17,464	30
Côte d'Ivoire	16.9	18.1	21.0	8.9	4.9	3.7	15.3	28.4	27.6	10	3,432	35
Croatia	36.9	17.4	8.7	9.6	23.5	0.0	0.0	3.6	6.8	35	8,758	..
Cuba	..	..	..	..	..	..	..	..	..	..	..	..
Czech Republic	32.3	..	21.1	..	11.3	..	0.0	..	1.4	32	9,134	31
Denmark	31.9	43.5	40.2	18.9	19.5	0.0	0.0	0.1	0.0	59	..	30
Dominican Republic	15.6	23.8	19.6	3.1	4.8	0.1	0.0	41.4	44.1	25	15,165	25
Ecuador	..	62.9	..	4.5	..	0.3	..	12.1	..	25	49,600	25
Egypt, Arab Rep.	..	26.4	..	4.1	..	0.0	..	18.9	..	32	10,823	40
El Salvador	1.6	..	18.6	..	0.8	..	0.0	..	7.3	..	..	..
Eritrea	..	..	..	..	..	..	..	..	..	..	..	..
Estonia	27.5	27.5	14.7	14.8	15.3	0.0	0.0	0.8	0.2	26	678	35
Ethiopia	13.0	40.9	33.1	9.1	7.4	2.8	2.9	18.0	26.3	..	..	..
Finland	..	34.5	..	17.7	..	0.0	..	1.0	..	37	50,940	29
France	..	18.7	..	13.1	..	0.0	..	0.0	..	..	..	33
Gabon	..	35.9	..	5.0	..	2.8	..	23.4	..	50	31,462	35
Gambia, The	..	13.7	..	12.2	..	0.2	..	45.6	..	..	..	..
Georgia	9.7	..	4.0	..	8.9	..	0.0	..	6.1	..	..	..
Germany	..	17.5	..	6.8	..	0.0	..	0.0	..	49	49,736	25
Ghana	..	25.1	..	6.8	..	12.4	..	28.7	..	30	7,059	33
Greece	..	23.3	..	14.5	..	0.0	..	0.1	..	40	21,157	35
Guatemala	..	..	..	..	..	..	..	..	..	31	38,155	31
Guinea	11.2	12.6	10.1	3.2	0.8	51.7	0.2	11.2	42.9	..	..	..
Guinea-Bissau	..	..	..	..	..	..	..	..	..	..	..	..
Haiti	..	..	..	..	..	..	..	..	..	..	..	..

	Tax revenue	Taxes on income, profits, and capital gains		Domestic taxes on goods and services		Export duties		Import duties		Highest marginal tax rate [a]		
											Individual		Corporate
	% of GDP	% of total taxes		% of value added in industry and services		% of tax revenue		% of tax revenue		rate %	on income over $	rate %
	2001	1990	2001	1990	2001	1990	2001	1990	2001	2002	2002	2002
Honduras	..	..	..	..	..	..	..	..	..	25	32,916	..
Hungary	32.1	21.2	23.4	22.6	..	1.3	0.0	5.6	3.3	40	4,373	18
India	10.0	18.6	37.4	7.4	5.6	0.1	0.1	35.8	24.1	30	3,124	36
Indonesia	13.2	65.4	48.0	5.6	6.3	0.1	0.3	6.6	4.6	35	19,231	30
Iran, Islamic Rep.	8.5	24.7	41.7	1.0	1.6	0.0	0.0	18.6	14.4	54	128,205	25
Iraq	..	..	..	..	..	..	..	..	..	..	..	..
Ireland	..	39.7	..	15.5	..	0.0	..	0.0	..	42	25,316	16
Israel	37.7	42.4	45.2	..	..	0.0	0.0	1.4	0.7	50	53,757	36
Italy	38.5	37.7	38.8	12.7	11.6	0.0	0.0	0.0	0.0	45	63,040	36
Jamaica	25.4	41.5	39.0	8.2	11.5	0.0	0.0	14.0	9.3	25	2,547	33
Japan	..	73.0	..	2.4	..	0.0	..	1.4	..	37	136,415	30
Jordan	19.0	22.9	16.4	6.8	10.6	0.0	0.0	34.7	20.4	..	..	..
Kazakhstan	9.5	..	28.9	..	6.8	..	0.3	..	5.7	30	..	30
Kenya	..	32.9	..	15.9	..	0.0	..	17.8	..	30	5,612	30
Korea, Dem. Rep.	..	..	..	..	..	..	..	..	..	..	..	..
Korea, Rep.	..	37.5	..	6.7	..	0.0	..	13.0	..	36	60,332	27
Kuwait	3.4	19.5	8.2	0.0	..	0.0	0.0	76.8	0.0	0	..	0
Kyrgyz Republic	11.7	..	18.0	..	15.7	..	..	..	..	..	..	..
Lao PDR	..	..	..	..	..	..	..	..	..	40	7,894	..
Latvia	24.4	..	15.4	..	13.6	..	0.0	..	1.3	25	..	22
Lebanon	14.1	..	15.1	..	4.9	..	..	..	39.0	..	..	..
Lesotho	..	12.7	..	12.8	..	0.2	..	63.6	..	..	..	..
Liberia	..	..	..	..	..	..	..	..	..	..	..	..
Libya	..	..	..	..	..	..	..	..	..	..	..	..
Lithuania	22.3	22.2	11.9	16.4	14.1	..	0.0	..	1.3	33	..	5
Macedonia, FYR	..	..	..	..	..	..	..	..	..	..	..	..
Madagascar	11.3	15.7	15.7	3.4	5.2	8.5	0.0	50.1	53.5	..	..	..
Malawi	..	42.5	..	13.9	..	0.0	..	18.7	..	38	948	38
Malaysia	..	42.5	..	6.3	..	9.7	..	15.1	..	28	65,789	28
Mali	..	..	..	..	..	..	..	..	..	..	..	..
Mauritania	..	..	..	..	..	..	..	..	..	..	..	..
Mauritius	17.4	15.2	14.0	7.0	9.2	4.6	0.0	45.7	29.3	25	828	25
Mexico	13.2	34.2	38.1	10.2	10.6	0.1	0.0	6.9	4.5	40	258,269	35
Moldova	19.0	..	3.3	..	16.0	..	0.0	..	5.1	..	..	..
Mongolia	23.0	28.2	10.5	9.3	18.2	0.0	0.4	19.6	9.8	..	..	..
Morocco	25.0	27.3	28.5	12.1	12.7	0.3	0.0	20.3	18.8	44	5,243	35
Mozambique	..	..	..	..	..	..	..	..	..	20	5,754	35
Myanmar	3.0	29.8	34.5	6.8	4.0	0.0	0.0	23.3	7.2	30	..	30
Namibia	29.9	39.4	35.3	8.4	8.8	3.6	..	26.9	..	36	17,241	35
Nepal	9.5	13.0	21.9	6.6	7.1	0.4	1.3	37.0	30.9	..	..	..
Netherlands	..	33.6	..	11.5	..	0.0	..	0.0	..	52	43,169	35
New Zealand	28.4	62.2	68.3	13.2	..	0.0	0.0	2.5	1.8	39	24,845	33
Nicaragua	..	20.0	14.1	16.9	..	0.0	0.0	21.3	7.8	25	31,545	25
Niger	..	..	..	..	..	..	..	..	..	..	..	30
Nigeria	..	..	..	..	..	..	..	..	..	25	1,553	28
Norway	33.2	21.7	24.5	17.0	17.8	0.1	0.0	0.6	0.6	..	..	28
Oman	7.2	87.6	77.1	0.3	..	0.0	0.0	7.8	10.3	0	..	12
Pakistan	12.4	12.8	29.0	8.6	8.5	0.0	0.0	44.4	15.4	35	11,111	..
Panama	16.8	24.4	29.4	4.8	..	1.3	0.0	15.8	..	30	200,000	30
Papua New Guinea	21.9	47.0	56.2	5.0	3.5	2.1	4.5	29.3	24.2	47	24,842	25
Paraguay	9.6	12.4	16.1	3.6	7.6	0.0	0.0	18.8	17.5	0	..	30
Peru	13.5	5.8	25.1	8.2	9.7	7.6	0.0	9.9	10.5	27	46,619	27
Philippines	13.4	32.5	45.6	6.4	4.7	0.0	0.0	28.4	19.6	32	9,727	32
Poland	27.3	..	18.8	..	13.5	..	0.0	..	2.1	40	18,596	28
Portugal	..	25.7	..	13.0	..	0.0	..	2.6	..	40	46,339	30
Puerto Rico	..	..	..	..	..	..	..	..	..	33	50,000	20

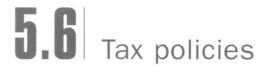

	Tax revenue	Taxes on income, profits, and capital gains		Domestic taxes on goods and services		Export duties		Import duties		Highest marginal tax rate [a]		
	% of GDP	% of total taxes		% of value added in industry and services		% of tax revenue		% of tax revenue		Individual rate %	on income over $	Corporate rate %
	2001	1990	2001	1990	2001	1990	2001	1990	2001	2002	2002	2002
Romania	23.1	21.0	12.0	16.0	10.7	0.0	0.0	0.6	3.4	40	3,743	25
Russian Federation	22.5	..	10.8	..	11.4	..	11.2	..	5.1	13	6,036	35
Rwanda	..	20.0	..	5.5	..	7.4	..	20.7	..	..	..	..
Saudi Arabia	..	..	..	..	..	..	..	..	..	0	..	0
Senegal	17.0	..	22.8	..	7.2	..	..	..	..	50	22,469	35
Sierra Leone	6.8	33.0	26.9	2.1	2.8	0.4	0.0	41.3	49.8	..	..	..
Singapore	15.3	44.6	52.7	4.3	4.7	0.0	0.0	3.5	2.6	26	223,003	25
Slovak Republic	29.6	..	19.7	..	10.9	..	0.0	..	1.3	38	11,637	25
Slovenia	36.3	12.3	15.5	12.7	17.6	..	0.0	..	1.8	50	..	25
Somalia	..	..	..	..	..	..	..	..	..	..	..	..
South Africa	26.5	55.0	57.0	10.3	10.8	0.0	0.0	3.9	2.9	42	18,534	30
Spain	..	34.0	..	7.5	..	0.0	..	1.7	..	32	60,971	35
Sri Lanka	14.6	12.0	16.9	14.7	13.4	4.2	0.0	27.4	12.7	35	4,170	35
Sudan	6.6	..	18.3	..	5.1	..	0.8	..	35.5	..	..	..
Swaziland	26.6	33.2	26.4	5.2	6.6	2.0	0.0	50.5	54.7	39	5,089	30
Sweden	34.9	20.6	15.5	14.5	12.2	0.0	0.0	0.6	0.0	..	..	28
Switzerland	23.6	17.0	17.7	..	..	0.0	0.0	6.9	1.1	..	..	..
Syrian Arab Republic	17.4	40.2	51.5	9.6	6.0	1.3	1.5	8.2	11.7	..	..	..
Tajikistan	10.5	..	3.0	..	9.5	..	0.0	..	17.1	..	..	..
Tanzania	..	..	..	..	..	..	..	..	..	30	7,074	30
Thailand	14.5	26.2	34.3	8.8	7.7	0.2	0.3	23.7	12.3	37	92,443	30
Togo	..	..	..	..	..	..	..	..	..	..	..	..
Trinidad and Tobago	..	..	..	..	..	..	..	..	..	35	7,937	35
Tunisia	26.0	16.0	22.3	7.1	12.5	0.4	0.1	35.1	12.5	..	..	..
Turkey	23.8	51.2	42.2	5.9	15.3	0.0	0.0	7.3	1.1	40	65,992	30
Turkmenistan	..	..	..	..	..	..	..	..	..	..	..	..
Uganda	10.7	..	20.1	..	5.3	..	0.0	..	50.3	30	2,860	30
Ukraine	21.9	..	14.3	..	10.7	..	0.0	..	4.4	40	3,850	30
United Arab Emirates	..	0.0	0.0	0.6	..	..	..	..	..	0	..	..
United Kingdom	34.3	43.2	41.8	11.3	12.8	0.0	0.0	0.0	0.0	40	43,302	30
United States	19.4	56.1	58.8	0.7	0.8	0.0	0.0	1.7	1.0	39	297,350	35
Uruguay	23.3	7.1	16.5	9.4	10.4	0.6	0.1	8.1	3.0	0	..	30
Uzbekistan	..	..	..	..	..	..	..	..	..	33	603	24
Venezuela, RB	12.3	82.2	34.0	0.8	5.8	0.0	0.0	7.1	12.1	34	102,406	34
Vietnam	16.8	..	32.7	..	8.9	..	0.0	..	21.4	..	..	32
West Bank and Gaza	..	..	..	..	..	..	..	..	..	..	..	..
Yemen, Rep.	9.3	44.9	45.9	2.5	2.6	0.0	0.0	29.2	25.9	..	..	..
Yugoslavia, Fed. Rep.	..	..	..	..	..	..	..	..	..	..	..	..
Zambia	..	..	..	..	..	..	..	..	..	30	557	35
Zimbabwe	..	49.7	..	8.4	..	0.0	..	18.8	..	46	15,273	30

a. These data are from PricewaterhouseCoopers's *Individual Taxes: Worldwide Summaries 2002–2003* and *Corporate Taxes: Worldwide Summaries 2002–2003*, copyright 2002 by PricewaterhouseCoopers by permission of John Wiley and Sons, Inc.

About the data

Taxes are the main source of revenue for many governments. The sources of the tax revenue received by governments and the relative contributions of these sources are determined by policy choices about where and how to impose taxes and by changes in the structure of the economy. Tax policy may reflect concerns about distributional effects, economic efficiency (including corrections for externalities), and the practical problems of administering a tax system. There is no ideal level of taxation. But taxes influence incentives and thus the behavior of economic actors and the economy's competitiveness.

Taxes are compulsory transfers to governments from individuals, businesses, or institutions. They include service fees that are clearly out of proportion to the costs of providing the services but exclude fines, penalties, and compulsory social security contributions. Taxes are considered unrequited because governments provide nothing specifically in return for them, although taxes typically are used to provide goods or services to individuals or communities on a collective basis.

The level of taxation is typically measured by tax revenue as a share of gross domestic product (GDP). Comparing levels of taxation across countries provides a quick overview of the fiscal obligations and incentives facing the private sector. In this table tax data in local currencies are normalized by scaling values in the same units to ease cross-country comparisons. The table shows only central government data, which may significantly understate the total tax burden, particularly in countries where provincial and municipal governments are large or have considerable tax authority.

Low ratios of tax revenue to GDP may reflect weak administration and large-scale tax avoidance or evasion. They may also reflect the presence of a sizable parallel economy with unrecorded and undisclosed incomes. Tax revenue ratios tend to rise with income, with higher-income countries relying on taxes to finance a much broader range of social services and social security than lower-income countries are able to provide.

As economies develop, their capacity to tax residents directly typically expands and indirect taxes become less important as a source of revenue. Thus the share of taxes on income, profits, and capital gains is one measure of an economy's (and tax system's) level of development. In the early stages of development governments tend to rely on indirect taxes because the administrative costs of collecting them are relatively low. The two main indirect taxes are international trade taxes (including customs revenues) and domestic taxes on goods and services. The table shows these domestic taxes as a percentage of value added in industry and services. Agriculture and mining are excluded from the denominator

because indirect taxes on goods originating from these sectors are usually negligible. What is missing here is a measure of the uniformity of these taxes across industries and along the value added chain of production. Without such data, no clear inferences can be drawn about how neutral a tax system is between subsectors. "Surplus" revenues raised by some governments by charging higher prices for goods produced under monopoly by state-owned enterprises are not counted as tax revenues. Similarly, losses from charging below-market prices for products are rarely identified as subsidies.

Export and import duties are shown separately because the burden they impose on the economy (and thus growth) is likely to be large. Export duties, typically levied on primary (particularly agricultural) products, often take the place of direct taxes on income and profits, but they reduce the incentive to export and encourage a shift to other products. High import duties penalize consumers, create protective barriers—which promote higher-priced output and inefficient production—and implicitly tax exports. By contrast, lower trade taxes enhance openness—to foreign competition, knowledge, technologies, and resources—energizing development in many ways. Seeing this pattern, some of the fastest growing economies have lowered import tariffs in recent years. The simple mean import tariff in India, for example, declined from almost 80 percent in 1990 to about 30 percent in 2001. In some countries, such as members of the European Union, most customs duties are collected by a supranational authority; these revenues are not reported in the individual countries' accounts.

The tax revenues collected by governments are the outcomes of systems that are often complex, containing many exceptions, exemptions, penalties, and other inducements that affect the incidence of taxes and thus influence the decisions of workers, managers, and entrepreneurs. A potentially important influence on both domestic and international investors is a tax system's progressivity, as reflected in the highest marginal tax rate on individual and corporate income. Figures for individual marginal tax rates generally refer to employment income. In some countries the highest marginal tax rate is also the basic or flat rate, and other surtaxes, deductions, and the like may apply. And in many countries several different corporate tax rates may be levied, depending on the type of business (mining, banking, insurance, agriculture, manufacturing), ownership (domestic or foreign), volume of sales, or whether surtaxes or exemptions are included. The corporate tax rates in the table are mainly general rates applied to domestic companies. For more detailed information, see the country's laws, regulations, and tax treaties.

Definitions

• **Tax revenue** comprises compulsory transfers to the central government for public purposes. Compulsory transfers such as fines, penalties, and most social security contributions are excluded. Refunds and corrections of erroneously collected tax revenue are treated as negative revenue. • **Taxes on income, profits, and capital gains** are levied on wages, salaries, tips, fees, commissions, and other compensation for labor services; interest, dividends, rent, and royalties; profits of businesses, estates, and trusts; and capital gains and losses. Social security contributions based on gross pay, payroll, or number of employees are not included, but taxable portions of social security, pension, and other retirement account distributions are included. • **Domestic taxes on goods and services** include all taxes and duties levied by central governments on the production, extraction, sale, transfer, leasing, or delivery of goods and rendering of services, or on the use of goods or permission to use goods or perform activities. These include value added taxes, general sales taxes, single-stage and multistage taxes (where *stage* refers to stage of production or distribution), excise taxes, motor vehicle taxes, and taxes on the extraction, processing, or production of minerals or other products. • **Export duties** include all levies collected on goods at the point of export. Rebates on exported goods that are repayments of previously paid general consumption taxes, excise taxes, or import duties are deducted from the gross amounts receivable from these taxes, not from amounts receivable from export duties. • **Import duties** comprise all levies collected on goods at the point of entry into the country. The levies may be imposed for revenue or protection purposes and may be determined on a specific or ad valorem basis as long as they are restricted to imported products. • **Highest marginal tax rate** is the highest rate shown on the schedule of tax rates applied to the annual taxable income of individuals and corporations. Also presented are the income levels above which the highest marginal tax rates for individuals apply.

Data sources

The definitions used here are from the International Monetary Fund's (IMF) *Manual on Government Finance Statistics* (2001). The data on tax revenues are from print and electronic editions of the IMF's *Government Finance Statistics Yearbook*. The data on individual and corporate tax rates are from PricewaterhouseCoopers's *Individual Taxes: Worldwide Summaries 2002–2003* and *Corporate Taxes: Worldwide Summaries 2002–2003*.

5.7 | Relative prices and exchange rates

	Exchange rate arrangements [a]		Official exchange rate	Purchasing power parity (PPP) conversion factor		Ratio of PPP conversion factor to official exchange rate	Real effective exchange rate	Interest rate		
			local currency units to $	local currency units to international $			1995 = 100	Deposit %	Lending %	Real %
	Classification 2001	Structure 2001	2001	1990	2001	2001	2001	2001	2001	2001
Afghanistan	IF	M	3,000.00	..	..	..	..	..	..	..
Albania	IF	U	143.48	2.0	50.7	0.4	..	7.7	19.7	16.4
Algeria	MF	U	77.22	4.3	22.5	0.3	110.5	6.3	9.5	6.5
Angola	MF	U	22.06	0.0	7.6	0.3	..	47.9	96.0	−13.9
Argentina	MF	U	1.00	0.3	0.6	0.6	..	16.2	27.7	29.1
Armenia	IF	U	555.08	..	116.2	0.2	105.3	14.9	26.7	21.8
Australia	IF	U	1.93	1.4	1.4	0.8	91.1	3.3	8.1	5.6
Austria	Euro	U	1.12	1.0	1.0	0.9	91.1	2.2	5.6	4.9
Azerbaijan	MF	U	4,656.58	..	1,061.4	0.2	..	8.5	19.7	16.5
Bangladesh	P	U	55.81	9.6	11.8	0.2	..	8.5	15.8	14.0
Belarus	P	M	1,390.00	..	222.7	0.2	..	34.2	47.0	−17.4
Belgium	Euro	U	1.12	0.9	1.0	0.9	89.3	3.4	8.5	6.0
Benin	EA/FF	U	733.04	158.9	275.3	0.4	..	3.5	..	..
Bolivia	P	U	6.61	1.4	2.7	0.4	117.8	9.8	20.1	19.3
Bosnia and Herzegovina	CB	U	..	..	0.4	..	..	..	..	..
Botswana	P	D	5.84	1.2	2.3	0.3	..	10.2	15.8	10.9
Brazil	IF	U	2.36	0.0	0.9	0.4	..	17.9	57.6	46.7
Bulgaria	CB	U	2.18	0.0	0.5	0.2	130.3	2.9	11.1	4.4
Burkina Faso	EA/FF	U	733.04	116.4	140.6	0.2	..	3.5	..	..
Burundi	MF	U	830.35	42.8	120.0	0.1	93.4	..	16.8	3.0
Cambodia	MF	D	3,916.33	58.4	585.9	0.1	..	4.4	16.5	19.9
Cameroon	EA/FF	U	733.04	194.5	247.2	0.3	98.7	5.0	20.7	17.2
Canada	IF	U	1.55	1.3	1.3	0.8	98.7	3.9	5.8	4.7
Central African Republic	EA/FF	U	733.04	117.9	144.6	0.2	92.3	5.0	20.7	17.2
Chad	EA/FF	U	733.04	93.5	138.8	0.2	..	5.0	20.7	11.8
Chile	IF	U	634.94	149.3	298.1	0.5	96.6	6.2	11.9	10.2
China	P	U	8.28	1.3	1.9	0.2	110.5	2.3	5.8	5.8
Hong Kong, China	CB	U	7.80	6.3	7.6	1.0	..	2.4	5.1	5.6
Colombia	IF	U	2,299.63	105.1	625.8	0.3	98.0	12.4	20.7	12.2
Congo, Dem. Rep.	IF	U	21.82	0.0	43.4	0.4	239.8	..	165.0	−63.7
Congo, Rep.	EA/FF	U	733.04	435.7	667.3	1.1	..	5.0	20.7	41.2
Costa Rica	P	U	328.87	28.4	144.9	0.4	111.9	11.8	23.8	15.6
Côte d'Ivoire	EA/FF	U	733.04	168.5	312.4	0.4	99.9	3.5	..	..
Croatia	MF	U	8.34	..	4.2	0.5	103.2	3.2	9.5	6.3
Cuba	..	..	..	..	..	..	..	..	..	..
Czech Republic	IF	U	38.04	7.9	14.3	0.4	121.3	3.0	7.1	1.7
Denmark	P	U	8.32	8.1	8.7	1.0	94.9	3.3	8.2	5.3
Dominican Republic	MF	D	16.95	2.2	6.0	0.4	117.0	15.6	24.3	14.1
Ecuador	EA/other	U	1.00	0.4	0.4	0.4	102.3	6.6	15.5	−7.7
Egypt, Arab Rep.	P	U	3.97	0.8	1.6	0.4	..	9.5	13.3	9.1
El Salvador	EA/other	U	8.75	2.1	3.6	0.4	..	9.3	14.0	10.5
Eritrea	P	U	..	..	1.7	..	..	..	..	..
Estonia	CB	U	17.56	0.1	7.0	0.4	..	4.0	7.8	2.3
Ethiopia	MF	U	8.46	0.6	1.0	0.1	..	7.0	10.9	19.2
Finland	Euro	U	1.12	1.0	1.1	1.0	89.1	1.9	5.8	3.6
France	Euro	U	1.12	1.0	1.0	0.9	88.4	3.0	7.0	5.5
Gabon	EA/FF	U	733.04	348.0	420.6	0.6	91.0	5.0	20.7	36.7
Gambia, The	IF	U	15.69	1.5	2.2	0.1	83.5	12.5	24.0	15.7
Georgia	IF	U	2.07	..	0.5	0.2	..	7.8	27.3	22.0
Germany	Euro	U	1.12	1.0	1.0	0.9	85.6	3.6	10.0	8.6
Ghana	MF	U	7,170.76	84.4	857.7	0.1	81.7	30.9	..	..
Greece	Euro	U	1.12	0.3	0.7	0.6	97.2	3.3	8.6	4.9
Guatemala	MF	U	7.86	1.2	3.1	0.4	..	8.8	19.0	11.7
Guinea	MF	U	1,950.56	223.8	392.4	0.2	..	8.0	19.4	9.6
Guinea-Bissau	EA/FF	U	733.04	10.1	123.0	0.2	..	3.5	..	..
Haiti	IF	U	24.43	1.0	5.9	0.2	..	13.7	28.6	10.1

	Exchange rate arrangements [a]		Official exchange rate	Purchasing power parity (PPP) conversion factor		Ratio of PPP conversion factor to official exchange rate	Real effective exchange rate	Interest rate		
	Classification	Structure	local currency units to $	local currency units to international $			1995 = 100	Deposit %	Lending %	Real %
	2001	2001	2001	1990	2001	2001	2001	2001	2001	2001
Honduras	P	U	15.47	1.1	5.3	0.3	..	14.5	23.8	13.0
Hungary	P	U	286.49	22.2	118.4	0.4	118.5	9.3	12.1	2.9
India	MF	U	47.19	4.2	7.8	0.2	..	..	12.1	8.3
Indonesia	MF	U	10,260.85	643.3	2,423.7	0.2	..	15.5	18.5	5.3
Iran, Islamic Rep.	MF	D	1,753.56	182.7	1,714.0	1.0	181.1	..	..	..
Iraq	MF	U	0.31	..	..	..	..	..	..	..
Ireland	Euro	U	1.12	0.8	0.9	0.8	94.5	0.1	4.8	−0.5
Israel	P	U	4.21	1.6	3.6	0.8	113.8	6.2	10.0	7.8
Italy	Euro	U	1.12	0.7	0.9	0.8	107.7	2.0	6.5	3.8
Jamaica	MF	U	46.00	4.2	37.1	0.8	..	9.6	20.6	12.8
Japan	IF	U	121.53	189.7	157.6	1.3	85.5	0.1	2.0	3.4
Jordan	P	U	0.71	0.3	0.3	0.5	..	5.8	10.9	10.6
Kazakhstan	MF	U	146.74	..	33.9	0.2	..	..	..	..
Kenya	MF	U	78.56	9.0	29.7	0.4	..	6.6	19.7	7.6
Korea, Dem. Rep.	..	..	..	..	..	..	..	..	..	..
Korea, Rep.	IF	U	1,290.99	567.9	763.1	0.6	..	5.8	7.7	6.3
Kuwait	P	U	0.31	0.3	0.3	0.9	..	4.5	7.9	16.7
Kyrgyz Republic	MF	U	48.38	..	5.4	0.1	..	12.5	37.3	27.9
Lao PDR	MF	D	8,954.58	173.3	1,790.3	0.2	..	6.5	26.2	14.8
Latvia	P	U	0.63	..	0.3	0.4	..	5.2	11.2	9.4
Lebanon	P	U	1,507.50	305.4	1,377.8	0.9	..	10.9	17.2	17.1
Lesotho	P	U	8.61	0.8	1.4	0.2	69.6	4.8	16.6	10.2
Liberia	IF	U	48.58	..	..	..	..	5.9	22.1	9.0
Libya	P	U	0.60	..	..	..	..	3.0	7.0	..
Lithuania	CB	U	4.00	..	1.6	0.4	..	3.0	9.6	9.2
Macedonia, FYR	P	U	68.04	..	18.7	0.3	73.2	10.0	19.4	16.1
Madagascar	IF	U	6,588.49	511.5	2,275.3	0.3	..	12.0	25.3	14.9
Malawi	IF	U	72.20	1.4	21.0	0.3	116.8	35.0	56.2	23.9
Malaysia	P	U	3.80	1.5	1.6	0.4	91.4	3.4	6.7	9.5
Mali	EA/FF	U	733.04	140.7	214.6	0.3	..	3.5	..	..
Mauritania	MF	U	255.63	30.6	47.2	0.2	..	..	..	..
Mauritius	MF	U	29.13	6.5	10.5	0.4	..	9.8	21.1	18.0
Mexico	IF	U	9.34	1.5	6.9	0.7	..	4.7	13.9	7.9
Moldova	IF	U	12.87	..	2.1	0.2	107.0	20.9	28.7	15.0
Mongolia	MF	U	1,097.70	2.7	273.8	0.2	..	14.3	30.2	19.8
Morocco	P	U	11.30	3.2	3.7	0.3	103.7	5.0	13.3	10.5
Mozambique	IF	U	20,703.64	274.3	3,622.5	0.2	..	15.0	22.7	10.3
Myanmar	MF	D	6.75	..	..	..	..	9.5	15.0	−6.2
Namibia	P	U	8.61	1.1	2.1	0.2	..	6.8	14.5	4.9
Nepal	P	U	74.95	6.8	13.3	0.2	..	4.8	7.7	4.4
Netherlands	Euro	U	1.12	0.9	1.0	0.9	92.7	3.1	5.0	0.3
New Zealand	IF	U	2.38	1.6	1.6	0.7	81.7	5.3	9.9	5.7
Nicaragua	P	U	13.37	0.0	..	..	116.5	9.0	22.8	..
Niger	EA/FF	U	733.04	104.0	144.3	0.2	..	3.5	..	..
Nigeria	MF	M	111.23	3.7	41.6	0.4	89.8	15.3	23.4	16.4
Norway	IF	U	8.99	9.1	11.2	1.2	99.6	6.7	8.9	5.2
Oman	P	U	0.38	0.3	0.3	0.6	..	4.5	9.2	−8.3
Pakistan	MF	U	61.93	5.8	12.8	0.2	87.2	..	..	..
Panama	EA/other	U	1.00	0.6	0.6	0.6	..	6.8	11.0	9.6
Papua New Guinea	IF	U	3.39	0.4	0.7	0.2	86.9	8.9	16.2	7.9
Paraguay	MF	U	4,105.92	342.2	1,007.2	0.2	93.1	16.2	28.3	19.9
Peru	IF	U	3.51	0.1	1.6	0.4	..	9.9	20.4	18.9
Philippines	IF	U	50.99	5.6	12.1	0.2	85.4	8.7	12.4	5.4
Poland	IF	U	4.09	0.3	2.0	0.5	138.3	11.8	18.4	13.5
Portugal	Euro	U	1.12	0.5	0.7	0.6	98.7	2.4	*5.2*	*1.9*
Puerto Rico	..	..	..	0.6	0.6	..	..	..	..	..

	Exchange rate arrangements [a]		Official exchange rate	Purchasing power parity (PPP) conversion factor		Ratio of PPP conversion factor to official exchange rate	Real effective exchange rate	Interest rate		
			local currency units to $	local currency units to international $			1995 = 100	Deposit %	Lending %	Real %
	Classification 2001	Structure 2001	2001	1990	2001	2001	2001	2001	2001	2001
Romania	P	U	29,060.79	7.1	8,832.0	0.3	108.8	..	..	..
Russian Federation	MF	M	29.17	..	8.8	0.3	105.5	4.8	17.9	0.0
Rwanda	MF	U	442.99	26.0	69.4	0.2	..	9.2	..	..
Saudi Arabia	P	U	3.74	2.3	2.4	0.7	111.8	3.9	..	..
Senegal	EA/FF	U	733.04	185.8	230.7	0.3	..	3.5	..	..
Sierra Leone	IF	D	1,986.15	29.8	615.1	0.3	116.2	7.7	24.3	17.2
Singapore	MF	U	1.79	1.8	1.6	0.9	96.2	1.5	5.7	7.8
Slovak Republic	MF	U	48.35	..	15.3	0.3	107.8	6.5	11.2	5.5
Slovenia	MF	U	242.75	..	133.8	0.6	..	9.8	15.1	4.7
Somalia	IF	D	..	..	..	..	..	..	..	..
South Africa	IF	U	8.61	0.9	2.0	0.2	73.2	9.4	13.8	5.9
Spain	Euro	U	1.12	0.6	0.8	0.7	95.9	3.1	5.2	1.2
Sri Lanka	MF	U	89.38	10.2	23.5	0.3	..	11.0	19.4	5.5
Sudan	MF	U	258.70	0.6	52.0	0.3	..	..	..	..
Swaziland	P	U	8.61	0.9	2.3	0.3	..	6.2	13.3	4.5
Sweden	IF	U	10.33	9.6	10.1	1.0	87.6	2.2	5.8	4.7
Switzerland	IF	U	1.69	2.0	2.1	1.2	89.8	1.7	4.3	2.5
Syrian Arab Republic	P	M	11.23	10.2	18.0	1.6	..	4.0	9.0	2.9
Tajikistan	IF	U	2.37	..	0.3	0.1	..	21.0	5.2	−16.6
Tanzania	IF	U	876.41	75.7	454.1	0.5	..	4.8	20.3	12.8
Thailand	MF	U	44.43	10.8	13.0	0.3	..	2.5	7.3	5.0
Togo	EA/FF	U	733.04	80.2	119.8	0.2	102.1	3.5	..	..
Trinidad and Tobago	MF	U	6.23	3.1	4.6	0.7	124.1	7.7	15.7	12.0
Tunisia	MF	U	1.44	0.4	0.5	0.3	97.3	..	..	..
Turkey	IF	U	1,225,588.00	1,638.1	464,782.5	0.4	125.3	74.7	..	..
Turkmenistan	P	D	5,200.00	..	1,321.7	0.3	..	..	..	..
Uganda	IF	U	1,755.66	97.1	295.0	0.2	81.7	8.5	22.7	14.2
Ukraine	MF	U	5.37	..	0.9	0.2	119.6	11.0	32.3	21.5
United Arab Emirates	P	U	3.67	2.9	..	..	..	..	..	..
United Kingdom	IF	U	0.69	0.6	0.7	1.0	129.5	..	5.1	2.6
United States	IF	U	1.00	1.0	1.0	1.0	134.5	..	6.9	4.5
Uruguay	P	U	13.32	0.6	8.8	0.7	112.0	14.3	51.7	43.6
Uzbekistan	MF	M	236.61	..	79.0	0.2	..	..	..	..
Venezuela, RB	IF	U	723.67	24.3	648.0	0.9	173.1	15.5	22.5	14.6
Vietnam	MF	U	14,725.17	641.0	2,945.8	0.2	..	5.3	9.4	6.6
West Bank and Gaza	..	..	..	..	..	..	..	..	..	..
Yemen, Rep.	IF	U	168.67	20.3	109.4	0.7	..	13.0	17.5	14.9
Yugoslavia, Fed. Rep.	MF	U	..	..	..	..	..	..	..	..
Zambia	MF	U	3,610.94	18.3	1,645.2	0.5	122.4	23.4	46.2	17.6
Zimbabwe	P	U	55.05	0.9	17.0	0.3	..	13.9	38.0	−18.9

a. Exchange rate arrangements are given for the end of the year in 2001. Exchange rate classifications include independent floating (IF), managed floating (MF), pegged (P), currency board (CB), and several exchange arrangements (EA): FF means that the currency is pegged to the French franc, and other that the currency of another country is used as legal tender. Exchange rate structures include dual exchange rates (D), multiple exchange rates (M), and unitary rate (U).

In a market-based economy the choices households, producers, and governments make about the allocation of resources are influenced by relative prices, including the real exchange rate, real wages, real interest rates, and a host of other prices in the economy. Relative prices also reflect, to a large extent, the choices of these agents. Thus relative prices convey vital information about the interaction of economic agents in an economy and with the rest of the world.

The exchange rate is the price of one currency in terms of another. Official exchange rates and exchange rate arrangements are established by governments (other exchange rates fully recognized by governments include market rates, which are determined largely by legal market forces, and, for countries maintaining multiple exchange arrangements, principal rates, secondary rates, and tertiary rates).

The official or market exchange rate is often used to compare prices in different currencies. Since exchange rates reflect at best the relative prices of tradable goods, the volume of goods and services that a U.S. dollar buys in the United States may not correspond to what a U.S. dollar converted to another country's currency at the official exchange rate would buy in that country. Since identical volumes of goods and services in different countries correspond to different values (and vice versa) when official exchange rates are used, an alternative method of comparing prices across countries has been developed. In this method national currency estimates of gross national income (GNI) are converted to a common unit of account by using conversion factors that reflect equivalent purchasing power. Purchasing power parity (PPP) conversion factors are based on price and expenditure surveys conducted by the International Comparison Program and represent the conversion factors applied to equalize price levels across countries. See *About the data* for table 1.1 for further discussion of the PPP conversion factor.

The ratio of the PPP conversion factor to the official exchange rate (also referred to as the national price level) makes it possible to compare the cost of the bundle of goods that make up gross domestic product (GDP) across countries. These national price levels vary systematically, rising with GNI per capita.

Real effective exchange rates are derived by deflating a trade-weighted average of the nominal exchange rates that apply between trading partners. For most high-income countries the weights are based on trade in manufactured goods with other high-income countries in 1989–91, and an index of relative, normalized unit labor costs is used as the deflator. (Normalization smooths a time series by removing short-term fluctuations while retaining changes of a large amplitude over the longer economic cycle.) For other countries the weights before 1990 take into account trade in manufactured and primary products in 1980–82, the weights from January 1990 onward take into account trade in 1988–90, and an index of relative changes in consumer prices is used as the deflator. An increase in the real effective exchange rate represents an appreciation of the local currency. Because of conceptual and data limitations, changes in real effective exchange rates should be interpreted with caution.

Many interest rates coexist in an economy, reflecting competitive conditions, the terms governing loans and deposits, and differences in the position and status of creditors and debtors. In some economies interest rates are set by regulation or administrative fiat. In economies with imperfect markets, or where reported nominal rates are not indicative of effective rates, it may be difficult to obtain data on interest rates that reflect actual market transactions. Deposit and lending rates are collected by the International Monetary Fund (IMF) as representative interest rates offered by banks to resident customers. The terms and conditions attached to these rates differ by country, however, limiting their comparability. Real interest rates are calculated by adjusting nominal rates by an estimate of the inflation rate in the economy. A negative real interest rate indicates a loss in the purchasing power of the principal. The real interest rates in the table are calculated as $(i - P)/(1 + P)$, where i is the nominal interest rate and P is the inflation rate (as measured by the GDP deflator).

• **Exchange rate arrangements** describe the arrangements furnished to the IMF by each member country under article IV, section 2(a) of the IMF's Articles of Agreement. **Exchange rate classification** indicates how the exchange rate is determined in the main market when there is more than one market: floating (managed or independent), pegged (conventional, within horizontal bands, crawling peg, or crawling band), currency board (implicit legislative commitment to exchange domestic currency for a specified foreign currency at a fixed exchange rate), and exchange arrangement (currency is pegged to the French franc, or another country's currency is used as legal tender). **Exchange rate structure** shows whether countries have a unitary exchange rate or dual or multiple rates. • **Official exchange rate** refers to the exchange rate determined by national authorities or to the rate determined in the legally sanctioned exchange market. It is calculated as an annual average based on monthly averages (local currency units relative to the U.S. dollar). • **Purchasing power parity (PPP) conversion factor** is the number of units of a country's currency required to buy the same amount of goods and services in the domestic market as a U.S. dollar would buy in the United States. • **Ratio of PPP conversion factor to official exchange rate** is the result obtained by dividing the PPP conversion factor by the official exchange rate. • **Real effective exchange rate** is the nominal effective exchange rate (a measure of the value of a currency against a weighted average of several foreign currencies) divided by a price deflator or index of costs. • **Deposit interest rate** is the rate paid by commercial or similar banks for demand, time, or savings deposits. • **Lending interest rate** is the rate charged by banks on loans to prime customers. • **Real interest rate** is the lending interest rate adjusted for inflation as measured by the GDP deflator.

Data sources

The information on exchange rate arrangements is from the IMF's *Exchange Arrangements and Exchange Restrictions Annual Report, 2002*. The official and real effective exchange rates and deposit and lending rates are from the IMF's *International Financial Statistics*. PPP conversion factors are from the World Bank. The real interest rates are calculated using World Bank data on the GDP deflator.

5.8 Defense expenditures and trade in arms

	Military expenditures				Armed forces personnel				Arms trade			
	% of GDP		% of central government expenditure		Total thousands		% of labor force		Exports % of total exports		Imports % of total imports	
	1992	2001	1992	2001	1992	1999	1992	1999	1992	1999	1992	1999
Afghanistan	..	..	..	..	45	..	0.6	..	..	..	0.7	..
Albania	4.6	1.2	..	3.7	65	18	4.1	1.2	0.0	0.0	0.0	2.6
Algeria	2.2	3.5	9.5	12.0	126	120	1.6	1.2	0.0	0.0	0.1	4.1
Angola	12.0	3.1	..	..	128	100	2.7	1.7	0.0	0.0	1.5	7.3
Argentina	1.4	1.4	12.0	8.1	65	73	0.5	0.5	0.0	0.0	0.3	0.4
Armenia	2.2	3.1	..	..	20	50	1.1	2.6	0.0	0.0	0.0	1.3
Australia	2.3	1.7	8.9	7.5	68	55	0.8	0.6	0.1	1.0	2.1	1.6
Austria	1.0	0.8	2.4	2.0	44	49	1.2	1.3	0.2	0.0	0.1	0.0
Azerbaijan	3.3	2.6	12.4	10.2	43	75	1.4	2.1	0.0	0.0	0.0	1.2
Bangladesh	1.1	1.3	..	11.2	107	110	0.2	0.2	0.0	0.0	1.1	1.0
Belarus	1.5	1.4	4.1	4.5	102	65	1.9	1.2	0.0	5.2	0.0	0.0
Belgium	1.8	1.3	3.7	3.2	79	42	1.9	1.0	0.3	0.0	0.2	0.2
Benin	..	..	..	..	7	8	0.3	0.3	0.0	0.0	0.0	0.8
Bolivia	2.1	1.6	10.6	6.1	32	33	1.2	1.0	0.0	0.0	0.9	0.6
Bosnia and Herzegovina	..	9.5	..	..	60	30	3.2	1.7	0.0	0.0	0.0	6.2
Botswana	4.3	3.5	11.7	..	7	8	1.2	1.1	0.0	0.0	1.1	1.8
Brazil	1.1	1.5	..	5.2	296	300	0.4	0.4	0.5	0.0	0.9	0.3
Bulgaria	2.7	2.7	6.6	7.9	99	70	2.3	1.7	3.1	5.1	0.0	0.2
Burkina Faso	2.3	1.6	14.0	..	9	9	0.2	0.2	0.0	0.0	1.1	0.0
Burundi	3.6	8.1	10.7	27.1	13	40	0.4	1.1	0.0	0.0	0.0	0.0
Cambodia	4.7	3.0	..	..	135	60	2.7	1.0	0.0	0.0	0.0	0.3
Cameroon	1.5	1.4	8.4	10.4	12	15	0.2	0.3	0.0	0.0	0.0	0.4
Canada	1.9	1.2	6.9	6.2	82	60	0.5	0.4	0.7	0.2	0.6	0.5
Central African Republic	1.6	..	..	..	4	3	0.3	0.2	0.0	0.0	0.0	0.0
Chad	2.7	1.5	..	..	38	30	1.3	0.8	0.0	0.0	4.1	3.2
Chile	3.4	2.9	16.2	12.4	92	88	1.8	1.4	0.0	0.1	1.0	0.7
China	2.7	2.3	32.5	19.2	3,160	2,400	0.5	0.3	1.3	0.2	1.6	0.4
Hong Kong, China	..	..	..	..	..	..	..	..	..	..	..	..
Colombia	2.4	3.8	15.8	18.8	139	155	0.9	0.9	0.0	0.0	1.7	0.6
Congo, Dem. Rep.	2.9	1.6	..	..	45	55	0.3	0.3	0.0	0.0	0.0	8.9
Congo, Rep.	..	..	..	..	10	10	1.0	0.8	0.0	0.0	0.0	0.0
Costa Rica	..	..	..	..	8	10	0.6	0.7	0.0	0.0	0.2	0.0
Côte d'Ivoire	1.4	0.9	4.0	3.7	15	15	0.3	0.2	0.0	0.0	0.0	0.0
Croatia	7.6	2.6	19.1	5.9	103	60	4.6	2.9	0.0	0.2	0.0	0.1
Cuba	..	..	..	..	175	50	3.5	0.9	0.0	0.0	4.5	0.0
Czech Republic	2.3	2.1	6.2	5.4	107	54	1.9	0.9	1.5	0.3	0.0	0.7
Denmark	1.9	1.6	4.8	4.3	28	27	1.0	0.9	0.0	0.0	0.5	0.7
Dominican Republic	..	..	..	..	22	30	0.7	0.8	0.0	0.0	0.2	0.3
Ecuador	2.7	2.1	16.9	..	57	58	1.5	1.2	0.0	0.0	1.2	0.7
Egypt, Arab Rep.	3.6	2.6	10.5	10.2	424	430	2.2	1.8	0.7	0.0	19.2	4.4
El Salvador	2.0	0.8	..	31.2	49	15	2.4	0.6	0.0	0.0	4.1	0.3
Eritrea	21.4	27.5	..	..	55	215	3.2	10.8	0.0	0.0	0.0	33.5
Estonia	0.5	0.0	2.2	5.6	3	7	0.4	0.9	0.0	0.0	1.2	0.2
Ethiopia	2.7	6.2	19.3	43.0	120	300	0.5	1.1	0.0	0.0	0.0	20.5
Finland	1.9	1.2	4.6	4.4	33	35	1.3	1.3	0.0	0.1	2.1	1.3
France	3.4	2.5	7.6	6.4	522	421	2.1	1.6	0.9	1.0	0.2	0.3
Gabon	..	0.3	..	..	7	7	1.5	1.3	0.0	0.0	0.0	0.0
Gambia, The	1.0	1.0	..	..	1	1	0.2	0.2	0.0	0.0	2.3	0.0
Georgia	..	0.7	..	6.6	25	14	0.9	0.5	0.0	6.2	0.0	1.0
Germany	2.1	1.5	6.3	4.7	442	331	1.1	0.8	0.3	0.3	0.6	0.3
Ghana	0.6	0.6	3.6	..	7	7	0.1	0.1	0.0	0.0	0.0	0.0
Greece	4.5	4.6	15.5	15.6	208	204	4.8	4.5	0.2	0.9	3.9	7.5
Guatemala	1.3	1.0	..	..	44	30	1.4	0.7	0.0	0.0	0.2	0.0
Guinea	1.9	1.7	9.0	8.5	15	12	0.5	0.3	0.0	0.0	0.0	0.0
Guinea-Bissau	0.3	3.1	..	..	11	7	2.3	1.3	0.0	0.0	0.0	0.0
Haiti	..	..	..	..	8	0	0.3	0.0	0.0	0.0	0.0	0.0

Defense expenditures and trade in arms

	Military expenditures				Armed forces personnel				Arms trade			
	% of GDP		% of central government expenditure		Total thousands		% of labor force		Exports % of total exports		Imports % of total imports	
	1992	2001	1992	2001	1992	1999	1992	1999	1992	1999	1992	1999
Honduras	..	..	..	..	17	8	0.9	0.3	0.0	0.0	2.9	0.4
Hungary	2.4	1.8	*4.3*	4.3	78	51	1.6	1.1	0.4	0.0	0.0	0.3
India	2.3	2.5	14.6	14.0	1,270	1,300	0.3	0.3	0.0	0.0	2.9	1.6
Indonesia	1.7	1.1	9.4	4.6	283	296	0.3	0.3	0.1	0.2	0.4	1.9
Iran, Islamic Rep.	1.9	4.8	11.2	*17.2*	528	460	3.2	2.4	0.1	0.1	3.3	0.9
Iraq	..	..	..	..	407	420	8.2	6.7	0.0	0.0	0.0	0.1
Ireland	1.2	0.7	3.0	*2.8*	13	14	1.0	0.9	0.0	0.0	0.1	0.1
Israel	10.5	7.7	21.6	16.6	181	173	8.8	6.6	6.2	2.3	10.3	7.2
Italy	0.0	2.0	3.9	*4.8*	471	391	1.9	1.5	0.3	0.2	0.2	0.3
Jamaica	..	..	..	..	3	3	0.2	0.2	0.0	0.0	0.6	0.3
Japan	0.9	1.0	4.5	..	242	240	0.4	0.4	0.0	0.0	0.9	1.0
Jordan	8.2	8.6	27.8	26.5	100	102	9.8	7.3	0.0	0.0	1.2	1.9
Kazakhstan	*1.0*	1.0	..	6.8	*15*	33	*0.2*	0.4	0.0	0.2	0.0	4.3
Kenya	1.9	1.8	7.9	*5.8*	24	24	0.2	0.2	0.0	0.0	1.1	0.2
Korea, Dem. Rep.	..	..	..	..	1,200	1,000	11.3	8.6	13.1	22.4	7.9	2.5
Korea, Rep.	3.4	2.8	20.6	*16.6*	750	665	3.6	2.8	0.1	0.0	1.5	1.8
Kuwait	31.8	11.3	31.5	*18.8*	12	21	2.1	2.7	0.2	0.0	13.8	9.5
Kyrgyz Republic	0.7	1.7	*3.2*	*10.0*	12	12	0.6	0.6	0.0	0.0	0.0	0.0
Lao PDR	..	2.1	..	..	37	50	1.7	2.0	0.0	0.0	3.7	0.0
Latvia	*0.8*	1.2	*3.4*	3.9	5	5	0.3	0.4	0.0	0.0	0.0	0.2
Lebanon	8.0	5.5	*25.7*	*14.0*	37	58	3.1	3.9	0.0	0.0	0.0	0.2
Lesotho	2.6	*3.1*	5.7	*6.4*	2	2	0.3	0.2	0.0	0.0	0.0	0.0
Liberia	10.6	..	..	..	2	..	0.2	..	0.0	0.0	0.0	0.0
Libya	..	..	..	..	85	85	6.6	5.8	0.1	0.8	1.7	0.2
Lithuania	*0.7*	1.8	*3.5*	6.8	10	12	0.5	0.7	0.0	0.0	0.0	0.4
Macedonia, FYR	..	7.0	..	..	10	16	1.1	1.7	0.0	0.0	0.0	1.1
Madagascar	1.2	*1.2*	6.6	*7.1*	21	20	0.4	0.3	0.0	0.0	0.0	0.0
Malawi	1.4	0.8	..	..	10	5	0.2	0.1	0.0	0.0	0.0	0.0
Malaysia	3.0	2.2	10.5	*10.6*	128	95	1.7	1.0	0.0	0.0	0.6	1.4
Mali	*2.4*	2.0	..	..	12	10	0.3	0.2	0.0	0.0	0.0	0.0
Mauritania	3.5	*2.1*	..	..	16	11	1.7	0.9	0.0	0.0	0.0	0.0
Mauritius	0.4	0.2	1.5	0.8	1	2	0.2	0.4	0.0	0.0	0.3	0.0
Mexico	0.5	0.5	3.3	*3.2*	175	255	0.5	0.6	0.0	0.0	0.5	0.1
Moldova	*0.5*	0.4	..	1.8	9	11	0.4	0.5	0.0	2.1	0.8	0.0
Mongolia	2.5	2.3	11.6	7.5	21	20	2.1	1.7	0.0	0.0	0.0	0.0
Morocco	4.3	4.1	14.4	*12.4*	195	195	2.1	1.7	0.0	0.0	1.4	1.3
Mozambique	5.1	2.3	..	..	50	8	0.6	0.1	0.0	0.0	0.6	0.4
Myanmar	3.4	*2.3*	30.1	*26.6*	286	345	1.3	1.4	0.0	*0.0*	23.0	*13.6*
Namibia	4.3	2.8	10.6	*9.1*	8	3	1.3	0.4	0.0	0.0	0.0	1.3
Nepal	0.9	1.1	6.4	6.5	35	35	0.4	0.3	0.0	0.0	0.0	0.0
Netherlands	2.4	1.6	4.7	*4.0*	90	54	1.3	0.7	0.1	0.1	0.4	0.4
New Zealand	1.6	1.2	4.3	4.0	11	10	0.6	0.5	0.0	0.0	1.2	4.0
Nicaragua	2.4	1.1	7.6	*3.1*	15	12	1.0	0.6	13.5	0.0	0.6	0.0
Niger	*1.2*	*1.1*	..	..	5	6	0.1	0.1	0.0	0.0	0.0	0.0
Nigeria	0.5	1.1	..	..	76	77	0.2	0.2	0.0	0.0	1.9	0.0
Norway	3.0	1.8	7.0	*5.9*	36	33	1.7	1.4	0.1	0.0	1.7	1.4
Oman	16.2	12.2	40.9	40.7	35	38	6.7	6.1	0.0	0.0	0.3	0.6
Pakistan	6.1	4.5	27.7	23.0	580	590	1.4	1.2	0.4	0.1	6.6	9.7
Panama	1.2	*1.2*	4.8	*4.2*	11	13	1.1	1.1	2.0	0.0	0.5	0.1
Papua New Guinea	1.3	*0.8*	4.2	*3.3*	4	4	0.2	0.2	0.0	0.0	4.0	0.0
Paraguay	1.6	0.9	11.8	5.0	16	17	1.0	0.8	0.0	0.0	0.7	0.6
Peru	2.2	1.7	11.9	9.2	112	115	1.4	1.2	0.0	0.0	1.4	0.4
Philippines	1.3	1.0	6.5	5.1	107	107	0.4	0.3	0.0	0.0	1.8	0.3
Poland	2.3	1.9	*5.5*	5.3	270	187	1.4	0.9	0.2	0.1	0.0	0.1
Portugal	2.7	2.1	6.2	*5.4*	80	71	1.6	1.4	0.1	0.0	0.6	0.2
Puerto Rico	..	..	..	..	..	..	..	..	..	..	..	..

	Military expenditures				Armed forces personnel				Arms trade			
	% of GDP		% of central government expenditure		Total thousands		% of labor force		Exports % of total exports		Imports % of total imports	
	1992	2001	1992	2001	1992	1999	1992	1999	1992	1999	1992	1999
Romania	4.3	2.5	10.7	8.1	172	170	1.6	1.6	0.5	0.5	0.6	1.9
Russian Federation	5.5	3.8	*21.1*	15.4	1,900	900	2.5	1.2	5.8	4.2	0.0	1.1
Rwanda	4.4	3.9	21.6	..	30	40	0.8	0.9	0.0	0.0	0.0	11.9
Saudi Arabia	11.7	11.3	..	..	172	190	3.1	2.9	0.0	0.0	25.2	27.5
Senegal	1.8	1.5	..	6.8	18	13	0.5	0.3	0.0	0.0	1.0	0.0
Sierra Leone	2.5	*3.6*	17.7	*6.5*	8	3	0.5	0.2	0.0	0.0	6.8	12.3
Singapore	4.8	5.0	24.0	22.8	56	60	3.4	3.0	0.0	0.0	0.4	0.9
Slovak Republic	*2.1*	1.9	..	4.9	*33*	36	*1.2*	1.2	*0.7*	0.1	*3.5*	0.2
Slovenia	2.2	1.4	5.8	3.5	15	10	1.5	1.0	0.0	0.0	0.0	0.1
Somalia	..	..	..	..	..	..	..	..	0.0	0.0	0.0	0.0
South Africa	..	..	8.8	5.4	75	68	0.5	0.4	0.4	0.1	1.3	0.2
Spain	1.6	1.2	4.4	*4.2*	198	155	1.2	0.9	0.3	0.1	0.4	0.5
Sri Lanka	3.0	3.9	11.3	14.7	110	110	1.6	1.4	0.0	0.0	0.3	0.7
Sudan	2.5	*3.0*	..	27.4	82	105	0.8	0.9	0.0	0.0	13.4	0.7
Swaziland	1.9	1.5	..	*5.2*	3	3	1.1	0.8	0.0	0.0	0.0	0.0
Sweden	2.6	2.0	5.6	*5.4*	70	52	1.5	1.1	1.5	0.8	0.3	0.3
Switzerland	1.8	1.1	7.0	*4.2*	31	39	0.8	1.0	1.2	0.1	0.7	1.5
Syrian Arab Republic	9.0	6.2	39.0	*24.2*	408	310	11.0	6.2	0.6	0.0	11.2	5.5
Tajikistan	0.4	1.2	..	10.1	3	7	0.1	0.3	0.0	0.0	0.0	0.0
Tanzania	1.9	*1.3*	..	..	46	35	0.3	0.2	0.0	0.0	0.3	0.3
Thailand	2.3	1.4	15.3	7.1	283	300	0.9	0.8	0.0	0.0	1.2	0.7
Togo	2.9	..	..	..	8	11	0.5	0.6	0.0	0.0	0.0	0.0
Trinidad and Tobago	..	..	..	..	2	2	0.4	0.4	0.0	0.0	0.0	0.0
Tunisia	1.9	1.6	5.8	*5.2*	35	35	1.1	0.9	0.0	0.0	0.3	0.1
Turkey	3.7	4.9	18.8	10.0	704	789	2.7	2.6	0.1	0.3	6.6	7.9
Turkmenistan	*1.8*	3.8	..	..	28	15	1.7	0.7	1.4	0.0	0.0	1.0
Uganda	1.6	2.1	..	10.1	70	50	0.8	0.5	0.0	0.0	2.0	2.2
Ukraine	*0.5*	2.7	..	9.8	430	340	1.6	1.3	0.0	4.7	0.0	0.1
United Arab Emirates	4.5	2.5	37.4	*30.1*	55	65	5.2	4.7	0.0	0.0	4.2	3.8
United Kingdom	3.8	2.5	8.7	*7.0*	293	218	1.0	0.7	3.3	1.9	1.3	0.8
United States	4.8	3.1	21.1	16.0	1,920	1,490	1.5	1.0	5.6	4.7	0.3	0.2
Uruguay	2.1	1.3	8.0	4.2	25	24	1.8	1.6	0.0	0.0	0.5	0.3
Uzbekistan	*1.5*	1.1	..	..	40	60	0.5	0.6	0.0	0.4	0.0	0.0
Venezuela, RB	1.6	1.5	8.2	6.1	75	75	1.0	0.8	0.0	0.0	0.9	2.2
Vietnam	3.4	..	*10.6*	..	857	485	2.4	1.2	0.4	0.0	0.4	0.6
West Bank and Gaza	..	..	..	..	..	..	..	..	..	..	..	..
Yemen, Rep.	9.1	6.1	30.7	*18.8*	64	69	1.5	1.3	0.0	0.0	0.2	1.5
Yugoslavia, Fed. Rep.	..	4.9	..	..	137	105	2.8	2.1	0.0	..	0.0	..
Zambia	3.0	*0.6*	..	..	16	17	0.5	0.4	0.0	0.0	0.0	0.0
Zimbabwe	3.7	3.2	11.3	*9.4*	48	40	1.0	0.7	0.3	0.0	4.1	0.5
World	**2.9 w**	**2.3 w**	**11.5 w**	**11.0 w**	**24,533 t**	**21,198 t**	**0.9 w**	**0.7 w**	**1.2 w**	**1.0 w**	**1.1 w**	**0.9 w**
Low income	2.4	2.3	14.4	12.9	6,490	6,259	0.7	0.6	0.1	0.4	2.0	1.9
Middle income	3.0	2.5	*15.8*	*11.7*	11,623	9,543	1.0	0.7	0.3	0.4	3.2	1.6
Lower middle income	3.6	2.8	19.8	14.8	9,931	7,806	1.0	0.7	0.6	0.8	2.8	1.4
Upper middle income	2.4	2.2	*13.1*	10.2	1,692	1,737	0.9	0.8	0.1	0.0	3.6	1.9
Low & middle income	2.9	2.5	*15.6*	*12.6*	18,113	15,802	0.9	0.7	0.3	0.4	3.0	1.7
East Asia & Pacific	2.4	2.1	23.7	*16.4*	6,506	5,166	0.7	0.5	0.5	0.1	1.2	0.6
Europe & Central Asia	4.4	3.0	*15.2*	9.6	4,303	3,192	2.1	1.3	*1.4*	1.8	*1.4*	1.8
Latin America & Carib.	1.2	1.3	*6.2*	6.9	1,443	1,371	0.8	0.6	0.2	0.0	0.7	0.3
Middle East & N. Africa	7.6	6.7	..	..	2,626	2,522	3.3	2.6	0.1	0.1	10.8	8.4
South Asia	2.7	2.6	16.8	14.7	2,152	2,153	0.4	0.4	0.1	0.0	3.3	2.4
Sub-Saharan Africa	2.3	2.0	*8.4*	..	1,083	1,398	0.5	0.5	0.2	0.0	1.3	1.4
High income	2.9	2.3	10.8	*10.4*	6,420	5,396	1.4	1.1	1.4	1.1	0.7	0.6
Europe EMU	1.9	1.8	5.7	*4.9*	2,181	1,768	1.6	1.3	0.4	0.3	0.4	0.4

Note: Data for some countries are based on partial or uncertain data or rough estimates; see SIPRI (2002) and U.S. Department of State (2002).

Defense expenditures and trade in arms | 5.8

About the data

Although national defense is an important function of government and security from external threats contributes to economic development, high levels of defense spending burden the economy and may impede growth. Comparisons of defense spending between countries should take into account the many factors that influence perceptions of vulnerability and risk, including historical and cultural traditions, the length of borders that need defending, the quality of relations with neighbors, and the role of the armed forces in the body politic.

Military expenditures as a share of gross domestic product (GDP) are a rough indicator of the portion of national resources used for military activities and of the burden on the national economy. As an "input" measure, military spending is not directly related to the "output" of military activities, capabilities, or military security. Data on defense spending from governments are often incomplete and unreliable. Even in countries where the parliament vigilantly reviews government budgets and spending, defense spending and trade in arms often do not receive close scrutiny. For a detailed critique of the quality of such data, see Ball (1984) and Happe and Wakeman-Linn (1994).

This edition of the *World Development Indicators* uses a new source of data for military expenditures, the Stockholm International Peace Research Institute (SIPRI). The data presented for military expenditures as a percentage of GDP and central government expenditure therefore differ from those in previous editions.

SIPRI's primary source of military expenditure data is official data provided by national governments. These data are derived from national budget documents, defense white papers, and other public documents from official government agencies, including governments' responses to questionnaires sent by SIPRI, the United Nations, or the Organization for Security and Co-operation in Europe. Secondary sources include international statistics, such as those of the North Atlantic Treaty Organization (NATO) and the International Monetary Fund's (IMF) *Government Finance Statistics Yearbook*. Other secondary sources include Europa Publications' *Europa World Yearbook*, country reports of the Economist Intelligence Unit, and country reports by IMF staff. Still others include specialist journals and newspapers.

Lack of sufficiently detailed data makes it difficult to apply a common definition of military expenditure globally, so SIPRI has adopted a definition (based on the NATO definition) as a guideline (see *Definitions*). This definition cannot be applied for all countries, however, since that would require much more detailed information

than is available about what is included in military budgets and off-budget military expenditure items. (For example, military budgets might or might not cover civil defense, reserves and auxiliary forces, police and paramilitary forces, dual-purpose forces such as military and civilian police, military grants in kind, pensions for military personnel, and social security contributions paid by one part of government to another.) In the many cases where SIPRI cannot make independent estimates, it uses the national data provided. Because of the differences in definitions and the difficulty in verifying the accuracy and completeness of data, the data on military spending are not strictly comparable across countries.

The data on armed forces refer to military personnel on active duty, including paramilitary forces. These data exclude civilians in the defense establishment and so are not consistent with the data on military spending on personnel. Moreover, because they exclude personnel not on active duty, they underestimate the share of the labor force working for the defense establishment. Because governments rarely report the size of their armed forces, such data typically come from intelligence sources. The data in the table are from the U.S. Department of State's Bureau of Verification and Compliance, which attributes its data to unspecified U.S. government sources.

The Standard International Trade Classification does not clearly distinguish trade in military goods. For this and other reasons, customs-based data on trade in arms are of little use, so most compilers rely on trade publications, confidential government information on third-country trade, and other sources. The construction of defense production facilities and the licensing fees paid for the production of arms are included in trade data when they are specified in military transfer agreements. Grants in kind are usually included as well. Definitional issues include treatment of dual-use equipment such as aircraft, use of military establishments such as schools and hospitals by civilians, and purchases by nongovernmental buyers.

Valuation problems arise when data are reported in volume terms and the purchase price must be estimated. Differences between sources may reflect reporting lags or differences in the period covered. Most compilers revise their time-series data regularly, so estimates for the same year may not be consistent between publication dates.

The data on arms trade are from the Bureau of Verification and Compliance, published in *World Military Expenditures and Arms Transfers 2000* (U.S. Department of State 2002). These data do not include arms supplied to subnational groups.

Definitions

• **Military expenditures** are based on the NATO definition, which includes all current and capital expenditures on the armed forces, including peacekeeping forces; defense ministries and other government agencies engaged in defense projects; paramilitary forces, if these are judged to be trained and equipped for military operations; and military space activities. Such expenditures include military and civil personnel, including retirement pensions of military personnel and social services for personnel; operation and maintenance; procurement; military research and development; and military aid (in the military expenditures of the donor country). Excluded are civil defense and current expenditures for previous military activities, such as for veterans' benefits, demobilization, conversion, and destruction of weapons. • **Armed forces personnel** refer to active duty military personnel, including paramilitary forces if these forces resemble regular units in their organization, equipment, training, or mission. • **Arms trade** comprises exports and imports of military equipment usually referred to as "conventional," including weapons of war, parts thereof, ammunition, support equipment, and other commodities designed for military use. See *About the data* for more details.

Data sources

The data on military expenditures are from SIPRI's *Yearbook 2002: Armaments, Disarmament and International Security*. The data on armed forces personnel and arms trade are from the Bureau of Verification and Compliance's *World Military Expenditures and Arms Transfers 2000* (U.S. Department of State 2002).

5.9 Transport infrastructure

	Roads			Railways					Ports	Air		
	Total road network km	Paved roads %	Goods hauled million ton-km	Rail lines Total km	Electric km	Traffic density traffic units per km	Employee productivity traffic units per employee	Ratio of passenger tariffs to freight tariffs	Container traffic thousand TEUs	Aircraft departures thousands	Passengers carried thousands	Air freight million ton-km
	1995–2000[a]	1995–2000[a]	1995–2000[a]	1996–2001[a]	1996–2001[a]	1996–2001[a]	1996–2001[a]	1996–2001[a]	2001	2001	2001	2001
Afghanistan	21,000	13.3	..	..	..	..	..	..	..	3	150	8
Albania	18,000	39.0	1,830	440	..	334	39	..	..	4	146	..
Algeria	104,000	68.9	..	3,793	283	419	230	..	311.1	44	3,240	19
Angola	51,429	10.4	..	..	..	..	..	..	..	4	193	51
Argentina	215,471	29.4	..	28,291	179	318	1,209	1.28	1,058.0	123	5,739	124
Armenia	15,918	96.3	40	842	784	465	80	0.23	..	3	369	8
Australia	811,603	38.7	..	..	..	..	..	..	3,619.7	389	33,477	1,678
Austria	200,000	100.0	16,100	5,780	3,493	4,261	482	1.14	..	133	6,514	356
Azerbaijan	24,981	92.3	3,513	..	..	..	..	..	..	8	544	66
Bangladesh	207,486	9.5	..	2,768	..	1,704	126	0.24	486.3	7	1,450	170
Belarus	74,385	89.0	8,982	5,512	874	7,857	630	..	..	6	222	2
Belgium	148,216	78.2	35,000	3,471	2,705	4,445	373	1.07	5,109.7	178	8,489	853
Benin	6,787	20.0	..	..	..	..	..	..	..	1	46	7
Bolivia	53,790	6.5	..	3,163	..	336	1,381	0.31	..	20	1,560	14
Bosnia and Herzegovina	21,846	52.3	..	..	..	..	..	..	..	5	65	1
Botswana	10,217	55.0	..	..	..	..	..	..	..	7	168	0
Brazil	1,724,929	5.5	..	25,652	1,220	1,805	3,970	..	2,616.1	654	34,286	1,467
Bulgaria	37,286	94.0	168	4,290	2,708	1,846	216	0.89	..	7	234	2
Burkina Faso	12,506	16.0	..	..	..	..	..	..	..	2	100	7
Burundi	14,480	7.1	..	..	..	..	..	..	..	..	..	..
Cambodia	12,323	16.2	412	601	..	228	69	0.39	..	..	..	..
Cameroon	34,300	12.5	..	1,006	..	1,333	496	0.34	..	5	247	42
Canada	901,903	..	82,500	39,400	..	7,479	7,600	6.63	2,870.7	292	24,204	1,605
Central African Republic	23,810	2.7	60	..	..	..	..	..	..	1	46	7
Chad	33,400	0.8	..	..	..	..	..	..	..	1	46	7
Chile	79,814	19.4	..	4,814	850	370	2,162	..	1,209.1	83	5,301	1,279
China	1,402,698	22.4	612,940	58,656	14,864	30,262	1,155	1.19	43,970.4[b]	841	72,661	4,232
Hong Kong, China	1,831	100.0	..	..	..	..	..	..	..	88	14,050	5,051
Colombia	112,988	14.4	31	3,154	..	..	1,795	..	531.3	190	9,566	625
Congo, Dem. Rep.	157,000	..	..	3,641	858	169	40	..	..	..	..	..
Congo, Rep.	12,800	9.7	..	900	..	188	55	..	..	5	95	7
Costa Rica	35,892	22.0	3,070	424	109	..	..	..	563.8	26	752	23
Côte d'Ivoire	50,400	9.7	..	639	..	986	540	0.67	543.8	1	46	7
Croatia	28,123	84.6	1,090	2,726	983	1,280	163	0.80	..	18	1,064	3
Cuba	60,858	49.0	..	4,667	132	468	81	..	..	12	882	54
Czech Republic	55,408	100.0	39,036	9,365	2,843	2,615	284	..	..	44	2,560	26
Denmark	71,591	100.0	11,696	2,047	625	3,648	770	..	549.1	111	6,382	184
Dominican Republic	12,600	49.4	..	..	..	..	..	..	466.0	..	..	..
Ecuador	43,197	18.9	4,176	..	..	..	..	..	414.4	17	1,251	14
Egypt, Arab Rep.	64,000	78.1	31,500	5,024	59	14,308	753	0.20	1,709.0	41	4,389	239
El Salvador	10,029	19.8	..	1,202	503	..	367	..	..	44	2,192	47
Eritrea	4,010	21.8	..	..	..	..	..	..	..	..	..	..
Estonia	51,411	20.1	3,689	968	132	7,999	1,358	2.36	..	8	278	2
Ethiopia	31,571	12.0	0	..	..	..	..	..	..	28	1,028	79
Finland	77,900	64.5	26,500	5,854	2,372	2,308	1,056	2.47	1,018.7	129	6,698	171
France	894,000	100.0	245,400	32,515	14,104	3,854	715	1.54	2,983.9	786	50,817	4,868
Gabon	8,464	9.9	..	814	..	2,087	894	..	..	8	374	49
Gambia, The	2,700	35.4	..	..	..	..	..	..	..	..	..	..
Georgia	20,362	93.5	475	1,562	1,544	2,794	276	0.37	..	2	111	2
Germany	230,735	99.1	226,982	36,652	19,079	4,128	681	2.77	8,299.2	782	57,334	7,026
Ghana	39,409	29.6	..	953	..	1,778	376	..	..	6	301	33
Greece	117,000	91.8	17,000	2,299	..	830	182	..	1,429.7	103	7,303	99
Guatemala	14,118	34.5	..	..	..	..	..	..	528.0	..	..	3
Guinea	30,500	16.5	..	..	..	..	..	..	..	..	..	1
Guinea-Bissau	4,400	10.3	..	..	..	..	..	..	..	..	..	..
Haiti	4,160	24.3	..	..	..	..	..	..	..	..	..	..

	Roads			Railways					Ports	Air		
	Total road network km 1995–2000[a]	Paved roads % 1995–2000[a]	Goods hauled million ton-km 1995–2000[a]	Rail lines Total km 1996–2001[a]	Rail lines Electric km 1996–2001[a]	Traffic density traffic units per km 1996–2001[a]	Employee productivity traffic units per employee 1996–2001[a]	Ratio of passenger tariffs to freight tariffs 1996–2001[a]	Container traffic thousand TEUs 2001	Aircraft departures thousands 2001	Passengers carried thousands 2001	Air freight million ton-km 2001
Honduras	13,603	20.4	..	..	..	..	..	..	406.4	..	..	..
Hungary	188,203	43.4	14	7,729	2,628	2,242	319	..	..	32	2,075	38
India	3,319,644	45.7	958	62,759	14,261	11,725	467	0.31	2,591.1	214	17,272	518
Indonesia	342,700	46.3	..	5,324	131	3,974	610	0.95	3,492.2	166	10,049	415
Iran, Islamic Rep.	167,157	56.3	..	6,688	148	3,185	758	..	..	86	9,318	77
Iraq	45,550	84.3	..	..	..	..	..	..	..	..	..	..
Ireland	92,500	94.1	5,900	1,915	37	982	171	..	750.3	164	16,374	147
Israel	16,281	100.0	..	925	..	2,112	1,628	..	..	52	3,990	734
Italy	479,688	100.0	219,800	16,499	10,937	4,102	618	1.42	7,131.0	395	31,031	1,521
Jamaica	18,700	70.1	..	..	..	..	..	..	888.9	24	1,946	26
Japan	1,161,894	46.0	307,149	20,165	12,080	13,048	1,528	..	12,980.6	641	107,870	7,627
Jordan	7,245	100.0	..	293	..	2,123	518	..	..	16	1,178	178
Kazakhstan	81,331	94.7	4,506	13,545	3,725	9,981	1,069	..	..	8	501	12
Kenya	63,942	12.1	..	2,634	..	699	184	..	..	25	1,418	93
Korea, Dem. Rep.	31,200	6.4	..	..	..	..	..	..	..	1	79	2
Korea, Rep.	86,990	74.5	74,504	3,123	668	12,456	1,323	1.43	9,887.6	226	32,638	6,957
Kuwait	4,450	80.6	..	..	..	..	..	..	..	17	2,085	226
Kyrgyz Republic	18,500	91.1	1,220	..	..	..	..	..	..	5	192	6
Lao PDR	21,716	..	..	..	..	..	..	..	..	7	211	2
Latvia	73,202	38.6	4,789	2,331	258	5,834	917	..	..	11	305	1
Lebanon	7,300	84.9	..	..	..	..	..	..	..	10	816	75
Lesotho	5,940	18.3	..	..	..	..	..	..	..	..	..	..
Liberia	10,600	6.2	..	..	..	..	..	..	..	..	..	..
Libya	83,200	57.2	..	..	..	..	..	..	..	6	583	0
Lithuania	75,243	91.3	7,769	1,905	122	4,171	611	..	..	10	304	2
Macedonia, FYR	8,684	63.8	1,210	699	233	972	162	0.39	..	5	316	1
Madagascar	49,827	11.6	..	..	..	..	..	..	..	21	624	34
Malawi	28,400	18.5	..	710	..	159	176	0.25	..	5	113	1
Malaysia	65,877	75.8	..	1,622	152	1,368	370	0.87	6,224.8	176	16,311	1,533
Mali	15,100	12.1	..	734	..	658	322	..	..	1	46	7
Mauritania	7,660	11.3	..	..	..	..	..	..	..	2	156	7
Mauritius	1,926	97.0	..	..	..	..	..	..	..	13	997	175
Mexico	329,532	32.8	197,958	17,697	250	2,660	3,925	..	1,358.2	291	20,043	269
Moldova	12,657	87.0	952	..	..	..	..	..	..	4	120	0
Mongolia	49,250	3.5	126	1,810	..	2,963	394	..	..	18	255	7
Morocco	57,707	56.4	3,035	1,907	1,003	3,425	610	0.86	346.7	44	3,681	63
Mozambique	30,400	18.7	110	..	..	..	..	..	..	7	264	7
Myanmar	28,200	12.2	..	..	..	..	..	..	..	10	398	1
Namibia	66,467	13.6	..	2,382	..	474	..	..	..	6	212	73
Nepal	13,223	30.8	..	..	..	..	..	..	..	12	641	16
Netherlands	116,500	90.0	32,700	2,802	2,061	6,631	752	2.56	6,227.3	227	20,474	4,116
New Zealand	92,053	62.8	..	3,913	519	938	1,120	1.46	1,144.3	266	11,095	763
Nicaragua	19,032	11.0	..	..	..	..	..	..	..	1	61	1
Niger	10,100	7.9	..	..	..	..	..	..	..	1	46	7
Nigeria	194,394	30.9	..	3,557	..	287	65	0.10	..	8	529	3
Norway	91,454	76.0	12,796	..	..	..	..	..	..	307	14,559	185
Oman	32,800	30.0	..	..	..	..	..	..	1,325.5	18	1,980	149
Pakistan	254,410	43.0	96,802	7,791	293	2,838	232	0.28	..	53	4,871	371
Panama	11,400	34.6	..	..	..	..	..	..	2,170.5	25	1,115	25
Papua New Guinea	19,600	3.5	..	..	..	..	..	..	..	30	1,188	22
Paraguay	29,500	9.5	..	..	..	..	..	..	..	8	281	..
Peru	72,900	12.8	..	1,691	..	406	363	..	537.6	30	1,605	56
Philippines	201,994	21.0	..	491	..	505	112	0.09	3,091.0	44	5,652	264
Poland	364,656	68.3	72,843	22,560	11,826	3,537	415	0.79	..	72	2,670	69
Portugal	68,732	86.0	14,200	2,814	904	2,066	465	..	804.2	96	6,651	209
Puerto Rico	14,400	100.0	..	..	..	..	..	..	1,886.0	..	..	..

	Roads			Railways					Ports	Air		
	Total road network km	Paved roads %	Goods hauled million ton-km	Rail lines Total km	Electric km	Traffic density traffic units per km	Employee productivity traffic units per employee	Ratio of passenger tariffs to freight tariffs	Container traffic thousand TEUs	Aircraft departures thousands	Passengers carried thousands	Air freight million ton-km
	1995–2000[a]	1995–2000[a]	1995–2000[a]	1996–2001[a]	1996–2001[a]	1996–2001[a]	1996–2001[a]	1996–2001[a]	2001	2001	2001	2001
Romania	198,603	49.5	13,457	11,364	3,929	2,467	267	1.24	..	20	1,135	10
Russian Federation	532,393	67.4	139	86,075	40,962	15,854	1,054	0.97	382.2	329	20,235	895
Rwanda	12,000	8.3	..	..	..	..	..	..	..	..	..	..
Saudi Arabia	151,470	30.1	..	1,390	..	799	555	..	1,677.4	108	12,836	1,000
Senegal	14,576	29.3	..	906	..	562	339	..	..	0	6	*14*
Sierra Leone	11,330	7.9	..	..	..	..	..	..	..	0	14	6
Singapore	3,066	100.0	..	..	..	..	..	..	15,603.8	76	16,374	5,774
Slovak Republic	42,717	86.7	8,474	3,662	1,536	3,851	302	1.11	..	2	43	0
Slovenia	20,177	99.9	4,407	..	..	2,746	..	..	..	13	690	4
Somalia	22,100	11.8	..	..	..	..	..	..	..	..	..	..
South Africa	362,099	20.3	..	22,657	10,430	5,018	2,933	..	1,817.8	122	7,948	747
Spain	663,795	99.0	98,145	13,866	7,523	2,295	842	..	6,153.4	518	41,470	879
Sri Lanka	96,695	..	30	1,447	..	2,271	189	0.11	1,726.6	11	1,719	218
Sudan	11,900	36.3	..	4,599	..	298	98	..	..	8	415	33
Swaziland	3,247	..	..	..	..	..	..	..	..	2	90	0
Sweden	212,402	78.4	32,000	10,068	7,405	2,492	2,144	2.34	856.6	234	13,123	264
Switzerland	71,011	..	22,000	..	..	..	..	..	..	285	16,915	1,642
Syrian Arab Republic	43,381	23.1	..	1,771	..	996	160	..	..	14	761	21
Tajikistan	27,767	..	..	..	..	..	..	..	..	5	274	3
Tanzania	88,200	4.2	..	2,722	..	598	181	0.41	..	5	171	3
Thailand	64,600	97.5	..	4,044	..	3,342	660	0.75	3,381.6	102	17,662	1,669
Togo	7,520	31.6	..	..	..	..	..	..	..	1	46	7
Trinidad and Tobago	8,320	51.1	..	..	..	..	..	..	352.8	28	1,124	26
Tunisia	18,997	64.8	..	2,260	60	1,010	341	1.87	..	19	1,926	20
Turkey	385,960	34.0	150,974	8,671	1,752	1,798	330	1.20	1,554.9	106	9,905	339
Turkmenistan	24,000	81.2	..	..	..	..	..	..	..	24	1,407	13
Uganda	27,000	6.7	..	261	..	805	131	..	..	0	41	21
Ukraine	169,491	96.7	18,206	22,302	9,170	9,535	598	..	..	39	996	12
United Arab Emirates	1,088	100.0	..	..	..	..	..	..	5,082.0	51	7,676	1,631
United Kingdom	371,913	100.0	150,700	17,067	5,225	3,500	2,678	..	6,212.7	985	72,772	4,549
United States	6,304,193	58.8	1,534,430	160,000	484	13,800	13,476	9.28	28,082.5	8,535[c]	619,262[c]	28,042[c]
Uruguay	8,983	90.0	..	3,003	..	127	191	..	..	10	559	13
Uzbekistan	81,600	87.3	..	..	619	4,830	304	..	..	40	2,256	104
Venezuela, RB	96,155	33.6	..	336	..	161	180	0.21	924.6	124	4,052	31
Vietnam	93,300	25.1	..	3,142	..	1,624	154	0.88	1,290.6	35	3,410	134
West Bank and Gaza	..	..	..	..	..	..	..	..	..	..	..	..
Yemen, Rep.	67,000	11.5	..	..	..	..	..	..	377.7	15	841	32
Yugoslavia, Fed. Rep.	49,805	62.3	630	4,058	1,103	522	94	..	..	16	1,117	4
Zambia	66,781	..	..	1,273	..	144	610	0.27	..	5	49	*1*
Zimbabwe	18,338	47.4	..	2,759	311	1,977	454	0.60	..	13	495	158
World	**43.4 m**			**.. s**		**.. m**	**.. m**	**.. m**	**230,671 s**	**21,496 s**	**1,621,061 s**	
Low income	16.1			..		..	..	..	..	841	52,262	
Middle income	52.7			..		..	..	..	84,636	4,383	306,292	
Lower middle income	53.0			..		..	..	..	62,064	2,369	186,767	
Upper middle income	51.1			..		..	611.0	..	22,573	2,014	119,525	
Low & middle income	30.9			..		..	..	..	93,418	5,223	358,554	
East Asia & Pacific	21.2			..		2,293.4	382.0	..	61,451	1,525	128,916	
Europe & Central Asia	91.3			..		..	304.0	..	..	832	49,444	
Latin America & Carib.	26.9			..		..	..	..	15,912	1,784	93,872	
Middle East & N. Africa	66.3			..		..	555.0	..	..	437	42,954	
South Asia	36.9			..		..	..	0.24	4,804	304	26,299	
Sub-Saharan Africa	12.9			..		..	..	..	..	342	17,069	
High income	91.8			..		3,648.3	770.0	..	137,253	16,272	1,262,508	
Europe EMU	92.9		124,467			3,853.9	618.0	..	39,907	3,548	254,040	

a. Data are for the latest year available in the period shown. b. Includes Hong Kong, China. c. Data cover only those carriers designated by the U.S. Department of Transportation as major and national air carriers.

About the data

Transport infrastructure—highways, railways, ports and waterways, and airports and air traffic control systems—and the services that flow from it are crucial to the activities of households, producers, and governments. Because performance indicators vary significantly by transport mode and by focus (whether physical infrastructure or the services flowing from that infrastructure), highly specialized and carefully specified indicators are required. The table provides selected indicators of the size, extent, and productivity of roads, railways, and air transport systems and of the volume of traffic in these modes as well as in ports.

Data for transport sectors are not always internationally comparable. Unlike for demographic statistics, national income accounts, and international trade data, the collection of infrastructure data has not been "internationalized." But data on roads are collected by the International Road Federation (IRF), and data on air transport by the International Civil Aviation Organization (ICAO).

National road associations are the primary source of IRF data. In countries where such an association is lacking or does not respond, other agencies are contacted, such as road directorates, ministries of transport or public works, or central statistical offices. As a result, the compiled data are of uneven quality. Even when data are available, they are often of limited value because of incompatible definitions (for example, in some countries a path used mainly by animals may be considered a road, while in others a road must be registered with a state agency responsible for its maintenance), inappropriate geographic units, lack of timeliness, and variations in the nature of the terrain.

Moreover, the quality of transport service (reliability, transit time, and condition of goods delivered) is rarely measured, though it may be as important as quantity in assessing an economy's transport system. Serious efforts are needed to create international databases whose comparability and accuracy can be gradually improved.

New indicators for railways focus on efficiency and productivity. Traffic density is an indication of the intensity of use of a railway's largest investment—its track. Traffic densities for branch lines tend to range around 500,000 traffic units per kilometer (see *Definitions*), while those for mainlines range from more than 5 million traffic units per kilometer to 100 million. (Note that kilometers of track may exceed kilometers of line because of double and triple tracking, yard tracks, and the like.) Railways whose traffic density averages less than 500,000 traffic units per kilometer need to operate at low costs and very high labor productivity to survive. Labor is the most expensive factor of production for a railway, and most railways have found that improving labor productivity is the most important factor in establishing economic viability. Employee productivity is heavily influenced by the balance of passenger and freight

service, with productivity far lower in passenger service. In developing countries a ratio of passenger tariffs to freight tariffs greater than 1 indicates an absence of significant cross-subsidies and a potential to provide higher-quality service. This ratio, like the other railway indicators, has no normative value and is intended for relative analysis only.

Measures of port container traffic, much of it commodities of medium to high value added, give some indication of economic growth in a country. But when traffic is merely transshipment, much of the economic benefit goes to the terminal operator and ancillary services for ships and containers rather than to the country more broadly. In transshipment centers empty containers may account for as much as 40 percent of traffic.

The air transport data represent the total (international and domestic) scheduled traffic carried by the air carriers registered in a country. Countries submit air transport data to ICAO on the basis of standard instructions and definitions issued by ICAO. In many cases, however, the data include estimates by ICAO for nonreporting carriers. Where possible, these estimates are based on previous submissions supplemented by information published by the air carriers, such as flight schedules.

The data represent the air traffic carried on scheduled services, but changes in air transport regulations in Europe have made it more difficult to classify traffic as scheduled or nonscheduled. Thus recent increases shown for some European countries may be due to changes in the classification of air traffic rather than actual growth. For countries with few air carriers or only one, the addition or discontinuation of a home-based air carrier may cause significant changes in air traffic.

Definitions

• **Total road network** includes motorways, highways, main or national roads, secondary or regional roads, and all other roads in a country. • **Paved roads** are those surfaced with crushed stone (macadam) and hydrocarbon binder or bituminized agents, with concrete, or with cobblestones. • **Goods hauled by road** are the volume of goods transported by road vehicles, measured in millions of metric tons times kilometers traveled. • **Total rail lines** refer to the length of the railway lines. • **Electric rail lines** refer to the length of line with electric traction. This line can include overhead catenary at various direct current (DC) or alternating current (AC) voltages and third-rail DC systems. • **Railway traffic density** is the sum of passenger-kilometers (passengers times kilometers traveled) and ton-kilometers (metric tons of freight times kilometers traveled)—together, traffic units—divided by kilometers of line. • **Employee productivity** is annual output (in traffic units) per employee. • **Ratio of passenger tariffs to freight tariffs** is the average passenger fare (total passenger revenue divided by total passenger-kilometers) divided by the average freight rate (total freight revenue divided by total ton-kilometers). A ratio less than 1 indicates a likelihood of cross-subsidy of passengers from freight tariffs. • **Port container traffic** measures the flow of containers from land to sea transport modes, and vice versa, in twenty-foot-equivalent units (TEUs), a standard-size container. Data refer to coastal shipping as well as international journeys. Transshipment traffic is counted as two lifts at the intermediate port (once to off-load and again as an outbound lift) and includes empty units. • **Aircraft departures** are domestic and international takeoffs of air carriers registered in the country. • **Air passengers carried** include both domestic and international passengers of air carriers registered in the country. • **Air freight** is the sum of the metric tons of freight, express, and diplomatic bags carried on each flight stage (the operation of an aircraft from takeoff to its next landing), multiplied by the stage distance, by air carriers registered in the country.

Data sources

The data on roads are from the International Road Federation's *World Road Statistics*. The data on railways are from a database maintained by the World Bank's Transportation, Water, and Urban Development Department, Transport Division. Those on port container traffic are from Containerisation International's *Containerisation International Yearbook*. And the data on air transport are from the International Civil Aviation Organization's *Civil Aviation Statistics of the World* and ICAO staff estimates.

Power and communications

	Electric power		Telephone mainlines[a]							Mobile phones[a]	International telecommunications[a]	
	Consumption per capita kwh	Transmission and distribution losses % of output	per 1,000 people	In largest city per 1,000 people	Waiting list thousands	Waiting time years	per employee	Revenue per line $	Cost of local call $ per 3 minutes	per 1,000 people	Outgoing traffic minutes per subscriber	Cost of call to U.S. $ per 3 minutes
	2000	2000	2001	2001	2001	2000	2001	2001	2001	2001	2001	2001
Afghanistan	..	..	1	8	..	..	..	..	..	..	..	..
Albania	1,073	51	50	94	11.8	4.5	53	853	0.02	88	361	5.92
Algeria	612	16	61	124	727.0	5.4	105	192	0.02	3	0	..
Angola	88	15	6	21	..	8.5	37	1,633	0.08	6	444	3.11
Argentina	2,038	13	224	..	93.1	0.2	337	931	0.09	193	58	..
Armenia	944	25	140	212	80.8	..	74	119	0.11	6	62	..
Australia	9,006	8	519	..	0.0	0.0	179	1,330	0.11	576	224	0.59
Austria	6,457	7	468	..	0.0	0.0	217	1,512	0.13	807	274	..
Azerbaijan	1,852	15	111	270	55.4	1.3	99	97	0.29	80	34	6.96
Bangladesh	96	16	4	30	199.1	3.3	29	593	0.03	4	77	2.47
Belarus	2,678	13	279	397	373.0	2.7	107	45	0.01	13	73	2.43
Belgium	7,564	4	498	..	..	..	180	1,269	0.13	746	344	..
Benin	64	72	9	..	23.0	4.5	62	1,044	0.09	19	294	..
Bolivia	387	18	62	109	..	0.2	171	756	0.09	90	27	..
Bosnia and Herzegovina	1,473	17	111	502	..	2.2	248	482	0.02	57	200	..
Botswana	..	..	91	..	..	0.5	..	..	0.02	165	..	..
Brazil	1,878	18	218	311	..	0.5	400	822	0.04	167	21	..
Bulgaria	2,962	15	359	..	181.7	3.6	116	0	0.00	191	254	2.46
Burkina Faso	..	..	5	42	12.3	2.2	45	998	0.10	3	145	..
Burundi	..	..	3	..	..	7.3	..	..	..	3	..	..
Cambodia	..	..	2	19	..	..	51	705	0.03	17	320	..
Cameroon	183	22	7	..	..	6.2	46	..	0.06	20	218	..
Canada	15,620	8	676	..	..	0.0	238	1,044	..	362	347	..
Central African Republic	..	..	2	..	..	>10.0	22	1,048	..	3	434	12.93
Chad	..	..	1	8	..	0.5	17	..	0.10	3	..	9.11
Chile	2,406	7	233	333	32.3	0.0	184	710	0.10	342	67	2.18
China	827	7	137	584	..	0.0	..	239	..	110	7	..
Hong Kong, China	5,447	13	580	577	0.0	0.0	150	1,907	0.00	859	932	2.62
Colombia	788	24	171	327	1,174.7	2.0	227	291	0.03	76	40	..
Congo, Dem. Rep.	40	4	0	..	..	..	..	..	..	3	..	..
Congo, Rep.	86	60	7	..	..	..	..	..	..	48	..	..
Costa Rica	1,630	7	230	..	19.6	0.3	190	369	0.03	76	138	1.93
Côte d'Ivoire	..	..	18	68	22.7	0.8	77	1,284	0.05	45	212	5.89
Croatia	2,695	19	365	..	..	0.9	..	..	0.08	377	129	..
Cuba	1,049	16	51	121	..	..	34	1,315	0.09	1	65	..
Czech Republic	4,807	7	375	666	30.5	0.2	157	683	0.11	675	93	0.79
Denmark	6,079	6	719	..	0.0	0.0	172	1,092	0.08	738	219	..
Dominican Republic	788	27	110	..	..	..	..	..	0.00	146	213	..
Ecuador	624	21	104	133	14.5	..	275	336	0.60	67	48	1.75
Egypt, Arab Rep.	976	12	104	..	583.3	1.9	122	383	0.01	43	33	2.91
El Salvador	587	13	93	..	38.2	..	155	985	0.07	125	264	1.23
Eritrea	..	..	8	43	27.0	7.2	66	437	0.03	..	114	..
Estonia	3,628	15	352	422	13.8	1.4	220	621	0.09	455	153	0.70
Ethiopia	22	10	4	60	155.2	7.8	39	329	0.02	0	47	7.14
Finland	14,588	4	548	..	0.0	0.0	114	1,472	0.12	778	190	0.17
France	6,539	6	573	..	0.0	0.0	223	860	0.14	605	120	..
Gabon	697	10	30	..	..	>10.0	32	1,796	..	205	673	..
Gambia, The	..	..	26	97	10.9	6.0	37	..	0.05	41	192	4.40
Georgia	1,212	15	159	233	104.8	2.2	72	114	..	54	74	1.88
Germany	5,963	4	634	696	0.0	0.0	216	1,083	0.09	682	168	0.33
Ghana	288	1	12	83	154.8	..	61	525	0.03	9	193	1.26
Greece	4,086	8	529	731	7.6	0.2	302	864	0.08	751	147	0.69
Guatemala	335	25	65	..	..	..	..	..	0.08	97	207	..
Guinea	..	..	3	..	1.4	0.1	32	1,119	0.09	7	180	4.61
Guinea-Bissau	..	..	10	..	5.1	4.4	46	..	..	..	271	..
Haiti	37	45	10	..	..	>10.0	18	..	..	11	..	..

Power and communications

	Electric power		Telephone mainlines [a]							Mobile phones [a]	International telecommunications [a]	
	Consumption per capita kwh	Transmission and distribution losses % of output	per 1,000 people	In largest city per 1,000 people	Waiting list thousands	Waiting time years	per employee	Revenue per line $	Cost of local call $ per 3 minutes	per 1,000 people	Outgoing traffic minutes per subscriber	Cost of call to U.S. $ per 3 minutes
	2000	2000	2001	2001	2001	2000	2001	2001	2001	2001	2001	2001
Honduras	499	19	47	..	..	7.8	50	1,115	0.07	36	144	3.72
Hungary	2,909	14	374	588	20.1	0.1	181	1,017	0.09	498	51	0.98
India	355	27	38	136	1,648.8	0.8	91	198	0.02	6	14	3.20
Indonesia	384	11	35	261	..	..	181	300	0.02	31	44	..
Iran, Islamic Rep.	1,474	16	169	381	1,155.5	1.2	229	398	0.02	32	25	7.70
Iraq	1,450	..	29	..	..	..	..	..	..	..	..	..
Ireland	5,324	9	485	..	..	..	116	1,536	0.14	729	786	..
Israel	6,188	3	476	..	..	0.3	253	1,407	0.02	808	323	..
Italy	4,732	7	471	..	0.0	0.0	358	1,288	0.11	839	169	..
Jamaica	2,328	9	197	..	209.1	6.5	175	..	..	269	144	..
Japan	7,628	3	597	554	0.0	0.0	508	1,552	0.07	588	36	1.67
Jordan	1,236	11	127	183	9.4	0.3	101	1,044	0.04	167	288	2.68
Kazakhstan	2,622	17	113	..	155.6	>10.0	60	147	..	36	57	..
Kenya	106	22	10	77	134.0	8.1	17	1,482	0.04	19	75	5.84
Korea, Dem. Rep.	..	..	22	..	..	..	..	..	..	..	..	..
Korea, Rep.	5,607	5	486	632	0.0	0.0	336	791	0.03	621	45	1.69
Kuwait	13,995	..	240	46	0.0	0.0	64	1,516	0.00	445	340	1.96
Kyrgyz Republic	1,606	25	78	168	37.7	6.9	50	83	..	5	61	8.92
Lao PDR	..	..	10	65	5.9	1.1	39	488	0.02	5	138	6.37
Latvia	1,887	24	308	500	14.7	3.3	179	321	0.11	279	67	1.99
Lebanon	1,814	18	195	..	..	..	..	..	0.07	212	..	..
Lesotho	..	..	10	64	19.0	>10.0	64	478	0.02	15	..	2.31
Liberia	..	..	2	..	..	>10.0	..	..	..	1	..	..
Libya	3,921	..	109	..	..	1.2	43	..	..	9	..	..
Lithuania	1,768	12	313	427	9.1	0.9	217	230	0.11	253	30	2.13
Macedonia, FYR	..	..	263	..	..	1.2	143	406	0.01	109	122	..
Madagascar	..	..	4	9	0.3	0.1	23	1,450	0.09	9	166	8.98
Malawi	..	..	5	41	20.1	9.1	9	625	0.02	5	435	0.06
Malaysia	2,628	8	196	..	91.0	0.7	219	958	0.02	314	146	2.37
Mali	..	..	4	24	..	..	37	1,187	0.07	4	307	12.64
Mauritania	..	..	7	..	..	>10.0	26	1,330	0.08	42	476	..
Mauritius	..	..	257	376	9.9	1.0	165	470	0.03	252	116	3.60
Mexico	1,655	14	137	156	..	0.1	139	1,055	0.16	217	148	3.04
Moldova	720	45	154	350	118.3	5.5	93	85	0.02	48	69	3.96
Mongolia	..	..	52	99	37.6	2.6	28	396	0.02	81	38	4.92
Morocco	447	6	41	..	5.0	0.1	74	1,189	0.08	164	172	..
Mozambique	53	10	4	..	21.3	3.2	39	1,319	0.07	8	246	..
Myanmar	69	31	6	32	79.9	5.3	37	61	0.01	0	34	23.71
Namibia	..	..	66	157	2.4	0.7	70	756	0.03	56	512	4.28
Nepal	56	21	13	315	286.0	6.7	64	246	0.01	1	109	..
Netherlands	6,152	5	621	..	0.0	0.0	169	1,313	0.11	767	260	..
New Zealand	8,813	10	477	..	0.0	0.0	325	958	0.00	599	521	..
Nicaragua	267	30	31	..	..	9.1	..	..	..	30	..	..
Niger	..	..	2	24	..	..	16	848	0.11	0	292	8.77
Nigeria	81	32	5	12	..	1.4	47	715	..	4	112	..
Norway	24,422	8	720	..	0.0	0.0	144	1,574	0.14	825	128	0.28
Oman	2,952	17	90	..	..	0.5	115	1,823	0.02	124	646	..
Pakistan	352	24	23	..	230.0	1.8	61	369	0.02	6	53	3.54
Panama	1,331	20	148	284	..	..	78	1,018	0.06	207	121	4.36
Papua New Guinea	..	..	12	115	0.2	..	36	1,221	0.06	2	402	4.31
Paraguay	838	2	51	91	..	0.7	25	1,068	0.09	204	110	0.82
Peru	668	11	78	..	..	1.2	271	..	0.07	59	58	..
Philippines	477	14	42	265	..	..	257	721	0.00	150	49	..
Poland	2,511	10	295	..	501.6	0.8	159	646	0.08	260	73	2.92
Portugal	3,834	8	427	..	..	0.2	236	1,170	0.11	774	125	0.87
Puerto Rico	..	..	336	..	..	..	261	1,480	..	306	..	..

	Electric power		Telephone mainlines [a]							Mobile phones [a]	International telecommunications [a]	
	Consumption per capita kwh	Transmission and distribution losses % of output	per 1,000 people	In largest city per 1,000 people	Waiting list thousands	Waiting time years	per employee	Revenue per line $	Cost of local call $ per 3 minutes	per 1,000 people	Outgoing traffic minutes per subscriber	Cost of call to U.S. $ per 3 minutes
	2000	2000	2001	2001	2001	2000	2001	2001	2001	2001	2001	2001
Romania	1,513	13	184	..	576.0	3.8	103	222	0.11	172	44	1.96
Russian Federation	4,181	12	243	..	6,020.0	5.1	75	195	..	38	29	..
Rwanda	..	..	3	..	..	4.0	61	934	0.04	8	245	..
Saudi Arabia	4,912	8	145	214	85.6	2.6	131	1,719	0.01	113	458	3.20
Senegal	121	17	25	71	9.8	0.8	152	852	0.11	31	294	1.81
Sierra Leone	..	..	5	..	..	>10.0	19	..	..	6	336	..
Singapore	6,948	4	471	471	0.0	0.0	221	1,411	0.02	724	961	0.68
Slovak Republic	4,075	6	288	665	7.0	0.7	106	604	0.12	397	111	0.79
Slovenia	5,290	6	401	..	1.0	0.1	194	7,820	0.05	760	124	0.52
Somalia	..	..	4	..	..	..	..	..	..	..	..	..
South Africa	3,745	8	112	..	50.0	1.1	125	1,262	0.07	252	100	0.58
Spain	4,653	9	431	..	..	0.0	415	954	0.07	655	150	..
Sri Lanka	293	20	44	299	257.7	1.9	73	373	0.04	36	58	2.66
Sudan	66	15	14	80	444.0	4.4	150	364	0.03	3	80	39.08
Swaziland	..	..	31	131	14.6	7.2	67	826	0.04	65	822	2.97
Sweden	14,471	8	739	..	0.0	0.0	254	1,062	0.11	790	191	0.32
Switzerland	7,294	6	746	..	0.0	0.0	217	1,593	0.12	731	481	..
Syrian Arab Republic	900	..	103	156	2,805.9	>10.0	79	253	0.01	12	96	20.04
Tajikistan	2,137	15	36	133	5.6	..	45	32	0.01	0	38	..
Tanzania	56	22	4	20	7.3	1.3	42	932	0.07	12	63	..
Thailand	1,448	8	99	452	544.2	1.6	198	579	0.07	123	52	1.49
Togo	..	..	10	35	16.8	2.9	55	908	0.10	20	239	7.67
Trinidad and Tobago	3,692	7	240	..	..	0.5	100	958	0.04	197	218	2.21
Tunisia	939	11	109	..	..	0.9	143	451	0.02	40	172	..
Turkey	1,468	19	285	388	198.5	0.5	270	275	0.12	302	36	3.06
Turkmenistan	1,071	14	80	..	61.1	8.5	52	127	..	2	50	..
Uganda	..	..	3	..	..	3.6	27	1,787	0.13	14	..	..
Ukraine	2,293	18	212	..	2,500.4	7.9	85	146	..	44	36	..
United Arab Emirates	10,725	9	340	348	0.3	0.0	118	1,956	0.00	616	1,326	1.73
United Kingdom	5,601	8	588	..	0.0	0.0	169	1,875	0.17	770	225	..
United States	12,331	6	667	..	..	0.0	163	1,566	0.00	451	156	..
Uruguay	1,924	19	283	335	0.0	0.0	168	837	0.17	155	87	4.88
Uzbekistan	1,612	9	66	248	33.1	0.9	69	118	0.01	2	34	13.95
Venezuela, RB	2,533	24	109	..	..	..	154	2,557	0.10	263	104	..
Vietnam	286	13	38	..	..	..	41	414	0.02	15	18	..
West Bank and Gaza	..	..	78	..	..	0.7	155	..	0.06	91	176	..
Yemen, Rep.	107	26	22	80	159.5	3.8	76	228	0.02	8	102	4.45
Yugoslavia, Fed. Rep.	..	..	229	424	143.0	1.8	174	..	..	187	114	..
Zambia	556	3	8	22	12.8	6.7	28	808	0.06	11	170	2.57
Zimbabwe	845	21	19	76	158.9	10.0	63	817	0.04	24	289	4.36
World	**2,176 w**	**9 w**	**172 w**	**296 w**	**.. w**	**1.1 m**	**227 m**	**784 m**	**0.05 m**	**158 m**	**118 m**	**3.13 m**
Low income	352	22	30	130	8,170.7	4.4	92	241	0.05	10	112	5.27
Middle income	1,391	11	152	406	..	1.0	..	397	0.04	129	90	2.86
Lower middle income	1,193	10	139	524	..	1.9	..	288	0.04	107	62	..
Upper middle income	2,252	14	208	289	..	0.5	278	859	0.09	224	108	2.46
Low & middle income	914	13	93	270	..	2.0	..	370	0.04	72	102	3.54
East Asia & Pacific	760	8	110	502	..	1.4	..	278	0.02	97	49	4.62
Europe & Central Asia	2,753	13	235	..	12,154.9	1.8	131	268	0.10	140	65	2.13
Latin America & Carib.	1,528	16	165	..	..	0.5	295	840	0.08	161	87	..
Middle East & N. Africa	1,346	12	100	..	5,366.8	1.2	158	585	0.02	53	102	..
South Asia	323	26	32	127	2,623.8	1.9	87	222	0.02	6	58	2.66
Sub-Saharan Africa	432	10	14	..	..	4.4	101	1,082	0.06	27	245	5.15
High income	8,617	6	593	..	..	0.0	244	1,338	0.08	609	204	0.81
Europe EMU	5,757	6	540	..	14.1	0.0	255	1,108	0.11	711	169	..

a. Data are from the International Telecommunication Union's (ITU) *World Telecommunication Development Report 2002*. Please cite the ITU for third-party use of these data.

STATES AND MARKETS

About the data

The quality of an economy's infrastructure, including power and communications, is an important element in investment decisions for both domestic and foreign investors. Government effort alone will not suffice to meet the need for investments in modern infrastructure; public-private partnerships, especially those involving local providers and financiers, will be critical in lowering costs and delivering value for money. In telecommunications, competition in the marketplace, along with sound regulation, is lowering costs and improving the quality of and access to services around the globe.

An economy's production and consumption of electricity is a basic indicator of its size and level of development. Although a few countries export electric power, most production is for domestic consumption. Expanding the supply of electricity to meet the growing demand of increasingly urbanized and industrialized economies without incurring unacceptable social, economic, and environmental costs is one of the great challenges facing developing countries.

Data on electric power production and consumption are collected from national energy agencies by the International Energy Agency (IEA) and adjusted by the IEA to meet international definitions (for data on electricity production, see table 3.9). Electricity consumption is equivalent to production less power plants' own use and transmission, distribution, and transformation losses. It includes consumption by auxiliary stations, losses in transformers that are considered integral parts of those stations, and electricity produced by pumping installations. It covers electricity generated by primary sources of energy—

coal, oil, gas, nuclear, hydro, geothermal, wind, tide and wave, and combustible renewables—where data are available. Neither production nor consumption data capture the reliability of supplies, including breakdowns, load factors, and frequency of outages.

Over the past decade new financing and technology, along with privatization and liberalization, have spurred dramatic growth in telecommunications in many countries. The table presents some common performance indicators for telecommunications, including measures of supply and demand, service quality, productivity, economic and financial performance, and tariffs. The quality of data varies among reporting countries as a result of differences in regulatory obligations for the provision of data.

Demand for telecommunications is often measured by the sum of telephone mainlines and registered applicants for new connections. (A mainline is normally identified by a unique number that is the one billed.) In some countries the list of registered applicants does not reflect real current pending demand, which is often hidden or suppressed, reflecting an extremely short supply that has discouraged potential applicants from applying for telephone service. And in some countries the waiting list may overstate demand because applicants have placed their names on the list several times to improve their chances. Waiting time is calculated by dividing the number of applicants on the waiting list by the average number of mainlines added each year over the past three years. The number of mainlines no longer reflects a telephone system's full capacity because mobile telephones—whose use has been expanding rapidly in most countries, rich and poor—provide an alternative point of access.

In addition to waiting list and waiting time, the table includes two other measures of efficiency in telecommunications: mainlines per employee and revenue per mainline. Caution should be used in interpreting the estimates of mainlines per employee because firms often subcontract part of their work. The cross-country comparability of revenue per mainline may also be limited because, for example, some countries do not require telecommunications providers to submit financial information; the data usually do not include revenues from mobile phones or radio, paging, and data services; and there are definitional and accounting differences between countries.

Definitions

- **Electric power consumption** measures the production of power plants and combined heat and power plants less transmission, distribution, and transformation losses and own use by heat and power plants.
- **Electric power transmission and distribution losses** are losses in transmission between sources of supply and points of distribution and in distribution to consumers, including pilferage. • **Telephone mainlines** are telephone lines connecting a customer's equipment to the public switched telephone network. Data are presented for the entire country and for the largest city.
- **Waiting list** shows the number of applications for a connection to a mainline that have been held up by a lack of technical capacity. • **Waiting time** is the approximate number of years applicants must wait for a telephone line. • **Mainlines per employee** are calculated by dividing the number of mainlines by the number of telecommunications staff (with part-time staff converted to full-time equivalents) employed by enterprises providing public telecommunications services.
- **Revenue per line** is the revenue received by firms per mainline for providing telecommunications services.
- **Cost of local call** is the cost of a three-minute, peak rate, fixed line call within the same exchange area using the subscriber's equipment (that is, not from a public phone). • **Mobile phones** refer to users of portable telephones subscribing to an automatic public mobile telephone service using cellular technology that provides access to the public switched telephone network, per 1,000 people. • **Outgoing traffic** is the telephone traffic, measured in minutes per subscriber, that originates in the country and has a destination outside the country. • **Cost of call to U.S.** is the cost of a three-minute peak rate call from the country to the United States.

5.10a

In many countries mobile phone subscribers now outnumber fixed-line subscribers

Per 1,000 people, 2001

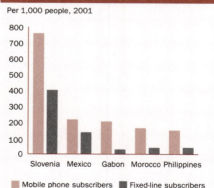

■ Mobile phone subscribers   ■ Fixed-line subscribers

Source: Table 5.10. Based on International Telecommunication Union data.

Data sources

The data on electricity consumption and losses are from the IEA's *Energy Statistics and Balances of Non-OECD Countries 1999–2000*, the IEA's *Energy Statistics of OECD Countries 1999–2000*, and the United Nations Statistics Division's *Energy Statistics Yearbook*. The telecommunications data are from the International Telecommunication Union's (ITU) *World Telecommunication Development Report 2002*.

	Daily newspapers per 1,000 people 2000	Radios per 1,000 people 2001	Television[a] Sets per 1,000 people 2001	Television[a] Cable subscribers per 1,000 people 2001	Personal computers per 1,000 people[a] 2001	Personal computers In education 2001	Internet Users thousands[a] 2001	Internet Monthly off-peak access charges[a] Service provider charge $ 2001	Internet Monthly off-peak access charges[a] Telephone usage charge $ 2001	Secure servers 2001	Information and communications technology expenditures % of gdp 2001	Information and communications technology expenditures per capita $ 2001
Afghanistan	5	114	14	0.0	..	..	..	..	..	1	..	..
Albania	35	260	123	..	7.6	..	10	19	0.20	1	..	..
Algeria	27	244	114	..	7.1	..	60	27	0.17	..	..	..
Angola	11	74	19	0.9	1.3	..	60	20	0.57	..	..	..
Argentina	37	681	326	162.9	91.1	140,053	3,300	78	0.47	238	4.0	310
Armenia	5	225	230	1.2	7.9	..	50	42	0.78	1	..	..
Australia	293	1,999	731	72.2	515.8	706,794	7,200	13	2.60	3,422	10.7	1,939
Austria	296	753	542	147.4	335.4	149,243	2,600	23	17.21	669	7.2	1,764
Azerbaijan	27	22	321	0.6	..	..	25	..	2.15	1	..	..
Bangladesh	53	49	17	..	1.9	..	250	17	0.33	1	..	..
Belarus	152	199	342	33.2	..	..	422	15	54.25	4	..	..
Belgium	160	793	543	370.0	232.8	193,997	3,200	23	27.52	342	8.1	1,870
Benin	5	441	44	..	1.7	..	25	129	0.93	1	..	..
Bolivia	55	676	121	9.7	20.5	..	150	..	..	5	..	..
Bosnia and Herzegovina	152	243	111	..	38.7	..	45	19	0.13	..	..	..
Botswana	27	150	30	7.3	38.7	..	50	15	0.14	..	..	..
Brazil	43	433	349	13.8	62.9	879,575	8,000	..	..	1,028	8.3	287
Bulgaria	116	543	453	131.3	44.3	22,078	605	8	0.02	18	3.8	65
Burkina Faso	1	433	103	0.0	1.5	..	19	29	0.84	..	..	..
Burundi	2	220	30	..	..	..	6	..	0.18	..	..	..
Cambodia	2	119	8	..	1.5	..	10	104	0.30	2	..	..
Cameroon	7	163	34	..	3.9	..	45	77	0.56	..	..	..
Canada	159	1,047	700	267.9	459.9	1,019,436	13,500	12	..	5,055	8.7	1,960
Central African Republic	2	80	6	..	1.9	..	2	166	1.40	..	..	..
Chad	0	236	1	..	1.6	..	4	..	..	..	..	..
Chile	98	759	286	46.0	106.5	123,595	3,102	..	..	141	8.1	371
China	..	339	312	68.6	19.0	2,092,119	33,700	7	0.14	184	5.7	53
Hong Kong, China	792	686	504	83.8	386.6	166,388	2,601	18	..	538	8.7	2,110
Colombia	46	549	286	13.6	42.1	118,796	1,154	..	0.25	71	12.0	231
Congo, Dem. Rep.	3	386	..	..	..	..	6	95	..	..	..	..
Congo, Rep.	8	123	..	..	3.9	..	1	..	..	..	..	..
Costa Rica	91	816	231	..	170.2	..	384	16	0.10	56	..	..
Côte d'Ivoire	16	183	60	0.0	7.2	..	70	183	0.25	..	..	..
Croatia	114	340	293	38.0	85.9	..	250	20	0.42	61	..	..
Cuba	118	185	251	..	19.6	..	120	..	..	2	..	..
Czech Republic	254	803	534	93.8	145.7	99,555	1,400	25	11.60	273	9.5	483
Denmark	283	1,400	857	200.9	540.3	154,797	2,900	21	..	396	9.3	2,912
Dominican Republic	27	181	..	..	..	..	186	18	..	8	..	..
Ecuador	96	413	225	33.8	23.3	..	328	..	..	11	..	..
Egypt, Arab Rep.	31	339	217	..	15.5	48,816	600	9	0.14	11	2.5	37
El Salvador	28	478	201	49.7	21.9	..	50	26	0.62	7	..	..
Eritrea	..	464	39	0.0	1.8	..	15	23	0.21	..	..	..
Estonia	176	1,136	629	97.9	174.8	..	430	..	0.57	80	..	..
Ethiopia	0	189	6	0.0	1.1	..	25	94	0.24	3	..	..
Finland	445	1,624	678	192.5	423.5	205,032	2,235	9	10.62	498	7.7	1,938
France	201	950	632	54.6	337.0	896,621	15,653	20	..	1,641	9.1	2,048
Gabon	30	501	326	..	11.9	..	17	35	1.26	1	..	..
Gambia, The	2	396	3	..	12.7	..	18	18	2.70	..	..	..
Georgia	5	556	474	2.7	..	..	25	20	0.00	10	..	..
Germany	305	570	586	264.5	382.2	1,054,871	30,800	13	..	5,156	7.9	1,880
Ghana	14	710	118	0.3	3.3	..	41	36	0.38	1	..	..
Greece	23	478	519	0.0	81.2	83,187	1,400	15	5.40	116	6.1	688
Guatemala	33	79	61	..	12.8	..	200	..	..	12	..	..
Guinea	..	52	44	0.0	4.0	..	15	58	0.86	..	..	..
Guinea-Bissau	5	204	36	..	..	..	4	..	..	1	..	..
Haiti	3	18	6	4.8	..	..	30	..	..	1	..	..

	Daily newspapers	Radios	Television [a]		Personal computers		Internet				Information and communications technology expenditures	
								Monthly off-peak access charges [a]				
			Sets	Cable subscribers			Users	Service provider charge	Telephone usage charge	Secure servers		per capita
	per 1,000 people	per 1,000 people	per 1,000 people	per 1,000 people	per 1,000 people [a]	In education	thousands [a]	$	$		% of gdp	$
	2000	2001	2001	2001	2001	2001	2001	2001	2001	2001	2001	2001
Honduras	55	413	96	7.7	12.2	..	40	15	0.61	4	..	..
Hungary	465	690	445	159.7	100.3	76,731	1,480	13	13.59	127	8.9	466
India	60	120	83	38.9	5.8	238,667	7,000	10	0.18	122	3.9	19
Indonesia	23	159	153	0.3	11.0	58,491	4,000	12	0.20	60	2.2	17
Iran, Islamic Rep.	28	281	163	..	69.7	..	1,005	..	..	1	..	..
Iraq	19	222	83	..	..	..	..	..	..	..	..	..
Ireland	150	695	399	159.4	390.7	60,008	895	21	16.45	350	6.2	1,704
Israel	290	526	335	185.0	245.9	..	1,800	11	0.18	301	7.4	..
Italy	104	878	494	1.4	194.8	852,612	16,400	23	17.62	1,041	5.7	1,117
Jamaica	62	796	194	..	50.0	..	100	49	..	5	..	..
Japan	578	956	731	147.4	348.8	2,172,000	55,930	17	27.67	5,153	9.6	3,256
Jordan	75	372	111	0.3	32.8	..	212	24	0.42	2	..	..
Kazakhstan	..	411	241	4.1	..	..	100	1	0.02	8	..	..
Kenya	10	221	26	0.4	5.6	..	500	66	0.46	1	..	..
Korea, Dem. Rep.	208	154	59	0.0	..	..	0	..	..	..	..	..
Korea, Rep.	393	1,034	363	182.5	256.5	610,724	24,380	8	..	345	7.4	676
Kuwait	374	624	482	..	131.9	..	200	32	0.00	4	..	..
Kyrgyz Republic	27	110	49	2.6	..	..	151	10	0.00	2	..	..
Lao PDR	4	148	52	0.0	3.0	..	10	50	0.17	..	..	..
Latvia	135	700	840	116.1	153.1	..	170	29	0.82	43	..	..
Lebanon	107	182	336	28.1	56.2	..	300	60	0.36	19	..	..
Lesotho	8	53	16	..	..	..	5	12	0.17	..	..	..
Liberia	12	274	25	..	..	..	1	..	..	..	..	..
Libya	15	273	137	..	..	..	20	108	0.20	..	..	..
Lithuania	29	524	422	89.4	70.6	..	250	45	0.38	43	..	..
Macedonia, FYR	21	205	282	..	..	..	70	12	0.04	..	..	..
Madagascar	5	216	24	..	2.4	..	35	66	0.44	..	..	..
Malawi	3	499	4	0.5	1.3	..	20	..	0.25	..	..	..
Malaysia	158	420	201	0.0	126.1	121,850	6,500	5	0.24	146	6.6	262
Mali	1	180	17	..	1.2	..	30	70	0.72	1	..	..
Mauritania	0	149	..	..	10.3	..	7	29	0.76	1	..	..
Mauritius	119	379	301	..	109.1	..	158	23	0.38	12	..	..
Mexico	94	330	283	24.8	68.7	515,871	3,636	11	..	259	3.2	196
Moldova	13	758	296	11.3	15.9	..	60	33	0.17	3	..	..
Mongolia	30	50	72	16.5	14.6	..	40	52	0.17	1	..	..
Morocco	28	243	159	..	13.7	..	400	26	0.75	5	..	..
Mozambique	2	44	5	..	3.5	..	15	..	..	..	..	..
Myanmar	9	65	8	..	1.1	..	10	..	..	..	..	..
Namibia	19	141	38	10.6	36.4	..	45	..	..	3	..	..
Nepal	12	39	8	..	3.5	..	60	16	0.07	..	..	..
Netherlands	306	980	553	392.4	428.4	773,332	7,900	23	16.40	798	9.3	2,327
New Zealand	362	997	557	7.1	392.6	195,483	1,092	11	..	609	14.4	1,835
Nicaragua	30	270	69	10.8	9.6	..	50	30	0.54	6	..	..
Niger	0	121	37	..	0.5	..	12	63	0.53	..	..	..
Nigeria	24	200	68	0.4	6.8	..	115	44	0.57	1	..	..
Norway	569	3,324	883	185.2	508.0	163,399	2,700	11	20.64	369	7.2	2,573
Oman	29	621	563	..	32.4	..	120	19	0.79	2	..	..
Pakistan	40	105	148	..	4.1	..	500	13	0.20	6	..	..
Panama	62	300	194	..	37.9	..	90	..	..	29	..	..
Papua New Guinea	14	86	19	3.9	56.7	..	50	34	2.52	..	..	..
Paraguay	43	182	218	21.3	14.2	..	60	..	..	4	..	..
Peru	0	269	148	16.7	47.9	..	3,000	..	..	35	..	..
Philippines	82	161	173	13.1	21.7	77,400	2,000	24	..	68	4.2	41
Poland	102	523	401	92.9	85.4	252,713	3,800	14	18.39	326	5.9	271
Portugal	32	304	415	108.6	117.4	48,511	2,500	19	13.00	138	6.5	735
Puerto Rico	126	761	330	..	..	..	600	43	1.30	63	..	..

5.11 The information age

	Daily newspapers per 1,000 people 2000	Radios per 1,000 people 2001	Television[a] Sets per 1,000 people 2001	Television[a] Cable subscribers per 1,000 people 2001	Personal computers per 1,000 people[a] 2001	Personal computers In education 2001	Internet Users thousands[a] 2001	Internet Service provider charge $ 2001	Internet Telephone usage charge $ 2001	Internet Secure servers 2001	ICT % of GDP 2001	ICT per capita $ 2001
Romania	300	358	379	120.6	35.7	36,754	1,000	15	0.37	53	2.2	43
Russian Federation	105	418	538	76.7	49.7	471,270	4,300	15	0.14	285	3.3	68
Rwanda	0	76	..	..	..	..	20	38	0.36	1	..	..
Saudi Arabia	326	326	264	..	62.7	..	300	31	0.13	11	..	..
Senegal	5	126	79	0.1	18.6	..	100	14	0.53	1	..	..
Sierra Leone	4	259	13	..	..	..	7	..	..	1	..	..
Singapore	298	672	300	73.1	508.3	150,702	1,500	15	0.12	525	9.9	2,110
Slovak Republic	131	965	407	122.9	148.1	27,729	674	9	0.54	79	7.5	325
Slovenia	169	405	367	160.8	275.7	28,842	600	29	0.31	102	4.7	496
Somalia	1	60	14	..	..	..	1	..	..	..	..	..
South Africa	32	338	152	0.0	68.5	364,722	3,068	30	0.33	521	9.2	269
Spain	100	330	598	14.2	168.2	306,320	7,388	17	..	938	5.1	769
Sri Lanka	29	215	117	0.3	9.3	..	150	6	0.05	6	..	..
Sudan	26	466	386	0.0	3.6	..	56	3	2.33	..	..	..
Swaziland	26	162	128	..	..	..	14	12	0.24	1	..	..
Sweden	410	2,811	965	224.5	561.2	548,698	4,600	2	21.35	1,033	11.3	2,804
Switzerland	373	1,002	554	370.0	540.2	175,431	2,223	18	30.87	1,079	10.2	3,618
Syrian Arab Republic	20	276	67	..	16.3	..	60	..	..	1	..	..
Tajikistan	20	141	326	..	..	..	3	..	..	..	..	..
Tanzania	4	406	42	0.2	3.3	..	300	69	0.79	..	..	..
Thailand	64	235	300	2.5	27.8	271,528	3,536	9	0.75	116	3.7	76
Togo	2	265	37	..	21.5	..	150	8	0.75	..	..	..
Trinidad and Tobago	123	532	340	..	69.2	..	120	1	0.37	12	..	..
Tunisia	19	158	198	..	23.7	..	400	25	0.22	4	..	..
Turkey	111	487	319	13.7	40.7	123,907	2,500	25	4.10	219	3.6	143
Turkmenistan	7	256	196	..	..	..	8	..	..	..	..	..
Uganda	2	127	27	0.2	3.1	..	60	30	0.82	..	..	..
Ukraine	175	889	456	52.3	18.3	..	600	7	0.04	44	..	..
United Arab Emirates	156	318	252	..	135.5	..	976	13	0.00	31	..	..
United Kingdom	329	1,446	950	64.1	366.2	1,824,106	24,000	14	..	6,467	9.7	2,319
United States	213	2,117	835	256.8	625.0	16,322,694	142,823	5	3.50	78,126	7.9	2,924
Uruguay	293	603	530	125.9	110.1	..	400	..	..	37	..	..
Uzbekistan	3	456	276	3.0	..	..	150	77	0.10	..	..	..
Venezuela, RB	206	294	185	40.2	52.8	100,663	1,265	27	..	92	4.0	199
Vietnam	4	109	186	..	11.7	26,957	1,010	20	0.25	6	6.7	26
West Bank and Gaza	..	..	134	0.0	..	..	60	700	0.28	..	..	..
Yemen, Rep.	15	65	283	..	1.9	..	17	45	0.09	..	..	..
Yugoslavia, Fed. Rep.	107	297	282	..	23.4	..	600	..	0.13	7	..	..
Zambia	12	169	113	..	7.0	..	25	19	0.31	..	..	..
Zimbabwe	18	362	..	..	12.1	..	100	46	0.34	1	..	..
World	.. w	419 w	242 w	64.3 w	86.5 w		501,478 s	20 w	0.38 w	121,223 s		
Low income	41	156	91	24.0	6.1		15,932	34	0.36	279		
Middle income	..	350	291	56.7	35.4		96,658	19	0.37	4,975		
Lower middle income	..	326	284	60.9	25.5		60,355	17	0.23	1,704		
Upper middle income	95	457	320	40.5	77.2		36,303	23	0.44	3,271		
Low & middle income	..	258	191	39.5	21.6		112,591	24	0.36	5,254		
East Asia & Pacific	..	287	266	54.8	19.1		50,902	22	0.24	595		
Europe & Central Asia	102	447	407	61.8	52.1		18,778	15	0.37	1,694		
Latin America & Carib.	71	413	274	34.8	59.3		26,282	..	..	2,199		
Middle East & N. Africa	33	277	171	..	32.0		3,356	27	0.22	79		
South Asia	60	112	81	37.3	5.3		7,973	13	0.18	135		
Sub-Saharan Africa	12	198	59	0.3	9.9		5,300	36	0.53	552		
High income	285	1,268	677	178.2	416.3		388,888	13	11.81	115,969		
Europe EMU	209	810	582	130.5	286.2		91,231	23	16.42	11,741		

a. Data are from the International Telecommunication Union's (ITU) *World Telecommunication Development Report 2002*. Please cite the ITU for third-party use of these data.

The digital and information revolution has changed the way the world learns, communicates, does business, and treats illnesses. New information and communications technologies offer vast opportunities for progress in all walks of life in all countries—opportunities for economic growth, improved health, better service delivery, learning through distance education, and social and cultural advances. This table presents indicators of the penetration of the information economy—newspapers, radios, television sets, personal computers, and Internet use—as well as some of the economics of the information age—Internet access charges, the number of secure servers, and spending on information and communications technology.

The data on the number of daily newspapers in circulation and radio receivers in use are from statistical surveys carried out by the United Nations Educational, Scientific, and Cultural Organization (UNESCO). In some countries definitions, classifications, and methods of enumeration do not entirely conform to UNESCO standards. For example, newspaper circulation data should refer to the number of copies distributed, but in some cases the figures reported are the number of copies printed. In addition, many countries impose radio and television license fees to help pay for public broadcasting, discouraging radio and television owners from declaring ownership. Because of these and other data collection problems, estimates of the number of newspapers and radios vary widely in reliability and should be interpreted with caution.

5.11a

Personal computers per 1,000 people

Source: World Development Indicators database based on International Telecommunication Union data.

The data for other electronic communications and information technology are from the International Telecommunication Union (ITU), the Internet Software Consortium, Netcraft, and the World Information Technology and Services Alliance. The ITU collects data on television sets and cable television subscribers through annual questionnaires sent to national broadcasting authorities and industry associations. Some countries require that television sets be registered. To the extent that households do not register their televisions or do not register all of them, the data on licensed sets may understate the true number.

The estimates of personal computers are derived from an annual questionnaire, supplemented by other sources. In many countries mainframe computers are used extensively. Since thousands of users can be connected to a single mainframe computer, the number of personal computers understates the total use of computers.

The data on Internet users are based on estimates derived from reported counts of Internet service subscribers or calculated by multiplying the number of Internet hosts by an estimated multiplier. Internet hosts are computers connected directly to the worldwide network, each allowing many computer users to access the Internet. This method may undercount the number of people actually using the Internet, particularly in developing countries, where many commercial subscribers rent out computers connected to the Internet or pre-paid cards are used to access the Internet. Although survey methods used to estimate the number of Internet hosts have improved in recent years, some measurement problems remain (see Zook 2000). For detailed analysis of Internet trends by country, it is best to use the original source data.

The table shows both the off-peak charge by the Internet service provider (ISP) and the telephone usage charge for logging on to the Internet. Some countries have peak rates that are higher. The number of secure servers, from the Netcraft Secure Server Survey, gives an indication of how many companies are conducting encrypted transactions over the Internet.

The data on information and communications technology expenditures cover the world's 55 largest buyers of such technology among countries and regions. These account for 98 percent of global spending.

Because of different regulatory requirements for the provision of data, complete measurement of the telecommunications sector is not possible. Telecommunications data are compiled through annual questionnaires sent to telecommunications authorities and operating companies. The data are supplemented by annual reports and statistical yearbooks of telecommunications ministries, regulators, operators, and industry associations. In some cases estimates are derived from ITU documents or other references.

• **Daily newspapers** refer to those published at least four times a week. • **Radios** refer to radio receivers in use for broadcasts to the general public. • **Television sets** refer to those in use. • **Cable television subscribers** are households that subscribe to a multichannel television service delivered by a fixed line connection. Some countries also report subscribers to pay-television using wireless technology or those cabled to community antenna systems. • **Personal computers** are self-contained computers designed to be used by a single individual. • **Personal computers in education** are those installed in primary and secondary schools and universities. • **Internet users** are people with access to the worldwide network. • **Internet service provider charge** is the cost of 30 off-peak hours of dial-up Internet access per month. It is the monthly Internet subscription rate plus extra charges once free hours have been used up. Some countries have peak rates that are higher. • **Telephone usage charge** refers to the amount payable to the telephone company for 30 off-peak hours of local telephone use while logged on to the Internet. Excluded is the monthly telephone line tariff. If a special Internet telephone tariff exists, it is used instead. Some countries have peak rates that are higher. • **Secure servers** are servers using encryption technology in Internet transactions. • **Information and communications technology expenditures** include external spending on information technology ("tangible" spending on information technology products purchased by businesses, households, governments, and education institutions from vendors or organizations outside the purchasing entity), internal spending on information technology ("intangible" spending on internally customized software, capital depreciation, and the like), and spending on telecommunications and other office equipment.

The data on newspapers and radios are compiled by the UNESCO Institute for Statistics. The data on television sets, cable television subscribers, personal computers, Internet users, and Internet access charges are from the ITU. They are reported in the ITU's *World Telecommunication Development Report 2002* and the *World Telecommunications Indicators Database* (2002b). The data on secure servers are from Netcraft (http://www.netcraft.com/). The data on personal computers in education and on information and communications technology expenditures are from *Digital Planet 2002: The Global Information Economy* by the World Information Technology and Services Alliance (WITSA), which uses data from the International Data Corporation.

	Scientists and engineers in R&D	Technicians in R&D	Scientific and technical journal articles	Expenditures for R&D	High-technology exports		Royalty and license fees		Patent applications filed[a]		Trademark applications filed[b]
					$ millions	% of manufactured exports	Receipts $ millions	Payments $ millions	Residents	Non-residents	
	per million people 1990–2000[c]	per million people 1990–2001[c]	1999	% of GDP 1989–2000[c]	2001	2001	2001	2001	2000	2000	2000
Afghanistan	..	..	0	..	..	..	..	..	..	..	..
Albania	..	..	17	..	2	1	..	..	1	111,609	2,166
Algeria	..	..	162	..	21	4	..	..	30	33,620	4,601
Angola	..	..	3	..	..	..	16	6	..	..	..
Argentina	713	158	2,361	0.45	807	9	23	465	..	6,634[d]	61,828
Armenia	1,313	223	142	..	4	4	..	..	123	58,154	3,014
Australia	3,353	792	12,525	1.51	2,671	10	298	868	10,367	70,354	71,496
Austria	2,313	979	3,580	1.80	7,471	14	138	602	3,115	197,915	20,334
Azerbaijan	2,799	160	66	0.24	9	8	..	..	0	58,076	2,140
Bangladesh	51	32	148	..	..	..	0	6	32	184	..
Belarus	1,893	273	564	..	373	8	1	4	1,003	58,427	5,982
Belgium	2,953	1,157	4,896	1.96	16,183	10	887	1,246	1,835	139,931	36,709
Benin	174	53	20	..	..	..	..	0	..	..	..
Bolivia	98	72	33	0.29	37	10	2	5	..	..	..
Bosnia and Herzegovina	..	..	9	..	..	..	..	..	31	59,157	4,219
Botswana	..	..	41	..	..	..	0	6	0	15	..
Brazil	323	129	5,144	0.77	6,110	18	112	1,245	41	64,645	..
Bulgaria	1,316	476	801	0.57	79	2	3	12	255	60,225	9,211
Burkina Faso	16	15	23	0.19	..	..	..	..	..	..	..
Burundi	21	32	3	..	0	0	0	..	..	..	..
Cambodia	..	..	5	..	..	..	..	..	..	..	1,303
Cameroon	..	..	61	..	1	0	..	..	..	..	..
Canada	2,985	1,038	19,685	1.84	27,000	15	1,499	3,474	5,518	80,408	46,252
Central African Republic	47	27	4	..	..	..	..	..	..	..	..
Chad	..	..	2	..	..	..	..	..	..	..	..
Chile	370	380	879	0.54	108	1	5	360	241	2,879	..
China	545	187	11,675	1.00	49,427	20	110	1,938	25,592	96,714	6,252
Hong Kong, China	93	100	1,817	0.44	3,716	20	107	461	51	8,244	28,114
Colombia	101	..	207	0.25	349	7	2	71	75	1,724	12,788
Congo, Dem. Rep.	..	..	6	..	..	..	..	..	..	..	..
Congo, Rep.	33	37	13	..	..	..	..	..	..	..	..
Costa Rica	533	..	69	0.20	1,071	36	1	49	0	52,437	..
Côte d'Ivoire	..	..	40	..	15	3	0	9	..	..	..
Croatia	1,187	347	545	0.98	357	10	106	63	368	58,568	7,197
Cuba	480	2,160	192	0.49	..	..	..	..	0	58,418	2,222
Czech Republic	1,349	682	2,005	1.35	3,066	10	36	93	598	62,047	19,457
Denmark	3,476	2,594	4,131	2.09	6,912	21	..	..	3,468	197,184	12,448
Dominican Republic	..	..	6	..	..	..	..	22	..	..	..
Ecuador	83	72	20	0.09	25	4	..	52	0	11	..
Egypt, Arab Rep.	493	366	1,198	0.19	12	1	46	361	534	1,081	3,155
El Salvador	47	303	0	..	51	7	1	22	..	..	..
Eritrea	..	..	2	..	..	..	..	..	..	..	..
Estonia	2,128	531	261	0.76	586	19	2	11	19	60,218	5,946
Ethiopia	..	..	95	..	0	0	..	0	3	4	..
Finland	5,059	..	4,025	3.37	9,254	23	584	534	2,965	195,328	10,470
France	2,718	2,878	27,374	2.15	67,191	23	2,504	1,879	21,471	138,707	111,781
Gabon	..	..	20	..	..	..	..	..	..	..	..
Gambia, The	..	..	17	..	0	3	..	..	0	115,420	..
Georgia	2,421	97	112	0.33	..	..	..	..	235	59,133	3,149
Germany	3,161	1,345	37,308	2.48	85,958	18	3,149	5,243	78,754	183,796	97,325
Ghana	..	..	73	..	1	1	..	0	0	115,543	..
Greece	1,400	554	2,241	0.67	548	8	14	225	59	140,481	10,583
Guatemala	..	..	14	..	70	8	..	..	13	213	9,821
Guinea	..	..	2	..	0	0	0	1	..	..	..
Guinea-Bissau	..	..	6	..	..	..	..	..	0	1	..
Haiti	..	..	1	..	..	..	..	..	1	5	1,456

	Scientists and engineers in R&D	Technicians in R&D	Scientific and technical journal articles	Expenditures for R&D	High-technology exports		Royalty and license fees		Patent applications filed [a]		Trademark applications filed [b]
	per million people	per million people		% of GDP	$ millions	% of manufactured exports	Receipts $ millions	Payments $ millions	Residents	Non-residents	
	1990–2000[c]	1990–2001[c]	1999	1989–2000[c]	2001	2001	2001	2001	2000	2000	2000
Honduras	..	..	11	..	4	1	0	11	8	148	5,045
Hungary	1,445	518	1,958	0.82	6,298	23	96	263	881	61,557	15,840
India	157	115	9,217	1.23	1,680	6	83	306	90	60,852	66,378
Indonesia	..	..	142	..	4,473	13	..	..	0	60,363	..
Iran, Islamic Rep.	590	174	624	..	40	2	0	0	366	177	..
Iraq	..	..	21	..	..	..	..	..	..	..	..
Ireland	2,184	590	1,237	1.21	35,898	48	346	8,770	278	140,241	4,518
Israel	1,563	516	5,025	3.62	7,456	25	432	457	2,460	65,398	11,730
Italy	1,128	808	17,149	1.04	21,486	10	443	1,312	3,667	138,248	11,392
Jamaica	..	..	44	..	1	0	6	38	11	90	1,775
Japan	5,095	667	47,826	2.98	99,389	26	10,462	11,099	388,879	97,325	145,834
Jordan	1,948	717	204	..	89	7	..	..	..	..	..
Kazakhstan	716	293	104	0.29	184	4	0	14	1,400	58,187	4,887
Kenya	..	..	252	..	13	4	5	62	2	115,934	1,545
Korea, Dem. Rep.	..	..	1	..	..	..	..	..	0	57,805	2,342
Korea, Rep.	2,319	564	6,675	2.68	40,427	29	688	3,221	73,378	98,806	110,073
Kuwait	212	53	260	0.20	35	1	0	0	..	..	..
Kyrgyz Republic	581	49	10	0.19	5	5	1	2	80	58,116	2,430
Lao PDR	..	..	2	..	..	..	..	..	..	..	701
Latvia	1,078	298	153	0.40	45	3	3	7	100	112,128	6,733
Lebanon	..	..	100	..	16	3	..	..	..	104[d]	3,774
Lesotho	..	..	1	..	..	..	11	0	0	115,822	1,080
Liberia	..	..	1	..	..	..	..	..	0	58,896	1,223
Libya	361	493	19	..	..	..	..	..	..	..	..
Lithuania	2,027	631	214	..	133	5	0	10	66	112,174	7,010
Macedonia, FYR	387	29	36	..	9	1	3	6	71	111,612	4,626
Madagascar	12	37	..	..	4	3	0	1	7	59,022	634
Malawi	..	..	36	..	..	..	..	..	3	115,891	723
Malaysia	160	45	416	0.40	40,939	57	21	751	..	..	..
Mali	..	..	11	..	..	..	..	..	..	..	..
Mauritania	..	..	2	..	..	..	..	..	..	..	..
Mauritius	360	157	16	0.28	14	1	0	1	3	12	..
Mexico	225	183	2,291	0.43	29,759	22	40	419	451	66,465	46,146
Moldova	334	1,665	92	..	5	3	1	1	240	58,178	3,694
Mongolia	531	116	8	..	..	..	0	..	0	58,983	1,479
Morocco	..	..	386	..	537	11	22	256	104	51,907	7,388
Mozambique	..	..	14	..	2	0	..	0	0	56,555	1,368
Myanmar	..	..	10	..	..	..	0	0	..	..	..
Namibia	..	..	13	..	..	..	..	..	..	..	..
Nepal	..	..	39	..	0	0	..	..	..	..	..
Netherlands	2,572	1,464	10,441	2.02	38,960	32	1,723	2,319	7,528	136,813	..
New Zealand	2,197	732	2,375	1.11	466	8	61	297	2,266	65,672	24,046
Nicaragua	73	33	8	0.15	2	3	..	..	9	136	..
Niger	..	..	21	..	0	8	..	..	..	..	..
Nigeria	..	..	397	..	0	1	..	..	..	..	..
Norway	4,112	1,836	2,598	1.70	2,082	12	155	329	1,842	66,213	16,341
Oman	4	0	73	..	42	3	..	..	..	..	2,822
Pakistan	69	12	277	..	24	0	2	19	..	..	8,320
Panama	124	244	37	0.35	2	1	0	31	7	153	13,223
Papua New Guinea	..	..	36	..	11	19	..	..	..	..	566
Paraguay	..	..	4	..	7	4	180	7	..	..	..
Peru	229	9	56	0.08	56	2	0	46	48	944	..
Philippines	156	22	164	..	21,032	70	1	158	154	3,482	10,780
Poland	1,429	463	4,523	0.70	936	3	48	508	2,419	62,454	28,197
Portugal	1,576	506	1,508	0.71	1,343	6	25	234	126	198,574	18,394
Puerto Rico	..	..	..	..	..	..	..	..	..	..	..

	Scientists and engineers in R&D	Technicians in R&D	Scientific and technical journal articles	Expenditures for R&D	High-technology exports		Royalty and license fees		Patent applications filed [a]		Trademark applications filed [b]
	per million people	per million people		% of GDP	$ millions	% of manufactured exports	Receipts $ millions	Payments $ millions	Residents	Non-residents	
	1990–2000 [c]	1990–2001 [c]	1999	1989–2000 [c]	2001	2001	2001	2001	2000	2000	2000
Romania	913	584	785	0.37	567	6	16	60	1,019	112,360	11,326
Russian Federation	3,481	551	15,654	1.00	3,257	8	60	343	23,658	65,771	42,806
Rwanda	..	6	4	..	..	..	0	0	0	4	129
Saudi Arabia	..	..	528	..	23	0	0	0	72	1,144	..
Senegal	2	3	66	0.01	12	5	2	5	..	..	..
Sierra Leone	..	..	3	..	..	..	..	..	0	116,129	1,209
Singapore	4,140	335	1,653	1.88	62,572	60	..	..	0	62,471	145
Slovak Republic	1,844	791	871	0.69	473	4	16	58	247	60,264	11,320
Slovenia	2,181	872	599	1.48	442	5	14	60	340	112,524	8,518
Somalia	..	..	0	..	..	..	..	..	..	..	..
South Africa	992	303	2,018	..	937	5	51	115	190	57,976	..
Spain	1,921	1,019	12,289	0.94	7,106	8	365	1,678	3,813	198,626	98,739
Sri Lanka	191	46	84	0.18	109	3	..	..	0	58,929	..
Sudan	..	..	43	..	..	..	0	0	5	115,855	1,243
Swaziland	..	..	6	..	..	..	0	46	0	58,033	1,187
Sweden	4,511	404	8,326	3.80	10,698	18	1,427	860	10,287	193,886	16,647
Switzerland	3,592	1,399	6,993	2.64	17,353	21	..	..	7,024	194,547	12,511
Syrian Arab Republic	29	24	55	0.18	2	1	..	..	249	47	0
Tajikistan	660	..	20	..	..	..	..	..	46	58,087	2,277
Tanzania	..	..	92	..	6	6	0	4	0	108,930	2
Thailand	74	74	470	0.10	15,286	31	9	823	1,117	4,548	27,055
Togo	102	65	11	..	1	1	0	1	..	..	..
Trinidad and Tobago	145	258	37	0.14	11	1	..	..	0	58,974	1,196
Tunisia	336	32	237	0.45	154	3	15	6	..	..	..
Turkey	306	38	2,761	0.63	1,100	5	0	119	333	67,289	33,731
Turkmenistan	..	..	0	..	9	5	..	..	0	58,061	1,254
Uganda	24	14	59	0.75	5	22	..	0	0	115,875	..
Ukraine	2,118	594	2,194	0.95	..	..	5	183	5,645	60,272	11,310
United Arab Emirates	..	..	118	..	..	..	..	..	0	56,158	..
United Kingdom	2,666	1,014	39,711	1.87	67,416	31	7,910	5,909	33,658	199,565	85,570
United States	4,099	..	163,526	2.69	178,906	32	38,660	16,360	175,582	156,191	292,464
Uruguay	219	21	144	0.26	19	2	0	7	44	572	9,741
Uzbekistan	1,754	312	236	..	..	..	..	..	757	59,102	3,344
Venezuela, RB	194	32	448	0.34	95	2	0	0	56	2,292	23,703
Vietnam	274	..	98	..	..	..	..	..	35	59,741	8,123
West Bank and Gaza	..	..	..	..	..	..	..	..	..	..	..
Yemen, Rep.	..	..	10	..	..	..	..	..	..	..	..
Yugoslavia, Fed. Rep.	2,389	515	546	..	..	..	..	..	396	59,273	6,150
Zambia	..	..	26	..	11	1	..	0	0	10	959
Zimbabwe	..	..	85	..	..	0	..	..	0	115,692	14
World	.. w	.. w	528,627 s	2.38 w	.. s	23 w	72,356 s	73,148 s	908,117 s	8,531,295 s	1,794,635 s
Low income	..	..	14,376	..	..	7	27	284	7,271	2,092,440	62,042
Middle income	778	245	62,409	..	..	22	1,026	8,828	61,798	2,367,259	410,686
Lower middle income	818	237	39,216	0.72	..	17	532	4,534	56,236	1,270,074	201,002
Upper middle income	453	171	23,193	..	100,096	22	494	4,294	5,562	1,097,185	209,684
Low & middle income	..	..	76,785	..	..	18	1,053	9,112	69,069	4,459,699	472,728
East Asia & Pacific	545	185	13,055	1.00	..	31	141	3,671	26,898	341,636	57,298
Europe & Central Asia	2,074	452	34,679	0.80	16,589	8	382	1,697	39,991	1,880,499	259,416
Latin America & Carib.	287	..	12,033	..	40,832	15	372	2,850	940	589,433	113,573
Middle East & N. Africa	..	..	3,637	..	..	4	84	634	940	86,748	23,781
South Asia	158	113	9,769	..	..	5	6	25	90	119,781	8,448
Sub-Saharan Africa	..	..	3,612	..	..	4	69	236	210	1,441,602	10,212
High income	3,281	..	451,842	2.61	834,173	24	71,303	64,037	839,048	4,071,596	1,321,907
Europe EMU	2,302	1,028	122,077	2.12	285,398	19	10,381	24,286	123,862	2,007,040	415,727

Note: The original information on patent and trademark applications was provided by the World Intellectual Property Organization (WIPO). The International Bureau of WIPO assumes no liability or responsibility with respect to the transformation of these data.
a. Other patent applications filed in 2000 include those filed under the auspices of the African Regional Industrial Property Organization (8 by residents, 58,044 by nonresidents), European Patent Office (61,637 by residents, 81,437 by nonresidents), and the Eurasian Patent Organization (460 residents, 58,438 by nonresidents). b. Other trademark applications filed in 2000 include those filed under the auspices of the Office for Harmonization in the Internal Market (57,324). c. Data are for the latest year available. See *Primary data documentation* for the year. d. Total for residents and nonresidents.

About the data

The best opportunities to improve living standards—including new ways of reducing poverty—will come from science and technology. Science, advancing rapidly in virtually all fields—particularly biotechnology—is playing a growing economic role: countries able to access, generate, and apply relevant scientific knowledge will have a competitive edge over those that cannot. And there is greater appreciation of the need for high-quality scientific input into public policy issues such as regional and global environmental concerns. Technological innovation, often fueled by government-led research and development (R&D), has been the driving force for industrial growth around the world.

Science and technology cover a range of issues too complex and too broad to be quantified by any single set of indicators, but those in the table shed light on countries' "technological base"—the availability of skilled human resources, the number of scientific and technical articles published, the competitive edge countries enjoy in high-technology exports, sales and purchases of technology through royalties and licenses, and the number of patent and trademark applications filed.

The United Nations Educational, Scientific, and Cultural Organization (UNESCO) collects data on scientific and technical workers and R&D expenditures from member states, mainly through questionnaires and special surveys as well as from official reports and publications, supplemented by information from other national and international sources. UNESCO reports either the stock of scientists, engineers, and technicians or the number of economically active people qualified as such. UNESCO supplements these data with estimates of qualified scientists and engineers by counting people who have completed education at ISCED (International Standard Classification of Education) levels 6 and 7; qualified technicians are estimated using the number of people who have completed education at ISCED level 5. The data are normally calculated in terms of full-time-equivalent staff. The information does not reflect the quality of training and education, which varies widely. Similarly, R&D expenditures are no guarantee of progress; governments need to pay close attention to the practices that make them effective.

The counts of scientific and technical journal articles include those published in a stable set of about 5,000 of the world's most influential scientific and technical journals, tracked since 1985 by the Institute of Scientific Information's Science Citation Index (SCI) and Social Science Citation Index (SSCI). (See *Definitions* for the fields covered.) The SCI and SSCI databases cover the core set of scientific journals but may exclude some of regional or local importance. They may also reflect some bias toward English-language journals.

The method used for determining a country's high-technology exports was developed by the Organisation for Economic Co-operation and Development in collaboration with Eurostat. Termed the "product approach" to distinguish it from a "sectoral approach," the method is based on the calculation of R&D intensity (R&D expenditure divided by total sales) for groups of products from six countries (Germany, Italy, Japan, the Netherlands, Sweden, and the United States). Because industrial sectors characterized by a few high-technology products may also produce many low-technology products, the product approach is more appropriate for analyzing international trade than is the sectoral approach. To construct a list of high-technology manufactured products (services are excluded), the R&D intensity was calculated for products classified at the three-digit level of the Standard International Trade Classification revision 3. The final list was determined at the four- and five-digit levels. At these levels, since no R&D data were available, final selection was based on patent data and expert opinion. This method takes only R&D intensity into account. Other characteristics of high technology are also important, such as know-how, scientific and technical personnel, and technology embodied in patents; considering these characteristics would result in a different list. (See Hatzichronoglou 1997 for further details.) Moreover, the R&D for high-technology exports may not have occurred in the reporting country.

Most countries have adopted systems that protect patentable inventions. Under most patent legislation, to be protected by law (patentable), an idea must be new in the sense that it has not already been published or publicly used; it must be nonobvious (involve an inventive step) in the sense that it would not have occurred to any specialist in the industrial field had such a specialist been asked to find a solution to the problem; and it must be capable of industrial application in the sense that it can be industrially manufactured or used. Information on patent applications filed is shown separately for residents and nonresidents of the country.

A trademark provides protection to its owner by ensuring the exclusive right to use it to identify goods or services or to authorize another to use it in return for payment. The period of protection varies, but a trademark can be renewed indefinitely by paying additional fees. The trademark system helps consumers identify and purchase a product or service whose nature and quality, indicated by its unique trademark, meet their needs.

Definitions

• **Scientists and engineers in R&D** are people engaged in professional R&D activity who have received tertiary-level training to work in any field of science. • **Technicians in R&D** are people engaged in professional R&D activity who have received vocational or technical training in any branch of knowledge or technology. Most such jobs require three years beyond the first stage of secondary education. • **Scientific and technical journal articles** refer to scientific and engineering articles published in the following fields: physics, biology, chemistry, mathematics, clinical medicine, biomedical research, engineering and technology, and earth and space sciences. • **Expenditures for R&D** are current and capital expenditures on creative, systematic activity that increases the stock of knowledge. Included are fundamental and applied research and experimental development work leading to new devices, products, or processes. • **High-technology exports** are products with high R&D intensity, such as in aerospace, computers, pharmaceuticals, scientific instruments, and electrical machinery. • **Royalty and license fees** are payments and receipts between residents and nonresidents for the authorized use of intangible, nonproduced, nonfinancial assets and proprietary rights (such as patents, copyrights, trademarks, franchises, and industrial processes) and for the use, through licensing agreements, of produced originals of prototypes (such as films and manuscripts). • **Patent applications filed** are applications filed with a national patent office for exclusive rights to an invention—a product or process that provides a new way of doing something or offers a new technical solution to a problem. A patent provides protection for the invention to the owner of the patent for a limited period, generally 20 years. • **Trademark applications filed** are applications for registration of a trademark with a national or regional trademark office. Trademarks are distinctive signs that identify goods or services as those produced or provided by a specific person or enterprise. A trademark provides protection to the owner of the mark by ensuring the exclusive right to use it to identify goods or services or to authorize another to use it in return for payment.

Data sources

The data on technical personnel and R&D expenditures are from UNESCO's *Statistical Yearbook*. The data on scientific and technical journal articles are from the National Science Foundation's *Science and Engineering Indicators 2002*. The information on high-technology exports is from the United Nations Statistics Division's Commodity Trade (COMTRADE) database. The data on royalty and license fees are from the International Monetary Fund's Balance of *Payments Statistics Yearbook*, and the data on patents and trademarks are from the World Intellectual Property Organization's *Industrial Property Statistics*.

6| GLOBAL LINKS

Global integration—the widening and intensifying of links between both high-income and developing economies—has accelerated, especially in the past 20 years. The reasons? Lower transport costs, lower trade barriers, faster communication of ideas, greater mobility of people, and growing capital flows.

These changes have provided new opportunities for a growing number of the world's people. But while progress has been rapid, it has been uneven across countries. The challenge this poses is reflected in the Millennium Development Goals, particularly goal 8, to develop a global partnership for development. This goal includes targets for expanding market access, encouraging debt sustainability, and increasing aid and improving its targeting. It also addresses needs of countries with particular challenges, including heavily indebted poor countries and small island states.

Trade for development

The exchange of goods and services across borders is a primary indicator of a country's integration with the global economy. Trade spurs economic growth by encouraging specialization in line with a country's comparative advantage while increasing potential capital inputs and consumer choice. Countries that have integrated more with the world trade system have on average enjoyed stronger growth: in the past decade countries that significantly increased their trade grew more than three times as fast as those that did not. Five tables in this section examine the role of trade in improving prospects for growth.

Trade flows

In the past decade trade between low- and middle-income countries grew by more than 13 percent, with East Asia and Pacific, Latin America and the Caribbean, and Sub-Saharan Africa leading the way. Developing countries' exports to high-income countries also grew from 1990 to 2000—by 11 percent—while trade between high-income countries grew at less than half that rate. A continuation of these trends would allow developing countries to fully reap the benefits of global integration (table 6.2).

The types of goods traded are changing. In 2001, 64 percent of OECD imports from low- and middle-income countries were manufactured goods, up from 45 percent a decade earlier (table 6.3). Greater internal trade facilitation, a commitment to lowering trade barriers, and better trade, production, and monetary policies will all help expand trade for low- and middle-income countries. Membership in trade blocs can often encourage countries to adopt these pro-trade policies (table 6.5).

For the many developing countries dependent on commodity exports, global commodity prices can have a significant impact on trade receipts. The volatility of these prices means unstable economic prospects—especially for some of the poorest countries. While the prices of some important commodities rose in 2002— those for cocoa by 65 percent, palm oil by 36 percent, and coconut oil by 32 percent—the prices of many commodities declined slightly (table 6.4). Diversifying exports leaves low- and middle-income countries less vulnerable to these external shocks.

Barriers to trade

Tariffs and nontariff barriers hamper growth prospects for developing countries, and reducing trade barriers is a key target under the Millennium Development Goal calling for a global partnership for development. The poorest countries depend on exports of agricultural goods and labor-intensive manufactures such as textiles and clothing—products highly protected in the European Union, Japan, and the United States because of domestic pressures. Average tariffs in high-income countries are low—the weighted mean tariffs in Japan and the United States are around 2 percent (table 6.6). But much higher peak tariffs on textiles and agricultural products are common. Lowering these barriers could boost annual growth in developing countries by an extra 0.5 percent over the long run—and lift

an additional 300 million people out of poverty by 2015. The 2001 ministerial meeting of the World Trade Organization in Doha, Qatar, articulated a commitment to lowering these barriers, and the new trade round agreed to at Doha is the first to put development at the top of the agenda (box 6a).

Developing countries have a similar responsibility to lower trade barriers. While low- and middle-income countries have cut average tariffs in half in the past 20 years (from 15 percent to 7 percent), more needs to be done. In 2001 China's tariffs averaged 15 percent, and India's 31 percent. Regional averages can also be high: 20 percent for South Asia and 13 percent for Latin America. High average rates in the developing world contribute to the fact that developing countries face tariffs twice as high on average as those faced by high-income countries (table 6.6).

These high tariffs have a dampening effect on trade between developing countries. And the practice of escalating tariffs— imposing higher tariffs on processed goods—constrains the development of manufacturing and industry. Tariff escalation has confined many Sub-Saharan African countries to exporting unprocessed goods such as cocoa, coffee, and cotton—and discouraged development of the labor-intensive manufacturing that has been a key vehicle for growth in several developing countries.

Financial flows weaker—except for foreign direct investment

Several trends have emerged in the world's financial markets in recent years: Cross-border capital flows have shifted from public transfers to primarily private sector flows. The flow of private lending to developing countries has declined, and capital flows other than foreign direct investment have become negative. And

6a

A global trade agenda focusing on development

The new trade round that emerged from the World Trade Organization negotiations at Doha, Qatar, in 2001 is the first to make development the primary goal. And China's accession to the World Trade Organization should help keep market access issues at the forefront. Although participants at Doha did not reach universal agreement on all points, the declaration emerging from the negotiations gave developing countries reason to hope for a more welcoming trading environment and promised a focus on implementation. Several key agreements at Doha relate to market access:

- An agreement to substantially improve market access, to reduce all forms of export subsidies (with a view to phasing them out), and to substantially reduce trade-distorting domestic support.
- An agreement to support growth in service trade for developing and least developed countries.
- An agreement to reduce or, as appropriate, eliminate tariffs. This includes reducing or eliminating tariff peaks, high tariffs, and tariff escalation as well as nontariff barriers, particularly on nonagricultural products of export interest to developing countries.

Source: World Trade Organization, Doha Declaration.

foreign direct investment has become the largest and most resilient form of capital flow, especially for developing countries, where it provides a stable alternative to debt financing. Foreign direct investment may also lead to many indirect benefits—through innovative ideas, new technologies, and improvements in human capital. But more capital does not automatically translate into higher growth. A country also needs good government policies and strong institutions (Stern 2002b).

The global economic slowdown has reduced financial flows in the past couple of years, and political and economic instability have exacerbated problems in some regions. Capital flows in Latin America dropped from a peak of $126 billion in 1998 to $72 billion in 2001, reflecting regional problems and global economic uncertainty. Private capital flows to Argentina fell from a peak of $21 billion in 1999 to negative flows in 2001, while its foreign direct investment flows declined from $24 billion to $3 billion. Turkey too saw private capital flows fall (from $10 billion in 1999 to less than $1 billion in 2001). But foreign direct investment has remained strong in East Asia and Pacific and in Europe and Central Asia (table 6.7).

Over the past two decades, as financial openness has increased across the world, global flows of foreign direct investment have more than doubled relative to gross domestic product (GDP). The flows increased in the 1990s, rising from $324 billion in 1995 to $1.5 trillion in 2000. East Asia and Pacific experienced the largest growth, thanks mostly to China, with investment flows to the region rising from $1 billion in 1980 to a peak of $62 billion in 1997. Growth was also strong in Latin America and the Caribbean, where foreign direct investment flows increased from about $6 billion in 1980 to $88 billion in 1999. The growth was due in large part to Brazil, Argentina, Mexico, and Chile, which accounted for 75 percent of the flows to the region (table 6.7).

New commitments on aid

Aid has increased in dollar amount since the Second World War, but as a share of donor countries' output it has fallen significantly. Between 1960 and 1990 official development assistance from major aid donors declined from 0.5 percent of their gross national income (GNI) to 0.34 percent. In 2001 it had fallen to 0.22 percent of GNI, half its share in 1960. Only 5 of the 22 Development Assistance Committee members gave more than 0.7 percent of GNI in official development assistance in 2001: Denmark, Luxembourg, the Netherlands, Norway, and Sweden (tables 6.8 and 6.9). And only 43 developing countries received more than $50 per capita (table 6.10).

At the United Nations International Conference on Financing for Development in 2002 many countries made new commitments to strengthen partnerships (box 6b). High-income countries committed additional aid, and all countries that attended confirmed their commitment to the goals of the Millennium Declaration.

6b

Aid after Monterrey

In March 2002 world leaders came together at the United Nations International Conference on Financing for Development in Monterrey, Mexico, to discuss new strategies for attacking global poverty. As part of this, high-income countries made new commitments on aid that would raise official development assistance (ODA) in real terms by about $15 billion by 2006—and from 0.22 percent of donor countries' gross national income (GNI) to 0.26 percent. The commitments are:

- Members of the European Union: to strive to raise ODA to at least 0.33 percent of GNI by 2006, with the European Union's average rising to 0.4 percent of GNI or more.
- United States: to increase its core development assistance over three years (2004–06) so as to achieve a $5 billion annual increase (almost 50 percent) over current levels by 2006.
- Canada: to increase its ODA budget by 8 percent annually so as to double its aid by 2010.
- Japan: to reduce its ODA budget in fiscal 2002 and 2003 as part of necessary fiscal consolidation.
- Norway: to increase its ODA to 1 percent of GNI by 2005.
- Switzerland: to increase its ODA to 0.4 percent of GNI by 2010.
- Australia: to increase its ODA by 3 percent in real terms in 2002–03.

Source: Development Assistance Committee, OECD.

For poor countries, especially those unable to attract significant private flows, aid is an important means of fostering change. According to World Bank research, an additional $10 billion in aid in 1998 would have enabled around 3 million more people to escape poverty (World Bank 2002b). But such outcomes depend on making aid more effective, a responsibility of both donors and recipients. Donor countries can help recipient countries build capacity to foster change. And recipient countries can continue to invest in their people and build their capacity in government and business.

More people moving across borders

The movement of people is another visible and increasingly important aspect of global integration. People moving across borders can be categorized into three groups—migrants (table 6.13), tourists (table 6.14), and refugees or displaced persons. Job creation in developing countries has generally failed to keep pace with population growth—a situation that grows more dire as populations become younger. Migration and labor flows ease unemployment pressures in the sending country and increase private financial flows through remittances. Migration to high-income countries has been increasing. In 2000 foreign population inflows in OECD countries rose by 13 percent (table 6.13). Such increases often result in higher population growth in host countries, and tighter controls and regulations on labor migration. In such cases illegal immigration is likely to rise as a result of the sending countries' greater dependence on remittance income.

6.1 Integration with the global economy

	Trade in goods				Change in trade	Growth in real trade less growth in real GDP	Gross private capital flows		Gross foreign direct investment	
	% of GDP		% of goods GDP		% of GDP	percentage points	% of GDP		% of GDP	
	1990	**2001**	**1990**	**2001**	**1990–2000**	**1990–2001**	**1990**	**2001**	**1990**	**2001**
Afghanistan	..	..	..	..	..	..	..	..	..	..
Albania	29.0	39.4	34.5	53.5	..	6.8	18.0	11.5	0.0	5.0
Algeria	36.6	54.4	55.0	81.5	−24.6	−0.7	2.6		0.0	..
Angola	53.5	106.1	91.0	141.9	..	..	10.1	20.4	3.3	9.9
Argentina	11.6	17.5	27.0	50.0	155.5	6.4	8.2	18.4	1.3	2.2
Armenia	..	57.1	..	86.9	..	−11.5	..	10.7	..	3.3
Australia	26.3	34.5	68.9	97.5	75.7	3.7	9.3	19.5	3.7	4.8
Austria	55.9	76.8	140.5	203.8	58.5	4.0	9.8	36.6	1.5	5.0
Azerbaijan	..	71.4	..	107.2	..	7.4	..	32.1	..	25.3
Bangladesh	17.6	32.0	..	..	130.6	6.0	0.9	2.2	0.0	0.2
Belarus	..	127.4	..	232.1	..	−4.3	..	4.9	..	0.8
Belgium	120.4	161.3	321.7	491.7	46.1	2.4	18.5	49.4	6.7	9.6
Benin	30.0	43.5	60.8	75.1	−44.2	−1.7	10.7	14.6	3.7	0.0
Bolivia	33.1	37.8	..	..	47.1	1.0	3.1	15.0	0.7	8.3
Bosnia and Herzegovina	..	81.6	..	235.9	..	−2.6	..	..	..	..
Botswana	98.4	91.6	..	..	−24.2	−0.5	9.0	6.9	4.4	1.4
Brazil	11.6	23.2	..	..	71.9	5.4	1.9	10.9	0.4	5.1
Bulgaria	48.9	91.1	70.8	186.7	..	5.4	39.2	16.6	0.0	5.2
Burkina Faso	24.9	33.4	44.4	55.3	−24.4	−3.5	1.1	..	0.0	..
Burundi	27.0	26.0	35.1	38.6	26.8	7.2	3.7	6.5	0.1	1.7
Cambodia	22.4	91.7	33.6	..	..	10.1	3.2	6.2	1.7	3.3
Cameroon	30.5	42.4	..	..	56.4	2.4	15.5	..	1.1	..
Canada	43.7	70.1	114.5	..	96.9	4.3	8.1	21.5	2.7	9.6
Central African Republic	18.4	27.0	26.4	37.3	..	..	2.2	..	0.5	..
Chad	27.2	49.8	54.9	92.6	−29.4	−1.9	5.6	..	0.0	..
Chile	53.1	52.2	100.5	105.1	65.5	3.3	15.0	24.1	2.2	9.2
China	32.5	44.0	47.4	66.3	..	6.2	2.5	10.4	1.2	4.9
Hong Kong, China	223.5	242.8	784.6	1,268.8	209.7	4.0	..	97.0	..	28.8
Colombia	30.7	30.4	..	..	80.7	3.7	3.1	14.1	1.3	2.9
Congo, Dem. Rep.	43.5	34.2	74.5	45.6	60.6	5.5	..	..	..	..
Congo, Rep.	57.2	109.8	107.0	152.4	−9.1	2.0	6.6	..	0.0	..
Costa Rica	60.2	71.9	..	..	69.0	4.1	7.0	8.5	2.9	4.2
Côte d'Ivoire	47.9	60.3	86.0	131.3	25.2	−0.8	3.5	9.1	0.4	2.5
Croatia	89.3	62.7	165.6	121.6	..	4.2	..	32.1	..	8.2
Cuba	..	..	..	..	..	..	..	..	..	..
Czech Republic	83.6	123.1	..	..	..	9.2	..	21.8	..	8.8
Denmark	52.6	60.2	144.1	167.2	56.9	2.8	15.1	26.2	2.0	10.4
Dominican Republic	73.2	66.6	163.2	..	52.5	−0.4	5.0	10.5	1.9	5.7
Ecuador	42.8	54.5	..	..	3.1	0.7	10.7	21.9	1.2	7.4
Egypt, Arab Rep.	36.8	17.1	72.9	32.3	−40.5	−1.2	6.8	6.7	1.7	0.5
El Salvador	38.4	57.4	88.5	146.7	48.5	7.4	2.0	14.7	0.8	2.0
Eritrea	65.0	72.6	117.2	167.6	..	−0.2	..	..	..	..
Estonia	..	137.7	..	320.7	..	11.0	3.7	29.8	2.0	15.4
Ethiopia	20.2	23.4	31.3	..	..	2.6	2.0	3.2	0.0	..
Finland	39.2	62.0	86.5	145.6	57.5	5.2	17.4	62.4	3.6	14.6
France	37.1	49.4	101.6	148.9	63.3	4.2	20.6	26.2	3.9	10.4
Gabon	52.5	82.3	97.7	..	2.8	−1.8	18.0	24.5	8.4	14.5
Gambia, The	69.1	53.5	134.4	107.7	−34.7	−1.8	0.9	..	0.0	..
Georgia	..	32.8	..	69.6	..	16.1	..	4.9	..	4.4
Germany	46.0	57.6	106.2	160.5	40.7	3.7	9.8	30.7	1.8	5.4
Ghana	35.7	89.2	58.0	146.0	−1.3	5.9	2.7	4.7	0.3	2.2
Greece	33.2	29.1	83.5	106.1	102.6	4.3	3.9	18.8	1.2	1.9
Guatemala	36.8	39.4	..	..	−12.9	3.4	2.9	29.7	0.6	12.0
Guinea	49.5	47.7	85.5	74.1	..	−1.2	3.9	3.2	0.6	0.1
Guinea-Bissau	43.0	60.3	53.3	72.9	−28.9	3.3	23.0	..	0.0	..
Haiti	17.2	34.5	..	..	168.1	8.1	1.1	..	0.3	..

	Trade in goods				Change in trade	Growth in real trade less growth in real GDP	Gross private capital flows		Gross foreign direct investment	
	% of GDP		% of goods GDP		% of GDP	percentage points	% of GDP		% of GDP	
	1990	2001	1990	2001	1990–2000	1990–2001	1990	2001	1990	2001
Honduras	57.9	66.3	106.4	127.1	−21.6	−0.4	7.2	5.9	1.4	3.1
Hungary	61.5	123.6	102.4	..	81.8	8.5	4.6	23.0	0.0	5.8
India	13.1	19.5	..	..	65.1	5.6	0.8	3.1	0.0	0.6
Indonesia	41.5	60.1	64.4	95.5	−16.6	1.2	4.1	6.5	1.0	3.2
Iran, Islamic Rep.	32.9	37.5	61.8	72.4	−63.3	−8.7	2.6	2.4	0.0	0.0
Iraq	41.2	..	..	..	..	..	..	..	..	..
Ireland	93.9	129.3	186.7	265.1	129.5	7.0	22.2	272.5	2.2	27.0
Israel	55.0	59.2	..	..	25.1	4.4	6.5	16.1	0.7	4.0
Italy	32.0	43.5	83.3	123.9	68.5	3.8	10.6	16.9	1.3	3.6
Jamaica	67.2	58.5	162.2	150.5	41.9	−0.6	8.4	25.1	3.0	9.0
Japan	17.1	18.2	44.4	61.7	39.4	2.7	5.4	12.3	1.7	1.1
Jordan	91.1	80.8	205.2	224.2	−7.9	−2.8	6.3	8.0	1.7	1.2
Kazakhstan	..	67.0	..	135.5	..	−3.1	..	25.7	..	12.4
Kenya	38.1	42.4	68.5	92.8	−9.1	2.2	3.6	5.4	0.7	0.0
Korea, Dem. Rep.	..	..	..	..	..	..	..	..	..	..
Korea, Rep.	53.4	69.1	102.7	152.6	121.6	7.1	5.6	11.4	0.7	1.5
Kuwait	59.8	72.8	112.9	..	..	..	19.3	39.9	1.3	1.1
Kyrgyz Republic	..	61.6	..	91.2	..	−2.1	..	11.1	..	3.5
Lao PDR	30.5	50.4	40.2	..	..	..	3.7	1.4	0.7	1.4
Latvia	..	72.9	..	185.6	..	2.5	1.7	23.8	0.5	7.2
Lebanon	106.5	48.8	..	..	..	−3.1	..	..	..	..
Lesotho	118.0	120.9	..	..	−13.5	−1.6	9.4	17.9	2.7	14.7
Liberia	143.1	173.1	..	..	..	..	..	..	..	..
Libya	64.2	62.0	..	..	..	..	7.3	2.2	0.9	1.2
Lithuania	..	90.6	..	191.8	..	8.9	..	13.5	..	3.8
Macedonia, FYR	103.8	81.7	168.9	161.6	..	5.9	..	42.0	..	13.0
Madagascar	31.5	45.7	53.7	81.9	−24.8	2.5	1.8	0.4	0.7	0.2
Malawi	52.7	49.2	70.6	87.6	−32.8	−2.8	3.2	..	0.0	..
Malaysia	133.4	184.0	232.3	..	125.4	3.7	10.3	6.6	5.3	5.7
Mali	39.7	52.8	63.4	75.3	121.4	1.2	2.0	..	0.2	..
Mauritania	84.1	61.1	134.0	103.4	−25.5	−1.8	48.8	..	0.7	..
Mauritius	118.0	78.1	219.8	174.2	..	0.0	8.0	19.7	1.7	1.1
Mexico	32.1	54.2	76.9	143.8	223.6	9.8	9.2	7.9	1.0	4.6
Moldova	..	99.0	..	175.3	..	12.2	..	18.0	..	10.1
Mongolia	..	67.8	..	143.1	..	..	..	8.4	..	6.0
Morocco	43.3	52.8	86.5	113.0	30.4	3.1	5.5	10.3	0.6	8.5
Mozambique	40.8	49.0	68.9	89.4	..	2.4	0.4	16.9	0.4	13.3
Myanmar	..	..	..	..	17.1	..	..	..	..	..
Namibia	80.7	94.8	166.1	188.8	..	−1.1	13.9	..	4.3	..
Nepal	24.1	39.7	..	..	..	..	3.5	3.2	0.0	0.0
Netherlands	87.6	114.9	230.9	354.0	57.8	3.8	29.8	105.5	8.3	26.0
New Zealand	43.3	53.7	121.0	..	69.3	2.6	17.8	15.0	11.5	8.5
Nicaragua	95.9	..	183.0	..	60.2	6.4	9.0	..	0.0	..
Niger	27.0	35.3	49.9	59.3	−46.9	−2.5	2.8	..	1.6	..
Nigeria	67.5	73.2	90.8	94.7	−39.9	2.4	5.9	13.0	2.1	2.9
Norway	53.1	54.3	127.8	119.5	14.8	1.7	11.9	31.4	2.1	3.6
Oman	77.7	80.2	127.4	..	..	..	3.8	2.0	1.4	0.4
Pakistan	32.6	33.8	..	..	−13.1	−1.7	4.2	2.8	0.6	0.7
Panama	35.4	38.1	..	..	..	−1.6	106.6	46.3	2.6	6.0
Papua New Guinea	73.6	97.3	123.9	143.1	−8.1	0.1	5.7	15.4	4.8	2.2
Paraguay	43.9	43.5	82.8	82.7	142.3	−2.4	5.4	5.2	1.5	2.3
Peru	25.5	29.1	..	..	45.9	3.9	3.2	5.1	0.2	2.2
Philippines	47.7	88.9	84.7	..	142.3	3.8	4.4	42.0	1.2	2.7
Poland	43.9	49.0	75.2	111.1	..	9.1	11.0	10.5	0.2	4.5
Portugal	58.3	56.4	140.8	144.4	113.1	3.8	11.4	46.3	3.9	12.9
Puerto Rico	..	..	..	..	32.8	−0.4	..	..	..	..

	Trade in goods				Change in trade	Growth in real trade less growth in real GDP	Gross private capital flows		Gross foreign direct investment	
	% of GDP		% of goods GDP		% of GDP	percentage points	% of GDP		% of GDP	
	1990	2001	1990	2001	1990–2000	1990–2001	1990	2001	1990	2001
Romania	32.8	69.6	45.2	126.3	..	8.1	2.9	9.1	0.0	3.0
Russian Federation	..	50.6	..	97.7	..	0.5	..	8.1	..	1.6
Rwanda	15.4	19.7	26.9	31.7	63.4	1.5	2.8	0.9	0.3	0.3
Saudi Arabia	65.4	53.3	106.7	..	..	..	9.8	9.3	1.8	0.0
Senegal	34.7	55.8	90.0	124.5	−21.0	−1.1	4.8	8.8	1.3	4.0
Sierra Leone	44.2	25.9	..	..	−71.1	−15.4	11.0	..	5.0	..
Singapore	309.5	277.6	891.3	..	..	..	54.6	60.2	20.7	22.0
Slovak Republic	110.8	133.9	192.1	302.4	..	9.0	..	29.6	..	11.8
Slovenia	102.4	103.1	196.5	209.6	..	0.3	3.4	15.6	0.9	3.8
Somalia	26.7	..	33.2	..	..	..	..	..	..	..
South Africa	37.5ᵃ	50.9ᵃ	75.2ᵃ	..	22.8	3.9	2.2	22.8	0.2	10.9
Spain	28.1	43.4	70.6	119.6	161.7	6.8	11.4	28.3	3.4	8.7
Sri Lanka	57.3	67.5	..	..	40.1	2.6	13.1	13.0	0.5	1.1
Sudan	7.5	25.6	..	43.8	−30.5	..	0.3	5.4	0.0	4.6
Swaziland	138.2	130.9	..	..	37.9	−0.5	10.7	12.9	5.0	3.6
Sweden	46.9	65.7	119.8	190.4	67.0	5.0	34.2	45.2	7.0	9.6
Switzerland	58.4	67.2	..	..	50.6	3.3	15.9	46.0	5.8	8.9
Syrian Arab Republic	53.7	45.1	102.4	78.0	−29.8	0.1	18.0	16.9	0.0	1.5
Tajikistan	..	127.0	..	203.0	..	..	..	..	..	..
Tanzania	31.9	26.1	47.8	41.1	..	0.7	0.2	3.3	0.0	2.1
Thailand	65.7	110.9	132.2	213.9	99.6	2.8	13.5	9.1	3.0	3.5
Togo	52.1	83.6	92.6	138.0	−22.3	−0.8	9.6	17.4	1.1	5.7
Trinidad and Tobago	65.9	93.3	130.7	204.0	43.4	2.0	11.4	..	3.1	..
Tunisia	73.5	80.8	161.6	199.6	9.3	0.2	9.5	6.2	0.6	2.3
Turkey	23.4	48.6	44.5	101.8	..	7.1	4.3	15.1	0.5	2.5
Turkmenistan	..	79.3	..	..	..	3.6	..	..	..	..
Uganda	10.2	36.1	14.7	59.6	..	6.8	1.1	4.2	0.0	2.5
Ukraine	..	85.2	..	143.4	..	4.0	..	11.9	..	2.2
United Arab Emirates	101.8	..	159.6	..	..	..	..	..	..	..
United Kingdom	41.2	42.5	102.6	126.6	57.2	4.1	35.3	69.2	7.4	12.7
United States	15.8	19.0	44.4	68.1	99.1	5.2	5.7	11.7	2.8	3.1
Uruguay	32.7	27.4	85.0	101.6	90.9	3.8	12.7	25.1	0.0	1.7
Uzbekistan	..	53.9	..	71.9	..	−2.8	..	..	..	..
Venezuela, RB	51.1	36.4	90.8	65.0	12.1	3.7	49.9	10.8	1.7	3.1
Vietnam	79.7	93.6	129.7	..	..	23.9	..	7.6	..	4.0
West Bank and Gaza	..	..	..	..	..	2.0	..	..	..	..
Yemen, Rep.	46.9	58.9	90.0	100.7	..	4.1	16.2	8.1	2.7	2.2
Yugoslavia, Fed. Rep.	..	62.1	..	..	..	..	..	..	..	..
Zambia	76.9	50.3	102.3	83.6	−45.1	1.8	64.7	9.3	6.2	3.8
Zimbabwe	40.7	36.5	74.5	98.9	139.6	5.3	1.7	..	0.1	..
World	**32.5 w**	**40.0 w**	**81.5 w**	**110.7 w**			**10.3 w**	**21.6 w**	**2.7 w**	**5.1 w**
Low income	27.4	39.8	..	..			3.0	5.1	0.5	1.7
Middle income	35.5	50.8	74.8	93.0			6.8	12.2	1.0	4.3
Lower middle income	37.6	50.3	66.9	80.5			5.0	12.1	0.9	4.3
Upper middle income	33.4	51.3	86.4	118.6			8.6	12.4	1.1	4.3
Low & middle income	33.8	48.9	74.4	93.7			6.0	11.8	0.9	4.2
East Asia & Pacific	47.0	61.0	77.8	69.7			5.0	11.1	1.7	4.6
Europe & Central Asia	..	65.9	..	119.4			..	13.2	..	3.9
Latin America & Carib.	23.3	37.6	66.2	110.4			7.9	12.1	0.9	4.4
Middle East & N. Africa	48.1	45.4	84.2	78.5			6.2	9.7	0.8	1.3
South Asia	16.5	23.4	..	..			1.4	3.2	0.1	0.6
Sub-Saharan Africa	42.3	56.0	77.1	97.5			5.1	17.0	1.0	8.1
High income	32.3	37.9	82.3	112.3			11.1	23.6	3.0	5.3
Europe EMU	44.9	56.3	112.6	141.9			14.1	49.3	2.9	14.8

a. Data refer to the South African Customs Union (Botswana, Lesotho, Namibia, South Africa, and Swaziland).

The growing integration of societies and economies has helped reduce poverty in many countries. Between 1990 and 1999 the number of poor people in developing countries declined by about 125 million. Although global integration is a powerful force in reducing poverty, more needs to be done—2 billion people are in danger of becoming marginal to the world economy. All countries have a stake in helping developing countries integrate with the global economy and gain better access to rich country markets.

One indication of increasing global economic integration is the growing importance of trade in the world economy. Another is the increased size and importance of private capital flows to developing countries that have liberalized their financial markets. This table presents standardized measures of the size of trade and capital flows relative to gross domestic product (GDP). The numerators are based on gross flows that capture the two-way flow of goods and capital. In conventional balance of payments accounting exports are recorded as a credit and imports as a debit. And in the financial account inward investment is a credit and outward investment a debit. Thus net flows, the sum of credits and debits, represent a balance in which many transactions are canceled out. Gross flows are a better measure of integration because they show the total value of financial transactions during a given period.

Trade in goods (exports and imports) is shown relative to both total GDP and goods GDP (GDP less services such as storage, transport, communications, retail trade, business services, public administration, restaurants and hotels, and social, community, and personal services). As a result of the growing share of services in GDP, trade as a share of total GDP appears to be declining for some

economies. Comparing merchandise trade with GDP after deducting value added in services thus provides a better measure of its relative size than does comparing it with total GDP, although this neglects the growing service component of most goods output.

Trade in services (such as transport, travel, finance, insurance, royalties, construction, communications, and cultural services) is an increasingly important element of global integration. The difference between the growth of real trade in goods and services and the growth of GDP helps to identify economies that have integrated with the global economy by liberalizing trade, lowering barriers to foreign investment, and harnessing their abundant labor to gain a competitive advantage in labor-intensive manufactures and services.

The change in trade gives an indication of the effectiveness of trade policy. This indicator measures the effect of trade on growth using the decade-over-decade change in a country's trade as a share of its GDP.

The indicators on capital flows—gross private capital flows and gross foreign direct investment—are calculated from detailed accounts, since higher-level aggregates would result in smaller totals by netting out credits and debits. The comparability of the data between countries and over time is affected by the accuracy and completeness of balance of payments records and by their level of detail.

Trade and capital flows are converted to U.S. dollars at the International Monetary Fund's average official exchange rate for the year shown. An alternative conversion factor is applied if the official exchange rate diverges by an exceptionally large margin from the rate effectively applied to transactions in foreign currencies and traded products.

• **Trade in goods as a share of GDP** is the sum of merchandise exports and imports divided by the value of GDP, all in current U.S. dollars. • **Trade in goods as a share of goods GDP** is the sum of merchandise exports and imports divided by the value of GDP after subtracting value added in services, all in current U.S. dollars. • **Change in trade as a share of GDP** is the decade-over-decade change in trade as a share of GDP. • **Growth in real trade less growth in real GDP** is the difference between annual growth in trade of goods and services and annual growth in GDP. Growth rates are calculated using constant price series taken from national accounts and are expressed as a percentage. • **Gross private capital flows** are the sum of the absolute values of direct, portfolio, and other investment inflows and outflows recorded in the balance of payments financial account, excluding changes in the assets and liabilities of monetary authorities and general government. The indicator is calculated as a ratio to GDP in U.S. dollars. • **Gross foreign direct investment** is the sum of the absolute values of inflows and outflows of foreign direct investment recorded in the balance of payments financial account. It includes equity capital, reinvestment of earnings, other long-term capital, and short-term capital. This indicator differs from the standard measure of foreign direct investment, which captures only inward investment (see table 6.7). The indicator is calculated as a ratio to GDP in U.S. dollars.

6.1a

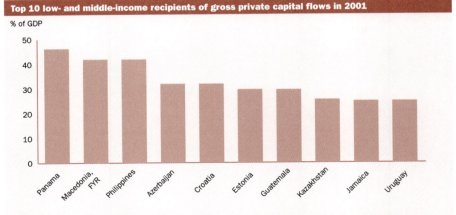

Top 10 low- and middle-income recipients of gross private capital flows in 2001

% of GDP

Countries: Panama, Macedonia FYR, Philippines, Azerbaijan, Croatia, Estonia, Guatemala, Kazakhstan, Jamaica, Uruguay

Private capital flows to low- and middle-income economies continued to grow in 2001, with Latin America and the Caribbean and Europe Central Asia capturing the largest shares.

Source: International Monetary Fund's Balance of Payments database.

The data on merchandise trade are from the World Trade Organization. The data on GDP come from the World Bank's national accounts files, converted from national currencies to U.S. dollars using the official exchange rate, supplemented by an alternative conversion factor if the official exchange rate is judged to diverge by an exceptionally large margin from the rate effectively applied to transactions in foreign currencies and traded products. The data on real trade and GDP growth come from the World Bank's national accounts files. Gross private capital flows and foreign direct investment were calculated using the International Monetary Fund's Balance of Payments database.

Direction of trade (% of world trade), 2001

High-income importers

Source of exports	European Union	Japan	United States	Other industrial	All industrial	Other high income	All high income
High-income economies	30.1	3.2	11.8	6.1	51.2	7.0	58.2
Industrial economies	28.4	2.0	9.6	5.7	45.7	5.1	50.8
European Union	22.9	0.7	3.5	2.1	29.1	1.7	30.8
Japan	1.1		2.0	0.3	3.3	1.5	4.9
United States	2.6	0.9		3.1	6.6	1.4	8.0
Other industrial economies	1.9	0.4	4.1	0.2	6.6	0.4	7.0
Other high-income economies	1.7	1.2	2.2	0.4	5.5	1.9	7.5
Low- and middle-income economies	6.3	2.0	6.2	0.7	15.2	3.4	18.6
East Asia & Pacific	1.4	1.4	1.7	0.2	4.8	2.3	7.0
Europe & Central Asia	2.5	0.1	0.2	0.1	2.9	0.2	3.1
Latin America & Caribbean	0.7	0.1	3.3	0.2	4.2	0.2	4.4
Middle East & N. Africa	0.9	0.3	0.4	0.1	1.7	0.5	2.2
South Asia	0.3	0.0	0.3	0.0	0.6	0.2	0.8
Sub-Saharan Africa	0.5	0.0	0.3	0.0	0.8	0.1	0.9
World	36.4	5.2	18.0	6.8	66.4	10.4	76.8

Low- and middle-income importers

Source of exports	East Asia & Pacific	Europe & Central Asia	Latin America & Caribbean	Middle East & N. Africa	South Asia	Sub-Saharan Africa	All low & middle income	World
High-income economies	5.8	3.2	4.1	1.5	0.7	0.9	17.1	75.3
Industrial economies	3.1	3.1	3.8	1.4	0.4	0.7	12.9	63.7
European Union	0.8	2.8	0.9	0.9	0.2	0.5	6.5	37.4
Japan	1.2	0.1	0.3	0.1	0.1	0.1	1.7	6.6
United States	0.7	0.2	2.6	0.2	0.1	0.1	3.9	11.9
Other industrial economies	0.3	0.1	0.1	0.1	0.0	0.0	0.8	7.8
Other high-income economies	2.8	0.1	0.2	0.1	0.3	0.1	4.2	11.6
Low- and middle-income economies	1.5	1.6	1.2	0.5	0.4	0.4	6.1	24.7
East Asia & Pacific	0.8	0.2	0.2	0.1	0.2	0.1	1.7	8.8
Europe & Central Asia	0.1	1.3	0.0	0.1	0.0	0.0	1.7	4.8
Latin America & Caribbean	0.1	0.1	0.9	0.1	0.0	0.0	1.3	5.7
Middle East & N. Africa	0.2	0.1	0.0	0.1	0.1	0.1	0.8	3.0
South Asia	0.1	0.0	0.0	0.0	0.1	0.0	0.3	1.1
Sub-Saharan Africa	0.1	0.0	0.0	0.0	0.0	0.2	0.4	1.3
World	7.3	4.3	5.4	2.1	1.2	1.3	23.2	100.0

Direction and growth of merchandise trade

Nominal growth of trade (annual % growth), 1991–2001

High-income importers

Source of exports	European Union	Japan	United States	Other industrial	All industrial	Other high income	All high income
High-income economies	3.5	2.9	6.8	4.5	4.3	5.4	4.4
Industrial economies	3.4	1.9	7.2	4.5	4.2	4.5	4.2
European Union	3.6	3.2	8.5	3.1	4.0	6.9	4.1
Japan	0.1		2.9	−0.5	1.6	2.6	1.9
United States	3.9	1.8		6.4	4.6	4.7	4.6
Other industrial economies	3.3	0.3	8.8	3.5	6.1	3.2	5.9
Other high-income economies	5.6	4.7	5.5	4.1	5.3	8.4	6.0
Low- and middle-income economies	7.0	6.7	12.3	9.6	8.9	8.5	8.9
East Asia & Pacific	12.8	9.8	15.7	13.8	12.7	8.1	11.0
Europe & Central Asiaa	9.8	2.1	12.1	5.2	9.6	8.6	9.5
Latin America & Caribbean	3.5	−1.0	12.6	8.9	9.8	9.4	9.7
Middle East & N. Africa	2.5	3.9	4.4	2.7	3.1	7.1	3.9
South Asia	7.0	0.5	12.6	7.5	8.2	9.6	8.5
Sub-Saharan Africa	6.1	9.0	9.1	7.5	7.2	24.6	8.0
World	4.0	4.2	8.4	4.9	5.2	6.3	5.3

Low- and middle-income importers

Source of exports	East Asia & Pacific	Europe & Central Asia	Latin America & Caribbean	Middle East & N. Africa	South Asia	Sub-Saharan Africa	All low & middle income	World
High-income economies	9.5	7.6	8.6	1.0	5.8	1.7	7.1	4.9
Industrial economies	8.0	7.7	8.6	0.8	3.1	1.7	6.4	4.6
European Union	8.4	8.7	7.6	0.9	3.5	1.8	6.1	4.4
Japan	7.5	−1.1	3.2	−2.2	−1.2	−2.7	4.5	2.5
United States	9.5	0.5	9.9	0.6	4.0	3.8	8.2	5.7
Other industrial economies	6.1	8.5	6.0	4.0	6.7	2.7	4.7	5.8
Other high-income economies	11.4	6.8	7.2	1.3	11.1	2.2	9.9	7.2
Low- and middle-income economies	15.8	13.7	11.0	5.7	11.1	11.4	9.6	9.0
East Asia & Pacific	17.0	7.1	20.8	9.2	14.4	16.4	15.1	11.7
Europe & Central Asia[a]	1.7	10.3	9.1	3.9	3.5	8.3	8.0	9.0
Latin America & Caribbean	12.7	8.3	10.0	5.1	9.9	7.7	9.2	9.6
Middle East & N. Africa	18.2	3.0	0.3	4.6	7.9	14.3	7.5	4.7
South Asia	15.5	0.1	24.1	5.2	12.1	11.6	8.8	8.6
Sub-Saharan Africa	22.0	16.3	16.7	9.5	18.2	12.2	14.7	9.6
World	10.5	8.8	9.1	2.0	7.4	4.0	7.7	5.8

a. Data are for 1993–2001.

About the data

This table provides estimates of the flow of trade in goods between groups of economies. The data are from the International Monetary Fund's (IMF) *Direction of Trade Statistics Yearbook* and Direction of Trade database, which cover 186 countries. All 33 high-income countries and 22 of the 153 developing countries report trade on a timely basis, covering about 80 percent of trade for recent years.

Trade by less timely reporters and by countries that do not report is estimated using reports of partner countries. Because the largest exporting and importing countries are reliable reporters, a large portion of the missing trade flows can be estimated from partner reports. Partner country data may introduce discrepancies due to smuggling, confidentiality, different exchange rates, overreporting of transit trade, inclusion or exclusion of freight rates, and different points of valuation and times of recording.

In addition, estimates of trade within the European Union (EU) have been significantly affected by changes in reporting methods following the creation of a customs union. The new system for collecting data on trade between EU members—Intrastat, introduced in 1993—has less exhaustive coverage than the previous customs-based system and has resulted in some asymmetry problems (estimated imports are about 5 percent less than exports). Despite these issues, only a small portion of world trade is estimated to be omitted from the IMF's *Direction of Trade Statistics Yearbook* and Direction of Trade database.

Most countries report their trade data in national currencies, which are converted using the IMF's published period average exchange rates (series rf or rh, monthly averages of the market or official rates) for the reporting country or, if those are not available, monthly average rates in New York. Because imports are reported at c.i.f. (cost, insurance, and freight) valuations, and exports at f.o.b. (free on board) valuations, the IMF adjusts country reports of import values by dividing those values by 1.10 to estimate equivalent export values. This approximation is more or less accurate, depending on the set of partners and the items traded. Other factors affecting the accuracy of trade data include lags in reporting, recording differences across countries, and whether the country reports trade according to the general or special system of trade. (For further discussion of the measurement of exports and imports, see *About the data* for tables 4.5 and 4.6.)

The regional trade flows shown in the table were calculated from current price values. The growth rates presented are in nominal terms; that is, they include the effects of changes in both volumes and prices.

Definitions

• **Merchandise trade** includes all trade in goods; trade in services is excluded. • **High-income economies** are those classified as such by the World Bank. • **Industrial economies** are those classified as such in the IMF's *Direction of Trade Statistics Yearbook*. They include the countries of the European Union, Japan, the United States, and the other industrial economies listed below. • European Union comprises Austria, Belgium, Denmark, Finland, France, Germany, Greece, Ireland, Italy, Luxembourg, the Netherlands, Portugal, Spain, Sweden, and the United Kingdom. • **Other industrial economies** include Australia, Canada, Iceland, New Zealand, Norway, and Switzerland. • **Other high-income economies** include Aruba, The Bahamas, Bermuda, Brunei, Cyprus, Faeroe Islands, French Polynesia, Greenland, Guam, Hong Kong (China), Israel, the Republic of Korea, Kuwait, Macao (China), Netherlands Antilles, New Caledonia, Qatar, Singapore, Slovenia, Taiwan (China), and the United Arab Emirates. • **Low- and middle-income regional groupings** are based on World Bank classifications and may differ from those used by other organizations.

Data sources

Intercountry trade flows are published in the IMF's *Direction of Trade Statistics Yearbook* and *Direction of Trade Statistics Quarterly*; the data in the table were calculated using the IMF's Direction of Trade database.

Exports to low- and middle-income economies

	High-income OECD countries		European Union		Japan		United States	
	1991	2001[a]	1991	2001[a]	1991	2001	1991	2001
$ billions								
Food	38.5	55.1	18.4	23.8	0.4	1.3	12.6	19.4
Cereals	14.6	14.1	4.2	4.6	0.1	1.0	6.1	6.1
Agricultural raw materials	9.6	15.9	3.1	4.9	0.7	1.1	3.7	5.8
Ores and nonferrous metals	9.6	16.2	2.9	6.3	0.5	2.2	4.2	3.6
Fuels	9.3	17.4	3.8	6.0	0.4	0.5	3.4	5.2
Crude petroleum	0.7	0.9	0.3	0.2	0.0	0.0	0.0	0.0
Petroleum products	6.7	12.8	3.2	5.2	0.2	0.5	2.4	4.3
Manufactured goods	341.4	670.6	171.8	327.3	64.3	96.4	75.7	175.7
Chemical products	45.2	94.5	25.9	49.1	4.1	8.0	10.1	23.5
Mach. and transport equip.	198.5	391.2	94.5	181.7	42.7	64.9	47.3	108.6
Other	97.6	184.9	51.4	96.5	17.5	23.5	18.2	43.7
Miscellaneous goods	10.3	16.7	4.4	4.4	0.7	2.9	4.9	8.6
Total	**419.9**	**795.8**	**204.3**	**372.7**	**67.0**	**104.5**	**104.4**	**218.3**
% of total exports								
Food	9.2	6.9	9.0	6.4	0.6	1.3	12.0	8.9
Cereals	3.5	1.8	2.0	1.2	0.1	0.9	5.8	2.8
Agricultural raw materials	2.3	2.0	1.5	1.3	1.0	1.1	3.5	2.7
Ores and nonferrous metals	2.3	2.0	1.4	1.7	0.8	2.1	4.0	1.6
Fuels	2.2	2.2	1.8	1.6	0.6	0.5	3.2	2.4
Crude petroleum	0.2	0.1	0.1	0.0	0.0	0.0	0.0	0.0
Petroleum products	1.6	1.6	1.6	1.4	0.4	0.4	2.3	1.9
Manufactured goods	81.3	84.3	84.1	87.8	96.0	92.3	72.4	80.5
Chemical products	10.8	11.9	12.7	13.2	6.1	7.6	9.7	10.7
Mach. and transport equip.	47.3	49.2	46.2	48.8	63.8	62.1	45.3	49.7
Other	23.3	23.2	25.1	25.9	26.1	22.5	17.4	20.0
Miscellaneous goods	2.4	2.1	2.2	1.2	1.0	2.8	4.7	4.0
Total	**100.0**	**100.0**	**100.0**	**100.0**	**100.0**	**100.0**	**100.0**	**100.0**

6.3 OECD trade with low- and middle-income economies

	High-income OECD countries		European Union		Japan		United States	
$ billions	**1991**	**2001**[a]	**1991**	**2001**[a]	**1991**	**2001**	**1991**	**2001**
Food	69.6	95.7	37.5	44.6	11.1	17.3	15.4	24.9
Cereals	1.9	3.5	0.5	1.2	0.6	0.6	0.2	0.7
Agricultural raw materials	19.8	22.8	10.3	12.4	5.1	3.7	2.3	4.3
Ores and nonferrous metals	32.8	50.5	15.5	21.4	9.8	10.1	4.6	10.5
Fuels	158.5	230.4	74.0	91.0	31.0	34.2	41.2	76.2
Crude petroleum	111.3	166.6	50.7	63.3	19.0	21.0	32.2	60.9
Petroleum products	25.6	31.6	11.4	13.5	4.1	2.0	8.4	13.2
Manufactured goods	205.5	745.2	91.8	268.9	20.3	80.5	75.0	334.2
Chemical products	15.8	38.7	8.7	16.6	2.1	4.0	3.1	12.7
Mach. and transport equip.	54.4	317.0	19.0	103.6	3.2	31.3	27.4	155.5
Other	135.3	389.5	64.1	148.7	15.0	45.2	44.5	166.0
Miscellaneous goods	7.1	14.6	4.0	1.9	0.5	1.7	2.6	11.0
Total	**493.6**	**1,159.5**	**233.0**	**440.1**	**77.9**	**147.4**	**141.1**	**461.2**
% of total imports								
Food	14.1	8.3	16.1	10.1	14.3	11.8	10.9	5.4
Cereals	0.4	0.3	0.2	0.3	0.8	0.4	0.1	0.1
Agricultural raw materials	4.0	2.0	4.4	2.8	6.5	2.5	1.6	0.9
Ores and nonferrous metals	6.7	4.4	6.6	4.9	12.5	6.8	3.3	2.3
Fuels	32.1	19.9	31.8	20.7	39.8	23.2	29.2	16.5
Crude petroleum	22.6	14.4	21.8	14.4	24.4	14.2	22.8	13.2
Petroleum products	5.2	2.7	4.9	3.1	5.2	1.4	6.0	2.9
Manufactured goods	41.6	64.3	39.4	61.1	26.1	54.6	53.2	72.5
Chemical products	3.2	3.3	3.7	3.8	2.6	2.7	2.2	2.8
Mach. and transport equip.	11.0	27.3	8.2	23.5	4.1	21.3	19.4	33.7
Other	27.4	33.6	27.5	33.8	19.3	30.6	31.5	36.0
Miscellaneous goods	1.4	1.3	1.7	0.4	0.7	1.1	1.8	2.4
Total	**100.0**	**100.0**	**100.0**	**100.0**	**100.0**	**100.0**	**100.0**	**100.0**

a. Data for Portugal are for 2000.

About the data

Developing countries are becoming increasingly important in the global trading system. Since the early 1990s trade between high-income members of the Organisation for Economic Co-operation and Development (OECD) and low- and middle-income economies has grown faster than trade between OECD members. The increased trade benefits consumers and producers. But as the World Trade Organization's (WTO) ministerial conference in Doha, Qatar, in October 2001 showed, achieving a more pro-development outcome from trade remains a major challenge. Meeting this challenge will require strengthening international consultation. Negotiations after the Doha meetings will be launched (or continued) on services, agriculture, manufactures, WTO rules, the environment, dispute settlement, intellectual property rights protection, and disciplines on regional integration. These negotiations are scheduled to be concluded by 2005.

For developing countries a key issue is better access to rich country markets. What do developing countries stand to gain? Improved access to rich country markets could increase their exports by $9 billion a year in textiles alone, and another $22.3 billion in other manufactures. They would also reap large benefits from better access to one another's markets: opening their own markets would lead to gains of about $27.6 billion a year for manufactures, and $31.4 billion for agricultural goods.

Trade flows between high-income members of the OECD and low- and middle-income economies reflect the changing mix of exports to and imports from developing economies. While food and primary commodities have continued to fall as a share of OECD imports, the share of manufactures in goods imports from developing countries has grown dramatically, from about

42 percent in 1991 to 64 percent in 2001. At the same time developing countries have increased their imports of manufactured goods from high-income countries—particularly capital-intensive goods such as machinery and transport equipment.

Moreover, trade between developing countries has grown substantially over the past decade, with 40 percent of exports going to other developing countries. This growth has resulted from many factors, including developing countries' increasing share of world output and the liberalization of their trade. Yet trade barriers remain high (more than 70 percent of the tariff burden faced by manufactured goods from developing countries is imposed by other developing countries). The growing trade between developing countries strengthens the case for reducing these barriers. Despite the growth in trade between developing countries, high-income OECD countries remain the developing world's most important partners.

The aggregate flows in the table were compiled from intercountry flows recorded in the United Nations Statistics Division's Commodity Trade (COMTRADE) database. Partner country reports by high-income OECD countries were used for both exports and imports. Exports are recorded free on board (f.o.b.); imports include insurance and freight charges (c.i.f.). Revisions have been made to the time-series data as far back as 1990. Because of differences in sources of data, timing, and treatment of missing data, the data in this table may not be fully comparable with those used to calculate the direction of trade statistics in table 6.2 or the aggregate flows shown in tables 4.4–4.6. For further discussion of merchandise trade statistics, see *About the data* for tables 4.4–4.6 and 6.2.

Definitions

The product groups in the table are defined in accordance with the Standard International Trade Classification (SITC) revision 1: food (0, 1, 22, and 4) and cereals (04); agricultural raw materials (2 excluding 22, 27, and 28); ores and nonferrous metals (27, 28, and 68); fuels (3), crude petroleum (331), and petroleum products (332); manufactured goods (5–8 excluding 68), chemical products (5), machinery and transport equipment (7), and other manufactured goods (6 and 8 excluding 68); and miscellaneous goods (9). • **Exports** are all merchandise exports by high-income OECD countries to low- and middle-income economies as recorded in the United Nations Statistics Division's COMTRADE database. • **Imports** are all merchandise imports by high-income OECD countries from low- and middle-income economies as recorded in the United Nations Statistics Division's COMTRADE database. • **High-income OECD countries** in 2001 were Australia, Austria, Belgium, Canada, Denmark, Finland, France, Germany, Greece, Iceland, Ireland, Italy, Japan, the Republic of Korea, Luxembourg, the Netherlands, New Zealand, Norway, Portugal, Spain, Sweden, Switzerland, the United Kingdom, and the United States. • **European Union** comprises Austria, Belgium, Denmark, Finland, France, Germany, Greece, Ireland, Italy, Luxembourg, the Netherlands, Portugal, Spain, Sweden, and the United Kingdom.

6.3a

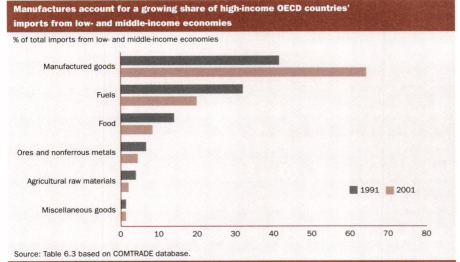

Manufactures account for a growing share of high-income OECD countries' imports from low- and middle-income economies

% of total imports from low- and middle-income economies

■ 1991 ■ 2001

Source: Table 6.3 based on COMTRADE database.

Data sources

COMTRADE data are available in electronic form from the United Nations Statistics Division. Although not as comprehensive as the underlying COMTRADE records, detailed statistics on international trade are published annually in the United Nations Conference on Trade and Development's (UNCTAD) *Handbook of International Trade and Development Statistics* and the United Nations Statistics Division's *International Trade Statistics Yearbook*.

6.4 Primary commodity prices

	1970	1980	1990	1995	1996	1997	1998	1999	2000	2001	2002
World Bank commodity price index											
(1990 = 100)											
Non-energy commodities	156	159	100	104	103	114	99	89	89	82	86
Agriculture	163	175	100	112	113	124	108	93	90	83	90
Beverages	203	230	100	129	113	165	141	108	91	75	88
Food	166	177	100	100	111	112	105	88	87	90	94
Raw materials	130	133	100	116	114	110	88	89	94	81	86
Fertilizers	108	164	100	89	108	116	123	115	109	103	104
Metals and minerals	144	120	100	87	80	87	76	74	85	78	75
Petroleum	19	205	100	64	80	81	57	79	127	111	113
Steel products [a]	111	100	100	91	86	86	75	69	79	70	70
MUV G-5 index	28	79	100	117	111	103	100	99	97	96	96
Commodity prices											
(1990 prices)											
Agricultural raw materials											
Cotton (cents/kg)	225	260	182	182	159	169	145	118	134	110	106
Logs, Cameroon ($/cu. m) [a]	153	319	343	290	255	275	288	271	283	277	..
Logs, Malaysian ($/cu. m)	154	248	177	218	227	230	163	188	195	166	169
Rubber (cents/kg)	145	181	86	135	125	98	72	63	71	63	80
Sawnwood, Malaysian ($/cu. m)	625	503	533	632	666	641	486	605	613	502	547
Tobacco ($/mt)	3,836	2,889	3,392	2,259	2,746	3,412	3,349	3,061	3,058	3,130	2,852
Beverages (cents/kg)											
Cocoa	240	330	127	122	131	156	168	114	93	111	184
Coffee, robustas	330	412	118	237	162	168	183	150	94	63	69
Coffee, Arabica	409	440	197	285	242	403	299	231	197	143	141
Tea, avg., 3 auctions	298	211	206	127	149	199	205	185	193	167	156
Energy											
Coal, Australian ($/mt)	..	50.01	39.67	33.64	34.21	33.92	29.35	26.13	26.97	33.68	28.05
Coal, U.S. ($/mt)	..	54.71	41.67	33.47	33.44	35.16	34.52	33.38	33.97	46.75	41.49
Natural gas, Europe ($/mmbtu)	..	4.32	2.55	2.33	2.55	2.65	2.43	2.14	3.97	4.23	3.16
Natural gas, U.S. ($/mmbtu)	0.59	1.97	1.70	1.47	2.45	2.40	2.09	2.28	4.43	4.12	3.48
Petroleum ($/bbl)	4.31	46.80	22.88	14.68	18.35	18.52	13.12	18.19	29.01	25.38	25.84

About the data

Primary commodities—raw or partially processed materials that will be transformed into finished goods—are often the most significant exports of developing countries, and revenues obtained from them have an important effect on living standards. Price data for primary commodities are collected from a variety of sources, including trade journals, international study groups, government market surveys, newspaper and wire service reports, and commodity exchange spot and near-term forward prices. This table is based on frequently updated price reports. When possible, the prices received by exporters are used; if export prices are unavail-

able, the prices paid by importers are used. Annual price series are generally simple averages based on higher-frequency data. The constant price series in the table is deflated using the manufactures unit value (MUV) index for the G-5 countries (see below).

The commodity price indexes are calculated as Laspeyres index numbers, in which the fixed weights are the 1987–89 export values for low- and middle-income economies, rebased to 1990. Each index represents a fixed basket of primary commodity exports. The non-energy commodity price index contains 37 price series for 31 non-energy commodities.

Separate indexes are compiled for petroleum and for steel products, which are not included in the non-energy commodity price index.

The MUV index is a composite index of prices for manufactured exports from the five major (G-5) industrial countries (France, Germany, Japan, the United Kingdom, and the United States) to low- and middle-income economies, valued in U.S. dollars. The index covers products in groups 5–8 of the Standard International Trade Classification (SITC) revision 1. To construct the MUV G-5 index, unit value indexes for each country are combined using weights determined by each country's export share.

	1970	1980	1990	1995	1996	1997	1998	1999	2000	2001	2002
Commodity prices (continued)											
(1990 prices)											
Fertilizers ($/mt)											
Phosphate rock	39	59	40	30	35	40	43	44	45	44	42
TSP	152	229	132	128	158	166	174	155	142	132	138
Food											
Fats and oils ($/mt)											
Coconut oil	1,417	855	336	573	675	635	661	742	462	332	436
Groundnut oil	1,350	1,090	964	847	806	976	913	793	733	709	712
Palm oil	927	741	290	537	477	527	674	439	319	298	405
Soybeans	417	376	247	221	274	285	244	203	218	204	220
Soybean meal	367	333	200	168	240	266	171	153	194	189	182
Soybean oil	1,021	759	447	534	496	546	628	430	347	369	471
Grains ($/mt)											
Grain sorghum	185	164	104	102	135	106	98	85	90	99	105
Maize	208	159	109	106	149	113	102	91	91	93	103
Rice	450	521	271	274	305	293	305	250	208	180	199
Wheat	196	219	136	151	187	154	127	113	117	132	154
Other food											
Bananas ($/mt)	590	481	541	380	422	500	491	376	436	608	548
Beef (cents/kg)	465	350	256	163	160	179	173	186	199	222	221
Oranges ($/mt)	599	496	531	454	442	443	444	434	373	621	597
Sugar, EU domestic (cents/kg)	40	62	58	59	61	61	60	60	57	55	57
Sugar, U.S. domestic (cents/kg)	59	84	51	43	44	47	49	47	44	49	48
Sugar, world (cents/kg)	29	80	28	25	24	24	20	14	19	20	16
Metals and minerals											
Aluminum ($/mt)	1,982	1,848	1,639	1,543	1,353	1,545	1,363	1,370	1,592	1,505	1,400
Copper ($/mt)	5,038	2,770	2,661	2,509	2,062	2,200	1,661	1,583	1,863	1,645	1,617
Iron ore (cents/dmtu)	35	36	32	24	27	29	31	28	30	31	30
Lead (cents/kg)	108	115	81	54	70	60	53	51	47	50	47
Nickel ($/mt)	10,148	8,274	8,864	7,031	6,741	6,694	4,648	6,050	8,876	6,196	7,021
Tin (cents/kg)	1,310	2,129	609	531	554	546	556	544	559	467	421
Zinc (cents/kg)	105	97	151	88	92	127	103	108	116	92	81

a. Series not included in the non-energy index.

Definitions

• **Non-energy commodity price index** covers the 31 non-energy primary commodities that make up the agriculture, fertilizer, and metals and minerals indexes. • **Agriculture** includes beverages, food, and agricultural raw material. • **Beverages** include cocoa, coffee, and tea. • **Food** includes rice, wheat, maize, sorghum, soybeans, soybean oil, soybean meal, palm oil, coconut oil, groundnut oil, bananas, beef, oranges, and sugar. • **Agricultural raw materials** include cotton, timber (logs and sawnwood), natural rubber, and tobacco. • **Fertilizers** include phosphate rock and triple superphosphate (TSP). • **Metals and minerals** include aluminum, copper, iron ore, lead, nickel, tin, and zinc. • **Petroleum price index** refers to the average spot price of Brent, Dubai, and West Texas Intermediate crude oil, equally weighted. • **Steel products price index** is the composite price index for eight steel products based on quotations f.o.b. (free on board) Japan excluding shipments to China and the United States, weighted by product shares of apparent combined consumption (volume of deliveries) for Germany, Japan, and the United States. • **MUV G-5 index** is the manufactures unit value index for G-5 country exports to low- and middle-income economies. • **Commodity prices**—for definitions and sources, see "Commodity Price Data" (also known as the "Pink Sheet") at the Global Prospects Web site (http://www.worldbank.org/prospects).

Data sources

Commodity price data and the G-5 MUV index are compiled by the World Bank's Development Prospects Group. Monthly updates of commodity prices are available on the Web at http://www.worldbank.org/prospects.

6.5 | Regional trade blocs

$ millions

	1970	1980	1990	1995	1996	1997	1998	1999	2000	2001
High-income and low- and middle-income economies										
APEC [a]	58,633	357,697	901,560	1,688,707	1,755,116	1,869,192	1,734,386	1,896,217	2,262,159	2,075,735
CEFTA	1,157	7,766	4,235	12,118	12,874	13,169	14,234	13,226	15,108	16,488
European Union	76,451	456,857	981,260	1,259,699	1,273,430	1,162,419	1,226,988	1,404,833	1,418,149	1,406,859
NAFTA	22,078	102,218	226,273	394,472	437,804	496,423	521,649	581,162	676,440	639,138
Latin America and the Caribbean										
ACS	758	4,892	5,401	11,013	10,847	11,985	12,547	11,663	13,908	13,631
Andean Group	97	1,161	1,312	4,812	4,762	5,524	5,408	3,929	5,136	5,444
CACM	287	1,174	671	1,595	1,723	1,973	2,038	2,161	2,541	2,648
CARICOM	52	576	448	867	900	968	1,020	1,136	1,050	1,176
Central American Group of Four	176	692	399	1,026	1,106	1,299	1,171	1,335	1,602	1,607
Group of Three	59	706	1,046	3,460	3,131	3,944	3,921	2,912	3,731	4,177
LAIA	1,263	10,981	12,331	35,299	38,384	44,814	42,974	34,785	42,833	40,921
MERCOSUR	451	3,424	4,127	14,199	17,075	20,772	20,352	15,313	17,910	15,295
OECS	..	8	29	39	33	34	36	37	38	40
Africa										
CEMAC	22	75	139	120	164	161	153	127	103	120
CEPGL	3	2	7	8	9	6	8	9	10	11
COMESA	412	616	963	1,386	1,610	1,545	1,501	1,348	1,519	1,622
Cross-Border Initiative	209	447	613	1,002	1,191	1,144	1,156	964	1,060	987
ECCAS	162	89	163	163	212	211	198	179	200	219
ECOWAS	86	692	1,557	1,936	2,293	2,244	2,361	2,382	2,969	2,898
Indian Ocean Commission	5	8	20	61	67	70	90	86	93	103
MRU	1	7	0	1	4	7	8	8	10	11
SADC	483	617	1,630	3,373	3,963	4,471	3,865	4,224	4,380	3,626
UDEAC	22	75	139	120	163	160	152	126	102	119
UEMOA	52	460	621	560	667	707	752	805	744	761
Middle East and Asia										
Arab Common Market	102	661	911	1,368	1,149	1,146	978	951	1,312	1,722
ASEAN	1,456	13,350	28,648	81,911	86,925	88,773	72,352	80,418	101,848	91,675
Bangkok Agreement	132	1,464	4,476	12,066	13,092	13,640	13,175	14,910	17,235	16,719
EAEC	9,197	98,532	281,067	636,973	651,379	673,244	551,553	614,945	776,209	706,378
ECO	63	15,891	1,243	4,746	4,773	4,929	4,031	3,903	4,495	4,422
GCC	156	4,632	6,906	6,832	7,624	8,124	7,358	7,306	9,234	9,137
SAARC	93	613	863	2,024	2,144	2,004	2,834	2,615	2,798	3,094
UMA	60	109	958	1,109	1,115	924	881	919	1,076	1,140

Note: Regional bloc memberships are as follows: **Asia Pacific Economic Cooperation (APEC),** Australia, Brunei Darussalam, Canada, Chile, China, Hong Kong (China), Indonesia, Japan, the Republic of Korea, Malaysia, Mexico, New Zealand, Papua New Guinea, Peru, the Philippines, the Russian Federation, Singapore, Taiwan (China), Thailand, the United States, and Vietnam; **Central European Free Trade Area (CEFTA),** Bulgaria, the Czech Republic, Hungary, Poland, Romania, the Slovak Republic, and Slovenia; **European Union (EU; formerly European Economic Community and European Community),** Austria, Belgium, Denmark, Finland, France, Germany, Greece, Ireland, Italy, Luxembourg, the Netherlands, Portugal, Spain, Sweden, and the United Kingdom; **North American Free Trade Area (NAFTA),** Canada, Mexico, and the United States; **Association of Caribbean States (ACS),** Antigua and Barbuda, the Bahamas, Barbados, Belize, Colombia, Costa Rica, Cuba, Dominica, the Dominican Republic, El Salvador, Grenada, Guatemala, Guyana, Haiti, Honduras, Jamaica, Mexico, Nicaragua, Panama, St. Kitts and Nevis, St. Lucia, St. Vincent and the Grenadines, Suriname, Trinidad and Tobago, and República Bolivariana de Venezuela; **Andean Group,** Bolivia, Colombia, Ecuador, Peru, and República Bolivariana de Venezuela; **Central American Common Market (CACM),** Costa Rica, El Salvador, Guatemala, Honduras, and Nicaragua; **Caribbean Community and Common Market (CARICOM),** Antigua and Barbuda, the Bahamas (part of the Caribbean Community but not of the Common Market), Barbados, Belize, Dominica, Grenada, Guyana, Jamaica, Montserrat, St. Kitts and Nevis, St. Lucia, St. Vincent and the Grenadines, Suriname, and Trinidad and Tobago; **Central American Group of Four,** El Salvador, Guatemala, Honduras, and Nicaragua; **Group of Three,** Colombia, Mexico, and República Bolivariana de Venezuela; **Latin American Integration Association (LAIA; formerly Latin American Free Trade Area),** Argentina, Bolivia, Brazil, Chile, Colombia, Ecuador, Mexico, Paraguay, Peru, Uruguay, and República Bolivariana de Venezuela; **Southern Cone Common Market (MERCOSUR),** Argentina, Brazil, Paraguay, and Uruguay; **Organization of Eastern Caribbean States (OECS),** Antigua and Barbuda, Dominica, Grenada, Montserrat, St. Kitts and Nevis, St. Lucia, and St. Vincent and the Grenadines; **Economic and Monetary Community of Central Africa (CEMAC),** Cameroon, the Central African Republic, Chad, the Republic of Congo, Equatorial Guinea, Gabon, and São Tomé and Principe; **Economic Community of the Countries of the Great Lakes (CEPGL),** Burundi, the Democratic Republic of Congo, and Rwanda; **Common Market for Eastern and Southern Africa (COMESA),** Angola, Burundi, Comoros, the Democratic Republic of Congo, Djibouti, the Arab Republic of Egypt, Eritrea, Ethiopia, Kenya, Madagascar, Malawi, Mauritius, Namibia, Rwanda, Seychelles, Sudan, Swaziland, Uganda, Tanzania, Zambia,

Merchandise exports within bloc

% of total bloc exports

	1970	1980	1990	1995	1996	1997	1998	1999	2000	2001
High-income and low- and middle-income economies										
APEC[a]	57.8	57.9	68.3	71.8	71.9	71.6	69.7	71.8	73.1	72.6
CEFTA	12.9	14.8	9.9	14.6	14.4	13.4	13.0	12.1	12.1	12.3
European Union	59.5	60.8	65.9	62.4	61.4	55.5	57.0	63.3	62.1	61.3
NAFTA	36.0	33.6	41.4	46.2	47.6	49.1	51.7	54.6	55.7	55.5
Latin America and the Caribbean										
ACS	9.6	8.7	8.4	8.5	6.9	6.9	7.2	5.8	5.6	5.9
Andean Group	1.8	3.8	4.1	12.0	9.7	10.8	12.8	8.8	8.4	10.9
CACM	26.0	24.4	15.4	21.7	22.0	18.1	16.1	12.8	13.7	15.0
CARICOM	4.2	5.3	8.1	12.1	13.0	14.4	17.3	16.9	14.6	13.3
Central American Group of Four	20.1	18.1	13.7	22.0	22.0	19.9	16.3	14.0	14.8	14.8
Group of Three	1.1	1.8	2.0	3.2	2.4	2.7	2.6	1.7	1.7	2.1
LAIA	9.9	13.7	10.8	17.1	16.2	17.0	16.7	12.7	12.9	13.0
MERCOSUR	9.4	11.6	8.9	20.3	22.6	24.8	25.0	20.6	20.9	17.3
OECS	..	9.1	8.1	12.6	10.6	10.7	12.0	13.1	10.0	5.3
Africa										
CEMAC	4.8	1.6	2.3	2.1	2.3	2.0	2.3	1.7	1.0	1.2
CEPGL	0.4	0.1	0.5	0.5	0.5	0.4	0.6	0.7	0.8	0.8
COMESA	9.1	6.1	6.6	7.7	8.0	7.8	8.7	7.4	5.6	6.9
Cross-Border Initiative	9.3	8.8	10.3	11.9	12.4	12.7	13.8	12.1	10.7	10.3
ECCAS	9.6	1.4	1.4	1.5	1.6	1.5	1.8	1.3	1.1	1.3
ECOWAS	2.9	10.1	7.9	9.0	8.5	8.6	10.6	10.9	9.6	9.7
Indian Ocean Commission	8.4	3.9	4.1	6.0	5.4	3.9	4.7	4.8	4.3	3.9
MRU	0.2	0.8	0.0	0.1	0.3	0.5	0.5	0.6	0.6	0.6
SADC	8.0	2.0	4.8	8.7	9.4	10.4	10.4	11.9	11.7	10.2
COMESA	4.9	1.6	2.3	2.1	2.3	2.0	2.3	1.7	1.0	1.2
UDEAC	4.9	1.6	2.3	2.1	2.3	2.0	2.3	1.7	1.0	1.2
UEMOA	6.5	9.6	13.0	10.3	9.6	11.8	11.0	13.2	13.3	13.9
Middle East and Asia										
Arab Common Market	2.2	2.4	2.7	6.7	4.4	4.1	4.8	3.3	3.0	4.5
ASEAN	22.9	18.7	19.8	25.4	25.4	24.9	21.9	22.4	23.9	23.3
Bangkok Agreement	2.7	3.7	3.7	5.0	5.2	5.1	5.0	5.2	5.2	5.5
EAEC	28.9	35.6	39.7	48.1	49.0	48.0	42.2	44.0	46.8	46.9
ECO	1.5	73.2	3.2	7.9	7.1	7.5	6.8	5.7	5.4	5.4
GCC	2.9	3.0	8.0	6.8	6.4	6.5	8.0	6.7	5.5	5.7
SAARC	3.2	4.8	3.2	4.4	4.3	4.0	5.2	4.6	4.3	4.8
UMA	1.4	0.3	2.9	3.8	3.4	2.7	3.3	2.5	2.2	2.5

and Zimbabwe; **Cross-Border Initiative,** Burundi, Comoros, Kenya, Madagascar, Malawi, Mauritius, Namibia, Rwanda, Seychelles, Swaziland, Tanzania, Uganda, Zambia, and Zimbabwe; **Economic Community of Central African States (ECCAS),** Angola, Burundi, Cameroon, the Central African Republic, Chad, the Democratic Republic of Congo, the Republic of Congo, Equatorial Guinea, Gabon, Rwanda, and São Tomé and Principe; **Economic Community of West African States (ECOWAS),** Benin, Burkina Faso, Cape Verde, Côte d'Ivoire, The Gambia, Ghana, Guinea, Guinea-Bissau, Liberia, Mali, Mauritania, Niger, Nigeria, Senegal, Sierra Leone, and Togo; **Indian Ocean Commission,** Comoros, Madagascar, Mauritius, Reunion, and Seychelles; **Mano River Union (MRU),** Guinea, Liberia, and Sierra Leone; **Southern African Development Community (SADC; formerly Southern African Development Coordination Conference),** Angola, Botswana, the Democratic Republic of Congo, Lesotho, Malawi, Mauritius, Mozambique, Namibia, Seychelles, South Africa, Swaziland, Tanzania, Zambia, and Zimbabwe; **Central African Customs and Economic Union (UDEAC; formerly Union Douanière et Economique de l'Afrique Centrale),** Cameroon, the Central African Republic, Chad, the Republic of Congo, Equatorial Guinea, and Gabon; **West African Economic and Monetary Union (UEMOA),** Benin, Burkina Faso, Côte d'Ivoire, Guinea-Bissau, Mali, Niger, Senegal, and Togo; **Arab Common Market,** the Arab Republic of Egypt, Iraq, Jordan, Libya, Mauritania, the Syrian Arab Republic, and the Republic of Yemen; **Association of South-East Asian Nations (ASEAN),** Brunei, Cambodia, Indonesia, the Lao People's Democratic Republic, Malaysia, Myanmar, the Philippines, Singapore, Thailand, and Vietnam; **Bangkok Agreement,** Bangladesh, India, the Republic of Korea, the Lao People's Democratic Republic, the Philippines, Sri Lanka, and Thailand; **East Asian Economic Caucus (EAEC),** Brunei, China, Hong Kong (China), Indonesia, Japan, the Republic of Korea, Malaysia, the Philippines, Singapore, Taiwan (China), and Thailand; **Economic Cooperation Organization (ECO),** Afghanistan, Azerbaijan, the Islamic Republic of Iran, Kazakhstan, the Kyrgyz Republic, Pakistan, Tajikistan, Turkey, Turkmenistan, and Uzbekistan; **Gulf Cooperation Council (GCC),** Bahrain, Kuwait, Oman, Qatar, Saudi Arabia, and the United Arab Emirates; **South Asian Association for Regional Cooperation (SAARC),** Bangladesh, Bhutan, India, Maldives, Nepal, Pakistan, and Sri Lanka; and **Arab Maghreb Union (UMA),** Algeria, Libya, Mauritania, Morocco, and Tunisia.
a. No preferential trade agreement.

Total merchandise exports by bloc

% of world exports

	1970	1980	1990	1995	1996	1997	1998	1999	2000	2001
High-income and low- and middle-income economies										
APEC [a]	36.0	33.7	39.0	46.3	46.0	47.3	46.1	46.6	48.5	46.5
CEFTA	3.2	2.9	1.3	1.6	1.7	1.8	2.0	1.9	2.0	2.2
European Union	45.6	41.0	44.0	39.7	39.1	37.9	39.9	39.2	35.8	37.4
NAFTA	21.7	16.6	16.2	16.8	17.3	18.3	18.7	18.8	19.0	18.7
Latin America and the Caribbean										
ACS	2.8	3.1	1.9	2.6	3.0	3.1	3.2	3.5	3.9	3.7
Andean Group	1.9	1.7	0.9	0.8	0.9	0.9	0.8	0.8	1.0	0.8
CACM	0.4	0.3	0.1	0.1	0.1	0.2	0.2	0.3	0.3	0.3
CARICOM	0.4	0.6	0.2	0.1	0.1	0.1	0.1	0.1	0.1	0.1
Central American Group of Four	0.3	0.2	0.1	0.1	0.1	0.1	0.1	0.2	0.2	0.2
Group of Three	1.8	2.1	1.5	2.1	2.5	2.7	2.8	3.0	3.3	3.2
LAIA	4.5	4.4	3.4	4.1	4.5	4.8	4.8	4.8	5.2	5.1
MERCOSUR	1.7	1.6	1.4	1.4	1.4	1.5	1.5	1.3	1.3	1.4
OECS	..	0.0	0.0	0.0	0.0	0.0	0.0	0.0	0.0	0.0
Africa										
CEMAC	0.2	0.3	0.2	0.1	0.1	0.1	0.1	0.1	0.2	0.2
CEPGL	0.3	0.1	0.0	0.0	0.0	0.0	0.0	0.0	0.0	0.0
COMESA	1.6	0.6	0.4	0.4	0.4	0.4	0.3	0.3	0.4	0.4
Cross-Border Initiative	0.8	0.3	0.2	0.2	0.2	0.2	0.2	0.1	0.2	0.2
ECCAS	0.6	0.3	0.3	0.2	0.3	0.3	0.2	0.2	0.3	0.3
ECOWAS	1.1	0.4	0.6	0.4	0.5	0.5	0.4	0.4	0.5	0.5
Indian Ocean Commission	0.1	0.1	0.1	0.0	0.0	0.0	0.0	0.0	0.0	0.0
MRU	0.1	0.0	0.1	0.0	0.0	0.0	0.0	0.0	0.0	0.0
SADC	2.2	1.6	1.0	0.8	0.8	0.8	0.7	0.6	0.6	0.6
UDEAC	0.2	0.3	0.2	0.1	0.1	0.1	0.1	0.1	0.2	0.2
UEMOA	0.3	0.3	0.1	0.1	0.1	0.1	0.1	0.1	0.1	0.1
Middle East and Asia										
Arab Common Market	1.6	1.5	1.0	0.4	0.5	0.5	0.4	0.5	0.7	0.6
ASEAN	2.3	3.9	4.3	6.4	6.5	6.4	6.1	6.3	6.7	6.4
Bangkok Agreement	1.8	2.2	3.6	4.8	4.8	4.9	4.9	5.0	5.2	4.9
EAEC	11.3	15.1	20.9	26.1	25.1	25.4	24.2	24.7	26.0	24.5
ECO	1.5	1.2	1.1	1.2	1.3	1.2	1.1	1.2	1.3	1.3
GCC	1.9	8.5	2.5	2.0	2.2	2.3	1.7	1.9	2.7	2.6
SAARC	1.1	0.7	0.8	0.9	0.9	0.9	1.0	1.0	1.0	1.1
UMA	1.5	2.3	1.0	0.6	0.6	0.6	0.5	0.6	0.8	0.7

Regional trade blocs

Trade blocs are groups of countries that have established special preferential arrangements governing trade between members. Although in some cases the preferences—such as lower tariff duties or exemptions from quantitative restrictions—may be no greater than those available to other trading partners, the general purpose of such arrangements is to encourage exports by bloc members to one another—sometimes called intratrade.

Most countries are members of a regional trade bloc, and more than a third of the world's trade takes place within such arrangements. While trade blocs vary widely in structure, they all have the same main objective: to reduce trade barriers among member countries. But effective integration requires more than reducing tariffs and quotas. Economic gains from competition and scale may not be achieved unless other barriers that divide markets and impede the free flow of goods, services, and investments are lifted. For example, many regional trade blocs retain contingent protections or restrictions on intrabloc trade. These include antidumping, countervailing duties, and "emergency protection" to address balance of payments problems or to protect an industry from surges in imports. Other barriers include differing product standards, discrimination in public procurement, and cumbersome and costly border formalities.

Membership in a regional trade bloc may reduce the frictional costs of trade, increase the credibility of reform initiatives, and strengthen security among partners. But making it work effectively is a challenge

for any government. All sectors of an economy may be affected, and some sectors may expand while others contract, so it is important to weigh the potential costs and benefits that membership may bring.

The table shows the value of merchandise intratrade for important regional trade blocs (service exports are excluded) as well as the size of intratrade relative to each bloc's total exports of goods and the share of the bloc's total exports in world exports. Although Asia Pacific Economic Cooperation (APEC) has no preferential arrangements, it is included in the table because of the volume of trade between its members.

The data on country exports are drawn from the International Monetary Fund's (IMF) Direction of Trade database and should be broadly consistent with those from other sources, such as the United Nations Statistics Division's Commodity Trade (COMTRADE) database. However, trade flows between many developing countries, particularly in Africa, are not well recorded. Thus the value of intratrade for certain groups may be understated. Data on trade between developing and high-income countries are generally complete.

Membership in the trade blocs shown is based on the most recent information available, from the World Bank Policy Research Report Trade Blocs (2000a) and from consultation with the World Bank's international trade unit. Although bloc exports have been calculated back to 1970 on the basis of current membership, most of the blocs came into existence

in later years and their membership may have changed over time. For this reason, and because systems of preferences also change over time, intratrade in earlier years may not have been affected by the same preferences as in recent years. In addition, some countries belong to more than one trade bloc, so shares of world exports exceed 100 percent. Exports of blocs include all commodity trade, which may include items not specified in trade bloc agreements. Differences from previously published estimates may be due to changes in bloc membership or to revisions in the underlying data.

• **Merchandise exports within bloc** are the sum of merchandise exports by members of a trade bloc to other members of the bloc. They are shown both in U.S. dollars and as a percentage of total merchandise exports by the bloc. • **Total merchandise exports by bloc as a share of world exports** are the ratio of the bloc's total merchandise exports (within the bloc and to the rest of the world) to total merchandise exports by all economies in the world.

6.5a

Exports within several trade blocs have remained a steady share of world exports

Note: For the full names and memberships of the trade blocs shown, see the note to table 6.5.
Source: Table 6.5.

6.6 Tariff barriers

	Year	All products					Primary products		Manufactured products	
		Simple mean tariff %	Standard deviation of tariff rates %	Weighted mean tariff %	Share of lines with international peaks %	Share of lines with specific tariffs %	Simple mean tariff %	Weighted mean tariff %	Simple mean tariff %	Weighted mean tariff %
Albania	1997	17.0	8.5	14.5	56.1	0.0	15.7	12.8	17.2	15.2
	2001	11.8	6.9	11.8	38.3	0.0	11.8	10.8	11.3	12.0
Algeria	1993	22.9	16.5	15.5	46.8	0.0	15.5	8.9	22.9	18.7
	2001	22.4	14.3	15.0	50.3	0.0	15.0	11.3	22.6	16.7
Argentina	1992	12.2	7.7	12.8	31.0	0.0	12.8	5.8	12.3	13.6
	2001	11.6	7.2	9.2	39.1	0.0	9.2	4.8	11.7	9.7
Armenia	2001	3.3	4.7	2.5	0.0	0.0	2.5	3.4	2.8	1.2
Australia	1991	13.1	14.3	9.5	30.5	1.2	9.5	1.6	14.2	10.5
	2001	5.4	6.7	3.9	6.5	1.5	3.9	0.8	5.8	4.4
Bangladesh	1989	106.2	79.2	88.2	98.5	1.0	88.2	53.6	108.7	109.6
	2000	21.6	13.6	21.0	52.9	0.0	21.0	18.6	21.5	22.3
Belarus	1996	12.4	8.7	8.9	31.4	0.0	8.9	6.5	12.9	10.5
	1997	13.1	8.3	9.6	32.5	0.0	9.6	7.0	13.8	11.2
Benin	2001	14.7	6.7	14.0	59.1	0.0	14.0	12.8	14.5	12.8
Bhutan	1996	17.7	14.1	15.3	51.9	5.3	15.3	9.7	17.0	16.8
Bolivia	1993	9.7	1.1	9.4	0.0	0.0	9.4	10.0	9.7	9.3
	1999	9.5	1.6	9.0	0.0	0.0	9.0	10.0	9.4	8.9
Bosnia and Herzegovina	2001	7.6	4.4	6.6	0.0	0.0	6.6	5.7	7.5	6.9
Brazil	1989	42.2	17.2	32.0	92.4	0.2	32.0	18.6	42.4	37.1
	2001	12.9	7.2	11.1	46.3	0.0	11.1	4.7	12.9	12.5
Bulgaria	2001	13.8	11.3	10.9	30.0	1.5	10.9	11.8	12.0	10.8
Burkina Faso	1993	25.6	10.0	19.9	73.6	0.0	19.9	23.1	25.5	20.3
	2001	12.8	7.0	10.1	45.9	0.0	10.1	14.8	12.4	8.9
Cameroon	1994	19.4	10.5	14.0	54.7	0.0	14.0	14.9	18.6	13.6
	2001	18.0	9.6	13.1	48.6	0.1	13.1	18.5	17.4	12.0
Canada	1989	8.6	7.4	6.1	14.6	3.4	6.1	2.6	9.2	6.6
	2001	4.5	6.7	0.9	9.6	4.8	0.9	0.5	4.7	0.9
Central African Republic	1995	18.3	10.7	13.7	53.6	0.4	13.7	13.7	16.8	13.1
	2001	18.4	9.9	16.0	52.4	0.2	16.0	26.9	17.5	11.9
Chad	1995	15.9	10.9	16.3	44.9	0.0	16.3	15.9	15.5	13.4
	2001	17.0	9.4	12.7	44.6	0.1	12.7	24.9	16.7	11.4
Chile	1992	11.0	0.5	11.0	0.0	0.0	11.0	11.0	11.0	10.9
	2001	8.0	0.0	8.0	0.0	0.0	8.0	8.0	8.0	8.0
China [†]	1992	41.2	30.6	32.5	78.2	0.0	32.5	14.0	41.6	35.6
	2001	15.3	10.0	14.3	40.5	0.5	14.3	18.6	15.0	12.9
Hong Kong, China	1988	0.0	0.0	0.0	0.0	0.0	0.0	0.0	0.0	0.0
	1998	0.0	0.0	0.0	0.0	0.0	0.0	0.0	0.0	0.0
Colombia	1991	5.7	8.2	6.4	1.6	0.0	6.4	7.5	5.5	6.1
	2001	11.8	6.2	11.0	23.2	0.0	11.0	12.7	11.6	10.5
Congo, Rep	1994	20.9	9.3	16.4	64.0	0.0	16.4	20.5	20.2	14.6
	2001	18.6	9.6	16.1	52.5	0.1	16.1	21.9	17.8	14.4
Costa Rica	1995	10.3	8.1	8.5	29.5	0.0	8.5	10.5	9.9	8.0
	2001	6.3	7.5	4.3	0.5	0.0	4.3	7.8	5.6	3.8
Côte d'Ivoire	1993	25.4	12.1	22.1	75.6	0.0	22.1	21.6	25.0	22.5
	2001	12.6	6.9	9.6	44.3	0.0	9.6	10.6	12.3	9.1
Croatia	2001	12.0	7.4	9.8	30.8	0.1	9.8	6.1	11.7	11.1
Cuba	1993	13.1	8.0	10.2	25.8	0.0	10.2	8.3	12.9	11.5
	1997	11.4	6.6	8.2	9.6	0.0	8.2	5.2	11.3	9.7
Czech Republic	1996	6.9	6.2	5.8	5.4	0.0	5.8	4.1	6.6	6.2
	1999	6.5	9.3	5.8	5.4	0.0	5.8	5.1	5.3	5.8
Dominican Republic	1997	15.0	9.1	16.3	33.8	0.0	16.3	10.4	14.6	17.7
	2000	19.5	10.0	20.3	55.0	0.1	20.3	13.8	19.0	21.9
Ecuador	1993	8.7	6.0	8.2	20.7	0.0	8.2	6.4	8.6	8.3
	1999	12.9	6.3	11.3	37.0	0.0	11.3	10.6	12.8	11.2
Egypt, Arab Rep.	1995	25.6	33.2	16.7	53.1	1.2	16.7	7.6	25.6	22.2
	1998	20.5	39.5	13.8	47.4	9.5	13.8	7.5	20.2	17.5
El Salvador	1995	10.3	7.8	9.3	27.8	0.0	9.3	10.2	9.8	8.7
	2001	7.4	8.4	6.4	10.1	0.0	6.4	7.6	6.7	5.5
Equatorial Guinea	1998	19.9	9.7	15.3	60.1	0.2	15.3	23.7	18.4	13.6
	2001	18.7	9.6	13.7	53.5	0.0	13.7	21.4	17.5	12.5
Ethiopia	1995	32.1	23.5	19.0	71.5	0.2	19.0	18.4	31.6	18.0
	2001	17.2	12.3	11.0	45.7	0.2	11.0	11.7	16.6	10.5
European Union	1988	3.7	5.9	3.7	4.1	12.8	3.7	2.7	2.5	4.3
	2001	3.9	4.9	2.6	2.6	7.4	2.6	1.7	3.2	2.9
Estonia	1995	0.1	1.0	0.4	0.1	0.0	0.4	0.0	0.1	0.5
Finland	1988	10.3	11.0	6.2	24.4	1.0	6.2	3.0	10.4	6.9
	1990	10.7	11.3	6.3	25.0	1.1	6.3	2.7	10.7	7.2
[†] Taiwan, China	1989	12.3	9.5	9.9	16.6	0.5	9.9	8.4	11.1	10.4
	2001	7.6	8.0	3.5	8.8	1.6	3.5	6.2	6.6	2.9

	Year	All products					Primary products		Manufactured products	
		Simple mean tariff %	Standard deviation of tariff rates %	Weighted mean tariff %	Share of lines with international peaks %	Share of lines with specific tariffs %	Simple mean tariff %	Weighted mean tariff %	Simple mean tariff %	Weighted mean tariff %
Gabon	1995	20.6	9.6	16.2	61.9	0.0	16.2	20.0	19.6	15.1
	2001	18.8	9.7	15.2	53.3	0.1	15.2	20.2	17.9	14.0
Georgia	1999	9.9	3.2	9.9	0.0	1.0	9.9	12.0	9.5	8.3
Ghana	1993	14.4	8.5	9.5	42.1	0.0	9.5	16.2	13.7	8.7
	2000	14.0	10.7	9.7	41.1	0.0	9.7	28.2	13.0	8.9
Guatemala	1995	10.0	7.5	8.6	25.7	0.0	8.6	10.2	9.5	8.0
	2001	7.0	7.7	5.6	9.6	0.0	5.6	7.4	6.6	5.0
Guinea-Bissau	2001	14.0	7.1	14.3	56.0	0.0	14.3	19.6	13.3	10.3
Guyana	1996	22.4	12.5	17.6	47.4	39.3	17.6	15.8	21.1	16.9
	2001	11.7	10.4	9.9	27.7	0.5	9.9	12.6	10.6	9.2
Honduras	1995	9.7	7.5	8.4	25.3	0.0	8.4	12.9	9.2	7.5
	2001	7.3	7.0	7.5	9.5	1.9	7.5	11.6	6.7	6.6
Hungary	1991	12.6	10.9	10.0	18.9	0.0	10.0	5.5	12.3	11.7
	1997	8.2	14.7	4.5	10.5	0.0	4.5	6.8	4.5	3.8
Iceland	1993	3.6	7.5	3.1	5.5	0.0	3.1	5.7	3.5	2.6
	2001	5.2	8.1	3.4	5.3	0.0	3.4	4.2	4.8	2.8
India	1990	79.0	43.6	56.2	97.1	0.9	56.2	25.4	79.9	70.8
	2001	30.9	12.4	28.2	91.8	0.1	28.2	28.5	30.6	29.0
Indonesia	1989	22.0	19.7	13.2	50.5	0.3	13.2	5.9	22.1	15.1
	2000	8.4	10.8	5.4	11.2	0.0	5.4	2.8	8.9	6.6
Iran, Islamic Rep.	2000	4.9	4.2	3.1	0.6	0.0	3.1	0.9	5.0	3.8
Israel	1993	7.8	12.3	4.0	15.8	0.0	4.0	1.9	7.9	4.4
Jamaica	1996	21.3	8.8	19.8	45.1	41.9	19.8	14.2	20.7	20.9
	2001	10.7	11.0	10.3	36.6	0.3	10.3	9.5	9.7	10.1
Japan	1988	6.0	8.1	3.6	8.7	11.3	3.6	4.4	4.7	2.7
	2001	5.1	7.5	2.1	7.6	2.1	2.1	2.5	3.9	1.7
Jordan	2000	22.8	16.6	18.6	63.1	0.4	18.6	16.9	22.1	19.8
	2001	16.2	15.6	13.5	46.1	0.3	13.5	13.9	15.4	13.3
Kenya	1994	32.1	13.7	21.5	88.3	0.1	21.5	17.0	31.9	23.3
	2001	20.2	13.6	15.5	44.3	0.1	15.5	19.6	19.9	12.5
Korea, Rep.	1988	18.8	7.9	13.8	73.0	10.3	13.8	8.2	18.6	17.0
	1999	8.7	5.9	6.0	4.8	0.8	6.0	5.6	7.8	6.1
Kyrgyz Republic	1995	0.0	0.0	0.0	0.0	15.9	0.0	0.0	0.0	0.0
Lao PDR	2000	9.4	7.5	14.2	11.4	2.1	14.2	14.7	8.6	12.7
Latvia	1996	4.4	7.5	2.5	2.2	0.0	2.5	1.5	3.2	2.6
	2001	4.0	7.4	2.6	2.9	0.0	2.6	4.3	2.4	1.6
Lebanon	1999	12.6	9.9	12.0	24.0	0.1	12.0	11.9	12.4	12.3
	2001	8.3	11.2	12.0	13.0	0.7	12.0	21.3	6.8	6.2
Libya	1996	27.4	37.1	21.3	58.8	0.4	21.3	9.7	27.3	25.6
Lithuania	1995	3.9	8.6	2.8	7.1	0.0	2.8	3.7	2.5	1.8
	1997	3.9	8.0	2.4	6.5	0.0	2.4	3.3	2.8	1.8
Macedonia, FYR	2001	15.9	11.6	13.8	47.4	0.0	13.8	16.4	14.9	12.4
Madagascar	1995	7.7	5.9	5.3	6.0	0.0	5.3	2.9	7.7	6.3
Malawi	1994	31.6	14.5	23.1	87.5	0.0	23.1	12.9	31.7	26.6
	2001	12.6	10.5	8.2	40.1	0.0	8.2	16.1	12.2	7.1
Malaysia	1988	17.0	15.1	9.9	46.4	6.7	9.9	4.6	17.3	10.8
	1997	9.2	33.3	5.8	24.7	0.4	5.8	10.0	10.2	5.5
Maldives	2000	22.1	15.8	19.6	65.2	0.0	19.6	14.9	23.2	21.5
	2001	22.1	15.8	19.6	65.2	0.0	19.6	14.9	23.2	21.5
Mali	1995	16.4	12.8	9.8	43.1	0.0	9.8	13.4	16.1	8.5
	2001	12.9	6.9	9.4	46.7	0.0	9.4	13.9	12.5	8.4
Malta	1997	8.7	5.6	8.8	6.0	0.0	8.8	6.2	8.9	9.3
	2000	8.8	5.7	9.8	6.9	0.4	9.8	6.8	8.8	10.3
Mauritania	2001	12.1	7.4	9.0	40.4	0.0	9.0	6.8	12.1	10.5
Mauritius	1995	36.2	28.4	20.7	64.7	0.0	20.7	25.7	37.2	22.9
	1998	31.2	27.8	24.5	58.0	0.0	24.5	15.3	32.0	27.0
Mexico	1991	13.4	4.3	12.0	20.9	0.0	12.0	8.3	13.4	13.0
	2001	16.2	9.3	15.4	50.8	0.5	15.4	19.9	16.1	14.7
Moldova	1996	6.5	9.3	2.1	20.6	1.2	2.1	0.8	4.7	2.7
	2001	4.5	5.5	2.6	0.1	0.7	2.6	1.6	3.9	2.7
Morocco	1993	66.6	29.5	45.3	96.8	0.1	45.3	30.2	67.3	55.2
	2001	32.6	20.5	25.4	79.1	0.0	25.4	29.0	31.1	24.6
Mozambique	1994	5.0	0.0	5.0	0.0	0.0	5.0	5.0	5.0	5.0
	2001	13.4	11.3	13.8	31.2	0.0	13.8	17.9	13.2	11.2
Nepal	1993	22.0	17.8	17.5	59.9	0.1	17.5	9.3	23.1	21.0
	2000	14.7	13.4	16.8	18.3	0.5	16.8	13.6	14.3	19.9
New Zealand	1992	10.5	11.0	8.5	36.2	2.7	8.5	4.0	11.0	9.4
	2000	3.4	4.4	2.4	0.0	5.8	2.4	0.5	3.6	2.8
Nicaragua	1995	7.4	7.9	5.0	19.5	0.0	5.0	7.1	7.3	4.6
	2001	3.8	5.9	3.0	0.2	0.0	3.0	4.2	3.4	2.6

6.6 Tariff barriers

		All products					Primary products		Manufactured products	
	Year	Simple mean tariff %	Standard deviation of tariff rates %	Weighted mean tariff %	Share of lines with international peaks %	Share of lines with specific tariffs %	Simple mean tariff %	Weighted mean tariff %	Simple mean tariff %	Weighted mean tariff %
Niger	2001	14.5	6.7	13.2	57.6	0.0	13.2	12.9	14.4	12.0
Nigeria	1988	26.0	16.7	23.8	63.0	0.3	23.8	32.4	25.3	21.4
	1995	21.8	15.7	20.0	9.7	80.5	20.0	20.8	19.9	19.6
Norway	1988	1.9	5.2	0.8	5.0	8.0	0.8	0.2	2.0	0.8
	2001	3.3	14.0	1.6	4.0	8.4	1.6	2.1	2.7	1.5
Oman	1992	5.5	8.2	7.6	1.5	0.0	7.6	14.2	5.1	5.4
	1997	4.7	1.2	4.5	0.0	0.0	4.5	3.6	4.9	4.9
Pakistan	1995	50.8	21.6	46.3	92.3	3.5	46.3	24.0	51.5	50.8
	2001	20.6	19.2	14.7	58.5	0.5	14.7	8.5	20.5	16.8
Panama	1997	15.2	13.2	10.5	36.5	0.1	10.5	9.6	14.6	11.0
	2001	9.3	7.2	7.1	1.2	0.2	7.1	6.0	8.8	7.5
Papua New Guinea	1997	21.2	18.5	15.3	33.4	1.4	15.3	21.8	19.4	13.7
Paraguay	1991	15.8	11.4	12.6	42.3	0.0	12.6	3.6	15.7	14.5
	2001	10.7	6.2	12.6	29.2	0.0	12.6	9.6	10.6	11.9
Peru	1993	17.4	4.2	15.9	23.5	0.0	15.9	15.5	17.2	16.1
	2000	13.1	2.9	12.9	12.3	0.0	12.9	13.9	12.9	12.3
Philippines	1988	28.0	14.2	22.4	77.2	0.1	22.4	18.5	27.5	23.4
	2001	7.0	7.3	4.0	6.9	0.0	4.0	5.9	6.5	3.4
Poland	1991	12.2	9.0	10.4	24.6	0.0	10.4	8.2	12.2	11.2
	2000	10.0	9.8	7.3	14.3	4.5	7.3	6.2	8.3	7.7
Romania	1991	19.2	8.3	12.0	55.7	0.0	12.0	8.1	18.9	17.9
	2001	18.1	15.9	13.7	45.9	0.0	13.7	11.4	15.7	14.1
Russian Federation	1993	7.8	9.9	6.3	3.3	0.0	6.3	3.9	9.3	7.4
	2001	11.1	5.4	8.4	11.0	17.3	8.4	7.6	11.0	8.7
Rwanda	1993	28.5	26.9	25.7	60.2	1.2	25.7	35.8	27.5	21.9
	2001	10.0	7.6	8.1	13.1	0.0	8.1	12.4	9.2	6.4
Saudi Arabia	1994	12.5	3.3	10.9	10.2	0.1	10.9	9.1	12.6	11.5
	2000	12.3	3.1	10.5	8.2	4.0	10.5	7.9	12.4	11.4
Senegal	2001	14.0	6.8	8.5	53.5	0.0	8.5	6.5	13.8	10.3
Singapore	1989	0.5	2.2	0.5	0.1	1.1	0.5	2.5	0.5	0.6
	2001	0.0	0.0	0.0	0.0	0.2	0.0	0.0	0.0	0.0
Slovenia	1999	11.9	6.6	11.5	21.0	3.2	11.5	7.5	11.7	12.1
	2001	11.4	7.0	9.9	23.1	0.0	9.9	7.4	11.1	10.4
Solomon Islands	1995	37.5	48.5	34.6	52.2	1.8	34.6	35.9	36.8	34.1
South Africa	1988	12.7	11.8	12.1	32.4	18.8	12.1	3.6	12.8	12.3
	2001	11.0	11.7	5.0	32.9	2.2	5.0	1.9	11.1	5.8
Sri Lanka	1990	28.3	24.5	26.9	51.6	1.4	26.9	32.3	27.7	24.2
	2001	9.8	9.3	7.2	21.8	0.7	7.2	14.6	9.2	5.2
Sudan	1996	5.3	11.9	4.4	8.9	0.0	4.4	3.4	4.7	4.0
Switzerland	1990	0.0	0.0	0.0	0.0	53.1	0.0	0.0	0.0	0.0
	2001	0.0	0.0	0.0	0.0	38.9	0.0	0.0	0.0	0.0
Tanzania	1993	14.4	10.7	15.6	42.6	0.0	15.6	19.9	13.8	15.0
	2000	18.2	8.4	14.5	71.2	0.0	14.5	16.1	18.0	13.6
Thailand	1989	38.5	19.5	33.0	72.9	21.8	33.0	24.3	39.0	34.9
	2000	17.0	14.3	9.7	47.1	1.2	9.7	7.7	15.9	10.1
Togo	2001	14.5	6.7	12.6	58.2	0.0	12.6	10.5	14.4	12.5
Trinidad and Tobago	1991	19.9	14.9	12.9	40.3	0.0	12.9	10.9	18.5	14.1
	2001	11.2	10.6	4.6	36.5	0.6	4.6	3.2	10.2	5.8
Tunisia	1990	28.4	10.0	26.6	97.3	0.0	26.6	17.4	28.6	28.5
	1998	30.6	12.6	26.3	91.9	0.0	26.3	18.5	30.5	27.9
Turkey	1993	7.4	5.0	6.1	5.9	0.0	6.1	7.9	7.6	5.3
	1999	8.4	14.7	5.4	9.8	0.7	5.4	5.5	6.3	5.3
Turkmenistan	1998	0.0	0.0	0.0	0.0	0.0	0.0	0.0	0.0	0.0
Uganda	1994	17.0	9.3	13.9	54.5	0.0	13.9	17.4	16.7	12.3
	2001	8.2	5.7	6.9	0.0	0.0	6.9	6.0	8.0	6.3
Ukraine	1995	9.1	9.5	9.8	14.7	0.0	9.8	15.7	7.5	6.3
	1997	10.5	11.0	5.3	24.1	0.0	5.3	3.4	8.1	7.2
United States	1989	5.6	6.8	3.8	8.1	12.4	3.8	2.0	5.9	4.1
	2001	4.0	11.1	1.8	5.7	7.6	1.8	1.2	3.9	1.9
Uruguay	1992	7.5	5.8	5.9	0.0	0.0	5.9	5.8	7.4	5.8
	2001	11.0	8.0	6.6	40.7	0.0	6.6	2.1	11.1	8.4
Uzbekistan	2001	9.6	12.2	4.2	24.1	0.0	4.2	4.6	9.7	4.3
Venezuela, RB	1992	15.7	11.4	16.4	47.7	0.4	16.4	14.7	15.4	16.5
	2000	12.6	5.9	13.5	25.6	0.0	13.5	13.6	12.5	13.3
Vietnam	1994	12.7	17.8	18.4	32.4	1.0	18.4	46.5	11.8	12.9
	2001	15.0	18.5	15.1	35.9	0.0	15.1	21.7	13.4	9.3
Zambia	1993	25.2	11.1	17.9	90.9	0.0	17.9	12.4	24.4	20.0
	1997	14.7	8.8	13.1	31.7	0.0	13.1	13.9	14.5	12.9
Zimbabwe	1996	40.8	15.0	38.2	94.4	1.5	38.2	40.4	41.3	38.8
	2001	19.0	18.6	15.6	37.5	1.7	15.6	20.8	17.6	15.3

About the data

Poor people in developing countries work primarily in agriculture and labor-intensive manufactures, the very sectors that confront the greatest trade barriers. Removing barriers to merchandise trade could increase growth by about 0.5 percent a year in these countries. If trade in services (retailing, business, financial, and telecommunications services) were also liberalized, growth would be even higher.

In general, tariffs in high-income countries on imports from developing countries, though low, are four times those collected from other high-income countries. But protection is also an issue for developing countries, which maintain high tariffs on agricultural commodities, labor-intensive manufactures, and other products and services. In some developing regions new trade policies could make the difference between achieving important Millennium Development Goals—such as reducing poverty, lowering maternal and child mortality, and improving educational attainment—and falling short by a large margin.

Countries use a combination of tariff and nontariff measures to regulate their imports. The most common form of tariff is an ad valorem duty, based on the value of the import, but tariffs may also be levied on a specific, or per unit, basis or may combine ad valorem and specific rates. Tariffs may be used to raise fiscal revenues or to protect domestic industries from foreign competition—or both. Nontariff barriers, which limit the quantity of imports of a particular good, take many forms. Some common ones are quotas, prohibitions, licensing schemes, export restraint arrangements, and health and quarantine measures.

Nontariff barriers are generally considered less desirable than tariffs because changes in an exporting country's efficiency and costs no longer result in changes in market share in the importing country. Further, the quotas or licenses that regulate trade become very valuable, and resources are often wasted in attempts to acquire these assets. A high percentage of products subject to nontariff barriers suggests a protectionist trade regime, but the frequency of nontariff barriers does not measure how much they restrict trade. Moreover, a wide range of domestic policies and regulations (such as health regulations) may act as nontariff barriers. Because of the difficulty of combining nontariff barriers into an aggregate indicator, they are not included in this table.

The tariff rates used in calculating the indicators in the table are effectively applied rates, which reflect the rates actually applied to partners in preferential trade agreements such as the North American Free Trade Agreement. Countries typically maintain a hierarchy of trade preferences applicable to specific trading partners. Where these rates were not available, most-favored-nation rates, which are equal to or higher than effectively applied rates, are used.

Two measures of average tariffs are shown: the simple and the weighted mean tariff. Weighted mean tariffs are weighted by the value of the country's trade with each of its trading partners. Simple averages are often a better indicator of tariff protection than weighted averages, which are biased downward because higher tariffs discourage trade and reduce the weights applied to these tariffs. Specific duties—duties not expressed as a proportion of the declared value—are not included in the table, but work is under way to estimate ad valorem equivalents.

Some countries set fairly uniform tariff rates across all imports. Others are more selective, setting high tariffs to protect favored domestic industries. The standard deviation of tariffs is a measure of the dispersion of tariff rates around their mean value. Highly dispersed rates increase the costs of protection substantially. But these nominal tariff rates tell only part of the story. The effective rate of protection—the degree to which the value added in an industry is protected—may exceed the nominal rate if the tariff system systematically differentiates among imports of raw materials, intermediate products, and finished goods.

Two other measures of tariff coverage are shown: the share of tariff lines with international peaks (those for which ad valorem tariff rates exceed 15 percent) and the share of tariff lines with specific duties (those not covered by ad valorem rates). Some countries—for example, Switzerland—apply only specific duties.

The indicators in the table were calculated from data supplied by the United Nations Conference on Trade and Development (UNCTAD) and the World Trade Organization (WTO). Data are classified using the Harmonized System of trade at the six- or eight-digit level. Tariff line data were matched to Standard International Trade Classification (SITC) revision 2 codes to define the commodity groups and import weights. Import weights were calculated for 1995 using the United Nations Statistics Division's Commodity Trade (COMTRADE) database. Data are shown only for the first and last year for which complete data are available. To conserve space, countries that are members of the European Union have not been included. Instead, data for the whole of the European Union are shown.

Definitions

• **Primary products** are commodities classified in SITC revision 2 sections 0–4 plus division 68 (nonferrous metals). • **Manufactured products** are commodities classified in SITC revision 2 sections 5–9 excluding division 68. • **Simple mean tariff** is the unweighted average of the effectively applied rates for all products subject to tariffs. • **Standard deviation of tariff rates** measures the average dispersion of tariff rates around the simple mean. • **Weighted mean tariff** is the average of effectively applied rates weighted by the product import shares corresponding to each partner country. • **International peaks** are tariff rates that exceed 15 percent. • **Specific tariffs** are tariffs that are set on a per unit basis or that combine ad valorem and per unit rates.

Data sources

All indicators in the table were calculated by World Bank staff using the World Integrated Trade Solution (WITS) system. Tariff data were provided by UNCTAD and the WTO. Data on global imports come from the United Nations Statistics Division's COMTRADE database.

	Net private capital flows		Foreign direct investment		Portfolio investment flows				Bank and trade-related lending	
					Bonds		Equity			
	$ millions		$ millions		$ millions		$ millions		$ millions	
	1990	2001	1990	2001	1990	2001	1990	2001	1990	2001
Afghanistan	..	..	..	..	..	..	..	..	31	–4
Albania	31	203	0	207	0	0	0	0	–409	–953
Algeria	–424	243	0	1,196	–16	0	0	0	570	–222
Angola	235	897	–335	1,119	0	0	0	0	–1,195	–3,216
Argentina	–135	–3,897	1,836	3,214	–857	–3,815	80	–81		4
Armenia	..	74	..	70	..	0	..	0	..	..
Australia	..	..	8,111	4,394	..	..	..	..	..	..
Austria	..	..	653	5,898	..	..	..	..	..	..
Azerbaijan	..	216	..	227	..	0	..	0	..	–11
Bangladesh	59	304	3	78	0	0	0	–4	55	230
Belarus	..	83	..	96	..	0	..	0	..	–13
Belgium [a]	..	..	8,047	73,635	..	..	..	..	..	..
Benin	62	131	62	131	0	0	0	0	0	0
Bolivia	3	637	27	662	0	0	0	0	–24	–26
Bosnia and Herzegovina	..	226	0	222	..	0	..	0	..	4
Botswana	77	55	96	57	0	0	0	0	–19	–2
Brazil	666	23,336	989	22,636	129	1,704	103	2,482	–555	–3,485
Bulgaria	–42	1,043	4	692	65	202	0	–9	–111	158
Burkina Faso	–1	26	0	26	0	0	0	0	–1	0
Burundi	–5	0	1	0	0	0	0	0	–6	0
Cambodia	0	113	0	113	0	0	0	0	0	0
Cameroon	–124	–16	–113	75	0	0	0	0	–12	–91
Canada	..	..	7,581	27,438	..	..	..	..	..	..
Central African Republic	0	8	1	8	0	0	0	0	–1	0
Chad	8	80	9	80	0	0	0	0	–1	–1
Chile	2,216	5,727	661	4,476	–7	1,527	367	–219	1,194	–57
China	8,258	43,238	3,487	44,241	–48	400	151	3,015	4,668	–4,417
Hong Kong, China	..	..	..	22,834	..	..	..	..	..	..
Colombia	345	3,597	500	2,328	–4	1,961	0	–43	–151	–650
Congo, Dem. Rep.	–27	32	–15	32	0	0	0	0	–12	0
Congo, Rep.	–93	59	7	59	0	0	0	0	–100	0
Costa Rica	22	630	163	454	–42	208	0	0	–99	–32
Côte d'Ivoire	57	137	48	246	–1	0	0	1	10	–110
Croatia	..	2,236	..	1,512	..	790	..	6	..	–72
Cuba	..	..	..	..	..	..	..	..	..	..
Czech Republic	741	5,194	72	4,924	0	–263	0	616	669	–83
Denmark	..	..	1,132	7,238	..	..	..	..	..	..
Dominican Republic	129	1,729	133	1,198	0	480	0	0	–3	50
Ecuador	184	1,444	126	1,330	0	0	0	1	58	113
Egypt, Arab Rep.	668	2,068	734	510	–1	1,500	0	39	–65	19
El Salvador	7	674	2	268	0	351	0	0	6	55
Eritrea	..	34	..	34	..	0	..	0	..	0
Estonia	..	624	..	539	..	62	..	32	..	–9
Ethiopia	–45	10	12	20	0	0	0	0	–57	–10
Finland	..	..	812	3,739	..	..	..	..	..	..
France	..	..	13,183	52,504	..	..	..	..	..	..
Gabon	103	170	74	200	0	0	0	0	29	–30
Gambia, The	–8	36	0	36	0	0	0	0	–8	0
Georgia	..	173	..	160	..	0	..	0	..	13
Germany	..	..	2,532	31,526	..	..	..	..	..	..
Ghana	–5	244	15	89	0	0	0	0	–20	154
Greece	..	..	1,005	1,585	..	..	..	..	..	..
Guatemala	44	403	48	456	–11	–31	0	0	7	–22
Guinea	–1	1	18	2	0	0	0	0	–19	0
Guinea-Bissau	2	30	2	30	0	0	0	0	0	0
Haiti	0	3	0	3	0	0	0	0	0	0

	Net private capital flows		Foreign direct investment		Portfolio investment flows				Bank and trade-related lending	
					Bonds		Equity			
	$ millions		$ millions		$ millions		$ millions		$ millions	
	1990	**2001**	**1990**	**2001**	**1990**	**2001**	**1990**	**2001**	**1990**	**2001**
Honduras	75	126	44	195	0	0	0	0	32	−69
Hungary	28	3,952	311	2,440	921	94	175	134	−1,379	1,284
India	1,947	3,534	237	3,403	147	−131	105	1,739	1,458	−1,477
Indonesia	3,386	−7,312	1,093	−3,278	26	−1,376	463	164	1,804	−2,822
Iran, Islamic Rep.	−392	1,049	−362	33	0	0	0	0	−30	1,016
Iraq	..	..	..	..	..	..	..	..	..	..
Ireland	..	..	627	9,865	..	..	..	..	..	..
Israel	..	..	151	3,224	..	..	..	..	..	..
Italy	..	..	6,411	14,874	..	..	..	..	..	..
Jamaica	92	1,385	138	614	0	819	0	0	−46	−48
Japan	..	..	1,777	6,191	..	..	..	..	..	..
Jordan	252	−114	38	100	0	−45	0	−145	214	−25
Kazakhstan	..	4,947	..	2,763	..	0	..	55	..	2,128
Kenya	122	−37	57	5	0	0	0	0	65	−43
Korea, Dem. Rep.	..	..	..	..	..	..	..	..	..	..
Korea, Rep.	1,038	9,279	788	3,198	151	530	518	10,165	−418	−4,614
Kuwait	..	..	..	−39	..	..	..	..	..	..
Kyrgyz Republic	..	−73	..	5	..	0	..	0	..	−78
Lao PDR	6	24	6	24	0	0	0	0	0	0
Latvia	..	880	..	177	..	179	..	6	..	518
Lebanon	13	2,757	7	249	0	2,500	0	0	6	7
Lesotho	17	113	17	117	0	0	0	0	0	−4
Liberia	0	13	0	13	0	0	0	0	0	0
Libya	..	..	..	..	..	..	..	..	..	..
Lithuania	..	521	..	446	..	179	..	−16	..	−88
Macedonia, FYR	..	466	..	443	..	0	..	0	..	23
Madagascar	7	9	22	11	0	0	0	0	−15	−2
Malawi	25	58	23	58	0	0	0	0	2	0
Malaysia	908	855	2,332	554	−1,239	1,464	432	−650	−617	−513
Mali	5	103	6	103	0	0	0	0	−1	0
Mauritania	5	27	7	30	0	0	0	0	−1	−3
Mauritius	86	−75	41	−48	0	0	0	0	45	−27
Mexico	9,600	28,079	2,549	24,731	661	−1,651	1,995	150	4,396	4,849
Moldova	..	70	..	94	..	−25	..	4	..	−2
Mongolia	..	62	..	63	..	0	..	0	..	−1
Morocco	341	2,633	165	2,658	0	−29	0	−8	176	12
Mozambique	35	450	9	480	0	0	0	0	26	−30
Myanmar	153	145	161	208	0	0	0	0	−8	−63
Namibia	..	..	..	..	..	..	..	..	..	..
Nepal	−8	19	6	19	0	0	0	0	−14	0
Netherlands	..	..	10,676	51,239	..	..	..	..	..	..
New Zealand	..	..	1,735	1,731	..	..	..	..	..	..
Nicaragua	20	13	0	132	0	0	0	0	20	−120
Niger	51	7	41	13	0	0	0	0	10	−6
Nigeria	467	920	588	1,104	0	0	0	0	−121	−184
Norway	..	..	1,003	2,166	..	..	..	..	..	..
Oman	−257	−867	142	42	0	0	0	−3	−400	−905
Pakistan	182	−308	245	383	0	−45	0	−130	−63	−516
Panama	130	1,799	136	513	−2	1,014	0	0	−4	273
Papua New Guinea	204	2	155	63	0	0	0	0	49	−61
Paraguay	68	−14	77	79	0	0	0	0	−9	−93
Peru	59	1,400	41	1,064	0	0	0	42	18	294
Philippines	779	2,076	530	1,792	395	761	139	383	−286	−859
Poland	71	9,611	89	5,713	0	667	0	−307	−18	3,537
Portugal	..	..	2,610	5,945	..	..	..	..	..	..
Puerto Rico	..	..	..	..	..	..	..	..	..	..

	Net private capital flows		Foreign direct investment		Portfolio investment flows				Bank and trade-related lending	
					Bonds		Equity			
	$ millions		$ millions		$ millions		$ millions		$ millions	
	1990	2001	1990	2001	1990	2001	1990	2001	1990	2001
Romania	4	2,633	0	1,157	0	375	0	8	4	1,094
Russian Federation	5,556	1,488	0	2,469	310	−679	0	543	5,246	−845
Rwanda	6	5	8	5	0	0	0	0	−2	0
Saudi Arabia	..	..	..	..	..	..	..	..	..	..
Senegal	42	167	57	126	0	0	0	0	−15	41
Sierra Leone	36	4	32	4	0	0	0	0	4	0
Singapore	..	..	5,575	8,609	..	..	..	..	..	..
Slovak Republic	278	303	0	1,475	0	−283	0	0	278	−889
Slovenia	..	..	..	503	..	..	..	..	..	..
Somalia	6	0	6	0	0	0	0	0	0	0
South Africa	..	6,627	..	7,162	..	1,938	..	−962	..	−1,511
Spain	..	..	13,984	21,540	..	..	..	..	..	..
Sri Lanka	54	243	43	172	0	159	0	0	10	−88
Sudan	0	574	0	574	0	0	0	0	0	0
Swaziland	28	35	30	21	0	0	0	0	−2	14
Sweden	..	..	1,982	13,085	..	..	..	..	..	..
Switzerland	..	..	5,987	8,628	..	..	..	..	..	..
Syrian Arab Republic	63	204	72	205	0	0	0	0	−9	−1
Tajikistan	..	39	..	22	..	0	..	0	..	17
Tanzania	3	197	0	224	0	0	0	0	3	−28
Thailand	4,371	−3,052	2,444	3,820	−87	−1,605	440	18	1,574	−5,285
Togo	18	67	18	67	0	0	0	0	0	0
Trinidad and Tobago	−68	830	109	835	−52	0	0	0	−126	−5
Tunisia	−116	1,108	76	457	−60	453	5	−15	−137	213
Turkey	1,836	906	684	3,266	597	−493	89	−79	466	−1,788
Turkmenistan	..	..	..	..	..	..	..	..	..	..
Uganda	16	147	0	145	0	0	0	0	16	2
Ukraine	..	426	..	792	..	−133	..	−734	..	502
United Arab Emirates	..	..	..	..	..	..	..	..	..	..
United Kingdom	..	..	33,504	63,109	..	..	..	..	..	..
United States	..	..	48,490	130,800	..	..	..	..	..	..
Uruguay	−192	796	0	318	−16	512	0	0	−176	−34
Uzbekistan	..	46	..	71	..	0	..	0	..	−25
Venezuela, RB	−126	2,644	451	3,448	345	240	0	−74	−922	−970
Vietnam	16	710	16	1,300	0	0	0	0	0	−590
West Bank and Gaza	..	..	..	..	..	..	..	..	..	..
Yemen, Rep.	30	−210	−131	−205	0	0	0	0	161	−5
Yugoslavia, Fed. Rep.	−837	10	67	0	0	0	0	0	−904	10
Zambia	194	126	203	72	0	0	0	0	−9	54
Zimbabwe	85	−28	−12	5	−30	0	0	0	127	−33
World	.. s	.. s	**202,547 s**	**746,470 s**	.. s	.. s	.. s	.. s	.. s	.. s
Low income	7,242	2,737	2,610	8,977	142	−1,711	568	1,040	3,923	−5,569
Middle income	36,978	165,240	21,494	161,690	889	11,791	3,979	4,918	10,617	−13,159
Lower middle income	20,486	79,848	9,157	82,262	1,140	6,513	827	2,843	9,362	−11,770
Upper middle income	16,493	85,392	12,337	79,427	−251	5,279	3,152	2,075	1,255	−1,389
Low & middle income	44,220	167,977	24,103	170,666	1,032	10,080	4,546	5,958	14,539	−18,728
East Asia & Pacific	18,210	36,817	10,341	48,913	−952	−357	1,625	2,930	7,197	−14,668
Europe & Central Asia	7,668	36,162	1,227	30,130	1,893	671	264	258	4,284	5,103
Latin America & Carib.	14,050	72,067	8,177	69,309	101	3,467	2,545	2,258	3,227	−2,967
Middle East & N. Africa	595	7,462	2,810	5,460	−126	4,379	5	−132	−2,094	−2,245
South Asia	2,240	3,798	542	4,066	147	−18	105	1,606	1,446	−1,856
Sub-Saharan Africa	1,458	11,670	1,008	12,788	−31	1,938	2	−961	480	−2,095
High income	..	..	178,443	575,804	..	..	..	..	..	..
Europe EMU	..	..	60,540	272,350	..	..	..	..	..	..

a. Includes Luxembourg.

About the data

The data on foreign direct investment are based on balance of payments data reported by the International Monetary Fund (IMF), supplemented by data on net foreign direct investment reported by the Organisation for Economic Co-operation and Development (OECD) and official national sources. The internationally accepted definition of foreign direct investment is provided in the fifth edition of the IMF's *Balance of Payments Manual* (1993).

Under this definition foreign direct investment has three components: equity investment, reinvested earnings, and short- and long-term intercompany loans between parent firms and foreign affiliates. But many countries fail to report reinvested earnings, and the definition of long-term loans differs among countries. Foreign direct investment, as distinguished from other kinds of international investment, is made to establish a lasting interest in or effective management control over an enterprise in another country. As a guideline, the IMF suggests that investments should account for at least 10 percent of voting stock to be counted as foreign direct investment. In practice, many countries set a higher threshold.

The OECD has also published a definition, in consultation with the IMF, Eurostat, and the United Nations. Because of the multiplicity of sources and differences in definitions and reporting methods, there may be more than one estimate of foreign direct investment for a country and data may not be comparable across countries.

Foreign direct investment data do not give a complete picture of international investment in an economy. Balance of payments data on foreign direct investment do not include capital raised locally, which has become an important source of financing for investment projects in some developing countries. In addition, foreign direct investment data capture only cross-border investment flows involving equity participation and thus omit nonequity cross-border transactions such as intrafirm flows of goods and services. For a detailed discussion of the data issues, see the World Bank's *World Debt Tables 1993–94* (volume 1, chapter 3).

Portfolio flow data are compiled from several market and official sources, including Euromoney databases and publications, Micropal, Lipper Analytical Services, published reports of private investment houses, central banks, national securities and exchange commissions, national stock exchanges, and the World Bank's Debtor Reporting System.

Gross statistics on international bond and equity issues are produced by aggregating individual transactions reported by market sources. Transactions of public and publicly guaranteed bonds are reported through the Debtor Reporting System by World Bank member economies that have received either loans from the International Bank for Reconstruction and Development or credits from the International Development Association. Information on private nonguaranteed bonds is collected from market sources, because official national sources reporting to the Debtor Reporting System are not asked to report the breakdown between private nonguaranteed bonds and private nonguaranteed loans. Information on transactions by nonresidents in local equity markets is gathered from national authorities, investment positions of mutual funds, and market sources.

The volume of portfolio investment reported by the World Bank generally differs from that reported by other sources because of differences in the sources, in the classification of economies, and in the method used to adjust and disaggregate reported information. Differences in reporting arise particularly for foreign investments in local equity markets because clarity, adequate disaggregation, and comprehensive and periodic reporting are lacking in many developing economies. By contrast, capital flows through international debt and equity instruments are well recorded, and for these the differences in reporting lie primarily in the classification of economies, the exchange rates used, whether particular tranches (installments) of the transactions are included, and the treatment of certain offshore issuances.

Definitions

• **Net private capital flows** consist of private debt and nondebt flows. Private debt flows include commercial bank lending, bonds, and other private credits, as well as foreign direct investment and portfolio equity investment. • **Foreign direct investment** is net inflows of investment to acquire a lasting management interest (10 percent or more of voting stock) in an enterprise operating in an economy other than that of the investor. It is the sum of equity capital, reinvestment of earnings, other long-term capital, and short-term capital, as shown in the balance of payments. • **Portfolio investment flows** are net and include non-debt-creating portfolio equity flows (the sum of country funds, depository receipts, and direct purchases of shares by foreign investors) and portfolio debt flows (bond issues purchased by foreign investors). • **Bank and trade-related lending** covers commercial bank lending and other private credits.

Data sources

The data are compiled from a variety of public and private sources, including the World Bank's Debtor Reporting System, the IMF's International Financial Statistics and Balance of Payments databases, and other sources mentioned in *About the data*. These data are also published in the World Bank's *Global Development Finance 2003*.

Net flows to part I countries

$ millions, 2001	Official development assistance				Other official flows	Private flows					Net grants by NGOs	Total net flows
	Total	Bilateral grants	Bilateral loans	Contributions to multilateral institutions		Total	Foreign direct investment	Bilateral portfolio investment	Multilateral portfolio investment	Private export credits		
Australia	873	660	..	212	56	43	357	−314	..	..	211	1,183
Austria	533	334	7	191	13	279	277	..	..	2	57	882
Belgium	867	507	−4	365	7	−712	530	−1,383	..	142	141	304
Canada	1,533	1,222	−22	333	−98	−12	633	−601	..	−44	116	1,538
Denmark	1,634	1,048	−14	600	−4	998	998	..	..	..	17	2,645
Finland	389	229	−4	165	5	915	624	−70	..	361	9	1,317
France	4,198	2,920	−325	1,602	−39	12,168	8,049	3,838	..	280	..	16,327
Germany	4,990	2,858	−5	2,136	−663	737	1,798	−748	−863	551	808	5,872
Greece	202	81	1	119	..	..	..	..	..	..	..	202
Ireland	287	184	..	102	..	347	..	347	..	..	101	735
Italy	1,627	546	−104	1,185	55	−1,903	1,221	−3,617	..	494	32	−189
Japan	9,847	4,742	2,716	2,389	−854	5,380	6,473	−354	−355	−384	235	14,608
Luxembourg	141	106	..	35	..	..	..	..	..	..	5	146
Netherlands	3,172	2,392	−167	948	42	−6,886	2,526	−8,462	−1,133	182	240	−3,432
New Zealand	112	85	..	27	..	16	16	..	..	..	11	139
Norway	1,346	938	2	406	..	−71	−131	..	..	60	210	1,485
Portugal	268	166	18	85	−1	1,503	1,273	..	..	230	5	1,775
Spain	1,737	966	184	588	146	9,640	10,160	..	..	−520	..	11,523
Sweden	1,666	1,185	20	461	1	1,394	507	..	..	888	16	3,077
Switzerland	908	643	1	263	6	−1,252	−1,107	..	−1	−144	180	−158
United Kingdom	4,579	2,643	−21	1,957	23	4,669	8,164	−3,001	..	−493	327	9,597
United States	11,429	8,954	−670	3,145	755	21,864	24,236	−1,773	−1,729	1,130	4,569	38,618
Total	**52,336**	**33,409**	**1,613**	**17,314**	**−549**	**49,117**	**66,602**	**−16,138**	**−4,082**	**2,735**	**7,289**	**108,193**

Net flows to part II countries

$ millions, 2001	Official aid				Other official flows	Private flows				Net grants by NGOs	Total net flows
	Total	Bilateral grants	Bilateral loans	Contributions to multilateral institutions		Total	Foreign direct investment	Bilateral portfolio investment	Private export credits		
Australia	5	2	..	3	3	−4,110	−2,816	−1,294	..	..	−4,102
Austria	212	161	..	50	..	2,453	2,453	..	..	6	2,671
Belgium	88	5	..	84	−16	−1,252	348	−1,614	14	10	−1,170
Canada	152	152	..	..	−67	4,548	4,489	59	..	..	4,633
Denmark	181	101	12	68	29	565	..	565	..	2	777
Finland	61	31	1	28	−3	1,106	307	787	12	..	1,164
France	1,334	1,021	−11	323	−75	21,705	5,400	16,615	−311	..	22,964
Germany	687	317	−72	442	3,258	10,925	5,685	5,975	−735	90	14,960
Greece	9	7	..	2	..	..	..	..	..	..	9
Ireland	..	..	..	..	..	3	..	3	..	..	3
Italy	281	22	−1	260	27	−1,030	634	−1,652	−12	..	−721
Japan	84	138	−113	59	−651	3,168	5,671	−3,670	1,167	..	2,602
Luxembourg	9	3	..	6	..	..	..	..	..	..	9
Netherlands	214	103	−7	117	−15	3,432	4,656	−1,175	−50	..	3,631
New Zealand	..	..	..	..	..	..	..	..	..	..	0
Norway	32	29	..	2	3	542	550	..	−8	..	577
Portugal	28	1	..	27	13	384	374	..	10	..	425
Spain	14	16	−2	..	..	1,056	1,056	..	..	..	1,070
Sweden	119	113	..	6	−1	295	361	..	−66	..	413
Switzerland	63	53	2	7	1	5,665	5,661	..	4	7	5,735
United Kingdom	461	87	..	374	..	−4,737	−2,074	−2,528	−135	4	−4,272
United States	1,542	1,605	−145	83	−266	19,371	15,972	3,360	39	3,031	23,678
Total	**5,574**	**3,967**	**−335**	**1,942**	**2,240**	**64,088**	**48,728**	**15,431**	**−70**	**3,151**	**75,053**

Note: Data may not sum to totals because of gaps in reporting.

Net financial flows from Development Assistance Committee members

6.8

About the data

The high-income members of the Development Assistance Committee (DAC) of the Organisation for Economic Co-operation and Development (OECD) are the main source of official external finance for developing countries. This table shows the flow of official and private financial resources from DAC members to official and private recipients in developing and transition economies.

DAC exists to help its members coordinate their development assistance and to encourage the expansion and improve the effectiveness of the aggregate resources flowing to recipient economies. In this capacity DAC monitors the flow of all financial resources, but its main concern is official development assistance (ODA). DAC has three criteria for ODA: It is undertaken by the official sector. It promotes the economic development and welfare of developing countries as a main objective. And it is provided on concessional terms, with a grant element of at least 25 percent on loans (calculated at a rate of discount of 10 percent).

This definition excludes nonconcessional flows from official creditors, which are classified as "other official flows," and military aid, which is not recorded in DAC statistics. The definition includes food aid, capital projects, emergency relief, technical cooperation, and postconflict peacekeeping efforts. Also included are contributions to multilateral institutions, such as the United Nations and its specialized agencies, and concessional funding to the multilateral development banks. In 1999, to avoid double counting extrabud-

getary expenditures reported by DAC countries and flows reported by the United Nations, all United Nations agencies revised their data to include only regular budgetary expenditures since 1990 (except for the World Food Programme and the United Nations High Commissioner for Refugees, which revised their data from 1996 onward).

DAC maintains a list of countries and territories that are aid recipients. Part I of the list comprises developing countries and territories considered by DAC members to be eligible for ODA. Part II comprises economies in transition: more advanced countries of Central and Eastern Europe, the countries of the former Soviet Union, and certain advanced developing countries and territories. Flows to these recipients that meet the criteria for ODA are termed official aid.

The data in the table were compiled from replies by DAC member countries to questionnaires issued by the DAC Secretariat. Net flows of ODA, official aid, and other official resources are defined as gross disbursements of grants and loans minus repayments of principal on earlier loans. Because the data are based on donor country reports, they do not provide a complete picture of the resources received by developing and transition economies, for two reasons. First, flows from DAC members are only part of the aggregate resource flows to these economies. Second, the data that record contributions to multilateral institutions measure the flow of resources made available to those institutions by DAC members, not the flow of resources from those institutions to developing and transition economies.

Definitions

• **Official development assistance** comprises grants and loans (net of repayments of principal) that meet the DAC definition of ODA and are made to countries and territories in part I of the DAC list of aid recipients. • **Official aid** comprises grants and loans (net of repayments) that meet the criteria for ODA and are made to countries and territories in part II of the DAC list of aid recipients. • **Bilateral grants** are transfers of money or in kind for which no repayment is required. • **Bilateral loans** are loans extended by governments or official agencies that have a grant element of at least 25 percent (calculated at a rate of discount of 10 percent). • **Contributions to multilateral institutions** are concessional funding received by multilateral institutions from DAC members in the form of grants or capital subscriptions. • **Other official flows** are transactions by the official sector whose main objective is other than development or whose grant element is less than 25 percent. • **Private flows** consist of flows at market terms financed from private sector resources in donor countries. They include changes in holdings of private long-term assets by residents of the reporting country. • **Foreign direct investment** is investment by residents of DAC member countries to acquire a lasting management interest (at least 10 percent of voting stock) in an enterprise operating in the recipient country. The data reflect changes in the net worth of subsidiaries in recipient countries whose parent company is in the DAC source country. • **Bilateral portfolio investment** covers bank lending and the purchase of bonds, shares, and real estate by residents of DAC member countries in recipient countries. • **Multilateral portfolio investment** records the transactions of private banks and nonbanks in DAC member countries in the securities issued by multilateral institutions. • **Private export credits** are loans extended to recipient countries by the private sector in DAC member countries to promote trade; they may be supported by an official guarantee. • **Net grants by NGOs** are private grants by nongovernmental organizations, net of subsidies from the official sector. • **Total net flows** comprise ODA or official aid flows, other official flows, private flows, and net grants by NGOs.

Data sources

The data on financial flows are compiled by DAC and published in its annual statistical report, *Geographical Distribution of Financial Flows to Aid Recipients*, and its annual *Development Co-operation Report*. Data are available in electronic format on the OECD's *International Development Statistics* CD-ROM and to registered users at http://www.oecd.org/dac/htm/online.htm.

6.8a

Official development assistance is one of several sources of financing to developing countries

Total net flows to recipient countries ($ billions), 2001

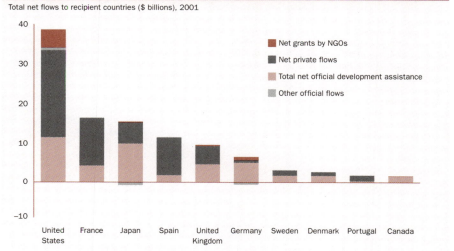

Net grants by NGOs
Net private flows
Total net official development assistance
Other official flows

Source: Organisation for Economic Co-operation and Development data.

6.9 Aid flows from Development Assistance Committee members

Net flows to part I countries

	Net official development assistance								Untied aid [a]	
	$ millions		% of GNI		average annual % change in volume [b] 1995–96 to	Per capita of donor country [b] $	$	% of general government disbursement		% of bilateral ODA commitments	
	1996	2001	1996	2001	2000–2001	1996	2001	1996	2001	1996	2001
Australia	1,074	873	0.27	0.25	0.6	46	49	0.76	0.74	78.1	59.3
Austria	557	533	0.24	0.29	0.2	51	66	0.46	0.57	..	..
Belgium	913	867	0.34	0.37	3.5	67	85	0.68	0.82	..	89.8
Canada	1,795	1,533	0.32	0.22	−2.6	59	51	0.68	0.57	31.5	31.7
Denmark	1,772	1,634	1.04	1.03	4.4	265	306	1.72	2.00	61.3	93.3
Finland	408	389	0.33	0.32	5.0	61	75	0.59	0.72	60.2	87.5
France	7,451	4,198	0.48	0.32	−6.6	95	72	0.93	0.66	38.7	66.6
Germany	7,601	4,990	0.32	0.27	−1.2	67	62	0.67	0.59	60.0	84.6
Greece	184	202	0.15	0.17	24.3	14	19	0.33	0.40	..	17.3
Ireland	179	287	0.31	0.33	11.9	43	74	0.67	0.92	..	100.0
Italy	2,416	1,627	0.20	0.15	−2.3	34	28	0.38	0.32	..	7.8
Japan	9,439	9,847	0.20	0.23	3.0	73	89	0.58	0.64	98.9	81.1
Luxembourg	82	141	0.44	0.82	18.1	156	325	1.05	1.89	94.4	..
Netherlands	3,246	3,172	0.81	0.82	5.0	161	195	1.73	1.97	82.2	91.2
New Zealand	122	112	0.21	0.25	5.6	22	30	0.49	0.61	..	..
Norway	1,311	1,346	0.84	0.83	1.7	278	299	1.82	1.95	88.4	98.9
Portugal	218	268	0.21	0.25	6.7	18	26	0.47	0.58	100.0	57.7
Spain	1,251	1,737	0.22	0.30	7.3	25	43	0.50	0.79	0.0	68.9
Sweden	1,999	1,666	0.84	0.81	4.4	173	207	1.27	1.52	78.9	86.5
Switzerland	1,026	908	0.34	0.34	3.0	108	123	..	..	92.9	96.1
United Kingdom	3,199	4,579	0.27	0.32	5.8	58	80	0.66	0.84	86.1	93.9
United States	9,377	11,429	0.12	0.11	3.2	38	39	0.37	0.36	28.4	..
Total or average	**55,622**	**52,336**	**0.25**	**0.22**	**1.8**	**59**	**63**	**0.63**	**0.61**	**71.3**	**79.1**

Net flows to part II countries

	Net official aid						
	$ millions		% of GNI		average annual % change in volume [b] 1995–96 to	Per capita of donor country [b] $	$
	1996	2001	1996	2001	2000–01	1996	2001
Australia	10	5	0.00	0.00	2.8	0	0
Austria	226	212	0.10	0.11	0.7	21	26
Belgium	70	88	0.03	0.04	7.0	5	9
Canada	181	152	0.03	0.02	−5.4	6	5
Denmark	120	181	0.07	0.11	10.3	18	34
Finland	57	61	0.05	0.05	3.6	9	12
France	711	1,334	0.05	0.10	22.4	9	23
Germany	1,329	687	0.06	0.04	−20.0	12	8
Greece	2	9	0.00	0.01	66.2	0	1
Ireland	1	0	0.00	0.00	−61.8	0	0
Italy	294	281	0.02	0.03	7.0	4	5
Japan	184	84	0.00	0.00	−35.9	1	1
Luxembourg	2	9	0.01	0.05	12.5	4	20
Netherlands	13	214	0.00	0.06	16.8	1	13
New Zealand	0	0	0.00	0.00	−1.4	0	0
Norway	50	32	0.03	0.02	−11.0	11	7
Portugal	18	28	0.02	0.03	10.8	1	3
Spain	98	14	0.02	0.00	−31.5	2	0
Sweden	178	119	0.07	0.06	−0.5	15	15
Switzerland	97	63	0.03	0.02	−3.7	10	9
United Kingdom	362	461	0.03	0.03	1.8	7	8
United States	1,694	1,542	0.02	0.02	4.6	7	5
Total or average	**5,696**	**5,574**	**0.03**	**0.02**	**0.2**	**6**	**7**

a. Excluding administrative costs and technical cooperation. b. At 2000 exchange rates and prices.

About the data

Effective aid supports institutional development and policy reforms, which are at the heart of successful development. To be effective, especially in reducing global poverty, aid requires partnerships between recipient countries, aid agencies, and donor countries. It also requires improvements in economic policies and institutions. Where traditional methods of nurturing such reforms have failed, aid agencies need to find alternative approaches and new opportunities.

As part of its work, the Development Assistance Committee (DAC) of the Organisation for Economic Co-operation and Development (OECD) assesses the aid performance of member countries relative to the size of their economies. As measured here, aid comprises bilateral disbursements of concessional financing to recipient countries plus the provision by donor governments of concessional financing to multilateral institutions. Volume amounts, at constant prices and exchange rates, are used to measure the change in real resources provided over time. Aid flows to part I recipients—official development assistance (ODA)—are tabulated separate from those to part II recipients—official aid (see *About the data* for table 6.8 for more information on the distinction between the two types of aid flows).

Measures of aid flows from the perspective of donors differ from recipients' perceived aid receipts for two main reasons. First, aid flows include expenditure items about which recipients may have no precise information, such as development-oriented research, stipends and tuition costs for aid-financed students in donor countries, or payment of experts hired by donor countries. Second, donors

record their concessional funding (usually grants) to multilateral agencies when they make payments, while the agencies make funds available to recipients with a time lag and in many cases in the form of soft loans where donors' grants have been used to reduce the interest burden over the life of the loan.

Aid as a share of gross national income (GNI), aid per capita, and ODA as a share of the general government disbursements of the donor are calculated by the OECD. The denominators used in calculating these ratios may differ from corresponding values elsewhere in this book because of differences in timing or definitions.

DAC members have progressively introduced the new United Nations System of National Accounts (adopted in 1993), which replaced gross national product (GNP) with GNI. Because GNI includes items not included in GNP, ratios of ODA to GNI are slightly smaller than the previously reported ratios of ODA to GNP.

The proportion of untied aid is reported here because tying arrangements may prevent recipients from obtaining the best value for their money and so reduce the value of the aid received. Tying arrangements require recipients to purchase goods and services from the donor country or from a specified group of countries. They may be justified on the grounds that they prevent a recipient from misappropriating or mismanaging aid receipts, but they may also be motivated by a desire to benefit suppliers in the donor country. The same volume of aid may have different purchasing power depending on the relative costs of suppliers in countries to which the aid is tied and the degree to which each recipient's aid basket is untied.

Definitions

• **Net official development assistance** and **net official aid** record the actual international transfer by the donor of financial resources or of goods or services valued at the cost to the donor, less any repayments of loan principal during the same period. Data are shown at current prices and dollar exchange rates. • **Aid as a percentage of GNI** shows the donor's contributions of ODA or official aid as a share of its gross national income. • **Average annual percentage change in volume** and **aid per capita of donor country** are calculated using 2000 exchange rates and prices. • **Aid as a percentage of general government disbursements** shows the donor's contributions of ODA as a share of public spending. • **Untied aid** is the share of ODA that is not subject to restrictions by donors on procurement sources.

6.9a

Official development assistance from selected non-DAC donors, 1997–2001

Net disbursements ($ millions)

	1997	1998	1999	2000	2001
OECD members (non-DAC)					
Czech Republic	..	16	15	16	26
Iceland	8	7	8	9	10
Korea, Rep.	186	183	317	212	265
Poland	..	19	20	29	36
Slovak Republic	..	..	7	6	8
Turkey	77	69	120	82	64
Arab countries					
Kuwait	373	278	147	165	73
Saudi Arabia	251	288	185	295	490
United Arab Emirates	115	63	92	150	127
Other donors					
Estonia	..	0	0	1	0
Israel	89	87	114	164 [a]	76 [a]

Note: China also provides aid but does not disclose the amount.
a. The figure for 2000 includes $66.8 million—and that for 2001, $50.1 million—for first-year sustenance expenses for people arriving from developing countries (many of which are experiencing civil war or severe unrest) or who have left their country for humanitarian or political reasons.
Source: OECD data.

Data sources

The data on financial flows are compiled by DAC and published in its annual statistical report, *Geographical Distribution of Financial Flows to Aid Recipients*, and its annual *Development Co-operation Report*. Data are available in electronic format on the OECD's *International Development Statistics* CD-ROM and to registered users at http://www.oecd.org/dac/htm/online.htm.

	Net official development assistance or official aid		Aid per capita		Aid dependency ratios							
					Aid as % of GNI		Aid as % of gross capital formation		Aid as % of imports of goods and services		Aid as % of central government expenditure	
	$ millions		$									
	1996	2001	1996	2001	1996	2001	1996	2001	1996	2001	1996	2001
Afghanistan	183	402	8	15	..	..	..	..	..	..	..	..
Albania	228	269	72	85	8.3	6.3	54.7	33.6	20.3	15.0	28.5	..
Algeria	304	182	11	6	0.7	0.3	2.6	1.3	2.5	1.2	2.2	1.1
Angola	473	268	40	20	8.1	3.4	18.1	8.3	7.9	3.6	..	..
Argentina	135	151	4	4	0.1	0.1	0.3	0.4	0.3	0.4	0.3	0.3
Armenia	293	212	78	56	18.3	9.7	91.8	53.8	31.8	20.9	..	..
Australia												
Austria												
Azerbaijan	96	226	12	28	3.1	4.3	10.5	19.3	5.3	8.9	18.1	..
Bangladesh	1,236	1,024	10	8	3.0	2.2	15.2	9.5	15.8	9.8	..	..
Belarus	77	39	8	4	0.5	0.3	2.2	1.4	1.0	0.4	1.6	1.1
Belgium												
Benin	288	273	51	42	13.3	11.6	76.3	60.1	36.1	36.0	..	..
Bolivia	832	729	110	86	11.6	9.4	69.2	70.5	42.3	31.3	48.9	34.2
Bosnia and Herzegovina	845	639	239	157	33.5	12.8	73.6	..	33.8	23.8	..	..
Botswana	75	29	48	17	1.6	0.6	6.2	2.5	2.9	1.0	4.3	..
Brazil	288	349	2	2	0.0	0.1	0.2	0.3	0.3	0.4	..	..
Bulgaria	182	346	22	43	1.9	2.6	22.6	12.5	2.8	3.7	3.8	7.4
Burkina Faso	420	389	41	34	16.9	15.7	61.8	61.7	55.0	57.4	..	..
Burundi	111	131	18	19	12.5	19.3	102.3	274.3	69.9	80.7	44.6	..
Cambodia	422	409	38	33	13.6	12.4	51.8	67.1	30.5	20.1	..	..
Cameroon	412	398	30	26	4.8	5.0	29.4	26.3	16.7	13.3	..	..
Canada												
Central African Republic	170	76	49	20	16.2	7.9	369.9	56.0	70.7	49.5	..	..
Chad	296	179	43	23	18.8	11.2	123.7	26.9	57.1	18.1	..	..
Chile	196	58	14	4	0.3	0.1	1.1	0.4	0.8	0.2	1.4	0.4
China	2,646	1,460	2	1	0.3	0.1	0.8	0.3	1.5	0.5	4.1	..
Hong Kong, China	13	4	2	1	0.0	0.0	0.0	0.0	0.0	0.0	..	..
Colombia	189	380	5	9	0.2	0.5	0.9	3.1	1.0	1.9	1.3	..
Congo, Dem. Rep.	166	251	4	5	3.1	5.3	10.3	95.1	9.0	18.1	24.7	..
Congo, Rep.	429	75	160	24	26.4	3.9	62.7	10.0	15.6	3.6	56.8	10.5
Costa Rica	–10	2	–3	1	–0.1	0.0	–0.5	0.1	–0.2	0.0	–0.4	0.1
Côte d'Ivoire	965	187	67	11	8.6	1.9	65.6	18.2	19.3	4.3	35.6	10.6
Croatia	133	113	29	26	0.7	0.6	3.1	2.3	1.3	1.0	1.5	1.3
Cuba	57	51	5	5	..	..	..	..	..	..	..	..
Czech Republic	129	314	12	31	0.2	0.6	0.6	1.8	0.4	0.7	0.6	1.4
Denmark												
Dominican Republic	100	105	13	12	0.8	0.5	3.9	2.1	1.3	0.9	4.8	..
Ecuador	253	171	22	13	1.4	1.1	7.7	3.8	4.1	2.1	..	..
Egypt, Arab Rep.	2,199	1,255	37	19	3.2	1.3	19.6	8.2	11.6	5.6	10.0	..
El Salvador	302	234	52	37	2.9	1.7	19.3	10.7	8.2	3.7	..	66.9
Eritrea	159	280	43	67	24.6	40.8	71.6	115.2	27.3	52.3	..	..
Estonia	59	69	42	50	1.4	1.3	4.9	4.5	1.7	1.2	4.0	4.1
Ethiopia	818	1,080	14	16	13.7	17.5	80.6	96.0	55.9	53.6	..	..
Finland												
France												
Gabon	127	9	114	7	2.6	0.2	9.4	0.6	4.7	0.3	..	..
Gambia, The	37	51	32	38	9.5	13.3	44.1	72.8	12.3	14.1	..	..
Georgia	310	290	57	55	10.3	9.2	93.3	49.2	..	22.1	..	82.7
Germany												
Ghana	651	652	37	33	9.6	12.7	32.2	51.2	25.5	19.2	..	..
Greece												
Guatemala	194	225	19	19	1.3	1.1	9.7	7.1	5.1	3.5	..	..
Guinea	299	272	44	36	7.9	9.4	44.6	41.3	28.4	27.4	..	..
Guinea-Bissau	181	59	164	48	71.8	32.0	290.0	135.6	172.7	52.5	..	..
Haiti	370	166	50	20	12.8	4.4	45.2	14.4	46.8	13.2	140.8	..

	Net official development assistance or official aid		Aid per capita		Aid dependency ratios							
					Aid as % of GNI		Aid as % of gross capital formation		Aid as % of imports of goods and services		Aid as % of central government expenditure	
	$ millions		$									
	1996	2001	1996	2001	1996	2001	1996	2001	1996	2001	1996	2001
Honduras	359	678	62	103	9.4	10.9	28.2	34.7	14.1	18.3	..	..
Hungary	204	418	20	41	0.5	0.8	1.7	3.0	0.9	1.1	1.0	..
India	1,897	1,705	2	2	0.5	0.4	2.2	1.6	3.2	2.2	3.3	2.0
Indonesia	1,123	1,501	6	7	0.5	1.1	1.6	6.1	1.7	2.5	3.4	4.3
Iran, Islamic Rep.	169	115	3	2	0.2	0.1	0.8	0.3	0.9	0.5	0.5	..
Iraq	348	122	16	5	..	..	..	..	..	..	..	..
Ireland												
Israel	2,217	172	389	27	2.3	0.2	9.4	..	5.2	0.3	4.7	0.3
Italy												
Jamaica	58	54	23	21	0.9	0.7	3.1	2.3	1.4	1.0	2.2	1.8
Japan												
Jordan	507	432	117	86	7.5	4.9	24.0	18.9	8.7	6.7	21.6	15.1
Kazakhstan	125	148	8	10	0.6	0.7	3.7	2.6	1.6	1.2	..	4.6
Kenya	597	453	22	15	6.6	4.0	38.4	31.1	16.1	10.8	22.3	..
Korea, Dem. Rep.	26	119	1	5	..	..	..	..	..	..	..	..
Korea, Rep.	−149	−111	−3	−2	0.0	0.0	−0.1	−0.1	−0.1	−0.1	−0.2	..
Kuwait	3	4	1	2	0.0	0.0	0.1	0.1	0.0	0.0	0.0	..
Kyrgyz Republic	231	188	50	38	12.9	12.9	50.1	75.2	21.4	29.2	56.5	..
Lao PDR	332	243	69	45	17.8	14.5	61.2	62.5	42.5	40.6	..	..
Latvia	72	106	29	45	1.4	1.4	7.5	5.1	2.3	2.4	4.5	4.8
Lebanon	232	241	57	55	1.7	1.4	6.0	7.7	2.9	..	4.7	..
Lesotho	104	54	55	26	8.2	5.5	18.9	18.4	8.9	6.9	21.9	..
Liberia	173	37	62	11	..	8.3	..	..	..	..	..	..
Libya	8	10	2	2	..	..	0.2	..	0.1	..	..	..
Lithuania	91	130	25	37	1.2	1.1	4.7	5.0	1.8	1.8	4.6	4.1
Macedonia, FYR	106	248	53	121	2.4	7.3	11.9	43.3	5.7	12.4	..	..
Madagascar	357	354	26	22	9.3	7.8	76.7	49.6	30.5	188.8	51.4	..
Malawi	492	402	52	38	20.5	23.4	174.9	210.2	42.8	38.3	..	..
Malaysia	−457	27	−22	1	−0.5	0.0	−1.1	0.1	−0.5	0.0	−2.1	..
Mali	491	350	50	32	19.1	13.9	81.9	62.7	49.1	28.4	..	..
Mauritania	272	262	116	95	25.7	26.6	131.3	97.4	43.7	56.6	..	..
Mauritius	20	22	17	18	0.5	0.5	1.9	2.0	0.7	0.8	2.0	2.1
Mexico	287	75	3	1	0.1	0.0	0.4	0.1	0.2	0.0	0.6	..
Moldova	36	119	8	28	2.1	7.5	8.9	40.2	2.8	9.7	7.6	35.4
Mongolia	201	212	87	88	19.4	20.6	71.8	67.5	33.5	28.7	90.8	65.9
Morocco	650	517	24	18	1.8	1.6	9.1	6.1	5.3	3.8	..	..
Mozambique	888	935	55	52	33.2	28.1	143.2	62.3	74.9	20.3	..	..
Myanmar	43	127	1	3	..	..	..	..	1.8	4.1	0.3	..
Namibia	188	109	116	61	5.3	3.4	23.3	14.4	8.0	5.1	14.8	..
Nepal	391	388	19	16	8.6	6.7	31.8	28.8	23.8	19.1	51.0	39.4
Netherlands												
New Zealand												
Nicaragua	934	928	205	178	58.4	..	180.0	..	57.2	41.3	137.9	..
Niger	255	249	27	22	13.0	12.8	132.7	111.0	51.2	47.9	..	..
Nigeria	190	185	2	1	0.6	0.5	3.8	1.6	1.3	1.0	..	..
Norway												
Oman	62	2	28	1	0.5	..	..	..	1.0	0.0	1.3	0.0
Pakistan	884	1,938	7	14	1.4	3.4	7.3	20.7	5.1	13.1	6.2	16.2
Panama	49	28	18	10	0.6	0.3	2.0	1.0	0.5	0.3	2.2	..
Papua New Guinea	381	203	82	39	7.6	7.2	32.2	..	13.9	11.0	27.1	..
Paraguay	89	61	18	11	0.9	0.9	3.9	3.6	1.7	1.7	5.9	4.8
Peru	329	451	14	17	0.6	0.9	2.6	4.5	2.6	4.0	3.3	4.6
Philippines	901	577	13	7	1.0	0.8	4.5	4.5	2.0	1.5	5.9	4.2
Poland	1,167	966	30	25	0.9	0.6	4.1	2.5	2.7	1.6	2.1	1.5
Portugal												
Puerto Rico												

	Net official development assistance or official aid		Aid per capita		Aid dependency ratios							
					Aid as % of GNI		Aid as % of gross capital formation		Aid as % of imports of goods and services		Aid as % of central government expenditure	
	$ millions		$									
	1996	2001	1996	2001	1996	2001	1996	2001	1996	2001	1996	2001
Romania	233	648	10	29	0.7	1.7	2.7	7.6	1.8	3.7	2.1	5.3
Russian Federation	1,282	1,110	9	8	0.3	0.4	1.2	1.6	1.3	1.3	..	1.5
Rwanda	467	291	69	33	34.1	17.3	234.9	92.7	120.6	62.0	..	..
Saudi Arabia	23	27	1	1	0.0	0.0	0.1	0.1	0.0	0.1	..	..
Senegal	580	419	68	43	12.7	9.2	67.5	45.0	32.0	21.7	58.8	41.6
Sierra Leone	184	334	40	65	20.0	45.8	195.2	563.9	51.2	110.1	132.3	..
Singapore	15	1	4	0	0.0	0.0	0.0	0.0	0.0	0.0	0.1	0.0
Slovak Republic	98	164	18	30	0.5	0.8	1.3	2.5	0.7	0.9	1.1	2.1
Slovenia	82	126	41	63	0.4	0.7	1.9	..	0.8	1.1	1.1	1.7
Somalia	88	149	12	16	..	..	..	..	..	..	..	..
South Africa	364	428	9	10	0.3	0.4	1.5	2.5	1.0	1.2	0.8	1.3
Spain												
Sri Lanka	487	330	28	18	3.6	2.0	14.4	9.4	7.5	4.4	12.6	8.0
Sudan	220	172	8	5	3.0	1.5	12.1	7.8	14.3	6.5	..	..
Swaziland	33	29	36	27	2.3	2.3	7.8	12.5	2.4	2.6	..	..
Sweden												
Switzerland												
Syrian Arab Republic	219	153	15	9	1.6	0.8	6.6	3.7	3.1	2.1	1.6	..
Tajikistan	103	159	17	25	10.5	15.5	44.0	..	11.7	18.4	..	129.1
Tanzania	877	1,233	29	36	13.8	13.3	81.2	77.7	38.6	53.5	..	..
Thailand	830	281	14	5	0.5	0.3	1.1	1.0	0.9	0.4	2.8	1.2
Togo	157	47	39	10	10.9	3.8	57.1	17.9	18.7	6.8	..	..
Trinidad and Tobago	17	−2	13	−1	0.3	0.0	1.2	−0.1	0.6	0.0	..	..
Tunisia	124	378	14	39	0.7	2.0	2.5	6.9	1.3	3.3	1.9	..
Turkey	238	167	4	3	0.1	0.1	0.5	0.7	0.4	0.3	0.5	0.2
Turkmenistan	24	72	5	13	1.0	1.2	..	3.3	1.2	2.3	..	..
Uganda	676	783	34	34	11.3	14.1	69.6	68.9	40.5	48.3	..	64.6
Ukraine	398	519	8	11	0.9	1.4	3.9	6.8	1.8	2.4	..	4.7
United Arab Emirates	7	3	3	1	0.0	..	..	..	..	..	0.1	..
United Kingdom												
United States												
Uruguay	35	15	11	5	0.2	0.1	1.1	0.6	0.8	0.3	0.6	0.3
Uzbekistan	88	153	4	6	0.6	1.4	2.2	7.0	1.8	4.5	..	..
Venezuela, RB	38	45	2	2	0.1	0.0	0.3	0.2	0.2	0.2	0.3	0.1
Vietnam	939	1,435	13	18	3.9	4.4	13.6	14.2	7.3	7.7	16.5	18.0
West Bank and Gaza	550	865	218	280	13.2	19.6	42.9	..	..	..	..	..
Yemen, Rep.	247	426	16	24	4.8	5.0	18.6	22.5	7.0	9.1	10.8	..
Yugoslavia, Fed. Rep. [a]	70	1,306	7	123	..	12.1	..	89.2	1.6	25.0	..	..
Zambia	610	374	66	36	19.9	10.7	145.1	51.2	35.8	20.9	..	..
Zimbabwe	371	159	32	12	4.5	1.8	23.4	22.5	10.5	7.3	12.5	..
World	**62,264 s**	**58,244 s**	**11 w**	**10 w**	**0.2 w**	**0.2 w**	**0.9 w**	**0.9 w**	**0.8 w**	**0.6 w**	**..**	**..**
Low income	25,309	25,342	11	10	2.5	2.4	10.2	11.0	8.9	8.1	..	..
Middle income	21,799	20,284	9	8	0.5	0.4	1.7	1.6	1.6	1.2	..	..
Lower middle income	17,598	16,086	9	7	0.7	0.6	2.3	2.1	2.5	1.9	..	..
Upper middle income	3,532	3,672	7	7	0.2	0.2	0.7	0.8	0.6	0.5	..	..
Low & middle income	59,015	57,217	12	11	1.0	0.9	3.9	3.8	3.6	2.9	..	..
East Asia & Pacific	8,040	7,394	5	4	0.6	0.5	1.4	1.3	1.6	1.2	..	..
Europe & Central Asia	8,670	9,783	18	21	0.8	1.0	3.3	4.4	2.4	2.3	..	..
Latin America & Carib.	7,446	5,992	15	11	0.4	0.3	1.9	1.6	1.9	1.2	..	..
Middle East & N. Africa	5,956	4,838	22	16	1.0	0.7	5.0	3.2	3.5	2.7	..	..
South Asia	5,169	5,871	4	4	1.0	1.0	4.6	4.4	5.5	5.1	..	..
Sub-Saharan Africa	16,552	13,933	28	21	5.2	4.6	27.3	23.4	14.2	10.9	..	..
High income	3,249	1,027	4	1	0.0	0.0	0.1	0.0	0.1	0.0	..	..
Europe EMU												

Note: Regional aggregates include data for economies not specified elsewhere. World and income group totals include aid not allocated by country or region. The 2001 data exclude aid from the World Food Programme.

a. Aid to the states of the former Socialist Federal Republic of Yugoslavia that is not otherwise specified is included in regional and income group aggregates.

Ratios of aid to gross national income (GNI), gross capital formation, imports, and public spending provide a measure of the recipient country's dependency on aid. But care must be taken in drawing policy conclusions. For foreign policy reasons some countries have traditionally received large amounts of aid. Thus aid dependency ratios may reveal as much about the donors' interests as they do about the recipients' needs. Ratios in Sub-Saharan Africa are generally much higher than those in other regions, and they increased in the 1980s. These high ratios are due only in part to aid flows. Many African countries saw severe erosion in their terms of trade in the 1980s, which, along with weak policies, contributed to falling incomes, imports, and investment. Thus the increase in aid dependency ratios reflects events affecting both the numerator and the denominator.

As defined here, aid includes official development assistance (ODA) and official aid. The data cover loans and grants from the Development Assistance Committee (DAC) member countries, multilateral organizations, and non-DAC donors. They do not reflect aid given by recipient countries to other developing countries. As a result, some countries that are net donors (such as Saudi Arabia) are shown in the table as aid recipients (see table 6.9a). The 2001 data exclude aid from the World Food Programme because the organization implemented an annual program budget in 2002, and the 2001 data are not yet consistent with the DAC reporting system.

The data in the table do not distinguish among different types of aid (program, project, or food aid; emergency assistance; postconflict peacekeeping assistance; or technical cooperation), each of which may have a very different effect on the economy. Expenditures on technical cooperation do not always directly benefit the economy to the extent that they defray costs incurred outside the country on the salaries and benefits of technical experts and the overhead costs of firms supplying technical services.

In 1999, to avoid double counting extrabudgetary expenditures reported by DAC countries and flows reported by the United Nations, all United Nations agencies revised their data to include only regular budgetary expenditures since 1990 (except for the World Food Programme and the United Nations High Commissioner for Refugees, which revised their data from 1996 onward). These revisions have affected net ODA and official aid and, as a result, aid per capita and aid dependency ratios.

Because the table relies on information from donors, it is not consistent with information recorded by recipients in the balance of payments, which often excludes all or some technical assistance—particularly payments to expatriates made directly by the donor. Similarly, grant commodity aid may not always be recorded in trade data or in the balance of payments. Moreover, DAC statistics exclude purely military aid.

The nominal values used here may overstate the real value of aid to the recipient. Changes in international prices and in exchange rates can reduce the purchasing power of aid. The practice of tying aid, still prevalent though declining in importance, also tends to reduce its purchasing power (see *About the data* for table 6.9).

The values for population, GNI, gross capital formation, imports of goods and services, and central government expenditure used in computing the ratios are taken from World Bank and International Monetary Fund databases. The ratios shown may therefore differ somewhat from those computed and published by the Organisation for Economic Co-operation and Development (OECD). Aid not allocated by country or region—including administrative costs, research on development issues, and aid to nongovernmental organizations—is included in the world total. Thus regional and income group totals do not sum to the world total.

• **Net official development assistance** consists of disbursements of loans made on concessional terms (net of repayments of principal) and grants by official agencies of the members of DAC, by multilateral institutions, and by non-DAC countries to promote economic development and welfare in countries and territories in part I of the DAC list of aid recipients. It includes loans with a grant element of at least 25 percent (calculated at a rate of discount of 10 percent). • **Net official aid** refers to aid flows (net of repayments) from official donors to countries and territories in part II of the DAC list of aid recipients: more advanced countries of Central and Eastern Europe, the countries of the former Soviet Union, and certain advanced developing countries and territories. Official aid is provided under terms and conditions similar to those for ODA. • **Aid per capita** includes both ODA and official aid. • **Aid dependency ratios** are calculated using values in U.S. dollars converted at official exchange rates. For definitions of GNI, gross capital formation, imports of goods and services, and central government expenditure, see *Definitions* for tables 1.1, 4.9, and 4.12.

The data on financial flows are compiled by DAC and published in its annual statistical report, *Geographical Distribution of Financial Flows to Aid Recipients*, and in its annual *Development Co-operation Report*. Data are available in electronic format on the OECD's *International Development Statistics* CD-ROM and to registered users at http://www.oecd.org/dac/htm/online.htm. The data on population, GNI, gross capital formation, imports of goods and services, and central government expenditure are from World Bank and International Monetary Fund databases.

6.11 Distribution of net aid by Development Assistance Committee members

$ millions, 2001	Total	Ten major DAC donors United States	Japan	France	Germany	United Kingdom	Netherlands	Canada	Sweden	Denmark	Norway	Other DAC donors
Afghanistan	322.9	7.7	0.6	9.6	44.1	35.4	72.0	14.2	20.6	2.4	39.7	76.5
Albania	149.8	42.3	6.7	2.0	24.6	5.3	11.5	2.5	3.8	3.9	3.0	44.2
Algeria	24.8	0.2	–4.0	63.5	0.6	0.2	0.5	–0.2	1.7	0.0	2.1	–39.9
Angola	179.4	34.0	20.7	5.9	9.9	7.9	20.5	2.3	13.4	3.0	17.5	44.4
Argentina	10.1	–0.5	16.5	5.9	9.2	0.0	0.5	0.7	0.2	0.0	0.0	–22.5
Armenia	124.2	78.0	5.2	4.1	16.8	2.4	7.9	0.4	0.9	0.3	2.4	5.9
Australia												
Austria												
Azerbaijan	148.4	30.9	101.0	1.5	6.8	1.2	2.6	0.3	0.1	..	2.7	1.4
Bangladesh	578.4	87.1	125.6	13.1	30.1	124.5	43.2	30.3	28.4	41.8	20.6	33.7
Belarus	22.1	8.8	0.3	1.1	6.1	0.1	1.7	0.1	1.5	0.7	0.1	1.6
Belgium												
Benin	144.5	27.4	8.3	42.5	21.9	0.1	8.0	1.8	0.1	22.9	0.1	11.4
Bolivia	530.2	119.1	65.9	8.4	51.7	45.6	73.3	8.8	20.2	26.4	3.2	107.6
Bosnia and Herzegovina	376.7	135.1	9.6	2.1	27.0	6.1	52.9	10.6	29.0	7.9	16.9	79.5
Botswana	24.2	–0.3	7.2	0.4	5.6	2.8	2.8	0.1	0.4	1.0	3.6	0.6
Brazil	156.8	–70.8	106.1	14.6	47.0	12.1	15.2	4.0	2.1	1.6	2.4	22.5
Bulgaria	173.4	39.8	48.4	11.0	37.1	5.3	4.3	0.4	0.2	4.6	0.1	22.4
Burkina Faso	220.9	13.1	20.4	44.0	23.6	1.7	44.4	5.9	6.0	28.8	0.3	32.7
Burundi	54.7	4.9	0.3	4.7	3.3	1.7	11.7	2.3	2.5	..	5.7	17.9
Cambodia	264.8	22.4	120.2	21.4	18.7	11.7	8.2	8.0	16.9	4.9	5.6	26.8
Cameroon	274.6	4.8	41.3	59.3	46.1	10.7	13.2	5.4	0.0	12.0	1.0	80.9
Canada												
Central African Republic	47.9	2.4	15.1	20.9	7.1	..	0.3	0.5	0.8	..	..	0.9
Chad	72.8	4.5	0.1	39.5	16.7	0.2	1.8	0.4	0.1	..	0.1	9.3
Chile	39.6	–18.1	21.9	8.0	18.0	..	4.0	0.7	2.3	0.0	0.8	2.2
China	1,075.1	4.8	686.1	42.8	163.8	50.7	26.5	24.3	10.1	10.2	9.7	46.0
Hong Kong, China	3.6	0.0	2.5	0.7	0.2	..	0.1	..	..	..	..	0.1
Colombia	372.3	274.7	7.1	8.2	15.0	2.6	15.5	4.8	6.2	0.0	7.4	30.8
Congo, Dem. Rep.	143.4	20.2	0.3	7.9	12.9	17.0	12.0	6.4	5.5	0.2	3.9	57.0
Congo, Rep.	29.6	10.6	0.2	11.2	1.7	..	1.4	0.3	1.7	..	0.3	2.2
Costa Rica	6.1	–29.6	–3.1	14.2	0.7	1.4	15.2	1.6	0.3	0.2	0.4	4.9
Côte d'Ivoire	158.5	2.0	4.3	110.4	19.0	1.2	7.6	1.5	0.1	..	0.2	12.3
Croatia	74.4	28.5	3.2	1.4	1.6	2.5	3.0	2.8	6.2	..	18.1	7.2
Cuba	33.7	3.6	1.9	1.4	2.2	3.2	1.1	2.6	0.8	0.1	1.7	15.2
Czech Republic	29.7	0.5	1.2	5.5	9.8	1.2	3.1	0.3	0.2	2.1	0.0	5.7
Denmark												
Dominican Republic	101.9	29.7	42.4	4.4	8.2	–0.9	2.4	0.8	0.1	0.3	0.4	14.1
Ecuador	147.6	55.2	16.5	5.1	13.7	1.0	13.6	6.2	0.4	0.9	2.8	32.2
Egypt, Arab Rep.	1,090.3	630.1	52.7	201.5	106.3	3.6	20.3	9.6	1.9	25.2	0.9	38.4
El Salvador	231.1	50.9	58.2	1.1	25.8	3.1	9.5	5.3	8.3	1.2	2.6	65.2
Eritrea	151.4	28.9	3.5	5.2	4.7	4.9	11.9	1.4	7.4	13.9	4.6	65.1
Estonia	25.6	0.5	0.9	0.9	2.4	0.1	1.8	0.2	5.2	7.3	2.5	3.8
Ethiopia	367.1	94.4	52.4	6.6	25.9	27.6	44.2	12.4	20.6	2.8	16.3	64.0
Finland												
France												
Gabon	–8.0	2.3	1.6	–14.0	0.5	..	0.8	0.9	..	..	..	0.0
Gambia, The	13.4	1.6	3.1	0.5	2.2	3.8	0.7	0.3	0.4	0.1	0.2	0.6
Georgia	151.6	94.3	15.5	1.9	20.1	5.7	3.3	0.6	2.0	0.1	3.1	5.0
Germany												
Ghana	396.0	53.5	34.6	4.5	23.8	97.8	114.2	11.2	2.0	39.7	0.5	14.0
Greece												
Guatemala	201.2	63.6	45.7	1.6	15.5	0.6	21.2	5.0	12.4	2.0	10.0	23.7
Guinea	120.3	34.9	17.4	20.4	17.9	1.1	2.3	7.7	0.6	..	3.0	15.1
Guinea-Bissau	30.4	0.1	0.2	3.9	0.7	0.0	8.0	0.1	2.1	0.2	0.0	15.2
Haiti	136.0	81.1	8.6	13.7	4.7	0.2	4.8	13.1	0.2	0.1	2.1	7.5

$ millions, 2001	Total	Ten major DAC donors										Other DAC donors
		United States	Japan	France	Germany	United Kingdom	Netherlands	Canada	Sweden	Denmark	Norway	
Honduras	422.3	201.3	76.3	4.1	17.3	1.2	10.1	6.0	31.3	3.4	21.8	49.6
Hungary	54.5	2.5	7.4	5.8	18.9	2.5	2.8	0.3	0.4	0.4	0.1	13.5
India	904.5	−17.3	528.9	−8.9	57.5	173.9	73.5	13.4	11.2	19.0	11.6	41.8
Indonesia	1,375.4	141.0	860.1	26.1	29.9	23.4	119.7	18.8	3.7	3.7	4.6	144.4
Iran, Islamic Rep.	90.8	..	34.4	6.8	32.6	2.5	3.8	..	0.0	0.1	3.7	7.0
Iraq	100.8	..	0.0	1.9	46.0	12.6	16.9	..	3.9	..	10.7	8.8
Ireland												
Israel	148.5	190.3	0.5	3.6	−47.7	..	0.7	0.1	0.0	..	..	0.9
Italy												
Jamaica	−1.0	−17.8	−4.3	−1.0	−4.7	6.7	1.8	19.8	0.4	..	0.3	−2.1
Japan												
Jordan	302.1	155.9	42.7	1.6	59.7	8.5	0.7	1.7	0.7	3.0	2.0	25.5
Kazakhstan	122.7	56.0	43.9	0.7	8.2	0.9	2.2	1.3	0.6	0.1	1.0	7.9
Kenya	270.5	43.4	46.7	9.9	32.5	55.1	23.1	3.8	13.6	12.3	4.0	26.1
Korea, Dem. Rep.	52.3	0.3	..	0.3	27.0	1.1	0.1	1.5	3.4	..	3.5	15.2
Korea, Rep.	−108.6	−44.3	−79.1	10.1	3.9	..	0.1	..	..	..	..	0.7
Kuwait	2.9	..	0.1	1.0	1.8	..	0.0	..	..	..	..	0.0
Kyrgyz Republic	71.3	28.1	23.2	0.2	7.4	2.4	1.8	0.8	0.9	0.7	0.5	5.4
Lao PDR	149.9	4.5	75.5	10.7	13.6	1.1	2.7	0.6	12.1	3.2	4.8	21.0
Latvia	49.6	1.7	1.2	0.9	4.6	0.1	2.1	0.5	12.7	21.3	0.7	3.8
Lebanon	101.7	46.8	7.4	27.1	5.6	0.4	0.5	1.5	0.9	..	4.3	7.3
Lesotho	29.5	1.7	5.2	−0.2	4.4	4.1	0.7	0.2	..	3.2	0.3	9.9
Liberia	15.6	12.6	0.1	1.5	−6.5	1.2	2.3	0.3	1.1	0.0	0.7	2.4
Libya	4.3	..	0.2	1.1	1.5	..	0.1	..	..	..	..	1.5
Lithuania	48.4	−1.2	1.8	1.3	6.8	0.2	2.0	0.2	14.8	19.7	0.6	2.2
Macedonia, FYR	164.2	37.3	20.2	1.0	12.2	7.4	43.9	10.8	6.2	0.4	6.3	18.6
Madagascar	137.9	37.2	25.5	41.7	10.0	2.5	1.5	0.2	..	0.1	4.2	15.1
Malawi	195.8	30.6	18.3	0.5	19.8	66.5	13.1	11.0	2.3	21.6	9.6	2.7
Malaysia	24.9	0.7	13.1	−3.3	4.1	0.6	0.6	0.6	0.0	10.8	0.5	−2.2
Mali	208.5	24.8	23.1	60.8	19.3	1.1	41.5	9.0	4.4	0.1	6.7	17.9
Mauritania	81.3	6.2	29.6	18.6	9.7	1.0	3.5	1.0	0.4	..	0.4	11.0
Mauritius	8.1	−0.4	1.3	3.2	−1.2	2.3	0.1	0.1	..	..	0.6	2.0
Mexico	40.7	41.8	−11.1	−2.7	14.2	1.3	2.7	1.5	0.3	−0.4	0.4	−7.3
Moldova	78.8	43.5	8.2	1.1	1.9	2.5	15.2	0.1	2.6	..	1.0	2.9
Mongolia	141.1	12.7	81.5	0.4	24.9	2.1	2.5	0.8	2.6	1.1	5.7	6.7
Morocco	342.1	−12.7	101.6	174.4	29.3	0.2	1.0	3.2	0.6	−0.7	0.1	45.2
Mozambique	720.2	91.8	33.5	15.3	40.7	185.2	86.6	13.9	42.6	48.3	32.6	129.7
Myanmar	89.2	2.9	69.9	1.2	1.8	1.7	2.2	1.3	0.6	1.0	2.8	3.8
Namibia	77.5	13.9	3.2	3.2	18.4	3.5	5.0	0.2	8.6	2.8	3.7	15.0
Nepal	270.2	20.2	84.4	−0.6	37.9	33.2	13.4	4.3	13.6	26.1	11.5	26.2
Netherlands												
New Zealand												
Nicaragua	714.7	100.6	62.0	2.8	31.8	1.0	18.5	6.5	22.7	28.0	14.6	426.3
Niger	113.6	8.0	13.0	37.0	15.7	0.5	4.2	2.3	..	5.6	2.6	24.6
Nigeria	107.5	24.7	8.9	14.8	13.3	32.8	2.8	4.5	0.7	−3.5	1.1	7.6
Norway												
Oman	8.1	−4.0	11.6	0.5	0.1	0.0	0.0	.	..	..	..	0.0
Pakistan	1,110.1	775.6	211.4	13.9	20.1	27.4	18.0	13.9	1.1	−0.8	5.5	24.0
Panama	17.1	0.8	3.5	0.4	1.7	0.3	0.6	0.7	..	1.7	..	7.4
Papua New Guinea	198.0	1.1	26.2	0.3	3.3	..	1.2	..	0.1	..	0.1	165.7
Paraguay	58.3	7.0	34.8	0.0	3.6	0.1	1.1	0.2	1.4	..	0.6	9.5
Peru	425.4	161.6	156.5	3.2	24.2	7.5	24.5	9.5	2.7	1.9	2.2	31.8
Philippines	505.0	83.0	298.2	0.7	19.1	6.0	20.6	14.4	2.5	5.5	1.7	53.2
Poland	486.9	8.0	−3.9	182.9	39.4	4.5	2.7	112.7	3.5	16.2	0.3	120.9
Portugal												
Puerto Rico												

6.11 Distribution of net aid by Development Assistance Committee members

	Total	Ten major DAC donors										Other DAC donors
$ millions, 2001		United States	Japan	France	Germany	United Kingdom	Netherlands	Canada	Sweden	Denmark	Norway	
Romania	142.1	41.8	9.7	24.5	24.8	6.8	8.1	3.3	0.5	5.2	0.1	17.3
Russian Federation	906.6	659.3	4.5	14.2	64.1	38.3	9.9	18.1	32.5	14.3	18.7	32.6
Rwanda	148.9	31.1	1.0	6.1	14.6	36.8	19.2	6.7	8.4	2.7	2.0	20.3
Saudi Arabia	10.5	..	7.2	2.9	0.4	..	0.0	..	..	..	..	0.0
Senegal	223.7	28.8	22.4	102.4	16.7	1.0	12.0	8.6	0.1	1.4	1.1	29.3
Sierra Leone	166.8	26.4	0.0	2.0	12.0	51.1	38.1	2.8	3.5	0.2	9.3	21.5
Singapore	0.7	..	2.4	1.3	–3.4	0.2	0.1	0.1	..	..	..	0.1
Slovak Republic	33.8	3.1	2.4	3.0	6.1	2.3	3.5	1.0	0.2	3.8	0.2	8.2
Slovenia	0.0	0.7	0.4	0.7	–6.7	0.2	0.8	1.0	0.5	..	0.0	2.5
Somalia	88.5	17.8	..	0.5	1.1	3.6	13.1	0.5	5.6	0.4	12.4	33.5
South Africa	313.3	85.9	13.4	1.3	36.9	41.8	34.8	7.5	26.5	15.3	17.0	33.0
Spain												
Sri Lanka	279.9	–9.7	184.7	0.8	31.1	15.0	15.8	2.8	18.3	–0.5	15.2	6.5
Sudan	107.6	17.5	0.7	1.8	11.3	9.9	23.6	4.7	7.9	1.5	13.1	15.7
Swaziland	4.2	–0.1	6.5	0.0	–1.3	–3.2	1.1	0.1	..	0.4	0.1	0.5
Sweden												
Switzerland												
Syrian Arab Republic	92.3	0.0	–19.5	14.6	83.3	0.1	2.8	0.1	0.1	..	0.9	9.8
Tajikistan	63.5	40.4	4.6	0.0	4.7	0.9	0.6	0.8	1.0	0.2	0.8	9.3
Tanzania	943.8	25.9	260.4	13.1	48.2	290.1	75.1	8.4	47.3	66.6	34.9	73.7
Thailand	270.9	24.7	209.6	–10.3	7.7	–0.2	3.3	2.6	3.2	11.8	1.4	16.9
Togo	28.5	2.3	2.9	10.3	7.3	0.5	1.0	0.2	0.3	..	0.0	3.6
Trinidad and Tobago	4.3	1.2	1.2	0.9	0.1	0.3	0.1	0.5	..	..	..	0.1
Tunisia	183.7	–18.8	88.5	87.6	8.0	0.1	0.1	0.1	0.4	..	0.0	17.8
Turkey	–31.4	–59.5	–64.6	3.1	66.3	–0.2	2.4	0.0	0.8	0.0	2.9	17.5
Turkmenistan	33.1	14.1	16.4	0.3	0.9	0.1	0.2	0.0	1.0	..	0.0	0.1
Uganda	386.3	66.5	14.6	6.5	33.2	82.2	40.8	2.6	29.4	58.7	19.7	32.1
Ukraine	342.5	247.0	7.1	4.3	33.5	13.7	3.6	13.8	5.9	6.2	0.2	7.3
United Arab Emirates	2.5	..	0.1	1.9	0.5	..	..	..	..	..	..	0.0
United Kingdom												
United States												
Uruguay	10.7	–1.7	5.9	1.4	4.2	..	0.1	0.2	0.1	..	0.0	0.5
Uzbekistan	106.7	50.2	30.9	3.7	13.7	0.8	1.1	0.3	0.0	..	0.8	5.0
Venezuela, RB	33.5	10.6	3.1	3.3	2.9	0.1	0.3	0.6	0.1	..	0.1	12.4
Vietnam	822.1	8.7	459.5	61.8	37.9	23.7	36.2	11.8	34.9	60.2	5.7	81.6
West Bank and Gaza	280.2	84.3	21.5	12.7	17.9	17.0	14.0	0.5	21.9	5.0	37.5	47.9
Yemen, Rep.	99.8	28.5	4.9	1.6	27.3	3.3	28.7	0.4	0.6	0.1	0.1	4.4
Yugoslavia, Fed. Rep.	631.1	210.2	0.1	21.4	78.3	17.0	51.6	0.3	35.0	0.9	35.8	180.5
Zambia	274.1	29.0	47.0	7.7	13.8	55.8	29.6	8.9	17.5	22.6	20.8	21.3
Zimbabwe	148.6	16.0	29.0	2.0	10.2	18.1	23.5	3.0	8.2	17.9	10.2	10.5
World	**38,660.0 s**	**9,743.4 s**	**7,482.5 s**	**3,606.6 s**	**3,104.2 s**	**2,708.4 s**	**2,320.7 s**	**1,351.4 s**	**1,317.8 s**	**1,147.4 s**	**969.8 s**	**4,907.9 s**
Low income	15,383.8	2,774.3	3,739.0	940.4	1,082.8	1,576.7	1,247.7	311.5	444.9	594.0	394.9	2,277.7
Middle income	12,714.5	3,512.7	2,642.7	1,210.8	1,448.9	453.0	632.0	356.7	349.3	265.3	298.2	1,544.9
Lower middle income	10,787.8	3,388.6	2,400.5	803.2	1,185.2	341.2	553.4	189.4	295.4	151.8	244.9	1,234.1
Upper middle income	1,543.4	44.0	240.4	388.4	203.8	91.8	65.4	132.4	49.8	85.5	35.5	206.3
Low & middle income	37,836.4	9,561.9	7,554.5	2,904.0	3,149.7	2,707.7	2,273.1	1,350.1	1,317.2	1,147.4	969.5	4,901.3
East Asia & Pacific	5,649.9	535.2	2,987.6	214.8	355.6	134.6	232.3	90.5	93.1	116.5	50.8	839.0
Europe & Central Asia	4,895.7	1,944.0	306.9	301.9	544.0	153.0	251.6	198.1	202.9	154.5	125.9	712.9
Latin America & Carib.	4,465.3	1,473.3	738.2	111.9	334.3	190.1	269.6	137.8	139.3	76.0	87.1	907.8
Middle East & N. Africa	2,815.1	920.6	352.4	623.8	422.9	48.8	91.3	29.6	37.6	33.1	65.0	190.1
South Asia	3,523.6	863.7	1,156.8	27.9	221.8	409.7	242.8	79.6	93.5	100.3	104.8	222.9
Sub-Saharan Africa	8,335.5	1,374.8	849.0	978.8	684.2	1,185.6	830.0	201.4	346.5	412.0	321.6	1,151.5
High income	823.6	181.4	–72.0	702.6	–45.6	0.7	47.6	1.4	0.6	0.0	0.3	6.7
Europe EMU												

Note: Regional aggregates include data for economies not specified elsewhere. World and income group totals include aid not allocated by country or region.

About the data

The data in the table show net bilateral aid to low- and middle-income economies from members of the Development Assistance Committee (DAC) of the Organisation for Economic Co-operation and Development (OECD). The DAC compilation of the data includes aid to some countries and territories not shown in the table and small quantities of aid to unspecified economies that are recorded only at the regional or global level. Aid to countries and territories not shown in the table has been assigned to regional totals based on the World Bank's regional classification system. Aid to unspecified economies has been included in regional totals and, when possible, in income group totals. Aid not allocated by country or region—including administrative costs, research on development issues, and aid to non-governmental organizations—is included in the world total; thus regional and income group totals do not sum to the world total.

In 1999 all United Nations agencies revised their data to include only regular budgetary expenditures since 1990 (except for the World Food Programme and the United Nations High Commissioner for Refugees, which revised their data from 1996 onward). They did so to avoid double counting extra-budgetary expenditures reported by DAC countries and flows reported by the United Nations.

The data in the table are based on donor country reports of bilateral programs, which may differ from reports by recipient countries. Recipients may lack access to information on such aid expenditures as development-oriented research, stipends and tuition costs for aid-financed students in donor countries, or payment of experts hired by donor countries. Moreover, a full accounting would include donor country contributions to multilateral institutions, the flow of resources from multilateral institutions to recipient countries, and flows from countries that are not members of DAC.

The expenditures that countries report as official development assistance (ODA) have changed. For example, some DAC members have reported as ODA the aid provided to refugees during the first 12 months of their stay within the donor's borders.

Some of the aid recipients shown in the table are also aid donors. See table 6.9a for a summary of ODA from non-DAC countries.

Definitions

• **Net aid** comprises net bilateral official development assistance to part I recipients and net bilateral official aid to part II recipients (see *About the data* for table 6.8). • **Other DAC donors** are Australia, Austria, Belgium, Finland, Greece, Ireland, Italy, Luxembourg, New Zealand, Portugal, Spain, and Switzerland.

6.11a

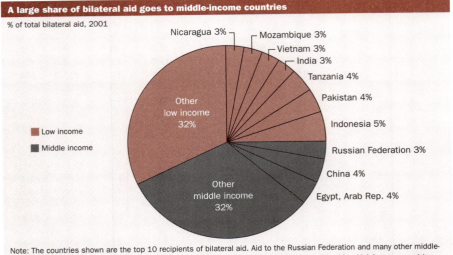

A large share of bilateral aid goes to middle-income countries

% of total bilateral aid, 2001

- Nicaragua 3%
- Mozambique 3%
- Vietnam 3%
- India 3%
- Tanzania 4%
- Pakistan 4%
- Indonesia 5%
- Russian Federation 3%
- China 4%
- Egypt, Arab Rep. 4%
- Other low income 32%
- Other middle income 32%

■ Low income
■ Middle income

Note: The countries shown are the top 10 recipients of bilateral aid. Aid to the Russian Federation and many other middle-income economies is not classified as official development assistance. The figure excludes aid to high-income countries (less than 1 percent of bilateral aid) and unallocated aid.
Source: OECD data.

Data sources

Data on financial flows are compiled by DAC and published in its annual statistical report, *Geographical Distribution of Financial Flows to Aid Recipients*, and its annual *Development Co-operation Report*. Data are available in electronic format on the OECD's *International Development Statistics* CD-ROM and to registered users at http://www.oecd.org/dac/htm/online.htm.

$ millions, 2001	International financial institutions							United Nations					Total
	World Bank		IMF		Regional development banks								
	IDA	IBRD	Concessional	Non-concessional	Concessional	Non-concessional	Others	UNDP	UNFPA	UNICEF	WFP	Others	
Afghanistan	..	..	..	..	..	..	..	3.9	0.8	9.0	6.7	13.6	27.2
Albania	34.3	0.0	4.1	−5.6	0.0	1.4	16.4	1.6	0.5	0.5	..	3.4	56.5
Algeria	0.0	−93.9	0.0	−140.6	0.0	42.8	−182.8	0.7	1.2	0.9	2.4	4.9	−366.8
Angola	10.8	0.0	0.0	0.0	−0.1	−1.5	2.7	1.0	1.7	7.2	38.4	9.8	31.6
Argentina	0.0	653.3	0.0	9,218.3	0.0	1,191.1	0.1	..	0.0	1.1	..	8.3	11,072.2
Armenia	55.0	−0.4	10.6	−7.2	0.0	−2.3	10.7	0.5	0.3	0.9	2.6	4.3	72.2
Australia													
Austria													
Azerbaijan	27.6	0.0	10.2	−39.3	0.0	−1.7	5.5	2.2	0.8	0.8	2.4	4.1	10.2
Bangladesh	217.9	−5.2	−60.1	0.0	122.7	0.2	22.9	12.2	13.7	12.8	8.9	14.0	351.3
Belarus	0.0	−7.3	0.0	−29.7	0.0	−16.3	−3.0	0.3	0.1	..	..	1.7	−54.2
Belgium													
Benin	43.6	0.0	0.5	0.0	25.0	−0.1	13.5	0.9	1.9	1.8	1.9	3.2	90.3
Bolivia	101.3	−0.2	3.6	0.0	68.4	−40.0	77.8	1.2	2.7	1.4	5.7	3.6	219.8
Bosnia and Herzegovina	61.7	−5.3	0.0	10.1	0.0	15.5	−177.4	0.2	0.1	0.4	..	23.4	−71.3
Botswana	−0.5	−4.5	0.0	0.0	−1.6	−13.3	−4.1	0.7	1.0	0.7	..	2.4	−19.1
Brazil	0.0	810.2	0.0	6,718.3	0.0	728.1	−12.5	0.3	1.2	1.6	..	123.9	8,371.3
Bulgaria	0.0	55.8	0.0	−167.6	0.0	−9.5	−15.4	0.7	0.1	..	..	1.7	−134.2
Burkina Faso	69.0	0.0	14.5	0.0	13.8	0.0	18.5	3.9	1.4	3.6	1.1	4.5	129.2
Burundi	2.2	0.0	−4.4	0.0	−0.3	−0.2	−0.9	4.5	0.8	2.5	2.1	7.2	11.5
Cambodia	39.6	0.0	10.6	−1.3	41.4	0.0	4.5	3.9	3.1	3.6	10.2	4.9	110.2
Cameroon	12.3	−8.6	20.3	−2.0	13.5	4.1	0.8	1.9	1.3	2.2	0.4	3.4	49.2
Canada													
Central African Republic	−5.5	0.0	10.2	0.0	0.0	0.0	−1.1	1.2	0.8	2.0	1.6	4.2	11.6
Chad	20.2	9.1	15.7	0.0	9.4	0.0	0.7	2.4	0.9	2.3	3.5	5.3	66.0
Chile	−0.7	−79.9	0.0	0.0	−1.3	11.7	−0.4	3.2	0.1	0.8	..	1.6	−65.0
China	223.7	663.1	0.0	0.0	0.0	643.7	−137.8	8.9	3.6	12.5	7.5	11.6	1,429.4
Hong Kong, China	..	..	..	..	..	..	..	..	..	..	..	0.0	0.0
Colombia	−0.7	136.1	0.0	0.0	−12.3	649.4	345.0	0.2	0.7	1.0	3.2	5.4	1,124.6
Congo, Dem. Rep.	0.0	0.0	0.0	0.0	0.0	0.0	0.0	3.7	1.7	18.0	2.1	42.8	66.2
Congo, Rep.	32.4	−48.2	0.0	−1.2	0.0	−0.7	0.0	2.1	0.3	1.0	0.1	7.7	−6.7
Costa Rica	−0.2	−18.6	0.0	0.0	−11.0	−34.9	43.9	0.1	0.2	0.7	..	2.3	−17.4
Côte d'Ivoire	5.0	−72.1	−66.7	0.0	0.1	−26.4	0.4	1.7	1.0	2.7	0.8	10.3	−144.0
Croatia	0.0	56.9	0.0	−30.8	0.0	5.6	1.4	0.2	..	..	..	10.1	43.4
Cuba	..	..	..	..	..	..	..	0.9	0.6	0.9	2.0	2.3	4.6
Czech Republic	0.0	−41.2	0.0	0.0	0.0	0.0	177.7	0.1	..	..	..	1.2	137.8
Denmark													
Dominican Republic	−0.7	25.6	0.0	0.0	−10.2	107.1	−1.6	0.1	1.0	0.9	1.0	1.9	124.0
Ecuador	−1.1	48.3	0.0	48.1	−16.0	68.4	−52.2	0.2	1.0	0.9	2.3	2.3	99.8
Egypt, Arab Rep.	2.5	−55.1	0.0	0.0	17.8	−1.0	−28.1	1.7	3.2	3.4	9.1	6.7	−49.0
El Salvador	−0.8	25.2	0.0	0.0	−17.9	128.4	0.6	−0.1	1.0	0.8	0.9	1.5	138.6
Eritrea	78.2	0.0	0.0	0.0	5.6	0.0	5.8	3.7	2.7	2.1	1.7	3.4	101.5
Estonia	0.0	−2.5	0.0	−4.9	0.0	−2.7	−3.4	0.1	0.1	..	..	0.2	−13.2
Ethiopia	433.1	0.0	32.4	0.0	24.7	−18.5	14.9	17.0	3.3	19.4	36.0	32.7	559.0
Finland													
France													
Gabon	0.0	−9.1	0.0	−11.1	0.0	−31.7	−0.6	0.1	0.2	0.8	0.0	3.2	−48.2
Gambia, The	6.9	0.0	8.5	0.0	3.1	0.0	6.3	1.9	0.4	0.9	1.6	1.7	29.7
Georgia	63.1	0.0	30.8	−11.8	0.0	5.8	−6.4	1.2	0.3	0.6	2.0	5.9	89.5
Germany													
Ghana	158.9	−3.3	1.5	0.0	46.2	−8.5	4.1	4.0	2.8	3.0	1.5	5.0	213.6
Greece													
Guatemala	0.0	34.7	0.0	0.0	−4.9	64.9	−7.8	0.4	0.6	1.1	2.7	0.8	89.8
Guinea	62.5	0.0	17.7	0.0	2.3	−0.5	−1.8	1.2	0.8	3.4	1.3	31.5	117.0
Guinea-Bissau	2.4	0.0	0.0	0.0	1.1	0.0	−1.8	1.0	0.5	1.0	0.2	1.7	5.8
Haiti	0.8	0.0	0.0	0.0	5.3	0.0	−0.1	2.5	2.9	2.2	6.1	1.4	14.9

	International financial institutions							United Nations					Total
	World Bank		IMF		Regional development banks								
	IDA	IBRD	Concessional	Non-concessional	Concessional	Non-concessional	Others	UNDP	UNFPA	UNICEF	WFP	Others	
$ millions, 2001													
Honduras	94.5	−5.0	13.2	0.0	94.1	−14.4	10.7	0.1	1.4	1.1	*0.9*	1.0	196.6
Hungary	0.0	−10.3	0.0	0.0	0.0	−12.2	7.5	0.4	..	..	..	1.8	−12.8
India	771.1	−79.0	0.0	0.0	0.0	91.2	103.4	17.7	11.1	30.8	*27.0*	32.4	1,136.7
Indonesia	12.3	−280.0	0.0	−1,357.5	10.5	230.4	−21.7	3.8	6.8	5.1	*0.0*	16.3	−1,373.9
Iran, Islamic Rep.	0.0	−25.4	0.0	0.0	0.0	0.0	0.0	1.2	2.1	1.8	*0.1*	17.2	−3.1
Iraq	..	..	..	..	..	..	..	0.8	0.3	2.4	*0.1*	5.9	9.4
Ireland													
Israel	..	..	..	..	..	..	..	..	..	..	..	0.5	0.5
Italy													
Jamaica	0.0	39.5	0.0	−18.4	−4.7	−9.0	−9.3	0.1	0.0	0.8	..	1.3	0.3
Japan													
Jordan	−2.6	106.4	0.0	−12.5	0.0	0.0	38.3	0.5	0.9	0.8	*1.2*	82.7	214.5
Kazakhstan	0.0	66.6	0.0	0.0	1.3	2.9	18.0	0.8	0.7	0.8	..	2.0	93.2
Kenya	80.9	−22.5	−23.7	0.0	7.1	−15.1	−15.5	5.2	2.1	4.7	*19.4*	25.4	48.6
Korea, Dem. Rep.	..	..	..	..	..	..	..	0.7	0.7	1.1	*0.6*	4.8	7.3
Korea, Rep.	−3.5	−140.2	0.0	−5,681.2	0.0	−29.9	0.1	−0.4	..	..	..	1.0	−5,854.1
Kuwait												0.7	0.7
Kyrgyz Republic	26.7	0.0	4.8	−6.8	58.3	−8.5	6.3	1.2	0.5	0.9	..	1.9	85.1
Lao PDR	26.9	0.0	−3.6	0.0	38.9	0.0	11.4	1.5	1.9	2.3	*1.0*	2.7	82.0
Latvia	0.0	10.7	0.0	−9.7	0.0	−14.1	21.2	0.2	0.1	..	..	0.4	8.8
Lebanon	0.0	23.9	0.0	0.0	0.0	0.0	53.9	0.6	1.1	0.8	..	50.1	130.3
Lesotho	9.5	−0.8	4.6	0.0	3.8	−2.4	−3.5	0.5	0.3	0.7	*1.2*	0.8	13.5
Liberia	0.0	0.0	0.0	−0.6	0.0	0.0	0.0	2.1	0.8	1.8	*12.7*	8.0	12.1
Libya	..	..	..	..	..	..	..	..	..	..	..	5.2	5.2
Lithuania	0.0	26.7	0.0	−34.0	0.0	−6.3	21.4	0.2	0.1	..	..	0.4	8.5
Macedonia, FYR	14.9	4.5	0.0	−7.6	0.0	−13.8	−0.7	0.6	..	0.8	..	6.1	4.7
Madagascar	86.8	0.0	28.1	0.0	19.0	0.0	12.0	5.9	1.8	3.6	*2.7*	2.1	159.2
Malawi	98.6	−4.5	−4.0	0.0	8.8	−0.7	0.0	1.7	2.5	4.3	*1.8*	3.1	109.7
Malaysia	0.0	−22.5	0.0	0.0	0.0	−24.5	−2.3	0.4	0.1	0.7	..	1.9	−46.3
Mali	64.6	0.0	8.4	0.0	5.8	0.0	10.8	2.6	2.1	4.9	*2.0*	3.8	103.0
Mauritania	45.4	0.0	17.9	0.0	4.3	0.0	−12.4	0.8	1.3	1.3	*2.2*	1.4	59.9
Mauritius	−0.6	−8.2	0.0	0.0	−0.3	−4.0	−3.8	0.2	0.2	0.6	..	1.0	−14.9
Mexico	0.0	−560.6	0.0	0.0	−0.4	300.4	0.0	0.5	1.6	1.4	..	8.3	−248.9
Moldova	14.2	−3.1	11.8	−14.3	0.0	3.2	−7.7	0.9	0.2	0.7	..	1.4	7.2
Mongolia	23.5	0.0	−1.7	0.0	30.4	0.0	0.7	1.2	2.2	1.1	..	3.4	60.8
Morocco	−1.4	−218.3	0.0	0.0	5.1	−5.3	99.4	1.1	0.8	1.8	*2.2*	3.7	−113.2
Mozambique	48.7	0.0	10.5	0.0	48.9	−3.9	4.4	6.5	5.8	8.4	*3.4*	4.0	133.2
Myanmar	0.0	0.0	0.0	0.0	0.0	0.0	−0.2	15.6	1.5	6.5	..	9.2	32.6
Namibia	..	..	..	..	..	..	..	0.3	0.6	0.8	*0.3*	4.8	6.5
Nepal	29.6	0.0	−4.3	0.0	34.1	0.0	4.3	8.4	4.9	6.0	*6.3*	11.4	94.5
Netherlands													
New Zealand													
Nicaragua	61.8	−4.6	−5.1	0.0	105.3	−8.5	0.2	1.5	2.4	1.0	*8.4*	1.8	155.9
Niger	61.5	0.0	10.1	0.0	8.3	0.0	−4.2	5.0	2.3	5.9	*3.0*	4.1	93.0
Nigeria	1.3	−189.1	0.0	0.0	10.1	−78.0	−1.7	8.6	5.6	22.8	..	21.0	−199.4
Norway													
Oman	0.0	−1.4	0.0	0.0	0.0	0.0	285.7	..	0.0	0.5	..	1.2	286.1
Pakistan	530.6	−161.4	37.9	297.5	432.5	9.7	8.7	5.9	3.3	12.4	*2.7*	24.7	1,201.8
Panama	0.0	0.0	0.0	−33.3	−10.6	44.7	4.4	0.2	0.4	0.6	..	1.4	7.8
Papua New Guinea	−3.2	40.3	0.0	70.9	−3.9	30.3	−2.4	0.3	0.5	1.1	..	1.9	135.8
Paraguay	−1.5	13.0	0.0	0.0	−10.2	32.7	−11.3	0.1	0.7	0.8	..	0.5	24.9
Peru	0.0	35.4	0.0	−153.4	−6.4	278.3	507.0	0.6	1.6	1.0	*3.9*	5.6	669.5
Philippines	1.7	−193.7	0.0	−7.7	14.4	94.9	−0.1	2.9	2.9	2.9	..	6.0	−75.8
Poland	0.0	93.4	0.0	0.0	0.0	0.0	0.0	0.3	0.1	..	..	1.3	95.1
Portugal													
Puerto Rico													

$ millions, 2001	World Bank IDA	World Bank IBRD	IMF Concessional	IMF Non-concessional	Regional development banks Concessional	Regional development banks Non-concessional	Others	UNDP	UNFPA	UNICEF	WFP	Others	Total
Romania	0.0	31.4	0.0	−50.6	0.0	4.5	207.6	0.6	0.5	0.7	..	2.1	196.8
Russian Federation	0.0	23.5	0.0	−3,816.7	0.0	26.8	0.0	0.5	0.6	..	..	17.3	−3,748.0
Rwanda	50.1	0.0	11.0	−0.9	10.2	0.0	−2.1	2.7	1.6	2.8	20.0	8.5	83.9
Saudi Arabia	..	..	..	..	..	..	..	..	..	0.4	..	15.9	16.3
Senegal	109.4	−1.3	7.1	0.0	20.9	−3.6	18.3	2.3	2.2	2.5	3.0	2.8	160.5
Sierra Leone	67.2	0.0	32.0	−47.7	12.4	−0.3	−1.1	3.1	0.5	2.8	0.0	5.6	74.3
Singapore	..	..	..	..	..	..	..	..	..	..	..	0.2	0.2
Slovak Republic	0.0	31.7	0.0	0.0	0.0	−1.1	64.4	0.3	..	..	..	1.1	96.4
Slovenia	..	..	..	..	..	..	..	0.1	..	..	..	1.0	1.0
Somalia	0.0	0.0	0.0	0.0	0.0	0.0	0.0	3.6	0.2	5.6	0.7	11.5	20.8
South Africa	0.0	4.0	0.0	0.0	0.0	0.0	0.0	1.5	1.6	2.0	..	7.1	16.1
Spain													
Sri Lanka	11.9	−4.3	−71.3	131.6	59.3	0.2	1.3	3.2	1.4	0.8	2.5	9.0	143.0
Sudan	−0.9	−0.5	0.0	0.0	0.0	0.0	−0.2	2.2	2.5	6.4	6.7	18.3	27.8
Swaziland	−0.3	0.0	0.0	1.6	5.2	8.0	0.3	0.2	0.6	..	1.4	17.0	
Sweden													
Switzerland													
Syrian Arab Republic	−1.5	−7.9	0.0	0.0	0.0	0.0	−43.6	0.9	2.5	0.9	4.6	28.5	−20.1
Tajikistan	34.8	0.0	15.3	−11.9	2.9	0.0	28.2	2.5	0.6	1.1	4.9	2.5	76.0
Tanzania	99.6	−3.5	48.6	0.0	9.3	0.0	4.2	5.2	4.1	5.9	2.5	29.9	203.3
Thailand	−3.4	105.5	0.0	−1,289.0	−2.2	70.5	−15.2	1.0	0.7	1.2	0.0	6.5	−1,124.4
Togo	1.4	0.0	0.0	0.0	0.0	0.0	12.0	2.3	1.2	1.6	..	2.1	20.6
Trinidad and Tobago	0.0	1.3	0.0	0.0	2.8	−8.9	−5.4	0.0	..	..	..	0.5	−9.7
Tunisia	−2.1	146.9	0.0	−31.5	0.0	47.4	120.1	0.5	0.8	0.8	..	2.4	285.3
Turkey	−5.9	1,105.7	0.0	10,219.8	0.0	0.0	547.3	0.8	0.7	0.9	..	5.6	11,874.9
Turkmenistan	0.0	2.2	0.0	0.0	0.0	−3.0	−0.7	0.9	0.7	1.0	..	1.0	2.1
Uganda	292.8	0.0	−3.3	0.0	34.1	−2.6	−0.4	4.3	4.8	5.4	8.6	17.6	352.6
Ukraine	0.0	304.8	0.0	−89.7	0.0	−22.9	−15.3	1.2	0.3	..	..	4.0	182.4
United Arab Emirates	..	..	..	..	..	..	..	−0.4	..	..	..	0.9	0.5
United Kingdom													
United States													
Uruguay	0.0	−7.8	0.0	0.0	−1.7	157.2	−3.8	0.3	0.1	0.9	..	1.0	146.1
Uzbekistan	0.0	31.2	0.0	−44.7	4.5	45.5	0.1	1.2	0.7	1.6	..	1.4	41.3
Venezuela, RB	0.0	−133.3	0.0	−198.1	0.0	119.1	102.9	0.2	0.6	0.8	0.2	2.9	−104.9
Vietnam	276.7	0.0	67.0	−5.1	138.9	0.0	14.1	7.4	3.9	4.4	10.1	7.1	514.3
West Bank and Gaza	..	..	..	..	..	..	..	2.4	1.2	1.5	1.1	211.9	217.0
Yemen, Rep.	59.8	0.0	113.0	−44.5	0.0	0.0	−16.2	5.7	4.0	3.8	7.1	8.9	134.5
Yugoslavia, Fed. Rep.	0.0	0.0	0.0	127.3	0.0	0.0	5.9	1.8	1.6	0.1	0.2	50.8	187.5
Zambia	121.6	−7.8	53.5	0.0	10.9	0.0	6.2	2.8	1.1	3.4	4.2	14.2	206.0
Zimbabwe	−2.2	−10.9	−1.3	−7.6	0.0	−2.0	1.2	1.7	1.6	3.4	..	5.1	−10.9
World	.. s	.. s	.. s	.. s	.. s	.. s	.. s	287.0 s	313.6 s	605.2 s	357.3 s	1,920.3 s	.. s
Low income	4,458.5	−363.3	473.4	−1,378.0	1,393.5	279.2	183.1	230.1	136.4	285.4	298.0	560.7	6,258.9
Middle income	556.8	2,862.2	−51.3	20,418.6	209.1	4,609.4	2,086.6	52.5	53.0	69.0	59.4	850.8	31,716.6
Lower middle income	557.3	2,053.8	−51.3	4,804.0	234.5	2,186.8	1,359.5	43.2	43.0	56.0	55.8	562.6	11,849.4
Upper middle income	−0.5	808.3	0.0	15,614.6	−25.5	2,422.6	727.0	9.3	7.3	12.2	0.2	251.8	19,827.3
Low & middle income	5,015.3	2,498.9	422.1	19,040.6	1,602.6	4,888.6	2,269.7	286.7	313.6	605.2	357.3	1,913.6	38,856.8
East Asia & Pacific	600.5	308.9	72.3	−2,589.8	269.0	1,045.8	−152.6	51.2	30.5	46.6	29.6	91.7	−226.0
Europe & Central Asia	326.3	1,774.8	87.6	5,974.2	67.0	−3.2	897.8	21.1	9.8	16.0	12.2	144.9	9,316.4
Latin America & Carib.	261.3	1,013.7	6.2	15,581.5	212.9	3,797.6	1,029.6	14.4	22.3	25.4	37.3	213.8	22,178.7
Middle East & N. Africa	63.1	−124.7	117.6	−231.1	24.7	83.8	321.0	16.4	18.5	21.1	28.8	448.6	758.9
South Asia	1,566.5	−91.8	−97.7	429.1	656.9	169.8	84.0	53.1	36.5	73.4	55.6	107.1	2,986.9
Sub-Saharan Africa	2,197.7	−382.1	236.1	−123.3	372.2	−205.4	89.8	126.5	75.6	181.2	190.6	562.4	3,130.8
High income							..	0.3	0.0	0.0	0.0	6.7	..
Europe EMU													

Note: The aggregates for the regional development banks, United Nations, and total net financial flows include amounts for economies not specified elsewhere. Because the World Food Programme implemented an annual program budget in 2002, its 2001 data are not yet consistent with the Development Assistance Committee's reporting system. The World Food Programme data in the table are for 2000 and are not included in the total column.

About the data

This table shows concessional and nonconcessional financial flows from the major multilateral institutions—the World Bank, the International Monetary Fund (IMF), regional development banks, United Nations agencies, and regional groups such as the Commission of the European Communities. Much of the data comes from the World Bank's Debtor Reporting System.

The multilateral development banks fund their nonconcessional lending operations primarily by selling low-interest, highly rated bonds (the World Bank, for example, has a AAA rating) backed by prudent lending and financial policies and the strong financial backing of their members. These funds are then on-lent at slightly higher interest rates, and with relatively long maturities (15–20 years), to developing countries. Lending terms vary with market conditions and the policies of the banks.

Concessional flows from bilateral donors are defined by the Development Assistance Committee (DAC) of the Organisation for Economic Co-operation and Development (OECD) as those containing a grant element of at least 25 percent. The grant element of loans is evaluated assuming a nominal market interest rate of 10 percent. The grant element of a loan carrying a 10 percent interest rate is nil, and for a grant, which requires no repayment, it is 100 percent. Concessional flows from multilateral development agencies are credits provided through their concessional lending facilities. The cost of these loans is reduced through subsidies provided by donors or drawn from other resources available to the agencies. Grants provided by multilateral agencies are not included in the net flows.

All concessional lending by the World Bank is carried out by the International Development Association (IDA).

Eligibility for IDA resources is based on gross national income (GNI) per capita; countries must also meet performance standards assessed by World Bank staff. Since July 1, 2002, the GNI per capita cutoff has been set at $745, measured in 2001 using the Atlas method (see *Users guide*). In exceptional circumstances IDA extends eligibility temporarily to countries that are above the cutoff and are undertaking major adjustment efforts but are not creditworthy for lending by the International Bank for Reconstruction and Development (IBRD). An exception has also been made for small island economies. Lending by the International Finance Corporation is not included in this table.

The IMF makes concessional funds available through its Poverty Reduction and Growth Facility, which replaced the Enhanced Structural Adjustment Facility in 1999, and through the IMF Trust Fund. Eligibility is based principally on a country's per capita income and eligibility under IDA, the World Bank's concessional window.

Regional development banks also maintain concessional windows for funds. Loans from the major regional development banks—the African Development Bank, Asian Development Bank, and Inter-American Development Bank—are recorded in the table according to each institution's classification.

In 1999 all United Nations agencies revised their data to include only regular budgetary expenditures since 1990 (except for the World Food Programme and the United Nations High Commissioner for Refugees, which revised their data from 1996 onward). They did so to avoid double counting extrabudgetary expenditures reported by DAC countries and flows reported by the United Nations.

Definitions

- **Net financial flows** in this table are disbursements of public or publicly guaranteed loans and credits, less repayments of principal. • **IDA** is the International Development Association, the soft loan window of the World Bank. • **IBRD** is the International Bank for Reconstruction and Development, the founding and largest member of the World Bank Group. • **IMF** is the International Monetary Fund. Its nonconcessional lending consists of the credit it provides to its members, mainly to meet their balance of payments needs. It provides concessional assistance through the Poverty Reduction and Growth Facility and the IMF Trust Fund. • **Regional development banks** include the African Development Bank, in Abidjan, Côte d'Ivoire, which lends to all of Africa, including North Africa; the Asian Development Bank, in Manila, Philippines, which serves countries in South and Central Asia and East Asia and Pacific; the European Bank for Reconstruction and Development, in London, England, which serves countries in Europe and Central Asia; the European Development Fund, in Brussels, Belgium, which serves countries in Africa, the Caribbean, and the Pacific; and the Inter-American Development Bank, in Washington, D.C., which is the principal development bank of the Americas. • **Others** is a residual category in the World Bank's Debtor Reporting System. It includes such institutions as the Caribbean Development Bank and the European Investment Bank. • **United Nations** includes the United Nations Development Programme (UNDP), United Nations Population Fund (UNFPA), United Nations Children's Fund (UNICEF), World Food Programme (WFP), and other United Nations agencies, such as the United Nations High Commissioner for Refugees, United Nations Relief and Works Agency for Palestine Refugees in the Near East, and United Nations Regular Programme for Technical Assistance. • **Concessional financial flows** cover disbursements made through concessional lending facilities. • **Nonconcessional financial flows** cover all other disbursements.

Data sources

The data on net financial flows from international financial institutions come from the World Bank's Debtor Reporting System. These data are published in the World Bank's *Global Development Finance 2003* and electronically as *GDF Online*. The data on aid from United Nations agencies come from the DAC annual *Development Co-operation Report*. Data are available in electronic format on the OECD's *International Development Statistics* CD-ROM and to registered users at http://www.oecd.org/dac/htm/online.htm.

6.12a

The International Monetary Fund responds to financial crises in developing countries

Net nonconcessional financial flows from the IMF ($ billions)

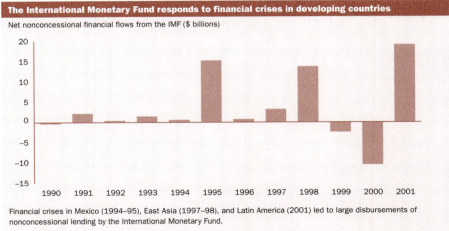

Financial crises in Mexico (1994–95), East Asia (1997–98), and Latin America (2001) led to large disbursements of nonconcessional lending by the International Monetary Fund.

Source: World Bank, Debtor Reporting System.

	Foreign population [a]				Foreign labor force [b]		Inflows of foreign population			
	thousands		% of total population		% of total labor force		Total thousands [c]		Asylum seekers thousands	
	1990	2000	1990	2000	1990	2000	1990	2000	1990	2000
Austria	456	758	5.9	9.3	7.4	10.5	..	66	23	18
Belgium	905	862	9.1	8.4	7.1	*8.9*	50	69	13	43
Denmark	161	259	3.1	4.8	2.4	3.4	15	*20*	5	10
Finland	26	91	0.5	1.8	..	*1.5*	6	9	3	3
France	3,597	*3,263*	6.3	*5.6*	6.2	6.0	102 [d]	119 [d]	55	39
Germany	5,343	7,297	8.4	8.9	..	8.8 [e]	842	649	193	79
Ireland	80	127	2.3	3.3	2.6	3.7	..	24 [d]	0	11
Italy	781	1,388	1.4	2.4	*1.3*	3.6	..	272 [d]	5	25
Japan	1,075	1,686	0.9	1.3	*0.1*	0.2	224	346	..	0
Luxembourg	113	165	29.4	37.3	45.2 [e]	57.3 [e]	9	11	0	1
Netherlands	692	668	4.6	4.2	3.1 [e]	*3.4* [e]	81	91	21	44
Norway	143	184	3.4	4.1	2.3	4.9	16	28	4	11
Portugal	108	208	1.1	2.1	1.0	2.0	*14* [d]	16 [d]	0	0
Spain	279	896	0.7	2.2	0.6	*1.2*	..	..	9	8
Sweden	484	477	5.6	5.4	5.4	5.0	53	34	29	16
Switzerland	1,100	1,384	16.3	19.3	18.9	18.3	101	87	36	18
United Kingdom	1,723	2,342	3.2	4.0	3.3	4.4	*204*	289	38	99

	Foreign population [a]				Foreign labor force [b]		Inflows of foreign population			
	thousands		% of total population		% of total labor force		Total thousands [c, d]		Asylum seekers thousands	
	1990	2000	1990	2000	1990	2000	1990	2000	1990	2000
Australia	3,886	4,517	22.8	23.6	*25.7*	24.5	121	316	4	12
Canada	*4,343*	..	*16.1*	..	*18.5*	..	214	313	37	36
United States	19,767 [f]	28,400 [g]	7.9 [f]	10.4 [g]	9.4	12.4	1,536	3,590	74	57

a. Data are from population registers or from registers of foreigners, except for Australia, Canada, France, and the United States (censuses), Portugal and Spain (residence permits), and Ireland and the United Kingdom (labor force surveys), and refer to the population on December 31 of the year indicated. b. Data include the unemployed, except in Italy, Luxembourg, the Netherlands, Norway, and the United Kingdom. Cross-border and seasonal workers are excluded unless otherwise noted. c. Inflow data are based on population registers and are not fully comparable because the criteria governing who gets registered differ from country to country. Counts for the Netherlands, Norway, and especially Germany include substantial numbers of asylum seekers. d. Data are based on residence permits or other sources. e. Includes cross-border workers. f. From the U.S. Census Bureau, *1990 Census of Population Listing*. g. From the U.S. Census Bureau, *Current Population Report* (March 2000).

About the data

The data in the table are based on national definitions and data collection practices and are not fully comparable across countries. Japan and the European members of the Organisation for Economic Co-operation and Development (OECD) have traditionally defined foreigners by nationality of descent. Australia, Canada, and the United States use place of birth, which is closer to the concept used in the United Nations' definition of the immigrant stock. Few countries, however, apply just one criterion in all circumstances. For this and other reasons, data based on the concept of foreign nationality and data based on the concept of foreign-born cannot be completely reconciled. See the notes to the table for other breaks in comparability between countries and over time.

Data on the size of the foreign labor force are also problematic. Countries use different permit systems to gather information on immigrants. Some countries issue a single permit for residence and work, while others issue separate residence and work permits. Differences in immigration laws across countries, particularly with respect to immigrants' access to employment, greatly affect the recording and measurement of migration and reduce the international comparability of raw data. The data exclude temporary visitors and tourists (see table 6.14).

OECD countries are not the only ones that receive substantial migration flows. Migrant workers make up a significant share of the labor force in Gulf countries and in southern Africa, and people are displaced by wars and natural disasters throughout the world. Systematic recording of migration flows is difficult, however, especially in poor countries and those affected by civil disorder.

Definitions

• **Foreign (or foreign-born) population** is the number of foreign or foreign-born residents in a country. • **Foreign (or foreign-born) labor force as a percentage of total labor force** is the share of foreign or foreign-born workers in a country's workforce. • **Inflows of foreign population** are the gross arrivals of immigrants in the country shown. The total does not include asylum seekers, except as noted. • **Asylum seekers** are those who apply for permission to remain in a country for humanitarian reasons.

6.13a

Foreign labor levels have remained steady over the past decade in many OECD countries

% of total labor force, 1990–2000

Source: Organisation for Economic Co-operation and Development.

Data sources

International migration data are collected by the OECD through information provided by national correspondents to the Continuous Reporting System on Migration (SOPEMI) network, which provides an annual overview of trends and policies. The data appear in the OECD's *Trends in International Migration 2002*.

	International tourism				International tourism receipts				International tourism expenditures			
	Inbound tourists thousands		Outbound tourists thousands		$ millions		% of exports		$ millions		% of imports	
	1990	2001	1990	2000	1990	2001	1990	2001	1990	2001	1990	2001
Afghanistan	..	..	..	..	..	..	..	..	1	..	..	..
Albania	30	34	..	18	4	389	1.1	55.3	4	258	0.8	14.5
Algeria	1,137	901	3,828	903	64	102	0.5	0.5	149	193	1.5	2.0
Angola	67	67	..	..	13	18	0.3	0.2	38	127	1.1	2.2
Argentina	1,930	2,629	2,398	4,786	1,131	2,534	7.6	8.2	1,505	3,890	22.0	14.1
Armenia	..	45	..	..	..	45	..	10.1	..	37	..	3.8
Australia	2,215	4,817	2,170	3,210	4,088	7,625	8.2	9.5	4,535	5,812	8.5	7.4
Austria	19,011	18,180	8,527	3,954	13,417	10,118	21.1	10.1	7,748	8,886	12.6	8.9
Azerbaijan	..	766	..	1,204	228	63	..	3.0	..	132	..	6.5
Bangladesh	115	207	388	1,103	11	48	0.6	0.7	78	163	1.9	1.6
Belarus	..	..	..	..	..	19	..	0.2	..	133	..	1.6
Belgium	5,204	6,452	3,835	7,773	3,721	6,917	2.7	3.2	5,477	9,766	4.1	4.8
Benin	110	..	418	..	28	..	7.7	..	12	..	2.6	..
Bolivia	254	300	242	196	91	156	9.3	10.3	130	118	12.0	5.9
Bosnia and Herzegovina	1	89	..	..	..	21	..	1.7	..	..	..	..
Botswana	543	995	192	..	117	313	5.8	10.4	56	143	2.8	6.0
Brazil	1,091	4,773	1,188	2,679	1,444	3,701	4.1	5.5	1,559	3,199	5.5	4.4
Bulgaria	1,322	3,186	2,395	2,592	320	1,201	4.6	16.0	189	569	2.4	6.6
Burkina Faso	74	126	..	..	11	..	3.2	..	32	..	4.2	..
Burundi	109	26	24	16	4	..	4.5	..	17	14	5.3	9.3
Cambodia	17	466	..	49	50	228	15.9	15.1	..	19	..	1.0
Cameroon	89	59	..	..	53	39	2.4	1.4	279	..	14.5	..
Canada	15,209	19,697	20,415	18,368	6,339	10,774	4.2	3.5	10,931	11,624	7.3	4.3
Central African Republic	8	10	..	..	3	..	1.4	..	51	..	12.4	..
Chad	9	56	24	..	8	..	3.0	..	70	..	14.4	..
Chile	943	1,723	768	1,567	540	788	5.3	3.5	426	1,040	4.6	4.9
China	..	33,167	2,134	10,473	2,218	17,792	3.9	5.9	470	13,114	1.0	5.2
Hong Kong, China	6,581	13,725	2,043	4,175	5,032	8,241	5.0	3.5	..	12,494	..	5.6
Colombia	813	616	781	1,098	406	1,209	4.7	8.1	454	1,160	6.6	7.3
Congo, Dem. Rep.	55	103	..	50	7	..	0.3	..	16	..	0.6	..
Congo, Rep.	33	19	..	..	8	12	0.5	0.7	113	58	8.8	4.2
Costa Rica	435	1,132	191	353	275	1,278	14.0	18.4	148	361	6.3	4.9
Côte d'Ivoire	196	..	2	..	51	57	1.5	1.3	169	226	4.9	6.2
Croatia	7,049	6,544	..	..	1,704	3,335	..	34.6	729	606	..	5.7
Cuba	327	1,736	12	56	243	1,692	..	..	..	..	..	..
Czech Republic	..	5,194	3,510	39,977	419	2,979	..	7.4	455	1,388	..	3.3
Denmark	..	2,028	3,929	4,841	3,322	3,923	6.8	5.0	3,676	4,684	8.9	6.9
Dominican Republic	1,305	2,778	137	364	900	2,689	49.1	32.3	144	286	6.4	2.8
Ecuador	362	609	181	386	188	430	5.8	7.4	175	340	6.9	5.0
Egypt, Arab Rep.	2,411	4,357	2,012	2,886	1,100	3,800	12.0	22.5	129	1,132	0.9	5.2
El Salvador	194	735	525	787	18	235	1.8	5.9	61	171	3.8	3.0
Eritrea	169	113	..	..	..	74	..	50.2	..	..	..	..
Estonia	372	1,320	..	1,780	27	507	4.1	10.2	19	191	2.7	3.7
Ethiopia	79	136	89	..	25	68	3.7	6.9	11	74	1.0	3.8
Finland	..	2,826	1,169	5,314	1,167	1,441	3.7	3.0	2,791	1,854	8.3	4.8
France	52,497	76,506	19,430	16,709	20,184	29,979	7.1	8.1	12,423	17,718	4.4	5.0
Gabon	109	169	161	..	3	7	0.1	0.2	137	170	7.6	8.7
Gambia, The	100	96	..	..	26	..	15.5	..	8	..	4.2	..
Georgia	..	302	..	373	..	413	..	62.1	..	110	..	9.3
Germany	17,045	17,861	56,261	73,400	14,288	17,225	3.0	2.6	33,771	46,222	8.0	7.5
Ghana	146	439	..	..	81	448	8.2	18.8	13	100	0.9	3.0
Greece	8,873	13,096	1,651	..	2,587	9,219	19.9	31.3	1,090	4,181	5.6	10.1
Guatemala	509	835	289	391	185	493	11.8	12.7	100	182	5.5	3.3
Guinea	..	37	..	..	30	14	3.6	1.7	30	15	3.1	1.7
Guinea-Bissau	..	8	..	..	..	..	..	..	..	..	..	..
Haiti	144	140	..	..	46	54	15.2	10.9	37	..	5.3	..

Travel and tourism

	International tourism				International tourism receipts				International tourism expenditures			
	Inbound tourists thousands		Outbound tourists thousands		$ millions		% of exports		$ millions		% of imports	
	1990	2001	1990	2000	1990	2001	1990	2001	1990	2001	1990	2001
Honduras	290	518	196	235	29	262	2.8	10.6	38	157	3.4	4.5
Hungary	20,510	15,340	13,596	10,622	824	3,933	6.8	11.0	477	1,309	4.3	3.7
India	1,707	2,537	2,281	3,811	1,513	3,042	6.6	4.7	393	2,567	1.2	3.4
Indonesia	2,178	5,154	688	..	2,105	5,411	7.2	8.6	836	3,197	3.0	5.8
Iran, Islamic Rep.	154	1,402	788	1,450	61	1,122	0.3	4.7	340	1,350	1.5	8.9
Iraq	748	127	239	..	..	..	..	..	..	..	..	..
Ireland	3,666	6,448	1,798	3,576	1,883	3,547	7.0	3.6	1,163	2,957	4.7	3.9
Israel	1,063	1,196	883	3,203	1,396	2,166	8.1	5.5	1,442	2,896	7.1	6.7
Italy	26,679	39,055	16,152	18,962	16,458	25,787	7.5	8.6	10,304	14,215	4.7	5.0
Jamaica	989	1,277	..	..	740	1,233	33.4	36.8	114	209	4.8	4.7
Japan	3,236	4,772	10,997	16,358	3,578	3,301	1.1	0.7	24,928	26,530	8.4	6.3
Jordan	572	1,478	1,143	1,560	512	700	20.4	18.5	336	420	9.4	7.0
Kazakhstan	..	1,845	..	..	..	396	..	3.8	..	474	..	4.4
Kenya	814	841	210	..	443	308	19.9	10.3	38	132	1.4	3.5
Korea, Dem. Rep.	115	..	..	..	..	..	..	..	..	..	..	..
Korea, Rep.	2,959	5,147	1,561	5,508	3,559	6,283	4.9	3.5	3,166	6,887	4.1	4.0
Kuwait	15	79	..	..	132	98	1.6	0.5	1,837	2,451	25.6	21.5
Kyrgyz Republic	..	69	..	32	..	15	..	2.6	..	16	..	2.4
Lao PDR	14	169	..	..	3	104	2.9	21.8	1	17	0.5	2.9
Latvia	..	591	..	2,256	7	120	0.6	3.5	13	224	1.3	5.3
Lebanon	210	837	..	1,650	..	837	..	43.6	..	..	..	..
Lesotho	171	231	..	..	17	24	17.0	9.5	12	9	1.6	1.2
Liberia	..	..	..	..	..	..	..	..	..	..	..	..
Libya	96	174	425	..	6	28	0.1	0.4	424	150	4.7	3.1
Lithuania	..	1,271	..	3,482	..	384	..	6.4	..	218	..	3.3
Macedonia, FYR	562	99	..	..	45	23	..	1.7	..	..	..	..
Madagascar	53	170	34	..	40	119	8.5	10.0	40	114	4.9	7.5
Malawi	130	228	..	..	16	27	3.6	5.5	16	..	2.9	..
Malaysia	7,446	12,775	14,920	26,067	1,667	4,936	5.1	4.4	1,450	1,973	4.6	2.6
Mali	44	89	..	..	47	71	11.2	11.3	62	41	7.5	4.4
Mauritania	..	30	..	..	9	28	1.9	7.7	23	55	4.4	13.3
Mauritius	292	660	89	154	244	625	14.2	22.0	94	182	4.9	6.7
Mexico	17,176	19,811	7,357	11,081	5,467	8,401	11.2	4.9	5,519	5,702	10.6	3.1
Moldova	226	16	49	37	4	46	..	6.2	..	88	..	8.0
Mongolia	147	192	..	..	5	36	1.0	6.8	1	41	0.1	6.2
Morocco	4,024	4,223	1,202	1,612	1,259	2,460	20.2	22.0	184	354	2.4	2.9
Mozambique	..	..	..	..	..	..	..	..	..	..	..	..
Myanmar	21	205	..	..	9	45	1.4	1.7	16	25	1.4	1.0
Namibia	213	861	..	..	85	..	7.0	..	63	..	4.0	..
Nepal	255	363	82	122	64	137	16.9	10.1	45	73	5.9	3.8
Netherlands	5,795	9,500	9,000	14,180	4,155	6,722	2.6	2.6	7,376	12,016	5.0	5.0
New Zealand	..	1,910	717	1,185	1,030	2,252	8.8	12.3	958	1,340	8.2	8.0
Nicaragua	106	483	173	452	12	109	3.1	11.7	15	76	2.2	3.8
Niger	21	52	18	10	17	24	3.2	7.5	44	28	6.0	6.1
Nigeria	190	955	56	..	25	156	0.2	0.7	576	730	8.3	5.2
Norway	1,955	4,244	2,667	..	1,570	2,042	3.3	2.6	3,679	4,305	9.5	8.8
Oman	149	562	..	..	69	118	1.2	1.0	47	341	1.4	5.5
Pakistan	424	500	..	..	156	92	2.5	0.9	440	255	4.7	2.0
Panama	214	519	151	221	172	626	3.9	8.1	99	176	2.4	2.2
Papua New Guinea	41	54	66	106	41	101	3.0	4.8	50	53	3.3	2.9
Paraguay	280	295	264	281	128	101	5.1	3.6	103	91	4.7	2.7
Peru	317	1,010	329	781	217	865	5.3	10.1	295	576	7.2	6.1
Philippines	1,025	1,797	1,137	1,755	1,306	1,723	11.4	5.0	111	1,005	0.8	2.8
Poland	11,350	15,000	22,131	55,097	358	4,815	1.9	9.4	423	3,500	2.8	6.0
Portugal	8,020	12,167	2,268	..	3,555	5,479	16.5	15.8	867	2,105	3.2	4.7
Puerto Rico	2,560	3,551	996	1,134	1,366	2,728	..	..	630	1,004	..	..

	International tourism				International tourism receipts				International tourism expenditures			
	Inbound tourists thousands		Outbound tourists thousands		$ millions		% of exports		$ millions		% of imports	
	1990	2001	1990	2000	1990	2001	1990	2001	1990	2001	1990	2001
Romania	3,099	2,820	11,247	6,274	106	362	1.7	2.7	103	449	1.0	2.7
Russian Federation	3,009	21,169	4,150	18,371	..	7,510	..	8.9	..	7,434	..	14.1
Rwanda	16	..	..	..	10	24	6.9	21.9	23	20	6.4	4.7
Saudi Arabia	2,209	6,295	..	..	..	..	..	..	..	..	..	..
Senegal	246	389	..	..	167	140	11.5	10.5	105	54	5.7	3.0
Sierra Leone	98	24	..	..	19	8	9.1	11.0	4	6	1.9	2.5
Singapore	4,842	6,726	1,237	3,971	4,937	6,018	7.3	3.6	1,893	4,647	2.9	3.6
Slovak Republic	822	1,219	188	343	70	639	..	4.2	181	287	..	1.7
Slovenia	616	1,219	..	..	671	996	8.5	8.8	282	519	4.1	4.5
Somalia	..	..	..	..	..	..	..	..	..	..	..	..
South Africa	1,029	5,908	616	3,363	992	2,707	3.6	7.4	1,117	2,004	5.3	6.1
Spain	34,085	49,519	10,698	4,794	18,593	32,873	22.2	18.7	4,254	5,974	4.2	3.3
Sri Lanka	298	337	297	524	132	211	5.8	3.4	74	245	2.5	3.4
Sudan	33	50	203	..	21	56	4.2	3.3	51	55	5.8	2.7
Swaziland	263	281	..	..	30	34	4.6	3.4	35	36	4.6	2.9
Sweden	..	2,894	6,232	10,500	2,906	4,162	4.1	4.2	6,286	6,803	8.9	8.0
Switzerland	13,200	10,700	9,627	12,009	7,411	7,618	7.6	6.2	5,873	6,180	6.1	5.6
Syrian Arab Republic	562	1,318	1,041	..	320	1,082	6.4	15.8	249	610	8.4	10.2
Tajikistan	..	4	..	..	..	0	..	0.0	..	..	..	..
Tanzania	..	501	301	..	65	725	12.1	51.7	23	330	1.6	15.1
Thailand	5,299	10,133	883	1,909	4,326	6,731	14.8	8.8	854	2,179	2.4	3.1
Togo	103	57	..	..	58	5	8.7	1.2	40	3	4.7	0.5
Trinidad and Tobago	195	399	254	..	95	210	4.2	6.2	122	..	8.6	..
Tunisia	3,204	5,387	1,727	1,480	948	1,605	18.2	16.9	179	263	3.0	2.8
Turkey	4,799	10,783	2,917	4,758	3,225	8,932	15.3	17.7	520	1,738	2.0	3.8
Turkmenistan	..	..	..	357	..	..	..	..	..	..	..	..
Uganda	69	205	..	..	10	149	4.1	20.5	8	141	1.2	9.4
Ukraine	..	5,791	..	7,399	..	2,725	..	12.9	..	2,179	..	10.6
United Arab Emirates	973	3,907	..	..	315	1,012	..	..	..	..	..	..
United Kingdom	18,013	22,833	31,150	53,881	13,762	16,283	5.8	4.2	17,560	36,483	6.6	8.7
United States	39,362	45,491	44,623	58,386	43,007	72,295	8.0	7.2	37,349	60,117	6.1	4.4
Uruguay	..	1,892	..	778	238	561	11.0	17.1	111	252	6.7	6.8
Uzbekistan	..	..	..	..	..	..	..	..	..	..	..	..
Venezuela, RB	525	469	309	891	496	563	2.6	1.6	1,023	1,801	10.8	8.2
Vietnam	250	1,383	..	168	85	..	..	..	..	..	..	..
West Bank and Gaza	..	330	..	..	..	155	..	..	..	..	..	..
Yemen, Rep.	52	76	..	..	20	38	1.3	0.9	64	136	2.9	4.8
Yugoslavia, Fed. Rep.	1,186	351	..	..	134	40	..	1.4	..	..	..	..
Zambia	141	457	..	..	41	85	3.0	9.7	54	..	2.8	..
Zimbabwe	605	1,868	200	331	60	125	3.0	5.9	66	110	3.3	4.8
World	**481,270 t**	**696,494 t**	**508,753 t**	**644,804 t**	**265,316 t**	**457,890 t**	**6.1 w**	**5.9 w**	**269,195 t**	**418,340 t**	**6.3 w**	**5.6 w**
Low income	13,437	28,833	..	..	10,970	16,709	4.9	6.5	..	13,100	3.8	5.1
Middle income	133,372	232,474	149,300	236,011	43,817	125,609	7.3	8.2	28,764	70,989	5.0	4.7
Lower middle income	64,533	125,664	43,815	63,822	22,403	71,418	8.0	8.9	..	34,596	2.7	4.6
Upper middle income	85,421	105,950	..	177,268	21,710	54,168	6.5	7.4	17,542	31,535	7.5	4.7
Low & middle income	151,524	264,322	..	294,863	51,846	142,306	6.8	8.0	35,180	84,218	4.8	4.8
East Asia & Pacific	..	67,164	21,567	45,404	12,218	38,207	7.3	6.7	3,946	22,600	2.3	4.7
Europe & Central Asia	64,476	98,720	..	176,460	9,975	40,747	7.4	11.1	..	21,727	2.6	4.6
Latin America & Carib.	33,957	49,861	17,586	28,743	15,622	32,562	8.2	7.1	13,049	21,299	9.0	5.0
Middle East & N. Africa	16,544	27,419	..	..	..	..	..	..	3,288	6,937	..	..
South Asia	3,054	4,496	3,503	6,255	1,968	3,873	5.8	4.3	1,048	3,491	2.1	3.3
Sub-Saharan Africa	7,168	17,931	..	..	3,093	7,030	3.8	6.0	3,683	5,507	5.5	5.7
High income	311,961	426,407	275,794	331,292	212,121	319,585	6.0	5.4	232,094	336,785	6.5	5.7
Europe EMU	184,004	253,706	..	..	100,058	149,258	6.6	6.2	88,497	127,959	6.0	5.8

About the data

Tourism is defined as the activities of people traveling to and staying in places outside their usual environment for no more than one consecutive year for leisure, business, and other purposes not related to an activity remunerated from within the place visited. The social and economic phenomenon of tourism has grown substantially over the past quarter of a century.

In the past, descriptions of tourism focused on the characteristics of visitors, such as the purpose of their visit and the conditions in which they traveled and stayed. Now there is a growing awareness of the direct, indirect, and induced effects of tourism on employment, value added, personal income, government income, and the like.

Statistical information on tourism is based mainly on data on arrivals and overnight stays along with balance of payments information. But these do not completely capture the economic phenomenon of tourism. Thus governments, businesses, and citizens may not receive the information needed for effective public policies and efficient business operations. Although the World Tourism Organization reports that progress has been made in harmonizing definitions and measurement units, differences in national practices still prevent full international comparability. Credible data are needed on the scale and significance of tourism. Information on the role tourism plays in national economies throughout the world is particularly deficient.

The data in the table are from the World Tourism Organization. The data on international inbound and outbound tourists refer to the number of arrivals and departures of visitors within the reference period, not to the number of people traveling. Thus a person who makes several trips to a country during a given period is counted each time as a new arrival. International visitors include tourists (overnight visitors), same-day visitors, cruise passengers, and crew members.

Regional and income group aggregates are based on the World Bank's classification of countries and differ from those shown in the World Tourism Organization's Yearbook of Tourism Statistics. Countries not shown in the table but for which data are available are included in the regional and income group totals. World totals are no longer calculated by the World Tourism Organization. The aggregates in the table are calculated using the World Bank's weighted aggregation methodology (see Statistical methods) and differ from aggregates provided by the World Tourism Organization.

Definitions

• **International inbound tourists** are the number of visitors who travel to a country other than that in which they have their usual residence for a period not exceeding 12 months and whose main purpose in visiting is other than an activity remunerated from within the country visited. • **International outbound tourists** are the number of departures that people make from their country of usual residence to any other country for any purpose other than a remunerated activity in the country visited. • **International tourism receipts** are expenditures by international inbound visitors, including payments to national carriers for international transport. These receipts include any other prepayment made for goods or services received in the destination country. They also may include receipts from same-day visitors, except in cases where these are important enough to justify a separate classification. Their share in exports is calculated as a ratio to exports of goods and services. • **International tourism expenditures** are expenditures of international outbound visitors in other countries, including payments to foreign carriers for international transport. These expenditures may include those by residents traveling abroad as same-day visitors, except in cases where these are so important as to justify a separate classification. Their share in imports is calculated as a ratio to imports of goods and services.

6.14a

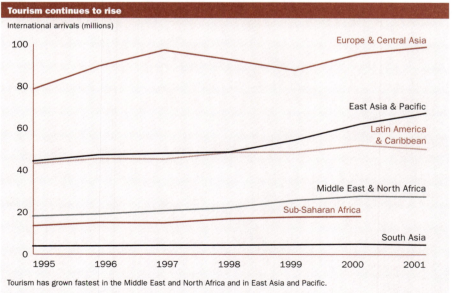

Tourism continues to rise

International arrivals (millions)

Europe & Central Asia

East Asia & Pacific

Latin America & Caribbean

Middle East & North Africa

Sub-Saharan Africa

South Asia

1995 1996 1997 1998 1999 2000 2001

Tourism has grown fastest in the Middle East and North Africa and in East Asia and Pacific.

Source: World Tourism Organization data.

Data sources

The visitor and expenditure data are available in the World Tourism Organization's *Yearbook of Tourism Statistics and Compendium of Tourism Statistics, 2001*. The data in the table were updated from electronic files provided by the World Tourism Organization. The data on exports and imports are from the International Monetary Fund's International Financial Statistics and World Bank staff estimates.

PRIMARY DATA DOCUMENTATION

The World Bank is not a primary data collection agency for most areas other than living standards surveys and debt. As a major user of socioeconomic data, however, the World Bank places particular emphasis on data documentation to inform users of data in economic analysis and policymaking. The tables in this section provide information on the sources, treatment, and currentness of the principal demographic, economic, and environmental indicators in the *World Development Indicators*.

Differences in the methods and conventions used by the primary data collectors—usually national statistical agencies, central banks, and customs services—may give rise to significant discrepancies over time both among and within countries. Delays in reporting data and the use of old surveys as the base for current estimates may severely compromise the quality of national data.

Although data quality is improving in some countries, many developing countries lack the resources to train and maintain the skilled staff and obtain the equipment needed to measure and report demographic, economic, and environmental trends in an accurate and timely way. The World Bank recognizes the need for reliable data to measure living standards, track and evaluate economic trends, and plan and monitor development projects. Thus, working with bilateral and other multilateral agencies, it continues to fund and participate in technical assistance projects to improve statistical organization and basic data methods, collection, and dissemination.

The World Bank is working at several levels to meet the challenge of improving the quality of the data that it collates and disseminates. At the country level the Bank is carrying out technical assistance, training, and survey activities— with a view to strengthening national capacity—in the following areas:

- Poverty assessments in most borrower member countries.
- Living standards measurement and other household and farm surveys with partner national statistical agencies.
- National accounts and inflation.
- Price and expenditure surveys for the International Comparison Program.
- Projects to improve statistics in the countries of the former Soviet Union.
- External debt management.
- Environmental and economic accounting.

PRIMARY DATA DOCUMENTATION

	National currency	Fiscal year end	National accounts					Balance of payments and trade			Government finance	IMF data dissemination standard
			Reporting period [a]	Base year	SNA price valuation	Alternative conversion factor	PPP survey year	Balance of Payments Manual in use	External debt	System of trade	Accounting concept	
Afghanistan	Afghan afghani	Mar. 20	FY	1975	VAB							
Albania	Albanian lek	Dec. 31	CY	1990 [b]	VAP		1996	BPM5	Actual	G	C	G
Algeria	Algerian dinar	Dec. 31	CY	1980	VAB			BPM5	Actual	S	B	
Angola	Angolan kwanza	Dec. 31	CY	1997	VAP	1991–96		BPM4	Estimate	S		
Argentina	Argentine peso	Dec. 31	CY	1993	VAB	1971–84	1996	BPM5	Preliminary	S	C	S*
Armenia	Armenian dram	Dec. 31	CY	1996 [b, c]	VAB	1990–95	1996	BPM5	Actual	G	C	S*
Australia	Australian dollar	Jun. 30	FY	1995 [b, c]	VAB		1999	BPM5		G	C	S*
Austria	Euro	Dec. 31	CY	1995 [b]	VAB		1999	BPM5		S	C	S*
Azerbaijan	Azeri manat	Dec. 31	CY	2000 [b, c]	VAB	1987–95	1996	BPM5	Actual	G	C	G
Bangladesh	Bangladesh taka	Jun. 30	FY	1996 [b]	VAB	1971–2000	1996	BPM5	Actual	G		G
Belarus	Belarussian rubel	Dec. 31	CY	1990 [b, c]	VAB	1987–94	1996	BPM5	Actual	G	C	
Belgium	Euro	Dec. 31	CY	1995 [b]	VAB		1999	BPM5		S	C	S*
Benin	CFA franc	Dec. 31	CY	1985	VAP	1992	1996	BPM5	Actual	S		G
Bolivia	Boliviano	Dec. 31	CY	1990 [b]	VAB	1960–85	1996	BPM5	Actual	S	C	G
Bosnia and Herzegovina	Convertible mark	Dec. 31	CY	1996 [c]	VAB			BPM5	Actual			
Botswana	Botswana pula	Jun. 30	FY	1994	VAB	1999	1996	BPM5	Actual	G	B	G
Brazil	Brazilian real	Dec. 31	CY	1995	VAB	1999	1996	BPM5	Preliminary	S	C	S*
Bulgaria	Bulgarian lev	Dec. 31	CY	1990 [b, c]	VAB	1978–89, 91–92	1999	BPM5	Actual	G	C	G
Burkina Faso	CFA franc	Dec. 31	CY	1985	VAB	1992–93		BPM4	Actual	S	C	G
Burundi	Burundi franc	Dec. 31	CY	1980	VAB			BPM5	Preliminary	S	C	
Cambodia	Cambodian riel	Dec. 31	CY	1989	VAP			BPM5	Preliminary	G		G
Cameroon	CFA franc	Jun. 30	FY	1990	VAB	1965–2002	1996	BPM5	Preliminary	S	C	
Canada	Canadian dollar	Mar. 31	CY	1995 [b]	VAB	1999	1999	BPM5		G	C	S*
Central African Republic	CFA franc	Dec. 31	CY	1987	VAB			BPM4	Estimate	S		
Chad	CFA franc	Dec. 31	CY	1995	VAB			BPM5	Preliminary	S	C	G
Chile	Chilean peso	Dec. 31	CY	1986	VAB		1996	BPM5	Actual	S	C	S*
China	Chinese yuan	Dec. 31	CY	1990	VAP	1987–93	1986	BPM5	Estimate	S	B	G
Hong Kong, China	Hong Kong dollar	Dec. 31	CY	1990	VAB		1993	BPM5		G		S*
Colombia	Colombian peso	Dec. 31	CY	1994	VAB	1992–94	1993	BPM5	Actual	S	B	S*
Congo, Dem. Rep.	Congo franc	Dec. 31	CY	1987	VAP	1999–2000		BPM5	Actual	S	C	
Congo, Rep.	CFA franc	Dec. 31	CY	1978	VAP	1993	1996	BPM4	Estimate	S	C	
Costa Rica	Costa Rican colon	Dec. 31	CY	1991 [b]	VAB			BPM5	Actual	S	C	S*
Côte d'Ivoire	CFA franc	Dec. 31	CY	1986	VAP		1996	BPM5	Estimate	S	C	G
Croatia	Croatian kuna	Dec. 31	CY	1997 [b]	VAB		1999	BPM5	Actual	G	C	S*
Cuba	Cuban peso	Dec. 31	CY	1984	VAP					G		
Czech Republic	Czech koruna	Dec. 31	CY	1995 [b]	VAB		1999	BPM5	Preliminary	G	C	S*
Denmark	Danish krone	Dec. 31	CY	1995 [b]	VAB		1999	BPM5		G	C	S*
Dominican Republic	Dominican peso	Dec. 31	CY	1990	VAP			BPM5	Actual	G	C	
Ecuador	U.S. dollar	Dec. 31	CY	1975	VAP	1999	1996	BPM5	Estimate	S	B	S*
Egypt, Arab Rep.	Egyptian pound	Jun. 30	FY	1992	VAB	1965–91	1993	BPM5	Actual	S	C	
El Salvador	Salvadoran colone	Dec. 31	CY	1990	VAP	1982–90		BPM5	Actual	S	B	S*
Eritrea	Eritrean nakfa	Dec. 31	CY	1992	VAB			BPM4	Actual			
Estonia	Estonian kroon	Dec. 31	CY	1995 [b]	VAB	1990–95	1999	BPM5	Actual	G	C	S*
Ethiopia	Ethiopian birr	Jul. 7	FY	1981	VAB	1989–92, 94		BPM5	Preliminary	G	B	G
Finland	Euro	Dec. 31	CY	1995 [b]	VAB		1999	BPM5		G	C	S*
France	Euro	Dec. 31	CY	1995 [b, c]	VAB		1999	BPM5		S	C	S*
Gabon	CFA franc	Dec. 31	CY	1991	VAP	1993	1996	BPM5	Actual	S	B	G
Gambia, The	Gambian dalasi	Jun. 30	CY	1987	VAB			BPM5	Actual	G	B	G
Georgia	Georgian lari	Dec. 31	CY	1994 [b, c]	VAB	1990–94	1996	BPM5	Actual	G	C	
Germany	Euro	Dec. 31	CY	1995 [b]	VAB		1999	BPM5		S	C	S*
Ghana	Ghanaian cedi	Dec. 31	CY	1975	VAP	1973–87		BPM5	Actual	G	B	
Greece	Euro	Dec. 31	CY	1995 [b, c]	VAB		1999	BPM4	Estimate	S	C	S*
Guatemala	Guatemalan quetzal	Dec. 31	CY	1958	VAP		1980	BPM5	Actual	S	B	
Guinea	Guinean franc	Dec. 31	CY	1994	VAB	1986	1993	BPM5	Estimate	S	C	
Guinea-Bissau	CFA franc	Dec. 31	CY	1986	VAB	1970–86		BPM5	Estimate	G		G
Haiti	Haitian gourde	Sep. 30	FY	1976	VAB	1991		BPM5	Preliminary	G		

PRIMARY DATA DOCUMENTATION

	Latest population census (including registration-based censuses)	Latest demographic, household, or health survey	Vital registration complete	Latest agricultural census	Latest industrial data	Latest water withdrawal data	Latest survey of scientists and engineers engaged in R&D	Latest survey of expenditure for R&D
Afghanistan		MICS, 2000				1987		
Albania	1989	MICS, 2000	Yes	1995	1990	1995		
Algeria	1998	MICS, 2000		1973	1996	1995		
Angola	1970	MICS, 2000		1964–65		1987		
Argentina	2001		Yes	1988	1996	1995	2000	2000
Armenia	2001	DHS, 2000	Yes		1991	1994	2000	
Australia	1996		Yes	1990	1997	1985	1998	1998
Austria	2001		Yes	1990	1998	1991	1998	2000
Azerbaijan	1999	MICS, 2000	Yes			1995	1997	1996
Bangladesh	1991	Special, 2001		1976	1997	1990	1995	
Belarus	1999		Yes	1994		1990	1997	
Belgium	2001		Yes	1990	1997	..	1999	1999
Benin	1992	DHS, 2001		1992–93	1981	1994	1989	
Bolivia	2001	MICS, 2000			1998	1987	2000	2000
Bosnia and Herzegovina	1991	MICS, 2000	Yes		1991	1995		
Botswana	1991	MICS, 2000		1993	1994	1992		
Brazil	2000	DHS, 1996		1996	1996	1992	2000	2000
Bulgaria	1992	LSMS, 1995	Yes		1998	1988	1999	1996
Burkina Faso	1996	DHS, 1998–99		1993	1997	1992	1997	1997
Burundi	1990	MICS, 2000			1991	1987	1989	
Cambodia	1998	DHS, 2000				1987		
Cameroon	1987	MICS, 2000		1972–73	1998	1987		
Canada	2001		Yes	1991	1997	1991	1998	2000
Central African Republic	1988	MICS, 2000			1993	1987	1996	
Chad	1993	MICS, 2000				1987		
Chile	1992		Yes	1997	1997	1987	2000	2000
China	2000	Population, 1995		1996	1998	1993	2000	2000
Hong Kong, China	2000		Yes		1998		1995	1998
Colombia	1993	DHS, 2000		1988	1997	1996	2000	2000
Congo, Dem. Rep.	1984	MICS, 2000		1990		1990		
Congo, Rep.	1996			1986	1988	1987	2000	
Costa Rica	2000	CDC, 1993	Yes	1973	1997	1997	1996	1998
Côte d'Ivoire	1998	MICS, 2000		1974–75	1997	1987		
Croatia	2001		Yes		1992	1996	1999	1999
Cuba	1981	MICS, 2000	Yes		1989	1995	2000	2000
Czech Republic	2001	CDC, 1993	Yes	..	1998	1991	2000	2000
Denmark	2001		Yes	1989	1998	1990	1999	1999
Dominican Republic	1993	DHS, 2002		1971	1984	1994		
Ecuador	2001	CDC, 1999		1997	1998	1997	1998	1998
Egypt, Arab Rep.	1996	DHS, 2000	Yes	1989–90	1997	1996	1991	2000
El Salvador	1992	CDC, 1994		1970–71	1998	1992	2000	
Eritrea	1984	DHS, 1995			1998			
Estonia	2000		Yes	1994		1995	1999	1999
Ethiopia	1994	DHS, 2000		1988–89	1998	1987		
Finland	2000		Yes	1990	1998	1991	2000	2000
France	1999		Yes	1988	1998	1999	1999	2000
Gabon	1993	DHS, 2000		1974–75	1982	1987		
Gambia, The	1993	MICS, 2000			1982	1982		
Georgia	1989	MICS, 2000	Yes			1990	1999	1999
Germany	..		Yes	1993		1991	2000	2000
Ghana	2000	SPA, 2000		1984	1995	1997		
Greece	2001		Yes	1993	1996	1980	1999	1999
Guatemala	1994	DHS, 1998–99	Yes	1979	1988	1992	1988	1988
Guinea	1996	DHS, 1999		1996		1987		
Guinea-Bissau	1991	MICS, 2000		1988		1991		
Haiti	1982	DHS, 2000		1971	1996	1991		

PRIMARY DATA DOCUMENTATION

	National currency	Fiscal year end	National accounts					Balance of payments and trade			Government finance	IMF data dissemination standard
			Reporting period [a]	Base year	SNA price valuation	Alternative conversion factor	PPP survey year	Balance of Payments Manual in use	External debt	System of trade	Accounting concept	
Honduras	Honduran lempira	Dec. 31	CY	1978	VAB	1988–89		BPM5	Actual	S		
Hungary	Hungarian forint	Dec. 31	CY	1994 [b]	VAB		1999	BPM5	Actual	S	C	S*
India	Indian rupee	Mar. 31	FY	1993	VAB	1971–2000		BPM5	Preliminary	G	C	S
Indonesia	Indonesian rupiah	Mar. 31	CY	1993	VAP		1996	BPM5	Preliminary	S	C	S*
Iran, Islamic Rep.	Iranian rial	Mar. 20	FY	1982	VAB	1980–90	1996	BPM5	Actual	G	C	
Iraq	Iraqi dinar	Dec. 31	CY	1969	VAB					S		
Ireland	Euro	Dec. 31	CY	1995 [b]	VAB		1999	BPM5		G	C	S*
Israel	Israeli new shekel	Dec. 31	CY	1995 [b]	VAP		1999	BPM5		S	C	S*
Italy	Euro	Dec. 31	CY	1995 [b]	VAB		1999	BPM5		S	C	S*
Jamaica	Jamaica dollar	Dec. 31	CY	1986	VAP		1996	BPM5	Preliminary	G		
Japan	Japanese yen	Mar. 31	CY	1995	VAB		1999	BPM5		G	C	S*
Jordan	Jordan dinar	Dec. 31	CY	1994	VAB		1996	BPM5	Actual	G	B	G
Kazakhstan	Kazakh tenge	Dec. 31	CY	1993 [b, c]	VAB	1987–95	1996	BPM5	Actual	G	C	G
Kenya	Kenya shilling	Jun. 30	CY	1982	VAB		1996	BPM5	Actual	G	B	G
Korea, Dem. Rep.	Democratic Republic of Korea won	Dec. 31	CY	..	..			BPM5				
Korea, Rep.	Korean won	Dec. 31	CY	1995 [b]	VAB		1999	BPM5	Actual	S	C	S*
Kuwait	Kuwaiti dinar	Jun. 30	CY	1984	VAP			BPM5		S	C	G
Kyrgyz Republic	Kyrgyz som	Dec. 31	CY	1995 [b, c]	VAB	1992–96	1996	BPM5	Actual	G	B	G
Lao PDR	Lao kip	Dec. 31	CY	1990	VAB	1960–89	1993	BPM5	Preliminary	G		
Latvia	Latvian lat	Dec. 31	CY	1995 [b]	VAB	1987–95	1999	BPM5	Actual	S	C	S*
Lebanon	Lebanese pound	Dec. 31	CY	1994	VAB		1996	BPM4	Actual	G	V	G
Lesotho	Lesotho loti	Mar. 31	CY	1995	VAB			BPM5	Actual	G	C	
Libya	Libyan dinar	Dec. 31	CY	1975	VAB	1986		BPM5		G		
Liberia	Liberian dollar	Dec. 31	CY	1971	VAB				Estimate			
Lithuania	Lithuanian litas	Dec. 31	CY	1995 [b]	VAB	1987–95	1999	BPM5	Actual	G	C	S*
Macedonia, FYR	Macedonian denar	Dec. 31	CY	1995 [b]	VAB		1999	BPM5	Actual	G		
Madagascar	Malagasy franc	Dec. 31	CY	1984	VAB		1996	BPM5	Preliminary	S	C	
Malawi	Malawi kwacha	Mar. 31	CY	1994	VAB		1996	BPM5	Estimate	G	B	G
Malaysia	Malaysian ringgit	Dec. 31	CY	1987	VAP		1993	BPM5	Estimate	G	C	S*
Mali	CFA franc	Dec. 31	CY	1987	VAB		1996	BPM4	Preliminary	G		G
Mauritania	Mauritanian ouguiya	Dec. 31	CY	1985	VAB			BPM4	Actual	G		
Mauritius	Mauritian rupee	Jun. 30	CY	1992	VAB		1996	BPM5	Actual	G	C	G
Mexico	Mexican new peso	Dec. 31	CY	1993 [b]	VAB		1999	BPM5	Actual	G	C	S*
Moldova	Moldovan leu	Dec. 31	CY	1996	VAB	1987–95	1996	BPM5	Actual	G	C	
Mongolia	Mongolian tugrik	Dec. 31	CY	1998	VAP		1996	BPM5	Actual	S	C	G
Morocco	Moroccan dirham	Dec. 31	CY	1980	VAP		1996	BPM5	Actual	S	C	
Mozambique	Mozambican metical	Dec. 31	CY	1995	VAB	1992–95		BPM5	Estimate	S		
Myanmar	Myanmar kyat	Mar. 31	FY	1985	VAP	1980–82		BPM5	Estimate	G	C	
Namibia	Namibia dollar	Mar. 31	CY	1995	VAB			BPM5	Estimate		B	G
Nepal	Nepalese rupee	Jul. 14	FY	1985	VAB	1973–2000	1996	BPM5	Actual	S	C	G
Netherlands	Euro	Dec. 31	CY	1995 [b, c]	VAB		1999	BPM5		S	C	S*
New Zealand	New Zealand dollar	Mar. 31	FY	1995	VAB		1999	BPM5		G	B	
Nicaragua	Nicaraguan gold cordoba	Dec. 31	CY	1998	VAP	1965–93		BPM5	Actual	S	C	
Niger	CFA franc	Dec. 31	CY	1987	VAP	1993		BPM5	Preliminary	S	G	
Nigeria	Nigerian naira	Dec. 31	CY	1987	VAB	1971–98	1996	BPM5	Estimate	G		
Norway	Norwegian krone	Dec. 31	CY	1995 [b, c]	VAB		1999	BPM5		G	C	S*
Oman	Rial Omani	Dec. 31	CY	1978	VAP		1996	BPM5	Actual	G	B	G
Pakistan	Pakistan rupee	Jun. 30	FY	1981	VAB	1972–2000	1996	BPM5	Preliminary	G	C	
Panama	Panamanian balboa	Dec. 31	CY	1982 [c]	VAP		1996	BPM5	Actual	S	C	G
Papua New Guinea	Papua New Guinea kina	Dec. 31	CY	1983	VAP	1989		BPM5	Actual	G	B	G
Paraguay	Paraguayan guarani	Dec. 31	CY	1982	VAP	1982–88		BPM5	Actual	S	C	G
Peru	Peruvian new sol	Dec. 31	CY	1994	VAB	1985–91	1996	BPM5	Actual	S	C	S*
Philippines	Philippine peso	Dec. 31	CY	1985	VAB		1996	BPM5	Actual	G	B	S*
Poland	Polish zloty	Dec. 31	CY	1990 [b, c]	VAB		1996	BPM5	Actual	S	C	S*
Portugal	Euro	Dec. 31	CY	1995 [b]	VAB		1999	BPM5		S	C	S*
Puerto Rico	U.S. dollar	Jun. 30	FY	1954	VAP					G		

PRIMARY DATA DOCUMENTATION

	Latest population census (including registration-based censuses)	Latest demographic, household, or health survey	Vital registration complete	Latest agricultural census	Latest industrial data	Latest water withdrawal data	Latest survey of scientists and engineers engaged in R&D	Latest survey of expenditure for R&D
Honduras	1988	CDC, 1994		1993	1997	1992		
Hungary	2001		Yes	1994	1997	1991	2000	2000
India	2001	Benchmark, 1998–2002		1986	1997	1990	1996	1996
Indonesia	2000	MICS, 2000		1993	1998	1990		
Iran, Islamic Rep.	1991	Demographic, 1995		1988	1996	1993	1994	1999
Iraq	1997	MICS, 2000		1981	1997	1990	1994	
Ireland	1996		Yes	1991	1997	1980	1999	1999
Israel	1995		Yes	1983	1996	1997	1997	1999
Italy	2001		Yes	1990	1994	1998	1999	1999
Jamaica	2001	CDC, 1997	Yes	1979	1996	1993		
Japan	2000		Yes	1990	1998	1992	2000	2000
Jordan	1994	DHS, 2002		1997	1997	1993	1998	
Kazakhstan	1999	DHS, 1999	Yes			1993	1999	1997
Kenya	1999	DHS, 2003		1981	1998	1990		
Korea, Dem. Rep.	1993	MICS, 2000				1987	2000	2000
Korea, Rep.	1995			1991	1997	1994	1999	1997
Kuwait	1995	FHS, 1996	Yes	1970	1997	1994	2000	1997
Kyrgyz Republic	1999	DHS, 1997	Yes			1994	1997	1997
Lao PDR	1995	MICS, 2000		1999		1987		
Latvia	2000		Yes	1994	1998	1994	1999	1999
Lebanon	1970	MICS, 2000		1999		1996		
Lesotho	1996	MICS, 2000		1989–90	1985	1987		
Libya	1995	MICS, 2000		1987	1997	1999	2000	
Liberia						1987		
Lithuania	2001		Yes	1994		1995	1996	
Macedonia, FYR	1994		Yes	1994	1996	1996	1999	
Madagascar	1993	DHS, 2003		1984	1988	1984	1994	
Malawi	1998	EdData, 2002		1992–93	1998	1994		
Malaysia	2000		Yes		1996	1995	1998	1998
Mali	1998	DHS, 2001		1978	1997	1987		
Mauritania	2000	PAPCHILD, 1990		1985		1985		
Mauritius	2000	CDC, 1991	Yes		1997	..	1992	1997
Mexico	2000	Population, 1995		1991	1995	1998	1999	1999
Moldova	1989	MICS, 2000	Yes			1992	1997	
Mongolia	2000	MICS, 2000			1998	1993	2000	
Morocco	1994	DHS, 1995		1997	1998	1998		
Mozambique	1997	Interim, 2003				1992		
Myanmar	1983	MICS, 2000		1993	1998	1987		
Namibia	1991	DHS, 2000		1995	1994	1991		
Nepal	1991	DHS, 2001		1992	1996	1994		
Netherlands	2001		Yes	1989	1998	1991	1999	1999
New Zealand	2001		Yes	1990	1997	1991	1997	1997
Nicaragua	1995	DHS, 2001		1963	1997	1998	1997	1997
Niger	1988	MICS, 2000		1980	1998	1988		
Nigeria	1991	DHS, 2003		1960	1994	1987	1987	
Norway	2001		Yes	1989	1998	1985	1999	1999
Oman	1993	FHS, 1995		1979	1998	1991	2000	
Pakistan	1998	RHS, 2000–01		1990	1996	1991	1997	
Panama	2000	LSMS, 1997		1990	1998	1990	1999	1999
Papua New Guinea	2000	DHS, 1996				1987		
Paraguay	1992	DHS, 1990; CDC, 1998		1991	1997	1987		
Peru	1993	DHS, 2000		1994	1994	1992	1997	1999
Philippines	2000	MICS, 2000		1991	1997	1995	1992	
Poland	1988		Yes	1990	1997	1991	2000	2000
Portugal	2001		Yes	1989	1997	1990	1999	2000
Puerto Rico	2000		Yes	1987	1998			

PRIMARY DATA DOCUMENTATION

	National currency	Fiscal year end	National accounts — Reporting period[a]	Base year	SNA price valuation	Alternative conversion factor	PPP survey year	Balance of payments and trade — Balance of Payments Manual in use	External debt	System of trade	Government finance — Accounting concept	IMF data dissemination standard
Romania	Romanian leu	Dec. 31	CY	1993[c]	VAB	1987–89, 92	1999	BPM5	Actual	S	C	G
Russian Federation	Russian ruble	Dec. 31	CY	1997[b,c]	VAB	1987–94	1999	BPM5	Estimate	G	C	
Rwanda	Rwanda franc	Dec. 31	CY	1995	VAP			BPM5	Estimate	G		
Saudi Arabia	Saudi Arabian riyal	hijri year	FY	1970	VAP		1993	BPM4	Estimate	G		
Senegal	CFA franc	Dec. 31	CY	1987	VAP		1996	BPM5	Estimate	S	B	G
Sierra Leone	Sierra Leonean leone	Jun. 30	CY	1990	VAB	1971–79, 87	1996	BPM5	Actual	G	B	
Singapore	Singapore dollar	Mar. 31	CY	1990	VAP		1996	BPM5		G	C	S*
Slovak Republic	Slovak koruna	Dec. 31	CY	1995[b]	VAB		1999	BPM5	Actual	G	C	S*
Slovenia	Slovenian tolar	Dec. 31	CY	1993[b]	VAB		1999	BPM5	Actual	S	C	S*
Somalia	Somali shilling	Dec. 31	CY	1985	VAB				Estimate			
South Africa	South African rand	Mar. 31	CY	1995	VAB			BPM5	Preliminary	S	C	S*
Spain	Euro	Dec. 31	CY	1995[b]	VAB		1999	BPM5		S	C	S*
Sri Lanka	Sri Lankan rupee	Dec. 31	CY	1996	VAB		1996	BPM5	Actual	G	B	G
Sudan	Sudanese dinar	Dec. 31	CY	1982	VAP	1985–91		BPM5	Preliminary	G	B	
Swaziland	Lilangeni	Jun. 30	FY	1985	VAB		1996		Actual		B	
Sweden	Swedish krona	Jun. 30	CY	1995[c]	VAB		1999	BPM5		G	C	S*
Switzerland	Swiss franc	Dec. 31	CY	1995	VAB		1999	BPM5	Estimate	S	C	S*
Syrian Arab Republic	Syrian pound	Dec. 31	CY	1995	VAP	1970–2000	1996	BPM5	Estimate	S	C	
Tajikistan	Tajik somoni	Dec. 31	CY	1985[b]	VAB	1987–95	1996	BPM5	Actual	G	C	
Tanzania	Tanzania shilling	Dec. 31	CY	1992	VAB		1996	BPM5	Estimate	S		G
Thailand	Thai baht	Sep. 30	CY	1988	VAP		1996	BPM5	Preliminary	G	C	S*
Togo	CFA franc	Dec. 31	CY	1978	VAP		1993	BPM5	Preliminary	S		G
Trinidad and Tobago	Trinidad and Tobago dollar	Dec. 31	CY	1985	VAP		1996	BPM5	Preliminary	S	C	
Tunisia	Tunisian dinar	Dec. 31	CY	1990	VAP		1996	BPM5	Actual	G	C	S*
Turkey	Turkish lira	Dec. 31	CY	1987	VAB		1999	BPM5	Actual	S	C	S*
Turkmenistan	Turkmen manat	Dec. 31	CY	1987[b]	VAB		1996	BPM5	Estimate	G		
Uganda	Uganda shilling	Jun. 30	FY	1998	VAB	1980–99		BPM5	Actual	G	B	G
Ukraine	Ukrainian hryvnia	Dec. 31	CY	1990[b]	VAB	1988–95	1999	BPM5	Actual	G	C	S*
United Arab Emirates	U.A.E. dirham	Dec. 31	CY	1985	VAB		1993	BPM4		G	B	
United Kingdom	Pound sterling	Dec. 31	CY	1995[b]	VAB		1999	BPM5		G	C	S*
United States	U.S. dollar	Sep. 30	CY	1995[c]	VAB		1999	BPM5		G	C	S*
Uruguay	Uruguayan peso	Dec. 31	CY	1983	VAB		1996	BPM5	Actual	S	C	
Uzbekistan	Uzbek sum	Dec. 31	CY	1997[c]	VAB	1991–94, 97–2000	1996	BPM5	Actual	G		
Venezuela, RB	Venezuelan bolivar	Dec. 31	CY	1984	VAB		1996	BPM5	Actual	G	C	G
Vietnam	Vietnamese dong	Dec. 31	CY	1994	VAP	1991	1996	BPM4	Preliminary	G	B	
West Bank and Gaza	Israeli new shekel	Dec. 31	CY	1997	VAB		1993					
Yemen, Rep.	Yemen rial	Dec. 31	CY	1990	VAP	1991–96	1996	BPM5	Preliminary	G	B	G
Yugoslavia, Fed. Rep.	Yugoslav new dinar	Dec. 31	CY	1998	VAB				Preliminary	S		
Zambia	Zambian kwacha	Dec. 31	CY	1994	VAB	1990–92	1996	BPM5	Preliminary	G	B	G
Zimbabwe	Zimbabwe dollar	Jun. 30	CY	1990	VAB	1991, 98	1996	BPM5	Preliminary	G	C	G

Note: For an explanation of the abbreviations used in the table, see the notes.
a. Also applies to balance of payments reporting. b. Country uses the 1993 System of National Accounts methodology. c. Original chained constant price data are rescaled.

	Latest population census (including registration-based censuses)	Latest demographic, household, or health survey	Vital registration complete	Latest agricultural census	Latest industrial data	Latest water withdrawal data	Latest survey of scientists and engineers engaged in R&D	Latest survey of expenditure for R&D
Romania	1992	CDC, 1999	Yes		1997	1994	2000	2000
Russian Federation	1989	LSMS, 1992	Yes	1994–95	1998	1994	2000	2000
Rwanda	1991	SPA, 2001		1984	1986	1993		
Saudi Arabia	1992	Demographic, 1999		1983		1992		
Senegal	1988	MICS, 2000		1960	1997	1987	1997	1997
Sierra Leone	1985	MICS, 2000		1985	1986	1987		
Singapore	2000	General household, 1995	Yes		1998	1975	1995	1995
Slovak Republic	1991		Yes		1998	1991	2000	2000
Slovenia	1991		Yes	1991	1998	1996	2000	1998
Somalia		MICS, 2000				1987		
South Africa	2001	DHS, 1998			1996	1990	1993	
Spain	2001		Yes	1989	1998	1997	2000	2000
Sri Lanka	2001	DHS, 1993	Yes	1982	1995	1990	1996	1996
Sudan	1993	MICS, 2000			1997	1995		
Swaziland		MICS, 2000				..		
Sweden	1990		Yes	1981	1997	1991	1999	1999
Switzerland	2000		Yes	1990	1998	1991	2000	2000
Syrian Arab Republic	1994	MICS, 2000		1981	1998	1995	1997	1997
Tajikistan	2000	MICS, 2000	Yes	1994		1994	1993	
Tanzania	1988	DHS, 1999		1995	1997	1994		
Thailand	2000	DHS, 1987		1993	1996	1990	1997	1997
Togo	1981	MICS, 2000		1996	1997	1987	1994	1995
Trinidad and Tobago	1990	MICS, 2000	Yes	1982	1997	1997	1997	1997
Tunisia	1994	MICS, 2000		1961	1998	1996	1999	2000
Turkey	1997	DHS, 1998		1991	1997	1997	1999	1999
Turkmenistan	1995	DHS, 2000	Yes			1994		
Uganda	1991	HIV, 2003		1991	1997	1970	2000	1999
Ukraine	2001	MICS, 2000	Yes			1992	2000	2000
United Arab Emirates	1995			1998	1981	1995		
United Kingdom	2001		Yes	1993	1998	1991	1998	1999
United States	2000	Current population, 1997	Yes	1997	1997	1990	1997	2000
Uruguay	1996		Yes	1990	1997	1965	1999	1999
Uzbekistan	1989	Special, 2002	Yes			1994	1992	
Venezuela, RB	2001	MICS, 2000	Yes	1997–98	1996	1970	2000	2000
Vietnam	1999	DHS, 2002		1994	1998	1990	1995	
West Bank and Gaza	1997	Demographic, 1995		1971				
Yemen, Rep.	1994	DHS, 1997		1982–85		1990		
Yugoslavia, Fed. Rep.	1991	MICS, 2000	Yes	1981	1998	1995	1999	
Zambia	2000	EdData, 2002		1990	1997	1994		
Zimbabwe	1997	DHS, 1999		1960	1997	1987		

• **Fiscal year end** is the date of the end of the fiscal year for the central government. Fiscal years for other levels of government and the reporting years for statistical surveys may differ, but if a country is designated as a fiscal year reporter in the following column, the date shown is the end of its national accounts reporting period. • **Reporting period** for national accounts and balance of payments data is designated as either calendar year (CY) or fiscal year (FY). Most economies report their national accounts and balance of payments data using calendar years, but some use fiscal years, which straddle two calendar years. In the *World Development Indicators* fiscal year data are assigned to the calendar year that contains the larger share of the fiscal year. If a country's fiscal year ends before June 30, the data are shown in the first year of the fiscal period; if the fiscal year ends on or after June 30, the data are shown in the second year of the period. Saudi Arabia follows a lunar year whose starting and ending dates change with respect to the solar year. Because the International Monetary Fund (IMF) reports most balance of payments data on a calendar year basis, balance of payments data for fiscal year reporters in the *World Development Indicators* are based on fiscal year estimates provided by World Bank staff. These estimates may differ from IMF data but allow consistent comparisons between national accounts and balance of payments data. • **Base year** is the year used as the base period for constant price calculations in the country's national accounts. Price indexes derived from national accounts aggregates, such as the GDP deflator, express the price level relative to prices in the base year. Constant price data reported in the *World Development Indicators* are rescaled to a common 1995 reference year. See *About the data* for table 4.1 for further discussion. • **SNA price valuation** shows whether value added in the national accounts is reported at basic prices (VAB) or at producers' prices (VAP). Producers' prices include the value of taxes paid by producers and thus tend to overstate the actual value added in production. See *About the data* for tables 4.1 and 4.2 for further discussion of national accounts valuation. • **Alternative conversion factor** identifies the countries and years for which a World Bank–estimated conversion factor has been used in place of the official exchange rate (line rf in the IMF's *International Financial Statistics*). See *Statistical methods* for further discussion of the use of alternative conversion factors. • **PPP survey year** refers to the latest available survey year for the International Comparison Program's estimates of purchasing power parities (PPPs). • **Balance of Payments Manual in use** refers to the classification system used

for compiling and reporting data on balance of payments items in table 4.15. BPM4 refers to the fourth edition of the IMF's *Balance of Payments Manual* (1977), and BPM5 to the fifth edition (1993). Since 1995 the IMF has adjusted all balance of payments data to BPM5 conventions, but some countries continue to report using the older system. • **External debt** shows the debt reporting status for 2001 data. *Actual* indicates that data are as reported, *preliminary* that data are preliminary and include an element of World Bank staff estimation, and *estimate* that data are World Bank staff estimates. • **System of trade** refers to the general trade system (G) or the special trade system (S). Under the general trade system both goods entering directly for domestic consumption and goods entering customs storage are recorded, at the time of their first arrival, as imports; under the special trade system goods are recorded as imports when declared for domestic consumption whether at the time of entry or on withdrawal from customs storage. Exports under the general trade system comprise outward-moving goods: (a) national goods wholly or partly produced in the country; (b) foreign goods, neither transformed nor declared for domestic consumption in the country, that move outward from customs storage; and (c) nationalized goods that have been declared from domestic consumption and move outward without having been transformed. Under the special trade system exports comprise categories (a) and (c). In some compilations categories (b) and (c) are classified as re-exports. Direct transit trade, consisting of goods entering or leaving for transport purposes only, is excluded from both import and export statistics. See *About the data* for tables 4.5 and 4.6 for further discussion. • **Government finance accounting concept** describes the accounting basis for reporting central government financial data. For most countries government finance data have been consolidated (C) into one set of accounts capturing all the central government's fiscal activities. Budgetary central government accounts (B) exclude central government units. See *About the data* for tables 4.11, 4.12, and 4.13 for further details. • **IMF data dissemination standard** shows the countries that subscribe to the IMF's Special Data Dissemination Standard (SDDS) or the General Data Dissemination System (GDDS). *S* refers to countries that subscribe to the SDDS; *S** indicates subscribers that have posted data on the IMF's Dissemination Standards Bulletin Board Web site; and *G* refers to countries that subscribe to the GDDS. (Posted data can be reached through the IMF's Dissemination Standards Bulletin Board at http://dsbb.imf.org.) The SDDS was established by the IMF for member countries that have

or that might seek access to international capital markets, to guide them in providing their economic and financial data to the public. The GDDS helps guide member countries in disseminating comprehensive, timely, accessible, and reliable economic, financial, and socio-demographic statistics. IMF member countries voluntarily elect to participate in either the SDDS or the GDDS. Both the SDDS and the GDDS are expected to enhance the availability of timely and comprehensive data and therefore contribute to the pursuit of sound macroeconomic policies; the SDDS is also expected to help improve the functioning of financial markets. • **Latest population census** shows the most recent year in which a census was conducted from which at least preliminary results have been released. • **Latest demographic, household, or health survey** gives information on the surveys used in compiling demographic and health data presented in the *People* section. CDC is U.S. Centers for Disease Control and Prevention, DHS is Demographic and Health Survey, EdData refers to education data collected in DHS surveys, FHS is Family Health Survey, HIV is HIV survey data, LSMS is Living Standards Measurement Study, MICS is Multiple Indicator Cluster Survey, PAPCHILD is Pan Arab Project for Child Development, RHS is Reproductive Health Survey, and SPA is Service Provision Assessments. • **Vital registration complete** identifies countries judged by the United Nations Statistics Division to have complete registries of vital (birth and death) statistics, with the statistics reported in the United Nations Statistics Division's *Population and Vital Statistics Report*. Countries with complete vital statistics registries may have more accurate and more timely demographic indicators. • **Latest agricultural census** shows the most recent year in which an agricultural census was conducted and reported to the Food and Agriculture Organization. • **Latest industrial data** refer to the most recent year for which manufacturing value added data at the three-digit level of the International Standard Industrial Classification (revision 2 or revision 3) are available in the United Nations Industrial Development Organization (UNIDO) database. • **Latest water withdrawal data** refer to the most recent year for which data have been compiled from a variety of sources. See *About the data* for table 3.5 for more information. • **Latest surveys of scientists and engineers engaged in R&D and expenditure for R&D** refer to the most recent year for which data are available from a data collection effort by the United Nations Educational, Scientific, and Cultural Organization (UNESCO) in science and technology and research and development (R&D). See *About the data* for table 5.12 for more information.

ACRONYMS AND ABBREVIATIONS

Technical terms

AIDS	acquired immunodeficiency syndrome
BOD	biochemical oxygen demand
CFC	chlorofluorocarbon
c.i.f.	cost, insurance, and freight
COMTRADE	United Nations Statistics Division's Commodity Trade database
CO₂	carbon dioxide
cu. m	cubic meter
DHS	Demographic and Health Survey
DMTU	dry metric ton unit
DOTS	directly observed treatment, short-course (strategy)
DPT	diphtheria, pertussis, and tetanus
DRS	World Bank's Debtor Reporting System
ESAF	Enhanced Structural Adjustment Facility
f.o.b.	free on board
FYR	former Yugoslav Republic
GDP	gross domestic product
GEMS	Global Environment Monitoring System
GIS	geographic information system
GNI	gross national income (formerly referred to as gross national product)
ha	hectare
HIPC	heavily indebted poor country
HIV	human immunodeficiency virus
ICD	International Classification of Diseases
ICSE	International Classification of Status in Employment
ICT	information and communications technology
IP	Internet Protocol
ISCED	International Standard Classification of Education
ISIC	International Standard Industrial Classification
ISP	Internet service provider
kg	kilogram
km	kilometer
kwh	kilowatt-hour
LIBOR	London interbank offered rate
LSMS	Living Standards Measurement Study
M0	currency and coins (monetary base)
M1	narrow money (currency and demand deposits)
M2	money plus quasi money
M3	broad money or liquid liabilities
MICS	Multiple Indicator Cluster Survey
mmbtu	millions of British thermal units
mt	metric ton
MUV	manufactures unit value
NEAP	national environmental action plan
NGO	nongovernmental organization
NO₂	nitrogen dioxide
ODA	official development assistance
PC	personal computer
PM10	particulate matter smaller than 10 microns
PPI	private participation in infrastructure
PPP	purchasing power parity
PRGF	Poverty Reduction and Growth Facility
R&D	research and development
SDR	special drawing right
SITC	Standard International Trade Classification
SNA	System of National Accounts
SOPEMI	Continuous Reporting System on Migration
SO2	sulfur dioxide
sq. km	square kilometer
STD	sexually transmitted disease
TB	tuberculosis
TEU	twenty-foot equivalent unit
TFP	total factor productivity
ton-km	metric ton-kilometer
TSP	total suspended particulates
TU	traffic unit

Organizations

ADB	Asian Development Bank
AfDB	African Development Bank
APEC	Asia Pacific Economic Cooperation
CDC	Centers for Disease Control and Prevention
CDIAC	Carbon Dioxide Information Analysis Center
CEC	Commission of the European Communities
DAC	Development Assistance Committee of the OECD
EBRD	European Bank for Reconstruction and Development
EDF	European Development Fund
EFTA	European Free Trade Area
EIB	European Investment Bank
EMU	European Monetary Union
EU	European Union
Eurostat	Statistical Office of the European Communities
FAO	Food and Agriculture Organization
G-5	France, Germany, Japan, United Kingdom, and United States
G-7	G-5 plus Canada and Italy
G-8	G-7 plus Russian Federation
GEF	Global Environment Facility
IBRD	International Bank for Reconstruction and Development
ICAO	International Civil Aviation Organization
ICP	International Comparison Programme
ICSID	International Centre for Settlement of Investment Disputes
IDA	International Development Association
IDB	Inter-American Development Bank
IDC	International Data Corporation
IEA	International Energy Agency
IFC	International Finance Corporation
ILO	International Labour Organization
IMF	International Monetary Fund
IRF	International Road Federation
ITU	International Telecommunication Union
IUCN	World Conservation Union
MIGA	Multilateral Investment Guarantee Agency
NAFTA	North American Free Trade Agreement
NATO	North Atlantic Treaty Organization
NSF	National Science Foundation
OECD	Organisation for Economic Co-operation and Development
PAHO	Pan American Health Organization
PARIS21	Partnership in Statistics for Development in the 21st Century
S&P	Standard & Poor's
UIP	Urban Indicators Programme
UIS	UNESCO Institute for Statistics
UN	United Nations
UNAIDS	Joint United Nations Programme on HIV/AIDS
UNCED	United Nations Conference on Environment and Development
UNCHS	United Nations Centre for Human Settlements (Habitat)
UNCTAD	United Nations Conference on Trade and Development
UNDP	United Nations Development Programme
UNECE	United Nations Economic Commission for Europe
UNEP	United Nations Environment Programme
UNESCO	United Nations Educational, Scientific, and Cultural Organization
UNFPA	United Nations Population Fund
UNHCR	United Nations High Commissioner for Refugees
UNICEF	United Nations Children's Fund
UNIDO	United Nations Industrial Development Organization
UNRISD	United Nations Research Institute for Social Development
UNSD	United Nations Statistics Division
USAID	U.S. Agency for International Development
WCMC	World Conservation Monitoring Centre
WFP	World Food Programme
WHO	World Health Organization
WIPO	World Intellectual Property Organization
WITSA	World Information Technology and Services Alliance
WTO	World Trade Organization
WWF	World Wildlife Fund

STATISTICAL METHODS

This section describes some of the statistical procedures used in preparing the World Development Indicators. It covers the methods employed for calculating regional and income group aggregates and for calculating growth rates, and it describes the World Bank's Atlas method for deriving the conversion factor used to estimate gross national income (GNI) (formerly referred to as GNP) and GNI per capita in U.S. dollars. Other statistical procedures and calculations are described in the About the data sections that follow each table.

Aggregation rules

Aggregates based on the World Bank's regional and income classifications of economies appear at the end of most tables. These classifications are shown on the front and back cover flaps of the book. Most tables also include aggregates for the member countries of the European Monetary Union (EMU). Members of the EMU on 1 January 2001 were Austria, Belgium, Finland, France, Germany, Ireland, Italy, Luxembourg, the Netherlands, Portugal, and Spain. Other classifications, such as the European Union and regional trade blocs, are documented in About the data for the tables in which they appear.

Because of missing data, aggregates for groups of economies should be treated as approximations of unknown totals or average values. Regional and income group aggregates are based on the largest available set of data, including values for the 148 economies shown in the main tables, other economies shown in table 1.6, and Taiwan, China. The aggregation rules are intended to yield estimates for a consistent set of economies from one period to the next and for all indicators. Small differences between sums of subgroup aggregates and overall totals and averages may occur because of the approximations used. In addition, compilation errors and data reporting practices may cause discrepancies in theoretically identical aggregates such as world exports and world imports.

Five methods of aggregation are used in the World Development Indicators:

- For group and world totals denoted in the tables by a t, missing data are imputed based on the relationship of the sum of available data to the total in the year of the previous estimate. The imputation process works forward and backward from 1995. Missing values in 1995 are imputed using one of several proxy variables for which complete data are available in that year. The imputed value is calculated so that it (or its proxy) bears the same relationship to the total of available data. Imputed values are usually not calculated if missing data account for more than a third of the total in the benchmark year. The variables used as proxies are GNI in U.S. dollars, total population, exports and imports of goods and services in U.S. dollars, and value added in agriculture, industry, manufacturing, and services in U.S. dollars.
- Aggregates marked by an s are sums of available data. Missing values are not imputed. Sums are not computed if more than a third of the observations in the series or a proxy for the series are missing in a given year.

- Aggregates of ratios are generally calculated as weighted averages of the ratios (indicated by w) using the value of the denominator or, in some cases, another indicator as a weight. The aggregate ratios are based on available data, including data for economies not shown in the main tables. Missing values are assumed to have the same average value as the available data. No aggregate is calculated if missing data account for more than a third of the value of weights in the benchmark year. In a few cases the aggregate ratio may be computed as the ratio of group totals after imputing values for missing data according to the above rules for computing totals.
- Aggregate growth rates are generally calculated as a weighted average of growth rates (and indicated by a w). In a few cases growth rates may be computed from time series of group totals. Growth rates are not calculated if more than half the observations in a period are missing. For further discussion of methods of computing growth rates see below.
- Aggregates denoted by an m are medians of the values shown in the table. No value is shown if more than half the observations for countries with a population of more than 1 million are missing.

Exceptions to the rules occur throughout the book. Depending on the judgment of World Bank analysts, the aggregates may be based on as little as 50 percent of the available data. In other cases, where missing or excluded values are judged to be small or irrelevant, aggregates are based only on the data shown in the tables.

Growth rates

Growth rates are calculated as annual averages and represented as percentages. Except where noted, growth rates of values are computed from constant price series. Three principal methods are used to calculate growth rates: least squares, exponential endpoint, and geometric endpoint. Rates of change from one period to the next are calculated as proportional changes from the earlier period.

Least-squares growth rate. Least-squares growth rates are used wherever there is a sufficiently long time series to permit a reliable calculation. No growth rate is calculated if more than half the observations in a period are missing. The least-squares growth rate, r, is estimated by fitting a linear regression trend line to the logarithmic annual values of the variable in the relevant period. The regression equation takes the form

$$\ln X_t = a + bt,$$

which is equivalent to the logarithmic transformation of the compound growth equation,

$$X_t = X_o (1 + r)^t.$$

In this equation X is the variable, t is time, and $a = \ln X_o$ and $b = \ln (1 + r)$ are parameters to be estimated. If b^* is the least-squares estimate of b, the average annual growth rate, r, is obtained as $[\exp(b*) - 1]$ and is multiplied by 100 for expression as a percentage.

The calculated growth rate is an average rate that is representative of the available observations over the entire period. It does not necessarily match the actual growth rate between any two periods.

Exponential growth rate. The growth rate between two points in time for certain demographic indicators, notably labor force and population, is calculated from the equation

$$r = \ln(p_n/p_1)/n,$$

where p_n and p_1 are the last and first observations in the period, n is the number of years in the period, and ln is the natural logarithm operator. This growth rate is based on a model of continuous, exponential growth between two points in time. It does not take into account the intermediate values of the series. Nor does it correspond to the annual rate of change measured at a one-year interval, which is given by $(p_n - p_{n-1})/p_{n-1}$.

Geometric growth rate. The geometric growth rate is applicable to compound growth over discrete periods, such as the payment and reinvestment of interest or dividends. Although continuous growth, as modeled by the exponential growth rate, may be more realistic, most economic phenomena are measured only at intervals, in which case the compound growth model is appropriate. The average growth rate over n periods is calculated as

$$r = \exp[\ln(p_n/p_1)/n] - 1.$$

Like the exponential growth rate, it does not take into account intermediate values of the series.

World Bank Atlas method

In calculating GNI and GNI per capita in U.S. dollars for certain operational purposes, the World Bank uses the Atlas conversion factor. The purpose of the Atlas conversion factor is to reduce the impact of exchange rate fluctuations in the cross-country comparison of national incomes.

The Atlas conversion factor for any year is the average of a country's exchange rate (or alternative conversion factor) for that year and its exchange rates for the two preceding years, adjusted for the difference between the rate of inflation in the country and that in the G-5 countries (France, Germany, Japan, the United Kingdom, and the United States). A country's inflation rate is measured by the change in its GDP deflator.

The inflation rate for G-5 countries, representing international inflation, is measured by the change in the SDR deflator. (Special drawing rights, or SDRs, are the IMF's unit of account.) The SDR deflator is calculated as a weighted average of the G-5 countries' GDP deflators in SDR terms, the weights being the amount of each country's currency in one SDR unit. Weights vary over time because both the composition of the SDR and the relative exchange rates for each currency change. The SDR deflator is calculated in SDR terms first and then converted to U.S. dollars using the SDR to dollar Atlas conversion factor. The Atlas conversion factor is then applied to a country's GNI. The resulting GNI in U.S. dollars is divided by the midyear population to derive GNI per capita.

When official exchange rates are deemed to be unreliable or unrepresentative of the effective exchange rate during a period, an alternative estimate of the exchange rate is used in the Atlas formula (see below).

The following formulas describe the calculation of the Atlas conversion factor for year t:

$$e_t^* = \frac{1}{3}\left[e_{t-2}\left(\frac{p_t}{p_{t-2}} \Big/ \frac{p_t^{S\$}}{p_{t-2}^{S\$}}\right) + e_{t-1}\left(\frac{p_t}{p_{t-1}} \Big/ \frac{p_t^{S\$}}{p_{t-1}^{S\$}}\right) + e_t\right]$$

and the calculation of GNI per capita in U.S. dollars for year t:

$$Y_t^\$ = (Y_t/N_t)/e_t^*,$$

where e_t^* is the Atlas conversion factor (national currency to the U.S. dollar) for year t, e_t is the average annual exchange rate (national currency to the U.S. dollar) for year t, p_t is the GDP deflator for year t, $p_t^{S\$}$ is the SDR deflator in U.S. dollar terms for year t, $Y_t^\$$ is the Atlas GNI per capita in U.S. dollars in year t, Y_t is current GNI (local currency) for year t, and N_t is the midyear population for year t.

Alternative conversion factors

The World Bank systematically assesses the appropriateness of official exchange rates as conversion factors. An alternative conversion factor is used when the official exchange rate is judged to diverge by an exceptionally large margin from the rate effectively applied to domestic transactions of foreign currencies and traded products. This applies to only a small number of countries, as shown in *Primary data documentation*. Alternative conversion factors are used in the Atlas methodology and elsewhere in the *World Development Indicators* as single-year conversion factors.

CREDITS

This book has drawn on a wide range of World Bank reports and numerous external sources, listed in the bibliography following this section. Many people inside and outside the World Bank helped in writing and producing the *World Development Indicators*. The team would like to particularly acknowledge the help and encouragement of Nicholas Stern, Senior Vice-President and Chief Economist. It is also grateful to those who provided valuable comments on the entire book, especially Jean Baneth and Jong-goo Park. This note identifies those who made specific contributions. Numerous others, too many to acknowledge here, helped in many ways for which the team is extremely grateful.

1. World view

was prepared by Eric Swanson and K. M. Vijayalakshmi. Eric Swanson wrote the introduction. Mona Fetouh, Amy Heyman, Masako Hiraga, and Sulekha Patel assisted in developing and preparing tables and figures. Valuable suggestions were received from members of the World Bank's Human Development Network. Yonas Biru and William Prince provided substantial assistance with the data, preparing the estimates of gross national income in purchasing power parity terms. Azita Amjadi, Aki Kuwahara (UNCTAD), and Jerzy Rozanski helped in preparing the market access indicators.

2. People

was prepared by Masako Hiraga in partnership with the World Bank's Human Development Network and the Development Research Group in the Development Economics Vice Presidency. Vivienne Wang provided invaluable assistance in data and table preparation. Sulekha Patel wrote the introduction, with input from Eric Swanson. Contributions to the section were provided by Eduard Bos and Emi Suzuki (demography, health, and nutrition); Raquel Artecona and Martin Rama (labor force and employment); Shaohua Chen and Martin Ravallion (poverty and income distribution); Montserrat Pallares-Miralles (vulnerability and security); and Barbara Bruns, Saida Mamodova, and Lianqin Wang (education). Comments and suggestions at various stages of production also came from Jean Baneth and Eric Swanson.

3. Environment

was prepared by M. H. Saeed Ordoubadi and Mona Fetouh in partnership with the World Bank's Environmentally and Socially Sustainable Development Network and in collaboration with the World Bank's Development Research Group and Transportation, Water, and Urban Development Department. Important contributions were made by Robin White and Christian Layke of the World Resources Institute, Orio Tampieri of the Food and Agriculture Organization, Laura Battlebury of the World Conservation Monitoring Centre, Gerhard Metchies of GTZ, and Christine Auclair, Moses Ayiemba, Bildad Kagai, Guenter Karl, Pauline Maingi, and Markanley Rai of the Urban Indicators Programme, United Nations Centre for Human Settlements. Mehdi Akhlaghi managed the databases for this section, and Mona Fetouh assisted with research and data preparation. The World Bank's Environment Department and Rural Development Department devoted substantial staff resources to the book, for which the team is very grateful. M. H. Saeed Ordoubadi wrote the introduction to the section with valuable comments from Eric Swanson and Bruce Ross-Larson, who edited the text. Other contributions were made by Susmita Dasgupta, Craig Meisner, Kiran Pandey, and David Wheeler (air and water pollution); Juan Blazquez Ancin, Jan Bojö, Katja Erickson, Surhid Gautam, and Kirsten Oleson (government commitment); and Katie Bolt and Kirk Hamilton (adjusted savings). Valuable comments were also provided by Jean Baneth, C. Fallert Kessides, Marianne Fay, Katie Bolt, Roberto Martin-Hurtado, Coralie Gevers, Erica Soler Hampejsek, and Marcin Jan Sasin.

4. Economy

was prepared by K. M. Vijayalakshmi in close collaboration with the Macroeconomic Data Team of the World Bank's Development Data Group, led by Soong Sup Lee. Eric Swanson and K. M. Vijayalakshmi wrote the introduction. Contributions to the section were provided by Azita Amjadi (trade) and Punam Chuhan and Ibrahim Levent (external debt). The national accounts and balance of payments data for low- and middle-income economies were gathered from the World Bank's regional staff through the annual Unified Survey. Maja Bresslauer, Victor Gabor, Barbro Hexeberg, Soong Sup Lee, and Naoko Watanabe worked on updating, estimating, and validating the databases for national accounts. The national accounts data for OECD countries were processed by Mehdi Akhlaghi. The team is grateful to Guy Karsenty and Andreas Maurer, at the World Trade Organization, and Sanja Blazevic, Arunas Butkevicius, and Aurelie von Wartensleben, at UNCTAD, for providing data on trade in goods; to Tetsuo Yamada for help in obtaining the UNIDO database; and to Jean Baneth for helpful comments.

5. States and markets

was prepared by David Cieslikowski and Mona Fetouh in partnership with the World Bank's Private Sector and Infrastructure Network, its Poverty Reduction and Economic Management Network, the World Bank Institute, the International Finance Corporation, and external partners. David Cieslikowski wrote the introduction to the section. Other contributors include Ada Karina Izaguirre and Kathy Khuu (privatization and infrastructure projects); Andrew Newby of Euromoney (credit ratings); Simeon Djankov (business environment); Isilay Cabuk and Shannon Laughlin (Standard & Poor's emerging stock market indexes); Yonas Biru (purchasing power parity conversion factors); Esperanza Magpantay and Michael Minges of the International Telecommunication Union (communications and information); Louis Thompson (railways); Jane Degerlund of Containerisation International (ports); Jens Johanson of the UNESCO Institute for Statistics (culture, research and development, scientists and engineers); Anders Halvorsen of the World Information Technology and Services Alliance (information and communications technology); Dan Gallik of the U.S. Department of State (military personnel and arms exports); Petter Stalenheim of the Stockholm International Peace Research Institute (military expenditures); and Lise McLeod of the World Intellectual Property Organization (patents data).

6. Global links

was prepared by Mona Fetouh and Amy Heyman. Substantial help came from Azita Amjadi and Francis Ng (trade); Betty Dow (commodity prices); Aki Kuwahara of UNCTAD and Jerzy Rozanski (tariffs); Shelly Fu, Ibrahim Levent, and Gloria Reyes (financial data); Cecile Thoreau of the OECD (migration); Yasmin Ahmad, Brian Hammond, Aimee Nichols, Rudolphe Petras, and Simon Scott of the OECD (aid flows); and Antonio Massieu and Azucena Pernia of the World Tourism Organization (tourism data). Valuable comments were also provided by Barbro Hexeberg.

Other parts

The preparation of the maps on the inside covers was coordinated by Jeff Lecksell and Greg Prakas of the World Bank's Map Design Unit. The *Users guide* was prepared by David Cieslikowski. *Partners* was prepared by Mona Fetouh. *Statistical methods* was written by Eric Swanson. *Primary data documentation* was coordinated by K. M. Vijayalakshmi, who served as database administrator, and Estela Zamora. Mehdi Akhlaghi was responsible for database updates and aggregation. *Acronyms and abbreviations* was prepared by Amy Heyman. The index was collated by Richard Fix and Gonca Okur.

Data management

Database management was coordinated by Mehdi Akhlaghi with cross-team participation of Development Data Group staff to create an integrated World Development Indicators database. This database was used to generate the tables for the *World Development Indicators* and related products such as WDI Online, *The World Bank Atlas*, *The Little Data Book*, and the *World Development Indicators* CD-ROM.

Administrative assistance and office technology support

Estela Zamora provided administrative assistance and assisted in updating the databases. Jean-Pierre Djomalieu, Nacer Megherbi, and Shahin Outadi provided information technology support.

Design, production, and editing

Richard Fix coordinated all aspects of production with Communications Development Incorporated. Communications Development Incorporated provided overall design direction, editing, and layout. Led by Meta de Coquereaumont and Bruce Ross-Larson, the editing and production team consisted of Joseph Costello, Wendy Guyette, Paul Holtz, Elizabeth McCrocklin, Alison Strong, and Elaine Wilson. Communications Development's London partner, Grundy & Northedge, provided art direction and design. Staff from External Affairs oversaw publication and dissemination of the book.

Client services

The Development Data Group's Client Services Team (Azita Amjadi, Elizabeth Crayford, Richard Fix, Anat Lewin, Gonca Okur, and William Prince) contributed to the design and planning of the *World Development Indicators* and the *Atlas* and helped coordinate work with the Office of the Publisher.

Publishing and dissemination

The Office of the Publisher, under the direction of Dirk Koehler, provided valuable assistance throughout the production process. Randi Park coordinated printing, and Carlos Rossel supervised marketing and distribution. Andrew Kircher of External Affairs managed the communications strategy, with assistance from Lawrence Macdonald, and the regional operations group headed by Paul Mitchell helped coordinate the overseas release.

The Atlas

Production and design were managed by Richard Fix. Content development for this year's *Atlas* was coordinated by a redesign team led by David Cieslikowski that included Elizabeth Crayford, Richard Fix, Amy Heyman, and Eric Swanson. The graphic design was realized with Communications Development Incorporated and their London partner, Grundy & Northedge. Valuable input was provided by many staff of the Development Data Group and the Office of the Publisher. The preparation of data benefited from the work on corresponding sections in the *World Development Indicators*. William Prince assisted with systems support and production of tables and graphs. Jeffrey Lecksell and Greg Prakas from the World Bank's Map Design Unit coordinated map production.

World Development Indicators CD-ROM

Programming and testing were carried out by Reza Farivari and his team: Azita Amjadi, Ying Chi, Elizabeth Crayford, Ramgopal Erabelly, Nacer Megherbi, Shahin Outadi, and William Prince. Masako Hiraga produced the social indicators tables. William Prince coordinated user interface design and overall production and provided quality assurance.

WDI Online

Design, programming, and testing were carried out by Reza Farivari and his team: Mehdi Akhlagi, Azita Amjadi, Ying Chi, Elizabeth Crayford, Shahin Outadi, and Nacer Megherbi. William Prince coordinated production and provided quality assurance. Cybèle Bourgougnon, Hafed Al-Ghwell, and Stacey Leonard-Frank of the Office of the Publisher were responsible for the implementation of the WDI Online and the management of the subscription service.

Client feedback

The team is also grateful to the many people who took the trouble to provide comments on its publications. Their feedback and suggestions have helped improve this year's edition.

BIBLIOGRAPHY

AbouZahr, Carla. 2000. "Maternal Mortality." *OECD Observer* (223): 29–30.

Ahmad, Sultan. 1992. "Regression Estimates of Per Capita GDP Based on Purchasing Power Parities." Policy Research Working Paper 956. World Bank, International Economics Department, Washington, D.C.

———. 1994. "Improving Inter-Spatial and Inter-Temporal Comparability of National Accounts." *Journal of Development Economics* 44: 53–75.

American Automobile Manufacturers Association. 1998. *World Motor Vehicle Data.* Detroit, Mich.

Ball, Nicole. 1984. "Measuring Third World Security Expenditure: A Research Note." *World Development* 12(2): 157–64.

Barro, Robert J. 1991. "Economic Growth in a Cross-Section of Countries." *Quarterly Journal of Economics* 106(2): 407–44.

Barro, Robert J., and Jong-Wha Lee. 2000. *International Data on Educational Attainment: Updates and Implications.* NBER Working Paper 7911. Cambridge, Mass.: National Bureau of Economic Research.

Beck, Thorsten, and Ross Levine. 2001. "Stock Markets, Banks, and Growth: Correlation or Causality?" Policy Research Working Paper 2670. World Bank, Development Research Group, Washington, D.C.

Behrman, Jere R., and Mark R. Rosenzweig. 1994. "Caveat Emptor: Cross-Country Data on Education and the Labor Force." *Journal of Development Economics* 44: 147–71.

Bhalla, Surjit. 2002. *Imagine There Is No Country: Poverty, Inequality, and Growth in the Era of Globalization.* Washington, DC: Institute for International Economics.

Bloom, David E., and Jeffrey G. Williamson. 1998. "Demographic Transitions and Economic Miracles in Emerging Asia." *World Bank Economic Review* 12(3): 419–55.

Brown, Lester R., and others. 1999. *Vital Signs 1999: The Environmental Trends That Are Shaping Our Future.* New York and London: W. W. Norton for Worldwatch Institute.

Brown, Lester R., Christopher Flavin, Hilary F. French, and others. 1998. *State of the World 1998.* Washington, D.C.: Worldwatch Institute.

Brown, Lester R., Michael Renner, Christopher Flavin, and others. 1998. *Vital Signs 1998.* Washington, D.C.: Worldwatch Institute.

Bulatao, Rodolfo. 1998. *The Value of Family Planning Programs in Developing Countries.* Santa Monica, Calif.: Rand.

Caiola, Marcello. 1995. *A Manual for Country Economists.* Training Series 1, vol. 1. Washington, D.C.: International Monetary Fund.

Centro Latinoamericano de Demografía. Various years. *Boletín Demográfico.* Santiago.

Chen, Shaohua, and Martin Ravallion. 2000. "How Did the World's Poorest Fare in the 1990s?" Policy Research Working Paper 2409. World Bank, Development Research Group, Washington, D.C.

Collier, Paul, and David Dollar. 1999. "Aid Allocation and Poverty Reduction." Policy Research Working Paper 2041. World Bank, Development Research Group, Washington, D.C.

———. 2001. "Can the World Cut Poverty in Half? How Policy Reform and Effective Aid Can Meet the International Development Goals." Policy Research Working Paper 2403. World Bank, Development Research Group, Washington, D.C.

Collins, Wanda W., Emile A. Frison, and Suzanne L. Sharrock. 1997. "Global Programs: A New Vision in Agricultural Research." *Issues in Agriculture* (World Bank, Consultative Group on International Agricultural Research, Washington, D.C.) 12: 1–28.

Commission of the European Communities, International Monetary Fund, Organisation for Economic Co-operation and Development, United Nations, and World Bank. 2002. *System of Environmental and Economic Accounts: SEEA 2000.* New York.

Containerisation International. 2003. *Containerisation International Yearbook 2003.* London.

Corrao, Marlo Ann, G. Emmanuel Guindon, Namita Sharma, and Donna Fakhrabadi Shokoohi, eds. 2000. *Tobacco Control Country Profiles.* Atlanta: American Cancer Society.

Deaton, Angus. 2002. "Counting the World's Poor: Problems and Possible Solutions." *World Bank Research Observer* 16(2): 125–47.

Demirgüç-Kunt, Asli, and Enrica Detragiache. 1997. "The Determinants of Banking Crises: Evidence from Developed and Developing Countries." Working paper. World Bank and International Monetary Fund, Washington, D.C.

Demirgüç-Kunt, Asli, and Ross Levine. 1996a. "Stock Market Development and Financial Intermediaries: Stylized Facts." *World Bank Economic Review* 10(2): 291–321.

———. 1996b. "Stock Markets, Corporate Finance, and Economic Growth: An Overview." *World Bank Economic Review* 10(2): 223–39.

———. 1999. "Bank-Based and Market-Based Financial Systems: Cross-Country Comparisons." Policy Research Working Paper 2143. World Bank, Development Research Group, Washington, D.C.

de Onis, Mercedes, and Monika Blossner. 2000. "Prevalence and Trends of Overweight among Preschool Children in Developing Countries." *American Journal of Clinical Nutrition* 72: 1032–39.

———. Forthcoming. "The WHO Global Database on Child Growth and Malnutrition: Methodology and Applications." *International Journal of Epidemiology.*

Devarajan, Shantayanan, David Dollar, and Torgny Holmgren, eds. 2001. *Aid and Reform in Africa: Lessons from Ten Case Studies.* World Bank: Washington, D.C.

Dixon, John, and Paul Sherman. 1990. *Economics of Protected Areas: A New Look at Benefits and Costs.* Washington, D.C.: Island Press.

Djankov, Simeon, Rafael La Porta, Florencio López-de-Silanes, and Andrei Shleifer. 2001. "The Regulation of Entry." Policy Research Working Paper 2661. World Bank, Financial Sector Strategy and Policy Department, Washington, D.C.

DKT International. 1998. *1997 Contraceptive Social Marketing Statistics.* Washington, D.C.

Doyle, John J., and Gabrielle J. Persley, eds. 1996. *Enabling the Safe Use of Biotechnology: Principles and Practice.* Environmentally Sustainable Development Studies and Monographs Series, no. 10. Washington, D.C.: World Bank.

Drucker, Peter F. 1994. "The Age of Social Transformation." *Atlantic Monthly* 274 (November).

Easterly, William. 2000. "Growth Implosions, Debt Explosions, and My Aunt Marilyn: Do Growth Slowdowns Cause Public Debt Crises?" Policy Research Working Paper 2531. World Bank, Development Research Group, Washington, D.C.

Economist. 2001. "Globalisation and Its Critics: A Survey of Globalisation." September 29, pp. 1–30.

Euromoney. 2002. September. London.

Europa Publications. Various years. *Europa World Year Book.* London.

Eurostat (Statistical Office of the European Communities). Various years. *Demographic Statistics.* Luxembourg.

———. Various years. *Statistical Yearbook.* Luxembourg.

Evenson, Robert E., and Carl E. Pray. 1994. "Measuring Food Production (with Reference to South Asia)." *Journal of Development Economics* 44: 173–97.

Faiz, Asif, Christopher S. Weaver, and Michael P. Walsh. 1996. *Air Pollution from Motor Vehicles: Standards and Technologies for Controlling Emissions.* Washington, D.C.: World Bank.

Fallon, Peter, and Zafiris Tzannatos. 1998. *Child Labor: Issues and Directions for the World Bank.* Washington, D.C.: World Bank.

Fankhauser, Samuel. 1995. *Valuing Climate Change: The Economics of the Greenhouse.* London: Earthscan.

FAO (Food and Agriculture Organization). 1986. "Inter-Country Comparisons of Agricultural Production Aggregates." Economic and Social Development Paper 61. Rome.

———. 1996. *Food Aid in Figures 1994.* Vol. 12. Rome.

———. 2001. *State of the World's Forests 2001.* Rome.

———. Various years. *Fertilizer Yearbook.* FAO Statistics Series. Rome.

———. Various years. *Production Yearbook.* FAO Statistics Series. Rome.

———. Various years. *The State of Food Insecurity in the World.* Rome.

———. Various years. *Trade Yearbook.* FAO Statistics Series. Rome.

Frankel, Jeffrey. 1993. "Quantifying International Capital Mobility in the 1990s." In Jeffrey Frankel, ed., *On Exchange Rates.* Cambridge, Mass.: MIT Press.

Frankhauser, Pierre. 1994. "Fractales, tissus urbains et reseaux de transport." *Revue d'economie politique* 104: 435–55.

Fredricksen, Birger. 1993. *Statistics of Education in Developing Countries: An Introduction to Their Collection and Analysis.* Paris: UNESCO.

French, Kenneth, and James M. Poterba. 1991. "Investor Diversification and International Equity Markets." *American Economic Review* 81: 222–26.

Gallup, John L., and Jeffrey D. Sachs. 1998. "The Economic Burden of Malaria." Harvard Institute for International Development, Cambridge, Mass.

Gannon, Colin, and Zmarak Shalizi. 1995. "The Use of Sectoral and Project Performance Indicators in Bank-Financed Transport Operations." TWU Discussion Paper 21. World Bank, Transportation, Water, and Urban Development Department, Washington, D.C.

Gardner, Robert. 1998. "Education." Demographic and Health Surveys, Comparative Study 29. Macro International, Calverton, Md.

Gardner-Outlaw, Tom, and Robert Engelman. 1997. "Sustaining Water, Easing Scarcity: A Second Update." Population Action International, Washington, D.C.

Goldfinger, Charles. 1994. *L'utile et le futile: L'économie de l'immatériel.* Paris: Editions Odile Jacob.

GTZ (German Agency for Technical Cooperation). 2002. *Fuel Prices and Taxation.* Eschborn, Germany.

Gupta, Sanjeev, Hamid Davoodi, and Erwin Tiongson. 2000. "Corruption and the Provision of Health Care and Education Services." IMF Working Paper 00/116. International Monetary Fund, Washington, D.C.

Gupta, Sanjeev, Brian Hammond, and Eric Swanson. 2000. "Setting the Goals." *OECD Observer* (223): 15–17.

Hamilton, Kirk, and Michael Clemens. 1999. "Genuine Savings Rates in Developing Countries." *World Bank Economic Review* 13(2): 333–56.

Happe, Nancy, and John Wakeman-Linn. 1994. "Military Expenditures and Arms Trade: Alternative Data Sources." IMF Working Paper 94/69. International Monetary Fund, Policy Development and Review Department, Washington, D.C.

Harrison, Ann. 1995. "Factor Markets and Trade Policy Reform." World Bank, Washington, D.C.

Hatzichronoglou, Thomas. 1997. "Revision of the High-Technology Sector and Product Classification." STI Working Paper 1997/2. OECD Directorate for Science, Technology, and Industry, Paris.

Heck, W. W. 1989. "Assessment of Crop Losses from Air Pollutants in the U.S." In J. J. McKenzie and M. T. El Ashry, eds., *Air Pollution's Toll on Forests and Crops.* New Haven, Conn.: Yale University Press.

Heggie, Ian G. 1995. *Management and Financing of Roads: An Agenda for Reform.* World Bank Technical Paper 275. Washington, D.C.

BIBLIOGRAPHY

Hellman, Joel S., Geraint Jones, Daniel Kaufmann, and Mark Schankerman. 2000. "Measuring Governance, Corruption, and State Capture: How Firms and Bureaucrats Shape the Business Environment in Transition Economies." Policy Research Working Paper 2312. World Bank, Washington, D.C.

Heston, Alan. 1994. "A Brief Review of Some Problems in Using National Accounts Data in Level of Output Comparisons and Growth Studies." *Journal of Development Economics* 44: 29–52.

Hettige, Hemamala, Muthukumara Mani, and David Wheeler. 1998. "Industrial Pollution in Economic Development: Kuznets Revisited." Policy Research Working Paper 1876. World Bank, Development Research Group, Washington, D.C.

Hill, Kenneth, Carla AbouZahr, and Tessa Wardlaw. 2001. "Estimates of Maternal Mortality for 1995." *Bulletin of the World Health Organization* 79(3): 182–93.

Hill, Kenneth, Rohini Pande, Mary Mahe, and Gareth Jones. 1999. *Trends in Child Mortality in the Developing World: 1960 to 1996.* New York: UNICEF.

IEA (International Energy Agency). 2002. *World Energy Outlook: Energy and Poverty.* Paris.

———. Various years. *Energy Balances of OECD Countries.* Paris.

———. Various years. *Energy Statistics and Balances of Non-OECD Countries.* Paris.

———. Various years. *Energy Statistics of OECD Countries.* Paris.

IFC (International Finance Corporation). 2001. *SME: World Bank Group Review of Small Business Activities.* Washington, D.C.

IFPRI (International Food Policy Research Institute). 1999. *Soil Degradation: A Threat to Developing-Country Food Security by 2020.* Washington, D.C.

ILO (International Labour Organization). 1990. *ILO Manual on Concepts and Methods.* Geneva: International Labour Office.

———. 2002. *Key Indicators of the Labour Market 2001–2002.* Geneva: International Labour Office.

———. Various years. *Sources and Methods: Labour Statistics* (formerly *Statistical Sources and Methods*). Geneva: International Labour Office.

———. Various years. *Yearbook of Labour Statistics.* Geneva: International Labour Office.

IMF (International Monetary Fund). 1977. *Balance of Payments Manual.* 4th ed. Washington, D.C.

———. 1993. *Balance of Payments Manual.* 5th ed. Washington, D.C.

———. 1995. *Balance of Payments Compilation Guide.* Washington, D.C.

———. 1996a. *Balance of Payments Textbook.* Washington, D.C.

———. 1996b. *Manual on Monetary and Financial Statistics.* Washington, D.C.

———. 2002. *Exchange Arrangements and Exchange Restrictions Annual Report, 2002.* Washington, D.C.

———. 2001. *A Manual on Government Finance Statistics.* Washington, D.C.

———. Various issues. *Direction of Trade Statistics.* Quarterly. Washington, D.C.

———. Various issues. *International Financial Statistics.* Monthly. Washington, D.C.

———. Various years. *Balance of Payments Statistics Yearbook.* Parts 1 and 2. Washington, D.C.

———. Various years. *Direction of Trade Statistics Yearbook.* Washington, D.C.

———. Various years. *Government Finance Statistics Yearbook.* Washington, D.C.

———. Various years. *International Financial Statistics Yearbook.* Washington, D.C.

IMF (International Monetary Fund), OECD (Organisation for Economic Co-operation and Development), United Nations, and World Bank. 2000. *A Better World for All: Progress towards the International Development Goals.* Washington, D.C.

Institutional Investor. 2002. September. New York.

International Civil Aviation Organization. 2002. *Civil Aviation Statistics of the World, 1999–2000.* Montreal.

International Road Federation. 2001. *World Road Statistics 2001.* Geneva.

International Working Group of External Debt Compilers (Bank for International Settlements, International Monetary Fund, Organisation for Economic Co-operation and Development, and World Bank). 1987. *External Debt Definitions.* Washington, D.C.

Inter-Secretariat Working Group on National Accounts (Commission of the European Communities, International Monetary Fund, Organisation for Economic Co-operation and Development, United Nations, and World Bank). 1993. *System of National Accounts.* Brussels, Luxembourg, New York, and Washington, D.C.

IPCC (Intergovernmental Panel on Climate Change). 2001. *Climate Change 2001.* Cambridge: Cambridge University Press.

Irwin, Douglas A. 1996. "The United States in a New Global Economy? A Century's Perspective." *American Economic Review, Papers and Proceedings of the 108th Annual Meeting of the American Economic Association* (May).

Isard, Peter. 1995. *Exchange Rate Economics.* Cambridge: Cambridge University Press.

ITU (International Telecommunication Union). 2002a. *World Telecommunication Development Report 2002.* Geneva.

———. 2002b. *World Telecommunications Indicators Database.* Geneva.

IUCN (World Conservation Union). 1998. *1997 IUCN Red List of Threatened Plants.* Gland, Switzerland.

———. 2000. *2000 IUCN Red List of Threatened Animals.* Gland, Switzerland.

Journal of Development Economics. 1994. Special issue on Database for Development Analysis. Edited by T. N. Srinivasan. Vol. 44, no. 1.

Kaminsky, Graciela L., Saul Lizondo, and Carmen M. Reinhart. 1997. "Leading Indicators of Currency Crises." Policy Research Working Paper 1852. World Bank, Latin America and the Caribbean Region, Office of the Chief Economist, Washington, D.C.

Klein, Michael, Carl Aaron, and Bita Hadjimichael. 2001. "Foreign Direct Investment and Poverty Reduction." Policy Research Working Paper 2613. World Bank, Private Sector Advisory Services Department, Washington, D.C.

Knetter, Michael. 1994. *Why Are Retail Prices in Japan So High? Evidence from German Export Prices.* NBER Working Paper 4894. Cambridge, Mass.: National Bureau of Economic Research.

Komives, Kristin, Dale Whittington, and Xun Wu. 2000. "Infrastructure Coverage and the Poor: A Global Perspective." Paper presented at the conference Infrastructure for Development: Private Solutions and the Poor, Public-Private Infrastructure Advisory Facility, World Bank, and government of United Kingdom, London, May 31–June 2.

Kunte, Arundhati, Kirk Hamilton, John Dixon, and Michael Clemens. 1998. "Estimating National Wealth: Methodology and Results." Environmental Economics Series, no. 57. World Bank, Environment Department, Washington, D.C.

Lanjouw, Jean O., and Peter Lanjouw. 2001. "The Rural Non-Farm Sector: Issues and Evidence from Developing Countries." *Agricultural Economics* 26: 1–23.

Lanjouw, Peter, and Gershon Feder. 2001. *Rural Nonfarm Activities and Rural Development: From Experience toward Strategy.* Rural Strategy Discussion Paper 4. Washington, D.C.: World Bank.

Lele, Uma, William Lesser, and Gesa Horstkotte-Wessler, eds. 2000. *Intellectual Property Rights in Agriculture: The World Bank's Role in Assisting Borrower and Member Countries.* Washington, D.C.: World Bank.

Lewis, Karen K. 1995. "Puzzles in International Financial Markets." In Gene Grossman and Kenneth Rogoff, eds., *Handbook of International Economics.* Vol. 3. Amsterdam: North Holland.

Lewis, Stephen R., Jr. 1989. "Primary Exporting Countries." In Hollis Chenery and T. N. Srinivasan, eds., *Handbook of Development Economics.* Vol. 2. Amsterdam: North Holland.

Lovei, Magdolna. 1997. "Toward Effective Pollution Management." *Environment Matters* (fall): 52–53.

Lucas, R. E. 1988. "On the Mechanics of Economic Development." *Journal of Monetary Economics* 22: 3–22.

Maddison, Angus. 1995. *Monitoring the World Economy 1820–1992.* Paris: OECD.

Mani, Muthukumara, and David Wheeler. 1997. "In Search of Pollution Havens? Dirty Industry in the World Economy, 1960–95." World Bank, Policy Research Department, Washington, D.C.

McCarthy, F. Desmond, and Holger Wolf. 2001. "Comparative Life Expectancy in Africa." Policy Research Working Paper 2668. World Bank, Development Research Group, Washington, D.C.

Midgley, Peter. 1994. *Urban Transport in Asia: An Operational Agenda for the 1990s.* World Bank Technical Paper 224. Washington, D.C.

Moody's Investors Service. 2002. *Sovereign, Sub-national and Sovereign-Guaranteed Issuers.* January. New York.

Morgenstern, Oskar. 1963. *On the Accuracy of Economic Observations.* Princeton, N.J.: Princeton University Press.

Morisset, Jacques. 2000. "Foreign Direct Investment in Africa: Policies Also Matter." Policy Research Working Paper 2481. World Bank, Washington, D.C.

Murray, Christopher J. L., and Alan D. Lopez. 1996. *The Global Burden of Disease.* Cambridge, Mass.: Harvard University Press.

———, eds. 1998. *Health Dimensions of Sex and Reproduction: The Global Burden of Sexually Transmitted Diseases, HIV, Maternal Conditions, Perinatal Disorders, and Congenital Anomalies.* Cambridge, Mass.: Harvard University Press.

National Science Foundation. 2002. *Science and Engineering Indicators 2002.* Arlington, Va.

Netcraft. 2002. *Netcraft Secure Server Survey.* [http://www.netcraft.com/].

Obstfeldt, Maurice. 1995. "International Capital Mobility in the 1990s." In P. B. Kenen, ed., *Understanding Interdependence: The Macroeconomics of the Open Economy.* Princeton, N.J.: Princeton University Press.

Obstfeldt, Maurice, and Kenneth Rogoff. 1996. *Foundations of International Macroeconomics.* Cambridge, Mass.: MIT Press.

OECD (Organisation for Economic Co-operation and Development). 1985. *Measuring Health Care 1960–1983: Expenditure, Costs, Performance.* Paris.

———. 1996. *Trade, Employment, and Labour Standards: A Study of Core Workers' Rights and International Trade.* Paris.

———. 1997. *Employment Outlook.* Paris.

———. 1999. *OECD Environmental Data: Compendium 1999.* Paris.

———. Various issues. *Main Economic Indicators.* Monthly. Paris.

———. Various years. *International Development Statistics.* CD-ROM. Paris.

———. Various years. *National Accounts.* Vol. 1, *Main Aggregates.* Paris.

———. Various years. *National Accounts.* Vol. 2, *Detailed Tables.* Paris.

———. Various years. *Trends in International Migration: Continuous Reporting System on Migration.* Paris.

OECD, Development Assistance Committee. Various years. *Development Co-operation.* Paris.

———. Various years. *Geographical Distribution of Financial Flows to Aid Recipients: Disbursements, Commitments, Country Indicators.* Paris.

O'Meara, Molly. 1999. "Reinventing Cities for People and the Planet." Worldwatch Paper 147. Worldwatch Institute, Washington, D.C.

Palacios, Robert, and Montserrat Pallares-Miralles. 2000. "International Patterns of Pension Provision." Social Protection Discussion Paper 0009. World Bank, Human Development Network, Washington, D.C.

Pandey, Kiran Dev, Katharine Bolt, Uwe Deichmann, Kirk Hamilton, Bart Ostro, and David Wheeler. 2003. "The Human Cost of Air Pollution: New Estimates

BIBLIOGRAPHY

for Developing Countries." World Bank, Development Research Group and Environment Department, Washington, D.C.

Pearce, David, and Giles Atkinson. 1993. "Capital Theory and the Measurement of Sustainable Development: An Indicator of Weak Sustainability." *Ecological Economics* 8: 103–08.

Pilling, David. 1999. "In Sickness and in Wealth." *Financial Times*, 22 October.

Plucknett, Donald L. 1991. "Saving Lives through Agricultural Research." *Issues in Agriculture* (World Bank, Consultative Group on International Agricultural Research, Washington, D.C.) 16.

Population Reference Bureau. 2002. *2002 Women of Our World.* Washington, D.C.

PricewaterhouseCoopers. 2002a. *Corporate Taxes 2002–2003: Worldwide Summaries.* New York.

———. 2002b. *Individual Taxes 2002–2003: Worldwide Summaries.* New York.

PRS Group, Inc. 2002. *International Country Risk Guide.* CD-ROM. December. East Syracuse, N.Y.

Rama, Martin, and Raquel Artecona. 2002. "A Database of Labor Market Indicators across Countries." World Bank, Development Research Group, Washington, D.C.

Ravallion, Martin. 1996. "Poverty and Growth: Lessons from 40 Years of Data on India's Poor." DECNote 20. World Bank, Development Economics Vice Presidency, Washington, D.C.

———. 2001. "Growth, Inequality and Poverty: Looking Beyond Averages." Policy Research Working Paper 2558. World Bank, Development Research Group, Washington, D.C.

———. 2002. "Counting the World's Poor: A Comment." *World Bank Research Observer* 16(2): 149–56.

Ravallion, Martin, and Shaohua Chen. 1996. "What Can New Survey Data Tell Us about the Recent Changes in Living Standards in Developing and Transitional Economies?" World Bank, Policy Research Department, Washington, D.C.

———. 1997. "Can High-Inequality Developing Countries Escape Absolute Poverty?" *Economic Letters* 56: 51–57.

Ravallion, Martin, Gaurav Datt, and Dominique van de Walle. 1991. "Quantifying Absolute Poverty in the Developing World." *Review of Income and Wealth* 37: 345–61.

Reddy, Sanjay, and Thomas Pogge. 2002. "How *Not* to Count The Poor." Working paper. Barnard College and Columbia University, New York.

Rodrik, Dani. 1996. "Labor Standards in International Trade: Do They Matter and What Do We Do about Them?" Overseas Development Council, Washington, D.C.

Romer, P. M. 1986. "Increasing Returns and Long-Run Growth." *Journal of Political Economy* 94: 1002–37.

Ruggles, Robert. 1994. "Issues Relating to the UN System of National Accounts and Developing Countries." *Journal of Development Economics* 44(1): 87–102.

Ryten, Jacob. 1998. "Fifty Years of ISIC: Historical Origins and Future Perspectives." ECA/STAT.AC. 63/22. United Nations Statistics Division, New York.

Sala-i-Martin, Xavier. 2002. *The Disturbing 'Rise' in Global Income Inequality.* NBER Working Paper 8904. Cambridge, Mass.: National Bureau of Economic Research.

Sen, Amartya. 1988. "The Concept of Development." In Hollis Chenery and T. N. Srinivasan, eds., *Handbook of Development Economics.* Vol. 1. Amsterdam: North Holland.

Serageldin, Ismail. 1995. *Toward Sustainable Management of Water Resources.* A Directions in Development book. Washington, D.C.: World Bank.

Shiklovanov, Igor. 1993. "World Fresh Water Resources." In Peter H. Gleick, ed., *Water in Crisis: A Guide to Fresh Water Resources.* New York: Oxford University Press.

SIPRI (Stockholm International Peace Research Institute). 2002. *SIPRI Yearbook 2002: Armaments, Disarmament, and International Security.* Oxford: Oxford University Press.

Srinivasan, T. N. 1994. "Database for Development Analysis: An Overview." *Journal of Development Economics* 44(1): 3–28.

Standard & Poor's. 2000. *The S&P Emerging Market Indices Methodology, Definitions, and Practices.* New York.

———. 2002. *Emerging Stock Markets Factbook 2002.* New York.

———. 2003. *Credit Week.* January. New York.

Stern, Nicholas. 2001. "A Strategy for Development." Keynote address, Annual World Bank Conference on Development Economics, Washington, D.C., May 1–2.

———. 2002a. "Development as a Process of Change: Toward a Dynamic Public Economics." Keynes Lecture, British Academy, London, November 21.

———. 2002b. "Dynamic Development: Innovation and Inclusion." Munich Lectures in Economics, Ludwig Maximilian University, Center for Economic Studies, Munich, November 19.

Taylor, Alan M. 1996a. *International Capital Mobility in History: Purchasing Power Parity in the Long Run.* NBER Working Paper 5742. Cambridge, Mass.: National Bureau of Economic Research.

———. 1996b. *International Capital Mobility in History: The Saving-Investment Relationship.* NBER Working Paper 5743. Cambridge, Mass.: National Bureau of Economic Research.

Thomas, Duncan, and John Strauss. 1977. "Health and Wages: Evidence on Men and Women in Urban Brazil." *Journal of Econometrics* 77(1): 159–86.

UNACC/SCN (United Nations Administrative Committee on Co-ordination, Subcommittee on Nutrition). Various years. *Update on the Nutrition Situation.* Geneva.

———. 2000. *Fourth Report on the World Nutrition Situation.* Geneva.

UNAIDS (Joint United Nations Programme on HIV/AIDS) and WHO (World Health Organization). 2002. *AIDS Epidemic Update*. December.

UNCTAD (United Nations Conference on Trade and Development). 2002. *The Least Developed Countries Report*. Geneva.

———. Various years. *Handbook of International Trade and Development Statistics*. Geneva.

UNEP (United Nations Environment Programme). 1991. *Urban Air Pollution*. Nairobi.

UNEP (United Nations Environment Programme) and WHO (World Health Organization). 1992. *Urban Air Pollution in Megacities of the World*. Cambridge, Mass.: Blackwell.

———. 1995. *City Air Quality Trends*. Nairobi.

UNESCO (United Nations Educational, Scientific, and Cultural Organization). 1998. *World Education Report 1998*. Paris: UNESCO Publishing and Bernan Press.

———. Various years. *Statistical Yearbook*. Paris: UNESCO Publishing and Bernan Press.

UNESCO (United Nations Educational, Scientific, and Cultural Organization) and OECD (Organisation for Economic Co-operation and Development). 2003. *Financing Education: Investments and Returns—Analysis of the World Education Indicators*. 2002 ed. Paris.

UNESCO Institute for Statistics. 2001. *Sub-Saharan Africa Regional Report*. Montreal.

UNICEF (United Nations Children's Fund). 2001. *Progress since the World Summit for Children: A Statistical Review*. New York.

———. Various years. *The State of the World's Children*. New York: Oxford University Press.

UNIDO (United Nations Industrial Development Organization). Various years. *International Yearbook of Industrial Statistics*. Vienna.

United Nations. 1947. *Measurement of National Income and the Construction of Social Accounts*. New York.

———. 1968. *A System of National Accounts: Studies and Methods*. Series F, no. 2, rev. 3. New York.

———. 1990. *International Standard Industrial Classification of All Economic Activities, Third Revision*. Statistical Papers Series M, no. 4, rev. 3. New York.

———. 1992. *Handbook of the International Comparison Programme*. Studies in Methods Series F, no. 62. New York.

———. 1993. *SNA Handbook on Integrated Environmental and Economic Accounting*. Statistical Office of the United Nations. Series F, no. 61. New York.

———. 1999. *Integrated Environmental and Economic Accounting: An Operational Manual*. Studies in Methods Series F, no. 78. New York.

———. 2000. *We the Peoples: The Role of the United Nations in the 21st Century*. New York.

United Nations Economic and Social Commission for Western Asia. 1997. *Purchasing Power Parities: Volume and Price Level Comparisons for the Middle East, 1993*. E/ESCWA/STAT/1997/2. Amman.

United Nations Population Division. 1996. *International Migration Policies 1995*. New York.

———. 2000. *World Population Prospects: The 2000 Revision*. New York.

———. 2002. *World Urbanization Prospects: The 2001 Revision*. New York.

———. Various years. *Levels and Trends of Contraceptive Use*. New York.

United Nations Statistics Division. 1985. *National Accounts Statistics: Compendium of Income Distribution Statistics*. New York.

———. Various issues. *Monthly Bulletin of Statistics*. New York.

———. Various years. *Energy Statistics Yearbook*. New York.

———. Various years. *International Trade Statistics Yearbook*. New York.

———. Various years. *National Accounts Statistics: Main Aggregates and Detailed Tables*. Parts 1 and 2. New York.

———. Various years. *National Income Accounts*. New York.

———. Various years. *Population and Vital Statistics Report*. New York.

———. Various years. *Statistical Yearbook*. New York.

U.S. Census Bureau. 1990. *1990 Census of Population Listing*. Washington, D.C.

———. 2000. *Current Population Report*. March. Washington, D.C.

U.S. Department of Health and Human Services. 1997. *Social Security Systems throughout the World*. Washington, D.C.

U.S. Department of State, Bureau of Verification and Compliance. 2002. *World Military Expenditures and Arms Transfers 2000*. Washington, D.C.

U.S. Environmental Protection Agency. 1995. *National Air Quality and Emissions Trends Report 1995*. Washington, D.C.

Wagstaff, Adam, and Harold Alderman. 2001. "Life and Death on a Dollar a Day: Does It Matter Where You Live?" World Bank, Washington, D.C.

Walsh, Michael P. 1994. "Motor Vehicle Pollution Control: An Increasingly Critical Issue for Developing Countries." World Bank, Washington, D.C.

Watson, Robert, John A. Dixon, Steven P. Hamburg, Anthony C. Janetos, and Richard H. Moss. 1998. *Protecting Our Planet, Securing Our Future: Linkages among Global Environmental Issues and Human Needs*. A joint publication of the United Nations Environment Programme, U.S. National Aeronautics and Space Administration, and World Bank, Nairobi and Washington, D.C.

WCMC (World Conservation Monitoring Centre). 1992. *Global Biodiversity: Status of the Earth's Living Resources*. London: Chapman and Hall.

———. 1994. *Biodiversity Data Sourcebook*. Cambridge: World Conservation Press.

WHO (World Health Organization). 1977. *International Classification of Diseases*. 9th rev. Geneva.

———. 1995. *Trends and Challenges in World Health: Report by the Secretariat*. WHO Executive Board Document EB 105/4. Geneva.

BIBLIOGRAPHY

———. 1997. *Coverage of Maternity Care*. Geneva.

———. 2002a. *Global Tuberculosis Control Report 2002*. Geneva.

———. 2002b. *The Tobacco Atlas*. Geneva.

———. Various years. *World Health Report*. Geneva.

———. Various years. *World Health Statistics Annual*. Geneva.

WHO (World Health Organization) and UNICEF (United Nations Children's Fund). 1992. *Low Birth Weight: A Tabulation of Available Information*. Geneva.

———. 2000. *Global Water Supply and Sanitation Assessment 2000 Report*. Geneva.

WITSA (World Information Technology and Services Alliance). 2002. *Digital Planet 2002: The Global Information Economy*. Based on research by International Data Corporation. Vienna, Va.

Wolf, Holger C. 1997. *Patterns of Intra- and Inter-State Trade*. NBER Working Paper 5939. Cambridge, Mass.: National Bureau of Economic Research.

World Bank. 1990. *World Development Report 1990: Poverty*. New York: Oxford University Press.

———. 1991. *World Development Report 1991: The Challenge of Development*. New York: Oxford University Press.

———. 1992. *World Development Report 1992: Development and the Environment*. New York: Oxford University Press.

———. 1993a. *The Environmental Data Book: A Guide to Statistics on the Environment and Development*. Washington, D.C.

———. 1993b. *Purchasing Power Parities: Comparing National Incomes Using ICP Data*. Washington, D.C.

———. 1993c. *World Development Report 1993: Investing in Health*. New York: Oxford University Press.

———. 1996a. *Environment Matters* (summer). Environment Department, Washington, D.C.

———. 1996b. *Livable Cities for the 21st Century*. A Directions in Development book. Washington, D.C.

———. 1996c. *National Environmental Strategies: Learning from Experience*. Environment Department, Washington, D.C.

———. 1997a. *Can the Environment Wait? Priorities for East Asia*. Washington, D.C.

———. 1997b. *Expanding the Measure of Wealth: Indicators of Environmentally Sustainable Development*. Environmentally Sustainable Development Studies and Monographs Series, no. 17. Washington, D.C.

———. 1997c. *Private Capital Flows to Developing Countries: The Road to Financial Integration*. A World Bank Policy Research Report. New York: Oxford University Press.

———. 1997d. *Rural Development: From Vision to Action*. Environmentally Sustainable Development Studies and Monographs Series, no. 12. Washington, D.C.

———. 1997e. *Sector Strategy: Health, Nutrition, and Population*. Human Development Network, Washington, D.C.

———. 1997f. *World Development Report 1997: The State in a Changing World*. New York: Oxford University Press.

———. 1998. *1998 Catalog: Operational Documents as of July 31, 1998*. Washington, D.C.

———. 1999a. *Fuel for Thought: Environmental Strategy for the Energy Sector*. Environment Department, Energy, Mining, and Telecommunications Department, and International Finance Corporation, Washington, D.C.

———. 1999b. *Greening Industry: New Roles for Communities, Markets, and Governments*. A World Bank Policy Research Report. New York: Oxford University Press.

———. 1999c. *Health, Nutrition, and Population Indicators: A Statistical Handbook*. Human Development Network, Washington, D.C.

———. 1999d. *Toward a Virtuous Circle: A Nutrition Review of the Middle East and North Africa*. Middle East and North Africa Working Paper Series, no. 17. Washington, D.C.

———. 1999e. *World Development Report 1999/2000: Entering the 21st Century—The Changing Development Landscape*. New York: Oxford University Press.

———. 2000a. *Trade Blocs*. A World Bank Policy Research Report. New York: Oxford University Press.

———. 2000b. *World Development Report 2000/2001: Attacking Poverty*. New York: Oxford University Press.

———. 2002a. "Achieving Education for All by 2015: Simulation Results for 47 Low-Income Countries." Africa Region and Human Development Network, Education Department, Washington, D.C.

———. 2002b. *A Case for Aid: Building a Consensus for Development Assistance*. Washington, D.C.

———. 2002c. *Financial Impact of the HIPC Initiative: First 24 Country Cases*. [http://www.worldbank.org/hipc].

———. 2002d. *Global Economic Prospects and the Developing Countries: Making Trade Work for the World's Poor*. Washington, D.C.

———. 2002e. *Globalization, Growth, and Poverty: Building an Inclusive World Economy*. A World Bank Policy Research Report. New York: Oxford University Press.

———. 2002f. *Private Sector Development Strategy: Directions for the World Bank Group*. Private Sector Development Network, Washington, D.C.

———. 2002g. *Social Protection in Latin America and the Caribbean*. Fact Sheet. Latin America and the Caribbean Region and Human Development Network, Washington, D.C.

———. 2002h. *World Development Report 2003: Transforming Growth—Neighbor, Nature, Future*. Draft. Washington, D.C.

————. 2002i. The Environment and the Millennium Development Goals. Washington, D.C.

————. Forthcoming. *Poverty Reduction and the World Bank: Operationalizing World Development Report 2000/2001*. Washington, D.C.

————. Various issues. *Global Commodity Markets*. Quarterly. Washington, D.C.

————. Various years. *Global Development Finance* (formerly *World Debt Tables*). Washington, D.C. (Also available on CD-ROM.)

————. Various years. *Global Economic Prospects and the Developing Countries*. Washington, D.C.

————. Various years. *World Development Indicators*. Washington, D.C.

World Energy Council. 1995. *Global Energy Perspectives to 2050 and Beyond*. London.

World Intellectual Property Organization. 2002. *Industrial Property Statistics*. Publication A. Geneva.

World Resources Institute, International Institute for Environment and Development, and IUCN (World Conservation Union). Various years. *World Directory of Country Environmental Studies*. Washington, D.C.

World Resources Institute, UNEP (United Nations Environment Programme), and UNDP (United Nations Development Programme). 1994. *World Resources 1994–95: A Guide to the Global Environment*. New York: Oxford University Press.

World Resources Institute, UNEP (United Nations Environment Programme), UNDP (United Nations Development Programme), and World Bank. Various years. *World Resources: A Guide to the Global Environment*. New York: Oxford University Press.

World Tourism Organization. 2001a. *Compendium of Tourism Statistics 2001*. Madrid.

————. 2001b. *Yearbook of Tourism Statistics*. Vols. 1 and 2. Madrid.

WTO (World Trade Organization). Various years. *Annual Report*. Geneva.

Zook, Matthew. 2000. "Internet Metrics: Using Host and Domain Counts to Map the Internet." *International Journal on Knowledge Infrastructure Development, Management and Regulation* (University of California at Berkeley) 24(6/7).

INDEX OF INDICATORS

INDEX OF INDICATORS

F

INDEX OF INDICATORS

INDEX OF INDICATORS

M

INDEX OF INDICATORS

INDEX OF INDICATORS

T

INDEX OF INDICATORS

V

W